uk:athletics

BRITISH ATHLETICS 2001

Compiled by the
National Union of Track Statisticians

Editors: Rob Whittingham & Peter Matthews
Assistant Editors: Ian Hodge, Tony Miller
and Martin Rix.

Published by: Umbra Athletics Limited,
Unit 1, Bredbury Business Park,
Bredbury Park Way, Bredbury, Stockport SK6 2SN
Tel: 0161 406 6320 Fax: 0161 406 6732

ISBN 0 9540390 0 9

Front Cover: DENISE LEWIS. Olympic Champion

All photos by: All photographs provided by Mark Shearman,
22 Grovelands Road, Purley, Surrey CR8 4LA
Tel: 020 8660 0156 Fax: 020 8660 3437
His help is greatly appreciated.

Distributed by: Umbra Athletics Limited,
Unit 1, Bredbury Business Park,
Bredbury Park Way, Bredbury, Stockport SK6 2SN
Tel: 0161 406 6320 Fax: 0161 406 6732

Printed in
Great Britain by: J.R. Davies (Printers) Limited,
The Old Bakehouse, Church Street, Abertillery, Gwent NP13 1EA
Tel: 01495 212600 Fax: 01495 216222

CONTENTS

NATIONAL UNION OF TRACK STATISTICIANS AND COMPILERS

Honorary President: Norris D McWhirter CBE

Vice Presidents: Peter E May Leonard F Gebbett Richard Hymans Martin H James Patrick E Brian Colin Young Andrew Huxtable Tim G Lynch-Staunton

Honorary Members: Roberto L Quercetani, John Bromhead

Executive Committee: Les Crouch (Chairman) Dr Shirley E Hitchcock (Hon Sec) John M Powell (Treasurer)

Stanley Greenberg	Peter J Matthews	Melvyn F Watman	Lionel Peters
Elizabeth Sissons	Bob Sparks	Alfred P Wilkins	Colin Young
Sally Gandee	Dr. Tim Grose	Joe Barrass	Justin Clouder

Annual

General Editors - Rob Whittingham, Peter Matthews

Assistant Editors - Ian Hodge, Tony Miller, Martin Rix

Records - Bob Sparks All Time Lists and Index - Martin Rix, Tony Miller

Results - Brian Hatch, Brian Webster and Peter Matthews

Men's Lists - Ian Hodge (HJ, PV and overall), Joe Barrass (sprints), Tim Grose (800m to 10,000m), Steve Mitchell (5000m, 10,000m), John Walsh (Marathon), Shirley Hitchcock (Hurdles), Bill Myers (LJ, TJ),Tony O'Neill (throws).

Under 20 & Under 17 Men - Ian Hodge with above compilers

Under 15 Men - Ian Hodge Under 13 Men - Liz Smart

Women's Lists - Liz Sissons, Peter Martin, Tony Miller (including U17), Bill Green (U15 & U13)

Walks - John Powell Relays - Keith Morbey Multi-Events - Alan Lindop

Also acknowledgements for specific help to Arnold Black (Scotland), John Glover and Alan Keys (Northern Ireland) and various other NUTS members.

ABBREVIATIONS & NOTES

A - mark set at altitude over 1000m
a - automatic timing only known to one tenth of a second
D - performance made in a Decathlon
dh - downhill
e - estimated time
et - extra trial
ex - exhibition
h - heat
H - performance made in a Heptathlon
hc - handicap race
i - indoor
jo - jump off
m - position in race when intermediate time taken
mx - performance in mixed race
O - performance made in an Octathlon
o - over age
P - performance made in a Pentathlon
Q - qualifying round
q - quarter final
r - race number
s - semi final
t - track
u - unofficial time
un - unconfirmed performance
w - wind assisted (> 2.0 m/sec)
W - wind assisted (over 4m/sec in decathlon/heptathlon)
x - relay team may include outside age-group members
+ - intermediate time
* - legal performance where best is wind assisted
" - photo electric cell time
- Unratified (may not be ratifiable)
& - as yet unratified
§ - now competes for another nation
¶ - drugs ban (as per IAAF)

AGE GROUP DESIGNATIONS

U13 - Under 13	(born 1.9.87 or later)	U15 - Under 15	(born 1.9.85 to 31.8.87)
U17 - Under 17	(born 1.9.83 to 31.8.85)	U20 - Under 20	(born 1.1.81 to 31.8.83)
Vxx - Veteran	(age 40 or over Men)	Vxx - Veteran	(age 35 or over Women)

Care must be taken with very young age groups for athletes with an unknown date of birth from Northern Ireland since their age groups differ slightly.

Italics indicates the athlete competes for a British club but is not eligible to represent Britain.

MULTI - EVENTS

Pentathlon, Heptathlon and Decathlon lists show the complete breakdown of individual performances in the following order:

Pentathlon (women) - 100mH, SP, HJ, LJ, 800m; Junior: LJ, SP, 75mH, HJ, 800m
Heptathlon (women) - 100mH, HJ, SP, 200m (1st day); LJ, JT, 800m (2nd day) (80mH - Inters)
Decathlon (men) - 100m, LJ, SP, HJ, 400m (1st day); 110mH, DT, PV, JT, 1500m (2nd day)

Totals which include performances made with following winds in excess of 4 m/s are denoted by W. The date shown is the second day of competition.

RANKING LISTS:

These show the best performances in each event recorded during the 1999 season.
For each performance the following details are shown:

Performance; wind reading (where appropriate); name (with, where appropriate, age-group category); date of birth (DDMMYY); position in competition; vcnuc; date.

The following numbers are used, although strength of performance or lack of information may vary the guidelines -

50 perfomances 100 athletes for each standard event

Age Groups - 40 Under 20, 30 Under 17, 20 Under 15, 10 Under 13

In the junior men, athletes are shown in older age groups if their performances merit this, e.g. an U15 can appear in the U17 list etc. For junior women, athletes are shown in their age group as per womens rules, although juniors of any age will be shown in the main list on merit.

INDEX

Club details and previous personal bests, where better than those recorded in 2000, are shown in the index for all athletes in the main lists.

VENUES

Tim Grose has done major research on all British Tracks and a full list was shown in last year's annual; this list will be repeated in some subsequent annuals - full details at www.runtrackdir.com

(London tracks for clarification)

LONDON (B)	Barn Elms Sports Ground, Rocks Lane, Barnes (6L, 8S)
LONDON (BP)	Battersea Park
LONDON (Cat)	Ladywell Arena, Silvermere Road, Catford (6L, 8S)
LONDON (Col)	Metropolitan Police (Hendon) Track, Hendon Police Training Coll, Colindale (6L, 6S)
LONDON (CP)	Crystal Palace National Sports Centre, Ledrington Road
LONDON (Cr)	Croydon Sports Arena, Albert Road
LONDON (DC)	Dulwich College, College Road, Dulwich (300m, 6L, 6S)
LONDON (Elt)	Sutcliffe Park, Eltham Road (6L, 8S)
LONDON (FP)	Finsbury Park, Endymion Road (6L, 10S)
LONDON (Ha)	New River Sports Centre, White Hart Lane, Wood Green, Haringey
LONDON (He)	Barnet Copthall Stadium, Great North Way, Hendon
LONDON (ME)	Mile End Stadium, Rhodeswell Road
LONDON (Nh)	Terence McMillan Stadium, Newham Leisure Centre, Plaistow
LONDON (Pa)	Paddington Recreation Ground, Randolph Avenue (6L, 6S)
LONDON (PH)	Parliament Hill Fields, Highgate Road, Hampstead
LONDON (SP)	Southwark Park, Hawkstone Road, Surrey Quays (7L, 7S)
LONDON (TB)	Tooting Bec Athletics Track, Tooting Bec Road
LONDON (WF)	Waltham Forest Track, Chingford Road, Walthamstow
LONDON (Wil)	Willesden Sports Stadium, Donnington Road (6L, 8S)
LONDON (WL)	Linford Christie Stadium, Du Cane Road, West London
LONDON (WP)	Wimbledon Park, Home Park Road (6L, 8S)

INTRODUCTION - by Rob Whittingham

An Olympic year has just past and everyone should feel proud of British Athletics and their successes in 2000. I was able to attend my first Olympics in Sydney and feel privileged to have seen the best Olympics and probably the greatest overall performance by a British Olympic Team including the athletes. True, larger medal totals have been achieved, but this was in the context of reduced competition. The two golds were excellent; Denise Lewis battling against injury and Jonathan Edwards battling against previous disappointments. All our medallists were superb but three other performances impressed me. Paula Radcliffe did everything she could to win a medal and fourth must be the worst position to finish, however success in the World Half Marathon Championships and recently in the 2001 World Cross Country, show her true ability. Dean Macey also finished fourth after an injury hit season, but my true hero finished last! How do you walk 49,600 metres injured, where you are certain to be last and there is every chance they will close the stadium doors and not let you finish the course? Chris Maddox did this, and It was a very special moment to be in the Stadium and witness the reception this remarkable athlete received.

UK Athletics continues its progress as the governing body and is slowly widening its influence in the general athletics arena. As an official body it has many detractors and speed is always difficult, but it is moving in the right direction. I am involved in the official website www.ukathletics.org and the enhancements planned for this year should contribute to the whole arena of British athletics.

The Annual would not be possible without contributions from many people and I am grateful for all the help. Some people deserve particular mention - Peter Matthews has contributed in all areas of the book, Tony Miller has put in even more effort this year to ensure as much accuracy as possible and Ian Hodge has again created most of the junior men's lists and helped with many senior lists and queries. A couple of junior compilers are also worthy of mention - Bill Green moved to U15 girls and provided U13 lists at the last minute and Liz Smart has brought the U13 boys lists up to a very good standard.

Staff within Umbra have helped, in particular Julie Fletcher has made a very large contribution to the book during the later stages of checking and typesetting.

Marty has endured my creation of the book for the twelfth time.

After the expansion of the book last year, this has been a year of consolidation and I look forward to new developments next year.

As usual any corrections are always welcome.

Rob Whittingham
March 2001

7 Birch Green Glossop SK13 8PR
e-mail rob@umbra.co.uk

UK ATHLETICS AND OTHER ADDRESSES

UK Athletics
Athletics House
10 Harborne Road
Edgbaston
Birmingham B15 3AA
Tel: 0121 456 5098

AAA of England
Edgbaston House
3 Duchess Place
Hagley Road
Birmingham B16 8NM
Tel: 0121 452 1500

SCOTLAND

Scotland A.F.
Caledonia House
South Gyle
Edinburgh
Tel: 0131 317 7320

WALES

A.A. of Wales
Morfa Stadium Landore
Swansea
West Glamorgan SA1 7DF
Tel: 01792 456237

NORTHERN IRELAND

Northern Ireland A.A.F.
Honorary Secretary: J.Allen
Athletics House
Old Coach Road
Belfast BT9 5PR
Tel: 01232 381222

Midland Counties A.A.
Edgbaston House
3 Duchess Place
Hagley Road
Birmingham
B16 8NM
Tel: 0121 452 1500

North of England A.A.
Studio 106, EMCO House
5/7 New York Road
Leeds LS2 7PJ
Tel: 01532 461835

South of England A.A.
Suite 106 City of London Fruit Exchange
Brushfield St
London E1 6EU
Tel: 0171 247 2963

Commonwealth Games Councils:

England
General Secretary: Miss A.Hogbin
1 Wandsworth Plain
London SW18 1EH
Tel: 0181 871 2677

Northern Ireland
Honorary Secretary: R.J.McColgan MBE
22 Mountcoole Park, Cave Hill
Belfast BT14 8JR
Tel: 01232 716558

Scotland
Honorary Secretary: G.A.Hunter OBE
139 Old Dalkeith Road
Little France
Edinburgh EH16 4SZ
Tel: 0131 664 1070

Wales
Honorary Secretary: M.John MBE
Pennant
Blaenau, Ammanford
Dyfed SA18 3BZ
Tel: 0269 850390

British Athletics League
Honorary Secretary: D. Jeacock
16 Church Street
Wotton Bassett
Wilts SN4 7BQ

National Young Athletes' League
Honorary Secretary: N. Bailey
15 Chaseley Avenue
Cannock
Staffs WS11 1JG
Tel: 01543 574624

Supporters Club - British Athletics Club
Honorary Secretary: Mrs M.Pieri
11 Railway Road
Newbury, Berks RG14 7PE
Tel: 01635 33400

Sports Council
The Sports Council
16 Upper Woburn Place
London WC1H OQP
Tel: 0171 388 1277

Athletics Weekly
Editor: Nigel Walsh
Descartes Publishing Limited
13 Clavell Court, Peterborough PE1 2RJ
Tel: 01733 898440

National Union of Track Statisticians
Secretary: Dr. S. Hitchcock
2 Chudleigh Close
Bedford
MK40 3AW

MAJOR OUTDOOR FIXTURES IN 2001

MAY		
5-7	British Universities Championships	Scotstoun, Glasgow
12-13	County Championships	Various
12-13	Scottish District Championships	Various
20	UK & AAA 100km Championship	Moreton in the Marsh
20	Aqua-Pura International	Loughborough
27-28	CAU Inter Counties Championships	Bedford
JUNE		
8-9	RUS v Eng v IRE	Moscow, RUS
9-10	International Combined Events	Arles, FRA
9	NU 10k World Trials/ AAA Track Championships	Watford
9	English County Schools Championships	Various
23-24	SPAR European Cup Super League	Bremen, GER
23-24	Scottish Championships	Scotstoun, Glasgow
23	Norwich Union International – U23 GBR v Spain	Liverpool
29-1Jul	Norwich Union AAA U23 & U20 Champs	Bedford
30-1Jul	European Cup Combined Events – Men, Women	Lithuania(M) Austria(W)
JULY		
4-15	World Veterans Championships	Brisbane, AUS
5	Throws International	Verazdin, CRO
6-7	English Schools Championships	Exeter
12-15	World Youth Championships	Debrecen, HUN
12-15	European U23 Championships	Amsterdam, HOL
13-15	Norwich Union World Trials & AAA Champs	Birmingham
14-15	AAA Combined Events Champs.	Bedford
18	Bedford International Games	Bedford
19-22	European Junior Championships	Grosseto, ITA
21	England v Wales v Estonia v Latvia	Tallin, EST
22	Norwich Union British Grand Prix 1	Crystal Palace, London
28	Northern Irish Championships	Belfast
AUGUST		
3/12	IAAF World Athletics Champs.	Edmonton, CAN
4/5	Norwich Union International Combined Events	Bedford
11	Norwich Union International - GBR v France	Ashford
11-12	AAA U17 & U15 Champs	Sheffield
19	UKA Half Marathon Champs.	Glasgow
19	Norwich Union Classic GP II	Gateshead
26	IAU 100km World Challenge	Cleder, FRA
27-1Sep	World Student Games	Beijing, CHN
SEPTEMBER		
9	IAAF Grand Prix Final	Melbourne, AUS
9	Fila AAA 10km Road Champs.	Cheltenham
16	The BUPA Great North Run	Tyneside
OCTOBER		
7	IAAF World Half Marathon Champs.	Bristol
27	AAAoE Road Relay Champs.	Sutton Park, Birmingham
DECEMBER		
9	European Cross Country Champs	Thun, SWZ

BEST AUTHENTIC PERFORMANCES (MEN)

(as at 31st December 2000)

W = World, E = European, C = Commonwealth, A = UK All-Comers, N = UK, J = Junior

Event	Record	Performance		Athlete	Nat	Date	Venue
100m	W	9.79		Maurice Greene	USA	16 Jun 99	Athens
	E,N	9.87		Linford Christie		15 Aug 93	Stuttgart
	C	9.84		Donovan Bailey	CAN	27 Jul 96	Atlanta
		9.84		Bruny Surin	CAN	22 Aug 99	Seville
	A	9.97		Maurice Greene	USA	7 Aug 99	London (CP)
	WJ	10.05	#	Davidson Ezinwa	NGR	4 Jan 90	Bauchi
	WJ,EJ,NJ	10.06		Dwain Chambers		25 Jul 97	Ljubljana
200m	W	19.32		Michael Johnson	USA	1 Aug 96	Atlanta
	E	19.72	A	Pietro Mennea	ITA	12 Sep 79	Mexico City
	C	19.68		Frank Fredericks	NAM	1 Aug 96	Atlanta
	A	19.85		Michael Johnson	USA	6 Jul 90	Edinburgh
	N	19.87	A#	John Regis		31 Jul 94	Sestriere
		19.94		John Regis		20 Aug 93	Stuttgart
	WJ	20.07	#	Lorenzo Daniel	USA	18 May 85	Starkville
		20.13		Roy Martin	USA	16 Jun 85	Indianapolis
	EJ,NJ	20.29		Christian Malcolm		19 Sep 98	Kuala Lumpur
300m	W	30.85	A	Michael Johnson	USA	24 Mar 00	Pretoria
	E,C,A,N	31.56		Doug Walker	Sco	19 Jul 98	Gateshead
	WJ	32.08	+	Steve Lewis	USA	28 Sep 88	Seoul
	EJ,NJ	32.53		Mark Richardson		14 Jul 91	London (Ha)
400m	W	43.18		Michael Johnson	USA	26 Aug 99	Seville
	E	44.33		Thomas Schönlebe	GER	3 Sep 87	Rome
	C	44.17		Innocent Egbunike	NGR	19 Aug 87	Zürich
	A	43.98		Michael Johnson	USA	10 Jul 92	London (CP)
	N	44.36		Iwan Thomas		13 Jul 97	Birmingham
	WJ	43.87		Steve Lewis	USA	28 Sep 88	Seoul
	EJ	45.01		Thomas Schönlebe	GER	15 Jul 84	Berlin
	NJ	45.36		Roger Black		24 Aug 85	Cottbus
600m	W	1:12.81		Johnny Gray	USA	24 May 86	Santa Monica
	E	1:14.41		Andrea Longo	ITA	30 Aug 00	Roverto
	C	1:13.2		John Kipkurgat	KEN	23 Mar 74	Pointe-à-Pierre
	A,N	1:14.95		Steve Heard		14 Jul 91	London (Ha)
	WJ	1:14.8	A	Mark Winzenreid	USA	31 Aug 68	Echo Summit
	NJ	1:16.79		Andrew Lill		24 Jul 90	Mansfield
800m	W,E	1:41.11		Wilson Kipketer	DEN	24 Aug 97	Cologne
	C,N	1:41.73"		Sebastian Coe	Eng	10 Jun 81	Florence
	A	1:43.22		Steve Cram		31 Jul 86	Edinburgh
	WJ	1:43.64		Japheth Kimutai	KEN	13 Aug 97	Zürich
	EJ	1:44.33		Yuriy Borzakovskiy	RUS	25 Sep 00	Sydney
	NJ	1:45.64		David Sharpe		5 Sep 86	Brussels
1000m	W,C	2:11.96		Noah Ngeny	KEN	17 Jul 99	Nice
	E,N	2:12.18		Sebastian Coe		11 Jul 81	Oslo
	A	2:12.88		Steve Cram		9 Aug 85	Gateshead
	WJ	2:15.00		Benjamin Kipkurui	KEN	17 Jul 99	Nice
	EJ	2:17.40		Yuriy Borzakovskiy	RUS	8 Jul 00	Nice
	NJ	2:18.98		David Sharpe		19 Aug 86	Birmingham
1500m	W	3:26.00		Hicham El Guerrouj	MAR	14 Jul 98	Rome
	E	3:28.95		Fermín Cacho	SPA	13 Aug 97	Zürich
	C	3:28.12		Noah Ngeny	KEN	11 Aug 00	Zurich
	A	3:30.2		Hicham El Guerrouj	MAR	5 Aug 00	London (CP)
	N	3:29.67		Steve Cram		16 Jul 85	Nice

Event	Record	Mark		Athlete	Nat	Date	Venue
1500m	WJ	3:32.91	#	Noah Ngeny	KEN	16 Aug 97	Monaco
		3:33.16		Benjamin Kipkurui	KEN	11 Aug 99	Zürich
	EJ	3:35.51		Reyes Estévez	SPA	16 Aug 95	Zürich
	NJ	3:36.6		Graham Williamson		17 Jul 79	Oslo
1 Mile	W	3:43.13		Hicham El Guerrouj	MAR	7 Jul 99	Rome
	E,N	3:46.32		Steve Cram	Eng	27 Jul 85	Oslo
	C	3:43.40		Noah Ngeny	KEN	7 Jul 99	Rome
	A	3:45.96		Hicham El Guerrouj	MAR	5 Aug 00	London (CP)
	WJ	3:50.41		Noah Ngeny	KEN	16 Jul 97	Nice
	EJ,NJ	3:53.15		Graham Williamson		17 Jul 79	Oslo
2000m	W	4:44.79		Hicham El Guerrouj	MAR	7 Sep 99	Berlin
	E,N	4:51.39		Steve Cram		4 Aug 85	Budapest
	C	4:48.74		John Kibowen	KEN	1 Aug 98	Hechtel
	A	4:48.36		Hicham El Guerrouj	MAR	19 Jul 98	Gateshead
	WJ	4:59.14		Ali Saïdi-Sief	ALG	29 Jun 97	Villeneuve d'Ascq
	EJ	5:04.4		Harald Hudak	GER	30 Jun 76	Oslo
	NJ	5:06.56		Jon Richards		7 Jul 82	Oslo
3000m	W,C	7:20.67		Daniel Komen	KEN	1 Sep 96	Rieti
	E	7:26.62		Mohammed Mourit	BEL	18 Aug 00	Monaco
	A	7:29.69		Haile Gebrselassie	ETH	7 Aug 99	London (CP)
	N	7:32.79		Dave Moorcroft		17 Jul 82	London (CP)
	WJ	7:33.00	#	Hailu Mekonnen	ETH	6 Jun 99	Stuttgart
		7:34.58		Sammy Kipketer	KEN	3 Sep 99	Brussels
	EJ	7:43.20		Ari Paunonen	FIN	22 Jun 77	Cologne
	NJ	7:48.28		Jon Richards		9 Jul 83	Oslo
2 Miles	W,C	7:58.61		Daniel Komen	KEN	19 Jul 97	Hechtel
	E	8:13.2	i#	Emiel Puttemans	BEL	18 Feb 73	Berlin
	E,N	8:13.51		Steve Ovett		15 Sep 78	London (CP)
	A	8:01.72		Haile Gebrselassie	ETH	7 Aug 99	London (CP)
	WJ	8:13.47		Richard Limo	KEN	30 May 99	Hengelo
	EJ,NJ	8:28.31		Steve Binns		31 Aug 79	London (CP)
5000m	W	12:39.36		Haile Gebreselassie	ETH	13 Jun 98	Helsinki
	E	12:49.71		Mohammed Mourit	BEL	25 Aug 00	Brussels
	C	12:39.74		Daniel Komen	KEN	22 Aug 97	Brussels
	A	12:50.38	i#	Haile Gebrselassie	ETH	14 Feb 99	Birmingham
		13:06.23		Haile Gebrselassie	ETH	5 Aug 00	London (CP)
	N	13:00.41		Dave Moorcroft		7 Jul 82	Oslo
	WJ	12:53.72		Philip Mosima	KEN	5 Jun 96	Rome
	EJ,NJ	13:27.04		Steve Binns		14 Sep 79	London (CP)
10000m	W	26:22.75		Haile Gebreselassie	ETH	1 Jun 98	Hengelo
	E	26:52.30		Mohammed Mourhit	BEL	3 Sep 99	Brussels
	C	26:27.85		Paul Tergat	KEN	22 Aug 97	Brussels
	A	27:20.38		Aloÿs Nizigama	BUR	7 Jul 95	London (CP)
	N	27:18.14	#	Jon Brown		28 Aug 98	Brussels
		27:23.06		Eamonn Martin		2 Jul 88	Oslo
	WJ	27:11.18		Richard Chelimo	KEN	25 Jun 91	Hengelo
	EJ	28:22.48		Christian Leuprecht	ITA	4 Sep 90	Koblenz
	NJ	29:21.9		Jon Brown		21 Apr 90	Walnut
20000m	W	56:55.6		Arturo Barrios	MEX	30 Mar 91	La Flèche
	E	57:18.4		Dionisio Castro	POR	31 Mar 90	La Flèche
	C,N	57:28.7		Carl Thackery	Eng	31 Mar 90	La Flèche
	A	58:39.0		Ron Hill		9 Nov 68	Leicester
1 Hour	W	21,101 m		Arturo Barrios	MEX	30 Mar 91	La Flèche
	E	20,944 m		Jos Hermens	HOL	1 May 76	Papendal
	C,N	20,855 m		Carl Thackery	Eng	31 Mar 90	La Flèche
	A	20,472 m		Ron Hill		9 Nov 68	Leicester
	NJ	18,221 m		Eddie Twohig		16 Jun 81	Leamington

Event	Record	Performance		Athlete	Nat	Date	Venue
25000m	W	1:13:55.8		Toshihiko Seko	JAP	22 Mar 81	Christchurch, NZL
	E	1:13:57.6		Stéphane Franke	GER	30 Mar 99	Walnut
	C,A,N	1:15:22.6		Ron Hill	Eng	21 Jul 65	Bolton
30000m	W	1:29:18.78		Toshihiko Seko	JAP	22 Mar 81	Christchurch, NZL
	E,C,A,N	1:31:30.4		Jim Alder	Sco	5 Sep 70	London (CP)
Half Marathon	W,C	59:06		Paul Tergat	KEN	26 Mar 00	Lisbon
	E	59:43		António Pinto	POR	15 Mar 98	Lisbon
	A	60:02		Benson Masya	KEN	18 Sep 94	South Shields
	N	60:09	#	Paul Evans		15 Jan 95	Marrakech
		60:59		Steve Jones		8 Jun 86	South Shields
	WJ	59:37		Faustin Baha	TAN	26 Mar 00	Lisbon
	NJ	66:41		Stuart Jones		12 Jun 88	Weaverham
Marathon	W	2:05:42		Khalid Khannouchi	MAR	24 Oct 99	Chicago
	E,A	2:06:36		António Pinto	POR	16 Apr 00	London
	C	2:06:16		Moses Tanui	KEN	24 Oct 99	Chicago
	N	2:07:13		Steve Jones		20 Oct 85	Chicago
	WJ	2:12:49		Negash Dube	ETH	18 Oct 87	Beijing
		2:12:49		Tesfaye Dadi	ETH	9 Oct 88	Berlin
	NJ	2:23:28		Eddie Twohig		28 Mar 82	Wolverhampton
2000m SC	W,C	5:14.43		Julius Kariuki	KEN	21 Aug 90	Rovereto
	E	5:18.36		Alessandro Lambruschini	ITA	12 Sep 89	Verona
	A	5:19.68		Samson Obwocha	KEN	19 Jul 86	Birmingham
	N	5:19.86		Mark Rowland		28 Aug 88	London (CP)
	WJ,EJ	5:25.01		Arsenios Tsiminos	GRE	2 Oct 80	Athens
	NJ	5:29.61		Colin Reitz		18 Aug 79	Bydgoszcz
3000m SC	W,C	7:55.72		Bernard Barmasai	KEN	24 Aug 97	Cologne
	E	8:07.62		Joseph Mahmoud	FRA	24 Aug 84	Brussels
	A	8:08.11		Patrick Sang	KEN	7 Jul 95	London (CP)
	N	8:07.96		Mark Rowland		30 Sep 88	Seoul
	WJ	8:03.74		Raymond Yator	KEN	18 Aug 00	Monaco
	EJ	8:29.50		Ralf Pönitzsch	GER	19 Aug 76	Warsaw
	NJ	8:29.85		Paul Davies-Hale		31 Aug 81	London (CP)
110m H	W,E,C,N	12.91		Colin Jackson	Wal	20 Aug 93	Stuttgart
	A	13.03		Colin Jackson		4 Sep 94	Sheffield
	WJ	13.23		Renaldo Nehemiah	USA	16 Aug 78	Zürich
	EJ,NJ	13.44		Colin Jackson		19 Jul 86	Athens
200m H	W,E	22.55		Laurant Ottoz	ITA	31 May 95	Milan
	C	22.59		Darryl Wohlsen	AUS	14 Mar 96	Brisbane
	A,N	22.63		Colin Jackson		1 Jun 91	Cardiff
	NJ	24.02		Paul Gray		13 Sep 87	London (CP)
400m H	W	46.78		Kevin Young	USA	6 Aug 92	Barcelona
	E	47.37		Stéphane Diagana	FRA	5 Jul 95	Lausanne
	C	47.10		Samuel Matete	ZAM	7 Aug 91	Zürich
	A	47.67		Kevin Young	USA	14 Aug 92	Sheffield
	N	47.82		Kriss Akabusi		6 Aug 92	Barcelona
	WJ	48.02		Danny Harris	USA	17 Jun 84	Los Angeles
	EJ	48.74		Vladimir Budko	RUS	18 Aug 84	Moscow
	NJ	50.22		Martin Briggs		28 Aug 83	Schwechat
High Jump	W	2.45		Javier Sotomayor	CUB	27 Jul 93	Salamanca
	E	2.42		Patrik Sjöberg	SWE	30 Jun 87	Stockholm
		2.42	i#	Carlo Thränhardt	GER	26 Feb 88	Berlin
	C,N	2.38	i#	Steve Smith	Eng	4 Feb 94	Wuppertal
	C	2.38		Troy Kemp	BAH	12 Jul 95	Nice

Event	Record	Mark		Athlete	Nat	Date	Venue
High	A	2.41		Javier Sotomayor	CUB	15 Jul 94	London (CP)
	N,WJ,EJ,NJ	2.37		Steve Smith		20 Sep 92	Seoul
Jump	N	2.37		Steve Smith		22 Aug 93	Stuttgart
	WJ,EJ	2.37		Dragutin Topic	YUG	12 Aug 90	Plovdiv
Pole	W,E	6.15	i#	Sergey Bubka	UKR	21 Feb 93	Donetsk
Vault		6.14	A	Sergey Bubka	UKR	31 Jul 94	Sestriere
	C	6.03		Okkert Brits	RSA	18 Aug 95	Cologne
	A	6.05		Sergey Bubka	UKR	10 Sep 93	London (CP)
	N	5.80		Nick Buckfield		27 May 98	Hania
	WJ,EJ	5.80		Maksim Tarasov	RUS	14 Jul 89	Bryansk
	NJ	5.50		Neil Winter		9 Aug 92	San GiulianoTerme
Long	W	8.95		Mike Powell	USA	30 Aug 91	Tokyo
Jump	E	8.86	A	Robert Emmiyan	ARM	22 May 87	Tsakhkadzor
	C	8.62		James Beckford	JAM	5 Apr 97	Orlando
	A	8.54		Mike Powell	USA	10 Sep 93	London (CP)
	N	8.23		Lynn Davies		30 Jun 68	Berne
	WJ	8.34		Randy Williams	USA	8 Sep 72	Munich
	EJ	8.24		Vladimir Ochkan	UKR	21 Jun 87	St. Petersburg
	NJ	7.98		Stewart Faulkner		6 Aug 88	Birmingham
Triple	W,E,C,N	18.29		Jonathan Edwards	Eng	7 Aug 95	Gothenburg
Jump	A	18.00		Jonathan Edwards		27 Aug 95	London (CP)
	WJ,EJ	17.50		Volker Mai	GER	23 Jun 85	Erfurt
	NJ	16.58		Tosi Fasinro		15 Jun 91	Espoo
Shot	W	23.12		Randy Barnes	USA	20 May 90	Los Angeles (Ww)
	E	23.06		Ulf Timmermann	GER	22 May 88	Hania
	C,N	21.68		Geoff Capes	Eng	18 May 80	Cwmbrân
	A	22.28	#	Brian Oldfield	USA	18 Jun 75	Edinburgh
		21.75		John Godina	USA	17 Aug 97	London (CP)
	WJ	21.05	i#	Terry Albritton	USA	22 Feb 74	New York
		20.65	#	Mike Carter	USA	4 Jul 79	Boston
		20.39	A	Janus Robberts	RSA	7 Mar 98	Germiston
	EJ	20.20		Udo Beyer	GER	6 Jul 74	Leipzig
	NJ	19.46		Carl Myerscough		6 Sep 98	Blackpool
Discus	W,E	74.08		Jürgen Schult	GER	6 Jun 86	Neubrandenburg
	C	69.75	A	Frantz Kruger	RSA	15 Sep 00	Bloemfontein
	A	68.32		John Powell	USA	30 Aug 82	London (CP)
	N	66.64		Perriss Wilkins		6 Jun 98	Birmingham (Un)
	WJ	65.62	#	Werner Reiterer	AUS	15 Dec 87	Melbourne
	WJ,EJ	63.64		Werner Hartmann	GER	25 Jun 78	Strasbourg
	NJ	60.97		Emeka Udechuku		5 Jul 98	Bedford
Hammer	W,E	86.74		Yuriy Sedykh	UKR/RUS	30 Aug 86	Stuttgart
	C	78.71	A	Chris Harmse	RSA	23 Sep 00	Pretoria
	A	85.60		Yuriy Sedykh	UKR/RUS	13 Jul 84	London (CP)
	N	77.54		Martin Girvan		12 May 84	Wolverhampton
	WJ,EJ	78.33		Olli-Pekka Karjalainen	FIN	5 Aug 99	Seinäjoki
	NJ	67.48		Paul Head		16 Sep 84	Karlovac
Javelin	W,E	98.48		Jan ZeleznΩ	CZE	25 May 96	Jena
	C,N	91.46		Steve Backley	Eng	25 Jan 92	Auckland (NS)
	A	95.66		Jan ZeleznΩ	CZE	29 Aug 93	Sheffield
	WJ,EJ	82.52		Harri Haatainen	FIN	25 May 96	Leppävirta
	NJ	79.50		Steve Backley		5 Jun 88	Derby
Pent.	W,A	4282		Bill Toomey	USA	16 Aug 69	London (CP)
	E	4273		Rein Aun	EST	18 Jul 68	Tartu
	C,N	3841		Barry King	Eng	20 May 70	Santa Barbara
	NJ	3112		Wayne Dubose		21 Jul 74	London (VP)

Dec.	W,E	8994		Tomás Dvorák	CZE	4 Jul 99	Prague
	C,N	8847		Daley Thompson	Eng	9 Aug 84	Los Angeles
	A	8663		Daley Thompson		28 Jul 86	Edinburgh
	WJ,EJ	8397		Torsten Voss	GER	7 Jul 82	Erfurt
	NJ	8082		Daley Thompson		31 Jul 77	Sittard
(with 1986 Javelin)							
	C,N	8811	#	Daley Thompson	Eng	28 Aug 86	Stuttgart
	WJ,EJ	8114	#	Michael Kohnle	GER	25 Aug 89	Varazdin
	NJ	7488	#	David Bigham		9 Aug 90	Plovdiv
4x100m	W	37.40		United States		8 Aug 92	Barcelona
		37.40		United States		21 Aug 93	Stuttgart
	E,N	37.73		UK National Team		29 Aug 99	Seville
	C	37.69		Canada		3 Aug 96	Atlanta
	A	37.95		United States		28 Aug 00	Gateshead
	WJ	39.00	A	United States		18 Jul 83	Colorado Springs
	EJ,NJ	39.05		UK National Team		22 Oct 00	Santiago
4x200m	W	1:18.68		Santa Monica T.C.	USA	17 Apr 94	Walnut
	E	1:21.10		Italy		29 Sep 83	Cagliari
	C	1:20.79		Jamaica		24 Apr 88	Walnut
	A,N	1:21.29		UK National Team		23 Jun 89	Birmingham
	NJ	1:25.40	i#	UK National Team		2 Mar 96	Liévin
		1:27.6		Borough of Enfield Harriers		13 Jun 82	London (He)
4x400m	W	2:54.20		United States		22 Jul 98	Uniondale
	E,N	2:56.60		UK National Team		3 Aug 96	Atlanta
	C	2:56.75		Jamaica		10 Aug 97	Athens
	A	2:59.85		UK National Team		19 Aug 96	Gateshead
	WJ	3:01.90		United States		20 Jul 86	Athens
	(EJ),NJ	3:03.80		UK National Team		12 Aug 90	Plovdiv
	EJ	3:04.58		East Germany		23 Aug 81	Utrecht
4x800m	WECAN	7:03.89		UK National Team	Eng	30 Aug 82	London (CP)
	NJ	7:26.2		BMC Junior Squad		2 Sep 95	Oxford
4x1500m	W,E	14:38.8		West Germany		16 Aug 77	Cologne
	C	14:40.4		New Zealand		22 Aug 73	Oslo
	A	15:04.7		Italy		5 Jun 92	Sheffield
	N	14:56.8	a#	BMC National Squad		23 Jun 79	Bourges
		15:04.6		UK National Team		5 May 76	Athens (NF)
	NJ	15:52.0		BMC Junior Squad		30 Apr 97	Watford
4x1Mile	W,E	15:49.08		Irish Republic		17 Aug 85	Dublin (B)
	C	15:59.57		New Zealand		1 Mar 83	Auckland
	A	16:21.1		BMC National Squad		10 Jul 93	Oxford
	N	16:17.4		Bristol A.C./Western Kentucky U		25 Apr 75	Des Moines
	NJ	16:56.8		BMC Junior Squad		10 Jul 93	Oxford

Track Walking

1500m	W,E	5:12.0		Algis Grigaliunas	LIT	12 May 90	Vilnius
	C	5:19.1		Dave Smith	AUS	7 Feb 83	Melbourne
	A,N	5:46.2	a	Roger Mills		29 Aug 75	London (CP)
	N	5:19.22	i#	Tim Berrett §		9 Feb 90	East Rutherford
1 Mile	W	5:33.53	i#	Tim Lewis	USA	5 Feb 88	New York
	W,E	5:36.9		Algis Grigaliunas	LIT	12 May 90	Vilnius
	C	5:54.6	i#	Marcel Jobin	CAN	16 Feb 80	Houston
	C,A,N	5:58.9	mx	Andy Penn	Eng	13 Aug 97	Rugby
	N	5:56.39	i#	Tim Berrett §		2 Feb 90	New York
	NJ	6:09.2		Phil Vesty		23 Jun 82	Leicester

Event	Cat.	Mark		Name	Nat.	Date	Venue
3000m	W,E	10:47.11		Giovanni DeBenedictis	ITA	19 May 90	S. G. Valdarno
	C	10:56.22		Andrew Jachno	AUS	7 Feb 91	Melbourne
	A	11:19.00	i#	Axel Noack	GER	23 Feb 90	Glasgow
		11:19.9		Tim Berrett	CAN	20 Apr 92	Tonbridge
	N	11:24.4		Mark Easton		10 May 89	Tonbridge
	WJ,EJ	11:13.2		Jozef Pribilinec	SVK	28 Mar 79	Banská Bystrica
	NJ	11:54.23		Tim Berrett §		23 Jun 84	London (CP)
5000m	W	18:05.49		Hatem Ghoula	TUN	1 May 97	Tunis
	E	18:07.08	i#	Mikhail Shchennikov	RUS	14 Feb 95	Moscow
		18:17.22		Robert Korzeniowski	POL	3 Jul 92	Reims
	C ·	18:47.56	i#	Tim Berrett	CAN	20 Feb 93	Winnipeg
		18:51.39		Nick A'Hern	AUS	21 Feb 98	Auckland (NS)
	A	18:56.27	i#	Axel Noack	GER	23 Feb 90	Glasgow
	A,N	19:35.0		Darrell Stone		16 May 89	Brighton
	WJ,EJ	19:19.3		Mikhail Shchennikov	RUS	9 Aug 86	Chemnitz
	NJ	20:16.40		Philip King		26 Jun 93	Lübeck
10000m	W,E	38:02.60		Jozef Pribilinec	SVK	30 Aug 85	Banská Bystrica
	C	38:06.6		Dave Smith	AUS	25 Sep 86	Sydney
	A	39:26.02		Guillaume Leblanc	CAN	29 Jun 90	Gateshead
	N	40:06.65		Ian McCombie		4 Jun 89	Jarrow
	WJ,EJ	38:46.4		Viktor Burayev	RUS	20 May 00	Moscow
	NJ	41:52.13		Darrell Stone		7 Aug 87	Birmingham
(Road)	W,E	37:11		Roman Rasskazov	RUS	28 May 00	Saransk
	NJ	41:47		Darrell Stone		26 Sep 87	Paris
1 Hour	W	15,577 m		Bernardo Segura	MEX	7 May 94	Fana
	E	15,447 m		Jozef Pribilinec	SVK	6 Sep 86	Hildesheim
	C	15,300 m		Dave Smith	AUS	6 Sep 86	Hildesheim
	A	14,383 m		Anatoliy Solomin	UKR	26 Aug 77	Edinburgh
	N	14,324 m	#	Ian McCombie		7 Jul 85	London (SP)
		14,158 m		Mark Easton		12 Sep 87	Woodford
	NJ	13,487 m		Darrell Stone		12 Sep 87	Woodford
20000m	W	1:17:25.6		Bernardo Segura	MEX	7 May 94	Fana
	E	1:18:35.2		Stefan Johansson	SWE	15 May 92	Fana
	C	1:20:12.3		Nick A'Hern	AUS	8 May 93	Fana
	A	1:24:07.6	#	Phil Vesty		1 Dec 84	Leicester
		1:24:22.0		José Marín	SPA	28 Jun 81	Brighton
	N	1:23:26.5		Ian McCombie		26 May 90	Fana
	WJ	1:22:16.0		Li Mingcai	CHN	3 Mar 90	Donetsk
	EJ	1:22:42		Andrey Perlov	RUS	6 Sep 80	Hefei
	NJ	1:31:34.4		Gordon Vale		28 Jun 81	Brighton
2 Hours	W,E	29,572 m		Maurizio Damilano	ITA	4 Oct 92	Cuneo
	C	28,800 m	#	Guillaume Leblanc	CAN	16 Jun 90	Sept Îles
		27,720 m		Craig Barratt	NZL	19 Jul 98	Auckland
	A,N	27,262 m	#	Chris Maddocks		31 Dec 89	Plymouth
	A	26,265 m		Jorge Llopart	SPA	28 Jun 81	Brighton
	N	26,037 m		Ron Wallwork		31 Jul 71	Blackburn
30000m	W,E	2:01:44.1		Maurizio Damilano	ITA	4 Oct 92	Cuneo
	C	2:04:55.7		Guillaume Leblanc	CAN	16 Jun 90	Sept Îles
	A,N	2:11:54	#	Chris Maddocks		31 Dec 89	Plymouth
	A	2:17:26.4		Jorge Llopart	SPA	28 Jun 81	Brighton
	N	2:19:18		Chris Maddocks		22 Sep 84	Birmingham
50000m	W,E	3:40:57.9		Thierry Toutain	FRA	29 Sep 96	Héricourt
	C	3:43:50.0		Simon Baker	AUS	9 Sep 90	Melbourne
	A	4:03:52		Gerhard Weidner	GER	1 Jun 75	Woodford
	N	4:05:44.6		Paul Blagg		26 May 90	Fana

Race Walking - Fastest Recorded Times

Event	Cat	Time	Athlete	Nat	Date	Venue
20km	W	1:17:25.6 t	Bernardo Segura	MEX	7 May 94	Fana
	E	1:17:46	Roman Rasskazov	RUS	19 May 00	Moscow
	C	1:19:22	Dave Smith	AUS	19 Jul 87	Hobart
	A	1:20:18	Francisco Fernández	SPA	23 Apr 00	Leamington
	N	1:22:03	Ian McCombie		23 Sep 88	Seoul
	WJ	1:19:38	Yu Guohui	CHN	10 Mar 96	Zhuhai
	EJ	1:21:14	Maris Putenis	LAT	21 Jul 00	Aizpute
	NJ	1:26:13	Tim Berrett §		25 Feb 84	Dartford
30km	W,E	2:01:44.1 t	Maurizio Damilano	ITA	4 Oct 92	Cuneo
	C	2:04:55.7 t	Guillaume Leblanc	CAN	16 Jun 90	Sept Îles
	A	2:07:47	Simon Baker	AUS	31 Jul 86	Edinburgh
	N	2:07:56	Ian McCombie		27 Apr 86	Edinburgh
	WJ,EJ	2:10:19.4 t	Ralf Kowalsky	GER	29 Mar 81	Berlin (E)
	NJ	2:30:46	Phil Vesty		31 Jul 82	London (VP)
50km	W,E	3:37:26	Valeriy Spitsyn	RUS	21 May 00	Moscow
	C	3:43:13	Simon Baker	AUS	28 May 89	L'Hospitalet
	A	3:47:31	Hartwig Gauder	GER	28 Sep 85	St. John's, IoM
	N	3:51:37	Chris Maddocks		28 Oct 90	Burrator
	WJ	4:00:04	Hao Huanquan	CHN	10 Apr 94	Beijing
	EJ	4:07:23	Aleksandr Volgin	RUS	27 Sep 86	Zhytomyr
	NJ	4:18:18	Gordon Vale		24 Oct 81	Lassing

RECORDS set in 2000

Event	Cat	Mark		Athlete	Nat	Date	Venue
300m	W	30.85	A	Michael Johnson	USA	24 Mar 00	Pretoria
600m	E	1:14.41		Andrea Longo	ITA	30 Aug 00	Roverto
800m	EJ	1:44.35	i#	Yuriy Borzakovskiy	RUS	30 Jan 00	Dortmund
	EJ	1:44.63		Yuriy Borzakovskiy	RUS	5 Jul 00	Lausanne
	EJ	1:44.33		Yuriy Borzakovskiy	RUS	25 Sep 00	Sydney
1000m	EJ	2:17.40		Yuriy Borzakovskiy	RUS	8 Jul 00	Nice
1500m	A	3:30.2		Hicham El Guerrouj	MAR	5 Aug 00	London (CP)
	C	3:28.12		Noah Ngeny	KEN	11 Aug 00	Zürich
1 Mile	A	3:45.96		Hicham El Guerrouj	MAR	5 Aug 00	London (CP)
3000m	E	7:26.62		Mohammed Mouthit	BEL	18 Aug 00	Monaco
5000m	A	13:06.23		Haile Gebrselassie	ETH	5 Aug 00	London (CP)
	E	12:49.71		Mohammed Mouthit	BEL	25 Aug 00	Brussels
H. Mar	W,C	59:06		Paul Tergat	KEN	26 Mar 00	Lisbon
	WJ	59:37		Faustin Baha	TAN	26 Mar 00	Lisbon
Mar	E,A	2:06:36		António Pinto	POR	16 Apr 00	London
3000mSc	WJ	8:03.74		Raymond Yator	KEN	18 Aug 00	Monaco
Discus	C	68.13		Frantz Kruger	RSA	23 Aug 00	Cottbus
	C	69.75	A	Frantz Kruger	RSA	15 Sep 00	Bloemfontein
Hammer	C	77.68	A	Stuart Rendell	AUS	18 Mar 00	Pietsburg
	C	77.92		Chris Harmse	RSA	31 Mar 00	Cape Town
	C	78.71	A	Chris Harmse	RSA	23 Sep 00	Pretoria
4x100m	A	37.95		United States		28 Aug 00	Gateshead
	EJ,NJ	39.14		UK National Team		22 Oct 00	Santiago
	EJ,NJ	39.05		UK National Team		22 Oct 00	Santiago

Track Walking

Event	Cat	Mark	Athlete	Nat	Date	Venue
10000m	WJ,EJ	38:46.4	Viktor Burayev	RUS	20 May 00	Moscow

Race Walking

Event	Cat	Mark	Athlete	Nat	Date	Venue
20 km	E	1:18:07	Roman Rasskazov	RUS	20 Feb 00	Adler
	A	1:20:18	Francisco Fernández	SPA	23 Apr 00	Leamington
	E	1:17:46	Roman Rasskazov	RUS	19 May 00	Moscow
	WJ,EJ	1:21:14	Maris Putenis	LAT	21 Jul 00	Aizpute
50 km	W,E	3:37:26	Valeriy Spitsyn	RUS	21 May 00	Moscow

BEST AUTHENTIC PERFORMANCES (WOMEN)

(as at 31st December 2000)

Event	Record	Performance		Athlete	Nation	Date	Venue
100m	W	10.49		Florence Griffith Joyner	USA	16 Jul 88	Indianapolis
	E	10.73		Christine Arron	FRA	19 Aug 98	Budapest
	C	10.74		Merlene Ottey	JAM	7 Sep 96	Milan
	A	10.78		Marion Jones	USA	5 Aug 00	London (CP)
	N	11.10		Kathy Smallwood/Cook		5 Sep 81	Rome
	WJ,EJ	10.88		Marlies Oelsner/Göhr	GER	1 Jul 77	Dresden
	NJ	11.27	A	Kathy Smallwood/Cook		9 Sep 79	Mexico City
200m	W	21.34		Florence Griffith Joyner	USA	29 Sep 88	Seoul
	E	21.71		Marita Koch	GER	10 Jun 79	Chemnitz
		21.71	#	Marita Koch	GER	21 Jul 84	Potsdam
		21.71		Heike Drechsler	GER	29 Jun 86	Jena
		21.71	#	Heike Drechsler	GER	29 Aug 86	Stuttgart
	C	21.64		Merlene Ottey	JAM	13 Sep 91	Brussels
	A	22.23		Merlene Ottey	JAM	9 Sep 94	London (CP)
	N	22.10		Kathy Cook		9 Aug 84	Los Angeles
	WJ,EJ	22.19		Natalya Bochina	RUS	30 Jul 80	Moscow
	NJ	22.70	A	Kathy Smallwood/Cook		12 Sep 79	Mexico City
300m	W,E	35.00	+	Marie-José Pérec	FRA	27 Aug 91	Tokyo
		34.1	+	Marita Koch	GER	6 Oct 85	Canberra
	C,A,N	35.46		Kathy Cook	Eng	18 Aug 84	London (CP)
	A	35.46		Chandra Cheeseborough	USA	18 Aug 84	London (CP)
	WJ,EJ	36.24	+	Grit Breuer	GER	29 Aug 90	Split
		35.4	+	Christina Brehmer/Lathan	GER	29 Jul 76	Montréal
	NJ	36.46		Linsey Macdonald		13 Jul 80	London (CP)
		36.2		Donna Murray/Hartley		7 Aug 74	London (CP)
400m	W,E	47.60		Marita Koch	GER	6 Oct 85	Canberra
	C	48.63		Cathy Freeman	AUS	29 Jul 96	Atlanta
	A	49.33		Tatána Kocembová	CZE	20 Aug 83	London (CP)
	N	49.43		Kathy Cook		6 Aug 84	Los Angeles
	WJ,EJ	49.42		Grit Breuer	GER	27 Aug 91	Tokyo
	NJ	51.16		Linsey Macdonald		15 Jun 80	London (CP)
600m	W	1:22.63		Ana Fidelia Quirot	CUB	25 Jul 97	Guadalajara
	E	1:23.5		Doina Melinte	ROM	27 Jul 86	Poiana Brasov
	C	1:25.37		Charmaine Howell	JAM	14 Sep 00	Sydney (OWT)
	A	1:25.90		Delisa Walton-Floyd	USA	28 Aug 88	London (CP)
	N	1:26.0		Kelly Holmes	Eng	13 Aug 95	Gothenburg
	WJ,EJ	1:25.2		Vera Nikolic	YUG	Jun 67	Belgrade
	NJ	1:27.33		Lorraine Baker		13 Jul 80	London (CP)
800m	W,E	1:53.28		Jarmila Kratochvílová	CZE	26 Jul 83	Munich
	C	1:55.29		Maria Lurdes Mutola	MOZ	24 Aug 97	Cologne
	A	1:57.14		Jarmila Kratochvílová	CZE	24 Jun 85	Belfast
	N	1:56.21		Kelly Holmes		9 Sep 95	Monaco
	WJ	1:57.18		Wang Yuan	CHN	8 Sep 93	Beijing
	EJ	1:57.45	#	Hildegard Ullrich	GER	31 Aug 78	Prague
		1:59.17		Birte Bruhns	GER	20 Jul 88	Berlin
	NJ	2:01.11		Lynne MacDougall		18 Aug 84	London (CP)
1000m	W,E	2:28.98		Svetlana Masterkova	RUS	23 Aug 96	Brussels
	C	2:29.66		Maria Lurdes Mutola	MOZ	23 Aug 96	Brussels
	A	2:32.08	i#	Maria Lurdes Mutola	MOZ	10 Feb 96	Birmingham
	A,N	2:32.55		Kelly Holmes		15 Jun 97	Leeds
	WJ,EJ	2:35.4	a	Irina Nikitina	RUS	5 Aug 79	Podolsk
		2:35.4		Kathrin Wühn	GER	12 Jul 84	Potsadam
	NJ	2:38.58		Jo White		9 Sep 77	London (CP)

Event	Record	Performance		Name	Nat	Date	Venue
1500m	W	3:50.46		Qu Yunxia	CHN	11 Sep 93	Beijing
	E	3:52.47		Tatyana Kazankina	RUS	13 Aug 80	Zürich
	C	3:57.41		Jackline Maranga	KEN	8 Aug 98	Monaco
	A,N	3:58.07		Kelly Holmes		29 Jun 97	Sheffield
	WJ	3:51.34		Lang Yinglai	CHN	18 Oct 97	Shanghai
	(EJ,)NJ	3:59.96		Zola Budd/Pieterse		30 Aug 85	Brussels
	EJ	4:03.45		Anita Weyermann	SWZ	3 Jul 96	Lausanne
1 Mile	W,E	4:12.56		Svetlana Masterkova	RUS	14 Aug 96	Zürich
	C,N,WJ,EJ,NJ	4:17.57		Zola Budd/Pieterse	Eng	21 Aug 85	Zürich
	A	4:19.59		Mary Slaney	USA	2 Aug 85	London (CP)
2000m	W,E,A	5:25.36		Sonia O'Sullivan	IRE	8 Jul 94	Edinburgh
	C,N	5:26.93		Yvonne Murray	Sco	8 Jul 94	Edinburgh
	WJ,EJ,NJ	5:33.15		Zola Budd/Pieterse		13 Jul 84	London (CP)
3000m	W	8:06.11		Wang Junxia	CHN	13 Sep 93	Beijing
	E,A	8:21.64		Sonia O'Sullivan	IRE	15 Jul 94	London (CP)
	C,N	8:27.40		Paula Radcliffe	Eng	11 Aug 99	Zürich
	WJ,EJ,NJ	8:28.83		Zola Budd/Pieterse		7 Sep 85	Rome
2 Miles	W	9:11.97	mx	Regina Jacobs	USA	12 Aug 99	Los Gatos
	W,E	9:19.56		Sonia O'Sullivan	IRE	27 Jun 98	Cork
	C	9:27.18		Kathy Butler	CAN	27 Jun 98	Cork
	A	9:28.6	e	Paula Radcliffe		7 Aug 99	London (CP)
	A,N	9:32.07		Paula Radcliffe		23 May 99	Loughborough
	N	9:27.5	e	Paula Radcliffe		22 Aug 97	Brussels
	NJ	9:29.6		Zola Budd/Peiterse		26 Aug 85	London (CP)
		10:35.10		Jane Potter		23 May 99	Loughborough
5000m	W	14:28.09		Jiang Bo	CHN	23 Oct 97	Shanghai
	E	14:31.48		Gabriela Szabo	ROM	1 Sep 98	Berlin
	C	14:39.83		Leah Malot	KEN	1 Sep 00	Berlin
	A	14:41.23		Ayelech Worku	ETH	5 Aug 00	London (CP)
	N	14:43.54		Paula Radcliffe		7 Aug 99	London (CP)
	WJ	14:39.96	#	Yin Lili	CHN	23 Oct 97	Shanghai
		14:45.90		Jiang Bo	CHN	24 Oct 95	Nanjing
	(EJ,)NJ	14:48.07		Zola Budd/Pieterse		26 Aug 85	London (CP)
	EJ	14:56.22		Annemari Sandell	FIN	8 Jul 96	Stockholm
10000m	W	29:31.78		Wang Junxia	CHN	8 Sep 93	Beijing
	E	30:13.74		Ingrid Kristiansen	NOR	5 Jul 86	Oslo
	C,N	30:26.97		Paula Radcliffe	Eng	30 Sep 00	Sydney
	A	30:52.51		Elana Meyer	RSA	10 Sep 94	London (CP)
	WJ	30:39.41		Lan Lixin	CHN	19 Oct 97	Shanghai
	EJ	31:40.42		Annemari Sandell	FIN	27 Jul 96	Atlanta
	NJ	34:31.41	#	Tanya Povey		3 Jun 98	Amherst
1 Hour	W,C	18,393 m	#	Tegla Loroupe	KEN	3 Sep 00	Borgholzhausen
	W,C	18,340 m		Tegla Loroupe	KEN	7 Aug 98	Borgholzhausen
	E	18,084 m		Silvana Cruciata	ITA	4 May 81	Rome
	A,N	16,460 m	i#	Bronwen Cardy-Wise		8 Mar 92	Birmingham
	N	16,495 m	#	Michaela McCallum		2 Apr 00	Asti
	A,N	16,364 m		Alison Fletcher		3 Sep 97	Bromley
	NJ	14,580 m		Paula Simpson		20 Oct 93	Bebington
20000m	W,C	1:05:26.6		Tegla Loroupe	KEN	3 Sep 00	Borgholzhausen
	W	1:06:48.8		Izumi Maki	JAP	19 Sep 93	Amagasaki
	E	1:06:55.5#		Rosa Mota	POR	14 May 83	Lisbon
	A,N	1:15:46		Caroline Hunter-Rowe	Eng	6 Mar 94	Barry
25000m	W,E	1:29:29.2		Karolina Szabó	HUN	22 Apr 88	Budapest
	C,A,N	1:35:16		Caroline Hunter-Rowe	Eng	6 Mar 94	Barry
30000m	W,E	1:47:05.6		Karolina Szabó	HUN	22 Apr 88	Budapest
	C,A,N	1:55:03		Caroline Hunter-Rowe	Eng	6 Mar 94	Barry

Event	Record	Performance	Athlete	Nat	Date	Venue
Half Marathon	W,E	66:40 #	Ingrid Kristiansen	NOR	5 Apr 87	Sandnes
	W	66:43	Masako Chiba	JAP	19 Jan 97	Tokyo
	E,A,N	67:07	Paula Radcliffe		22 Oct 00	South Shields
	C	66:44	Elana Meyer	RSA	15 Jan 99	Tokyo
	WJ	69:05	Delillah Asiago	KEN	5 May 91	Exeter
	NJ	77:52	Kathy Williams		28 Mar 82	Barry
Marathon	W,C	2:20:43	Tegla Loroupe	KEN	26 Sep 99	Berlin
	E,A	2:21:06	Ingrid Kristiansen	NOR	21 Apr 85	London
	N	2:25:56	Véronique Marot		23 Apr 89	London
	WJ	2:27:30	Ai Dongmei	CHN	4 Oct 97	Beijing
	NJ	2:50:09	Siobhan Quenby		16 Oct 83	Milan
2000m SC	W,E	6:11.84	Marina Pluzhnikova	RUS	25 Jul 94	St. Petersburg
	C, WJ	6:25.77	Melissa Rollison	AUS	1 May 00	Sydney
	A,N	6:36.02	Jayne Spark		8 Aug 00	Stretford
	EJ	6:31.31	Yelena Sayko	UKR	13 Jul 97	Kiyev
	NJ	7:27.99	Lois Joslin		2 May 98	Bath
3000m SC	W,E	9:40.20	Christina Iloc-Casandra	ROM	30 Aug 00	Reims
	C,A,N	10:08.11	Tara Krzywicki	Eng	5 Sep 00	Stretford
	WJ	10:10.73	Melissa Rollison	AUS	25 Feb 00	Sydney
	EJ	10:20.32 #	Tamara Cojocar	ROM	2 Aug 98	Bucharest
	EJ	10:22.92	Ida Nilsson	SWE	2 Jun 00	Högby
	NJ	12:11.1	Lindsey Oliver		22 Aug 93	Horsham
100m H	W,E	12.21	Yordanka Donkova	BUL	20 Aug 88	Stara Zagora
	C	12.44	Glory Alozie	NGR	28 Aug 99	Seville
	A	12.51	Ginka Zagorcheva	BUL	12 Sep 86	London (CP)
	N	12.80	Angie Thorp		31 Jul 96	Atlanta
	WJ	12.76 #	Liu Jing	CHN	18 Oct 97	Shanghai
		12.84	Aliuska López	CUB	16 Jul 87	Zagreb
	EJ	12.88	Yelena Ovcharova	UKR	25 Jun 95	Villeneuve d'Ascq
	NJ	13.25	Diane Allahgreen		21 Jul 94	Lisbon
400m H	W	52.61	Kim Batten	USA	11 Aug 95	Gothenburg
	E,C,N	52.74	Sally Gunnell	Eng	19 Aug 93	Stuttgart
	A	53.69	Sandra Farmer-Patrick	USA	10 Sep 93	London (CP)
	WJ	54.93 #	Li Rui	CHN	22 Oct 97	Shanghai
		55.20	Leslie Maxie	USA	9 Jun 84	San Jose
		55.20 A	Jana Piiman	AUS	18 Mar 00	Pietersburg
	EJ	55.26	Ionela Tîrlea	ROM	12 Jul 95	Nice
	NJ	57.27	Vicki Jamison		28 Jul 96	Bedford
High Jump	W,E	2.09	Stefka Kostadinova	BUL	30 Aug 87	Rome
	C	2.04	Hestrie Cloete	RSA	4 Aug 99	Monaco
	A	2.03	Ulrike Meyfarth	GER	21 Aug 83	London (CP)
		2.03	Tamara Bykova	RUS	21 Aug 83	London (CP)
	N	1.95	Diana Elliott/Davies		26 Jun 82	Oslo
		1.95 i#	Debbie Marti		23 Feb 97	Birmingham
	WJ,EJ	2.01 #	Olga Turchak	KZK/UKR	7 Jul 86	Moscow
		2.01	Heike Balck	GER	18 Jun 89	Chemnitz
	NJ	1.91	Lea Haggett		2 Jun 91	Hania
		1.91	Susan Jones		31 Aug 97	Catania
Pole Vault	W	4.70 #	Stacy Dragila	USA	11 Jun 00	Santa Barbara
		4.63	Stacy Dragila	USA	23 Jul 00	Sacramento
	E	4.56 i#	Nicole Humbert	GER	25 Feb 99	Stockholm
		4.56	Anzhela Balakhonova	UKR	8 Aug 00	Linz
	C	4.60	Emma George	AUS	20 Feb 99	Sydney

Pole Vault	A	4.41	i#	Elmarie Gerryts	RSA	20 Feb 00	Birmingham
		4.35		Svetlana Feofanova	RUS	15 Jul 00	Gateshead
	N	4.35		Janine Whitlock		5 Jun 00	Prague
	WJ,EJ	4.45	i#	Yelena Isinbayeva	RUS	4 Feb 00	Volgograd
		4.42	#	Yvonne Buschbaum	GER	27 Jun 99	Rheinau-Freistatt
		4.40		Yelena Isinbayeva	RUS	24 Jul 00	Tula
	NJ	3.90		Ellie Spain		6 May 00	Eton
Long Jump	W,E	7.52		Galina Chistyakova	RUS	11 Jun 88	St. Petersburg
	C,N,NJ	6.90		Beverly Kinch	Eng	14 Aug 83	Helsinki
	A	7.14		Galina Chistyakova	RUS	24 Jun 89	Birmingham
	WJ,EJ	7.14	#	Heike Daute/Drechsler	GER	4 Jun 83	Bratislava
Triple Jump	W,E	15.50		Inessa Kravets	UKR	10 Aug 95	Gothenburg
	C,N	15.16	i#	Ashia Hansen	Eng	28 Feb 98	Valencia
		15.15		Ashia Hansen	Eng	13 Sep 97	Fukuoka
	A	14.98		Tatyana Lebedyeva	RUS	16 Jul 00	Gateshead
	WJ,EJ	14.62		Tereza Marinova	BUL	25 Aug 96	Sydney
	NJ	13.05		Michelle Griffith		16 Jun 90	London (CP)
Shot	W,E	22.63		Natalya Lisovskaya	RUS	7 Jun 87	Moscow
	C	19.74		Gael Mulhall/Martin	AUS	14 Jul 84	Berkeley
	A	21.95		Natalya Lisovskaya	RUS	29 Jul 88	Edinburgh
	N	19.36		Judy Oakes		14 Aug 88	Gateshead
	WJ,EJ	20.54		Astrid Kumbernuss	GER	1 Jul 89	Orimattila
	NJ	17.10		Myrtle Augee		16 Jun 84	London (CP)
Discus	W,E	76.80		Gabriele Reinsch	GER	9 Jul 88	Neubrandenburg
	C	68.72		Daniela Costian	AUS	22 Jan 94	Auckland
	A	73.04		Ilke Wyludda	GER	5 Aug 89	Gateshead
	N	67.48		Meg Ritchie		26 Apr 81	Walnut
	WJ,EJ	74.40		Ilke Wyludda	GER	13 Sep 88	Berlin
	NJ	54.78		Lynda Whiteley/Wright		4 Oct 82	Brisbane
Hammer	W,E	76.07		Mihaela Melinte	ROM	29 Aug 99	Rüdingen
	C	67.95		Debbie Sosimenko	AUS	29 Sep 00	Sydney
	A	70.20	dq?	Mihaela Melinte	ROM	15 Jul 00	Gateshead
		70.20		Olga Kuzenkova	RUS	15 Jul 00	Gateshead
	N	67.44		Lorraine Shaw		15 Jul 00	Gateshead
	WJ,EJ	71.16		Kamila Skolimowska	POL	29 Sep 00	Sydney
	NJ	57.97		Rachael Beverley		25 Jul 98	Birmingham
Javelin	W,E	69.48		Trine Hattestad	NOR	28 Jul 00	Oslo
	C	66.80		Louise Currey	AUS	5 Aug 00	Gold Coast (RB)
	A	63.23		Ana Mirela Termure	ROM	15 Jul 00	Gateshead
	N	59.50		Karen Martin		14 Jul 99	Cosford
	WJ	61.99		Wang Yaning	CHN	14 Oct 99	Huizhou
	EJ	61.79		Nikolett Szabó	HUN	23 May 99	Schwechat
	NJ	54.61		Kelly Morgan		4 Sep 99	Exeter
Hept.	W	7291		Jackie Joyner-Kersee	USA	24 Sep 88	Seoul
	E	7007		Larisa Nikitina	RUS	11 Jun 89	Bryansk
	C,N	6831		Denise Lewis	Eng	30 Jul 00	Talence
	A	6419		Birgit Clarius	GER	21 Jul 91	Sheffield
	WJ,EJ	6465		Sybille Thiele	GER	28 Aug 83	Schwechat
	NJ	5833		Joanne Mulliner		11 Aug 85	Lons-le-Saunier
(with 1999 Javelin)							
	W,E	6861		Eunice Barber	FRA	22 Aug 99	Seville
	A	5719		Barbora Potáková	CZE	21 May 00	Hexham
	WJ,EJ	6056		Carolina Klüft	SWE	21 Oct 00	Santiago
	NJ	5283		Chloe Cozens		23 May 99	Alhama de Murcia

Event	Record	Time	Name	Nat	Date	Venue
4x100m	W,E	41.37	East Germany		6 Oct 85	Canberra
	C	41.92	Bahamas		29 Aug 99	Seville
	A	41.87	East Germany		5 Aug 89	Gateshead
	N	42.43	UK National Team		1 Aug 80	Moscow
	WJ,EJ	43.33 #	East Germany		20 Jul 88	Berlin
	WJ	43.38	United States		11 Jul 99	Tampa
	EJ	43.48	East Germany		31 Jul 88	Sudbury
	NJ	44.16	UK National Team		12 Aug 90	Plovdiv
4x200m	W	1:27.46	United States		29 Apr 00	Philadelphia
	E	1:28.15	East Germany		9 Aug 80	Jena
	C,N	1:31.57	UK National Team	Eng	20 Aug 77	London (CP)
	A	1:31.49	Russia		5 Jun 93	Portsmouth
	NJ	1:38.34 i#	UK National Team		2 Mar 96	Liévin
		1:42.2	London Olympiades AC		19 Aug 72	Bracknell
4x400m	W,E	3:15.17	U.S.S.R.		1 Oct 88	Seoul
	C	3:21.21 #	Canada		11 Aug 84	Los Angeles
		3:21.30	Jamaica		10 Aug 97	Athens
	A	3:20.79	Czechoslovakia		21 Aug 83	London (CP)
	N	3:22.01	UK National Team		1 Sep 91	Tokyo
	WJ,EJ	3:28.39	East Germany		31 Jul 88	Sudbury
	NJ	3:33.82	UK National Team		22 Oct 00	Santiago
4x800m	W,E	7:50.17	U.S.S.R.		5 Aug 84	Moscow
	C	8:20.73	UK National Team	Eng	5 Jun 93	Portsmouth
	A	7:57.08	Russia		5 Jun 93	Portsmouth
	N	8:19.9	UK National Team		5 Jun 92	Sheffield
	NJ	8:39.6	BMC Junior Squad		17 Jul 96	Watford
4x1500m	W,C,A	17:09.75	Australia		25 Jun 00	London (BP)
	E	17:19.09	Irish Republic		25 Jun 00	London (BP)
	N	17:41.0	BMC National Squad	Eng	30 Apr 97	Watford
	NJ	18:38.0	BMC Junior Squad		30 Apr 97	Watford
4x1Mile	W	18:39.58	University of Oregon		3 May 85	Eugene
	ECAN	19:17.3	BMC National Squad	Eng	10 Jul 93	Oxford
	NJ	20:16.2	BMC Junior Squad		11 Jun 97	Watford

Track Walking

Event	Record	Time	Name	Nat	Date	Venue
1500m	W,C	5:50.41	Kerry Saxby-Junna	AUS	20 Jan 91	Sydney
	E	5:53.0	Sada Eidikyte	LIT	12 May 90	Vilnius
	A	6:04.5 i#	Beate Anders/Gummelt	GER	4 Mar 90	Glasgow
	A,NJ	6:58.5	Carol Tyson		5 Sep 76	Gateshead
	N	6:32.16	Niobe Menendez		13 Aug 00	Tullamore
1 Mile	W,E	6:16.72 i#	Sada Eidikyte	LIT	24 Feb 90	Kaunas
		6:19.31	Ileana Salvador	ITA	15 Jun 91	Siderno
	C	6:35.47 i#	Ann Peel	CAN	15 Feb 87	Fairfax
		6:47.9	Sue Cook	AUS	14 Mar 81	Canberra
	A	6:30.7 i#	Beate Anders/Gummelt	GER	4 Mar 90	Glasgow
	N	7:08.9 mx#	Catherine Charnock		22 Aug 00	Rugby
	A,N	7:14.3	Carol Tyson		17 Sep 77	London (PH)
	NJ	7:31.6	Kate Horwill		22 Aug 93	Solihull
3000m	W,E	11:40.33 i#	Claudia Iovan	ROM	30 Jan 99	Bucharest
		11:48.24	Ileana Salvador	ITA	29 Aug 93	Padua
	C	11:51.26	Kerry Saxby-Junna	AUS	7 Feb 91	Melbourne
	A	12:32.37	Yelena Nikolayeva	RUS	19 Jun 88	Portsmouth
	N	12:49.16	Betty Sworowski		28 Jul 90	Wrexham
	WJ,EJ	12:21.7 i#	Susana Feitór	POR	19 Feb 94	Braga
		12:24.47	Claudia Iovan	ROM	24 Jul 97	Ljubljana
	NJ	13:03.4	Vicky Lupton/White		18 May 91	Sheffield

5000m	W,C	20:03.0	#	Kerry Saxby-Junna	AUS	11	Feb	96	Sydney
		20:13.26		Kerry Saxby-Junna	AUS	25	Feb	96	Hobart
	E	20:07.52	#	Beate Anders/Gummelt	GER	23	Jun	90	Rostock
		20:21.69		Annarita Sidoti	ITA	1	Jul	95	Cesenatico
	A	21:08.65		Yelena Nikolayeva	RUS	19	Jun	88	Portsmouth
	N	21:52.4	#	Vicky Lupton/White		9	Aug	95	Sheffield (?)
		22:01.53		Lisa Kehler		26	Jul	98	Birmingham
	WJ,EJ	20:31.4		Irina Stankina	RUS	10	Feb	96	Adler
	NJ	22:36.81		Vicky Lupton/White		15	Jun	91	Espoo
(Road)	W,E	20:05		Olga Polyakova	RUS	28	May	00	Saransk
	WJ,EJ	20:24		Lyudmila Yefimkina	RUS	28	May	00	Saransk
	N	21:36		Vicky Lupton/White		18	Jul	92	Sheffield
10000m	W,E	41:56.23		Nadezhda Ryashkina	RUS	24	Jul	90	Seattle
	C	41:57.22		Kerry Saxby-Junna	AUS	24	Jul	90	Seattle
	A,N	45:09.57		Lisa Kehler		13	Aug	00	Birmingham
	WJ	42:49.7		Gao Hongmiao	CHN	15	Mar	92	Jinan
	EJ	43:35.2		Lyudmila Yefimkina	RUS	20	May	00	Moscow
	NJ	47:04		Vicky Lupton		30	Mar	91	Sheffield (W)
1 Hour	W	13,194 m		Victoria Herazo	USA	5	Dec	92	Santa Monica
	E	12,913 m		Valentina Sachuk	UKR	24	Jun	99	Belaya Tserkov
	C	12,805 m		Wendy Muldoon	AUS	25	Jun	94	Melbourne
	A,N,NJ	11,590 m		Lisa Langford/Kehler		13	Sep	86	Woodford
20000m	W,E	1:30:48.3	#	Rossella Giordano	ITA	4	Aug	00	Almada
	W	1:34:56.7		Maria del Rosario Sánchez	MEX	16	Jul	00	Xalapa
	E	1:35:23.7		Kristina Saltanovic	LIT	3	Aug	00	Kaunas
	C	1:39:23.0		Jenny Jones	AUS	19	Nov	94	East Coast Bays
	A,N	1:56:59.7		Cath Reader		21	Oct	95	Loughborough
	WJ	1:37:33.9		Gao Kelian	CHN	18	Sep	99	Xian
	EJ	1:39:20.5		Vera Santos	POR	4	Aug	00	Almada
2 Hours	W,C	22,747 m		Carolyn Vanstan	AUS	20	Jun	92	Melbourne
	E	22,239 m		Jana Zárubová	CZE	12	Oct	85	Prague
	A,N	20,502 m		Cath Reader		21	Oct	95	Loughborough
30000m	W,E	2:56:36.0		Cinzia Chianda	ITA	18	Oct	86	Limbiate
50000m	W,E	4:55:19.4		Svetlana Bychenkova	RUS	27	Jun	98	St. Petersburg
	C,N	5:26:59		Sandra Brown	Eng	27	Oct	90	Étréchy

Road Walking - Fastest Recorded Times

10km	W,E	41:04		Yelena Nikolayeva	RUS	20	Apr	96	Sochi
	C	41:30		Kerry Saxby-Junna	AUS	27	Aug	88	Canberra
	A	44:04		Sari Essayah	FIN	23	Jul	91	Sheffield
	N	45:03		Lisa Kehler		19	Sep	98	Kuala Lumpur
	WJ,EJ	41:55		Irina Stankina	RUS	11	Feb	95	Adler
	NJ	47:04	t	Vicky Lupton/White		30	Mar	91	Sheffield (W)
20km	W,E	1:25:18		Tatyana Gudkova	RUS	19	May	00	Moscow
	C	1:28:56		Jane Saville	AUS	6	May	00	Vallensbæk
	A	1:28:40		Liu Hongyu	CHN	23	Apr	00	Leamington
	N	1:33:57		Lisa Kehler		17	Jun	00	Eisenhüttenstadt
	WJ,EJ	1:27:35		Natalya Fedoskina	RUS	2	May	99	Mézidon-Canon
	NJ	1:52:03		Vicky Lupton/White		13	Oct	91	Sheffield
50km	W,E	4:41:57		Kora Boufflért	FRA	17	Sep	95	Ay-Champagne
	C,A,N	4:50:51		Sandra Brown	Eng	13	Jul	91	Basildon
	WJ,EJ	5:17:45	t	Maria Baranova	RUS	15	Oct	00	St. Petersburg

RECORDS set in 2000

100m	A	10.78	Marion Jones	USA	5	Aug	00	London (CP)
600m	C	1:25.37	Charmaine Howell	Jam	14	Sep	00	Sydney (OWT)
5000m	A	14:41.23	Avelech Worku	ETH	5	Aug	00	London (CP)
	C	14:39.83	Leah Malot	KEN	1	Sep	00	Berlin
10000m	C,N	30:26.97	Paula Radcliffe	Eng	30	Sep	00	Sydney

Event	Records	Mark		Athlete	Nat	Date	Venue
20000m	W,C	1:05:26.6		Tegla Loroupe	KEN	3 Sep 00	Borgholzhausen
1 Hour	N	16495m	#	Michaela McCallum		2 Apr 00	Asti
H.Mar	E,A,N	67:07		Paula Radcliffe		22 Oct 00	South Shields
2000m SC	C,WJ	6:25.77		Melissa Rollison	AUS	1 May 00	Sydney
	A,N	6:36.49		Tara Krzywicki		21 May 00	Loughborough
	A,N	6:36.02		Jayne Spark		8 Aug 00	Stretford
3000m SC	C,WJ	10:10.73		Melissa Rollison	AUS	25 Feb 00	Sydney
	EJ	10:22.92		Ida Nilsson	SWE	2 Jun 00	Högby
	W,E	9:43.64		Christina Iloc-Casandra	ROM	7 Aug 00	Bucharest
	W,E	9:40.20		Christina Iloc-Casandra	ROM	30 Aug 00	Reims
	C,A,N	10:08.11		Tara Krzywicki	Eng	5 Sep 00	Stretford
400m H	WJ	55.20	A	Jana Pittman	AUS	18 Mar 00	Pietersburg
Pole	WJ,EJ	4.45	i#	Yelena Isinbayeva	RUS	4 Feb 00	Volgograd
Vault	W	4.60	Ai#	Stacy Dragila	USA	19 Feb 00	Pocatello
	N	4.31	i#	Janine Whitlock		20 Feb 00	Birmingham
	A	4.41	i#	Elmaine Gerryts	RSA	20 Feb 00	Birmingham
	NJ	3.80		Ellie Spain		6 May 00	Eton
	NJ	3.90		Ellie Spain		6 May 00	Eton
	W	4.60		Stacy Dragila	USA	13 May 00	Modesto
	W	4.62		Stacy Dragila	USA	26 May 00	Phoenix
	N	4.35		Janine Whitlock		5 Jun 00	Prague
	W	4.70	#	Stacy Dragila	USA	11 Jun 00	Santa Barbara
	A	4.35		Svetlana Feofanova	RUS	15 Jul 00	Gateshead
	W	4.63		Stacy Dragila	USA	23 Jul 00	Sacramento
	WJ,EJ	4.40		Yelena Isinbayeva	RUS	24 Jul 00	Tula
	E	4.56		Anzhela Balakhonova	UKR	8 Aug 00	Linz
Triple J	A,	14.98		Tatyana Lebedyeva	RUS	16 Jul 00	Gateshead
Hammer	WJ,EJ	69.13		Kamila Skolimoska	POL	10 Jun 00	Warsaw
	A	70.20	dq?	Mihaela Melinte	ROM	15 Jul 00	Gateshead
	A	70.20		Olga Kurenkova	RUS	15 Jul 00	Gateshead
	C,N	67.44		Lorraine Shaw		15 Jul 00	Gateshead
	WJ,EJ	70.62		Kamila Skolimoska	POL	13 Aug 00	Rüdlingen
	C	67.95		Debbie Sosimenko	AUS	29 Sep 00	Sydney
	WJ,EJ	71.16		Kamila Skolimoska	POL	29 Sep 00	Sydney
Javelin	W,E	68.22		Trine Hattestad	NOR	30 Jun 00	Rome
	A	63.23		Ana Mirela Termure	ROM	15 Jul 00	Gateshead
	W,E	69.48		Trine Hattestad	NOR	28 Jul 00	Oslo
	C	66.80		Louise Currey	AUS	5 Aug 00	Gold Coast (RB)
Hept.	C,N	6831		Denise Lewis	Eng	30 Jul 00	Talence
4x200m	W	1:27.46		United States		29 Apr 00	Philadelphia
4x400m	NJ	3:33.82		UK National Team		22 Oct 00	Santiago
4x1500m	W,C,A	17:09.75		Australia		25 Jun 00	London (BP)
	E	17:19.09		Irish Republic		25 Jun 00	London (BP)
Track Walking							
1500m	N	6:32.16		Niobe Menendez		13 Aug 00	Tullamore
1 Mile	N	7:08.9	mx#	Catherine Charnock		22 Aug 00	Rugby
10000m	EJ	43:35.2		Lyudmila Yefimkina	RUS	20 May 00	Moscow
	A,N	45:09.57		Lisa Kehler		13 Aug 00	Birmingham
20000m	W	1:34:56.7		Maria del Rosario Sánchez	MEX	16 Jul 00	Xalapa
	E	1:35:23.7		Kristina Saltanovic	LIT	3 Aug 00	Kaunas
	W,E	1:30:48.3	#	Rosella Giordano	ITA	4 Aug 00	Almada
	EJ	1:39:20.5		Vera Santos	POR	4 Aug 00	Almada
Race Walking							
20 km	N	1:37:31		Sara Cattermole		23 Jan 00	Perth
	N	1:36:40		Sara Cattermole		4 Mar 00	Perth
	A	1:28:40		Liu Hongyu	CHN	23 Apr 00	Leamington
	N	1:35:35		Lisa Kehler		23 Apr 00	Leamington
	C	1:29:36		Kerry Saxby-Junna	AUS	30 Apr 00	Naumburg
	C	1:28:56		Jane Saville	AUS	6 May 00	Vallensbæk
	W,E	1:25:18		Tatyana Gudkova	RUS	19 May 00	Moscow
	N	1:33:57		Lisa Kehler		17 Jun 00	Eisenhüttenstadt
50 km	WJ,EJ	5:17:45	t	Maria Baranova	RUS	15 Oct 00	St. Petersburg

NATIONAL RECORDS OF THE UNITED KINGDOM (MEN)

(as at 31st December 2000)

These are the best authentic performances for the four home countries of the U.K.
E = England S = Scotland W = Wales NI = Northern Ireland

Event		Performance		Name	Date	Venue
100m	E	9.87		Linford Christie	15 Aug 93	Stuttgart, GER
	S	10.11		Allan Wells	24 Jul 80	Moscow, RUS
	W	10.12		Christian Malcolm	29 Jul 98	Annecy, FRA
	NI	10.46		Mark Forsythe	17 Jun 89	Tel Aviv, ISR
200m	E	19.87	A#	John Regis	31 Jul 94	Sestriere, ITA
		19.94		John Regis	20 Aug 93	Stuttgart, GER
	W	20.19		Christian Malcolm	27 Sep 00	Sydney, AUS
		20.19		Christian Malcolm	28 Sep 00	Sydney, AUS
	S	20.21		Allan Wells	28 Jul 80	Moscow, RUS
	NI	20.81		Paul McBurney	24 Aug 94	Victoria, CAN
300m	S	31.56		Dougie Walker	19 Jul 98	Gateshead
	E	31.67		John Regis	17 Jul 92	Gateshead
	W	32.06		Jamie Baulch	31 May 97	Cardiff
	NI	33.77		Simon Baird	24 Jun 85	Belfast
400m	W	44.36		Iwan Thomas	13 Jul 97	Birmingham
	E	44.37		Roger Black	3 Jul 96	Lausanne, SWZ
		44.37		Mark Richardson	9 Jul 98	Oslo, NOR
		44.37		Mark Richardson	8 Aug 98	Monaco, MON
	S	44.93		David Jenkins	21 Jun 75	Eugene, USA
	NI	45.85		Paul McBurney	13 Jul 97	Birmingham
600m	E	1:14.95		Steve Heard	14 Jul 91	London (Ha)
	S	1:15.4		Tom McKean	21 Jul 91	Grangemouth
	W	1:17.8	i	Bob Adams	20 Dec 69	Cosford
		1:18.02		Glen Grant	2 Aug 78	Edmonton, CAN
	NI	1:18.3	i	Joe Chivers	14 Dec 74	Cosford
		1:20.1		Kenneth Thompson	24 May 80	Belfast
800m	E	1:41.73	"	Sebastian Coe	10 Jun 81	Florence, ITA
	S	1:43.88		Tom McKean	28 Jul 89	London (CP)
	W	1:45.44		Neil Horsfield	28 Jul 90	Wrexham
	NI	1:45.96		James McIlroy	5 Aug 00	London (CP)
		1:45.32		while representing IRE	16 Jul 98	Nice
1000m	E	2:12.18		Sebastian Coe	11 Jul 81	Oslo, NOR
	S	2:16.82		Graham Williamson	17 Jul 84	Edinburgh
	W	2:17.36		Neil Horsfield	9 Aug 91	Gateshead
	NI	2:19.05		Mark Kirk	5 Aug 87	Oslo, NOR
		2:15.57		James McIlroy (IRE perIAAF)	5 Sep 99	Rieti, ITA
1500m	E	3:29.67		Steve Cram	16 Jul 85	Nice, FRA
	S	3:33.83		John Robson	4 Sep 79	Brussels, BEL
	NI	3:34.76		Gary Lough	9 Sep 95	Monaco, MON
	W	3:35.08		Neil Horsfield	10 Aug 90	Brussels, BEL
1 Mile	E	3:46.32		Steve Cram	27 Jul 85	Oslo, NOR
	S	3:50.64		Graham Williamson	13 Jul 82	Cork, IRE
	W	3:54.39		Neil Horsfield	8 Jul 86	Cork, IRE
	NI	3:55.0		Jim McGuinness	11 Jul 77	Dublin (B), IRE
2000m	E	4:51.39		Steve Cram	4 Aug 85	Budapest, HUN
	S	4:58.38		Graham Williamson	29 Aug 83	London (CP)
	NI	5:02.61		Steve Martin	19 Jun 84	Belfast
	W	5:05.32		Tony Simmons	4 Jul 75	London (CP)

Event		Performance		Athlete	Date	Venue
3000m	E	7:32.79		Dave Moorcroft	17 Jul 82	London (CP)
	S	7:45.81		John Robson	13 Jul 84	London (CP)
	W	7:46.40		Ian Hamer	20 Jan 90	Auckland, NZL
	NI	7:49.1		Paul Lawther	27 Jun 78	Oslo, NOR
2 Miles	E	8:13.51		Steve Ovett	15 Sep 78	London (CP)
	S	8:19.37		Nat Muir	27 Jun 80	London (CP)
	W	8:20.28		David James	27 Jun 80	London (CP)
	NI	8:30.6		Paul Lawther	28 May 77	Belfast
5000m	E	13:00.41		Dave Moorcroft	7 Jul 82	Oslo, NOR
	W	13:09.80		Ian Hamer	9 Jun 92	Rome, ITA
	S	13:17.9		Nat Muir	15 Jul 80	Oslo, NOR
	NI	13:27.63		Dermot Donnelly	1 Aug 98	Hechtel, BEL
10000m	E	27:18.14	#	Jon Brown	28 Aug 98	Brussels, BEL
		27:23.06		Eamonn Martin	2 Jul 88	Oslo, NOR
	W	27:39.14		Steve Jones	9 Jul 83	Oslo, NOR
	S	27:43.03		Ian Stewart	9 Sep 77	London (CP)
	NI	28:38.56		Dermot Donnelly	29 Jun 97	Sheffield
20000m	E	57:28.7		Carl Thackery	31 Mar 90	La Flèche, FRA
	S	59:24.0		Jim Alder	9 Nov 68	Leicester
	W	69:37.0		Mick McGeoch	4 Mar 90	Barry
	NI	77:16.0		Ian Anderson	5 Mar 00	Barry
1 Hour	E	20,855 m		Carl Thackery	31 Mar 90	La Flèche, FRA
	S	20,201 m		Jim Alder	9 Nov 68	Leicester
	W	18,898 m		Mike Rowland	7 Aug 73	Stockholm, SWE
	NI	18,354 m		Dave Smyth	19 Sep 65	Bristol (?)
25000m	E	1:15:22.6		Ron Hill	21 Jul 65	Bolton
	S	1:15:34.3		Jim Alder	5 Sep 70	London (CP)
	W	1:27:01.0	e	Mick McGeoch	4 Mar 90	Barry
	NI	1:37:18.0	e	Ian Anderson	5 Mar 00	Barry
30000m	S	1:31:30.4		Jim Alder	5 Sep 70	London (CP)
	E	1:31:56.4		Tim Johnston	5 Sep 70	London (CP)
	W	1:33:49.0		Bernie Plain	1 Dec 73	Bristol
	NI	1:57:30.0		Ian Anderson	5 Mar 00	Barry
Half Marathon	E	60:09	#	Paul Evans	15 Jan 95	Marrakesh, MAR
		61:03		Nick Rose	15 Sep 85	Philadelphia, USA
	W	60:59		Steve Jones	8 Jun 86	South Shields
	S	61:34	#	Paul Evans	15 Mar 92	Lisbon, POR
		62:28		Allister Hutton	21 Jun 87	South Shields
	NI	62:16		Jim Haughey	20 Sep 87	Philadelphia, USA
Marathon	W	2:07:13		Steve Jones	20 Oct 85	Chicago, USA
	E	2:08:33		Charlie Spedding	21 Apr 85	London
	S	2:09:16		Allister Hutton	21 Apr 85	London
	NI	2:13:06		Greg Hannon	13 May 79	Coventry
2000m SC	E	5:19.86		Mark Rowland	28 Aug 88	London (CP)
	S	5:21.77		Tom Hanlon	11 Jun 92	Caserta, ITA
	W	5:23.6		Roger Hackney	10 Jun 82	Birmingham
	NI	5:31.09		Peter McColgan	5 Aug 86	Gateshead
3000m SC	E	8:07.96		Mark Rowland	30 Sep 88	Seoul, SKO
	S	8:12.58		Tom Hanlon	3 Aug 91	Monaco, MON
	W	8:18.91		Roger Hackney	30 Jul 88	Hechtel, BEL
	NI	8:27.93		Peter McColgan	25 Jun 91	Hengelo, HOL

Event		Mark		Athlete	Date	Venue
110m H	W	12.91		Colin Jackson	20 Aug 93	Stuttgart, GER
	E	13.00		Tony Jarrett	20 Aug 93	Stuttgart, GER
	S	13.66		Ross Baillie	20 Feb 99	Sydney, AUS
	NI	14.19		C.J. Kirkpatrick	16 Jun 73	Edinburgh
200m H	W	22.63		Colin Jackson	1 Jun 91	Cardiff
	E	22.79		John Regis	1 Jun 91	Cardiff
	S	23.76		Angus McKenzie	22 Aug 81	Edinburgh
	NI	24.81		Terry Price	31 Aug 92	Belfast
400m H	E	47.82		Kriss Akabusi	6 Aug 92	Barcelona, SPA
	W	49.16		Paul Gray	18 Aug 98	Budapest, HUN
	NI	49.60		Phil Beattie	28 Jul 86	Edinburgh
	S	50.43		Charles Robertson-Adams	17 Aug 97	London (CP)
High Jump	E	2.38	i	Steve Smith	4 Feb 94	Wuppertal, GER
		2.37		Steve Smith	20 Sep 92	Seoul, SKO
		2.37		Steve Smith	22 Aug 93	Stuttgart, GER
	S	2.31		Geoff Parsons	26 Aug 94	Victoria, CAN
	W	2.24		John Hill	23 Aug 85	Cottbus, GER
	NI	2.20		Floyd Manderson	14 Jul 85	London (CP)
		2.20		Floyd Manderson	21 Jun 86	London (CP)
		2.20		Floyd Manderson	16 Aug 86	Leiden, HOL
Pole Vault	E	5.80		Nick Buckfield	27 May 98	Hania, GRE
	W	5.60		Neil Winter	19 Aug 95	Enfield
	NI	5.25		Mike Bull	22 Sep 73	London (CP)
	S	5.21		Graham Eggleton	10 Jul 82	Grangemouth
Long Jump	W	8.23		Lynn Davies	30 Jun 68	Berne, SWZ
	E	8.15		Stewart Faulkner	16 Jul 90	Belfast
	NI	8.14		Mark Forsythe	7 Jul 91	Rhede, GER
	S	7.88		Darren Ritchie	20 Aug 00	Bedford
Triple Jump	E	18.29		Jonathan Edwards	7 Aug 95	Gothenburg, SWE
	S	16.17		John Mackenzie	17 Sep 94	Bedford
	W	15.99		Steven Shalders	20 Oct 00	Santiago, CHI
	NI	15.78		Michael McDonald	31 Jul 94	Corby
Shot	E	21.68		Geoff Capes	18 May 80	Cwmbrân
	W	20.45		Shaun Pickering	17 Aug 97	London (CP)
	S	18.93		Paul Buxton	13 May 77	Los Angeles(Ww), USA
	NI	16.35		Mike Atkinson	18 Jul 81	Dublin (S), IRE
		16.35		John Reynolds	16 Aug 86	Leiden, HOL
Discus	E	66.64		Perriss Wilkins	6 Jun 98	Birmingham (Un)
	W	60.43		Lee Newman	12 Aug 98	Enfield
	S	59.84	#	Colin Sutherland ¶	10 Jun 78	San Jose, USA
		58.58		Darrin Morris	22 Jun 91	Enfield
	NI	51.76		John Moreland	1 Jul 95	Antrim
Hammer	NI	77.54		Martin Girvan	12 May 84	Wolverhampton
	E	77.30		David Smith	13 Jul 85	London (CP)
	S	75.40		Chris Black	23 Jul 83	London (CP)
	W	68.64		Shaun Pickering	7 Apr 84	Stanford, USA
Javelin	E	91.46		Steve Backley	25 Jan 92	Auckland(NS), NZL
	W	81.70		Nigel Bevan	28 Jun 92	Birmingham
	NI	70.34	#	Damien Crawford	20 Jul 91	Hayes
		67.60		Dean Smahon	9 Jul 94	King's Lynn
	S	69.20		Roddy James	28 Apr 89	Des Moines, USA

Event		Performance		Name	Date	Venue
Dec.	E	8847		Daley Thompson	9 Aug 84	Los Angeles, USA
	S	7885	#h	Brad McStravick	6 May 84	Birmingham
		7856	#	Brad McStravick	28 May 84	Cwmbrân
	NI	7874		Colin Boreham	23 May 82	Götzis, AUT
	W	7308	h	Clive Longe	29 Jun 69	Kassel, GER
		7268		Paul Edwards ¶	14 Aug 83	Bonn, GER
(with 1986 Javelin)						
	E	8811	#	Daley Thompson	28 Aug 86	Stuttgart, GER
	S	7739		Jamie Quarry	30 May 99	Arles, FRA
	W	7071	#	Paul Jones	4 Jun 00	Arles, FRA
	NI	6839	#	Matt Douglas	25 Aug 96	Worcester
4x100m	E	37.73		J. Gardener, D.Campbell (UK)		
				M.Devonish, D.Chambers	29 Aug 99	Seville, SPA
	W	38.73		K. Williams, D. Turner,		
				C. Malcolm, J. Henthorn	21 Sep 98	Kuala Lumpur, MAL
	S	39.24		D. Jenkins, A. Wells,		
				C. Sharp, A. McMaster	12 Aug 78	Edmonton, CAN
	NI	40.71		J. McAdorey, I. Craig,		
				P. Brizzell, M. Allen	22 Jun 96	Belfast
4x400m	E	2:57.53		R. Black, D. Redmond, (UK)		
				J. Regis, K. Akabusi	1 Sep 91	Tokyo, JAP
	W	3.01.86		P. Gray, J. Baulch,		
				D. Turner, I. Thomas	21 Sep 98	Kuala Lumpur, MAL
	S	3:04.68		M. Davidson, T. McKean,		
				D. Strang, B. Whittle	3 Feb 90	Auckland, NZL
	NI	3:07.27		B. Forbes, M. Douglas,		
				E. King, P. McBurney	21 Sep 98	Kuala Lumpur, MAL
Track Walking						
3000m	E	11:24.4		Mark Easton	10 May 89	Tonbridge
	W	11:45.77		Steve Johnson	20 Jun 87	Cwmbrân
	S	11:53.3	#	Martin Bell	9 Aug 95	Birmingham
		11:59.47		Martin Bell	25 May 98	Bedford
	NI	13:15.0		David Smyth	5 Sep 70	Plymouth
5000m	E	19:22.29	i	Martin Rush	8 Feb 92	Birmingham
		19:35.0		Darrell Stone	16 May 89	Brighton
	W	20:08.04	i	Steve Barry	5 Mar 83	Budapest, HUN
		20:22.0		Steve Barry	20 Mar 82	London (WL)
	S	20:13.0		Martin Bell	2 May 92	Enfield
	NI	23:50.0		Jimmy Todd	28 Aug 68	Ballyclare
10000m	E	40:06.65		Ian McCombie	4 Jun 89	Jarrow
	W	41:13.62		Steve Barry	19 Jun 82	London (CP)
	S	41:13.65		Martin Bell	22 Jul 95	Cardiff
	NI	47:37.6		David Smyth	26 Apr 70	Bournemouth
1 Hour	E	14,324 m	#	Ian McCombie	7 Jul 85	London (SP)
		14,158 m		Mark Easton	12 Sep 87	Woodford
	W	13,987 m		Steve Barry	28 Jun 81	Brighton
	S	13,393 m		Bill Sutherland	27 Sep 69	London (He)
	NI	12,690 m	#	David Smyth	26 Apr 70	Bournemouth
		12,646 m		David Smyth	23 Sep 67	London (PH)
20000m	E	1:23:26.5		Ian McCombie	26 May 90	Fana, NOR
	W	1:26:22.0		Steve Barry	28 Jun 81	Brighton
	S	1:38:53.6		Alan Buchanan	6 Jul 75	Brighton
2 Hours	E	27,262 m	#	Chris Maddocks	31 Dec 89	Plymouth
		26,037 m		Ron Wallwork	31 Jul 71	Blackburn

Road Walking

10km	E	40:17		Chris Maddocks	30 Apr 89	Burrator
	W	40:35		Steve Barry	14 May 83	Southport
	S	41:28		Martin Bell	24 Apr 99	Sheffield
	NI	44:49	#	David Smyth	20 Jun 70	Clevedon
		51:53		Arthur Agnew	6 Aug 80	Helsinki, FIN
		51:53		G. Smyth	6 Aug 80	Helsinki, FIN
20km	E	1:22:03		Ian McCombie	23 Sep 88	Seoul, SKO
	W	1:22:51		Steve Barry	26 Feb 83	Douglas, I of M
	S	1:25:42		Martin Bell	9 May 92	Lancaster
	NI	1:39:01		David Smyth	Jul 67	Cardiff
30km	E	2:07:56		Ian McCombie	27 Apr 86	Edinburgh
	W	2:10:16		Steve Barry	7 Oct 82	Brisbane, AUS
	S	2:22:21		Martin Bell	8 May 94	Cardiff
	NI	2:41:15		David Smyth	26 Apr 69	Winterbourne
50km	E	3:51:37		Chris Maddocks	28 Oct 90	Burrator
	W	4:11:59		Bob Dobson	22 Oct 81	Lassing, AUT
	S	4:13:18		Graham White	27 Jun 98	Stockport
	NI	4:45:48		David Smyth	3 May 69	Bristol

NATIONAL RECORDS OF THE UNITED KINGDOM (WOMEN)

(as at 31st December 2000)

100m	E	11.10		Kathy Smallwood/Cook	5 Sep 81	Rome, ITA
	W	11.39		Sallyanne Short	12 Jul 92	Cwmbrân
	S	11.40		Helen Golden/Hogarth	20 Jul 74	London (CP)
	NI	11.91	#	Joan Atkinson	1 Sep 61	Sofia, BUL
		11.93		Vicki Jamison	2 Aug 97	Belfast
200m	E	22.10		Kathy Cook	9 Aug 84	Los Angeles, USA
	W	22.80		Michelle Scutt	12 Jun 82	Antrim
	S	22.98		Sandra Whittaker	8 Aug 84	Los Angeles, USA
	NI	23.62		Linda McCurry	8 Aug 78	Edmonton, CAN
300m	E	35.46		Kathy Cook	18 Aug 84	London (CP)
	W	36.01		Michelle Probert/Scutt	13 Jul 80	London (CP)
	S	36.46		Linsey Macdonald	13 Jul 80	London (CP)
	NI	38.20		Linda McCurry	2 Aug 78	Edmonton, CAN
400m	E	49.43		Kathy Cook	6 Aug 84	Los Angeles, USA
	W	50.63		Michelle Scutt	31 May 82	Cwmbrân
	S	50.71		Allison Curbishley	18 Sep 98	Kuala Lumpur, MAL
	NI	52.54		Stephanie Llewellyn	9 Jul 95	Cwmbrân
		52.4		Stephanie Llewellyn	1 Jul 95	London (He)
600m	E	1:26.0		Kelly Holmes	13 Aug 95	Gothenburg, SWE
	W	1:26.5		Kirsty McDermott/Wade	21 Aug 85	Zürich, SWZ
	S	1:27.4	i	Linsey Macdonald	12 Dec 81	Cosford
		1:29.88		Anne Clarkson/Purvis	25 Sep 82	Brisbane, AUS
	NI	1:29.46		Jo Latimer	19 May 93	Birmingham
800m	E	1:56.21		Kelly Holmes	9 Sep 95	Monaco, MON
	W	1:57.42		Kirsty McDermott/Wade	24 Jun 85	Belfast
	S	2:00.15		Rosemary Stirling/Wright	3 Sep 72	Munich, GER
	NI	2:01.83		Amanda Crowe	18 Sep 98	Kuala Lumpur, MAL
1000m	E	2:32.55		Kelly Holmes	15 Jun 97	Leeds
	W	2:33.70		Kirsty McDermott/Wade	9 Aug 85	Gateshead
	S	2:37.05		Christine Whittingham	27 Jun 86	Gateshead
	NI	2:48.59		Jane Ewing	26 Jun 90	Antrim

Event		Performance		Athlete	Date	Venue
1500m	E	3:58.07		Kelly Holmes	29 Jun 97	Sheffield
	W	4:00.73		Kirsty Wade	26 Jul 87	Gateshead
	S	4:01.20		Yvonne Murray	4 Jul 87	Oslo, NOR
	NI	4:10.68		Amanda Crowe	21 Sep 98	Kuala Lumpur, MAL
1 Mile	E	4:17.57		Zola Budd	21 Aug 85	Zürich, SWZ
	W	4:19.41		Kirsty McDermott/Wade	27 Jul 85	Oslo, NOR
	S	4:22.64		Yvonne Murray	22 Jul 94	Oslo, NOR
	NI	4:32.99		Amanda Crowe	30 Aug 98	Glasgow (S)
2000m	S	5:26.93		Yvonne Murray	8 Jul 94	Edinburgh
	E	5:30.19		Zola Budd	11 Jul 86	London (CP)
	W	5:45.81	i	Kirsty Wade	13 Mar 87	Cosford
		5:50.17		Susan Tooby/Wightman	13 Jul 84	London (CP)
	NI	5:57.24		Ursula McKee/McGloin	25 Jun 90	Antrim
3000m	E	8:27.40		Paula Radcliffe	11 Aug 99	Zürich, SWZ
	S	8:29.02		Yvonne Murray	25 Sep 88	Seoul, SKO
	W	8:47.59		Hayley Tullett	15 Jul 00	Gateshead
	NI	9:16.25		Ursula McKee/McGloin	7 Jun 90	Helsinki, FIN
2 Miles	E	9:27.5	e	Paula Radcliffe	22 Aug 97	Brussels, BEL
		9:32.07		Paula Radcliffe	23 May 99	Loughborough
	S	9:36.85	i	Yvonne Murray	15 Mar 87	Cosford
		9:51.38		Hayley Haining	23 May 99	Loughborough
	W	9:49.73		Hayley Tullett	23 May 99	Loughborough
5000m	E	14:43.54		Paula Radcliffe	7 Aug 99	London (CP)
	S	14:56.94		Yvonne Murray	7 Jul 95	London (CP)
	W	15:13.22		Angela Tooby/Tooby-Smith	5 Aug 87	Oslo, NOR
	NI	16:50.22	#	Teresa Duffy	30 May 99	Bedford
		16:54.47		Ann Terek	23 Jul 95	Cardiff
10000m	E	30:26.97		Paula Radcliffe	30 Sep 00	Sydney, AUS
	S	30:57.07		Liz McColgan	25 Jun 91	Hengelo, HOL
	W	31:55.30		Angela Tooby/Tooby-Smith	4 Sep 87	Rome, ITA
	NI	36:19.98	#	Teresa Kidd	25 Aug 85	Dublin (S), IRE
1 Hour	E	16,495 m	#	Michaela McCallum	2 Apr 00	Asti
		16,364 m		Alison Fletcher	3 Sep 97	Bromley
	W	16,460 m	i#	Bronwen Cardy-Wise	8 Mar 92	Birmingham
		14,400 m		Ann Franklin	5 Mar 89	Barry
	S	12,800 m		Leslie Watson	12 Mar 83	London (He)
20000m	E	1:15:46		Carolyn Hunter-Rowe	6 Mar 94	Barry
	W	1:23:56		Ann Franklin	9 Mar 86	Barry
25000m	E	1:35:16	e	Carolyn Hunter-Rowe	6 Mar 94	Barry
	W	1:44:58	e	Ann Franklin	9 Mar 86	Barry
	S	1:54:55		Leslie Watson	12 Mar 83	London (He)
30000m	E	1:55:03		Carolyn Hunter-Rowe	6 Mar 94	Barry
	W	2:05:59		Ann Franklin	9 Mar 86	Barry
	S	2:16:44		Leslie Watson	12 Mar 83	London (He)
Half Marathon	E	1:07:07		Paula Radcliffe	22 Oct 00	South Shields
	S	1:07:11		Liz McColgan	26 Jan 92	Tokyo, JAP
	W	1:09:56		Susan Tooby/Wightman	24 Jul 88	South Shields
	NI	1:15:57	#	Moira O'Boyle/O'Neill	23 Mar 86	Cavan, IRE
		1:16:23		Moira O'Neill	24 Sep 88	Londonderry
Marathon	E	2:25:56		Véronique Marot	23 Apr 89	London
	S	2:26:52		Liz McColgan	13 Apr 97	London
	W	2:31:33		Susan Tooby/Wightman	23 Sep 88	Seoul, SKO
	NI	2:37:06		Moira O'Neill	31 Oct 88	Dublin, IRE

Event		Mark		Athlete	Date	Venue
2000mSC	E	6:36:02		Jayne Spark	8 Aug 00	Stretford
	W	7:34.66		Claire Martin	2 May 98	Bath
	S	7:43.55		Samantha Marshall	6 Sep 00	Grangemouth
3000mSC	E	10:08.11		Tara Krzywicki	5 Sep 00	Stretford
100m H	E	12.80		Angie Thorp	31 Jul 96	Atlanta, USA
	W	12.91		Kay Morley-Brown	2 Feb 90	Auckland, NZL
	NI	13.29		Mary Peters	2 Sep 72	Munich, GER
	S	13.35		Pat Rollo	30 Jul 83	London (CP)
400m H	E	52.74		Sally Gunnell	19 Aug 93	Stuttgart, GER
	S	55.24		Sinead Dudgeon	24 Jul 99	Birmingham
	NI	55.91		Elaine McLaughlin	26 Sep 88	Seoul, SKO
	W	56.43		Alyson Layzell	16 Jun 96	Birmingham
High Jump	E	1.95		Diana Elliott/Davies	26 Jun 82	Oslo, NOR
		1.95	i	Debbie Marti	23 Feb 97	Birmingham
	NI	1.92		Janet Boyle	29 Sep 88	Seoul, SKO
	S	1.91		Jayne Barnetson	7 Jul 89	Edinburgh
	W	1.85	i	Julie Crane	13 Feb 00	Cardiff
		1.84		Sarah Rowe	22 Aug 81	Utrecht, HOL
		1.84		Sarah Rowe	31 May 82	Cwmbrân
Pole Vault	E	4.35		Janine Whitlock	5 Jun 00	Prague, CZE
	W	4.15		Rhian Clarke	7 Apr 00	Austin, USA
	S	3.95	A&	Alison Jessee	25 Jun 99	El Paso, USA
		3.95	A&	Alison Jessee	11 Jul 99	Albuquerque, USA
		3.60		Alison Jessee	4 Aug 98	Cardiff
		3.60		Alison Jessee	21 Apr 00	Tucson, USA
		3.60		Alison Jessee	8 Jul 00	Glasgow
		3.60		Alison Jessee	12 Aug 00	Birmingham
	NI	3.00		Zoe Brown	15 Jul 00	Blackpool
Long Jump	E	6.90		Bev Kinch	14 Aug 83	Helsinki, FIN
	W	6.52		Gillian Regan	28 Aug 82	Swansea
	S	6.43	#	Moira Walls/Maguire	18 Sep 70	Bucharest, ROM
		6.43		Myra Nimmo	27 May 73	Edinburgh
	NI	6.11		Thelma Hopkins	29 Sep 56	Budapest, HUN
		6.11		Michelle Rea	11 Aug 90	Maia, POR
Triple Jump	E	15.16	i	Ashia Hansen	28 Feb 98	Valencia, SPA
		15.15		Ashia Hansen	13 Sep 97	Fukuoka, JAP
	S	12.89		Karen Hambrook/Skeggs	17 May 92	London (CP)
	W	12.14		Jayne Ludlow	21 May 94	Istanbul, TUR
	NI	11.93		Sharon Oakes	13 Aug 00	Edinburgh
Shot	E	19.36		Judy Oakes	14 Aug 88	Gateshead
	S	18.99		Meg Ritchie	7 May 83	Tucson, USA
	W	19.06	i	Venissa Head	7 Apr 84	St. Athan
		18.93		Venissa Head	13 May 84	Haverfordwest
	NI	16.40	i	Mary Peters	28 Feb 70	Bucharest, ROM
		16.31		Mary Peters	1 Jun 66	Belfast (PP)
Discus	S	67.48		Meg Ritchie	26 Apr 81	Walnut, USA
	W	64.68		Venissa Head	18 Jul 83	Athens, GRE
	E	60.82		Shelley Drew	25 Jul 98	Birmingham
	NI	60.72		Jackie McKernan	18 Jul 93	Buffalo, USA
Hammer	E	67.44		Lorraine Shaw	15 Jul 00	Gateshead
	W	56.60		Sarah Moore	12 Jul 97	Birmingham
	S	54.03		Mhairi Walters	27 May 00	Nicosia, CYP
	NI	48.90		Julie Kirkpatrick	15 Jun 96	Dublin (S), IRE
Javelin	E	59.50		Karen Martin	14 Jul 99	Cosford
	S	57.19		Lorna Jackson	9 Jul 00	Peterborough
	NI	47.72		Alison Moffitt	21 Aug 99	Belfast
	W	46.89		Caroline White	19 Jun 99	Colwyn Bay

Event		Mark		Athlete	Date	Venue
Hept.	E	6831		Denise Lewis	30 Jul 00	Talence, FRA
	S	5803		Jayne Barnetson	20 Aug 89	Kiyev, UKR
	W	5642		Sarah Rowe	23 Aug 81	Utrecht, HOL
	NI	5065	h	Catherine Scott	13 Sep 87	Tullamore, IRE
		4564		Wendy Phillips	18 Jul 82	Birmingham
(with 1999 Javelin)						
	S	5257		Chloe Cozens	24 Sep 00	Watford
	W	5186		Rebecca Jones	4 Jun 00	Arles, FRA
4x100m	E	42.43		H. Oakes, K. Cook, (UK) B. Callender, S. Lannaman	1 Aug 80	Moscow, RUS
	S	45.37		J. Booth, K. Hogg, J. Neilson, S. Whittaker	8 Jun 86	Lloret de Mar, SPA
		45.2		A. MacRitchie, S. Pringle, (ESH) H. Hogarth, E. Sutherland	27 Jun 70	London (CP)
	W	45.37		H. Miles, S. Lewis, S. Short, C. Smart	2 Aug 86	Edinburgh
	NI	46.36		K. Graham, H. Gourlay, J. Robinson, R. Gaylor	31 Aug 85	Tel Aviv, ISR
4x400m	E	3:22.01		L. Hanson, P. Smith, (UK) S. Gunnell, L. Staines	1 Sep 91	Tokyo, JAP
	S	3:32.92		S. Whittaker, A. Purvis, A. Baxter, L. Macdonald	9 Oct 82	Brisbane, AUS
	W	3:35.60		C. Smart, K. Wade, D. Fryar, M. Scutt	4 Jul 82	Dublin (S), IRE
	NI	3:40.12		Z. Arnold, V. Jamison, J. Latimer, S. Llewellyn	22 Jun 96	Belfast
Track Walking						
3000m	E	12:49.16		Betty Sworowski	28 Jul 90	Wrexham
	S	13:16.23		Verity Snook	27 May 96	Bedford
	W	14:28.2		Karen Dunster	18 May 91	Portsmouth
5000m	E	21:52.4	#	Vicky Lupton/White	9 Aug 95	Sheffield (?)
		22:01.53		Lisa Kehler	26 Jul 98	Birmingham
	S	23:22.52		Verity Snook	19 Jun 94	Horsham
	W	24:32.92		Karen Nipper	21 Jul 84	Lyngby, DEN
10000m	E	45:09.57		Lisa Kehler	13 Aug 00	Birmingham
	S	47:10.07		Verity Larby/Snook	19 Jun 93	Horsham
	W	50:25.0	mx	Lisa Simpson	1 Apr 87	Hornchurch
		51:00.0		Karen Nipper	21 Feb 81	Leicester
1 Hour	E	11,590 m		Lisa Langford/Kehler	13 Sep 86	Woodford
20000m	E	1:56:59.7		Cath Reader	21 Oct 95	Loughborough
2 Hours	E	20,502 m		Cath Reader	21 Oct 95	Loughborough
50000m	E	5:26:59		Sandra Brown	28 Oct 99	Étréchy, FRA
Road Walking						
5km	E	21:36		Vicky Lupton/White	18 Jul 92	Sheffield
	S	22:45		Verity Snook	25 Aug 94	Victoria, CAN
	W	23:35		Lisa Simpson	31 Oct 87	Cardiff
10km	E	45:03		Lisa Kehler	19 Sep 98	Kuala Lumpur, MAL
	S	46:06		Verity Snook	25 Aug 94	Victoria, CAN
	W	49:33		Lisa Simpson	14 Mar 87	Ham
20km	E	1:33:57		Lisa Kehler	17 Jun 00	Eisenhüttenstadt, GER
	S	1:36:40		Sara Cattermole	4 Mar 00	Perth, AUS
50km	E	4:50:51		Sandra Brown	13 Jul 91	Basildon
	S	5:53.41		Kath Crilley	2 May 93	Burrator
	NI	7:04:10		A. Telford	20 May 72	Isle of Man

UNITED KINGDOM INDOOR RECORDS
(as at 31st March 2001)

MEN

Event	Mark	Name	Date	Venue
50m	5.61 +	Jason Gardener	16 Feb 00	Madrid, SPA
60m	6.46	Jason Gardener	7 Mar 99	Maebashi, JAP
200m	20.25	Linford Christie	19 Feb 95	Liévin, FRA
300m	32.90	Ade Mafe	31 Jan 92	Karlsruhe, GER
400m	45.39	Jamie Baulch	9 Feb 97	Birmingham
800m	1:44.91	Sebastian Coe	12 Mar 83	Cosford
1000m	2:17.86	Matthew Yates	22 Feb 92	Birmingham
1500m	3:34.20	Peter Elliott	27 Feb 90	Seville, SPA
1 Mile	3:52.02	Peter Elliott	9 Feb 90	East Rutherford, USA
2000m	4:57.09	John Mayock	25 Feb 01	Liévin, FRA
3000m	7:43.31	John Mayock	23 Feb 97	Birmingham
5000m	13:21.27	Nick Rose	12 Feb 82	New York, USA
50m Hurdles	6.40	Colin Jackson	5 Feb 99	Budapest, HUN
60m Hurdles	7.30	Colin Jackson	6 Mar 94	Sindelfingen, GER
High Jump	2.38	Steve Smith	4 Feb 94	Wuppertal, GER
Pole Vault	5.61	Nick Buckfield	3 Feb 96	Birmingham
Long Jump	8.05	Barrington Williams	11 Feb 89	Cosford
	8.05 #	Stewart Faulkner	27 Feb 90	Seville, SPA
Triple Jump	17.64	Jonathan Edwards	15 Feb 98	Birmingham
Shot	20.98	Geoff Capes	16 Jan 76	Los Angeles, USA
	20.98 #	Geoff Capes	14 Feb 76	Winnipeg, CAN
Heptathlon	5978	Alex Kruger	12 Mar 95	Barcelona, SPA
		(7.16, 7.23, 14.79, 2.16, 8.36, 4.90, 2:48.66)		
5000m Walk	19:22.29	Martin Rush	8 Feb 92	Birmingham
4 x 200m Relay	1:22.11	UK National Team	3 Mar 91	Glasgow
		(Linford Christie, Darren Braithwaite, Ade Mafe, John Regis)		
4 x 400m Relay	3:03.20	UK National Team	7 Mar 99	Maebashi, JAP
		(Allyn Condon, Solomon Wariso, Adrian Patrick, Jamie Baulch)		

WOMEN

Event	Mark	Name	Date	Venue
50m	6.21	Wendy Hoyte	22 Feb 81	Grenoble, FRA
60m	7.13	Bev Kinch	23 Feb 86	Madrid, SPA
200m	22.83	Katharine Merry	14 Feb 99	Birmingham
300m	37.46 A	Sharon Colyear/Danville	14 Mar 81	Pocatello, USA
400m	50.53	Katharine Merry	18 Feb 01	Birmingham
800m	2:01.12	Jane Colebrook/Finch	13 Mar 77	San Sebastián, SPA
1000m	2:38.95	Kirsty Wade	1 Feb 87	Stuttgart, GER
1500m	4:06.75	Hayley Tullett	19 Mar 01	Glasgow
1 Mile	4:23.86	Kirsty Wade	5 Feb 88	New York, USA
2000m	5:40.86	Yvonne Murray	20 Feb 93	Birmingham
3000m	8:34.80	Liz McColgan	4 Mar 89	Budapest, HUN
5000m	15:03.17	Liz McColgan	22 Feb 92	Birmingham
50m Hurdles	7.03	Yvette Wray/Luker	21 Feb 81	Grenoble, FRA
60m Hurdles	7.99	Diane Allahgreen	26 Feb 00	Ghent, BEL
High Jump	1.95	Debbie Marti	23 Feb 97	Birmingham
Pole Vault	4.31	Janine Whitlock	2 Feb 00	Birmingham
Long Jump	6.70	Sue Hearnshaw/Telfer	3 Mar 84	Gothenburg, SWE (r3)
	6.70	Sue Hearnshaw/Telfer	3 Mar 84	Gothenburg, SWE (r6)
	6.70	Jo Wise	9 Mar 97	Paris (B), FRA
Triple Jump	15.16	Ashia Hansen	28 Feb 98	Valencia, SPA
Shot	19.06	Venissa Head	7 Apr 84	St. Athan
Pentathlon	4392	Julie Hollman	28 Jan 01	Prague, CZE
		(8.78, 1.81, 12.98, 6.13, 2:19.57)		
3000m Walk	13:12.01	Julie Drake	12 Mar 93	Toronto, CAN
4 x 200m Relay	1:33.96	UK National Team	23 Feb 90	Glasgow
		(Paula Thomas, Jenni Stoute, Linda Staines, Sally Gunnell)		
4 x 400m Relay	3:32.25	UK National Team	9 Mar 97	Paris (B), FRA
		(Phylis Smith, Sally Gunnell, Michelle Thomas, Donna Fraser)		

UK ALL TIME LISTS - MEN

as at 31 December 2000

100 METRES

	9.87	Linford Christie ¶	15 Aug 93
	9.91	Christie	23 Aug 94
	9.92	Christie	25 Aug 91
	9.96	Christie	1 Aug 92
	9.97	Christie	24 Sep 88
	9.97	Christie	15 Aug 93
	9.97 A	Christie	23 Sep 95
	9.97	Dwain Chambers	22 Aug 99
	9.98	Christie	23 Aug 94
	9.98	Jason Gardener	2 Jul 99
	10.04	Darren Campbell	19 Aug 98
	10.09	Jason Livingston ¶	13 Jun 92
	10.10	Mark Lewis-Francis	5 Aug 00
	10.11	Allan Wells	24 Jul 80
	10.12	Darren Braithwaite	15 Jul 95
	10.12	Christian Malcolm	29 Jul 98
10	10.13	Marlon Devonish	17 Sep 98
	10.15	Michael Rosswess	15 Sep 91
	10.15	John Regis	29 May 93
	10.17	Ian Mackie	25 Aug 96
	10.20	Cameron Sharp	24 Aug 83
	10.20	Elliot Bunney	14 Jun 86
	10.21 A	Ainsley Bennett	8 Sep 79
	10.21	Jamie Henderson	6 Aug 87
	10.21	Allyn Condon	14 Aug 99
	10.22	Mike McFarlane	20 Jun 86
20	10.23	Marcus Adam	26 Jul 91
	10.23	Jason John	15 Jul 94
	10.23	Terry Williams	22 Aug 94
	10.26	Daley Thompson	27 Aug 86
	10.26	Ernest Obeng	1 Aug 87
	10.28	Julian Golding	22 Jul 97
	10.28	Jon Barbour	17 Jun 00
	10.29	Peter Radford (10.31?)	13 Sep 58
	10.29	Colin Jackson	28 Jul 90
	10.30	Clarence Callender	26 Jul 91
30	10.30 A	Doug Bignall	6 Jul 00
	10.31	Doug Walker ¶	11 Jun 97
	10.31	Chris Lambert	21 Aug 99
	10.31	Owusu Dako	16 Apr 00
	10.32	Buster Watson	1 Jul 83
	10.32	Donovan Reid	4 Aug 84
	10.32	Lincoln Asquith	11 Aug 86
	10.32	Lenny Paul	29 May 93
	10.32	Toby Box	28 Jun 95
	10.32	Daniel Money	28 Aug 97
40	10.32	Josephus Thomas ¶	25 Jul 98
	10.33	Brian Green	15 Jul 72
	10.33	Solomon Wariso	19 Jun 94
	10.34	Drew McMaster	9 Jul 83
	10.34	Barrington Williams	5 Aug 88
	10.34	Kevin Williams	11 Jun 97
	10.35 A	Barrie Kelly	13 Oct 68
	10.35	Brian Taylor	29 May 93
	10.35	Owusu Dako	8 Jul 96
	10.35	Mark Richardson	2 May 98
50	10.35 A	Akinola Lashore	10 Apr 99
	10.35	Mark Findlay ¶	19 Jun 99

wind assisted

	9.90	Christie	24 Aug 91
	9.91	Christie	11 Jun 94
	9.93	Christie	28 Jan 90
	9.95	Christie	22 Jun 90
	10.00	Ian Mackie	18 Jul 98
	10.01	Doug Walker ¶	18 Jul 98
	10.02	Allan Wells	4 Oct 82
	10.07	Cameron Sharp	4 Oct 82
	10.07	John Regis	28 Aug 90
	10.07	Toby Box	11 Jun 94
	10.07	Michael Rosswess	11 Jun 94
	10.08	Mike McFarlane	27 May 84
	10.08	Jason John	11 Jun 94
10	10.10	Donovan Reid	26 Jun 83
	10.10	Christian Malcolm	18 Jul 98
	10.11	Drew McMaster	26 Jun 83
	10.12	Buster Watson	27 May 84
	10.14	Ernest Obeng	20 Jun 87
	10.14	Marcus Adam	28 Jan 90
	10.16	Daniel Money	21 Jun 97
	10.17	Terry Williams	23 Aug 94
	10.17	Owusu Dako	5 Jul 98
	10.19	Josephus Thomas ¶	23 Apr 98
20	10.20	Lincoln Asquith	6 Jul 85
	10.22	Jamie Henthorn	29 Aug 97
	10.22	Danny Joyce	30 Aug 97
	10.25	Lenny Paul	14 Jul 91
	10.26	Peter Little	21 May 80
	10.26	Doug Turner	13 Jul 96
	10.27	Barrington Williams	2 Jul 88
	10.27	Clarence Callender	22 Jun 91
	10.27	Doug Bignall	4 Jul 00
	10.28	Du'aine Ladejo	23 May 98
30	10.29	Trevor Cameron	11 Jun 94
	10.30	Kevin Williams	27 Jul 97
	10.31	Jim Evans	22 Aug 81
	10.32	Brian Green	16 Jun 72
	10.32	Harry King	22 Aug 81
	10.32	Uvie Ugono	23 Apr 98
	10.33	Steve Gookey	20 Jul 91
	10.34	Phil Davies	13 Jul 86
	10.34	Jason Fergus	5 Jun 94
	10.35	Nigel Walker	26 Aug 89
40	10.35	Ross Baillie	18 Jul 98

hand timing

10.1	David Jenkins	20 May 72
10.1	Brian Green	3 Jun 72

hand timing - wind assisted

10.0	Allan Wells	16 Jun 79
10.0	Drew McMaster	1 Jun 80
10.1	David Roberts	17 Jul 82

200 METRES

	Mark	Name	Date
	19.87 A	John Regis	31 Jul 94
	19.94	Regis	20 Aug 93
	20.01	Regis	2 Aug 94
	20.09	Regis	5 Aug 92
	20.09	Linford Christie ¶	28 Sep 88
	20.11	Regis	30 Aug 90
	20.11	Christie	25 Jun 95
	20.12	Regis	10 Jul 91
	20.13	Darren Campbell	27 Sep 00
	20.14	Campbell	28 Sep 00
	20.18	Julian Golding	19 Sep 98
	20.19	Christian Malcolm	27 Sep 00
	20.21	Allan Wells	28 Jul 80
	20.25	Marlon Devonish	25 Aug 99
	20.35	Doug Walker ¶	26 Jul 98
	20.36	Todd Bennett	28 May 84
10	20.41	Marcus Adam	13 Jun 92
	20.42 A	Ainsley Bennett	12 Sep 79
		20.84	31 Aug 80
	20.43	Mike McFarlane	7 Oct 82
	20.43	Doug Turner	9 Jun 96
	20.47	Cameron Sharp	9 Sep 82
	20.47	Darren Braithwaite	13 May 95
	20.50	Terry Williams	24 Aug 94
	20.50	Tony Jarrett	16 Jul 95
	20.50	Solomon Wariso	16 Jul 95
	20.51	Michael Rosswess	28 Sep 88
20	20.53 i	Allyn Condon	8 Feb 98
		20.63	19 Jul 97
	20.54	Ade Mafe	25 Aug 85
	20.56	Roger Black	4 May 96
	20.57	Owusu Dako	16 Jul 95
	20.62	Buster Watson	5 Jun 83
	20.62	Donovan Reid	28 May 84
	20.62	Mark Richardson	24 Aug 97
	20.63	Chris Lambert	21 Aug 99
	20.65	Jason Gardener	11 Jul 99
	20.66 A	Dick Steane	15 Oct 68
30	20.66	David Jenkins	27 Aug 73
	20.68	Dwain Chambers	22 Apr 99
	20.70	Chris Monk	20 Aug 73
	20.72	Toby Box	24 Aug 94
	20.72	Tim Benjamin	18 Jul 99
	20.73 A	Ralph Banthorpe	15 Oct 68
	20.75	Dave Clark	20 Jan 90
	20.76	Andy Carrott	5 Jul 88
	20.76	Clarence Callender	24 Jun 91
	20.77	Drew McMaster	9 Jul 83
40	20.79	Phil Goedluck	6 Aug 94
	20.79	Paul White	27 May 96
	20.79	Jon Barbour	9 Sep 00
	20.81	Mike St. Louis	21 Jun 86
	20.81	Paul McBurney	24 Aug 94
	20.83	Martin Reynolds	22 Jul 70
	20.83	Claude Moseley	23 Aug 81
	20.83	John Stewart	9 Sep 00
	20.84	Brian Green	4 Sep 71
	20.84	Earl Tulloch	25 May 81
50	20.84	Jamie Baulch	24 Aug 94

wind assisted (* 220 yards time less 0.12)

Mark	Name	Date	
20.08	Regis	2 Jul 93	
20.10	Marcus Adam	1 Feb 90	
20.11	Allan Wells	20 Jun 80	
20.26	Ade Mafe	1 Feb 90	
20.36	Doug Turner	27 Jul 97	
20.48	Michael Rosswess	9 Sep 90	
20.49	Josephus Thomas ¶	23 Apr 98	
20.51	Jason John	2 Jul 93	
20.55	Buster Watson	10 Aug 85	
20.59	Allyn Condon	25 Jul 99	
20.60	Tim Benjamin	7 Aug 99	10
20.61	Martin Reynolds	22 Jul 70	
20.61	Ed White	11 Jul 99	
20.62	Adrian Patrick	10 Jun 95	
20.64	Drew McMaster	23 Aug 80	
20.68	Ian Mackie	29 May 00	
20.70 *	Dave Jones	20 May 61	
20.70	Trevor Hoyte	14 Sep 79	
20.73	Phil Goedluck	23 Apr 95	
20.75	Daniel Money	26 May 97	
20.76	Paul McBurney	26 May 97	20
20.80	Ben Lewis	11 Jul 99	

hand timing (* 220 yards time less 0.1)

Mark	Name	Date
20.3	David Jenkins	19 Aug 72
20.4 *	Peter Radford	28 May 60
20.6	Donovan Reid	1 Jul 84
20.7 *	Menzies Campbell	10 Jun 67
20.7	Martin Reynolds	2 Aug 70
20.7	Brian Green	3 Jun 72
20.7	Drew McMaster	16 Aug 80
20.7	Claude Moseley	28 Aug 81

wind assisted

Mark	Name	Date
20.4	Buster Watson	11 Aug 85
20.5	Roger Black	6 Jul 96
20.6	Ainsley Bennett	22 Jun 74
20.6	Mark Richardson	6 Jul 96

300 METRES

Mark	Name	Date	
31.56	Doug Walker ¶	19 Jul 98	
31.67	John Regis	17 Jul 92	
31.87	Mark Richardson	19 Jul 98	
31.98	Regis	19 Jun 93	
31.99	Regis	21 Jun 91	
32.06	Jamie Baulch	31 May 97	
32.08	Roger Black	8 Aug 86	
32.14	Todd Bennett	18 Aug 84	
32.23	Solomon Wariso	19 Jul 98	
32.26	Mark Hylton	19 Jul 98	
32.32	Derek Redmond	16 Jul 88	
32.36	Iwan Thomas	19 Jul 98	10
32.44	David Jenkins	4 Jul 75	
32.45	David Grindley	19 Jun 93	
32.59	Kriss Akabusi	14 Jul 91	
32.61	Brian Whittle	16 Jul 88	

during 400m

Mark	Name	Date
32.06 +	Roger Black	29 Aug 91
32.08 +	Iwan Thomas	5 Aug 97
32.26 +	Derek Redmond	1 Sep 87
32.35 +	David Grindley	26 Jun 93

400 METRES

	44.36	Iwan Thomas	13	Jul	97
	44.37	Roger Black	3	Jul	96
	44.37	Mark Richardson	9	Jul	98
	44.37	Richardson	8	Aug	98
	44.38	Thomas	8	Aug	98
	44.39	Black	16	Jun	96
	44.41	Black	29	Jul	96
	44.46	Thomas	2	Jul	97
	44.47	David Grindley	3	Aug	92
	44.47	Richardson	5	Aug	97
	44.47	Richardson	24	Aug	99
	44.50	Derek Redmond	1	Sep	87
	44.57	Jamie Baulch	3	Jul	96
	44.66	Du'aine Ladejo	16	Jun	96
	44.68	Solomon Wariso	26	Jul	98
	44.93	David Jenkins	21	Jun	75
10	44.93	Kriss Akabusi	7	Aug	88
	45.20	Sean Baldock	12	Aug	00
	45.22	Brian Whittle	25	Sep	88
	45.24	Mark Hylton	12	Aug	98
	45.26	Phil Brown	26	May	85
	45.27	Todd Bennett	7	Aug	88
	45.30	Ade Mafe	23	Jul	93
	45.33	Paul Sanders	15	Jun	91
	45.37	Daniel Caines	23	Sep	00
	45.47	David McKenzie	12	Jun	94
20	45.48	John Regis	17	Apr	93
	45.49	Glen Cohen	21	May	78
	45.63	Adrian Patrick	5	Jul	95
	45.64	Paul Harmsworth	7	Aug	88
	45.65	Alan Bell	14	Jun	80
	45.67	Roger Hunter	19	May	85
	45.69	Jared Deacon	29	Jul	00
	45.74	Steve Heard	26	May	85
	45.75	Robbie Brightwell	19	Oct	64
	45.76	Guy Bullock	16	Jun	96
30	45.81	Terry Whitehead	14	Jun	80
	45.83	Geoff Dearman	29	Jul	00
	45.84	Richard Knowles	18	May	97
	45.85	Paul McBurney	13	Jul	97
	45.88	Wayne McDonald	17	Aug	91
	45.91 A	Martin Winbolt-Lewis	17	Oct	68
	45.92	Mark Thomas	27	Jun	87
	45.94	Paul Slythe	26	Jul	98
	45.97	Steve Scutt	14	Sep	79
	46.03	Peter Crampton	8	Aug	87
40	46.04	Alan Slack	27	Jun	85
	46.08	Tim Graham	19	Oct	64
	46.08	Rod Milne	15	Jun	80
	46.10	Peter Gabbett	7	Sep	72
	46.11	Martin Reynolds	4	Sep	72
	46.15	Ainsley Bennett	29	Aug	75
	46.16	Gary Armstrong	15	Jul	72
	46.16	Claude Moseley	1	Jul	83
	46.18	Garry Cook	14	Jun	80
	46.19	Roy Dickens	28	May	84
50	46.20	Dave Nolan	9	Jun	96
	46.22	Mark Sesay	25	May	97
	46.23 i	Allyn Condon	14	Feb	99

hand timing (* 440 yards time less 0.3)

45.6 *	Robbie Brightwell	14	Jul	62
45.7	Adrian Metcalfe	2	Sep	61
45.9	Colin Campbell	2	Jul	68
46.0	Garry Cook	20	May	81

600 METRES

1:14.95	Steve Heard	14	Jul	91
1:15.0 +	Sebastian Coe	10	Jun	81
1:15.4	Garry Cook	30	Jul	84
1:15.4	Tom McKean	21	Jul	91
1:15.6	David Jenkins	3	Aug	74
1:15.94	Brian Whittle	28	Jul	92

800 METRES (* 880 yards time less 0.60)

1:41.73"	Sebastian Coe	10	Jun	81	
1:42.33	Coe	5	Jul	79	
1:42.88	Steve Cram	21	Aug	85	
1:42.97	Peter Elliott	30	May	90	
1:43.07	Coe	25	Aug	85	
1:43.19	Cram	7	Sep	86	
1:43.22	Cram	31	Jul	86	
1:43.38	Coe	29	Aug	89	
1:43.41	Elliott	1	Sep	87	
1:43.42	Cram	17	Aug	88	
1:43.84	Martin Steele	10	Jul	93	
1:43.88	Tom McKean	28	Jul	89	
1:43.98	David Sharpe	19	Aug	92	
1:44.09	Steve Ovett	31	Aug	78	
1:44.55	Garry Cook	29	Aug	84	
1:44.59	Tony Morrell	2	Jul	88	
1:44.65	Ikem Billy	21	Jul	84	10
1:44.65	Steve Heard	26	Aug	92	
1:44.92	Curtis Robb	15	Aug	93	
1:45.05	Matthew Yates	26	Aug	92	
1:45.12	Andy Carter	14	Jul	73	
1:45.14	Chris McGeorge	28	Jun	83	
1:45.14	John Gladwin	22	Jul	86	
1:45.31	Rob Harrison	21	Jul	84	
1:45.32	James McIlroy (IRE)	16	Jul	98	
1:45.35	Kevin McKay	16	Aug	92	
1:45.44	Neil Horsfield	28	Jul	90	20
1:45.47	Brian Whittle	20	Jul	90	
1:45.6	Graham Williamson	12	Jun	83	
1:45.64	Paul Herbert	5	Jun	88	
1:45.66	Paul Forbes	8	Jun	83	
1:45.68	Mark Sesay	7	Aug	99	
1:45.69	Steve Crabb	17	Aug	88	
1:45.69	Craig Winrow	21	Jun	96	
1:45.71	Andy Hart	19	Sep	98	
1:45.76	Frank Clement	10	Jul	76	
1:45.81	David Strang	12	Jul	96	30
1:45.81	Anthony Whiteman	5	Aug	00	
1:45.82	Jason Lobo	7	Aug	99	
1:46.10	Gary Marlow	10	Jul	87	
1:46.1	Colin Campbell	26	Jul	72	
1:46.16	Gareth Brown	2	Jul	84	
1:46.20	David Warren	29	Jun	80	
1:46.21	Pete Browne	14	Jul	73	
1:46.26	Phil Lewis	27	Jan	74	

	Mark	Athlete	Date
	1:46.3 a	Chris Carter	4 Sep 66
40	1:46.37	Andrew Lill	28 Jun 92
	1:46.4	Paul Walker	22 Jul 97
	1:46.51	John Boulter	18 Jun 66
	1:46.6	Derek Johnson	9 Aug 57
	1:46.63	Peter Hoffmann	11 Jun 78
	1:46.64	Dave Moorcroft	25 Jul 82
	1:46.65	Steve Caldwell	31 May 82
	1:46.72	Mal Edwards	13 Sep 87
	1:46.80 *	John Davies I	3 Jun 68
	1:46.8	Bob Adams	9 Aug 69
50	1:46.8	Dave Cropper	1 Jul 73
	1:46.8	Dave McMeekin	6 Jun 74

1000 METRES

	Mark	Athlete	Date
	2:12.18	Sebastian Coe	11 Jul 81
	2:12.88	Steve Cram	9 Aug 85
	2:13.40	Coe	1 Jul 80
	2:14.90	Coe	16 Jul 86
	2:15.57	James McIlroy	5 Sep 99
	2:15.91	Steve Ovett	6 Sep 79
	2:16.30	Peter Elliott	17 Jan 90
	2:16.34	Matthew Yates	6 Jul 90
	2:16.82	Graham Williamson	17 Jul 84
	2:16.99	Tony Morrell	28 Aug 88
10	2:17.14	John Gladwin	6 Jul 90
	2:17.20	Rob Harrison	18 Aug 84
	2:17.36	Neil Horsfield	9 Aug 91
	2:17.43	Gareth Brown	18 Aug 84
	2:17.45	Chris McGeorge	20 Aug 84
	2:17.63	Kevin McKay	14 Jul 89
	2:17.75	Steve Crabb	5 Aug 87
	2:17.79	David Sharpe	31 Aug 92
	2:17.95	Mark Scruton	17 Jul 84
	2:17.96	Ikem Billy	14 Jul 89
20	2:18.18	Mal Edwards	11 Jul 86
	2:18.2	John Boulter	6 Sep 69
	2:18.28	Garry Cook	23 Aug 81
	2:18.31 i	David Strang	30 Jan 93
	2:18.33	Gary Marlow	5 Aug 87
	2:18.35	Paul Larkins	27 Jun 86
	2:18.48	John Mayock	11 Aug 96

1500 METRES (+ during 1 mile)

	Mark	Athlete	Date
	3:29.67	Steve Cram	16 Jul 85
	3:29.77	Sebastian Coe	7 Sep 86
	3:30.15	Cram	5 Sep 86
	3:30.77	Steve Ovett	4 Sep 83
	3:30.95	Cram	19 Aug 88
	3:31.34	Cram	27 Jun 85
	3:31.36	Ovett	27 Aug 80
	3:31.43	Cram	19 Aug 87
	3:31.57	Ovett	29 Jul 81
	3:31.66	Cram	26 Aug 83
	3:31.86	John Mayock	22 Aug 97
	3:31.95	Coe	7 Jul 81
	3:31.95	Ovett	8 Jul 81
	3:32.34	Anthony Whiteman	16 Aug 97
	3:32.69	Peter Elliott	16 Sep 90
	3:33.34	Steve Crabb	4 Jul 87
	3:33.79	Dave Moorcroft	27 Jul 82
10	3:33.83	John Robson	4 Sep 79
	3:34.00	Matthew Yates	13 Sep 91
	3:34.01	Graham Williamson	28 Jun 83
	3:34.1 +	Tony Morrell	14 Jul 90
	3:34.50	Adrian Passey	4 Jul 87
	3:34.53	Mark Rowland	27 Jul 88
	3:34.59	Kevin McKay	24 Aug 97
	3:34.76	Gary Lough	9 Sep 95
	3:35.08	Neil Horsfield	10 Aug 90
	3:35.26	John Gladwin	5 Sep 86
20	3:35.28	Jack Buckner	1 Jul 86
	3:35.66	Frank Clement	12 Aug 78
	3:35.74	Rob Harrison	26 May 86
	3:35.94	Paul Larkins	10 Jul 87
	3:36.18	Andrew Graffin	20 Aug 00
	3:36.53	David Strang	15 Jul 94
	3:36.81	Mike Kearns	26 Jul 77
	3:37.55	Colin Reitz	27 Jun 85
	3:37.64	Brendan Foster	2 Feb 74
	3:37.75	Jon McCallum	1 Aug 00
30	3:37.88	Jason Dullforce	17 Jul 92
	3:37.97	Rod Finch	30 Jul 93
	3:37.99	Rob Denmark	5 Jun 95
	3:38.05	Glen Grant	12 Aug 78
	3:38.06	Tim Hutchings	31 Aug 84
	3:38.08	Tom Hanlon	28 Jun 92
	3:38.1	Jim McGuinness	1 Aug 77
	3:38.2 a	James Espir	11 Jul 80
	3:38.22	Peter Stewart	15 Jul 72
	3:38.31	Matt Barnes	23 Jul 93
40	3:38.52	Ray Smedley	15 Jul 72
	3:38.56	Curtis Robb	26 Jun 93
	3:38.64	Simon Fairbrother	17 Jun 92
	3:38.65	Ian Stewart II	8 Aug 81
	3:38.66	Glen Stewart	26 May 96
	3:38.68	John Kirkbride	15 Jul 72
	3:38.7	Jim Douglas	27 Jun 72
	3:38.78	Mark Scruton	17 Jun 84
	3:38.8	Paul Lawther	12 Jun 77
	3:38.9	Ian Hamer	5 Aug 89
50	3:38.93	Brian Treacy	28 Aug 94
	3:39.0	David Lewis	9 Aug 83
	3:39.03	Neil Caddy	22 Jul 00
	3:39.06	Andy Keith	5 Jun 93

ONE MILE

Mark	Athlete	Date
3:46.32	Steve Cram	27 Jul 85
3:47.33	Sebastian Coe	28 Aug 81
3:48.31	Cram	5 Jul 86
3:48.40	Steve Ovett	26 Aug 81
3:48.53	Coe	19 Aug 81
3:48.8	Ovett	1 Jul 80
3:48.85	Cram	2 Jul 88
3:48.95	Coe	17 Jul 79
3:49.20	Peter Elliott	2 Jul 88
3:49.22	Coe	27 Jul 85
3:49.25	Ovett	11 Jul 81
3:49.34	Dave Moorcroft	26 Jun 82
3:49.46	Elliott	6 Jul 91

	3:49.49	Cram	12 Sep 86
	3:49.57	Ovett	31 Aug 79
	3:49.65	Cram	29 Aug 84
	3:49.66	Ovett	14 Jul 81
	3:49.76	Elliott	14 Jul 90
	3:49.90	Cram	13 Jul 82
	3:49.95	Cram	19 Aug 81
	3:50.32	John Mayock	5 Jul 96
	3:50.64	Graham Williamson	13 Jul 82
	3:51.02	John Gladwin	19 Aug 87
	3:51.31	Tony Morrell	14 Jul 90
10	3:51.57	Jack Buckner	29 Aug 84
	3:51.76hc	Steve Crabb	14 Aug 87
		3:52.20	1 Jul 89
	3:51.90	Anthony Whiteman	16 Jul 98
	3:52.44	John Robson	11 Jul 81
	3:52.75	Matthew Yates	10 Jul 93
	3:52.99	Mark Rowland	10 Sep 86
	3:53.20	Ian Stewart II	25 Aug 82
	3:53.64	Kevin McKay	22 Jul 94
	3:53.82	Gary Staines	12 Aug 90
	3:53.85	Rob Harrison	15 Jul 86
20	3:54.2	Frank Clement	27 Jun 78
	3:54.30	David Strang	22 Jul 94
	3:54.39	Neil Horsfield	8 Jul 86
	3:54.53	Tim Hutchings	31 Jul 82
	3:54.9	Adrian Passey	20 Aug 89
	3:55.0	Jim McGuinness	11 Jul 77
	3:55.3	Peter Stewart	10 Jun 72
	3:55.38	Rob Denmark	12 Aug 90
	3:55.41	Colin Reitz	31 Jul 82
	3:55.68	Alan Simpson	30 Aug 65
30	3:55.8	Geoff Smith	15 Aug 81
	3:55.84	Neil Caddy	25 Aug 96
	3:55.9	Brendan Foster	10 Jun 72
	3:55.91	Gary Lough	27 Aug 95
	3:55.96	David Lewis	23 Aug 83
	3:56.0	Jim Douglas	10 Jun 72
	3:56.04	Mike Downes	25 Aug 82
	3:56.1	Neill Duggan	11 Jun 66
	3:56.13	Andrew Graffin	5 Aug 00
	3:56.19	Ian Hamer	5 Jul 91
40	3:56.29 i	Andy Keith	22 Jan 94
	3:56.36	Steve Martin	5 Aug 86
	3:56.38	Mike McLeod	31 Aug 79
	3:56.5	John Kirkbride	10 Jun 72
	3:56.5	Paul Davies-Hale	20 Aug 89
	3:56.6	Walter Wilkinson	31 May 71
	3:56.65	Paul Larkins	17 Jul 87
	3:56.7	James Espir	15 Aug 81
	3:56.71	Chris McGeorge	5 Jul 88
	3:56.8	Ian McCafferty	11 Jun 69
50	3:56.83	Simon Fairbrother	17 Aug 90
	3:56.9 a	Ron Speirs	30 Apr 77
	3:56.95	Sean Cahill	31 Aug 79
	3:56.95	Dave Clarke	17 Jul 82
	3:56.90	Alan Salter	9 Jul 85
	3:57.07	Neil Ovington	11 Jul 86
	3:57.15	Gary Taylor	5 Jul 88

2000 METRES

	4:51.39	Steve Cram	4 Aug 85
	4:52.82	Peter Elliott	15 Sep 87
	4:53.06	Jack Buckner	15 Sep 87
	4:53.69	Gary Staines	15 Sep 87
	4:55.20	Cram	28 Aug 88
	4:55.72	Elliott	28 Aug 88
	4:56.75	John Mayock	30 Jul 99
	4:57.71	Steve Ovett	7 Jul 82
	4:57.82	Ovett	3 Jun 78
	4:58.38	Graham Williamson	29 Aug 83
	4:58.57	Mayock	7 Sep 99
	4:58.84	Sebastian Coe	5 Jun 82
	4:59.57	Nick Rose	3 Jun 78
10	5:00.37	Tim Hutchings	29 Aug 83
	5:01.09	Eamonn Martin	19 Jun 84
	5:01.28	Andrew Graffin	25 Jun 00
	5:01.48	Paul Larkins	5 Jun 88
	5:02.35	Sean Cahill	4 Aug 85
	5:02.61	Steve Martin	19 Jun 84
	5:02.8 a	Frank Clement	10 Sep 78
	5:02.86	David Moorcroft	19 Jul 86
	5:02.90	Allen Graffin	25 Jun 00
	5:02.93	Brendan Foster	4 Jul 75
20	5:02.98	Ian Stewart I	4 Jul 75
	5:02.98	Gary Lough	11 Aug 96
	5:02.99	Neil Caddy	11 Aug 96
	5:03.16	Dave Bedford	8 Jul 72
	5:03.8	Lawrie Spence	26 May 78
	5:04.11	Rob Denmark	11 Aug 96

3000 METRES (+ during 2 Miles)

	7:32.79	Dave Moorcroft	17 Jul 82
	7:35.1	Brendan Foster	3 Aug 74
	7:36.40	John Nuttall	10 Jul 96
	7:39.55	Rob Denmark	1 Aug 93
	7:39.72	Denmark	15 Jul 92
	7:40.4	Nick Rose	27 Jun 78
	7:40.43	Jack Buckner	5 Jul 86
	7:40.94	Eamonn Martin	9 Jul 83
	7:41.3	Steve Ovett	23 Sep 77
	7:41.79	Gary Staines	14 Jul 90
10	7:42.26	Graeme Fell	9 Jul 83
	7:42.47	David Lewis	9 Jul 83
	7:42.77	Billy Dee	18 Jul 92
	7:43.03	Tim Hutchings	14 Jul 89
	7:43.1 +	Steve Cram	29 Aug 83
	7:43.31 i	John Mayock	23 Feb 97
		7:47.28	23 Jul 95
	7:43.61	Anthony Whiteman	27 Jun 98
	7:43.90	Ian Stewart II	26 Jun 82
	7:44.40	Colin Reitz	9 Jul 83
	7:44.76	Paul Davies-Hale	20 Jul 85
20	7:45.2 +	Geoff Turnbull	12 Sep 86
	7:45.29	Dennis Coates	9 Sep 77
	7:45.41	Jon Brown	1 Aug 98
	7:45.81	John Robson	13 Jul 84
	7:46.22 i	Mark Rowland	27 Feb 90
		7:49.82	28 Jul 89
	7:46.39	Adrian Royle	28 Jun 83

	Time	Athlete	Date
	7:46.40	Ian Hamer	20 Jan 90
	7:46.4	David Bedford	21 Jun 72
	7:46.6 +	Dave Black	14 Sep 73
	7:46.83	Ian Stewart I	26 May 76
30	7:46.85 i	Ricky Wilde	15 Mar 70
	7:46.95	David James	26 May 80
	7:47.12	Simon Mugglestone	27 Jun 88
	7:47.54	Paul Larkins	14 Jul 89
	7:47.56	Dick Callan	15 Jul 83
	7:47.6	Dick Taylor	6 Sep 69
	7:48.00	Richard Nerurkar	15 Jul 92
	7:48.09	Adrian Passey	28 Jul 89
	7:48.18	Mike McLeod	9 Jul 78
	7:48.28	Jon Richards	9 Jul 83
40	7:48.28	Ian Gillespie	25 May 97
	7:48.6 +	Nat Muir	27 Jun 80
	7:48.66	Julian Goater	26 May 80
	7:48.76	Neil Caddy	2 Aug 98
	7:48.81	Tim Redman	18 Aug 84
	7:49.1	Paul Lawther	27 Jun 78
	7:49.45	Gary Lough	30 May 95
	7:49.47	Roger Hackney	13 Jul 84
	7:49.64	Barry Smith	26 Jul 81
	7:49.72	Ray Smedley	9 Jul 78
50	7:49.80	Steve Jones	13 Jul 84
	7:49.83 i	Andy Keith	6 Feb 94
	7:50.04	Karl Keska	2 Aug 98
	7:50.20	Jon Solly	8 Aug 86

2 MILES

	Time	Athlete	Date
	8:13.51	Steve Ovett	15 Sep 78
	8:13.68	Brendan Foster	27 Aug 73
	8:14.93	Steve Cram	29 Aug 83
	8:15.53	Tim Hutchings	12 Sep 86
	8:15.98	Geoff Turnbull	12 Sep 86
	8:16.75	Dave Moorcroft	20 Aug 82
	8:16.94	Foster	17 Jul 79
	8:17.12	Jack Buckner	12 Sep 86
	8:17.79	Cram	16 Jul 88
	8:18.4 i	Nick Rose	17 Feb 78
		8:22.41	15 Sep 78
	8:18.57	Moorcroft	27 Jun 80
	8:18.98	Eamonn Martin	16 Jul 88
10	8:19.37	Nat Muir	27 Jun 80
	8:20.28	David James	27 Jun 80
	8:20.66	David Lewis	7 Sep 84
	8:21.09	Barry Smith	27 Jun 80
	8:21.86	David Black	14 Sep 73
	8:21.97	Rob Denmark	9 Aug 91
	8:22.0	Ian Stewart I	14 Aug 72
	8:22.65	Ian Hamer	17 Jul 92
	8:22.7 i	Graeme Fell	19 Feb 82
	8:22.98	Geoff Smith	27 Jun 80
20	8:23.16	Gary Staines	9 Aug 91
	8:23.80	Billy Dee	9 Aug 91
	8:23.92	Ray Smedley	6 Aug 76
	8:24.58	Adrian Royle	16 May 82
	8:24.82	Eddie Wedderburn	16 Jul 88
	8:25.02	Tony Simmons	6 Aug 76
	8:25.52	Colin Reitz	19 Aug 86

5000 METRES

Time	Athlete	Date	
13:00.41	Dave Moorcroft	7 Jul 82	
13:09.80	Ian Hamer	9 Jun 92	
13:10.15	Jack Buckner	31 Aug 86	
13:10.24	Rob Denmark	9 Jun 92	
13:10.47	Buckner	9 Jun 92	
13:10.48	Buckner	19 Aug 87	
13:11.50	Tim Hutchings	11 Aug 84	
13:12.88	Hutchings	31 Aug 86	
13:13.01	Denmark	17 Jul 91	
13:13.77	Denmark	15 Jun 95	
13:14.28	Gary Staines	15 Aug 90	
13:14.6 a	Brendan Foster	29 Jan 74	
13:15.59	Julian Goater	11 Sep 81	
13:16.70	John Nuttall	8 Jun 95	
13:17.21	Dave Bedford	14 Jul 72	10
13:17.21	Keith Cullen	19 Jul 97	
13:17.84	Eamonn Martin	14 Jul 89	
13:17.9	Nat Muir	15 Jul 80	
13:18.06	Ian Gillespie	19 Jul 97	
13:18.6	Steve Jones	10 Jun 82	
13:18.91	Nick Rose	28 Jun 84	
13:19.03	Jon Brown	5 Aug 98	
13:19.66	Ian McCafferty	14 Jul 72	
13:20.06	Steve Ovett	30 Jun 86	
13:20.09	Adrian Passey	19 Jul 97	20
13:21.13	David Lewis	4 Jul 85	
13:21.14	Barry Smith	7 Jun 81	
13:21.2	Tony Simmons	23 May 76	
13:21.60	Paul Davies-Hale	8 Jul 88	
13:21.73	Geoff Turnbull	5 Sep 86	
13:21.83	Mark Rowland	1 Jun 88	
13:22.17 i	Geoff Smith	12 Feb 82	
	13:26.33	8 Aug 81	
13:22.39	Jon Solly	7 Jul 86	
13:22.54	Dave Clarke	28 Jun 83	
13:22.8 a	Ian Stewart I	25 Jul 70	30
13:23.07	Karl Keska	7 Aug 99	
13:23.26	Mike McLeod	24 Jun 80	
13:23.36	Richard Nerurkar	10 Aug 90	
13:23.48	John Doherty	1 Jun 85	
13:23.52	Dave Black	29 Jan 74	
13:23.71	Steve Binns	1 Jun 88	
13:25.38	Paul Evans	28 Jun 95	
13:26.0	Bernie Ford	30 Jul 77	
13:26.19	Adrian Royle	4 Jul 83	
13:26.2	Dick Taylor	13 Jun 70	40
13:26.74	Craig Mochrie	25 Aug 89	
13:26.97	John Mayock	9 Jun 92	
13:27.14	Dick Callan	25 Aug 82	
13:27.41	Billy Dee	10 Jul 92	
13:27.63	Dermot Donnelly	1 Aug 98	
13:27.75	Rod Finch	1 Aug 98	
13:28.15	Malcolm Prince	14 Sep 79	
13:28.22	Kris Bowditch	25 Jun 00	
13:28.29	Simon Mugglestone	8 Jul 88	
13:28.58	Steve Cram	3 Jun 89	50
13:28.7 a	Charlie Spedding	13 Aug 78	
13:28.99	Steve Emson	4 Sep 79	
13:29.8 a	Allan Rushmer	25 Jul 70	

10000 METRES

	Time	Name	Date
	27:18.14	Jon Brown	28 Aug 98
	27:23.06	Eamonn Martin	2 Jul 88
	27:27.47	Brown	31 May 97
	27:30.3	Brendan Foster	23 Jun 78
	27:30.80	Dave Bedford	13 Jul 73
	27:31.19	Nick Rose	9 Jul 83
	27:32.65	Foster	29 Aug 78
	27:34.58	Julian Goater	26 Jun 82
	27:36.27	David Black	29 Aug 78
	27:36.62	Foster	9 Sep 77
	27:39.14	Steve Jones	9 Jul 83
	27:39.76	Mike McLeod	4 Sep 79
10	27:40.03	Richard Nerurkar	10 Jul 93
	27:43.03	Ian Stewart I	9 Sep 77
	27:43.59	Tony Simmons	30 Jun 77
	27:43.74	Bernie Ford	9 Sep 77
	27:43.76	Geoff Smith	13 Jun 81
	27:44.09	Karl Keska	25 Sep 00
	27:47.16	Adrian Royle	10 Apr 82
	27:47.79	Paul Evans	5 Jul 93
	27:48.73	Gary Staines	6 Jul 91
	27:50.33	Keith Cullen	10 Apr 99
20	27:51.76	Jon Solly	20 Jun 86
	27:55.66	Steve Binns	9 Jul 83
	27:55.77	Dave Clarke	25 May 82
	27:57.77	Ian Hamer	13 Sep 91
	27:59.12	Allister Hutton	30 May 86
	27:59.24	Carl Thackery	16 Jul 87
	27:59.33	Steve Harris	22 Jul 86
	28:00.50	Andres Jones	22 Jul 00
	28:00.62	Jim Brown	1 Aug 75
	28:00.64	Billy Dee	13 Sep 91
30	28:03.31	Rob Denmark	22 Jul 00
	28:04.04	Andy Bristow	17 Aug 90
	28:04.2	Ian Robinson	20 Apr 96
	28:04.48	Mark Steinle	22 Jul 00
	28:05.2	Dave Murphy	10 Apr 81
	28:06.13	Barry Smith	7 Aug 81
	28:06.6	Dick Taylor	22 Jun 69
	28:07.43	John Nuttall	25 Aug 95
	28:07.57	Tim Hutchings	7 Jul 90
	28:08.12	Charlie Spedding	23 Jul 83
40	28:08.44	David Lewis	5 Jun 88
	28:09.39	Mark Dalloway	5 Jun 88
	28:11.07	Karl Harrison	20 Jun 86
	28:11.71	Lachie Stewart	18 Jul 70
	28:11.85	Lawrie Spence	29 May 83
	28:13.04	Gerry Helme	29 May 83
	28:13.13	Colin Moore	29 Jun 90
	28:13.36	Jack Buckner	13 Sep 91
	28:14.08	Jon Richards	20 Jun 86
	28:14.65	Mike Tagg	10 Aug 71
50	28:14.89	Bernie Plain	1 Aug 75
	28:15.58	Martin McLoughlin	20 Jun 86
	28:16.0	Mike Baxter	23 May 74
	28:16.73	Neil Coupland	11 Jun 77
	28:17.00	Justin Hobbs	29 Jun 94
	28:18.6	John Davies II	11 Apr 79
	28:18.68	Terry Thornton	17 Aug 90

10 KILOMETRES ROAD

Time	Name	Date	
27:34	Nick Rose	1 Apr 84	
27:53	Mike O'Reilly	19 Oct 86	
27:55	Mark Scrutton	5 Mar 84	
27:56	John Doherty	4 Jul 86	
27:58	Steve Harris	5 Apr 86	
27:59	Steve Jones	28 Apr 84	
28:02	Steve Binns	15 Apr 89	
28:03	Jon Solly	5 Apr 86	
28:03	Jack Buckner	28 Feb 87	
28:05	Jon Brown	17 Oct 93	10
28:06	Geoff Smith	2 Mar 85	
28:07	Colin Reitz	28 Apr 84	
28:07	Peter Whitehead	4 Jul 96	
28:09	Dave Moorcroft	16 May 82	
28:10	Adrian Leek	10 Mar 84	
28:10	Dave Clarke	5 May 85	
28:11	Jon Richards	5 May 85	
28:12	Dave Murphy	19 May 85	
28:13	Allister Hutton	28 Apr 84	
28:13	Paul Evans	8 Jan 95	20
28:14	Karl Harrison	5 May 85	
28:14	David Lewis	5 Apr 86	
28:14	Eamonn Martin	30 Apr 89	
28:17	Paul Davies-Hale	21 Apr 85	
28:17	Colin Moore	5 May 85	
28:18	Steve Kenyon	15 Sep 85	
28:19	Peter Tootell	28 Apr 84	
28:19	Nigel Gates	5 May 85	
28:19	Terry Greene	4 Apr 87	

course measurement uncertain

Time	Name	Date
27:56	Steve Harris	4 Dec 83
28:00	Roger Hackney	4 Dec 83
28:01	Barry Smith	4 Dec 83
28:01	Steve Kenyon	21 Sep 86
28:04	Dave Bedford	27 Mar 77
28:08	Kevin Forster	15 Jul 84
28:08	Dave Clarke	15 Jul 84
28:10	John McLaughlin	19 May 84

downhill

Time	Name	Date
27:20	Jon Brown	24 Sep 95
27:57	Malcolm East	25 Sep 82

short (50m)

Time	Name	Date
27:50	Mark Scrutton	6 Dec 81

10 MILES ROAD

Time	Name	Date	
46:02	Richard Nerurkar	17 Oct 93	
46:11	Gary Staines	10 Oct 93	
46:19	Nerurkar	23 Jul 95	
46:25	Carl Thackery	7 Apr 91	
46:35	Paul Evans	21 Sep 97	
46:41	Roger Hackney	6 Apr 86	
46:42	Dave Murphy	28 Apr 84	
46:43	Nick Rose	25 Apr 87	
46:48	Geoff Smith	2 May 82	
46:49	Steve Jones	2 Apr 89	
47:00	Paul Davies-Hale	10 Oct 93	10
47:02	Martin McLoughlin	10 Oct 93	
47:10	Colin Moore	6 Nov 88	
47:10	Jack Buckner	11 Oct 92	

intermediate times

46:10 +	Paul Evans	14 Sep 97
46:21 +	Nigel Adams	15 Sep 91
46:21 +	Carl Thackery	15 Sep 91
46:23 +	Allister Hutton	1 Jan 85

estimated times

46:02 +	Steve Jones	8 Jun 86

course measurement uncertain

45:13	Ian Stewart I	8 May 77
45:37	Barry Smith	22 Mar 81
45:44	Mike McLeod	9 Apr 78
46:03	Colin Moore	29 Aug 83
46:08	Nick Rose	26 Apr 81
46:11	Steve Kenyon	20 Jun 81
46:14	Charlie Spedding	12 Oct 86
46:17	Brendan Foster	9 Apr 78

downhill

46:05	Allister Hutton	3 Apr 82

HALF MARATHON

	1:00:59	Steve Jones	8 Jun 86
	1:01:03	Nick Rose	15 Sep 85
	1:01:04	Carl Thackery	12 Apr 87
	1:01:06	Richard Nerurkar	14 Apr 96
	1:01:13	Thackery	3 Oct 93
	1:01:14	Jones	11 Aug 85
	1:01:17	David Lewis	20 Sep 92
	1:01:18	Paul Evans	14 Sep 97
	1:01:28	Steve Brooks	23 Mar 97
	1:01:31	Steve Kenyon	8 Jun 86
	1:01:39	Geoff Smith	25 Sep 83
10	1:01:39	Paul Davies-Hale	15 Sep 91
	1:01:49	Jon Brown	14 Sep 97
	1:01:53	Nigel Adams	15 Sep 91
	1:01:56	Mark Flint	22 Aug 93
	1:01:57	Gary Staines	14 Sep 97
	1:02:07	Kevin Forster	5 Apr 87
	1:02:07	Martyn Brewer	20 Sep 87
	1:02:07	Andrew Pearson	14 Sep 97
	1:02:08	Steve Harris	20 Oct 85
	1:02:11	Dave Clarke	5 Apr 92
20	1:02:11	Keith Cullen	20 Aug 00
	1:02:15	Dave Murphy	16 Sep 84
	1:02:16	Jim Haughey	20 Sep 87
	1:02:19	Dave Long I	11 Dec 81
	1:02:22	Colin Moore	26 May 85
	1:02:23	Mark Steinle	10 Oct 99
	1:02:24	Jimmy Ashworth	8 Jun 86
	1:02:25	Barry Royden	18 Sep 94
	1:02:28	Terry Greene	12 Apr 86
	1:02:28	Allister Hutton	21 Jun 87
30	1:02:28	Andy Coleman	22 Oct 00

course measurement uncertain

1:00:09	Paul Evans	15 Jan 95
1:01:47	Dave Long II	17 Mar 91
1:02:08	Ray Smedly	28 Mar 82
1:02:09	Steve Anders	25 Sep 88
1:02:19	Mike Carroll	3 Jun 90
1:02:23	Charlie Spedding	15 Mar 87

MARATHON

2:07:13	Steve Jones	20 Oct 85	
2:08:05	Jones	21 Oct 84	
2:08:16	Jones	21 Apr 85	
2:08:20	Jones	6 Nov 88	
2:08:33	Charlie Spedding	21 Apr 85	
2:08:36	Richard Nerurkar	13 Apr 97	
2:08:52	Paul Evans	20 Oct 96	
2:09:08	Geoff Smith	23 Oct 83	
2:09:12	Ian Thompson	31 Jan 74	
2:09:16	Allister Hutton	21 Apr 85	
2:09:24	Hugh Jones	9 May 82	
2:09:28	Ron Hill	23 Jul 70	
2:09:28	John Graham	23 May 81	10
2:09:43	Mike Gratton	17 Apr 83	
2:09:44	Jon Brown	18 Apr 99	
2:09:54	Tony Milovsorov	23 Apr 89	
2:10:12	Gerry Helme	17 Apr 83	
2:10:30	Dave Long II	21 Apr 91	
2:10:35	Steve Brace	21 Jan 96	
2:10:39	Mike O'Reilly	5 Dec 93	
2:10:48	Bill Adcocks	8 Dec 68	
2:10:50	Eamonn Martin	18 Apr 93	
2:10:51	Bernie Ford	2 Dec 79	20
2:10:52	Kevin Forster	17 Apr 88	
2:10:55	Chris Bunyan	18 Apr 83	
2:11:06	Dave Buzza	31 Oct 93	
2:11:18	Dave Murphy	12 Jun 83	
2:11:18	Mark Steinle	16 Apr 00	
2:11:22	Dave Cannon	6 Sep 80	
2:11:25	Paul Davies-Hale	29 Oct 89	
2:11:25	Gary Staines	20 Oct 96	
2:11:35	Malcolm East	20 Apr 81	
2:11:36	Kenny Stuart	15 Jan 89	30
2:11:40	Steve Kenyon	13 Jun 82	
2:11:43	Jimmy Ashworth	29 Sep 85	
2:11:44	Jim Dingwall	17 Apr 83	
2:11:50	Fraser Clyne	2 Dec 84	
2:11:54	Martin McCarthy	17 Apr 83	
2:11:58	Mark Hudspith	2 Apr 95	
2:12:04	Jim Alder	23 Jul 70	
2:12:07	Jon Solly	14 Oct 90	
2:12:07	Mark Flint	17 Apr 94	
2:12:12	Dennis Fowles	13 May 84	40
2:12:12	Andy Green	25 Apr 93	
2:12:13	John Wheway	17 Apr 88	
2:12:17	Dave Long I	16 Jan 82	
2:12:19	Don Faircloth	23 Jul 70	
2:12:23	Peter Whitehead	2 Apr 95	
2:12:32	Trevor Wright	3 Dec 78	
2:12:33	Tony Simmons	7 May 78	
2:12:37	Carl Thackery	25 Oct 92	
2:12:41	Derek Stevens	16 Jun 84	
2:12:50	Jeff Norman	7 May 78	50
2:13:06	Greg Hannon	13 May 79	
2:13:12	Chris Stewart	8 Dec 74	
2:13:15	Ray Crabb	17 Apr 83	
2:13:16	Norman Wilson	20 Apr 81	
2:13:17	Mike Hurd	26 Sep 82	
2:13:17	Geoff Wightman	29 Sep 91	

2000 METRES STEEPLECHASE

	5:19.86	Mark Rowland	28 Aug 88
	5:20.56	Rowland	17 Aug 90
	5:21.77	Tom Hanlon	11 Jun 92
	5:22.37	Rowland	16 Sep 90
	5:22.96	Hanlon	16 Sep 90
	5:23.56	Tom Buckner	17 Jul 92
	5:23.6	Roger Hackney	10 Jun 82
	5:23.71	Colin Walker	28 Aug 88
	5:23.87	Colin Reitz	28 Jun 84
	5:24.91	Eddie Wedderburn	19 Aug 86
	5:26.24	Paul Davies-Hale	26 Aug 85
	5:26.64	Nick Peach	19 Aug 86
10	5:26.82 "	David Lewis	12 Jun 83
	5:30.6	Dennis Coates	23 Apr 78
	5:30.86	Tony Staynings	26 May 76
	5:31.04	John Hartigan	17 Aug 90
	5:31.09	Peter McColgan	5 Aug 86
	5:31.43	John Bicourt	26 May 76
	5:31.59	Mick Hawkins	20 Jan 90
	5:32.45	Neil Smart	17 Aug 90
	5:33.09	Spencer Duval	17 Jul 92
	5:33.59	Mark Sinclair	10 Aug 86
20	5:33.76	Graeme Fell	9 Sep 79

3000 METRES STEEPLECHASE

	8:07.96	Mark Rowland	30 Sep 88
	8:12.11	Colin Reitz	5 Sep 86
	8:12.58	Tom Hanlon	3 Aug 91
	8:13.27	Rowland	30 Aug 90
	8:13.50	Reitz	4 Aug 85
	8:13.65	Hanlon	4 Jul 92
	8:13.78	Reitz	21 Jul 84
	8:14.73	Hanlon	15 Jul 92
	8:14.95	Reitz	27 Jul 85
	8:15.16	Graeme Fell	17 Aug 83
	8:18.32	Eddie Wedderburn	5 Jul 88
	8:18.91	Roger Hackney	30 Jul 88
	8:18.95	Dennis Coates	25 Jul 76
	8:20.83	Paul Davies-Hale	10 Jun 84
	8:22.48	John Davies II	13 Sep 74
10	8:22.82	John Bicourt	8 Jun 76
	8:23.90	Justin Chaston	18 Jul 94
	8:24.64	Spencer Duval	16 Jul 95
	8:25.15	Colin Walker	28 Jun 92
	8:25.37	Christian Stephenson	19 Aug 00
	8:25.50	Tom Buckner	28 Aug 92
	8:26.05	Keith Cullen	21 Aug 95
	8:26.33	Rob Hough	6 Jul 96
	8:26.4	Andy Holden	15 Sep 72
	8:26.6	Gordon Rimmer	4 Jun 80
20	8:27.21	Tony Staynings	15 Jun 80
	8:27.8	Steve Hollings	5 Aug 73
	8:27.93	Peter McColgan	25 Jun 91
	8:28.6	Dave Bedford	10 Sep 71
	8:29.46	Julian Marsay	14 Jul 79
	8:29.72	David Lewis	29 May 83
	8:30.6 a	Peter Griffiths	17 Jul 77
	8:30.8	Gerry Stevens	1 Sep 69
	8:31.09	Ian Gilmour	16 Jul 78
	8:31.22	Dave Lee	19 Jun 92
30	8:32.00	Steve Jones	8 Aug 80
	8:32.06	David Camp	10 Aug 74
	8:32.13	Barry Knight	25 Jul 82
	8:32.4 a	Maurice Herriott	17 Oct 64
	8:33.0	John Jackson	13 Aug 69
	8:33.61	Stuart Stokes	14 Jun 00
	8:33.8 a	Gareth Bryan-Jones	23 Jul 70
	8:33.8	Peter Morris	4 Aug 73
	8:33.83	Richard Charleston	24 May 80
	8:33.89	Nick Peach	21 Jun 86
40	8:33.97	John Hartigan	20 Jul 90
	8:34.67	Craig Wheeler	9 Jun 99
	8:34.77	Kevin Capper	18 Aug 85
	8:34.83	Ken Baker	1 Jul 84
	8:35.49	Micky Morris	14 Aug 76
	8:35.52	Neil Smart	28 Aug 89
	8:35.6	Ron McAndrew	9 Jul 71
	8:35.8	John Wild	3 Aug 77
	8:36.2 a	Bernie Hayward	26 Jan 74
	8:36.55	Mick Hawkins	16 Jul 95
50	8:37.0	Ernie Pomfret	15 Jul 67

110 METRES HURDLES

	12.91	Colin Jackson	20 Aug 93
	12.97 A	Jackson	28 Jul 93
	12.98	Jackson	15 Sep 94
	12.99	Jackson	3 Sep 93
	12.99	Jackson	6 Sep 94
	13.00	Tony Jarrett	20 Aug 93
	13.02	Jackson	30 Aug 94
	13.02	Jackson	22 Aug 98
	13.03	Jackson	4 Sep 94
	13.04	Jackson	16 Aug 92
	13.04	Jackson	12 Aug 94
	13.04	Jarrett	12 Aug 95
	13.04	Jackson	25 Aug 99
	13.29	Jon Ridgeon	15 Jul 87
	13.42	David Nelson	27 Aug 91
	13.43	Mark Holtom	4 Oct 82
	13.44	Hugh Teape	14 Aug 92
	13.49	Andy Tulloch	30 Jun 99
	13.51	Nigel Walker	3 Aug 90
	13.53	Paul Gray	22 Aug 94
10	13.60	Wilbert Greaves	21 Aug 85
	13.60	Neil Owen	28 Jun 95
	13.62	Damien Greaves	30 Jul 00
	13.66	Ross Baillie	20 Feb 99
	13.69	Berwyn Price	18 Aug 73
	13.72	David Hemery	1 Aug 70
	13.75	Lloyd Cowan	17 Jul 94
	13.79	Alan Pascoe	17 Jun 72
	13.82	Mensah Elliott	30 Jul 00
	13.84	Chris Baillie	27 Aug 00
20	13.86	Ken Campbell	23 Aug 94
	13.95	Robert Newton	27 Aug 00
	13.96	Steve Buckeridge	31 May 86
	14.00	Matt Douglas	23 May 99
	14.02	Mark Lambeth	9 Jul 95
	14.03	Brett St Louis	27 Jun 87

	14.03	Brian Taylor	19 May 96
	14.04	Daley Thompson	28 Aug 86
	14.04	Mike Robbins	1 May 99
	14.05	Liam Collins	4 Jun 00
30	14.08	Paul Brice	26 Aug 83
	14.09	Colin Hamplett	11 Aug 90
	14.10	Graham Gower	15 Jul 72
	14.10	Bob Danville	4 Jul 76
	14.10	Jamie Quarry	25 Jun 94
	14.10	Duncan Malins	1 Jul 00
	14.11	Neil Fraser	11 Jul 87
	14.11	Ererton Harrison	31 Jul 91
	14.12	Matthew Clements	17 May 98
	14.13	Mark Stern	22 Jun 96
40	14.14	Mike Hogan	5 Sep 63
	14.14	Max Robertson	7 Jun 86
	14.14	Martin Nicholson	12 Jun 94
	14.16 A	Mike Parker	16 Oct 68
	14.16	Martyn Hendry	25 Aug 97
	14.17	Colin Bovell	23 Jul 94
	14.18	Chris Breen	13 Jul 75
	14.18	James Archampong	21 Jul 94
	14.19	C. J. Kirkpatrick	16 Jun 73
	14.20 A	Stuart Storey	16 Oct 68
50	14.20	Kevin Lumsdon	16 Jul 94
	14.21	David Wilson	15 Jul 72
	14.21	Alan Cronin	13 Jul 75
	14.21	Mark Whitby	14 Jun 85
	14.23	Alan Tapp	14 Jun 86
	14.24	Kieran Moore	7 Jun 86
	14.25	Ben Warmington	31 Jul 98

wind assisted

	12.94 A	Jackson	31 Jul 94
	12.95	Jackson	10 Sep 89
	12.99	Jackson	23 Jun 89
	13.01	Jackson	2 Jul 93
	13.49	Nigel Walker	3 Jun 89
	13.65	Berwyn Price	25 Aug 75
	13.66	David Hemery	18 Jul 70
	13.69	Mensah Elliott	19 Aug 00
	13.93	Robert Newton	7 Aug 99
	13.96	Mike Robbins	28 Mar 98
	13.97	Brett St Louis	30 Jul 88
	13.99	Bob Danville	14 Aug 76
	14.06	Tony James	22 Aug 81
10	14.07	Dominic Bradley	24 May 98
	14.08	David Wilson	15 Jul 72
	14.08	Duncan Malins	18 Jun 00
	14.11	Mark Stern	20 Jun 93
	14.14	James Archampong	25 May 96
	14.16	Mark Hatton	14 Jul 79
	14.17	C. J. Kirkpatrick	13 Jul 74
	14.19	Alan Cronin	25 Aug 75
	14.19	Norman Ashman	15 Aug 92
	14.22	Phil Barthropp	1 Jul 84
20	14.22	Dave Sweetman	24 May 98
	14.22	Tony Gill	14 Aug 99
	14.23	Gus McKenzie	21 May 80
	14.23	John Wallace	26 Jul 86
	14.23	Greg Dunson	10 Jun 89
	14.24	Ben Warmington	5 Jul 98
	14.25	Stuart Storey	18 Jul 70
	14.25	Glenn MacDonald	13 Jun 82
	14.25	Anthony Brannen	30 Apr 95
	14.25	Chris Rawlinson	28 Jun 97

hand timing

	13.5	Berwyn Price	1 Jul 73
	13.6	David Hemery	5 Jul 69
	13.7	Alan Pascoe	5 Jul 69
	13.7	C. J. Kirkpatrick	29 Jun 74
	13.7	Mensah Elliott	2 Sep 00
	13.8	Martin Nicholson	25 Jun 94
	13.9	Mike Parker	2 Oct 63
	13.9	David Wilson	29 Jun 74
	13.9	Brian Taylor	8 May 93
10	14.1	Stuart Storey	2 Aug 67
	14.1	Colin Bovell	17 Jul 94
	14.1 y	Laurie Taitt	13 Jul 63
		14.2	2 Oct 63
	14.2	Bob Birrell	6 Sep 61
	14.2	Andy Todd	27 Oct 67
	14.2	Mark Whitby	12 May 84
	14.2	James Hughes	2 Jul 94
	14.2	Anthony Brannen	6 May 95
	14.2	Chris Rawlinson	3 May 97
	14.2 y	Rodney Morrod	13 Jun 64

wind assisted

	12.8	Colin Jackson	10 Jan 90
	13.0	Jarrett	2 Jun 96
	13.4	Berwyn Price	7 Jul 76
	13.5	Neil Owen	2 Jun 96
	13.7	Lloyd Cowan	27 Apr 95
	14.0	Laurie Taitt	13 Sep 62
	14.0 y	Bob Birrell	9 Sep 61

400 METRES HURDLES

	47.82	Kriss Akabusi	6 Aug 92
	47.86	Akabusi	27 Aug 91
	47.91	Akabusi	26 Aug 91
	47.92	Akabusi	29 Aug 90
	48.01	Akabusi	5 Aug 92
	48.12 A	David Hemery	15 Oct 68
		48.52	2 Sep 72
	48.14	Chris Rawlinson	11 Aug 99
	48.22	Rawlinson	7 Jun 00
	48.22	Rawlinson	5 Jul 00
	48.26	Akabusi	10 Jul 92
	48.59	Alan Pascoe	30 Jun 75
	48.73	Jon Ridgeon	6 Sep 92
	49.03 A	John Sherwood	15 Oct 68
		49.88	13 Aug 69
	49.07	Gary Cadogan	22 Jul 94
	49.11	Gary Oakes	26 Jul 80
	49.16	Paul Gray	18 Aug 98
10	49.25	Max Robertson	28 Aug 90
	49.26	Peter Crampton	8 Aug 94
	49.26	Matt Douglas	30 Aug 00
	49.49	Mark Holtom	20 Jul 85
	49.60	Phil Beattie	28 Jul 86

	49.65	Bill Hartley	2 Aug 75
	49.68	Anthony Borsumato	2 Jul 00
	49.82	Martin Gillingham	14 Aug 87
	49.82	Gary Jennings	27 Jun 95
	49.86	Martin Briggs	6 Jun 84
20	49.95	Steve Sole	24 Jul 83
	49.96	Tony Williams	24 Jul 99
	50.01	Phil Harries	5 Jun 88
	50.05	Lawrence Lynch	15 Jun 96
	50.09	Du'aine Ladejo	6 Aug 00
	50.16	Paul Thompson	17 May 96
	50.1 a	John Cooper	16 Oct 64
	50.19	Steve Coupland	12 Jun 94
	50.37	Bob Danville	27 Jul 82
	50.38	Andy Todd	18 Sep 69
30	50.43	Charles Robertson-Adams	17 Aug 97
	50.49	Eddie Betts	13 Jul 97
	50.52	Paul Hibbert	30 Jun 96
	50.58	Colin O'Neill	29 Jan 74
	50.58	Mike Whittingham	7 Aug 82
	50.68	Peter Warden	18 Jun 66
	50.70	Noel Levy	8 Jul 94
	50.71	Steve Hawkins	4 Jun 89
	50.79	Mark Davidson	17 Jun 89
	50.79	Lloyd Cowan	3 Jun 95
40	50.82 "	Paul Atherton	12 Jun 83
		50.91	6 Jun 84
	50.84	Mark Whitby	6 Jun 84
	50.84	Matthew Elias	29 Jul 99
	50.86	Wilbert Greaves	18 May 80
	50.88	Greg Dunson	7 Jun 92
	50.91	Brian Whittle	5 Jun 93
	50.94	Trevor Burton	17 Jul 87
	50.97	Dave Savage	15 Jun 96
	50.98	Tom Farrell	15 Jun 60
50	50.98	Stan Devine	14 Jul 82
	51.04	Peter Kelly	12 Jun 76
	51.08	Tim Gwynne	30 May 94
	51.09	Steve Black	14 Jul 73
	51.09	Richard McDonald	22 Aug 00

hand timing

49.9	Andy Todd	9 Oct 69
50.5	Wilbert Greaves	12 Feb 80
50.7	Steve Black	20 Aug 74
50.7	Stewart McCallum	21 Mar 76
50.8	Dave Schärer	26 Jun 71
51.0	Chris Surety	2 Sep 61
51.0	Richard McDonald	24 Jul 99

HIGH JUMP

2.38 i	Steve Smith	4 Feb 94	
	2.37	20 Sep 92	
2.37 i	Smith	14 Mar 93	
2.37	Smith	22 Aug 93	
2.37 i	Dalton Grant	13 Mar 94	
	2.36	1 Sep 91	
2.36 i	Smith	5 Feb 93	
2.36 i	Smith	24 Feb 94	
2.36 i	Smith	10 Feb 96	
2.36 i	Smith	8 Feb 98	
2.36	Smith	27 Jun 99	
2.32 i	Brendan Reilly	24 Feb 94	
	2.31	17 Jul 92	
2.31	Geoff Parsons	26 Aug 94	
2.30	Ben Challenger	13 Jul 99	
2.28 i	John Holman	28 Jan 89	
	2.24	27 May 89	
2.26	James Brierley	3 Aug 96	
2.25	Floyd Manderson	20 Aug 88	
2.24	Mark Naylor	28 Jun 80	
2.24	John Hill	23 Aug 85	10
2.24	Phil McDonnell	26 Aug 85	
2.23	Mark Lakey	29 Aug 82	
2.23 i	David Abrahams	12 Mar 83	
	2.19	7 Oct 82	
2.22	Danny Graham	20 May 00	
2.21	Fayyaz Ahmed	29 Jun 86	
2.21	Steve Chapman	30 Jul 89	
2.20	Brian Burgess	11 Jun 78	
2.20	Trevor Llewelyn	15 Jul 83	
2.20	Byron Morrison	14 Jul 84	
2.20 i	Henderson Pierre	10 Jan 87	20
	2.18	16 Aug 86	
2.20	Alex Kruger	18 Jun 88	
2.20	Ossie Cham	21 May 89	
2.20 i	Warren Caswell	10 Mar 90	
	2.18	2 Sep 90	
2.20	Colin Bent	16 Jun 96	
2.20 i	Stuart Ohrland	1 Feb 97	
	2.18	28 Aug 99	
2.20	Stuart Smith	13 Apr 97	
2.20	David Barnetson	3 Aug 97	
2.20 i	Robert Mitchell	16 Jan 00	
	2.20	19 Aug 00	
2.19 i	Mike Robbins	3 Feb 96	
	2.17	5 Aug 95	
2.18	Tim Foulger	23 Sep 79	30
2.18	Rupert Charles	25 Jul 82	
2.18	Steve Ritchie	15 Jul 89	
2.18	Hopeton Lindo	23 Jul 89	
2.18	Andrew Lynch	9 Jul 95	
2.18 i	Tony Gilhooly	9 Mar 97	
	2.18	12 Sep 99	
2.17 i	Richard Aspden	11 Feb 99	
	2.16	7 Jul 95	
2.16 i	Mike Butterfield	23 Jan 76	
2.16 i	Claude Moseley	13 Apr 80	
	2.16	19 Jul 81	
2.16 i	David Watson	13 Mar 82	
	2.15	19 Aug 84	
2.16	Andy Hutchinson	2 Sep 84	40
2.16	Mike Powell	3 Sep 88	
2.16	John Wallace	29 Jul 90	
2.16	Rob Brocklebank	7 Jul 95	
2.16	Ian Holliday	8 Aug 98	
2.16 i	Jason McDade	24 Jan 99	
	2.15	30 Aug 98	
2.16 i	Andrew Penk	20 Feb 00	
	2.15	31 May 97	

POLE VAULT

Rank	Mark	Athlete	Date
	5.80	Nick Buckfield	27 May 98
	5.75	Buckfield	7 Sep 97
	5.71	Buckfield	16 Jun 96
	5.70	Buckfield	23 Jul 95
	5.70	Buckfield	8 Aug 97
	5.70	Buckfield	10 Aug 97
	5.65	Keith Stock	7 Jul 81
	5.65	Buckfield	26 May 96
	5.62	Buckfield	29 May 97
	5.61	Kevin Hughes	28 Jul 99
	5.61 i	Buckfield	3 Feb 96
	5.60	Neil Winter	19 Aug 95
	5.59	Brian Hooper	6 Sep 80
	5.55	Paul Williamson	13 May 00
	5.52	Mike Edwards	13 May 93
	5.45 i	Andy Ashurst	16 Feb 92
		5.40	19 Jun 88
	5.45	Mike Barber	27 Jul 97
10	5.40 A	Jeff Gutteridge ¶	23 Apr 80
		5.40	5 Jun 83
	5.40 i	Matt Belsham	10 Feb 96
		5.35	26 Jun 93
	5.40	Tim Thomas	2 Aug 97
	5.40	Ben Flint	25 Jul 99
	5.35	Ian Tullett	26 Jul 98
	5.30	Dean Mellor	17 Jun 95
	5.30	Christian North	25 Jul 99
	5.26	Mark Johnson	31 Aug 91
	5.25	Mike Bull	22 Sep 73
	5.25	Allan Williams	29 Aug 77
20	5.25	Daley Thompson	15 Jun 86
	5.25	Tom Richards	8 Aug 99
	5.21	Graham Eggleton	10 Jul 82
	5.21 i	Christian Linskey	20 Feb 99
		5.20	24 May 98
	5.20	Billy Davey	5 Jun 83
	5.20	Warren Siley	4 Aug 90
	5.20	Mark Hodgkinson	24 Aug 96
	5.20	Neil Young	2 Aug 97
	5.20	Mark Davis	25 Jul 99
	5.18	Steve Chappell	15 Jun 78
30	5.11	Andrew Gayle	10 Aug 91
	5.10	Darren Wright	12 Jun 88
	5.10	Paul Phelps	9 Jul 89
	5.10	Mark Grant	20 May 95
	5.10 i	Scott Simpson	13 Feb 00
		5.00	26 Jun 99
	5.02	Bob Kingman	29 Aug 94
	5.02 i	Craig Guite	11 Jan 97
	5.01	Paul Hoad	16 Aug 86
	5.00	Richard Gammage	19 Aug 84
	5.00	Brian Taylor	5 May 91
40	5.00	Dan Gilby	20 Jul 91
	5.00	Paul Wray	26 Jul 91
	5.00	Alex Greig	31 May 92
	5.00	Barry Thomas	23 Aug 92
	5.00	Ian Wilding	1 Jun 96
	5.00	Andrew Weston	29 Jul 98
	5.00	Matt Weaver	25 Jul 99
	5.00 i	Ashley Swain	16 Aug 00

LONG JUMP

Rank	Mark	Athlete	Date
	8.23	Lynn Davies	30 Jun 68
	8.18 A	Davies	9 Apr 66
	8.15	Stewart Faulkner	16 Jul 90
	8.14	Davies	18 Jun 69
	8.14	Faulkner	25 Aug 89
	8.14	Mark Forsythe	7 Jul 91
	8.13 A	Davies	6 Apr 66
	8.13 A	Davies	19 Oct 67
	8.13	Faulkner	12 Aug 89
	8.11	Nathan Morgan	24 Jul 98
	8.10	Fred Salle	9 Sep 94
	8.08	Roy Mitchell	27 Sep 80
	8.05 i	Barrington Williams	11 Feb 89
		8.01	17 Jun 89
	8.03	Steve Phillips	5 Aug 98
	8.01	Daley Thompson	8 Aug 84
10	8.00	Derrick Brown	7 Aug 85
	7.98	Alan Lerwill	29 Jun 74
	7.94 i	Paul Johnson	10 Mar 89
		7.85	3 Jun 89
	7.91	John King	26 Sep 87
	7.90	Ian Simpson	3 Jun 89
	7.90	Chris Davidson	19 Jun 99
	7.90	Darren Ritchie	19 Aug 00
	7.89	George Audu	12 Aug 00
	7.87	Keith Fleming	7 Jun 87
	7.84	Wayne Griffith	25 Aug 89
20	7.83	Phil Idowu	25 Jul 00
	7.79	John Morbey	11 Jul 64
	7.79	Geoff Hignett	31 May 71
	7.79	Don Porter	13 Jul 75
	7.77	Len Tyson	25 Jul 82
	7.77	Dean Macey	27 Sep 00
	7.76	Carl Howard	31 Jul 93
	7.75	Ken Cocks	2 Jul 78
	7.75	Trevor Hoyte	6 May 84
	7.75	Michael Morgan	30 Jul 94
30	7.74	Fred Alsop	6 Jun 64
	7.74 i	Phil Scott	17 Feb 73
		7.68	27 May 73
	7.74 i	Aston Moore	10 Jan 81
	7.74	John Herbert	14 Jul 85
	7.74	David Burgess	4 Jul 87
	7.73	Jason Canning	20 Apr 88
	7.72	Femi Abejide	20 Jun 86
	7.71	Billie Kirkpatrick	2 Jun 78
	7.71 i	Keith Connor	20 Feb 81
	7.70	Kevin Liddington	27 Aug 88
40	7.70	Julian Flynn	19 Jun 99
	7.68	Garry Slade	1 Aug 92
	7.67	Dave Walker	14 Sep 68
	7.67	Oni Onuorah	15 Jun 96
	7.66	Tony Henry	12 Jun 77
	7.66	Barry Nevison	7 Jul 85
	7.66	John Shepherd	18 Jun 88
	7.65 i	John Munroe	11 Feb 95
		7.64	24 Jun 95
	7.64	Gus Udo	6 Sep 80
	7.64	Eddie Starrs	11 Jul 81
50	7.64 i	Enyinna Chukukere	6 Mar 94

wind assisted

	Mark	Athlete	Date
	8.17	Mark Forsythe	11 Jun 89
	8.16	Roy Mitchell	26 Jun 76
	8.15	Alan Lerwill	29 May 72
	8.15	Lerwill	15 Jul 72
	8.14	Forsythe	23 Jun 89
	8.12	Derrick Brown	14 Jun 86
	8.11	Daley Thompson	7 Aug 78
	8.07	Steve Phillips	11 Jul 99
	8.04	Ian Simpson	3 Jun 89
	7.96	Colin Jackson	17 May 86
	7.94	John Herbert	25 Jul 82
10	7.94	John King	20 Jun 86
	7.94	Chris Davidson	21 Jun 97
	7.93	David Burgess	15 Jun 86
	7.92	Darren Ritchie	26 Jun 99
	7.91	Steve Ingram	18 Jun 94
	7.89	John Shepherd	20 Jun 86
	7.87	Paul Johnson	15 May 88
	7.84	George Audu	22 May 99
	7.82	Peter Reed	20 Jul 68
	7.82	Femi Abejide	20 Jun 86
20	7.82	Kevin Liddington	25 Jun 89
	7.81	Enyinna Chukukere	9 Apr 94
	7.81	Oni Onuorah	21 Aug 95
	7.76	Aston Moore	7 Aug 77
	7.76	Julian Flynn	19 Jun 99
	7.72	Ken McKay	21 Jun 85
	7.72	Nick Riley	18 Jun 88
	7.70	Derek Cole	29 May 72
	7.69	Garry Slade	12 Jun 88

TRIPLE JUMP

	Mark	Athlete	Date
	18.29	Jonathan Edwards	7 Aug 95
	18.01	Edwards	9 Jul 98
	18.00	Edwards	27 Aug 95
	17.99	Edwards	23 Aug 98
	17.98	Edwards	18 Jul 95
	17.88	Edwards	27 Jul 96
	17.82	Edwards	25 Jun 96
	17.79	Edwards	14 Aug 96
	17.75	Edwards	12 Aug 98
	17.57 A	Keith Connor	5 Jun 82
		17.31 i	13 Mar 81
		17.30	9 Jun 82
	17.41	John Herbert	2 Sep 85
	17.30	Larry Achike	23 Sep 00
	17.21	Tosi Fasinro	27 Jul 93
	17.18	Francis Agyepong	7 Jul 95
	17.12	Phil Idowu	23 Sep 00
	17.06	Julian Golley	10 Sep 94
	17.01	Eric McCalla	3 Aug 84
10	16.87	Mike Makin	2 Aug 86
	16.86	Aston Moore	16 Aug 81
	16.75	Vernon Samuels	7 Aug 88
	16.63 A	Femi Akinsanya	10 Apr 99
		16.58	15 Jun 96
	16.57	Tosin Oke	8 Aug 99
	16.46	Fred Alsop	16 Oct 64
	16.32	Tayo Erogbogbo	21 Aug 95
	16.30	Nick Thomas	22 Jul 00
	16.30	Femi Abejide	27 Jun 85
	16.29 i	David Johnson	1 Mar 78
		16.18	22 Jun 75
20	16.26	Joe Sweeney	3 Aug 91
	16.22	Derek Boosey	15 Jun 68
	16.20	Rez Cameron	5 Jun 88
	16.18	Tony Wadhams	6 Jul 69
	16.17	John Mackenzie	17 Sep 94
	16.16	Conroy Brown	19 Sep 81
	16.15	Wayne Green	10 Jul 88
	16.15	Michael Brown	23 Jul 89
	16.13	Steven Anderson	11 Jun 83
	16.10	Alan Lerwill	28 Aug 71
30	16.09	Courtney Charles	17 Jun 90
	16.08	Craig Duncan	21 Jun 86
	16.02	Peter Akwaboah	15 Jun 89
	16.02	Jonathan Moore	13 Aug 00
	15.99	Steven Shalders	20 Oct 00
	15.98	Frank Attoh	5 Sep 80
	15.97	Mike Ralph	23 Jul 64
	15.97	Carl Howard	6 May 95
	15.95	Derek Browne	12 Jun 93
	15.92	John Slaney	15 Oct 77
40	15.92	Lawrence Lynch	13 Jul 85
	15.91 i	Akin Oyediran	3 Mar 84
	15.91	Dave Emanuel	31 Aug 91
	15.90	David Wood	16 Sep 84
	15.88	John Phillips	14 May 78
	15.87	Chris Colman	15 Jul 78
	15.87	Stewart Faulkner	22 Aug 87
	15.86 i	Donovan Perkins	23 Jan 81
	15.86	Joe Allison	24 Aug 85
	15.82	Graham Hamlyn	12 Jul 68
50	15.82 i	Charles Madeira-Cole	15 Mar 98
	15.82	Jon Wallace	11 Jul 98
	15.80	Richard Edwards	21 Mar 87

wind assisted

	Mark	Athlete	Date
	18.43	Jonathan Edwards	25 Jun 95
	18.08	Edwards	23 Jul 95
	18.03	Edwards	2 Jul 95
	17.81	Keith Connor	9 Oct 82
	17.31	Larry Achike	15 Jul 00
	17.30	Tosi Fasinro	12 Jun 93
	17.29 A	Francis Agyepong	29 Jul 95
		17.24	2 Jul 95
	17.02	Aston Moore	14 Jun 81
	16.82	Vernon Samuels	24 Jun 89
	16.65	Fred Alsop	13 Aug 65
	16.49	Tony Wadhams	16 Sep 69
10	16.44	Tayo Erogbogbo	31 May 97
	16.38	Femi Abejide	10 Jun 89
	16.38	Courtney Charles	22 Jul 90
	16.33	David Johnson	28 May 78
	16.32	Craig Duncan	20 Jun 87
	16.32	Rez Cameron	21 May 89
	16.21	Alan Lerwill	28 Aug 71
	16.17	Chris Colman	15 Jul 78
	16.12	Donovan Perkins	21 Sep 80
	16.00	Frank Attoh	14 Jun 80

SHOT

	Mark	Name	Date
	21.68	Geoff Capes	18 May 80
	21.55	Capes	28 May 76
	21.50	Capes	24 May 80
	21.37	Capes	10 Aug 74
	21.36	Capes	19 Jun 76
	21.35	Capes	5 Jun 80
	21.30	Capes	3 Jul 77
	21.20	Capes	22 Aug 76
	21.18	Capes	8 May 76
	21.15	Capes	23 May 76
	20.85 i	Mark Proctor	25 Jan 98
		20.40	7 Jul 99
	20.45	Shaun Pickering	17 Aug 97
	20.43	Mike Winch	22 May 74
	20.33	Paul Edwards ¶	9 Jul 91
	19.72	Mark Edwards	16 Aug 00
	19.56	Arthur Rowe	7 Aug 61
	19.49	Matt Simson	28 Aug 94
	19.46	Carl Myerscough ¶	6 Sep 98
10	19.44 i	Simon Williams	28 Jan 89
		19.17	18 May 91
	19.43	Bill Tancred	18 May 74
	19.18	Jeff Teale ¶	7 Aug 68
	19.01	Billy Cole	21 Jun 86
	18.94	Bob Dale	12 Jun 76
	18.93	Paul Buxton	13 May 77
	18.85	Lee Newman	2 Jun 96
	18.79	Steph Hayward	6 Sep 00
	18.62	Martyn Lucking	2 Oct 62
	18.59 i	Alan Carter	11 Apr 65
		18.26	1 May 65
20	18.50	Mike Lindsay	2 Jul 63
	18.46	Roger Kennedy	22 May 77
	18.46 i	Simon Rodhouse	20 Feb 82
		18.20	25 Jul 82
	18.35	Peter Tancred	9 Jul 74
	18.34	Richard Slaney	3 Jul 83
	18.14 i	Neal Brunning ¶	26 Jan 92
		17.45	17 Aug 91
	18.10	Emeka Udechuku	9 Sep 00
	18.05	John Watts	19 Aug 72
	18.04	Andy Vince	30 Apr 83
	17.96	Nigel Spratley	28 Aug 94
30	17.95	Graham Savory	4 Jun 88
	17.92	Nick Tabor	9 Apr 83
	17.87	Bill Fuller	15 Jul 72
	17.87 i	Ian Lindley	15 Mar 81
		17.58	25 May 81
	17.87 i	Antony Zaidman	22 Jan 83
		17.22	4 Jul 81
	17.79	John Alderson	31 Jul 74
	17.78	Steve Whyte	11 Feb 89
	17.62	Neil Gray	7 Jun 89
	17.55	David Callaway	1 Aug 93
	17.54	Eric Irvine	16 Aug 86
40	17.50	David Readle	25 Mar 00
	17.47	Carl Jennings	13 Sep 87
	17.45	Abi Ekoku	3 Feb 90
	17.44	Hamish Davidson	3 Jun 78
	17.41	Lee Wiltshire	1 May 94
	17.41	Jamie Cockburn	12 May 96
	17.40	Barry King	11 Apr 70
	17.40	Allan Seatory	27 Apr 75
	17.36 i	Chris Ellis	8 Dec 84

DISCUS

	Mark	Name	Date
	66.64	Perris Wilkins	6 Jun 98
	65.22	Wilkins	30 Aug 97
	65.16	Richard Slaney	1 Jul 85
	65.11	Glen Smith	18 Jul 99
	65.08	Robert Weir	19 Aug 00
	64.94	Bill Tancred	21 Jul 74
	64.87	Wilkins	12 Jun 99
	64.68	Slaney	6 Jul 84
	64.65	Wilkins	22 Jul 00
	64.64	Slaney	30 Apr 82
	62.36	Peter Tancred	8 May 80
	62.07	Emeka Udechuku	19 Aug 00
	61.86	Paul Mardle	13 Jun 84
	61.62	Peter Gordon	15 Jun 91
10	61.14	Simon Williams	18 Apr 92
	61.10	Kevin Brown	30 Aug 97
	61.00	Allan Seatory	6 Oct 74
	60.92	Graham Savory	10 May 86
	60.48	Lee Newman	10 May 97
	60.42	Mike Cushion	16 Aug 75
	60.19	Carl Myerscough ¶	8 Aug 98
	60.08	Abi Ekoku	16 May 90
	59.84	Colin Sutherland ¶	10 Jun 78
	59.76	John Hillier	27 Jul 74
20	59.70	John Watts	14 Jul 72
	58.64	Steve Casey	19 May 91
	58.58	Darrin Morris	22 Jun 91
	58.36	Paul Reed	11 Jul 99
	58.34	Geoff Capes	29 Sep 73
	58.08	Mike Winch	7 Sep 75
	57.58	Arthur McKenzie	17 Aug 69
	57.14	Mark Proctor	24 Jun 00
	57.12	Paul Edwards ¶	10 Aug 88
	57.10	Dennis Roscoe	3 May 80
30	57.00	Gerry Carr	17 Jul 65
	56.71	Roy Hollingsworth	14 Sep 63
	56.66	Gary Herrington	15 Jun 96
	56.42	Paul Buxton	6 Aug 76
	56.40	Guy Dirkin	1 Aug 75
	55.68	Neville Thompson	12 Jun 93
	55.68	Leith Marar	24 Jul 96
	55.60	Jeff Clare	25 Jul 88
	55.52	Jamie Murphy	29 Jul 95
	55.42	Geoff Tyler	3 May 80
40	55.34	Nick Woolcott	27 Jul 88
	55.32	Mike Lindsay	4 May 60
	55.04	Denzil McDonald	28 Aug 95
	54.78	Colin Bastien	29 Mar 87
	54.38	Shaun Pickering	26 Aug 89
	54.36	Matt Symonds	24 Jun 95
	54.27	Mark Pharoah	27 Nov 56
	54.16	Scott Hayes	23 Mar 97
	54.01	Eric Cleaver	21 Oct 62
	53.76	John Turton	18 May 79
50	53.76	Robert Russell	8 Sep 96

HAMMER

	Mark	Name	Date
	77.54	Martin Girvan	12 May 84
	77.30	Dave Smith I	13 Jul 85
	77.16	Girvan	13 Jul 84
	77.04	Smith I	25 May 85
	77.02	Matt Mileham	11 May 84
	76.92	Girvan	5 May 84
	76.60	Smith I	6 Sep 86
	76.38	Girvan	25 Apr 84
	76.36	Smith I	5 May 85
	76.36	Smith I	29 Jun 85
	75.94	Mick Jones	6 Sep 00
	75.40	Chris Black	23 Jul 83
	75.10	Dave Smith II	27 May 96
	75.08	Robert Weir	3 Oct 82
	74.02	Paul Head	30 Aug 90
	73.86	Barry Williams	1 Jul 76
10	73.80	Jason Byrne	19 Sep 92
	73.20	Paul Dickenson	22 May 76
	72.63	Bill Beauchamp	25 Jul 99
	71.60	Shane Peacock	24 Jun 90
	71.28	Peter Vivian	25 Jun 95
	71.00	Ian Chipchase	17 Aug 74
	70.88	Howard Payne	29 Jun 74
	70.33	John Pearson	30 Jul 00
	70.30	Stewart Rogerson	14 Aug 88
	70.28	Paul Buxton	19 May 79
20	69.52	Jim Whitehead	23 Sep 79
	69.38	Mike Floyd	18 Jun 00
	68.64	Shaun Pickering	7 Apr 84
	68.18	Ron James	2 Jun 82
	67.82	Steve Whyte	15 Apr 89
	67.45	Steve Pearson	27 Jun 98
	67.32	Gareth Cook	1 Jun 91
	66.97	Chris Howe	6 Jun 98
	66.00	Russell Devine	28 Jan 99
	65.32	Simon Bown	20 Jun 99
30	65.30	Karl Andrews	2 Jul 94
	64.95	Mike Ellis	4 Jun 59
	64.80	Bruce Fraser	30 Sep 73
	64.64	Iain Park	22 Jul 98
	64.54	Michael Petra	30 May 79
	64.39	Craig Ellams	19 Aug 00
	64.36	Andrew Tolputt	27 Jun 87
	63.74	Mark Sterling	18 Jul 84
	63.71	David Allen	26 Jun 99
	63.59	Matthew Bell	25 Jul 99
40	63.20	Peter Gordon	17 Sep 82
	63.16	Graham Callow	29 May 89
	62.88	Anthony Swain	13 Apr 97
	62.70	Paul Barnard	19 Jul 95
	62.60	Peter Weir	2 Aug 87
	62.60	Rob Earle	1 Aug 95
	62.56	Adrian Palmer	6 Aug 94
	62.54	Tony Elvin	25 May 70
	62.42	Malcolm Fenton	16 May 82
	62.40	Lawrie Nisbet	5 Jul 86
50	62.32	Peter Aston	6 Sep 75
	62.28	Lawrie Bryce	13 Oct 73

JAVELIN

Mark	Name	Date	
91.46	Steve Backley	25 Jan 92	
89.89	Backley	19 Jul 98	
89.85	Backley	23 Sep 00	
89.72	Backley	23 Aug 98	
89.58	Backley	2 Jul 90	
89.22	Backley	11 Jun 98	
89.02	Backley	30 May 97	
88.80	Backley	2 Aug 98	
88.71 A	Backley	13 Sep 98	
88.54	Backley	7 Jul 95	
86.94	Mick Hill	13 Jun 93	
85.67	Mark Roberson	19 Jul 98	
85.09	Nick Nieland	13 Aug 00	
83.84	Roald Bradstock	2 May 87	
82.38	Colin Mackenzie	7 Aug 93	
81.70	Nigel Bevan	28 Jun 92	
80.98	Dave Ottley	24 Sep 88	
78.54	Gary Jenson	17 Sep 89	
78.24	David Parker	27 May 00	10
77.84	Peter Yates	21 Feb 87	
76.66 i	Stuart Faben	3 Mar 96	
	75.37	22 Apr 00	
75.52	Marcus Humphries	25 Jul 97	
75.32	Steve Harrison	9 Jul 95	
75.28	Nigel Stainton	5 Aug 89	
74.90	Daryl Brand	27 Jun 86	
74.72	Chris Crutchley	13 Jul 86	
74.70	Myles Cottrell	16 May 92	
73.88	Keith Beard	12 May 90	
73.56	Dan Carter	16 Sep 00	20
73.26	David Messom	25 Apr 87	
72.92	Stefan Baldwin	8 May 93	
71.86	Tony Hatton	3 May 93	
71.79	Phill Sharpe	27 Aug 00	
70.90	Shane Lewis	6 Jun 98	
70.30	Tim Newenham	11 Jun 89	
70.12	Paul Morgan	12 Sep 87	
70.10	Richard Hooper	21 May 89	
70.00	Paul Bushnell	22 Jul 90	
70.00	Phil Parry	2 Jul 94	30
69.90	Ken Hayford	5 Jul 87	
69.90	Tony Smith	6 Jul 96	
69.20	Roddy James	28 Apr 89	
69.02	Kevin Murch	2 Sep 89	
68.91	Stuart Loughran	26 Jul 98	
68.84	James Hurrion	12 Jul 91	
68.74	Jon Clarke	14 Jun 86	
68.74	Tony Norman	23 May 87	
68.70	Robert Mullen	2 Jul 96	
68.38	James Drennen	12 Jul 91	40
68.30	Mark Lawrence	31 Jul 88	
68.27	Neil McLellan	1 Jul 00	
68.10	Paul Edgington	12 Oct 86	
68.08	Tim Kitney	13 Sep 98	
68.02	Mark Francis	12 Jul 97	
67.62	Alan Holloway	25 Jun 89	
67.60	Dean Smahon	9 Jul 94	
67.48	Rob Laing	31 May 87	
67.44	John Guthrie	17 May 89	
67.22	Richard Atkinson	14 Aug 93	50

DECATHLON (1985 Tables)

	8847	Daley Thompson	9 Aug 84
	8811	Thompson	28 Aug 86
	8774	Thompson	8 Sep 82
	8730	Thompson	23 May 82
	8714	Thompson	13 Aug 83
	8667	Thompson	18 May 86
	8663	Thompson	28 Jul 86
	8648	Thompson	18 May 80
	8567	Dean Macey	28 Sep 00
	8556	Macey	25 Aug 99
	8131	Alex Kruger	2 Jul 95
	7980	Simon Shirley	24 Aug 94
	7922 w	Brad McStravick	28 May 84
		7885	6 May 84
	7904	David Bigham	28 Jun 92
	7901	Peter Gabbett	22 May 72
	7889	Eugene Gilkes	18 May 86
	7874	Colin Boreham	23 May 82
10	7861	Anthony Brannen	30 Apr 95
	7787	Brian Taylor	30 May 93
	7766	Barry Thomas	2 Sep 95
	7748	Eric Hollingsworth	30 May 93
	7740	Greg Richards	7 Jun 87
	7739	Jamie Quarry	30 May 99
	7713	James Stevenson	5 Jun 93
	7708	Fidelis Obikwu	28 May 84
	7663	Rafer Joseph	24 Aug 94
	7643 w	Tom Leeson	8 Sep 85
		7565	11 Aug 85
20	7635 w	Du'aine Ladejo	24 May 98
		7633	18 Sep 98
	7596	Mike Corden	27 Jun 76
	7594	Mark Bishop	3 Sep 89
	7579	Mark Luscombe	8 May 88
	7571	Alexis Sharp	17 Apr 98
	7535	Duncan Mathieson	24 Jun 90
	7515	Ken Hayford	9 Jun 85
	7500	Barry King	22 May 72
	7500	Pan Zeniou	2 Aug 81
	7439	Kevan Lobb	19 Aug 84
30	7431	Alan Drayton	8 Aug 78
	7425	Anthony Southward	16 Jun 96
	7425 w	Paul Field	21 May 95
		7295	2 Jul 95
	7367	John Garner	8 May 88
	7363	Mike Bull	27 Jan 74
	7363	Nick Phipps	27 Jun 76
	7335	Stewart McCallum	19 Aug 73
	7308	Clive Longe	29 Jun 69
	7295	Stephen Rogers	4 Jun 95
	7275	Buster Watson	18 Jun 78
40	7268	Paul Edwards ¶	14 Aug 83
	7240	Paul Allan	25 Aug 91
	7221	Andy Lewis	19 Jun 94
	7198	Robert Betts	7 Aug 83
	7172	Dave Kidner	20 Aug 72
	7159	Roger Hunter	20 Jul 97
	7147	Justin Whitfield	12 May 85
	7146	Steve Bonnett	30 May 99
	7136	Billy Jewers	3 Sep 89
	7116	Fyn Corcoran	23 May 99
50	7112	Gavin Sunshine	30 Jul 93

3000 METRES TRACK WALK

	11:24.4	Mark Easton	10 May 89
	11:28.4	Phil Vesty	9 May 84
	11:29.6 i	Tim Berrett	21 Jan 90
		11:54.23	23 Jun 84
	11:31.0	Andi Drake	22 Jul 90
	11:32.2	Ian McCombie	20 Jul 88
	11:33.4	Steve Partington	12 Jul 95
	11:35.5	Andy Penn	10 May 97
	11:39.0 i+	Martin Rush	8 Feb 92
		11:49.48	1 Jul 84
	11:44.68	Roger Mills	7 Aug 81
10	11:45.1	Chris Maddocks	9 Aug 87
	11:45.77	Steve Johnson	20 Jun 87
	11:47.12 i	Philip King	26 Feb 95
		11:49.64	29 May 95
	11:49.0	Darrell Stone	10 Jul 90
	11:51.1	Paul Nihill	5 Jun 71
	11:52.51	Sean Martindale	28 Jul 90
	11:53.3	Martin Bell	9 Aug 95
	11:53.46	Steve Barry	21 Aug 82
	11:54.7	Mike Parker	20 Apr 82
	11:55.0	Phil Embleton	24 May 71

10000 METRES TRACK WALK

	40:06.65	Ian McCombie	4 Jun 89
	40:39.77	McCombie	5 Jun 88
	40:42.53	McCombie	28 Aug 89
	40:45.87	McCombie	25 May 87
	40:47.5 +	McCombie	26 May 90
	40:53.60	Phil Vesty	28 May 84
	40:55.6	Martin Rush	14 Sep 91
	41:06.57	Chris Maddocks	20 Jun 87
	41:10.11	Darrell Stone	16 Jul 95
	41:13.62	Steve Barry	19 Jun 82
	41:13.65	Martin Bell	22 Jul 95
	41:14.3	Mark Easton	5 Feb 89
	41:14.61	Steve Partington	16 Jul 95
10	41:18.64	Andi Drake	5 Jun 88
	41:49.06	Sean Martindale	26 Jun 90
	41:55.5	Phil Embleton	14 Apr 71
	41:59.10	Andy Penn	27 Jul 91
	42:06.35	Gordon Vale	2 Aug 81
	42:08.57	Paul Blagg	28 Aug 89
	42:23.0	Mike Parker	2 Feb 86
	42:28.0	Philip King	17 May 95
	42:34.6	Paul Nihill	28 May 72
	42:35.6	Ken Matthews	1 Aug 60
20	42:40.0	Brian Adams	29 Mar 75
	42:41.6	Mick Greasley	25 May 80
	42:42.18	Steve Johnson	5 Jun 88
	42:44.0	George Nibre	2 Apr 80
	42:45.0	Tim Berrett	22 Jul 88
	42:54.6	Roger Mills	25 May 80

track short

	40:54.7	Steve Barry	19 Mar 83

20 KILOMETRES ROAD WALK

	Time	Name	Date
	1:22:03	Ian McCombie	23 Sep 88
	1:22:12	Chris Maddocks	3 May 92
	1:22:35	Maddocks	27 May 89
	1:22:37	McCombie	11 May 85
	1:22:51	Steve Barry	26 Feb 83
	1:22:58	McCombie	27 May 89
	1:23:15	Barry	14 May 83
	1:23:24	McCombie	24 May 86
	1:23:26	McCombie	28 Feb 87
	1:23:26.5t	McCombie	26 May 90
	1:23:34	Andy Penn	29 Feb 92
	1:23:34	Martin Rush	29 Feb 92
	1:23:58	Darrell Stone	24 Feb 96
	1:24:04	Mark Easton	25 Feb 89
	1:24:04.0t	Andi Drake	26 May 90
	1:24:07.6t	Phil Vesty	1 Dec 84
10	1:24:09	Steve Partington	24 Sep 94
	1:24:25	Tim Berrett	21 Apr 90
	1:24:50	Paul Nihill	30 Jul 72
	1:25:42	Martin Bell	9 May 92
	1:25:53.6t	Sean Martindale	28 Apr 89
	1:26:53	Chris Cheeseman	21 Mar 99
	1:27:00	Roger Mills	30 Jun 80
	1:27:04.0t	Steve Hollier	9 Jan 00
	1:27:16	Les Morton	25 Feb 89
	1:27:35	Olly Flynn	3 Oct 76
20	1:27:46	Brian Adams	11 Oct 75
	1:27:59	Phil Embleton	3 Apr 71
	1:28:02	Paul Blagg	27 Feb 82
	1:28:15	Ken Matthews	23 Jul 60
	1:28:26	Chris Harvey	29 Sep 79
	1:28:30	Allan King	11 May 85
	1:28:34	Chris Smith	11 May 85
	1:28:37	Dave Jarman	30 Jun 80
	1:28:46	Jimmy Ball	4 Apr 87
	1:28:46	Steve Taylor	20 Dec 92
30	1:28:46	Jamie O'Rawe	21 Mar 99
	1:28:50	Amos Seddon	3 Aug 74
	1:29:07	Philip King	20 Aug 95
	1:29:19	Stuart Phillips	31 May 92
	1:29:24	George Nibre	6 Apr 80
	1:29:27	Graham White	19 Apr 97
	1:29:29 +	Steve Johnson	16 Apr 89
	1:29:37	John Warhurst	28 Jul 73
	1:29:42	Dennis Jackson	10 May 86
	1:29:48	Mike Parker	8 May 82
40	1:29:48	Martin Young	31 Mar 96
	1:29:49	Peter Marlow	3 Aug 74
	1:30:00	John Webb	18 May 68
	1:30:02	Bob Dobson	3 Aug 74
	1:30:15	Gareth Brown	13 May 89
	1:30:16	Roy Thorpe	28 Jul 73
	1:30:22	Roy Sheppard	26 Apr 80
	1:30:27.38t	Steve Gower	10 Jun 78
	1:30:30	Graham Morris	23 Feb 80
	1:30:35	Peter Fullager	4 Apr 70
50	1:30:38	Matthew Hales	21 Mar 99
	1:30:51	Mick Greasley	4 May 80
	1:30:52	Mike Smith	27 Jun 87

50 KILOMETRES ROAD WALK

Time	Name	Date	
3:51:37	Chris Maddocks	28 Oct 90	
3:53:14	Maddocks	25 Nov 95	
3:57:10	Maddocks	12 Mar 00	
3:57:48	Les Morton	30 Apr 89	
3:58:25	Morton	20 Mar 88	
3:58:36	Morton	11 Oct 92	
3:59:30	Morton	30 Sep 88	
3:59:55	Paul Blagg	5 Sep 87	
4:00:02	Maddocks	11 Oct 92	
4:00:07	Blagg	30 Sep 88	
4:03:08	Dennis Jackson	16 Mar 86	
4:03:53	Mark Easton	25 Apr 98	
4:06:14	Barry Graham	20 Apr 85	
4:07:18	Steve Hollier	18 Jun 00	
4:07:23	Bob Dobson	21 Oct 79	
4:07:49	Chris Cheesman	2 May 99	
4:07:57	Ian Richards	20 Apr 80	10
4:08:41	Adrian James	12 Apr 80	
4:09:15un	Don Thompson	10 Oct 65	
	4:12:19	20 Jun 59	
4:09:22	Mike Smith	27 Mar 89	
4:10:23	Darrell Stone	6 May 90	
4:10:42	Amos Seddon	9 Mar 80	
4:11:32	Paul Nihill	18 Oct 64	
4:12:00	Sean Martindale	16 Oct 93	
4:12:02	Martin Rush	28 Jul 91	
4:12:37	John Warhurst	27 May 72	
4:12:50	Darren Thorn	6 May 90	20
4:13:18	Graham White	27 Jun 98	
4:13:25	Allan King	16 Apr 83	
4:14:03	Tom Misson	20 Jun 59	
4:14:25	Dave Cotton	15 Jul 78	
4:15:14	Shaun Lightman	13 Oct 73	
4:15:22	Brian Adams	17 Sep 78	
4:15:52	Ray Middleton	27 May 72	
4:16:30	Karl Atton	20 Apr 97	
4:16:47	George Nibre	9 Mar 80	
4:17:24	Andi Drake	18 Oct 87	30
4:17:34	Gordon Vale	9 Oct 83	
4:17:52	Stuart Elms	17 Apr 76	
4:18:30	Peter Ryan	10 Apr 82	
4:19:00	Carl Lawton	17 Jul 71	
4:19:13	Bryan Eley	19 Jul 69	
4:19:26	Roger Mills	9 Apr 83	
4:19:55	Mick Holmes	4 Aug 73	
4:19:57	Barry Ingarfield	21 Oct 79	
4:20:05	George Chaplin	27 May 72	
4:20:43	Tim Watt	8 Oct 95	40
4:20:48	Andrew Trigg	1 May 88	
4:20:51	Murray Lambden	18 Jul 82	
4:21:02	Ron Wallwork	17 Jul 71	
4:22:05	Mel McCann	14 Sep 86	
4:22:41.0t	Charley Fogg	1 Jun 75	
4:23:12	Peter Hodkinson	21 Jul 79	
4:23:22	Chris Berwick	12 Jul 86	
4:23:32	John Lees	19 Mar 78	
4:23:43	Roy Thorpe	17 Jul 76	
4:23:50	Paul Jarman	18 Jul 81	50
4:24:02	Howard Timms	15 Jul 72	

4 x 100 METRES RELAY

37.73 Great Britain & NI 29 Aug 99
Gardener, Campbell, Devonish, Chambers
37.77 Great Britain & NI 22 Aug 93
Jackson, Jarrett, Regis, Christie ¶
37.98 Great Britain & NI 1 Sep 90
Braithwaite, Regis, Adam, Christie ¶
38.05 Great Britain & NI 21 Aug 93
John, Jarrett, Braithwaite, Christie ¶
38.08 Great Britain & NI 8 Aug 92
Adam, Jarrett, Regis, Christie ¶
38.09 Great Britain & NI 1 Sep 91
Jarrett, Regis, Braithwaite, Christie ¶
38.09 A Great Britain & NI 12 Sep 98
Condon, Devonish, Golding, Chambers
38.14 Great Britain & NI 10 Aug 97
Braithwaite, Campbell, Walker, Golding
38.16 Great Britain & NI 19 Jun 99
Gardener, Campbell, Devonish, Golding
10 38.17 Great Britain & NI 'A' 7 Aug 99
Gardener, Campbell, Devonish, Golding
38.20 England 21 Sep 98
Chambers, Devonish, Golding, Campbell
38.25 Great Britain & NI 9 Aug 97
Chambers, Campbell, Braithwaite, Golding
38.28 Great Britain & NI 1 Oct 88
Bunney, Regis, McFarlane, Christie ¶
38.31 Great Britain & NI 28 Aug 99
Gardener, Campbell, Condon, Chambers
38.34 Great Britain & NI 9 Sep 89
Callender, Regis, Adam, Christie ¶
38.35 Great Britain & NI 28 Aug 00
Chambers, Campbell, Devonish, Gardener
38.36 Great Britain & NI 31 Aug 91
Jarrett, Regis, Braithwaite, Christie ¶
38.39 Great Britain & NI 5 Aug 89
Jarrett, Regis, Adam, Christie ¶
38.41 Great Britain & NI 15 Jul 00
Malcolm, Campbell, Devonish, Chambers
20 38.46 Great Britain & NI 10 Sep 94
Braithwaite, Jarrett, Regis, Christie ¶
38.47 Great Britain & NI 9 Aug 97
Campbell, Devonish, Braithwaite, Golding
38.47 Great Britain & NI 22 Aug 98
Condon, Campbell, Devonish, Chambers
38.52 Great Britain & NI 1 Oct 88
Bunney, Regis, McFarlane, Christie ¶
38.52 Great Britain & NI 22 Aug 98
Condon, Campbell, Walker, Golding
38.53 Great Britain & NI 26 Jun 93
John, Jarrett, Regis, Christie ¶
38.56 Great Britain & NI 27 Jun 98
Condon, Campbell, Walker, Golding
38.58 Great Britain & NI 'B' 7 Aug 99
Condon, Mackie, Regis, Chambers
38.62 Great Britain & NI 1 Aug 80
McFarlane, Wells, Sharp, McMaster
38.62 England 20 Sep 98
Gardener, Devonish, Chambers, Campbell

4 x 400 METRES RELAY

2:56.60 Great Britain & NI 3 Aug 96
Thomas, Baulch, Richardson, Black
2:56.65 Great Britain & NI 10 Aug 97
Thomas, Black, Baulch, Richardson
2:57.53 Great Britain & NI 1 Sep 91
Black, Redmond, Regis, Akabusi
2:58.22 Great Britain & NI 1 Sep 90
Sanders, Akabusi, Regis, Black
2:58.68 Great Britain & NI 23 Aug 98
Hylton, Baulch, Thomas, Richardson
2:58.86 Great Britain & NI 6 Sep 87
Redmond, Akabusi, Black, Brown
2:59.13 Great Britain & NI 11 Aug 84
Akabusi, Cook, Bennett, Brown
2:59.13 Great Britain & NI 14 Aug 94
McKenzie, Whittle, Black, Ladejo
2:59.46 Great Britain & NI 22 Jun 97
Black, Baulch, Thomas, Richardson
2:59.49 Great Britain & NI 31 Aug 91 10
Mafe, Redmond, Richardson, Akabusi
2:59.71 A Great Britain & NI 13 Sep 98
Hylton, Baulch, Baldock, Thomas
2:59.73 Great Britain & NI 8 Aug 92
Black, Grindley, Akabusi, Regis
2:59.84 Great Britain & NI 31 Aug 86
Redmond, Akabusi, Whittle, Black
2:59.85 Great Britain & NI 19 Aug 96
Baulch, Hylton, Richardson, Black
3:00.19 Great Britain & NI 9 Aug 97
Hylton, Black, Baulch, Thomas
3:00.25 Great Britain & NI 27 Jun 93
Ladejo, Akabusi, Regis, Grindley
3:00.34 Great Britain & NI 25 Jun 95
Thomas, Patrick, Richardson, Black
3:00.46 Great Britain & NI 10 Sep 72
Reynolds, Pascoe, Hemery, Jenkins
3:00.58 Great Britain & NI 30 Jun 91
Sanders, Akabusi, Whittle, Black
3:00.61 Great Britain & NI 20 Jun 99 20
Hylton, Baulch, Wariso, Richardson
3:00.68 Great Britain & NI 11 Sep 82
Jenkins, Cook, Bennett, Brown
3:00.82 England 21 Sep 98
Slythe, Wariso, Hylton, Richardson
3:00.93 Great Britain & NI 19 Jun 92
Redmond, Akabusi, Ladejo, Black
3:00.95 Great Britain & NI 28 Jun 98
Black, Baulch, Thomas, Richardson
3:01.03 Great Britain & NI U23 19 Jul 92
McKenzie, Grindley, Richardson, Ladejo
3:01.12 Great Britain & NI 28 Jun 87
Harmsworth, Whittle, Bennett, Black
3:01.20 Great Britain & NI 7 Aug 92
Richardson, Akabusi, Black, Ladejo
3:01.21 A Great Britain & NI 20 Oct 68
Winbolt-Lewis, Campbell, Hemery, Sherwood
3:01.22 Great Britain & NI 12 Aug 95
McKenzie, Patrick, Hylton, Richardson
3:01.22 Great Britain & NI 30 Sep 00 30
Deacon, Caines, Thomas, Baulch

UNDER 23

100 METRES

9.97	Dwain Chambers	22 Aug 99
10.09	Jason Livingston ¶	13 Jun 92
10.13	Marlon Devonish	17 Sep 98
10.17	Ian Mackie	25 Aug 96
10.20	Elliot Bunney	14 Jun 86
10.22	Christian Malcolm	29 Jul 99
10.28	Marcus Adam	11 Aug 89
10.28	Darren Braithwaite	3 Aug 90
10.28	Julian Golding	22 Jul 97
10.28	Jon Barbour	17 Jun 00
wind assisted		
10.07	Toby Box	11 Jun 94
10.10	Donovan Reid	26 Jun 83
10.11	Mike McFarlane	4 Oct 82
10.12	Jason John	29 Aug 93
10.14	Marcus Adam	28 Jan 90
10.16	Daniel Money	21 Jun 97
10.17	Jason Gardener	7 Sep 97
hand timing		
10.1	David Jenkins	20 May 72
10.2	Derek Redmond	2 May 87
wind assisted		
10.1	Drew McMaster	16 Jun 79

200 METRES

20.18	John Regis	3 Sep 87
20.19	Christian Malcolm	27 Sep 00
20.36	Todd Bennett	28 May 84
20.38	Julian Golding	24 Aug 97
20.43	Mike McFarlane	7 Oct 82
20.57	Owusu Dako	16 Jul 95
20.62	Donovan Reid	28 May 84
20.63	Roger Black	12 Sep 86
20.63	Marcus Adam	4 Aug 90
20.65	Marlon Devonish	25 Aug 97
wind assisted		
20.10	Marcus Adam	1 Feb 90
20.51	Jason John	2 Jul 93
20.53	Dougie Walker	8 May 95
20.55	Darren Campbell	2 Jul 93
hand timing		
20.3	David Jenkins	19 Aug 72

400 METRES

44.47	David Grindley	3 Aug 92
44.50	Derek Redmond	1 Sep 87
44.59	Roger Black	29 Aug 86
44.66 A	Iwan Thomas	14 Apr 96
	44.69	16 Jun 96
45.09	Mark Richardson	10 Jul 92
45.14	Jamie Baulch	23 Aug 95
45.18	David Jenkins	16 Aug 74
45.24	Mark Hylton	12 Aug 98
45.25	Du'aine Ladejo	3 Jun 92
45.37	Daniel Caines	23 Sep 00
hand timing		
45.2	Du'aine Ladejo	1 May 93

800 METRES

1:43.97	Sebastian Coe	15 Sep 78
1:43.98	Peter Elliott	23 Aug 83
1:44.45	Steve Cram	17 Jul 82
1:44.65	Ikem Billy	21 Jul 84
1:44.92	Curtis Robb	15 Aug 93
1:45.14	Chris McGeorge	28 Jun 83
1:45.44	Steve Ovett	25 Jul 76
1:45.64	Paul Herbert	5 Jun 88
1:45.70	David Sharpe	2 Jul 88
1:45.80	Steve Crabb	18 Aug 84
1:45.80	Kevin McKay	15 Sep 91

1000 METRES

2:15.12	Steve Cram	17 Sep 82
2:16.34	Matthew Yates	6 Jul 90

1500 METRES

3:33.66	Steve Cram	18 Aug 82
3:33.83	John Robson	4 Sep 79
3:34.00	Matthew Yates	13 Sep 91
3:34.45	Steve Ovett	3 Sep 77
3:35.16	Steve Crabb	28 Jun 84
3:35.72	Graham Williamson	15 Jul 80
3:36.70	Kevin McKay	20 Jul 90
3:36.97	Peter Elliott	1 Jul 84
3:37.25	Jack Buckner	31 Aug 83
3:37.38	Frank Clement	30 Jul 74

ONE MILE

3:49.90	Steve Cram	13 Jul 82
3:50.64	Graham Williamson	13 Jul 82
3:52.74	John Robson	17 Jul 79
3:53.20	Ian Stewart II	25 Aug 82
3:53.44	Jack Buckner	13 Jul 82
3:54.36	Steve Crabb	21 Jul 84
3:54.39	Neil Horsfield	8 Jul 86
3:54.69	Steve Ovett	26 Jun 77
3:55.38	Rob Denmark	12 Aug 90
3:55.41	Colin Reitz	31 Jul 82

2000 METRES

5:01.90	Jack Buckner	29 Aug 83
5:02.67	Gary Staines	4 Aug 85
5:02.99	Neil Caddy	11 Aug 96

3000 METRES

7:41.3	Steve Ovett	23 Sep 77
7:42.47	David Lewis	9 Jul 83
7:43.90	Ian Stewart II	26 Jun 82
7:45.45	Paul Davies-Hale	13 Jul 84
7:46.6+	David Black	14 Sep 73
7:47.12	Simon Mugglestone	27 Jun 88
7:47.82	Steve Cram	26 Jul 81
7:48.6+	Nat Muir	27 Jun 80
7:48.47 i	John Mayock	1 Mar 92
7:49.45	Paul Lawther	9 Sep 77

TWO MILES

8:19.37	Nat Muir	27 Jun 80
8:21.86	David Black	14 Sep 73

5000 METRES

13:17.9	Nat Muir	15 Jul 80
13:19.78	Jon Brown	2 Jul 93
13:22.2	Dave Bedford	12 Jun 71
13:22.85	Ian Stewart I	25 Jul 70
13:23.52	David Black	29 Jan 74
13:24.59	Paul Davies-Hale	1 Jun 84
13:25.0	Steve Ovett	30 Jul 77
13:26.97	John Mayock	9 Jun 92
13:28.29	Simon Mugglestone	8 Jul 88
13:29.28 i	Steve Binns	12 Feb 82

10000 METRES

27:47.0	Dave Bedford	10 Jul 71
27:48.49	David Black	25 Jan 74
28:09.95	Bernie Ford	6 Oct 73
28:12.42	Dave Murphy	13 Jul 79
28:14.08	Jon Richards	20 Jun 86
28:18.8	Nicky Lees	7 May 79
28:19.6	Jon Brown	17 Apr 92
28:20.71	Jim Brown	12 Jul 74
28:20.76	Steve Binns	27 Aug 82
28:24.01	Jack Lane	10 Aug 71

MARATHON

2:12:19	Don Faircloth	23 Jul 70
2:16:04	Ian Ray	27 Oct 79
2:16:21	Norman Wilson	10 Sep 77
2:16:47	Ieuan Ellis	19 Sep 82
2:17:13	Brent Jones	13 May 84

3000 METRES STEEPLECHASE

8:16.52	Tom Hanlon	23 Aug 89
8:18.80	Colin Reitz	6 Jul 82
8:20.83	Paul Davies-Hale	10 Jun 84
8:22.48	John Davies	13 Sep 74
8:28.6	Dave Bedford	10 Sep 71
8:29.72	David Lewis	29 May 83
8:29.86	Tony Staynings	2 Aug 75
8:30.64	Dennis Coates	2 Aug 75
8:31.72	Keith Cullen	28 Jun 92
8:31.80	Graeme Fell	8 Aug 81

110 METRES HURDLES

13.11 A	Colin Jackson	11 Aug 88
	13.11	14 Jul 89
13.21	Tony Jarrett	31 Aug 90
13.29	Jon Ridgeon	15 Jul 87
13.57	David Nelson	11 Aug 89
13.60	Neil Owen	28 Jun 95
13.66	Ross Baillie	20 Feb 99
13.69	Berwyn Price	18 Aug 73
13.71	Mark Holtom	6 Sep 80
13.78	Nigel Walker	24 Jun 84
13.82	Damien Greaves	21 Jun 97
wind assisted		
12.95	Colin Jackson	10 Sep 89
13.70	Nigel Walker	6 Jul 85
hand timing		
13.5	Berwyn Price	1 Jul 73

400 METRES HURDLES

49.11	Gary Oakes	26 Jul 80
49.75	Max Robertson	30 Aug 85
49.86	Martin Briggs	6 Jun 84
50.01	Phil Harries	5 Jun 88
50.20	Matt Douglas	17 Sep 98
50.24	Martin Gillingham	24 Jun 84
50.38	Andy Todd	18 Sep 69
50.43	Philip Beattie	6 Jun 84
50.43	Charles Robertson-Adams	17 Aug 97
50.60	Gary Jennings	21 Jul 94
hand timing		
49.9	Andy Todd	9 Oct 69
50.2	John Sherwood	2 Sep 67

HIGH JUMP

2.38 i	Steve Smith	4 Feb 94
	2.37	22 Aug 93
2.32 i	Brendan Reilly	24 Feb 94
	2.31	17 Jul 92
2.31	Dalton Grant	25 Sep 88
2.30 i	Geoff Parsons	25 Jan 86
	2.28	18 May 86
2.30	Ben Challenger	13 Jul 99
2.28 i	John Holman	28 Jan 89
	2.24	27 May 89
2.23	Phil McDonnell	29 Jul 84
2.22 i	Mark Naylor	3 Feb 79
2.22	Danny Graham	20 May 00
2.21	Fayyaz Ahmed	29 Jun 86

POLE VAULT

5.70	Nick Buckfield	23 Jul 95
5.60	Neil Winter	19 Aug 95
5.50	Paul Williamson	6 Jul 96
5.42	Mike Barber	26 Aug 95
5.40	Ben Flint	25 Jul 99
5.35	Andy Ashurst	29 Jun 85
5.35	Matt Belsham	26 Jun 93
5.31	Mike Edwards	10 Jun 90
5.30 i	Kevin Hughes	25 Feb 95
	5.30	28 Aug 95
5.25	Keith Stock	15 Jul 78
5.25	Ian Tullett	2 Feb 90
5.25	Tom Richards	8 Aug 99

LONG JUMP

8.15	Stewart Faulkner	16 Jul 90
8.11	Nathan Morgan	24 Jul 98
8.07	Lynn Davies	18 Oct 64
8.04	Roy Mitchell	25 Jun 77
8.00	Daley Thompson	25 Jul 80
8.00	Derrick Brown	7 Aug 85
7.97	Fred Salle	13 Jul 86
7.94 i	Paul Johnson	10 Mar 89
7.89	John King	26 Jul 85
7.87	Keith Fleming	7 Jun 87
wind assisted		
8.16	Roy Mitchell	26 Jun 76
8.11	Daley Thompson	7 Aug 78
7.94	John Herbert	25 Jul 82
7.94	Chris Davidson	21 Jun 97

TRIPLE JUMP

17.21	Tosi Fasinro	27 Jul 93
17.12	Phil Idowu	23 Sep 00
17.05	John Herbert	8 Jul 83
16.95	Julian Golley	10 Jul 92
16.76	Keith Connor	12 Aug 78
16.74	Jonathan Edwards	23 Jul 88
16.71	Vernon Samuels	18 May 86
16.69	Aston Moore	12 Aug 78
16.54	Eric McCalla	17 Sep 82
16.47	Mike Makin	1 Jul 84
16.41	Francis Agyepong	2 Aug 87
wind assisted		
17.30	Tosi Fasinro	12 Jun 93
17.21	Keith Connor	12 Aug 78
16.76	Aston Moore	25 Sep 78
16.44	Tayo Erogbogbo	31 May 97

SHOT

19.48	Geoff Capes	21 Aug 71
19.44 i	Simon Williams	28 Jan 89
	18.93	23 Jul 89
19.23	Matt Simson	20 May 01
19.01	Billy Cole	21 Jun 86
18.97	Carl Myerscough ¶	25 Jul 99
18.93	Paul Buxton	13 May 77
18.59 i	Alan Carter	11 Apr 65
	18.26	1 May 65
18.46	Lee Newman	9 Jul 95
18.40	Steph Hayward	9 Jun 96
18.14 i	Neal Brunning ¶	26 Jan 92
17.96	Arthur Rowe	3 Sep 58

DISCUS

62.07	Emeka Udechuku	19 Aug 00
61.86	Paul Mardle	13 Jun 84
60.48	Robert Weir	13 May 83
59.78	Glen Smith	5 Jun 94
58.99	Carl Myerscough ¶	2 Jul 99
58.52	Colin Sutherland ¶	1 May 77
58.34	Lee Newman	9 Jun 94
58.08	Simon Williams	11 Jun 89
57.04	Richard Slaney	23 Jul 77
56.42	Paul Buxton	6 Aug 76
55.90	Peter Tancred	13 Aug 69
downhill		
57.56	Peter Tancred	26 Jul 69

HAMMER

75.10	Dave Smith II	27 May 96
75.08	Robert Weir	3 Oct 82
74.62	David Smith I	15 Jul 84
74.18	Martin Girvan	31 May 82
73.80	Jason Byrne	19 Sep 92
71.08	Paul Head	1 Sep 85
71.00	Ian Chipchase	17 Aug 74
69.34	Paul Buxton	26 Aug 77
68.30	Mick Jones	1 Jul 84
67.60	Ron James	19 Sep 81
67.32	Gareth Cook	1 Jun 91

JAVELIN (1986 Model)

89.58	Steve Backley	2 Jul 90
80.92	Mark Roberson	12 Jun 88
79.70	Nigel Bevan	3 Feb 90
78.56	Mick Hill	2 Aug 86
78.54	Gary Jenson	17 Sep 89
78.24	David Parker	27 May 00
76.66 i	Stuart Faben	3 Mar 96
	74.24	29 Jul 95
76.28	Nick Nieland	9 Jul 94
74.70	Myles Cottrell	16 May 92
71.94	Steve Harrison	9 Jul 94
71.86	Stefan Baldwin	17 May 92
71.16	Tony Hatton	28 Jun 92

DECATHLON (1985 Tables)

8648	Daley Thompson	18 May 80
8556	Dean Macey	25 Aug 99
7904	David Bigham	28 Jun 92
7723 w	Eugene Gilkes	8 Jul 84
	7660	8 Jul 84
7713	Jim Stevenson	5 Jun 93
7668	Fidelis Obikwu	5 Oct 82
7643 w	Tom Leeson	8 Sep 85
	7565	11 Aug 85
7616	Barry Thomas	23 Aug 92
7610	Jamie Quarry	24 Aug 94
7594	Mark Bishop	3 Sep 89
7567	Brian Taylor	8 Jul 90
7535	Duncan Mathieson	24 Jun 90

3000 METRES TRACK WALK

11:28.4	Phil Vesty	9 May 84

10000 METRES TRACK WALK

40:53.60	Phil Vesty	28 May 84
41:24.7	Martin Rush	6 Jul 86
41:51.55	Andi Drake	25 May 87
41:55.6	Darrell Stone	7 Feb 88
42:24.61	Ian McCombie	29 May 83
42:28.0	Philip King	17 May 95
43:00.67	Sean Martindale	5 Jun 88
43:10.4	Gareth Holloway	2 May 92
43:12.85	Matt Hales	12 Aug 00
43:26.2	Gordon Vale	20 Mar 82

20 KILOMETRES ROAD WALK

1:24:07.6t	Phil Vesty	1 Dec 84
1:24:53	Andi Drake	27 Jun 87
1:26:14	Darrell Stone	27 Mar 89
1:26:21	Ian McCombie	8 Aug 82
1:26:32	Martin Rush	25 Feb 84
1:28:02	Paul Blagg	27 Feb 82
1:28:15	Mark Easton	11 May 85
1:28:17	Andy Penn	21 May 88
1:29:01	Steve Partington	11 May 85
1:29:07	Philip King	20 Aug 95

50 KILOMETRES ROAD WALK

4:10:23	Darrell Stone	6 May 90

UNDER 20

100 METRES

	Mark	Athlete	Date
	10.06	Dwain Chambers	25 Jul 97
	10.10	Mark Lewis-Francis	21 Aug 99
	10.12	Christian Malcolm	29 Jul 98
	10.21	Jamie Henderson	6 Aug 87
	10.25	Jason Livingston ¶	9 Aug 90
	10.25	Jason Gardener	21 Jul 94
	10.29	Peter Radford (10.31?)	13 Sep 58
	10.31	Chris Lambert	21 Aug 99
	10.32	Mike McFarlane	6 Aug 78
10	10.34	Lincoln Asquith	25 Aug 83
	10.37	Darren Campbell	26 Jul 91
	10.38	Elliot Bunney	22 Aug 85
	10.39	Jason John	28 Jul 90
	10.39	Tyrone Edgar	7 Oct 00
	10.41	Jamie Henthorn	28 Jul 95
	10.43	Julian Golding	20 Jul 94
	10.44	Steve Gookey	3 Aug 90
	10.44	Jason Fergus	16 Sep 92
	10.45	Luke Davis	21 Jul 97
20	10.46	Marcus Adam	6 Aug 87

wind assisted

	Mark	Athlete	Date
	10.10	Christian Malcolm	18 Jul 98
	10.22	Lincoln Asquith	26 Jun 83
	10.28	Darren Campbell	26 Jul 91
	10.29	Mike McFarlane	7 Aug 78
	10.29	Elliot Bunney	27 May 84
	10.29	Trevor Cameron	11 Jun 94
	10.34	Darren Braithwaite	25 Jun 88
	10.34	Julian Golding	17 Sep 94
	10.37	Courtney Rumbolt	25 Jun 88
10	10.37	Allyn Condon	3 Jul 93

hand timing

	Mark	Athlete	Date
	10.3	Martin Reynolds	29 Jun 68

200 METRES

	Mark	Athlete	Date
	20.29	Christian Malcolm	19 Sep 98
	20.54	Ade Mafe	25 Aug 85
	20.63	Chris Lambert	21 Aug 99
	20.67	David Jenkins	4 Sep 71
	20.72	Tim Benjamin	18 Jul 99
	20.73 A	Ralph Banthorpe	15 Oct 68
		20.94	3 Aug 68
	20.78	John Regis	29 Sep 85
	20.80	Mike McFarlane	1 Jul 79
	20.85	Richard Ashby	25 Aug 85
10	20.86	Lincoln Asquith	28 Aug 83
	20.86	Roger Hunter	5 May 84
	20.87	Donovan Reid	7 Oct 82
	20.87	Mark Smith	28 Jul 90
	20.87	Darren Campbell	19 Sep 92
	20.88	Dwayne Grant	20 Oct 00
	20.91	Jamie Baulch	18 Sep 92
	20.91	Ian Mackie	23 Jul 94
	20.92	Marcus Adam	8 Aug 87
	20.94	Marlon Devonish	6 Aug 95
20	20.95	Allyn Condon	26 Jun 93

wind assisted

	Mark	Athlete	Date
	20.60	Tim Benjamin	7 Aug 99
	20.61	Darren Campbell	11 Aug 91
	20.73	Julian Golding	17 Sep 94
	20.80	Ben Lewis	11 Jul 99
	20.85	Mark Smith	1 Jul 90

hand timing

	Mark	Athlete	Date
	20.6	David Jenkins	19 Sep 71

wind assisted

	Mark	Athlete	Date
	20.7	Lincoln Asquith	2 Jul 83

300 METRES

	Mark	Athlete	Date
	32.53	Mark Richardson	14 Jul 91

400 METRES

	Mark	Athlete	Date
	45.36	Roger Black	24 Aug 85
	45.41	David Grindley	10 Aug 91
	45.45	David Jenkins	13 Aug 71
	45.53	Mark Richardson	10 Aug 91
	45.83	Mark Hylton	16 Jul 95
	46.03	Peter Crampton	8 Aug 87
	46.13	Guy Bullock	31 Jul 93
	46.22	Wayne McDonald	17 Jun 89
	46.32	Derek Redmond	9 Sep 84
10	46.46	Adrian Metcalfe	19 Sep 61
	46.48	Roger Hunter	20 May 84
	46.53	Mark Thomas	15 Sep 84
	46.54	Michael Parper	7 Jun 97
	46.56	Roy Dickens	6 Sep 80
	46.59	Carl Southam	17 Sep 92
	46.63	Melvin Fowell	18 Aug 79
	46.64	Alloy Wilson	31 Jul 98
	46.65	Darren Bernard	20 May 88
	46.66	Du'aine Ladejo	9 Aug 90
20	46.77	Paul Dunn	31 May 82

hand timing

	Mark	Athlete	Date
	45.7	Adrian Metcalfe	2 Sep 61

800 METRES (* 880 yards time less 0.60)

	Mark	Athlete	Date
	1:45.64	David Sharpe	5 Sep 86
	1:45.77	Steve Ovett	4 Sep 74
	1:46.46	John Gladwin	7 Jul 82
	1:46.63	Curtis Robb	6 Jul 91
	1:46.80*	John Davies I	3 Jun 68
	1:47.0	Ikem Billy	12 Jun 83
	1:47.02	Chris McGeorge	8 Aug 81
	1:47.22	Kevin McKay	5 Jun 88
	1:47.27	Tom Lerwill	22 Aug 96
10	1:47.35	Peter Elliott	23 Aug 81
	1:47.53	Graham Williamson	1 Aug 79
	1:47.6	Julian Spooner	24 Apr 79
	1:47.69	Simon Lees	5 Sep 98
	1:47.70	Darryl Taylor	13 Jul 84
	1:47.71	Dane Joseph	15 Sep 78
	1:47.73	Colin Szwed	9 Sep 77
	1:47.75	Garry Cook	3 Jul 77
	1:47.79	Craig Winrow	20 Jul 90
	1:47.85	Steve Crabb	17 Sep 82
20	1:47.96*	Dave Wilcox	8 Jul 66

1000 METRES

	2:18.98	David Sharpe	19 Aug 86
	2:19.92	Graham Williamson	8 Jul 79
	2:20.0	Steve Ovett	17 Aug 73
	2:20.02	Darryl Taylor	18 Aug 84
	2:20.37	Johan Boakes	17 Jun 84
	2:21.17	Curtis Robb	16 Sep 90
	2:21.41	Stuart Paton	17 Sep 82
	2:21.7 A	David Strang (GBR?)	26 Jan 87
	2:21.71	Kevin Glastonbury	18 Jun 77

1500 METRES

	3:36.6 +	Graham Williamson	17 Jul 79
	3:40.09	Steve Cram	27 Aug 78
	3:40.68	Brian Treacy	24 Jul 90
	3:40.72	Gary Taylor	8 Jul 81
	3:40.90	David Robertson	28 Jul 92
	3:41.59	Chris Sly	22 Jul 77
	3:42.2	Paul Wynn	9 Aug 83
	3:42.5	Colin Reitz	8 Aug 79
	3:42.67	Matthew Hibberd	28 Jul 92
10	3:42.7	David Sharpe	17 Oct 85
	3:42.86	Stuart Paton	29 Aug 82
	3:42.89	Alistair Currie	17 Jul 84
	3:43.1 a	Paul Lawther	31 Jan 74
	3:43.24	Nick Hopkins	15 Jun 85
	3:43.37	Davey Wilson	4 Jul 87
	3:43.39	Johan Boakes	30 May 87
	3:43.4	Tom Mayo	5 Jun 96
	3:43.5	Matt Dixon	7 Aug 97
	3:43.69	Jon Richards	1 Jul 83
20	3:43.8	John Nuttall	24 Jun 86

ONE MILE

	3:53.15	Graham Williamson	17 Jul 79
	3:57.03	Steve Cram	14 Sep 79
	3:58.68	Steve Flint	26 May 80
	3:59.4	Steve Ovett	17 Jul 74
	4:00.31	Johan Boakes	5 Aug 86
	4:00.6	Simon Mugglestone	16 Sep 87
	4:00.67	Brian Treacy	22 Aug 90
	4:01.0	David Sharpe	3 May 86

2000 METRES

	5:06.56	Jon Richards	7 Jul 82

3000 METRES

	7:48.28	Jon Richards	9 Jul 83
	7:51.84	Steve Binns	8 Sep 79
	7:56.28	John Doherty	13 Jul 80
	7:59.55	Paul Davies-Hale	8 Aug 81
	8:00.1 a	Micky Morton	11 Jul 78
	8:00.7	Graham Williamson	29 Jul 78
	8:00.73	David Black	24 Jul 71
	8:00.8	Steve Anders	1 Aug 78
	8:00.88	Paul Taylor	12 Jun 85
10	8:01.2	Ian Stewart I	7 Sep 68
	8:01.26	Darius Burrows	21 Aug 94
	8:01.43	Nat Muir	28 Aug 77
	8:01.44	Colin Reitz	16 May 79

5000 METRES

	13:27.04	Steve Binns	14 Sep 79
	13:35.95	Paul Davies-Hale	11 Sep 81
	13:37.4	David Black	10 Sep 71
	13:43.82	Simon Mugglestone	24 May 87
	13:44.64	Julian Goater	14 Jul 72
	13:48.74	Jon Richards	28 May 83
	13:48.84	John Doherty	8 Aug 80
	13:49.1 a	Nat Muir	21 Aug 77
	13:53.30	Ian Stewart I	3 Aug 68
10	13:53.3 a	Nicky Lees	21 Aug 77
	13:54.2	Mick Morton	1 Jul 78
	13:54.52	Keith Cullen	8 Jun 91
	14:00.7	Peter Tootell	19 Jun 82
	14:00.7	Mike Chorlton	19 Jun 82
	14:00.85	Paul Taylor	15 Sep 84
	14:03.0	Steve Anders	1 Jul 78
	14:03.09	Jon Brown	11 Aug 90
	14:03.4	Jim Brown	26 Jun 71
	14:05.0	Paul Bannon	24 Jun 72

10000 METRES

	29:21.9	Jon Brown	21 Apr 00
	29:38.6	Ray Crabb	18 Apr 73
	29:44.0	Richard Green	27 Sep 75
	29:44.8	Jack Lane	23 Sep 69
	29:45.8	Dave Murphy	17 Jul 76

2000 METRES STEEPLECHASE

	5:29.61	Colin Reitz	18 Aug 79
	5:31.12	Paul Davies-Hale	22 Aug 81
	5:32.84	Tom Hanlon	20 Jul 86
	5:34.8 a	Micky Morris	24 Aug 75
	5:38.01	Ken Baker	1 Aug 82
	5:38.2	Spencer Duval	8 Jul 89
	5:39.3 a	Graeme Fell	11 Jul 78
	5:39.93	Eddie Wedderburn	9 Sep 79
	5:40.2	Paul Campbell	31 Jul 77
10	5:40.2	John Hartigan	27 Jun 84

3000 METRES STEEPLECHASE

	8:29.85	Paul Davies-Hale	31 Aug 81
	8:42.75	Colin Reitz	6 Jun 79
	8:43.21	Kevin Nash	2 Jun 96
	8:44.68	Alastair O'Connor	12 Aug 90
	8:44.91	Ken Baker	30 May 82
	8:45.65	Spencer Duval	17 Jun 89
	8:47.49	Tom Hanlon	8 Jun 86
	8:48.43	Graeme Fell	16 Jul 78
	8:50.14	Dave Long I	13 Jul 73
10	8:51.02	Tony Staynings	14 Jul 72
	8:54.15	Stuart Kefford	18 Sep 92
	8:54.6	Micky Morris	7 Sep 75
	8:54.92	Mark Wortley	4 Jun 88
	8:56.0	John Davies	13 Jun 71
	8:56.0	Eddie Wedderburn	3 Jun 79
	8:56.36	Dave Robertson	15 Jun 91
	8:57.4	Keith Cullen	8 May 91
	8:57.83	Iain Murdoch	3 May 99
	8:59.09	Ben Whitby	27 Jul 96
20	8:59.2	Maurice Herriott	3 Sep 58

110 METRES HURDLES (3'3")

	13.57	Chris Baillie	21 Aug 99
	13.77	Kevin Lumsdon	8 Aug 92
	13.90	Robert Newton	10 Jul 99
	14.01	Jamie Quarry	13 Jul 91
	14.06	Neil Owen	4 Jul 92
	14.07	Leo Barker	12 Jul 97
	14.08	Liam Collins	12 Jul 97
	14.11	Nathan Palmer	22 Aug 99
	14.13	Derek Wilson	25 Jun 83
10	14.14	James Hughes	30 May 93
	wind assisted		
	13.92	Matthew Clements	27 Aug 94
	13.96	Dominic Girdler	8 Jul 00
	hand timing		
	13.8	Jon Ridgeon	13 Jul 84
	13.8	Paul Gray	16 Jul 88
	wind assisted		
	13.6	Mark Holtom	9 Jul 77
	13.8	Paul Brice	9 Jul 83
	13.8	Colin Jackson	15 Jul 84
	13.8	Brett St Louis	11 Jul 87

110 METRES HURDLES (3'6")

	13.44	Colin Jackson	19 Jul 86
	13.46	Jon Ridgeon	23 Aug 85
	13.72	Tony Jarrett	24 May 87
	13.84	Chris Baillie	27 Aug 00
	13.91	David Nelson	21 Jun 86
	13.95	Robert Newton	4 Sep 00
	13.97	Paul Gray	30 Jul 88
	14.01	Ross Baillie	25 Aug 96
	14.03	Brett St Louis	27 Jun 87
10	14.04	Damien Greaves	25 Aug 96
	14.06	Mark Holtom	7 Aug 77
	14.08	Paul Brice	26 Aug 83
	14.14	Neil Owen	17 Sep 92
	14.18	James Archampong	21 Jul 94
	14.21	Berwyn Price	12 Sep 70
	14.24	Nigel Walker	17 Sep 82
	14.25	Ben Warmington	31 Jul 98
	14.29	Andy Tulloch	13 Jul 85
	14.30	Dominic Girdler	27 Aug 00
	wind assisted		
	13.42	Colin Jackson	27 Jul 86
	13.82	David Nelson	5 Jul 86
	13.92	Chris Baillie	7 Aug 99
	13.93	Robert Newton	7 Aug 99
	14.24	Ben Warmington	5 Jul 98

400 METRES HURDLES

50.22	Martin Briggs	28 Aug 83	
50.70	Noel Levy	8 Jul 94	
51.07	Philip Beattie	20 Aug 82	
51.15 A	Andy Todd	18 Oct 67	
	51.70	23 Sep 67	
51.31	Gary Oakes	9 Sep 77	
51.39	Richard McDonald	19 Jun 99	
51.48	Bob Brown	19 Jun 88	
51.51	Max Robertson	24 Jul 82	
51.55	Mark Whitby	26 Aug 83	
51.63	Mark Rowlands	21 Jun 97	10
51.66	Paul Goacher	2 Aug 80	
51.71	Matthew Elias	7 Jun 97	
51.73	Matt Douglas	29 Jul 95	
51.91	Peter Campbell	19 Jun 88	
51.97	Bel Blik	17 Aug 85	
52.24	Andrew Abrahams	11 Aug 84	
52.26	Gary Jennings	30 Jun 91	
52.26	Charles Robertson-Adams	15 Jun 96	
52.44	Philip Parkinson	17 Aug 85	
52.48	Andrew Nelson	21 Jun 87	20
hand timing			
51.0	Richard McDonald	24 Jul 99	
51.5	Max Robertson	10 Jul 82	
51.5	Matthew Elias	6 Jun 98	
52.1	Michael Bryars	30 Apr 83	
52.2	Phil Harries	20 Jul 85	

HIGH JUMP

2.37	Steve Smith	20 Sep 92	
2.27	Brendan Reilly	27 May 90	
2.26	James Brierley	3 Aug 96	
2.25	Geoff Parsons	9 Jul 83	
2.24	John Hill	23 Aug 85	
2.23	Mark Lakey (U17)	29 Aug 82	
2.23 i	Ben Challenger	1 Mar 97	
	2.21	24 Aug 96	
2.22	Dalton Grant	3 Jul 85	
2.20	Byron Morrison	14 Jul 84	
2.18	Ossie Cham	14 Jun 80	10
2.18	Alex Kruger	26 Jun 82	
2.18	Steve Ritchie	15 Jul 89	
2.18	Hopeton Lindo	23 Jul 89	
2.17	Stuart Ohrland	27 Aug 94	
2.17	Mike Robbins	5 Aug 95	
2.16 i	Claude Moseley	13 Apr 80	
2.16	Andy Hutchison	2 Sep 84	
2.16	John Holman	4 Jul 87	
2.16	Andrew Lynch	18 Sep 93	
2.16	Richard Aspden	7 Jul 95	20
2.16	Rob Brocklebank	7 Jul 95	
2.16 i	Jason McDade	24 Jan 99	

POLE VAULT

5.50	Neil Winter	9 Aug 92	
5.30	Matt Belsham	16 Sep 90	
5.21	Andy Ashurst	2 Sep 84	
5.21 i	Christian Linskey	20 Feb 99	
	5.20	24 May 98	
5.20	Billy Davey	5 Jun 83	
5.20	Warren Siley	4 Aug 90	
5.20	Nick Buckfield	31 May 92	
5.20	Ben Flint	2 Aug 97	
5.10	Brian Hooper	1 Oct 72	
5.10	Mike Edwards	20 Jun 87	10
5.10	Mark Davis	9 Jun 96	
5.05	Ian Tullett	22 Aug 87	
5.05	Dean Mellor	7 Jul 90	
5.02	Paul Williamson	29 May 93	

	5.00	Keith Stock	3 Jul 76
	5.00	Bob Kingman	2 May 92
	5.00	Tim Thomas	17 Jun 92
	5.00	Mike Barber	1 Jul 92
	5.00 sq	Ian Wilding	16 Jul 94
20	5.00	Neil Young	18 May 96

LONG JUMP

	7.98	Stewart Faulkner	6 Aug 88
	7.91	Steve Phillips	10 Aug 91
	7.90	Nathan Morgan	25 Jul 97
	7.84	Wayne Griffith	25 Aug 89
	7.76	Carl Howard	31 Jul 93
	7.73	Jason Canning	20 Apr 88
	7.72	Daley Thompson	21 May 77
	7.70	Kevin Liddington	27 Aug 88
	7.66	Barry Nevison	7 Jul 85
10	7.62	Colin Mitchell	11 Jul 78
	7.62	Chris Tomlinson	21 Oct 00
	7.61	Darren Gomersall	19 Jul 87
	7.58	Fred Salle	11 Jun 83
	7.56	John Herbert	11 Jul 81
	7.56	Colin Jackson	31 Aug 85
	7.56	Stuart Wells	12 Jul 97
	7.56	Darren Thompson	30 May 98
	7.54	Derrick Brown	26 Jun 82
	7.53	Paul Johnson	19 Jul 87
20	7.53	Brian Robinson (U17)	21 Jul 97

wind assisted

	8.04	Stewart Faulkner	20 Aug 88
	7.97	Nathan Morgan	13 Jul 96
	7.96	Colin Jackson	17 May 86
	7.82	Kevin Liddington	25 Jun 89
	7.72	John Herbert	15 Jun 80
	7.60	Brian Robinson (U17)	21 Jul 97
	7.58	Gus Udo	8 Jul 78
	7.58	Garry Slade	6 Jun 87
	7.56	Eddie Starrs	22 Jul 79

TRIPLE JUMP

	16.58	Tosi Fasinro	15 Jun 91
	16.57	Tosin Oke	8 Aug 99
	16.53	Larry Achike	24 Jul 94
	16.24	Aston Moore	11 Jun 75
	16.22	Mike Makin	17 May 81
	16.13	Steven Anderson	11 Jun 83
	16.03	John Herbert	23 Jun 81
	16.02	Jonathan Moore (U17)	13 Aug 00
	15.99	Steven Shalders	20 Oct 00
10	15.95	Keith Connor	30 Aug 76
	15.94	Vernon Samuels	27 Jun 82
	15.93	Tayo Erogbogbo	17 Sep 94
	15.92	Lawrence Lynch	13 Jul 85
	15.88	Julian Golley	28 Jul 90
	15.87	Stewart Faulkner	22 Aug 87
	15.86	Phillips Idowu	5 Jul 97
	15.84	Francis Agyepong	29 Sep 84
	15.82	Jon Wallace	11 Jul 98
	15.80	David Johnson	14 Jul 72
20	15.79	Paul Johnson	27 Jun 87

wind assisted

16.81	Tosi Fasinro	15 Jun 91	
16.67	Larry Achike	24 Jul 94	
16.43	Mike Makin	14 Jun 81	
16.34	Phillips Idowu	27 Jul 97	
16.31	Aston Moore	9 Aug 75	
16.07	Vernon Samuels	14 Aug 82	
16.01	Julian Golley	22 Jul 90	
15.96	Paul Johnson	27 Jun 87	
15.95	Lawrence Lynch	26 May 86	
15.81	Junior Campbell	28 May 89	10

SHOT (7.26kg)

19.46	Carl Myerscough ¶	6 Sep 98	
18.21 i	Matt Simson	3 Feb 89	
	18.11	27 Aug 89	
17.78 i	Billy Cole	10 Mar 84	
	17.72	2 Jun 84	
17.36 i	Chris Ellis	8 Dec 84	
	17.10	7 Jul 85	
17.26 i	Geoff Capes	16 Nov 68	
	16.80	30 Jul 68	
17.25	Emeka Udechuku	20 Sep 97	
17.22	Antony Zaidman	4 Jul 81	
16.69	Gregg Beard	30 Sep 00	
16.61	Simon Williams	10 Aug 86	
16.60	Alan Carter	11 May 63	10
16.48	Martyn Lucking	24 Aug 57	
16.47	Paul Buxton	25 May 75	
16.23 i	David Readle	30 Jan 99	
	16.15	3 Jul 99	
16.21	Mike Lindsay	29 Jul 57	
16.20 i	Nigel Spratley	19 Mar 89	
	16.04	20 May 89	
16.18	Tony Satchwell	23 Apr 72	
16.10	Martin Fletcher	19 Jun 88	
16.03	Jon Wood	26 Sep 70	
15.94	Andy Vince	5 May 78	
15.94	Mitchell Smith	23 Mar 85	20

SHOT (6.25kg)

21.03	Carl Myerscough ¶	13 May 98	
19.47	Matt Simson	20 May 89	
19.15	Billy Cole	19 May 84	
18.66 i	Simon Williams	15 Nov 86	
	18.52	11 Jul 86	
18.20 i	Chris Ellis	16 Feb 85	
	18.13	14 Jul 84	
17.81	Antony Zaidman	16 May 81	
17.74	Emeka Udechuku	9 Aug 98	
17.67	David Readle	22 Aug 99	
17.58	Nigel Spratley	28 May 89	10
17.32	Andy Vince	15 May 77	
17.31	Mitchell Smith	11 Jun 85	
17.31	Lyndon Woodward	10 Jul 99	
17.30	Jamie Cockburn	20 Sep 92	
17.26	Neil Gray	19 May 84	
17.26 i	Neal Brunning ¶	9 Dec 89	
	17.08	21 Aug 88	
17.22	Richard Slaney	20 Jul 75	

DISCUS (2kg)

	60.97	Emeka Udechuku	5 Jul 98
	60.19	Carl Myerscough ¶	8 Aug 98
	55.10	Glen Smith	31 Aug 91
	53.42	Paul Mardle	25 Jul 81
	53.40	Robert Weir	10 Aug 80
	53.32	Paul Buxton	9 Aug 75
	53.02	Simon Williams	16 Aug 86
	52.94	Lee Newman	29 Aug 92
	52.84	Jamie Murphy	14 Jun 92
10	52.14	Robert Russell	4 Jul 93
	51.70	Richard Slaney	27 Jul 75
	51.66	Neal Brunning ¶	30 Jul 89
	51.28	Adam Major	10 Sep 00
	51.10	Mike Lindsay	29 May 57
	51.08	Peter Weir	1 Aug 82
	51.05	Luke Rosenberg	4 Jul 99
	50.74	Tony Satchwell	21 Aug 72
	50.64	Colin Bastien	9 Jun 85
	50.46	Neil Boyton	16 Jul 83
20	50.07	Scot Thompson	27 Aug 00

DISCUS (1.75kg)

	64.35	Emeka Udechuku	21 Jun 98
	61.81	Carl Myerscough ¶	18 Aug 98
	60.76	Glen Smith	26 May 91
	56.64	Jamie Murphy	19 May 90
	56.10	Lee Newman	4 Jul 92
	56.00	Simon Williams	17 May 86
	55.94	Mark Davies	19 Aug 90
	55.44	Neal Brunning ¶	8 Jul 89
	55.16	Adam Major	10 Sep 00
10	55.00	Robert Russell	16 May 93

HAMMER (7.26kg)

	67.48	Paul Head	16 Sep 84
	67.10	Jason Byrne	6 Aug 89
	66.14	Martin Girvan	21 Jul 79
	65.86	Robert Weir	6 Sep 80
	65.30	Karl Andrews	2 Jul 94
	64.14	Ian Chipchase	25 Sep 71
	63.84	Andrew Tolputt	7 Sep 86
	63.72	Gareth Cook	10 Jul 88
	62.82	Mick Jones	29 Aug 82
10	62.02	Peter Vivian	1 Jul 89
	61.34	Ron James	22 Apr 78
	61.22	Malcolm Croad	25 Aug 92
	61.10	Vaughan Cooper	5 May 84
	60.86	David Smith I	2 Aug 81
	60.34	Tony Kenneally	1 Aug 82
	60.24	Paul Buxton	17 Jun 75
	60.04	Eric Berry	16 Jun 73
	59.98	David Smith II	3 Jul 93
	59.80	Matthew Bell	7 Jun 97
20	59.12	Andrew Grierson	18 Jul 98

HAMMER (6.25kg)

	74.92	Jason Byrne	17 Dec 89
	73.28	Robert Weir	14 Sep 80
	72.66	Paul Head	2 Sep 84
	71.84	Gareth Cook	28 May 88
	70.36	Andrew Tolputt	21 Sep 86
	69.10	Karl Andrews	3 Aug 94
	67.80	Martin Girvan	7 Jul 79
	67.52	Vaughan Cooper	19 May 84
	67.48	Mick Jones	2 Jun 82
10	66.38	Tony Kenneally	10 Jul 82

JAVELIN

	79.50	Steve Backley	5 Jun 88
	77.48	David Parker	14 Aug 99
	74.54	Gary Jenson	19 Sep 86
	74.24	Mark Roberson	18 Jul 86
	73.76	Nigel Bevan	29 Aug 87
	71.79	Phill Sharpe	27 Aug 00
	71.74	Myles Cottrell	29 Jul 89
	71.14	Dan Carter	11 Jul 98
	69.62	Stefan Baldwin	8 Jul 89
10	68.84	James Hurrion	12 Jul 91
	68.74	Jon Clarke	14 Jun 86
	68.38	James Drennen	12 Jul 91
	68.30	Mark Lawrence	31 Jul 88
	68.08	Tim Kitney	13 Sep 98
	67.22	Richard Atkinson	14 Aug 93
	66.74	Stuart Faben	22 Jul 94
	66.62	Mark Francis	13 Jul 96
	66.21	Clifton Green	4 May 98
	65.70	Duncan MacDonald	17 Jul 93
20	65.34	Paul Cooper	11 Jun 95

DECATHLON (1985 Tables)

	Points	Name	Date
	8082	Daley Thompson	31 Jul 77
	7488	David Bigham	9 Aug 90
	7480	Dean Macey	22 Aug 96
	7299	Eugene Gilkes	24 May 81
	7274	Jim Stevenson	24 Jun 90
	7247	Brian Taylor	7 May 89
	7169	Barry Thomas	5 Aug 90
	7126	Fidelis Obikwu	16 Sep 79
	7112	Gavin Sunshine	30 Jul 93
10	7018	Jamie Quarry	30 Jun 91
	6958	Roy Mitchell	29 Sep 74
	6936	Anthony Brannen	24 May 87
	6925	Roger Hunter	4 Jun 95
	6843	Ed Coats	30 May 99
	6839	Mark Bushell	30 Apr 95
	6812	Nigel Skinner	19 Aug 84
	6809	Rafer Joseph	26 Jul 87
	6801 w	Kevan Lobb	18 Jun 78
	6774	Jason McDade	30 May 99
20	6766	Ken Hayford	18 Jul 82

Junior Implements

	Points	Name	Date
	7134	Dean Macey	17 Sep 95
	6958 w	Roger Hunter	18 Sep 94
	6789	Jamie Quarry	16 Sep 90
	6762	Fyn Corcoran	22 Sep 96
	6678	Darren Hatton	21 Sep 97
	6674	John Heanley	19 Sep 99
	6672	Martin Troy	17 Sep 95
	6636	Jason McDade	19 Sep 99

3000 METRES TRACK WALK

11:54.23	Tim Berrett	23 Jun 84
12:01.89 i	Philip King	21 Feb 93
	12:02.0	12 May 92
12:02.04	Phil Vesty	24 Jul 82
12:16.5	David Hucks	5 Aug 84
12:19.8	Gordon Vale	11 Mar 81

5000 METRES TRACK WALK

20:16.40	Philip King	26 Jun 93
20:33.4 +	Darrell Stone	7 Aug 87
20:55.4	Tim Berrett	9 Jun 84
21:00.5 +	Phil Vesty	19 Jun 82
21:10.5 +	Gordon Vale	2 Aug 81

10000 METRES TRACK WALK

	41:52.13	Darrell Stone	7 Aug 87
	42:06.35	Gordon Vale	2 Aug 81
	42:46.3	Phil Vesty	20 Mar 82
	42:47.7	Philip King	2 May 92
	43:04.09	Tim Berrett	25 Aug 83
	43:42.75	Martin Rush	29 May 83
	43:54.25	Gareth Brown	7 Aug 87
	44:22.12	Gareth Holloway	5 Jun 88
	44:22.4	Jon Vincent	1 Apr 89
10	44:30.0	Andy Penn	15 Mar 86
	44:38.0	Ian McCombie	29 Mar 80
	44:53.0	Michael Kemp	4 Apr 98
	45:04.28	Andi Drake	1 Jul 84
	45:04.37	Ian Ashforth	3 Aug 85
	45:06.19	Jon Bott	25 May 87
	45:13.50	Kirk Taylor	23 Aug 87
	45:17.0	Bob Chaplain	28 Jun 75
	45:20.0	Jacky Lord	3 Aug 74
	45:20.42	Steve Hollier	2 Jul 95
20	45:22.2	Pat Chichester	7 Jul 85

10k Road - *where superior to track time*

	41:47	Darrell Stone	26 Sep 87
	42:29	Steve Hollier	10 Dec 95
	42:39	Martin Rush	7 May 83
	42:40	Tim Berrett	18 Feb 84
	43:18	Richard Dorman	18 Oct 80
	43:35	Gareth Brown	12 Apr 87
	43:38 hc	Lloyd Finch (U17)	20 Nov 99
	43:50	Kirk Taylor	12 Apr 87
	43:53	Michael Kemp	25 Apr 98
10	44:08	Nathan Kavanagh	5 May 85
	44:08	Gareth Holloway	8 Jul 89
	44:09	Jimmy Ball	16 Oct 82
	44:18	Ian McCombie	16 Feb 80

20 KILOMETRES ROAD WALK

1:26:13	Tim Berrett	25 Feb 84
1:29:10	Phil Vesty	18 Jul 82
1:31:34.4t	Gordon Vale	28 Jun 81
1:32:46	Graham Morris	26 Feb 77
1:33:03	Darrell Stone	10 May 86

50 KILOMETRES ROAD WALK

4:18:18	Gordon Vale	24 Oct 81

UNDER 17

100 METRES

10.31	Mark Lewis-Francis	21 Aug 99	
10.60	Tyrone Edgar	16 Aug 98	
10.64	Jon Barbour	12 Jul 97	
10.66	Ben Lewis	7 Sep 97	
10.67	Michael Nartey	28 Sep 91	
10.69	Mike McFarlane	13 Aug 76	
10.70	Steve Green	15 Jul 72	
10.70	Karl Forde	3 Jul 99	
10.71	Luke Davis	12 Jul 96	
10.71	Tim Benjamin	16 Aug 98	10
10.72	Peter Little	6 Aug 77	
10.72	Trevor Cameron	7 Aug 93	
10.73	Danny Joyce	17 Aug 91	
10.75	Elliot Bunney	28 May 83	
10.75	Dwain Chambers	28 May 94	

wind assisted

10.26	Mark Lewis-Francis	5 Aug 99	
10.38	Kevin Mark	3 Jul 93	
10.44	Luke Davis	13 Jul 96	
10.51	Tim Benjamin	4 Jul 98	
10.56	Dwain Chambers	8 Jul 94	
10.57	Trevor Cameron	3 Jul 93	
10.58	Tyrone Edgar	16 Aug 98	
10.62	Elliot Bunney	25 Jun 83	
10.62	Jamie Nixon	7 Jul 85	
10.65	Mike Williams	20 Jun 87	10

hand timing

10.5	Michael Powell	17 Sep 78

200 METRES

20.92	Ade Mafe	27 Aug 83	
21.19	Tim Benjamin	31 Jul 98	
21.24	Peter Little	21 Aug 77	
21.25	Mark Richardson	24 Jul 88	
21.44	Roger Hunter	2 Aug 81	
21.45	Monu Miah	29 Jul 00	
21.51	Darren Campbell	15 Sep 90	
21.51	Ben Lewis	19 Jul 97	
21.53	Steve Eden	2 Aug 81	
21.56	Trevor Cameron	8 Aug 93	10
21.58	Christian Malcolm	9 Jul 95	
21.62	Tyrone Edgar	24 May 98	
21.63	Richard Ashby	7 Aug 83	
21.64	Elliot Bunney	7 Aug 83	
21.64	Adam Rogers	14 Aug 99	

wind assisted

20.98	Tim Benjamin	18 Jul 98
21.17	Mark Richardson	20 Aug 88
21.25	Trevor Cameron	25 Sep 93
21.31	Monu Miah	15 Jul 00
21.32	Graham Beasley	9 Jul 94
21.38	Elliot Bunney	13 Aug 83
21.38	Ben Lewis	12 Jul 97
21.39	Laurence Oboh	15 Jul 00

hand timing wind assisted

21.0	Peter Little	30 Jul 77

400 METRES

46.43 Mark Richardson 28 Jul 88
46.74 Guy Bullock 17 Sep 92
47.81 Mark Hylton 17 Jul 93
47.86 Kris Stewart 13 Jul 96
48.05 David Naismith 10 Aug 96
48.11 Gary Thomas 18 Sep 82
48.22 Robert Tobin 8 Jul 00
48.25 Adrian Patrick 2 Sep 89
48.34 Richard McNabb 27 Aug 95
10 48.35 James Hilston 6 Aug 95
48.36 David Simpson 29 May 89
48.41 Mark Tyler 11 Aug 84
48.46 Phil Harvey 24 Jun 79
48.46 Simon Tunnicliffe 29 May 99
48.50 Russell Nicholls 10 Jul 99

hand timing

47.6 Kris Stewart 3 Aug 96
48.2 David Simpson 8 Jul 89
48.3 David McKenzie 21 Sep 86
48.4 Steve Ovett 20 Aug 72
48.4 Chris Thompson 1 Aug 81
48.4 Martin Bradbury 31 Jul 99

800 METRES

1:49.9 Mark Sesay 18 Jul 89
1:50.7 Peter Elliott 16 Sep 79
1:50.90 Craig Winrow 21 Aug 88
1:51.0 Chris McGeorge 1 Jul 78
1:51.05 Mal Edwards 20 Sep 74
1:51.3 Julian Spooner 3 Aug 77
1:51.4 Kevin McKay 19 Aug 85
1:51.6 Neil Horsfield 31 Aug 83
1:51.6 David Gerard 21 Jul 84
10 1:51.8 Paul Burgess 14 Jul 87
1:51.9 + Johan Boakes 17 Jun 84
1:52.0 Paul Causey 21 Jul 84
1:52.21 Malcolm Hassan 21 Aug 99
1:52.29 Simon Young 7 Aug 90
1:52.5 Steve Ovett 17 Jun 72
1:52.5 Michael Combe 1 Aug 95

1000 METRES

2:20.37 Johan Boakes 17 Jun 84

1500 METRES

3:47.7 Steve Cram 14 May 77
3:48.49 Johan Boakes 28 Jun 84
3:49.9 Kelvin Newton 20 Jun 79
3:51.1 Jason Lobo 30 Aug 86
3:51.4 Darren Mead 26 Jul 85
3:51.7 Martin Forder 19 Sep 86
3:51.8 Mark Sesay 22 Aug 89
3:52.0 Stuart Poore 6 Sep 89
3:52.47 Simon Young 4 Aug 90
10 3:52.6 Glen Stewart 19 Sep 87
3:52.78 Clifton Bradeley 2 Aug 81
3:52.9 Steve Johnson 8 Jul 89
3:53.0 Mark Bateman 31 Aug 74
3:53.16 Robert Farish 2 Aug 81
3:53.3 Richard Bunn 8 Jul 89

ONE MILE

4:06.7 Barrie Williams 22 Apr 72

2000 METRES

5:28.2 + Kevin Steere 10 Jul 71

3000 METRES

8:13.42 Barrie Moss 15 Jul 72
8:15.34 Kevin Steere 30 Aug 71
8:16.18 Mohammed Farah 21 Aug 99
8:19.08 Darren Mead 26 Aug 85
8:19.38 Johan Boakes 24 Jun 84
8:24.2 Simon Goodwin 16 Jul 80
8:24.2 Jason Lobo 13 Aug 86
8:25.2 Colin Clarkson 3 Aug 77
8:26.3 Paul Williams 10 Aug 83
8:26.6 Jon Dennis 23 Apr 86 10
8:26.92 Jon Richards 5 Sep 80
8:29.09 Steve Fury 18 Aug 84
8:29.4 Darrell Smith 16 Jul 83
8:30.4 Nicky Lees 15 Jul 74
8:30.4 David Lewis 13 Aug 78
8:30.4 David Thompson 8 Jul 89

5000 METRES

14:41.8 Nicky Lees 24 Aug 74

1500 METRES STEEPLECHASE

4:11.2 Steve Evans 15 Jul 74
4:12.3 Chris Sly 15 Jul 74
4:13.1 John Crowley 15 Jul 74
4:13.2 David Lewis 1 Jul 78
4:13.7 Danny Fleming 31 Jul 77
4:13.9 Eddie Wedderburn 31 Jul 77
4:14.0 Dave Robertson 8 Jul 89
4:14.4 Stephen Arnold 7 Sep 85
4:15.0 David Caton 9 Jun 84
4:15.0 Spencer Duval 12 Jul 86 10
4:15.2 Garrie Richardson 8 Jul 89
4:15.3 John Wilson 26 Jul 75
4:16.6 Adrian Green 9 Jun 84
4:17.4 Spencer Newport 9 Jul 83
4:17.7 Kevin Capper 8 Aug 76
4:17.7 Stuart Kefford 8 Jul 89

2000 METRES STEEPLECHASE

5:55.0 David Lewis 20 Aug 78

3000 METRES STEEPLECHASE

9:16.6 Colin Reitz 19 Sep 76

100 METRES HURDLES (3'0")

12.60 Tristan Anthony 14 Aug 99
12.68 Matthew Clements 8 Aug 93
12.90 Steve Markham 17 Aug 91
12.91 Allan Scott 14 Aug 99
12.97 Jon Snade 8 Aug 93
12.97 Andy Turner 16 Aug 97
12.98 Robert Newton 16 Aug 97
12.99 Dominic Girdler 11 Jul 98

	13.01	Hugh Teape	3 Aug 80
10	13.05	Brett St Louis	4 Aug 85
	13.07	Jon Ridgeon	7 Aug 83
	13.07	David O'Leary	3 Aug 96
	13.09	Damien Greaves	8 Jul 94
	13.09	Chris Baillie	16 Aug 97
	13.10	Ricky Glover	17 Aug 91
	wind assisted		
	12.47	Matthew Clements	9 Jul 94
	12.70	Damien Greaves	9 Jul 94
	12.88	Nick Csemiczky	13 Jul 91
	12.90	Ricky Glover	13 Jul 91
	12.90	Ben Warmington	8 Jul 95
	12.96	Nathan Palmer	15 Aug 98
	12.96	Dominic Girdler	15 Aug 98
	12.99	Neil Owen	1 Jul 90
	hand timing		
	12.8	Brett St Louis	28 Jul 85
	12.8	Richard Dunn	29 Jun 91
	12.9	Hugh Teape	31 Aug 80
	wind assisted		
	12.6	Brett St Louis	20 Jul 85
	12.9	Jon Ridgeon	9 Jul 83
	12.9	Dominic Girdler	13 Sep 98

110 METRES HURDLES (3'0")

13.71	Matthew Clements	19 May 94
14.16	Ben Warmington	12 Jul 95
14.19	Ross Baillie	19 May 94
hand timing		
13.6	Jon Ridgeon	16 Jul 83

110 METRES HURDLES (3'3")

15.07	Edward Dunford	10 Sep 00
wind assisted		
13.92	Matthew Clements	27 Aug 94
hand timing		
14.5	Kieran Moore	30 Aug 80

110 METRES HURDLES (3'6")

14.89	Tristan Anthony	4 Jul 99

400 METRES HURDLES (2'9")

	52.20	Tristan Anthony	18 Jul 99
	52.69	Jeffrey Christie	18 Jul 99
	52.81	Richard McDonald	10 Aug 96
	53.14	Martin Briggs	2 Aug 80
	53.26	Nange Ursell	11 Jul 98
	53.30	Mark Rowlands	31 Jul 94
	53.55	Charles Robertson-Adams	31 Jul 94
	53.58	Noel Levy	13 Jul 91
	53.64	Dean Park	17 May 94
10	53.69	Max Robertson	2 Aug 80
	53.69	Bob Brown	9 Aug 86
	53.71	Andrew Bargh	11 Jul 92
	53.82	Robert Taylor	9 Aug 86
	53.84	Rhys Williams	5 Aug 00
	hand timing		
	53.2	Phil Beattie	24 May 80
	53.8	Carl McMullen	20 Jul 96

400 METRES HURDLES (3'0")

53.06	Phil Beattie	2 Aug 80
53.31	Richard McDonald	28 Jul 96

HIGH JUMP

2.23	Mark Lakey	29 Aug 82	
2.15	Ossie Cham	14 Jul 79	
2.15	Brendan Reilly	7 May 89	
2.15	Stanley Osuide	1 Sep 91	
2.15	Chuka Enih-Snell	10 Sep 00	
2.12	Femi Abejide	11 Jul 81	
2.11	Leroy Lucas	6 Aug 83	
2.11 i	Ken McKeown	12 Jul 98	
	2.11	18 Jul 98	
2.10	Dalton Grant	18 Sep 82	
2.10	Tim Blakeway	29 Aug 87	10
2.10	James Brierley	16 May 93	
2.10	Martin Lloyd	28 Sep 96	
2.10	Martin Aram	23 Jul 00	
2.09	Steve Smith	10 Sep 89	
2.09	Samuel Hood	27 Aug 00	

POLE VAULT

5.20	Neil Winter	2 Sep 90	
5.15	Christian Linskey	23 Aug 96	
4.90	Warren Siley	8 Sep 89	
4.80	Billy Davey	14 Sep 80	
4.76	Nick Buckfield	11 Jun 89	
4.72	Ian Lewis	24 Aug 85	
4.70	Richard Smith	7 Jun 97	
4.66	Mike Edwards	24 Aug 85	
4.60	Ben Flint	10 Jun 95	
4.53	Keith Stock	5 Sep 73	10
4.50	Christian North	26 Aug 90	
4.50	Mike Barber	15 Sep 90	
4.50	Neil Young	5 Jun 93	
4.50	Chris Type	4 Jul 98	
4.50	Cameron Johnston	15 Aug 99	
4.50	Paul Stevens	8 Jul 00	

LONG JUMP

7.53	Brian Robinson	21 Jul 97	
7.46	Jonathan Moore	30 Jul 00	
7.32	Kevin Liddington	16 May 87	
7.25	Alan Slack	12 Jun 76	
7.21	Hugh Teape	17 May 80	
7.21	Jordan Lau	8 Jul 00	
7.21	Onew Eyong	30 Jul 00	
7.20	Hugh Davidson	21 Jun 80	
7.19	Oni Onuorah	8 Jul 89	
7.18	Barry Nevison	1 May 83	10
7.17	Hugh Whyte	15 Jul 79	
7.17	Mark Awanah	4 Jul 99	
7.15	Matthew John	29 Jun 86	
7.14	Stewart Faulkner	17 Aug 85	
7.13	Mark Findlay ¶	24 Sep 94	
wind assisted			
7.60	Brian Robinson	21 Jul 97	
7.40	Matthew John	10 May 86	
7.27	David Mountford	25 Jul 98	

	Mark	Athlete	Date
	7.25	Nathan Morgan	27 Aug 94
	7.25	Mark Awanah	25 Jul 98
	7.23	Oni Onuorah	26 May 90
	7.23	Andy Turner	20 Sep 97
	7.22	Paul Hanson	7 Jul 78
	7.18	Nicki Gordon	12 Sep 93
10	7.18	Kevin Hibbins	21 Jul 96
	7.16	Marcellas Peters	18 Jun 94

TRIPLE JUMP

	Mark	Athlete	Date
	16.02	Jonathan Moore	13 Aug 00
	15.65	Vernon Samuels	18 Jul 81
	15.50	Junior Campbell	18 May 86
	15.45	Steven Anderson	2 Aug 81
	15.28	Larry Achike	22 Jun 91
	note resident but not British citizen at this time		
	15.14	Marvin Bramble	8 Aug 93
	15.14	Steven Shalders	18 Jul 98
	14.94	Hugh Teape	17 May 80
	14.93	Mark Whitehead	26 Aug 85
10	14.90	Lawrence Lynch	21 Jul 84
	14.84	Peter Vaughan	2 May 83
	14.83	Malwyn Gordon	10 Jul 98
	14.82	Philip Ferdinand	5 Sep 99
	14.77	Carl Howard	13 Jul 90
	14.76	Delroy Ricketts	13 Jul 90
	14.76	Jon Wallace	3 Sep 95

wind assisted

	Mark	Athlete	Date
	15.46	Jonathan Moore	17 Jul 99
	15.40	Steven Shalders	18 Jul 98
	15.25	Marvin Bramble	3 Jul 93
	15.08	Lawrence Lynch	29 Apr 84
	15.06	Craig Duncan	7 Aug 82
	15.01	Malwyn Gordon	15 Aug 98
	14.93	Chris Tomlinson	18 Jul 98
	14.88	Carl Howard	13 Jul 90
	14.87	Darren Gomersall	3 Aug 85
10	14.84	Nick Leech	8 Jul 78

SHOT (7.26kg)

	Mark	Athlete	Date
	17.30	Carl Myerscough ¶	3 Aug 96

SHOT (6.25kg)

	Mark	Athlete	Date
	16.88	Gregg Beard	29 Aug 99

SHOT (5kg)

	Mark	Athlete	Date
	21.20	Carl Myerscough ¶	22 Sep 96
	19.22	Chris Ellis	4 Jun 82
	18.91	Gregg Beard	19 Sep 99
	18.90	Neal Brunning ¶	6 Sep 87
	18.44	Matt Simson	27 Jul 86
	18.43	Emeka Udechuku	28 May 95
	18.25	Billy Cole	1 Aug 81
	17.91	Antony Zaidman	28 May 78
	17.76	George Brocklebank	22 Jul 79
10	17.61	Derrick Squire	15 Jul 00
	17.40	Osita Iwenjiora	20 Sep 89
	17.36	Piers Selby	10 Jul 92
	17.34	Carl Saggers	30 Jul 00
	17.30	Jason Mulcahy	7 Jul 89
	17.24	Mark Edwards	20 Aug 91

DISCUS (2kg)

	Mark	Athlete	Date
	50.60	Carl Myerscough ¶	28 Jul 96
	48.96	Emeka Udechuku	19 Aug 95

DISCUS (1.75kg)

	Mark	Athlete	Date
	54.70	Emeka Udechuku	18 Jun 95
	52.50	Paul Mardle	7 Jul 79

DISCUS (1.5kg)

	Mark	Athlete	Date
	62.22	Emeka Udechuku	10 Jul 95
	58.14	Carl Myerscough ¶	12 May 96
	56.14	Chris Symonds	6 Sep 87
	55.94	Simon Williams I	9 Sep 84
	55.90	Guy Litherland	14 Sep 85
	55.72	Keith Homer	27 Jun 82
	55.52	Glen Smith	14 May 88
	55.36	Neal Brunning ¶	7 Jun 87
	55.17	Gregg Beard	30 May 99
10	54.18	Matt Symonds	21 Jul 84
	53.98	Felice Miele	10 Jul 98
	53.80	Paul Mardle	19 May 79
	53.69	Carl Saggers	17 Sep 00
	52.84	Simon Williams II	31 Aug 97
	52.76	Julian Willett	17 Jun 89
	52.76	James South	1 Sep 91
	52.62	Ashley Knott	22 Sep 91
	52.40	Guy Dirkin	28 Jun 69

HAMMER (7.26kg)

	Mark	Athlete	Date
	59.94	Andrew Tolputt	30 Sep 84
	57.04	Peter Vivian	27 Jun 87

HAMMER (6.25kg)

	Mark	Athlete	Date
	66.70	Andrew Tolputt	2 Sep 84
	64.00	Matthew Sutton	22 Aug 98

HAMMER (5kg)

	Mark	Athlete	Date
	76.28	Andrew Tolputt	11 Aug 84
	73.90	Paul Head	29 Aug 81
	73.76	Matthew Sutton	14 Jun 98
	73.00	Nick Steinmetz	17 Jul 93
	71.34	Tony Kenneally	7 Sep 80
	70.82	Jason Byrne	20 Jun 87
	68.62	Peter Vivian	16 May 87
	68.27	Carl Saggers	17 Jun 00
	67.64	Gareth Cook	22 Sep 85
10	67.48	Chris Howe	24 Jun 84
	67.21	Ross Thompson	22 Aug 98
	66.92	Paul Murden	8 May 85
	66.30	Malcolm Croad	21 Jul 90
	65.70	Ross Kidner	26 May 97
	64.82	Vaughan Cooper	13 May 82
	64.40	Jonathan Bond	14 May 89
	64.32	Neil Homer	18 Aug 84
	64.18	Charles Beresford	1 May 89
	63.64	Graeme Allan	19 Jul 97

JAVELIN (800g -1986 model)

	Mark	Athlete	Date
	68.26	David Parker	19 May 96
	61.00	Phill Sharpe	6 Jul 97

JAVELIN (800g Original model)

72.78	Gary Jenson	10 Sep 83
69.84	Colin Mackenzie	12 May 79
66.14	David Messom	14 May 81
65.32	Marcus Humphries	26 Aug 78
64.80	Paul Bushnell	1 Sep 85
64.34	Steve Backley	1 Sep 85
63.44	Michael Williams	16 Sep 79

JAVELIN (700g)

73.56	David Parker	20 Jul 96
72.48	Gary Jenson	3 Jul 83
70.30	Colin Mackenzie	6 Jul 79
68.88	Phill Sharpe	19 Jul 97
68.26	Ian Marsh	30 Jul 77
68.18	James Hurrion	3 Jun 90
66.88	David Messom	4 Jul 81
66.86	Michael Williams	16 Jul 79
66.52	Marcus Humphries	17 Sep 78
10 66.00	Dan Carter	1 Sep 96
65.92	Tim Kitney	10 Aug 96
65.68	Tim Eldridge	18 Aug 91
65.16	Mark Wells	31 May 77
64.92	Jason Beaumont	11 Jun 83
64.92	Paul Bushnell	20 Sep 85
64.80	Justin Rubio	1 Sep 85
64.68	Paul Godwin	19 May 90

DECATHLON (Senior Implements)

6484	David Bigham	27 Sep 87
6299	Tom Leeson	21 Sep 80

DECATHLON (Junior Implements)

6554	Jim Stevenson	25 Sep 88
6093	Robert Hughes	28 May 89

DECATHLON (U17 Implements)

6712	Edward Dunford	3 Sep 00
6706	David Bigham	28 Jun 87
6047	Jeremy Lay	30 Jun 85

OCTATHLON

5550	Dominic Girdler	20 Sep 98
5426	John Holtby	20 Sep 98
5423	Leo Barker	17 Sep 95
5420	Edward Dunford	18 Jun 00
5378	Matthew Lewis	20 Sep 92
5311	Dean Macey	18 Sep 94
5238	Neil Scrivener	21 Sep 97
5208	Fyn Corcoran	18 Sep 94
5158	Ed Coats	25 Aug 96
10 5149	Paul Hourihan	19 Sep 93
5144	Marc Newton	17 Sep 95
5136	Jamie Russell	20 Sep 98
5121	Chris Hindley	20 Sep 92
5102	Matt Douglas	22 Aug 93
5093	Robert Hollinger	21 Sep 97
5059	Mark Bushell	19 Sep 93
5051	Scott Walker	18 Sep 94

with 100m

5531	Jim Stevenson	18 Sep 88
5304	Tom Leeson	28 Sep 80
5194	Bryan Long	26 Sep 76
5106	Jeremy Lay	29 Sep 85
5096	Onochie Onuorah	17 Sep 89
5090	David Vidgen	22 Sep 91

3000 METRES TRACK WALK

12:04.9	Philip King	18 May 91
12:29.90	Andy Parker	2 Jul 00
12:34.98	Lloyd Finch	17 Jul 99
12:35.94	David Hucks	30 Aug 82
12:50.9	Jon Vincent	8 Jul 87
12:50.67 i	Stuart Monk	18 Feb 95
	12:52.9	12 Jul 95
13:03.5	Ian Ashforth	16 Sep 84
13:05.18	Cameron Smith	3 Sep 00
13:05.8	Sean Maxwell	8 Aug 76

5000 METRES TRACK WALK

20:46.5	Philip King	29 Sep 91
21:52.7	Stuart Monk	22 Jul 95
22:17.5	Russell Hutchings	27 Sep 86
22:19.11	Lloyd Finch	18 Sep 99
22:32.5	Gareth Holloway	27 Sep 86
22:35.0	Ian Ashforth	6 Jun 84
22:37.0	Jon Bott	27 Sep 86
22:42.0	Martin Young	20 Aug 88
22:42.19	Jon Vincent	6 Jun 86 10
22:48.91	Andy Parker	30 Jul 00
22:50.51	Dom King	18 Sep 99
22:53.7	Tim Berrett	28 Jun 81
22:53.8	David Hucks	10 Mar 82
22:57.7	Michael Kemp	31 Aug 96
23:01.0	Karl Atton	19 Apr 88
23:16.1	Thomas Taylor	31 May 97
23:16.5	Nathan Kavanagh	10 Jul 83

5k Road - *where superior to track time*

21:33	Jon Vincent	1 Nov 86
21:47	Lloyd Finch	20 Jun 99
22:04	Gareth Holloway	14 Sep 86
22:05	Karl Atton	19 Mar 88
22:30	Gordon Vale	15 Oct 77
22:31	Jon Bott	3 May 86
22:39	Matthew Hales	23 Jun 96
22:41	Thomas Taylor	26 Apr 97

10000 METRES TRACK WALK

43:56.5	Philip King	2 Feb 91
45:47.0	Ian Ashforth	12 Sep 84
45:52.39	Lloyd Finch	4 Jul 99
46:11.0	Jon Vincent	20 May 87

10k Road - *where superior to track time*

43:38 hc	Lloyd Finch	20 Nov 99
	44:21	13 Nov 99
43:49	Philip King	29 Jun 91
45:43	Jon Vincent	7 Mar 87

UNDER 15

100 METRES

10.93	Mark Lewis-Francis	12	Jul	97
11.05	Jamie Nixon	21	Jul	84
11.11	Tristan Anthony	17	Aug	97
11.20	Jamie McNiel	29	May	99
11.21	Kevin Mark	13	Jul	91
11.22	Chris Blake	7	Aug	93
11.23	Ray Burke	11	Aug	84
11.23	Charles Gordon	12	Aug	90
11.24	Mike Williams II	19	Jul	86
11.24	Jamie Gill	30	Jul	00
11.25	André Duffus	31	Jul	94
11.27	Tom Hyde	16	Aug	98
11.27	Alex Coley	30	Jul	00
11.27	Richard Davenport	28	Aug	00
wind assisted				
11.00	Steve Wiggans	9	Jul	94
11.04	Joe Brown	13	Jul	96
11.05	Ray Burke	11	Aug	84
11.06	Duncan Game	5	Jul	86
11.06	Paul Chantler	9	Jul	94
11.11	Andrew Rose	13	Jul	96
11.17	Tony Cairns	5	Jul	86
11.17	Steven Fowles	15	Aug	99
hand timing				
11.0	Norman Ellis	23	Jul	89
hand timing wind assisted				
11.0	Malcolm James	24	Jun	77
11.0	Ian Strange	24	Jun	77
11.0	John Burt	6	Sep	80
11.0	Hilton Thompson	6	Aug	89
11.0	Jeffrey Anderson	6	Aug	89
11.0	Matthew Clements	15	Sep	91

200 METRES

22.30	Jamie Nixon	29	Sep	84
22.31	Mike Williams II	10	Aug	86
22.35	Tristan Anthony	12	Jul	97
22.40	Ben Lewis	8	Jul	95
22.54	Matthew Clements	16	Aug	92
22.64	Martin Blencowe	8	Jul	00
22.65	Daniel Angus	12	Jul	96
22.65	Simon Farenden	25	Jun	00
22.69	Chris Blake	8	Aug	93
22.74	Laurence Oboh	11	Jul	98
22.79	Jermaine Williams	16	Aug	92
22.80	Joe Brown	8	Sep	96
22.80	James Ellington	8	Jul	00
wind assisted				
22.26	Steven Daly	9	Jul	94
22.26	Simon Farenden	8	Jul	00
22.39	André Duffus	9	Jul	94
22.40	Tom Hyde	15	Aug	98
22.43	Martin Blencoe	8	Jul	00
22.46	Robert Allenby	9	Jul	94
22.46	James Ellington	29	Jul	00
hand timing				
22.2	Mike Williams II	12	Jul	86
22.3	Tony Cairns	12	Jul	86
wind assisted				
21.9	Tony Cairns	21	Jun	86

300 METRES

37.45	Matthew Petty	5	Jul	97
hand timing				
35.9	Richard Davenport	26	Jul	00
during 400m				
35.7 +	Richard Davenport	23	Aug	00

400 METRES

49.74	Richard Davenport	23	Aug	00
49.96	Craig Erskine	18	Jul	98
49.97	David McKenzie	23	Jun	85
49.98	Ryan Preddy	11	Jul	98
50.65	Ian Lowthian	29	Jul	95
50.67	Fola Onibije	10	Jul	99
50.78	Mike Snow	12	Jul	97
50.88	Aaron Evans	17	Aug	96
50.99	Cephas Howard	13	Jul	91
51.00	Paul Roberts	22	Jul	84
51.09	David Vass	8	Jul	00
51.11	Leon Connikie	29	Jul	95
hand timing				
49.8	Mark Tyler	25	Aug	82
49.9	David McKenzie	11	Aug	85
50.0	Simon Heaton	7	Jul	79
50.1	Ade Mafe	6	Sep	81
50.3	Malcolm James	29	Aug	77
50.7	Cephas Howard	19	May	91
50.9	Alan Leonard	30	Aug	78
50.9	Noel Goode	7	Jul	79

600 METRES

1:23.6	Chris Davies	26	Jul	00

800 METRES

1:55.56	Michael Rimmer	25	Jul	00
1:56.1	Craig Winrow	12	Jul	86
1:56.6	Paul Burgess	13	Jul	85
1:57.1	Delroy Smith	12	Jul	86
1:57.12	Michael Combe	14	Aug	93
1:57.24	Tony Jarman	15	Sep	78
1:57.5	Noel Goode	11	Jul	79
1:57.5	Ryan Preddy	7	Jun	98
1:57.7	Eric Kimani	15	Sep	81
1:57.7	Mark Sesay	11	Aug	87
1:57.87	Austin Finn	7	Jul	91
1:58.1	Piers Counsell	12	Jul	86

1000 METRES

2:38.2	Eric Kimani	11	Sep	81

1500 METRES

4:03.0	Glen Stewart	28	Aug	85
4:03.0	Scott West	28	Aug	90
4:03.52	Mike Isherwood	17	Sep	82
4:03.56	Richard Youngs	17	Sep	82
4:03.6	Doug Stones	7	Jul	79
4:03.7	David Gerard	31	Jul	83

4:04.52	Chris Reynolds	10	Jul	99
4:04.63	Lee Bowron	29	Jul	00
4:05.7	Ben Mabon	1	Sep	85
4:05.8	Graham Green	19	Jun	79
4:05.9	Glen Coppin	25	Jun	97
4:06.0	Eric Kimani	29	Jul	81

ONE MILE

4:21.9	Glen Stewart	11	Sep	85

2000 METRES

5:45.8	Richard Slater	16	Jun	74

3000 METRES

8:47.0	Ben Mabon	16	Jul	85
8:47.48	Mohammed Farah	5	Jul	97
8:48.8	Dale Smith	14	Aug	85
8:51.1	Mark Slowikowski	4	Jun	80
8:53.66	Tom Snow	7	Jun	00
8:54.6	Gary Taylor	14	Sep	77
8:54.6	David Bean	22	Jul	79
8:56.0	Paul Ryder	29	Aug	79
8:56.4	Stuart Bond	10	Sep	91
8:57.0	Philip Hennessy	28	Jul	82
8:57.6	Chris Taylor	16	Jul	69
8:58.4	James Clarke	30	Sep	81

80 METRES HURDLES (2'9")

10.71	Matthew Clements	15	Aug	92
10.99	Edward Dunford	14	Aug	99
11.04	Leon McRae	8	Jul	95
11.07	Robert Hollinger	8	Jul	95
11.10	Seb Bastow	13	Jul	96
11.10	Chris Tye-Walker	12	Jul	97
11.15	Matthew Hansford	16	Sep	00
11.20	Tony Lashley	13	Jul	91
11.21	Joe Maxwell	8	Jul	95
11.21	Sam Bibby	12	Jul	97
11.21	Phillip Parnell	9	Jul	99
11.21	Richard Alexis-Smith	30	Jul	00
wind assisted				
11.00	Tom Benn	9	Jul	94
11.02	Nick Dowsett	10	Jul	93
11.12	Sam Allen	10	Jul	93
11.16	Sean Ashton	8	Jul	00
hand timing				
11.0	Austin Drysdale	22	Jun	75
hand timing wind assisted				
11.0	Tim Greenwood	29	Jun	97

100 METRES HURDLES (3'0")

13.3	Matthew Clements	23	Aug	92

400 METRES HURDLES (2'6")

60.1	Jonathan Gorrie	17	Jun	78

HIGH JUMP

2.04	Ross Hepburn	22	Aug	76
2.01	Ken McKeown	10	Aug	96
1.97	Andrew Lynch	29	Aug	88
1.97	Wayne Gray	3	Sep	95
1.96	Chuka Enih-Snell	29	Aug	98
1.95	Mark Lakey	14	Sep	80
1.95	Mark Bidwell	26	Sep	99
1.94	Brian Hall	16	Aug	97
1.93	Ewan Gittins	21	Jul	84
1.91	Mark Smith	15	Jul	89
1.91	Ed Willers	9	Jul	94
1.91	Matthew Brereton	9	Jul	94
1.91	Jamie Russell	21	Sep	96

POLE VAULT

4.31	Richard Smith	28	Aug	95
4.30	Neil Winter	2	Jul	88
4.30	Christian Linskey	18	Jun	94
4.18	Ian Lewis	24	May	83
4.00	Jimmy Lewis	9	Sep	79
3.90	Peter Eyre	2	Jul	89
3.90	Martin Parley	6	Jun	92
3.90	Steve Francis	12	Sep	93
3.90	Andrew Corey	17	Aug	96
3.85	Steven Brown	2	Jun	96
3.80	Steve Fuller	12	May	80
3.80	Mark Davis	9	Jul	91
3.80	Daniel Broadhead	17	Aug	96

LONG JUMP

6.79	Oni Onuorah	17	Sep	88
6.77	Barry Nevison	30	Aug	81
6.74	Kevin Hibbins	17	Jun	95
6.71	Mark Awanah	17	Aug	97
6.68	Onew Eyong	9	Jul	99
6.67	Gary Wilson	27	Aug	00
6.65	Edward Dunford	25	Sep	99
6.65	Bernard Yeboah	27	Aug	00
6.62	Martin Giraud	25	May	92
6.59	Danny Smith	29	Aug	87
6.58	Tony Allen	8	Aug	82
6.55	Jonathan Moore	17	May	98
6.54	Jordon Lau	11	Jul	98
wind assisted				
7.12	Oni Onuorah	17	Sep	88
6.72	David Gilkes	6	Apr	92
6.72	Onew Eyong	15	Aug	99
6.68	Jordon Lau	16	Aug	98
6.63	Ian Strange			77
downhill				
6.77	Eric Wood	25	Aug	58

TRIPLE JUMP

13.86	Jamie Quarry	10	Jul	87
13.79	Paul Dundas	11	Jun	88
13.77	Eugene Hechevarria	16	Sep	78
13.71	Larry Achike	10	Jun	89
note resident but not British citizen at this time				
13.69	Vernon Samuels	25	Aug	79
13.60	Steven Anderson	9	Jun	79
13.60	Steve Folkard	11	Jul	80
13.57	Errol Burrows	11	Jul	80
13.56	Delroy Ricketts	18	Jun	88
13.55	Darren Yeo	15	Jul	89
13.55	Michael Duberry	14	Jul	90
13.43	Michael Powell	12	Sep	76
13.43	Marvin Bramble	8	Sep	91

wind assisted

13.92	Eugene Hechevarria	7	Jul	78
13.87	Vernon Samuels	20	Sep	79
13.83	Chris Tomlinson	12	Jul	96
13.73	Donovan Fraser	6	Jul	79
13.69	Kevin O'Shaughnessy	7	Jul	78
13.60	Dean Taylor	12	Jul	96
13.58	Daniel Puddick	26	May	93

SHOT (5kg)

15.62	Chris Ellis	18	Jun	80

SHOT (4kg)

18.71	Chris Ellis	14	Jun	80
16.54	Geoff Hodgson	7	Jul	72
16.50	Carl Saggers	14	Jul	98
16.39	Pete Waterman	2	Jul	94
16.39	Gregg Beard	25	Aug	97
16.29	Neal Brunning ¶	11	Sep	85
16.11	Billy Cole	6	Jul	79
16.11	Andrae Davis	29	Jul	00
16.05	John Nicholls	29	Jun	80
16.01	Ian McLaughlin	18	Sep	91
15.96	James Muirhead	14	Sep	85
15.95	Spencer English	3	Aug	86

DISCUS (1.5kg)

44.20	Matt Symonds	18	Sep	82

DISCUS (1.25kg)

53.08	Emeka Udechuku	5	Sep	93
50.80	Paul Mardle	3	Sep	77
50.32	Chris Symonds	23	Jul	85
50.04	Keith Homer	11	Jul	80
49.36	James Muirhead	12	May	85
49.32	Lucan Douglas	16	Sep	79
49.22	Spencer English	1	Jun	86
49.10	Simon Bissell	27	Aug	00
48.84	Witold Leonowicz	23	Aug	80
48.78	Neville Lynch	7	Sep	80
48.76	Ben Walker	15	Aug	92
48.48	Simon Cooke	8	Jul	00

HAMMER (5kg)

60.10	Andrew Tolputt	5	Sep	82

HAMMER (4kg)

70.78	Andrew Tolputt	9	Jul	82
67.24	Peter Vivian	22	Sep	85
65.42	Matthew Sutton	29	Sep	96
64.28	Jason Byrne	22	Sep	85
63.68	Paul Binley	29	Sep	85
63.60	Richard Fedder	26	Aug	79
63.16	Tony Kenneally	29	May	78
62.06	Nick Steinmetz	4	Aug	91
61.32	John Barnes	8	Jun	96
61.08	Neil Curtis	11	Sep	88
60.52	Ian McLaughlin	21	Aug	91
60.15	Carl Saggers	16	Aug	98

JAVELIN (700g)

58.76	Dan Carter	29	Aug	94

JAVELIN (600g 1999 Model)

58.27	Mark Lindsay	30	Aug	99
54.11	Thomas Rees	5	Aug	00
53.93	Faron Paul	9	Apr	00

JAVELIN (600g pre 1999 Model)

62.70	Paul Godwin	21	May	89
60.56	David Messom	6	Jul	79
60.56	Clifton Green	3	Jul	94
60.34	Richard Lainson	18	Aug	96
59.88	James Hurrion	17	Sep	88
59.52	Paul Brice	19	Aug	79
58.94	Dan Carter	7	Aug	94
58.74	Philips Olweny	6	Aug	95
58.58	Justin Rubio	11	Jun	83
58.58	Rhys Williams	10	Aug	96

DECATHLON (Under 15 implements)

5341	Jamie Quarry	28	Jun	87

OCTATHLON (Under 15 implements)

3933	Aidan Turnbull	1	Oct	95

PENTATHLON (80H,SP,LJ,HJ,800)

3403	Edward Dunford	22	Aug	99
3281	Andrae Davis	16	Sep	00
3272	Chris Dack	20	Sep	97
3187	Marc Newton	27	Aug	94
3163	Kevin Drury	27	Aug	94
3129	Mark Awanah	24	Aug	97
3039	Chuka Enih-Snell	23	Aug	98
3024	Tom Benn	17	Sep	94
3014	Chris Jenkins	21	Sep	96
3001	Louis Moore	16	Sep	00
2995	Marcellas Peters	18	Sep	93
2993	Sam Allen	18	Sep	93
(100,SP,LJ,HJ,800)				
3199	Onochie Onuorah	17	Sep	88
3085 w	Cephas Howard	21	Sep	91

3000 METRES TRACK WALK

12:44.64	Lloyd Finch	24	May	98
13:19.57	Philip King	29	May	89
13:35.0	Russell Hutchings	7	Sep	85
13:45.0	John Murphy	14	May	95
13:51.0	Robert Mecham	12	May	92
13:57.06	James Davis	29	Aug	99
13:58.0	Jon Vincent	7	Sep	85
14:03.0	Neil Simpson	1	Apr	89
14:03.5	Nathan Kavanagh	20	Sep	81
14:09.93	Luke Finch	30	Jul	00
3k Road - *where superior to track time*				
13:20	Jonathan Deakin	18	Sep	88
13:29	Robert Mecham	20	Apr	92
13:32	Russell Hutchings	10	Nov	84
13:39	Neil Simpson	6	May	89
13:43	Nathan Kavanagh	21	Feb	81

5000 METRES TRACK WALK

22:54.0	Lloyd Finch	15	Jul	98

UNDER 13

75 METRES

9.7	A. White	1 Sep 96

80 METRES

10.17	Ricky Jasper	12 Aug 95
hand timing		
10.0	Adam Rogers	15 Jul 95

100 METRES

11.86	Chris Julien	3 Sep 00
12.14	Mark Lewis-Francis	3 Sep 95
12.29	Paul Moore	28 Aug 99
wind assisted		
12.25	Leon Cameron	8 Sep 96
hand timing		
11.6	Tristan Anthony	28 Aug 95
11.8	Cephas Howard	2 Jul 89
11.9	Stephen Buttler	26 Sep 87
12.0	Michael Tietz	22 Jul 90
12.0	Paul Twidale	11 Sep 99
wind assisted		
11.9	Michael Tietz	3 Jun 90

150 METRES

18.5	Tom Rayner	5 Jul 00

200 METRES

24.79	Leon Cameron	8 Sep 96
25.36	Mark Lewis-Francis	3 Sep 95
wind assisted		
24.28	Chris Julien	3 Sep 00
24.86	Tom Rayner	3 Sep 00
hand timing		
24.0	Stephen Buttler	26 Jul 87
24.1	Tristan Anthony	30 Jul 95
24.4	Cephas Howard	3 Sep 89
24.8	Michael Brown	8 Sep 85
24.8	Paul Twidale	16 May 99
24.9	Joelle Powell	4 Jun 00
25.0	Tyrone Keating	4 Sep 94
25.0	Jamaal Dixon	16 Aug 98
25.0	Chris Julien	2 Jul 00

300 METRES

41.8	Dominic Jones	5 Jul 97

400 METRES

58.06	Sam Allen	25 May 91
hand timing		
55.1	Cephas Howard	2 Jul 89
56.5	Craig Erskine	22 Sep 96
57.1	Wayne McDonald	17 Aug 83
57.3	E. Francis	18 May 74
57.4	David Tucker	78
57.6	Frank Adesoyan	27 Aug 90

600 METRES

1:34.7+	Eric Kimani	9 Sep 79

800 METRES

2:04.1	Ben Mabon	8 Jul 83
2:06.4	Eric Kimani	11 Aug 79
2:11.0	Brendan Waters	17 Jun 89
2:11.2	Chris Perrington	6 Aug 78
2:11.2	Gerry Maley	7 Jul 82
2:11.3	Ahmed Ali	10 May 98

1000 METRES

2:54.1	Stephen Holmes	1 Aug 93

1500 METRES

4:18.4	Eric Kimani	26 Sep 79
4:20.5	Ben Mabon	18 Jun 83
4:22.3	David Gerard	12 Aug 81
4:23.9	Mark Slowikowski	12 Jul 78
4:28.0	Ciaran Murphy	16 Jun 84
4:29.3	Dylan Gregory	21 Aug 83
4:29.7	Adam Hickey	28 Aug 00

ONE MILE

4:52.0	Tom Quinn	20 Jul 69

3000 METRES

9:31.4	Ben Mabon	24 Jul 83
9:41.4	Mark Slowikowski	21 May 78
9:47.99	Robert Pickering	25 Jun 00
9:49.5	John Tilley	9 Jul 86
9:50.45	Adam Hickey	30 Aug 00
9:50.7	Jacob McCulloch	31 May 00
9:51.1	Sam Hall	23 Sep 98

70 METRES HURDLES (2'3")

11.2	Brendan Kennedy	12 Jun 99
11.2	Elliot Donaldson	17 Jun 99

75 METRES HURDLES (2'3")

11.7	Stephen Cotterill	16 Jul 78
11.7	Sean Ashton	12 Sep 98
11.8	Edward Dunford	28 Sep 97

75 METRES HURDLES (2'6")

wind assisted		
11.98	Chris Douglas	2 Sep 00

80 METRES HURDLES (2'6")

12.74	Jermaine Bernard	14 Sep 97
hand timing		
11.9	Matthew Clements	27 Aug 90
12.1	Sean Ashton	27 May 98
12.4	Jon Crawshaw	14 Aug 94
12.5	Leo Cotterell	26 Sep 87
12.5	Tristan Anthony	9 Jul 95
12.6	James Dunford	2 Aug 98

80 METRES HURDLES (2'9")

12.92	Sam Allen	18 Aug 91
hand timing		
12.6	James Dunford	27 Sep 98
12.7	James Shipp	9 Jun 90

HIGH JUMP

1.70 Adrian Pettigrew 22 Jun 99
1.68 Sam Allen 22 Sep 91
1.68 James Dunford 29 Sep 98
1.67 Glen Carpenter 3 Jul 83
1.67 Jamie Dalton 28 Jun 92
1.66 Shane Smith 11 May 86
1.66 Tim Greenwood 95

POLE VAULT

3.40 Neil Winter 27 Jul 86
3.20 Ian Lewis 8 Sep 81
3.00 Luke Cutts 14 May 00

LONG JUMP

5.65 Sam Allen 14 Sep 91
5.64 Kevin Hibbins 18 Jul 93
5.62 Paul Twidale 31 Jul 99
5.61 Robert Creese 23 Jun 90
5.58 Edward Dunford 27 Sep 97
5.58 Matthew Hislop 5 Sep 99
5.55 Jason Davis 9 Jul 95
5.53 Jermaine Bernard 21 Sep 97

wind assisted

5.76 Seamas Cassidy 5 Sep 99
5.74 Edward Dunford 21 Sep 97

TRIPLE JUMP

12.57 Rigsby Agoreyo 9 Aug 69
11.78 Edward Dunford 27 Sep 97
11.52 Daniel Hutchinson 2 Jul 92

SHOT (4kg)

11.99 Mark Griffiths 70

SHOT (3.25kg)

13.36 Chris Hughes 21 Aug 91
13.11 Tony Quinn 28 Aug 93
12.60 Carl Saggers 7 Jul 96
12.58 Daniel Hepplewhite 15 Aug 99
12.58 Sam Herrington 5 Sep 99
12.46 Paul Beard 31 Aug 86
12.42 Edward Dunford 28 Sep 97
12.40 Shane Birch 23 Jul 00

SHOT (2.72kg)

13.49 Martin Wilson 13 Sep 92

DISCUS (1.25kg)

36.98 Sam Herrington 5 Sep 99

DISCUS (1kg)

42.50 Sam Herrington 12 Sep 99
42.38 Ben Barnes 1 Sep 91
38.92 Chris Hughes 28 Jul 91
38.58 Carl Saggers 15 Sep 96
38.30 Liam Walsh 13 Aug 94
35.50 Edward Dunford 20 Sep 97
34.46 Simon Bulley 6 Sep 97
34.14 James Dunford 5 Sep 98

DISCUS (750g)

43.70 Sam Herrington 8 Jul 99

HAMMER (4kg)

38.72 Adrian Johnson 30 Sep 84
38.64 Ross Thompson 14 Aug 94

HAMMER (3.25kg)

44.38 Ross Thompson 4 Sep 94
36.96 Edward Dunford 24 Sep 97
35.22 Sean Lewis 30 Sep 00

JAVELIN (600g Pre 1999 Model)

39.62 P. Shearing 23 May 76

JAVELIN (400g)

43.02 Max Shale 8 Aug 93
42.29 Edward Dunford 27 Sep 97
41.86 James Dunford 29 Sep 98
41.32 A. Westergren 5 Jul 80
41.20 S. Ahma 2 Jul 92
40.91 Adam Akehurst 30 Jul 00
40.60 Philip Mann 13 Sep 98

PENTATHLON (80H,SP,LJ,HJ,800 U15)

2444 James Dunford 27 Sep 98

PENTATHLON (75H,SP,LJ,HJ,800)

2562 Edward Dunford 28 Sep 97

1000 METRES TRACK WALK

4:46.0 Luke Finch 15 Jul 98
4:48.0 Dan King 21 Sep 95
4.48.0 Dom King 21 Sep 95

1k Road - *where superior to track time*

4:34 Luke Finch 27 Sep 97
4:42 Dom King 23 Sep 95
4:44 Nick Ball 16 Jul 00

2000 METRES TRACK WALK

9:40.0 Luke Finch 12 Nov 97
9:40.3 Thomas Taylor 19 Jun 93
9:51.0 Lloyd Finch 11 Aug 96
9:57.0 Jamie Nunn 7 Feb 88
10:06.0 Grant Ringshaw 23 Jul 78
10:10.0hc Dom King 23 Mar 95
10:11.0 John Griffiths 1 Jul 84
10:11.0 Philip King 30 Jun 87

2k Road - *where superior to track time*

9:16 Lloyd Finch 28 Sep 96
9:38 Luke Finch 12 Sep 98
9:55 hc Nick Ball 5 Sep 00
9:56 Grant Ringshaw 27 Oct 79
10:01 Gareth Brown 27 Oct 79
10:01 Paul Miles 28 Sep 96

3000 METRES TRACK WALK

15:02.62 Lloyd Finch 21 Sep 96

3k Road - *where superior to track time*

14:44 Martin Young 22 Sep 84

UK ALL TIME LISTS - WOMEN

100 METRES

	Perf	Name	Day	Month	Year
	11.10	Kathy Cook	5	Sep	81
	11.13	Cook	29	Aug	83
	11.15	Paula Thomas	23	Aug	94
	11.16	Andrea Lynch	11	Jun	75
	11.20	Sonia Lannaman	25	Jul	80
	11.20	Heather Oakes	26	Sep	80
	11.22	Lynch	21	Aug	76
	11.22	Lannaman	13	Aug	77
	11.22	Lynch	20	Aug	77
	11.22 A	Bev Callender	8	Sep	79
		11.35	22	Jul	81
	11.22	Oakes	27	Jul	86
	11.24	Joice Maduaka	19	Jun	99
	11.27	Stephi Douglas	26	Jul	91
	11.29	Bev Kinch	6	Jul	90
10	11.31	Wendy Hoyte	4	Oct	82
	11.31	Shirley Thomas	3	Jul	83
	11.31	Simmone Jacobs	24	Sep	88
	11.32	Joan Baptiste	24	Aug	83
	11.32	Christine Bloomfield	3	Jul	99
	11.34	Katharine Merry	25	Jun	94
	11.34	Shani Anderson	26	Aug	00
	11.35	Sharon Danville	20	Aug	77
	11.35	Marcia Richardson	4	Jun	00
	11.36 A	Della Pascoe	14	Oct	68
20	11.39 A	Val Peat	14	Oct	68
	11.39	Sallyanne Short	12	Jul	92
	11.40	Helen Hogarth	20	Jul	74
	11.41	Jayne Andrews	27	May	84
	11.43	Donita Benjamin	11	Aug	00
	11.44	Sam Davies	11	Aug	00
	11.45	Helen Burkart	26	Aug	83
	11.46 A	Donna Hartley	22	Mar	75
	11.46	Eleanor Cohen	30	Jul	82
	11.47	Mary Agyepong	20	Jun	87
30	11.48	Carmen Smart	26	Aug	89
	11.48	Geraldine McLeod	26	May	96
	11.48	Andrea Coore	1	Jun	97
	11.49	Sophia Smith	25	Aug	96
	11.49	Sarah Wilhelmy	17	Sep	00
	11.50	Sandra Whittaker	14	Jun	86
	11.50	Helen Miles	5	Aug	88
	11.51	Kaye Scott	28	May	83
	11.51	Sarah Reilly	21	Jun	97
	11.52	Pippa Windle	6	Jun	86
40	11.52	Abi Oyepitan	11	Jun	00
	11.53	Sharon Williams	31	Aug	95
	11.54	Dorothy Hyman	15	Oct	64
	11.54	Janis Neilson	24	May	87
	11.54	Aileen McGillivary	27	Jun	92
	11.55	Anita Neil	1	Sep	72
	11.55	Amanda Forrester	9	Sep	00
	11.56	Janine Whitlock	14	Aug	99
	11.57	Michelle Scutt	2	Sep	84
	11.57	Donna Fraser	29	May	00
50	11.5 a	Daphne Slater	15	Oct	64
	11.59	Rebecca Drummond	8	Jul	95

wind assisted

Perf	Name	Day	Month	Year	
10.93	Sonia Lannaman	17	Jul	77	
11.01	Heather Oakes	21	May	80	
11.06	Lannaman	21	May	80	
11.08	Oakes	27	May	84	
11.08	Kathy Cook	24	Aug	83	
11.10	Cook	13	Sep	80	
11.11	Lannaman	5	Jun	80	
11.11	Cook	26	Jun	83	
11.13	Bev Kinch	6	Jul	83	
11.13	Shirley Thomas	27	May	84	
11.13	Paula Thomas	20	Aug	88	
11.18	Wendy Hoyte	4	Oct	82	
11.18	Simmone Jacobs	11	Jun	97	
11.19	Bev Callender	21	May	80	
11.23	Joan Baptiste	24	Aug	83	10
11.23	Jayne Andrews	17	Jul	84	
11.27	Katharine Merry	11	Jun	94	
11.29	Marcia Richardson	29	May	00	
11.32	Donna Fraser	25	Apr	97	
11.34	Sandra Whittaker	22	May	83	
11.36	Sallyanne Short	26	Aug	89	
11.37	Val Peat	17	Jul	70	
11.37	Kaye Scott	22	May	83	
11.37	Helen Burkart	11	Sep	83	
11.39	Pippa Windle	24	Jul	87	20
11.40	Phylis Smith	3	Jun	90	
11.41	Helen Miles	20	Aug	88	
11.43	Dorothy Hyman	2	Sep	60	
11.43	Aileen McGillivary	10	Jul	93	
11.43	Clova Court	26	May	97	
11.45	Michelle Scutt	12	Jun	82	
11.45	Rebecca White	4	Jul	98	
11.45	Abi Oyepitan	4	Jul	98	
11.46	Geraldine McLeod	9	Jul	93	
11.48	Jakki Harman	23	Jul	88	30
11.48	Angie Thorp	7	Jul	96	
11.49	Ellena Ruddock	29	May	00	
11.50	Margot Wells	15	Jul	78	
11.50	Rebecca Drummond	9	Jul	94	
11.51	Anita Neil	17	Jul	70	
11.52	Zoe Wilson	29	May	00	

hand timing

Perf	Name	Day	Month	Year
10.9	Andrea Lynch	28	May	77
11.1	Sonia Lannaman	29	Jun	80
11.1	Heather Oakes	29	Jun	80
11.1	Joan Baptiste	16	Jul	85
11.2	Helen Golden	29	Jun	74
11.2	Sharon Danville	25	Jun	77
11.2	Bev Kinch	14	Jul	84
11.2	Geraldine McLeod	21	May	94

hand timing - wind assisted

Perf	Name	Day	Month	Year
10.8	Sonia Lannaman	22	May	76
11.1	Sharon Danville	22	May	76
11.1	Bev Kinch	9	May	87
11.2	Margaret Williams	15	May	76
11.2	Donna Fraser	31	Jan	98

200 METRES

	22.10	Kathy Cook	9	Aug	84
	22.13	Cook	9	Sep	82
	22.21	Cook	20	Aug	84
	22.25	Cook	22	Aug	84
	22.26	Cook	24	Aug	83
	22.31	Cook	8	Aug	80
	22.37	Cook	14	Aug	83
	22.38	Cook	9	Aug	84
	22.53	Cook	25	Aug	82
	22.57	Cook	13	Aug	83
	22.58	Sonia Lannaman	18	May	80
	22.69	Paula Thomas	26	Aug	94
	22.72	Bev Callender	30	Jul	80
	22.73	Jenni Stoute	3	Aug	92
	22.75	Donna Hartley	17	Jun	78
	22.76	Katharine Merry	25	Jul	00
	22.80	Michelle Scutt	12	Jun	82
	22.83	Joice Maduaka	25	Jul	99
10	22.85	Christine Bloomfield	25	Jul	99
	22.86	Joan Baptiste	9	Aug	84
	22.92	Heather Oakes	28	Aug	86
	22.95	Simmone Jacobs	25	Apr	96
	22.96 i	Donna Fraser	23	Feb	97
		23.08	22	Jul	00
	22.98	Sandra Whittaker	8	Aug	84
	23.06	Sam Davies	28	Aug	00
	23.10	Diane Smith	11	Aug	90
	23.14	Helen Hogarth	7	Sep	73
	23.14	Helen Burkart	17	Jul	82
20	23.15	Andrea Lynch	25	Aug	75
	23.17	Stephi Douglas	12	Jun	94
	23.18	Joslyn Hoyte-Smith	9	Jun	82
	23.20	Sarah Reilly	21	Jun	97
	23.20	Shani Anderson	10	Sep	00
	23.23	Sarah Wilhelmy	13	Jun	98
	23.24	Sallyanne Short	28	Jun	92
	23.28	Catherine Murphy	25	Jul	99
	23.29	Verona Elder	17	Jun	78
	23.29	Aileen McGillivary	25	Jul	93
30	23.30	Sally Gunnell	13	Jun	93
	23.30	Janine Whitlock	25	Jul	99
	23.33	Linsey Macdonald	9	Jun	82
	23.33	Allison Curbishley	8	Jun	98
	23.34	Val Peat	19	Sep	69
	23.35	Melanie Neef	2	Jul	95
	23.36	Shirley Thomas	10	Jun	84
	23.36	Louise Stuart	4	Aug	90
	23.40	Dorothy Hyman	18	Aug	62
	23.40	Sharon Danville	9	Sep	77
40	23.40	Phylis Smith	6	Jun	92
	23.42 A	Lillian Board	17	Oct	68
	23.42	Debbie Bunn	17	Jun	78
	23.43	Sue Hearnshaw	16	Jun	84
	23.46	Janine MacGregor	22	Aug	81
	23.47 A	Angela Baxter	10	May	86
	23.47	Geraldine McLeod	24	Aug	94
	23.48	Wendy Hoyte	7	Jun	75
	23.48	Denise Ramsden	21	Aug	76
	23.48	Margaret Williams	21	Aug	76
50	23.49	Wendy Addison	16	Jun	84
	23.49 i	Vernicha James	30	Jan	00

wind assisted

22.21	Cook	7	Oct	82	
22.48	Michelle Scutt	4	Jul	82	
22.69	Bev Callender	24	Jun	81	
22.90	Andrea Lynch	11	Jun	75	
22.90	Donna Fraser	25	Apr	97	
22.90	Allison Curbishley	17	Jul	98	
22.97	Helen Golden	26	Jul	74	
23.00	Joslyn Hoyte-Smith	13	Jun	82	
23.11	Linsey Macdonald	5	Jul	80	
23.14	Shirley Thomas	28	May	84	
23.15	Margaret Williams	22	Jul	70	10
23.19	Sallyanne Short	29	Jan	90	
23.20	Sarah Wilhelmy	18	Jul	98	
23.23	Sinead Dudgeon	29	Jul	00	
23.32	Louise Stuart	4	Jun	89	
23.36	Lorna Boothe	30	Mar	80	
23.39 A	Angela Baxter	12	Apr	86	
23.41	Louise Fraser	16	Jun	91	
23.46	Maureen Tranter	21	Jul	70	
23.48	Vernicha James	21	Aug	99	

hand timing

22.9	Heather Oakes	3	May	80
22.9	Helen Barnett	6	Aug	83
23.0	Helen Golden	30	Jun	74
23.1	Andrea Lynch	21	May	77
23.1	Linda Keough	5	Jul	89
23.2	Dorothy Hyman	3	Oct	63
23.2	Margaret Williams	2	Aug	70
23.3	Sharon Danville	30	Jun	74
23.3	Linsey Macdonald	8	May	82
23.3	Louise Stuart	25	Aug	91

wind assisted

23.1	Margaret Williams	14	Jul	74
23.1	Sharon Danville	17	Sep	77
23.1	Linda McCurry	2	Jul	78
23.2	Debbie Bunn	2	Jul	78
23.2	Sybil Joseph	1	Jun	85

300 METRES

35.46	Kathy Cook	18	Aug	84	
35.51	Cook	9	Sep	83	
35.71	Donna Fraser	28	Aug	00	
36.00	Katharine Merry	28	Aug	00	
36.01	Michelle Scutt	13	Jul	80	
36.44	Sally Gunnell	30	Jul	93	
36.45	Joslyn Hoyte-Smith	5	Jul	80	
36.46	Linsey Macdonald	13	Jul	80	
36.65	Joan Baptiste	18	Aug	84	
36.69	Helen Burkart	9	Sep	83	
36.92	Phylis Smith	11	Aug	96	10
36.95	Jenni Stoute	21	Jul	91	
36.97	Donna Hartley	4	Jul	75	
37.30	Verona Elder	26	May	76	
37.33	Melanie Neef	8	Jul	94	
37.40	Tracey Lawton	18	Aug	84	

hand timing

36.2	Donna Hartley	7	Aug	74
37.0	Linda Keough	22	Jul	89

400 METRES

	49.43	Kathy Cook	6 Aug 84
	49.72	Katharine Merry	25 Sep 00
	49.79	Donna Fraser	25 Sep 00
	50.05	Merry	8 Jul 00
	50.21	Merry	24 Aug 99
	50.21	Fraser	24 Sep 00
	50.28	Merry	25 Jun 00
	50.32	Merry	24 Sep 00
	50.40	Phylis Smith	3 Aug 92
	50.45	Merry	5 Aug 00
	50.63	Michelle Scutt	31 May 82
	50.71	Allison Curbishley	18 Sep 98
	50.75	Joslyn Hoyte-Smith	18 Jun 82
	50.93	Lorraine Hanson	26 Aug 91
	50.98	Linda Staines	26 Aug 91
10	51.04	Sally Gunnell	20 Jul 94
	51.16	Linsey Macdonald	15 Jun 80
	51.18	Melanie Neef	6 Aug 95
	51.28	Donna Hartley	12 Jul 75
	51.41	Sandra Douglas	2 Aug 92
	51.53	Jenni Stoute	12 Aug 89
	51.70	Verona Elder	10 Jun 78
	51.93	Janine MacGregor	28 Aug 81
	51.97	Linda Forsyth	31 May 82
	52.05	Sinead Dudgeon	3 Jul 99
20	52.12 A	Lillian Board	16 Oct 68
		53.00	2 Sep 68
	52.13	Helen Burkart	28 Jun 84
	52.20	Ann Packer	17 Oct 64
	52.26	Pat Beckford	14 Aug 88
	52.40	Helen Frost	17 Sep 00
	52.43	Gladys Taylor	2 Sep 84
	52.47	Michelle Thomas	3 Jul 99
	52.48	Georgina Oladapo	16 Jun 96
	52.52	Sybil Joseph	14 Sep 85
	52.54	Stephanie Llewellyn	9 Jul 95
30	52.57 A	Janet Simpson	16 Oct 68
	52.65	Jane Parry	11 Jun 83
	52.67	Tracey Lawton	8 Jul 84
	52.71	Loreen Hall	18 Jun 88
	52.72	Catherine Murphy	17 Sep 00
	52.75	Sandra Leigh	12 Jul 91
	52.77	Michelle Pierre	20 Jul 97
	52.79	Angela Piggford	2 Jul 89
	52.80	Sian Lewis	18 Jun 83
	52.83	Ruth Patten	10 Jul 79
40	52.85	Jannette Roscoe	3 Sep 74
	52.89	Janet Smith	6 Aug 88
	52.97	Vicki Jamison	1 Aug 98
	52.98	Karen Ford	6 Aug 78
	52.98	Dyanna Clarke	28 Jul 79
	52.99	Angela Baxter	24 Jul 82
	53.01 i	Marilyn Neufville	14 Mar 70
	53.02	Lesley Owusu	20 May 00
	53.08	Bev Callender	21 Aug 76
	53.16	Joy Grieveson	14 Sep 63
50	53.23	Tracy Joseph	15 Jun 91
	53.24	Rosemary Wright	28 Aug 71
	53.24	Dawn Higgins	16 Jul 00

hand timing

51.2	Donna Hartley	28 Jul 78
51.4	Verona Elder	22 May 76
52.2	Liz Barnes	22 May 76
52.4	Stephanie Llewellyn	1 Jul 95
52.6	Marilyn Neufville	20 Jun 70

600 METRES

1:26.0 +	Kelly Holmes	13 Aug 95
1:26.18	Diane Modahl	22 Aug 87
1:26.5 +	Kirsty Wade	21 Aug 85

800 METRES

1:56.21	Kelly Holmes	9 Sep 95	
1:56.80	Holmes	25 Sep 00	
1:56.95	Holmes	13 Aug 95	
1:57.14	Holmes	7 Jul 97	
1:57.42	Kirsty Wade	24 Jun 85	
1:57.45	Wade	21 Aug 85	
1:57.48	Wade	17 Aug 85	
1:57.56	Holmes	16 Jul 95	
1:57.84	Holmes	15 Jun 96	
1:57.88	Wade	9 Jul 85	
1:58.65	Diane Modahl	14 Jul 90	
1:58.97	Shireen Bailey	15 Sep 87	
1:59.05	Christina Cahill	4 Aug 79	
1:59.67	Lorraine Baker	15 Aug 86	
1:59.76	Paula Fryer	17 Jul 91	
1:59.81	Ann Griffiths	10 Aug 94	
2:00.10	Tanya Blake	31 May 98	
2:00.15	Rosemary Wright	3 Sep 72	10
2:00.20	Anne Purvis	7 Jul 82	
2:00.30	Cherry Hanson	25 Jul 81	
2:00.39	Bev Nicholson	28 Aug 88	
2:00.55mx	Zola Budd	21 Jun 86	
2:00.6 a	Jane Finch	9 Jul 77	
2:00.80	Yvonne Murray	10 Jul 87	
2:01.1 a	Ann Packer	20 Oct 64	
2:01.11	Lynne MacDougall	18 Aug 84	
2:01.2	Joan Allison	1 Jul 73	
2:01.2	Christine Whittingham	26 Aug 78	20
2:01.24	Chris Benning	28 Jul 79	
2:01.25	Hayley Tullett	22 Jul 00	
2:01.35	Liz Barnes	10 Jul 76	
2:01.36	Gillian Dainty	31 Aug 83	
2:01.40	Janet Bell	10 Jul 87	
2:01.48	Lesley Kiernan	11 Jun 77	
2:01.50	Lillian Board	18 Sep 69	
2:01.65	Teena Colebrook	21 Jul 84	
2:01.66	Pat Cropper	12 Aug 71	
2:01.67	Sonya Bowyer	24 Jun 95	30
2:01.7	Ann Middle	28 Aug 91	
2:01.82	Linda Keough	1 Aug 93	
2:01.83	Amanda Crowe	18 Sep 98	
2:01.86	Helen Daniel	10 Jul 87	
2:01.87	Dawn Gandy	19 Jun 88	
2:01.93	Sue Bevan	19 Jul 91	
2:02.0	Margaret Coomber	1 Jul 73	
2:02.0	Jo White	13 Aug 77	
2:02.0	Lynne Robinson	26 Jul 89	

40	2:02.34	Lynn Gibson	14 Aug 92
	2:02.39	Emma Davies	17 Sep 98
	2:02.47	Abigail Hunte	16 Jul 95
	2:02.6	Evelyn McMeekin	20 Aug 78
	2:02.69	Natalie Tait	16 Jul 95
	2:02.70	Janet Marlow	15 Jun 80
	2:02.79	Sue Morley	27 Jul 85
	2:02.83	Mary Kitson	21 Jul 91
	2:02.89	Wendy Sly	30 Jul 83
	2:02.9	Sheila Carey	10 Sep 71
50	2:02.91	Carol Sharp	7 Jul 82

1000 METRES

	2:32.55	Kelly Holmes	15 Jun 97
	2:32.82	Holmes	23 Jul 95
	2:33.18	Holmes	25 Aug 95
	2:33.70	Kirsty Wade	9 Aug 85
	2:34.92	Christina Cahill	9 Aug 85
	2:35.32	Shireen Bailey	19 Jul 86
	2:35.51	Lorraine Baker	19 Jul 86
	2:35.86	Diane Modahl	29 Aug 93
	2:37.05	Christine Whittingham	27 Jun 86
	2:37.29	Yvonne Murray	14 Jul 89
	2:37.61	Bev Hartigan	14 Jul 89
	2:37.82	Gillian Dainty	11 Sep 81
10	2:38.44	Evelyn McMeekin	23 Aug 78
	2:38.58	Jo White	9 Sep 77
	2:38.67	Lynne MacDougall	19 Jul 86
	2:38.83	Lynn Gibson	29 Aug 93
	2:39.23	Teena Colebrook	24 Jul 90
	2:39.29	Ann Griffiths	16 Sep 90
	2:39.42	Mary Cotton	26 May 76
	2:39.78	Liz Barnes	26 May 76

1500 METRES

	3:58.07	Kelly Holmes	29 Jun 97
	3:59.96	Zola Budd	30 Aug 85
	4:00.57	Christina Cahill	6 Jul 84
	4:00.64	Cahill	1 Oct 88
	4:00.73	Kirsty Wade	26 Jul 87
	4:01.13	Holmes	5 Jul 96
	4:01.20	Yvonne Murray	4 Jul 87
	4:01.23	Hayley Tullett	28 Jul 00
	4:01.38	Liz McColgan	4 Jul 87
	4:01.41	Wade	5 Sep 87
	4:01.53	Chris Benning	15 Aug 79
	4:02.32	Shireen Bailey	1 Oct 88
10	4:03.17	Alison Wyeth	7 Aug 93
	4:04.14	Wendy Sly	14 Aug 83
	4:04.81	Sheila Carey	9 Sep 72
	4:04.82	Helen Pattinson	25 Jul 00
	4:05.66	Bev Hartigan	20 Jul 90
	4:05.75	Lynn Gibson	20 Jul 94
	4:05.81	Paula Radcliffe	1 Jun 98
	4:05.96	Lynne MacDougall	20 Aug 84
	4:06.0	Mary Cotton	24 Jun 78
	4:06.24	Christine Whittingham	5 Jul 86
20	4:07.11	Janet Marlow	18 Aug 82
	4:07.28	Joanne Pavey	29 Jun 97
	4:07.59	Ann Griffiths	9 Jun 92
	4:07.69	Teena Colebrook	19 Aug 90
	4:07.90	Gillian Dainty	16 Jun 84
	4:09.26	Lisa York	13 Jun 92
	4:09.29	Angela Newport	20 Jul 94
	4:09.37	Joyce Smith	7 Sep 72
	4:09.46	Karen Hargrave	4 Sep 89
	4:09.5	Penny Forse	6 Aug 80
30	4:10.07	Maxine Baker	28 Jun 92
	4:10.10	Cherry Hanson	30 Aug 81
	4:10.21	Kathy Carter	31 Jul 82
	4:10.22	Kelly Caffel	20 Aug 00
	4:10.32	Lynne Robinson	30 Jul 94
	4:10.41	Jo White	10 Jun 84
	4:10.66	Joan Allison	2 Feb 74
	4:10.68	Amanda Crowe	21 Sep 98
	4:10.7 mx	Sonya Bowyer	16 Jul 96
	4:10.75	Sonia McGeorge	20 Jul 90
40	4:10.76	Ruth Partridge	16 Jun 84
	4:11.00	Sue Morley	6 Jul 85
	4:11.12	Bridget Smyth	26 May 85
	4:11.23	Paula Fudge	31 Jul 81
	4:11.24 i	Nicky Morris	7 Jan 89
	4:11.46	Ursula McGloin	20 Jan 90
	4:11.51	Jane Shields	4 Sep 83
	4:11.57	Sue Lamb	18 Jun 96
	4:11.75	Debbie Peel	31 Jul 82
	4:11.82	Una English	28 Jun 92
50	4:11.85	Jo Dering	28 Jul 90
	4:11.94	Lorraine Baker	5 Jul 90

ONE MILE

	4:17.57	Zola Budd	21 Aug 85
	4:19.41	Kirsty Wade	27 Jul 85
	4:21.61	Wade	5 Sep 86
	4:22.64	Christina Cahill	7 Sep 84
	4:22.64	Yvonne Murray	22 Jul 94
	4:24.57	Chris Benning	7 Sep 84
	4:24.87	Alison Wyeth	6 Jul 91
	4:24.94	Paula Radcliffe	14 Aug 96
	4:26.11	Liz McColgan	10 Jul 87
	4:26.16	Teena Colebrook	14 Jul 90
10	4:26.50 i	Hayley Tullett	6 Feb 00
	4:26.52	Bev Hartigan	14 Aug 92
	4:27.80	Lisa York	14 Aug 92
	4:28.04	Kelly Holmes	30 Aug 98
	4:28.07	Wendy Sly	18 Aug 84
	4:28.8	Karen Hargrave	20 Aug 89
	4:29.15	Sue Morley	18 Aug 84
	4:30.08	Lynne MacDougall	7 Sep 84
	4:30.29	Jane Shields	9 Sep 83
	4:30.77	Joanne Pavey	30 Aug 97
20	4:30.89	Ruth Partridge	18 Aug 84
	4:31.17	Lynn Gibson	1 Jul 94
	4:31.24 i	Jo White	5 Feb 83
	4:31.45	Shireen Bailey	17 Sep 89
	4:31.65	Gillian Dainty	26 Jun 82
	4:31.83	Angela Davies	1 Jul 94
	4:32.00	Carole Bradford	18 Aug 84
	4:32.32	Debbie Gunning	5 Jul 91
	4:32.82	Monica Joyce	10 May 81

2000 METRES

	Time	Athlete	Date
	5:26.93	Yvonne Murray	8 Jul 94
	5:29.58	Murray	11 Jul 86
	5:30.19	Zola Budd	11 Jul 86
	5:33.85	Christina Cahill	13 Jul 84
	5:37.00	Chris Benning	13 Jul 84
	5:38.50	Alison Wyeth	29 Aug 93
	5:39.20	Paula Radcliffe	29 Aug 93
	5:40.24	Liz McColgan	22 Aug 87
	5:42.15	Wendy Sly	17 Sep 82
	5:43.24	Sue Morley	13 Jul 84
10	5:45.0 i	Bev Hartigan	20 Feb 93

estimated

	Time	Athlete	Date
	5:44.0 +	Joanne Pavey	28 Aug 00

3000 METRES

	Time	Athlete	Date
	8:27.40	Paula Radcliffe	11 Aug 99
	8:28.83	Zola Budd	7 Sep 85
	8:28.85	Radcliffe	11 Aug 00
	8:29.02	Yvonne Murray	25 Sep 88
	8:29.60	Murray	15 Jul 94
	8:30.30	Murray	10 Jul 93
	8:31.61	Radcliffe	7 Jul 99
	8:32.43	Murray	3 Sep 93
	8:34.43	Budd	30 Jun 86
	8:34.80 i	Liz McColgan	4 Mar 89
		8:38.23	15 Jul 91
	8:36.70	Joanne Pavey	28 Aug 00
	8:37.06	Wendy Sly	10 Aug 83
	8:38.42	Alison Wyeth	16 Aug 93
	8:44.46	Chris Benning	22 Aug 84
	8:45.39	Hayley Tullett	15 Jul 00
10	8:45.69	Jane Shields	10 Aug 83
	8:47.36	Jill Boltz	17 Aug 88
	8:47.59	Angela Tooby-Smith	5 Jul 88
	8:47.7	Kirsty Wade	5 Aug 87
	8:47.71	Lisa York	31 Jul 92
	8:48.72	Karen Hargrave	28 Jan 90
	8:48.74	Paula Fudge	29 Aug 78
	8:49.89	Christina Cahill	20 Jul 85
	8:50.52	Debbie Peel	7 Aug 82
	8:51.33	Sonia McGeorge	29 Aug 90
20	8:51.40	Ruth Partridge	7 Aug 82
	8:52.79	Ann Ford	28 Aug 77
	8:53.52 i	Nicky Morris	4 Mar 89
		8:59.46	24 Jun 89
	8:55.53	Joyce Smith	19 Jul 74
	8:56.09	Andrea Wallace	10 Jul 92
	8:56.39	Sue Morley	21 Jul 84
	8:57.17	Susan Wightman	6 Jun 84
	8:57.2	Kathy Carter	7 Apr 84
	8:57.75 mx	Sarah Wilkinson	27 Jun 00
	8:58.44	Kath Binns	26 May 80
30	8:58.59	Andrea Whitcombe	26 Jul 91
	8:59.39	Regina Joyce	8 May 81
	8:59.45	Jo Dering	11 Aug 90
	8:59.65	Gillian Dainty	20 Jul 83
	9:00.21	Carole Bradford	9 Jul 85
	9:00.3	Bridget Smyth	20 Apr 91
	9:00.68	Alison Wright	23 Jun 81
	9:01.67	Melissa Watson	27 Jun 88
	9:02.25	Julie Holland	11 Aug 90
	9:02.47	Laura Adam	4 Jun 94
40	9:02.67 mx	Amanda Parkinson	22 Aug 00

5000 METRES

	Time	Athlete	Date
	14:43.54	Paula Radcliffe	7 Aug 99
	14:44.36	Radcliffe	5 Aug 00
	14:45.51	Radcliffe	22 Aug 97
	14:46.76	Radcliffe	16 Aug 96
	14:48.07	Zola Budd	26 Aug 85
	14:48.79	Radcliffe	20 Jun 99
	14:49.27	Radcliffe	7 Jul 95
	14:50.32	Radcliffe	26 Aug 97
	14:51.27	Radcliffe	5 Aug 98
	14:51.71	Radcliffe	12 Jul 96
	14:56.94	Yvonne Murray-Mooney	7 Jul 95
	14:58.27	Joanne Pavey	25 Sep 00
	14:59.56	Liz McColgan	22 Jul 95
	15:00.37	Alison Wyeth	7 Jul 95
	15:09.98	Jill Boltz	18 Jul 92
	15:13.22	Angela Tooby-Smith	5 Aug 87
	15:14.51	Paula Fudge	13 Sep 81
10	15:21.45	Wendy Sly	5 Aug 87
	15:28.63	Andrea Wallace	2 Jul 92
	15:29.04	Sonia McGeorge	27 May 96
	15:31.78	Julie Holland	18 Jul 90
	15:32.19	Susan Wightman	26 May 85
	15:32.34	Jane Shields	5 Jun 88
	15:32.62	Andrea Whitcombe	25 Jun 00
	15:34.16	Jill Harrison	26 May 85
	15:34.40	Lucy Elliott	2 Jun 97
	15:36.27	Hayley Yelling	16 Jul 00
20	15:36.35	Birhan Dagne	5 Aug 00
	15:38.84	Ann Ford	5 Jun 82
	15:40.14	Helen Titterington	17 Jul 89
	15:40.85	Sarah Wilkinson	11 Jul 00
	15:41.11	Angie Hulley	18 Jul 90
	15:41.68	Debbie Peel	27 Jun 85
	15:43.99	Angela Newport	9 Jun 99
	15:45.03	Lynne MacDougall	29 Jun 97
	15:46.05	Hayley Haining	7 Aug 99
	15:48.1 mx	Tara Krzywicki	5 Aug 98
		15:53.28	25 Jul 98
30	15:49.6	Kath Binns	5 Apr 80
	15:50.85	Liz Yelling	1 Aug 98
	15:51.62	Carol Greenwood	26 May 85
	15:52.2	Ruth Partridge	23 Aug 89
	15:53.84	Heather Knight	6 Jul 96
	15:53.86	Sarah Bentley	22 Jul 95
	15:55.64	Katie Skorupska	9 Jun 99
	15:56.0	Lucy Taylor	15 May 90
	15:56.04	Vikki McPherson	25 Jul 98
	15:56.4+	Sue Crehan	4 Jul 87
40	15:56.58	Gillian Palmer	13 Aug 00
	15:56.64	Amanda Parkinson	11 Jul 00
	15:56.83	Suzanne Rigg	30 Jul 94
	15:57.06	Louise Watson	24 Jun 95
	15:57.45	Amy Waterlow	25 Jul 98
	15:58.8	Teresa Dyer	21 Jul 93

10000 METRES

	Time	Name	Day	Month	Year
	30:26.97	Paula Radcliffe	30	Sep	00
	30:27.13	Radcliffe	26	Aug	99
	30:40.70	Radcliffe	10	Apr	99
	30:48.58	Radcliffe	4	Apr	98
	30:57.07	Liz McColgan	25	Jun	91
	31:06.99	McColgan	2	Jul	88
	31:07.88	Jill Hunter	30	Jun	91
	31:08.44	McColgan	30	Sep	88
	31:14.31	McColgan	30	Aug	91
	31:19.82	McColgan	4	Sep	87
	31:53.36	Wendy Sly	8	Oct	88
	31:55.30	Angela Tooby-Smith	4	Sep	87
	31:56.97	Yvonne Murray-Mooney	24	Aug	94
	32:20.95	Susan Wightman	2	Jul	88
	32:21.61	Andrea Wallace	6	Jun	92
	32:24.63	Sue Crehan	4	Jul	87
10	32:30.4	Birhan Dagne	22	Jul	00
	32:32.42	Vikki McPherson	15	Jul	93
	32:34.7	Sarah Wilkinson	22	Jul	00
	32:36.09	Helen Titterington	29	Aug	89
	32:41.29	Jenny Clague	20	Jun	93
	32:42.0	Jane Shields	24	Aug	88
	32:42.84	Angie Hulley	6	Aug	89
	32:44.06	Suzanne Rigg	27	Jun	93
	32:47.78	Julie Holland	31	Aug	90
	32:52.5	Hayley Yelling	22	Jul	00
20	32:57.17	Kath Binns	15	Aug	80
	32:58.2	Claire Lavers	20	Apr	91
	33:04.55	Tara Krzywicki	10	Apr	99
	33:05.43	Elspeth Turner	1	Jun	88
	33:07.9	Liz Yelling	22	Jul	00
	33:10.25	Shireen Barbour	5	Jul	86
	33:10.94	Marina Stedman	28	Jul	86
	33:12.8	Lucy Elliott	5	Jun	99
	33:17.88	Karen Macleod	1	Jul	89
	33:19.19	Bernadette Madigan	27	Apr	85
30	33:19.48	Heather Knight	6	Jun	92
	33:21.46	Louise Watson	14	Jun	96
	33:23.25	Zahara Hyde-Peters	12	Jun	94
	33:26.79	Amanda Allen	6	Jun	92
	33:27.69	Jill Harrison	22	Jun	86
	33:30.0	Annette Bell	10	Aug	91
	33:30.27	Angie Joiner	4	Apr	98
	33:34.03	Lynn Everington	26	May	86
	33:34.7	Priscilla Welch	2	Jun	84
	33:34.77	Debbie Peel	22	Jun	86
40	33:34.96	Carol Greenwood	12	Jun	94
	33:38.36	Jo Thompson	29	Jun	97
	33:39.0	Veronique Marot	5	Apr	86
	33:40.3	Sandra Branney	3	Sep	89
	33:40.6	Andrea Paolillo	5	Apr	86
	33:41.16	Lucy Wright	29	Jun	97
	33:46.1	Vicki Vaughan	15	May	91
	33:47.47	Cathy Newman	22	Jun	90
	33:49.8	Bev Jenkins	22	Jul	00
	33:53.4 mx	Nicky McCracken	19	Sep	89
50	33:57.86	Alison Rose	12	Jun	94
	33:59.69	Sarah Bentley	4	Apr	98
	33:59.90	Christine Price	28	Jul	86

10 KILOMETRES ROAD

Time	Name	Day	Month	Year	
30:39	Liz McColgan	11	Mar	89	
30:59	McColgan	6	Feb	88	
31:07	McColgan	21	Feb	87	
31:13	McColgan	10	Oct	87	
31:19	McColgan	4	Apr	93	
31:29	Wendy Sly	27	Mar	83	
31:42	Jill Hunter	21	Jan	89	
31:47	Paula Radcliffe	29	Mar	97	
31:56	Andrea Wallace	4	Aug	91	
32:14	Priscilla Welch	23	Mar	85	
32:15	Angela Tooby-Smith	31	Mar	84	
32:20	Zola Budd	2	Mar	85	
32:24	Yvonne Murray-Mooney	2	Nov	97	
32:27	Ruth Partridge	11	Mar	89	10
32:31	Heather Knight	6	Nov	94	
32:35	Suzanne Rigg	15	Aug	92	
32:38	Jane Shields	23	Mar	85	
32:38	Marian Sutton	28	Sep	97	
32:41	Jill Harrison	21	Feb	87	
32:43	Teresa Dyer	1	Jan	93	
32:44	Carole Bradford	14	Oct	85	
32:44	Paula Fudge	13	Mar	88	
32:45	Sarah Wilkinson	4	Dec	99	
32:46	Kirsty Wade	28	Feb	87	20
32:47	Chris Benning	15	Mar	87	
32:52	Susan Wightman	29	Oct	89	
32:55	Hayley Yelling	4	Jun	00	
32:56	Alison Wyeth	20	Mar	94	
33:00	Sheila Catford	24	Aug	88	
33:02	Bev Hartigan	8	Apr	95	
33:02	Lucy Elliott	19	Apr	98	
33:03	Cathy Newman	6	Feb	88	
33:04	Glynis Penny	1	Jan	86	
33:04	Gillian Stacey	24	Jan	93	30

course measurement uncertain

Time	Name	Day	Month	Year
31:43	Zola Budd	6	May	84
31:58	Sandra Branney	10	May	89
32:03	Paula Fudge	29	Aug	82
32:29	Yvonne Danson	13	Nov	94
32:36	Mary Cotton	5	Aug	84
32:41	Susan Wightman	4	Mar	84
32:42	Veronique Marot	30	Sep	84
32:46	Amanda Allen	25	Feb	96
32:47	Debbie Peel	15	Apr	84
32:54	Shireen Barbour	3	Aug	86
32:59	Sharon Astley	20	Sep	87

10 MILES ROAD

Time	Name	Day	Month	Year	
51:41	Jill Hunter	20	Apr	91	
51:56	Hunter	7	Apr	91	
51:51	Angie Hulley	18	Nov	89	
52:00	Liz McColgan	5	Oct	97	
52:15	Marian Sutton	5	Oct	97	
53:42	Suzanne Rigg	10	Oct	93	
53:44	Paula Fudge	21	Sep	85	
53:44	Andrea Wallace	7	Mar	93	
53:49	Véronique Marot	25	Aug	85	
53:50	Yvonne Murray	6	Oct	96	
53:51	Priscilla Welch	5	Apr	87	10

intermediate times

51:41 +	Paula Radcliffe	22	Oct	00
53:00 +	Andrea Wallace	5	May	91

course measurement uncertain

53:17	Joyce Smith	12	Oct	80
53:44	Sarah Rowell	10	Mar	84

downhill

53:42	Karen Macleod	11	Apr	93

HALF MARATHON

1:07:07	Paula Radcliffe	22	Oct	00
1:07:11	Liz McColgan	26	Jan	92
1:08:42	McColgan	11	Oct	92
1:08:53	McColgan	20	Sep	92
1:09:07	Radcliffe	12	Nov	00
1:09:39	Andrea Wallace	21	Mar	93
1:09:41	Marian Sutton	14	Sep	97
1:09:56	Susan Wightman	24	Jul	88
1:10:54	Alison Wyeth	29	Mar	98
1:11:17	Veronique Marot	21	Jun	87
1:11:33	Vikki McPherson	14	Sep	97
1:11:36	Ann Ford	30	Jun	85
1:11:37	Paula Fudge	24	Jul	88
1:11:38	Sally Ellis	20	Mar	88
1:11:44	Jill Harrison	29	Mar	87
1:11:44	Lorna Irving	6	Sep	87
1:12:06	Sarah Rowell	11	Nov	84
1:12:07	Suzanne Rigg	3	Oct	93
1:12:22	Sandra Branney	4	May	86
1:12:24	Jill Boltz	15	Sep	91
1:12:25	Angie Hulley	1	Apr	90
1:12:25	Yvonne Murray-Mooney	15	Sep	96
1:12:29	Cathy Newman	25	Aug	90
1:12:31	Liz Yelling	22	Oct	00
1:12:49	Sheila Catford	11	Sep	88
1:12:53	Birhan Dagne	22	Aug	99
1:13:04	Sue Reinsford	22	Aug	99

intermediate times

1:11:44 +	Sally-Ann Hales	21	Apr	85
1:11:59 +	Angie Hulley	1	Jan	89
1:12:17 +	Priscilla Welch	1	Nov	87

estimated time

1:11:57 +	Priscilla Welch	10	May	87

course measurement uncertain

1:11:44	Karen Macleod	15	Jan	95
1:12:23	Lynn Everington	6	Sep	87
1:12:32	Yvonne Danson	31	Jul	94

MARATHON

2:25:56	Véronique Marot	23	Apr	89
2:26:51	Priscilla Welch	10	May	87
2:26:52	Liz McColgan	13	Apr	97
2:26:54	McColgan	26	Apr	98
2:27:32	McColgan	3	Nov	91
2:27:38	McColgan	15	Nov	92
2:27:54	McColgan	21	Apr	96
2:28:04	Marot	20	Oct	85
2:28:06	Sarah Rowell	21	Apr	85
2:28:38	Sally-Ann Hales	21	Apr	85
2:28:42	Marian Sutton	24	Oct	99
2:29:29	Sally Eastall	8	Dec	91
2:29:43	Joyce Smith	9	May	82
2:29:47	Paula Fudge	30	Oct	88
2:30:38	Ann Ford	17	Apr	88
2:30:51	Angie Hulley	23	Sep	88
2:30:53	Yvonne Danson	17	Apr	95
2:31:33	Susan Wightman	23	Sep	88
2:31:33	Andrea Wallace	12	Apr	92
2:31:45	Lynn Harding	23	Apr	89
2:32:53	Gillian Castka	2	Dec	84
2:33:04	Sheila Catford	23	Apr	89
2:33:07	Nicky McCracken	22	Apr	90
2:33:16	Karen Macleod	27	Aug	94
2:33:22	Carolyn Naisby	6	Dec	87
2:33:24	Sally Ellis	23	Apr	89
2:33:38	Lynda Bain	21	Apr	85
2:33:41	Sue Reinsford	16	Apr	00
2:34:11	Sally Goldsmith	3	Mar	96
2:34:19	Jill Harrison	23	Apr	89
2:34:21	Suzanne Rigg	24	Sep	95
2:34:26	Heather MacDuff	16	Oct	88
2:35:03	Sandra Branney	23	Apr	89
2:35:10	Sue Crehan	17	Apr	88
2:35:18	Karen Holdsworth	29	Sep	85
2:35:18	Debbie Noy	13	Oct	91
2:35:32	Rose Ellis	23	Apr	89
2:35:39	Hayley Nash	27	Aug	94
2:35:53	Julie Coleby	13	May	84
2:36:06	Margaret Lockley	13	May	84
2:36:12	Kath Binns	12	Jun	82
2:36:21	Glynis Penny	17	Apr	83
2:36:29	Danielle Sanderson	7	Aug	94
2:36:31	Julia Cornford	20	Apr	86
2:36:32	Marina Stedman	23	Apr	89
2:36:34	Lorna Irving	1	Aug	86
2:36:40	Teresa Dyer	17	Apr	94
2:36:52	Gillian Horovitz	20	Jun	92
2:37:06	Moira O'Neill	31	Oct	88
2:37:14	Cath Mijovic	22	Oct	95
2:37:26	Caroline Horne	21	Apr	85
2:37:36	Sandra Mewett	17	Jan	88
2:37:37	Anne Roden	20	Apr	92
2:37:49	Alison Gooderham	17	Apr	88
2:37:53	Carol Gould	12	Jun	82

course measurement uncertain

2:35:05	Carol Gould	26	Oct	80

100 KILOMETRES ROAD

7:27:19	Carolyn Hunter-Rowe	8	Aug	93
7:42:17	Trudi Thomson	26	Jun	94
7:48:33	Eleanor Robinson	7	Oct	89

2000 METRES STEEPLECHASE (2'6")

6:36.02	Jayne Spark	8	Aug	00
6:36.49	Tara Krzywicki	21	May	00
6:53.7	Sharon Dixon	8	May	94
6:57.42	Clare Martin	8	Aug	00
7:00.7	Sally Young	8	May	94

3000 METRES STEEPLECHASE (2'6")

10:08.11	Tara Krzywicki	5	Sep	00

100 METRES HURDLES

	Time	Name	Date
	12.80	Angie Thorp	31 Jul 96
	12.82	Sally Gunnell	17 Aug 88
	12.87	Shirley Strong	24 Aug 83
	12.88	Strong	10 Aug 84
	12.90	Jacqui Agyepong	25 Jun 95
	12.91	Strong	12 Aug 83
	12.91	Kay Morley-Brown	2 Feb 90
	12.93	Agyepong	6 Jul 94
	12.93	Agyepong	8 Jul 94
	12.93	Thorp	29 Jul 96
	12.95	Keri Maddox	25 Aug 99
	12.99	Diane Allahgreen	26 Aug 99
	13.03	Lesley-Ann Skeete	3 Aug 90
	13.04	Clova Court	9 Aug 94
10	13.05	Judy Simpson	29 Aug 86
	13.07	Lorna Boothe	7 Oct 82
	13.08	Sam Farquharson	4 Jul 94
	13.11	Sharon Danville	22 Jun 76
	13.13	Denise Lewis	29 Jul 00
	13.16	Wendy Jeal	27 Aug 86
	13.17	Melanie Wilkins	18 Jun 00
	13.20	Natasha Danvers	2 May 98
	13.24	Kim Hagger	31 Aug 87
	13.26	Michelle Campbell	3 Aug 90
20	13.29	Mary Peters	2 Sep 72
	13.32	Sam Baker	29 Aug 93
	13.34	Judy Vernon	7 Sep 73
	13.35	Pat Rollo	30 Jul 83
	13.36	Louise Fraser	17 Aug 91
	13.40	Julie Pratt	1 Aug 99
	13.44	Judith Robinson	1 Jul 89
	13.45	Lorna Drysdale	20 Jul 74
	13.46	Tessa Sanderson	25 Jul 81
	13.46	Nathalie Byer	26 Aug 83
30	13.46	Rachel King	3 Jul 99
	13.47	Heather Ross	16 Jun 84
	13.49	Blondelle Caines	17 Jul 77
	13.49	Liz Fairs	30 Jul 00
	13.50A	Yvette Wray-Luker	8 Sep 79
		13.57	15 Jul 79
	13.52	Bianca Liston	30 Jul 00
	13.53	Ann Simmonds	4 Sep 72
	13.53	Lynne Green	27 Jun 88
	13.54	Debbie Brennan	7 Aug 88
	13.57	Bethan Edwards	29 Aug 92
40	13.58	Lauraine Cameron	19 Jun 90
	13.59	Jane Hale	19 May 96
	13.59	Sarah Claxton	31 Jul 99
	13.60	Elaine McMaster	7 Oct 82
	13.60	Joanne Mulliner	25 Jul 87
	13.62	Gillian Evans	1 Jul 83
	13.62	Jill Kirk	3 Jul 83
	13.62	Danielle Freeman	3 Jun 00
	13.68	Heather Platt	7 Jul 85
	13.70	Yinka Idowu	14 Jun 92
50	13.71	Margot Wells	4 Aug 82
	13.73	Ann Girvan	7 Aug 82
	13.74	Kerry Robin-Millerchip	6 Jun 86
	13.75	Sue Reeve	21 Jul 70
	13.75	Maureen Prendergast	5 May 84

wind assisted

Time	Name	Date	
12.78	Shirley Strong	8 Oct 82	
12.78	Strong	13 Aug 83	
12.80	Sally Gunnell	29 Jul 88	
12.83	Strong	13 Sep 81	
12.84 A	Kay Morley-Brown	8 Aug 90	
12.86	Strong	9 Aug 84	
12.86	Gunnell	5 Jun 88	
12.90	Lorna Boothe	8 Oct 82	
13.01	Lesley-Ann Skeete	1 Feb 90	
13.06	Sharon Danville	14 Jul 84	
13.08	Michelle Campbell	26 May 95	
13.12	Pat Rollo	27 May 84	
13.19	Natasha Danvers	22 Apr 00	
13.22	Heather Ross	27 May 84	10
13.28	Sarah Claxton	5 Jul 98	
13.28	Julie Pratt	23 May 99	
13.36	Judith Robinson	11 Jul 87	
13.39	Debbie Brennan	29 Jul 88	
13.39	Lauraine Cameron	1 Jul 90	
13.44	Yvette Wray-Luker	21 May 80	
13.44	Kerry Robin-Millerchip	27 May 84	
13.44	Rachel King	28 May 98	
13.48	Elaine McMaster	12 Jun 82	
13.48	Joanne Mulliner	25 Jul 87	20
13.54	Jill Kirk	7 Jun 86	
13.56	Ann Girvan	15 Jul 84	
13.57	Katy Sketchley	14 Jun 98	
13.61	Clare Milborrow	28 May 00	
13.62	Yinka Idowu	17 Sep 94	
13.63	Heather Platt	1 Jul 84	
13.66	Maureen Prendergast	14 Apr 84	
13.71	Sue Longden	21 May 80	
13.71	Manndy Laing	12 Jun 82	
13.71	Kerry Jury	22 May 99	30
13.72	Myra Nimmo	20 Jul 74	
13.72	Kate Forsyth	6 Jul 97	

hand timing

Time	Name	Date	
13.0	Judy Vernon	29 Jun 74	
13.0	Blondelle Caines	29 Jun 74	
13.1	Melanie Wilkins	2 Jul 95	
13.2	Pat Rollo	11 Jun 83	
13.3	Ann Simmonds	29 Jul 72	
13.3	Debbie Brennan	16 Jul 89	
13.4	Christine Bell	2 Aug 70	
13.4	Bianca Liston	15 Jul 00	
13.5	Pat Pryce	26 Jul 72	
13.5	Liz Sutherland	29 Mar 76	10
13.5	Sue Longden	26 Jun 76	
13.5	Yvette Wray-Luker	7 Jun 80	
13.5	Jill Kirk	7 Aug 83	

wind assisted

Time	Name	Date
12.7	Kay Morley-Brown	10 Jan 90
12.8	Natasha Danvers	3 Apr 99
12.9	Judy Vernon	18 May 74
13.1	Mary Peters	19 Aug 72
13.2	Ann Simmonds	19 Aug 72
13.2	Liz Sutherland	8 May 76
13.3	Kerry Robin-Millerchip	9 May 87
13.5	Myra Nimmo	24 Jul 74

400 METRES HURDLES

	52.74	Sally Gunnell	19 Aug 93
	53.16	Gunnell	29 Aug 91
	53.23	Gunnell	5 Aug 92
	53.33	Gunnell	12 Aug 94
	53.51	Gunnell	24 Jul 94
	53.52	Gunnell	4 Aug 93
	53.62	Gunnell	7 Aug 91
	53.73	Gunnell	26 Jun 93
	53.78	Gunnell	3 Aug 91
	53.78	Gunnell	3 Aug 92
	54.63	Gowry Retchakan	3 Aug 92
	54.95	Natasha Danvers	25 Sep 00
	55.22	Keri Maddox	12 Aug 00
	55.24	Sinead Dudgeon	24 Jul 99
	55.91	Elaine McLaughlin	26 Sep 88
	56.04	Sue Chick	10 Aug 83
	56.05	Wendy Cearns	13 Aug 89
	56.06	Christine Warden	28 Jul 79
10	56.15	Jacqui Parker	27 Jul 91
	56.26	Louise Fraser	7 Jun 92
	56.42	Vicki Jamison	20 Jun 98
	56.43	Alyson Layzell	16 Jun 96
	56.46	Yvette Wray-Luker	11 Jul 81
	56.61	Louise Brunning	16 Jun 96
	56.70	Lorraine Hanson	13 Aug 89
	56.72	Gladys Taylor	6 Aug 84
	57.00	Simone Gandy	6 Aug 88
	57.07	Verona Elder	15 Jul 83
20	57.38	Sarah Dean	27 Jul 91
	57.41	Jennie Matthews	6 Aug 88
	57.43	Liz Sutherland	6 Jul 78
	57.49	Maureen Prendergast	16 Jun 84
	57.52	Clare Sugden	3 Jun 90
	57.55	Sharon Danville	8 May 81
	57.76	Aileen Mills	5 Aug 86
	57.79	Susan Cluney	15 Jun 80
	57.81	Margaret Southerden	10 Jul 82
	57.86	Teresa Hoyle	29 Jul 83
30	57.92	Tracey Duncan	29 Jul 00
	58.02	Vyv Rhodes	28 Jun 92
	58.04	Clare Bleasdale	16 Jul 94
	58.09	Stephanie McCann	12 Jun 94
	58.16	Diane Fryar	9 Jul 83
	58.19	Sara Elson	4 Jul 92
	58.28	Carol Dawkins	14 Sep 85
	58.31	Jannette Roscoe	19 Jul 75
	58.31	Fiona Laing	18 Sep 81
	58.35	Debbie Skerritt	11 Jul 81
40	58.41	Lynn Edwards	19 Jun 88
	58.43	Jane Low	24 Aug 94
	58.44	Maggie Still	19 Jun 88
	58.50	Nicola Sutton	23 May 99
	58.51	Julie Vine	17 Jun 90
	58.55	Jackie Stokoe	19 Jul 75
	58.62	Sharon Allen	3 May 97
	58.68	Kay Simpson	15 Jul 83
	58.68	Vicky Lee	5 Aug 86
	58.75	Katie Jones	29 Jul 00
50	58.79	Sheila Peak	25 Jul 87

hand timing

57.5	Vicky Lee	28 Jun 86	
57.8	Teresa Hoyle	26 Jul 86	
58.0	Fiona Laing	28 Aug 81	
58.2	Debbie Skerritt	6 Jun 81	
58.6	Jane Finch	21 Sep 80	
58.8	Veronica Boden	28 Jun 87	
58.8	Allison Curbishley	5 May 96	
HIGH JUMP			
1.95	Diana Davies	26 Jun 82	
1.95 i	Debbie Marti	23 Feb 97	
	1.94	9 Jun 96	
1.94	Louise Gittens	25 May 80	
1.94 i	Davies	7 Mar 82	
1.94 i	Marti	3 Feb 91	
1.94 i	Jo Jennings	13 Mar 93	
	1.91	20 Sep 98	
1.94	Marti	9 Jun 96	
1.94	Marti	15 Jun 96	
1.93	Susan Jones	2 Sep 00	
1.93	Michelle Dunkley	2 Sep 00	
1.92	Barbara Simmonds	31 Jul 82	
1.92	Judy Simpson	8 Aug 83	
1.92	Janet Boyle	29 Sep 88	
1.92 i	Julia Bennett	10 Mar 90	10
	1.89	11 Jun 94	
1.92	Lea Goodman	15 Jun 96	
1.91	Ann-Marie Cording	19 Sep 81	
1.91	Gillian Evans	30 Apr 83	
1.91	Jayne Barnetson	7 Jul 89	
1.90	Kim Hagger	17 May 86	
1.90	Sharon Hutchings	1 Aug 86	
1.88 i	Debbie McDowell	17 Jan 88	
	1.82	7 May 88	
1.88 i	Kerry Roberts	16 Feb 92	
	1.86	6 Jun 92	
1.88 i	Kelly Thirkle	16 Feb 92	
	1.85	10 Aug 91	
1.88	Lee McConnell	19 Aug 00	20
1.87	Barbara Lawton	22 Sep 73	
1.87	Moira Maguire	11 May 80	
1.87	Louise Manning	6 May 84	
1.87	Rachael Forrest	7 Jul 95	
1.87	Denise Lewis	21 Aug 99	
1.86	Claire Summerfield	7 Aug 82	
1.86	Jennifer Farrell	11 May 86	
1.86	Catherine Scott	8 May 87	
1.86	Michele Marsella	31 May 87	
1.85	Brenda Flowers	20 Aug 77	30
1.85	Gillian Cadman	3 Jun 78	
1.85	Julie Peacock	8 Jul 94	
1.85	Hazel Melvin	3 Aug 97	
1.85 i	Julie Crane	13 Feb 00	
	1.83	30 May 98	
1.84	Sarah Rowe	22 Aug 81	
1.84	Ursula Fay	6 Aug 83	
1.84	Tonia Schofield	20 Aug 83	
1.83	Linda Hedmark	4 Jul 71	
1.83	Val Rutter	19 Jun 74	
1.83 i	Ros Few	25 Feb 75	40

	1.83	Denise Hinton	8 Aug 80
	1.83	Joanne Brand	4 Jun 83
	1.83	Rhona Scobie	4 Aug 85
	1.83	Marion Hughes	19 Jul 86
	1.83	Tracey Clarke	2 Aug 87
	1.83	Kay Fletcher	17 Jun 89
	1.83	Gillian Black	25 Jul 99
	1.83 i	Rebecca Jones	4 Mar 00
		1.83	3 Jun 00
	1.83	Aileen Wilson	8 Jul 00
50	1.82	Mary Peters	2 Sep 72
	1.82	Wendy Phillips	19 Jul 80
	1.82	Elaine Hickey	9 Aug 80
	1.82	Natasha Danvers	24 May 98

POLE VAULT

	4.35	Janine Whitlock	5 Jun 00
	4.31	Whitlock	30 May 98
	4.31 i	Whitlock	20 Feb 00
	4.30	Whitlock	27 May 98
	4.30	Whitlock	27 Jun 98
	4.30 i	Whitlock	6 Feb 00
	4.30 i	Whitlock	25 Feb 00
	4.30 i	Whitlock	27 Feb 00
	4.30	Whitlock	8 Aug 00
	4.30	Whitlock	17 Sep 00
	4.20	Irie Hill	6 Aug 00
	4.15	Rhian Clarke	7 Apr 00
	4.04	Lucy Webber	15 Jul 00
	4.00	Alison Davies	12 Aug 00
	3.95A	Allie Jessee	25 Jun 99
		3.60	4 Aug 98
	3.91	Emma Hornby	27 Jun 98
	3.90	Kate Staples	26 May 96
	3.90	Ellie Spain	6 May 00
10	3.90	Tracey Bloomfield	4 Jun 00
	3.80	Paula Wilson	25 Jul 98
	3.76A	Krissy Owen	1 May 99
		3.55	16 Apr 99
	3.75	Louise Schramm	19 Jul 98
	3.72	Linda Stanton	11 Jun 95
	3.70	Liz Hughes	29 Jul 00
	3.65 i	Lindsay Hodges	6 Feb 00
		3.55	14 Aug 99
	3.60	Fiona Harrison	25 May 98
	3.60	Clare Ridgley	25 May 98
	3.55	Kim Rothman	17 Jun 98
20	3.55	Gael Davies	20 Aug 00
	3.50	Noelle Bradshaw	25 Jul 98
	3.50	Becky Ridgley	23 May 99
	3.50	Larissa Lowe	17 Jun 00
	3.50	Hilary Smith	26 Jul 00
	3.50	Helen Roscoe	9 Sep 00
	3.45	Laura Patterson	4 Sep 99
	3.41	Louise Gauld	2 Aug 00
	3.40 i	Claire Adams	26 Feb 95
		3.30	18 Jun 95
	3.40	Maria Newton	10 May 98
30	3.40	Danielle Codd	4 Jul 98
	3.40	Nicole Green	24 Jun 00
	3.40	Ruth Anness	22 Jul 00
	3.35	Kathryn Dowsett	24 Apr 99
	3.35	Kirsty Maguire	25 Jun 00
	3.30	Kate Alexander	20 Jul 96
	3.30	Stacey Dicker	7 Sep 96
	3.30	Kate Rowe	14 Aug 99
	3.30	Eugenie Lewis	29 Apr 00
	3.30	Gillian Cooke	6 Aug 00
40	3.25 i	Anna Leyshon	16 Aug 00
		3.20	6 Aug 00
	3.20 i	Samantha Stapleton	3 Aug 94
		3.20	17 Aug 96
	3.20	Rebecca Roles	31 Aug 96
	3.20	Jenny Wood	5 Oct 97
	3.20 i	Suzanne Woods	15 Mar 98
		3.20	10 Jun 98
	3.20 i	Catherine MacRae	12 Mar 00
		3.20	6 Aug 00
	3.20	Kate Dennison	15 Jul 00
	3.20	Janet Vousden	6 Aug 00
	3.20	Kath Callaghan	12 Aug 00
	3.20	Helen Webb	28 Aug 00
50	3.20	Natalie Olson	9 Sep 00

LONG JUMP

	6.90	Bev Kinch	14 Aug 83
	6.88	Fiona May	18 Jul 90
	6.86	May	6 Jul 90
	6.86 A	May	28 Jul 93
	6.85	May	12 Jul 90
	6.83	Sue Hearnshaw	6 May 84
	6.82	May	30 Jul 88
	6.82	May	29 Jun 90
	6.80	May	6 Aug 89
	6.80	Hearnshaw	26 Jun 84
	6.76	Mary Rand	14 Oct 64
	6.76	Jo Wise	2 Aug 99
	6.75	Joyce Hepher	14 Sep 85
	6.73	Sheila Sherwood	23 Jul 70
	6.73	Yinka Idowu	7 Aug 93
	6.70	Kim Hagger	30 Aug 86
10	6.69	Sue Reeve	10 Jun 79
	6.69	Denise Lewis	30 Jul 00
	6.63	Mary Agyepong	17 Jun 89
	6.58	Jade Johnson	4 Jun 00
	6.56	Sarah Claxton	23 May 99
	6.55	Ann Simmonds	22 Jul 70
	6.52	Gill Regan	29 Aug 82
	6.52	Georgina Oladapo	16 Jun 84
	6.51 i	Ruth Howell	23 Feb 74
		6.49	16 Jun 72
	6.51	Julie Hollman	3 Sep 00
20	6.47A	Ashia Hansen	26 Jan 96
		6.27	26 Jun 94
	6.45	Carol Zeniou	12 May 82
	6.45	Margaret Cheetham	18 Aug 84
	6.44	Sharon Danville	15 Jun 77
	6.44	Barbara Clarke	13 Sep 81
	6.43	Myra Nimmo	27 May 73
	6.40	Judy Simpson	26 Aug 84

	6.40	Sharon Bowie	28 Jun 86
	6.39	Moira Maguire	22 Jul 70
	6.39	Maureen Chitty	28 Jun 72
30	6.39	Sue Longden	12 Sep 76
	6.39	Tracy Joseph	27 Jun 98
	6.37	Kelly Wenlock	24 Apr 82
	6.36	Andrea Coore	19 Jul 98
	6.34 i	Barbara-Anne Barrett	20 Feb 71
		6.31	14 Aug 71
	6.33 i	Barbara Lawton	21 Nov 70
	6.33	Glenys Morton	19 Jul 81
	6.33	Joanne Mulliner	13 Sep 86
	6.33	Jo Dear	19 May 93
	6.32	Helen Garrett	7 Jun 87
40	6.32	Jo Willoughby	28 May 89
	6.31	Lorraine Campbell	19 May 85
	6.28	Janet Robson	4 May 77
	6.28	Ruth Irving	14 May 94
	6.28	Vikki Schofield	16 Jul 95
	6.27	Alix Stevenson	13 Jun 70
	6.27	Anita Neil	29 Aug 70
	6.27	Sandra Green	14 Jun 80
	6.27	Allison Manley	18 Aug 80
	6.27	Liz Ghojefa	23 Jul 95
50	6.26	Maria Smallwood	14 Jun 80
	6.26	Donita Benjamin	19 Aug 00

wind unconfirmed

	6.43	Moira Maguire	18 Sep 70

wind assisted

	7.00	Sue Hearnshaw	27 May 84
	6.98	Fiona May	4 Jun 89
	6.93	Bev Kinch	14 Aug 83
	6.84	Sue Reeve	25 Jun 77
	6.80	Joyce Hepher	22 Jun 85
	6.77	Denise Lewis	1 Jun 97
	6.65	Mary Agyepong	4 Jun 89
	6.57	Ann Simmonds	22 Aug 70
	6.56	Judy Simpson	30 Aug 86
10	6.54	Ruth Howell	16 Jun 72
	6.54	Myra Nimmo	19 Jun 76
	6.49	Margaret Cheetham	4 Sep 83
	6.48	Moira Maguire	17 May 70
	6.45	Donita Benjamin	23 Jul 00
	6.44	Tracy Joseph	21 Jun 97
	6.41	Allison Manley	28 Jul 79
	6.40	Barbara-Anne Barrett	17 Jul 71
	6.39	Alix Stevenson	6 Jun 70
	6.39	Carolyn Ross	19 Apr 87
20	6.38	Joanne Mulliner	1 Jun 85
	6.38	Jo Willoughby	6 Aug 89
	6.38	Ann Danson	7 Aug 94
	6.36	Karen Murray	9 Jul 77
	6.34	Janet Frank-Lynch	8 Jul 78
	6.34	Jill Moreton	8 Jul 78
	6.32	Diana Davies	22 May 88
	6.32	Liz Ghojefa	16 Jul 94
	6.29	Evette Finikin	1 May 89
	6.29	Karen Skeggs	17 Jun 89
30	6.27	Lorraine Lynch	24 Jun 90
	6.26	Sheila Turner	7 Jul 56

TRIPLE JUMP

15.16 i	Ashia Hansen	28 Feb 98	
	15.15	13 Sep 97	
15.02 i	Hansen	7 Mar 99	
14.96	Hansen	11 Sep 99	
14.94	Hansen	29 Jun 97	
14.85 i	Hansen	15 Feb 98	
14.81 i	Hansen	21 Feb 99	
14.78	Hansen	25 Aug 96	
14.77	Hansen	2 Aug 97	
14.76 i	Hansen	14 Feb 99	
14.08	Michelle Griffith	11 Jun 94	
13.95	Connie Henry	27 Jun 98	
13.64	Rachel Kirby	7 Aug 94	
13.56	Mary Agyepong	5 Jun 92	
13.46	Evette Finikin	26 Jul 91	
13.03	Shani Anderson	4 May 96	
13.03	Kate Evans	26 Apr 97	
12.97	Debbie Rowe	22 Jul 00	
12.94	Lorna Turner	9 Jul 94	10
12.92	Liz Patrick	5 Aug 00	
12.89	Karen Skeggs	17 May 92	
12.84	Anna-Maria Thorpe	23 May 99	
12.67	Caroline Stead	1 Jun 96	
12.64	Liz Ghojefa	4 Sep 93	
12.64	Jodie Hurst	23 Jul 00	
12.61	Kerensa Denham	14 Jun 98	
12.55	Pamela Anderson	29 Jun 96	
12.52	Leandra Polius	1 Jul 00	
12.50	Julia Johnson	21 Jun 98	20
12.45	Lea Goodman	11 Nov 95	
12.42	Liz Gibbens	2 Jul 95	
12.41 i	Judy Kotey	28 Feb 98	
	12.33	17 May 98	
12.24	Rebecca White	5 Aug 00	
12.22	Mary Rand	18 Jun 59	
12.22	Allison Forbes	9 Sep 89	
12.22	Nikki Barr	16 Aug 92	
12.22	Angela Williams	16 Sep 00	
12.18	Justina Cruickshank	26 May 96	
12.15 i	Fiona Davidson	22 Jan 95	30
	11.91	29 Jun 96	
12.14	Jayne Ludlow	21 May 94	
12.13 i	Maggie Still	21 Jan 96	
	12.03	2 Jun 96	
12.11 i	Caroline Warden	21 Jan 96	
	12.06	1 May 94	
12.10	Jane Falconer	30 Aug 93	
12.03	Stephanie Aneto	17 May 97	
11.97	Jo Morris	24 Jun 00	
11.93	Sharon Oakes	13 Aug 00	
11.91	Lisa Brown	30 Jul 95	
11.90 i	Joanne Stanley	12 Dec 99	
11.88	Rachel Atkinson	9 May 98	40
11.88	Emily Parker	7 Jul 00	
11.87	Kirsty Payne	15 Aug 98	
11.86	Kerry Jury	19 Jul 98	
11.86	Rebecca Bates	8 Jul 00	
11.85	Lauraine Cameron	16 Jul 94	
11.85	Hayley Warrilow	13 Jun 98	

	11.84	Jayne Green	7 Sep 91
	11.83	Marcia Richardson	4 Sep 93
	11.83	Susan Furlonger	4 Jul 99
50	11.83	Carly Robson	7 Jul 00

wind assisted

	14.78 A	Hansen	1 Feb 97
	14.14	Michelle Griffith	25 Jul 00
	13.14	Debbie Rowe	22 Jul 00
	13.04	Kate Evans	23 Jul 00
	12.93	Karen Skeggs	13 Jun 92
	12.61	Judy Kotey	5 Jul 98
	12.55	Lauraine Cameron	30 Aug 93
	12.42	Nikki Barr	28 Jun 97
	12.37	Jane Falconer	30 Aug 93
	12.31	Caroline Warden	23 Jul 94
	12.21	Justina Cruickshank	19 May 96
10	12.20	Rachel Atkinson	28 Jul 96
	12.18	Michelle Rea	29 Jun 91
	12.07	Jo Morris	13 Jul 96
	12.07	Rachel Peacock	18 Jul 98
	12.07	Susan Furlonger	28 May 00
	12.06	Fiona Davidson	2 Jun 96
	12.06	Stephanie Aneto	7 Jun 97
	11.98	Ruth Irving	25 Feb 95
	11.96	Lisa Brown	24 Jun 95

SHOT

	19.36	Judy Oakes	14 Aug 88
	19.33	Oakes	3 Sep 88
	19.26	Oakes	29 Jul 88
	19.13	Oakes	20 Aug 88
	19.06 i	Venissa Head	7 Apr 84
		18.93	13 May 84
	19.05	Oakes	16 Jul 88
	19.03	Myrtle Augee	2 Jun 90
	19.01	Oakes	17 Sep 88
	19.01	Oakes	11 Jun 89
	19.01	Oakes	11 May 96
	18.99	Meg Ritchie	7 May 83
	17.53	Angela Littlewood	24 Jul 80
	17.45	Yvonne Hanson-Nortey	28 Jul 89
	16.57	Maggie Lynes	20 Jul 94
	16.40 i	Mary Peters	28 Feb 70
		16.31	1 Jun 66
	16.40	Julie Dunkley	12 Aug 00
10	16.29	Brenda Bedford	26 May 76
	16.12	Jo Duncan	10 Jul 99
	16.12	Denise Lewis	21 Aug 99
	16.05	Janis Kerr	15 May 76
	15.95 i	Philippa Roles	6 Feb 99
	15.85 i	Alison Grey	12 Feb 94
		15.69	11 Jun 94
	15.81	Tracy Axten	19 Jul 98
	15.80	Sharon Andrews	30 Jul 93
	15.75 i	Caroline Savory	23 Feb 83
		15.50	19 Jun 83
	15.60 i	Justine Buttle	27 Feb 88
		15.45	25 Aug 88
20	15.55	Christina Bennett	13 Jun 99
	15.48	Mary Anderson	8 Sep 85
	15.46	Vanessa Redford	14 Jun 80
	15.45	Susan King	27 Mar 83
	15.44	Vickie Foster	14 May 00
	15.41	Fatima Whitbread	29 Apr 84
	15.32 i	Helen Hounsell	13 Feb 82
		14.91	22 May 82
	15.23	Judy Simpson	18 Jun 88
	15.21	Uju Efobi	23 Apr 94
	15.18	Suzanne Allday	18 May 64
30	15.18 i	Lana Newton	Jan 79
		15.09	6 Sep 78
	15.09	Jayne Berry	22 Jul 93
	15.09	Nicola Gautier	1 Jul 00
	15.08	Janet Kane	3 Jun 79
	15.08	Susan Tudor	30 May 82
	14.98 i	Sandra Smith	21 Dec 85
		14.95	18 Aug 85
	14.88 i	Jenny Kelly	10 Mar 90
		14.73	18 May 91
	14.88	Debbie Callaway	15 May 93
	14.77	Gay Porter	11 Apr 70
	14.76 i	Carol Parker	14 Dec 91
		14.71	1 Sep 90
40	14.75 i	Cynthia Gregory	12 Dec 81
		14.70	29 Aug 81
	14.68	Eleanor Gatrell	18 Jul 98
	14.67	Rosemary Payne	23 Apr 74
	14.66 i	Terri Salt	7 Jan 84
	14.66 i	Eva Massey	26 Feb 00
		14.56	29 Apr 00
	14.62	Kathryn Farr	7 Jun 92
	14.59	Dawn Grazette	19 May 91
	14.53	Emma Beales	12 Sep 92
	14.51	Pauline Richards	4 Jul 98
	14.46 i	Heather Yule	3 Feb 73
		14.20	8 Jul 72
50	14.44	Irene Duffin	2 Jun 90
	14.44	Clova Court	25 May 97

DISCUS

	67.48	Meg Ritchie	26 Apr 81
	67.44	Ritchie	14 Jul 83
	66.04	Ritchie	15 May 82
	65.96	Ritchie	19 Jul 80
	65.78	Ritchie	17 Jul 81
	65.34	Ritchie	24 Apr 83
	65.18	Ritchie	17 May 81
	65.08	Ritchie	26 Apr 80
	65.02	Ritchie	5 May 84
	65.00	Ritchie	24 Apr 82
	64.68	Venissa Head	18 Jul 83
	60.82	Shelley Drew	25 Jul 98
	60.72	Jackie McKernan	18 Jul 93
	60.00	Philippa Roles	9 May 99
	58.56	Debbie Callaway	19 May 96
	58.18	Tracy Axten	31 May 97
	58.02	Rosemary Payne	3 Jun 72
	57.75	Emma Merry	9 Aug 99
10	57.32	Lynda Wright	16 Jun 84
	56.24	Sharon Andrews	12 Jun 94

56.06	Kathryn Farr	27	Jun	87
55.52	Jane Aucott	17	Jan	90
55.42	Lesley Bryant	12	Sep	80
55.06	Janet Kane	17	Jun	78
55.04	Lorraine Shaw	14	May	94
54.72	Karen Pugh	27	Jul	86
54.68	Emma Beales	10	Jun	95
54.46	Ellen Mulvihill	14	May	86
54.46	Janette Picton	17	Aug	90
54.24	Nicola Talbot	15	May	93
53.96	Julia Avis	27	Apr	86
53.66	Rosanne Lister	22	Jun	91
53.44	Judy Oakes	20	Aug	88
53.16	Sarah Winckless	18	Jun	94
52.52	Alison Grey	18	Jun	94
52.46	Vanessa Redford	4	Jul	82
52.31	Lauren Keightley	18	Jul	98
52.21	Emma Carpenter	17	Jun	00
52.19	Claire Smithson	7	Oct	00
51.82	Catherine Bradley	20	Jul	85
51.79	Rebecca Roles	31	May	99
51.60	Dorothy Chipchase	20	Jul	73
51.18	Angela Sellars	12	Aug	00
51.12	Joanne Brand	26	May	86
50.98	Sarah Henton	30	Aug	97
50.57	Brenda Bedford	24	Aug	68
50.06	Joanne Jackson	7	May	89
50.04	Morag Bremner	27	Apr	86
49.92	Fiona Condon	10	Apr	82
49.84	Janis Kerr	15	May	77
49.84	Denise Sturman	12	Apr	81
49.66	Gay Porter	19	Aug	70
49.58	Jackie Wright	2	Aug	75
49.48	Gwen Bird	20	Jul	91
49.44	Myrtle Augee	14	May	95
49.30	Amanda Barnes	18	Jun	88
49.25	Vickie Foster	20	May	00
49.20	Jane Tabor	5	Apr	86
49.12	Jean Robertson	14	Jul	74
downhill				
51.04	Fiona Condon	7	Jul	79

HAMMER

67.44	Lorraine Shaw	15	Jul	00
67.10	Shaw	9	Aug	99
66.87	Shaw	22	Jul	00
66.85	Shaw	12	Aug	00
66.75	Shaw	30	May	99
66.68	Shaw	8	May	99
66.65	Shaw	10	Jul	99
66.37	Shaw	23	May	99
66.21	Shaw	26	Feb	00
66.19	Shaw	5	Aug	00
63.96	Lyn Sprules	20	Aug	00
63.61	Liz Pidgeon	27	May	00
60.88	Rachael Beverley	23	May	99
58.83	Suzanne Roberts	9	Sep	00
57.95	Diana Holden	18	Jul	98
56.76	Esther Augee	15	May	93
56.60	Sarah Moore	12	Jul	97

55.60	Ann Gardner	9	May	98
55.57	Zoe Derham	19	Aug	00
55.10	Mhairi Walters	27	May	00
55.09	Philippa Roles	9	May	99
54.72	Helen Arnold	26	Jul	97
54.15	Sarah Harrison	4	Jul	99
54.03	Catherine Garden	25	Apr	99
53.80	Carys Parry	17	Oct	00
53.74	Christina Bennett	20	Aug	00
53.19	Vicci Scott	11	Jul	00
52.28	Samantha Burns-Salmond	3	May	97
51.86	Lesley Brannan	17	Jun	00
51.62	Fiona Whitehead	24	Apr	93
51.62	Julie Lavender	15	May	94
51.54	Lucy Marshall	3	Sep	00
50.62	Janet Smith	16	Aug	97
50.42	Katy Lamb	20	Aug	00
50.38	Irene Duffin	31	May	97
50.34	Jean Clark	27	Jul	97
50.33	Andrea Jenkins	14	May	00
49.68	Sue Last	12	Aug	00
49.10	Lindsey Jones	25	Aug	97
48.90	Julie Kirkpatrick	15	Jun	96
48.66	Karen Chambers	8	Apr	00
48.63	Laura Douglas	13	Aug	00
48.32	Helen McCreadie	9	Jun	96
48.31	Helen Wilding	1	Jul	00
47.89	Helen Taylor	24	Sep	00
47.70	Angela Bonner	11	May	96
47.62	Nicola Dudman	11	Jun	00
47.52	Vicki Clark	1	Aug	98
47.38	Belinda Heil	2	Jul	00
47.33	Shirley Webb	7	Jul	00
47.06	Caroline Manning	22	Jul	95
46.86	Leanne Taylor	12	Jun	97
46.64	Myrtle Augee	5	Jul	95
46.39	Karen Bell	25	Jun	00
46.01	Janette Brown	15	Jul	00
46.00	Diane Smith	24	Aug	96
45.90	Joanne John	12	Aug	00
45.70	Rachel Clough	19	Jun	99
45.46	Vickie Foster	10	Aug	97

JAVELIN (1999 Model)

59.50	Karen Martin	14	Jul	99
58.45	Martin	12	Aug	00
58.07	Martin	4	Jun	00
57.99	Martin	5	Aug	00
57.75	Martin	12	Aug	00
57.31	Martin	6	Aug	00
58.45	Kelly Morgan	12	Aug	00
57.19	Lorna Jackson	9	Jul	00
55.91	Kirsty Morrison	23	May	99
54.58	Goldie Sayers	19	Oct	00
53.06	Shelley Holroyd	7	May	00
52.54	Jenny Kemp	3	Jul	99
51.79	Chloe Cozens	3	Sep	00
51.13	Denise Lewis	19	Aug	00
50.85	Sharon Gibson	18	Jul	99
48.77	Linda Gray	8	Jul	00

	48.24	Tammie Francis	29 Apr 00
	47.72	Alison Moffitt	21 Aug 99
	47.57	Amy Harvey	7 Oct 00
	47.26	Joanne Bruce	18 Jul 99
	46.89	Caroline White	19 Jun 99
	46.81	Noelle Bradshaw	19 Aug 00
	46.75	Katie Amos	19 Jun 99
	46.02	Clova Court	12 Aug 00
20	45.84	Suzanne Finnis	24 Jun 00
	45.37	Katherine Evans	3 Jul 99
	45.29	Lucy Stevenson	30 Aug 99
	45.24	Katy Watts	10 Jul 99
	45.24	Samantha Redd	27 May 00
	44.67	Nicola Gautier	2 May 99
	43.70	Chrissie Head	13 Aug 00
	43.41	Melanie Burrows	20 May 00
	43.17	Wendy Newman	30 May 99
	43.11	Charlotte Rees	28 Aug 00
30	42.94	Liz Pidgeon	4 Dec 99

JAVELIN (pre 1999)

	77.44	Fatima Whitbread	28 Aug 86
	76.64	Whitbread	6 Sep 87
	76.34	Whitbread	4 Jul 87
	76.32	Whitbread	29 Aug 86
	75.62	Whitbread	25 May 87
	74.74	Whitbread	26 Aug 87
	73.58	Tessa Sanderson	26 Jun 83
	73.32	Whitbread	20 Jun 87
	62.32	Sharon Gibson	16 May 87
	62.22	Diane Royle	18 May 85
	60.12	Shelley Holroyd	16 Jun 96
	60.00	Julie Abel	24 May 87
	59.40	Karen Hough	28 Aug 86
	59.36	Kirsty Morrison	4 Sep 93
	58.60	Jeanette Rose	30 May 82
10	58.39	Lorna Jackson	6 Jun 98
	57.90	Anna Heaver	1 Jul 87
	57.84	Mandy Liverton	3 Jun 90
	57.82	Karen Martin	19 Sep 98
	56.96	Nicky Emblem	1 Feb 90
	56.50	Caroline White	8 Jun 91
	56.50	Denise Lewis	11 Aug 96
	55.70	Lynn Hayhoe	31 May 92
	55.60	Sue Platt	15 Jun 68
	55.38	Catherine Garside	19 May 84
20	55.36	Jackie Zaslona	30 Aug 80
	55.30	Clova Court	27 Aug 91
	55.04	Joanne Harding	24 May 87
	54.50	Karen Costello	11 Jun 94
	54.19	Rosemary Morgan	25 Apr 64
	54.02	Janeen Williams	29 Mar 80
	53.88	Sharon Avann	21 Jul 73
	53.32	Maxine Jervis	27 Aug 78
	53.04	Kelly Morgan	17 May 98
	52.58	Shona Urquhart	17 Jun 83
30	52.48	Gail Hornby	22 Jun 90
	52.40	Noelle Bradshaw	30 Jun 93
	52.16	Sandra O'Toole	5 Apr 78
	52.14	Amanda Caine	25 May 87
	52.14	Jo Burton	25 Jun 94

HEPTATHLON (1985 Tables)

6831	Denise Lewis	30 Jul 00	
6736	Lewis	1 Jun 97	
6724	Lewis	22 Aug 99	
6654	Lewis	4 Aug 97	
6645	Lewis	26 May 96	
6623	Judy Simpson	30 Aug 86	
6584	Lewis	24 Sep 00	
6559	Lewis	22 Aug 98	
6513	Lewis	17 Sep 98	
6347	Simpson	11 Sep 83	
6259	Kim Hagger	18 May 86	
6125	Tessa Sanderson	12 Jul 81	
6094	Joanne Mulliner	7 Jun 87	
6022	Clova Court	27 Aug 91	
6005 w	Kerry Jury	24 May 98	
	5908	1 Aug 99	
5826	Jenny Kelly	3 Jul 94	
5816 w	Julie Hollman	24 May 98	
	5685	20 Aug 00	
5803	Jayne Barnetson	20 Aug 89	10
5776	Kathy Warren	12 Jul 81	
5760	Nicola Gautier	23 May 99	
5747 w	Julia Bennett	5 May 96	
	5538	4 Jun 00	
5702	Yinka Idowu	21 May 95	
5700	Vikki Schofield	5 May 96	
5691 w	Pauline Richards	24 May 98	
	5563	5 Jul 98	
5644	Danielle Freeman	4 Jun 00	
5642	Sarah Rowe	23 Aug 81	
5633	Marcia Marriott	18 May 86	
5632	Emma Beales	1 Aug 93	20
5618 w	Sarah Damm	5 May 96	
	5392	30 Apr 95	
5594	Gillian Evans	22 May 83	
5585	Kelly Sotherton	13 Jul 97	
5555 w	Diana Bennett	24 May 98	
	5550	1 Jun 97	
5548	Val Walsh	18 May 86	
5517	Shona Urquhart	21 Aug 88	
5495	Charmaine Johnson	24 May 92	
5493	Sally Gunnell	28 May 84	
5455	Claire Phythian	19 May 95	
5446	Manndy Laing	7 Aug 83	30
5434 w	Debbie Woolgar	8 Jul 90	
	5380	18 Jun 89	
5424	Lisa Gibbs	1 Aug 93	
5409	Uju Efobi	19 Jun 94	
5391 w	Jackie Kinsella	22 Jun 86	
	5331	19 Jul 86	
5389	Sarah Owen	15 Aug 82	
5384	Sue Longden	8 May 82	
5358 w	Chloe Cozens	24 May 98	
	5283	23 May 99	
5353	Emma Lindsay	23 Aug 94	
5351	Wendy Laing	1 Aug 93	
5339	Tracy Joseph	4 Aug 96	40
5297	Kim Crowther	24 Aug 86	
5279	Fiona Harrison	21 Oct 00	

	5273 w	Debbie Marti	11 Aug 85
		5216	7 Jul 85
	5259 w	Anne Hollman	8 Aug 99
		5258	26 May 96
	5244	Val Lemoignan	19 Apr 84
	5242	Allison Manley	28 Mar 81
	5239 w	Katherine Livesey	22 May 99
		5215	1 Jun 97
	5208	Michelle Stone	30 Sep 84
	5208	Mary Anderson	24 Aug 86
50	5190	Wendy Jeal	2 Jun 91

3000 METRES TRACK WALK

	12:49.16	Betty Sworowski	28 Jul 90
	12:50.61	Lisa Kehler	29 Jul 00
	12:59.3	Vicky Lupton	13 May 95
	13:12.01 i	Julie Drake	12 Mar 93
		13:16.0	11 Dec 90
	13:13.3	Cal Partington	12 Jul 95
	13:16.23	Verity Snook	27 May 96
	13:21.5	Catherine Charnock	8 May 99
	13:25.2	Carol Tyson	6 Jul 79
	13:28.0	Helen Elleker	22 Jul 00
10	13:37.1	Bev Allen	16 May 87

5000 METRES TRACK WALK

	21:52.4	Vicky Lupton	9 Aug 95
	21:57.68	Lisa Kehler	25 Jun 90
	22:01.53	Kehler	26 Jul 98
	22:02.06	Betty Sworowski	28 Aug 89
	22:08.69	Kehler	30 May 98
	22:37.47	Julie Drake	17 Jul 93
	22:41.19	Cal Partington	16 Jul 95
	22:51.23	Helen Elleker	25 Jun 90
	23:11.2	Carol Tyson	30 Jun 79
	23:11.7	Catherine Charnock	19 Jun 99
	23:15.04	Bev Allen	25 May 87
10	23:19.2	Marion Fawkes	30 Jun 79
	23:20.00	Ginney Birch	25 May 85
	23:22.52	Verity Snook	19 Jun 94
	23:34.43	Sylvia Black	5 Jul 92
	23:35.54	Nicky Jackson	25 May 87
	23:38.3	Irene Bateman	28 Jun 81
	23:46.7	Lillian Millen	28 Jun 81
	23:47.6	Melanie Wright	29 May 94
	23:51.1	Jill Barrett	5 May 84
	23:55.27	Susan Ashforth	25 May 85
20	24:00.0	Sarah Brown	21 May 91

5k Road - *where superior to track time*

21:36	Vicky Lupton	18 Jul 92
21:50	Betty Sworowski	6 May 90
21:55 hc	Lisa Kehler	13 Jul 98
22:45 +	Verity Snook	25 Aug 94
22:51	Marion Fawkes	29 Sep 79
22:59	Carol Tyson	29 Sep 79
23:00 +	Bev Allen	1 Sep 87
23:09	Catherine Charnock	5 Jun 99
23:13	Sylvia Black	13 Feb 93

10000 METRES TRACK WALK

45:09.57	Lisa Kehler	13 Aug 00	
45:18.8	Vicky Lupton	2 Sep 95	
45:53.9	Julie Drake	26 May 90	
46:23.08	Betty Sworowski	4 Aug 91	
46:25.2	Helen Elleker	26 May 90	
47:10.07	Verity Snook	19 Jun 93	
47:56.3	Ginney Birch	15 Jun 85	
47:58.3	Bev Allen	21 Jun 86	
48:11.4	Marion Fawkes	8 Jul 79	
48:20.0	Cal Partington	7 May 94	10
48:34.5	Carol Tyson	22 Aug 81	
48:35.8	Melanie Wright	2 Sep 95	
48:56.5	Sarah Brown	18 Apr 91	
48:57.6	Irene Bateman	20 Mar 82	
49:27.0	Sylvia Black	22 Apr 95	
49:39.0	Karen Ratcliffe	22 May 91	
49:41.0	Elaine Callanin	22 Apr 95	
50:08.0 +	Niobe Menendez	9 Jan 00	
50:10.2	Brenda Lupton	17 Mar 84	
50:25.0 mx	Lisa Simpson	1 Apr 87	20

track short

48:52.5	Irene Bateman	19 Mar 83

Road - *where superior to track time*

45:03	Lisa Kehler	19 Sep 98	
45:59	Betty Sworowski	24 Aug 91	
46:06	Verity Snook	25 Aug 94	
46:26	Cal Partington	1 Jul 95	
47:47	Sara Cattermole	23 Jul 00	
47:51	Catherine Charnock	5 Sep 99	
47:58	Nicky Jackson	27 Jun 87	
47:59	Sylvia Black	29 Mar 92	
48:18	Melanie Wright	9 May 92	
48:30	Karen Ratcliffe	16 Apr 94	10
48:36	Kim Braznell	25 Apr 98	
48:47	Irene Bateman	20 Jun 81	

20 KILOMETRES ROAD WALK

1:33:57	Lisa Kehler	17 Jun 00	
1:36:40	Sara Cattermole	4 Mar 00	
1:37:44	Vicky Lupton	27 Jun 99	
1:38:29	Catherine Charnock	11 Sep 99	
1:40:12	Niobe Menendez	21 Mar 99	
1:40:45	Irene Bateman	9 Apr 83	
1:42:02 hc	Lillian Millen	9 Apr 83	
	1:44:42	2 Apr 83	
1:43:50	Betty Sworowski	22 Feb 88	
1:43:52	Sylvia Black	14 Jun 97	
1:44:29	Kim Braznell	21 Mar 99	10
1:45:11	Elaine Callanin	16 Oct 93	
1:46:48	Lisa Crump	27 Jun 99	
1:47:10	Liz Corran	29 Jun 96	
1:47:21	Debbie Wallen	17 Apr 99	
1:48:00	Brenda Lupton	4 Sep 83	
1:48:22	Cath Reader	31 May 92	
1:48:24	Jane Kennaugh	11 Sep 99	

50 KILOMETRES ROAD WALK

4:50:51	Sandra Brown	13 Jul 91
5:01:52	Lillian Millen	16 Apr 83

4 x 100 METRES RELAY

42.43 Great Britain & NI 1 Aug 80
Oakes, Cook, Callender, Lannaman
42.66 Great Britain & NI 11 Sep 82
Hoyte, Cook, Callender, S.Thomas
42.71 Great Britain & NI 10 Aug 83
Baptiste, Cook, Callender, S.Thomas
42.72 Great Britain & NI 3 Sep 78
Callender, Cook, Danville, Lannaman
43.02 Great Britain & NI 26 Sep 80
Oakes, Cook, Callender, Scutt
43.03 Great Britain & NI 15 Aug 81
Hoyte, Cook, Callender, S.Thomas
43.06 Great Britain & NI 10 Aug 83
Baptiste, Cook, Callender, S.Thomas
43.11 Great Britain & NI 11 Aug 84
Jacobs, Cook, Callender, Oakes
43.15 England 9 Oct 82
Hoyte, Cook, Callender, Lannaman
10 43.18 Great Britain & NI 4 Aug 79
Barnett, Hoyte, Cook, Oakes
43.18 Great Britain & NI 20 Aug 83
Baptiste, Cook, Callender, S.Thomas
43.19 Great Britain & NI 20 Sep 80
Oakes, Cook, Callender, Scutt
43.19 Great Britain & N.I. 29 Sep 00
Maduaka, Richardson, Davies, Anderson
43.21 Great Britain & NI 18 Aug 82
Hoyte, Cook, Callender, S.Thomas
43.26 A Great Britain & NI Students 13 Sep 79
Wray, Cook, Patten, Callender
43.26 Great Britain & N.I. 29 Sep 00
Maduaka, Richardson, Wilhelmy, Anderson
43.30 Great Britain & NI 30 Aug 86
P.Thomas, Cook, Baptiste, Hoyte
43.3 Great Britain & NI 1 Jul 80
Oakes, Cook, Callender, Lannaman
43.31 Great Britain & NI 28 Aug 99
Richardson, Anderson, Bloomfield, Maduaka
20 43.32 Great Britain & NI 5 Jun 80
Oakes, Cook, Callender, Lannaman
43.32 Great Britain & NI 1 Sep 90
Douglas, Kinch, Jacobs, P.Thomas
43.35 Great Britain & NI 17 Aug 85
Andrews, Baptiste, Joseph, Oakes
43.36 Great Britain & NI'A' 13 Jul 80
Oakes, Cook, Callender, Lannaman
43.36 Great Britain & NI 23 Jun 81
Hoyte, Cook, Callender, S.Thomas
43.37 Great Britain & NI'A' 30 Aug 82
Hoyte, Cook, Callender, S.Thomas
43.38 Great Britain & NI 8 Aug 86
P.Thomas, Cook, Baptiste, Oakes
43.39 England 2 Aug 86
P.Thomas, Cook, Baptiste, Oakes
43.43 Great Britain & NI 31 Aug 91
Douglas, Kinch, Jacobs, P.Thomas
43.44 Great Britain & NI 30 Jul 76
Hoyte, Ramsden, Danville, Lynch
30 43.44 Great Britain & NI 31 Aug 86
P.Thomas, Cook, Baptiste, Hoyte

4 x 400 METRES RELAY

3:22.01 Great Britain & NI 1 Sep 91
Hanson, Smith, Gunnell, Keough
3:23.41 Great Britain & NI 22 Aug 93
Keough, Smith, Joseph, Gunnell
3:23.89 Great Britain & NI 31 Aug 91
Smith, Hanson, Keough, Gunnell
3:24.14 Great Britain & NI 14 Aug 94
Neef, Keough, Smith, Gunnell
3:24.23 Great Britain & NI 8 Aug 92
Smith, Douglas, Stoute, Gunnell
3:24.25 Great Britain & NI 30 Jun 91
Gunnell, Hanson, Stoute, Keough
3:24.36 Great Britain & NI 5 Jun 93
Smith, Joseph, Stoute, Gunnell
3:24.78 Great Britain & NI 1 Sep 90
Gunnell, Stoute, Beckford, Keough
3:25.20 Great Britain & NI 7 Aug 92
Douglas, Smith, Stoute, Gunnell
3:25.28 Great Britain & N.I. 29 Sep 00 10
Frost, D.Fraser, Curbishley, Merry
3:25.50 Great Britain & NI 12 Aug 95
Neef, Llewellyn, Hanson, Oladapo
3:25.51 Great Britain & NI 11 Aug 84
Scutt, Barnett, Taylor, Hoyte-Smith
3:25.66 Great Britain & NI 23 Aug 98
Fraser, Jamison, Merry, Curbishley
3:25.67 Great Britain & N.I. 30 Sep 00
(Danvers, D.Fraser, Curbishley, Merry)
3:25.78 Great Britain & NI 9 Aug 97
Curbishley, Pierre, Thomas, Fraser
3:25.82 Great Britain & NI 11 Sep 82
Cook, Macdonald, Taylor, Hoyte-Smith
3:25.87 Great Britain & NI 19 Jun 82
Forsyth, Hoyte-Smith, Elder, Scutt
3:26.27 Great Britain & NI 10 Aug 97
Curbishley, Pierre, Thomas, Fraser
3:26.48 Great Britain & NI 22 Jun 97
Curbishley, Fraser, Thomas, Gunnell
3:26.54 Great Britain & NI 6 Aug 89 20
Keough, Stoute, Piggford, Gunnell
3:26.6 a Great Britain & NI 17 Aug 75
Roscoe, Taylor, Elder, Hartley
3:26.89 Great Britain & NI 1 Oct 88
Keough, Stoute, Piggford, Gunnell
3:26.89 Great Britain & NI 13 Aug 95
Neef, Llewellyn, Hanson, Oladapo
3:27.04 Great Britain & NI 21 Aug 93
Keough, Smith, Joseph, Gunnell
3:27.06 England 28 Aug 94
Smith, Joseph, Keough, Gunnell
3:27.09 Great Britain & NI 30 Jul 76
Barnes, Taylor, Elder, Hartley
3:27.17 Great Britain & NI 3 Sep 78
Williams, Hoyte-Smith, Elder, Hartley
3:27.19 England 12 Aug 78
Patten, Hoyte-Smith, Elder, Hartley
3:27.25 Great Britain & NI 13 Aug 94
Neef, Keough, Smith, Gunnell
3:27.27 Great Britain & NI 16 Aug 81 30
Forsyth, Scutt, Elder, Hoyte-Smith

UNDER 23

100 METRES

11.10	Kathy Smallwood	5 Sep 81
11.20	Heather Hunte	26 Sep 80
11.22	Sonia Lannaman	13 Aug 77
11.25	Paula Dunn	27 Aug 86
11.27	Andrea Lynch	20 Jul 74
11.27	Stephi Douglas	26 Jul 91
11.31	Shirley Thomas	3 Jul 83
11.31	Simmone Jacobs	24 Sep 88
11.34	Katharine Merry	25 Jun 94
11.35	Sharon Colyear	20 Aug 77
wind assisted		
10.93	Sonia Lannaman	17 Jul 77
11.01	Heather Hunte	21 May 80
11.13	Shirley Thomas	27 May 84
11.14	Paula Dunn	27 Jul 86
11.23	Jayne Andrews	17 Jul 84
11.25	Andrea Lynch	27 Jul 74
11.27	Katharine Merry	11 Jun 94
11.30	Bev Goddard	15 Jul 78
11.34	Sandra Whittaker	22 May 00
hand timing		
11.1	Andrea Lynch	29 Jun 74
11.1	Heather Hunte	29 Jun 80
wind assisted		
10.8	Sonia Lannaman	22 May 76
10.9	Andrea Lynch	18 May 74
11.1	Sharon Colyear	22 May 76

200 METRES

22.13	Kathy Smallwood	9 Sep 82
22.80	Michelle Scutt	12 Jun 82
22.81	Sonia Lannaman	2 May 76
22.85	Katharine Merry	12 Jun 94
22.98	Sandra Whittaker	8 Aug 84
23.06	Heather Hunte	15 Jun 80
23.06	Sam Davies	28 Aug 00
23.11	Bev Goddard	17 Jun 78
23.14	Helen Golden	7 Sep 73
23.18	Andrea Lynch	26 May 74
wind assisted		
22.48	Michelle Scutt	4 Jul 82
22.69	Sonia Lannaman	10 Jul 77
22.90	Allison Curbishley	17 Jul 98
22.95	Bev Goddard	10 Aug 78
22.97	Helen Golden	26 Jul 74
23.14	Shirley Thomas	28 May 84
23.15	Margaret Critchley	22 Jul 70
hand timing		
22.9	Heather Hunte	3 May 80
wind assisted		
22.6	Sonia Lannaman	23 May 76

300 METRES

36.01	Michelle Probert	13 Jul 80

during 400m

35.8+	Kathy Smallwood	17 Sep 82

400 METRES

50.46	Kathy Smallwood	17 Sep 82
50.63	Michelle Scutt	31 May 82
50.71	Allison Curbishley	18 Sep 98
51.28	Donna Murray	12 Jul 75
51.77 i	Sally Gunnell	6 Mar 88
51.93	Janine MacGregor	28 Aug 81
51.94	Verona Bernard	26 Jan 74
51.97	Linda Forsyth	31 May 82
52.12A	Lillian Board	16 Oct 68
52.20	Ann Packer	17 Oct 64

600 METRES

1:26.18	Diane Edwards	22 Aug 87

800 METRES

1:59.05	Christina Boxer	4 Aug 79
1:59.30	Diane Edwards	4 Jul 87
1:59.67	Lorraine Baker	15 Aug 86
1:59.76	Paula Fryer	17 Jul 91
2:00.39	Bev Nicholson	28 Aug 88
2:00.55 mx	Zola Budd	21 Jun 86
2:00.56	Kirsty McDermott	17 Sep 82
2:00.6a	Jane Colebrook	9 Jul 77
2:01.1a	Ann Packer	20 Oct 64
2:01.2	Christine McMeekin	26 Aug 78

1000 METRES

2:35.51	Lorraine Baker	19 Jul 86

1500 METRES

4:01.93	Zola Budd	7 Jun 86
4:05.76	Yvonne Murray	5 Jul 86
4:06.0	Mary Stewart	24 Jun 78
4:06.84	Paula Radcliffe	2 Jul 95
4:07.06	Christina Boxer	15 Aug 79
4:07.98	Bev Nicholson	7 Jul 89
4:08.92	Janet Marlow	12 Jul 80
4:09.26	Lisa York	13 Jun 92
4:09.7a	Chris Benning	23 Aug 77
4:10.07	Maxine Newman	28 Jun 92

ONE MILE

4:23.08	Yvonne Murray	5 Sep 86

2000 METRES

5:29.58	Yvonne Murray	11 Jul 86
5:30.19	Zola Budd	11 Jul 86

3000 METRES

8:34.43	Zola Budd	30 Jun 86
8:37.15	Yvonne Murray	28 Aug 86
8:40.40	Paula Radcliffe	16 Aug 93
8:46.53	Liz Lynch	18 Jul 86
8:47.36	Jill Hunter	17 Aug 88
8:47.71	Lisa York	31 Jul 92
8:51.40	Ruth Smeeth	7 Aug 82
8:53.78	Wendy Smith	26 May 80
8:53.98	Jane Furniss	30 May 82
8:58.44	Kath Binns	26 May 80

5000 METRES

14:49.27	Paula Radcliffe	7 Jul 95
15:17.77	Jill Hunter	26 Aug 88
15:34.92	Jane Furniss	26 Jun 82
15:36.35	Birhan Dagne	5 Aug 00
15:40.14	Helen Titterington	17 Jul 89
15:41.58+	Liz Lynch	30 Aug 86
15:49.6	Kath Binns	5 Apr 80
15:50.54	Yvonne Murray	28 May 84
15:55.64	Katie Skorupska	9 Jun 99
15:56.58	Gillian Palmer	13 Aug 00

10000 METRES

31:41.42	Liz Lynch	28 Jul 86
32:30.4	Birhan Dagne	22 Jul 00
32:32.42	Vikki McPherson	15 Jul 93
32:36.09	Helen Titterington	29 Aug 89
32:41.29	Jenny Clague	20 Jun 93
32:57.17	Kath Binns	15 Aug 80
33:40.6	Andrea Everett	5 Apr 86
33:43.80	Yvonne Murray	27 Jul 85
34:11.2	Lisa Hollick	15 May 91
34:15.52	Elspeth Turner	1 Apr 87

2000 METRES STEEPLECHASE

7:04.20	Lois Joslin	8 Aug 99

3000 METRES STEEPLECHASE

10:52.6	Tanya Blake	22 Aug 93

100 METRES HURDLES

12.82	Sally Gunnell	17 Aug 88
13.03	Diane Allahgreen	11 Jul 97
13.06	Shirley Strong	11 Jul 80
13.07	Lesley-Ann Skeete	14 Aug 87
13.11	Sharon Colyear	22 Jun 76
13.17	Jacqui Agyepong	3 Aug 90
13.20	Natasha Danvers	2 May 98
13.22	Judy Livermore	3 Oct 82
13.24	Keri Maddox	12 Jun 93
13.26	Michelle Edwards	3 Aug 90

wind assisted

12.80	Sally Gunnell	29 Jul 88
13.20	Keri Maddox	2 Jul 93
13.22	Heather Ross	27 May 84

hand timing

13.0	Blondelle Thompson	29 Jun 74

hand timing wind assisted

12.8	Natasha Danvers	3 Apr 99

400 METRES HURDLES

54.03	Sally Gunnell	28 Sep 88
55.69	Natasha Danvers	19 Jul 98
56.26	Louise Fraser	7 Jun 92
56.42	Vicki Jamison	20 Jun 98
57.03	Sue Morley	12 Jun 82
57.45	Jacqui Parker	5 Aug 88
57.56	Simone Gandy	14 Jun 86
57.79	Susan Dalgoutte	15 Jun 80
57.81	Wendy Griffiths	7 Aug 82
57.86	Teresa Hoyle	29 Jul 83

hand timing

57.5	Vicky Lee	28 Jun 86
57.5	Simone Gandy	28 Jun 86

HIGH JUMP

1.95	Diana Elliott	26 Jun 82
1.94	Louise Miller	25 May 80
1.93	Susan Jones	2 Sep 00
1.93	Michelle Dunkley	2 Sep 00
1.92	Barbara Simmonds	31 Jul 82
1.92 i	Julia Bennett	10 Mar 90
1.91	Ann-Marie Cording	19 Sep 81
1.91	Jayne Barnetson	7 Jul 89
1.90 i	Lea Haggett	3 Jan 92
	1.89	6 May 92
1.89	Judy Livermore	9 Sep 82

POLE VAULT

3.90 i	Rhian Clarke	8 Mar 97
	3.90	31 May 97
3.90	Tracey Bloomfield	4 Jun 00
3.72	Linda Stanton	11 Jun 95
3.60 i	Janine Whitlock	30 Dec 95
	3.41	17 Sep 95
3.60	Clare Ridgley	25 May 98
3.55	Gael Davies	20 Aug 00
3.50	Helen Roscoe	9 Sep 00
3.41	Hilary Smith	20 Sep 98
3.41	Louise Gauld	2 Aug 00
3.40	Ruth Anness	22 Jul 00
3.40	Becky Ridgley	12 Aug 00

LONG JUMP

6.88	Fiona May	18 Jul 90
6.79	Bev Kinch	7 Jul 84
6.75	Joyce Oladapo	14 Sep 85
6.73	Yinka Idowu	7 Aug 93
6.58	Mary Berkeley	14 Sep 85
6.58	Jade Johnson	4 Jun 00
6.57	Jo Wise	25 May 92
6.56	Denise Lewis	12 Jun 94
6.56	Sarah Claxton	23 May 99
6.55	Ann Wilson	22 Jul 70

wind assisted

6.98	Fiona May	4 Jun 89
6.80	Joyce Oladapo	22 Jun 85
6.59	Jo Wise	2 Jul 93
6.57	Ann Wilson	22 Aug 70

TRIPLE JUMP

13.75	Michelle Griffith	18 Jul 93
13.48 i	Ashia Hansen	13 Feb 93
	13.31	18 Jul 92
13.31	Connie Henry	9 Jul 94
13.16	Rachel Kirby	26 Jul 91
13.03	Shani Anderson	4 May 96
12.94	Lorna Turner	9 Jul 94
12.81	Karen Hambrook	15 Jun 91
12.61	Liz Patrick	28 Aug 99
12.59	Jodie Hurst	4 Jul 99
12.55	Pamela Anderson	29 Jun 96

wind assisted

13.93	Michelle Griffith	2 Jul 93
13.55	Ashia Hansen	2 Jul 93
12.69	Liz Patrick	18 Jul 99
12.59	Liz Ghojefa	22 Sep 91
12.58	Kate Evans	31 Aug 96
12.55	Lauraine Cameron	30 Aug 93

SHOT

18.19	Myrtle Augee	14 Aug 87
17.20	Judy Oakes	8 Aug 80
16.55	Yvonne Hanson-Nortey	15 Jun 86
16.40	Julie Dunkley	12 Aug 00
15.95 i	Philippa Roles	6 Feb 99
15.85 i	Alison Grey	12 Feb 94
	15.69	11 Jun 94
15.72	Venissa Head	12 Jun 77
15.55	Christina Bennett	13 Jun 99
15.32 i	Helen Hounsell	13 Feb 82
15.21	Uju Efobi	23 Apr 94

DISCUS

60.00	Philippa Roles	9 May 99
57.32	Lynda Whiteley	16 Jun 84
56.06	Kathryn Farr	27 Jun 87
55.70	Shelley Drew	25 Jun 95
55.52	Jane Aucott	17 Jan 90
54.72	Karen Pugh	27 Jul 86
54.46	Ellen Mulvihill	14 May 86
54.24	Nicola Talbot	15 May 93
54.16	Janet Thompson	15 May 76
53.78	Emma Beales	30 Aug 93

HAMMER

61.70	Lyn Sprules	12 Jul 97
60.88	Rachael Beverley	23 May 99
60.37	Liz Pidgeon	31 Jul 99
58.83	Suzanne Roberts	9 Sep 00
55.86	Diana Holden	21 Jun 97
55.57	Zoe Derham	19 Aug 00
55.09	Philippa Roles	9 May 99
54.15	Sarah Harrison	4 Jul 99
54.03	Catherine Garden	25 Apr 99
53.74	Christina Bennett	20 Aug 00

JAVELIN (1999 Model)

58.45	Kelly Morgan	12 Aug 00
52.20	Jenny Kemp	29 Apr 00
51.79	Chloe Cozens	3 Sep 00
48.24	Tammie Francis	29 Apr 00
47.26	Joanne Bruce	18 Jul 99
46.75	Katie Amos	19 Jun 99
45.37	Katherine Evans	3 Jul 99
44.67	Nicola Gautier	2 May 99
43.70	Chrissie Head	13 Aug 00
42.94	Liz Pidgeon	4 Dec 99

JAVELIN (pre 1999 Model)

69.54	Fatima Whitbread	3 Jul 83
67.20	Tessa Sanderson	17 Jul 77
60.10	Shelley Holroyd	16 Jul 93
60.00	Julie Abel	24 May 87
59.88	Sharon Gibson	3 Jul 83
58.20	Lorna Jackson	16 Jun 96
57.82	Mandy Liverton	21 Jun 92
56.28	Anna Lockton	20 Jul 85
55.42	Kirsty Morrison	14 Jun 97
55.34	Caroline White	20 Jan 90

HEPTATHLON (1985 Tables)

6325	Denise Lewis	23 Aug 94
6259	Judy Livermore	10 Sep 82
6094	Joanne Mulliner	7 Jun 87
5816 w	Julie Hollman	24 May 98
5803	Jayne Barnetson	20 Aug 89
5765	Kim Hagger	17 Jul 83
5765	Jenny Kelly	5 Aug 90
5760	Nicola Gautier	23 May 99
5671	Vikki Schofield	3 Jul 94
5644	Danielle Freeman	4 Jun 00

3000 METRES TRACK WALK

13:15.16+	Vicky Lupton	28 Jun 92

5000 METRES TRACK WALK

22:12.21	Vicky Lupton	28 Jun 92
22:19.04	Lisa Langford	25 May 87
22:40.0	Julie Drake	21 May 91
5k Road - *where superior to track time*		
21:36	Vicky Lupton	18 Jul 92
22:09	Lisa Langford	8 Apr 89

10000 METRES TRACK WALK

45:53.9	Julie Drake	26 May 90
46:30.0	Vicky Lupton	14 Sep 94
49:59.0	Carol Tyson	25 Mar 78
10k Road - *where superior to track time*		
45:42	Lisa Langford	3 May 87
45:48	Vicky Lupton	25 Aug 94

20 KILOMETRES ROAD WALK

1:38:25	Sara Cattermole	31 Oct 99
1:44:48	Vicky Lupton	3 Sep 94
1:47:21	Debbie Wallen	17 Apr 99
1:49:12	Nikki Huckerby	26 Sep 99
1:49:18	Helen Sharratt	16 Oct 93
1:52:37	Sally Warren	23 Apr 00
1:59:33	Melanie Brookes	9 Aug 86
2:00:26	Elaine Allen	4 Sep 83
2:08:23	Suzanne Ford-Dunn	16 Oct 93
2:09:23	Diane Wood	4 Sep 83

UNDER 20

100 METRES

	11.27A	Kathy Smallwood	9 Sep 79
		11.42	11 Aug 79
	11.30	Bev Kinch	5 Jul 83
	11.36A	Della James	14 Oct 68
	11.43	Shirley Thomas	7 Aug 82
	11.45	Sonia Lannaman (U17)	1 Sep 72
	11.45	Simmone Jacobs	6 Jul 84
	11.52	Katharine Merry	16 Sep 92
	11.53	Marcia Richardson	21 Jul 91
	11.54	Wendy Clarke	8 Jun 75
10	11.59	Heather Hunte	9 Sep 77
	11.59	Stephi Douglas	23 Jul 88
	11.59	Rebecca Drummond	8 Jul 95
	11.61	Diane Smith (U17)	9 Aug 90
	11.61	Donna Hoggarth	16 Sep 92
	11.62	Helen Miles	22 Aug 85
	11.63	Jane Parry	29 May 82
	11.63	Sallyanne Short	23 Aug 87
	11.63	Tatum Nelson	25 Jul 97
	11.64	Helen Barnett	21 Aug 76
20	11.64	Georgina Oladapo	22 Aug 85

wind assisted

	11.13	Bev Kinch	6 Jul 83
	11.25	Shirley Thomas	20 Aug 81
	11.26	Simmone Jacobs	27 May 84
	11.40	Katharine Merry	3 Jul 93
	11.43	Dorothy Hyman	2 Sep 60
	11.45	Stephi Douglas	25 Jun 88
	11.45	Rebecca White	4 Jul 98
	11.45	Abi Oyepitan	4 Jul 98
	11.47	Helen Golden	17 Jul 70
10	11.50	Rebecca Drummond (U17)	9 Jul 94
	11.50	Sam Davies	18 Jul 98
	11.53	Wendy Clarke	22 Aug 75
	11.53	Sharon Dolby	16 Aug 86
	11.55	Donna Hoggarth	29 Aug 92

hand timing

11.3	Sonia Lannaman	9 Jun 74
11.3	Heather Hunte	15 Jul 78
11.4	Della James	2 Aug 67

wind assisted

11.2	Wendy Clarke	22 May 76
11.3	Helen Golden	30 May 70
11.3	Linsey Macdonald (U17)	3 May 80
11.4	Anita Neil	30 Jun 68
11.4	Helen Barnett	16 May 76
11.4	Jane Parry (U17)	5 Jul 80

downhill

11.3 w	Denise Ramsden	28 Jun 69

200 METRES

22.70 A	Kathy Smallwood	12 Sep 79	
	22.84	5 Aug 79	
23.10	Diane Smith (U17)	11 Aug 90	
23.20	Katharine Merry	13 Jun 93	
23.23	Sonia Lannaman	25 Aug 75	
23.23	Sarah Wilhelmy	13 Jun 98	
23.24	Sandra Whittaker	12 Jun 82	
23.28	Simmone Jacobs (U17)	28 Aug 83	
23.33	Linsey Macdonald	9 Jun 82	
23.35	Donna Murray	26 May 74	
23.42	Debbie Bunn (U17)	17 Jun 78	10
23.46	Shirley Thomas	31 May 82	
23.48	Wendy Clarke	7 Jun 75	
23.49 i	Vernicha James (U17)	30 Jan 00	
	23.59	20 Oct 00	
23.51	Sharon Colyear	26 May 74	
23.54	Jane Parry	30 Jul 83	
23.57	Sophia Smith	30 Jul 93	
23.59	Eleanor Thomas	17 Jul 77	
23.60	Michelle Probert (U17)	12 Sep 76	
23.63	Helen Barnett	21 Aug 76	
23.65	Georgina Oladapo	20 Jul 85	20

wind assisted

23.01	Simmone Jacobs	28 May 84
23.11	Linsey Macdonald (U17)	5 Jul 80
23.16	Donna Murray	27 Jul 74
23.20	Sarah Wilhelmy	18 Jul 98
23.42	Helen Golden	22 Jul 70
23.48	Vernicha James (U17)	21 Aug 99
23.54	Janine MacGregor	17 Jun 78
23.55	Sallyanne Short	25 Jul 87

hand timing

23.1	Sonia Lannaman	7 Jun 75
23.3	Donna Murray	9 Jun 74
23.3	Sharon Colyear	30 Jun 74
23.3	Linsey Macdonald	8 May 82
23.4	Helen Barnett	17 Jul 76

wind assisted

22.9	Donna Murray	14 Jul 74
23.2	Debbie Bunn (U17)	2 Jul 78
23.3	Angela Bridgeman	15 Aug 82

300 METRES

36.46	Linsey Macdonald (U17)	13 Jul 80

400 METRES

51.16	Linsey Macdonald (U17)	15 Jun 80	
51.77	Donna Murray	30 Jul 74	
52.54	Donna Fraser	10 Aug 91	
52.65	Jane Parry	11 Jun 83	
52.80	Sian Morris	18 Jun 83	
52.98	Karen Williams	6 Aug 78	
52.99	Angela Bridgeman	24 Jul 82	
53.01 i	Marilyn Neufville	14 Mar 70	
53.08	Loreen Hall	29 Jul 84	
53.14	Michelle Probert	28 Jul 79	10
53.20	Verona Bernard	8 Jul 72	
53.48	Lillian Board	22 Sep 67	
53.52	Ruth Kennedy	25 Sep 74	
53.59	Janine MacGregor	11 Jul 78	
53.73	Paulette McLean	24 Aug 89	
53.75	Linda Keough (U17)	8 Aug 80	
53.84	Jenny Meadows	12 Aug 00	
53.86	Lisa Miller	18 Oct 00	
53.92	Alison Reid	25 Jul 81	
54.00	Heather Brookes	12 Aug 00	20

hand timing

52.6 Marilyn Neufville 20 Jun 70
52.8 Lillian Board 9 Jul 67
52.9 Verona Bernard 15 Sep 72
53.3 Tracey Burges 5 Sep 81
53.5 Ruth Kennedy 30 Jun 74
53.7 Linda Keough (U17) 2 Aug 80
53.8 Alison Reid 28 May 81

600 METRES

1:27.33 Lorraine Baker (U17) 13 Jul 80

800 METRES (*880yds less 0.7)

2:01.11 Lynne MacDougall 18 Aug 84
2:01.66 Lorraine Baker 26 Jun 82
2:02.00 Diane Edwards 14 Sep 85
2:02.0 Jo White (U17) 13 Aug 77
2:02.18 Lynne Robinson 18 Jul 86
2:02.8 a Lesley Kiernan 2 Sep 74
2:02.88 i Kirsty McDermott 22 Feb 81
 2:04.01 29 Jul 81
2:03.11 Janet Prictoe 19 Aug 78
2:03.18 Paula Newnham 17 Jun 78
10 2:03.53 Christine McMeekin 25 Aug 75
2:04.30 Bridget Smyth 19 Aug 86
2:04.6 Janet Lawrence 26 Jul 77
2:04.7* Rosemary Stirling 13 Aug 66
2:04.85 Louise Parker 28 Jul 79
2:04.95 Denise Kiernan 3 Jun 78
2:05.0 i Jane Colebrook 11 Dec 76
2:05.07 Bev Nicholson 25 May 86
2:05.1 Paula Fryer 14 Jun 88
2:05.1 Natalie Tait 22 Jul 89
20 2:05.14 Angela Creamer 19 Jul 75

1000 METRES

2:38.58 Jo White (U17) 9 Sep 77

1500 METRES

3:59.96 Zola Budd 30 Aug 85
4:05.96 Lynne MacDougall 20 Aug 84
4:11.12 Bridget Smyth 26 May 85
4:13.40 Wendy Smith 19 Aug 78
4:14.40 Janet Lawrence 20 Aug 77
4:14.50 Wendy Wright 20 Jun 87
4:14.56 Andrea Whitcombe 22 Aug 90
4:14.58 Ruth Smeeth 16 Jul 78
4:14.73 Mary Stewart 2 Feb 74
10 4:15.1 Yvonne Murray 18 Jul 82
4:15.39 Lisa York 26 Aug 89
4:15.55 Sandra Arthurton (U17) 29 Jul 78
4:16.10 Katie Fairbrass 29 May 83
4:16.12 Elise Lyon 3 Jul 83
4:16.13 Bernadette Madigan 12 Aug 79
4:16.2 i Jo White 28 Jan 78
 4:16.8 (U17) 30 Jul 77
4:16.4 Julie Holland 15 May 84
4:16.51 Maxine Newman 26 Aug 89
4:16.8 Norine Braithwaite 20 Jun 70
20 4:16.82 Paula Radcliffe 4 Jul 92

ONE MILE

4:17.57 Zola Budd 21 Aug 85

2000 METRES

5:33.15 Zola Budd 13 Jul 84

3000 METRES

8:28.83 Zola Budd 7 Sep 85
8:51.78 Paula Radcliffe 20 Sep 92
9:03.35 Philippa Mason 19 Jul 86
9:04.14 Yvonne Murray 28 May 83
9:06.16 Helen Titterington 19 Jun 88
9:07.02 Carol Haigh 24 Jun 85
9:09.14 Lisa York 19 Jul 89
9:10.9 Julie Holland 7 Apr 84
9:12.28 Hayley Haining 20 Jul 91
9:12.97 Bernadette Madigan 30 Jun 79 10
9:13.4 mx Caroline Walsh 30 Jun 99
 9:20.38 7 Aug 99
9:13.81 Andrea Whitcombe 12 Aug 90
9:14.10 Maxine Newman 19 Jul 89
9:15.82 Ruth Smeeth 17 Jun 78
9:17.70 i Alice Braham 3 Dec 94
9:18.07 Heidi Moulder 1 Aug 93
9:20.0 Judith Shepherd 13 Aug 77
9:20.9 Wendy Wright 26 Apr 86
9:21.20 Nikki Slater 3 Jul 94
9:21.8 Wendy Smith 12 Aug 78 20

5000 METRES

14:48.07 Zola Budd 26 Aug 85
15:51.62 Carol Haigh 26 May 85
15:52.55 Yvonne Murray 29 May 83
16:11.61 i Jenny Clague 22 Feb 92
16:16.77 i Paula Radcliffe 22 Feb 92
16:15.36 Louise Kelly 31 Jul 98
16:35.56 Gillian Stacey 22 Aug 90
16:37.18 Henrietta Freeman 19 Aug 00
16:41.9 Katie Skorupska 22 Jun 96
16:47.4 Sally James 7 Sep 83 10
16:47.44 Collette Fagan 16 Sep 00
16:48.44 Claire Forbes 21 Apr 90
16:49.2 Sam Baines 6 Jun 87
16:50.4 Amanda Tremble 9 Aug 95
16:50.84 Fiona Truman 30 Apr 88
16:58.87 Tanya Povey 23 Apr 98
17:09.8 Karen Fletcher 23 Aug 98
17:09.97 Alison Hollington 30 Jul 82
17:10.92 Donna Rutherford 3 May 92
17:13.74 Charlotte Coffey 9 Jun 99 20

10000 METRES

34:31.41 Tanya Povey 3 Jun 98

2000 METRES STEEPLECHASE

7:27.99 Lois Joslin 2 May 98
7:43.55 Samantha Marshall 6 Sep 00
7:51.32 Esther Merchant 6 May 95

3000 METRES STEEPLECHASE

12:11.1 Lindsey Oliver 22 Aug 93

100 METRES HURDLES

13.25	Diane Allahgreen	21 Jul 94	
13.30	Sally Gunnell	16 Jun 84	
13.32	Keri Maddox	21 Jul 91	
13.45	Natasha Danvers	6 Aug 95	
13.46	Nathalie Byer	26 Aug 83	
13.47	Sam Baker	30 Jun 91	
13.49	Angie Thorp	30 Jun 91	
13.50	Lesley-Ann Skeete	6 Jun 86	
13.52	Julie Pratt	5 Jul 98	
10 13.56	Wendy McDonnell	3 Jun 79	
13.57	Bethan Edwards	29 Aug 92	
13.58	Lauraine Cameron	19 Jun 90	
13.62	Sarah Claxton	18 Jul 98	
13.68	Jacqui Agyepong	7 Aug 87	
13.72	Judy Livermore	15 Jul 79	
13.73	Ann Girvan (U17)	7 Aug 82	
13.73	Yinka Idowu	10 Aug 91	
13.75	Sue Scott	21 Jul 70	
13.76	Shirley Strong	20 Aug 77	
20 13.80	Louise Fraser	25 Aug 89	

wind assisted

13.24	Lesley-Ann Skeete	7 Jun 86
13.28	Sarah Claxton	5 Jul 98
13.39	Lauraine Cameron	1 Jul 90
13.45	Louise Fraser	30 Jul 89
13.45	Sam Baker	30 Jun 91
13.46	Wendy McDonnell	30 Jun 79
13.48	Julie Pratt	5 Jul 98
13.55	Shirley Strong	10 Jul 77
13.56	Ann Girvan	15 Jul 84
13.72	Kate Forsyth	6 Jul 97

hand timing

13.5	Christine Perera	19 Jul 68

hand timing wind assisted

13.1	Sally Gunnell	7 Jul 84
13.3	Keri Maddox	14 Jul 90
13.4	Judy Livermore	27 May 79
13.4	Sam Baker	14 Jul 90

400 METRES HURDLES

57.27	Vicki Jamison	28 Jul 96
58.02	Vyv Rhodes	28 Jun 92
58.37	Alyson Evans	1 Sep 85
58.68	Kay Simpson	15 Jul 83
58.76	Simone Gandy	28 May 84
58.91	Rachael Kay	6 Aug 99
58.96	Nicola Sanders	17 Jul 99
59.00	Diane Heath	19 Jul 75
59.01	Sara Elson	24 Aug 89
10 59.04	Allison Curbishley	31 Jul 93
59.12	Tracy Allen	29 Jul 89
59.13	Sue Morley	12 Aug 79
59.39	Tracey Duncan	29 Jul 98
59.52	Debbie Church	25 Jul 81
59.56	Lucy Elliott	26 Jul 85
59.65	Debbie Duncan	7 Aug 87
60.07	Michelle Cooney	6 Jul 85
60.15	Kate Norman	2 Jul 95
60.20	Teresa Hoyle	24 May 82
20 60.21	Kate Williams	10 Aug 96

hand timing

58.3	Simone Gandy	14 Jul 84
58.7	Sara Elson	18 Jun 89
59.0	Tracy Allen	9 Jul 88
59.3	Michelle Cooney	13 Jul 85
59.4	Diane Wade	21 Jul 79
59.5	Samantha Flynn	12 Jul 86
59.7	Keri Maddox (U17)	9 Jul 88
59.9	Denise Kiernan	6 Sep 78
60.0	Jacqui Parker	13 Jul 85

HIGH JUMP

1.91	Lea Haggett	2 Jun 91
1.91	Susan Jones	31 Aug 97
1.90	Jo Jennings	29 Sep 88
1.89	Debbie Marti (U17)	2 Jun 84
1.89 i	Michelle Dunkley	16 Feb 97
	1.87	7 Jul 95
1.88	Jayne Barnetson	3 Aug 85
1.87	Louise Manning	6 May 84
1.87	Rachael Forrest	7 Jul 95
1.86	Barbara Simmonds	9 Sep 79
1.86	Claire Summerfield	7 Aug 82 10
1.86	Michele Wheeler	31 May 87
1.85	Gillian Hitchen	3 Jun 78
1.85	Sharon McPeake	22 Sep 81
1.85	Julia Bennett	15 Apr 89
1.84	Louise Miller	12 May 79
1.84	Sarah Rowe	22 Aug 81
1.84	Ursula Fay (U17)	6 Aug 83
1.83	Diana Elliott	15 Jun 80
1.83	Jennifer Little	30 Jun 84
1.83	Kerry Roberts	22 Jun 86 20
1.83	Tracey Clarke (U17)	2 Aug 87
1.83 i	Rebecca Jones	4 Mar 00
	1.83	3 Jun 00
1.83	Aileen Wilson (U17)	8 Jul 00

POLE VAULT

3.90	Ellie Spain	6 May 00
3.75	Tracey Bloomfield	9 Aug 98
3.70	Rhian Clarke	10 Aug 96
3.65 i	Lindsay Hodges	6 Feb 00
	3.55 (U17)	14 Aug 99
3.60	Fiona Harrison (U17)	25 May 98
3.51 i	Clare Ridgley	17 Feb 96
	3.50	6 May 96
3.50	Becky Ridgley	23 May 99
3.45	Laura Patterson	4 Sep 99
3.40	Danielle Codd	4 Jul 98
3.35	Kirsty Maguire	25 Jun 00 10
3.30	Louise Gauld	23 May 99
3.30	Gillian Cooke	6 Aug 00
3.20	Rebecca Roles (U17)	31 Aug 96
3.20	Kate Dennison	15 Jul 00
3.20	Natalie Olson	9 Sep 00
3.15	Sarah Hartley (U17)	9 Aug 97
3.15	Caroline Nutt	6 Aug 00
	11 athletes at 3.10	

LONG JUMP

	Mark	Name	Date
	6.90	Bev Kinch	14 Aug 83
	6.82	Fiona May	30 Jul 88
	6.68	Sue Hearnshaw	22 Sep 79
	6.63	Yinka Idowu	21 May 89
	6.55	Joyce Oladapo	30 Jul 83
	6.52	Georgina Oladapo	16 Jun 84
	6.52	Sarah Claxton	31 Jul 98
	6.52	Jade Johnson	23 May 99
	6.47	Jo Wise	30 Jul 88
10	6.45	Margaret Cheetham (U17)	18 Aug 84
	6.43	Myra Nimmo	27 May 73
	6.39	Moira Walls	22 Jul 70
	6.35	Sharon Bowie	1 Jun 85
	6.34	Ann Wilson	3 Aug 68
	6.33	Jo Dear	19 May 93
	6.31	Joanne Mulliner	1 Jun 85
	6.27	Sheila Parkin	3 Aug 64
	6.26	Maria Smallwood	14 Jun 80
	6.25	Lisa Armstrong	15 Jul 92
20	6.24	Karen Murray	16 Jul 77

wind unconfirmed

Mark	Name	Date
6.43	Moira Walls	18 Sep 70

wind assisted

Mark	Name	Date
6.93	Bev Kinch	14 Aug 83
6.88	Fiona May	30 Jul 88
6.71	Yinka Idowu	15 Jun 91
6.69	Jo Wise	30 Jul 88
6.53	Sarah Claxton	12 Jul 97
6.49	Margaret Cheetham (U17)	4 Sep 83
6.48	Moira Walls	17 May 70
6.41	Ann Wilson	30 Jun 68

TRIPLE JUMP

	Mark	Name	Date
	13.05	Michelle Griffith	16 Jun 90
	12.50	Julia Johnson	21 Jun 98
	12.43	Shani Anderson	26 Jun 93
	12.42	Liz Gibbens	2 Jul 95
	12.41 i	Judy Kotey	28 Feb 98
		12.33	17 May 98
	12.27	Lorna Turner	26 May 91
	12.22	Mary Bignal	18 Jun 59
	12.22	Angela Williams	16 Sep 00
	12.20	Jodie Hurst	8 Jun 96
10	12.18	Justina Cruickshank	26 May 96
	12.14	Jayne Ludlow (U17)	21 May 94
	12.10	Jane Falconer	30 Aug 93
	12.10	Pamela Anderson	2 Jul 95
	11.93	Sharon Oakes	13 Aug 00
	11.91	Lisa Brown	30 Jul 95
	11.88	Emily Parker	7 Jul 00
	11.86	Rebecca Bates	8 Jul 00
	11.85	Jo Morris	30 Jun 96
	11.85	Hayley Warrilow	13 Jun 98
20	11.85	Leandra Polius	4 Jul 99

wind assisted

Mark	Name	Date
12.61	Judy Kotey	5 Jul 98
12.48	Lorna Turner	30 Jun 91
12.44	Shani Anderson	9 Jul 94
12.37	Jane Falconer	30 Aug 93
12.21	Justina Cruickshank	19 May 96

SHOT

Mark	Name	Date	
17.10	Myrtle Augee	16 Jun 84	
16.24 i	Judy Oakes	26 Feb 77	
	16.05	26 Aug 77	
15.72 i	Alison Grey	29 Feb 92	
	15.26	13 Jul 91	
15.60 i	Justine Buttle	27 Feb 88	
	15.45	25 Aug 88	
15.48	Mary Anderson	8 Sep 85	
15.45	Susan King	27 Mar 83	
15.27	Julie Dunkley	21 Jun 98	
14.75 i	Cynthia Gregory	12 Dec 81	
	14.70	29 Aug 81	
14.71 i	Nicola Gautier	26 Jan 97	
	14.37	12 Jul 97	
14.66 i	Terri Salt	7 Jan 84	10
14.60	Philippa Roles	4 Sep 96	
14.59	Dawn Grazette	19 May 91	
14.59 i	Christina Bennett	16 Mar 97	
	14.27	11 May 97	
14.54	Carol Cooksley	9 Jul 88	
14.54 i	Jayne Berry	18 Mar 89	
	14.45	17 Jun 88	
14.49	Eva Massey	9 Aug 99	
14.36	Venissa Head	4 Jul 75	
14.33	Jenny Kelly	27 May 89	
14.27	Uju Efobi	4 Sep 93	
14.23	Sharon Andrews	8 May 85	20

DISCUS

Mark	Name	Date	
54.78	Lynda Whiteley	4 Oct 82	
53.10	Kathryn Farr	19 Jul 86	
52.58	Emma Merry	22 Aug 93	
52.31	Lauren Keightley	18 Jul 98	
52.21	Emma Carpenter	17 Jun 00	
52.19	Claire Smithson	7 Oct 00	
51.82	Catherine Bradley	20 Jul 85	
51.60	Philippa Roles	24 Jul 97	
51.24	Jane Aucott	11 Jun 86	
51.12	Janette Picton	6 Jun 82	10
50.44	Karen Pugh	8 Jul 83	
50.34	Angela Sellars	27 Jul 86	
50.30	Julia Avis	19 Sep 82	
49.74	Shelley Drew	10 May 92	
49.60	Fiona Condon	3 Jun 79	
49.56	Sarah Winckless	2 May 92	
49.42	Rosanne Lister	29 Aug 88	
49.30	Amanda Barnes	18 Jun 88	
49.24	Lesley Mallin	31 May 75	
49.00	Tracey Whincup	26 Jun 84	20

HAMMER

Mark	Name	Date	
57.97	Rachael Beverley	25 Jul 98	
55.10	Mhairi Walters	27 May 00	
54.72	Helen Arnold	26 Jul 97	
54.48	Lyn Sprules	2 Jul 94	
53.80	Carys Parry	17 Oct 00	
53.34	Diana Holden	13 Aug 94	
52.33	Zoe Derham	13 Jun 99	
51.62	Julie Lavender	15 May 94	
51.54	Lucy Marshall	3 Sep 00	
50.66	Vicci Scott	12 Sep 99	10

	50.52	Catherine Garden	3 Aug 97
	50.50	Sarah Harrison	2 Aug 97
	50.42	Katy Lamb	20 Aug 00
	49.48	Samantha Burns-Salmond	13 Aug 95
	48.98	Liz Pidgeon	21 Sep 96
	48.63	Laura Douglas	13 Aug 00
	48.18	Suzanne Roberts	1 Jun 97
	47.89	Helen Taylor	24 Sep 00
	47.62	Nicola Dudman	11 Jun 00
20	47.52	Vicki Clark	1 Aug 98

JAVELIN (1999 Model)

	54.61	Kelly Morgan	4 Sep 99
	54.58	Goldie Sayers	19 Oct 00
	52.54	Jenny Kemp	3 Jul 99
	48.15	Chloe Cozens	19 Jun 99
	47.57	Amy Harvey	7 Oct 00
	45.84	Suzanne Finnis	24 Jun 00
	45.24	Katy Watts	10 Jul 99
	45.24	Samantha Redd	27 May 00
	43.11	Charlotte Rees	28 Aug 00
10	42.73	Carol Wallbanks	10 Jul 00
	41.99	Sarah Ellis	27 May 00
	41.62	Georgina Hogsden	2 Sep 00

JAVELIN (pre 1999 Model)

	60.14	Fatima Whitbread	7 May 80
	59.40	Karen Hough	28 Aug 86
	59.36	Kirsty Morrison	4 Sep 93
	57.84	Mandy Liverton	3 Jun 90
	57.82	Shelley Holroyd	9 Aug 92
	57.80	Julie Abel	5 Jun 83
	56.96	Nicky Emblem	1 Feb 90
	55.72	Karen Martin	25 Jul 92
	55.38	Catherine Garside	19 May 84
10	55.04	Tessa Sanderson	26 Sep 74

HEPTATHLON (1985 Tables)

	5833	Joanne Mulliner	11 Aug 85
	5642	Sarah Rowe	23 Aug 81
	5496	Yinka Idowu	3 Sep 89
	5493	Sally Gunnell	28 May 84
	5484	Denise Lewis	30 Jun 91
	5459	Jenny Kelly	30 Jul 88
	5391 w	Jackie Kinsella	22 Jun 86
		5331	19 Jul 86
	5377	Uju Efobi	18 Jul 93
	5358 w	Chloe Cozens	24 May 98
		5283	23 May 99
10	5311	Nicola Gautier	21 Sep 97
	5299	Emma Beales	26 Aug 90
	5279	Fiona Harrison	21 Oct 00
	5273 w	Debbie Marti	11 Aug 85
		5216	7 Jul 85
	5258 w	Danielle Freeman	23 May 99
		5237	19 Jul 98
	5246	Val Walsh	7 Aug 83
	5215	Katherine Livesey	1 Jun 97
	5208	Michelle Stone (U17)	30 Sep 84
	5208	Mary Anderson	24 Aug 86
	5187 w	Anne Hollman	2 May 93
20	5186	Rebecca Jones	4 Jun 00

3000 METRES TRACK WALK

13:03.4	Vicky Lupton	18 May 91	
13:47.0	Julie Drake	5 Jul 88	
13:53.0 e+	Lisa Langford	23 Aug 85	
	14:01.0	17 Aug 85	
14:04.1	Susan Ashforth (U17)	19 May 85	
14:09.81	Amy Hales (U17)	19 Sep 98	

5000 METRES TRACK WALK

22:36.81	Vicky Lupton	15 Jun 91	
23:31.67	Lisa Langford	23 Aug 85	
23:55.27	Susan Ashforth (U17)	25 May 85	
23:56.9	Julie Drake	24 May 88	
24:02.15	Nicky Jackson	27 May 84	
24:08.4	Jill Barrett	28 May 83	
24:19.0	Vicky Lawrence	13 Jun 87	
24:24.31	Andrea Crofts	4 Jun 89	
24:27.73	Carolyn Brown	29 Aug 92	
24:28.60	Debbie Wallen	26 Jul 98	10
24:34.6	Tracy Devlin	17 Sep 89	
24:35.0	Joanne Pope	16 Dec 90	

5k Road - *where superior to track time*

23:05	Lisa Langford	2 Nov 85	
23:18	Julie Drake	27 Feb 88	
23:35	Lisa Simpson	31 Oct 87	
23:44	Nicky Jackson	12 May 84	
23:46	Jill Barrett	14 May 83	
23:54	Vicky Lawrence	26 Sep 87	

10000 METRES TRACK WALK

47:04.0	Vicky Lupton	30 Mar 91	
48:34.0mx	Lisa Langford	15 Mar 86	
	49:07.8	21 Jun 86	
49:48.7	Julie Drake	7 Feb 88	
50:25.0mx	Lisa Simpson	1 Apr 87	
	51:54.5	27 Sep 86	
51:00.0	Karen Nipper (U17)	21 Feb 81	
51:31.2	Helen Ringshaw	17 Mar 84	
52:09.0	Elaine Cox	8 Apr 78	
52:10.4	Sarah Brown	20 Mar 82	
52:48.5	Kate Horwill	22 Aug 92	
53:11.4	Jill Barrett	28 Mar 81	10
53:36.0mx	Suzie Pratt	15 Mar 86	
53:39.0	Karen Eden	22 Mar 80	

short

50:11.2	Jill Barrett	19 Mar 83

10k Road - *where superior to track time*

49:10	Vicky Lawrence	14 Mar 87
49:14	Carolyn Brown	29 Mar 92
49:26	Julie Drake	21 May 88
49:33	Lisa Simpson	14 Mar 87
49:47	Jill Barrett	24 Sep 83
51:15	Nicky Jackson	18 Nov 84
51:36	Nicola Phillips	23 Apr 00
51:51	Elaine Cox	2 Sep 79
52:00	Theresa Ashman	9 May 92

Note: LJ, Hep. Although Idowu competed for UK Juniors, she was a Nigerian citizen at the time.

UNDER 17

100 METRES

	11.45	Sonia Lannaman	1	Sep	72	
	11.59	Simmone Jacobs	25	Aug	83	
	11.60	Katharine Merry	28	Jul	90	
	11.61	Diane Smith	9	Aug	90	
	11.69	Jane Parry	6	Jun	81	
	11.70	Linsey Macdonald	24	May	80	
	11.73	Etta Kessebeh	20	Aug	81	
	11.77	Hayley Clements	26	Jul	85	
	11.78	Tatum Nelson	16	May	94	
10	11.79	Janet Smith	26	Jul	85	
	11.80	Sharon Dolby	26	Jul	85	
	11.81	Lisa Goreeph	6	Jun	82	
	11.83"	Sarah Wilhelmy	13	May	95	
	11.84	Jakki Harman	30	Jul	82	
	11.85	Renate Chinyou	2	Sep	89	
	11.85	Sophia Smith	20	Jul	91	
	11.85	Vernicha James	11	Jun	00	
	wind assisted					
	11.47	Katharine Merry (U15)	17	Jun	89	
	11.50	Rebecca Drummond	9	Jul	94	
	11.61	Linsey Macdonald	16	Jun	79	
	11.62	Kathleen Lithgow	25	Jun	88	
	11.62	Donna Maylor	4	Jul	98	
	11.63	Sharon Dolby	10	Aug	85	
	11.67	Tatum Nelson (U15)	10	Jul	93	
	hand timing					
	11.6	Denise Ramsden	19	Jul	68	
	11.6	Linsey Macdonald	25	May	80	
	11.6	Jane Parry	2	Aug	80	
	wind assisted					
	11.3	Linsey Macdonald	3	May	80	
	11.4	Sonia Lannaman	3	Jun	72	
	11.4	Jane Parry	5	Jul	80	
	11.5	Sharon Dolby	20	Jul	85	

200 METRES

	23.10	Diane Smith	11	Aug	90	
	23.28	Simmone Jacobs	28	Aug	83	
	23.42	Debbie Bunn	17	Jun	78	
	23.43	Linsey Macdonald	20	Aug	80	
	23.49 i	Vernicha James	30	Jan	00	
		23.62	8	Jul	00	
	23.50	Katharine Merry	20	Jul	91	
	23.60	Michelle Probert	12	Sep	76	
	23.66	Jane Parry	15	Jun	80	
	23.69	Donna Fraser	1	Jul	89	
10	23.79	Sharon Colyear	5	Sep	71	
	23.90	Angela Bridgeman	20	Aug	80	
	23.95	Helen Golden	30	Aug	69	
	23.97	Lisa Goreeph	31	Jul	82	
	24.06	Fay Nixon	4	Jun	76	
	wind assisted					
	23.11	Linsey Macdonald	5	Jul	80	
	23.41	Katharine Merry	15	Jun	91	
	23.48	Vernicha James	21	Aug	99	
	23.64	Jane Parry	5	Jul	80	
	23.70	Sonia Lannaman	16	Jun	72	
	23.85	Helen Golden	1	Sep	69	
	hand timing (* 220 yards less 0.1)					
	23.8 *	Marilyn Neufville	27	Jul	68	
	23.8	Janis Walsh (U15)	23	Jun	74	
	23.8	Janet Smith	1	Jun	85	
	23.9	Fay Nixon	24	Jul	76	
	23.9	Hayley Clements	1	Jun	85	
	wind assisted					
	23.2	Debbie Bunn	2	Jul	78	
	23.4	Hayley Clements	10	Aug	85	

300 METRES

	36.46	Linsey Macdonald	13	Jul	80	
	38.19	Eleanor Caney	22	Jul	00	
	38.21	Lesley Owusu	27	Aug	95	
	38.49	Kim Wall	24	May	98	
	38.60	Karlene Palmer	12	Jul	97	
	38.75	Gabi Howell	24	May	98	
	38.90	Liza Parry	15	Jul	00	
	38.95	Maria Bolsover	8	Jul	95	
	39.04	Heather McKay	19	Jun	98	
	39.07	Nicola Sanders	24	May	98	10
	39.21	Lisa Miller	10	Jul	99	
	39.22	Jenny Meadows	11	Jul	97	
	39.25	Rebecca White	17	Aug	96	
	39.34	Ruth Watson	12	Jul	96	
	39.36	Olivia Hines	29	Jul	00	
	hand timing					
	38.2	Marilyn Neufville	6	Sep	69	
	38.4	Kim Wall	10	May	98	
	38.6	Fay Nixon	10	Sep	77	
	38.7	Katharine Merry	1	Sep	91	

400 METRES

	51.16	Linsey Macdonald	15	Jun	80	
	53.08	Loreen Hall	29	Jul	84	
	53.75	Linda Keough	8	Aug	80	
	54.01	Angela Bridgeman	16	Aug	80	
	54.25	Emma Langston	19	Jun	88	
	54.57	Lesley Owusu	9	Sep	95	
	hand timing					
	53.7	Linda Keough	2	Aug	80	

600 METRES

	1:27.33	Lorraine Baker	13	Jul	80	

800 METRES

	2:02.0	Jo White	13	Aug	77	
	2:03.66	Lesley Kiernan	26	Aug	73	
	2:03.72	Lorraine Baker	15	Jun	80	
	2:04.85	Louise Parker	28	Jul	79	
	2:06.5	Rachel Hughes (U15)	19	Jul	82	
	2:06.5	Emma Langston	10	Aug	88	
	2:06.53	Lynne Robinson	6	Jul	85	
	2:06.72	Jemma Simpson	19	Aug	00	
	2:06.8	Jayne Heathcote	31	May	87	
	2:07.0	Bridget Smyth	27	Jun	84	10
	2:07.1	Charlotte Moore	12	Aug	00	
	2:07.3	Amanda Alford	7	May	80	
	2:07.32	Amanda Pritchard	22	Jun	96	
	2:07.53	Sandra Arthurton	17	Sep	78	
	2:07.57	Mary Sonner	13	Sep	70	

1000 METRES

	2:38.58	Jo White	9 Sep 77

1500 METRES

	4:15.20	Bridget Smyth	29 Jul 84
	4:15.55	Sandra Arthurton	29 Jul 78
	4:16.8	Jo White	30 Jul 77
	4:21.88	Jeina Mitchell	20 Jul 91
	4:22.25	Karen Hughes	24 May 81
	4:22.25	Clare Keller	7 Jul 85
	4:22.51	Elise Lyon	31 Jul 82
	4:23.11	Gillian Stacey	2 Sep 89
	4:23.25	Denise Kiernan	20 Aug 77
10	4:23.37	Dawn Hargan	14 Jun 87
	4:23.45	Isabel Linaker (U15)	7 Jul 90
	4:23.6	Janette Howes	5 Sep 81
	4:23.61	Charlotte Moore	15 Jul 00
	4:23.75	Lynne MacDougall	24 May 81
	4:23.96	Zoe Jelbert	19 Aug 00

1 MILE

	4:46.0	Sandra Arthurton	13 May 78

3000 METRES

	9:28.9	Bridget Smyth	21 Apr 84
	9:30.0	Yvonne Murray	4 Jul 81
	9:32.20	Nikki Slater	28 Aug 93
	9:33.1	Alison Hollington	6 Jun 81
	9:34.5	Louise Watson	28 Aug 88
	9:34.79	Helen Titterington	28 Jun 86
	9:34.9 mx	Charlotte Dale	16 Jul 00
		9:35.25	19 Aug 00
	9:35.52	Courtney Birch	15 Jul 00
	9:36.8	Karen Hughes	4 Jun 80
10	9:37.54 i	Zoe Jelbert	5 Feb 00
	9:38.1	Elise Lyon	12 Sep 81
	9:38.2	Amanda Alford	7 Mar 79
	9:39.9	Sharon Willicombe	8 Jul 88
	9:40.0	Julie Adkin	12 Sep 87
	9:40.5	Sharon Murphy	24 Jun 92

5000 METRES

	17:45.2	Kathy Williams	10 May 80

80 METRES HURDLES (2'6")

	11.02	Helen Worsey	15 Aug 98
	11.07	Amanda Parker	7 Jun 86
	11.12	Sam Farquharson	7 Jun 86
	11.13	Claire St. John	2 Jun 79
	11.16	Ann Girvan	4 Jul 81
	11.16	Stephi Douglas	27 Jul 85
	11.17	Sara McGreavy	14 Aug 99
	11.20	Ann Wilson	11 Aug 66
	11.20	Louise Brunning	25 Jul 87
10	11.20	Symone Belle	30 Jul 00
	11.22	Sharon Davidge	18 Jul 98
	11.23	Rachel Rigby	25 Jul 87
	11.25	Louise Fraser	25 Jul 87
	11.26	Liz Fairs	17 Jul 93
	11.29	Nina Thompson	7 Aug 88

wind assisted

10.96	Helen Worsey	11 Jul 98
11.00	Sharon Davidge	11 Jul 98
11.03	Wendy McDonnell	20 Aug 77

hand timing

11.0	Wendy McDonnell	2 Jul 77

wind assisted

10.9	Ann Wilson	16 Jul 66
10.9	Wendy McDonnell	9 Jul 77
10.9	Sam Farquharson	20 Jul 85

100 METRES HURDLES (2'6")

13.66	Ann Girvan	25 Jul 81

100 METRES HURDLES (2'9")

13.73	Ann Girvan	7 Aug 82
13.88	Natasha Danvers	28 Aug 93
13.98	Claire St. John	11 Aug 79
14.04	Lauraine Cameron	7 Aug 88
14.24	Pam St. Ange	2 Oct 82
14.24	Angie Thorp	9 Jul 89
14.39	Michelle Stone	18 Aug 84
14.40	Vicki Jamison	22 Jun 93

wind assisted

13.67	Ann Girvan	4 Jul 82
13.76	Natasha Danvers	27 Aug 94
14.10	Sue Mapstone	25 Aug 73
14.27	Heather Ross	27 Aug 78

hand timing

13.7	Ann Girvan	29 Aug 81
14.1	Pam St Ange	7 Aug 83

wind assisted

13.7	Nathalie Byer	4 Sep 82
13.9	Angie Thorp	9 Sep 89

300 METRES HURDLES

41.98	Rachael Kay	3 Aug 97	
41.99	Natasha Danvers	10 Jul 93	
42.58	Syreeta Williams	12 Jul 97	
42.67	Vicki Jamison	17 Jul 93	
42.68	Gemma Dooney	15 Jul 00	
42.87	Nusrat Ceesay	12 Jul 97	
42.91	Allison Curbishley	18 Aug 91	
43.03	Val Theobalds	13 Aug 89	
43.03	Wendy Davidson	15 Aug 99	
43.06	Claire Griffiths	18 Aug 91	10
43.08	Yewande Ige	13 Jul 96	
43.12	Keri Maddox	6 Aug 88	
43.12	Sian Scott	30 Jul 00	
43.28	Denise Bolton	5 Sep 93	
43.32	Symone Belle	27 May 00	

hand timing

41.8	Rachael Kay	17 Aug 97
42.4	Keri Maddox	8 May 88
42.4	Syreeta Williams	17 Aug 97
42.5	Louise Brunning	8 May 88
42.6	Sian Scott	10 Jun 00
42.8	Rachel Stafford	8 Jul 89
42.8	Vyv Rhodes	8 Jul 89
42.9	Val Theobalds	17 Jun 89

400 METRES HURDLES

	Mark	Athlete	Date
	60.87	Karin Hendrickse	31 Jul 82
	60.93	Rachael Kay	21 Jul 97
	61.02	Claire Edwards	8 Sep 91
	61.04	Allison Curbishley	26 Jul 92
	61.10	Vicki Jamison	26 Jun 93

hand timing

	Mark	Athlete	Date
	59.7	Keri Maddox	9 Jul 88
	60.8	Jayne Puckeridge	9 Jul 88

HIGH JUMP

	Mark	Athlete	Date
	1.89	Debbie Marti	2 Jun 84
	1.85	Louise Manning	11 Sep 82
	1.85	Jayne Barnetson	21 Jul 84
	1.84	Ursula Fay	6 Aug 83
	1.83	Jo Jennings	26 Jul 85
	1.83	Tracey Clarke	2 Aug 87
	1.83	Aileen Wilson	8 Jul 00
	1.82	Elaine Hickey	9 Aug 80
	1.82	Kerry Roberts	16 Jul 83
10	1.82	Susan Jones	20 May 94
	1.81	Barbara Simmonds	22 Jul 78
	1.81	Lea Haggett (U15)	6 Jun 86
		1.80	3 Sep 88
	1.80	Carol Mathers	10 Jun 73
	1.80	Susan Brown	28 Jul 79

POLE VAULT

	Mark	Athlete	Date
	3.60	Fiona Harrison	25 May 98
	3.55	Lindsay Hodges	14 Aug 99
	3.44	Clare Ridgley	10 Sep 94
	3.30	Rhian Clarke	4 Jul 93
	3.20	Rebecca Roles	31 Aug 96
	3.20	Ellie Spain	13 Sep 98
	3.20 i	Kirsty Maguire	20 Feb 99
		3.11	25 Jul 99
	3.20	Kate Dennison	15 Jul 00
	3.15	Sarah Hartley	9 Aug 97
10	3.15	Laura Patterson	7 Sep 97
	3.10	Zoe Parsons	22 May 99
	3.10	Amy Rennison	23 May 99
	3.03	Anna Watson	13 Sep 98

LONG JUMP

	Mark	Athlete	Date
	6.45	Margaret Cheetham	18 Aug 84
	6.32	Georgina Oladapo	23 Jul 83
	6.30	Fiona May (U15)	7 Jul 84
		6.27	14 Jun 86
	6.26	Jo Wise	31 May 87
	6.25	Sue Hearnshaw	9 Jul 77
	6.24	Sarah Claxton	15 Jun 96
	6.23	Sue Scott	27 Jul 68
	6.22	Ann Wilson	18 Sep 66
	6.22	Michelle Stone	28 Apr 84
10	6.18	Sheila Parkin	4 Aug 62
	6.15	Zainab Ceesay	20 Aug 00
	6.14	Bev Kinch	26 Jul 80
	6.13	Sonya Henry	7 Jul 85
	6.13	Jade Johnson	28 May 95
	6.12	Karen Glen	10 Aug 80

wind assisted

Mark	Athlete	Date
6.49	Margaret Cheetham (U15)	4 Sep 83
	6.49	23 Sep 84
6.47	Fiona May	28 Jun 86
6.41	Sue Hearnshaw	9 Jul 77
6.34	Sarah Claxton	12 Jul 96
6.33	Sue Scott	27 Aug 68
6.28	Bev Kinch	6 Sep 80
6.24	Jade Johnson	28 May 95
6.15	Sue Mapstone	27 May 72
6.15	Karen Glen	5 Jul 80

TRIPLE JUMP

Mark	Athlete	Date	
12.14	Jayne Ludlow	21 May 94	
11.88	Emily Parker	7 Jul 00	
11.83	Carly Robson	7 Jul 00	
11.82	Julia Johnson	30 Jun 96	
11.71	Hayley Warrilow	30 Jun 96	
11.68 i	Syreeta Williams	16 Feb 97	
	11.45	22 Jun 97	
11.64	Rachel Peacock	19 Jul 97	
11.61	Aisha Myton	30 Jul 00	
11.59	Tolu Jegede	30 Jun 96	
11.58 i	Linsi Robinson	6 Feb 00	10
11.50	Michelle Johansen	20 Aug 00	
11.48	Emma Hughes	10 Aug 96	
11.44	Donna Quirie	8 Aug 93	
11.44	Rachel Hogg	23 May 98	
11.41	Shani Anderson	8 Sep 91	

wind assisted

Mark	Athlete	Date
12.07	Rachel Peacock	18 Jul 98
11.69	Claire Quigg	18 Jul 98
11.68	Rachel Hogg	18 Jul 98
11.60	Lara Richards	15 Aug 99
11.58	Natalie Brant	17 Jul 99
11.50	Pamela Anderson	8 Aug 93
11.45	Nicky Ladrowski	13 Aug 95
11.44	Kim Goodall	15 Aug 99
11.43	Linsi Robinson	15 Aug 99

SHOT

Mark	Athlete	Date	
15.08	Justine Buttle	16 Aug 86	
14.40	Susan King	17 May 81	
14.04	Mary Anderson	6 May 84	
14.03 i	Terri Salt	19 Mar 83	
	13.77	17 Sep 83	
13.94	Jenny Bloss	13 May 67	
13.89 i	Alison Grey	11 Feb 89	
	13.83	20 May 89	
13.68 i	Philippa Roles	26 Feb 94	
	13.65	6 Aug 94	
13.64	Cynthia Gregory	20 Aug 80	
13.58 i	Natalie Hart	19 Mar 88	
	13.32	28 Aug 88	
13.49	Lana Newton	11 Jul 75	10
13.46	Julie Dunkley	22 Jun 96	
13.35	Carol Cooksley	6 Sep 86	
13.35	Claire Smithson	4 Jul 99	
13.24	Myrtle Augee	2 Aug 81	
13.20	Jayne Thornton	9 Jul 86	

DISCUS

51.60 Emma Merry 27 Jun 90
49.56 Jane Aucott 3 Aug 85
49.36 Claire Smithson 10 Jul 99
48.88 Philippa Roles 13 Aug 94
48.84 Karen Pugh 7 Aug 82
47.58 Catherine Bradley 14 Jul 84
47.54 Lauren Keightley 12 Jul 95
47.50 Sarah Symonds 16 May 90
47.24 Amanda Barnes 3 Aug 85
10 46.76 Fiona Condon 6 Aug 77
46.55 Emma Carpenter 5 Sep 98
46.34 Janette Picton 25 Mar 79
45.93 Joanne Street 3 Jul 99
45.72 Sarah Winckless 1 Jul 90
45.52 Jayne Thornton 12 May 86

HAMMER

48.66 Zoe Derham 16 Aug 97
47.68 Diana Holden 31 Jul 91
47.62 Nicola Dudman 11 Jun 00
46.98 Helen Arnold 29 Jul 95
46.82 Carys Parry 30 Aug 97
45.58 Julie Lavender 13 Sep 92
45.54 Laura Douglas 26 Jun 99
44.70 Rachael Beverley 15 Jul 95
43.64 Catherine Garden 30 Apr 95
10 43.36 Vicki Clark 16 Aug 97
43.19 Frances Miller 30 Apr 00
43.10 Lucy Marshall 15 Aug 98
42.14 Louise Kay 22 Jul 94
41.34 Katy Lamb 5 Sep 98
41.26 Sarah Harrison 5 Jul 95

JAVELIN (1999 Model)

45.24 Samantha Redd 27 May 00
43.11 Charlotte Rees 28 Aug 00
41.99 Sarah Ellis 27 May 00
41.47 Jo Chapman 20 Aug 00
41.11 Alison Siggery 5 Aug 00
40.98 Lisa Fryer 20 Jun 00
39.78 Joanna McGilchrist 14 Aug 99
39.55 Louise Matthews 27 Aug 00
39.54 Becky Bartlett 28 May 00
10 38.47 Helen Davis 17 Sep 00
38.39 Colette Doran 19 Jul 00
38.36 Helen Mounteney 23 Sep 00

JAVELIN (pre 1999 Model)

56.02 Mandy Liverton 11 Jun 89
53.42 Karen Hough 15 Jul 84
53.22 Kirsty Morrison 15 Aug 92
51.92 Goldie Sayers 17 May 98
51.50 Shelley Holroyd 22 Jul 89
50.82 Nicky Emblem 19 Jun 87
50.04 Kim Lisbon 19 Feb 84
50.02 Angelique Pullen 31 Aug 85
49.24 Jacqui Barclay 7 Aug 82
10 49.00 Kelly Morgan 27 Apr 96
48.34 Fatima Whitbread 29 Aug 77

HEPTATHLON (1985 Tables) Senior

5208 Michelle Stone 30 Sep 84
5184 Claire Phythian 20 Aug 89
4815 w Julie Hollman 2 May 93
4807 30 May 93
4784 Jackie Kinsella 12 May 85
4721 Joanne Taylor 21 Sep 80

HEPTATHLON (1985 Tables) with 80mH

5037 Michelle Stone 1 Jul 84
5031 Yinka Idowu 18 Sep 88
4915 Denise Lewis 24 Jul 88
4861 Clover Wynter-Pink 26 Jun 94
4841 Rebecca Lewis 18 Sep 94
4839 Jackie Kinsella 21 Jul 85
4830 w Katherine Livesey 22 Sep 96
4790 28 Jul 96
4794 Claire Phythian 22 May 88
4780 Danielle Freeman 23 Jun 96
4746 Chloe Cozens 22 Sep 96 10
4742 Julie Hollman 26 Sep 93
4673 Denise Bolton 19 Sep 93
4666 Tina Thirwell 20 Sep 98
4657 Rebecca Jones 4 Jul 99
4654 Aileen Wilson 27 Jun 99

with 100mH

5071 Debbie Marti 5 Jun 83
4661 Suzanne Sherratt 23 Aug 81

3000 METRES TRACK WALK

14:04.1 Susan Ashforth 19 May 85
14:09.81 Amy Hales 19 Sep 98
14:17.96 i Katie Ford 28 Feb 98
14:21.0 Julie Drake 25 Jun 85
14:24.6 Becky Tisshaw 19 Jul 97
14:26.4 Sarah Brown 29 Oct 80

5000 METRES TRACK WALK

23:55.27 Susan Ashforth 25 May 85
24:22.3 Vicky Lawrence 21 Jun 86
24:34.6 Tracy Devlin 17 Sep 89
24:45.4 Karen Eden 9 Jul 78
24:57.5 Angela Hodd 24 Jun 86
25:11.46 Nicola Phillips 21 Aug 99
25:13.8 Carla Jarvis 2 Jun 91
25:15.3 Vicky Lupton 3 Sep 88
25:18.5 Jill Barrett 16 Aug 80
25:20.0 Katie Ford 10 Sep 97 10
25:25.02 Nina Howley 31 Jul 94
25:25.80 Kim Macadam 25 May 85
25:26.41 Becky Tisshaw 6 Jul 97
25:31.14 Zena Lindley 4 Jun 89
25:33.94 Kerry Woodcock 26 Jun 88

5k Road - *where superior to track time*

23:57 Sarah Brown 6 Dec 80
24:20 Karen Eden 3 Dec 78

10000 METRES TRACK WALK

51:00.0 Karen Nipper 21 Feb 81
53:34.1 Vicky Lupton 5 Sep 87

UNDER 15

100 METRES
11.67 Katharine Merry 13 May 89
11.86 Hayley Clements 2 Jul 83
11.89 Joanne Gardner 20 Aug 77
11.92 Jane Parry (U13) 20 Aug 77
11.95 Tatum Nelson 7 Aug 93
12.00 Diane Smith 15 Sep 89
12.02 Renate Chinyou 28 Aug 88
12.02 Sarah Wilhelmy 28 May 94
12.02 Amy Spencer 29 Jul 00
12.07 Margaret Cheetham 29 Jul 83
12.09 Libby Alder 8 Jul 95
12.10 A Helen Seery 25 Jul 91
12.10 Lesley Owusu 7 Aug 93

wind assisted
11.47 Katharine Merry 17 Jun 89
11.67 Tatum Nelson 10 Jul 93
11.78 Jane Parry 8 Aug 78
11.84 Janis Walsh 26 May 74
11.88 Sarah Claxton 9 Jul 94
11.97 Yvonne Anderson 16 Jun 79
11.97 Renate Chinyou 20 Aug 88

hand timing
11.8 Janis Walsh 7 Jul 74
11.8 Joanne Gardner 2 Jul 77
11.9 Sonia Lannaman 9 Aug 69
11.9 Linsey Macdonald 26 Aug 78
11.9 Jane Perry 22 Apr 79
11.9 Etta Kessebeh 11 Jul 80

wind assisted
11.7 Diane Smith 30 Jul 89
11.8 Sonia Lannaman 30 May 70
11.8 Debbie Bunn (U13) 28 Jun 75
11.8 Delmena Doyley 6 Jul 79

200 METRES
23.72 Katharine Merry 17 Jun 89
23.90 Diane Smith 3 Sep 89
24.05 Jane Parry 16 Jul 78
24.31 Amy Spencer 8 Jul 00
24.39 Hayley Clements 3 Jul 83
24.44 Rachael Kay 8 Jul 95
24.51 Tatum Nelson 8 Aug 93
24.54 Sarah Wilhelmy 31 Jul 94
24.58 Simmone Jacobs 25 Jul 81
24.58 Donna Fraser 22 Aug 87
24.59 Janet Smith 30 Jul 83

wind assisted
23.54 Katharine Merry 30 Jul 89
23.99 Sarah Wilhelmy 9 Jul 94
24.24 Amy Spencer 8 Jul 00
24.25 Vernicha James 11 Jul 98
24.35 Tatum Nelson 27 Jun 93

hand timing
23.8 Janis Walsh 23 Jun 74
24.1 Sonia Lannaman 29 Aug 70

wind assisted
23.6 Jane Parry (U13) 9 Jul 77
23.8 Diane Smith 9 Sep 89

300 METRES
41.1 Maria Bolsover 10 Apr 94

400 METRES
56.7 Jane Colebrook 25 Jun 72

800 METRES
2:06.5 Rachel Hughes 19 Jul 82
2:08.7 Emma Langston 12 Jul 86
2:09.58 Sally Ludlam 8 Jun 75
2:09.6 Isabel Linaker 1 Aug 90
2:09.77 Lorraine Baker 19 Aug 78
2:09.80 Hannah Curnock 15 Aug 92
2:10.1 Lesley Kiernan 9 Jul 71
2:10.3 Carol Pannell 9 Jul 71
2:10.6 Christina Boxer 10 Jul 71
2:10.6 Natalie Tait 12 Jul 86
2:10.66 Amanda Pritchard 15 Jul 94
2:10.76 Carolyn Wells 19 Aug 78

1000 METRES
2:51.4 Hayley Haining 20 Aug 86

1500 METRES
4:23.45 Isabel Linaker 7 Jul 90
4:27.9 Joanne Davis 9 Jul 88
4:29.0 Claire Allen 8 Jul 89
4:29.6 Lynne MacDougall 16 Jul 79
4:29.9 Heidi Hosking 9 Jul 88
4:30.4 Claire Nicholson 18 Jun 87
4:31.12 Karen Hughes 31 Aug 79
4:31.45 Amanda Alford 22 Jul 78
4:31.6 Michelle Lavercombe 13 Jun 81
4:31.70 Jennifer Mockler 4 Aug 96
4:32.0 Elise Lyon 2 Apr 80
4:32.0 Jojo Tulloh 13 Jul 85
4:32.0 Julie Adkin 13 Aug 86
4:32.0 Katrina Wootton 15 Jul 00

ONE MILE
4:54.7 Hannah Curnock 9 Sep 92

75 METRES HURDLES (2'6")
10.93 Rachel Halstead-Peel 27 Jul 85
11.00 Louise Fraser 27 Jul 85
11.00 Danielle Selley 20 Jun 98
11.01 Nathalie Byer 16 Aug 80
11.06 Jessica Ennis 30 Jul 00
11.06 Phyllis Agbo 17 Sep 00
11.07 Symone Belle 10 Jul 99
11.08 Nicola Hall 29 May 94
11.08 Sara McGreavy 12 Jul 97
11.09 Catherine Murphy 6 Aug 88
11.09 Orla Bermingham 25 Aug 90
11.13 Lydia Chadwick 7 Jun 86
11.13 Naomi Hodge-Dallaway 30 Jul 95
11.14 Serena Bailey 30 Jul 95

wind assisted
10.95 Symone Belle 9 Jul 99
11.01 Naomi Hodge-Dallaway 8 Jul 95
11.05 Helen Worsey 13 Jul 96
11.06 Kate Forsyth 10 Jul 93
11.07 Melissa Harris 11 Jul 98

hand timing

10.8	Symone Belle	29 Aug 99

wind assisted

10.7	Orla Bermingham	14 Jul 90
10.8	Nathalie Byer	12 Jul 80
10.8	Ann Girvan	12 Jul 80

80 METRES HURDLES (2'6") U17

11.44	Catherine Crawford	4 Jul 99

HIGH JUMP

1.83	Ursula Fay	5 Jun 82
1.81	Debbie Marti	18 Sep 82
1.81	Lea Haggett	6 Jun 86
1.80	Jo Jennings	12 Aug 84
1.79 i	Julia Charlton	24 Feb 80
	1.78	13 Jul 80
1.79	Aileen Wilson	4 Jul 98
1.78	Claire Summerfield	28 Jul 79
1.75	Anne Gilson	2 Jun 73
1.75	Claire Smith	8 Aug 82
1.75	Jane Falconer	10 Jun 89
1.74	Lorinda Matthews	19 Aug 77
1.74	Janice Anderson	27 Jun 87
1.74	Katharine Merry	18 Sep 88

POLE VAULT

3.50	Fiona Harrison	24 Aug 96
3.20	Natalie Olson	9 Sep 00
3.10	Cariann Cutts	14 Aug 99
3.10	Hannah Olson (U13)	9 Sep 00
2.85	Zoe Holland	25 Jul 99

LONG JUMP

6.34	Margaret Cheetham	14 Aug 83
6.30	Fiona May	7 Jul 84
6.07	Georgina Oladapo	21 Jun 81
5.98	Sandy French	22 Jul 78
5.93	Jackie Harris	10 Jul 87
5.91	Symone Belle	29 Aug 99
5.88	Sue Scott	11 Aug 66
5.86	Tammy McCammon	18 Aug 91
5.85	Kim Hagger	20 Aug 76
5.81	Yvonne Hallett	24 Aug 86
5.80	Monique Parris	23 May 98
5.78	Pam St. Ange	15 Aug 81
5.76	Debbie Marti	31 Jul 82
5.75	Lyn Connolly	16 Jun 85

wind assisted

6.49	Margaret Cheetham	4 Sep 83
6.05	Katharine Merry	18 Sep 88
6.02	Michelle Stone	10 Jul 82
5.99	Sandy French	8 Jul 78
5.86	Donna Maylor	13 Jul 96
5.85	Karen Glen	8 Jul 78
5.80	Sue Mapstone	26 Jun 71

TRIPLE JUMP

10.77 w?	Angela Barratt	16 Sep 00
10.71	Kate Todd	30 Apr 94

SHOT (4kg)

12.16	Susan King	8 Sep 79

SHOT (3.25kg)

14.27	Susan King	19 May 79
13.69	Gloria Achille	21 Jun 80
13.61	Justine Buttle	4 Aug 84
13.22	Emily Steele	23 Jul 89
13.11	Amy Wilson	2 Sep 95
13.08	Ashley Morris	11 Aug 84
13.05	Tracy Page	21 Jun 86
13.04	Navdeep Dhaliwal	17 May 92
12.97	Alison Grey	23 Aug 87
12.96	April Kalu	23 Jun 96
12.95	Cynthia Gregory	7 Jul 78
12.91	Terri Salt	24 Jul 81
12.86	Lucy Rann	28 May 95

DISCUS

44.12	Philippa Roles	30 Aug 92
41.92	Catherine Garden	12 Sep 93
40.92	Sandra McDonald	24 Jun 78
40.84	Natalie Kerr	24 Jul 94
40.54	Claire Smithson	25 May 97
40.44	Catherine MacIntyre	12 Sep 82
40.34	Natalie Hart	23 Mar 86
40.22	Emma Merry	27 Aug 88
40.18	Kelly Mellis	17 Sep 94
40.14	Clare Tank	29 Aug 88
39.76	Alix Gallagher	6 Jun 87
39.38	Charladee Clarke	1 Sep 85
39.38	Alex Hajipavlis	13 Aug 95

HAMMER (4kg)

38.00	Catherine Garden	14 Mar 93

HAMMER (3.25kg)

40.54	Laura Chalmers	9 Jul 00
39.75	Shaeleen Bruce	9 Jul 00
39.35	Kirsty Walters	8 May 99
38.32	Sarah Holt	15 Jul 00
38.21	Frances Miller	19 Sep 99

JAVELIN (1999 Model)

38.01	Lauren Therin	15 Aug 99
37.40	Rebecca Pyne	20 Jun 99
36.03	Kelly-Jane Berry	28 Aug 00
35.98	Debbie Collinson	24 Jun 00
35.61	Louise Watton	17 Jun 00
34.84	Christine Lawrence	26 Aug 00
34.16	Jo Blair	8 Jul 00
34.14	Helen Davis	19 Sep 99

JAVELIN (pre 1999 Model)

48.40	Mandy Liverton	31 Aug 87
46.98	Kirsty Morrison	30 Jun 90
43.16	Shelley Holroyd	27 Jun 87
43.08	Karen Hough	4 Sep 82
42.70	Emily Steele	23 Sep 89
41.56	Goldie Sayers	12 Jul 96
41.50	Kelly Morgan	9 Jul 94
41.22	Maxine Worsfold	12 Jul 80
41.06	Heather Derbyshire	15 Aug 93

PENTATHLON (with 800m & 75m hdls)

3518	Katharine Merry	18 Sep 88
3509	Aileen Wilson	20 Sep 98
3333	Jackie Harris	27 Jun 87
3296	Claire Everett	19 Sep 93
3236	Emma Perkins	10 Sep 00
3225	Amy Nuttell	26 Jun 94
3216	Sally Gunnell	23 Aug 80
3213	Julie Hollman	22 Sep 91
3207	Louise Hazel	17 Sep 00
3195	Julia Charlton	10 May 80
3193	Sam Foster	26 Jun 94
3186	Lauraine Cameron	16 Aug 86
with 80mH		
3444	Jane Shepherd	16 Jul 83
3350	Claire Smith	3 Jul 82
3295	Paula Khouri	16 Jul 83
3283	Jackie Kinsella	16 Jul 83
3260	Debbie Marti	14 Aug 82
3186	Michelle Stone	3 Jul 82

2000 METRES TRACK WALK

9:35.0	Karen Eden	17 Jun 77

2500 METRES TRACK WALK

11:50.0	Susan Ashforth	12 Sep 84

3000 METRES TRACK WALK

14:56.4	Sarah Bennett	26 Sep 93
15:00.0	Susan Ashforth	19 Jun 84
15:00.6	Sally Wish	16 Sep 72
15:06.69	Kelly Mann	30 May 98
15:14.6	Amy Hales	31 Aug 96
15:16.4	Natalie Watson	31 Aug 96
15:18.3	Vicky Lawrence	17 Jul 83
15:19.0	Tracy Devlin	28 Mar 87
15:25.06	Sophie Hales	18 Sep 99
15:26.63	Nicola Phillips	20 Sep 97
15:28.0	Kim Macadam	3 Sep 83
15:30.0	Nikola Ellis	1 Sep 84
15:31.0	Philippa Savage	3 Sep 88
short track		
15:18.7	Sharon Tonks	19 Mar 83
3k Road - *where superior to track time*		
14:47	Amy Hales	23 Jun 96
14:48	Nikola Ellis	16 Sep 84
14:55	Lisa Langford	6 Dec 80
14:58	Carolyn Brown	19 Aug 87
14:59	Julie Snead	16 Sep 84
15:07	Stephanie Cooper	10 Dec 83
15:09	Angela Hodd	29 Jul 84
15:10	Vicky Lawrence	15 Apr 84
15:13	Jill Barrett	28 Jan 78

5000 METRES TRACK WALK

26:47.0hc	Amy Hales	15 Dec 96
26:52.0	Nina Howley	14 Sep 92
5k Road - *where superior to track time*		
26:20	Tracy Devlin	14 Feb 87

UNDER 13

75 METRES

9.83	Amy Spencer	6 Sep 98
9.98	Jenny Igbokwe	3 Sep 00
10.01	Jane Chadwick	3 Sep 00
10.02	Charlene Lashley	6 Sep 98
10.07	Lauren Duncan	3 Sep 00
wind assisted		
9.96	Joanne Wainwright	8 Sep 96
hand timing		
9.7	Carley Wenham	12 Jul 00
9.8	Amy Spencer	19 Jul 98
9.9	Cherie Pierre	21 Jul 96
9.9	Charlene Lashley	17 May 98
9.9	Nicola Gossman	2 May 99
9.9	Leah McGuire	30 Aug 99

80 METRES

10.2	Jane Riley	1 Jun 85
10.2	Helen Seery	20 May 89

100 METRES

11.92	Jane Parry	20 Aug 77
12.32	Katharine Merry	24 Jul 87
12.65	Sarah Claxton	4 Jul 92
hand timing		
12.1	Katharine Merry	26 Sep 87
12.3	Joanne Gardner	24 Aug 75
12.3	Debbie Bunn	30 Aug 75
wind assisted		
11.8	Debbie Bunn	28 Jun 75

150 METRES

19.47	Amy Spencer	6 Sep 98
19.69	Louise Dickson	4 Sep 99
19.78	Rebecca Smith	3 Sep 95
19.78	Jane Chadwick	3 Sep 00
hand timing		
19.1	Emma Ania	7 Sep 91
19.2	Helen Seery	19 Feb 89
19.2	Amy Spencer	28 Jun 98
19.2	Stacey Simpson	21 May 00
19.2	Laura Cox	21 May 00
19.3	Alanna Wain	29 Jun 97
19.3	Natalie Pearson	21 May 00
19.4	Vernicha James	1 Sep 96
19.4	Emma Burrows	18 Jul 99

200 METRES

24.49	Jane Parry	20 Aug 77
25.87	Amy Spencer	2 Aug 98
25.88	Myra McShannon	4 Sep 88
hand timing		
24.2	Jane Parry	28 May 77
25.4	Katharine Merry	21 Jun 87
25.4	Myra McShannon	8 May 88
25.6	Debbie Bunn	5 Jul 75
25.6	Joanne Gardner	24 Aug 75
25.6	Jane Riley	30 Jun 85
wind assisted		
23.6	Jane Parry	9 Jul 77

600 METRES

1:37.3	Lisa Lanini	19 Mar 00
1:37.5	Hannah Wood	17 Jul 94
1:38.5	Jenny Meadows	4 Apr 93

800 METRES

2:14.8	Janet Lawrence	10 Jul 71
2:15.05	Rachel Hughes	11 Sep 81
2:16.1	Lisa Lanini	5 Aug 00
2:16.8	Angela Davies	25 Jul 83
2:17.20	Emma Langston	7 Sep 84
2:17.6	Michelle Wilkinson	22 Jun 85
2:17.9	Melissa Rooney	20 Jun 81
2:18.1	Lileath Rose	19 Jun 76
2:18.50	Jenny Meadows	3 Jul 93
2:18.6	Jayne Heathcote	11 Jun 83

1000 METRES

3:00.1	Charlotte Moore	25 Aug 97
3:06.4	Charlotte Browning	6 Aug 00
3:08.1	Cheryl Hammond	4 Jul 99

1200 METRES

3:46.4	Lisa Lanini	18 Jul 99
3:49.1	Megan Foley	2 Jul 00
3:50.4	Lynsey Jepson	1 Aug 99
3:50.9	Charlotte Browning	4 Jul 00
3:51.3	Stephanie Bloor	2 Jul 00
3:52.9	Emma Hunt	17 May 98
3:53.1	Sara Luck	11 Jul 99
3:53.6	Natalie Real	2 Jul 00
3:55.5	Katie Harrison	18 Jul 99
3:55.5	Carolyn Plateau	23 Jul 00

1500 METRES

4:36.9	Rachel Hughes	20 Jul 81
4:39.3	Charlotte Moore	2 Aug 97
4:42.1	Stacey Washington	18 Jul 84

ONE MILE

5:24.6	Louise Ireland	9 Sep 90
5:24.6	Jacqueline Elliott	7 Aug 91

70 METRES HURDLES (2'3")

11.17	Anne-Marie Massey	3 Sep 95
11.24	Alana Watson	8 Sep 96
11.46	Sandra Gunn	13 Aug 88
11.50	Nafalya Francis	28 Aug 00
11.51	Kelly Marshall	11 Jul 98
wind assisted		
11.21	Sandra Gunn	4 Sep 88
11.26	Catriona Burr	4 Sep 88
11.32	Joanne Baker	3 Sep 00
hand timing		
11.0	Katharine Merry	20 Sep 87
11.0	Justine Roach	13 Sep 97
11.1	Sarah Claxton	14 Jun 92
11.1	Emma Makin	26 May 98
11.1	Leah McGuire	9 May 99
11.2	Clare Stuart	19 Jun 88

75 METRES HURDLES (2'6")

11.78	Caroline Pearce	7 Aug 93
hand timing		
11.3	Katharine Merry	26 Sep 87

HIGH JUMP

1.69	Katharine Merry	26 Sep 87
1.68	Julia Charlton	6 Aug 78
1.65	Debbie Marti	20 Sep 80
1.65	Jane Falconer	20 Sep 87
1.63	Lindsey Marriott	11 Aug 79
1.63	Paula Davidge	13 Sep 81
1.60	Denise Wilkinson	17 Jul 76
1.59	Julie O'Dell	28 Jul 74
1.59	Julia Cockram	18 May 80
1.59	Bev Green	30 Aug 86

POLE VAULT

3.10	Hannah Olson	9 Sep 00
2.80	Kim Skinner	24 May 00
2.30	Lauren Stoney	5 Aug 96

LONG JUMP

5.71	Sandy French	20 Aug 76
5.45	Sarah Wilhelmy	31 Aug 92
5.43	Margaret Cheetham	19 Sep 81
5.42	Katharine Merry	7 Jun 87
5.40	Kerry Gray	1 Sep 84
5.38	Toyin Campbell	6 Aug 77
5.35	Debbie Bunn	7 Sep 75
5.34	Fiona May	12 Jun 82
5.33	Kathryn Dowsett	7 Sep 91
5.32	Ann Flannery	18 Sep 82
wind assisted		
5.55	Katharine Merry	10 Jul 87

TRIPLE JUMP

9.55	Fiona Ferbrache	14 Jul 94

SHOT (3.25kg)

12.20	Susan King	3 Sep 77
10.77	Michele Morgan	19 Jun 82
10.54	Claire Burnett	1 Sep 85
10.49	Alison Grey	3 Aug 85

SHOT (2.72kg)

11.50	Nimi Iniekio	5 Sep 99
11.42	Candee Rhule	29 Jul 00
11.04	Amy Wilson	12 Sep 93
10.91	Catherine Garden	8 Sep 91
10.72	Kayleigh Southgate	3 Sep 00
10.60	Lucy Rann	29 Aug 93
10.56	Candace Schofield	17 Aug 97
10.52	Faye Brennan	18 Aug 96
10.50	Lynne Stewart	12 Jul 97
10.49	Sarah McRobbie	28 Aug 99

DISCUS (1kg)

34.22	Catherine Garden	25 Aug 91
31.34	Sandra Biddlecombe	9 Sep 90
30.54	Fiona Condon	15 Sep 73
30.02	Alison Moffitt	6 Jul 82
29.88	Iona Doyley	2 Sep 78

DISCUS (750g)

39.44	Catherine Garden	8 Sep 91
37.64	Sandra Biddlecombe	4 Jul 90
34.80	Rebecca Saunders	28 Aug 00
32.70	Claire Smithson	26 Aug 95
32.52	Candace Schofield	7 Sep 97
32.16	Christina Carding	25 Jul 99
31.46	Sian Howe	21 Sep 96
30.54	Eleanor Garden	10 Sep 89
29.76	Navdeep Dhaliwal	19 Aug 90
29.62	Helen Gates	3 Jul 93

HAMMER (3.25kg)

22.76	Ruth Hay	7 Sep 00

JAVELIN (600g original model)

32.02	Claire Lacey	20 Sep 87
31.60	Emma Langston	2 Sep 84
31.44	Alison Moffitt	6 Jul 82
31.28	Eve Russell	2 Sep 95

JAVELIN (400g)

38.07	Louise Watton	12 Sep 99
36.06	Samantha Redd	1 Sep 96
33.90	Lauren Therin	6 Sep 98
33.46	Emma Claydon	26 Jul 92
33.32	Melanie Vaggers	27 Sep 94
32.60	Candace Schofield	10 Aug 97
32.38	Eve Russell	30 Jul 95
31.87	Georgina Field	31 Aug 98
31.74	Josie Jamieson	28 Aug 99
31.58	Louise Telford	20 Aug 94

PENTATHLON (Under 15 implements)

2607	Jane Shepherd	6 Jun 81
2604	Alison Kerboas	19 Sep 93
2541 ?	Jane Falconer	23 Aug 87

PENTATHLON

2811	Katharine Merry	20 Sep 87
2551	Sarah Wilhelmy	2 Aug 92
2519	Naida Bromley	30 Aug 99
2505	Caroline Pearce	26 Sep 93
2451	Seonaid Ferry	17 Jul 94
2419	Donna Medlock	7 Aug 94

1000 METRES TRACK WALK

5:11.1	Amy Hales	4 Sep 94
5:14.6	Natasha Fox	31 Aug 98
5:17.0	Elizabeth Ryan	10 Jun 79
5:18.0	Margaret O'Rawe	28 Sep 80
5:19.3	J. Black	15 Oct 95
5:21.0	Sarah Bennett	30 Sep 90
5:22.6	Carley Tomlin	29 May 00
5:23.0	Hayley Dyke	15 Jul 98
5:27.0	Katrina Todd	27 Nov 77
5:29.0	Jo Pickett	30 Sep 90
5:29.0	E. Winstanley	11 Jun 00

1k Road - *where superior to track time*

4:42	Kelly Mann	23 Sep 95
4:43	Natalie Watson	23 Sep 95
4:50	Sarah Bennett	23 Sep 90

2000 METRES TRACK WALK

10:09.0	Kelly Mann	10 Sep 95
10:17.0	Sarah Bennett	27 Sep 92
10:19.0	Joanne Ashforth	7 Sep 85
10:31.0	Claire Walker	7 Sep 85
10:31.0	Jo Pickett	25 Apr 92
10:32.0	Karen Eden	25 Aug 75
10:37.0	Karen Bowers	29 Sep 79
10:41.0	Amy Hales	7 May 94
10:41.2	Linda Callow	22 Sep 73
10:45.0	Vicky Firmstone	17 Sep 83

2k Road - *where superior to track time*

10:03	Kelly Mann	23 Jun 96
10:36	Yvette Eden	24 Jan 76
10:38	Hayley Hutchings	28 Sep 96
10:39	Laura Fryer	23 Jun 96
10:42	Natalie Evans	28 Sep 96

2500 METRES TRACK WALK

12:48.9	Claire Walker	20 Jul 85
12:50.5	Vicky Lawrence	4 Jul 82

2.5k Road - *where superior to track time*

12:39	Amy Hales	16 Oct 93
12:41	Stephanie Cooper	1 May 82

3000 METRES TRACK WALK

15:41.0	Kelly Mann	30 Jul 95

3k Road - *where superior to track time*

15:25	Nicola Greenfield	21 Mar 87
15:44	Sarah Bennett	1 Mar 92

UK CLUB RELAY RECORDS

MEN

Seniors

4 x 100m	39.49	Haringey	1 Jun 91
4 x 200m	1:23.5	Team Solent	19 Jul 87
4 x 400m	3:04.48	Team Solent	29 Jun 90
1600m Medley	3:20.8	Wolverhampton & Bilston	1 Jun 75
4 x 800m	7:24.4*	North Staffs and Stone	27 Jul 65
4 x 1500m	15:12.6	Bristol	5 Aug 75

* = 4 x 880y time less 2.8sec

Under 20

4 x 100m	41.30	Victoria Park	14 Aug 76
4 x 200m	1:27.6	Enfield	13 Jun 82
4 x 400m	3:15.3	Enfield	5 Sep 82
1600m Medley	3:31.6	Cardiff	14 Aug 71
4 x 800m	7:35.3	Liverpool H	14 Aug 90
4 x 1500m	16:04.3	Blackburn	15 Sep 79
4 x 110H	1:04.8	Oundle Sch	19 May 79

Under 17

4 x 100m	42.22	Thames V H	24 Jun 89
4 x 200m	1:31.2	Herc Wimb	12 Jul 78
4 x 400m	3:23.1 o	Enfield	1 Oct 80
	3:23.2	Haringey	26 Jul 88
1600m Medley	3:36.1	Thurrock	13 Jun 84
4 x 800m	7:52.1	Clydebank	29 Aug 87
4 x 1500m	16:27.0	Liverpool H	14 Sep 88

Under 15

4 x 100m	44.62	Sale	29 Aug 93
4 x 200m	1:36.9	Belgrave	19 Sep 93
4 x 400m	3:31.5o?	Ayr Seaforth	5 Sep 82
	3:31.6	Shaftesbury B	26 Jul 88
1600m Medley	3:48.4	Blackheath	28 Sep 86
4 x 800m	8:13.28o?	Clydebank	2 Sep 89
	8:16.8	Shaftesbury B	14 Sep 88
4 x 1500m	17:52.4 o	Stretford	22 Oct 85
	18:18.4	Tonbridge	6 Jul 80

Under 13

4 x 100m	50.32	Shaftesbury B	5 Sep 99
4 x 200m	1:49.7	Braintree	29 Aug 94
4 x 400m	4:04.5	Blackheath	12 Sep 93
1600m Medley	4:13.7	Blackheath	28 Sep 86
4 x 800m	9:29.8	Sale	28 Jun 88

WOMEN

Seniors

4 x 100m	43.79	Hounslow	18 Sep 82
4 x 200m	1:35.15	Stretford	14 Jul 91
4 x 400m	3:31.62	Essex Ladies	31 May 92
1600m Medley	3:50.6	Coventry Godiva	5 May 84
3 x 800m	6:32.4	Cambridge H	29 Jun 74
4 x 800m	8:41.0	Cambridge H	26 May 75

Under 20

4 x 100m	46.80	Birchfield	26 Sep 98
4 x 200m	1:46.4	Millfield School	11 May 00
4 x 400m	3:51.6	Birchfield	23 Aug 98
	3:51.67	Sale Harriers	23 Sep 89
3 x 800m	7:33.2	Essex Ladies	12 Jun 94

Under 17

4 x 100m	47.52o	Hounslow	2 Oct 82
	47.8	B of Enfield	20 Jul 75
	47.8	Croydon	15 Sep 82
	48.08	Wigan & D	6 Sep 92
4 x 200m	1:42.2	London Oly.	19 Aug 72
4 x 400m	3:52.1	City of Hull	3 Jul 82
1600m Medley	4:07.8	Warrington	14 Aug 75
3 x 800m	6:46.5	Haslemere	15 Sep 79
	6:46.5	Bromley L	1 Jul 84
4 x 800m	8:53.1	Havering	24 May 80

Under 15

4 x 100m	48.5	Haringey	15 Sep 79
	49.08	Radley L	16 Jul 83
4 x 200m	1:44.0	Bristol	15 Sep 79
3 x 800m	6:39.8	Havering	13 Sep 78
4 x 800m	9:21.4	Sale	5 Aug 78

Under 13

4 x 100m	53.09	Wigan	5 Sep 99
4 x 200m	1:52.5	Mitcham	24 Jul 82
3 x 800m	7:18.0	Mid Hants	14 Sep 83
4 x 800m	10:02.4	Warrington	16 Sep 75

o overage by current rules

AAA INDOOR CHAMPIONSHIPS & CGU EUROPEAN INDOOR TRIALS

Birmingham 29 - 30 January 2000

The performance of the championship was Jason Gardener's 6.53 for 60 metres, 0.17 ahead of the opposition. On the women's side, Judy Oakes retained the Shot title, an event she first won in 1977. Daniel Cains' performances in the 400m, run as fast as you can for as long as you can, were the most spectacular and his winning time of 46.89 represented the first of many breakthroughs he would make in the year. 18 year old Chris Tomlinson won the men's long jump and 19 year old Jade Johnson the women's title. A 17 year old, Mark Lewis-Francis, made the 60 metre final.

MEN

60 Metres (29 Jan)

1.	Jason Gardener		6.53
2.	Josephus Thomas		6.70
3.	Jamie Henthorn		6.71
4.	Marlon Devonish		6.71
5.	Mark Lewis-Francis		6.72
6.	Jason John		6.74

200 Metres (30 Jan)

1.	Christian Malcolm		20.74
2.	Marlon Devonish		20.83
3.	Julian Golding		20.87
4.	Jamie Henthorn		21.24
	John Regis		dns
	Marcus Adam		dns

400 Metres (30 Jan)

1.	Daniel Caines		46.89
2.	Paul Slythe		47.60
3.	Adrian Patrick		47.90
4.	Mark Hylton		49.25
	Sean Baldock		dns
	Richard Knowles		dns

800 Metres (30 Jan)

1.	Luke Kipkoech	KEN	1:51.72
2.	Dominic Hall		1:52.14
3.	Neil Speaight		1:52.18
4.	James Parker		1:53.05
5.	Alistair McLean-Foreman		1:54.44
6.	Bradley Donkin		1:56.52

1500 Metres (30 Jan)

1.	Gareth Turnbull	IRE	3:44.06
2.	Eddie King		3:44.39
3.	Chris Bolt		3:47.52
4.	Justin Swift-Smith		3:47.57
5.	James Thie		3:48.12
6.	James Mayo		3:51.40

3000 Metres (30 Jan)

1.	Rob Whalley		8:02.40
2.	Andrew Graffin		8:04.64
3.	Matt Smith		8:06.33
4.	Darius Burrows		8:07.84
5.	Ian Grime		8:09.73
6.	Chris Davies		8:16.45

60 Metres Hurdles (30 Jan)

1.	Tony Jarrett		7.65
2.	Damien Greaves		7.76
3.	William Erese	NGR	7.91
4.	Mensah Elliott		7.93
5.	Liam Collins		7.94
6.	Martin Nicholson		8.00

High Jump (30 Jan)

1.	Stuart Ohrland		2.19
2.	Samson Oni	NGR	2.19
3.	Ben Challenger		2.19
4.	Robert Mitchell		2.14
5.	Tyron Peacock	RSA	2.14
6=	Robert Brocklebank		2.09
6=	Antoine Burke	IRE	2.09

Pole Vault (29 Jan)

1.	Ben Flint		5.35
2.	Paul Williamson		5.30
3.	Kevin Hughes		5.10
4.	Tim Thomas		5.10
5.	Mark Davis		5.00

Long Jump (30 Jan)

1.	Chris Tomlinson		7.57
2.	Steve Phillips		7.51
3.	Stuart Wells		7.40
4.	Chris Davidson		7.28
5.	Darren Ritchie		7.25
6.	Levi Edwards		7.16

Triple Jump (29 Jan)

1.	Julian Golley		16.56
2.	Nicholas Thomas		16.27
3.	Farel Mepandy	CGO	15.54
4.	Martin Rossiter		14.62
5.	Paul Weston		14.31
6.	John Wiggans		13.61

Shot (29 Jan)

1.	Steph Hayward		17.67
2.	Emeka Udechuku		17.06
3.	Scott Rider		16.28
4.	Mark Proctor		16.07
5.	Lyndon Woodward		15.44
6.	Anthony Soalla-Bell	SLE	15.23

3000 Metres Walk (29 Jan)

1.	Robert Heffernan	IRE	11:38.20
2.	Martin Bell		12:03.12
3.	Andrew Penn		12:10.08
4.	James Gibbons	IRE	12:48.55
5.	David Kibb	IRE	13:21.78
6.	Nathan Adams		13:37.69

Heptathlon (Birmingham 22/23 Jan)

1.	Paul Jones		5277
2.	Duncan Mathieson		5271
3.	Dominic Shepherd		5095
4.	James Holder		4888
5.	Alex Kruger		4807
6.	John Healey		4694

WOMEN

60 Metres (29 Jan)

1.	Marcia Richardson		7.25
2.	Joice Maduaka		7.34
3.	Janine Whitlock		7.36
4.	Christine Bloomfield		7.37
5.	Diane Allahgreen		7.38
6.	Catherine Murphy		7.46

200 Metres (30 Jan)

1.	Christine Bloomfield		23.31
2.	Donna Fraser		23.43
3.	Joice Maduaka		23.65
4.	Sarah Oxley		24.11
5.	Shani Anderson		24.17
6.	Zoe Wilson		24.25

400 Metres (29 Jan)

1.	Michelle Thomas		55.26
2.	Carey Easton		55.58
3.	Michelle Pierre		55.74
4.	Karen Gear		55.76
5.	Kim Goodwin		56.07
6.	Kim Wall		57.03

800 Metres (30 Jan)

1.	Emma Davies		2:07.34
2.	Jeina Mitchell		2:07.61
3.	Sally Evans		2:08.78
4.	Sarah Knights		2:10.07
5.	Emily Hathaway		2:11.29
6.	Kathryn Bright		2:12.90

1500 Metres (30 Jan)

1.	Shirley Griffiths		4:25.69
2.	Joanne Colleran		4:26.37
3.	Maria Lynch	IRE	4:28.23
4.	Valerie Bothams		4:32.00
5.	Catherine Dugdale		4:33.31
6.	Hayley Parkinson-Ovens		4:34.34

3000 Metres (Birmingham 23 Jan)

1.	Zahara Hyde-Peters		9:16.89
2.	Joanne Colleran		9:21.26
3.	Sarah Bull		9:22.68
4.	Sarah Salmon		9:27.75
5.	Shirley Griffiths		9:32.38

60 Metres Hurdles (30 Jan)

1.	Diane Allahgreen		8.24
2.	Melanie Wilkins		8.29
3.	Clova Court		8.40
4.	Julie Pratt		8.43
5.	Sarah Claxton		8.54
6.	Kerry Jury		8.56

High Jump (29 Jan)

1.	Wanita May	CAN	1.84
2=	Susan Jones		1.79
2=	Aileen Wilson		1.79
2=	Jo Jennings-Steele		1.79
5=	Julie Crane		1.79
5=	Dalia Mikneviciute		1.79

Pole Vault (30 Jan)

1.	Janine Whitlock		4.20
2.	Irie Hill		3.95
3.	Alison Daives		3.80
4.	Ellie Spain		3.60
5.	Lindsay Hodges		3.60
6=	Noelle Bradshaw		3.40
6=	Emma Hornby		3.40
6=	Linda Stanton		3.40

Long Jump (30 Jan)

1.	Jade Johnson		6.46
2.	Ann Danson		6.21
3.	Sarah Claxton		6.19
4.	Julie Hollman		6.09
5.	Kerry Jury		5.79
6.	Margaret Veldman	HOL	5.73

Triple Jump (29 Jan)

1.	Deborah Rowe		12.47
2.	Anna-Maria Thorpe		12.26
3.	Caroline Stead		12.18
4.	Jodie Hurst		12.00
5.	Julia Johnson		11.69

Shot (30 Jan)

1.	Judy Oakes		18.30
2.	Philippa Roles		15.62
3.	Maggie Lynes		15.45
4.	Julie Dunkley		15.41
5.	Vickie Foster		15.21
6.	Eleanor Gattrell		14.60

3000 Metres Walk (29 Jan)

1.	Gillian O'Sullivan	IRE	12:33.11
2.	Sharon Tinks		14:17.50
3.	Kate Horwill		14:17.50
4.	Anne McGill	IRE	16:34.54

Pentathlon (Birmingham 23 Jan)

1.	Julia Bennett		4216
2.	Kerry Jury		4044
3.	Julie Hollman		4016
4.	Diana Bennett		3977
5.	Anne Hollman		3770

CGU AAA INDOOR JUNIOR CHAMPIONSHIPS
Birmingham 5 - 6 February 2000

Tim Benjamin completed a fine U20 sprint double and Chris Tomlinson, fresh from senior championships, doubled with both Long and Triple Jumps. Aileen Wilson was best U20, winning the women's High Jump, although both Ellie Spain and Lyndsay Hodges equalled the junior indoor record for the Pole Vault. Best performance by an U17 athlete was Zoe Jelbert's British Record in the U20 3000m. Amy Spencer scored an easy double in the U15 Women's sprints.

MEN	**Under 20**			**Under 17**		**Under 15**	
60	Tim Benjamin	6.83		Monu Miah	7.06	Alexander Coley	7.35
200	Tim Benjamin	21.06		Aaron Aplin	22.35	James Ellington	23.18
400	Sam Ellis	49.1		Craig Erskine	50.24		
800	Paul Gilbert	1:54.07		Adam Davies	1:58.86	Luke Hopson	2:11.08
1500	Mark Pollard	3:58.56		Stephen Davies	4:06.02		
3k	Richard Ward	8:33.06		Ahmed Ali	9:04.38		
60H	Chris Baillie	7.95		Edward Dunford	8.10	Kevin Sempers	9.10
HJ	Jamie Russell	2.05		Chuka Enih-Snell	2.07	Matthew Chetwynd	1.69
PV	Mark Beharrell	4.80		Oliver Mahoney	4.20	Steven Lewis	3.10
LJ	Chris Tomlinson	7.48		Marlon Lewis	6.61	Alistair Hinze	5.91
TJ	Chris Tomlinson	15.31		Kevin Thompson	13.82		
SP	Greg Beard	15.39		Carl Saggers	16.21	Simon Cooke	13.82
3kW	Dominic King	12:44.51					
Hept	Jamie Russell	4725	Pent	Edward Dunford	3608	Louis Moore	2865

Hept/Pent Birmingham 22/23 January

WOMEN	**Under 20**			**Under 17**		**Under 15**	
60	Donna Maylor	7.65		Vernicha James	7.58	Amy Spencer	7.75
200	Lowri Jones	24.60		Samantha Gamble	24.93	Amy Spencer	25.03
400	Jennifer Meadows	55.34	300	Samantha Gamble	40.22		
800	Iona McIntyre	2:13.88		Jemma Simpson	2:12.92	Rachael Thompson	2:19.78
1500	Lisa Dobriskey	4:33.95		Emma King	4:52.70		
3k	Zoe Jelbert	9:37.54					
60H	Helen Worsey	8.69		Symone Belle	8:61	Amy Beighton	9.07
HJ	Aileen Wilson	1.79		Claire Wright	1.73	Jessica Ennis	1.60
PV	Ellie Spain	3.65		Natalie Olson	2.90		
LJ	Rachel Hogg	5.64		Zainab Ceesay	5.63	Leah McGuire	5.41
TJ	Angela Williams	12.00		Linsi Robinson	11.58		
SP	Claire Smithson	13.09		Shelley Moles	11.01	Debbie Collinson	10.63
3kW	Nicola Phillips	14:38.22					
Pent	Rebecca Jones	3236		Aileen Wilson	3527	Louise Hazel	3194

Pent Birmingham 22/23 January

EUROPEAN INDOOR CHAMPIONSHIPS

Ghent, BEL 25 - 27 February 2000

5 medals - 2 gold, 1 silver and 2 bronze was a good result for Britain. Jason Gardener had an excellent win in the 60 metres equalling Colin Jackson's championship record, Christian Malcolm completed the sprint double for Britain with Julian Golding picking up third. Tony Jarrett showed some of his old form and John Mayock won bronze in a hard race. Although the women won no medals there were some encouraging performances - Diane Allahgreen broke the British record in the hurdles and Janine Whitlock was unlucky to miss a medal, clearing 4.30 in both qualifying and the final.

MEN

60 Metres (27 Feb)

1.	**Jason Gardener**		**6.49**
2.	Georgios Theodoridis	GRE	6.51
3.	Angelos Pavlakakis	GRE	6.54
4.	Stefano Tilli	ITA	6.59
5.	Roland Nemeth	HUN	6.61
6.	Kostyantin Rurak	UKR	6.62
5h1	**Jamie Henthorn**		**6.84**

200 Metres (26 Feb)

1.	**Christian Malcolm**		**20.54**
2.	Patrick Stevens	BEL	20.70
3.	**Julian Golding**		**21.06**
4.	Christophe Cheval	FRA	21.37
5	Kostadinos Kenteris	GRE	21.79
	Anninos Marcoullides	CYP	dnf
5s3	**Tim Benjamin**		**21.54**

400 Metres (27 Feb)

1.	Ilya Tsevontov	BUL	46.63
2.	David Canal	ESP	46.85
3.	Marc Raquil	FRA	47.28
4.	Lars Figura	GER	47.53
5.	Alain Rohr	SUI	47.98
6.	**Daniel Caines**		**48.36**

800 Metres (27 Feb)

1.	Yuriy Borzakovskiy	RUS	1:47.92
2.	Nils Schumann	GER	1:48.41
3.	Balazs Koranyi	HUN	1:48.42
4.	Wilson Kirwa	FIN	1:48.69
5.	Roberto Parra	ESP	1:49.80
6.	Marco Chiavarini	ITA	1:51.27

1500 Metres (26 Feb)

1.	Jose Redolat	ESP	3:40.51
2.	James Nolan	IRE	3:41.59
3.	Medhi Baala	FRA	3:42.27
4.	Marko Koers	NED	3:42.46
5.	Vyacheslav Shabunin	RUS	3:43.44
6.	Juan Higuero	ESP	3:44.07
8s2	**Eddie King**		**3:49.18**

3000 Metres (27 Feb)

1.	Mark Carroll	IRE	7:49.24
2.	Rui Silva	POR	7:49.70
3.	**John Mayock**		**7:49.97**
4.	Mohammed Mourhit	BEL	7:49.99
5.	Andres Diaz	ESP	7:53.97
6.	Yusef El Nasri	ESP	7:55.37
8s1	**Rob Whalley**		**8:06.59**

60 Metres Hurdles (26 Feb)

1.	Stanislavs Olijars	LAT	7.50
2.	**Tony Jarrett**		**7.53**
3.	Tomasz Scigaczewski	POL	7.56
4.	Elmar Lichtenegger	AUT	7.56
5.	Falk Balzer	GER	7.63
6.	Robert Kronberg	SWE	7.64
5s2	**Damien Greaves**		**7.68**

High Jump (27 Feb)

1.	Vyacheslav Voronin	RUS	2.34
2.	Martin Buss	GER	2.34
3.	Dragutin Topic	YUG	2.34
4.	Stefan Holm	SWE	2.32
5.	Pyotr Brayko	RUS	2.27
6.	Oskari Frosen	FIN	2.24
14=Q	**Ben Challenger**		**2.16**

Pole Vault (26 Feb)

1.	Alex Averbukh	ISR	5.75
2.	Martin Eriksson	SWE	5.70
3.	Rens Blom	NED	5.60
4=	Thibaut Duval	BEL	5.60
4=	Richard Spiegelburg	GER	5.60
6.	Bjorn Otto	GER	5.50
9Q	**Paul Williamson**		**5.40**

Long Jump (26 Feb)

1.	Petar Dachev	BUL	8.26
2.	Bogdan Tarus	ROM	8.20
3.	Vitaliy Shkurlatov	RUS	8.10
4.	Alexei Lukashevych	UKR	8.02
5.	Gregor Cankar	SLO	7.94
6.	Emmanuel Banque	FRA	7.82

Triple Jump (27 Feb)

1.	Charles Friedek	GER	17.28
2.	Rotislav Dimitrov	BUL	17.22
3.	Paolo Camossi	ITA	17.05
4.	Zsolt Czingler	HUN	17.00
5.	Ketill Hanstveit	NOR	16.72
6.	Fabrizio Donato	ITA	16.57
8.	**Julian Golley**		**16.16**

Shot (27 Feb)

1.	Aleksandr Bagach	UKR	21.18
2.	Timo Aaltonen	FIN	20.62
3.	Manuel Martinez	ESP	20.38
4.	Miroslav Menc	CZE	20.23
5.	Gheorghe Guset	ROM	20.21
6.	Roman Virastyuk	UKR	20.07
10Q	**Mark Proctor**		**19.42**

Heptathlon (25/26 Feb)

1.	Tomas Dvorak	CZE	6424
2.	Roman Sebrle	CZE	6271
3.	Erki Nool	EST	6200
4.	Attila Zsovotzky	HUN	6033
5.	Mario Anibal	POR	5930
6.	Prodromos Korkizoglou	GRE	5855

4 x 400 Metres (27 Feb)

1.	Czech Republic	3:06.10
2.	Germany	3:06.64
3.	Hungary	3:09.35
4.	**Great Britain & NI**	**3:09.79**
	(White, Slythe, Naismith, Knowles)	
	France	dnf
	Russia	dq

WOMEN

60 Metres (27 Feb)

1.	Ekaterini Thanou	GRE	7.05
2.	Patia Pendareva	BUL	7.11
3.	Irina Pukha	UKR	7.11
4.	Anzhela Kravchenko	UKR	7.14
5.	Alenka Bikar	SLO	7.20
6.	Kim Gevaert	BEL	7.22
8.	**Marcia Richardson**		**7.27**
6s2	**Joice Maduaka**		**7.30**

200 Metres (26 Feb)

1.	Muriel Hurtis	FRA	23.06
2.	Alenka Bikar	SLO	23.16
3.	Yekaterina Leshchova	RUS	23.20
4.	Birgit Rockmeier	GER	23.29
5.	Irina Khabarova	RUS	23.64
6.	Fabe Dia	FRA	24.38
3s1	**Catherine Murphy**		**23.60**
4s3	**Joice Maduaka**		**23.63**
3h5	**Christine Bloomfield**		**23.99**

400 Metres (27 Feb)

1.	Svetlana Pospelova	RUS	51.68
2.	Natalya Nazarova	RUS	51.69
3.	Helena Fuchsova	CZE	52.32
4.	Karen Shinkins	IRE	53.15
	Daniela Georgieva	BUL	dq
	Claudia Marx	GER	dnf

800 Metres (27 Feb)
1. Stephanie Graf AUT 1:59.70
2. Natalya Tsyganova RUS 2:00.17
3. Sandra Stals BEL 2:01.34
4. Jolanda Ceplak SLO 2:02.10
5. Yvonne Teichmann GER 2:02.26
6. Stella Jongmans NED 2:03.11

1500 Metres (26 Feb)
1. Violeta Szekely ROM 4:12.82
2. Olga Kuznetsova RUS 4:13.45
3. Yulia Kosenkova RUS 4:13.60
4. Sinead Delahunty IRE 4:15.87
5. Patricia Djate-Taillard FRA 4:17.69
6. D. Briand-Calenic FRA 4:18.70

3000 Metres (27 Feb)
1. Gabriela Szabo ROM 8:42.06
2. Lidia Chojecka POL 8:42.42
3. Marta Dominguez ESP 8:44.08
4. Jelena Prokopchuka LAT 8:44.66
5. Daniela Yordanova BUL 8:47.45
6. Olga Yegorova RUS 8:49.18
7. Hayley Parry-Tullett 8:55.31

60 Metres Hurdles (26 Feb)
1. Linda Ferga FRA 7.88
2. Patricia Girard FRA 7.98
3. Yelena Krasovska UKR 8.03
4. Yuliya Graudyn RUS 8.03
5. Diane Allahgreen 8.04
6. Susanna Kallur SWE 8.19

High Jump (26 Feb)
1. Kajsa Bergqvist SWE 2.00
2. Zuzana Hlavonova CZE 1.98
3. Olga Kaliturina RUS 1.96
4. Venelina Veneva BUL 1.92
5. Viktoria Palamar UKR 1.92
6. Viktoria Slivka RUS 1.92

Pole Vault (27 Feb)
1. Pavla Hamackova CZE 4.40
2. Yelena Belyakova RUS 4.35
3. Christine Adams GER 4.35
4. Vala Flossadottir ICE 4.30
5. Janine Whitlock 4.30
6. Sabine Schulte GER 4.20

Long Jump (27 Feb)
1. Erica Johansson SWE 6.89
2. Heike Drechsler GER 6.86
3. Iva Prandzheva BUL 6.80
4. Olga Rublyoba RUS 6.67
5. Tunde Vaszi HUN 6.58
6. Tatyana Ter-Mesrobyan RUS 6.57
13QJade Johnson 6.18

Triple Jump (26 Feb)
1. Tatyana Lebedeva RUS 14.68
2. Cristina Nicolau ROM 14.63
3. Iva Prandzheva BUL 14.63
4. Yelena Govorova UKR 14.55
5. Oksana Rogova RUS 14.28
6. Rodica Petrescu-Mateescu ROM 14.16

Shot (26 Feb)
1. Larisa Peleshenko RUS 20.15
2. Nadine Kleinert-Schmitt GER 19.23
3. Astrid Kumbernuss GER 19.12
4. Svetlana Krivelyova RUS 18.96
5. Krystyna Danilczyk-Zabawska POL 18.88
6. Nadezhda Ostapchuk BLR 18.65
13QJudy Oakes 17.25

Pentathlon (25 Feb)
1. Karin Ertl GER 4671
2. Irina Vostrikova RUS 4615
3. Urszula Wlodarczyk POL 4590
4. Tiia Hautala FIN 4580
5. Yelena Prokhorova RUS 4555
6. Sonja Kesselschlager GER 4468

4 x 400 Metres (27 Feb)
1. Russia 3:32.53
2. Italy 3:35.01
3. Romania 3:36.28

GER v GB & NI v FRA (U20) Indoors

Neubrandenburg, GER 4 March 2000

Germany won easily, with Britain only winning two men's and three women's events, although one winner in women's 4 x 400 relay would repeat victory in a bigger arena later. Mohammed Farah's win was probably the best and Mark Lewis-Francis came second twice to further warn of more to come in the summer.

MEN

60 Metres Race 1
1. Tim Goebel GER 6.65
2. Mark Lewis-Francis 6.67
3. Tim Benjamin 6.77

60 Metres Race 2
1. Tim Goebel GER 6.65
2. Mark Lewis-Francis 6.69
3. Tim Benjamin 6.79

200 Metres Race A
1. Daniel Abenzoar-Foule FRA 21.52
2. Normen Ney GER 21.78
3. Ben Lewis 21.92

200 Metres Race B
1. Sebastian Gatzka GER 21.50
2. Tyrone Edgar 21.81

400 Metres Race A
1. David Brackstone 49.19

400 Metres Race B
1. Christian Duma GER 48.25
2. Sam Ellis 49.53

800 Metres
1. Wolfram Muller GER 1:49.00
3. Paul Gilbert 1:53.34
4. Alisdair McLean-Foreman 1:53.60

1500 Metres
1. Martin Uhlich GER 4:01.63
3. Richard Ward 4:01.91
5. Mark Pollard 4:03.08

3000 Metres
1. Mohammed Farah 8:32.64
4. Matthew Jones 8:47.62

60 Metres Hurdles Race 1
1. Thomas Blaschek GER 7.94
2. Chris Baillie 8.04
4. Robert Newton 8.18

60 Metres Hurdles Race 2
1. Thomas Blaschek GER 7.92
2. Chris Baillie 7.96
6. Robert Newton 10.35

High Jump
1. Jerome Tourre FRA 2.14
3. Jamie Russell 2.08
6. Chuka Enih-Snell 1.85

Pole Vault
1. Sebastien Homo FRA 5.25
3. Mark Beharrell 4.80
5. Chris Type 4.50

Long Jump
1. Ladji Doucoure FRA 7.55
3. Chris Tomlinson 7.47
6. Leigh Smith 7.15

Triple Jump
1. Rudolf Helpling GER 15.98
4. Chris Tomlinson 15.13
6. Alan Saulters 13.38

Shot
1. Alexander Heydemuller GER 16.46
2. Greg Beard 15.76
6. Scott Thompson 14.73

5000 Metres Walk
1. Andre Katzinski GER 21:03.88
3. Dominic King 21:25.17
5. Lloyd Finch 22:23.45

4 x 400 Metres
1. Germany 3:16.39
2. Great Britain & NI 3:20.89
(Ellis, Tunnicliffe, Tobin, Brackstone)

Match Result Men
1. Germany 125
2. Great Britain & NI 85
3. France 84

WOMEN

60 Metres Race 1

1. Sina Schielke GER 7.46
3= Donna Maylor 7.57
6. Siobahn McVie 7.77

60 Metres Race 2

1. Katchi Habel GER 7.44
3. Donna Maylor 7.52
6. Siobahn McVie 7.80

200 Metres Race A

1. Kerstin Grotzinger GER 24.07
2. Lowri Jones 24.38

200 Metres Race B

1. Sina Schielke GER 23.74
2. Vernicha James 24.02

400 Metres Race A

1. Helen Thieme 56.11

400 Metres Race B

1. Claudia Hoffmann GER 55.22
2. Jenny Meadows 55.52

800 Metres

1. Natalie Lewis 2:10.97
4. Iona McIntyre 2:13.96

1500 Metres

1. Kerstin Werner GER 4:31.75
3. Lisa Dobriskey 4:36.40
4. Louise Damen 4:37.08

3000 Metres

1. Katharina Splinter GER 9:55.69
2. Gemma Greenfield 10:04.35
3. Kate Bailey 10:04.96

60 Metres Hurdles Race 1

1. Corinna Rehwagen GER 8.50
4. Helen Worsey 8.90
5. Zoe McKinnon 9.08

60 Metres Hurdles Race 2

1. Adrianna Lamalle FRA 8.50
4. Helen Worseu 8.62
6. Zoe McKinnon 8.93

High Jump

1. Sophia Sagonas GER 1.88
4. Aileen Wilson 1.78
6. Natalie Clark 1.70

Pole Vault

1. Martina Strutz GER 4.00
5. Ellie Spain 3.60
6. Lindsay Hodges 3.40

Long Jump

1. Korinna Fink GER 6.36
5. Fiona Westwood 5.66
6. Rachel Hogg 5.61

Triple Jump

1. Claudia Ender GER 12.83
5. Angela Williams 11.73
6. Linsi Robinson 11.25

Shot

1. Kathleen Kluge GER 16.58
5. Claire Smithson 13.08
6. Kara Nwindobie 12.81

3000 Metres Walk

1. Stephanie Panzig GER 13:39.30
4. Nicola Phillips 14:29.37
6. Laura Fryer 16:29.82

4 x 400 Metres

1. Great Britain & NI 3:44.28
(Meadows, Clarkson, Wood, Thieme)

Match Result Women

1. Germany 144
2. Great Britain & NI 77
3. France 74

Match Result Combined

1. Germany 269
2. Great Britain & NI 162
3. France 158

GB & NI v RUS v CAN v FRA v ALL STARS (AS) Indoors

Glasgow 5 March 2000

A disappointing international for Britain with only two winners, the gold medallists from the European Championships.The Russians were dominant with many excellent performances from a quality team.

MEN

60 Metres

1. Jason Gardener 6.57
5. Jamie Henthorn AS 6.85

200 Metres

1. Christian Malcolm 21.06
3. Julian Golding AS 21.26

400 Metres

1. Andrey Semyonov RUS 46.91
4. Daniel Caines 47.45

800 Metres

1. Yuriy Barzakovskiy RUS 1:50.83
3. Dominic Hall 1:51.94

1500 Metres

1. Vyacheslav Shabunin RUS 3:42.70
5. Chris Bolt 3:47.65

60 Metres Hurdles

1. Tony Jarrett AS 7.58
2. Colin Jackson 7.62

High Jump

1. Vyacheslav Voronin RUS 2.37
3. Dalton Grant AS 2.25
Ben Challenger nh

Pole Vault

1. Martin Erikson SWE 5.72
4. Paul Williamson 5.17

Shot

1. Oliver-Sven Buder GER/AS 19.43
2. Mark Proctor 19.15
5. Steph Hayward gst 17.92

4 x 400 Metres

1. Russia 3:04.96
3. Great Britain & NI 3:08.38
(White, Slythe, Caines, Knowles)
4. All Stars 3:08.39
(3rd leg Golding)

WOMEN

60 Metres

1. Philomena Mensah RUS 7.22
2. Marcia Richardson 7.29
4. Joice Maduaka AS 7.36

200 Metres

1. Myriam Mani CMR/AS 23.62
3. Donna Fraser 23.96

400 Metres

1. Svetlana Pospelova RUS 52.41
5. Vicki Day 55.52

800 Metres

1. Stephanie Graf AUT/AS 2:00.62
3. Emma Davies 2:06.27

1500 Metres

1. Olga Kuznetsova RUS 4:13.28
5. Susan Scott 4:29.26

60 Metres Hurdles

1. Patricia Girard FRA 8.00
3. Diane Allahgreen 8.05

High Jump

1. Viktoria Seryogina RUS 1.97
4. Julia Bennett 1.81

Long Jump

1. Tatyana Ter-Mesrobyan RUS 6.62
3. Jade Johnson 6.24

4 x 400 Metres

1. Russia 3:30.23
2. All Stars 3:30.51
(2nd leg Murphy)
4. Great Britain & NI 3:39.54
(Day, Pierre, Fraser, Thomas)

Match Result

1. Russia 73.5
2. All Stars 64
3. Great Britain & NI 48
4. Canada 41
5. France 40.5

FRA v GB & NI v ITA Combined Indoors
Vittel, FRA 18 - 19 March 2000

MEN Heptathlon
1. Lionel Marceny FRA 5662
4. Jamie Quarry 5461
10. Dominic Shepherd 5035
11. Duncan Mathieson 4621
Alex Kruger dnf

Team
1. France 16453
2. Italy 16200
3. Great Britain & NI 15117

WOMEN Pentathlon
1. Julia Bennett 4222
2. Julie Hollman 4135
7. Kerry Jury 3794
Diana Bennett dnf

Team
1. Great Britain & NI 12151
2. Italy 11712
3. France 11214

MEN U23 Heptathlon (v FRA)
1. Romain Barras FRA 5369
5. Paul Jones 5136
6. Jamie Russell 4650
7. Fyn Corcoran 4440

Team
1. France 15902
2. Great Britain & NI 14226

WOMEN U23 Pentathlon (v FRA)
1. Nicola Gautier 4118
2. Danielle Freeman 3878
3. Chloe Cozens 3634

Team
1. Great Britain & NI 11630
2. France 9864

REEBOK CAU INTER-COUNTIES CHAMPIONSHIPS & WORLD TRIALS
Nottingham 12 February 2000

Both Keith Cullen and Dominic Bannister elected to run early season marathons and declined selection for the World Championships. Chris Thompson had to be on his best form to beat 16 year old Mohammed Farah. Tara Kryzwicki scored her first major cross country win in the long race, Hayley Tullett used the short race as training for her indoor races and left a disappointing Kelly Holmes back in 9th place. 17 year old Fagan beat 16 year old Freeman in the Junior race.

MEN 12k
1. Keith Cullen 37:10
2. Dominic Bannister 37:15
3. Nicky Comerford 37:22
4. Glynn Tromans 37:23
5. Jon Wild 37:31
6. Rob Denmark 37:34

WOMEN 8k
1. Tara Kryzwicki 27:54
2. Liz Yelling 28:01
3. Hayley Yelling 28:09
4. Hayley Haining 28:13
5. Sharon Morris 28:21
6. Angela Joiner 28:30

JUNIOR MEN 8k
1. Chris Thompson 25:28
2. Mohammed Farah 25:44
3. Robert Maycock 25:55
4. Andrew Sherman 26.28
5. Paul Shaw 26:29
6. Nick McCormick 26:38

MEN 4k
1. Rob Whalley 12:04
2. Spencer Barden 12:06
3. Phil Mowbray 12:07
4. Allen Graffin 12:09
5. Andrew Graffin 12:12
6. David Heath 12:16

WOMEN 4k
1. Hayley Tullett 14:00
2. Caroline Walsh 14:10
3. Angela Newport 14:18
4. Lucy Wright 14:21
5. Diane Henaghan 14:30
6. Jilly Ingman 14:32

JUNIOR WOMEN 6k
1. Collette Fagan 21:27
2. Henrietta Freeman 21:29
3. Emma Ward 21:33
4. Jane Potter 21:45
5. Zoe Jelbert 21:51
6. Kate Reed 21:56

ENGLISH NATIONAL CROSS COUNTRY CHAMPIONSHIPS
Stowe School Park, Bucks 26 February 2000

MEN 12k
1. Glynn Tromans 40:19
2. Ian Hudspith 41:02
3. Rob Birchall 41:13

MEN U20 10k
1. Chris Thompson 31:39

MEN U17 6k
1. Mohammed Farah 19:11

WOMEN 8k
1. Tara Krzywicki 27:21
2. Andrea Whitcombe 27:36
3. Birhan Dagne 27:52

WOMEN U20 5k
1. Caroline Walsh 17:06

WOMEN U17 5k
1. Henrietta Freeman 17:38

WOMEN U15 3.6k
1. Courtney Birch 12:58

WOMEN U13 3k
1. Lynsey Jepson 11:40

REGIONAL CROSS COUNTRY CHAMPIONSHIPS

Wales
Cardiff 17 February 2000

MEN
1. Nick Comerford 40:30

WOMEN
1. Catherine Dugdale 24:30

Scotland
Irvine 26 February 2000

MEN
1. Robert Quinn 41:16

WOMEN
1. Hayley Haining 31:19

Northern Ireland
Coleraine 4 March 2000

MEN
1. John Ferrin 40:08

WOMEN
1. Catriona McGranaghan 18:46

IAAF WORLD CROSS COUNTRY CHAMPIONSHIPS

Vilamoura, POR 18 - 19 March 2000

A very flat course and hot conditions did not help the British cause and in the main performances were disappointing. Paula Radcliffe was magnificent, but even in very good form could not match the speed of the Africans. Karl Keska ran well in the long race and Mohammed Farah gives hope for the future.

MEN (4k) 18 Mar

1.	John Kibowen	KEN	11:11
2.	Sammy Kipketer	KEN	11:12
3.	Paul Kosgei	KEN	11:15
4.	Leonard Mucheru	KEN	11:21
5.	Abraham Chebii	KEN	11:25
6.	Hailu Mekonnen	ETH	11:27
38.	**David Heath**		**11:57**
64.	**Rob Whalley**		**12:08**
65.	**Phil Mowbray**		**12:08**
78.	**Andrew Graffin**		**12:17**
89.	**Spencer Barden**		**12:27**
97.	**Matthew Smith**		**12:34**

Team

1.	Kenya	10
2.	Ethiopia	46
3.	Morocco	68
10.	**Great Britain & NI**	**245**

MEN (12k) 19 Mar

1.	Mohammed Mourhit	BEL	35:00
2.	Assefa Mezegebu	ETH	35:01
3.	Paul Tergat	KEN	35:02
4.	Patrick Ivuti	KEN	35:03
5.	Wilberforce Kapkeny Talel	KEN	35:06
6.	Paul Koech	KEN	35:22
13.	**Karl Keska**		**36:13**
34.	**Glynn Tromans**		**37:03**
47.	**Matthew O'Dowd**		**37:26**
62.	**Jonathan Wild**		**37:43**
88.	**Nick Comerford**		**38:45**
107.	**Rob Denmark**		**39:43**

Team

1.	Kenya	18
2.	Ethiopia	68
3.	Portugal	69
6.	**Great Britain & NI**	**156**

JUNIOR MEN (8k) 19 Mar

1.	Robert Kipchumba	KEN	22:49
2.	Duncan Kipkorir Lebo	KEN	22:52
3.	John Cheruiyot Korir	KEN	22:55
4.	Philmon Kemei	KEN	23:04
5.	Martin Sulle	TAN	23:14
6.	Phaustin Baha Sulle	TAN	23:27
25.	**Mohammed Farah**		**24:37**
41.	**Chris Thompson**		**25:14**
49.	**Robert Maycock**		**25:25**
101.	**Paul Shaw**		**26:29**
111.	**Andrew Sherman**		**26:42**
116.	**Nick McCormick**		**26:54**

Team

1.	Kenya	10
2.	Ethiopia	47
3.	Uganda	68
12.	**Great Britain & NI**	**216**

WOMEN (4k) 19 Mar

1.	Kutre Dulecha	ETH	13:00
2.	Zahra Ouaziz	MAR	13:00
3.	Margaret Ngotho	KEN	13:00
4.	**Paula Radcliffe**		**13:01**
5.	Fatima Yvelain	FRA	13:06
6.	Yemenashu Taye	ETH	13:07
34.	**Helen Pattinson**		**13:38**
39.	**Hayley Parry-Tullett**		**13:40**
61.	**Angela Newport**		**13:54**
76.	**Lucy Wright**		**14:09**
94.	**Caroline Walsh**		**14:34**

Team

1.	Portugal	46
2.	Ethiopia	55
3.	France	57
7.	**Great Britain & NI**	**138**

WOMEN (8k) 18 Mar

1.	Derartu Tulu	ETH	25:42
2.	Gete Wami	ETH	25:48
3.	Susan Chepkemei	KEN	25:50
4.	Lydia Cheromei	KEN	26:02
5.	**Paula Radcliffe**		**26:03**
6.	Leah Malot	KEN	26:09
34.	**Hayley Yelling**		**27:43**
44.	**Liz Yelling**		**28:02**
54.	**Sharon Morris**		**28:27**
56.	**Hayley Haining**		**28:37**
59.	**Tara Kryzwicki**		**28:39**

Team

1.	Ethiopia	20
2.	Kenya	23
3.	United States	98
6.	**Great Britain & NI**	**137**

JUNIOR WOMEN (6k) 18 Mar

1.	Vivian Cheruiyot	KEN	20:34
2.	Alice Timbilil	KEN	20:35
3.	Viola Kibiwot	KEN	20:36
4.	Hareg Sidelil	ETH	20:38
5.	Merima Hashim	ETH	20:41
6.	Fridah Domongole	KEN	20:43
55.	**Henrietta Freeman**		**22:56**
63.	**Emma Ward**		**23:09**
66.	**Collette Fagan**		**23:14**
75.	**Kate Reed**		**23:24**
84.	**Jane Potter**		**23:44**
95.	**Zoe Jelbert**		**24:19**

Team

1.	Kenya	12
2.	Ethiopia	24
3.	Japan	78
10.	**Great Britain & NI**	**259**

EUROPEAN CHALLENGE 10000 Metres

Lisbon, POR 1 April 2000

Karl Keska was not put off by the bad weather conditions and achieved the Sydney qualifying time and placed an excellent second, the highest place secured by a British man in the four runnings of this challenge.

MEN - Race A

1.	Enrique Molina	ESP	27:59.80
2.	**Karl Keska**		**28:00.56**
3.	Alberto Garcia	ESP	28:01.11
10.	**Rob Denmark**		**28:17.70**
12.	**Keith Cullen**		**28:22.06**

MEN - Race B

1.	Dmitriy Maksimov	RUS	28:15.85
2.	Francesco Bennici	ITA	28:18.55
3.	Jirka Arndt	GER	28:42.85
14.	**John Nuttall**		**29:35.48**
	Matthew O'Dowd		**dnf**

Team Result - Men

1.	Spain	1:24:06.77
2.	Portugal	1:24:16.38
3.	**Great Britain & NI**	**1:24:40.32**

Team Result - Women

1.	Portugal	1:36:43.78
2.	Norway	1:37:14.73
3.	Spain	1:37:24.41
7.	**Great Britain & NI**	**1:39:57.88**

WOMEN - Race A

1.	Fatima Yvelain	FRA	31:43.29
2.	Gunild Haugen	NOR	31:47.89
3.	Agata Balsamo	ITA	31:56.56
23.	**Tara Kryzwicki**		**33:10.89**
24.	**Liz Yelling**		**33:11.84**

WOMEN - Race B

1.	Jelena Prokopchuka	LAT	31:27.86
2.	Chantal Dallenbach	SUI	32:40.21
3.	Melanie Kraus	GER	32:41.15
8.	**Birhan Dagne**		**33:35.15**

Andrea Whitcombe/Sarah Young dnf

LONDON MARATHON 16 April 2000

(including AAA Championships)

Great performances by the winners but the British standards remain low. At least Mark Steinle and Keith Cullen made the all important Olympic qualifying time, albeit more than a mile behind the winner.

MEN

1.	Antonio Pinto	POR	2:06:36
2.	Abdelkader El Mouaziz	MAR	2:07:33
3.	Khalid Khannouchi	MAR	2:08:36
4.	William Kiplagat	KEN	2:09:06
5.	Hendrick Ramaala	RSA	2:09:43
6.	Stefano Baldini	ITA	2:09:45
7.	Mathias Ntawulikura	RWA	2:09:55
8.	Josia Thugwane	RSA	2:10:29
9.	Mohammed Nazipov	RUS	2:10:35
10.	Danilo Goffi	ITA	2:10:54
11.	**Mark Steinle**		**2:11:18**
15.	**Keith Cullen**		**2:13:37**
18.	**Mark Hudspith** (1 AAA)		**2:15:16**
20.	**Billy Burns** (2 AAA)		**2:15:42**
22.	**Mark Croasdale** (3 AAA)		**2:16:02**
24.	**Rhodri Jones**		**2:18:34**
25.	**Ian Hudspith**		**2:18:40**
26.	**N Cullen**		**2:18:43**

WOMEN

1.	Tegla Loroupe	KEN	2:24:33
2.	Lidia Simon	ROM	2:24:46
3.	Joyce Chepchumba	KEN	2:24:57
4.	Adriana Fernandez	MEX	2:25:42
5.	Kerryn McCann	AUS	2:25:59
6.	Derartu Tulu	ETH	2:26:09
7.	Maria Guida	ITA	2:26:12
8.	Lyubov Morgunova	RUS	2:26:33
9.	Manuela Machado	POR	2:26:41
10.	Svetlana Zakharova	RUS	2:28:11
20.	**Lynne MacDougall**		**2:38:32**
21.	**Alison Wyeth**		**2:39:01**
22.	**Trudi Thomson**		**2:40:39**
23.	**Jo Lodge** (1 AAA)		**2:40:51**
24.	**Angie Joiner** (2 AAA)		**2:44:07**
25.	**J Newcombe** (3 AAA)		**2:46:17**
26.	**Sharon Dixon**		**2:46:30**
27.	**Louise Watson**		**2:49:19**

EUROPEAN IAU 100K Championships

Belves, FRA

30 April 2000

MEN

1.	Farid Ganiyev	RUS	6:33:36
2.	Piotr Sekowski	POL	6:44:28
3.	Oleg Kharitonov	RUS	6:47:00
29.	**Ian Anderson**		**7:49:31**
	Takahiro Sunada	JPN/gst	6:17:17

WOMEN

1.	Edit Berces	HUN	7:53:12
2.	Karrine Herry	FRA	8:06:46
3.	Alzira Lario	POR	8:16:53
9.	**Hilary Walker**		**9:06:56**

THROWS INTERNATIONAL Halle, GER 27 May 2000

MEN

Shot

1.	Detlef Bock	GER	20.16
	Mark Proctor		**nm**

Shot B

1.	Rene Sack	GER	18.79
4.	**Mark Edwards**		**18.26**

Discus

1.	Lars Riedel	GER	66.89
8.	**Glen Smith**		**61.15**

Discus B

1.	Torsten Schmidt	GER	61.10
3.	**Emeka Udechuku**		**58.84**

Hammer

1.	Karsten Kobs	GER	79.13
6.	**Mick Jones**		**73.38**

Javelin

1.	Manuel Nau	GER	83.04
4.	**Nick Nieland**		**80.90**

Javelin B

1.	**David Parker**		**78.24**

WOMEN

Shot

1.	Astrid Kumbernuss	GER	19.93

Discus

1.	Franka Dietzsch	GER	67.13

Discus B

1.	**Philippa Roles**		**55.48**

Hammer

1.	Yipsi Moreno	CUB	69.09
7.	**Lorraine Shaw**		**65.00**

Hammer B

1.	**Liz Pidgeon**		**63.61**
3.	**Lyn Sprules**		**60.76**

Javelin

1.	Steffi Nerius	GER	65.47

Javelin B

1.	Yanuris La Montana	CUB	58.61
2.	**Karen Martin**		**55.73**

EUROPEAN CUP FOR COMBINED EVENTS

Esbjerg, DEN 1 - 2 July 2000

MEN (League 2)

1.	Rojs Piziks	LAT	7744
2.	Klaus Ambrosch	AUT	7604
3.	Michael Schnallinger	AUT	7423
7.	**Barry Thomas**		**7117**
11.	**Paul Jones**		**6920**
16.	**Stephen Bonnet**		**6756**
	Fyn Corcoran		**dnf**

Team Result

1.	Austria	22366
4.	**Great Britain & NI**	**20793**

Schwyz/Ibach, SWZ 1 - 2 July 2000

WOMEN (League 1)

1.	Natalya Sazanovich	BLR	6288
2.	Rita Inancsi	HUN	6177
3.	Tatiana Alisevich	BLR	6146
9.	**Kerry Jury**		**5667**
13.	**Julia Bennett**		**5444**
14.	**Danielle Freeman**		**5442**
	Nicola Gautier		**dnf**

Team Result

1.	Belarus	18248
4.	**Great Britain & NI**	**16553**

AAA 100K Championships

Edinburgh

9 July 2000

MEN

1.	Stephen Moore	7:14:57
2.	Alan Reid	7:27:24
3.	Chris Finill	7:37:11
4.	Ian Anderson	7:46:59

WOMEN

1.	Jackie Leak	9:00:15
2.	Victoria Musgrove	9:20:44
3.	Carol Cadger	9:23:09
4.	Hilary Walker	9:31:09

EAA EUROPEAN CUP OF RACE WALKING

Eisenhuttenstadt, GER 17 - 18 June 2000

Leading British performance was a new UK record for Lisa Kehler in the 20k, taking 92 seconds off the previous best. Steve Hollier improved his PB by 7 minutes but missed the Sydney qualifying time in the 50k and Dominic King showed promise in the junior 10k race.

MEN (50k) 18 Jun
1. Jesus Garcia ESP 3:42:51
2. Yevgeniy Shmaliuk RUS 3:44:33
3. Denis Langlois FRA 3:47:38
28. Steve Hollier 4:07:18
43. Chris Cheeseman 4:23:19
45. Don Bearman 4:36:15
Tim Watt dnf

Team
1. France 12
2. Spain 15
3. Germany 30
12. Great Britain & NI 116

MEN (20k) 17 Jun
1. Robert Korzeniowski POL 1:18:29
2. Andreas Erm GER 1:18:42
3. Francisco Fernandez ESP 1:18:56
50. Chris Maddocks 1:31:39
51. Andy Penn 1:33:10
Darrell Stone dq
Andrew Drake dq

Team (20k)
1. Spain 32
2. Poland 35
3. Germany 43
Great Britain & NI dnf

MEN U20 (10k) 17 Jun
1. Alexander Kuzmin BLR 41:16
2. Jan Albrecht GER 41:17
3. Andre Katzinski GER 41:59
27. Dominic King 45:03
31. Lloyd Finch 45:29
39. Thomas Taylor 48:55

Team (2 to score)
1. Germany 5
2. Belarus 5
3. Italy 15
12. Great Britain & NI 58

WOMEN (20k) 17 Jun
1. Olimpiada Ivanova RUS 1:26:48
2. Elisabetta Perrone ITA 1:27:42
3. Kjersti Platzer NOR 1:27:53
23. Lisa Kehler 1:33:57
46. Niobe Menendez 1:43:18
50. Kim Braznell 1:46:24
Sara-Jane Cattermole dnf

Team
1. Italy 11
2. Romania 29
3. Ukraine 38
11. Great Britain & NI 119

WOMEN U20 (10k)
1. Tatyana Koblova RUS 45:28
2. Marina Tikhonova BLR 45:33
3. Alena Benkova RUS 45:35
36. Clare Reeves 59:11

Team (2 to score)
1. Russia 4
2. Belarus 11
3. Germany 18

NORWICH UNION CHALLENGE GB & NI v USA Glasgow 2 July 2000

The headline result was Maurice Greene 5th in the 100 metres! There were some fine performances by the British, leading the men, Christian Malcolm in the 200 and Katharine Merry for the women with a fine win in the 400.

MEN

100 Metres wind -3.8
1. Jason Gardener 10.40
3. Darren Campbell 10.52
4. Dwain Chambers 10.54

200 Metres wind -3.8
1. Christian Malcolm 20.65
3. Marlon Devonish 20.75
5. Julian Golding 20.89

400 Metres
1. Danny McCray USA 45.59
3. Jamie Baulch 46.08
4. Iwan Thomas 46.19
6. Sean Baldock 47.25

800 Metres
1. Derrick Peterson USA 1:46.95
2. James McIlroy 1:47.40
5. Alasdair Donaldsongst **1:47.84**
6. Justin Swift-Smith 1:49.46
7. Jason Lobo 1:52.67

1 Mile
1. John Mayock 4:00.65
2. Matt Dixon 4:01.61
4. Michael East 4:04.65

110 Metres Hurdles wind -3.2
1. Colin Jackson 13.65
5. Chris Baillie 14.30
6. Mensah Elliott 14.39

400 Metres Hurdles
1. Chris Rawlinson 49.12
4. Matt Douglas 49.65
5. Anthony Borsumato 49.68

High Jump
1. Charles Austin USA 2.28
3= Ben Challenger 2.14
5. Danny Graham 2.14
6. Dalton Grant 2.09

Discus
1. Tony Washington USA 61.19
3. Bob Weir 59.14
4. Glen Smith 57.84
5. Emeka Udechuku 56.84

Javelin
1. Steve Backley 82.19
3. Mick Hill 79.90
4. Nick Nieland 79.46

4 x 100 Metres Relay
1. United States 38.90
2. Great Britain & NI 39.07
(Browne, Campbell, Devonish, Chambers)
Great Britain Juniors dsq
(Benjamin, Edgar, Lewis, Lewis-Francis)

WOMEN

100 Metres wind -3.3
1. Inger Miller USA 11.55
2. Joice Maduaka 11.82
4. Sam Davies 12.02
6. Zoe Wilson 12.25

400 Metres
1. Katharine Merry 50.99
4. Donna Fraser 52.17
6. Sinead Dudgeon 52.78

1500 Metres
1. Helen Pattinson 4:12.05
3. Kelly Caffel 4:14.91
5. Angela Newport 4:19.48

100 Metres Hurdles wind -1.2

1. Anjanette Kirkland USA 12.96
3. **Keri Maddox 13.24**
4. **Diane Allahgreen 13.45**
6. **Melanie Wilkins 13.74**
7. **Denise Lewis** gst **14.14**

High Jump

1. **Jo Jennings-Steele 1.88**
3. **Debbie Marti 1.85**
5. **Susan Jones 1.82**
6. **Denise Lewis** gst **1.78**

Shot

1. Connie Price-Smith USA 18.02
2. **Judy Oakes 17.81**
4. **Julie Dunkley 15.96**
6. **Denise Lewis** gst **15.50**
7. **Joanne Duncan 14.71**

4 x 100 Metres Relay

1. United States 44.56
2. **Great Britain & NI 44.65**

(Wilson, Anderson, Davies, Maduaka)

Match Result

1. United States 179.5
2. **Great Britain & NI 170.5**

SPAR EUROPEAN CUP SUPER-LEAGUE Gateshead 15 - 16 July 2000

The Britsh men scored an incredible win by half a point whilst missing eight first choice athletes. The women avoided relagation by their performance in the last event, the 4 x 400 relay. Darren Campbell's was probably the most dramatic win having only been brought into the race about 30 minutes before the start of his race. Victory was secured by a combination of good wins, inspired performances to achieve extra points and an extraordinary 110 hurdles race with 3 disqualified. The women's performances were disappointing with Lorraine Shaw's British record in the hammer by far the best.

MEN

100 Metres wind 2.3 (15 Jul)

1. **Darren Campbell 10.09w**
2. Roland Nemeth HUN 10.19w
3. Andrea Colombo ITA 10.23w
4. Aleksander Ryabov RUS 10.31w
5. Angelos Pavlakakis GRE 10.36w
6. Marc Blume GER 10.37w
7. David Patros FRA 10.44w
8. Matias Ghansah SWE 10.52w

200 Metres wind 0.0 (16 Jul)

1. **Christian Malcolm 20.45**
2. Alessandro Cavallaro ITA 20.48
3. Kostas Kenderis GRE 20.48
4. Christophe Cheval FRA 20.59
5. Miklos Gyulai HUN 20.97
6. Anton Galkin RUS 21.14
7. Johan Engberg SWE 21.18
8. Mathias Mertens GER 21.22

400 Metres (15 Jul)

1. **Jamie Baulch 46.64**
2. Alessandro Attene ITA 46.71
3. Jimisola Laursen SWE 46.93
4. Andrey Semyonov RUS 47.10
5. Anastasios Goussis GRE 47.12
6. Bruno Wavelet FRA 47.29
7. Zsolt Szeglet HUN 47.43
8. Lars Figura GER 47.90

800 Metres (16 Jul)

1. Mehdi Baala FRA 1:47.90
2. Nils Schumann GER 1:47.94
3. Balazs Koranyi HUN 1:48.52
4. Andrea Longo ITA 1:49.01
5. **Alasdair Donaldson 1:49.17**
6. Rizak Dirsche SWE 1:49.58
7. Panayiotis Stroubakos GRE 1:49.81
8. Boris Kaveshnikov RUS 1:50.24

1500 Metres (15 Jul)

1. Mehdi Baala FRA 3:41.75
2. **John Mayock 3:42.32**
3. Vyacheslav Shabunin RUS 3:42.44
4. Panayiotis Stroubakos GRE 3:42.95
5. Dirk Heinze GER 3:42.95
6. Andrea Abelli ITA 3.45.79
7. Balazs Tolgyesi HUN 3:49.40
8. Patrik Johansson SWE 3:49.79

3000 Metres (16 Jul)

1. Driss Maazouzi FRA 7:58.7
2. Vyacheslav Shabunin RUS 7:59.0
3. **Anthony Whiteman 8:01.0**
4. Jirka Arndt GER 8:02.2
5. Salvatore Vincenti ITA 8:04.8
6. Erik Sjoqvist SWE 8:16.6
7. Adonios Papantonis GRE 8:19.4
8. Balazs Csillag HUN 8:21.0

5000 Metres (15 Jul)

1. Mustapha Essaid FRA 13:47.44
2. Dmitriy Maksimov RUS 13:48.43
3. Sebastian Hallmann GER 13:49.95
4. Gennaro Di Napoli ITA 13:51.34
5. Adonios Papantonis GRE 14:01.01
6. **Kris Bowditch 14:03.10**
7. Claes Nyberg SWE 14:03.49
8. Imre Berkovics HUN 14:20.66

3000 Metres Steeplechase (16 Jul)

1. Bouabdallah Tahri FRA 8:27.28
2. Damian Kallabis GER 8:29.16
3. Giuseppe Maffei ITA 8:34.47
4. Georgios Giannelis GRE 8:34.80
5. Vladimir Pronin RUS 8:45.69
6. Henrik Skoog SWE 8:47.64
7. **Stuart Stokes 8:53.90**
8. Levente Timar HUN 9:07.19

110 Metres Hurdles wind 1.4 (16 Jul)

1. Falk Balzer GER 13.52
2. Emiliano Pizzoli ITA 13.54
3. Robert Kronberg SWE 13.67
4. **Damien Greaves 13.80**
5. Dimitrios Siatounis GRE 14.08

Jean-Marc Grava FRA dsq
Yevgeniy Pechyonkin RUS dsq
Levente Csillag HUN dsq

400 Metres Hurdles (15 Jul)

1. **Chris Rawlinson 48.84**
2. Ruslan Mashchenko RUS 49.19
3. Fabrizio Mori ITA 49.98
4. Periklis Iakovakis GRE 50.02
5. Tibor Bedi HUN 50.27
6. Jimmy Coco FRA 50.71
7. Steffen Kolb GER 50.82
8. Magnus Norberg SWE 52.18

High Jump (15 Jul)

1. Stefan Holm SWE 2.28
2. Wolfgang Kreissig GER 2.25

3= Sergey Klyugin RUS 2.20
3= Lambros Papakostas GRE 2.20
5. Mustapha Raifak FRA 2.20
6= Ivan Bernasconi ITA 2.15
6= Ben Challenger 2.15
Istvan Kovacs HUN nh

Pole Vault (16 Jul)

1. Yevgeniy Smiryagin RUS 5.85
2. Tim Lobinger GER 5.75
3. Patrik Kristiansson SWE 5.70
4. Giuseppe Gibilisco ITA 5.70
5. Romain Mesnil FRA 5.60
6. **Tim Thomas 5.40**
7. Marios Evangelou GRE 5.10
8. Mark Vaczi HUN 4.70

Long Jump (15 Jul)

1. Vitaliy Shkurlatov RUS 8.22
2. Kofi Amoah Prah GER 8.15w
3. Peter Haggstrom SWE 8.08w
4. Cheikh Toure FRA 7.96
5. Kostas Koukodimos GRE 7.64
6. Milko Campus ITA 7.62w
7. **Nathan Morgan 7.57**
8. Tamas Margl HUN 7.51

Triple Jump (15 Jul)

1. **Larry Achike 17.31w**
2. Fabrizio Donato ITA 17.17w
3. Stamatis Lenis GRE 17.01
4. Christian Olsson SWE 16.88w

5. Hrvoje Verzi GER 16.75w
6. Colomba Fofana FRA 16.69w
7. Sergey Kochkin RUS 16.48
8. Tibor Ordina HUN 15.96

Shot (15 Jul)
1. Paolo Dal Soglio ITA 19.99
2. Michael Mertens GER 19.71
3. Jimmy Nordin SWE 19.46
4. Szilard Kiss HUN 18.83
5. Yves Niare FRA 18.76
6. Vaios Tigas GRE 18.74
7. Sergey Lyakhov RUS 18.62
8. **Mark Edwards 17.59**

Discus (16 Jul)
1. Lars Riedel GER 63.30
2. Robert Fazekas HUN 62.15
3. Vitaliy Sidorov RUS 60.91
4. **Bob Weir 60.78**
5. Diego Fortuna ITA 59.81
6. Mattias Borrman SWE 57.95
7. Jean-Claude Retel FRA 57.10
8. Stefanos Konstas GRE 56.59

Hammer (16 Jul)
1. Christophe Epalle FRA 78.51
2. Alexandros Papadimitriou GRE 77.64
3. Karsten Kobs GER 77.55
4. Tibor Gecsek HUN 76.18
5. Sergey Kirmasov RUS 76.16
6. Bengt Johansson SWE 73.19
7. **Paul Head 67.75**

Loris Paoluzzi ITA nm

Javelin (16 Jul)
1. Sergey Makarov RUS 89.92
2. Kostas Gatsioudis GRE 84.56
3. Boris Henry GER 82.83
4. Patrik Boden SWE 82.39
5. **Mick Hill 80.24**
6. Gergely Horvath HUN 76.22
7. Laurent Dorique FRA 74.55
8. Armin Kerer ITA 72.43

4 x 100 Metres Relay (15 Jul)
1. **Great Britain & NI 38.41**

(Malcolm, Campbell, Devonish, Chambers)
2. Greece 38.67
3. Italy 39.17
4. Hungary 39.37
5. France 39.40
6. Germany 39.52
7. Sweden 39.82

Russia dnf

4 x 400 Metres Relay (16 Jul)
1. France 3:04.50
2. **Great Britain & NI 3:05.24**

(Knowles, Baldock, Rawlinson, Baulch)
3. Hungary 3:05.88
4. Greece 3:05.89
5. Italy 3:06.02
6. Sweden 3:06.35
7. Germany 3:07.15

Russia dsq

Match Results
1. **Great Britain & NI 101.5**
2. Germany 101
3. France 97
4. Italy 96.5
5. Russia 88.5
6. Greece 88.5
7. Sweden 75
8. Hungary 62

WOMEN

100 Metres wind 2.9 (15 Jul)
1. Ekaterini Thanou GRE 10.84w
2. Christine Arron FRA 11.02w
3. Manuela Levorato ITA 11.13w
4. Andrea Philipp GER 11.15w
5. Irina Pukha UKR 11.23w
6. Marina Trandenkova RUS 11.24w
7. **Marcia Richardson 11.47w**
8. Evelina Lisenco ROM 11.67w

200 Metres wind -0.3 (16 Jul)
1. Muriel Hurtis FRA 22.70
2. Natalya Voronova RUS 22.81
3. Andrea Philipp GER 22.88
4. Manuela Levorato ITA 22.89
5. Victoryna Fomenko UKR 23.03
6. **Donna Fraser 23.14**
7. Ekaterinin Koffa GRE 23.32
8. Evalina Lisenco ROM 23.96

400 Metres (15 Jul)
1. Svetlana Pospelova RUS 50.63
2. **Donna Fraser 51.78**
3. Uta Rohlander GER 52.17
4. Virna De Angeli ITA 52.85
5. Olena Rurak UKR 53.04
6. Chryssoula Goudenoudi GRE 53.20
7. Otilia Ruicu ROM 53.43
8. Marie Louise Bevis FRA 54.25

800 Metres (15 Jul)
1. Irina Mistyukevich RUS 2:02.52
2. Linda Kisabaka GER 2:03.88
3. Patricia Djate FRA 2:04.44
4. **Tanya Blake 2:04.71**
5. Patricia Spuri ITA 2:04.75
6. Simona Ionescu ROM 2:06.24
7. Marina Makarova UKR 2:08.15
8. Katerina Koutala GRE 2:09.76

1500 Metres (16 Jul)
1. **Helen Pattinson 4:12.05**
2. Yelena Zadorozhnaya RUS 4:12.20
3. Kristina da Fonseca GER 4:13.11
4. Fatima Yvelain FRA 4:13.97
5. Oksana Meltsayeva UKR 4:15.05
6. Elena Buhaianu ROM 4:15.70
7. Maria Tsirmba GRE 4:18.90
8. Elisabetta Artuso ITA 4:21.09

3000 Metres (15 Jul)
1. Gabriela Szabo ROM 8:43.33
2. Galina Bogomolova RUS 8:43.45
3. **Hayley Tullett 8:45.39**
4. Luminita Zaituc GER 9:03.20
5. Marina Dubrova UKR 9:03.90
6. Silvia Sommaggio ITA 9:06.75
7. Laurence Duquenoy FRA 9:12.76
8. Maria Protopappa GRE 9:21.68

5000 Metres (16 Jul)
1. Tatyana Tomashova RUS 14:53.00
2. Irina Mikitenko GER 14:54.30
3. Yamna Belkacem FRA 14:57.05
4. Maura Viceconte ITA 15:18.80
5. Elena Fidatov ROM 15:25.42
6. **Hayley Yelling 15:36.27**
7. Tatyana Byelovol UKR 15:37.32
8. Maria Protopappa GRE 16:12.24

100 Metres Hurdles wind 0.2 (16 Jul)
1. Linda Ferga FRA 12.93
2. Maya Shemchishina UKR 12.95
3. Yulia Graudyn RUS 13.08
4. **Keri Maddox 13.15**
5. Birgit Hamann GER 13.24
6. Viorica Tigau ROM 13.36
7. Christina Tambaki GRE 13.42
8. Margaret Macchiut ITA 13.92

400 Metres Hurdles (15 Jul)
1. Tatyana Tereshchuk UKR 54.68
2. Ulrike Urbansky GER 56.10
3. Monika Niederstatter ITA 56.33
4. **Keri Maddox 56.36**
5. Corinne Tafflet FRA 57.74
6. Yulia Nosova RUS 58.81
7. Chryssoula Goudenoudi GRE 60.02
8. Ana Maria Barbu ROM 64.04

High Jump (16 Jul)
1. Monica Dinescu ROM 1.93
2. Yulia Lyakhova RUS 1.92
3. **Jo Jennings-Steele 1.86**
4. Amewu Mensah GER 1.83
5. Stefania Cadamuro ITA 1.83
6. Tatyana Nikolayeva UKR 1.80
7. Marie Collonville FRA 1.80
8. Maria Chotokouridou GRE 1.75

Pole Vault (15 Jul)
1. Svetlana Feofanova RUS 4.35
2. Yvonne Buschbaum GER 4.30
3. Francesca Dolcini ITA 4.20
4. **Janine Whitlock 4.10**
5. Gabriela Mihalcea ROM 4.10
6. Maria Poissonnier FRA 4.00
7. Georgia Tsiligiri GRE 3.80

Yevhenia Savina UKR dns

Long Jump (16 Jul)
1. Olga Rublyova RUS 6.87
2. Olena Shekhovtsova UKR 6.79
3. Fiona May ITA 6.74w
4. Susan Tiedtke GER 6.46
5. Christina Athanasiou GRE 6.29w
6. Viorica Tigau ROM 6.19w
7. **Jade Johnson 6.15**
8. Marie Collonville FRA 6.12w

Triple Jump (16 Jul)

1.	Tatyana Lebedeva	RUS	14.98
2.	Olena Govorova	UKR	14.31
3.	Barbara Lah	ITA	13.86
4.	Adelina Gavrila	ROM	13.85
5.	Sandrine Domain	FRA	13.54
6.	Nicole Herschmann	GER	13.51
7.	**Michelle Griffith**		**13.50**
8.	Ioanna Kafetzi	GRE	13.40

Shot (16 Jul)

1.	Astrid Kumbernuss	GER	18.94
2.	Kaliopi Ouzouni	GRE	18.16
3.	**Judy Oakes**		**18.08**
4.	Lucica Ciobanu	ROM	17.57
5.	Laurence Manfredi	FRA	17.30
6.	Olena Dementiy	UKR	16.65
7.	Mara Rosolen	ITA	16.62
8.	Lyudmila Sechko	RUS	16.42

Discus (15 Jul)

1.	Nicoleta Grasu	ROM	63.35
2.	Ilke Wyludda	GER	62.45
3.	Anastasia Kelesidou	GRE	62.30
4.	Olga Chernyavskaya	RUS	62.20
5.	Nelina Robert-Michon	FRA	57.74
6.	Olena Antonova	UKR	57.69
7.	Agnese Maffeis	ITA	52.98
8.	**Shelley Drew**		**52.74**

Hammer (15 Jul)

1.	Mihaela Melinte	ROM	70.20
2.	Olga Kuzenkova	RUS	70.20
3.	Kirsten Munchow	GER	68.31
4.	Manuela Montebrun	FRA	67.73
5.	**Lorraine Shaw**		**67.44**
6.	Ester Balassini	ITA	65.13
7.	Irina Sekachova	UKR	64.44
8.	Evdokia Tsamoglou	GRE	62.25

Javelin (15 Jul)

1.	Ana Mirela Termure	ROM	63.23
2.	Tatyana Shikolenko	RUS	60.41
3.	Mirela Tzelili	GRE	57.84
4.	Claudia Coslovich	ITA	57.33
5.	Nadine Auzeil	FRA	57.21
6.	Karen Forkel	GER	52.89
7.	Olga Ivankova	UKR	51.58
8.	**Karen Martin**		**51.08**

4 x 100 Metres Relay (15 Jul)

1.	France	42.97
2.	Russia	43.38
3.	Germany	43.51
4.	Greece	43.76
5.	Ukraine	43.89
6.	Italy	44.00
7.	Romania	44.42
	Great Britain & NI	**dsq**

(Richardson, Anderson, Davies, Maduaka)

4 x 400 Metres Relay (16 Jul)

1.	Russia	3:25.50
2.	Germany	3:27.70
3.	**Great Britain & NI**	**3:28.12**
4.	Italy	3:32.23
5.	France	3:33.16
6.	Romania	3:34.65
	Greece	dsq
	Ukraine	dsq

(Danvers, Dudgeon, Curbishley, Fraser) (after 3rd place)

Match Result

1.	Russia	123
2.	Germany	110
3.	France	86
4.	Romania	80
5.	Italy	78
6.	**Great Britain & NI**	**77**
7.	Ukraine	70
8.	Greece	55

GB & NI v GER v FRA (U23) Liverpool 22 July 2000

This match was a mixture of very good and very mediocre performances. Daniel Caines recaptured his indoor form wth a new PB, and Alex Carter set a PB in coming second in the women's 800m. Susan Jones came close to the Olympic qualifying height of 1.93 in the high jump.

MEN

100 Metres wind 3.9

1.	**Jon Barbour**		**10.34w**
4.	**John Skeete**		**10.59w**

100 Metres B wind 0.5

1.	**Mark Findlay**		**10.63**

200 Metres wind 1.8

1.	**John Stewart**		**20.91**
6.	**Mark Findlay**		**21.52**

400 Metres

1.	**Daniel Caines**		**46.49**
2.	**David Naismith**		**47.00**

800 Metres

1.	**Chris Moss**		**1:48.68**
3.	**Neil Speaight**		**1:48.86**

1500 Metres

1.	Franek Haschke	GER	3:47.44
3.	**Angus Maclean**		**3:48.12**
4.	**James Thie**		**3:48.20**

3000 Metres

1.	Mario Krockert	GER	8:04.30
4.	**Stephen Hepples**		**8:15.40**
6.	**Oliver Laws**		**8:45.97**

110 Metres Hurdles wind -0.9

1.	Tylan Elmas	GER	14.00
4.	**Duncan Malins**		**14.32**
6.	**Liam Collins**		**14.39**

400 Metres Hurdles

1.	Naman Keita	FRA	50.63
2.	**Robert Lewis**		**51.29**
5.	**James Hillier**		**52.28**

3000 Metres Steeplechase

1.	Kevin Paulsen	FRA	8:47.95
2.	**Dave Mitchinson**		**8:48.93**
5.	**Iain Murdoch**		**8:56.61**

High Jump

1.	**Danny Graham**		**2.14**
3.	**Robert Mitchell**		**2.14**

Pole Vault

1.	Fabrice Fortin	FRA	5.35
5.	**Tom Richards**		**5.10**

Long Jump

1.	Salim Sdiri	FRA	7.79
4.	**Stuart Wells**		**7.41**
6.	**Dominique Richards**		**7.35**

Triple Jump

1.	**Tosin Oke**		**16.37w**
2.	**Nicholas Thomas**		**16.31**

Shot

1.	Ralf Bartels	GER	19.29
3.	**Emeka Udechuku**		**17.17**
5.	**David Readle**		**16.27**

Discus

1.	**Emeka Udechuku**		**56.30**
6.	**Andrew Rollins**		**45.46**

Hammer

1.	Markus Esser	GER	76.02
5.	**Graeme Allan**		**53.44**
6.	**Matthew Bell**		**47.58**

Javelin

1.	Bjorn Lange	GER	80.72
2.	**David Parker**		**72.84**
6.	**Dan Carter**		**66.42**

4 x 100 Metres Relay

1.	**Great Britain & NI**	**39.61**
2.	Germany	39.65
3.	France	40.28

(Malcolm, Barbour, Stewart, Skeete)

4 x 400 Metres Relay

1.	**Great Britain & NI**	**3:07.36**
2.	Germany	3:11.31
3.	France	3:11.34

WOMEN

100 Metres wind -0.2

1.	**Abiodun Oyepitan**		**11.58**
2.	**Amanda Forrester**		**11.59**

100 Metres B wind -1.2

1.	**Samantha Davies**		**11.63**

200 Metres wind 0.3

1.	Sabrina Mulrain	GER	23.01
2.	**Samantha Davies**		**23.31**
4.	**Melanie Purkiss**		**23.83**

400 Metres

1.	Claudia Marx	GER	52.60
2.	**Lesley Owusu**		**53.61**
6.	**Ruth Watson**		**56.54**

800 Metres

1.	Kerstin Werner	GER	2:04.86
2.	**Alex Carter**		**2:05.48**
5.	**Jennifer Ward**		**2:08.43**

1500 Metres

1.	**Kelly Caffel**		**4:13.23**
2.	**Ellen O'Hare**		**4:26.19**

3000 Metres

1.	Sabrina Mockenhaupt	GER	9:12.84
2.	**Gillian Palmer**		**9:18.64**
4.	**Karen Hind**		**9:45.39**

100 Metres Hurdles wind -0.3

1.	Joanna Bujak	FRA	13.42
4.	**Julie Pratt**		**13.56**
5.	**Sarah Claxton**		**13.67**

400 Metres Hurdles

1.	Anika Ahrens	GER	57.33
4.	**Tracey Duncan**		**58.22**
6.	**Rachael Kay**		**60.84**

High Jump

1.	**Susan Jones**		**1.90**
3.	**Michelle Dunkley**		**1.80**

Pole Vault

1.	Aurore Pignot	FRA	4.05
2.	**Tracey Bloomfield**		**3.80**
6.	**Becky Ridgley**		**3.20**

Long Jump

1.	Deborah Grapotte	FRA	6.28
5.	**Deborah Harrison**		**5.68**
6.	**Sarah Claxton**		**5.56**

Triple Jump

1.	Yasmina Soulhia	FRA	13.14
5.	**Leandra Polius**		**12.20**
6.	**Julia Johnson**		**11.54**

Shot

1.	Kathleen Kluge	GER	16.42
3.	**Julie Dunkley**		**15.96**
5.	**Christina Bennett**		**14.90**

Discus

1.	**Philippa Roles**		**55.39**
6.	**Rebecca Roles**		**44.33**

Hammer

1.	Susanne Keil	GER	61.27
2.	**Suzanne Roberts**		**57.07**
4.	**Zoe Derham**		**53.26**

Javelin

1.	Bina Ramesh	FRA	54.10
5.	**Chloe Cozens**		**50.49**
6.	**Jennifer Kemp**		**47.39**

5000 Metres Walk

1.	Stephanie Panzig	GER	23:30.50
4.	**Sally Warren**		**25:11.33**
5.	**Nichola Huckerby**		**25:33.09**

4 x 100 Metres Relay

1.	Germany	44.58
2.	Guest Team	45.46
3.	France	45.48
	Great Britain & NI	**dnf**

4 x 400 Metres Relay

1.	Germany	3:36.83
2.	France	3:43.65
3.	**Great Britain & NI**	**3:45.19**

Match Result

1.	Germany	257
2.	**Great Britain & NI**	**235**
3.	France	235

AAA CHAMPIONSHIPS Birmingham 11 - 13 August 2000
Including Norwich Union Olympic Trials

Some top athletes chose not to compete and the general level of performances was not of the highest quality. Steve Backley produced the best performance for the men and Paula Radcliffe had a good 'training' run. The men's sprints were strong with Mark Lewis-Franicis helping the selectors by sticking to his season's plan of making the World Juniors his focus for the year. Kelly Holmes showed some nice form and a pointer for the Olympics.

MEN

100 Metres wind -0.8 (12 Aug)

1.	Dwain Chambers	10.11
2.	Darren Campbell	10.12
3.	Mark Lewis-Francis	10.24
4.	Jason Gardener	10.29
5.	Ian Mackie	10.38
6.	Allyn Condon	10.44
7.	Doug Bignall	10.44
8.	Curtis Browne	10.69

200 Metres wind -1.2 (13 Aug)

1.	Darren Campbell	20.49
2.	Christian Malcolm	20.59
3.	Marlon Devonish	20.78
4.	Ian Mackie	20.92
5.	Tim Benjamin	20.96
6.	Marcus Adam	21.13
7.	Allyn Condon	21.50
	Dwain Chambers	dns

400 Metres (13 Aug)

1.	Mark Richardson	45.55
2.	Sean Baldock	45.71
3.	Jamie Baulch	46.07
4.	Daniel Caines	46.45
5.	Jared Deacon	46.60
6.	Solomon Wariso	46.95
7.	Richard Knowles	47.06
8.	Cori Henry	47.36

800 Metres (13 Aug)

1.	James McIlroy	1:50.08
2.	Andy Hart	1:50.09
3.	Alasdair Donaldson	1:50.57
4.	Chris Moss	1:50.84
5.	Neil Speaight	1:50.88
6.	Neil Dougal	1:51.17
7.	James Mayo	1:58.00
	Justin Swift-Smith	dnf

1500 Metres (13 Aug)

1.	John Mayock	3:45.29
2.	Tony Whiteman	3:45.57
3.	John McCallum	3:46.14
4.	Andrew Graffin	3:46.80
5.	Kevin McKay	3:47.16
6.	James Thie	3:47.23
7.	Richard Ashe	3:47.79
8.	Joseph Mills	3:48.67

5000 Metres (13 Aug)

1.	Andres Jones	13:45.86
2.	Michael Openshaw	13:49.34
3.	Mark Hudspith	13:52.74
4.	Ian Hudspith	13:55.54
5.	John Nuttall	13:56.35
6.	Julian Moorehouse	14:00.03
7.	Kris Bowditch	14:03.45
8.	Adrian Passey	14:04.53

10000 Metres (Watford 22 Jul)

	Kameil Maase	NED	27:56.94
1.	Andres Jones		28:00.50
2.	Rob Denmark		28:03.31
3.	Mark Steinle		28:04.48
	Michael Aish	NZL	28:08.46
	Hendrick Raamala	RSA	28:13.44
	Michael Buchleitner	AUT	28:18.58
	Seamus Power	IRE	28:23.11

3000 Metres Steeplechase (13 Aug)

1.	Christian Stephenson	8:28.21
2.	Justin Chaston	8:32.21
3.	Craig Wheeler	8:39.72
4.	Charlie Low	8:41.43
5.	Ben Whitby	8:44.68
6.	Dave Mitchinson	8:45.06
7.	Alastair O'Connor	8:49.03
8.	Donald Naylor	8:51.23

110 Metres Hurdles wind -2.3 (13 Aug)

1.	Colin Jackson	13.54
2.	Tony Jarrett	13.78
3.	Damien Greaves	13.85
4.	Mensah Elliott	14.10
5.	Ncil Owen	14.33
6.	Duncan Malins	14.42
7.	Liam Collins	14.52
8.	Chris Baillie	14.73

400 Metres Hurdles (13 Aug)

1.	Chris Rawlinson	48.95
2.	Anthony Borsumato	49.71
3.	Matthew Douglas	49.89
4.	Paul Hibbert	50.95
5.	Gary Jennings	51.08
6.	James Hillier	51.49
7.	Paul Gray	52.47
8.	Noel Levy	52.76

High Jump (13 Aug)

1.	Ben Challenger		2.22
2.	Brendan Reilly	IRE	2.22
3.	Stuart Ohrland		2.17
4=	Danny Graham		2.12
4=	Robert Mitchell		2.12
6.	James Brierley		2.12
7.	Dan Turner		2.12
8.	Tyron Peacock	RSA	2.12

Pole Vault (13 Aug)

1.	Kevin Hughes	5.50
2.	Paul Williamson	5.40
3.	Ben Flint	5.30
4.	Matt Belsham	5.20
5.	Tim Thomas	5.20
6.	Ian Tullett	5.00
7.	Mark Davis	5.00
8=	Christian North	4.80
8=	Matthew Weaver	4.80

Long Jump (12 Aug)

1.	George Audu	7.89
2.	Darren Ritchie	7.84
3.	Darren Thompson	7.48
4.	Julian Flynn	7.33
5.	Christopher Tomlinson	7.23
6.	Anthony Malcolm	7.08
7.	Dominique Richards	7.03
8.	Levi Edwards	6.89

Triple Jump (13 Aug)

1.	Phillips Idowu	16.87
2.	Larry Achike	16.83
3.	Francis Agyepong	16.40
4.	Julian Golley	16.38
5.	Tayo Erogbogbo	15.97
6.	Tosin Oke	15.87
7.	Tosi Fasinro	15.70
8.	Nicholas Thomas	15.47

Shot (13 Aug)

1.	Steph Hayward	18.24
2.	Emeka Udechuku	17.47
3.	Mark Proctor	17.21
4.	Lee Newman	17.03
5.	David Condon	17.03
6.	Scott Rider	16.72
7.	Iain McMullan	16.20
8.	Bruce Robb	15.88

Discus (12 Aug)

1.	Bob Weir	62.13
2.	Glen Smith	60.84
3.	Emeka Udechuku	59.58
4.	Perriss Wilkins	55.97
5.	Lee Newman	55.44
6.	Abi Ekoku	53.28
7.	Bruce Robb	52.30
8.	Scott Rider	51.65

Hammer (13 Aug)

1.	Mick Jones	71.51
2.	Paul Head	69.63
3.	John Pearson	67.22
4.	Mike Floyd	65.38
5.	Simon Bown	63.81
6.	Craig Ellams	62.32
7.	Shane Peacock	62.14
8.	Chris Howe	60.72

Javelin (13 Aug)

1.	Steve Backley	86.70
2.	Nick Nieland	85.09
3.	Mick Hill	80.28
4.	Mark Roberson	76.10
5.	Stuart Faben	73.60
6.	David Parker	72.31
7.	Dan Carter	70.11
8.	Neil McLellan	65.49

10000 Metres Walk (12 Aug)

1.	Matthew Hales	43:12.85
2.	Steve Partington	43:30.50
3.	Jamie O'Rawe	43:54.49
4.	Chris Cheeseman	44:29.51
5.	Andrew Parker	47:47.95
6.	Andrew Goudie	48:42.87
7.	Brian Adams	52:43.05
8.	Nathan Adams	53:55.17

Decathlon (Stoke 29-30 Jul)

1.	Alex Kruger	6975
2.	Mark Sweeney	6652
3.	Bill Wynn	6563
4.	John Heanley	6476
5.	Richard Czernik	6113
6.	Brian Hughes	6105

WOMEN

100 Metres wind -2.2 (12 Aug)

1.	Marcia Richardson		11.41
2.	Joice Maduaka		11.47
3.	Sam Davies		11.47
4.	Sarah Reilly	IRE	11.50
5.	Donita Benjamin		11.56
6.	Christine Bloomfield		11.67
7.	Catherine Murphy		11.80
8.	Ellena Ruddock		11.88

200 Metres wind -1.0 (13 Aug)

1.	Sarah Wilhelmy		23.39
2.	Sam Davies		23.42
3.	Shani Anderson		23.53
4.	Joice Maduaka		23.67
5.	Sarah Reilly	IRE	23.73
6.	Catherine Murphy		23.81
7.	Christine Bloomfield		23.99
8.	Susan Williams		24.39

400 Metres (13 Aug)

1.	Donna Fraser	50.94
2.	Allison Curbishley	51.50
3.	Helen Frost	53.33
4.	Louise Whitehead	53.68
5.	Lesley Owusu	54.11
6.	Michelle Pierre	54.20
7.	Linda Staines	54.33
8.	Jennifer Stoute	56.97

800 Metres (13 Aug)

1.	Kelly Holmes	2:02.08
2.	Claire Raven	2:05.12
3.	Jo Fenn	2:05.48
4.	Emma Davies	2:06.23
5.	Jennifer Ward	2:06.48
6.	Rachel Newcombe	2:06.65
7.	Alex Carter	2:07.36
8.	Sarah Knights	2:07.73

1500 Metres (13 Aug)

1.	Hayley Tullett	4:06.44
2.	Helen Pattinson	4:11.40
3.	Kelly Caffel	4:15.29
4.	Amanda Parkinson	4:19.68
5.	Susan Scott	4:21.15
6.	Emma Ward	4:21.86
7.	Clare Martin	4:22.52
8.	Sue Lamb	4:22.87

5000 Metres (13 Aug)

1.	Paula Radcliffe	15:05.48
2.	Joanne Pavey	15:21.15
3.	Hayley Yelling	15:50.41
4.	Gillian Palmer	15:56.58
5.	Catherine Berry	16:00.97
6.	Tara Krzywicki	16:02.48
7.	Lucy Wright	16:02.97
8.	Deborah Sullivan	16:07.51

10000 Metres (Watford 22 Jul)

	Elana Meyer	RSA	31:41.1
1.	Birhan Dagne		32:30.4
	Rosemary Ryan	IRE	32:31.9
2.	Sarah Young-Wilkinson		32:34.7
3.	Hayley Yelling		32:52.5
	Bente Landoy	NOR	32:57.3
	Ann Keenan-Buckley	IRE	33:05.5
4.	Liz Yelling		33:07.9

100 Metres Hurdles wind -2.1 (12 Aug)

1.	Diane Allahgreen	13.24
2.	Melanie Wilkins	13.35
3.	Julie Pratt	13.57
4.	Rachel King	13.58
5.	Bianca Liston	13.58
6.	Clova Court	13.81
7.	Liz Fairs	13.86
8.	Kerry Jury	14.27

400 Metres Hurdles (12 Aug)

1.	Keri Maddox	55.22
2.	Natasha Danvers	55.34
3.	Sinead Dudgeon	55.74
4.	Tracey Duncan	58.27
5.	Katie Jones	58.83
6.	Jenny Matthews	59.14
7.	Celia Brown	61.01
8.	Nusrat Ceesay	61.65

High Jump (12 Aug)

1.	Jo Jennings-Steele	1.89
2.	Michelle Dunkley	1.89
3.	Lee McConnell	1.86
4.	Susan Jones	1.86
5.	Debbie Marti	1.78
6.	Dahlia Mikneviciute	1.78
7.	Julie Crane	1.78
8.	Gillian Black	1.78

Pole Vault (12 Aug)

1.	Janine Whitlock	4.10
2.	Irie Hill	4.00
3.	Alison Davies	4.00
4=	Tracey Bloomfield	3.80
4=	Lucy Webber	3.80
6.	Rhian Clarke	3.80
7.	Alison Murray-Jessee	3.60
8.	Liz Hughes	3.60

Long Jump (13 Aug)

1.	Jo Wise	6.44
2.	Jade Johnson	6.34
3.	Donita Benjamin	6.28w
4.	Sarah Claxton	6.26
5.	Ann Danson	6.12
6.	Julie Hollman	6.09
7.	Joyce Hepher	5.95
8.	Kimberley Rothman	5.90

Triple Jump (12 Aug)

1.	Michelle Griffith	13.67
2.	Liz Patrick	12.79
3.	Connie Henry	12.75
4.	Judie Hurst	12.54
5.	Deborah Rowe	12.51
6.	Katie Evans	12.34
7.	Caroline Stead	12.25
8.	Rebecca White	12.23

Shot (12 Aug)

1.	Judy Oakes		17.91
2.	Julie Dunkley		16.40
3.	Joanne Duncan		16.00
4.	Maggie Lynes		14.64
5.	Christina Bennet		14.39
6.	Eva Massey	IRE	14.35
7.	Vicki Foster		14.27
8.	Eleanor Gatrell		13.82

Discus (13 Aug)

1.	Shelley Drew	59.03
2.	Philippa Roles	54.74
3.	Emma Merry	53.00
4.	Debbie Callaway	50.59
5.	Nicola Talbot	48.43
6.	Alison Grey	47.79
7.	Vicki Foster	46.12
8.	Susan Backhouse	44.09

Hammer (12 Aug)

1.	Lorraine Shaw	66.85
2.	Lynn Sprules	62.48
3.	Liz Pidgeon	59.95
4.	Suzanne Roberts	58.11
5.	Rachael Beverley	55.25
6.	Zoe Derham	54.49
7.	Diana Holden	53.42
8.	Sarah Moore	53.39

Javelin (12 Aug)

1.	Kelly Morgan	58.45
2.	Karen Martin	57.75
3.	Shelley Holroyd	51.96
4.	Goldie Sayers	51.11
5.	Jenny Kemp	48.73
6.	Sharon Gibson	47.76
7.	Kirsty Morrison	46.30
8.	Clova Court	46.02

10000 Metres Walk (13 Aug)

1.	Lisa Kehler	45:09.57
2.	Nicola Huckerby	54:53.35
3.	Kath Horwill	55:59.54
4.	Jo Hesketh	56:34.13

Heptathlon (Stoke 29-30 Jul)

1.	Julie Hollman	5560
2.	Kelly Sotherton	5388
3.	Anne Hollman	5028
4.	Sarah Still	4903

FRA v GB & NI v GER (U23 & U20) Combined Events

Val-de-Reuil, FRA 12 - 13 August 2000

MEN (U23)

1.	Stephan Zeyen	GER	7830
4.	**Paul Jones**		**6948**
8.	**Anthony Sawyer**		**6622**
9.	**John Heanley**		**6563**
10.	**Brendan McConville**		**5763**

Team Result

1.	Germany	21816
3.	**Great Britain & NI**	**20133**

MEN (U20)

1.	Dennis Leyckes	GER	7802
6.	**John Holtby**		**6471**
7.	**Jamie Russell**		**6388**
8.	**Adrian Hemery**		**6301**
	Martin Taylor		**dnf**

Team Result

1.	Germany	21155
3.	**Great Britain & NI**	**19160**

WOMEN (U23)

1.	Gabriela Kouassi	FRA	5464
4.	**Chloe Cozens**		**5205**
6.	**Danielle Freeman**		**5014**
11.	**Kirsty Roger**		**3713**
	Katherine Livesey		**dnf**

Team Result

1.	Germany	15798
3.	**Great Britain & NI**	**13932**

WOMEN (U20)

1.	Marene Freisen	GER	5555
7.	**Laura Redmond**		**4911**
8.	**Paula Hendriks**		**4906**
10.	**Lara Carty**		**4538**
	Fiona Harrison		**dnf**

Team Result

1.	Germany	16245
3.	**Great Britain & NI**	**14355**

IAU 100K World Challenge

Winschoten, HOL 9 September 2000

MEN

1.	Pascal Fetizon	FRA	6:23:15
2.	Dmitriy Radiuchenko	RUS	6:29:13
3.	Oleg Kharitonov	RUS	6:29:29
40.	**Steve Moore**		**7:20:55**
41.	**Ian Anderson**		**7:21:51**
43.	**Chris Finill**		**7:22:50**
60.	**Don Ritchie**		**7:54:45**
98.	**Brian Davidson**		**8:58:11**

WOMEN

1.	Edit Berces	HUN	7:25:21
2.	Elvira Kolpakova	RUS	7:35:01
3.	Magali Maggiolini	FRA	7:46:05
20.	**Hilary Walker**		**9:04:29**
23.	**Sharon Gayter**		**9:44:19**

FRA v GB & NI 'B' INTERNATIONAL Vittel, FRA 2 September 2000

Both Susan Jones and Michelle Dunkley reached the Olympic standard in the women's high jump, but too late for selection.

MEN

100 Metres wind -0.3
1. Jonathan Barbour 10.60
4. Curtis Browne 10.66
6. Jason Fergus 10.72

200 Metres wind 0.3
1. Jonathan Barbour 21.18
3. John Stewart 21.25
5. Brendon Ghent 21.52

400 Metres
1. David Naismith 46.65
2. Richard Knowles 46.78
4. Adam Buckley 47.34

800 Metres
1. Neil Speaight 1:51.42
2. Chris Moss 1:51.55
5. Justin Swift-Smith 1:52.82

1500 Metres
1. Fouad Chouki FRA 3:48.74
2. Michael East 3:48.76
5. Chris Bolt 3:51.68
6. Richard Ashe 3:52.29

3000 Metres
1. Michael Openshaw 8:17.02
2. Julian Moorehouse 8:25.00
4. Sam Haughian 8:26.43

110 Metres Hurdles wind 0.8
1. Eric Ciolfi FRA 13.5
2. Mensah Elliott 13.7
3. Neil Owen 13.8
6. Liam Collins 14.4

400 Metres Hurdles
1. Paul Hibbert 50.52
2. Du'aine Thorne-Ladejo 50.97
6. Steve Surety 52.50

3000 Metres Steeplechase
1. Stephane Desaulty FRA 8:54.79
2. Charlie Low 8:55.93
5. Craig Wheeler 9:02.03
6. Dave Mitchinson 9:09.06

High Jump
1. Stuart Ohrland 2.17
3. James Brierley 2.10
5= Danny Graham 2.05

Pole Vault
1. Gerald Baudouin FRA 5.15
Ben Flint nh
Matt Belsham nh
Paul Williamson nh

Long Jump
1. Nathan Morgan 7.90
3. Chris Davidson 7.46
4. Julian Flynn 7.38

Triple Jump
1. Jimmy Gabriel FRA 16.21
2. Tosin Oke 16.17w
5. Nick Thomas 15.47
6. Tayo Erogbogbo 15.05

Shot
1. Emeka Udechuku 17.52
5. David Condon 16.63
6. Paul Reed 14.42

Discus
1. Emeka Udechuku 56.99
5. Paul Reed 48.87

Hammer
1. Raphael Piolanti FRA 75.12
3. Mick Jones 74.37
5. Paul Head 69.46
6. Matthew Bell 59.63

Javelin
1. David Brisseault FRA 75.23
2. Mark Roberson 74.50
3. David Parker 71.42
5. Stuart Fabem 69.38

5000 Metres Walk
1. Pascal Servanty FRA 19:31.97
3. Matthew Hales 20:06.66
5. Dominic King 22:22.45
6. Andrew Goudie 22:39.26

4 x 100 Metres Relay
1. Great Britain & NI 40.26
(Fergus, Browne, Stewart, Barbour)

4 x 400 Metres Relay
1. Great Britain & NI 3:08.93
(Naismith, Knowles, Buckley, Ladejo)

Match Result Men
1. France 202
2. Great Britain & NI 188

WOMEN

100 Metres wind 1.0
1. Donita Benjamin 11.52
2. Christine Bloomfield 11.59
5. Amanda Forrester 11.72

200 Metres wind 0.8
1. Christine Bloomfield 23.67
3. Melanie Purkiss 24.15
5. Emma Whitter 24.58

400 Metres
1. Marie Louise Bevis FRA 53.49
3. Karen Gear 54.46
5. Ruth Watson 58.13

800 Metres
1. Tanya Blake 2:05.93
3. Claire Raven 2:07.48
6. Lucy Chaffe 2:11.80

1500 Metres
1. Latifa Essarokh FRA 4:21.32
2. Angela Newport 4:21.69
3. Amanda Parkinson 4:22.40

3000 Metres
1. Liz Yelling 9:24.95
3. Tara Krzywicki 9:36.25
6. Karen Hind 9:53.72

100 Metres Hurdles wind 0.6
1. Reina Okori FRA 13.28
4. Melanie Wilkins 13.42
5. Julie Pratt 13.65
6. Bianca Liston 14.01

400 Metres Hurdles
1. Olivia Abderrhamanne FRA 57.50
2. Katie Jones 58.92
5. Tracey Duncan 59.45
6. Rachel Kay 63.30

High Jump
1. Susan Jones 1.93
2. Michelle Dunkley 1.93
3. Jo Jennings-Steele 1.85

Pole Vault
1= Emilie Becot FRA 3.80
1= Aurore Pignot FRA 3.80
4. Alison Davies 3.70
5. Tracey Bloomfield 3.70

Long Jump
1. Ann Danson 6.07
2. Donita Benjamin 6.04
3. Sarah Claxton 6.03

Triple Jump
1. Michelle Griffiths 13.49w
4. Liz Patrick 12.50
6. Leandra Polius 11.90

Shot
1. Natalia Lisovskaya FRA 17.24
2. Julie Dunkley 15.99
4. Joanne Duncan 14.97
6. Maggie Lynes 14.26

Discus
1. Isabelle Devaluez FRA 53.77
3. Debbie Callaway 48.17
5. Tracey Axten 47.04
6. Joanne Bradley 41.46

Hammer
1. Florence Ezeh FRA 64.74
2. Liz Pidgeon 61.26
3. Suzanne Roberts 56.52
5. Zoe Derham 54.65

Javelin
1. Kelly Morgan 54.96
2. Shelley Holroyd 51.61
4. Jennifer Kemp 48.69

3000 Metres Walk
1. Tatiana Boulanger FRA 13:46.91
3. Catherine Charnock 13:58.96
4. Niobe Menendez 14:08.52
6. Sally Warren 14:54.39

4 x 100 Metres Relay
1. France 44.35
2. Great Britain & NI 44.93
(Forrester, Purkiss, Benjamin, Bloomfield)

4 x 400 Metres Relay
1. France 3:39.99
2. Great Britain & NI 3:48.50
(Gear, Watson, ??)

Match Result Women
1. France 196
2. Great Britain & NI 176

ESP v GB & NI (U23) Getafe, SPA 9 September 2000

Unusually, most of the best performances were set in the field events. See Nathan Morgan, Emeka Udechuku, David Parker and Suzanne Roberts below.

MEN

100 Metres wind -0.3
1. Jon Barbour 10.36
4. Marlon Dickson 10.74
7. Nick Thomas 10.89

200 Metres wind -0.8
1. Jon Barbour 20.79
2. John Stewart 20.83

400 Metres
1. David Naismith 46.47
3. Adam Buckley 47.04
4. Matthew Elias 47.25

800 Metres
1. Chris Moss 1:50.49
2. Neil Speaight 1:50.52

1500 Metres
1. Michael East 3:44.72
3. Angus Maclean 3:45.85

3000 Metres
1. Pablo Villalobos ESP 8:34.16
3. James Thie 8:37.87
4. Stephen Hepples 8:48.24

5000 Metres
1. Ivan Hierro ESP 14:23.63
3. Sam Haughian 14:26.96
4. Oliver Laws 15:28.82

110 Metres Hurdles wind -0.6
1. Felix Belmar ESP 14.36
2. Duncan Malins 14.46
4. Robert Lewis 15.51

400 Metres Hurdles
1. Constantino Navarro ESP 51.63
2. James Hillier 51.99
3. Robert Lewis 52.90

3000 Metres Steeplechase
1. Antonio Martinez ESP 8:49.78
3. David Mitchinson 9:11.40
4. Simon Delroy 9:33.24

High Jump
1. David Antona ESP 2.17
2. Robert Mitchell 2.14
3. Danny Graham 2.10

Pole Vault
1. Alberto Martinez ESP 5.30
2. Ben Flint 5.15
4. Tom Richards 5.10

Long Jump
1. Nathan Morgan 8.00
4. Darren Thompson 7.25

Triple Jump
1. Nick Thomas 15.89
2. Tosin Oke 15.85

Shot
1. Iker Sukia ESP 18.46
2. Emeka Udechuku 18.10
4. Iain McMullen 15.97

Discus
1. Emeka Udechuku 61.91
4. David Lovett 47.43

Hammer
1. Moises Campeny ESP 69.34
2. Matthew Bell 60.02
4. Chris Walsh 58.77

Javelin
1. David Parker 76.31
2. Dan Carter 72.48

4 x 100 Metres Relay
1. Great Britain & NI 39.86
(Thomas, Morgan, Stewart, Barbour)

4 x 400 Metres Relay
1. Great Britain & NI 3:08.02
(Buckley, Elias, Lewis, Naismith)

Match Result Men
1. Great Britain & NI 113
2. Spain 99

WOMEN

100 Metres wind 0.0
1. Amanda Forrester 11.55
2. Emma Whitter 11.86

200 Metres wind -2.4
1. Melanie Purkiss 24.03
2. Helen Roscoe 24.42

400 Metres
1. Karen Gear 54.48
2. Leigh Newton 55.78
3. Ruth Watson 56.61

800 Metres
1. Emma Davies 2:04.54
2. Jennifer Ward 2:05.92

1500 Metres
1. Kelly Caffel 4:21.59
2. Alex Carter 4:25.17

3000 Metres
1. Karen Hind 9:37.43
5. Sonia Thomas 9:59.97

5000 Metres
1. Alexandra Aguilar ESP 16:36.19
2. Amy Waterlow 16:54.04
Henrietta Freeman dnf

100 Metres Hurdles wind -1.2
1. Julie Pratt 13.49
3. Bianca Liston 13.85

400 Metres Hurdles
1. Cicely Hall 62.13
Rachel Kay dnf

High Jump
1. Michelle Dunkley 1.89
2. Susan Jones 1.86
3. Lee McConnell 1.83

Pole Vault
1. Vanesa Rios ESP 4.01
2. Tracey Bloomfield 3.60
4. Helen Roscoe 3.50

Long Jump
1. Sarah Claxton 6.23
4. Debbie Harrison 5.74

Triple Jump
1. Rebeca Azcona ESP 12.69
4. Rebecca White 12.00
5. Leandra Polius 11.61

Shot
1. Julie Dunkley 16.19
4. Christina Bennett 14.64

Discus
1. Philippa Roles 55.44
4. Joanna Bradley 45.68

Hammer
1. Suzanne Roberts 58.83
2. Rachel Beverley 56.40
4. Christina Bennett 50.05

Javelin
1. Mercedes Chilla ESP 57.00
2. Kelly Morgan 55.44
3. Chloe Cozens 50.39
5. Jennifer Kemp 43.29

4 x 100 Metres Relay

1.	**Great Britain & NI**	45.27

(Forrester, Purkiss, Roscoe, Whitter)

4 x 400 Metres Relay

1.	**Great Britain & NI**	**3:41.62**

(Watson, Newton, McConnell, Gear)

Match Result Women

1.	**Great Britain & NI**	**116**
2.	Spain	83

OLYMPIC GAMES

Sydney, AUS 22 September - 1 October 2000

2 Gold, 2 Silver and 2 Bronze was a good result. Jonathan Edwards secured his gold after some seasons missing the top prize and Denise Lewis was magnificent in winning carrying an injury. Darren Campbell was second in a strange 200m and Steve Backley held an early lead in the javelin with his best throw for years. Kelly Holmes made a dramatic return from injury and Katharine Merry secured a medal in the race of the games. There were also 5 close fourth places, with both Dean Macey and Paula Radcliffe showing great resolve even in defeat. Jon Brown, Karl Keska and Jo Pavey returned some pride to British distance running. The men's triple jump showed 3 British athletes in the top six - not a regular occurance in a field event. The one disappointment was the men's 4 x 100 metres relay where a medal looked to be available from the previous performances of the team.

MEN

100 Metres wind -0.3 (23 Sep)

1.	Maurice Greene	USA	9.87
2.	Ato Boldon	TRI	9.99
3.	Obadele Thompson	BAR	10.04
4.	**Dwain Chambers**		**10.08**
5.	Jon Drummond	USA	10.09
6.	**Darren Campbell**		**10.13**
7.	Kim Collins	STK	10.17
	Abdul Aziz Zakari	GHA	dnf
4q2	**Jason Gardener**		**10.27**

200 Metres wind -0.6 (28 Sep)

1.	Konstadinos Kederis	GRE	20.09
2.	**Darren Campbell**		**21.14**
3.	Ato Boldon	TRI	20.20
4.	Obadele Thompson	BAR	20.20
5.	**Christian Malcolm**		**20.23**
6.	Claudinei da Silva	BRA	20.28
7.	Coby Miller	USA	20.35
8.	John Capel	USA	20.49
7q4	**Marlon Devonish**		**20.82**

400 Metres (25 Sep)

1.	Michael Johnson	USA	43.84
2.	Alvin Harrison	USA	44.40
3.	Greg Haughton	JAM	44.70
4.	Sanderlei Parrela	BAR	45.01
5.	Robert Mackowiak	POL	45.14
6.	Hendrik Mokganyetsi	RSA	45.26
7.	Antonio Pettigrew	USA	45.42
8.	Danny McFarlane	JAM	45.55
5s2	**Daniel Caines**		**45.55**
5h7	**Sean Baldock**		**46.45**
7h5	**Jamie Baulch**		**46.52**

800 Metres (27 Sep)

1.	Nils Schumann	GER	1:45.08
2.	Wilson Kipketer	DEN	1:45.14
3.	Djabir Said-Guerni	ALG	1:45.16
4.	Hezekiel Sepeng	RSA	1:45.29
5.	Andre Bucher	SUI	1:45.40
6.	Yuriy Borzakovskiy	RUS	1:45.83
7.	Glody Dobe	BOT	1:46.24
	Andrea Longo	ITA	dsq
6s1	**James McIlroy**		**1:46.39**
6h2	**Andy Hart**		**1:48.78**

1500 Metres (29 Sep)

1.	Noah Ngeny	KEN	3:32.07
2.	Hicham El Guerrouj	MAR	3:32.32
3.	Bernard Lagat	KEN	3:32.44
4.	Mehdi Baala	FRA	3:34.14
5.	Kevin Sullivan	CAN	3:35.50
6.	Daniel Zegeye	ETH	3:36.78
7.	Andres Diaz	ESP	3:37.27
8.	Juan Carlos Higuero	ESP	3:38.91
9.	**John Mayock**		**3:39.41**
10s1	**Andrew Graffin**		**3:42.72**
h2	**Anthony Whiteman**		**dnf**

5000 Metres (25 Sep)

1.	Million Wolde	ETH	13:35.49
2.	Ali Saidi-Sief	ALG	13:36.20
3.	Brahim Lahlafi	MAR	13:36.47
4.	Fita Bayissa	ETH	13:37.03
5.	David Chelule	KEN	13:37.13
6.	Dagne Alemu	ETH	13:37.17
7.	Sergey Lebed	UKR	13:37.80
8.	Jirka Arndt	GER	13:38.57
15s1	**Kris Bowditch**		**14:08.92**

10000 Metres (25 Sep)

1.	Haile Gebrselassie	ETH	27:18.20
2.	Paul Tergat	KEN	27:18.29
3.	Assefa Mezgebu	ETH	27:19.75
4.	Patrick Ivuti	KEN	27:20.44
5.	John Korir	KEN	27:24.75
6.	Said Berioui	MAR	27:37.83
7.	Toshinari Takaoka	JPN	27:40.44
8.	**Karl Keska**		**27:44.09**
9s1	**Andres Jones**		**28:11.20**
13s1	**Rob Denmark**		**28:43.74**

Marathon (1 Oct)

1.	Gezahegne Abera	ETH	2:10:11
2.	Eric Wainaina	KEN	2:10:31
3.	Tesfaye Tola	ETH	2:11:10
4.	**Jon Brown**		**2:11:17**
5.	Giacomo Leone	ITA	2:12:14
6.	Martin Fiz	ESP	2:13:06
7.	Abdelkader El Mouaziz	MAR	2:13:49
8.	Mohamed Ouaadi	FRA	2:14:04
19.	**Keith Cullen**		**2:16:59**
56.	**Mark Steinle**		**2:24:42**

3000 Metres Steeplechase (29 Sep)

1.	Reuben Kosgei	KEN	8:21.43
2.	Wilson Boit Kipketer	KEN	8:21.77
3.	Ali Ezzine	MAR	8:22.15
4.	Bernard Barmasai	KEN	8:22.23
5.	Luis Martin	ESP	8:22.75
6.	Elisio Martin	ESP	8:23.00
7.	Brahim Boulami	MAR	8:24.32
8.	Gunther Weidlinger	AUT	8:26.70
7s3	**Justin Chaston**		**8:31.01**
10s1	**Christian Stephenson**		**8:46.66**

110 Metres Hurdles wind 0.6 (25 Sep)

1.	Anier Garcia	CUB	13.00
2.	Terrence Trammell	USA	13.16
3.	Mark Crear	USA	13.22
4.	Allen Johnson	USA	13.23
5.	**Colin Jackson**		**13.28**
6.	Florian Schwarthoff	GER	13.42
7.	Dudley Dorival	HAI	13.49
8.	Robert Kronberg	SWE	13.61
8q1	**Damien Greaves**		**14.08**
h1	**Tony Jarrett**		**dsq**

400 Metres Hurdles (27 Sep)

1.	Angelo Taylor	USA	47.50
2.	Hadi Al-Somaily	KSA	47.53
3.	Llewellyn Herbert	RSA	47.81
4.	James Carter	USA	48.04
5.	Eronilde de Araujo	BRA	48.34
6.	Pawel Januszewski	POL	48.44
7.	Fabrizio Mori	ITA	48.78
8.	Gennadiy Gorbenko	UKR	49.01
6s2	**Chris Rawlinson**		**49.25**
6s3	**Matt Douglas**		**49.53**
5h6	**Tony Borsumato**		**50.73**

High Jump (24 Sep)

1.	Sergey Klyugin	RUS	2.35
2.	Javier Sotomayor	CUB	2.32
3.	Abderahmane Hammad	ALG	2.32
4.	Stefan Holm	SWE	2.32
5.	Konstantin Matusevich	ISR	2.32
6=	Staffan Strand	SWE	2.32
6=	Mark Boswell	CAN	2.32
8.	Wolfgang Kreissig	GER	2.29
27=Q	**Ben Challenger**		**2.15**

Pole Vault (29 Sep)

1.	Nick Hysong	USA	5.90
2.	Lawrence Johnson	USA	5.90
3.	Maksim Tarasov	RUS	5.90
4.	Michael Stolle	GER	5.90
5=	Dmitriy Markov	AUS	5.80
5=	Viktor Chistyakov	AUS	5.80
7.	Okkert Brits	RSA	5.80
8.	Danny Ecker	GER	5.80
16=Q	**Kevin Hughes**		**5.55**

Long Jump (28 Sep)

1.	Ivan Pedroso	CUB	8.55
2.	Jai Taurima	AUS	8.49
3.	Roman Shchurenko	UKR	8.31
4.	Aleksey Lukashevich	UKR	8.26
5.	Kofi Amoah Prah	GER	8.19
6.	Peter Burge	AUS	8.15
7.	Luis Felipe Meliz	CUB	8.08
8.	Dwight Phillips	USA	8.06

Triple Jump (25 Sep)

1.	**Jonathan Edwards**		**17.71**
2.	Yool Garcia	CUB	17.47
3.	Denis Kapustin	RUS	17.46
4.	Yoelbi Quesada	CUB	17.37
5.	**Larry Achike**		**17.29**
6.	**Phillips Idowu**		**17.08**
7.	Robert Howard	USA	17.05
8.	Paolo Camossi	ITA	16.96

Shot (22 Sep)

1.	Arsi Harju	FIN	21.29
2.	Adam Nelson	USA	21.21
3.	John Godina	USA	21.20
4.	Andy Bloom	USA	20.87
5.	Yuriy Belonog	UKR	20.84
6.	Manuel Martinez	ESP	20.55
7.	Janus Robberts	RSA	20.32
8.	Oliver-Sven Buder	GER	20.18
31Q	**Mark Proctor**		**18.49**

WOMEN

100 Metres wind-0.4 (24 Sep)

1.	Marion Jones	USA	10.75
2.	Ekaterini Thanou	GRE	11.12
3.	Tanya Lawrence	JAM	11.18
4.	Merlene Ottey	JAM	11.19
5.	Zhanna Pintusevich	UKR	11.20
6.	Chandra Sturrrup	BAH	11.21
7.	Sevatheda Fynes	BAH	11.22
8.	Debbie Ferguson	BAH	11.29
5h1	**Joice Maduaka**		**11.51**
5h6	**Shani Anderson**		**11.55**
4h7	**Marcia Richardson**		**11.62**

200 Metres wind 0.7 (28 Sep)

1.	Marion Jones	USA	21.84
2.	Pauline Davis-Thompson	BAH	22.27
3.	Susanthika Jayasinghe	SRI	22.28
4.	Bev McDonald	JAM	22.35
5.	Debbie Ferguson	BAH	22.37
6.	Meilissa Gainsford-Taylor	AUS	22.42
7.	Cathy Freeman	AUS	22.53
8.	Zhanna Pintusevich	UKR	22.66
7q2	**Samantha Davies**		**23.20**
7q1	**Joice Maduaka**		**23.57**

Discus (25 Sep)

1.	Virgilijus Alekna	LIT	69.30
2.	Lars Riedel	GER	68.50
3.	Frantz Kruger	RSA	68.19
4.	Vasiliy Kaptyukh	BLR	67.59
5.	Adam Setliff	USA	66.02
6.	Jason Tunks	CAN	65.80
7.	Vladimir Dubrovshchik	BLR	65.13
8.	Jurgen Schult	GER	64.41
28Q	**Bob Weir**		**60.01**
38Q	**Glen Smith**		**56.22**

Hammer (24 Sep)

1.	Szymon Ziolkowski	POL	80.02
2.	Nicola Vizzoni	ITA	79.64
3.	Igor Astapkovich	BLR	79.17
4.	Ivan Tikhon	BLR	79.17
5.	Ilya Konovalov	RUS	78.56
6.	Loris Paoluzzi	ITA	78.18
7.	Tibor Gecsek	HUN	77.70
8.	Vladimir Maska	CZE	77.32

Javelin (23 Sep)

1.	Jan Zelezny	CZE	90.17
2.	**Steve Backley**		**89.85**
3.	Sergey Makarov	RUS	88.67
4.	Raymond Hecht	GER	87.76
5.	Aki Parviainen	FIN	86.62
6.	Konstadinos Gatsioudis	GRE	86.53
7.	Boris Henry	GER	85.78
8.	Emeterio Gonzalez	CUB	83.33
11.	**Mick Hill**		**81.00**
13Q	**Nick Nieland**		**82.12**

Decathlon (27-28 Sep)

1.	Erki Nool	EST	8641
2.	Roman Sebrle	CZE	8606
3.	Chris Huffins	USA	8595
4.	**Dean Macey**		**8567**
5.	Tom Pappas	USA	8425
6.	Tomas Dvorak	CZE	8385
7.	Frank Busemann	GER	8351
8.	Attila Zsivoczky	HUN	8277

400 Metres (25 Sep)

1.	Cathy Freeman		49.11
2.	Lorraine Graham	JAM	49.58
3.	**Katharine Merry**		**49.72**
4.	**Donna Fraser**		**49.79**
5.	Ana Guevara	MEX	49.96
6.	Heide Seyerling	RSA	50.05
7.	Falilat Ogunkoya	NGR	50.12
8.	Olga Kotlyarova	RUS	51.04
7q3	**Alison Curbishley**		**52.50**

800 Metres (25 Sep)

1.	Maria Mutola	MOZ	1:56.15
2.	Stephanie Graf	AUT	1:56.64
3.	**Kelly Holmes**		**1:56.80**
4.	Brigita Langerholc	SLO	1:58.51
5.	Helena Fuchsova	CZE	1:58.56
6.	Zulia Calatayud	CUB	1:58.66
7.	Hazel Clark	USA	1:58.75
8.	Hasna Benhassi	MAR	1:59.27

20 Kilometres Walk (22 Sep)

1.	Robert Korzeniowski	POL	1:18:59
2.	Noe Hernandez	MEX	1:19:03
3.	Vladimir Andreyev	RUS	1:19:27
4.	Jefferson Perez	ECU	1:20:18
5.	Andreas Erm	GER	1:20:25
6.	Roman Rasskazov	RUS	1:20:57
7.	Francisco Fernandez	ESP	1:21:01
8.	Nathan Deakes	AUS	1:21:03

50 Kilometres Walk (29 Sep)

1.	Robert Korzeniowski	POL	3:42:22
2.	Aigars Fadejevs	LAT	3:43:40
3.	Joel Sanchez	MEX	3:44:36
4.	Valenti Massana	ESP	3:46:01
5.	Nikolay Matyukhin	RUS	3:46:37
6.	Nathan Deakes	AUS	3:47:29
7.	Miguel Rodriguez	MEX	3:48:12
8.	Roman Magdziarczyk	POL	3:48:17
39.	**Chris Maddocks**		**4:52:12**

4 x 100 Metres Relay (30 Sep)

1.	United States	37.61
2.	Brasil	37.90
3.	Cuba	38.04
4.	Jamaica	38.20
5.	France	38.49
6.	Japan	38.66
7.	Italy	38.67
8.	Poland	38.96
h1	**Great Britain & NI**	**dsq**

(Condon, Gardener, Devonish, Chambers)

4 x 400 Metres Relay (30 Sep)

1.	United States	2:56.35
2.	Nigeria	2:58.68
3.	Jamaica	2:58.78
4.	Bahamas	2:59.23
5.	France	3:01.02
6.	**Great Britain & NI**	**3:01.22**
	(Deacon, Caines, Thomas, Baulch)	
7.	Poland	3:03.22
8.	Australia	3:03.91

1500 Metres (30 Sep)

1.	Nouria Merah-Benida	ALG	4:05.10
2.	Violeta Szekely	ROM	4:05.15
3.	Gabriela Szabo	ROM	4:05.27
4.	Kutre Dulecha	ETH	4:05.33
5.	Lidia Chojecka	POL	4:06.42
6.	Anna Jakubczak	POL	4:06.49
7.	**Kelly Holmes**		**4:08.02**
8.	Marla Runyan	USA	4:08.30
11.	**Hayley Tullett**		**4:22.29**
9s2	**Helen Pattinson**		**4:09.60**

5000 Metres (25 Sep)

1.	Gabriela Szabo	ROM	14:40.79
2.	Sonia O'Sullivan	IRE	14:41.02
3.	Gete Wami	ETH	14:42.23
4.	Ayelech Worku	ETH	14:42.67
5.	Irina Mikitenko	GER	14:43.59
6.	Lydia Cheromei	KEN	14:47.35
7.	Werknesh Kidane	ETH	14:47.40
8.	Olga Yegorova	RUS	14:50.31
12.	**Jo Pavey**		**14:58.27**
15s2	**Andrea Whitcombe**		**16:15.82**

10000 Metres (30 Sep)

1.	Derartu Tulu	ETH	30:17.49
2.	Gete Wami	ETH	30:22.48
3.	Fernanda Ribeiro	POR	30:22.88
4.	**Paula Radcliffe**		**30:26.97**
5.	Tegla Loroupe	KEN	30:37.26
6.	Sonia O'Sullivan	IRE	30:53.37
7.	Li Ji	CHN	31:06.94
8.	Elana Meyer	RSA	31:14.70

Marathon (24 Sep)

1.	Naoko Takahashi	JPN	2:23:14
2.	Lidia Simon	ROM	2:23:22
3.	Joyce Chepchumba	KEN	2:24:45
4.	Esther Wanjiru	KEN	2:26:17
5.	Madina Biktagirova	RUS	2:26:33
6.	Elfenesh Alemu	ETH	2:26:54
7.	Eri Yamaguchi	JPN	2:27:03
8.	Ham Bong-sil	PRK	2:27:07
26.	**Marian Sutton**		**2:34:33**

100 Metres Hurdles wind 0.0 (27 Sep)

1.	Olga Shishigina	KZK	12.65
2.	Glory Alozie	NGR	12.68
3.	Melissa Morrison	USA	12.76
4.	Delloreen Ennis-London	JAM	12.80
5.	Aliuska Lopez	CUB	12.83
6.	Nicole Ramalalanirina	FRA	12.91
7.	Linda Ferga	FRA	13.11
8.	Brigitte Foster	JAM	13.49
8q3	**Diana Allahgreen**		**13.22**

400 Metres Hurdles (27 Sep)

1.	Irina Privalova	RUS	53.02
2.	Deon Hemmings	JAM	53.45
3.	Nezha Bidouane	MAR	53.57
4.	Daimi Pernia	CUB	53.68
5.	Tatyana Tereshchuk	UKR	53.96
6.	Ionela Tirlea	ROM	54.35
7.	Gudrun Arnardottir	ISL	54.63
8.	**Natasha Danvers**		**55.00**
5h5	**Keri Maddox**		**57.44**
4h1	**Sinead Dudgeon**		**57.82**

High Jump (30 Sep)

1.	Yelena Yelesina	RUS	2.01
2.	Hestrie Cloete	RSA	2.01
3=	Kajsa Berqvist	SWE	1.99
3=	Oana Pantelimon	ROM	1.99
5.	Inga Babakova	UKR	1.96
6.	Svetlana Zalevskaya	KZK	1.96
7.	Viktoriiya Palamar	UKR	1.96
8.	Amewu Mensah	GER	1.93

Pole Vault (25 Sep)

1.	Stacy Dragila	USA	4.60
2.	Tatiana Grigorieva	AUS	4.55
3.	Vala Flosadottir	ISL	4.50
4.	Daniela Bartova	CZE	4.50
5.	Nicole Humbert	GER	4.45
6.	Yvonne Buschbaum	GER	4.40
7.	Monika Pyrek	POL	4.40
8.	Marie Rasmussen	DEN	4.35
20Q	**Janine Whitlock**		**4.15**

Long Jump (29 Sep)

1.	Heike Drechsler	GER	6.99
2.	Fiona May	ITA	6.92
3.	Marion Jones	USA	6.92
4.	Tatyana Kotova	RUS	6.83
5.	Olga Rublyova	RUS	6.79
6.	Susen Tiedtke	GER	6.74
7.	Jackie Edwards	BAH	6.59
8.	Tunde Vaszi	HUN	6.59
13Q	**Jo Wise**		**6.59**

Triple Jump (24 Sep)

1.	Tereza Marinova	BUL	15.20
2.	Tatyana Lebedeva	RUS	15.00
3.	Yelena Govorova	UKR	14.96
4.	Yamile Aldama	CUB	14.30
5.	Baya Rahouli	ALG	14.17
6.	Cristina Nicolau	ROM	14.17
7.	Olga Vasdeki	GRE	14.15
8.	Oxana Rogova	RUS	13.97
11.	**Ashia Hansen**		**13.44**

Shot (28 Sep)

1.	Yanina Korolchik	BLR	20.56
2.	Larisa Peleshenko	RUS	19.92
3.	Astrid Kumbernuss	GER	19.62
4.	Svetlana Krivelyova	RUS	19.37
5.	Krystyna Zabawska	POL	19.18
6.	Yumileidi Cumba	CUB	18.70
7.	Kalliopi Ouzouni	GRE	18.63
8.	Nadine Kleinert-Schmitt	GER	18.49
13Q	**Judy Oakes**		**17.81**

Discus (27 Sep)

1.	Ellina Zvereva	BLR	68.40
2.	Anastasia Kelesidou	GRE	65.71
3.	Irina Yatchenko	BLR	65.20
4.	Natalya Sadova	RUS	65.00
5.	Stiliani Tsikouna	GRE	64.08
6.	Franka Dietzsch	GER	63.18
7.	Ilke Wyludda	GER	63.16
8.	Lisa-Marie Vizaniari	AUS	62.57

Hammer (29 Sep)

1.	Kamila Skolimowska	POL	71.16
2.	Olga Kuzenkova	RUS	69.77
3.	Kirsten Munchow	GER	69.28
4.	Yipsi Moreno	CUB	68.33
5.	Debbie Sosimenko	AUS	67.95
6.	Lyudmila Gubkina	BLR	67.08
7.	Dawn Ellerbe	USA	66.80
8.	Amy Palmer	USA	66.15
9.	**Lorraine Shaw**		**64.27**

Javelin (30 Sep)

1.	Trine Hattestad	NOR	68.91
2.	Mirela Tzelili	GRE	67.51
3.	Osleidys Menendez	CUB	66.18
4.	Steffi Nerius	GER	64.84
5.	Sonia Bisset	CUB	63.26
6.	Xiomara Rivero	CUB	62.92
7.	Tatyana Shikolenko	RUS	62.91
8.	Nikola Tomeckova	CZE	62.10

Heptathlon (23-24 Sep)

1.	**Denise Lewis**		**6584**
2.	Yelena Prokhorova	RUS	6531
3.	Natalya Sazanovich	BLR	6527
4.	Urszula Wlodarczyk	POL	6470
5.	Sabine Braun	GER	6355
6.	Natalya Roshchupkina	RUS	6237
7.	Karin Ertl	GER	6209
8.	Tiia Hautala	FIN	6173

20 Kilometres Walk (28 Sep)

1.	Wang Liping	CHN	1:29:05
2.	Kjersti Platzer	NOR	1:29:33
3.	Maria Vasco	ESP	1:30:23
4.	Erica Alfridi	ITA	1:31:25
5.	Guadalupe Sanchez	MEX	1:31:33
6.	Norica Cimpean	ROM	1:31:50
7.	Kerry Saxby-Junna	AUS	1:32:02
8.	Tatyana Gudkova	RUS	1:32:35
33.	**Lisa Kehler**		**1:37:47**

4 x 100 Metres Relay (30 Sep)

1.	Bahamas	41.95
2.	Jamaica	42.12
3.	United States	42.20
4.	France	42.42
5.	Russia	43.02
6.	Germany	43.11
7.	Nigeria	44.05
8.	China	44.87
5s2	**Great Britain & NI**	**43.19**

(Maduaka, Richardson, Davies, Anderson)

4 x 400 Metres Relay (30 Sep)

1.	United States	3:22.62
2.	Jamaica	3:23.25
3.	Russia	3:23.46
4.	Nigeria	3:23.80
5.	Australia	3:23.81
6.	**Great Britain & NI**	**3:25.67**
	(Danvers, Fraser, Curbishley, Merry)	
7.	Czech Republic	3:29.17
8.	Cuba	3:29.47

ITA v GB & NI v ESP v FRA (U19) Grosseto, ITA 7 October 2000

The women out ran their male counterparts winning from 100 metres to 1500 metres, also a good win in the 4 x 400 metres was an omen for the World Juniors.

MEN

100 Metres wind 1.2
1. **Tyrone Edgar** **10.39**
5. **Ben Lewis** **10.70**

200 Metres wind 1.9
1. **Dwayne Grant** **21.27**
4. **Ben Lewis** **21.43**

400 Metres
1. Urel Lacroix FRA 47.72
3. **Russell Nicholls** **48.32**
8. **Martin Bradbury** **49.57**

800 Metres
1. Florent Lacasse FRA 1:47.41
6. **Andrew Fulford** **1:53.36**
8. **Raymond Adams** **1:54.71**

1500 Metres
1. Guillaume Eraud FRA 3:45.82
6. **Richard Ward** **3:50.54**
7. **Andrew Baddeley** **3:59.00**

3000 Metres
1. **Mohamed Farah** **8:12.53**
8. **Lee McCash** **8:43.09**

110 Metres Hurdles wind -0.3
1. Ladji Doucoure FRA 13.93
2. **Chris Baillie** **14.12**
3. **Rob Newton** **14.17**

400 Metres Hurdles
1. Federico Rubeca ITA 51.79
2. **Jeff Christie** **52.74**
7. **Nange Ursell** **54.80**

3000 Metres Steeplechase
1. Yuri Floriani ITA 9:01.09
2. **Adam Bowden** **9:04.43**
6. **Richard Williams** **9:25.75**

High Jump
1. Mickael Hanany FRA 2.14
2. **Luke Crawley** **2.14**
4. **Chuka Enih-Snell** **2.05**
Samson Oni gst **1.95**

Pole Vault
1. Giorgio Piantella ITA 5.05
Mark Beharrell **nm**
Richard Smith **nm**

Long Jump
1. Julien Ruiz FRA 7.41w
3. **Chris Tomlinson** **7.16**
8. **Martin Taylor** **6.45w**

Triple Jump
1. Dhabi Manga FRA 15.75
3. **Steven Shalders** **15.33**
7. **Nathan Douglas** **14.62**

Shot
1. Jose Ecija ESP 16.19
3. **Greg Beard** **15.87**
6. **Adam Major** **14.23**

Discus
1. Manuel Florido ESP 53.49
3. **Scot Thompson** **49.98**
4. **Adam Major** **48.36**

Hammer
1. Alessandro Beschi ITA 62.22
4. **Andy Frost** **55.56**
6. **David Little** **52.74**

Javelin
1. Jerome Haefler FRA 65.12
2. **Philip Sharpe** **64.93**
6. **Jonathon Lundman** **59.24**

10000 Metres Walk
1. Patrick Ennemoser ITA 44:47.76
6. **Dominic King** **47:29.37**
7. **Andrew Parker** **49:12.46**

4 x 100 Metres Relay
1. France 39.65
2. **Great Britain & NI** **39.71**

(Edgar, Grant, Benjamin, Lewis-Francis)

4 x 400 Metres Relay
1. France 3:12.22
2. **Great Britain & NI** **3:12.69**

(Bryan, Nicholls, Christie, Bradbury)

Match Result Men
1. France 188
2. Italy 167
3. **Great Britain & NI** **158**
4. Spain 148

WOMEN

100 Metres wind 1.9
1. **Donna Maylor** **11.72**
4. **Kelly Thomas** **11.86**

200 Metres wind 1.6
1. **Vernicha James** **23.65**
3. **Kim Wall** **24.06**

400 Metres
1. **Jennifer Meadows** **54.19**
3. **Lisa Miller** **54.38**

800 Metres
1. **Rebecca Lyne** **2:08.32**
5. **Joanna Ross** **2:11.81**

1500 Metres
1. **Emma Ward** **4:24.33**
3. **Charlotte Moore** **4:25.90**

3000 Metres
1. Sonia Bejarano ESP 9:29.76
3. **Collette Fagan** **9:32.11**
4. **Jane Potter** **9:34.43**

100 Metres Hurdles wind 0.9
1. Adriana Lamalle FRA 13.44
6. **Helen Worsey** **14.25**
7. **Sarah McGreavy** **14.41**

400 Metres Hurdles
1. Lara Damian ITA 59.90
2. **Nicola Sanders** **60.05**
4. **Nusrat Ceesay** **61.62**

High Jump
1. Anna Visigalli ITA 1.80
3. **Aileen Wilson** **1.78**
5. **Rebecca Jones** **1.70**

Pole Vault
1. Vanesa Boslak FRA 4.10
4. **Ellie Spain** **3.50**
6. **Kirsty Maguire** **3.30**

Long Jump
1. Mariachiara Baccini ITA 6.19
2. **Symone Belle** **6.07**
3. **Fiona Westwood** **5.89**

Triple Jump
1. Giovanna Franzon ITA 13.32
7. **Angela Williams** **11.67**
8. **Rachel Peacock** **11.45**

Shot
1. Eloise Villeneuve FRA 15.08
6. **Claire Smithson** **12.31**
8. **Kara Nwidobie** **11.76**

Discus
1. **Claire Smithson** **52.19**
3. **Emma Carpenter** **49.17**

Hammer
1. Federica Bertini ITA 54.59
4. **Carrys Parry** **49.94**
8. **Lucy Marshall** **43.78**
Mhairi Walters gst **48.90**

Javelin
1. **Goldie Sayers** **53.79**
3. **Amy Harvey** **47.57**

5000 Metres Walk
1. Beatriz Pascual ESP 22:41.59
7. **Natalie Evans** **29:00.58**

4 x 100 Metres Relay
1. France 45.07
3. **Great Britain & NI** **45.43**

(Selley, Thomas, Maylor, James)

4 x 400 Metres Relay
1. **Great Britain & NI** **3:38.99**

(Wall, Brookes, Thieme, Miller)

Match Result Women
1. Italy 180
2. **Great Britain & NI** **174**
3. France 157.5
4. Spain 119.5

IAAF WORLD JUNIOR CHAMPIONSHIPS
Santiago, CHI 17 - 22 October 2000

Mark Lewis-Francis showed that his season's strategy was perfect with two gold medals. The other gold medal was more surprising with the women's 4 x 400 producing a real team effort. Tim Benjamin's silver was the only other medal but many athletes set PBs including some in the qualifiers to reach the final, Steven Shalder set a PB in both qualifying and final.

MEN

100 Metres wind 0.1 (18 Oct)
1. Mark Lewis-Francis 10.12
2. Salem Al-Yami KSA 10.38
3. Marc Burns TRI 10.40
5q4 Tyrone Edgar 10.62

200 Metres wind 1.3 (21 Oct)
1. Paul Gorries RSA 20.64
2. Marek Jedrusinski POL 20.87
3. Tim Benjamin 20.94
7. Dwayne Grant 21.33

400 Metres (20 Oct)
1. Hamdan Al-Bishi KSA 44.66
2. Brandon Simpson JAM 45.73
3. Shinji Ishikawa JPN 45.77

800 Metres (20 Oct)
1. Nicholas Wachira KEN 1:47.16
2. Florent Lacasse FRA 1:47.61
3. Antonio Reina ESP 1:47.90
5h3 Raymond Adams 1:56.93

1500 Metres (22 Oct)
1. Cornelius Chirchir KEN 3:38.80
2. Wolfram Muller GER 3:39.37
3. Philemon Kibet KEN 3:40.77

5000 Metres (21 Oct)
1. Gordon Mugi KEN 13:44.93
2. Kenenisa Bekele ETH 13:45.43
3. Cyrus Kataron KEN 13:46.12
10. Mohamed Farah 14:12.21
11. Chris Thompson 14:13.91

10000 Metres (17 Oct)
1. Robert Kipchumba KEN 28:54.37
2. Duncan Lebo KEN 28:58.39
3. Abraha Hadush ETH 29:44.65

3000 Metres Steeplechase (21 Oct)
1. Raymond Yator KEN 8:16.34
2. David Chemweno KEN 8:31.95
3. Abdellatif Chemlal MAR 8:43.57

110 Metres Hurdles wind -0.1 (20 Oct)
1. Yunier Hernandez CUB 13.60
2. Thomas Blaschek GER 13.80
3. Ladji Doucoure FRA 13.84
7. Robert Newton 14.22
8. Chris Baillie 14.28

400 Metres Hurdles (21 Oct)
1. Marek Plawgo POL 49.23
2. Ter de Villiers RSA 50.52
3. Okkert Cilliers RSA 50.58
h2 Jeff Christie dsq

High Jump (19 Oct)
1. Jacques Freitag RSA 2.24
2. Germaine Mason JAM 2.24
3. Tomasz Smialek POL 2.21
10. Luke Crawley 2.10
20QChuka Enih-Snell 2.00

Pole Vault (22 Oct)
1. Aleksey Khanafin RUS 5.30
2. Aleksandr Korchmyd UKR 5.30
3. Rocky Danners USA 5.20

Long Jump (21 Oct)
1. Cai Peng CHN 7.88
2. Vladimir Zyuskov UKR 7.84
3. Yoelmis Pacheco CUB 7.71
12. Chris Tomlinson 7.29

Triple Jump (20 Oct)
1. Marian Oprea ROM 16.41
2. Yoandri Betanzos CUB 16.34
3. Mohammed Awadh QAT 16.29
10. Steven Shalders 15.99

Shot (19 Oct)
1. Rutger Smith NED 19.48
2. Ivan Yushkov RUS 19.06
3. Tomasz Chrzanowski POL 19.00
16QGreg Beard 16.49

Discus (21 Oct)
1. Hannes Hopley RSA 59.51
2. Niklas Arrhenius SWE 59.19
3. Rutger Smith NED 58.70
29QAdam Major 45.34

Hammer (18 Oct)
1. Esraf Apak TUR 69.97
2. Dylan Armstrong CAN 67.50
3. Aaron Fish AUS 67.44

Javelin (22 Oct)
1. Hardus Pienaar RSA 78.11
2. Andreas Thorkildsen NOR 76.34
3. Park Jae-myong KOR 72.36
22QPhil Sharpe 65.58

Decathlon (18-19 Oct)
1. Dennis Leyckes GER 7897
2. David Gomez ESP 7772
3. Andre Niklaus GER 7712

10000 Metres Walk (19 Oct)
1. Cristian Berdeja MEX 40:56.47
2. Yevgeniy Demkov RUS 40:56.53
3. Viktor Burayev RUS 40:56.97

4 x 100 Metres Relay (22 Oct)
1. Great Britain & NI 39.05
(Edgar, Grant, Benjamin, Lewis-Francis)
2. France 39.33
3. Japan 39.47

4 x 400 Metres Relay (22 Oct)
1. Jamaica 3:06.06
2. Germany 3:06.79
3. Poland 3:07.05

WOMEN

100 Metres wind 2.0 (18 Oct)
1. Veronica Campbell JAM 11.12
2. Katchi Habel GER 11.39
3. Fana Ashby TRI 11.47
8q2 Donna Maylor 12.22

200 Metres wind 0.7 (21 Oct)
1. Veronica Campbell JAM 22.87
2. Sina Schielke GER 23.20
3. Vida Anim GHA 23.81
5. Vernicha James 23.96
8. Kim Wall 24.46

400 Metres (20 Oct)
1. Jana Pittman AUS 52.45
2. Aneta Lemiesz POL 52.78
3. Norma Gonzalez COL 53.30
6s1 Lisa Miller 53.86
5s2 Jenny Meadows 54.27

800 Metres (20 Oct)
1. Chebet Langat KEN 2:01.51
2. Georgie Clarke AUS 2:02.28
3. Lucia Klocova SVK 2:04.00
4h4 Joanna Ross 2:10.56
6h3 Rebecca Lyne 2:20.17

1500 Metres (21 Oct)
1. Abebech Negussie ETH 4:19.93
2. Rose Kosgei KEN 4:20.16
3. Georgie Clarke AUS 4:20.21
6s2 Emma Ward 4:24.47

3000 Metres (22 Oct)
1. Beatrice Chepchumba KEN 9:08.80
2. Jane Chepkoech KEN 9:10.05
3. Etalemahu Kidane ETH 9:11.55

5000 Metres (6 Aug)
1. Dorcus Inzikuru UHA 16:21.32
2. Meseret Defaru ETH 16:23.69
3. Sharon Cherop KEN 16:23.73

100 Metres Hurdles wind -1.7 (19 Oct)

1.	Susanna Kallur	SWE	13.02
2.	Fanny Gerance	FRA	13.21
3.	Adrianna Lamalle	FRA	13.27
5h3	**Helen Worsey**		**14.11**
8h6	**Sara McGreavy**		**14.34**

400 Metres Hurdles (21 Oct)

1.	Jana Pittman	AUS	56.27
2.	Marjolein de Jong	NED	56.50
3.	Melanie Walker	JAM	56.96
6h1	**Nicola Sanders**		**60.07**

High Jump (20 Oct)

1.	Blanka Vlasic	CRO	1.91
2.	Marina Kuptsova	RUS	1.88
3.	Marisa Gertenbach	RSA	1.88
9=	**Aileen Wilson**		**1.80**
22=Q	**Rebecca Jones**		**1.75**

Pole Vault (18 Oct)

1.	Yelena Isinbayeva	RUS	4.20
2.	Annika Becker	GER	4.10
3=	Vanessa Bosiak	FRA	4.10
3=	Fanni Juhasz	HUN	4.10
14.	**Ellie Spain**		**3.50**

Long Jump (18 Oct)

1.	Concepcion Montaner	ESP	6.47
2.	Zhou Yangxia	CHN	6.45w
3.	Kumiko Ikeda	JPN	6.43

Triple Jump (21 Oct)

1.	Anastasiya Ilyina	RUS	14.24
2.	Anna Pyatykh	RUS	14.18
3.	Dana Veldakova	SVK	13.92

Shot (17 Oct)

1.	Kathleen Kluge	GER	17.37
2.	Li Meiju	CHN	16.57
3.	Natalya Kharaneko	BLR	16.40

Discus (19 Oct)

1.	Seema Antil	IND	55.27
2.	Xu Shaoyang	CHN	54.41
3.	Jana Tucholke	GER	53.97
8.	**Claire Smithson**		**50.18**
14Q	**Emma Carpenter**		**47.30**

Hammer (18 Oct)

1.	Ivana Brkljajcic	CRO	62.22
2.	Virginia Balut	ROM	60.23
3.	Yunaika Crawford	CUB	59.98
14Q	**Carys Parry**		**53.80**
29Q	**Mhairi Walters**		**48.77**

Javelin (20 Oct)

1.	Jarmila Klimesova	CZE	54.82
2.	Inga Kozarenoka	LAT	54.64
3.	Galina Kakhava	BLR	54.26
6.	**Goldie Sayers**		**51.52**

Heptathlon (19-20 Oct)

1.	Carolina Kluft	SWE	6056
2.	Lidiya Bashlyakova	RUS	5898
3.	Sanna Saarman	FIN	5707
11.	**Fiona Harrison**		**5279**

5000 Metres Walk (20 Oct)

1.	Lyudmila Yefimkina	RUS	44:07.74
2.	Tatyana Kozlova	RUS	44:24.43
3.	Sabine Zimmer	GER	46:49.97

4 x 100 Metres Relay (22 Oct)

1.	Germany	43.91
2.	Jamaica	44.05
3.	Sweden	44.78
h1	**Great Britain & NI**	**dsq**

(Selley, Casey, Maylor, James)

4 x 400 Metres Relay (22 Oct)

1.	**Great Britain & NI**	**3:33.82**

(Wall, Meadows, Thieme, Miller)

2.	Jamaica	3:33.99
3.	Romania	3:34.39

RWA NATIONAL WALK CHAMPIONSHIPS

20 Kilometres
Nottingham 12 March 2000

MEN

1.	Darrell Stone	1:27:08
2.	Andrew Penn	1:28:47
3.	Matthew Hales	1:31:50
4.	Don Bearman	1:32:38
5.	Gareth Brown	1:32:43
6.	Andrew O'Rawe	1:37:19

Team

1. Steyning 13

WOMEN

1.	Lisa Kehler	1:39:28
2.	Niobe Menendez	1:40:53
3.	Kim Braznell	1:48:14
4.	Sharon Tonks	1:49:51
5.	Sally Warren	1:53:17
6.	Katherine Horwill	1:54:46

Team

1. Dudley & Stourbridge 23

35 & 10 Kilometres
Dartford 7 May 2000

MEN (35k)

1.	Chris Cheeseman	2:51:20
2.	Don Bearman	2:53:10
3.	Gareth Brown	2:55:59
4.	Michael Smith	3:11:00
5.	Chris Berwick	3:14:41
6.	David Ratcliffe	3:24:43

Team

1. Steyning 19

WOMEN (10k)

1.	Sharon Tonks		52:00
	Sally Warren	gst	52:37
2.	Nikki Huckerby		54:15
3.	Katie Horwill		54:25
4.	Lisa Crump		54:56
5.	Joanne Hesketh		55:42

Team

1. Steyning 27

50 & 5 Kilometres
Victoria Park 7 September 2000

MEN (50k)

1.	Darrell Stone	4:21:23
2.	Gareth Brown	4:27:23
3.	Don Bearman	4:32:42
4.	Peter Kaneen	4:50:47
5.	Michael Smith	4:51:31
6.	Chris Berwick	4:52:15

Team

1. Steyning 6

WOMEN (5k)

1.	Niobe Menendez	24:19
2.	Sharon Tonks	24:59
3.	Lisa Crump	26:01
4.	Nikki Huckerby	26:28
5.	Joanne Hesketh	27:05
6.	V White	27:32

Team

1. City of Sheffield A 16

AAA & UK HALF MARATHON CHAMPIONSHIPS

Bristol 8 October 2000

MEN

1.	Nick Wetheridge		64:09
2.	Stephen Ariga	KEN	64:11
3.	Hilary Lelei	KEN	64:22
4.	Matthew Vaux-Harvey		64:28
5.	Simon Kasimili	KEN	64:58
6.	Ian Grime		65:38
7.	Nathaniel Lane		65:40
8.	Tony O'Brien		65:50

Team

1. Morpeth 57

WOMEN

1.	Andrea Green		73:28
2.	Sue Reinsford	1-AAA	74:21
3.	Misati	KEN	75:19
4.	Vicky Pincombe		75:49
5.	SharonDixon	2-AAA	76:16
6.	Jo Newcombe	3-AAA	76:21
7.	Louise Watson		76:25
8.	Lynne Williams		77:25

N.B. Green & Pincombe did not wear club vests.

Team

1. Arena 80 49

IAAF WORLD HALF MARATHON CHAMPIONSHIPS
Veracruz, MEX 12 November 2000

Paula Radcliffe made up a little for her disappointment in Sydney with a magnificent win and set something of a statistical poser. Has there ever been an international athletics competition where the leading Britsh woman beat all her male counterparts? (They did have worse weather !)

MEN

1.	Paul Tergat	KEN	63:47
2.	Phaustin Baha	TAN	63:48
3.	Tesfaye Jifar	ETH	63:50
4.	Joseph Kimani	KEN	63:52
5.	David Ruto	KEN	63:59
6.	John Gwako	KEN	64:16
7.	Amnaay Bayo	TAN	64:25
8.	Oscar Fernandez	ESP	64:25
9.	Marco Mazza	ITA	64:26
10.	Noureddine Betim	ALG	64:40
52.	**Matthew Vaux-Harvey**		**69:20**
70.	**Nick Wetheridge**		**72:00**
81.	**Nick Jones**		**74:23**

Team

1.	Kenya	3:11:38
2.	Ethiopia	3:14:45
3.	Belgium	3:18:35
17.	**Great Britain & NI**	**3:35:43**

WOMEN

1.	**Paula Radcliffe**		**69:07**
2.	Susan Chepkemei	KEN	69:40
3.	Lidia Slavuteanu-Simon	ROM	70:24
4.	Mizuki Noguchi	JAP	71:11
5.	Pamela Chepchumba	KEN	71:33
6.	Mihaela Botezan	ROM	71:52
7.	Cristiana Pomacu	ROM	72:06
8.	Yukiko Okamoto	JAP	72:20
9.	Yasuko Hashimoto	JAP	72:54
10.	Milena Glusac	USA	73:53
19.	**Sarah Young-Wilkinson**		**75:55**
45.	**Andrea Green**		**84:53**

Team

1.	Romania	3:34:22
2.	Japan	3:36:25
3.	Russia	3:45:41
6.	**Great Britain & NI**	**3:49:55**

EKIDEN RELAY
Chiba, JAP
24 November 2000

MEN (10k, 5k, 10k, 5k, 12.195k)

1.	Japan	1:59:47
2.	South Africa	2:01:28
3.	Australia	2:03:07
5.	**Great Britain & NI**	**2:03:49**
	Mike Openshaw	**28:40**
	Tom Hanlon	**14:12**
	Andy Coleman	**29:25**
	Rob Whalley	**14:33**
	Ian Hudspith	**36:59**

WOMEN (10k, 5k, 10k, 5k, 4.767k, 7.428k)

1.	Japan	2:15:30
2.	Ethiopia	2:17:30
3.	Kenya	2:18:18
12.	**Great Britain & NI**	**2:23:47**
	Birhan Dagne	**33:16**
	Emma Fisher	**17:22**
	Lucy Wright	**34:06**
	Debra Curley	**16:52**
	Debbie Sullivan	**16:25**
	Heather Knight	**25:46**

EUROPEAN CROSS COUNTRY CHAMPIONSHIPS
Malmo, SWE 10 December 2000

This was a good championship for Britain with three of the four teams gaining medals including the junior women with a surprise gold. The only individual medal was Chis Thompson's silver, but it could have been better with both he and Mohamed Farah claiming they were tripped.

MEN (9750m)

1.	Paolo Guerra	POR	29:29
2.	Sergey Lebed	UKR	29:39
3.	Driss El Himer	FRA	29:45
4.	Lyes Ramoul	FRA	29:47
5.	Mustapha El Ahmadi	FRA	29:47
6.	Carlos Adan	ESP	29:48
7.	Kamiel Maase	NED	29:49
8.	Tom Van Hooste	BEL	29:51
9.	Jose Martinez	ESP	29:52
10.	Peter Matthews	IRE	29:53
16.	**Matt O'Dowd**		**30:03**
18.	**Dominic Bannister**		**30:13**
32.	**Alan Buckley**		**30:40**
37.	**Dave Taylor**		**30:45**
38.	**Glynn Tromans**		**30:50**
	Spencer Duval		**dnf**

Team

1.	France	23
2.	Spain	51
3.	Ireland	72
6.	**Great Britain & NI**	**103**

JUNIOR MEN (6135m)

1.	Wolfram Muller	GER	18:58
2.	**Chris Thompson**		**19:00**
3.	Martin Proll	AUT	19:05
7.	**Mohamed Farah**		**19:12**
16.	**Lee McCash**		**19:34**
20.	**Robert Maycock**		**19:40**
62.	**Robert Smith**		**20:24**

Team

1.	Portugal	21
2.	**Great Britain & NI**	**25**
3.	France	30

JUNIOR WOMEN (3755m)

1.	Jessica Augusto	POR	12:55
2.	Nicola Spirig	SUI	12:56
3.	Elvan Can	TUR	12:56
5.	**Juliet Potter**		**13:02**
7.	**Jane Potter**		**13:14**
9.	**Collette Fagan**		**13:15**
15.	**Sally Oldfield**		**13:26**
44.	**Jessica Nugent**		**13:51**

Team

1.	**Great Britain & NI**	**21**
2.	Turkey	40
3.	Sweden	49

WOMEN (4945m)

1.	Katalin Szentgyorgyi	HUN	16:34
2.	Analidia Torre	POR	16:35
3.	Olivera Jevtic	YUG	16:39
4.	Zahia Dahmani	FRA	16:49
5.	**Kathy Butler**		**16:51**
6.	Monica Rosa	POR	16:55
7.	Anja Smolders	BEL	16:55
8.	**Liz Yelling**		**16:55**
9.	Anne Keenan-Buckley	IRE	16:56
10.	Analia Rosa	POR	16:57
20.	**Tara Krzywicki**		**17:08**
25.	**Helen Pattinson**		**17:16**
30.	**Hayley Yelling**		**17:20**

Team

1.	Portugal	18
2.	**Great Britain & NI**	**33**
3.	Germany	54

REGIONAL CHAMPIONSHIPS

	SCOTLAND **Scotstoun, Glasgow 28 - 29 July**		**WALES** **Cwmbran 17 - 18 June**		**NORTHERN IRELAND** **Belfast 8 July**	
MEN						
100	John Skeete	10.6	Christian Malcolm	10.4	Jonathan Carleton	11.05
200	Nigel Stickings	21.03w	Christian Malcolm	21.09	Jonathan Carleton	21.97
400	Paul Slythe	47.71	Jamie Baulch	46.35	Paul McBurney IRE	47.69
800	Jonathan McCallum	1:50.6	Matthew Shone	1:49.90	Niall Dunne IRE	1:56.08
1500	Glen Stewart	3:46.28	Chritian Stephenson	3:52.0	John Rogers	3:51.76
5000	Alistair Hart	15:04.25	Andres Jones (short)	14:09.8	Dermot Kerr IRE	15:36.0
10000	Thomas Murray	29:57.58			Donal Gallagher	31:43.3
3kSt	Andrew Lemoncello	9:26.5	Steven Smith	9:53.24	Dean Fisher	9:44.92
110H	Chris Baillie	14.03	Paul Gray	14.36	Trevor McGlynn IRE	15.24
400H	Richard McDonald	51.61	Matthew Elias	54.48	Stephen McDonnell IRE	54.83
HJ	Colin McMaster	2.00	Robert Mitchell	2.15	not contested	
PV	Iain Black	4.40	Egryn Jones	4.50	Neil Young	4.45
LJ	Darren Ritchie	7.80	Anthony Malcolm	7.55	John Donnelly	6.69
TJ	not contested		Charles Madeira-Cole	15.38	John Donnelly	14.52
SP	Stephan Hayward	17.59	Andrew Turner	14.59	Iain McMullen	15.18
DT	Bruce Robb	51.72	Lee Newman	55.14	John Farrelly IRE	43.51
HT	Iain Park	61.72	Graham Holder	61.44	Richard Murphy	41.02
JT	Thomas Dobbing	63.23	Derek Hormann	57.41	Michael Allen IRE	68.34
Dec	Brian Hughes	5726	Ben Roberts	5479	Philip McIlfatrick	4056
3kW			Mark Williams	14:21.7	James Gibbons IRE	13:30.4

10000 Antrim 1 July
Dec Antrim 1 - 2 July

WOMEN						
100	Joanna Hill	12.1	Catherine Murphy	12.14w	Vicki Jamison	12.53
200	Sinead Dudgeon	23.23w	Catherine Murphy	24.23w	Vicki Jamison	25.14
400	Allison Curbishley	51.96	Louise Whitehead	53.37	Jennifer McKenna IRE	55.87
800	Jennifer Ward	2:05.6	Natalie Lewis	2:12.04	Maura Prendiville IRE	2:14.58
1500	Kathy Butler CAN	4:17.28	Emma Brady	4:37.60	Pauline Thom	4:30.84
3000					Clare Quinn IRE	10:29.75
5000	Hayley Haining	16:29.8				
100H	Lorna Silver	14.3	Rachel King	14.12w	Rebecca Mitchell	15.24
400H	Alison Currie	62.22	Kathryn Williams	62.77	Geraldine Finegan IRE	65.11
HJ	Lee McConnell	1.83	Julie Crane	1.82	Ursula Fay	1.65
PV	Alison Murray-Jessee	3.50	Anna Leyshon	2.90	Zoe Brown	2.85
LJ	Kirsty Roger	5.41	Lara Richards	5.80	Shauna Colhoun IRE	5.74
TJ	Nicola Barr	11.97	not contested		Melissa Moss AUS	12.34
SP	Navdeep Dhaliwal	11.89	Liz Brannan	12.61	Claire McAleese	10.68
DT	Alison Grey	46.57	Rebecca Roles	45.56	not contested	
HT	Victoria Scott	50.39	Sarah Moore	53.74	Shirley Roberts	32.55
JT	Lorna Jackson	53.48	Alison Siggery	36.23	Linda Gray	48.77
Hept	not contested		Amanda Wale	4039	Danea Herron IRE	3342
5kW			P Reilly	26:37.2		

Hept Antrim 1 - 2 July

AREA CHAMPIONSHIPS

	SOUTH Brighton 17 - 18 June		MIDLANDS Stoke 17 - 18 June		NORTH Grantham 18 June	
MEN						
100	Jonathan Barbour	10.28	Brendon Ghent	10.88	Allyn Condon	11.08
200	Uvie Ugono	20.89w	Richard Knowles	21.56	Daniel Money	21.88
400	Sean Baldock	45.91	Bradley Yiend	48.74	Geoffrey Djan	47.93
800	Michael East	1:48.95	Gary Vickers	1:52.15	Garth Watson	1:53.50
1500	Patrick Davoren	3:48.27	Rob Scanlon	3:53.53	David Anderson	3:58.18
3000	Michael East	8:09.3	Steve Edmonds	8:37.2		
5000	Chris Thompson	14:30.33	Steve Edmonds	15:05.50	Alan Buckley	14:52.86
10000	Charles Herrington	31:00.13				
3kSt	Paul Farmer	9:09.17	Ben Trapnell	9:52.39	Darren Barton	9:19.99
110H	Mensah Elliott	14.03	Perry Batchelor	14.89	Dominic Bradley	14.75
400H	Richard Lewis	52.7	Paul Hibbert	53.26	David Savage	53.19
HJ	Tyron Peacock RSA	2.15	Khaled El Sheikh EGY	2.00	Rob Brocklebank	2.08
PV	Ian Tullett	4.80	Mark Davis	4.80	Alan Richardson	4.40
LJ	Andrew Lewis	7.20	T Sercombe	6.48w	Simon Roper	7.24w
TJ	Phillips Idowu	16.57	Matthew Muggeridge	13.61w	John Wiggans	13.84w
SP	Emeka Udechuku	17.74	Lyndon Woodward	16.30	Guy Marshall	15.55
DT	Emeka Udechuku	57.46	Gary Herrington	47.53	Peter Gordon	53.21
HT	Paul Head	68.92	Steve Pearson	64.47	Michael Floyd	69.38
JT	Dan Carter	66.76	Mike Tarran	62.24	Ian Burns	63.22
Dec	Scott Exley	6540	William Wynn	6652	Ashley Pritchard	5471
3kW	Andrew Goudie	13:29.0				
10kW	Jamie O'Rawe	46:21.75				

3000 Brighton 17 August
10000 Bedford 19 August
HT Enfield 30 July
Dec Enfield 29 - 30 July
10kW Enfield 30 July

3000 Nuneaton 15 July

Dec Jarrow 24 - 25 June

	SOUTH		MIDLANDS		NORTH	
WOMEN						
100	Sarah Reilly IRE	11.49	Amanda Forrester	11.84	Nicole Crosby	12.46
200	Sarah Reilly IRE	23.50w	Ellena Ruddock	24.45	Nicole Crosby	25.29
400	Linda Staines	55.31	Rosie Thorner	56.40	Kim Goodwin	54.72
800	Lorraine Phillips	2:07.85	Emma Ward	2:09.09	Paula Fryer	2:09.19
1500	Kelly Caffel	4:17.67	Tina Brown	4:33.0	Kerry Smithson	4:25.96
3000	Louise Damen	9:38.4	Emma Ward	9:27.63		
5000	Liz Yelling	16:47.58	Susan Harrison	17:21.37	Bev Jenkins	17:19.69
100H	Melanie Wilkins	13.17	Keri Maddox	13.52	Nicola Gautier	14.78
400H	Tracey Duncan	59.17	Celia Brown	61.38	Rachael Kay	62.92
HJ	Debbie Marti	1.85	Kelly Sotherton	1.65	Gayle O'Connor	1.70
PV	Tracey Bloomfield	3.60	Irie Hill	3.70	Caroline Nutt	3.00
LJ	Joyce Hepher	6.18	Kelly Sotherton	6.09	Ann Danson	6.32w
TJ	Michelle Griffiths	13.52	Debbie Rowe	12.78	Rebecca White	11.90w
SP	Judy Oakes	17.87			Nicola Gautier	14.07
DT	Deborah Callaway	50.53	Nicola Talbot	45.36	Susan Backhouse	45.02
HT	Lyn Sprules	56.67	Ann Gardener	51.26	Suzanne Roberts	56.16
JT	Tammie Francis	46.09	Sharon Gibson	44.56	Linda Gray	45.63
Hept	Hannah Staires	4553	Belinda Samuels	4506	Jacqueline Elliott	3560
3kW	Sally Warren	14:49.6				
5kW	Sigrun Sanvik	27:08.35				

3000 Brighton 17 August
Hept Enfield 29 - 30 July
5kW Enfield 30 July

3000 Solihull 28 May

Hept Jarrow 24 - 25 June

AGE CHAMPIONSHIPS

MEN	Under 20 Bedford 26 - 27 August Incorporating World Junior Trials			Under 17 Sheffield 29 - 30 July			Under 15 Sheffield 29 - 30 July	
100	Mark Lewis-Francis	10.46		Monu Miah	10.79		Jamie Gill	11.24
200	Tim Benjamin	20.95w		Monu Miah	21.45		James Ellington	22.46w
400	Ian Tinsley	48.19		Craig Erskine	50.01		Richard Davenport	51.4
800	Chris Mulvaney	1:51.40		Adam Davies	1:56.50		Michael Rimmer	1:56.9
1500	Chris Thompson	3:48.93		Ian Munro	3:58.62		Lee Bowron	4:04.63
3000				Glenn Raggett	8:59.46		Tom Snow	9:16.98
5000	Nicholas Goodliffe	14:47.15						
3kSt	Adam Bowden	9:14.12	1500St	Daniel Lewis	4:26.26			
110H	Chris Baillie	13.84	100H	Brendon Harmse	12.83	80H	Richard Alexis-Smith	11.21
400H	Jeffrey Christie	52.83		Rhys Williams	54.91			
HJ	Luke Crawley	2.15		Chuka Enih-Snell	2.06		Daniel Segerson	1.79
PV	Mark Beharrell	4.90		Mark Christie	4.30		Steven Lewis	3.70
LJ	Chris Tomlinson	7.59		Jonathan Moore	7.46		Gary Wilson	6.67
TJ	Steven Shalders	15.12		Jonathan Moore	15.67		Graham Jackson	12.59
SP	Greg Beard	15.59		Carl Saggers	17.34		Andrae Davis	16.11
DT	Scot Thompson	50.07		Carl Saggers	50.07		Simon Bissell	47.10
HT	John Osazuma NGR	62.87		Carl Saggers	63.69		Simon Bissell	54.47
JT	Phil Sharpe	71.79		Alex Van Der Merwe	60.08		Thomas Rees	47.33
Dec	James Wright	6007	Oct	Edward Dunford	5420	Pen	Louis Moore	2838
10kW	Colin Griffin IRE	46:45.31	5kW	Andrew Parker	22:48.91	3kW	Luke Finch	14:09.93
Dec	Stoke-on-Trent 29 - 30 July		3000	Bedford 1 July		3000	Bedford 1 July	
			1500St	Bedford 26 August		LJ	Bedford 27 August	

WOMEN	Incorporating World Junior Trials							
100	Kelly Thomas	12.06		Danielle Selley	12.00		Amy Spencer	12.02
200	Vernicha James	23.81w		Eleanor Caney	24.29		Amy Spencer	24.50
400	Jenny Meadows	54.53	300	Eleanor Caney	38.41			
800	Jemma Simpson	2:08.37		Charlotte Best	2:11.52		Hayley Beard	2:10.89
1500	Emma Ward	4:21.58		Charlotte Dale	4:30.87		Melissa Wall	4:39.80
3000	Jane Potter	9:30.13						
100H	Helen Worsey	13.76w	80H	Symone Belle	11.20	75H	Heather Jones	11.1
400H	Nicola Sanders	59.68	300H	Gemma Donney	42.96			
HJ	Aileen Wilson	1.79		Stephanie Higham	1.78		Jessica Ennis	1.60
PV	Ellie Spain	3.55		Kate Dennison	3.20			
LJ	Fiona Westwood	5.77		Symone Belle	5.74		Aimee Palmer	5.23
TJ	Rachel Peacock	11.98w		Emily Parker	11.70w			
SP	Claire Smithson	13.72		Frances Miller	11.37		Lucy Sutton	11.57
DT	Claire Smithson	48.65		Angela Lockley	36.44		Christina Carding	33.33
HT	Mhairi Walters	52.88		Nicola Dudman	44.40			
JT	Goldie Sayers	51.37		Samantha Redd	42.23		Christine Lawrence	34.84
Hept	Lara Carty	4491		Hannah Barnes	4338	Pen	Jessica Ennis	3109
5kW	Serena O'Keefe IRE	25:07.32		Natalie Evans	27:24.88	3kW	Carol Burtonshaw IRE	16:43.43
Hept	Stoke-on-Trent 29 - 30 July					LJ	Bedford 27 August	
						JT	Bedford 27 August	

AGE CHAMPIONSHIPS

The 1999 results were omitted from BA2000 and are shown on the right

MEN

	Under 23 Bedford 1 July		1999 Under 23 Bedford 3 - 4 July	
100	Jonathan Barbour	10.32	Christian Malcolm	10.20w
200	Jonathan Barbour	21.04	Christian Malcolm	21.01
400	Daniel Caines	46.82	David Naismith	46.95
800	Chris Moss	1:50.11	Alasdair Donaldson	1:49.02
1500	Angus MacLean	3:47.21	Matthew Dixon	3:47.38
5000	Stephen Hepples	14:40.85	Sam Haughian	14:09.21
3kSt	Iain Murdoch	9:01.32	Ben Whitby	8:59.29
110H	Duncan Malins	14.10	Duncan Malins	14.29
400H	Matthew Elias	51.51	James Hillier	51.30
HJ	Robert Mitchell	2.19	Daniel Graham	2.11
PV	Ben Flint	5.25	Mark Davis	5.10
LJ	Stuart Wells	7.28	Darren Thompson	7.52
TJ	Nicholas Thomas	15.93	Phillips Idowu	16.09w
SP	Emeka Udechuku	17.66	Carl Myerscough	17.99
DT	Emeka Udechuku	53.87	Carl Myerscough	58.99
HT	Matthew Bell	61.51	Matthew Bell	60.42
JT	Daniel Carter	71.90	Robert Charlesworth	60.92
10kW			Robert Hefferman IRE	43:49.80

WOMEN

	Under 23 Bedford 1 July		1999 Under 23 Bedford 3 - 4 July	
100	Amanda Forrester	11.71	Susan Williams	11.61
200	Melanie Purkiss	24.00	Susan Williams	23.95
400	Karen Gear	54.03	Louretta Thorne	54.37
800	Emma Davies	2:07.38	Emma Davies	2:15.26
1500	Ellen O'Hare	4:24.40	Susan Scott	4:25.87
3000	Gillian Palmer	9:35.03	Emma Ford	9:33.06
100H	Julie Pratt	13.50	Julie Pratt	13.62
400H	Tracey Duncan	58.84	Tracey Duncan	60.48
HJ	Michelle Dunkley	1.89	Susan Jones	1.82
PV	Tracey Bloomfield	3.80	Jenny Dryburgh NZL	4.00
LJ	Jade Johnson	6.48	Sarah Claxton	5.99
TJ	Leandra Polius	12.52	Jodie Hurst	12.59
SP	Julie Dunkley	15.96	Julie Dunkley	16.11
DT	Philippa Roles	51.79	Philippa Roles	55.08
HT	Suzanne Roberts	54.03	Rachael Beverley	60.27
JT	Chloe Cozens	49.24	Joanne Bruce	45.58
5kW			Nicola Huckerby	25:30.07

UK MERIT RANKINGS 2000 Compiled by Peter Matthews

This is the 33rd successive year that I have compiled annual merit rankings of British athletes. As usual they are based on an assessment of form during the outdoor season. The major factors by which the rankings are determined are win-loss record, performances in the major meetings, and sequence of marks.

I endeavour to be as objective as possible, but form can often provide conflicting evidence, or perhaps an athlete may not have shown good enough results against leading rivals, or in very important competition, to justify a ranking which his or her ability might otherwise warrant.

I can only rank athletes on what they have actually achieved. Much depends on having appropriate opportunities and getting invitations for the prestige meetings. Difficulties also arise when athletes reach peak form at different parts of the season or, through injury, miss significant competition. Also, increasingly, many of our top athletes are competing overseas instead of in domestic meetings, which makes comparisons of form difficult.

Once again it should be pointed out that the rankings are by no means necessarily the order in which I think the athletes would have finished in an idealised contest, but simply my attempt to assess what has actually happened in 2000.

I hope that I have not missed many performances, but I would be very pleased to receive any missing results at 10 Madgeways Close, Great Amwell, Herts SG12 9RU.

For each event the top 12 are ranked. On the first line is shown the athletes name, then their date of birth followed, in brackets, by the number of years ranked in the top 12 (including 2000), their ranking last year (1999) and their best mark prior to 2000. There follows their best performances (normally six) of the year followed, for completeness, by significant indoor marks indicated by 'i' (although indoor performances are not considered in the rankings). Then following lines show placings at major meetings, providing a summary of the athlete's year at the event.

Abbreviations include

AAA-23	AAA Under-23 Championships
AAA-20	AAA Under-20 Championships
BedI	Bedford International
BGP	British Grand Prix at London (CP)
BL	British League
BRS	Bedford 'Road to Sydney'
B.Univs	British Universities at Stoke-on-Trent
CAU	Inter-Counties at Bedford
Comm-Y	Commonwealth Youth Games
Croydon	Southern Inter-Counties
Cup	BAL Cup Final at Bedford (also major clashes in semis – sf)
E.Clubs	European Clubs Cup
ECp	European Cup
E.Sch	English Schools
GhCI	NU Gateshead Classic
GPF	Grand Prix Final
HCI	U23 Home Countries International at Derby
IR	Inter-Regional at Solihull
IS	Inter-Services
JI4	Junior International v France Italy and Spain at Grosseto
JLF	Junior League Final
Jnr IA	Junior Inter-Area
LI	Loughborough International
Lough	Loughborough 30 July
OG	Olympic Games
U23L	Under 23 International v France and Germany at Liverpool
v FRA	Eng v FRA at Vittel
v SPA-23	Under 23 International v SPA at Getafe
v USA	UK v USA at Glasgow
WG	Welsh Games at Wrexham
WJ	World Junior Championships at Santiago de Chile

UK RANKINGS 2000 - MEN

100 METRES

1. **Dwain Chambers** 5.4.78 (5y, 1) 9.97 '99 10.08, 10.11, 10.11, 10.12, 10.14, 10.18
6 Nuremberg, 9 Rome, 8 Lausanne, 4 v USA, 2 Dortmund, 5h Stockholm, 7 BGP, 1 BL1 (4), 1 AAA, 4 Monaco, 1 GhCl, 4 OG
2. **Darren Campbell** 12.9.73 (9y, 3) 10.04 '98 10.06, 10.09w, 10.10w, 10.12, 10.13, 10.13, 10.14, 10.19, 10.19
1 BL1 (1), 2 LI, 1 E.Clubs, 4 Helsinki, 2 Lille, 3 Nuremberg, 3 v USA, 2 Nice, 1 ECp, 3 Stockholm, 3 BGP, 2 AAA, 5 Monaco, 5 Brussels, 4 GhCl, 6 OG, 1 GPF
3. **Mark Lewis-Francis** 4.9.82 (2y, 8) 10.31/10.26w '99 10.10, 10.12, 10.13, 10.24, 10.24, 10.25
1 Mid-J, 1 LI, 3 BRS, 1 sf Cudworth, 1B BGP, 3 AAA, 1 Cup, 1 AAA-J, 1 JLF, 1 Bath, 1 WJ
4. **Jason Gardener** 18.9.75 (6y, 2) 9.98 '99 10.04w, 10.09, 10.16, 10.18, 10.25, 10.27
6 Athens, 1 v USA, 3 Lausanne, 4 AAA, 7 GhCl, 1 R.Bay 10/9, 4qf OG
5. **Ian Mackie** 27.2.75 (5y, 6) 10.17 '96, 10.00w '98 10.05w, 10.24, 10.36, 10.38, 10.39, 10.40
1 BRS, 3h4 Budapest, 5 AAA, 6 GhCl, 2 R.Bay 10/9
6. **Jonathan Barbour** 3.11.80 (1y, -) 10.64 '97, 10.45w '98 10.28, 10.30, 10.32, 10.34w, 10.36, 10.36w
3r2 Los Angeles 1r2 Bedl, 1 South, 1 AAA-23, 1 U23L, 4B BGP, 5s1 AAA, 2 Cup, 1 v FRA, 1 v SPA-23
7. **Christian Malcolm** 3.6.79 (4y, 5) 10.12/10.10w '98 10.29, 10.31, 10.32, 10.36, 10.37, 10.37
3 LI, 8 Helsinki, 1 Welsh, 4h Nuremberg, 7B Rome, 3 Dortmund, 2r1 R.Bay 17/9
8. **Marlon Devonish** 1.6.76 (4y, 4) 10.13 '98 10.27, 10.32, 10.32, 10.45, 10.48, 10.49
1r1 Fullerton, 2r2 Eagle Rock, 4 BRS, 5 Lille, 2 Rhede, 3 Budapest, 6 Rieti
9. **Allyn Condon** 24.8.74 (5y, 7) 10.21 '99 10.42, 10.44, 10.47, 10.49, 10.51, 10.52; 10.5
5 LI, 1 North, 4h4 Budapest, 3B Ljubljana, 6 AAA, 4r2 R.Bay 17/9
10. **Doug Bignall** 20.10.74 (1y, -) 10.49 '97 10.27Aw, 10.30A, 10.43, 10.44, 10.59; 10.8 7 AAA, 1 Croydon
11. **Curtis Browne** 11.9.75 (1y, -) 10.42/10.38w '99 10.42, 10.43w, 10.46w, 10.49, 10.52, 10.66
2r1 Riga, 3h3 Budapest, 2B Ljubljana, 8 AAA, 4 v FRA, BL1: -,2,1,-
12. **Uvie Ugono** 8.3.78 (1y, -) 10.40/10.32w '98 10.36, 10.45w, 10.47, 10.51, 10.51w, 10.51w
1 BL2 (1), 1B LI, dns CAU, 5 BRS, 2 South, 2 AAA-23

– **Owusu Dako** 23,5,75 (3y, -) 10.35 '96, 10.17w '98 10.31, 10.42, 10.79 1 Walnut, 1r2 Eagle Rock

Campbell had a terrific season, including wins in the European Cup and the Grand Prix Final and 6th at the Olympics. Chambers started the season in moderate form but came through to win the AAA title and place 4th in the Olympic Final. He retains his top ranking for these major championhip results and for the fact that he beat Campbell 4-3. Lewis-Francis is next as he beat Gardener at the AAAs and he showed immense ability and yet more potential for the future with his win in the B race at the British Grand Prix and at the World Juniors. Barbour is the top newcomer to the rankings. The 10th best performer is again 10.31, to equal the record high set in 1997, 1998 and 1999.

200 METRES

1. **Darren Campbell** 12.9.73 (6y, -) 20.48 '98 20.13, 20.14, 20.23, 20.49, 20.71, 20.71
1 BL1 (1), 1 Amsterdam, 1 LI, 1 E.Clubs, 7 Rome, 1 AAA, 2 OG
2. **Christian Malcolm** 3.6.79 (4y, 3) 20.29 '98 20.19, 20.19, 20.23, 20.45, 20.45, 20.51
1 Welsh, 3 Luzern, 1 v USA, 1 Dortmund, 1 ECp, 3 BGP, 2 AAA, 6 Brussels, 1 GhCl, 5 OG
3. **Marlon Devonish** 1.6.76 (5y, 2) 20.25 '98 20.59, 20.66, 20.69, 20.72, 20.75, 20.78
1 BRS, 1 Rhede, 5 Rome, 3 v USA, 1r4 Budapest, 7 BGP, 3 AAA, 5 GhCl, 3 Rieti, 7qf OG
4. **Ian Mackie** 27.2.75 (3y, 11) 20.91 '94 20.68w, 20.79w, 20.90, 20.92, 20.94, 21.05 2 LI, 1 CAU, 4 AAA
5. **Tim Benjamin** 2.5.82 (2y, 7) 20.72/20.60w '99 20.76, 20.76, 20.77, 20.89, 20.91, 20.92
4 LI, 1J Bedl, 2 Welsh, 5 Braga, 1 BL2 (3), 1r1 Budapest, 2 Berne, 5 AAA, 1 AAA-J, 1 U20HI, 1 Bath, 3 WJ
6. **Marcus Adam** 28.2.68 (12y, 9) 20.41 '92, 20.10w '90 20.65, 20.77, 20.89, 21.13, 21.20, 21.29; 21.02i
1r3 Budapest, 1r1 Ljubljana, 6 AAA, BL2: -,1B,3,1B
7. **Julian Golding** 17.2.75 (7y, 1) 20.18 '98 20.64, 20.84, 20.84, 20.88, 20.89, 20.97; 20.70i, 20.87i, 20.87i
2 Lille, 2 Riga, 5 v USA, 2r4 Budapest, 4 Barcelona, 6 BGP, 7s2 AAA
8. **Allyn Condon** 24.8.74 (6y, 5) 20.63 '97, 20.53i '98 20.80, 20.98, 21.04, 21.11, 21.19, 21.50
6 Dublin, 2r1 Budapest, 3r1 Ljubljana, 7 AAA
9. **Doug Turner** 2.12.66 (6y, 4) 20.43 '96, 20.36w '97 20.88w, 21.01, 21.04, 21.06, 21.08, 21.21
6r4 Budapest, 5r2 Ljubljana, 1 BL2 (4), 5s1 AAA, 4 Karlstad, 5 Rieti, 2 Bath
10. **Jonathan Barbour** 3.11.80 (1y, -) 21.6w '98 20.79, 21.04, 21.18, 21.22, 21.43, 21.71
1 AAA-23, 5 BL2 (3), 8s1 AAA, 1 v FRA, 1 v SPA-23
11. **John Stewart** 30.12.79 (2y, 10) 20.84 '99 20.83, 20.91, 21.07, 21.08, 21.09w, 21.14
1 B.Univs, 3 LI, 3 BRS, 1r3 Bed I, 6 Braga, 2 AAA-23, 1B BL1 (3), 1 U23L, 6s2 AAA, 3 v FRA, 2 v SPA-23
12. **Dwain Chambers** 5.4.78 (2y, 12) 20.68 '99 20.78, 20.87; 21.10i, 21.56i dns AAA

Campbell's Olympic silver medal was a huge delight as was Malcolm's fifth place. Campbell had won the world silver medal back in 1992, but had since only run the longer sprint occasionally. Malcom had an excellent record against the world's top 200m men. The top six follow the AAA order. Last year's 1st and 2nd Golding and Devonish slipped this year, but Benjamin, World Junior bronze medallist and still a junior in 2001, moved up to fifth ranking, just behind Mackie, whose season was thinner but who beat Benjamin at the AAAs and also won the CAU title. Barbour is the one newcomer to the rankings. John Regis is not ranked and retires after a record 14 years in the top ten.

400 METRES

1. **Mark Richardson** 26.7.72 (11y, 1) 44.37 '98 44.72, 45.11, 45.14, 45.16, 45.20, 45.46
   3 BGP, 1 AAA, 2 Brussels, 2 GhCl, 2 Berlin, 2 Rieti, 1 GPF
2. **Jamie Baulch** 3.5.73 (7y, 2) 44.57 '96 45.06, 45.38, 45.69, 45.86, 46.07, 46.08
   1 Welsh, 3 Nuremberg, 1 Haapsalu, 3 v USA, 3 Nice, 1 ECp, 8 BGP, 3 AAA, 8 Brussels, 7h OG
3. **Daniel Caines** 15.5.79 (1y, -) 47.13 '98 45.37, 45.39, 45.55, 45,79, 45.91, 46.31
   1 AAA-23, 1 U23L, 3r2 Ljubljana, 4 AAA, 1 Karlstad, 5sf OG
4. **Sean Baldock** 3.12.76 (4y, 12) 45.42 '97 45.20, 45.71, 45.91, 46.09, 46.19, 46.45
   1 E.Clubs, 1 South, 1 Haapsalu, 1b BL1 (2), 6 v USA, 7r4 Budapest, 2r3 Ljubljana, 2 AAA, 5h OG
5. **Jared Deacon** 15.10.75 (6y, 5) 45.88 '99 45.69, 46.04, 46.10, 46.15, 46.22, 46.48
   2 BRS, 3 Geneva, 2 Riga, 1r2 Budapest, 2r1 Dublin, 5 AAA, 6 GhCl
6. **Iwan Thomas** 5.1.74 (6y, -) 44.36 '97 45.82, 45.85, 46.19, 46.19, 46.24, 46.52
   4 v USA, 4 Falköping, 3 Karlstad, 7 GhCl
7. **Geoff Dearman** 4.8.77 (3y, 6) 46.05 '99 45.83, 46.15, 46.42, 46.43, 46.59, 46.7
   dnf B.Univs, 1 LI, 3 BRS, 1 Bedl, 1 Florø, 1 sf Rugby, 1r2 Dublin, BL1: -,1,-,1
8. **Solomon Wariso** 11.11.66 (3y, 3) 44.68 '98 46.14, 46.63, 46.86, 46.95, 47.8 2 sf Enfield, 6 AAA, 2 Azevvano
9. **Richard Knowles** 12.11.75 (3y, 9) 45.84 '97 46.14, 46.25, 46.49, 46.49, 46.54, 46.78
   1 Riga, 1 Fana, 3r4 Budapest, 5r2 Ljubljana, 7 AAA, 1 Cup, 2 v FRA
10. **Mark Hylton** 24.9.76 (7y, 4) 45.24 '98 46.24. 46.42, 47.02; 46.85i, 47.14i, 48.53i
    2r3 Budapest, 7r1 Dublin, 7 Leverkusen
11. **Adrian Patrick** 15.6.73 (8y, 10) 45.63 '95 46.19, 46.82, 46.93, 47.03, 47.25, 47.29
    3r1 Irvine, 2 Bedl, 2 South, 6r3 Budapest, 5s1 AAA
12. **David Naismith** 15.12.79 (1y, 8) 46.27 '99 46.47, 46.65, 46.88, 47.00, 47.01, 47.18; 47.05i
    4 LI, 2 Batt.Pk, 2 AAA-23, 2 U23L, 7s1 AAA, 1 v FRA, 1 vSPA-23, BL1: -,3,2,2

– **Du'aine Thorne-Ladejo** 14.2.71 (8y, 7) 44.66 '96 46.4, 46.61, 46.79 3 Fana, 1r2 Leverkusen

nr **Paul McKee** IRE 15.10.77 46.73 '99 45.92, 46.06, 46.10, 46.53, 46.62, 46.82
1 B.Univs, 1 BRS, 3 Riga, 4 Fana, 1 ECp 2B, 5r1 Dublin, 1 Antrim, dns Irish

Richardson, with a possible suspension hanging over him, did very well on his return to competition. He had to miss the Olympics while delaying his IAAF arbitration hearing, but excelled to win the Grand Prix Final, as he had in 1998; he ranks top for the third time. Caines is the only newcomer to the rankings; he made a superb breakthrough and was easily our best at the Olympics, both in the individual races and the relay. However, Baulch just takes second ranking as he was ahead of Caines in their only meeting, at the AAAs, and, as well as a faster time, had an important win in the European Cup. Baldock and Deacon follow ahead of Thomas, who made a most welcome reappearance without being able to recapture prime form. Note that Dean Macey, in his one 400m of the year, ran 46.41 in Sydney – faster than Baulch or Baldock managed there!

800 METRES

1. **James McIlroy** 30.12.76 (2y, 5) 1:45.32 '98 1:45.96, 1:46.39, 1:46.58, 1:47.01, 1:47.15, 1:47.24
   1 Bratislava, 2 v USA, 2 Caorle, 5B Oslo, 3 BGP, 1 AAA, 7 GhCl, 6sf OG
2. **Anthony Whiteman** 13.11.71 (4y, -) 1:47.16 '97 1:45.81, 1:47.32, 1:47.61A, 1:47.71A, 1:47.81
   6/7 in RSA, 1 Watford, 1 BGP, 11 GhCl
3. **Andy Hart** 13.9.69 (5y, 4) 1:45.71 '98 1:46.52, 1:46.54, 1:46.97, 1;47.08, 1:48.09, 1:48.21
   3 Batt.Pk, 1r2 Cardiff, dnf Lapinlahti, 4r2 Budapest, 4 Ljubljana, 7 BGP, 2 AAA, 9 GhCl, 6h OG
4. **Alasdair Donaldson** 21.6.77 (3y, 8) 1:48.10 '99 1:47.32, 1:47.58, 1:47.65, 1:47.69, 1:47.84, 1:49.17
   4 LI, 1 BRS, 2 Lough 14/6, 5g v USA, 3r2 Cardiff, 1 BL1 (3), 5 ECp, 2r1 Budapest, 8 BGP, 3 AAA, 2 Solihull
5. **Chris Moss** 17.6.79 (2y, -) 1:48.43 '98 1:47.75, 1:47.80, 1:48.68, 1:49.3, 1:49.77, 1:50.11
   1B LI, 5 BRS, 1 Lough 14/6, 1 AAA-23, 7r1 Cardiff, 1 U23L, 9 BGP, 4 AAA, 3 Solihull, 2 v FRA, 1 v SPA-23
6. **Neil Speaight** 9.9.78 (2y, 11) 1:48.1 '99 1:48.74, 1:48.86, 1:49.12, 1:49.46, 1:49.8, 1:50.24; 1:49.63i
   6 Wyth, 2 AAA-23, 5r1 Cardiff, 3 U23L, 2 Stretford 25/7, 1 Watford 2/8, 5 AAA, 6 Solihull, 1 v FRA, 2 v SPA-23
7. **Justin Swift-Smith** 28.8.74 (3y, 7) 1:47.9 '97 1:48.28, 1:48.61, 1:49.25, 1:49.46, 1;50.01, 1:50.1
   1 Wyth, 6 v USA, 2BL1 (3), 2 Watford, 11 BGP, 2 Watford 2/8, dnf AAA, 5 v FRA
8. **Jason Lobo** 18.9.69 (5y 3) 1:45.82 '99 1:47.81, 1;49.12, 1:49.44, 1:49.66, 1;50.21, 1:51.16
   1 E.Clubs, 2 Dessau, 9 Jena, 7 Kassel, 7 v USA, 1 sf Rugby, 6sf AAA, 3B Leverkusen
9. **Andrew Graffin** 20.12.77 (1y, -) 1:50.0 -97 1:49.1, 1:49.15; 1 TB, 1 BMC-F
10. **James Mayo** 24.2.75 (1y, -) 1:48.2 '96 1:49.07, 1:49.39, 1:49.49, 1:49.98, 1:50.10, 1:50.17
    1B Batt.Pk, 3 Watford, 7 AAA, 10 Karlstad, 8 Rovereto, 6 BMC-F
11. **Kevin McKay** 9.2.69 (8y, -) 1:45.35 '92 1:48.56, 1:49.17, 1:49.47, 1:49.69, 1:51.24
    3 Dessau, 10 Jena, 3 Wyth, 1 BL1 (2), 4 Stretford 11/7, 7 Cuxhaven
12. **Bradley Donkin** 6.12.71 (4y, 10) 1:46.86 '98 1:48.72, 1:49.28, 1:49.30, 1:49.99, 1:51.23, 1:51.24
    7 LI, 1 Stretford 30/5, 4 Wyth, 9 Batt.Pk, 3 Stretford 11/7, 8 Watford, 9 Dublin, 5sf AAA, 1 Cup, 2 BMC-F, BL1: -,-,3,3

- **Neil Caddy** 18.3.75 (0y, -) 1:49.5 '98 1:47.89; 5r2 Cardiff
- **John Mayock** 26.10.70 (0y, -) 1:47.8 '98 1:48.45, 1:50.37; 4 BRS, 2 Wyth
- **Mark Sesay** 13.12.72 (2y, 1) 1:45.68 '99 1:48.55, 1:50.82, 1:53.79 2 LI, dnf Riga, 12r2 Budapest, 1 BL2 (4)

Whiteman ran the fastest time of the year when winning the special race to help our athletes get OG qualifying times at the British Grand Prix. This was a remarkable breakthrough for him, taking 1.35 sec off his pb. McIlroy, who achieved the Olympic qualifying standard in third place in this race, was ahead of Whiteman in their other meeting at Gateshead and takes the top ranking with a solid season. He did not quite return to his form of 1998, when he competed for Ireland and was 4th in the European Championships, but he still stood out from the rest of the British runners. Hart, who had been top ranked in 1997 and 1998, moves up a place to third. Donaldson made notable progress, improving his personal best in four successive races in mid-season. Moss beat Speaight 5-2 in clashes between the top two U23s. The tenth best of 1:48.55 was the worst since 1978. Neil Caddy's 1:47.89 (5r2 Cardiff) made his seventh fastest, but it was his only race at the distance.

1500 METRES - 1 MILE

1. **John Mayock** 26.10.70 (9y, 1) 3:31.86 '97, 3:50.32M '96 3:50.61M (3:36,14), 3:34.69, 3:52.15M, 3:35.98, 3:53.44M, 3:36.98 5 Seville, 9 Paris, 1 v USA, 6 Nice, 2 ECp, 6 Oslo, 3 BGP, 1 AAA, 8 Monaco, 8 Brussels, 7 GhCl, 9 OG, 8 GPF
2. **Anthony Whiteman** 13.11.71 (5y, 2) 3:32.34 '97, 3:51.90M '98 3:34.93, 3:36.39, 3:36.39, 3:38.12, 3:41.34, 3:42.44; 3:42.36i 4/1/1 in RSA, 1 Dortmund, 3 Barcelona, 7 Stockholm, 2 AAA, dnf ht OG
3. **Andrew Graffin** 20.12.77 (2y, 7) 3:42.0/3:59.64M '99 3:36.18, 3:56.13M (3:39.6), 3:39.75, 3:39.79, 3:42.72, 3:43.68 2 Amsterdam, 1 Watford 22/7, 9 BGP, 4 AAA, 3 Leverkusen, 10sf OG
4. **Kevin McKay** 9.2.69 (11y, -) 3:34.59 '97, 3:53.64M '94 3:37.34, 3:55.07M (3:40.0), 3:38.94, 3:41.19, 3:42.10, 3:44.30 7 Kassel, 1 BL1 (2), 11 Zagreb, 7 BGP, 9 Linz, 5 AAA, 10 Leverkusen
5. **Jonathan McCallum** 19.11.75 (2y, 4) 3:40.87 '99 3:37.75, 3:38.87, 3:43.84, 3:44.06, 3:45.61, 3:46.14 10 LI, 7 Amsterdam, 3 BRS, 1 Fana, 1 Budapest, 11 Stockholm, 3 AAA, 15 Leverkusen
6. **Matt Dixon** 26.12.78 (2y, 10) 3:43.34 '99 3:39.80, 3:40.42, 4:01.61M, 3:45.60 1 B.Univs, 4 LI, 1 Wyth, 2 v USA
7. **Neil Caddy** 18.3.75 (6y, 3) 3:39.1/3:55.84M '96 3:39.03, 3:39.99, 3:58.31M (3:42.1), 3:41.24, 3:46.28, 3:51.92 6 LI, 2 Budapest, 3 Funchal, 12 BGP, 11 AAA
8. **Michael East** 20.1.78 (1y, -) 3:42.37 '99 3:40.13, 3:40.59, 3:42.57, 3:43.99, 3:44.723:45.36 5 LI, 2 Wyth, 4 v USA, 5 Budapest, 1 Dublin, 8h AAA, 2 v FRA, 1 v SPA-23
9. **Richard Ashe** 5.10.74 (2y, 5) 3:41.2/3:59.98M '96 3:41.36, 3:42.51, 3:44.82, 3:46.47, 3:47.79, 3:49.13 5 South, 11 Cardiff, 1 Watford 12/7, 2 Watford 22/7, 7 AAA, 6 v FRA
10. **Allen Graffin** 20.12.77 (1y, -) 3:43.76 '99, 4:04.0M '98 3:40.14, 3:59.86M (3:43.1), 3:43.29, 3:46.36, 3:46.92, 3:47.46 6 Amsterdam, 5 Watford 22/7, 13 BGP, 4h AAA, 10 GhCL, 3 BMC-F
11. **Angus Maclean** 20.9.80 (1y, -) 3:46.14 '99 3:41.19, 3:43.9, 3:45.85, 3:46.42, 3:47.21, 3:47.93 5 B.Univs, 1B LI, 1 AAA-23, 3 U23L, 1 Watford 2/8, 7h AAA, 1 Cup, 2 BMC-F, 3 v SPA-23, BL1: -,1,1,-
12. **James Thie** 27.6.78 (1y, -) 3:43.15 '99, 4:03.9M '98 3:42.85, 3:43.16, 3:43.39, 4:01.7M, 3:44.81, 3:45.20 2 B.Univs, 9 LI, 4 BRS, 4 Wyth, 2 AAA-23, 12 Cardiff, 4 U23L, 2 Dublin, 6 AAA, 2 Stretford 22/8, 2 Yeovil

M = 1 mile time (1500m times in brackets).

Mayock was top for the sixth successive year (tieing Steve Cram's event record) and Whiteman second for the fifth successive year, with Andrew Graffin making a major step forward and McKay returning after a year out. Seven men under 3:40 meant a big improvement in our standards and the 10th best of 3:41.19 compared to 1999's 3:42.37. McCallum improved his best by three seconds and Dixon and East looked especially impressive in early season races.

3000 METRES (Not ranked)

Kris Bowditch 14.1.75 7:55.61 '99 7:52.27, 8:01.84; 3 Wyth, 1 Solihull
Julian Moorhouse 13.11.71 7:56.88 '99 7:53.11, 8:08.80; 1 Stretford 30/5, 4 Wyth, 2 v FRA
Christian Stephenson 22.7.74 7:54.5 '97 7:53.23; 4 Cardiff
John Nuttall 11.1.67 7:36.40 '96 7:53.54, 7:59.20; 12 Wyth, 5 Cardiff
Adrian Passey 2.9.64 7:48.09 '89 7:53.68; 5 Wyth
Andres Jones 3.2.77 8:26.66 '96 7:54.12, 8:04.42; 1B Wyth, 6 Cardiff
Michael Openshaw 8.4.72 7:55.35 '99 7:55.12, 7:57.71; 6 Wyth, 1 Stretford 25/7, 1 v FRA
Glen Stewart 7.12.70 7:55.15 '99 7:56.80; 7 Wyth

5000 METRES

1. **Andres Jones** 3.2.77 (1y, -) 14:09.22 '99 13:39.43, 13:45.86, 13:54.3, c.14:04+, 14:12.4 1 Welsh, 14 BGP, 1 AAA, BL2: 1,1,1,-
2. **Michael Openshaw** 8.4.72 (2y, 10) 13:51.26 '99 13:37.97, 13:42.02, 13:49.34, 13:55.01 6 Batt.Pk, 6 Stretford, 16 BGP, 2 AAA, 7 Solihull
3. **Kris Bowditch** 14.1.75 (4y, -) 13:36.24 '98 13:28.22, 14:03.10, 14:03.45, 14:08.92 2 Batt.Pk, 6 ECp, 7 AAA, 15h OG
4. **Glen Stewart** 7.12.70 (1y, -) 13:53.55 '98 13:38.37, 13:43.89, 13:58.32, 13:58.40 5 LI, 4 Stretford, 17 BGP, 13 AAA, 4 Solihull
5. **John Nuttall** 11.1.67 (10y, 7) 13:16.70 '95 13:39.02, 13:56.35, 13:57.79 5 Stretford, 26 Heusden, 5 AAA
6. **Mark Hudspith** 19.1.69 (1y, -) 13:51.73 '91 13:49.37, 13:52.74; 7 Stretford, 3 AAA

7. **Julian Moorhouse** 13.11.71 (2y, -) 13:48.5 '98 13:42.35, 13:50.05, 13:53.90, 14:00.03
8 Batt.Pk, 8 Stretford, 4 Dublin, 6 AAA
8. **Allen Graffin** 20.12.77 (1y, -) 14:16.8 '95 13:41.42, 13:57.85; 4 LI, 2 Solihull
9. **Adrian Passey** 2.9.64 (4y, 6) 13:20.09 '97 13:30.67, 13:51.26, 13:52.97, 13:54.31, 14:02.11, 14:04.53
11 LI, 11 Batt.Pk, 9 Stretford, 2 Dublin, 13 Heusden, 8 AAA, 5 Solihull
10. **Karl Keska** 7.5.72 (4y, 3) 13:23.07 '99 13:42.13, c13:54+ in OG; 7 Eugene
11. **Ian Hudspith** 23.9.70 (2y, -) 13:52.8 '97 13:55.54, 13:57.37, 13:57.64 12 Stretford, 4 AAA, 6 Solihull
12. **Christian Nicolson** 19.9.73 (1y, -) 13:46.00 '99 13:45.26, 13:51.79, 14:06.63
11/15 Stanford, dnf Batt.Pk, 9 Lapinlahti

This was a poor year for British 5000m running. Bowditch headed the rankings with 13:28.22 at Battersea Park, a time which bettered the Olympic qualifying standard of 13:29.00, but did not break 14 minutes in three subsequent races. Jones took 30 secs off his best and won the AAA title all too easily to complete a 5k/10k double that had not been done since David Bedford in 1972. Despite a season's best of only 13:39.43 he takes top ranking on his debut in these lists for 5000m.

10,000 METRES

1. **Karl Keska** 7.5.72 (2y, -) 29:10.40 '96 8 OG 27:44.09 (27:48.29 ht), 2 Eur Challenge 28:00.56
2. **Andres Jones** 3.2.77 (2y, 8) 29:17.69 '99 2 (1) AAA 28:00.50, 9h OG 28:11.20, 1 CAU 29:51.73
3. **Rob Denmark** 23.11.68 (5y, -) 28:03.34 '94 3 AAA 28:03.31, 10 Eur Challenge 28:17.70, 13h OG 28:43.74
4. **Mark Steinle** 22.11.74 (4y, 10) 29:07.33 '95 4 AAA 28:04.48
5. **Keith Cullen** 13.6.72 (3y, 1) 27:53.52 '98 12 Eur Challenge 28:22.06
6. **Mark Hudspith** 19.1.69 (3y, -) 29:02.35 '92 11 AAA 28:43.08
7. **Ben Noad** 6.5.76 (1y, -) 0 15 Stanford 28:47.94
8. **Ian Hudspith** 23.9.70 (2y, -) 28:36.11 '97 12 AAA 28:50.98
9. **Glynn Tromans** 17.3.69 (4y, 2) 28:21.07 '99 14 AAA 29:05.28
10. **Adrian Mussett** 14.4.72 (2y, -) 29:40.96 '98 2 Batt.Pk 29:10.86
11. **John Nuttall** 11.1.67 (3y, -) 28:07.43 '95 14r2 Eur Challenge 29:35.48
12. **Nathaniel Lane** 10.4.76 (2y, 6) 29:01.17 '99 17 AAA 29:38.93

Keska stepped up to 10,000m and met with great success. First he achieved the Olympic qualifying time despite poor weather in Lisbon, and then he was the best European at the Olympic Games. Like Keska, Jones took over a minute off his pre-season best, and ran well in Sydney after winning the AAA title (2nd in the race to Maase NED). After 10th best in 29:10.86 there was a gap of nearly 25 seconds to the next best.

HALF MARATHON

1. **Keith Cullen** 13.6.72 (1y, -) 0 6 Gt.Scot 62:11
2. **Andy Coleman** 29.9.74 (1y, -) 2 GNR 62:28
3. **Paul Evans** 13.4.61 (1y, -) 60:09? '95, 61:18 ;97 8 Gt.Scot 62:58
4. **Nick Jones** 10.7.74 (2y, 3) 63:54 '99 1 Lake Vrynwy 63:12, 1 Wilmslow 63:51, 11 Gt.Scot 64:45, 81 World 74:23
5. **Ian Hudspith** 23.9.70 (2y, 5) 62:53 '96 3 Reading 63:19
6. **John Nuttall** 11.1.67 (1y, -) 0 12 GNR 63:49
7. **Dominic Bannister** 1.4.68 (1y, -) 0 1 Leyland 63:54
8. **Nick Wetheridge** 11.10.72 (1y, -) 64:46 '97 1 AAA 64:09, 70 World 72:00
9. **Matthew Vaux-Harvey** 30.3.76 (1y, -) 2 AAA 64:28, 52 World 69:20
10 **Karl Keska** 7.5.72 (1y, -) 0 13 GNR 64:07
11= **Alan Shepherd** 28.4.69 (1y, -) 64:52 '97 1 Chester 64:36
11= **Mark Steinle** 22.11.74 (2y, 1) 62:23 '99 1 Fleet 64:40
nr **John Mutai** KEN 22.4.76 60:52 '99 3 GNR 62:34

This event was ranked for the first time in 1999.

MARATHON

1. **Jon Brown** 27.2.71 (4y, 1) 2:09:44 '99 4 OG 2:11:17
2. **Keith Cullen** 13.6.72 (1y, -) 0 15 London 2:13:37, 19 OG 2:16:59
3. **Mark Steinle** 22.11.74 (1y, -) 0 11 London 2:11:18, 56 OG 2:24:42
4. **Dominic Bannister** 1.4.68 (1y, -) 0 8 Hamburg 2:14:39
5. **Mark Hudspith** 19.1.69 (6y, 2) 2:11:58 '95 18 London (1 AAA) 2:15:16
6. **Billy Burns** 13.12.69 (2y, -) 2:16:11 '98 20 London (2 AAA) 2:15:42
7. **Mark Croasdale** 10.1.65 (1y, -) 2:17:45 '93 22 London (3 AAA) 2:16:02, dnf Berlin, 1 Arlington 2:29:38
8. **Simon Pride** 20.7.67 (1y, -) 2:24:24 '99 10 Houston 2:21:35, 33 London 2:21:00, 1 Scot 2:21:17, 1 Dublin 2:18:49
9. **Ian Hudspith** 23.9.70 (2y, 3) 2:15:47 '99 25 London 2:18:40
10. **Rhodri Jones** 14.8.66 (2y, 11) 2:20:55 '99 24 London 2:18:34, 19 Frankfurt 2:19:10
11. **Barry Royden** 15.12.66 (1y, -) 2:19:00 '97 38 Rotterdam 2:18:54
12. **Alan Shepherd** 28.4.69 (1y, -) 2:22:15 '99 27 London 2:19:29
nr **John Mutai** KEN 22.4.76 2:13:37 '98 2 Dubai 2:13:20, 16 London 2:14:55, 10 Stockholm 2:27:19, 2 Dublin 2:19:53

Brown ran splendidly at the Olympics to rank top for the third successive year and there were encouraging debuts from Steinle, Cullen and Bannister, with four other men ranked for the first time at this event. We remain in a different age from 1983, when 102 men ran under 2:20, but this year's 13 is at least better than 1999's 8. It was good to see Pride moving down from 100km to the marathon, not least because he is prepared to run the distance more than once a year, which has become the norm for far too many British runners.

3000 METRES STEEPLECHASE

1. **Christian Stephenson** 22.7.74 (3y, 1) 8:29.09 '99 8:25.37, 8:28.21, 8:29.33, 8:46.66, 8:47.71
   1 Wyth, dnf Batt.Pk, 1 AAA, 1 Solihull, 10h1 OG
2. **Justin Chaston** 4.11.68 (10y, 3) 8:23.90 '94 8:26.07, 8:31.01, 8:32.21, 8:33.93, 8:36.27, 8:39.83
   5 Walnut, 2 Stanford, 12 Portland, 1 BL1 (4), 2 AAA, 2 Solihull, 7h OG
3. **Stuart Stokes** 15.12.76 (4y, 5) 8:48.21 '99 8:33.61, 8:41.45, 8:44.25, 8:53.90, 8:57.66, 8:57.70
   2 BL1 (1), 3 Wyth, 10 Zagreb, 7 ECp, 11 AAA
4. **Charlie Low** 9.10.74 (3y, 7) 8:54.46 '97 8:37.63, 8:41.43, 8:50.44, 8:53.65, 8:55.93, 9:01.17
   3 Watford, 4 AAA, 4 Solihull, 2 v FRA, BL1: -,1,1,-
5. **Craig Wheeler** 14.6.76 (3y, 2) 8:34.67 '99 8:39.72, 8:51.15, 8:57.04, 8:59.17, 9:02.03, 9:07.82
   4 AUS Ch, 1 sf Cudworth, 1 BL2 (4), 3 AAA, 7 Solihull, 5 v FRA
6. **David Heath** 22.5.65 (1y, -) 9:23.3 '97 8:42.04, 8:42.98, 8:52.92, 8:59.47, 9:03.98, 9:08.95
   4 Wyth, 2 Batt.Pk, 2 Watford, 11 Malmö, 7h2 AAA, 8 Solihull
7. **David Mitchinson** 4.9.78 (2y, 10) 8:52.58 '99 8:45.06, 8:46.05, 8:48.06, 8:48.93, 8:54.47, 8:59.32
   1 B.Univs, 7 LI, 6 Wyth, 2 U23L, 6 AAA, 6 v FRA, 3 v SPA-23
8. **Alistair O'Connor** 22.6.71 (1y, -) 8:42.88 '92 8:44.18, 8:49.03, 8:50.97, 8:53.62, 8:54.40, 8:56.2
   6 LI, 7 Wyth, 1 BL3 (2), 4 IR, 7 AAA, 5 Solihull
9. **Donald Naylor** 5.9.71 (2y, 8) 8:47.89 '99 8:44.03, 8:51.02, 8:51.23, 8:54.5, 8:56.5, 9:01.92
   1 CAU, 5 Wyth, 1 BL3 (3), 1 sf Rugby. 8 AAA
10. **Iain Murdoch** 10.7.80 (1y, -) 8:57.83 '99 8:42.79, 8:47.64, 8:51.99, 8:56.61, 8:59.67, 9:01.32
    2 B.Univs, 4 LI, 1 AAA-23, 5 U23L, 9 AAA
11. **Ben Whitby** 6.1.77 (3y, 9) 8:41.79 '98 8:44.68, 8:49.27, 8:57.3 (1 barrier missing) 5 AAA
12. **Andy Morgan-Lee** 1.3.69 (4y, 12) 8:50.40 '96 8:43.95, 8:47.65, 8:53.84, 9:00.0, 9:00.0 10 AAA, 6 Solihull

Stephenson retains his top ranking, making it top in each of his three years in these rankings, and both he and Chaston did well to make the Olympic qualifying standard of 8:27.0. The standard in depth was much better as 10th best of 8:44.18 compared to 8:54.46 to 8:55.74 each year 1997-9, although it was sub-8:40 in 1986 and 1989. Low improved by 17 seconds and Heath make his debut in the rankings at this event at the age of 35, making several brave bids to run much faster times.

110 METRES HURDLES

1. **Colin Jackson** 18.2.67 (17y, 1) 12.91 '93, 12.8w '90 13.10, 13.20, 13.27, 13.27, 13.28, 13.28, 13.29, 13.33, 13.34, 13.38 1 v USA, 1 Dortmund, 1 Chemnitz, 1 AAA, 3 Monaco, 1 Leverkusen, 3 GhCl, 5 OG
2. **Anthony Jarrett** 13.8.68 (15y, 2) 13.00 '93 13.53, 13.61, 13.64, 13.73, 13.78, 13.79
   2 Budapest, 4 BGP, 2 AAA, 8 Monaco, 2 Karlstad, 6GhCl, dq ht OG, BL2: -,-,1,1
3. **Damien Greaves** 19.9.77 (6y, 6) 13.82 '97 13.62, 13.64w, 13.66w, 13.75, 13.77, 13.80 1 LI, 1 BRS, 1r2 Bedl, 3 Rhede, 2 Dormagen, 4 ECp, 3 Budapest, 1 Lough, 3 AAA, 6 Namur, 1 Cup, 8 GhCl, 8qf OG, BL1: 1,-,1,-
4. **Mensah Elliott** 29.8.76 (2y, 10) 14.26/14.08w '99 13.69w, 13.82, 13.91, 13.92, 13.99w, 14.03; 13.7
   dq LI, 1r1 Bedl, 1 South, 3 Riga, 6 v USA, 5 Budapest, 1 IR, 2 Lough, 4 AAA, 2 Cup, 2 v FRA, BL2: 3,1,2,3
5. **Neil Owen** 18.10.73 (7y, -) 13.60 '95, 13.5w '96 13.87w, 13.89w, 13.93, 13.96w, 13.97w, 13.99w; 13.8
   1 E.Clubs, 3r2 Bedl, 3 South, 1 sf Rugby, 5 AAA, 3 Cup, 3 v FRA, BL1: 1B, 1, -,1
6. **Chris Baillie** 21.4.81 (2y, 7) 14.03/13.92w '99 13.84, 13.85w, 13.86, 13.95, 14.02w, 14.03
   2 LI, 1 Bedl-J, 2 BL1 (2), 5 v US, 1 Scot, 8 AAA, 1 AAA-J, 2 JI4N, 8 WJ
7. **Robert Newton** 10.5.81 (2y, 9) 14.19/13.93w '99 13.95, 14.01, 14.07, 14.09, 14.13, 14.13
   dnf B.Univs, 7 LI, 4J Bedl, 7 Budapest, 2 IR, 3 Lough, 2 Mannheim, 2h1 AAA, 2 AAA-J, 1 U20HI, 1 Bath, 2 JI4N, 7 WJ, BL1: 2B, 3,2,2
8. **Paul Gray** 25.5.69 (11y, 5) 13.53 '94 13.93, 14.22, 14.36; 13.9w 1 Welsh, 5 Riga, 1 Dublin, 2 BL2 (4)
9. **Duncan Malins** 12.6.78 (1y, -) 14.18 '99 14.08w, 14.10, 14.10w, 14.14w, 14.16, 14.17 3 B.Univs, 5 LI, 2r1 Bedl, 2 South, 1 AAA-23, 2 sf Eton, 4 U23L, 2 Dublin, 6 AAA, 1 Croydon, 2 v SPA-23, BL1: -,-,1B,3
10. **Liam Collins** 23.10.78 (1y, -) 14.43 '97, 14.35w '98 14.05, 14.06w, 14.08, 14.12, 14.29, 14.39
    3 LI, 4 BRS, 4r2 Bedl, 2 AAA-23, 6 U23L, 2=h3 AAA, 2 Croydon, 4 v FRA, BL1: 4,-,-,2B
11. **Martin Nicholson** 9.12.70 (5y, -) 14.14, 13.8 '94 14.14w, 14.18, 14.19w, 14.53; 14.4
    2 BL1 (1), 4 LI, 1 CAU
12. **Dominic Bradley** 22.12.76 (2y, -) 14.26, 14.07w '98 14.15w, 14.16w, 14.24w, 14.28w, 14.29, 14.30; 14.2
    1B LI, 2 CAU, 5r2 Bedl, 1 North, 1 sf Cudworth, 3 IR, 2h Lough, 3h1 AAA, 4 Cup, BL1: -,1B,3,-

– **Matt Douglas** 26.11.76 (2y, 8) 14.00 '99 14.08, 14.33, 14.54, 14.62, 14.92 1 B.Univs, 6 LI, BL1: 3,-,-,1B

Jackson is UK No. 1 for a record 13th time and ninth year in succession; he has now ranked in the world's top ten for 15 successive seasons. He competed less often than usual and won 5 of his 8 competitions. Jarrett is again number two, but he will have been most disappointed by his poor run at his fourth Olympics; in the last 13 years he has 12 second places and one first (in 1991). Greaves and Elliott both made progress and Baillie and Newton both made the World Junior final. The 10th best of 14.05 ties the record set in 1999.

400 METRES HURDLES

1. **Chris Rawlinson** 19.5.72 (6y, 1) 48.14 '99 48.22, 48.22, 48.35, 48.52, 48.68, 48.84 1 Walnut, 1 Milan, 4 Rome, 1 v USA, 2 Lausanne, 1 ECp, 5 Oslo, 3 BGP, 1 AAA, 2 Monaco, 8 Brussels, 6s2 OG, 6 GPF
2. **Matthew Douglas** 26.11.76 (6y, 5) 50.20 '98 49.26, 49.38, 49.53, 49.53, 49.62, 49.65
   1 B.Univs, 3 LI, 1 E.Clubs, 4 v USA, 7 BGP, 3 AAA, 1 Cup, 2 Rovereto, 1 R.Bay, 6sf OG, BL1: 1,1,-,1
3. **Anthony Borsumato** 13.12.73 (4y, 2) 49.78 '99 49.68, 49.71, 49.84, 49.95, 50.06, 50.17
   2 LI, 1 CAU, 1 Florø, 1 Riga, 5 v USA, 2r3 Budapest, 8 BGP, 2 AAA, 2 R.Bay, 5h OG
4. **Paul Hibbert** 31.3.65 (6y, 9) 50.52 '96 50.52, 50.83, 50.95, 51.07, 51.32, 51.32
   1B LI, 2 CAU, 1 Bedl, 1 Mid, 6 Dublin, 2 Lough, 4 AAA, 2 Cup, 1 v FRA, BL1: 4,2,-,2
5. **Gary Jennings** 21.2.72 (7y, -) 49.82 '95 50.11, 50.39, 50.60, 51.08, 51.09, 51.10
   1 LI, 1 Andorra, 2 Braga, 6 Chemnitz, 4 Lough, 5 AAA, 3 Cup, 4 Nivelles, BL1: 2,-,-,3
6. **Du'aine Thorne-Ladejo** 14.2.71 (1y, -) 0 50.09, 50.34, 50.97, 51.43
   1 IR, dnf ht AAA, 2 v FRA, BL1: -,-,1,1B
7. **Paul Gray** 25.5.69 (6y, 3) 49.16 '98 51.18, 51.26, 51.53, 51.65, 51.75, 51.97
   2 Batt.Pk, 2 Haapsalu, dnf Riga, 1 BL2 (2), 5r2 Budapest, 4 Ljubljana, 5 Dublin, 7 AAA
8. **Richard McDonald** 11.1.80 (2y, 8) 51.0/51.39 '99 51.09, 51.33, 51.47, 51.61, 51.82, 51.93
   4 LI, 2B Braga, 3r1 Budapest, 1 Scot, 3 Lough, 2 Tønsberg, BL1: -,-,3,4
9. **Matt Elias** 25.4.79 (3y, 7) 50.84 '99 51.16, 51.51, 52.79, 54.48
   1 Welsh, 3 Haapsalu, 1r2 Riga, 1 AAA-23
10. **James Hillier** 3.4.78 (2y, 12) 51.30 '99 51.49, 51.58, 51.70, 51.90, 51.99, 52.07
   2 B.Univs, 2B LI, 3 Batt.Pk, 5r1 Riga, 2 AAA-23, 5 U23L, 1B Lough, 6 AAA, 2B Nivelles, 2 v SPA-23
11. **Robert Lewis** 2.9.78 (1y, -) 52.07 '99 51.29, 52.33, 52.40, 52.7, 52.8, 52.8
   3 CAU, 1 South, 2 U23L, 3 IR, 5h2 AAA, 3 v SPA-23, BL4: 1,1,1,-
12. **Noel Levy** 22.6.75 (5y, -) 50.70 '94 51.58, 51.80, 51.85, 52.51, 52.76, 52.8
   1 sf Rugby, 7 Dublin, 8 AAA, BL1: -,1B,2, -

Rawlinson retained his top ranking and made good progress in world class, although not able to maintain his best form right through to the end of the season. Douglas made a major step forward and ran eight times under 50 seconds. Ladejo made a tantalising debut at the event, while Hibbert, at the age of 35, matched his best mark of 1996 and beat Jennings 4-1.

HIGH JUMP

1. **Ben Challenger** 7.3.78 (5y, 1) 2.30 '99 2.22, 2.20, 2.20, 2.20, 2.15, 2.15; 2.25i, 2.24i
   3= v USA, 5 Caorle, 6= ECp, 8 Jumpsl, 9 Oslo, 7= Stockholm, 9 BGP, 1 AAA, 1 Cup, dnq 27= OG
2. **Robert Mitchell** 14.9.80 (2y, 9) 2.14 '99 2.20, 2.19, 2.15, 2.15, 2.15, 2.15; 2.20i 1 CAU, 1 Batt.Pk, 1 Bedl, 1 Welsh, 2 Riga, 2 Haapsalu, 1 AAA-23, 3 U23L, 4= AAA, 2 Cup, 2 U23HI, 2 v SPA-23, BL1: 1,-,2,1=
3. **Stuart Ohrland** 6.9.75 (7y, 4=) 2.18 '99, 2.20i '97 2.17, 2.17, 2.10, 2.10, 2.10, 2.10; 2.19i, 2.18i, 2.17i
   2 Bedl, 2= South, 1 sf Eton, 4 Dublin, 3 AAA, 4 Cup, 1 Croydon, 1 v FRA, BL1: -,5,5=,5=
4. **James Brierley** 31.7.77 (6y, 6) 2.26 '96 2.15, 2.15, 2.14, 2.12, 2.10, 2.10
   2 CAU, 1 O/C v D/B, 6= Budapest, 6= AAA, 3 v FRA, BL4: -,1,1,-
5. **Danny Graham** 3.8.79 (4y, 3) 2.21 '99 2.22, 2.15, 2.15, 2.14, 2.14, 2.12; 2.16i, 2.15i
   1= LI, 5 v USA, 12 Jumpsl, 1 U23L, 4 Eur23, 5 Dublin, 4= AAA, 5= v FRA, 3 v SPA-23, BL3: 1,-,1,-
6. **Dalton Grant** 10.4.66 (16y, -) 2.37i '94, 2.36 '91 2.23, 2.18, 2.15, 2.15, 2.10, 2.09; 2.25i, 2.20i, 2.20i, 2.20i, 2.20i 6 v USA, 15 BL2 (3), 7 Leverkusen, nh Monaco, 1 Luton
7. **Luke Crawley** 5.9.81 (1y, -) 2.05 '99 2.15, 2.14, 2.14, 2.11, 2.10, 2.10
   3 Jnr IR, 1 E.Sch, 4 Mannheim, 1 AAA-J, 4 Bath, 2 JI4N, 10 WJ
8. **Dan Turner** 27.11.78 (3y, 8) 2.15 '97 2.12, 2.11, 2.10, 2.10, 2.10, 2.10
   3 CAU, 5 Riga, 2 AAA-23, 1 IR, 6= AAA, 5= Cup, 1 U23HI, BL1: 4/5,-,4,8
9. **Ian Holliday** 9.12.73 (4y, -) 2.16 '98 2.12, 2.10, 2.10, 2.10, 2.05, 2.05 4 CAU, 3 IR, 9 AAA, BL1: 2=,3/4,7,5=
10. **Chuka Enih-Snell** 2.3.84 (1y, -) 2.06 '99 2.15, 2.11, 2.10, 2.10, 2.09, 2.09
   1 Welsh-J, 2 BL3 (3), 1 Sch Int, 1 AAA-17, 3 Comm-Y, 5 AAA-J, 1 Bath, 4 JI4N, dnq 20 WJ
11. **Jamie Russell** 1.10.81 (1y, -) 2.10 '99 2.12, 2.12, 2.11, 2.10, 2.08, 2.06; 2.14i, 2.10i
   1 Nth-J, 1 Jnr IR, 2 IR, 4 AAA-J, BL3: -,1,-,1
12. **Darryl Stone** 6.6.83 (1y, -) 2.08 '99 2.10, 2.10, 2.10, 2.08, 2.06, 2.05
   3 Bedl, 1 U18 Int, 2 E.Sch, 2 Bath

nr **Brendan Reilly** IRE 23.12.72 (10y, -) 2.31 '92, 2.32i '94 2.24, 2.22, 2.20, 2.20, 2.20, 2.20; 2.28i, 2.25i, 2.25i, 2.24i, 2.24i 1 E.Clubs, 2 ECp 2A, 4 Budapest, 7 BGP, 2 AAA, 1 Irish, dnq 23 OG, BL1: 9,1,-,-

nr **Tyron Peacock** RSA 16.12.76 2.17 '99 2.16, 2.15, 2.12, 2.10, 2.10, 2.10; 2.15i, 2.14i
3= RSA Ch, 1 South, 1 sf Enfield, 8 AAA, BL1: 4/5,2,1,7

nr **Samson Oni** NGR 25.6.81 2.16 '99 2.15, 2.12, 2.10, 2.05, 2.00; 2.19i, 2.05i
2 AAA-J, 1 JLF, 5 Bath, BL1: -,-,3,4

This was a disapppointing year for British high jumping, with Steve Smith unable to compete after ten years always in the top four. Grant, after an encouraging return indoors, struggled to find any form outdoors, although he ties Geoff Parsons's record of 16 years in the rankings. Challenger was well below his best but takes top ranking; his 2.23 to head the outdoor rankings, was the lowest top UK mark since 1982. Reilly, now Irish, was the best of the home competitors and Mitchell made the most encouraging progress.

POLE VAULT

1. **Kevin Hughes** 30.4.73 (8y, 1) 5.61 '99 5.55, 5.50, 5.45, 5.22, 5.20, 5.20
   1 LI, 6= Cuxhaven, 2 sf Enfield, 1 AAA, dnq 16= OG
2. **Paul Williamson** 16.6.74 (8y, 3) 5.50 '96 5.55, 5.51, 5.40, 5.40, 5.40, 5.30; 5.50i
   1=B Modesto, 1 CAU, 4 Arles, 3 Bedl, nh BL1 (2), 1 sf Enfield, nh Jumpsl, 8 BGP, 2 AAA, 1 Cup, nh v FRA
3. **Tim Thomas** 18.11.73 (6y, 12) 5.40 '97 5.40, 5.40, 5.30, 5.20, 5.20, 5.20; 5.32i, 5.30i
   1 BL2 (1), 11= Arles, 1 Bedl, 4 Caorle, 6 ECp, 9 BGP, 5 AAA, 2 Cup, 1 Plate
4. **Ben Flint** 16.9.78 (4y, 4) 5.40 '99 5.30, 5.25, 5.20, 5.20, 5.15, 5.00; 5.35i 2 LI, nh E.Clubs, 11= Arles,
   2 Bedl, 1 AAA-23, 2 IR, nh Jumpsl, 4 Stoke, 3 AAA, 6 Cup, nh v FRA, 2 v SPA-23, BL1: -,1,-,3
5. **Matt Belsham** 11.10.71 (10y, 9) 5.35 '93, 5.40i '96 5.21, 5.20, 5.20, 5.20, 5.00
   3 Irvine, nh LI, nh CAU, 11= Arles, 1 BL1 (4), 4 AAA, nh Cup
6. **Ian Tullett** 15.8.69 (12y, -) 5.35 '98 5.20, 5.00, 5.00, 5.00, 5.00, 5.00
   3 LI, 2 CAU, 8= Arles, 4 Bedl, 1 South, 2 Stoke, 6 AAA, BL1: 1,2,1,2
7. **Mark Davis** 1.3.77 (3y, 6) 5.20 '99 5.20, 5.10, 5.10, 5.00, 5.00, 5.00
   nh CAU, 1 Batt.Pk, 5 Bedl, 1 Mid, 4 IR, 7 AAA
8. **Tom Richards** 13.11.78 (2y, 8) 5.25 '99 5.10, 5.10, 5.10, 5.00, 5.00, 4.90; 5.00i
   1 Cam v Ox, 2 B.Univs, 2 O/C v D/B, 5 U23L, 1B IR, 10= AAA, 4= Cup, 4 v SPA-23, BL1: 2,3,2,4=
9. **Nick Buckfield** 5.6.73 (9y, 11) 5.80 '98 5.40, 4.60; 1= Lewes, 1 Stoke, nh AAA, nh Cup
10. **Michael Barber** 19.10.73 (8y, -) 5.45 '97 5.10, 5.00, 4.80 1 sf Cudworth, 3 Cup, BL1: nh,nh,nh,4=
11. **Matt Weaver** 14.11.73 (1y, -) 5.00 '99 5.00, 5.00, 4.85, 4.80, 4.80, 4.80
    2= South, 1 O/C v D/B, 3 sf Enfield, 1 IR, 8= AAA, 2 Croydon, BL2: 3=,1,2,1
12. **Ashley Swain** 3.10.80 (1y, -) 4.90 '99 4.90, 4.90, 4.80, 4.80, 4.80, 4.80
    1 B.Univs, nh CAU, 2= South, 3 AAA-23, 1 sf Eton, 4= Cup, 1 Croydon, 1 U23HI, BL1: 6,6,3,6

\- **Mark Beharrel** 10.1.81 (1y, -) 4.91 '99 4.90, 4.90, 4.80, 4.80, 4.80, 4.70; 4.80i, 4.80i
  1 North-J, nh LI, 6 CAU, 1 Jnr IR, 3 sf Cudworth, 3 Stoke, 2 Plate, 1 AAA-J, 1 U20HI, nh JI4N

Hughes, who achieved the best ever height by a British vaulter at an Olympic Games, retains his top ranking, although Williamson had a much deeper set of marks. Buckfield struggled to return to fitness and had one clearance of 5.40, but that one mark is not enough for other than a rather token ranking. Overall standards were down, as the 10th best of 5.10 was well below 1999's record level of 5.25.

LONG JUMP

1. **Nathan Morgan** 30.6.78 (6y, 1) 8.11 '98 8.05w, 8.00, 7.98, 7.97, 7.97w, 7.90
   2 Arles, 7 ECp, 2 Budapest, 1 Ljubljana, 1 Lough, 4 Gothenburg, 2 Cup, 1 v FRA, 1 v SPA-23, BL1: -,-,2,2
2. **Darren Ritchie** 14.2.75 (4y, -) 7.86 '96, 7.92w '99 7.92w, 7.90, 7.88, 7.84, 7.81, 7.80
   1 Bedl, 1 Riga, 1 Scot, 2 AAA, 1 Cup, 1 Plate, BL1: -,-,1,1
3. **George Audu** 18.1.77 (3y, 5) 7.22/7.84w '99 7.89, 7.75, 7.63, 7.56w. 7.55
   1 BL1 (2), 1 AAA, 3 Cup, 2 Plate
4. **Steve Phillips** 17.3.72 (10y, 3) 8.03 '98, 8.07w '99 7.86w, 7.81w/7.63, 7.79, 7.63, 7.62, 7.61
   1 CAU, 2 Bedl, 1 sf Rugby, 2 Scot, 4 Cup, BL4: 1,1,-,1
5. **Dean Macey** 12.12.77 (2y, 9) 7.51/7.52w '99 7.77, 7.69; 1 BL2 (4)
6. **Phillips Idowu** 30.12.78 (1y, -) 6.16 '9x 7.83, 7.62, 7.34, 7.21w
   1 Batt.Pk, 2 Ljubljana, 6 BL1 (4), 5 R.Bay
7. **Chris Davidson** 4.12.75 (5y, 4) 7.90 '99, 7.94w '97 7.64w/7.50, 7.58w/7.51, 7.54, 7.46, 7.46, 7.45
   1 B.Univs, 1 LI, 1 sf Eton, 1 Dublin, 5 Cup, 3 Croydon, 3 v FRA, BL1: 3,-,3,3
8. **Julian Flynn** 3.7.72 (5y, 6) 7.70/7.76w '99 7.62, 7.47, 7.38, 7.34, 7.33, 7.31w
   5 Bedl, 2 sf Rugby, 1 IR, 2 Lough, 4 AAA, 6 Cup, 4 v FRA, BL1: -,2,4,4
9. **Darren Thompson** 6.11.79 (3y, 8) 7.56 '98 7.48, 7.45, 7.40, 7.38, 7.25, 7.23
   5 E.Clubs, 4 Bedl, 4 South, 3 AAA-23, 3 Lough, 3 AAA. 4 v Spa-23, BL1: -,3,8,-
10. **Chris Tomlinson** 15.9.81 (2y, 10) 7.40/7.44i '99 7.62, 7.59, 7.44, 7.29, 7.28w, 7.23; 7.57i, 7.48i, 7.47i
    1 North-J, 3 LI, 1 Jnr IR, 5 AAA, 1 AAA-J, 2 U20HI, 1 Bath, 3 JI4N, 12 WJ
11. **Stuart Wells** 26.7.79 (4y, 7) 7.56 '9, 7.68w '99 7.57w/7.51, 7.42, 7.41, 7.28, 7.16, 7.15; 7.40i, 7.38i, 7.34i
    1 Essex, 2 LI, 1 AAA-23, 4 U23L, 3 Dublin, 1 BL3 (3), nj AAA, 1 U23HI
12. **Jonathan Moore** 31.5.84 (1y, -) 6.58 '99 7.46, 7.45, 7.37; 1 AAA-17

\- **Dominique Richards** 12.9.79 (0y, -) 7.52i/7.29' '99 7.66w, 7.35, 7.33, 7.28, 7.17w, 7.14
  2 CAU, 2 South, 2 AAA-23, 6 U23L, 7 AAA, 4 Plate

Morgan is top for the third time and was challenged by Ritchie, who beat him 3-1 and set a Scottish record, but both fell short of the Olympic qualifying standard of 8.05. Flynn beat Thompson 3-2. The two newcomers, Idowu amd Moore (at 16) are difficult to rank, but both made huge improvements. The tenth best of 7.55 tied that of 1992, the best since 1989.

TRIPLE JUMP

1. **Jonathan Edwards** 10.5.66 (14y, 1) 18.29/18.43w '95 17.71, 17.62, 17.48, 17.36, 17.34, 17.32
   1 Tallahassee, 1 Fana, 4 Rome, 1 Tel Aviv, 1 BGP, 1 Zürich, 1 Leverkusen, 1 GhCl, nj Berlin, 1 Yokohama, 1 OG, 1 GPF
2. **Larry Achike** 31.1.75 (9y, 2) 17.10 '98 17.31w/16.91, 17.30, 17.29, 17.16, 17.03, 16.99w
   1/3/2/1/1 in AUS, 3 St Petersburg, 2 Fana, 1 Zagreb, 1 ECp, 2 Stockholm, 2 BGP, 2 AAA, 3 GhCl, 5 Berlin, 2 Yokohama, 5 OG, 3 GPF, BL1: -,1,3,-
3. **Phillips Idowu** 30.12.78 (4y, 6) 16.41 '99 17.12, 17.08, 17.05, 16.87, 16.83, 16.71w
   3 LI, 1 E.Clubs, 2 Bedl, 1 South, 3 Fana, 1 Budapest, 1 AAA, 2 GhCl, 6 OG, BL1: -,-,4,3
4. **Julian Golley** 12.9.71 (11y, 3) 17.06 '94 16.95, 16.82, 16.47, 16.38, 16.36w, 16.29 1 LI, 1 Bedl, 2 South, 5 Fana, 2 Zagreb, 2 BL1 (3), 7 Budapest, 8 Stockholm, 6 BGP, 4 AAA, 4 GhCl, 7 Rovereto, 8 Rieti, 4 Yokohama
5. **Francis Agyepong** 16.6.65 (17y, 4) 17.18/17.29Aw/17.24w '95 16.40, 16.38, 16.29, 16.19, 15.97, 15.73w
   4 Bedl, 3 South, 1 sf Enfield, 3 AAA, 6 Cup, BL1: 3-,-,1,1
6. **Femi Akinsanya** 29.11.69 (8y, 5) 16.63A '99, 16.58 '96 16.40w/16.18, 16.17w, 15.97, 15.81w/15.73, 15.59, 15.46 3 Bedl, 4 South, 9 AAA, BL2: 1,-,1,1
7. **Tosin Oke** 1.10.80 (2y, 7) 16.57 '99 16.37w, 16.17w, 16.04, 15.87, 15.85, 15.04
   2 LI, 1 U23L, 6 AAA, 2 v FRA, 2 v SPA-23
8. **Nicholas Thomas** 4.4.79 (3y, 9) 15.73/15.77w '99 16.31, 16.05w, 15.99, 15.93, 15.91, 15.89; 16.27i
   4 LI, 1 CAU, 7 Bedl, 5 South, 1 AAA-23, 2 U23L, 8 AAA, 5 v FRA, 1 v SPA-23, BL1: -,6,9,2
9. **Jonathan Moore** 31.5.84 (1y, -) 14.79/15.46w '99 16.02, 15.91, 15.67, 15.62, 15.58, 15.29
   1 E.Sch-I, 1 Sch.Int, 1 AAA-17, 1 Comm-Y
10. **Steven Shalders** 24.12.81 (2y, 11) 15.74 '99 15.99, 15.84, 15.73, 15.35, 15.30, 15.20
    3 BL2 (3), 1 Welsh JI, 1 sf Rugby, 3 Mannheim, 1 AAA-J, 1 Bath, 3 JI4N, 10 WJ
11. **Toyo Erogbogbo** 8.3.75 (8y, -) 10.02/10.44w '06 15.97, 15.58, 15.34, 15.05, 14.45
    2 Belgian Ch, 5 AAA, 5 Cup, 6 v FRA
12. **Tosi Fasinro** 28.3.72 (10y, -) 7.21/17.30w '93 15.70, 15.66, 15.57, 15.49w, 15.28, 15.24
    6 Bedl, 6 South, 2 sf Enfield, 7 AAA, BL2: -,2,2,2

Edwards capped his brilliant career with Olympic gold and is UK no.1 for the 11th time and tenth year in succession. He won ten of his 12 competitions and was over 17m in all but when he jumped 16.81 in Rome and had three no-jumps in Berlin. History was made when Achike and Idowu also placed in the Olympic top six and all three were ranked in the world's top eight. The top six are the same as last year, except that Idowu moves up from 6th to 3rd. Agyepong has an event record with 17 years in the rankings. Oke beat Thomas 4-1. Moore, son of Aston, makes his debut in the rankings at the age of 16, passing 16m to win the Commonwealth Youth title, and Shalders set Welsh junior records in both qualifying and final of the World Juniors. Tenth best of 15.99 is an all-time record.

SHOT

1. **Mark Proctor** 15.1.63 (10y, 1) 20.40 '99, 20.85i '98 20.11, 19.14, 19.04, 18.69, 18.55, 18.49; 20.57i, 19.77i, 19.42i, 19.15i 1 LI, nt Halle, 1 IS, 3 AAA, 1 Cup, 1 Plate, dnq 31 OG; BL1: -,1,-,nt
2. **Stephan Hayward** 30.7.74 (6y, 3) 18.40 '96 18.79, 18.38, 18.31, 18.24, 18.23, 18.22; 18.30i, 18.28i
   1 Scot-E, 2 LI, 1 CAU, 1 BRS, 1 Scot, 1 AAA, BL1: -,2,1,1
3. **Mark Edwards** 2.12.74 (5y, 3) 19.21 '99 19.72, 19.66, 19.66, 19.55, 19.32, 19.15
   3 LI, 4B Halle, 2 BRS, 8 ECp, 1 BLQ
4. **Emeka Udechuku** 10.7.79 (4y, 5) 17.25 '97 18.10, 17.95, 17.82, 17.81, 17.74, 17.65; 17.90i, 17.81i
   1 B.Univs, 4 LI, 3 BRS, 1 Bedl, 1 South, 1 AAA-23, 1 sf Rugby, 3 U23L, 3 Dublin, 2 AAA, 2 Cup, 2 Plate, 1 Croydon, 2 v FRA, 2 v SPA-23, BL2: 1,1,2,1
5. **Lee Newman** 1.5.73 (8y, 6) 18.85 '96 17.81, 17.38, 17.33, 17.03, 16.92, 16.84
   2 sf Rugby, 1 Lough, 4 AAA, 4 Cup, 3 Plate, BL1: -,3,3,2
6. **David Condon** 11.4.72 (4y, 12) 16.41 '94 17.16, 17.03, 16.80, 16.73, 16.70, 16.66
   6 LI, 2 CAU, 2 South, 8 Budapest, 1 IR, 5 AAA, 2 Croydon, 6 v FRA
7. **Scott Rider** 22.9.77 (1y, -) 16.11 '99 17.04, 16.72, 16.50, 16.33, 16.31, 16.29; 17.04i
   4 CAU, 4 Bedl, 1 sf Enfield, 2 IR, 3 Lough, 6 AAA, BL2: 2,2,3,2
8. **Bruce Robb** 27.7.77 (1y, -) 15.99 '97 16.55, 16.49, 16.47, 16.40, 16.35, 16.27
   2 Scot-E, 5 LI, 3 CAU, 2 Scot, 2 Lough, 8 AAA, 2 BLQ
9. **David Readle** 10.2.80 (2y, 9) 16.23i/16.15 '99 17.50, 16.84, 16.61, 16.27, 16.07, 15.90; 16.69i, 16.18i
   3 North, 2 AAA-23, 5 U23L, 12 AAA, BL1: -,4,2,3
10. **Gary Sollitt** 13.1.72 (7y, 8) 17.14 '97 16.95, 16.21, 16.12, 16.11, 16.11, 15.96 5 CAU, 1 sf Eton, 3 Cup, BL1: 2,-,5,4
11. **Greg Beard** 10.9.82 (1y, -) 15.28 '99 16.69, 16.49, 16.04, 15.99, 15.87, 15.82
    7 LI, 8 CAU, 5 Bedl, 3 South, 1 AAA-J, 1 U20HI, 3 JI4N, dnq 16 WJ, BL4: -,1,1,1
12. **Iain McMullen** 15.6.78 (1y, -) 15.45 '99 16.20, 16.03, 15.97, 15.78, 15.77, 15.65
    1 NI, 3 AAA-23, 3 Irish, 5 Dublin, 7 AAA, 1 U23HI, 4 vSPA-23, BL2: 5,4,-,4

Proctor was number one for the fourth time, although he struggled to come back from injury. Edwards had much the next best set of marks, ahead of Hayward's best in 11 competitions – but he was unable to show such form in any meeting that really mattered, as his best against top opposition was 18.26 in Halle. Hayward, who ended the year with a Scottish native record, was 2-2 v Proctor, beat Edwards on the two occasions they met and was also AAA champion, a meeting missed by Edwards.

DISCUS

1. **Robert Weir** 4.2.61 (13y, 1) 64.60 '97 65.08, 63.65, 63.58, 62,13, 61.87, 61.51
   3 v USA, 1 BL1 (3), 4 ECp, 6/1B Budapest, 1 Lough, 3 Helsingborg, 1 AAA, 1 Cup, dnq 28 OG
2. **Glen Smith** 21.5.72 (10y, 2) 65.11 '99 63.08, 62.92, 62.68, 61.92, 61.80, 61.62
   4 Modesto, 7 Salinas, 8 Halle, 1 Arles, 1 Lough 14/6, 1 Istanbul, 4 v USA, 7 Budapest, 1 IR, 3 Lough, 1 BL1 (4), 2 AAA, 5 Helsingborg, dnq 38 OG
3. **Emeka Udechuku** 10.7.79 (4y, 6) 60.97 '98 62.07, 61.91, 59.58, 59.55, 58.84, 58.83
   1 B.Univs, 1 LI, 3B Halle, 2 Bedl, 3 Lough 14/6, 1 South, 1 AAA-23, 5 v USA, 1 U23L, 1 sf Rugby, 3 Dublin, 2 Lough, 3 AAA, 9 Helsingborg, 2 Cup, 1 Plate, 2 Croydon, 3 v FRA, 1 v SPA-23, BL2: 1,1,1,1
4. **Perriss Wilkins** 12.12.69 (5y, 3) 66.64 '98 64.65, 60.21, 60.02, 59.06, 58.42, 57.72
   2 CAU, 3 Bedl, 2 South, 4 Dublin, 4 AAA, 4 Cup, 2 Plate, 1 Croydon
5. **Kevin Brown UK/JAM** 10.9.64 (16y, 4) 61.10 '97 62.10, 59.70, 58.00, 56.24, 56.18, 55.68
   2 E.Clubs, 6 Arles, 2 Lough 14/6, 1 Jamaican, 5 Lough, BL1: 1,2,3,3
6. **Lee Newman** 1.5.73 (8y, 5) 60.48 '97 57.44, 57.38, 57.32, 57.28, 57.10, 56.75 6 Walnut, 2 LI, 1 CAU, 8 Arles, 1 Bedl, 1 Welsh, 2 sf Rugby, 2 IR, 4 Lough, 5 AAA, 3 Cup, 1 Bath, BL1: 2,3,2,2
7. **Bruce Robb** 27.7.77 (1y, -) 50.04 '99 53.31, 52.40, 52.30, 51.72, 51.69, 51.20
   1 Scot-E, 3 LI, 4 CAU, 5B Budapest, 1 Scot, 7 Lough, 7 AAA, 1 BLQ
8. **Paul Reed** 2.6.62 (8y, 7) 58.36 '99 54.11, 53.10, 52.58, 52.02, 51.14, 51.03
   4 LI, 2 Police, 1 sf Cudworth, 7 v FRA, BL1: 3,5,5,5
9. **Neville Thompson** 28.3.55 (20y, 9) 55.68 '93 53.00, 52.21, 51.20, 51.05, 51.01, 50.79
   1 sf Enfield, 1 B.Vets, 9 AAA, 5 Cup, 3 Croydon, BL1: 6,6,4,6
10. **Scott Rider** 22.9.77 (2y, 12) 50.95 '99 52.81, 51.65, 51.55, 51.15, 50.69, 50.46
    5 CAU, 5 Bedl, 2 sf Enfield, 4 IR, 6 Lough, 8 AAA, BL2: 2,6,2,2
11. **Peter Gordon** 2.7.51 (18y, -) 61.62 '91 53.93, 53.21, 51.74, 51.65, 51.09, 51.02
    1 North, 1 Eur Vets, 2 Scot

12 **Denzil McDonald** 11.10.65 (4y, 11) 55.04 '95 52.49, 52.32, 52.09, 50.88, 50.13, 50.09
6 CAU, 10 AAA, 7 Cup, BL1: 5,4,nt,4

- **Mark Proctor** 15.1.63 (3y, 1) 55.08 '97 57.14, 51.26, 50.90, 46.10; 1 BL1 (2)
- **Abi Ekoku** 13.4.66 (7y, 8) 60.08 '90 53.28, 50.42; 6 AAA
- **Gary Herrington** 31.3.61 (11y, -) 56.66 '96 52.42, 50.83, 50.63, 50.62, 50.60, 50.40
  3 CAU, 5 Lough 14/6, 1 Mid, 1 Police, 3 sf Rugby, 2 IR, 8 Lough, 11 AAA, BL4: -,-,1,1

Weir is top for the eighth successive year and 10th in all, the record for the event. It was a delight that, at the Cup Final, he at last found the conditions to exceed 65m. Smith is 2nd for the fifth successive year and Udechuku moved up for third. I have again kept Kevin Brown in the rankings (for the 16th year) as he remains an integral part of the British discus scene despite his dual British/Jamaican citizenship. He was 3-3 with Newman, who was splendidly consistent. The final places in the rankings were closely contested. Thompson, at 45. achieved a 22-year span in the rankings and that would have been a record except that 49 year-old Gordon fought his way back in, and has a 23-year span (Weir also has a 20-year span). Ekoku was 6th at the AAAs, but only competed twice, and Proctor, did not have enough to back up his pb 57.14 in the second BL1 match.

HAMMER

1. **Michael Jones** 23.7.63 (19y, 1) 75.20 '99 75.94, 74.98, 74.89, 74.39, 74.37, 73.86
   1 Perivale, 1 Colindale, 1 E.Clubs, 6 Halle, 1 BRS. 1 Lough, 1 AAA, 1 Cup, 4 v FRA, BL1: 1,1,1,1
2. **Paul Head** 1.7.65 (18y, 3) 74.02 '90 70.90, 70.79, 69.63, 69.49, 69.46, 69.42
   1 Essex, 1 CAU, 7 ECp, 7B Budapest, 1 IR, 1 South, 2 AAA, 2 Cup, 1 Croydon, 6 v FRA, BL1: 2,2,2,2
3. **John Pearson** 30.4.66 (12y, 4) 70.24 '97 70.33, 69.49, 68.40, 68.36, 68.18, 68.18
   2 LI, 5 CAU, 2 Dublin, 2 Lough, 3 AAA
4. **Michael Floyd** 26.9.76 (3y, 8) 66.46 '99 69.38, 68.18, 67.71, 67.29, 67.13, 66.98
   3 Colindale, 1 LI, 2 CAU, 1 North, 1 sf Cudworth, 3 Dublin, 3 Lough, 4 AAA, 1 NthIC, BL1: 3,3,3,3
5. **Bill Beauchamp** 9.9.70 (6y, 2) 72.63 '99 71.76, 70.75, 70.37, 67.57, 67.16, 65.89
   2 Perivale, 2 Colindale, 3 LI, 4 CAU
6. **David Smith** 2.11.74 (7y, 5) 75.10 '96 68.02, 67.69, 67.01, 66.15 3 CAU, 2 North
7. **Simon Bown** 21.11.74 (3y, 7) 65.32 '99 65.22, 65.15, 64.84, 64.77, 64.61, 64.36
   6 Colindale, 2 Essex, 6 CAU, 1 sf Eton, 2 IR, 2 South, 5 AAA, 2 Croydon, BL1: 4,4,4,4
8. **Shane Peacock** 5.3.63 (15y, 6) 71.60 '90 63.60, 62.91, 62.70, 62.20, 62.14, 61.96
   3 North, 2 sf Cudworth, 5 Lough, 7 AAA, 3 Cup, BL1: 5,5,5,5
9. **Steve Pearson** 13.9.59 (10y, 9) 67.45 '98 64.47, 63.08, 62.64, 62.48, 62.36, 62.29
   4 Colindale, 2 Staffs, 7 CAU, 1 Mid, 3 IR, 4 Lough, 9 AAA, BL1: 10,-,6,nt
10. **Craig Ellams** 24.11.72 (4y, 11) 63.98 '97 64.39, 62.68, 62.32, 61.83, 60.90, 60.53
    8 Colindale, 1 Staffs, 12 CAU, 3 Mid, 1 sf Rugby, 6 AAA, BL3: 1,1,1,1
11. **Russell Devine** 24.4.68 (6y, 10) 66.00 '99 65.09, 63.99, 63.94, 63.89, 63.51, 63.44 all in Melbourne
12. **Chris Howe** 17.11.67 (11y, -) 66.97 '98 62.92, 61.87, 60.72, 60.28, 60.10, 60.06
    2 sf Eton, 8 AAA, BL2: 1,1,1,1

The horrid escalation of standards set by the IAAF will make it even harder for Jones to compete at the World Champs in 2001, but he was desperately unfortunate that his throw over this year's standard of 75.50 (a 74cm improvement on his pb) came a week too late for the British Olympic Committee deadline. He could still have gone ... and should. He retained the no.1 ranking for the third year and sets an event record with 19 years in the rankings. Beauchamp got injured in May after three 70m competitions and did not compete again and Head returned to second ranking. The greatest progress was made by Floyd, who added three metres to his best; he was just behind Pearson, who beat him 3-2, but beat Beauchamp 2-1. The consistency of our throwers was shown by the BL1 results where in all four fixtures the 1-2-3-4-5 was the same. There were no newcomers to the rankings, although Graham Holder was close.

JAVELIN

1. **Steve Backley** 12.2.69 (14y, 1) 91.46 '92 89.85, 86.70, 85.84, 83.74, 82.19, 82.13
   1 v USA, 2 BGP, 1 AAA, 1 GhCl, 2 OG
2. **Nick Nieland** 31.1.72 (9y, 4) 83.68 '99 85.09, 82.51, 82.33, 82.12, 81.25, 80.90
   4 Halle, 1 LI, 4 v USA, 2 Budapest, 5 Oslo, 5 BGP, 2 AAA, 2 GhCl, dnq 13 OG
3. **Mick Hill** 22.10.64 (17y, 2) 86.94 '93 83.71, 83.06, 82.42, 82.29, 82.24, 81.07
   5/6/1 in RSA, 3 v USA, 5 ECp, 9 Stockholm, 7 BGP, 3 AAA, 3 GhCl, 1 Rovereto, 11 OG
4. **Mark Roberson** 13.3.67 (15y, 3) 85.67 '98 79.40. 76.10, 74.70, 74.56, 74.50, 73.70 1 CAU, 4 Fana,
   5 Karlstad, 5 Budapest, 1 sf Eton, 2 Dublin, 4 AAA, 1 Cup, 6 GhCl, 5 Rovereto, 2 v FRA, BL1: -,-,2,1
5. **David Parker** 28.2.80 (5y, 5) 77.48 '99 78.24, 77.30, 76.60, 76.31, 75.94, 75.12 1 B.Univs, 3 LI, 1B Halle,
   5 CAU, 2 Karlstad, 2 U23L, 3 Dublin, 6 AAA, 2 Cup, 7 GhCl, 3 v FRA, 1 vSPA-23, BL1: 1,-,-,2
6. **Stuart Faben** 28.2.75 (6y, 6) 75.22 '99, 76.66i '96 75.37, 75.30, 74.67, 73.60, 73,29, 72.82
   2 LI, 3 E.Clubs, 4 Karlstad, 1 sf Rugby, 5 AAA, 3 Cup, 5 v FRA, BL1: 2,-,1,3
7. **Dan Carter** 15.4.80 (3y, 10) 71.14 '98 73.56, 72.46, 71.90, 70.98, 70.39, 70.11
   4 CAU, 1 South, 1 AAA-23, 6 U23L, 7 AAA, 1 U20HI, 2 vSPA-23, 1 Bath, BL2: 2,1,1,1
8. **Phill Sharpe** 6.3.81 (2y, 7) 70.17 '99 71.79, 71.77, 70.15, 69.99, 69.73, 68.36
   4 LI, 2 CAU, 3 Mannheim, 1 AAA-J, 1 U20HI, 2 JI4N, dnq 22 WJ, BL1: 3,-,-,5
9. **Neil McLellan** 10.9.78 (1y, -) 63.00 '99 68.27, 68.22, 65.49, 65.42, 64.26, 63.73
   6 CAU, 3 South, 2 AAA-23, 1 IR, 8 AAA
10. **Keith Beard** 8.11.61 (10y, 11) 76.10 '91 67.48, 66.85, 66.42, 64.19 4th Dutch Champs
11. **Michael Allen** UK/IRE 7.3.80 (1y, -) 66.65 '98 68.34, 64.27, 63.93, 63.71, 63.51, 61.77
    1 NI, 2 Scot, 2 U23HI, BL1: 6,2,-,7
12. **Gary Jensen** 14.2.67 (10y. -) 79.54R- 91, 78.54- 89 68.91, 68.53, 65.28, 58.77

Backley is number one for the 11th time (beating David Ottley's record for the event) and excelled with his best throw for eight years at the Olympic Games only to be passed by the world's greatest ever javelin thrower, Jan Zelezny. Hill made his 16th major championship final by relegating Nieland by just 12cm at the Olympics, but Nieland beat him 3-2 overall and his 85.09 at the AAAs perhaps just helps to give him the edge over Hill for second ranking. Roberson and Parker follow to make up the same top five as in 1998 and 1999 and Faben retains sixth place. There is all too large a gap after the top eight before the top newcomer, McLellan, and tenth best at 68.27 is the worst ever with the current javelin specification (introduced in 1986).

DECATHLON

1. **Dean Macey** 12.12.77 (3y, 1) 8556 '99 4 OG 8567
2. **Jamie Quarry** 15.11.72 (8y, 2) 7739 '99 10 Arles 7667
3. **Barry Thomas** 28.4.72 (10y, -) 7766 '95 4 Spanish 7407, 16 Arles 7209, 7 ECp2 7121
4. **Alexis Sharp** 31.10.72 (3y, -) 7354 '97 20 Arles 7133, dnf Spanish
5. **Paul Jones** 11.4.78 (3y, 7) 6940 '99 22 Arles 7071, 1 HCl 7002w, 4 U23V 6948, 11 ECp2 6930
6. **Alex Kruger** 18.11.63 (12y, -) 8131 '95 1 AAA 6975, 33 Arles 6499
7. **Mark Sweeney** 26.2.77 (1y, -) 6067 '97 2 HCl 6862w, 1 B.Univs 6752, 2 AAA 6652, 2 (1) Mid 6499
8. **Stephen Bonnett** 13.7.78 (2y, 4) 7146 '99 16 ECp2 6754, 24 (nh PV) Arles 6458
9. **Fyn Corcoran** 17.3.78 (2y, 6) 7116 '99 29 Arles 6761, dnf ECp2
10. **Brendan McConville** 3.1.79 (1y, -) 6530 '99 3 HCl 6720w, 32 Arles 6561, 3 B.Univs 6124 (nh PV),
    10 U23V 5763 (dq 400)
11. **Bill Wynn** 15.2.73 (5y, 9=) 6800w/6790 '96 4 HCl 6696w, 1g Mid 6652, 3 AAA 6563
12. **Anthony Sawyer** 29.4.80 (1y, -) 5861 '99 1 Gateshead 6680, 8 U23V 6622, 3g Mid 6425

HCl – Home Countries International at Waterford
U23V/U20V – International at Val-de-Reuil

The marvellous Macey went to Sydney with just one day of competition in 2000 behind him (LJ, SP and 400m relay leg at Enfield) and yet improved his pb while so narrowly and unluckily missing a medal. Sadly the 10th best on the UK lists, at 6720, is the second worst in the past 23 years.

20 KILOMETRES WALK

1. **Chris Maddocks** 28.3.57 (18y, 1) 1:22:12 '92
   1= Plymouth 1:27:04t*, 2 Manx 1:27:38, 18 Leamington 1:31:10, 50 ECp 1:31:39
2. **Andrew Penn** 31.3.67 (10y, -) 1:23:34 '92
   3 Manx 1:29:24, 2 RWA 1:28:47, 17 Leamington 1:30:26, 51 ECp 1:33:10
3. **Darrell Stone** 2.2.68 (12y, 4) 1:23:58 '96, 1:23:27sh '93 1 RWA 1:27:08, dq Leamington, dq ECp
4. **Andi Drake** 6.2.65 (9y, 3) 1:24:04.0t '90 2 Irish 1:25:56, dq ECp, dnf Dublin
5. **Matthew Hales** 6.10.79 (2y, 8) 1:30:38 '99 3 RWA 1:31:50, 20 Leamington 1:31:57
6. **Steve Hollier** 27.2.76 (3y, 9) 1:28:34 '99 1= Plymouth 1:27:04t* (* not subject to full judging controls)
7. **Mark Easton** 24.5.63 (11y, 7) 1:24:04 '89 1 Leamington 12/2 1:30:54
8. **Jamie O'Rawe** 3.2.73 (5y, 5) 1:28:46 '99 1 Basildon 1:35:33, 6 Dublin 1:30:56
9. **Steve Partington** 17.9.65 (14y, -) 1:24:19 '90 4 Manx 1:31:14
10. **Don Bearman** 16.4.66 (1y, -) 1:34:56 '98
    5 Manx 1:32:33, 4 RWA 1:32:38, 21 Leamington 1:34:01, dnf Dublin
11. **Gareth Brown** 10.5.68 (4y, -) 1:30:15 '89 5 RWA 1:32:43, 1 Sussex 1:41:29
12. **Andy O'Rawe** 8.9.63 (2y, -) 1:34:05 '96 6 RWA 1:37:19, 22 Leamington 1:34:41, 1 Basildon 1:34:23

This was an undistinguished year for the event, with nobody approaching international standards and very difficult to rank, because there was a lack of clear cut evidence. Drake produced the fastest time, but that was his only finish and was not against his main rivals. Stone won the RWA title, but was disqualified in the other two big races, in the Leamington GP and the European Cup. Top ranking goes to the man who was our first finisher in the European Cup – 43 year-old Maddocks, top for the fifth time at 20k and included for a record 18th year. Penn was beaten 2-1 by Maddocks and had a consistent set of results. 20 year-old Hales made encouraging progress, but Bearman, at the age of 34, is the only newcomer to the rankings.

50 KILOMETRES WALK

1. **Chris Maddocks** 28.3.57 (12y, -) 3:51:37 '90 1 Dutch 3:57:10, 39 OG 4:52:12
2. **Steve Hollier** 27.2.76 (3y, 3) 4:14:37 '98 dq Dutch, 9 Leamington 4:15:18, 28 ECp 4:07:18
3. **Chris Cheeseman** 11.12.58 (5y, 1) 4:07:49 '99 dnf POR Ch, dnf Essex, 10 Leamington 4:17:57,
   43 ECp 4:23:19, 6 Dublin 4:13:07, dnf RWA
   Note 35km: 1 RWA 2:51:20
4. **Mark Easton** 24.5.63 (5y, -) 4:03:53 '98 2 Dutch 4:07:33, dnf Naumburg, dnf Essex
5. **Darrell Stone** 2.2.68 (2y, -) 4:10:23 '90 1 RWA 4:21:23
6. **Tim Watt** 19.9.66 (5y, -) 4:20:43 '95 11 Leamington 4:23:18, dnf ECp
7. **Gareth Brown** 10.5.68 (3y, -) 4:27:22 '96 2 RWA 4:27:23
   Note 35km: 3 RWA 2:55:59
8. **Don Bearman** 16.4.66 (1y, -) 0 45 ECp 4:36:15, 3 RWA 4:32:42
   Note 35km: 2 RWA 2:53:10
9. **Peter Kaneen** 12.7.61 (1y, -) 4:55:36 '98 4 RWA 4:50:47
10. **Mike Smith** 20.4.63 (7y, -) 4:09:22 '89 5 RWA 4:51:31
    Note 35km: 4 RWA 3:11:00

It is good to report that this year, with three men in the world top 100, was a far better one for 50k walk in Britain after 1999 when I could find only five men to rank and when we had just one under 4:10, two under 4:20 and three under 4:40. Maddocks broke 4 hours for the first time since 1995 and, making history by being the first British male athlete to compete at five Olympic Games, was heroic in fighting injury to finish to a reception which he will always treasure and which crowned a most disintingushed career; he is top having previously taken that position in 1980 (tie), 1983-4, and 1995-7. Hollier set a pb when he was our top placer at the European Cup and was unfortunate to be disqualified when about to break 4 hours at the Dutch Championships. Cheeseman's depth of marks give him third over Easton, and Stone returned to the event (at which he had ranked 4th in 1990) to win the RWA title.

UK MERIT RANKINGS 2000 - WOMEN

100 METRES

1. **Marcia Richardson** 10.2.72 (10y, 3) 11.40, 11.36w '98 11.29w, 11.35, 11.38, 11.39w, 11.41, 11.43; 11.3w
   1 Fullerton, 1 CAU, 2 BRS, 1r3 Bedl, 7 ECp, 2 Budapest, 8 BGP, 1 AAA, 2 Cup, 5 GhCl, 4h7 OG
2. **Joice Maduaka** 30.9.73 (4y, 1) 11.24 '99 11.42, 11.44, 11.46, 11.46, 11.47, 11.47
   2 Riga, 3 Fana, 2 v USA, 4 Caorle, 1 Budapest, 2 Ljubljana, 1B Linz, 2 AAA, 7 GhCl, 5h1 OG
3. **Shani Anderson** 7.8.75 (4y, 4) 11.45/11.36w '99 11.34, 11.50, 11.52, 11.55, 11.55, 11.57; 11.3w
   5 v USA, 3 Budapest, 1 Lough, 1 BL1 (3), 1 Cup, 1 Plate inv, 1 Nitra, 6 GhCl, 5r1 R.Bay, 5h6 OG
4. **Samantha Davies** 20.9.79 (2y, -) 11.72 '99, 11.50w '98 11,44, 11.47, 11.51, 11.55, 11.55, 11.56; 11,4w
   1 LI, 3 CAU, 4 BRS, 1r2 Bedl, 3 Riga, 2 Fana, 4 v USA, 1 IR, 3 AAA, 3 Cup, 5h1 Leverkusen
5. **Donita Benjamin** 7.3.72 (1y, -) 12.0/12.15w '98 11.43, 11.50, 11.52, 11.56, 11.57w, 11.60
   1B LI, 2 South, 1 IS, 2 BL1 (2), 1 sf Eton, 1r2 Dublin, 5 AAA, 2 Cup inv, 2 Plate inv, 1 v FRA

6. **Christine Bloomfield** 12.2.68 (4y, 2) 11.32 '99 11.49w, 11.58, 11.59, 11.60, 11.64, 11.64 3r1 Irvine, 1 Basel, 7 Kiev, 6 Budapest, 4 Ljubljana, 1 Gothenburg, 6 AAA, 1 Cup inv, 1 Växjö, 2 v FRA, BL2: -,1,1
7. **Donna Fraser** 7.11.72 (2y, -) 11.66, 11.32w '97, 11.2w '98 11.45w, 11.51w, 11.53w, 11.57, 11.57w, 11.59 4r1 Irvine, 3 Fullerton, 2 CAU, 4r3 Bedl, 3 Cup inv
8. **Abi Oyepitan** 30.12.79 (3y, 8) 11.65 '99, 11.45w '98 11.52, 11.53, 11.58, 11.71, 11.71, 11.72 2 LI, 2r3 Bedl, 8 South, 2 AAA-23, 1 BL1 (2), 1 U23L, dns s1 AAA
9. **Amanda Forrester** 29.9.78 (1y, -) 11.97, 11.69w '99 11.55, 11.59, 11.71, 11.71, 11.72. 11.73 2 B.Univs, 4B LI, 1 Mid, 1 AAA-23, 2 U23L, 2r2 Dublin, 5 v FRA, 1 v SPA-23
10. **Catherine Murphy** 21.9.75 (4y. 9) 11.67 '99, 11.6 '96, 11.63w '94 11.68, 11.71A, 11.72, 11.73, 11.76, 11.76 4 Fullerton, 6 BRS, 5r3 Bedl, 1 Welsh, 3 Haapsalu, 1B BL1 (2), 4h1 Budapest, 7r1 Dublin, 7 AAA
11. **Ellana Ruddock** 23.2.76 (2y, -) 11.63A '99, 11.67/11.53w '98 11.49w, 11.66w, 11.77, 11.85w, 11.88, 11.95; 11.8, 11.8w, 11.8w 1 Warwicks, 2B LI, 4 CAU, 2 Mid, 2 sf Rugby, 4 IR, 8 AAA, 5 Cup, BL3: 1,1,1
12. **Zoe Wilson** 28.8.76 (1y, -) 11.82, 11.67w '99 11.52w, 11.52w, 11.66, 11.71w, 11.75, 11.75w 2 Fullerton, 1B BL1 (1), 2 Warwicks, 4 LI, 5 CAU, 1r1 Bedl, 3 South, 6h1 Budapest, 6s2 AAA, 4 Cup inv

– **Sarah Wilhelmy** 2.2.80 (1y, -) 11.71, 11.6w '98 11.49, 11.53; 1 Barbados Ch, 1r2 R.Bay

nr **Sarah Reilly** IRE 3.7.73 (1y, -) 11.51 '97 11.45w, 11.49, 11.50, 11.53, 11.53, 11,53w 6 Fullerton, 3r3 Bedl, 1 South, 4 Budapest, 1r1 Dublin, 5 Ljubljana, 2 BL1 (3), 4 AAA, 1 Irish, 7q4 OG

After three seconds and two thirds, Richardson is ranked top for the first time. Maduaka beat Anderson, who recorded the fastest legal time of the year, 2-1, but all these three went out in the first round at the Olympics. There Sarah Reilly (née Oxley) made it to the quarter-finals having switched to Ireland on her marriage to Brendan in March. Davies was 1-1 with Anderson. Benjamin made a big improvement and is the highest newcomer to the 100m rankings. After 17 successive years in the rankings, Simmone Jacobs misses out, although she had an early season 11.59w before injury. The tenth best of 11.58 has only once been bettered (11.57 in 1984).

200 METRES

1. **Katharine Merry** 21.9.74 (10y, 3) 22.77 '97 22.76, 23.17, 23.22 1 LI, 1 BRS, 2 Barcelona
2. **Donna Fraser** 7.11.72 (9y, 8) 23.13 '99, 22.96i/22.90w '97 23.08, 23.08w, 23.14, 23.15, 23.19, 23.29 1 Azusa, 3r1 Irvine, 1 Fullerton, 1r3 Bedl, 6 ECp, 1r2 Budapest, 1 Cup inv, 2 Thessaloniki
3. **Samantha Davies** 20.9.79 (1y, -) 24.22 '97, 24.02w '98 23.06, 23.20, 23.31, 23.36, 23.42, 23.47 4 Riga, 3 Fana, 2 U23L, 2 AAA, 5 GhCl, 7q2 OG
4. **Sarah Wilhelmy** 2.2.80 (3y, -) 23.23/23.20w '98 23.26, 23.29, 23.39, 23.61, 23.62, 23.73 2 Barbados Ch, 1r1 Dublin 1 AAA, 7 GhCl
5. **Shani Anderson** 7.8.75 (2y, 4) 23.22 '99 23.20, 23.27w, 23.36, 23.43, 23.49, 23.51 5r1 Irvine, 1 E.Clubs, 3r2 Budapest, 3 AAA, 1/2inv Cup, 2 Plate inv, 3 R.Bay, BL1: -,2,1
6. **Joice Maduaka** 30.9.73 (5y, 1) 22.83 '99 23.17, 23.27, 23.33w, 23.36, 23.44, 23.57; 23.52i 6 Turin, 3 Riga, 2 Fana, 3r3 Budapest, 1 Ljubljana, 3 Linz, 4 AAA, 7q1 OG
7. **Catherine Murphy** 21.9.75 (7y, 6) 23.28 '99 23.48w, 23.59, 23.72w, 23.74, 23.78, 23.81; 23.46i, 23.57i, 23.57i, 23.60i 5r4 Walnut, 4 Fullerton, 6r1 Irvine, 1 Welsh, 1 Haapsalu, 1B BL1 (2), 1= Jona, 6r2 Budapest, 1r2 Dublin, 6 AAA, 1 Tønsberg
8. **Vernicha James** 6.6.84 (1y, -) 24.42/24.37i, 23.48w '99 23.59, 23.62, 23.65, 23.76, 23.81w, 23.86; 23.49i 6 LI, 1r1 Bedl, 1 ES-I, 1 Comm-Y, 1 AAA-J, 1 Bath, 1 JI4N, 5 WJ
9. **Christine Bloomfield** 12.2.68 (2y, 2) 22.85 '99 23.62, 23.67, 23.73, 23.77, 23.80, 23.85; 23.31i, 23.40i, 23.6i 1 Basel, 7r3 Budapest, 5 Ljubljana, 7 AAA, 3 Cup inv, 1 Plate inv, 1 v FRA, BL2: -,1,1B
10. **Marcia Richardson** 10.2.72 (8y, -) 23.53 '95, 23.4 '93 23.53, 23.67; 24.1 2 Fullerton, 2r3 Bedl, 1 BL1 (2)
11. **Jennifer Stoute** 16.4.65 (11y, -) 22.73 '92 23.57, 23.72w, 23.75, 24.08w, 24.60; 24.75i 8r1 Irvine, 1= Jona, 6r3 Budapest, 3 Ljubljana, BL2: -,1B,1
12. **Susan Williams** 2.6.77 (2y, 10) 23.59 '99 23.90w, 24.05w, 24.09, 24.19w, 24.19, 24.32 4 LI, 2 CAU, 7r3 Bedl, 3 South, 3 Lewes, 1 IR, 8 AAA, 1 Croydon

– **Melanie Purkiss** 11.3.79 (3y, 9) 23.80/23.64w '99 23.83, 23.94, 24.00, 24.01, 24.03, 24.05 3 LI, 7 CAU, 6 BRS, 8 South, 1 AAA-23, 2 BL2 (2), 4 U23L, 2r2 Dublin, 5s2 AAA, 3 v FRA, 1 v SPA-23

– **Sinead Dudgeon** 9.7.76 (1y, 11) 23.59 '99 23.23w, 24.13; 1 Scot

nr **Sarah Reilly** 3.7.73 (2y, 7) 23.20 '97 23.12, 23.23, 23.43, 23.43, 23.50w, 23.53 3r3 Bedl, 1 South, 1 Lewes, 2r2 Budapest, 5 AAA, 1 Irish; 5h2 OG

The top two 400m runners were top at this event as well. As in 1999, Merry, had only three outdoor races at this distance, but her best time came in Barcelona ahead of European Cup winner, Muriel Hurtis FRA, and she had two good domestic victories, so she regains her number one ranking (fifth year at the top). Fraser was also superior to the other sprinters and Murphy is a third woman to rank at 100, 200 and 400. Wilhelmy came back to win the AAA title, but just failed to get the Olympic qualifying time of 23.20. Last year's top woman, Maduaka, was, as in the 100, quite a bit slower than in 1999, but made the Olympic quarter-finals, as did Davies, who had not broken 24 secs before the year started. Maduaka beat Davies 2-1, but Davies was ahead at the AAAs, beat Wihelmy to get the qualifying time in Gateshead and ran faster in Sydney. James comes in at age 16 and, as she did not meet those ranked around her, slots in on the basis of her times. Sinead Dudgeon ran 23.23w (24.13 in heat) to win the Scottish title but is not ranked as that was her only competition. The tenth best on legal marks, 23.59, was exactly the same as in 1999, and not bettered since 1984.

400 METRES

1. **Katharine Merry** 21.9.74 (3y, 1) 50.21 '99 49.72, 50.05, 50.28, 50.32, 50.45, 50.50
   1 Helsinki, 1 Nuremberg, 1 v USA, 1 Nice, 3 BGP, 5 Brussels, 3 OG
2. **Donna Fraser** 7.11.72 (8y, 2) 50.85 '98 49.79, 50.21, 50.77, 50.94, 51.06, 51.62
   3r2 Walnut, 4 Bratislava, 4 v USA, 2 ECp, 2A Budapest, 4 Oslo, 7 BGP, 1 AAA, 4 OG
3. **Allison Curbishley** 3.6.76 (5y, 3) 50.71 '98 51.50, 51.96, 52.04, 52.20, 52.50, 53.12
   1 Scot, 1 Lignano, 2 AAA, 7qf OG
4. **Helen Frost** 12.3.74 (4y, 4) 52.42 '99 52.40, 52.54, 52.62, 53.28, 53.33, 53.40
   1 CAU, 4 Riga, 2 Fana, 7A Budapest, 1 BL1 (3), 3 AAA, 1 Cup, 1r2 R.Bay
5. **Sinead Dudgeon** 9.7.76 (2y, 6) 52.05 '99 52.71, 52.78; 6 v USA, 2r1 R.Bay
6. **Catherine Murphy** 21.9.75 (1y, -) 0 52.72, 52.82, 53.30, 54.37, 54.69
   2 Azusa, 1 E.Clubs, 2 Cup, 1 Plate inv, 3r2 R.Bay
7. **Lesley Owusu** 21.12.78 (2y, 9) 53.84 '99 53.02, 53.06, 53.08, 53.13, 53.30, 53.47
   1r3 Walnut, 6 Austin, 4 Big 12, 8 NCAA, 2 U23L, 2 IR, 2 BL1 (3), 5 AAA, 2 Plate inv
8. **Louise Whitehead** 26.3.75 (2y, 8) 53.34 '9 53.37, 53.55, 53.57, 53.68, 53.74, 53.87
   1 LI, 2 Bedl, 1 Welsh, 1B Budapest, 5r1 Dublin, 4 AAA, 3 Plate inv, BL3: 1,1,-
9. **Dawn Higgins** 10.12.75 (3y, 12) 53.79 '98 53.24, 53.59, 53.63, 53.87, 53.90, 53.93
   1B LI, 3 BRS, 6 Riga, 2 Welsh, 1 BL4 (2), 1 Jona, 3B Budapest, 1r2 Dublin, 2h AAA, 4 Plate inv
10. **Jennifer Stoute** 16.4.65 (8y, -) 51.53 '89 53.41, 53.42, 53.72, 53.97, 54.85, 56.97
    2 Jona, 2B Budapest, 8 Ljubljana, 8 AAA, 7 Plate inv
11. **Karen Gear** 30.9.79 (1y, -) 55.13 '98 54.03, 54.27, 54.46, 54.48, 54.52, 54.68
    2 CAU, 5 BRS, 1 Bedl, 1 AAA-23, 4h2 AAA, 3 v FRA, 1 v SPA-23, 1 Bath
12. **Jennifer Meadows** 17.4.81 (1y, -) 54.88 '89 53.84, 53.85, 54.19, 54.24, 54.27, 54.36
    3 CAU, 2 Bedl-J, 1 Jnr IR, 1 IR, 1 AAA-J, 1 Mannheim, 4 Bath, 1 JI4N, 5s2 WJ

\- **Lisa Miller** 13.1.83 (1y, -) 55.73 '99 53.86, 53.91, 54.31, 54.38, 54.59, 54.99
  1 Batt.Pk, 5 Bedl-J, 1 U18 Int, 2 E.Sch, 2 Comm-Y, 2 AAA-J, 2 Bath, 3 JI4N, 6s1 WJ

\- **Michelle Pierre** 30.9.73 (5y, 7) 52.77 '97 53.98, 54.20, 54.36, 54.54, 54.8, 55.57
  4 Basel, 2 BL1 (2), 1 sf Enfield, 6r1 Dublin, 6 AAA

Merry and Fraser broke through the 50-second barrier when it really mattered, in the Olympic final, and both now have Kathy Cook's long-standing British record in their sights. Merry had looked an Olympic medal candidate all season, but Fraser (ranked 2nd for the fourth successive year) was a revelation. Benefitting from training with Cathy Freeman, she had got close to her pb of 50.85 when winning the AAA title in 50.94, then in Sydney she had successive runs of 50.77, 50.21 and 49.79. With Curbishley at 3, Frost at 4 and Dudgeon just doing enough for 5, the top five are the same as in 1999. Murphy made a most encouraging debut at the event to rank sixth. Stoute is ranked for the first time since 1993. Two of our brilliant World Junior gold medal-winning 4x400 team, Meadows and Miller vie to complete the top 12. Miller, with two years left as a junior, made exceptional progress during the year, but just misses these rankings. Natasha Danvers had no flat 400m races in the year, but ran c.53.2 on the first leg in the Olympic 4x400 final. The tenth best of 53.41 has been bettered only by 1982 (53.0) and 1983 (53.4).

800 METRES

1. **Kelly Holmes** 19.4.70 (8y, 1) 1:56.21 '95 1:56.80, 1:58.45, 2:00.35, 2:00.53, 2:01.76, 2:02.08
   1 AAA, 1 Karlstad, 3 GhCl, 1 Rovereto, 3 OG
2. **Hayley Tullett** 17.2.73 (5y, 9) 2:02.18 '97, 2:01.52i]98 2:01.25, 2:01.53, 2:02.92, 2:05.65mx
   1r1 Budapest, 1 Malmö, 6 GhCl
3. **Diane Modahl** 17.6.66 (16y, 2) 1:58.65 '90 2:00.53, 2:02.41, 2:02.73mx, 2:03.13, 2:03.94, 2:04.16
   3 Jena, 3 Kassel, 10 Leverkusen, 10 GhCl, 5h OG
4. **Tanya Blake** 16.1.71 (4y, 3) 2:00.10 '98 2:01.06, 2:02.47, 2:02.56, 2:02.92, 2:04.69, 2:04.71
   1 Irvine & LA, 6 Stanford, 4 ECp, 2 Ljubljana, 1r2 Budapest, 4 Leverkusen, 1 v FRA, 1 Biella
5. **Emma Davies** 9.10.78 (3y, 7) 2:02.39 '98 2:04.07, 2:04.42, 2:04.44, 2:04.54, 2:05.04, 2:05.67
   4 LI, 1 Basel, 3 Riga, 1 AAA-23, dnf r2 Budapest, 2 Gothenburg, 4 AAA, 4 Namur, 1 v SPA-23
6. **Joanne Fenn** 19.10.74 (3y, -) 2:05.2 '98 2:04.19, 2:05.48, 2:05.54, 2:05.60, 2:06.13, 2:06.14
   1 LI, 5 BRS, 4 Wyth, 4r2 Budapest, 2 IR, 3 AAA, 1 Solihull, 1 Växjö, 2 Biella
7. **Claire Raven** 15.6.72 (3y, -) 2:03.15 '97 2:04.58, 2:05.12, 2:05.52, 2:05.92, 2:06.41, 2:07.48
   3 Lough 10/5, 3 LI, 2 Watford 12/7, 6r1 Budapest, 6 Dublin, 2 Watford 2/8, 2 AAA, 1 Tønsberg, 3 v FRA
8. **Rachel Newcombe** 25.2.67 (3y, 5) 2:03.28 '98 2:05.60, 2:05.67, 2:05.69, 2:06.30, 2:06.50, 2:06.53
   5 Wyth, 4 Haapsalu,1 Riga, 2 BL2 (2), 1 Watford 12/7, 4r1 Budapest, 7 Dublin, 6 AAA, 2 Solihull, 2 BMC-F
9. **Jeina Mitchell** 21.1.75 (4y, 6) 2:03.36 '97 2:04.15, 2:04.24, 2:04.74, 2:05.3, 2:06.2, 2:06.23
   2 Tartu, dnf r1 Budapest, 2h3 AAA, 4 Solihull, 5 Karlstad, 1 Croydon, 8 Rovereto, 8 Rieti
10. **Alex Carter** 1.4.80 (1y, -) 2:07.33 '99 2:03.78mp, 2:05.48, 2:05.81, 2:06.21, 2:07.22, 2:07.3
    1 B.Univs, 1 Lough 10/5, 2 LI, 6 Riga, 2 AAA-23, 2 U23L, 7 AAA
11. **Mary McClung** 19.12.71 (2y, 12) 2:05.64 '95 2:03.92, 2:05.28, 2:05.67, 2:07.39, 2:07.60, 2:08.1
    1 Scot E/W, 1 CAU, 1 BRS, 3 Wyth, 1 Police, dnf Riga, 2r1 Budapest, 2h4 AAA, 8 Solihull, BL2: 1,1,-

12= **Kelly Caffel** 10.2.79 (1y, -) 2:06.91 '99 2:03.48mp, 2:04.35, 2:06.59 1 Cardiff, 1 Watford 30/8 & 6/9

12= **Helen Pattinson** 2.1.74 (1y, -) 2:06.1 '99 2:03.75, 2:04.27, 2:05.0mx 10 Jena, 9 GhCl

Holmes returned to run at the AAAs, but few then could have dreamed of how well she would run at the Olympic Games – just marvellous and she is top ranked for the sixth time at 800m. Tullett only had four races at this distance, but beat Modahl at Gateshead. Blake might be higher, but did not meet Modahl (who completes an event record 16 years in the rankings) or run at the AAAs. Newcombe and Raven were 2-2, but the latter ran faster times and was second at the AAAs. That was a place ahead of Fenn, but Fenn beat Newcombe 3-0. McClung is difficult to rank as she did not sustain her fine early season form, and Caffel and Patttinson only had three 800m races each. 10th best at 2:04.15 was much better than 1999's 2:06.1. mp = male pacemaker, mx = mixed race

1500 METRES

1. **Hayley Tullett** 17.2.73 (4y, 2) 4:05.72 '99 4:01.23, 4:05.19, 4:05.34, 4:05.52, 4:06.44, 4:09.23
   3 Luzern, 3 Nice, 7 Oslo, 1 AAA, 4 Berlin, 11 (fell) OG
2. **Kelly Holmes** 19.4.70 (7y, 1) 3:58.07 '97, 4:28.04M '98 4:05.35, 4:08.02, 4:10.38; 7 OG
3. **Helen Pattinson** 2.1.74 (3y, 4) 4:06.72 '99 4:04.82, 4:06.27, 4:07.61, 4:08.80, 4:09.60, 4:10.33
   2 Dessau, 4 Kassel, 4 Seville, 1 v USA, 1 ECp. 5 Nice, 2 Barcelona, 2 AAA, 13 Brussels, 9sf OG
4. **Kelly Caffell** 10.2.79 (2y, 10) 4:16.64 '99 4:10.22, 4:13.23, 4:14.40, 4:14.91, 4:15.29, 4:17.67
   4 Wyth, 1 South, 3 v USA, 1 U23L, 10 BGP, 3 AAA, 6 Leverkusen, 1 v SPA-23
5. **Paula Radcliffe** 17.12.73 (7y, 3) 4:05.81 '98, 4:24.94M '96 4:11.45; 11 Barcelona
6. **Kathy Butler** 22.10.73 (1y, -) 4:07.68 '97 4:15.46, 4:17.28, 4:18.47, 4:19.78
   2 Des Moines, 9 Raleigh, 8 Eugene, 1 Scot
7. **Angela Newport** 21.10.70 (8y, 6) 4:09.29 '94 4:15.28, 4:19.48, 4:21.69, 4:24.38mx, 4:24.9, 4:31.1
   2 Lough 10/5, 1 BL4 (1), 2 Wyth, 5 v USA, 2 v FRA
8. **Amanda Parkinson** 21.7.71 (3y, -) 4:132.9mx '95, 4:14.19 '98 4:17.45, 4:19.68, 4:19.70, 4:22.40, 4:22.76
   5 Watford, 1 BL1 (3), 4 AAA, 3 v FRA
9. **Alex Carter** 1.4.80 (2y, 11) 4:19.23 '99 4:17.98, 4:19.87, 4:22.91, 4:24.2, 4:25.13
   1 Lough 10/5, 3 Wyth, 3 Cardiff, 4 Dublin, 2 v SPA-23
10. **Dianne Henaghan** 6.8.65 (2y, -) 4:16.17 '97 4:18.04, 4:19.63, 4:20.04, 4:23.94
   2 LI, 3 BRS, 5 Dublin, 7 Watford
11. **Susan Scott** 26.9.77 (2y, 9) 4:16.16 '99 4:18.42, 4:18.63, 4:18.73, 4:20.07, 4:20.07, 4:20.47
   3 LI, 4 BRS, 5 Wyth, 8 Watford, 2 Scot, 5 AAA
12. **Liz Yelling** 5.12.74 (1y, -) 4:19.09 '95 4:16.75, 4:17.50, 4:21.5
   2 Solihull 19/8, 1 Watford 30/8, dnf v FRA

– **Diane Modahl** 17.6.66 (1y, -) 4:12.3 '89 4:14.41, 4:18.36mx; 8 Dessau

Holmes was seventh at the Olympics but that was her only competition of the year, and after six years at the top she yields top ranking to Tullett, who confirmed her breakthrough into world class but who had the misfortune to fall in the Olympic final. Pattinson also maintained her progress with two personal bests and fine wins in the European Cup and against the USA, and Caffel made an encouraging return after a year out through injury. It was difficult to select the final places in the rankings, not least because so many contenders had very few races at the distance. Sadly the tenth best of 4:17.45 was the second worst in the last 23 years.

3000 METRES (Not ranked)

Paula Radcliffe 17.12.73 8:27.40 '99 8:28.85, 8:36.11, c.8:52.0+, 9:01.99+. 9:02.09+ 4 Zürich, 3 GhCl
Jo Pavey 20.9.73 8:58.2 '98 8:36.70, 8:53.7mx, 8:57.00mx, 8:59.2e+, 9:02.6+, c.9:06+ 2 Cardiff, 1 Solihull, 4 GhCl
Hayley Tullett 17.2.73 9:14.5 '99 8:45.39; 8:54.63i, 8:55.31i, 9:00.62i 3 ECp
Sarah Young/Wilkinson 2.1.70 9:04.27 '98 8:57.75mx, 9:04.05mx, 9:12.03, c.9:16+, 9:20.8+ 8 GhCl
Amanda Parkinson 21.7.71 9:17.4mx '94, 9:19.6 '96 9:02.67mx, 9:12.75mx
Hayley Yelling 3.1.74 9:19.52 '99 9:02.88mp, 9:11.20, 9:12.4+, 9:18.9+, 9:20.6+, c.9:22+ 1 Wyth, 4 Cardiff
Angela Newport 21.10.70 9:07.5mx/9:12.6 '99 9:05.86mx, 9:08.46, c.9:26+, 9:29.0+ 1 BL4 (1), 6 GhCl
Helen Pattinson 2.1.74 9:16.3mx/9:17.3 '99 9:09.18; 1 LI
Liz Yelling 5.12.74 9:15.25 '98 9:11.4mx, 9:19.98, 9:24.95; 2 IR, 1 v FRA
Andrea Whitcombe 8.6.71 8:58.59 '91 9:12.45mx, 9:14.2mx, 9:16.2+, 9:34.3

5000 METRES (Previously ranked 1982-90, 1992 and 1995-9)

1. **Paula Radcliffe** 17.12.73 (6y, 1) 14:43.54 '99 14:44.36, 15:05.48, 15:05.70+, 16:39.3+ 2 BGP, 1 AAA
2. **Jo Pavey** 20.9.73 (1y, -) 0 14:58.27, 15:08.82, 15:18.51, 15:21.15 10 BGP, 2 AAA, 12 OG
3. **Hayley Yelling** 3.1.74 (1y, -) 16:23.05 '99 15.36.27, 15:42.93, 15:50.41, 15:59.53, 16:09.54, 16:12.6+e
   4 Batt.Pk, 6 ECp, 14 BGP, 3 AAA, 3 Solihuil
4. **Sarah Wilkinson (Young)** 2.1.70 (4y, 7) 15:45.08 '98 15:40.85, 15:41.75, c.16:12+
   4 Stretford, 13 BGP, dnf AAA
5. **Andrea Whitcombe** 8.6.71 (5y, -) 15:43.03 '98 15:32.62, 16:15.82 2 Batt.Pk, 15h OG
6. **Birhan Dagne** 8.4.78 (3y, 8) 15:55.81 '98 15:36.35, 16:12.2+e 12 BGP, dnf AAA
7. **Kathy Butler** (ex CAN) 22.10.73 (1y, -) 15:10.69 '98 15:42.22, 15:45.14
   2 Long Beach, 4r2 Walnut, dnf BGP, dnf AAA
8. **Angela Newport** 21.10.70 (3y, 3) 15:43.99 '99 15:48.50, 16:16.56 dnf Batt.Pk, 10 AAA, 1 Solihull
9. **Gillian Palmer** 30.12.80 (1y, -) 0 15:56.58, 16:08.54, 16:19.17, 16:33.82 B.Univs, 1 CAU, 4 AAA, 2 Solihull

10. **Catherine Berry** 8.10.75 (1y, -) 16:52.92 '99 16:00.97, 16:18.07, 16:19.44, 16:28.24
5 Raleigh, 14 Stanford, 8 NCAA, 5 AAA
11. **Amanda Parkinson** 21.7.71 (1y, -) 17:12.9 '96 5 Stretford 15:56.64
12. **Tara Krzywicki** 9.3.74 (3y, 6) 15:48.1mx/15:53.28 '98 16:02.48, 16:10.95 6 AAA, 4 Solihull
– **Lucy Wright** 17.11.69 (2y, -) 15:59.51 '98 7 Stretford 16:06.49, 7 AAA 16:02.97

Radcliffe was less than a second outside her Commonwealth record at Crystal Palace, and is top for the sixth time. Behind her comes Pavey, who had a brilliant first season at the event with personal bests in each round at the Olympics, and for whom no praise can be too high at the way she has come back from two years out of competition through injury. Although Whitcombe's OG qualifying time at Battersea Park (paced every inch of the way by Sonia O'Sullivan) was faster, Hayley Yelling ranks third due to her depth of marks; she made a huge improvement on her previous best. Palmer, with no track races before this year, showed great potential. The tenth best of 15:56.64 is a record, although ten under 16 minutes is one less than in 1998.

10000 METRES

1. **Paula Radcliffe** 17.12.73 (3y, 1) 30:27.13 '99 4 OG 30:26.97 (32:34.73 ht)
2. **Birhan Dagne** 8.4.78 (3y, 4) 33:24.46 '99 2 AAA 32:30.4, 8r2 Eur Challenge 33:35.15
3. **Sarah Wilkinson (Young)** 2.1.70 (1y, -) 0 4 AAA 32:34.7, dnf r2 Eur Challenge
4. **Hayley Yelling** 3.1.74 (1y, -) 0 5 AAA 32:52.5
5. **Liz Yelling** 5.12.74 (1y, -) 8 AAA 33:07.9, 24 Eur Challenge 33:11.84
6. **Tara Krzywicki** 9.3.74 (3y, 2) 33:04.55 '99 23 Eur Challenge 33:10.89, dnf AAA
7. **Bev Jenkins** 6.2.70 (2y, 5) 33:58.81 '99 9 AAA 33:49.8
8. **Debbie Sullivan** 24.1.72 (2y, 8) 34:30.16 '99 10 AAA 34:30.9
9. **Bronwen Cardy-Wise** 26.1.52 (1y, -) 35:08.33 '89 11 AAA 34:37.3
10. **Andrea Green** 14.12.68 (1y, -) 0 34:39.8mx Catford
11. **Sheila Fairweather** 24.11.77 (3y, 9) 34:32.70 '99 1 B.Univs 34:56.04

Radcliffe was disappointed by her fourth place at the Olympics, and perhaps she could have held back for a while, but she was simply wonderful, as ever, and is top for the third year at this event. The second fastest British runner was Dagne, who just missed the Olympic qualifying standard, but she was over two minutes slower than Radcliffe. At 48, Cardy-Wise becomes the oldest ever ranking debutante at any event (previous best men's walker Ted Shillabeer at 46).

HALF MARATHON

1. **Paula Radcliffe** 17.12.73 (2y, 1) 69:37 '99 1 GNR 67:07, 1 Worlds 69:07
2. **Liz Yelling** 5.12.74 (1y, -) 75:06 '98 1 Stroud 72:31
3. **Sarah Wilkinson** 2.1.70 (1y, -) 0 1 Manchester 74:33, 19 Worlds 75:55
4. **Birhan Dagne** 8.4.78 (2y, 3) 72:53 '99 1 Reading 74:23, 5 GNR 74:29
5. **Andrea Green** 14.12.68 (1y, -) 1 Bristol 73:28, 1 Dartford 75:27, 1 Paddock Wood 76:05, 45 Worlds 84:53
6. **Sue Reinsford** 24.3.69 (2y, 4) 73:04 '99 2 Bristol (1 AAA) 74:21, 6 Gt.Scot 74:52
7. **Beth Allott** 9.2.77 (2y, 6) 74:38 '99 1 Wilmslow 73:40
8. **Lynne MacDougall** 18.2.65 (1y, -) 3 Reading 74:50, 7 Gt.Scot 75:43
9. **Angela Joiner** 14.2.69 (1y, -) 73:44 '97 4 Reading 75:14
10. **Vicky Pincombe** 19.6.73 (1y, -) 75:14 '98 4 Bristol 75:49, 8 GNR 76:07
11. **Louise Watson** 13.12.71 (1y, -) 7 GNR 75:45

nr **Teresa Duffy** IRE 6.7.69 76:41 '98 1 Omagh 74:51

This event was ranked for the first time last year. Radcliffe's brilliant wins in the Great North Run (GNR) and World Champiomships ensured her of the world top ranking, with a new European best in the former.

MARATHON

1. **Sue Reinsford** 24.3.69 (2y, 2) 2:36:43 3 Rotterdam 2:33:41, 13 Berlin 2:36:57
2. **Marian Sutton** 7.10.63 (10y, 1) 2:28:42 '99 26 OG 2:34:33
3. **Lynne MacDougall** 18.2.65 (1y, -) 0 20 London 2:38:32
4. **Alison Wyeth** 26.5.64 (2y, 4) 2:38:26 21 London 2:39:01
5. **Michaela McCallum** 2.6.66 (2y, 3) 2:38:28 '99 1 Copenhagen 2:42:25, 3 Padua 2:42:44
6. **Trudi Thomson** 18.1.59 (5y, 5) 2:38:23 '95
6 Dubai 2:50:37, 22 London 2:40:39, 6 Stockholm 2:45:35, 5 Dublin 2:49:37
7. **Jo Lodge** 6.1.68 (2y, 9) 2:45:46 '99 23 London (1 AAA) 2:40:51
8. **Shona Crombie-Hick** 1.6.71 (1y, -) 2:58:51 '99 1 Manchester 2:42:44
9. **Anne Buckley** 20.6.67 (1y, -) 1 Hamilton 2:43:54
10. **Angela Joiner** 14.2.69 (1y, -) 0 24 London 2:44:07
11. **Joanne Newcombe** 20.2.65 (1y, -) 2:49:49 '97 25 London 2:46:16, 2 Florence 2:46:42
12. **Sharon Dixon** 22.4.68 (1y, -) 0 26 London 2:46:30, 6 Dublin 2:49:58

– **Gillian Horovitz** 7.6.55 (14y, 6) 2:36:52 '92
25 Boston 2:47:49, 20 New York 2:48:17, 15 Twin Cities 2:52:13, 11 Green Bay 2:56:42
nr **Teresa Duffy** 6.7.69 IRE 2:39:40 '99 2 Dublin 2:37:36, 19 London 2:38:38

For top ranking it is hard to judge between Sutton's Olympic run and Reinsford's pair of marathons; but two good performances and a faster time gave the place to Reinsford, who won three English Schools titles at age 12-13 in 1981-2 (as Sue Jordan).

100 METRES HURDLES

1. **Keri Maddox** 4.7.72 (11y, 2) 12.95 '99 13.13, 13.15, 13.24, 13.24, 13.26, 13.52; 13.2
   1 LI, 1 Mid, 3 v USA, 4 ECp, 1 Cup, BL1: -,1,1
2. **Diane Allahgreen** 21.2.75 (7y, 2) 12.99 '99 13.11, 13.15, 13.18, 13.22, 13.24, 13.26 6 Tartu,
   8 St Petersburg, 2 Riga, 4 v USA, 1r3 Lausanne, 1 Budapest, 1 Ljubljana, 1 Dublin, 1 BL2 (3), 1 AAA, 8q3 OG
3. **Melanie Wilkins** 18.1.73 (7y, 6) 13.34/13.1 '95, 13.23w '96 13.17, 13.23, 13.27w, 13.28, 13.32, 13.35
   1 Fullerton, 2 LI, 1 CAU, 1 Basel, 1 South, 2 Riga, 6 v USA, 3 Budapest, 2 AAA, 4 v FRA, BL1: 1,-,2
4. **Natasha Danvers** 19.9.77 (7y, 7) 13.20 '98, 12.8w '99 13.19w, 13.20, 13.23w, 13.27w, 13.38, 13.38
   7 Austin, 2 Westwood, 2 Pac-10, 2 Cup
5. **Julie Pratt** 20.3.79 (4y, 5) 13.40/13.28w '99 13.28w, 13.40, 13.41, 13.43, 13.45, 13.49 1 Essex, 3 LI,
   1 Bedl, 2 South, 1 AAA-23, 4 U23L, 2 Dublin, 3 AAA, 1 Croydon, 5 v FRA, 1 v SPA-23, BL2: 1,1,2
6. **Denise Lewis** 27.8.72 (9y, 9) 13.18 '96 13.13, 13.23, 13.49, 13.56, 14.14 2 E.Clubs, 7g v USA, 2 BL1 (2)
7. **Rachel King** 11.5.76 (4y, 10) 13.46 '99, 13.44w '98 13.51, 13.56, 13.58, 13.72, 13.74, 13.76
   3 Basel, 1 Welsh, 4 Riga, 4 Budapest, dnf Dublin, 4 AAA, BL4: 1,1,-
8. **Bianca Liston** 28.5.78 (2y, 12) 13.79/13.71w '99 13.52, 13.58, 13.58w, 13.61w, 13.63, 13.69; 13.4
   2 B.Univs, 2 Lough 10/5, 4 LI, 1 Batt.Pk, 2 Bedl, 3 South, 3 AAA-23, 1 Hendon, 1 sf Eton, 1 IR, 2 Lough,
   5 AAA, 6 v FRA, 3 v SPA-23, BL1: 1B,3,1B
9. **Liz Fairs** 1.12.77 (2y, -) 13.52 '98 13.49, 13.57, 13.70w, 13.78, 13.78, 13.81
   1 B.Univs, 1 Lough 10/5, 2 sf Eton, 2 IR, 1 Lough, 7 AAA, 4 Cup, BL1: 2.4.3
10. **Clova Court** 10.2.60 (10y, 3) 13.04 '94 13.55, 13.81, 13.84, 13.91 3 IR, 6 AAA, 3 Cup
11. **Sarah Claxton** 23.9.79 (4y, 8) 13.59 '99, 13.28w '98 13.67, 13.70w, 13.71, 13.72, 13.88w, 13.90
    2 Essex, 6 CAU, 3 Bedl, 4 South, 2 AAA-23, 5 U23L, 4 Dublin, 1B Croydon
12. **Helen Worsey** 29.8.82 (1y, -) 14.44, 14.1w '99 13.76w, 13.77w, 13.89, 13.92, 13.95w
    0 LI, 4 CAU, 1 Bedl-J, 1 Jnr IRT, 2 E.Sch, 4 IR, 4 Lough, 5h Mannheim, 1 AAA-J, 2 bath, 6 JI4N, 5h3 WJ

\- **Jacqui Agyepong** 5.1.69 (11y, 11) 12.90 '95 13.5; 2 Hendon

Only 0.09 sec separated the top five on their best times. Maddox just holds on for her third successive top ranking as she beat Allahgreen clearly in their one clash, the match v USA, but Allahgreen had the best depth of times. Pratt's bests of 13.40 and 13.28w were exactly as in 1999 and she ranks fifth for the third time, she headed Lewis, who contested the event only three times outside heptathlons. Liston was 4-3 v Fairs. Court set world W40 records in each of her four races. It was close for the final ranking with Clare Milborrow, Kerry Jury and Danielle Freeman just missing out. Tenth best at 13.55 has only once been bettered (13.47 in 1991).

400 METRES HURDLES

1. **Natasha Danvers** 19.9.77 (4y, 3) 55.69 '98 54.95, 55.00, 55.26, 55.34, 55.62, 55.68
   2 Walnut, 1 Westwood, 1 Pac-10, 1 NCAA, 7 Nice, 3 Budapest, 4 BGP, 2 AAA, 5 GhCl, 8 OG
2. **Keri Maddox** 4.7.72 (5y, 2) 55.33 '99 55.22, 55.46, 55.70, 56.04, 56.20, 56.36
   2 LI, 1 CAU, 1 BRS. 3 Haniá, 1 Riga, 4 ECp, 1AAA, 1 Cup, 4 GhCl, 5h5 OG
3. **Sinead Dudgeon** 9.7.76 (4y, 1) 55.24 '00 55.45, 55.56, 55.74, 55.92, 56.60, 56.88
   1 LI, 2 Kalamata, 1 Bedl, 5 Haniá, 5 Nice, 1 Budapest, 7 BGP, 3 AAA, 4h1 OG
4. **Tracey Duncan** 16.5.79 (2y, 8) 58.99 '99 57.92, 58.22, 58.27, 58.43, 58.84, 59.17
   2 B.Univs, 4 LI, 2 CAU, 4 Bedl, 1 South, 1 AAA-23, 4 U23L, 2 Dublin, 1 Lough, 4 AAA, 5 v FRA
5. **Katie Jones** 4.1.77 (1y, -) 61.19 '96 58.75, 58.83, 58.92, 59.11, 59.79, 59.96
   1B LI, 3 CAU, 4 BRS, 1 sf Eton, 3 Dublin, 5 AAA, 2 Cup, 2 v FRA, BL1: 1,1,1
6. **Jennie Matthews** (Pearson) 3.7.62 (14y, 4) 57.41 '88 59.14, 59.48, 59.79, 60.1, 60.13, 60.27
   5 LI, 4 CAU, 2 South, 1 IR, 6 AAA, BL2: 1,1,1
7. **Nicola Sanders** 23.6.82 (2y, 6) 58.96 '99 59.68, 59.79, 60.05, 60.07, 60.79, 60.84
   dns South, 1 Jnr IA, 1 E.Sch, 1 Comm-Y, 1 U20HI, 1 AAA-J, 1 Bath, 2 JI4N, 6h WJ
8. **Gowry Hodge** 26.6.60 (11y, -) 54.63 '92 58.3, 58.9, 60.1
9. **Celia Brown** 22.1.77 (1y, -) 562.2 '99 60.08, 60.26, 61.01, 61.38, 61.70, 62.2
   2 E.Clubs, 1 Mid, 2 sf Enfield, 7 AAA, 3 Cup, BL1: 3,2.-
10. **Clare Wise** 22.8.69 (3y, 11) 59.07 '98 60.61, 60.86, 60.90, 60.98, 61.1, 61.2
    6 Bedl, 3 South, 1 sf Enfield, 3 IR, 1B Lough, 5h2 AAA, BL1: -,3,2
11. **Rachael Kay** 8.9.80 (2y, 7) 58.91 '99 60.37, 60.54, 60.55, 60.84, 60.94, 61.7
    7 Bedl, 1 North, 2 AAA-23, 6 U23L, 2 IR, 5 Lough, 6h2 AAA, 1 Nth IC, 6 v FRA, dnf v SPA-23, BL3: -,1,2
12. **Hannah Wood** 17.11.81 (1y, -) 61.72 '99 60.86, 61.4, 61.44, 61.69, 61.70, 61.7
    6 LI, 5 CAU, 2 E.Sch, 6 IR, 2 U20HI, 2 AAA-J, 4 Bath

nr **Mari Bjone** NOR 11.9.70 57.06 '96 58.12, 58.16, 58.20, 58.65, 58.78, 59.37
1 B.Univs, 3 LI, 3 Bedl, 2 ECp1A, 3 Lough, 1 NOR Ch

As in 1999, the top three were closely matched, but Danvers made the Olympic final and takes the top spot for the first time. Maddox beat Dudgeon 2-1, but both disapppointed in Sydney. There is again a big gap after the top three, but Duncan and Jones made good progress to rank fourth and fifth. Two veterans make the top ten, Matthews, ranking for an event record 14th time, and Hodge (formerly Retchakan), who set UK W40 records in each of her three races and would surely have ranked higher if she had wanted to contest the major races. The 10th best of 60.37 is the worst since 1978.

HIGH JUMP

1. **Susan Jones** 8.6.78 (7y, 2) 1.91 '97, 1.92i '98 1.93, 1.90, 1.89, 1.89, 1.89, 1.88 1 LI, 1 CAU, 1 BRS, 2 Jumps-I, 5 v USA, 1 BL3 (2), 1 U23L, 3 Lough, 6= Malmö, 4 AAA, 1 Cup, 1 Plate, 1 v FRA, 2 v SPA-23
2. **Michelle Dunkley** 26.1.78 (5y, -) 1.88 '98, 1.89i '97 1.93, 1.90, 1.89, 1.89, 1.89, 1.85 1 AAA-23, 3 U23L, 1 Lough, 1 BL2 (3), 2 AAA, 3= Cup, 3 Plate, 2 v FRA, 1 v SPA-23
3. **Jo Jennings** 20.9.69 (12y, 1) 1.94i '93, 1.91 '98 1.89, 1.88, 1.86, 1.85, 1.85, 1.85 1 Yorks, 7 Jumps-I, 1 v USA, 3 ECp, 5 Budapest, 1 sf Rugby, 1 AAA, 4 Falköping, 3= Cup, 2 Plate, 4 Växjö, 3 v FRA, BL3: 1,2,1
4. **Lee McConnell** 9.10.78 (4y, 3) 1.86 '99 1.88, 1.86, 1.84, 1.84, 1.83, 1.83 2= LI, 6= Bedl, 4 Riga, 6 Budapest, 1 Scot, 3 AAA, 2 Cup, 4 Plate, 3 v SPA-23, BL1: -,2,1
5. **Dalia Mikneviciuté** (ex-LTU) 5.9.70 (1y, -) 1.89 '97 1.86, 1.85, 1.84, 1.83, 1.82, 1.81; 1.86i, 1.83i 2= LI, 1 E.Clubs, 3 BRS, 2 Riga, 1 BL1 (2), 1 sf Enfield, 2 Lough, 6 AAA
6. **Debbie Marti** 14.5.68 (15y, 4) 1.94 '96, 1.95i '97 1.85, 1.85, 1.84, 1.82, 1.80, 1.80 1 South, 3 v USA, 7 Budapest, 5 AAA, 1 Croydon
7. **Aileen Wilson** 30.3.84 (3y, 8=) 1.80 '99 1.83, 1.83, 1.82, 1.82, 1.82, 1.80 1 Nicosia, 3 Bedl, 1 E.Sch-I, 10= Budapest, 1 Sc JI, 2 Comm-Y, 1 AAA-J, 3 JI4N, 9= WJ
8. **Lea Goodman** 9.5.72 (8y, -) 1.92 '96 1.82, 1.81, 1.80, 1.80, 1.80, 1.80 1 Surrey, 4 BRS, 4 Bedl
9. **Julie Crane** 26.9.76 (5y, 10) 1.83 '98 1.82, 1.81, 1.80, 1.79, 1.79, 1.78; 1.85i, 1.83i, 1.80i 5 BRS, 5 Bedl, 1 Welsh, 3 Riga, 3 Haapsalu, 10= Budapest, 7 AAA, 5 Cup, BL1: 1,-,4
10. **Rebecca Jones** 17.1.83 (2y, 11=) 1.79 '99 1.83, 1.79, 1.79, 1.78, 1.77, 1.76; 1.83i 6= Bedl, 1 Welsh Sch, 1 Welsh-J, 8= Budapest, 4 Comm-Y, 2 AAA-J, 1 Bath, 5 JI4N, dnq 21= WJ
11. **Julia Bennett** 26.3.70 (13y, 6) 1.89 '94, 1.92i '90 1.83, 1.81, 1.75, 1.75, 1.73, 1.70; 1.85, 1.83i, 1.83i, 1.81i 2 CAU, 2 sf Enfield, 9 AAA, 5 Plate
12. **Denise Lewis** 27.8.72 (8y, 5) 1.87 '99 1.84, 1.78, 1.75, 1.73; 6g v USA

Jones and Dunkley achieved the Olympic qualifying height of 1.93 a week too late for selection and Jones ranks first for the first time; she beat Dunkley 4-3 and Jennings-Steele 5-2. Jennings-Steele was best in mid-season with a fine European Cup third and AAA win, but Dunkley had the better marks overall. I decided to change my policy and to rank Mikneviciuté, although she is still not GB-qualified, as she is otherwise stateless; she beat McConnell 2-1, but jumped only 1.78 to 1.86 at the AAAs. Wilson maintained her progress, and is ranked for the third time but still has three more seasons as a junior. Goodman (née Haggett) returns after two years out. Eleven women over 1.83 returns us to the standards of 1982-9.

POLE VAULT

1. **Janine Whitlock** 11.8.73 (6y, 1) 4.31 '98 4.35, 4.30, 4.30, 4.21, 4.20, 4,15; 4.31i, 4.30i, 4.30i, 4.30i; 15 outdoors and 13 indoor competitions at 4.00 or better 1 BL1 (1), 1 LI, 5 Jena, 2= Prague, 1 Bedl, 9 Nuremburg, 12 Athens, 4 ECp, 6 Linz, 3 GhCl, 1 AAA, 1 Cup, 5 R.Bay, dnq 20 OG
2. **Irie Hill** 16.1.69 (2y, 2) 4.05 '99 4.20, 4.10, 4.02, 4.00, 4.00, 4.00; 4.13ex; 4.10i, 4.01i 1 Mid, 3 Budapest, 2 Lough, 2 AAA
3. **Rhian Clarke** 19.4.77 (8y, 4) 3.90 '97 4.15, 4.11, 4.00, 4.00, 4.00, 3.97 1/2 Austin, 7 NCAA, 6 Budapest, 10 Gothenburg, 1 BL2 (3), 6 AAA
4. **Tracey Bloomfield** 13.9.79 (3y, 5) 3.75 '98 3.90, 3.90, 3.80, 3.80, 3.80, 3.80 2 CAU, 3 BRS, 2 Bedl, 1 South, 1 AAA-23, 2 U23L, 1 IR, 3= Lough, 4= AAA, 1 Horsham, 1 Croydon, 5 v FRA, 2 v SPA-23
5. **Lucy Webber** 5.2.72 (3y, 3) 3.89 '99 4.04, 3.90, 3.90, 3.82, 3.80, 3.80; 4.00i 8 Irvine, 4= Arles, 3 Bed I, 5 Jumpsl, 3= Lough, 4= AAA, BL2: -,2,2
6. **Alison Davies** 6.4.61 (3y, 7) 3.70 '99 4.00, 3.95, 3.90, 3.80, 3.80, 3.70; 3.80i 2 LI, 1 CAU, 4 BRS, 4 Bedl, 7 Jumpsl, 1 sf Eton, 2 IR, 5 Lough, 3 AAA, 4 v FRA, BL1: 3,-,2
7. **Ellie Spain** 23.8.82 (1y, -) 3.20 '98 3.90, 3.70, 3.70, 3.70, 3.65, 3.61; 3.65i 3 LI, nh E.Clubs, 8 Arles, 1 E.Sch, 1 sf Enfield, 6 Lough, 2 Stoke, 9 AAA, 2 Cup, 1 AAA-J, 1 U20HI, 4 JI4N, 14= WJ, BL1: 2,-,1
8. **Emma Hornby** 12.12.73 (4y, -) 3.91 '98 3.70, 3.70, 3.70, 3.60, 3.60, 3.60 4 CAU, 5 Bedl, 2 Mid, 1 sf Cudworth, 3 IR, nh Lough, 10= AAA, BL1: 4,2,-
9. **Alison Murray-Jessee** 13.1.67 (5y, 8) 3.95A '99 3.71A, 3.70A, 3.60, 3.60, 3.60, 3.50 4 LI, 1 Scot, nh Budapest, 7 AAA, BL1: -,1,3
10. **Elizabeth Hughes** 9.6.77 (1y, -) 3.00 '96 3.70, 3.60, 3.60, 3.60, 3.60, 3.60 2 South, 3 sf Enfield, 8 AAA, 2 Horsham, 2 Croydon
11. **Clare Ridgley** 11.9.77 (7y, -) 3.60 '98 3.60, 3.60, 3.60, 3.50, 3.40, 3.40 5 CAU, 1 O/C v D/B, 2 sf Eton, 10= AAA, 3 Croydon, BL2: 1,1,3
12. **Fiona Harrison** 30.11.81 (4y, -) 3.60 '98 3.51, 3.50, 3.46, 3.45, 3.40, 3.30 1 Nth-J, 3 CAU, 7 Arles, 1 Jnr IR, nh Lough

\- **Linda Stanton** 22.6.73 (7y, -) 3.72 '95 3.50, 3.40, 3.40, 3.40, 3.40, 3.40 11 CAU, 6 Bedl, nh North, 1 sf Rugby, 4/5 IR, 3 Stoke, 12 AAA, 3 Cup, 1 Nth IC, BL1: 5,5,4

Whitlock was top ranked for the fourth time, but, although she pushed her British record up to 4.35, was a little inconsistent outdoors after two more British records indoors. Clarke (uniquely included in all the eight years of rankings for this event), Webber and Davies took the number of British athletes over 4m to five. Bloomfield did not get so high, but beat Webber 1-0 with two ties and Davies 4-3, and Webber beat Davies 3-1. Spain looked terrific when raising the British junior record to 3.80 and 3.90 at the start of the season, but had a mid-season dip in form due to exams. Ten women over 3.70 is easily a record.

LONG JUMP

1. **Denise Lewis** 27.8.72 (9y, 2) 6.67 '95, 6.77w '97 6.69, 6.56w/6.18, 6.48, 6.39 1 BL1 (2), 2 Dutch Ch
2. **Joanne Wise** 15.3.71 (11y, 1) 6.76 '99 6.59, 6.45, 6.44, 6.39w/6.21, 6.36
   5 Budapest, 7 Malmö, 9 Monaco, 1 AAA, dnq 13 OG
3. **Jade Johnson** 7.6.80 (4y, 4) 6.52 '99 6.58, 6.53, 6.48, 6.36w/6.32, 6.35, 6.34; 6.46i
   1 LI, 1 Arles, 7 Helsinki, 1 Riga, 1 AAA-23. 7 ECp, 4 Budapest, 3 Ljubljana, 2 AAA, 3 Falköping, 4 Rovereto
4. **Sarah Claxton** 23.9.79 (5y, 3) 6.56 '99 6.45w, 6.44, 6.41w, 6.35, 6.27, 6.26
   3 LI, 1 CAU, 8 Arles, 1 Bedl, 2 AAA-23, 6 U23L, 1 Dublin, 7 BGP, 4 AAA, 1 Cup, 3 v FRA, 1 v SPA-23
5. **Donita Benjamin** 7.3.72 (2y, -) 6.09/6.28w '98 6.45w/6.24, 6.28w/6.26, 6.28w/6.17, 6.26w, 6.04, 6.00
   3 South, 1 IS, 1 sf Eton, 3 AAA, 2 Cup, 2 v FRA, BL1: 6,2,-
6. **Ann Danson** 4.5.71 (7y, 7) 6.16 '95, 6.38w '94 6.32w, 6.31w, 6.23w, 6.21, 6.20w, 6.18; 6.21i
   2 LI, 7 Arles, 2 Bedl, 1 North, 2 sf Rugby, 2 Dublin, 5 AAA, 3 Cup, 1 v FRA, BL1: 1,3,-
7. **Julie Hollman** 16.2.77 (4y, 5) 6.23/6.38w '99 6.51, 6.32w/6.21, 6.09, 6.07, 6.06w, 6.02w; 6.09i
   1 sf Rugby, 6 AAA, BL2: 1,-,1
8. **Joyce Hepher** 11.2.64 (13y, 6) 6.75, 6.80w '85 6.32, 6.25, 6.24, 6.24. 6.21, 6.19
   2 CAU, 1 South, 7 Budapest, 7 AAA, 1 Croydon
9. **Tracy Joseph** 29.11.69 (3y, -) 6.39 '98, 6.44w '97 6.37w, 6.16, 6.12, 6.10, 6.09, 6.07
   1 Hants, 2 South, 1 BL4 (2), 2 sf Eton
10. **Kelly Sotherton** 13.11.76 (2y, -) 6.10/6.16w '97 6.24w/6.07, 6.09, 6.07w/6.06, 6.06w/6.04, 6.04, 6.03
    2 Hants, 3 CAU, 1 Mid, 1 sf Cudworth, 9 AAA, 4 Cup
11. **Symone Belle** 12.11.84 (1y, -) 5.91 '99 6.11, 6.07, 6.02, 5.92w, 5.87w, 5.85
    1 South-17, 1 Jnr IR, 1 AAA-17, 2 Bath, 2 JI4N
12. **Kim Rothman** 6.9.64 (1y, -) ? 6.19, 5.94, 5.93w, 5.92, 5.90, 5.87
    5 CAU, 4 South, 2 IR, 2 Croydon, 1 Biella, BL1: 2,4,4

With a limited competitive programme behind her, Wise did well to record a season's best in just missing the Olympic final by one place, but Lewis, with slightly better marks, just regains top ranking. Johnson is a close third. Benjamin was 3-2 v Danson. Belle, at 15, showed great promise, while Hepher, over 20 years older, had a consistent set of marks and ranks for an event record 13th time over a 19-year span. The tenth best of 6.16 is the best since 1987, although well short of the record 6.30 set in 1984.

TRIPLE JUMP

1. **Ashia Hansen** 5.12.71 (9y, 1) 15.15 '97, 15.16i '98 14.29, 13.44; 14.11i; 11 OG
2. **Michelle Griffith** 6.10.71 (11y, 3) 14.08 '94 14.14w, 13.71, 13.67, 13.64, 13.63, 13.62 1 Bedl, 1 South,
   6 Bratislava, 7 ECp, 2 Budapest, 1 Ljubljana, 1 AAA, 1 Cup, 1 Plate, 2 GhCl, 1 v FRA, BL1: -,1,1
3. **Connie Henry** 15.4.72 (8y, 3) 13.95 '98 13.66w, 13.52, 13.48, 13.45, 13.39w, 13.31
   2/2/2 in AUS, 2 AUS Ch, 8 Bratislava, 2 South, 5 Budapest, 3 Ljubljana, 3 AAA
4. **Elizabeth Patrick** 29.8.77 (2y, 5) 12.61/12.69w '99 12.92, 12.89, 12.79, 12.77, 12.71, 12.70
   2 LI, 1 CAU, 3 South, 1 Dublin, 2 AAA, 3 Cup, 1 Croydon, 4 v FRA, BL1; 1,2,2
5. **Debbie Rowe** 8.9.72 (7y, 8) 12.61 '98, 12.76w '97 13.14w/12.97, 12.92, 12.89, 12.78, 12.73, 12.71
   2 CAU, 2 Bedl, 1 Mid, 1 Stoke, 3 BL1 (2), 1 sf Cudworth, 2 Dublin, 5 AAA
6. **Katie Evans** 4.2.74 (6y, 7) 13.03 '97 13.04w, 12.91w/12.63, 12.87, 12.67, 12.61, 12.47
   5 CAU, 2 Stoke, 1 sf Rugby, 6 AAA, 2 Cup, BL3: 1,1,1
7. **Jodie Hurst** 21.6.77 (4y, 6) 12.59 '99 12.64, 12.54, 12.45, 12.39, 12.29w, 12.27
   4 CAU, 4 Bedl, 2 sf Rugby, 1 IR, 4 AAA, 4 Cup, BL1: 2,4,-
8. **Anna-Maria Thorpe** 15.7.71 (3y, 4) 12.84 '99 12.83, 12.47, 12.39, 12.37w, 12.31, 12.29w
   1 LI, 3 CAU, 3 Bedl, 4 South, 1 sf Enfield, 9 AAA, 2 Plate, 2 Croydon
9. **Caroline Stead** 14.9.71 (7y, 12) 12.67 '96 12.47, 12.25, 12.25, 12.25, 12.15, 12.13; 12.18i
   5 Bedl, 5 South, 2 IR, 7 AAA, 5 Croydon, BL2: -,1,1
10. **Leandra Polius** 14.5.80 (1y, -) 11.85 '99 12.52, 12.24, 12.20, 11.90, 11.84, 11.61; 11.65i
    7 South, 1 AAA-23, 5 U23L, nj AAA, 3 Plate, 6 v FRA, 5 v SPA-23
11. **Rebecca White** 5.6.80 (1y, -) 11.67 '98 12.24, 12.23, 12.22, 12.00, 11.90w, 11.73
    4 B.Univs, 1 North, 3 IR, 8 AAA, 1 Nth IC, 1 U23HI, 4 v SPA-23, BL1: -,6,3
12. **Julia Johnson** 21.9.79 (4y, 9) 12.50 '98 12.12, 11.96, 11.54, 11.51 1 B.Univs, 3 LI, 6 U23L, 3 Croydon

Hansen competed only twice, indoors in Birmingham and at the Olympics, where she did well in the circumstances to make the final; she ranks top for the sixth time, with Griffith, ranking in the top three for the tenth time, regaining second place from Henry. The top eight are the same as last year, but with some changes in order. Patrick moves up to 4th, beating Rowe 4-0. The tenth best of 12.47 is just short of the record of 12.49 set in 1996.

SHOT

1. **Judy Oakes** 14.2.58 (24y, 1) 19.36 '88 18.22, 18.16, 18.08, 17.99, 17.92, 17.91; 18.30i, 18.12i
   1 Surrey, 1 LI, 1 Arles, 1 South, 2 v USA, 3 ECp, 1 IR, 1 AAA, 1 Cup, dnq 13 OG
2. **Julie Dunkley** 11.9.79 (4y, 3) 16.16 '99 16.40, 16.19, 16.05, 16.05, 15.99, 15.96; 16.13i 1 Kent, 1 E.Clubs,
   3 Arles, 2 South, 1 Woodford, 1 AAA-23, 4 v USA, 3 U23L, 2 AAA, 2 Cup, 3 v FRA, 1 v SPA-23, BL1: 1,1,1
3. **Joanne Duncan** 27.12.66 (7y, 4) 16.12 '99 16.09, 16.00, 15.92, 15.92, 15.84, 15.67
   1 Essex, 1 CAU, 3 South, 2 Woodford, 7 v USA, 2 IR, 3 AAA, 1 Croydon, 5 v FRA, BL2: 1,1,1

4. **Denise Lewis** 27.8.72 (5y, 5) 16.12 '99 15.55, 15.50, 15.47, 15.21, 15.11, 15.07
2 E.Clubs, 6g v USA, 3 Dutch Ch, 3 Cup
5. **Christina Bennett** 27.2.78 (4y, 6) 15.55 '99 15.51, 15.31, 15.14, 15.12, 15.11, 15.05
2 Surrey, 2 LI, 2 CAU, 4 South, 3 Woodford, 2 AAA-23, 5 U23L, 5 AAA, 2 Plate, 4 v SPA-23
6. **Vickie Foster** 1.4.71 (5y, 8) 15.24 '99 15.44, 14.91, 14.81, 14.74, 14.73, 14.59; 15.21i, 15.01i
3 CAU, 5 South, 1 sf Enfield, 7 AAA, 5 Cup, 2 Bath, BL1: 3,2,3
7. **Maggie Lynes** 19.2.63 (13y, -) 16.57 '94 14.73, 14.64, 14.59, 14.38, 14.32, 14.26; 15.45i, 15.31i, 15.28i, 15.08i, 15.03i 6 Arles, 6 South, 4 Woodford, 4 AAA, 7 v FRA, BL2: -,2,2
8. **Philippa Roles** 1.3.78 (5y, 10) 15.00i '98, 14.75 '99 14.84, 14.54, 14.29, 14.27, 14.24, 14.21; 15.62i, 15.39i, 14.97i, 14.86i, 14.75i 1 B.Univs, 3 LI, 1 sf Rugby, 4 Cup, 1 Bath, BL1: 5,5,2
9. **Eleanor Gatrell** 5.10.76 (3y, 12=) 14.68 '98 14.42, 14.42, 14.40, 14.25, 14.24, 13.82; 14.60i, 14.33i
3 Surrey, 7 CAU, 7 South, 1 sf Eton, 8 AAA, 1 Plate
10. **Tracy Axten** 20.7.63 (6y, 7) 15.81 '98 14.38, 14.25, 14.17, 14.01, 13.59, 13.38
5 CAU, 1 Police, 5 Woodford, 2 sf Enfield, BL1: 4,3,4
11. **Alison Grey** 12.5.73 (9y, 12=) 15.85i, 15.69 '94 14.30, 14.09, 13.96, 13.72, 13.55
1 Scot E, 4 LI, 6 CAU, 3 BL2 (2), 1 sf Cudworth
12. **Nicola Gautier** 21.3.78 (2y, 9) 15.01 '99 15.09, 14.07, 13.94, 13.69, 13.56, 13.15; 14.33i, 13.94i
1 Yorks, 1 North, BL1: 6,-,6
nr **Eva Massey** IRE 22.12.80 (1y, 11) 14.49 '99 14.90, 14.61, 14.56, 14.52, 14.49, 14.48; 14.66i
4 CAU, 6 ECp1B, 3 AAA-23, 6 AAA, 1 Irish, BL1: 2,-,5

We bid farewell to Oakes, who ended her extraordinary career with a record 18 number one rankings from 24 years in which she has been in the top five. Sadly she was just one place off qualifying for the Olympic final. She was again a class apart from the rest, although it was encouraging that Dunkley maintains her progress. Myrtle Augee did not compete in 2000 after 18 successive years in the rankings. There were no newcomers this year.

DISCUS

1. **Shelley Drew** 8.8.73 (9y, 1) 60.82 '98 59.03, 57.79, 57.43, 57.28, 57.03, 56.94
6 Walnut, 3 Lancaster, 1 LI, 1 CAU, 3 Arles, 1 Bedl, 8 ECp, 1 IR, 1 Lough, 1 AAA, 1 Cup, 1 Plate, 7 GhCl
2. **Philippa Roles** 1.3.78 (6y, 2) 60.00 '99 57.04, 56.35, 55.87, 55.59, 55.48, 55.44
1 B.Univs, 3 LI, 1B Halle, 2 Bedl, 1 AAA-23, 1 U23L, 1 sf Rugby, 2 Dublin, 3 Lough, 2 AAA, 2 Cup, 2 Plate, 8 GhCl, 1 v SPA-23, 1 Bath, BL1: 1,1,1
3. **Emma Merry** 2.7.74 (11y, 3) 57.75 '99 55.60, 54.50, 53.73, 53.69, 53.08, 53.03
2 LI, 2 CAU, 2 sf Rugby, 2 IR, 2 Lough, 3 AAA, 3 Cup, BL3: 1,1,1
4. **Debbie Callaway** 15.7.64 (17y, 8) 58.56 '96 52.34, 50.59, 50.53, 50.45, 50.11, 49.97
3 CAU, 1 South, 1 sf Enfield, 4 Lough, 4 AAA, 4 Cup, 2 Brighton, 1 Croydon, 4 v FRA, BL1: 2,2,2
5. **Tracy Axten** 20.7.63 (12y, 5) 58.18 '97 51.72, 51.45, 50.96, 50.04, 49.98, 49.64
4 CAU, 3 E.Clubs, 2 South, 1 Police, 2 sf Enfield, 3 Dublin, 5 Cup, 2 Croydon, 6 v FRA BL1: 4,3,3
6. **Claire Smithson** 3.8.83 (2y, 10) 49.36 '99 52.19, 51.38, 50.18, 49.98, 49.12, 48.95
1 Sth-J, 5 LI, 5 Bedl, 3 South, 1 E.Sch, 5 Lough, 4 Mannheim, 1 Brighton, 1 AAA-J, 2 Bath, 1 JI4N, 8 WJ
7. **Emma Carpenter** 16.5.82 (1y, -) 46.55 '98 52.21, 50.31, 50.09, 49.37, 49.24, 49.21
4 Bedl, 1 Jnr IR, 2 E.Sch, 4 Dublin, 1 Comm-Y, 2 AAA-J, 1 U20HI, 3 JI4N, dnq 14 WJ
8. **Judy Oakes** 14.2.58 (13y, -) 53.44 '88 49.82, 48.45, 48.20, 45.70 1 Surrey, 3 IR
9. **Lorraine Shaw** 2.4.68 (7y, 7) 55.04 '94 49.77, 49.15, 46.64, 46.64, 44.30 1 West, BL1: 3,5,5
10. **Nicola Talbot** 17.2.72 (8y, 11) 54.24 '93 48.84, 48.43, 48.26, 48.03, 47.47, 47.29
1 Mid, 1 sf Cudworth, 4 IR, 5 AAA, 6 Cup, BL1: 5,6,4
11. **Alison Grey** 12.5.73 (7y, 9) 52.52 '94 47.79, 47.51, 47.18, 46.57, 46.41, 46.39
4 LI, 5 CAU, 1 Scot, 2 sf Cudworth, 6 AAA, BL2: -,1,2
12. **Vickie Foster** 1.4.71 (3y, 12) 48.62 '93 49.25, 48.64, 47.69, 47.50, 46.15, 46.12
2 West, 6 CAU, 4 South, 7 AAA, 3 Brighton, 3 Bath, BL1: 7,4,6

Drew ranks first for the fourth successive year and had a good year despite the distractions of working to remodel her technique. She was unbeaten by a British athlete. P Roles and Merry are again second and third, with Roles ahead 3-2 on win-loss. Jacqui McKernan was missed after 15 successive years in the rankings. Although they had a similar series of best marks, Callaway beat Axten 9-0. Carpenter and Smithson went to 5th and 6th on the British all-time junior lists with one and two years respectively remaining as juniors and Smithson did well to make the World Junior final.

HAMMER

1. **Lorraine Shaw** 2.4.68 (7y, 1) 64.90 '95 67.44, 66.87, 66.85, 66.21, 66.19, 65.74
2/1/1 in SA, 1 Perivale, 1 Colindale, 1 West, 2 LI, 7 Halle, 1 Batt.Pk, 1 Bedl, 1 Leuven, 5 ECp, 3 Szom, 2 Budapest, 1 Dublin, 1 AAA, 1 Cup, 9 OG, BL1: 1,1,1
2. **Lyn Sprules** 11.9.75 (8y, 2) 63.05 '99 63.96, 63.35, 63.34, 62.71, 62.48, 62.47
3 LI, 3B Halle, 1 BRS, 2 Bedl, 1 South, 5 Budapest, 3 Dublin, 2 AAA, 3 Cup, 1 Plate, BL1: 2,2,2
3. **Elizabeth Pidgeon** 27.4.77 (5y, 4) 60.37 '99 63.61, 62.27, 62.09, 61.39, 61.26, 60.88
2 Colindale, 1B Halle, 5 Szom, 7 Budapest, 4 Dublin, 3 AAA, 2 Cup, 2 Plate, 1 Croydon, 3 v FRA, BL2: 1,1,1

4. **Suzanne Roberts** 19.12.78 (1y, -) 48.18 '97 58.83, 58.11, 57.36, 57.35, 57.07, 56.52
1 Yorks, 3 CAU, 1 North, 1 AAA-23, 2 U23L, 4 AAA, 4 Cup, 1 Nth IC, 4 v FRA, 1 v SPA-23, BL1: 5,4,-
5. **Rachael Beverley** 23.7.79 (5y, 3) 60.88 '99 57.09, 56.99, 56.40, 56.20, 55.25, 54.38
1 B.Univs, 4 LI, 5 BRS, nt AAA-23, 7 Dublin, 5 AAA, 2 v SPA-23, BL1: 3,3,-
6. **Zoe Derham** 24.11.80 (3y, 10) 52.33 '99 55.57, 54.65, 54.49, 54.43, 54.11, 53.94
6 Colindale, 3 West, 2 Mid, 2 AAA-23, 4 U23L, 1 sf Rugby, 2 IR, 6 AAA, 6 v FRA, BL4: 1,2,1
7. **Sarah Moore** 15.3.73 (9y, 7) 56.60 '97 55.74, 54.95, 54.82, 54.09, 53.91, 53.89
2 West, 4 BRS, 1 Welsh, 3B Budapest, 6 Dublin, 8 AAA, 1 Bath, BL4: -,1,2
8. **Esther Augee** 1.1.64 (8y, 6) 56.76 '93 54.68, 54.45, 54.45, 54.15, 53.69, 53.65
4 Colindale, 1 Kent, 4 CAU, 2 Batt.Pk, 4 Bedl, 2 South, 1 IR, 9 AAA, 2 Croydon, BL2: 2,2,2
9. **Diana Holden** 12.2.75 (10y, 5) 57.95 '98 55.62, 54.00, 53.79, 53.70, 53.59, 53.42 2 B.Univs, 3 Perivale,
3 Colindale, 5 LI, 3 Batt.Pk, 5 Bedl, 2 Leuven, 1 sf Enfield, 7 AAA, 5 Cup, 3 Croydon, BL1: 4,5,-
10. **Carys Parry** 24.7.81 (2y, 12) 51.09 '99 53.80, 53.08, 52.65, 52.10, 52.07, 51.88 3 B.Univs, 6 LI, 2 CAU,
1 Welsh-J, 2 Welsh, 1 Wrexham, 5B Budapest, 10 Dublin, 6 Mannheim, 2 U20HI, 2 AAA-J, 5 Bath, 4 JI4N, dnq 14 WJ
11. **Mhairi Walters** 19.6.81 (1y, -) 50.68 '99 55.10, 53.85, 53.79, 52.88, 52.31, 52.21
1 Nicosia, 1 Scot-J, 15 Budapest, 2 Scot, 5 Mannheim, 1 AAA-J, 3 Bath, 9 JI4N, dnq 29 WJ, BL1: 6,6,-
12. **Christina Bennett** 27.2.78 (1y, -) 50.43 '99 53.74, 52.70, 52.68, 52.12, 51.03, 50.64
1 CAU, 4 South, 3 Leuven, 5 AAA-23, 3 IR, 10 AAA, 3 Plate, 4 v SPA-23
nr **Olivia Kelleher** IRE 9.10.75 57.53 '99 55.50, 53.72, 53.24, 52.48, 52.44, 52.36
2 Perivale, 5 Colindale, 6 BRS, 3 Bedl, 7B Budapest, 4 Ljubljana, 1 Irish, BL1: 7,7,3

Shaw, who set her 13th British record and regained the Commonwealth record, ranks top for the seventh time. She had 13 competitions over 65m and had all 23 competitions at 62.53 or better. Sprules, second for the sixth time in the last seven years (she was 1st in 1997), was 4-2 against Pidgeon, and these two had 12 and 11 competitions respectively over 60m. The greatest progress was made by Roberts, who added over ten metres to her pre-season best. Those ranked 6-9 were very closely matched. Augee was 3-2 v Holden, although Holden (the only athlete to be included in all ten years of these rankings) beat both Moore and Augee at the AAAs. Parry and Walters were 3-3, but Parry was well ahead with a pb at the World Juniors. The tenth best at 54.68 improved the record level set in 1999 at 53.60.

JAVELIN

1. **Kelly Morgan** 17.6.80 (3y, 4) 54.61 '99 58.45, 57.99, 57.18, 55.44, 54.96, 53.41
1 AAA, 1 Cup, 1 Plate, 1 v FRA, 2 v SPA-23, BL1: 1,-,1
2. **Karen Martin** 24.11.74 (9y, 2) 59.50 '00 58.54, 58.07, 57.75, 57.31, 55.73, 55.30
2/1 in RSA, 1 LI, 2B Halle, 1 BRS, 2 Karlstad, 1 IS, 8 ECp, 5 Budapest, 1 BL4 (3), 2 AAA, 2 Cup
3. **Lorna Jackson** 9.1.74 (8y, 3) 56.00 '99, 58.39# '98 57.19, 53.57, 53.48, 53.38, 53.19, 51.68
3 LI, 1 CAU, 6 Kiev, 1 Scot, 1 sf Cudworth, BL2: -,1,1
4. **Goldie Sayers** 16.7.82 (3y, 6=) 51.06 '99, 51.92# '98 54.58, 53.79, 52.69, 51.64, 51.52, 51.37
4 LI, 2 CAU, 2 BRS, 2 IR, 4 AAA, 1 AAA-J, 1 U20HI, 1 Bath, 1 JI4N, 6 WJ, BL2: -,4,2
5. **Shelley Holroyd** 17.5.73 (12y, 9) 49.30 '99, 60.12# '96 53.06, 52.10, 51.96, 51.61, 51.58, 48.89
2 LI, 3 AAA, 2 v FRA, BL2: 1,2,-
6. **Jennifer Kemp** 18.2.80 (2y, 6=) 52.54 '99 52.20, 52.13, 50.49, 49.05, 48.73, 48.69
1 B.Univs, 6 LI, 4 CAU, 3 BRS, 3 AAA-23, 6 U23L, 5 AAA, 4 v FRA, 5 v SPA-23, BL2: 2,5,3
7. **Chloe Cozens** 9.4.80 (2y, 8) 48.15 '99 51.79, 51.67, 50.49, 50.45, 50.39, 49.63
2 B.Univs, 5 LI, 1 AAA-23, 5 U23L, 2, Plate, 3 v SPA-23
8. **Kirsty Morrison** 28.10.75 (8y, 1) 55.91 '99, 59.36# '93 51.22, 51.13A, 50.98A, 49.27, 48.52, 48.51
4/3 in RSA, 6 Budapest, 2 Ljubljana, 7 AAA, BL3: 1,1,1
9. **Denise Lewis** 27.8.72 (6y, 10) 47.44 '99, 56.50# '96 51.13, 50.19, 49.42, 48.21 4 Dutch Ch, 3 Cup
10. **Sharon Gibson** 31.12.61 (21y, 5) 50.85 '99, 62.32# '87 48.00, 47.76, 46.72, 45.50, 44.56, 41.70
1 Mid, 1 IR, 6 AAA
11. **Linda Gray** 23.3.71 (1y, -) 45.87 '99 48.77, 48.22, 47.75, 47.17, 47.07, 46.53
1 North, 1 NI, 1 sf Rugby, 3 IR, 9 AAA, BL2: -,3,4
12. **Tammie Francis** 14.11.78 (2y, -) 47.16 '99, 48.30# '97 48.24, 47.32, 46.76, 46.42, 46.31, 46.09
3 CAU, 1 South, 2 AAA-23, 1 sf Eton, 5 IR, BL4: 1,1,2

= old specification

Morgan set British U23 records with the new specification javelin on successive weekends in August, the second to win the AAA title, and 6 wins in seven competitions gets her top ranking from Martin (second for the fourth successive year) and Jackson. Sayers was sixth in the World Juniors after a pb in qualifying, and that gets her fourth ranking from Holroyd, although the latter was ahead at the AAAs. Gibson is ranked for the 21st successive year.

HEPTATHLON

1. **Denise Lewis** 27.8.72 (12y, 1) 6736 '97 1 Talence 6831, 1 OG 6584
2. **Kerry Jury** 19.11.68 (11y, 2) 6005w '98, 5908 '99
2 Spanish 5735, 9 ECp1 5667, 13 Arles 5638, 3 Watford 4647, dnf North
3. **Julie Hollman** 16.2.77 (4y, 4) 5816w '98, 5595 '97 3 Spanish 5685, 1 HCI 5622, 1 AAA 5560
4. **Danielle Freeman** 11.2.80 (3y, 8) 5258w '99, 5237 '98 12 Arles 5644, 14 ECp1 5442, 6 U23V 5014, dnf North

5. **Nicola Gautier** 21.3.78 (5y, 3) 5760 '99 15 Arles 5602, dnf ECp1 (4687)
6. **Julia Bennett** 26.3.70 (9y, 6) 5747w '96, 5496 '95 19 Arles 5538, 13 ECp1 5444
7. **Kelly Sotherton** 13.11.76 (2y, -) 5585 '97 20 Arles 5428, 2 HCI 5411, 2 AAA 5388
8. **Diana Bennett** 14.6.74 (8y, 5) 5555w '98, 5550 '97 23 Arles 5308, dnf AAA
9. **Chloe Cozens** 9.4.80 (3y,7) 5358w '98, 5283 '99 1 Watford 5257, 3 HCI 5246, 4 U23V 5205, 28 Arles 5098
10. **Fiona Harrison** 30.11.81 (2y, 11) 5140 '99
11 WJ 5279, 2 Watford 5250, 1 York 4859, 3 ES 4355 (dnf 800), dnf U20V
11. **Anne Hollman** 18.2.74 (5y, 9) 5259w '99, 5258 '96 27 Arles 5151, 3 AAA 5028, 4 HCI 5028
12. **Katherine Livesey** 15.12.79 (4y, 10) 5239w '99, 5215 '97 6 Big 12 5173, 4 Des Moines 5079h, dnf U23V
- **Rebecca Jones** 17.1.83 (0y, -) 4695 '99 25 Arles 5186, 4752, 3 HCI-J 4666

Lewis is top for the seventh successive year, improving her Commonwealth record at Talence and taking Olympic gold despite suffering from an ankle injury. Jury is second for the third successive year and Hollman moves up after two years at number four.

WALKS

Priority is given to form at the standard international distance of 20 kilometres, although performances at other distances are also taken into account. 3000m and 5000m performances are on the track, unless indicated by R for road marks (+ indicates intermediate time). All distances from 10k up are on the road unless shown by t. Previous bests are shown for track 5000m and road or track 10km and 20km.

1. **Lisa Kehler** 15.3.67 (15y, -) 21:57.68 '90, 45:03 '98, 0
3000m: 12:50.61, 12:59, 13:17.79+; 1 IR 5km: 22:22.94, 23:24R, 23:31R, 23:37+R; 1 Mid, 1 AAA
10km: 45:09.57t, 46:30+, 46:42, 46:51+, 47:23+; 1 AAA, 1 Leicester
20km: 1:33:57, 1:35:35, 1:37:47, 1:39:28; 1 RWA, 14 Leamington, 23 ECp, 33 OG
2. **Niobe Menendez** 1.9.66 (3y, 3) 25:11.75 '98, 49:10 '99, 1:40:12 '99
3000m: 14:08.52; 4 v FRA 5km: 24:22.84; 24:05+R, 24.19R; I Irish, 1 RWA
10km: 49:11+, 50:08+, 50:48+ 20km: 1:43:18, 1:44:55, 1:45:48, 1:52:27; 3 Manx, 2 RWA, 19 Leamington, 46 ECp
3. **Sara-Jane Cattermole** 29.1.77 (2y, 4) 24:59.0 '99, 49:05 '99, 1:38:25 '99
3000m: 14:10.9, 14:12.70mx, 14:29.2, 14:43.89mx 5000m: 25:23.1mx, 23:32+R, 23:53+R, 24:50R
10km: 47:47, 48:05+, 48:48; 47:28+ short 20km: 1:36:40, 1:37:31, 1:39:56, 1:41:55, 1:48:43;
1:35:52 (180m short); 21 Leamington, dnf ECp, 5 wins in Perth
4. **Sharon Tonks** 18.4.70 (3y, 12) 25:35.15 '89, 50:32 '99, 1:49:41 '99
3000m: 14:07.8, 14:24.11; 14:17.50i; 1 Worcs, 2 IR
5km: 24:59R, 24:59R, 25:28R, 25:33R; 2 Mid, 2 Worcester, 2 RWA
10km: 49:46, 52:00, 52:35, 53:04+; 1 RWA, 1 Tamworth
20km: 1:42:10 short, 1:49:19, 1:49:51; 4 RWA, 22 Leamington, 1 Yverdon
5. **Kim Braznell** 28.2.56 (8y, 5) 24:16.4 '95, 48:36 '98, 1:44:29 '99 5000m: 24:38.4
10km: 52:11+, 52:20; 2 Leicester 20km: 1:46:24, 1:48:14, 1:50:34; 3 RWA, 23 Leamington, 50 ECp
6. **Jane Kennaugh** 26.1.73 (2y, 9) 51:34 '99, 1:48:24 '99 3000m: 15:18.5; 1 Manx 10km: 53:35; 1 Isle of Man
20km: 1:50:13, 1:50:28, 1:51:57, 1:55:31; 8 RWA, 25 Leamington, 1 Isle of Man, 4 Dublin
7. **Sally Warren** 29.1.78 (1y, -) 25:36.61 '98, 51:20 '98 3000m: 14:49.6, 14:53.39; 1 South, 7 v FRA
5km: 25:11.33, 25:22.68; 4 U23L, 2 AAA-23/20 10km: 52:37; 2g RWA 20km: 1:52:37, 1:53:17; 5 RWA, 26 Leamington
8. **Nikki Huckerby** 27.2.78 (4y, 11) 24:56.69 '98, 51:07 '98, 1:49:12 '00 3000m: 15:13.68; 2 HCU23
5km: 25:33.09, 25:41.38; 25:53R, 26:22R, 26:28R; 4 Mid, 2 IC, 5 U23L, 3 AAA-23/20, 4 RWA
10km: 54:15, 54:53.35t, 55:24; 1 Mid, 4 RWA, 2 AAA 20km: 1:51:25, 1:54:04; 24 Leamington, 6 Dublin
9. **Lisa Crump** 30.3.76 (4y 6) 24:26.41 '99, 49:51 '98, 1:46:48 '99
5km: 24:44R, 25:57R, 26:01R; 3 IC, 3 RWA 10km: 49:50, 54:56; 5 RWA, 2 Tamworth
10. **Catherine Charnock** 3.5.75 (4y, 2) 23:11.7 '99, 47:51 '99, 1:38:29 '99 3000m: 13:58.96; 3 v FRA
5km: 26:24R 10km: dq E.Molesey, dq RWA, dq AAA 20km: dnf RWA, dq Leamington, dq Swiss
11. **Katherine Horwill** 26.1.75 (2y, 10) 25:08.24 '99, 49:38 '99, 1:51:38 '99
3000m: 14:30.3; 14:35.64i; 2 Worcs 10km: 53:22, 54:25, 55:59.54t; 4 RWA, 3 AAA, 3 Tamworth
20km: 1:54:46, 1:55:36; 6 RWA, 8 Dublin
12. **Bridget Kaneen** 15.8.65 (1y, -) 55:06 '99, 1:57:15 '99 5km: 26:57R, 10km: 55:54
20km: 1:54:21, 1:54:55, 1:55:23,. 1:59:03; 4 Manx, 7 RWA, 27 Leamington, 7 Dublin
- **Nicola Phillips** 23.4.83 (1y, -) 25:11.46 '99, 52:37 '99 3000m: 14:29.37i, 14:38.22i
5000m: 27:13.02, 25:33R, 25:59R; 4 IC, 5 AAA23/20, 1 E.Sch
10km: 51:36, 52:20, 55:09; 1 E.Molesey, 8 Leamington-J, 1 RWA-J

Kehler made a fine return after a year out, with a British record for 10,000m on the track and two road bests at 20km. She ranks at number one for the seventh time (previously 1987, 1989-90, 1995, 1997-8). Menendez was clearly second as Cattermole could not reproduce elsewhere the fast times she recorded in Perth. Charnock, second ranked last year, got into severe trouble with the judges and was disqualified in five of her six major races at 10k and 20k; she just gets a ranking by her third place in the A international at 3000m. Vicky Lupton was missed after eleven years in the rankings. The sad decline in walking is shown by tenth best for 10km being 54:15, the worst since 1982.

With thanks to Tony Miller, Alan Lindop, Ian Hodge, Ian Tempest, Martin Rix, Matthew Fraser-Moat, John Powell and Rob Whittingham for their comments.

2000 LISTS - MEN

60 METRES - Indoors

6.48	Jason Gardener		18.09.75	1	Madrid, SPA	16 Feb
	6.49			1	Stuttgart, GER	6 Feb
	6.49			1	Ghent, BEL	27 Feb
	6.50			1h2	Madrid, SPA	16 Feb
	6.51			1r3	Piraeus, GRE	9 Feb
	6.53			1	Birmingham	29 Jan
	6.54			1s1	Ghent, BEL	27 Feb
	6.55			1s1	Birmingham	29 Jan
	6.55			1h2	Stuttgart, GER	6 Feb
	6.57			1	Glasgow	5 Mar
	6.60			1h5	Birmingham	29 Jan
	6.63			1h5	Ghent, BEL	26 Feb
6.55	Dwain Chambers	U23	5.04.78	5	Ghent, BEL	11 Feb
	6.58			3	Lievin, FRA	13 Feb
	6.61			1h2	Lievin, FRA	13 Feb
	6.62			5r3	Piraeus, GRE	9 Feb
	6.62			2h2	Ghent, BEL	11 Feb
	6.64			1s3	Birmingham	29 Jan
	6.71			1	Birmingham	15 Jan
6.67	Mark Lewis-Francis	U20	4.09.82	2r1	Neubrandenburg, GER	4 Mar
	6.69			2s3	Birmingham	29 Jan
	6.69			2r2	Neubrandenburg, GER	4 Mar
	6.70			1h2	Birmingham	29 Jan
	6.72			5	Birmingham	29 Jan
6.71	Jamie Henthorn		20.02.77	2h2	Birmingham	28 Jan
	6.71			3	Birmingham	29 Jan
	6.76			1h4	Birmingham	29 Jan
6.71	Jason John		17.10.71	2s1	Birmingham	29 Jan
	6.74			6	Birmingham	29 Jan
	6.75			5h1	Birmingham	20 Feb
6.71	Marlon Devonish		1.06.76	3s2	Birmingham	29 Jan
	6.71			4	Birmingham	29 Jan
	6.76			2h4	Birmingham	29 Jan
6.74	John Skeete	U23	8.09.78	1s1	Glasgow	23 Jan
	6.74			1	Cardiff	26 Feb
	6.76			1	Glasgow	23 Jan
6.75	Tim Benjamin	U20	2.05.82	6h1	Birmingham	20 Feb
6.75	Doug Bignall		20.10.74	4h2	Birmingham	20 Feb
	(10)					
6.76	Christian Malcolm	U23	3.06.79	6h2	Piraeus, GRE	9 Feb
	6.76			7h1	Birmingham	20 Feb
6.76	Kevin Williams		15.12.71	2	Cardiff	26 Feb
	41 performances to 6.76 by 11 athletes					
6.78	Akinola Lashore		28.03.73	2	Birmingham	15 Jan
6.78	Uvie Ugono	U23	8.03.78	1h8	Birmingham	29 Jan
6.78	Ian Mackie		27.02.75	3s1	Birmingham	29 Jan
6.79	Jason Fergus		11.10.73	1h2	Birmingham	15 Jan
6.79	Brian Doyle		12.03.77	1	Glasgow	15 Jan
6.80	Julian Golding		17.02.75	7h2	Birmingham	20 Feb
6.81	Michael Tietz		14.09.77	1	Birmingham	8 Jan
6.82	Marlon Dickson	U23	17.11.78	7s2	Birmingham	29 Jan
6.82	John Stewart	U23	30.12.79	1s1	Cardiff	11 Mar
	(20)					
6.84	Jonathon Oparka	U23	27.01.80	2	Glasgow	15 Jan
6.85	Ray Salami		11.04.75	4	Glasgow	23 Jan
6.86	Nick Thomas	U23	4.04.79	4s2	Birmingham	15 Jan
6.86	Daniel Money		17.10.76	6s3	Birmingham	29 Jan

6.87	Brendon Ghent		7.09.76	1h9	Birmingham	15	Jan
6.88	Tyrone Edgar	U20	29.03.82	1J	Bedford	22	Jan
6.88	Terence Stamp		18.02.70	4s1	Glasgow	23	Jan
6.88	Dominic Bradley		22.12.76	1	Sheffield	23	Jan
6.89	Aiah Yambasu		10.11.73	1s1	Bedford	22	Jan
6.89	Kevin Ellis		18.06.76	4s2	Glasgow	23	Jan
	(30)						
6.89	Tony Jarrett		13.08.68	4h3	Birmingham	29	Jan
6.89	Ayo Falola		29.07.68	3h6	Birmingham	29	Jan
6.89	Richard Pinnock		31.10.70	3h7	Birmingham	29	Jan
6.90	Dominique Richards	U23	12.09.79	3	Bedford	22	Jan
6.90	Darren Burley	U23	13.01.80	4h5	Birmingham	29	Jan
6.91	Gary Jones		6.01.72	5h5	Birmingham	29	Jan
6.92	Darren Chin	U20	30.06.81	1s2	Birmingham	5	Feb
6.92	Luke Davis	U23	1.01.80	2	Birmingham	12	Feb
6.92	James Miller	U23	29.03.80	3s1	Glasgow	11	Mar
6.93	Henry Richards	U20	15.05.81	1	Birmingham	9	Jan
	(40)						
6.93	Nigel Stickings		1.04.71	4h7	Birmingham	29	Jan
6.93	Tim Barton		3.10.70	1r3	Birmingham	17	Feb
6.94	Matthew Russell	U20	20.01.81	3	Birmingham	5	Feb
6.94	Ruben Tabares	U23	22.10.78	2h1	Cardiff	12	Feb
6.94	Andy Hughes		10.07.67	3	Birmingham	17	Feb
6.95	Colin Wilson		30.10.77	2s1	Bedford	22	Jan
6.95	Tyrone Swaray		7.11.77	5h3	Birmingham	29	Jan
6.96	Graham Beasley		24.10.77	4h9	Birmingham	29	Jan
6.96	Andrew Parker	U23	1.08.80	1	Cardiff	4	Mar
6.97	Maclean Okotie		31.07.69	2s2	Bedford	22	Jan
	(50)						
6.97	Mark McIntyre		14.10.70	3h8	Birmingham	29	Jan
6.97	Dwayne Grant	U20	17.07.82	4	Birmingham	5	Feb
6.98	Ed White		16.11.73	7rB	Birmingham	8	Jan
6.98	Joshua Wood		19.04.74	1h3	Bedford	22	Jan
6.99	Richard Agyemang	U20	5.08.82	5	Birmingham	5	Feb
6.99	Tristan Anthony	U20	16.12.82	1s3	Birmingham	5	Feb

Doubtful Timing

6.86	Adam Potter	U23	12.04.80	1	Cardiff	23	Jan
6.86	Robert Newton	U20	10.05.81	2	Cardiff	23	Jan

Hand Timing

6.8	Nick Thomas	U23	(6.86)	1A1	London (CP)	12	Jan
6.8	Marlon Dickson	U23	(6.82)	1A2	London (CP)	13	Dec
6.9	Akeem Ogunyemi		4.06.74	3h1	London (Ha)	9	Jan
6.9	Maclean Okotie		(6.97)	4	London (Ha)	9	Jan
6.9	Alloy Wilson	U23	25.01.80	1rC	London (Ha)	9	Jan
6.9	Tyrone Swaray		(6.95)	3	London (CP)	12	Jan
6.9	Dwayne Grant	U20	(6.97)	1A2	London (CP)	9	Feb
6.9	Joshua Wood		(6.98)	2r2	London (CP)	9	Feb
6.9	Ian Clarke		6.11.72	3A2	London (CP)	13	Dec

Outdoor

6.62	0.6	Dwain Chambers	U23	5.04.78	1	Gold Coast (S), AUS	15	Sep
6.65	0.6	Christian Malcolm	U23	3.06.79	2	Gold Coast (S), AUS	15	Sep
6.68	0.6	Allyn Condon		24.08.74	3	Gold Coast (S), AUS	15	Sep
6.93	0.6	Marlon Devonish		1.06.76	4	Gold Coast (S), AUS	15	Sep

Foreign

6.69	*Josephus Thomas ¶ (SLE)*	*11.07.71*	*1s2*	*Birmingham*	*29*	*Jan*
	6.66 rolling start		*3h2*	*Birmingham*	*20*	*Feb*
6.80	*Joselyn Thomas (SLE)*	*11.07.71*	*5s1*	*Birmingham*	*29*	*Jan*
6.82	*Sylvain Reboul (FRA)*	*4.10.76*	*2*	*Cardiff*	*6*	*Feb*
	6.73 doubtful timing		*1*	*Cardiff*	*23*	*Jan*

100 METRES

10.06	0.4	Darren Campbell		12.09.73	3	Stockholm, SWE	1 Aug
		10.12 -0.8			2	Birmingham	12 Aug
		10.13 -0.1			2	Nice, FRA	8 Jul
		10.13 -0.3			6	Sydney, AUS	23 Sep
		10.14 0.9			3h1	Stockholm, SWE	1 Aug
		10.19 -0.1			5	Monaco, MON	18 Aug
		10.19 0.4			3s1	Sydney, AUS	23 Sep
		10.20 0.4			3	Nuremberg, GER	25 Jun
		10.20 -0.1			3	London (CP)	5 Aug
		10.21 0.4			4	Helsinki, FIN	15 Jun
		10.21 0.2			1q5	Sydney, AUS	22 Sep
		10.25 0.5			1	Doha, QAT	7 Oct
		10.27 -0.3			4	Gateshead	28 Aug
		10.28 0.4			5	Paris (Saint-Denis), FRA	23 Jun
		10.28 -0.5			1h5	Sydney, AUS	22 Sep
		10.29 0.8			3h1	Nuremberg, GER	25 Jun
		10.30 1.9			2	Loughborough	21 May
		10.30 0.7			2	Villeneuve d'Ascq, FRA	17 Jun
		10.31 0.2			1h2	Birmingham	11 Aug
		10.34 1.7			1	Liege, BEL	27 May
		10.34 0.5			1s1	Birmingham	12 Aug
		10.37 0.2			2h1	Helsinki, FIN	15 Jun
10.08	-0.3	Dwain Chambers	U23	5.04.78	4	Sydney, AUS	23 Sep
		10.11 -0.8			1	Birmingham	12 Aug
		10.11 -0.3			1	Gateshead	28 Aug
		10.12 0.8			1q4	Sydney, AUS	22 Sep
		10.14 0.4			1s1	Sydney, AUS	23 Sep
		10.18 -0.1			4	Monaco, MON	18 Aug
		10.24 0.4			5h2	Stockholm, SWE	1 Aug
		10.26 1.0			8r1	Lausanne, SWZ	5 Jul
		10.28 0.4			2	Dortmund, GER	8 Jul
		10.28 0.7			1h5	Birmingham	11 Aug
		10.28 0.0			1s2	Birmingham	12 Aug
		10.30 -0.1			7	London (CP)	5 Aug
		10.31 1.3			1	London (He)	6 Aug
		10.36 -0.2			2h3	Nuremberg, GER	25 Jun
		10.38 0.3			2h7	Sydney, AUS	22 Sep
		10.40 0.4			6	Nuremberg, GER	25 Jun
10.09	1.0	Jason Gardener		18.09.75	3r1	Lausanne, SWZ	5 Jul
		10.16 1.3			1h1	Gold Coast (RB), AUS	10 Sep
		10.18 0.5			3h1	Athens, GRE	28 Jun
		10.25 -0.8			6	Athens, GRE	28 Jun
		10.27 0.3			4q2	Sydney, AUS	22 Sep
		10.29 -0.8			4	Birmingham	12 Aug
		10.32 -0.1			1h3	Birmingham	11 Aug
		10.38 0.5			2s1	Birmingham	12 Aug
		10.38 -0.7			1h10	Sydney, AUS	22 Sep
		10.40 -3.8			1	Glasgow (S)	2 Jul
		10.40 -0.3			7	Gateshead	28 Aug
10.10	1.9	Mark Lewis-Francis	U20	4.09.82	1rB	London (CP)	5 Aug
		10.12 0.1			1	Santiago, CHI	18 Oct
		10.13 -0.6			1q2	Santiago, CHI	17 Oct
		10.24 -0.8			3	Birmingham	12 Aug
		10.24 -0.3			1s1	Santiago, CHI	18 Oct
		10.25 1.9			1	Loughborough	21 May
		10.29 1.1			3	Bedford	4 Jun
		10.30 0.8			1r2	Tallahassee, USA	15 Apr
		10.33 0.7			1h1	Birmingham	11 Aug
		10.35 0.0			2s2	Birmingham	12 Aug

10.24	1.1	Ian Mackie		27.02.75	1	Bedford	4	Jun
		10.36 1.0			2h2	Gold Coast (RB), AUS	10	Sep
		10.38 -0.8			5	Birmingham	12	Aug
		10.39 -0.3			6	Gateshead	28	Aug
		10.40 0.7			1h4	Birmingham	11	Aug
10.27	1.1	Marlon Devonish		1.06.76	1r1	Fullerton, USA	27	Apr
		10.32 1.1			4	Bedford	4	Jun
		10.32 0.0			3r1	Budapest, HUN	22	Jul
10.28	0.3	Jon Barbour	U23	3.11.80	1	Brighton	17	Jun
		10.30 1.9			4rB	London (CP)	5	Aug
		10.32 -0.4			1	Bedford	1	Jul
		10.36 -0.3			1	Getafe, SPA	9	Sep
10.29	0.6	Christian Malcolm	U23	3.06.79	2r1	Gold Coast (RB), AUS	17	Sep
		10.31 0.4			3h2	Helsinki, FIN	15	Jun
		10.32 1.9			3	Loughborough	21	May
		10.36 0.4			8	Helsinki, FIN	15	Jun
		10.37 0.7			7rB	Rome, ITA	30	Jun
		10.37 1.0			2h2	Dortmund, GER	8	Jul
		10.37 0.4			3	Dortmund, GER	8	Jul
10.30 A	1.4	Doug Bignall		20.10.74	1r5	Flagstaff, USA	6	Jul
		10.43 0.5			3s1	Birmingham	12	Aug
10.31	1.7	Owusu Dako		23.05.73	1rA1	Walnut, USA	16	Apr
	(10)							
10.36	-0.4	Uvie Ugono	U23	8.03.78	2	Bedford	1	Jul
10.38	1.3	Julian Golding		17.02.75	1r2	Irvine, USA	7	May
10.39	1.2	Tyrone Edgar	U20	29.03.82	1	Grosseto, ITA	7	Oct
10.40	2.0	John Stewart	U23	30.12.79	2	Stoke-on-Trent	29	Apr
		84 performances to 10.40 by 14 athletes						
10.42	0.2	Curtis Browne		11.09.75	2h2	Birmingham	11	Aug
10.42	0.0	Allyn Condon		24.08.74	3s2	Birmingham	12	Aug
10.43	1.8	Marcus Adam		28.02.68	1rB	Ljubljana, SLO	25	Jul
10.44	0.2	Nathan Morgan	U23	30.06.78	1rB	Bath	16	Sep
10.48	1.1	Adrian Patrick		15.06.73	2r1	Fullerton, USA	27	Apr
10.48	0.5	Tim Benjamin	U20	2.05.82	2	Bath	16	Sep
	(20)							
10.49	1.5	Jason John		17.10.71	2	Loughborough	30	Jul
10.50	0.7	Akinola Lashore		28.03.73	2h5	Birmingham	11	Aug
10.51	0.3	John Skeete	U23	8.09.78	3	Brighton	17	Jun
10.52	1.3	Jamie Henthorn		20.02.77	2	London (He)	6	Aug
10.53	1.7	Luke Davis	U23	1.01.80	1r3	Bedford	11	Jun
10.53	0.7	Doug Turner		2.12.66	4h2	Budapest, HUN	22	Jul
10.53	1.5	Kevin Williams		15.12.71	1	Dublin (S), IRE	29	Jul
10.56	1.5	Brendon Ghent		7.09.76	4	Dublin (S), IRE	29	Jul
10.57		Andy Hughes		10.07.67	1	Berlin, GER	10	May
10.58		Jason Fergus		11.10.73	1r1	Eagle Rock, USA	13	May
	(30)							
10.59	0.3	Mark Findlay ¶	U23	20.03.78	4	Brighton	17	Jun
10.59	0.2	Nigel Stickings		1.04.71	3h2	Birmingham	11	Aug
10.60	1.0	Marlon Dickson	U23	17.11.78	1rB	London (He)	6	Aug
10.61	0.3	Nick Thomas	U23	4.04.79	5	Brighton	17	Jun
10.61	-0.1	Tony Waddington		30.06.75	3h3	Birmingham	11	Aug
10.61	1.8	Dwayne Grant	U20	17.07.82	1h1	Bedford	26	Aug
10.63	0.0	Chris Lambert	U20	6.04.81	1h3	Mannheim, GER	12	Aug
10.63	1.3	Tim Abeyie	U20	7.11.82	2h3	Bedford	26	Aug
10.63	0.2	Darren Chin	U20	30.06.81	3rB	Bath	16	Sep
10.64	1.1	John Regis		13.10.66	4r1	Fullerton, USA	27	Apr
	(40)							
10.66	1.3	Terence Stamp		18.02.70	1h1	Brighton	17	Jun
10.66	-0.5	David Samuyiwa		4.08.72	3h2	Madrid, SPA	18	Jul
10.66	1.8	Ben Lewis	U20	6.03.81	2h1	Bedford	26	Aug

10.69	-2.1	Daniel Money		17.10.76	2	Solihull	29	Jul
10.70	1.3	Jonathon Oparka	U23	27.01.80	3	London (He)	6	Aug
10.70	0.7	Dominique Richards	U23	12.09.79	3h4	Birmingham	11	Aug
10.74	2.0	James Chatt	U23	11.02.80	3	Stoke-on-Trent	29	Apr
10.74	1.3	Ayo Falola		29.07.68	3h1	Brighton	17	Jun
10.75		Richard Rubenis		10.11.73	1	Colwyn Bay	3	Sep
10.76	1.7	Graham Beasley		24.10.77	4r3	Bedford	11	Jun
	(50)							
10.77	-0.3	Chris Stobart	U20	27.03.82	1	Cleckheaton	27	May
10.77	0.2	Dominic Bradley		22.12.76	1	Stretford	27	Jun
10.77	0.5	Dan Donovan		8.10.70	1	Watford	26	Jul
10.77	1.9	Anthony Noel		8.09.63	1	Watford	9	Aug
10.78	0.6	Kevin Ellis		18.06.76	2	Alfaz del Pi, SPA	29	Apr
10.78	0.6	Gavin Eastman	U23	28.06.80	2ro	Bedford	1	Jul
10.78	1.5	Andrew Parker	U23	1.08.80	5	Loughborough	30	Jul
10.79	0.4	Ian Clarke		6.11.72	3h4	Brighton	17	Jun
10.79	0.4	Joshua Wood		19.04.74	4h4	Brighton	17	Jun
10.79	0.3	Monu Miah	U17	10.01.84	1	Sheffield	30	Jul
	(60)							
10.79	0.5	Gary Jones		6.01.72	5h6	Birmingham	11	Aug
10.80	0.3	Laurence Oboh	U17	14.05.84	2	Sheffield	30	Jul
10.81	2.0	Ian Deeth	U23	25.06.79	4	Stoke-on-Trent	29	Apr
10.81	-0.5	Michael Champion		3.01.75	6s1	Brighton	17	Jun
10.81	-1.1	Dean Macey		12.12.77	2D	Sydney, AUS	27	Sep
10.82	-0.7	Darren Burley	U23	13.01.80	3h7	Brighton	17	Jun
10.83	1.9	Jamie Quarry		15.11.72	2D1	Arles, FRA	3	Jun
10.83	1.7	Sam Omonua		16.06.76	5r3	Bedford	11	Jun
10.83	-1.5	Alasdair McFarlane	U23	13.02.78	1h2	Riga, LAT	23	Jun
10.83	0.7	Richard Pinnock		31.10.70	5h5	Birmingham	11	Aug
	(70)							
10.84	1.6	Tony Gill		19.09.77	3s3	Stoke-on-Trent	29	Apr
10.84	0.6	Karl Forde	U20	15.04.83	1h2	Sheffield	7	Jul
10.84	1.0	Tim Barton		3.10.70	2rB	Loughborough	30	Jul
10.84	-0.7	Seriashe Childs	U20	2.09.82	2h1	Edinburgh	13	Aug
10.84	0.3	Henry Richards	U20	15.05.81	3h5	Bedford	26	Aug
10.85	0.3	Rikki Fifton	U17	17.06.85	3	Sheffield	30	Jul
10.85		Michael Smith	U23	3.06.79	2	Colwyn Bay	3	Sep
10.86	1.0	Maclean Okotie		31.07.69	3rB	London (He)	6	Aug
10.88	0.2	Vincent Davis	U20	1.11.81	2	Stretford	27	Jun
10.88	0.6	Alex Golding	U20	3.12.81	2h2	Sheffield	7	Jul
	(80)							
10.88	1.2	Ricky Alfred		20.12.77	1rB	Bedford	5	Aug
10.89	0.7	Aidan Syers	U20	29.06.83	3	Watford	2	Jul
10.89		Essop Merrick		24.05.74	1	Aldershot	16	Jul
10.91	1.3	Elisha Newell	U23	10.06.79	4h1	Brighton	17	Jun
10.92	2.0	Daniel Cummins		10.12.76	6	Stoke-on-Trent	29	Apr
10.92	1.8	Jared Deacon		15.10.75	1r7	Irvine, USA	7	May
10.92	-4.0	Du'aine Thorne-Ladejo		14.02.71	2h1	Stoke-on-Trent	18	Jun
10.92	0.7	Chris Tomlinson	U20	15.09.81	4	Watford	2	Jul
10.93	1.1	Gary Carr	U20	24.09.82	2	Nicosia, CYP	27	May
10.93	1.2	Ugochi Anomelechi	U17	29.10.83	1	Sheffield	8	Jul
	(90)							
10.93	1.2	Phillip Delbaugh	V40	25.01.60	1	Jyvaskyla, FIN	9	Jul
10.94		Quentin Diamond		25.09.74	2	Watford	7	Jun
10.94	1.3	Mark Hanson	U20	13.05.81	5h1	Brighton	17	Jun
10.94	1.0	Richard David		15.08.77	4h7	Brighton	17	Jun
10.94	1.1	Andrew Lewis		9.03.68	4	Diekirch, LUX	5	Aug
10.94	0.7	Tyrone Swaray		7.11.77	5h1	Birmingham	11	Aug
10.95	1.0	Mark McIntyre		14.10.70	2h6	Brighton	17	Jun
10.95	-0.1	Jason Jeffrey	U23	16.11.78	6h3	Birmingham	11	Aug
10.96	-1.0	Cori Henry		9.12.76	4	Loughborough	21	May

10.96	0.5 (100)	Ejike Wodu		15.12.74	6r2	Geneva, SWZ	24	Jun
10.97		Darren Scott		7.03.69	1h1	Stretford	2	May
10.97		Rob Harle	U23	1.06.79	3	Watford	7	Jun
10.97	1.0	Steven Fowles	U17	16.05.85	2s2	Sheffield	30	Jul
10.98	1.6	Paul Nwaolise		31.05.73	3	Cudworth	19	Aug
10.98	-0.6	Jonathan Carleton	U23	4.11.79	8	Dublin (S), IRE	20	Aug
10.99	0.2	Tony Leigh		27.12.65	4	Stretford	27	Jun
10.99	1.6	James Miller	U23	29.03.80	4	Cudworth	19	Aug
10.99	1.8	Dominic Papura	U20	12.02.81	3h1	Bedford	26	Aug
10.99		Adam Buckley	U23	6.12.80	1	Stretford	5	Sep

Wind Assisted

10.04	3.1	Jason Gardener		(10.09)	1	Gold Coast (RB), AUS	10	Sep
10.05	3.1	Ian Mackie		(10.24)	2	Gold Coast (RB), AUS	10	Sep
10.09	2.3	Campbell		(10.06)	1	Gateshead	15	Jul
		10.10 2.1			5	Brussels, BEL	25	Aug
10.25	2.2	Lewis-Francis	U20	(10.10)	1h1	Santiago, CHI	17	Oct
		10.28 2.4			1	Bedford	19	Aug
10.27 A	7.0	Doug Bignall		(10.30A)	2r2	Flagstaff, USA	4	Jul
10.34	3.9	Barbour	U23	(10.28)	1	Liverpool	22	Jul
		10.36 2.8			1r2	Bedford	11	Jun
		10.36 2.4			2	Bedford	19	Aug
10.36	3.9	Brendon Ghent		(10.56)	1h4	Bedford	28	May
		11 performances to 10.40 by 7 athletes						
10.45	2.4	Jason Fergus		(10.58)	3	Bedford	19	Aug
10.46	2.4	Marlon Dickson	U23	(10.60)	4	Bedford	19	Aug
10.48	2.7	Jamie Henthorn		(10.52)	1r4	Bedford	11	Jun
10.49	3.9	Kevin Ellis		(10.78)	2h4	Bedford	28	May
10.51	6.3	Daniel Money		(10.69)	3	Wigan	24	Jun
10.52	2.7	Mark Findlay ¶	U23	(10.59)	2r4	Bedford	11	Jun
10.53	6.3	Andy Hughes		(10.57)	4	Wigan	24	Jun
10.53	4.0	David Samuyiwa		(10.66)	5	La Laguna, SPA	15	Jul
10.57	2.2	Dwayne Grant	U20	(10.61)	1	London (CP)	13	May
10.58	2.4	Terence Stamp		(10.66)	6	Bedford	19	Aug
10.61	4.2	Graham Beasley		(10.76)	1h3	Bedford	28	May
10.61	2.7	John Regis		(10.64)	4r4	Bedford	11	Jun
10.63	4.3	Tim Barton		(10.84)	3h2	Bedford	28	May
10.65	4.3	Srdjan Dragutinovic		7.08.74	4h2	Bedford	28	May
10.67	3.7	Gavin Eastman	U23	(10.78)	3h3	Brighton	17	Jun
10.68	3.8	Ray Salami		11.04.75	3	Kortrijk, BEL	24	Jun
10.69	3.9	Mark Woodhouse		1.11.75	3h4	Bedford	28	May
10.69	2.7	Alex Golding	U20	(10.88)	2	Sheffield	8	Jul
10.71	4.2	Gary Jones		(10.79)	3h3	Bedford	28	May
10.71	2.3	Aidan Syers	U20	(10.89)	2	Watford	28	May
10.71	3.7	Michael Champion		(10.81)	4h3	Brighton	17	Jun
10.72	2.3	Jonathan Carleton	U23	(10.98)	7	Castleisland, IRE	11	Jun
10.72	4.7	Henry Richards	U20	(10.84)	3r1	Bedford	11	Jun
10.72	2.7	Karl Forde	U20	(10.84)	3	Sheffield	8	Jul
10.72	2.8	Andrew Parker	U23	(10.78)	3h1	Loughborough	30	Jul
10.74	2.7	Richard Agyemang	U20	5.08.82	4	Sheffield	8	Jul
10.79		Geoff Walismbi		27.02.74	1	Watford	12	Jul
10.82	2.4	Richard Pinnock		(10.83)	7	Bedford	19	Aug
10.83	2.3	Mark McIntyre		(10.95)	5s2	Bedford	28	May
10.86	2.8	Graeme Welsh		8.10.75	8	London (He)	8	Jul
10.87	3.0	Ricky Alfred		(10.88)	2h5	Brighton	17	Jun
10.88	2.7	Aki Abiola	U20	18.06.83	6	Sheffield	8	Jul
10.88	3.5	Ugochi Anomelechi	U17	(10.93)	1	Birmingham	3	Sep

10.90	2.3	Mark Hanson	U20	(10.94)	3	Watford	28 May
10.90	2.8	Sunny Adepegba		6.06.71	4r2	Bedford	11 Jun
10.91	2.2	Daniel Cummins		(10.92)	3s1	Stoke-on-Trent	29 Apr
10.91	2.1	Paul Nwaolise		(10.98)	3h1	Bedford	28 May
10.91	2.7	Ross Grant	U20	28.10.82	7	Sheffield	8 Jul
10.95	2.7	Ejike Wodu		(10.96)	5r4	Bedford	11 Jun
10.95	2.8	Aaron Aplin	U17	25.11.83	1	Birmingham	2 Sep
10.96	3.5	Clive Turner	U17	24.11.84	2	Birmingham	3 Sep

Hand Timing

10.4	-1.2	Malcolm	U23	(10.29)	1	Cwmbran	18 Jun
10.4	2.0	Brendon Ghent		(10.56)	1	Rugby	23 Jul
10.4	1.6	Edgar	U20	(10.39)	1	Enfield	6 Aug
		3 performances to 10.4 by 3 athletes					
10.5	1.6	Kevin Williams		(10.53)	3	Enfield	6 Aug
10.6	2.0	Terence Stamp		(10.66)	3	Glasgow (S)	29 Jul
10.6	2.0	Jonathon Oparka	U23	(10.70)	4	Glasgow (S)	29 Jul
10.6	1.6	Ian Clarke		(10.79)	4	Enfield	6 Aug
10.6 w		Graham Beasley		(10.76)	1	London (PH)	6 May
10.6 w		Dan Donovan		(10.77)	1rB	London (He)	22 Jul
10.6 w	2.4	Dominic Bradley		(10.77)	1rB	Cudworth	22 Jul
10.6 w	3.8	Richard Pinnock		(10.00)	2	Cudworth	22 Jul
		10.7 1.6			6	Enfield	6 Aug
10.7		Monu Miah	U17	(10.79)	1	Watford	27 May
10.7		Gary Jones		(10.79)	1	Eton	11 Jun
10.7	1.0	Kevin Ellis		(10.78)	4	Peterborough	8 Jul
10.7		Gavin Eastman	U23	(10.78)	1	Hayes	19 Jul
10.7	2.0	Richard Rubenis		(10.75)	5	Rugby	23 Jul
10.7	2.0	Chris Baillie	U20	21.04.81	5	Glasgow (S)	29 Jul
10.7		Scott Exley	U23	9.02.78	1	Eton	22 Aug
10.7 w	3.8	Du'aine Thorne-Ladejo		(10.92)	4rB	Wigan	24 Jun
10.7 w		Derek Morgan		4.04.69	1	Gloucester	29 Jul
10.7 w		James Miller	U23	(10.99)	1	Mansfield	25 Aug
		10.8			1	Grantham	3 Jun
10.7 w		Ricky Alfred		(10.88)	2	Ware	3 Sep
10.8		Darren Scott		(10.97)	1	Bebington	19 Apr
10.8		Chris Smith	U23	26.04.79	2	Bebington	19 Apr
10.8		Rob Kerry	U23	20.03.80	1	Pennsylvania, USA	22 Apr
10.8		Michael Otubambo		6.07.73	1rB	Woodford	22 Apr
10.8		Graham Hedman	U23	6.02.79	1rB	Woodford	29 Apr
10.8		Cori Henry		(10.96)	1h	Nottingham	13 May
10.8		Alasdair McFarlane	U23	(10.83)	1	Grantham	3 Jun
10.8		Gavin Stephens		12.09.77	1	Eton	11 Jun
10.8		Ben Ellis	U20	16.11.81	1	Hayes	24 Jun
10.8		Stephen Payne	U23	30.01.78	1	Aldershot	24 Jun
10.8		Rob Harle	U23	(10.97)	1	Oxford	28 Jun
10.8		Ray Salami		(10.68w)	1	London (TB)	8 Jul
10.8		Luke Bowling	U20	4.11.81	1	Ware	16 Jul
10.8	2.0	Dominic Papura	U20	(10.99)	6	Rugby	23 Jul
10.8	2.0	Tony Leigh		(10.99)	7	Rugby	23 Jul
10.8	2.0	Graeme Welsh		(10.86w)	6	Glasgow (S)	29 Jul
10.8		Michael Smith	U23	(10.85)	1	Rotherham	5 Aug
10.8		Jonathan Carleton	U23	(10.98)	1	Belfast	23 Aug
10.8		Brian Darby		14.10.72	1	London (FP)	27 Aug
10.8		Alex Fugallo		28.01.70	2	London (B)	10 Sep
10.8 w	2.9	Dominic Girdler	U20	6.03.82	1	Peterborough	31 May
10.8 w		Lee Holehouse	U20	23.12.81	1	Telford	10 Jun

10.8 w	3.8	Craig Townsend	U23	1.12.80	3	Cudworth	22 Jul
10.8 w		Darren Jackson	U23	21.10.78	2rB	Ware	3 Sep

Rolling Start

10.38	2.0	Akinola Lashore		(10.50)	1	Stoke-on-Trent	29 Apr

Drugs Test

10.43	1.5	Mark Findlay ¶	U23	20.03.78	1	Loughborough	30 Jul
		10.37 1.9	after positive		5rB	London (CP)	5 Aug

Additional Under 20

10.9		Aki Abiola		(10.88w)	1	Eton	10 Jun
10.9		Bradley Gelman		18.01.82	1	Ware	16 Jul
10.9		Alan Stuart		14.08.81	2	Glasgow	16 Jul

Additional Under 17 (1 -7 above)

11.0	1.3	Daniel Buss	10.10.83	3	London (BP)	10 Jun
11.0	1.4	Matthew Ouche	6.03.85	2	London (WF)	17 Sep
11.03	1.0	Devlin Williams	8.12.83	3s2	Sheffield	30 Jul
	(10)					
11.04	1.2	Peter Vickers	11.06.84	3	Sheffield	8 Jul
11.07	1.1	Lloyd Rice	13.02.85	1s1	Sheffield	8 Jul
11.07 w	2.8	Stuart Halcy	9.12.84	2	Birmingham	2 Sep
11.08		Tom Hyde	7.10.83	1	Bedford	10 Jun
11.10	-1.7	Clive Turner	(10.96w)	3rB	Birmingham	10 Sep
11.1		Adam Charlton	11.05.84	1	Peterborough	8 Apr
11.1		John Sherratt	18.10.83	1	Stafford	31 May
11.1		Matt Hopton	2.03.84	1	Portsmouth	10 Jun
11.1	1.3	Reginald Uzor	19.02.85	4	London (BP)	10 Jun
11.1		Ryan Morrison	16.12.83	1	Liverpool	2 Jul
11.1		James Graham	10.09.84	1	Sutton Coldfield	2 Jul
	(20)					
11.1		A. Riley		1	Banbury	13 Aug
11.1		Jason Rogers	19.07.84	1	Ayr	22 Aug
11.1		Simon Gardiner	14.02.84	1	Dublin (S), IRE	24 Aug
11.1 w		Jack Wilkie	30.07.84	1	Bromley	4 May
11.1 w		Michael Burgess	11.05.84	1	Derby	11 Jun
11.11	1.7	Martin Roberts	20.09.83	1	Cudworth	19 Aug
11.15	0.3	Fabian Collymore	19.10.84	6	Sheffield	30 Jul

Under 15

11.24	-0.5	Jamie Gill	29.10.85	1	Sheffield	30 Jul
11.27	-0.5	Alex Coley	8.02.86	2	Sheffield	30 Jul
11.27		Richard Davenport	12.09.85	1	Tamworth	28 Aug
11.32	1.0	James Ellington	6.09.85	1h3	Sheffield	30 Jul
11.38	1.7	Sam Huggins	30.11.85	2	Sheffield	8 Jul
11.40	0.7	Matthew Kelsey	20.11.85	1h5	Sheffield	7 Jul
11.4		Simon Farenden	6.10.85	1	Nottingham	13 May
		11.47 -1.1		1	Wigan	25 Jun
11.4		Oliver van Well	16.12.85	1h1	Glasgow (S)	7 Jun
		11.55 1.3		1rB	Grangemouth	5 Aug
11.4		Bernard Yeboah	7.01.86	1	London (BP)	19 Aug
11.4 w		Victor Barzey	10.01.86	1	Bournemouth	21 May
	(10)					
11.4 w		Andrew Owens	5.11.85	2	Derby	17 Jun
11.4 w		Paul Judson	20.06.86	2	Sutton Coldfield	2 Jul
11.43 w	2.2	Derek McShannock	2.11.85	2	Grangemouth	5 Aug
		11.54 1.0		2h3	Sheffield	30 Jul
11.49	0.8	Mark Small	17.10.85	1s2	Sheffield	7 Jul
11.5		Ross O'Donovan	12.03.86	1	Reading	21 May
		11.52 1.7		4	Sheffield	8 Jul

11.5	1.6	Martin Blencowe		11.04.86	1	Watford	27 May
11.5		Tristan Trigell		7.12.85	2	Portsmouth	10 Jun
11.5		Dorian Wood		8.10.85	1	Carmarthen	6 Aug
11.5 w	2.3	Donovan James		30.11.85	1	London (BP)	10 Jun
11.51	1.7	Ben Hamblin		2.11.85	3	Sheffield	8 Jul
	(20)						
11.56	-0.2	David Aguirreburualde		29.11.85	1	Cudworth	19 Aug
11.57 w	3.1	Louis Moisey		9.08.86	1	Birmingham	2 Sep
11.58	1.0	Jonathan Regis		7.07.86	3h3	Sheffield	30 Jul
11.6		Richard Gadd		30.07.86	1	Peterborough	13 May
11.6		Gary Hosking		25.11.85	1	Exeter	13 May
11.6		James Feasy		11.12.86	3	Portsmouth	10 Jun
11.6		James Boreham		27.11.86	2	Carmarthen	6 Aug
11.6		Allistair Tatton		9.01.86	1	Glasgow (S)	20 Aug

Uncertain age

11.59	1.8	Nathan Martin	U17	10.05.84	2	Birmingham	3 Sep
		competed as U15 - date of birth correct ?					

Under 13

11.86	1.4	Chris Julien	14.09.87	1	Birmingham	3 Sep
12.3		Joelle Powell	2.03.88	1	Derby	4 Jun
12.3		Denzil Davidson	16.00.87	1	Barking	4 Jul
12.3		Steven Horsburgh	11.11.87	1	Gateshead	16 Jul
12.3		Thomas Rayner	26.01.88	1	Burnley	27 Aug
12.46	2.0	Paul Crawford	4.10.87	1	Birmingham	2 Sep
12.48	1.4	Ben Wilson	27.10.87	3	Birmingham	3 Sep
12.5		Andrew Norton	14.12.87	1	Macclesfield	14 May
12.55	1.4	Emlyn Akoto	15.09.87	4	Birmingham	3 Sep
12.57	-0.3	Sean James	8.01.88	1rB	Birmingham	3 Sep

Foreign

10.28 w	*3.1*	*Paul Brizzel (IRE)*	*3.10.76*	*3*	*Fana, NOR*	*27 Jun*
		10.35 0.8		*2*	*Haapsalu, EST*	*20 Jun*
10.28 w	*4.5*	*John McAdorey (IRE)*	*16.09.74*	*1*	*Newcastle, AUS*	*9 Sep*
		10.52 0.9		*2r4*	*Sydney, AUS*	*14 Sep*
10.6	*2.0*	*Sylvain Reboul (FRA)*	*4.10.76*	*3*	*Rugby*	*23 Jul*
10.78 w	*2.8*	*Sanusi Turay (SLE)*	*14.04.68*	*7*	*London (He)*	*8 Jul*
		10.81 1.3		*6*	*London (He)*	*6 Aug*
10.8		*Paul McBurney (IRE)*	*14.03.72*	*2*	*Belfast*	*23 Aug*
10.8 w		*Joselyn Thomas (SLE)*	*11.07.71*	*1*	*Blandford*	*18 Jul*

Drugs Test

10.65		*Josephus Thomas (SLE) ¶*	*11.07.71*	*1*	*Aldershot*	*5 Jul*
		10.5 1.0 after positive test		*1*	*Peterborough*	*8 Jul*

200 METRES

20.13	0.3	Darren Campbell		12.09.73	1q1	Sydney, AUS	27 Sep
		20.14 -0.6			2	Sydney, AUS	28 Sep
		20.23 0.3			2s2	Sydney, AUS	28 Sep
		20.49 -1.2			1	Birmingham	13 Aug
		20.71 0.9			7	Rome, ITA	30 Jun
		20.71 -0.8			2s1	Birmingham	13 Aug
		20.71 0.2			2h4	Sydney, AUS	27 Sep
		20.82 1.8			1h1	Birmingham	12 Aug
		20.83 -1.4			1	Amsterdam, HOL	13 May
		20.85 -0.8			1	Loughborough	21 May
20.19	-0.2	Christian Malcolm	U23	3.06.79	2q3	Sydney, AUS	27 Sep
		20.19 -1.1			2s1	Sydney, AUS	28 Sep
		20.23 -0.6			5	Sydney, AUS	28 Sep

(Malcolm)		20.45 0.0			1	Gateshead	16	Jul
		20.45 0.3			1	Gateshead	28	Aug
		20.51 -0.5			3	London (CP)	5	Aug
		20.52 0.4			2h8	Sydney, AUS	27	Sep
		20.54 i			1	Ghent, BEL	26	Feb
		20.59 -1.2			2	Birmingham	13	Aug
		20.65 -3.8			1	Glasgow (S)	2	Jul
		20.65 -0.2			6	Brussels, BEL	25	Aug
		20.68 i			1	Birmingham	20	Feb
		20.68 -1.9			1s2	Birmingham	13	Aug
		20.71 0.7			3	Lucerne, SWZ	27	Jun
		20.73 i			2r3	Lievin, FRA	13	Feb
		20.74 i			1	Birmingham	30	Jan
		20.76 0.3			1	Dortmund, GER	8	Jul
		20.77 i			1s1	Ghent, BEL	25	Feb
		20.85 i			1h6	Ghent, BEL	25	Feb
		20.96 i			1s3	Birmingham	30	Jan
20.59	0.9	Marlon Devonish		1.06.76	5	Rome, ITA	30	Jun
		20.66 -0.5			1r4	Budapest, HUN	22	Jul
		20.69 -0.8			1s1	Birmingham	13	Aug
		20.72			1	Rhede, GER	23	Jun
		20.75 -3.8			3	Glasgow (S)	?	Jul
		20.78 2.0			1	Bedford	4	Jun
		20.78 -1.2			3	Birmingham	13	Aug
		20.79 0.3			3	Rieti, ITA	3	Sep
		20.82 i			1s2	Birmingham	30	Jan
		20.82 0.4			7q4	Sydney, AUS	27	Sep
		20.83 i			2	Birmingham	30	Jan
		20.88 i			3	Birmingham	20	Feb
		20.89 0.3			3h5	Sydney, AUS	27	Sep
		20.92 -0.5			7	London (CP)	5	Aug
		20.92 0.3			5	Gateshead	28	Aug
		20.93 -0.3			1h3	Birmingham	12	Aug
		20.95 i			1s1	Birmingham	16	Jan
20.64	-1.2	Julian Golding		17.02.75	2	Villeneuve d'Ascq, FRA	17	Jun
		20.70 i			2	Birmingham	20	Feb
		20.84 -0.5			2r4	Budapest, HUN	22	Jul
		20.84 0.0			4	Barcelona, SPA	25	Jul
		20.87 i			3	Birmingham	30	Jan
		20.87 i			2s2	Ghent, BEL	25	Feb
		20.88 -0.5			6	London (CP)	5	Aug
		20.89 i			1s1	Birmingham	30	Jan
		20.89 -3.8			5	Glasgow (S)	2	Jul
		20.91 i			3r2	Lievin, FRA	13	Feb
		20.96 i			2h3	Ghent, BEL	25	Feb
		20.97 -1.2			2r1	Riga, LAT	22	Jun
20.65	1.7	Marcus Adam		28.02.68	1r1	Ljubljana, SLO	25	Jul
		20.77 1.1			1r3	Budapest, HUN	22	Jul
		20.89 1.8			2h1	Birmingham	12	Aug
20.76	0.0	Tim Benjamin	U20	2.05.82	2	Berne, SWZ	5	Aug
		20.76 -0.5			3s2	Santiago, CHI	21	Oct
		20.77 0.1			2q3	Santiago, CHI	20	Oct
		20.89 1.1			1	Bath	16	Sep
		20.91 -1.5			2h4	Birmingham	12	Aug
		20.92 0.0			1r1	Budapest, HUN	22	Jul
		20.92 -0.8			3s1	Birmingham	13	Aug
		20.94 1.3			3	Santiago, CHI	21	Oct
		20.96 -1.2			5	Birmingham	13	Aug
20.78	-1.5	Dwain Chambers	U23	5.04.78	1h4	Birmingham	12	Aug
		20.87 -1.9			2s2	Birmingham	13	Aug

20.79	-0.8	Jon Barbour	U23	3.11.80	1	Getafe, SPA	9 Sep
20.80	1.7	Allyn Condon		24.08.74	3r1	Ljubljana, SLO	25 Jul
		20.98 -0.8			4s1	Birmingham	13 Aug
20.83	-0.8	John Stewart	U23	30.12.79	2	Getafe, SPA	9 Sep
		20.91 1.8			1	Liverpool	22 Jul
	(10)						
20.88	1.2	Dwayne Grant	U20	17.07.82	4s1	Santiago, CHI	21 Oct
20.90	-0.8	Ian Mackie		27.02.75	2	Loughborough	21 May
		20.92 -1.2			4	Birmingham	13 Aug
		20.94 -1.5			3h4	Birmingham	12 Aug
21.00 i		John Regis		13.10.66	2s1	Birmingham	16 Jan
		21.30 1.5			1h1	Brighton	18 Jun
		83 performances to 21.00 by 13 athletes including 18 indoors					
21.01	-0.5	Doug Turner		2.12.66	6r4	Budapest, HUN	22 Jul
21.04 i		Jason Fergus		11.10.73	3s3	Birmingham	30 Jan
		21.25 1.1			2	London (He)	6 Aug
21.08	0.4	Uvie Ugono	U23	8.03.78	3	Bedford	1 Jul
21.21	1.1	Jamie Henthorn		20.02.77	1	London (He)	6 Aug
21.24	-1.9	Brendon Ghent		7.09.76	5s2	Birmingham	13 Aug
21.26 i		Richard Knowles		12.11.75	3	Birmingham	16 Jan
		21.53 1.9			1r2	Bedford	11 Jun
21.26	-0.8	Daniel Caines	U23	15.05.79	2	Stoke-on-Trent	1 May
	(20)						
21.29	1.6	Nigel Stickings		1.04.71	2s2	Brighton	18 Jun
21.32	1.6	Michael Champion		3.01.75	3s2	Brighton	18 Jun
21.32	-0.1	Daniel Money		17.10.76	1	Solihull	29 Jul
21.33	1.1	Jamie Baulch		3.05.73	4r2	Budapest, HUN	22 Jul
21.40	1.6	Dominique Richards	U23	12.09.79	4s2	Brighton	18 Jun
21.40	0.8	Tim Abeyie	U20	7.11.82	1	Watford	2 Jul
21.41	1.1	Ed White		16.11.73	3	London (He)	6 Aug
21.42	1.1	Ben Lewis	U20	6.03.81	4	London (He)	6 Aug
21.44	2.0	Adrian Patrick		15.06.73	4	Bedford	4 Jun
21.45	1.6	John Skeete	U23	8.09.78	5s2	Brighton	18 Jun
	(30)						
21.45	0.5	Monu Miah	U17	10.01.84	1	Sheffield	29 Jul
21.48 i		Brian Doyle		12.03.77	3s2	Birmingham	30 Jan
		21.64 -1.0			2	Grangemouth	14 May
21.48	-0.3	Doug Bignall		20.10.74	5h3	Birmingham	12 Aug
21.51	0.0	Chris Lambert	U20	6.04.81	3r2	Mannheim, GER	12 Aug
21.52	-0.8	Akinola Lashore		28.03.73	3	Stoke-on-Trent	1 May
21.52	0.9	Jared Deacon		15.10.75	1r3	Irvine, USA	7 May
21.52	1.8	Mark %Findlay	U23	20.03.78	6	Liverpool	22 Jul
21.53	1.9	Chris Rawlinson		19.05.72	2r2	Fullerton, USA	27 Apr
21.53	-0.8	Michael Afilaka		16.11.71	4	Stoke-on-Trent	1 May
21.54	-0.1	Alan Stuart	U20	14.08.81	1	Grangemouth	14 May
	(40)						
21.57 i		Graham Beasley		24.10.77	3s2	Birmingham	16 Jan
21.57	0.8	Kevin Williams		15.12.71	4r2	Dublin, IRE	29 Jul
21.63	-0.1	Curtis Browne		11.09.75	2r2	Riga, LAT	22 Jun
21.63	1.5	Vincent Davis	U20	1.11.81	2h1	Sheffield	7 Jul
21.65	2.0	Laurence Oboh	U17	14.05.84	2	Sheffield	8 Jul
21.66 i		Darren Scott		7.03.69	3	Birmingham	9 Jan
		21.86			1	Stretford	2 May
21.66	0.4	Steve Webb	U23	17.07.78	6	Bedford	1 Jul
21.66	1.4	Jonathan Carleton	U23	4.11.79	6	Dublin (S), IRE	19 Aug
21.67 i		Mark Hylton		24.09.76	4	Birmingham	9 Jan
21.67 i+		Du'aine Thorne-Ladejo		14.02.71	1h4	Birmingham	29 Jan
	(50)						
21.68	1.5	Luke Bowling	U20	4.11.81	3h1	Sheffield	7 Jul
21.68	-1.3	Tony Waddington		30.06.75	2	Bedford	20 Aug
21.69 i		Tony Jarrett		13.08.68	3s3	Birmingham	16 Jan

Mark	Wind	Name	Age	DOB	Pos	Venue	Day	Month
21.69	-1.1	Iwan Thomas		5.01.74	2rB	London (He)	8	Jul
21.71	-0.2	David Samuyiwa		4.08.72	2	Valladolid, SPA	22	Jul
21.73 i		Marlon Dickson	U23	17.11.78	3h6	Birmingham	30	Jan
21.75	-0.4	Darren Burley	U23	13.01.80	1h4	Bedford	1	Jul
21.76	0.5	Aaron Aplin	U17	25.11.83	2	Sheffield	29	Jul
21.79	1.3	Dominic Papura	U20	12.02.81	2	Vilvoorde, BEL	6	Aug
21.81 i		Tyrone Edgar	U20	29.03.82	2rB	Neubrandenburg, GER	4	Mar
	(60)							
21.84 i		Matt Elias	U23	25.04.79	1	Cardiff	23	Jan
		21.96 -0.8			6	Stoke-on-Trent	1	May
21.84	-0.8	Paul Campbell	U23	26.03.80	5	Stoke-on-Trent	1	May
21.85	0.8	Ben Ellis	U20	16.11.81	3	Watford	2	Jul
21.85		Andy Hughes		10.07.67	1	Aldershot	5	Jul
21.87	1.5	Nigel Lowther	U20	4.05.83	4h1	Sheffield	7	Jul
21.88	-3.4	Cori Henry		9.12.76	3	Stoke-on-Trent	18	Jun
21.88		Richard Rubenis		10.11.73	2	Colwyn Bay	3	Sep
21.89		Adam Martin	U20	12.10.81	2	Watford	6	Sep
21.92	0.2	Ian Horsburgh	U23	10.01.78	2rB	Enfield	6	Aug
21.93	0.4	Dominic Bradley		22.12.76	1	Stretford	27	Jun
	(70)							
21.94 i		Ruben Tabares	U23	22.10.78	1rB	Birmingham	9	Jan
		21.94 0.2			3rB	Enfield	6	Aug
21.94		Matthew Bridle		11.08.76	2	Stretford	2	May
21.94	1.6	Michael Parper	U23	20.05.78	1r1	Bedford	11	Jun
21.94	1.4	Ian Deeth	U23	25.06.79	h	Glasgow	29	Jul
21.95	1.1	Peter Brend		2.02.77	6	Bath	16	Sep
21.98	-0.4	Andrew Parker	U23	1.08.80	2h4	Bedford	1	Jul
21.98	0.5	Fola Onibije	U17	25.09.84	3	Sheffield	29	Jul
21.99		Gary Jones		6.01.72	1	Watford	12	Jul
22.00	-0.8	Gavin Stephens		12.09.77	8	Stoke-on-Trent	1	May
22.01	1.9	Liam Collins	U23	23.10.78	3r2	Bedford	11	Jun
	(80)							
22.01	1.5	Joshua Wood		19.04.74	h	Brighton	18	Jun
22.04 i		David Naismith	U23	15.12.79	2	Cardiff	12	Mar
22.04		Ayo Falola		29.07.68	1r5	Eagle Rock, USA	13	May
22.04	1.6	Jonathon Oparka	U23	27.01.80	7r3	Bedford	11	Jun
22.06	2.0	Tom Hyde	U17	7.10.83	4	Sheffield	9	May
22.06	-0.3	Mark Lloyd		28.09.71	7h3	Birmingham	12	Aug
22.07		Rob Harle	U23	1.06.79	2	Watford	7	Jun
22.07		Essop Merrick		24.05.74	1	Watford	14	Jun
22.07	2.0	Mike Groves	U17	21.03.84	3h1	Edinburgh	13	Aug
22.08	0.2	Darren Chin	U20	30.06.81	4rB	Berne, SWZ	5	Aug
	(90)							
22.09	0.3	Gavin Eastman	U23	28.06.80	2	Derby	3	Sep
22.10	1.5	Alastair Gordon	U23	16.04.78	3h4	Brighton	18	Jun
22.10	0.7	Ray Salami		11.04.75	2	Kortrijk, BEL	24	Jun
22.10		Chris Bennett	U23	18.10.80	1	Aldershot	28	Jun
22.10	-0.9	Ricky Alfred		20.12.77	7h2	Birmingham	12	Aug
22.13	1.5	Ian Clarke		6.11.72	4h4	Brighton	18	Jun
22.15		Trevor Painter		10.08.71	1	Stretford	25	Jul
22.16	1.6	Sunny Adepegba		6.06.71	8r3	Bedford	11	Jun
22.16	-2.0	Gary Carr	U20	24.09.82	5	Edinburgh	13	Aug
22.17 i		Wayne Martin		12.08.76	1r1	Cardiff	5	Feb
	(100)							
22.18 i		Michael Tietz		14.09.77	2rB	Birmingham	9	Jan
22.20		Lawrence Baird		14.12.77	1	Bolton	6	May
22.20		Sam Ellis	U20	23.06.82	1	Cudworth	13	May
22.20	0.8	James Marshall	U20	6.02.81	4	Watford	2	Jul

Doubtful

Mark	Wind	Name	Age	DOB	Pos	Venue	Day	Month
21.60		Jonathan Carleton	U23	(21.66)		Dublin (S), IRE	16	Jul
22.07		Steve Buttler		20.02.75	1	Nuneaton	20	May

Wind Assisted

20.68	2.9	Ian Mackie		(20.90)	1	Bedford	29 May
		20.79 3.7			1s1	Bedford	29 May
20.88	2.2	Doug Turner		(21.01)	1	Enfield	6 Aug
20.89	2.5	Uvie Ugono	U23	(21.08)	1	Brighton	18 Jun
20.95	2.7	Benjamin	U20	(20.76)	1	Bedford	27 Aug
		5 performances to 21.00 by 4 athletes					
21.01	4.0	Graham Beasley		(21.57i)	1s2	Bedford	29 May
21.03	2.4	Nigel Stickings		(21.29)	1	Glasgow (S)	29 Jul
21.07	2.5	John Regis		(21.00i)	2	Brighton	18 Jun
21.07	3.8	Jason Fergus		(21.04i)	1	Bedford	19 Aug
21.12	4.0	Michael Champion		(21.32)	2s2	Bedford	29 May
21.15	4.0	Brian Doyle		(21.48i)	3s2	Bedford	29 May
21.16	6.6	Richard Knowles		(21.26i)	2rB	Wigan	24 Jun
21.19	3.7	Adrian Patrick		(21.44)	3s1	Bedford	29 May
21.19	4.0	Jared Deacon		(21.52)	4s2	Bedford	29 May
21.20	2.4	Ed White		(21.41)	1rB	Loughborough	21 May
21.21	2.3	Brendon Ghent		(21.24)	3r3	Bedford	11 Jun
21.26	4.0	Mark Woodhouse		1.11.75	5s2	Bedford	29 May
21.30	2.7	Ben Lewis	U20	(21.42)	2	Bedford	27 Aug
21.31	3.7	Steve Webb	U23	(21.66)	4s1	Bedford	29 May
21.31	3.0	Monu Miah	U17	(21.45)	1	Blackpool	15 Jul
21.36	3.8	Marlon Dickson	U23	(21.73i)	3s1	Brighton	18 Jun
21.37	2.4	John Skeete	U23	(21.45)	3	Glasgow (S)	29 Jul
21.39	3.0	Laurence Oboh	U17	(21.65)	2	Blackpool	15 Jul
21.40	2.9	Curtis Browne		(21.63)	3	London (He)	8 Jul
21.43	2.1	David Samuyiwa		(21.71)	2	Girona, SPA	21 Aug
21.53	2.4	Darren Scott		(21.66i)	4	Glasgow (S)	29 Jul
21.57	4.0	Gavin Stephens		(22.00)	6s2	Bedford	29 May
21.58	2.3	Tyrone Edgar	U20	(21.81i)	2h2	Bedford	27 Aug
21.60	5.0	Alex Fugallo		28.01.70	4	Wigan	24 Jun
21.61	2.7	Henry Richards	U20	15.05.81	5	Bedford	27 Aug
21.63	4.0	Ian Deeth	U23	(21.94)	7s2	Bedford	29 May
21.63	3.8	Ricky Alfred		(22.10)	4s1	Brighton	18 Jun
21.64	3.7	Lawrence Baird		(22.20)	5s1	Bedford	29 May
21.69	2.6	Cori Henry		(21.88)	1	Bedford	5 Aug
21.74	6.6	Luke Davis	U23	1.01.80	3rB	Wigan	24 Jun
21.75	6.6	Andrew Walcott		11.01.75	4rB	Wigan	24 Jun
21.76	4.1	David Naismith	U23	(22.04i)	4h4	Bedford	29 May
21.84	2.4	Cypren Edmunds		20.06.70	6	Glasgow (S)	29 Jul
21.87	4.1	Kevin Ellis		18.06.76	5h4	Bedford	29 May
21.91	3.4	Mark Brown		3.11.76	3h3	Bedford	29 May
21.94	5.0	Sean Baldock		3.12.76	6	Wigan	24 Jun
22.01	3.2	Philip Ellershaw		9.02.76	5h1	Bedford	29 May
22.04	2.2	Ian Clarke		(22.13)	5	Enfield	6 Aug
22.06	2.4	Sandy Scott		1.09.76	7	Glasgow (S)	29 Jul
22.08	2.9	Adam Rogers	U20	10.04.83	7	Sheffield	8 Jul
22.09	3.8	Alastair Gordon	U23	(22.10)	8s1	Brighton	18 Jun
22.10	2.1	Barry Middleton		10.03.75	5rB	London (He)	6 Aug
22.12	2.1	Andre Fernandez	U23	2.03.80	6rB	London (He)	6 Aug
22.12	2.2	Anthony Noel		8.09.63	1	Watford	8 Aug
22.14	3.4	Ben Watkins	U23	12.11.78	4h3	Bedford	29 May

Hand Timing

21.0	-1.3	Brendon Ghent	(21.24)	1	Crawley	24 Jun
21.3	2.0	Michael Champion	(21.32)	1	Enfield	24 Jun

21.3	-1.0	John Skeete	U23	(21.45)	2	Peterborough	8 Jul
21.3 w	2.1	Tim Abeyie	U20	(21.40)	2	Rugby	23 Jul
21.5		Cori Henry		(21.88)	1	Nottingham	13 May
21.5	-0.3	Ricky Alfred		(22.10)	2	Derby	9 Jul
21.5		Brian Darby		14.10.72	1	Loughborough	7 Sep
21.5		Alex Fugallo		(21.60w)	1	London (B)	10 Sep
21.6		Geoff Dearman		4.08.77	1	Watford	26 Apr
21.6		Graham Beasley		(21.57i)	1	Luton	13 May
21.6		Andrew Parker	U23	(21.98)	1	Newport	11 Jun
21.6	2.0	Steve Webb	U23	(21.66)	2	Enfield	24 Jun
21.6		Gary Jones		(21.99)	6	Enfield	20 Aug
21.7		Adam Buckley	U23	6.12.80	1	Riyadh, KSA	13 Apr
21.7		David Naismith	U23	(22.04i)	1	Nottingham	13 May
21.7	2.0	Solomon Wariso		11.11.66	3	Enfield	24 Jun
21.7	2.0	Darren Scott		(21.66i)	4	Enfield	24 Jun
21.7		Gavin Eastman	U23	(22.09)	2	Enfield	20 Aug
21.7		Darren Jackson	U23	21.10.78	1	Ware	3 Sep
21.7 w		Lee Holehouse	U20	23.12.81	1	Telford	10 Jun
21.7 w		David Brackstone	U20	13.03.82	1	Derby	17 Jun
		22.0			1	Macclesfield	10 Jun
21.7 w	2.7	Darren Burley	U23	(21.75)	2rB	Enfield	24 Jun
21.7 w	3.1	Mark Lloyd		(22.06)	3	Cudworth	22 Jul
		21.9			1	Warrington	3 Apr
21.8		Lawrence Baird		(22.20)	1	Grimsby	14 May
21.8	1.4	Mark Woodhouse		(21.26w)	3	Watford	20 May
21.8		Rob Harle	U23	(22.07)	1	Loughborough	14 Jun
21.8		Ray Salami		(22.10)	1	London (FP)	9 Jul
21.8	-0.3	Philip Ellershaw		(22.01w)	3	Derby	9 Jul
21.8		Michael Otubambo		6.07.73	3	Enfield	20 Aug
21.9	-0.7	Philip Sadler		22.04.77	1	Chelmsford	13 May
21.9	-0.7	Nick Thomas	U23	4.04.79	2	Chelmsford	13 May
21.9		Henry Richards	U20	(21.61w)	1	Loughborough	13 May
21.9		Alasdair McFarlane	U23	13.02.78	1	Grantham	16 Jul
21.9		Kevin Ellis		(21.87w)	2	Ware	3 Sep
21.9		Wayne Martin		(22.17i)	2	London (B)	10 Sep
21.9 w		Karl Forde	U20	15.04.83	3	Derby	17 Jun
		22.0			1	Banbury	10 Sep
22.0		James Chatt	U23	11.02.80	1	Loughborough	8 Apr
22.0		Matt Douglas		26.11.76	2	Watford	26 Apr
22.0		Andrew Mitchell		30.07.76	1	Coatbridge	30 Apr
22.0		Dalton Powell		20.08.63	2	Nottingham	13 May
22.0	1.4	Mike Rey		19.07.68	4	Watford	20 May
22.0		Sam Ellis	U20	(22.20)	1	Grantham	3 Jun
22.0		James Marshall	U20	(22.20)	1	Newport	11 Jun
22.0		Jon Hassain	U23	16.06.80	2	Loughborough	14 Jun
22.0		Jonathon Oparka	U23	(22.04)	1	Coatbridge	18 Jun
22.0		Colin Philip	U23	8.06.79	3	Giussano, ITA	18 Jun
22.0		Lee Bryan	U20	24.11.81	1	Coventry	16 Jul
22.0		Joshua Wood		(22.01)	1	Welwyn	22 Jul
22.0		Chris Smith	U23	26.04.79	1	Bebington	5 Aug
22.0		Adam Potter	U23	12.04.80	1	Yate	20 Aug
22.0 w		Simon Ciaravella		24.11.73	2	London (PH)	6 May
22.0 w		Daniel Brandwood	U20	1.10.82	1	Derby	18 Jun
22.0 w	2.1	Ben Watkins	U23	(22.14w)	6	Rugby	23 Jul

Additional Under 17 (1 - 6 above)

Perf	Wind	Name		Born	Pos	Venue	Date
22.1		Robert Tobin		20.12.83	1	Basingstoke	22 Jul
22.2	1.2	Martin Davolls		2.09.83	1	London (WF)	17 Sep
22.2	0.7	Rikki Fifton		17.06.85	1rB	London (WF)	17 Sep
22.21	2.0	James Bridge		28.11.83	2s1	Sheffield	29 Jul
	(10)						
22.23 w	3.0	Jason Rogers		19.07.84	4	Blackpool	15 Jul
		22.58 1.1			1	Grangemouth	5 Aug
22.26 w	4.1	Simon Farenden	U15	6.10.85	1	Sheffield	8 Jul
		22.6			1	Leeds	23 Jul
		22.65 -0.7			1	Wigan	25 Jun
22.29 w	2.2	Martin Roberts		20.09.83	2h2	Sheffield	29 Jul
		22.40 2.0			3s1	Sheffield	29 Jul
22.40	1.0	Ugochi Anomelechi		29.10.83	1	Birmingham	3 Sep
22.43 w	4.1	Martin Blencowe	U15	11.04.86	2	Sheffield	8 Jul
		22.64 1.7			1s2	Sheffield	8 Jul
22.46	2.0	Adam Charlton		11.05.84	4s1	Sheffield	29 Jul
22.46 w	2.5	James Ellington	U15	6.09.85	1	Sheffield	29 Jul
		22.80 1.7			2s2	Sheffield	8 Jul
22.5		Gavin Dublin		5.10.83	1	Bromley	30 Apr
22.5		Clive Turner		24.11.84	1	Enfield	20 Aug
		22.55 -0.6			2rB	Birmingham	10 Sep
22.51	1.7	Kamil Tojan Cole		21.01.85	3h3	Sheffield	7 Jul
	(20)						
22.55 w	2.3	Stuart Haley		9.12.84	2	Birmingham	2 Sep
22.58	1.3	Daniel Cossins		22.12.84	2h4	Sheffield	29 Jul
22.59 w	2.5	Alex Coley	U15	8.02.86	2	Birmingham	29 Jul
		22.9 1.8			1h1	Sheffield	29 Jul
		23.10 -1.4			2h4	Sheffield	7 Jul
22.6		Daniel Bray		6.09.83	1	Bournemouth	16 Jul
22.6		A. McIntyre			1	Leeds	23 Jul
22.6		Steven Cavanagh		9.07.85	1	Antrim	25 Jul
22.6		Leon Baptiste		23.05.85	2	Enfield	20 Aug

Unconfirmed

Perf	Wind	Name		Born	Pos	Venue	Date
22.3 w?		Christopher Kayes		14.04.84			

Additional Under 15 (1 - 4 above)

Perf	Wind	Name	Born	Pos	Venue	Date
22.6 w		Victor Barzey	10.01.86	1	Erith	6 Aug
		22.91 w 4.1		5	Sheffield	8 Jul
		22.94 1.7		3s2	Sheffield	8 Jul
22.7		Richard Davenport	12.09.85	2	Gloucester	26 Aug
22.75 w	2.5	Jonathan Regis	7.07.86	3	Sheffield	29 Jul
		23.34 1.1		1	London (He)	20 Aug
22.99	1.7	Marimba Odundo-Mendez	30.09.86	4s2	Sheffield	8 Jul
22.99 w	2.4	Kyle Pacey Vigo	10.04.86	1h3	Sheffield	7 Jul
22.99 w	2.5	Matthew Kelsey	20.11.85	5	Sheffield	29 Jul
		23.1		1	Cambridge	25 Jun
	(10)					
22.99 w	2.5	Derek McShannock	2.11.85	6	Sheffield	29 Jul
		23.21		1	Inverness	9 Jul
23.04	1.8	Jamie Gill	29.10.85	2	Birmingham	3 Sep
23.21 w	2.1	Richard Gadd	30.07.86	5s2	Sheffield	8 Jul
		23.37 -1.4		3h4	Sheffield	7 Jul
23.27	0.5	Gary Hosking	25.11.85	3h2	Sheffield	7 Jul
23.3		Ashley George	23.05.86	1		19 Apr
23.3		Sam Huggins	30.11.85	1		23 Jul
23.3 w		Andrew Owens	5.11.85	1	Derby	17 Jun
23.33		Oliver van Well	16.12.85	1	Grangemouth	21 Jun
23.38	1.9	Julian Thomas	28.12.86	1	Birmingham	2 Sep
23.46	1.7	James Milton	26.09.85	6s2	Sheffield	7 Jul

23.53	1.9	Louis Moisey		9.08.86	2	Birmingham	2 Sep
23.6		Donovan James		30.11.85	1rB	Barking	3 Jul
23.64	1.9	Craig Glanville		21.09.86	3	Birmingham	2 Sep
23.69	1.8	Bernard Yeboah		7.01.86	3	Birmingham	3 Sep

Uncertain age

22.98	1.8	Nathan Martin	U17	10.05.84	1	Birmingham	3 Sep
		competed as U15 - date of birth correct ?					

Under 13

24.28 w 2.5	Chris Julien	14.09.87	1	Birmingham	3 Sep
	25.0		1	Barking	2 Jul
24.86 w 2.5	Thomas Rayner	26.01.88	2	Birmingham	3 Sep
	25.9		1	Burnley	27 Aug
24.9	Joelle Powell	2.03.88	1	Derby	4 Jun
25.3	Anthony Burton	3.02.88	1	Bournemouth	13 May
25.50	Ben Ferriby	9.09.87	1	Watford	9 Jul
25.84 w 2.5	Jordan Roye	3.11.87	3	Birmingham	3 Sep
25.89 1.4	Richard Johnson	25.10.87	1	Birmingham	2 Sep

Foreign

20.54 A 2.0	*Paul Brizzel (IRE)*	*3.10.76*	*2rB*	*Pietersburg, RSA*	*18 Mar*
	20.65 0.5		*1r2*	*Ljubljana, SLO*	*25 Jul*
20.87 w 2.9	*Paul McKee (IRE)*	*15.10.77*	*2*	*Bedford*	*29 May*
	21.1 1.4		*1*	*Watford*	*20 May*
	21.20		*1*	*Haapsalu, EST*	*20 Jun*
21.21 1.3	*John McAdorey (IRE)*	*16.09.74*	*2*	*Tullamore, IRE*	*13 Aug*
21.5	*Paul McBurney (IRE)*	*14.03.72*	*1*	*Belfast*	*23 Aug*
	21.73 0.7		*2*	*Bedford*	*19 Aug*
21.6 1.4	*Sylvain Reboul (FRA)*	*4.10.76*	*2*	*Watford*	*20 May*
	22.08 i		*1r9*	*Birmingham*	*9 Jan*

After Positive Drugs Test

22.0 w	*Josephus Thomas ¶ (SLE)*	*11.07.71*	*1*	*Blandford*	*19 Jul*

300 METRES

33.49	Jared Deacon		15.10.75	1	Lewes	20 Jun
33.5 i+	Daniel Caines	U23	15.05.79	1	Birmingham	20 Feb
33.51	Ed White		16.11.73	1	Loughborough	30 Jul
33.56	Sean Baldock		3.12.76	2	Lewes	20 Jun
33.81	Mark Brown		3.11.76	2	Loughborough	30 Jul
33.84	Adrian Patrick		15.06.73	3	Lewes	20 Jun
34.05 i	Chris Rawlinson		19.05.72	1rB	Birmingham	17 Feb
34.2	Matthew Bridle		11.08.76	1	Stretford	23 Mar
34.29	Matt Douglas		26.11.76	4	Lewes	20 Jun
34.4	Brian Darby		14.10.72	1rB	Loughborough	30 Jul
(10)						
34.63 i	John Stewart	U23	30.12.79	1	Birmingham	17 Feb
34.64 i	Wayne Martin		12.08.76	2	Birmingham	17 Feb

400 METRES

44.72	Mark Richardson	26.07.72	2	Brussels, BEL	25 Aug
	45.11		3	London (CP)	5 Aug
	45.14		2	Rieti, ITA	3 Sep
	45.16		2	Gateshead	28 Aug
	45.20		1	Doha, QAT	5 Oct
	45.46		2	Berlin, GER	1 Sep
	45.55		1	Birmingham	13 Aug
	45.57		1s2	Birmingham	12 Aug

45.06	Jamie Baulch		3.05.73	1s1	Birmingham	12 Aug
	45.38			3	Nice, FRA	8 Jul
	45.69			3	Nuremberg, GER	25 Jun
	45.86			8	London (CP)	5 Aug
	46.07			3	Birmingham	13 Aug
	46.08			3	Glasgow (S)	2 Jul
	46.32			8	Brussels, BEL	25 Aug
	46.35			1	Cwmbran	18 Jun
45.20	Sean Baldock		3.12.76	2s1	Birmingham	12 Aug
	45.71			2	Birmingham	13 Aug
	45.91			1	Brighton	18 Jun
	46.09			2r3	Ljubljana, SLO	25 Jul
	46.19			1h3	Birmingham	11 Aug
	46.45			5h7	Sydney, AUS	22 Sep
45.37	Daniel Caines	U23	15.05.79	3q4	Sydney, AUS	23 Sep
	45.39			2h1	Sydney, AUS	22 Sep
	45.55			5s2	Sydney, AUS	24 Sep
	45.79			2s2	Birmingham	12 Aug
	45.91			1	Karlstad, SWE	23 Aug
	46.31			3r2	Ljubljana, SLO	25 Jul
	46.42			2h3	Birmingham	11 Aug
	46.45			4	Birmingham	13 Aug
	46.49			1	Liverpool	22 Jul
45.69	Jared Deacon		15.10.75	2	Dublin (S), IRE	29 Jul
	46.04			3s2	Birmingham	12 Aug
	46.10			1r2	Budapest, HUN	22 Jul
	46.15			6	Gateshead	28 Aug
	46.22			2	Riga, LAT	22 Jun
	46.48			2	Bedford	4 Jun
45.82	Iwan Thomas		5.01.74	4	Falkoping, SWE	15 Aug
	45.85			1	Budapest, HUN	16 Jun
	46.19			4	Glasgow (S)	2 Jul
	46.19			3	Leverkusen, GER	20 Aug
	46.24			3	Karlstad, SWE	23 Aug
45.83	Geoff Dearman		4.08.77	1rB	Dublin (S), IRE	29 Jul
	46.15			1	Bedford	11 Jun
	46.42			1	Floro, NOR	8 Jun
	46.43			1	London (He)	6 Aug
46.14	Richard Knowles		12.11.75	1	Riga, LAT	22 Jun
	46.25			3r4	Budapest, HUN	22 Jul
	46.49			1	Fana, NOR	27 Jun
	46.49			5r3	Ljubljana, SLO	25 Jul
46.14	Solomon Wariso		11.11.66	4s2	Birmingham	12 Aug
46.19	Adrian Patrick		15.06.73	2	Brighton	18 Jun
(10)						
46.24	Mark Hylton		24.09.76	7	Dublin (S), IRE	29 Jul
	46.42			2r3	Budapest, HUN	22 Jul
46.4	Du'aine Thorne-Ladejo		14.02.71	1	Birmingham	16 Aug
	46.61			1r2	Leverkusen, GER	20 Aug
46.41	Dean Macey		12.12.77	1D4	Sydney, AUS	27 Sep
46.47	David Naismith	U23	15.12.79	1	Getafe, SPA	9 Sep
	57 performances to 46.49 by 14 athletes					
46.54	Mark Brown		3.11.76	5s2	Birmingham	12 Aug
46.56	Ed White		16.11.73	2r1	Ljubljana, SLO	25 Jul
46.65 A	Matt Douglas		26.11.76	1	Font Romeu, FRA	9 Jul
46.81	Nick Budden		17.11.75	6s2	Birmingham	12 Aug
46.83	Marlon Devonish		1.06.76	1r1	Irvine, USA	7 May
46.83	Cori Henry		9.12.76	4s1	Birmingham	12 Aug
(20)						
46.91	Michael Parper	U23	20.05.78	3	Brighton	18 Jun

47.04	Adam Buckley	U23	6.12.80	2	Stoke-on-Trent	1 May
47.08	Peter Brend		2.02.77	6s1	Birmingham	12 Aug
47.15	Alex Fugallo		28.01.70	5	Brighton	18 Jun
47.22	Clayton Archer		29.05.76	2h4	Brighton	17 Jun
47.25	Matt Elias	U23	25.04.79	4	Getafe, SPA	9 Sep
47.36 i	Paul Slythe		5.09.74	4	Stockholm, SWE	17 Feb
	47.53			8s2	Birmingham	12 Aug
47.4	Brian Darby		14.10.72	1	Watford	17 Sep
	47.99			5h4	Birmingham	11 Aug
47.51	Chris Page	U23	13.11.80	2	Cwmbran	18 Jun
47.60	Jonathan Edwards	U23	6.11.78	3	Stoke-on-Trent	1 May
	(30)					
47.72	Robert Lewis	U23	2.09.78	5	Bedford	1 Jul
47.77	Neil Jennings		18.09.77	4	Stoke-on-Trent	1 May
47.84	Alasdair Donaldson		21.06.77	2	Glasgow	29 Jul
47.90	Russell Nicholls	U20	8.03.83	1	Birmingham	10 Sep
47.9	Ian McGurk		17.10.71	1	Montefiascone, ITA	16 Jul
	49.10			1rB	Enfield	6 Aug
47.93	Geoffrey Djan	U20	21.07.82	1	Grantham	18 Jun
47.94	Michael Afilaka		16.11.71	3	Glasgow	29 Jul
47.94	Sandy Scott		1.09.76	3h2	Birmingham	11 Aug
47.94	Martin Bradbury	U20	20.10.82	1	Bath	16 Sep
47.96	Philip Octave	U23	12.06.78	1h4	Bedford	1 Jul
	(40)					
47.98	Alastair Gordon	U23	16.04.78	5h3	Birmingham	11 Aug
48.0	Andrew Corey	U20	15.10.81	1	Derby	17 Jun
	48.65			4	Bedford	27 Aug
48.10 i	Wayne Martin		12.08.76	1	Cardiff	11 Mar
	48.21			2rB	Eton	6 May
48.1	Barry Middleton		10.03.75	1	Glasgow (S)	16 Jul
	48.53			7	Glasgow (S)	29 Jul
48.15	Lee Bryan	U20	24.11.81	1h1	Bedford	26 Aug
48.16	Alan Stuart	U20	14.08.81	4	Glasgow	29 Jul
48.16	Chris Smith	U23	26.04.79	2	Derby	3 Sep
48.17	Tony Borsumato		13.12.73	2rB	Wigan	24 Jun
48.18 i	John Stewart	U23	30.12.79	3	Birmingham	16 Jan
48.18	Darrell Maynard		21.08.61	3	Cwmbran	18 Jun
	(50)					
48.18	Ian Tinsley	U20	23.01.81	6h3	Birmingham	11 Aug
48.20	Sam Ellis	U20	23.06.82	1	Watford	2 Jul
48.22	Robert Tobin	U17	20.12.83	1	Sheffield	8 Jul
48.27	Graham Hedman	U23	6.02.79	2h1	Brighton	17 Jun
48.31	Stephen Payne	U23	30.01.78	3h5	Brighton	17 Jun
48.33	Lee Fairclough		23.06.70	3h3	Brighton	17 Jun
48.35 i	Lawrence Baird		14.12.77	2h7	Birmingham	29 Jan
	48.6			1	Darlington	9 Jul
	48.79			2	Stretford	25 Jul
48.35	Colin Philip	U23	8.06.79	2	Cernusco, ITA	14 Jun
48.4	Ruben Tabares	U23	22.10.78	1	Wigan	20 May
48.4	Tom Nimmo		9.05.71	1	Grangemouth	16 Jul
	(60)					
48.45	Ben Caldwell	U20	3.03.82	1	Stretford	25 Jul
48.47	Tony Williams		1.05.72	6	Fullerton, USA	27 Apr
48.47	Andrew Mitchell		30.07.76	5h5	Birmingham	11 Aug
48.5	Richard Workman		31.05.71	1	Stretford	2 May
48.5	Martyn Morant	U23	26.06.78	1	Bath	14 May
	48.65			6	Bath	16 Sep
48.5	Barry O'Brien		3.07.76	1	Lancaster	1 Jul
	49.01			3	Gateshead	13 May
48.52	Trevor Painter		10.08.71	6	Glasgow	29 Jul
48.53	Lee Holehouse	U20	23.12.81	2rB	Loughborough	21 May

48.53	Andrew Walcott		11.01.75	2rB	London (He)	8 Jul
48.6	Eddie Williams		1.10.70	1	Luton	11 Jun
(70)						
48.6	Nic Andrews	U20	3.10.81	1	Exeter	17 Jun
48.7	Simon Ciaravella		24.11.73	3	Peterborough	8 Jul
	49.05			3h1	Brighton	17 Jun
48.74	Bradley Yiend	U23	25.10.80	1	Stoke-on-Trent	17 Jun
48.75	Anders Lustgarten		9.02.74	2	Woerden, HOL	24 Jun
48.76 i	Darren Scott		7.03.69	1h1	Birmingham	29 Jan
48.80	Lee Wiscombe	U23	12.07.80	2	Gateshead	13 May
48.8	James Hillier	U23	3.04.78	1	Philadelphia, USA	22 Apr
48.8	Dean Clark		20.12.73	1	Guildford	3 Jun
48.8	Martin Davolls	U17	2.09.83	1	London (BP)	13 Aug
	48.99			2	Sheffield	9 Jul
48.8	Andre Fernandez	U23	2.03.80	1	London (Cr)	27 Aug
(80)						
48.8	Adam Rogers	U20	10.04.83	1	Carlisle	3 Sep
48.81	Nigel Carlisle		30.12.75	4	Dublin (S), IRE	19 Aug
48.86	Mark Sesay		13.12.72	3s3	Stoke-on-Trent	30 Apr
48.86	Jonathan Simpson	U20	27.05.82	1	Grangemouth	13 May
48.88	Paul May		31.10.77	3h2	Brighton	17 Jun
48.88	Joe Lloyd		9.04.73	4	Cwmbran	18 Jun
48.80	Russell Frost	U23	23.06.80	1	London (CP)	13 May
48.90	Nicholas Dawson	U23	11.05.78	3h1	Bedford	1 Jul
48.92	Tim Bayley	U20	4.10.81	7	Bedford	27 Aug
48.92	Greg McEwan	U20	9.04.81	2	Ljubljana, SLO	23 Sep
(90)						
49.0	Tom Lerwill		17.05.77	2	Riyadh, KSA	14 Apr
49.0	Lee Notman			1	Middlesbrough	6 May
49.0	Wayne Ellwood		26.09.74	1	Lancaster	13 May
49.0	David Brackstone	U20	13.03.82	1rB	Sheffield	24 Jun
	49.19 i			2	Neubrandenburg, GER	4 Mar
49.0	Steve Surety	U23	18.02.80	1	Luton	22 Jul
49.0	Jon Hassain	U23	16.06.80	1	Erith	5 Aug
49.0	Philip Sadler		22.04.77	1	Jarrow	6 Aug
49.0	Ryan Palmer	U20	21.06.83	1	Dumfries	13 Aug
49.0	Adam Potter	U23	12.04.80	1	Yate	3 Sep
49.03	Richard David		15.08.77	3rB	Eton	6 May
(100)						
49.04	John Regis		13.10.66	7r1	Irvine, USA	7 May
49.04	Matthew Still	U23	1.12.79	7h3	Birmingham	11 Aug
49.08	Simon Lees	U23	19.11.79	2	Stoke-on-Trent	18 Jun
49.09 i	Ian Lowthian	U23	10.10.80	4h2	Birmingham	29 Jan
	49.1			1	Watford	20 May
49.09	Mike Snow	U20	5.09.82	1	Watford	2 Aug
49.1	Chris Iddon	U20	8.10.82	2	Darlington	9 Jul
49.1	Scott McDiarmid	U23	15.11.80	3	Glasgow (S)	16 Jul

Additional Under 20 (1 - 21 above)

49.20	Richard Castillo		3.12.81	2	Solihull	27 May
49.2	Kofi Appiah		15.05.81	4	Peterborough	8 Jul
49.33 i	Simon Tunnicliffe		2.03.83		Neubrandenburg, GER	4 Mar
	49.4			1	Leamington	13 May
49.40	Daniel Pachter	U17	24.03.84	1h2	Sheffield	7 Jul
49.4	Emmanuel Farrugia		19.07.82	1	Erith	7 May

Additional Under 17 (1 - 3 above)

49.44	Gavin Dublin	5.10.83	8	Sheffield	8 Jul
49.48 i	Aaron Aplin	25.11.83	2	Birmingham	20 Feb
	49.94		1	Solihull	27 May

49.74	Richard Davenport	U15	12.09.85	3	Bedford	23	Aug
49.87	Rhys Williams		27.02.84	3h2	Edinburgh	13	Aug
49.97	Adam Davies		27.07.84	4h1	Edinburgh	13	Aug
50.01	Craig Erskine		26.09.83	1	Sheffield	29	Jul
50.04	Robert Smith		3.03.85	2h2	Sheffield	7	Jul
	(10)						
50.1	Chris Stoves		20.02.84	1	Lancaster	13	May
50.22	Mark Holloway		6.10.83	3h2	Sheffield	7	Jul
50.3	Liam Goodall		15.01.84	1	Corby	13	May
50.33	Daniel Bray		6.09.83	1O	Birmingham	16	Sep
50.4	Graham Blackman		25.03.85	1	Nottingham	13	May
50.5	Neil Burnside		7.08.84	1	Grangemouth	10	Sep
50.51	Neil Simpson		11.09.83	6	Sheffield	8	Jul
50.71	Stephen Gill		25.09.84	4h2	Sheffield	7	Jul
50.75	Daniel Petros		8.08.85	4h1	Sheffield	7	Jul
50.80	Liam McGowan		27.01.84	4	Solihull	27	May
	(20)						
50.92	Jonathon Hall		18.11.83	1	Grangemouth	25	Jun
51.0	Tom Carey		26.02.84	1	St. Ives	9	Jul
51.0	Mike Groves		21.03.84	1	Newport	23	Aug
51.05	Lee Whitehead		7.03.84	1	Wigan	25	Jun

Additional Under 15 (1 above)

51.09	David Vass	31.12.85	2	Sheffield	8	Jul
51.1	Chris Davies	7.09.85	1	Gloucester	1	Jul
51.46	Craig Glanville	21.09.86	3	Sheffield	8	Jul
52.05	Bob Thanda	22.09.85	4	Sheffield	8	Jul
52.1	Andrae Davis	27.09.85	1	Basildon	1	Jul
52.20	Richard Sheeran	27.11.85	5	Sheffield	8	Jul
52.36	Simon Toye	24.09.85	3h2	Sheffield	29	Jul
52.5	Ahmed Ali	31.03.86	1	Chelmsford	13	May
52.5	Adam Rodgers	19.01.86	1	London (BP)	10	Jun
	(10)					
52.6	Richard Parry	23.05.86	2	Derby	17	Jun
52.7	Simon Farenden	6.10.85	1	Leeds	23	Jul
52.9	Chris Baldwin	10.06.86	3	Derby	17	Jun
52.9	Aston Edwards	29.11.85	1	Basildon	23	Jul
	52.94		5s1	Sheffield	7	Jul
52.99	Thomas Franks	8.11.85	6	Sheffield	8	Jul
53.03	Paul Twidale	30.09.86	1	Wigan	25	Jun
53.1	Andrew Starnes	18.09.85	1	Ipswich	17	Jun
53.1	Lee Walters	1.06.86				
53.2	Ross Pratt	2.06.86	1h3	Sheffield	7	Jul
53.2	Ross Glover	2.11.85	3	Sheffield	29	Jul
	(20)					
53.4	Giles Freeman	19.11.85	4	Derby	17	Jun
53.4	Chris Gowell	26.09.85	1	Newport	23	Aug
53.41	Peter Warke	22.05.86	1	Antrim	10	Jun
53.6	James Milton	26.09.85	1	Barking	10	Sep
53.61	Chris Philpott	14.12.85	2	Birmingham	3	Sep

Under 13

61.4	Thomas Ashby	12.11.87	1	Dunfermline	15	Jun
61.5	Jake McCulloch	21.12.87	1	Newport	8	Jul
61.8	Robert Bates	29.10.87	1	Birmingham (Un)	25	Jul
61.9	Ian Horn	23.09.87	1	London (Cr)	28	Jun
62.2	Vito Tomasi	17.01.88	1	Guernsey	10	Aug
62.4	Sam Brasier	5.11.87	1	Milton Keynes	6	Aug
62.5	Sean McQueen	28.02.88	2	Dunfermline	15	Jun
62.8	Adam Hickey	30.05.88	1	Southend	7	May
62.8	Ross Finlayson	26.09.87	1	Grangemouth	1	Jul

Foreign

45.92	*Paul McKee (IRE)*		*15.10.77*	*1*	*Stoke-on-Trent*	*1 May*
47.61	*Paul McBurney (IRE)*		*14.03.72*	*4*	*Antrim*	*31 Jul*
47.8	*Brian Forbes (IRE)*		*6.09.74*	*1*	*Antrim*	*1 Jul*
	47.85			*2*	*Belfast*	*8 Jul*

800 METRES

1:45.81	Anthony Whiteman		13.11.71	1	London (CP)	5 Aug
	1:47.32			11	Gateshead	28 Aug
	1:47.61 A			7	Pretoria, RSA	24 Mar
	1:47.71 A			6	Potchefstroom, RSA	14 Feb
	1:47.81			1	Watford	22 Jul
1:45.96	James McIlroy		30.12.76	3	London (CP)	5 Aug
	1:46.39			6s1	Sydney, AUS	25 Sep
	1:46.58			7	Gateshead	28 Aug
	1:47.01			1	Bratislava, SVK	22 Jun
	1:47.18			5rB	Oslo, NOR	28 Jul
	1:47.24			2	Caorle, ITA	8 Jul
	1:47.40			2	Glasgow (S)	2 Jul
	1:47.44			3h1	Sydney, AUS	23 Sep
	1:48.54			8	Melbourne, AUS	2 Mar
	1:49.00			1s1	Birmingham	12 Aug
1:46.52	Andy Hart		13.09.69	4r2	Budapest, HUN	22 Jul
	1:46.54			7	London (CP)	5 Aug
	1:46.97			1r2	Cardiff	5 Jul
	1:47.08			9	Gateshead	28 Aug
	1:48.09			3	London (BP)	25 Jun
	1:48.21			4	Ljubljana, SLO	25 Jul
	1:48.78			6h1	Sydney, AUS	23 Sep
1:47.32	Alasdair Donaldson		21.06.77	8	London (CP)	5 Aug
	1:47.58			2rB	Budapest, HUN	22 Jul
	1:47.65			2	Solihull	19 Aug
	1:47.69			3r2	Cardiff	5 Jul
	1:47.84			5	Glasgow (S)	2 Jul
1:47.75	Chris Moss	U23	17.06.79	3	Solihull	19 Aug
	1:47.80			9	London (CP)	5 Aug
	1:48.68			1	Liverpool	22 Jul
1:47.81	Jason Lobo		18.09.69	3rB	Leverkusen, GER	20 Aug
1:47.89	Neil Caddy		18.03.75	5r2	Cardiff	5 Jul
1:48.28	Justin Swift-Smith		28.08.74	1	Manchester	14 Jun
	1:48.61			11	London (CP)	5 Aug
1:48.45	John Mayock		26.10.70	2	Manchester	14 Jun
1:48.55	Mark Sesay		13.12.72	2	Loughborough	21 May
	(10)					
1:48.56	Kevin McKay		9.02.69	3	Manchester	14 Jun
1:48.72	Brad Donkin		6.12.71	4	Manchester	14 Jun
1:48.74	Neil Speaight	U23	9.09.78	6	Solihull	19 Aug
	1:48.86			3	Liverpool	22 Jul
1:48.78	Tony Draper		23.04.74	1	Watford	7 Jun
1:48.95	Michael East	U23	20.01.78	1	Brighton	18 Jun
1:48.98	Grant Cuddy		6.01.77	3	Cardiff	5 Jul
	43 performances to 1:49.0 by 16 athletes					
1:49.05	Garth Watson		20.04.73	1	Stretford	25 Jul
1:49.07	James Mayo		24.02.75	1	Watford	12 Jul
1:49.1	Andrew Graffin		20.12.77	1	London (TB)	19 Jul
	1:49.15			1	Glasgow (S)	3 Sep
1:49.24	Dean Clark		20.12.73	7	London (BP)	25 Jun
(20)						
1:49.25	Matt Shone		10.07.75	6r2	Cardiff	5 Jul
1:49.26	Simon Lees	U23	19.11.79	2	Watford	7 Jun

1:49.33	Raymond Adams	U20	5.11.81	3	Glasgow (S)	3 Sep
1:49.45	Eddie Williams		1.10.70	2	Brighton	18 Jun
1:49.46	Stuart Bailey	U23	6.08.78	3	Stretford	25 Jul
1:49.53	Jon Stewart	U23	22.05.80	4	Stretford	25 Jul
1:49.55	Eddie King		26.11.75	7	Manchester	14 Jun
1:49.61	John Rogers		30.07.73	4	Glasgow (S)	3 Sep
1:49.67	Nic Andrews	U20	3.10.81	4	Cardiff	5 Jul
1:49.74	Matt Dixon	U23	26.12.78	7r2	Cardiff	5 Jul
	(30)					
1:49.76	Phillip Tulba		20.09.73	2	Watford	12 Jul
1:49.80	James Parker	U23	28.10.79	3	Brighton	18 Jun
1:49.82	Angus Maclean	U23	20.09.80	2	Watford	30 Aug
1:49.86	Dominic Hall		21.02.71	4	Brighton	18 Jun
1:49.86	Chris Mulvaney	U20	5.05.81	3	Watford	12 Jul
1:49.9	Tom Nimmo		9.05.71	2	Wigan	20 May
1:50.1	Allen Graffin		20.12.77	2	London (TB)	19 Jul
1:50.21	Steve Rees-Jones		24.12.74	6	Stretford	11 Jul
1:50.31	Michael Coltherd	U20	28.12.82	5	Stretford	25 Jul
1:50.36	Richard Ashe		5.10.74	3	Watford	30 Aug
	(40)					
1:50.39	Joe Mills		9.07.72	7	Riga, LAT	22 Jun
1:50.40	Jon McCallum		19.11.75	5	Watford	12 Jul
1:50.4	Chris Bolt	U23	21.09.80	1	Solihull	19 Jul
1:50.47	Noel Edwards		16.12.72	3rB	Manchester	14 Jun
1:50.50	Stewart Reid		15.11.73	1	Eton	6 May
1:50.51	Gary Vickers		26.02.71	5s1	Birmingham	12 Aug
1:50.52	James Thie	U23	27.06.78	4	Watford	30 Aug
1:50.63	Gregg Taylor		1.08.77	5	Watford	30 Aug
1:50.68	Tom Mayo		2.05.77	6	Watford	30 Aug
1:50.79	Michael Skinner	U23	21.11.79	7	Watford	12 Jul
	(50)					
1:50.8	Paul Walker		2.12.73	1	Sydney (B), AUS	24 Jun
1:50.86	Grant Graham		27.12.72	6rB	Manchester	14 Jun
1:50.87	Andi Knight		26.10.68	9	Watford	12 Jul
1:50.89	Andrew Brown		17.06.77	7	Glasgow (S)	3 Sep
1:50.91	Adam Zawadski		19.12.74	7	Watford	30 Aug
1:50.92	Peter Walsh	U23	5.05.80	1rC	Manchester	14 Jun
1:51.01	Neil Dougal	U23	7.03.80	4	Bedford	1 Jul
1:51.10	Pat Davoren		13.03.72	5	Watford	2 Aug
1:51.10	Andrew Ingle	U23	19.02.80	8	Watford	30 Aug
1:51.12	Steve Turvill		17.02.75	4	Watford	7 Jun
	(60)					
1:51.16	Andy Young		20.06.77	6	Loughborough	21 May
1:51.22	Ricky Soos	U20	28.06.83	1rB	Watford	30 Aug
1:51.26	Andrew Fulford	U20	23.06.82	2	Watford	2 Jul
1:51.3	Stuart Overthrow		13.06.75	1	Ghent, BEL	8 Jul
1:51.41	Rob Jefferies	U23	4.10.79	1rC	Solihull	19 Aug
1:51.48	Greg McEwan	U20	9.04.81	2rB	Glasgow (S)	3 Sep
1:51.51	Malcolm Hassan	U20	27.11.82	3rB	Watford	22 Jul
1:51.55	Steve Sharp		31.12.75	6	Watford	2 Aug
1:51.55	Terry Feasey		5.08.77	4rB	Solihull	19 Aug
1:51.60	Chris Bryan		12.01.77	6	Stretford	25 Jul
	(70)					
1:51.63	Chris Watson	U20	22.05.83	3rB	Glasgow (S)	3 Sep
1:51.64	Steve Tompson	U20	5.12.82	1	Watford	6 Sep
1:51.7	Lee Garrett	U23	2.09.78	2	Solihull	19 Jul
1:51.71	Kevin Corr	U23	17.04.79	3	Stretford	8 Aug
1:51.76	Robert Whittle	U20	14.06.81	6rB	Solihull	19 Aug
1:51.77	James Nasrat	U20	10.01.83	2	Sarajevo, BSH	4 Jun
1:51.88	Nathan Dosanjh	U23	13.02.79	8	Watford	7 Jun
1:51.89	Chris Livesey	U23	8.08.80	3	Providence, USA	15 Apr

1:51.92	Andy Baddeley	U20	20.06.82	1rD	Stretford	30 May
1:52.15	Nick McCormick	U20	11.09.81	7	Stretford	25 Jul
(80)						
1:52.21	Matt Thompson	U20	20.09.81	8rB	Watford	22 Jul
1:52.22	Vince Wilson		1.04.73	4rC	Manchester	14 Jun
1:52.23	Tony Thompson		9.11.77	2rB	London (He)	6 Aug
1:52.23	Andrew Sherman	U20	28.09.81	2rC	Solihull	19 Aug
1:52.24	Alan McDougall		9.11.75	4	Bedford	23 Aug
1:52.28	Andrew Walling		3.04.73	3	Cwmbran	18 Jun
1:52.3	Jon Goodwin		22.09.76	2	Brighton	16 Aug
1:52.32 i	Alasdair Mclean-Foreman	U20	10.11.81	3h2	Birmingham	29 Jan
1:52.34	Carl Tipton		4.02.77	7	Stretford	30 May
1:52.36	Ben Hyman		28.08.74	1rB	Stretford	25 Jul
(90)						
1:52.40	Martin Flook	U20	20.12.81	3rC	Solihull	19 Aug
1:52.43	Scott Hughes	U23	20.11.78	5rC	Manchester	14 Jun
1:52.46	Neil Bangs	U23	28.03.80	4rC	London (BP)	25 Jun
1:52.46	Andy Prophett		10.06.74	5	Stretford	8 Aug
1:52.51	James Scarth		3.10.73	4rC	Watford	22 Jul
1:52.53 i	Ben Reese		29.03.76	1r2	Mount Pleasant, USA	12 Feb
1:52.60	Denis Murphy	U23	14.09.79	4	Eton	6 May
1:52.6	Simon Stebbings		23.04.71	1	Bedford	14 May
1:52.64	Damien Moss	U20	2.09.82	2	Sheffield	8 Jul
1:52.65	Jeremy Bradley		5.02.77	2rB	Watford	12 Jul
(100)						
1:52.66	Paul Laslett	U23	12.05.80	1rD	Cardiff	5 Jul
1:52.69	Chris Stoves	U17	20.02.84	6	Stretford	8 Aug
1:52.69	Roger Morley		20.09.77	6	Bedford	23 Aug
1:52.70	Clive Gilby		24.02.66	3rB	London (He)	6 Aug
1:52.80	Alex Tanner	U23	29.12.78	4rC	Solihull	19 Aug
1:52.8	Louis Wells	U23	6.02.78	1	Watford	14 May
1:52.8	Phil Tedd		7.11.76	1	Derby	5 Aug
1:52.86	Richard Ward	U20	5.05.82	2rB	Watford	30 Aug
1:52.88	Nick Davy		26.12.74	1rD	Watford	22 Jul
1:52.90	Darren Middleton	U23	14.10.80	2rB	Stretford	25 Jul
(110)						
1:52.94	Brian Stopher	U23	8.04.80	3rB	Watford	30 Aug

Additional Under 20 (1 - 21 above)

1:52.96	Paul Gilbert		21.06.81	2rD	Watford	22 Jul
1:52.99	Dan Hermann		3.03.81	4	Bedford	27 Aug
1:52.99	Stephen Redshaw		11.11.81	2rC	Glasgow (S)	3 Sep
1:53.12	Royston Green		4.01.82	5	Watford	6 Sep
1:53.2	Sam Coombes		8.08.81	1	Erith	7 May
1:53.33	Ben Cooke		10.04.81	6rC	Solihull	19 Aug
1:53.4	Jermaine Mays		23.12.82	1	Watford	30 Aug
1:53.48	Michael Chisholm	U17	25.02.84	3rC	Glasgow (S)	3 Sep
1:53.5	Chris Thompson		17.04.81	1	Abingdon	10 Sep
(30)						
1:53.5	Mohammed Farah		23.03.83	2	Abingdon	10 Sep
1:53.72	Robert Barton		5.11.82	1rC	Stretford	27 Jun
1:53.78	Chris Burrows		23.11.82	2	Gateshead	14 May
1:53.9	David Moulton		7.09.81	1	Watford	28 Jun
1:54.0	Adam Bowden		5.08.82	1	Enfield	16 Jul
1:54.1	Mark Glennie		19.02.82	1	Perivale	5 Aug
1:54.20	Simon Rusbridge			2s2	Sheffield	8 Jul
1:54.25	Glen Coppin		16.01.83	3s2	Sheffield	8 Jul
1:54.29	Tom Carter		20.08.82	4h1	Sheffield	8 Jul
1:54.3	Robert Smith		3.12.82	2rB	Basildon	3 Jun

Additional Under 17 (1 - 2 above)

1:54.35	Ian Munro		5.09.83	4rC	Glasgow (S)	3 Sep
1:54.96	Robert Tobin		20.12.83	4rC	Watford	30 Aug
1:55.56	Michael Rimmer	U15	3.02.86	1D	Stretford	25 Jul
1:55.6	Adam Davies		27.07.84	2	Gloucester	3 Jun
1:55.90	Rory Smith		12.12.84	3rD	Stretford	25 Jul
1:55.9	Liam McGowan		27.01.84	3	Gloucester	3 Jun
1:56.06	Adam Vandenberg		2.06.84	2	Aldershot	28 Jun
1:56.2	Chris Reynolds		23.01.85	1	Chelmsford	13 May
	(10)					
1:56.3	Andrew Moreton		1.11.83	1rB	Watford	30 Aug
1:56.5	James Boxell		21.10.83	1	Wakefield	8 Jul
1:56.65	Joseph Godsell		27.10.83	2	Sheffield	30 Jul
1:56.98	Graeme Oudney		11.04.85	4rD	Glasgow (S)	3 Sep
1:57.0	Andrew Dean		25.09.83	2	Portsmouth	7 May
1:57.02	Darren Malin		19.06.85	2rD	Stretford	8 Aug
1:57.10	Jamie Atkinson		12.02.84	1	London (CP)	14 May
1:57.13	Richard Weir		7.08.84	4	Sheffield	30 Jul
1:57.37	Phillip Winfield		10.02.84	1rB	Watford	12 Jul
1:57.43	Richard Dowse		3.01.85	2h1	Sheffield	7 Jul
	(20)					
1:57.5	Chris Stoker		11.12.83	1	Gateshead	8 Jul
1:57.63	Matt Farmer		18.11.84	2h3	Sheffield	7 Jul
1:57.7	Stephen Davies		16.02.84	1	Neath	6 May
1:57.84	Matthew Rose		14.09.83	3h3	Sheffield	7 Jul
1:57.87	James Stephenson		16.10.84	3h1	Sheffield	7 Jul
1:57.91	Robert Goodwin		19.04.84	2h2	Sheffield	7 Jul
1:57.91	Dan Foley		11.09.84	3h2	Sheffield	7 Jul
1:57.92	Chris Parr		13.11.84	1	Gateshead	14 May
1:57.93	Ian Carter		19.09.83	5	Nantes, FRA	23 Jul

Additional Under 15 (1 above)

1:58.5	Ahmed Ali		31.03.86	5rB	Watford	2 Aug
1:58.69	Richard Davenport		12.09.85	7rE	Solihull	19 Aug
1:59.2	Tom Snow		7.09.85	8rB	Watford	30 Aug
1:59.7	Lee Bowron		2.10.85	1	Enfield	10 Jun
2:00.3	Chris Davies		7.09.85	1rB	Solihull	21 Jun
2:00.91	Richard Sheeran		27.11.85	4rD	Stretford	5 Sep
2:02.38	Luke Hopson		2.12.85	3	Sheffield	8 Jul
2:02.66	Jason Atkinson		28.10.85	7rF	Cardiff	5 Jul
2:02.7	Michael Smart		18.11.85	7	Watford	17 Sep
	(10)					
2:02.72	Peter Warke		22.05.86	2	Grangemouth	5 Aug
2:02.78	Craig Stewart		24.11.85	8rE	Glasgow (S)	3 Sep
2:03.0	Daryl Rogers		3.12.85	2	Basildon	10 Jun
2:03.3	Peter Bains		3.10.85	4rC	Solihull	19 Jul
2:03.85	Andrew Donaldson		23.01.86	2rG	Stretford	30 May
2:03.9	Ross Glover		2.11.85	1	Northampton	24 Aug
2:04.07	Stuart Morelands		16.06.86	6	Sheffield	8 Jul
2:04.7	Craig Glanville		21.09.86	1P	York	25 Jun
2:05.00	Colm O'Neill		7.11.85	2	Tullamore, IRE	3 Jun
2:05.00	Rhian Hastey		5.08.86	1	Cudworth	9 Sep
	(20)					
2:05.0	Michael Sawrey		30.05.86	1	Blackpool	10 Sep

Overage

1:58.65 i	Richard Davenport	U17	(1:58.69)	1	Cardiff	17 Dec
2:02.38 i	Jason Atkinson	U17	(2:02.66)	2	Cardiff	17 Dec
2:02.61 i	Chris Gowell	U17	26.09.85	1rB	Cardiff	17 Dec

Under 13

2:14.3	Jake McCulloch		21.12.87	1	Bedford	3 Jul
2:14.4	Adam Hickey		30.05.88	1	Bedford	6 Aug

2:15.3	Lewis Robson		9.01.88	1	Bebington	23	Jul
2:16.3	Abdi Igi		12.12.87	1	Perivale	2	Jul
2:16.4	Michael Garside			1	Eton	19	Jun
2:16.5	Laurence Cox		15.03.88	1	Crawley	23	Apr
2:17.8	Robert Bates		29.10.87	1	Rugby	22	Aug
2:17.96	Ross Finlayson		26.09.87	4	Grangemouth	16	Jun

Foreign

1:48.53	*Colm McLean (IRE)*	*U23*	*7.06.80*	*6*	*London (BP)*	*25*	*Jun*
1:48.8	*Gareth Turnbull (IRE)*	*U23*	*14.05.79*	*1*	*Loughborough*	*10*	*May*
1:52.19	*Karim Bouchamia (ALG)*	*U23*	*14.03.78*	*1rB*	*Watford*	*12*	*Jul*

1000 METRES

2:19.20 i	John Mayock		26.10.70	3	Birmingham	20	Feb
	2:20.75			1	Goldcoast (RB), AUS	17	Sep
2:22.05 i	Eddie King		26.11.75	5	Birmingham	20	Feb

1500 METRES

3:34.69	John Mayock		26.10.70	8	Monaco, MON	18	Aug
	3:35.98			6	Nice, FRA	8	Jul
	3:36.14 +			8m	Oslo, NOR	28	Jul
	3:36.98			9	Paris (Saint-Denis), FRA	23	Jun
	3:37.53			7	Gateshead	28	Aug
	3:37.66			5	Seville, SPA	9	Jun
	3:38.05 i			5	Stuttgart, GER	6	Feb
	3:38.18 i			5	Stockholm, SWE	17	Feb
	3:38.68			7s2	Sydney, AUS	27	Sep
	3:38.7 +			3m	London (CP)	5	Aug
	3:39.08			4h1	Sydney, AUS	25	Sep
	3:39.41			9	Sydney, AUS	29	Sep
	3:41.22 i+			2m	Lievin, FRA	13	Feb
	3:42.32			2	Gateshead	15	Jul
3:34.93	Anthony Whiteman		13.11.71	7	Stockholm, SWE	1	Aug
	3:36.39			1	Cape Town, RSA	31	Mar
	3:36.39			3	Barcelona, SPA	25	Jul
	3:38.12			1	Dortmund, GER	8	Jul
	3:41.34			1	Port Elizabeth, RSA	25	Feb
	3:42.36 i			5	Dortmund, GER	30	Jan
	3:42.44			4	Stellenbosch, RSA	18	Feb
3:36.18	Andrew Graffin		20.12.77	3	Leverkusen, GER	20	Aug
	3:39.6 +			9m	London (CP)	5	Aug
	3:39.75			11h3	Sydney, AUS	25	Sep
	3:39.79			1	Watford	22	Jul
	3:42.72			10s1	Sydney, AUS	27	Sep
3:37.34	Kevin McKay		9.02.69	9	Linz, AUT	8	Aug
	3:38.94			11	Zagreb, CRO	3	Jul
	3:40.0 +			7m	London (CP)	5	Aug
	3:41.19			10	Leverkusen, GER	20	Aug
	3:42.10			7	Kassel, GER	7	Jun
3:37.75	Jon McCallum		19.11.75	11	Stockholm, SWE	1	Aug
	3:38.87			1	Budapest, HUN	22	Jul
3:39.03	Neil Caddy		18.03.75	2	Budapest, HUN	22	Jul
	3:39.99			3	Funchal, POR	29	Jul
	3:41.24			6	Loughborough	21	May
	3:42.1 +			12m	London (CP)	5	Aug
3:39.80	Matt Dixon	U23	26.12.78	4	Loughborough	21	May
	3:40.42			1	Manchester	14	Jun
3:40.13	Michael East	U23	20.01.78	5	Loughborough	21	May
	3:40.59			2	Manchester	14	Jun
	3:42.57			5	Budapest, HUN	22	Jul
3:40.14	Allen Graffin		20.12.77	10	Gateshead	28	Aug

3:41.19	Angus Maclean	U23	20.09.80	2	Glasgow (S)	3 Sep
	(10)					
3:41.36	Richard Ashe		5.10.74	2	Watford	22 Jul
	3:42.51			1	Watford	12 Jul
3:42.36	Chris Bolt	U23	21.09.80	3	Watford	22 Jul
3:42.59	Justin Swift-Smith		28.08.74	7	Loughborough	21 May
3:42.59	Kris Bowditch		14.01.75	1	Stretford	22 Aug
3:42.76	Rob Denmark		23.11.68	12	Gateshead	28 Aug
3:42.85	James Thie	U23	27.06.78	4	Manchester	14 Jun
	51 performances to 3:43.0 by 16 athletes including 4 indoors					
3:43.13	Pat Davoren		13.03.72	4	Watford	22 Jul
3:43.41	Julian Moorhouse		13.11.71	3	Stretford	22 Aug
3:43.52	Mick Morris		16.07.74	4	Stretford	22 Aug
3:43.54	Phil Tedd		7.11.76	7	Manchester	14 Jun
	(20)					
3:43.56	Phillip Tulba		20.09.73	4	Cardiff	5 Jul
3:43.73	Joe Mills		9.07.72	7	Budapest, HUN	22 Jul
3:43.88	Steve Sharp		31.12.75	8	Manchester	14 Jun
3:44.07	Tom Mayo		2.05.77	2	Watford	12 Jul
3:44.39 i	Eddie King		26.11.75	2	Birmingham	30 Jan
	3:52.48			11	Amsterdam, HOL	13 May
3:44.66	Chris Thompson	U20	17.04.81	3	Watford	12 Jul
3:44.70	Christian Nicolson		19.09.73	10	Cardiff	5 Jul
3:44.79	Gregg Taylor		1.08.77	5	Stretford	22 Aug
3:44.88	Andy Renfree		18.05.75	9	Manchester	14 Jun
3:44.93	Steve Rees-Jones		24.12.74	10	Manchester	14 Jun
	(30)					
3:45.19	Nick McCormick	U20	11.09.81	1	Stretford	8 Aug
3:45.24	Chris Davies		19.10.76	4h2	Birmingham	12 Aug
3:45.67	Adam Zawadski		19.12.74	3	Solihull	19 Aug
3:45.79	Ian Grime		29.09.70	2	Stretford	25 Jul
3:45.88	Vince Wilson		1.04.73	5h2	Birmingham	12 Aug
3:45.90	Spencer Barden		31.03.73	13	Watford	22 Jul
3:46.04	John Rogers		30.07.73	3	Stretford	25 Jul
3:46.28	Glen Stewart		7.12.70	1	Glasgow (S)	29 Jul
3:46.36	Andy Baddeley	U20	20.06.82	4	Stretford	25 Jul
3:46.57	Ian Gillespie		18.05.70	3	Eugene, USA	29 Apr
	(40)					
3:46.66	Michael Skinner	U23	21.11.79	4	Stoke-on-Trent	1 May
3:46.75	Iain Murdoch	U23	10.07.80	2	Glasgow (S)	29 Jul
3:46.83	Jason Lobo		18.09.69	6	Cuxhaven, GER	19 Jul
3:46.84	Lee Garrett	U23	2.09.78	7h3	Birmingham	12 Aug
3:47.0	Chris Moss	U23	17.06.79	1	Solihull	21 Jun
3:47.20	Rob Scanlon		13.04.74	8h3	Birmingham	12 Aug
3:47.21	Alister Moses	U23	5.07.78	9h3	Birmingham	12 Aug
3:47.25	David Anderson		2.10.77	1	Stretford	27 Jun
3:47.28	Matt Davies		23.07.71	16	Cardiff	5 Jul
3:47.31	Simon Lees	U23	19.11.79	1rB	Manchester	14 Jun
	(50)					
3:47.36	Matt Smith		26.12.74	4	Eugene, USA	29 Apr
3:47.36	Ricky Soos	U20	28.06.83	6	Watford	12 Jul
3:47.61	Andrew Walling		3.04.73	13	Manchester	14 Jun
3:47.63	Adrian Passey		2.09.64	17	Watford	22 Jul
3:47.68	Alastair O'Connor		22.06.71	2	Stretford	27 Jun
3:47.77	Nathan Dosanjh	U23	13.02.79	2	Stretford	8 Aug
3:47.82	Gareth Price	U23	27.11.79	1rB	Cardiff	5 Jul
3:47.86 i	James Mayo		24.02.75	1	Cardiff	26 Feb
3:47.90	Ian Mitchell		10.03.76	5	Stretford	25 Jul
3:47.94	Kevin Farrow		8.09.75	1	Stretford	30 May
	(60)					
3:47.94	John Nuttall		11.01.67	3	Stretford	27 Jun
3:48.0	Mark Hudspith		19.01.69	1	Jarrow	5 Aug

3:48.1	Ian Hudspith		23.09.70	2	Jarrow	5 Aug
3:48.13	Chris Mulvaney	U20	5.05.81	3	Stretford	8 Aug
3:48.14	Michael Green		12.10.76	2	Gainesville, USA	24 Mar
3:48.27	Stuart Stokes		15.12.76	2	Stretford	30 May
3:48.35 i	Rob Whalley		11.02.68	1	Cardiff	23 Jan
3:48.41	Graeme Reid	U23	14.04.79	2	New York, USA	15 Apr
3:48.44	Yacin Yusuf		20.12.77	11	Loughborough	21 May
3:48.49	Stewart Reid		15.11.73	12	Loughborough	21 May
	(70)					
3:48.7	Donald Naylor		5.09.71	3	Jarrow	6 Aug
3:48.78	Alasdair Donaldson		21.06.77	2	Stretford	5 Sep
3:48.81	Simon Stebbings		23.04.71	1h1	Brighton	17 Jun
3:48.87	Andrew Ingle	U23	19.02.80	3rB	Cardiff	5 Jul
3:48.95	Chris Stephenson		22.07.74	1	Enfield	6 Aug
3:49.09	Neil Bangs	U23	28.03.80	3	Bedford	1 Jul
3:49.13	Michael Gregory		5.11.76	7	Watford	12 Jul
3:49.37	Sam Haughian	U23	9.07.79	12	Solihull	19 Aug
3:49.4	Richard Ward	U20	5.05.82	6	Watford	2 Aug
3:49.45	Grant Cuddy		6.01.77	4	London (He)	8 Jul
	(80)					
3:49.49	Paul Bennett		9.08.71	10	Raleigh, USA	27 May
3:49.55	James Bowler	U23	2.09.79	8	Watford	12 Jul
3:49.60	Mohammed Farah	U20	23.03.83	2	Bedford	27 Aug
3:49.68	Craig Wheeler		14.06.76	3	Stretford	5 Sep
3:49.87	Scott Hughes	U23	20.11.78	10	Princeton, USA	21 May
3:50.0	Nick Wetheridge		11.10.72	7	Watford	2 Aug
3:50.11	Stephen Patmore	U23	9.07.79	7	Stretford	22 Aug
3:50.30	Simon Deakin		5.10.77	6	Stretford	27 Jun
3:50.3	Andy Coleman		29.09.74	8	Watford	2 Aug
3:50.46	Stuart Overthrow		13.06.75	6rB	Manchester	14 Jun
	(90)					
3:50.51	Ray Ward		22.08.75	1rC	Manchester	14 Jun
3:50.51	Dave Mitchinson	U23	4.09.78	9	Watford	12 Jul
3:50.51	Jonathon Prowse		15.11.75	7	Stretford	25 Jul
3:50.64	Guy Amos		15.06.63	1	Watford	30 Aug
3:50.65	Gavin Thompson	U23	9.04.80	12h3	Birmingham	12 Aug
3:50.70	Martin Airey		28.10.70	10	Watford	12 Jul
3:50.87	David Peters		30.07.71	3h1	Brighton	17 Jun
3:50.87	Andy Caine		17.06.77	5	Stretford	5 Sep
3:51.04	Martin Yelling		7.02.72	2	Watford	30 Aug
3:51.12	Gareth Raven		9.05.74	4	Stretford	8 Aug
	(100)					
3:51.17	Bradley Yewer	U23	10.02.79	11	Watford	12 Jul
3:51.23	Matt Skelton		8.11.72	1	Bedford	23 Aug
3:51.32	Brett Stocks		16.06.74	9rB	Manchester	14 Jun
3:51.35	Andy Young		20.06.77	9	Stretford	25 Jul
3:51.37	Steffan North		19.07.76	5	Stretford	8 Aug
3:51.39	Jeremy Bradley		5.02.77	1rD	Watford	22 Jul
3:51.42	Steven Body		6.01.75	4	Watford	30 Aug
3:51.55 i	Michael Openshaw		8.04.72	3h2	Birmingham	29 Jan
3:51.56	Robert Barton	U20	5.11.82	2rC	Manchester	14 Jun
3:51.56	Matt Shone		10.07.75	4	Enfield	6 Aug
	(110)					
3:51.57	James Fewtrell	U23	22.12.80	3rB	Solihull	19 Aug
3:51.62	Matt O'Dowd		15.04.76	9rB	Watford	22 Jul
3:51.8	Philip McCrack	U20	11.03.82	1	Leicester	1 Jul
3:51.8	Dave Heath		22.05.65	1	Peterborough	8 Jul
3:51.86	Andy Hart		13.09.69	4	Stretford	30 May
3:51.86	Simon MacIntyre	U20	13.10.81	4rB	Solihull	19 Aug
3:51.88	Darius Burrows		8.08.75	6	London (He)	8 Jul
3:51.94	Andrew Norman	U23	19.08.80	10	Stretford	25 Jul

Additional Under 20 (1 - 10 above)

3:52.33	Matthew Jones		10.10.82	3rC	Manchester	14 Jun
3:52.5	Robert Whittle		14.06.81	6rC	Watford	22 Jul
3:52.91	Derek Watson		22.05.83	6	Bedford	27 Aug
3:53.06	Adam Bowden		5.08.82	2	London (He)	20 Aug
3:53.81	Robert Smith		3.12.82	3	London (He)	20 Aug
3:53.82	Matthew Simkins		9.05.82	12rB	Solihull	19 Aug
3:54.00	Ben Tickner		13.07.81	5h2	Columbia, USA	20 May
3:54.00	Stephen Murphy		6.01.83	1rE	Watford	22 Jul
3:54.25	Malcolm Hassan		27.11.82	4	Sheffield	9 Jul
3:54.89	Nicholas Goodliffe		12.05.82	12	Stretford	25 Jul
(20)						
3:55.08	Tom Carter		20.08.82	1	Stretford	22 Aug
3:55.12	Andrew Sherman		28.09.81	1rB	Watford	30 Aug

Under 17

3:55.79	Michael Chisholm		25.02.84	2rB	Stretford	5 Sep
3:57.70	Chris Stoves		20.02.84	2rB	Glasgow (S)	3 Sep
3:58.62	Ian Munro		5.09.83	1	Sheffield	30 Jul
3:59.60	Adam Vandenberg		2.06.84	10rB	Watford	12 Jul
3:59.7	Phil Nicholls		29.09.83	7	Solihull	19 Jul
3:59.96	Mark Draper		28.06.84	9rB	Watford	30 Aug
4:00.13	Stephen Davies		16.02.84	3	Sheffield	30 Jul
4:00.67	Chris Reynolds		23.01.85	1	Watford	28 May
4:01.07	Richard Kinsey		15.10.83	6rC	Cardiff	5 Jul
4:01.28	Rory Smith		12.12.84	4	Sheffield	30 Jul
(10)						
4:01.33	Steven Ablitt		16.11.83	6	Watford	6 Sep
4:01.82	Ray Edgar		15.05.84	5	Sheffield	30 Jul
4:01.83	David Jones		19.02.84	11h2	Bedford	26 Aug
4:02.4	Jon Graham		10.10.83	5	Jarrow	30 Jul
4:02.66	Mark Shankey		19.12.84	7	Sheffield	30 Jul
4:03.07	James Tydeman		4.10.83	1	Sheffield	9 Jul
4:03.99	Colin Hawkins		23.03.84	6rF	Watford	22 Jul
4:04.39	Tom Holden		2.02.84	1rB	Street	1 May
4:04.40	Ian Carter		19.09.83	4	Sheffield	9 Jul
4:04.4	Henry Stewart		16.12.83	1	Stretford	4 Jun
(20)						
4:04.63	Lee Bowron	U15	2.10.85	1	Sheffield	29 Jul
4:04.68	Philip Williams		28.09.84	9	Sheffield	30 Jul
4:05.0	Robert Spencer		4.10.83	9	Stretford	8 Aug
4:05.74	Chris Parr		13.11.84	4h2	Sheffield	29 Jul
4:06.0	Guy Thompson		20.09.84	1	Carlisle	7 Jun
4:06.16	Terry Hawkey		6.01.84	14rB	Watford	30 Aug
4:06.25	John Geary		30.09.83	2h1	Sheffield	8 Jul
4:06.6	Paul Moores		3.08.84	1	Coventry	16 Jul
4:06.69	Jack Vail		30.09.83	5h1	Sheffield	8 Jul
4:06.7	Daniel Lewis		16.10.83	1	London (He)	10 May
(20)						
4:06.74	Jamie Atkinson		12.02.84	11	Watford	6 Sep
4:06.85	Chris Ramsey		2.11.84	3	Solihull	28 May
4:06.9	Neil Siner		27.01.84	2	Stretford	4 Jun

Additional Under 15 (1 above)

4:07.8	Michael Rimmer	3.02.86	10	Stretford	8 Aug
4:08.6	Ahmed Ali	31.03.86	1	Chelmsford	1 May
4:09.08	Tom Snow	7.09.85	3rC	Watford	9 Aug
4:12.60	Michael Smart	18.11.85	2	London (He)	20 Aug
4:15.51	Paul Simner	13.12.85	3	Sheffield	29 Jul
4:16.11	Anthony Moran	8.01.86	4	Sheffield	29 Jul
4:17.18	Iskender Ibrahim	15.03.86	7rB	Watford	6 Sep

4:17.2	James Ellis		6.09.85	1	Horsham	17 Jun
4:17.68	Graham Welsh		24.09.85	8rB	Glasgow (S)	3 Sep
	(10)					
4:18.25	Tom Russell		3.10.85	3h1	Sheffield	8 Jul
4:18.56	Martin Edwards		13.10.85	4h1	Sheffield	8 Jul
4:18.8	Ashley Humphries		2.01.86	2	Colchester	28 Aug
4:18.87	Christopher Knights		17.10.85	4	London (He)	20 Aug
4:18.96	Sam Hall		15.10.85	5h1	Sheffield	8 Jul
4:19.2	Andrew Rolfe		25.10.85	2	Basildon	10 Jun
4:19.25 i	Alex Felce		11.09.86	1	Cardiff	9 Dec
4:19.68	Tom Michaelson		3.01.87	2	Wigan	25 Jun
4:19.8	Joe Hemsted		29.12.85	2	Horsham	17 Jun
4:19.92	Safeer Khan		1.11.85	4h2	Sheffield	8 Jul
	(10)					
4:20.07	Alistair Watts		12.06.86	5	Sheffield	29 Jul
4:20.34	Joe Sweeney		8.10.85	5h2	Sheffield	8 Jul
4:20.64	Paul Erwood		26.03.86	6	Sheffield	29 Jul
4:21.95	Kirk Wilson		21.12.85	7h2	Sheffield	8 Jul

Under 13

4:29.7	Adam Hickey		30.05.88	1	Colchester	28 Aug
4:32.5	Jake McCulloch		21.12.87	2	Kingston	30 Jul
4:33.34	Abdi Igi		12.12.87	2rD	Watford	6 Sep
4:34.6	Laurence Cox		15.03.88	3	Kingston	30 Jul
4:36.2	Matthew Williams		1.02.89			
4:38.8	Ben Wilson		1.07.88	4	Kingston	30 Jul
4:42.4	Andrew Livingstone		3.05.88	2	Chelmsford	1 May
4:42.9	Mark Mitchell		23.05.88	1	Glasgow (S)	20 Aug
4:45.0	Sean Ryder		12.12.87	1	Sutton Coldfield	2 Jul
4:45.6	Daniel Roberts		17.02.88	1	Ormskirk	2 Jul

Foreign

3:39.08	*Gareth Turnbull (IRE)*	*U23*	*14.05.79*	*2*	*Loughborough*	*21 May*
3:40.42	*Colm McLean (IRE)*	*U23*	*7.06.80*	*13*	*Barcelona, SPA*	*25 Jul*
3:43.34	*Karim Bouchamia (ALG)*	*U23*	*14.03.78*	*5*	*Manchester*	*14 Jun*
3:49.83	*Craig Kirkwood (NZL)*		*8.10.74*	*6rB*	*Watford*	*22 Jul*
3:51.04	*Gary Murray IRE)*	*U23*	*31.01.80*	*4rB*	*Cardiff*	*5 Jul*

1 MILE

3:50.61	John Mayock		26.10.70	6	Oslo, NOR	28 Jul
	3:52.15			8	Brussels, BEL	25 Aug
	3:53.44			3	London (CP)	5 Aug
	3:56.68 i			4	Lievin, FRA	13 Feb
	4:00.65			1	Glasgow (S)	2 Jul
3:55.07	Kevin McKay		9.02.69	7	London (CP)	5 Aug
3:56.13	Andrew Graffin		20.12.77	9	London (CP)	5 Aug
3:58.31	Neil Caddy		18.03.75	12	London (CP)	5 Aug
3:59.86	Allen Graffin		20.12.77	13	London (CP)	5 Aug
4:00.4	Chris Stephenson		22.07.74	1	Yeovil	28 Aug
4:00.60	Tom Mayo		2.05.77	4	London (BP)	4 Jun
4:00.77	Michael Openshaw		8.04.72	5	London (BP)	4 Jun
4:01.06	Dave Heath		22.05.65	6	London (BP)	4 Jun
4:01.61	Matt Dixon	U23	26.12.78	2	Glasgow (S)	2 Jul
	(10)					
4:01.7	James Thie	U23	27.06.78	2	Yeovil	28 Aug
4:01.76 i	Ben Reese		29.03.76	3	Fayetteville, USA	11 Mar
4:02.0	Steve Sharp		31.12.75	3	Yeovil	28 Aug
	17 performances to 4:02.0 by 13 athletes including 2 indoors					
4:02.35	Julian Moorhouse		13.11.71	7	London (BP)	4 Jun
4:02.45	Justin Swift-Smith		28.08.74	8	London (BP)	4 Jun

4:03.81 i	Chris Livesey	U23	8.08.80	1	Boston, USA	26 Feb
4:04.64	Chris Bolt	U23	21.09.80	3	Watford	6 Sep
4:04.65	Michael East	U23	20.01.78	4	Glasgow (S)	2 Jul
4:05.22	Ian Gillespie		18.05.70	9	Eugene, USA	13 May
4:06.7	Andrew Ingle	U23	19.02.80	5	Yeovil	28 Aug
	(20)					
4:07.52	Phil Tedd		7.11.76	1	Bedford	29 May
4:07.53	Alister Moses	U23	5.07.78	2	Bedford	29 May
4:07.95	Pat Davoren		13.03.72	1rB	London (BP)	4 Jun
4:07.97	Steven Body		6.01.75	2rB	London (BP)	4 Jun
4:08.16	Chris Davies		19.10.76	3	Bedford	29 May
4:08.41	Rob Whalley		11.02.68	11	London (BP)	4 Jun
4:08.60	Andy Hart		13.09.69	12	London (BP)	4 Jun
4:08.90 i	Paul Bennett		9.08.71	8	Roxbury, USA	11 Mar
4:08.92	Nick Wetheridge		11.10.72	4	Bedford	29 May
4:09.6	Matt Skelton		8.11.72	1	London (TB)	16 Aug

Under 20

4:10.93	Chris Mulvaney		5.05.81	4rB	London (BP)	4 Jun
4:14.20	Robert Smith		3.12.82	8	Watford	6 Sep
4:14.84 i	Nick McCormick		11.09.81	2	Boston, USA	2 Dec

Under 17

4:18.40	Mark Draper		28.06.84	2	Solihull	19 Aug

Under 15

4:47.0	Joe Hemsted		29.12.85	1	Tipton	24 Sep

Foreign

3:57.89	*Gareth Turnbull (IRE)*	*U23*	*14.05.79*	*2*	*Philadelphia, USA*	*29 Apr*
4:04.30	*Karim Bouchamia (ALG)*	*U23*	*14.03.78*	*10*	*London (BP)*	*4 Jun*

2000 METRES

5:01.28	Andrew Graffin	20.12.77	2	London (BP)	25 Jun
5:02.53 i	John Mayock	26.10.70	1	Ghent, BEL	11 Feb
5:02.90	Allen Graffin	20.12.77	3	London (BP)	25 Jun

3000 METRES

7:49.97 i	John Mayock		26.10.70	3	Ghent, BEL	27 Feb
	7:55.10 i			3h2	Ghent, BEL	25 Feb
7:52.27	Kris Bowditch		14.01.75	3	Manchester	14 Jun
7:53.11	Julian Moorhouse		13.11.71	4	Manchester	14 Jun
7:53.23	Chris Stephenson		22.07.74	4	Cardiff	5 Jul
7:53.54	John Nuttall		11.01.67	5	Cardiff	5 Jul
	7:59.20			12	Manchester	14 Jun
7:53.63 i	Rob Whalley		11.02.68	1	Cardiff	6 Feb
7:53.68	Adrian Passey		2.09.64	5	Manchester	14 Jun
7:54.12	Andres Jones		3.02.77	6	Cardiff	5 Jul
7:55.12	Michael Openshaw		8.04.72	6	Manchester	14 Jun
	7:57.1			1	Stretford	25 Jul
7:56.80	Glen Stewart		7.12.70	7	Manchester	14 Jun
	(10)					
7:57.48	Chris Davies		19.10.76	9	Manchester	14 Jun
7:58.15 i	Anthony Whiteman		13.11.71	1	Birmingham	16 Jan
	8:01.0			3	Gateshead	16 Jul
7:59.35	Nick Wetheridge		11.10.72	13	Manchester	14 Jun
	16 performances to 8:00.0 by 13 athletes including 4 indoors					
8:03.8	Mark Hudspith		19.01.69	1	Jarrow	2 Aug
8:03.91	Darius Burrows		8.08.75	13	Cardiff	5 Jul
8:04.27	Michael East	U23	20.01.78	1	Street	1 May

8:04.63 i	Andrew Graffin		20.12.77	2	Birmingham	30	Jan
8:04.93	Chris Thompson	U20	17.04.81	2rB	Manchester	14	Jun
8:05.45	Glynn Tromans		17.03.69	14	Manchester	14	Jun
8:05.7	Ian Hudspith		23.09.70	2	Jarrow	2	Aug
	(20)						
8:05.74	Mick Morris		16.07.74	3rB	Manchester	14	Jun
8:06.33 i	Matt Smith		26.12.74	3	Birmingham	30	Jan
8:06.6	Ian Grime		29.09.70	1	Loughborough	14	Jun
8:07 e+	Paul Evans		13.04.61	m	London (BP)	25	Jun
8:08.8	Kevin Farrow		8.09.75	2	Solihull	24	May
8:09.49 i	Ben Noad		6.05.76	2	Allston, USA	23	Jan
8:09.67	Robert Maycock	U20	21.02.81	5rB	Manchester	14	Jun
8:10.74	Andy Morgan-Lee		1.03.69	6rB	Manchester	14	Jun
8:11.27	Alan Buckley		25.10.74	15	Cardiff	5	Jul
8:11.68	Ian Mitchell		10.03.76	7rB	Manchester	14	Jun
	(30)						
8:11.8	Chris Bolt	U23	21.09.80	2	Brighton	16	Aug
8:11.9	Sam Haughian	U23	9.07.79	3	Brighton	16	Aug
8:12.53	Mohammed Farah	U20	23.03.83	1	Grosseto, ITA	7	Oct
8:12.68 i	Matt Dixon	U23	26.12.78	1	Cardiff	12	Mar
8:13.32	Justin Swift-Smith		28.08.74	2	Street	1	May
8:13.39 i	Nathaniel Lane		10.04.76	2	Cardiff	12	Mar
8:14.06	Gareth Raven		9.05.74	8rB	Manchester	14	Jun
8:14.8	Phillip Tulba		20.09.73	2	Loughborough	14	Jun
8:15.00 i	Adam Sutton	U20	22.03.81	2	Boston, USA	2	Dec
8:15.40	Stephen Hepples	U23	6.01.80	4	Liverpool	22	Jul
	(40)						
8:15.44	Allen Graffin		20.12.77	1	Glasgow (S)	3	Sep
8:15.60	Peter Riley	U23	6.07.79		New York, USA	11	Feb
8:16.2	Jerome Brooks		9.08.73	3rB	Cardiff	5	Jul
8:16.32 i	James Thie	U23	27.06.78	3	Birmingham	16	Jan
8:16.51	Martin Yelling		7.02.72	1	Watford	6	Sep
8:16.60	Andy Caine		17.06.77	2	Glasgow (S)	3	Sep
8:16.7	Steven Body		6.01.75	2	Watford	28	Jun
8:16.8	Andrew Hennessy		24.08.77	4rB	Cardiff	5	Jul
8:17.16	Mick Hill		2.09.75	9rB	Manchester	14	Jun
8:17.58	Michael Green		12.10.76	2	Troy, USA	8	Apr
	(50)						
8:18.25 i	Matt Hibberd		23.06.73	4	Birmingham	16	Jan
8:18.47	Spencer Duval		5.01.70	10rB	Manchester	14	Jun
8:18.55	Tom Mayo		2.05.77	3	Street	1	May
8:18.82 i	James Tonner		3.06.75	4	Cardiff	12	Mar
8:18.91 i	Ian Gillespie		18.05.70	4	New York, USA	4	Feb
8:19.08 i	Graeme Reid	U23	14.04.79		New York, USA	11	Feb
8:19.47 i	Lee Garrett	U23	2.09.78	5	Cardiff	12	Mar
8:19.75	Martin Hilton		9.05.75	3	Stretford	30	May
8:19.81 i	Robert Gould		16.01.76	5	Birmingham	16	Jan
8:20.0	Stuart Stokes		15.12.76	1	Stretford	16	May
	(60)						
8:20.24	Eric Crowther		23.01.75	4	Stretford	30	May
8:20.35	Tony O'Brien		14.11.70	1	Stretford	5	Sep
8:20.4	Daniel Dalmedo	U23	14.03.80	6	Brighton	16	Aug
8:20.80	Nick Francis		29.08.71	1	Watford	12	Jul
8:20.8	Alister Moses	U23	5.07.78	7	Brighton	16	Aug

Additional Under 20 (1 - 4 above)

8:21.2	Antony Brewer	3.06.81	8	Brighton	16	Aug
8:21.69	Stephen Murphy	6.01.83	2	Watford	12	Jul
8:22.74	Martyn Cryer	16.10.81	4	Glasgow (S)	3	Sep
8:24.73	Richard Ward	5.05.82	1	Sheffield	29	Jul
8:26.7	Dan Ledgerwood	24.03.83	9	Brighton	16	Aug

8:27.1	Lee McCash		22.10.81	8rB	Cardiff	5 Jul
	(10)					
8:28.73	Antony Ford		26.05.83	7	Glasgow (S)	3 Sep
8:33.54	Nicholas Goodliffe		12.05.82	2	Stretford	8 Aug
8:35.6	Ed Prickett		28.01.83	1	Watford	1 Jun
8:37.6	Phil Nicholls	U17	29.09.83	2	Coventry	5 Aug
8:37.61	Paul Murphy		13.04.81	3	Watford	2 Aug
8:38.0	Joseph Byrne		1.02.82	4	Belfast	23 Aug
8:38.3	Robert Smith		3.12.82	1	Watford	20 Sep
8:38.87	Richard Lee		25.12.81	1	Watford	10 Jun
8:39.8	Chris Mulvaney		5.05.81	5	Loughborough	10 May

Additional Under 17 (1 above)

8:40.00	David Jones		19.02.84	2	Blackpool	15 Jul
8:44.8	Paul Moores		3.08.84	5	Solihull	24 May
8:46.40	Richard Kinsey		15.10.83	4	Blackpool	15 Jul
8:46.80	Daniel Lewis		16.10.83	5	Watford	2 Aug
8:48.46	Glenn Raggett		3.07.84	1	Watford	2 Jul
8:51.78	Ray Edgar		15.05.84	1	Cleckheaton	27 May
8:52.77	Steven Ablitt		16.11.83	1	Cudworth	19 Aug
8:53.05	Chris Parr		13.11.84	2	Cleckheaton	27 May
8:53.09	Jon Graham		10.10.83	3	Cleckheaton	27 May
	(10)					
8:53.66	Tom Snow	U15	7.09.85	1	Watford	10 Jun
8:53.7	Chris Reynolds		23.01.85	1		23 Jul
8:56.53	Frank Tickner		12.10.83	3	Sheffield	8 Jul
8:56.87	Stephen Enright		5.09.84	17	Stretford	22 Aug
8:57.67	Philip McGlory		2.09.83	1	Stretford	5 Sep
8:57.77	Tom Bedford		12.12.83	4	Watford	26 Jul
8:58.32	Tom Fahey		27.09.84	4	Sheffield	9 Jul
8:58.60	James Henry		31.07.84	18	Stretford	22 Aug
8:59.81	Rory Smith		12.12.84	19	Stretford	22 Aug
9:00.3	Aaron Frazer		10.05.84	1	Stretford	10 Jun
	(20)					
9:00.56	Lee Pickering		16.09.83	4	Cleckheaton	27 May
9:00.57	Donald Macaulay		25.06.84	1	Grangemouth	25 Jun

Under 15 (1 above)

9:01.80	Michael Smart	18.11.85	7	Watford	6 Sep
9:03.54	Ashley Humphries	2.01.86	9	Watford	10 Sep
9:04.38 i	Ahmed Ali	31.03.86	1	Birmingham	6 Feb
9:10.29	Anthony Moran	8.01.86	1rB	Stretford	8 Aug
9:13.35	Andrew Rolfe	25.10.85	2	Enfield	29 Jul
9:16.6	Daniel Patten	11.07.86	1	Woodford	19 Jul
9:16.7	Oliver Holden	20.05.86	1	Banbury	10 Sep
9:22.67	Tom Michaelson	3.01.87	1	Stretford	5 Sep
9:22.8	Alex Felce	11.09.86	3	Gloucester	3 Jun
	(10)				
9:23.27	Ben Jones	14.01.86	1	Wigan	25 Jun
9:23.39	James Ellis	6.09.85	2	Bedford	1 Jul
9:29.9	Joe Hemsted	29.12.85	5rB	Watford	2 Aug
9:31.8	Ryan Hughes	1.11.85	1	Gateshead	21 May
9:31.9	David McQuarrie	28.11.85	1	Sheffield	15 Apr
9:31.98	Andrew McLeod	7.09.85	1	Birmingham	2 Sep
9:33.43	Sam Hall	15.10.85	4	Enfield	29 Jul
9:35.5	Wesley Gordon	9.11.85	1	Chester-le-Street	21 May
9:36.1	Andrew Friend	2.08.87	2	Portsmouth	13 May
9:36.3	Tom Compey	21.01.86	1	London (WP)	4 Jun
9:38.4	Tim Haughian	29.11.86	8rB	Watford	2 Aug
	(20)				
9:39.8	Christopher Knights	17.10.85	1	Reading	21 May

Under 13

9:47.99	Robert Pickering		3.11.87	5	Wigan	25 Jun
9:50.45	Adam Hickey		30.05.88	1	Bedford	23 Aug
9:50.7	Jake McCulloch		21.12.87	1	Watford	31 May
9:59.0	Ben Wilson		1.07.88	13rB	Watford	2 Aug
10:10.1	Matthew Vandeschans			8rB	Watford	30 Aug
10:10.8	Laurence Cox		15.03.88	1	Portsmouth	13 May
10:24.1	Stephen Blake		29.09.87	16rB	Watford	2 Aug

Foreign

7:58.03	*Dermot Donnelly (IRE)*		*23.09.70*	*10*	*Manchester*	*14 Jun*
8:01.84	*Craig Kirkwood (NZL)*		*8.10.74*	*11*	*Cardiff*	*5 Jul*
8:03.58	*Mohammed Fatihi (MOR)*		*16.06.73*	*12*	*Cardiff*	*5 Jul*
8:08.03 i	*Gareth Turnbull (IRE)*	*U23*	*14.05.79*	*1*	*Nenagh, IRE*	*9 Jan*

2 MILES

8:40.44 i	Kris Bowditch	14.01.75	8	Birmingham	20 Feb
8:49.39 i	Ian Gillespie	18.05.70	7	Roxbury, USA	7 Feb

5000 METRES

13:28.22	Kris Bowditch	14.01.75	2	London (BP)	25 Jun
13:30.67	Adrian Passey	2.09.64	10	Heusden, BEL	5 Aug
	13:51.26		2	Dublin (S), IRE	29 Jul
	13:52.97		5	Solihull	19 Aug
	13:54.31		9	Stretford	11 Jul
13:37.97	Michael Openshaw	8.04.72	6	London (BP)	25 Jun
	13:42.02		6	Stretford	11 Jul
	13:49.34		2	Birmingham	13 Aug
	13:55.01		16	London (CP)	5 Aug
13:38.37	Glen Stewart	7.12.70	4	Stretford	11 Jul
	13:43.89		4	Solihull	19 Aug
	13:58.32		17	London (CP)	5 Aug
	13:58.40		5	Loughborough	21 May
13:39.02	John Nuttall	11.01.67	5	Stretford	11 Jul
	13:56.35		5	Birmingham	13 Aug
	13:57.79		26	Heusden, BEL	5 Aug
13:39.43	Andres Jones	3.02.77	14	London (CP)	5 Aug
	13:45.86		1	Birmingham	13 Aug
	13:54.3		1	Peterborough	8 Jul
13:41.42	Allen Graffin	20.12.77	2	Solihull	19 Aug
	13:57.85		4	Loughborough	21 May
13:42.13	Karl Keska	7.05.72	7	Eugene, USA	24 Jun
	13:54 +		m	Sydney, AUS	25 Sep
13:42.35	Julian Moorhouse	13.11.71	8	London (BP)	25 Jun
	13:50.05		8	Stretford	11 Jul
	13:53.90		4	Dublin (S), IRE	29 Jul
13:45.26	Christian Nicolson	19.09.73	15	Palo Alto, USA	5 May
	13:51.79		11	Palo Alto, USA	25 Mar
(10)					
13:47.9	Keith Cullen	13.06.72	1	Hayes	5 Aug
13:48.98 i	Ben Noad	6.05.76	3	Boston, USA	29 Jan
	13:57.93		7r2	Walnut, USA	14 Apr
13:49.37	Mark Hudspith	19.01.69	7	Stretford	11 Jul
	13:52.74		3	Birmingham	13 Aug
13:52.06	Rob Denmark	23.11.68	3	Lapinlahti, FIN	16 Jul
13:55.54	Ian Hudspith	23.09.70	4	Birmingham	13 Aug
	13:57.37		12	Stretford	11 Jul
	13:57.64		6	Solihull	19 Aug
13:56.98	Paul Evans	13.04.61	10	London (BP)	25 Jun

13:57.01	Peter Riley	U23	6.07.79	4	Philadelphia, USA	27	Apr
13:57.31	Glynn Tromans		17.03.69	11	Stretford	11	Jul
13:57.50	Dave Heath		22.05.65	3	Loughborough	21	May
13:58.44	Nathaniel Lane		10.04.76	14	Stretford	11	Jul
(20)							
13:58.88	Donald Naylor		5.09.71	15	Stretford	11	Jun
13:59.28	Nick Wetheridge		11.10.72	6	Loughborough	21	May
	44 performances to 14:00.0 by 22 athletes						
14:02.69	Spencer Barden		31.03.73	18	London (CP)	5	Aug
14:03.01	Matt O'Dowd		15.04.76	7	Lapinlahti, FIN	16	Jul
14:03.30	Ian Mitchell		10.03.76	16	Stretford	11	Jul
14:04 e	Mark Steinle		22.11.74		Watford	22	Jul
14:04.50	Justin Chaston		4.11.68	1	Houston, USA	31	Mar
14:04.85	Sam Haughian	U23	9.07.79	9	Birmingham	13	Aug
14:05.72	Mohammed Farah	U20	23.03.83	8	Solihull	19	Aug
14:05.74	Alan Buckley		25.10.74	18	Stretford	11	Jul
(30)							
14:06.40	Andrew Graffin		20.12.77	7	Loughborough	21	May
14:06.52	Chris Thompson	U20	17.04.81	13	London (BP)	25	Jun
14:08.26	Martin Palmer		5.04.77	5	Chiba, JPN	24	Nov
14:09.89	Chris Davies		19.10.76	7	Dublin (S), IRE	29	Jul
14:12.99	Steffan White		21.12.72	11	Birmingham	13	Aug
14:13.30	Matthew Vaux-Harvey		30.03.76	12	Birmingham	13	Aug
14:14.3	Andy Coleman		29.09.74	2	Enfield	24	Jun
14:15.11	Martin Cox			5	Christchurch, NZL	18	Mar
14:16.79	Mark Miles		24.03.77	10	Loughborough	21	May
14:19.48	Nick Francis		29.08.71	2	London (He)	6	Aug
(40)							
14:19.56	Ian Grime		29.09.70	14	Birmingham	13	Aug
14:19.8	Adrian Mussett		14.04.72	1	Chelmsford	13	May
14:21.9	Mark Morgan		19.08.72	1	Sheffield (W)	24	Jun
14:22.64	Dave Mitchinson	U23	4.09.78	3	London (He)	6	Aug
14:22.71	Jerome Brooks		9.08.73	12	Solihull	19	Aug
14:22.82	Rob Whalley		11.02.68	15	Birmingham	13	Aug
14:25.0	Dominic Bannister		1.04.68	1	Bedford	19	Aug
14:25.3	Steve O'Gara		3.12.69	1	Jarrow	6	May
14:26.01	Martin Yelling		7.02.72	13	Solihull	19	Aug
14:26.91	Stephen Hepples	U23	6.01.80	16	Birmingham	13	Aug
(50)							
14:28.0	Michael East	U23	20.01.78	1	Feltham	6	May
14:28.47	Dave Wardle		1.10.75	14	Solihull	19	Aug
14:29.06	Robert Gould		16.01.76	1	Cudworth	28	Aug
14:30.34	Michael Green		12.10.76	12	Knoxville, USA	13	Apr
14:31.29	Richard Taylor		5.12.73	15	London (BP)	25	Jun
14:31.40	Gareth Raven		9.05.74	1rB	Stretford	11	Jul
14:32.47	Andy Morgan-Lee		1.03.69	20	Stretford	11	Jul
14:32.53	Andrew Norman	U23	19.08.80	2rB	Stretford	11	Jul
14:33.5	Darren Daniels		2.09.70	1	Stretford	28	Jun
14:33.68	Andrew Hennessy		24.08.77	1	Eton	6	May
(60)							
14:33.69	Simon Lessing		12.02.71	5rB	London (BP)	25	Jun
14:33.86	Alan Shepherd		28.04.69	1	Aldershot	5	Jul
14:34.19	Andy Caine		17.06.77	3	Stoke-on-Trent	1	May
14:34.88	Mark Flint		19.02.63	2	Aldershot	5	Jul
14:36.84	Richard Findlow		4.12.66	2	Bedford	29	May
14:36.9	Andy Arrand		20.01.66	2	Wigan	20	May
14:37.02	Robert Maycock	U20	21.02.81	2	Eton	6	May
14:38.06	Andy Beevers		3.05.73	3rB	Stretford	11	Jul
14:39.64	Paul Howarth		30.10.77	4rB	Stretford	11	Jul
14:40.2	Matthew Jones	U20	10.10.82	3	Sheffield (W)	24	Jun
(70)							

14:40.56	Alan Barnes	U23		4	Stoke-on-Trent	1 May
14:41.11	Darius Burrows		8.08.75	10	Dublin (S), IRE	29 Jul
14:41.22	Martin Hilton		9.05.75	5rB	Stretford	11 Jul
14:41.24	Colin Jones		8.04.74	2	Indianapolis, USA	4 May
14:42.16	Craig Wheeler		14.06.76	4	Sydney, AUS	20 Feb
14:42.22	Lee McCash	U20	22.10.81	6rB	London (BP)	25 Jun
14:42.41	Carl Warren		28.09.69	2	London (He)	8 Jul
14:42.85	Nicholas Goodliffe	U20	12.05.82	6rB	Stretford	11 Jul
14:43.5	Tony O'Brien		14.11.70	2	Watford	20 May
14:44.50	Michael Bulstridge		23.01.73	3	Eton	6 May
(80)						
14:44.66	James Fitzsimmons		20.04.74	2	Brighton	17 Jun

Additional Under 20 (1 - 6 above)

14:53.24	Martyn Cryer	16.10.81	3	Bedford	26 Aug
15:00.16	Ben Tickner	13.07.81	18	Columbia, USA	21 May
15:03.70	Thomas Frazer	10.09.81	2	Tullamore, IRE	3 Jun
15:12.20	Robert Russell	13.07.82	4	Bedford	26 Aug
(10)					
15:12.6	Richard Lee	25.12.81	6	Watford	20 May
15:19.29	Nick Samuels	13.06.81	6	Bedford	26 Aug
15:28.00	Joseph Byrne	1.02.82	2	Antrim	20 Jun
15:28.6	Benjamin Fish	21.05.82	2	Liverpool	3 Jun
15:31.68	Owain Matthews	4.11.81	7	Bedford	26 Aug
15:31.7	Paul Shaw	7.08.82	1	Stretford	5 Aug
15:33.00	Richard Ward	5.05.82	12	Bedford	29 May
15:34.0	Alex Haines	27.10.82	3	Newport	28 Jun
15:34.2	Martin Fielding	19.05.83	1rB	Redditch	22 Jul
15:34.8	Peter Willis	4.05.82	3rB	Cardiff	8 Jul

Foreign

13:56.74	*Dermot Donnelly (IRE)*		*23.09.70*	*1*	*Kaunas, LIT*	*9 Jul*
13:57.58	*Craig Kirkwood (NZL)*		*8.10.74*	*13*	*Stretford*	*11 Jul*
14:10.9	*Alan Merriman (IRE)*		*26.07.70*	*2*	*Peterborough*	*9 Jul*
14:26.41	*Joe McAllister (IRE)*	*U23*	*23.12.80*	*2*	*Dublin (S), IRE*	*20 Aug*

5 KILOMETRES Road - where better than track best

14:04	Ian Gillespie	18.05.70	1	Portland, USA	9 Apr
14:07	Anthony Whiteman	13.11.71	3	Stevenage	28 May
14:21	Rob Whalley	11.02.68	1	Street	13 Dec
14:23	Paul Freary	3.04.68	2	Chester	12 May

Foreign

14:15	*Mohammed Fatihi (MAR)*	*16.06.73*	*4*	*Stevenage*	*28 May*

5 MILES Road

22:57	Karl Keska	7.05.72	5	Balmoral	22 Apr
23:20	Chris Davies	19.10.76	1	Wolverhampton	10 Dec
23:21	Matt O'Dowd	15.04.76	1	Hillingdon	5 Mar
23:27	Mark Miles	24.03.77	1	Alsager	6 Feb
23:29	Tommy Murray	18.05.61	1	Irvine	19 Apr
23:31	John Nuttall	11.01.67	2	Alsager	6 Feb
23:31	Andy Coleman	29.09.74	11	Balmoral	22 Apr
23:35	Nick Wetheridge	11.10.72	12	Balmoral	22 Apr
23:36	Mark Morgan	19.08.72	3	Alsager	6 Feb
23:39	Andrew Graffin	20.12.77	1	Welwyn	24 Apr
(10)					
23:41	Alan Buckley	25.10.74	14	Balmoral	22 Apr
23:45	Steven Conaghan	18.05.67	2	Irvine	19 Apr
23:47	Gary Staines	3.07.63	2	Hackney	1 Apr

23:49	Nick Jones		10.07.74	4	Alsager	6 Feb
23:49	Tom Hearle		5.06.67	3	Irvine	19 Apr
23:49	Paul Evans		13.04.61	15	Balmoral	22 Apr
23:49	Adrian Mussett		14.04.72	2	Welwyn	24 Apr
23:49	Glynn Tromans		17.03.69	1	Blisworth	18 Aug
23:50	Barry Royden		15.12.66	2	Hackney	1 Apr
23:53	Alan Shepherd		28.04.69	5	Alsager	6 Feb
(20)						
23:53	John Mayock		26.10.70	1	Loughrea, IRE	15 Nov
23:54	Steve Sharp		31.12.75	5	Hillingdon	5 Mar
23:56	Matthew Vaux-Harvey		30.03.76	6	Alsager	6 Feb

Foreign

23:36	*Craig Kirkwood (NZL)*		*8.10.74*	*3*	*Hillingdon*	*5 Mar*
23:39	*Karim Bouchamia (ALG)*	*U23*	*14.03.78*	*4*	*Hillingdon*	*5 Mar*
23:48	*John Ferrin (IRE)*		*20.02.67*	*1*	*Belfast*	*14 Oct*

10000 METRES

27:44.09	Karl Keska		7.05.72	8	Sydney, AUS	25 Sep
	27:48.29			6h2	Sydney, AUS	22 Sep
	28:00.56			2	Lisbon, POR	1 Apr
28:00.50	Andres Jones		3.02.77	2	Watford	22 Jul
	28:11.20			9h1	Sydney, AUS	22 Sep
	29:51.73			1	Bedford	28 May
28:03.31	Rob Denmark		23.11.68	3	Watford	22 Jul
	28:17.70			10	Lisbon, POR	1 Apr
	28:43.74			13h1	Sydney, AUS	22 Sep
28:04.48	Mark Steinle		22.11.74	4	Watford	22 Jul
28:22.06	Keith Cullen		13.06.72	12	Lisbon, POR	1 Apr
28:43.08	Mark Hudspith		19.01.69	11	Watford	22 Jul
28:47.94	Ben Noad		6.05.76	15	Palo Alto, USA	5 May
28:50.98	Ian Hudspith		23.09.70	12	Watford	22 Jul
29:05.28	Glynn Tromans		17.03.69	14	Watford	22 Jul
29:10.86	Adrian Mussett		14.04.72	2	London (BP)	4 Jun
(10)						
29:35.48	John Nuttall		11.01.67	14rB	Lisbon, POR	1 Apr
29:38.93	Nathaniel Lane		10.04.76	17	Watford	22 Jul
29:40.17	Christian Nicolson		19.09.73	9	Melbourne, AUS	4 Dec
29:57.58	Tommy Murray		18.05.61	1	Glasgow	28 Jul
29:58.65	Richard Findlow		4.12.66	18	Watford	22 Jul
29:58.72	Alan Buckley		25.10.74	19	Watford	22 Jul
	22 performances to 30:00.0 by 16 athletes					
30:06.17	Colin Jones		8.04.74	6	Raleigh, USA	31 Mar
30:12.17	David Cunningham		24.10.70	20	Watford	22 Jul
30:15.80	Martin Palmer		5.04.77	1	Stoke-on-Trent	29 Apr
30:16.84	Martin Hula		2.01.66	4	London (BP)	4 Jun
(20)						
30:16.89	Will Levett		6.09.75	2	Stoke-on-Trent	29 Apr
30:30.4	Rob Birchall		14.06.70	1	Cudworth	22 Jul
30:33.07	Alaister Russell		17.06.68	2	Glasgow	28 Jul
30:37.96	Daniel Hyde		5.10.77	5	London (BP)	4 Jun
30:43.04	Richard Gardiner		11.06.73	21	Watford	22 Jul
30:43.63	Robert Gould		16.01.76	3	Stoke-on-Trent	29 Apr
30:47.7	Bill Foster	V40	9.08.58	1	Rugby	23 Jul
30:58.93	Ian Grime		29.09.70	2	Bedford	19 Aug
30:59.8	Gareth Deacon		8.08.66	1	Loughborough	17 May
31:00.13	Charles Herrington		28.09.71	3	Bedford	19 Aug
(30)						
31:01.18	Stephen Platts		12.03.66	23	Watford	22 Jul
31:04.5	Rhodri Jones		14.08.66	1	Newport	11 Jun
31:05.85	Peter Grime		8.11.69	4	Stoke-on-Trent	29 Apr

31:07.33	A. C. Muir		20.06.73	5	Stoke-on-Trent	29	Apr
31:08.76	Andrew Norman	U23	19.08.80	6	Stoke-on-Trent	29	Apr
31:10.12	James Fitzsimmons		20.04.74	3	Bedford	28	May
31:15.18	Andrew Mckenna	U23	3.01.80	7	Stoke-on-Trent	29	Apr
31:18.05	Nick Francis		29.08.71	4	Bedford	19	Aug
31:23.4	Andy Lyons		24.12.69	2	Cudworth	22	Jul
31:23.96	Mike Boyle		29.12.60	1	Bedford	20	Aug
	(40)						
31:24.4	Shaun Tobin		13.10.62	2	Rugby	23	Jul
31:25.2	Nathan Vengdasalam		11.03.64	1	Cudworth	28	Aug
31:28.7	Matthew Plano		8.10.76	2	Cudworth	28	Aug
31:31.8	Steve Gisbourne		24.03.68	3	Cudworth	28	Aug
31:33.1	Rod Leach		29.05.72	1	Aldershot	5	Jul
31:33.4	Tom Hart		7.12.77	1	Eton	23	Jul
31:35.12	Martin Ferguson		17.09.64	3	Glasgow	28	Jul
31:35.3	Terry Wall		12.06.70	1	Middlesbrough	1	Jul
31:36.35	Stuart Major		5.05.70	24	Watford	22	Jul
31:36.97	Tim Cook	U23	16.10.78	7	New York, USA	15	Apr
	(50)						
31:40.3	Tim Wright			1	Hull	17	Oct
31:42.0	Justin Reid		26.09.69	7	Dedham, USA	20	May
31:42.2	Colin Palmer		27.07.67	2	Aldershot	5	Jul
31:43.3	Donal Gallagher		5.12.72	1	Antrim	2	Jul
31:44.91	Carl Morris	U23	5.05.80	8	Stoke-on-Trent	29	Apr
31:45.63	Duncan Scobie		5.07.67	4	Glasgow (S)	28	Jul
31:46.6	David Brady		5.07.62	2	Antrim	2	Jul
31:50.3	Noel Thatcher		13.05.66	2	Ilford	25	Jul
31:51.89	Ian Johnston		12.02.68	5	Glasgow	28	Jul
31:53.0	Jamie Jones		8.12.71	1	Portsmouth	1	May
	(60)						
31:53.7	Tony Jackson		28.02.67	1	Enfield	23	Jul
31:54.4	Alan McCullough		9.08.63	3	Antrim	2	Jul
31:56.0	Tim Field		30.05.65	2	Middlesbrough	1	Jul
31:59.00	Robert Malseed		16.09.71	7rB	London (BP)	4	Jun
31:59.31	Justin Fowler			9	Stoke-on-Trent	29	Apr
32:00.3	Roy Smith		5.10.62	1	Blackheath	12	Jul
32:01.2	Keith Chapman	U20	15.02.81	1	Cudworth	1	Jul
32:01.2	Steve Murdoch		16.04.61	1	Middlesbrough	1	Jul

Foreign

29:36.91	*Dermot Donnelly (IRE)*		*23.09.70*	*16*	*Birmingham*	*22*	*Jul*
29:58.61	*Craig Kirkwood (IRE)*		*8.10.74*	*3*	*London (BP)*	*4*	*Jun*
30:57.1	*Amin Kokai (KEN)*		*5.01.74*	*1*	*Ilford*	*25*	*Jul*
31:54.3	*Paul O'Callaghan (IRE)*		*1.06.64*	*1*	*Nuneaton*	*11*	*Jun*

10 KILOMETRES Road

29:05	Michael Openshaw		8.04.72	1	Leeds	3	Dec
	29:13			2	Bradford	10	Sep
29:19	Andres Jones		3.02.77	1	Swansea	26	Mar
29:21	Ian Grime		29.09.70	1	Dewsbury	13	Feb
	29:22			2	Swansea	26	Mar
29:21	Nick Wetheridge		11.10.72	2	Swansea	26	Mar
29:22	Andrew Graffin		20.12.77	2	Dewsbury	13	Feb
29:23	Mark Hudspith		19.01.69	3	Dewsbury	13	Feb
29:23	Michael East	U23	20.01.78	1	Winchester	14	Oct
29:24	Ian Hudspith		23.09.70	4	Dewsbury	13	Feb
29:25	Andy Coleman		29.09.74	1	Eastleigh	19	Mar
29:26	Glen Stewart		7.12.70	14	Swansea	26	Mar
	(10)						
29:28	Adrian Mussett		14.04.72	1	Thetford	30	Apr
	13 performances to 29:30 by 11 athletes						

Where better than track best

29:31	Nick Jones	10.07.74	2	Eastleigh	19 Mar
29:31	Billy Burns	13.12.69	1	Wakefield	9 Apr
29:31	Matthew Vaux-Harvey	30.03.76	3	Bradford	10 Sep
29:35	Allen Graffin	20.12.77	2	Dewsbury	13 Feb
29:35	Nick Francis	29.08.71	5	Swansea	26 Mar
29:35	Paul Evans	13.04.61	4	Bishop Auckland	8 Oct
29:36	Matt Smith	26.12.74	5	Bradford	10 Sep
29:38	John Nuttall	11.01.67	7	Swansea	24 Sep
29:41	Nick Comerford	23.04.66	1	Langport	27 Aug
29:42	Mark Morgan	19.08.72	2	Leeds	3 Dec
29:45	Paul Taylor	9.01.66	2	Wakefield	9 Apr
29:48	Rob Birchall	14.06.70	9	Bradford	10 Sep
29:50	Rhodri Jones	14.08.66	5	Cardiff	3 Sep
29:51	Chris Davies	19.10.76	1	Telford	17 Dec
29:52	Malcolm Campbell	3.01.71	10	Tucker GA, USA	11 Mar
29:54	Tommy Murray	18.05.61	2	Dumbarton	9 Jun
29:54	Dominic Bannister	1.04.68	11	Bradford	10 Sep
29:55	Matt O'Dowd	15.04.76	7	Bishop Auckland	8 Oct
29:58	Dave Taylor	9.01.64	12	Bradford	10 Sep

Uncertain Distance

29:13	Carl Warren	28.09.69	1	Fradley	26 Mar
29:17	Robert Gould	16.01.76	2	Fradley	26 Mar

Foreign

29:29	*Dermot Donnelly (IRE)*	*23.09.70*	*2*	*Belfast*	*16 Apr*
29:44	*Jamie Lewis (IRE)*	*8.03.69*	*6*	*Swansea*	*26 Mar*
29:44	*Craig Kirkwood (NZL)*	*8.10.74*	*2*	*Basingstoke*	*15 Oct*

10 MILES Road

48:36	Glynn Tromans	17.03.69	3	Erewash	20 Aug
48:38	Nick Comerford	23.04.66	1	Peterborough	3 Dec
48:49	Nick Jones	10.07.74	1	Leyland	9 Jul
49:02	Andy Coleman	29.09.74	4	Erewash	20 Aug
49:06	Alan Shepherd	28.04.69	1	Blyth	30 Apr
49:07	Mark Croasdale	10.01.65	5	Erewash	20 Aug
49:20	John Nuttall	11.01.67	3	Ballycotton, IRE	12 Mar
49:21	Paul Evans	13.04.61	3	Portsmouth	26 Nov
49:26	Will Levett	6.09.75	2	Woking	5 Mar
49:31	Billy Farquharson	14.04.75	6	Erewash	20 Aug
	(10)				
49:32	Matthew Vaux-Harvey	30.03.76	7	Erewash	20 Aug
49:39	Rhodri Jones	14.08.66	8	Erewash	20 Aug
49:52	Mark Steinle	22.11.74	9	Erewash	20 Aug
49:54	Simon Pride	20.07.67	5	Portsmouth	26 Nov
49:55	Martin Hula	2.01.66	6	Portsmouth	26 Nov

Downhill

48:28	Allan Adams	11.09.72	1	Motherwell	9 Apr
48:47	Tommy Murray	18.05.61	2	Motherwell	9 Apr
49:12	Billy Coyle	3.10.62	3	Motherwell	9 Apr
49:27	Alex Robertson	6.05.63	4	Motherwell	9 Apr

Foreign

47:57	*Jamie Lewis (IRE)*	*8.03.69*	*2*	*Ballycotton, IRE*	*12 Mar*

HALF MARATHON

1:02:11	Keith Cullen	13.06.72	6	Glasgow	20 Aug
1:02:28	Andy Coleman	29.09.74	2	South Shields	22 Oct
1:02:58	Paul Evans	13.04.61	8	Glasgow	20 Aug

1:03:12	Nick Jones		10.07.74	1	Lake Vyrnwy	17 Sep
	1:03:51			1	Wilmslow	26 Mar
	1:04:45			11	Glasgow	20 Aug
1:03:19	Ian Hudspith		23.09.70	3	Reading	12 Mar
1:03:49	John Nuttall		11.01.67	12	South Shields	22 Oct
1:03:54	Dominic Bannister		1.04.68	1	Leyland	12 Mar
1:04:07	Karl Keska		7.05.72	13	South Shields	22 Oct
1:04:09	Nick Wetheridge		11.10.72	1	Bristol	8 Oct
1:04:28	Matthew Vaux-Harvey		30.03.76	4	Bristol	8 Oct
(10)						
1:04:36	Alan Shepherd		28.04.69	1	Chester	21 May
1:04:40	Mark Steinle		22.11.74	1	Fleet	19 Mar
1:04:46	Guy Amos		15.06.63	17	South Shields	22 Oct
1:04:50	Steve Hope		8.02.72	2	Wilmslow	26 Mar
	16 performances to 1:05:00 by 14 athletes					
1:05:17	Duncan Mason		8.12.68	4	Wilmslow	26 Mar
1:05:25	Simon Pride		20.07.67	18	South Shields	22 Oct
1:05:30	Carl Thackery		14.10.62	4	Hastings	19 Mar
1:05:37	Barry Royden		15.12.66	5	Hastings	19 Mar
1:05:38	Ian Grime		29.09.70	6	Bristol	8 Oct
1:05:40	Nathaniel Lane		10.04.76	7	Bristol	8 Oct
(20)						
1:05:40	Carl Warren		28.09.69	4	Stroud	22 Oct
1:05:44	Rob Holladay		10.01.75	5	Wilmslow	26 Mar
1:05:50	Jimmy Newnes		9.09.67	6	Wilmslow	26 Mar
1:05:50	Tony O'Brien		14.11.70	8	Bristol	8 Oct
1:05:51	Allan Adams		11.09.72	9	Bristol	8 Oct
1:05:51	Dave Taylor		9.01.64	1	Florence, ITA	26 Nov
1:06:00	Martin Yelling		7.02.72	6	Stroud	22 Oct
1:06:04	Mark Flint		19.02.63	1	Wokingham	13 Feb
1:06:10	Spencer Duval		5.01.70	19	South Shields	22 Oct
1:06:11	Mike Proudlove		26.01.70	7	Wilmslow	26 Mar
(30)						
1:06:13	Malcolm Price		18.06.62	6	Reading	12 Mar
1:06:14	Andy Arrand		20.01.66	2	Fleet	19 Mar
1:06:15	Steve Cairns		3.11.67	20	South Shields	22 Oct
1:06:27	Rhodri Jones		14.08.66	10	Bristol	8 Oct
1:06:29	Michael Green		12.10.76	1	Leyland	2 Jan
1:06:35	Ian Fisher		15.09.70	1	York	30 Jan
1:06:35	Stephen Platts		12.03.66	8	Wilmslow	26 Mar
1:06:41	Paul Farmer		23.11.77	22	South Shields	22 Oct
1:06:41	Tony Graham		15.10.63	7	Stroud	22 Oct
1:06:43	Terry Wall		12.06.70	11	Bristol	8 Oct
(40)						
1:06:43	Paul Green		7.04.72	23	South Shields	22 Oct
1:06:46	Bashir Hussain		20.12.64	2	Helsby	23 Jan
1:06:49	Colin Moore		25.11.60	15	Glasgow	20 Aug
1:06:50	Bobby Quinn		10.12.65	1	Alloa	26 Mar
1:06:52	Daniel Robinson		13.01.75	8	Stroud	22 Oct
1:06:54	Stuart Hall		21.12.64	24	South Shields	22 Oct
1:06:54	Martin Rees	V45	28.02.53	9	Stroud	22 Oct
1:06:56	Dale Rixon		8.07.66	3	Bath	19 Mar

Foreign

1:02:34	*John Mutai (KEN)*	*26.05.66*	*2*	*South Shields*	*22 Oct*
1:03:43	*Craig Kirkwood (NZL)*	*8.10.74*	*11*	*South Shields*	*22 Oct*
1:05:39	*Paul O'Callaghan (IRE)*	*1.06.64*	*5*	*Reading*	*12 Mar*
1:06:03	*Mohammed Fatihi (MAR)*	*16.06.73*	*1*	*Uxbridge*	*19 Mar*
1:06:43	*Amin Kokai (KEN)*	*5.01.74*	*8*	*Hastings*	*19 Mar*
1:06:59	*John Ferrin (IRE)*	*20.02.67*	*3*	*Londonderry*	*30 Sep*

MARATHON

2:11:17	Jon Brown		27.02.71	4	Sydney, AUS	1 Oct
2:11:18	Mark Steinle		22.11.74	11	London	16 Apr
2:13:37	Keith Cullen		13.06.72	15	London	16 Apr
	2:16:59			19	Sydney, AUS	1 Oct
2:14:39	Dominic Bannister		1.04.68	8	Hamburg, GER	16 Apr
2:15:16	Mark Hudspith		19.01.69	18	London	16 Apr
2:15:42	Billy Burns		13.12.69	20	London	16 Apr
2:16:02	Mark Croasdale		10.01.65	22	London	16 Apr
2:18:34	Rhodri Jones		14.08.66	24	London	16 Apr
	2:19:10			19	Frankfurt, GER	29 Oct
2:18:40	Ian Hudspith		23.09.70	25	London	16 Apr
2:18:49	Simon Pride		20.07.67	1	Dublin, IRE	30 Oct
	2:21:00			33	London	16 Apr
	2:21:17			1	Elgin	3 Sep
	2:21:35			10	Houston, USA	16 Jan
	(10)					
2:18:54	Barry Royden		15.12.66	38	Rotterdam, HOL	16 Apr
2:19:29	Alan Shepherd		28.04.69	27	London	16 Apr
2:19:57	Carl Thackery		14.10.62	28	London	16 Apr
2:20:26	Ian Fisher		15.09.70	32	London	16 Apr
2:21:10	Duncan Mason		8.12.68	34	London	16 Apr
2:21:15	Jamie Reid		1.01.75	35	London	16 Apr
2:21:57	Dave Buzza		6.12.62	21	Prague, CZE	21 May
2:22:04	Carl Warren		28.09.69	37	London	16 Apr
2:22:47	Dave Taylor		9.01.64	38	London	16 Apr
2:23:35	Dale Rixon		8.07.66	39	London	16 Apr
	(20)					
2:23:53	Robert Deakin		21.10.66	1	Manchester	8 Oct
2:24:02	Dan Rathbone		9.04.69	40	London	16 Apr
2:24:06	Allan Adams		11.09.72	8	Dublin, IRE	30 Oct
2:24:31	Andy Wetherill	V40	6.12.57	1	Nottingham	24 Sep
2:24:40	Andy Arrand		20.01.66	2	Manchester	8 Oct
2:24:42	Kenny Butler		17.09.63	42	London	16 Apr
2:24:50	Dave Cavers		9.04.63	43	London	16 Apr
2:24:52	Darren Bilton		9.03.72	24	Chicago, USA	22 Oct
2:24:57	Ronnie Adams		6.06.62	3	Manchester	8 Oct
	34 performances to 2:25:00 by 29 athletes					
2:25:14	Nathan Vengdasalam		11.03.64	4	Manchester	8 Oct
	(30)					
2:25:25	Chris Cariss		1.03.75	46	London	16 Apr
2:25:32	Craig McBurney		8.09.68	47	London	16 Apr
2:25:54	Mike Scott		4.11.65	50	London	16 Apr
2:25:57	Colin Deasy			7	Busseto, ITA	13 Feb
2:26:05	Scott Cohen		6.12.64	14	Duluth, USA	17 Jun
2:26:09	Dave Robertson		11.09.61		London	16 Apr
2:26:38	Tony Duffy	V40	26.06.56	6	Manchester	8 Oct
2:26:51	Shane Snow		31.10.66		London	16 Apr
2:26:57	Toby Tanser		21.07.68	31	New York, USA	5 Nov
2:27:06	Mike Thompson		14.09.68	55	London	16 Apr
	(40)					
2:27:10	Shaun Milford		13.07.63	56	London	16 Apr
2:27:16	Richard Mason		25.09.69	57	London	16 Apr
2:27:16	Robin Nash	V40	9.02.59	58	London	16 Apr
2:27:17	Terry Field		26.11.61	59	London	16 Apr
2:27:17	Andrew Weir		22.08.67	60	London	16 Apr
2:27:19	Peter Embleton	V45	16.04.54	61	London	16 Apr
2:28:32	Mike Feighan		5.11.65	62	London	16 Apr
2:28:36	Wayne Oxborough		10.11.66	63	London	16 Apr
2:28:39	Terry Mitchell	V40	23.08.59	2	Belfast	1 May
2:28:48	John Cox		17.09.63	64	London	16 Apr

2:28:53	David Rodgers			1	Fort William	30 Apr
2:28:54	Andrew Wright		30.12.65	65	London	16 Apr
2:28:59	Jeff Pyrah		6.07.72	66	London	16 Apr
2:29:09	Bill Speake		24.01.71	67	London	16 Apr
2:29:12	Michael Coleman	U23	14.05.78	68	London	16 Apr
2:29:14	Kevin Blake		29.05.67	57	Rotterdam, HOL	16 Apr
2:29:16	James Fitzsimmons		20.04.74	70	London	16 Apr
2:29:18	Alan McCullough		9.08.63	69	London	16 Apr
2:29:28	Dave Thomson	V40	18.09.59	71	London	16 Apr
2:29:28	Robin Bentley		17.02.65	58	Rotterdam, HOL	16 Apr
	(60)					
2:29:35	Simon Bell		26.12.66	72	London	16 Apr
2:29:36	Steve Payne	V40	1.12.55	73	London	16 Apr
2:29:37	Darren Hale	V40	2.10.59	1	Leyland	2 Jan
2:29:39	Paul Harwood		19.07.71	74	London	16 Apr
2:29:42	Warren Birchall		18.01.65	7	Manchester	8 Oct
2:29:43	John McFarlane		9.06.72	75	London	16 Apr
2:29:54	Gary Bishop		3.08.63	76	London	16 Apr
2:29:55	Paul Simons		4.04.64	15	Dublin, IRE	1 Nov
2:29:58	Chris Starbuck		8.12.60	77	London	16 Apr
2:30:03	Huw Lobb		29.08.76	78	London	16 Apr
	(70)					
2:30:13	Andy Holt		23.02.64	80	London	16 Apr
2:30:21	Paul Froud		6.04.66	82	London	16 Apr
2:30:31	Bill Gristwood	V40	20.03.59	83	London	16 Apr
2:30:34	Dennis Walmsley		5.09.62	3	Belfast	1 May
2:30:55	Garry Payne	V40	31.01.57	84	London	16 Apr
2:31:05	Ian Crampton		28.01.62	85	London	16 Apr
2:31:12	Ronnie James		14.12.64	7	Benidorm, SPA	26 Nov
2:31:26	Shane Downes		9.08.66	87	London	16 Apr
2:31:53	Malcolm Campbell		3.01.71	89	London	16 Apr
2:31:56	Richard Gay	V45	26.10.50	90	London	16 Apr
	(80)					
2:31:59	Alistair Hart		25.09.71	91	London	16 Apr
2:32:00	Mark Brown			92	London	16 Apr
2:32:04	Alex Rowe	V40	10.04.57	93	London	16 Apr
2:32:05	Martin Ferguson		17.09.64	52	Boston, USA	17 Apr
2:32:09	Mark Healey			94	London	16 Apr
2:32:15	Alasdair Kean	V50	5.11.47	95	London	16 Apr
2:32:18	Colin Hutt		18.11.66	96	London	16 Apr
2:32:43	Brian Cole			97	London	16 Apr
2:32:56	Steve Moore	V50	17.12.47	98	London	16 Apr
2:33:01	Shaun Tobin		13.10.62	99	London	16 Apr
	(90)					
2:33:12	Ginge Gough	V40	10.02.56	100	London	16 Apr
2:33:15	Andrew Pead		18.02.66	102	London	16 Apr
2:33:16	Stewart MacDonald		10.12.65	8	Manchester	8 Oct
2:33:22	Ian Kelly		3.12.64	103	London	16 Apr
2:33:35	Alan Ruben	V40	9.03.57	106	London	16 Apr
2:33:48	Mark Arridge		25.09.72	107	London	16 Apr
2:33:53	Nigel Payne			110	London	16 Apr
2:33:56	John Kerr	V50	1.06.49	111	London	16 Apr
2:34:09	Richard Jordan	V40	14.07.57	112	London	16 Apr
2:34:11	Mark Oakes		19.11.60	113	London	16 Apr
	(100)					
2:34:11	Steve Brunt	V40	22.07.60		Sydney, AUS	29 Oct
2:34:13	Wayne Thomas		21.02.68	114	London	16 Apr

Foreign

2:13:20	*John Mutai (KEN)*	*26.05.66*	*2*	*Dubai, UAE*	*14 Jan*
2:15:07	*Jamie Lewis (IRE)*	*8.03.69*	*17*	*London*	*16 Apr*
2:20:16	*Paul O'Callaghan (IRE)*	*1.06.64*	*30*	*London*	*16 Apr*

100 KILOMETRES Road

7:14:57	Steve Moore	V50	17.12.47	1	Edinburgh	9	Jul
	7:20:55			38	Winschoten, HOL	9	Sep
7:21:51	Ian Anderson		23.03.71	39	Winschoten, HOL	9	Sep
7:22:50	Chris Finill	V40	31.12.58	41	Winschoten, HOL	9	Sep
	7:37:11			3	Edinburgh	9	Jul
7:27:24	Alan Reid		19.04.66	2	Edinburgh	9	Jul
7:37:36	Shane Downes		9.08.66	1	Bruhl, GER	25	Jun
7:48:24	Brian Davidson		5.06.64	5	Edinburgh	9	Jul
7:54:45	Don Ritchie	V55	6.07.44	60	Winschoten, HOL	9	Sep

24 HOURS (Road)

246.704 km	William Sichel	V45	1.10.53	1	Basel, SWZ	14	May
230.667 km	Adrian Stott	V45	5.08.54	8	Uden, HOL	22	Oct
220.371 km	Don Ritchie	V55	6.07.44	16	Uden, HOL	22	Oct
216.650 km	Walter Hill	V45	19.06.53	17	Uden, HOL	22	Oct

1500 METRES STEEPLECHASE - Under 17

4:22.7	Daniel Lewis		16.10.83	1	Enfield	10	Jun
4:24.92	Tom Bedford		12.12.83	3	Blackpool	15	Jul
4:28.19	Paul Moores		3.08.84	1	Solihull	27	May
4:28.32	Oliver Brewer		14.09.83	1	Wigan	25	Jun
4:28.84	Ian Bowles		6.01.84	3	Bedford	26	Aug
4:29.59	Mark Donoghue		27.09.83	1	Stretford	30	May
4:29.77	Graham Dobbs		27.06.84	3	Sheffield	8	Jul
4:30.14	Peter Kellie		2.01.84	4	Sheffield	8	Jul
4:30.33	William Docherty		2.04.85	4	Bedford	26	Aug
4:31.5	Tim Lawrence		31.03.84	1	Derby	4	Jun
(10)							
4:31.53	Alistair Smith		22.02.84	5	Bedford	26	Aug
4:32.0	Tom Wade		31.12.83	1r2	Stretford	4	Jun
4:34.0	Adam Watt		29.10.84	1	Aberdeen	23	Jul
	4:34.08			7	Bedford	26	Aug
4:34.52	Ryan Armstrong		11.07.85	2	Birmingham	3	Sep
4:35.0	James Nickless		27.10.84	1	Worcester	10	Jun
4:35.39	Michael Targatt		1.02.84	5	Blackpool	15	Jul
4:36.4	Robert Neal		14.09.83	1	Crawley	10	Jun
4:36.6	Alex Hayward		29.11.83	1	Basildon	10	Jun
4:36.85	Thomas Bark		18.10.83	2	Solihull	27	May
4:37.03	John Gillam		15.10.84	4	Wigan	25	Jun
4:37.60	Jamie Stephen		27.09.83	6	Blackpool	15	Jul
(20)							
4:38.0	Henry Stewart		16.12.83	2	Gateshead	21	May
4:38.1	Darren Malin		19.06.85	2	Grangemouth	10	Sep
4:39.05	Chris Ward		8.04.84	9	Sheffield	8	Jul
4:39.2	Steven Ablitt		16.11.83	1	Tipton	4	Jun
4:39.44	John Walker		4.03.85	1	Birmingham	2	Sep
4:39.57	James Henry		31.07.84	10	Sheffield	8	Jul
4:39.68	Alan Wales		7.08.85	7	Blackpool	15	Jul
4:39.7	Greg Morris		27.09.83	1	Grantham	30	Apr
4:40.3	Tom Holden		2.02.84	1	Stafford	21	May
4:40.43	Chris Jones			2	Birmingham	2	Sep
4:40.5	Chris Parr		13.11.84	2	Rotherham	30	Apr

Senior and Under 20

4:16.57	Lee Hurst		29.07.72	1	Stretford	25	Jul
4:18.65	Andy Williams		21.01.77	2	Stretford	2	May
4:18.81	Dave Lee		16.09.65	1	Watford	26	Jul
4:19.98	Daniel Yates	U20	7.06.81	3	Stretford	2	May

2000 METRES STEEPLECHASE

5:36.6	Justin Chaston		4.11.68	1	Houston, USA	8 Jun
5:45.9	Simon Bell		26.12.66	1	Watford	2 Aug
5:49.9	Ricky Soos	U20	28.06.83	1	Derby	16 Jul
5:50.6	Stephen Murphy	U20	6.01.83	2	Watford	2 Aug
5:51.01	Spencer Duval		5.01.70	1	Stretford	11 Jul
5:52.90	Richard Williams	U20	22.10.81	1	Lewes	20 Jun
5:52.94	Michael Noyce		31.10.77	1	Aldershot	28 Jun
5:53.1	Adam Bowden	U20	5.08.82	1	Watford	10 Jun
5:53.32	Kevin Sheppard	U23	21.01.79	2	Aldershot	28 Jun
5:53.5	Andrew Mitchell	U23	30.07.80	3	Watford	2 Aug
	(10)					
5:54.08	Jermaine Mays	U20	23.12.82	2	Lewes	20 Jun
5:54.4	Mark Griffith	U20	25.11.81	4	Watford	2 Aug
5:55.72	Mohammed Farah	U20	23.03.83	1	Watford	27 May
5:56.0	Andrew Hennessy		24.08.77	5	Watford	2 Aug
5:57.10	Tim Watson		28.06.73	3	Lewes	20 Jun

Additional Under 20 (1 - 7 above)

5:59.1	Chris Thompson		17.04.81	1	Guildford	18 Jun
5:59.97	Andrew Lemoncello		12.10.82	1	Grangemouth	25 Jun
6:00.89	Bruce Raeside		2.12.81	2	Grangemouth	25 Jun
	(10)					
6:01.16	John Rice		29.08.81	1	Watford	2 Jul
6:02.22	Daniel Yates		7.06.81	2	Watford	2 Jul
6:03.2	Grant Ritchie		25.12.81	1	Grangemouth	13 May
6:03.87	Andrew Thomas		29.01.81	5	Watford	27 May
6:06.5	Dan Moore		8.11.81	1	London (He)	7 May
6:07.08	Andrew Lingard		12.09.81	3	Watford	2 Jul
6:07.7	Stewart Payne		15.03.82	1	Wakefield	16 Jul
6:12.0	James Bailey		1.10.82	1	Dumfries	13 Aug
6:12.4	James Williams		17.07.82	2	Wrexham	18 Jul
6:13.29	Aaron Frazer	U17	10.05.84	3	Birmingham	10 Sep
	(20)					
6:13.34	David Ragan		26.03.83	3	London (He)	20 Aug
6:14.5	Robert Smith		3.12.82	1	Ilford	13 Aug
6:14.71	Mark Harris		2.06.82	4	London (He)	20 Aug
6:14.84	Chris Norris		8.10.82	4	Birmingham	10 Sep

3000 METRES STEEPLECHASE

8:25.37	Chris Stephenson		22.07.74	1	Solihull	19 Aug
	8:28.21			1	Birmingham	13 Aug
	8:29.33			1	Manchester	14 Jun
	8:46.66			10h1	Sydney, AUS	27 Sep
	8:47.71			1h2	Birmingham	11 Aug
8:26.07	Justin Chaston		4.11.68	2	Solihull	19 Aug
	8:31.01			7h3	Sydney, AUS	27 Sep
	8:32.21			2	Birmingham	13 Aug
	8:33.93			2	Palo Alto, USA	5 May
	8:36.27			5	Walnut, USA	14 Apr
	8:39.83			12	Portland, USA	25 Jun
	8:41.97			1h1	Birmingham	11 Aug
	8:45.68			1	London (He)	6 Aug
8:33.61	Stuart Stokes		15.12.76	3	Manchester	14 Jun
	8:41.45			10	Zagreb, CRO	3 Jul
	8:44.25			4h1	Birmingham	11 Aug
	8:53.90			7	Gateshead	16 Jul
8:37.63	Charlie Low		9.10.74	4	Solihull	19 Aug
	8:41.43			4	Birmingham	13 Aug
	8:50.44			4h2	Birmingham	11 Aug
	8:53.65			3	Watford	22 Jul

8:39.72	Craig Wheeler		14.06.76	3	Birmingham	13 Aug
	8:51.15			4	Sydney, AUS	27 Feb
8:42.04	Dave Heath		22.05.65	4	Manchester	14 Jun
	8:42.98			2	London (BP)	25 Jun
	8:52.92			2	Watford	22 Jul
8:42.79	Iain Murdoch	U23	10.07.80	2h1	Birmingham	11 Aug
	8:47.64			4	Loughborough	21 May
	8:51.99			9	Birmingham	13 Aug
8:43.95	Andy Morgan-Lee		1.03.69	3h1	Birmingham	11 Aug
	8:47.65			6	Solihull	19 Aug
	8:53.84			10	Birmingham	13 Aug
8:44.03	Donald Naylor		5.09.71	5	Manchester	14 Jun
	8:51.02			6h2	Birmingham	11 Aug
	8:51.23			8	Birmingham	13 Aug
	8:54.5			1	Rugby	23 Jul
8:44.18	Alastair O'Connor		22.06.71	5	Solihull	19 Aug
	8:49.03			7	Birmingham	13 Aug
	8:50.97			5h2	Birmingham	11 Aug
	8:53.62			7	Manchester	14 Jun
	8:54.40			6	Loughborough	21 May
	(10)					
8:44.68	Ben Whitby		6.01.77	5	Birmingham	13 Aug
	8:49.27			3h2	Birmingham	11 Aug
8:45.06	Dave Mitchinson	U23	4.09.78	6	Birmingham	13 Aug
	8:46.05			6	Manchester	14 Jun
	8:48.06			2h2	Birmingham	11 Aug
	8:48.93			2	Liverpool	22 Jul
	8:54.47			7	Loughborough	21 May
8:45.27	Andy Coleman		29.09.74	5h1	Birmingham	11 Aug
8:53.23	Matt Smith		26.12.74	5	Palo Alto, USA	12 May
	50 performances to 8:55.00 by 14 athletes					
8:55.50	Lee Hurst		29.07.72	1	Eton	6 May
8:59.63	Simon Bell		26.12.66	7h1	Birmingham	11 Aug
9:00.53	Matthew Plano		8.10.76	3	Stoke-on-Trent	30 Apr
9:00.81	Delroy Simon	U23	27.11.78	8h1	Birmingham	11 Aug
9:01.23	Andrew Hennessy		24.08.77	8h2	Birmingham	11 Aug
9:01.85	Martin Yelling		7.02.72	9h1	Birmingham	11 Aug
	(20)					
9:03.29	Steve Cairns		3.11.67	2	London (He)	8 Jul
9:04.06	Colin Palmer		27.07.67	10h1	Birmingham	11 Aug
9:04.43	Adam Bowden	U20	5.08.82	2	Grosseto, ITA	7 Oct
9:04.77	Andrew Franklin	U23	13.09.80	7	Watford	22 Jul
9:05.7	Steve Smith		23.10.74	2	Sheffield (W)	24 Jun
9:06.49	Gary Blackman	U23	24.09.80	1	Derby	3 Sep
9:08.38	Mark Warmby	U23	12.12.78	3	Eton	6 May
9:08.83	Tim Watson		28.06.73	1	Aldershot	5 Jul
9:09.0	Dave Lee		16.09.65	1	Enfield	24 Jun
9:09.17	Paul Farmer		23.11.77	1	Brighton	17 Jun
	(30)					
9:10.5	Andrew Mitchell	U23	30.07.80	1	Peterborough	8 Jul
9:12.73	Darren Barton		11.10.69	1	Gateshead	14 May
9:13.02	Nick Talbot		14.12.77	6	Stoke-on-Trent	30 Apr
9:13.54	Chris Sampson		30.09.75	11h2	Birmingham	11 Aug
9:13.69	Kevin Nash		6.02.77	2	Bedford	28 May
9:14.01	Andy Beevers		3.05.73	12h2	Birmingham	11 Aug
9:14.11	Simon Wurr		7.01.77	13h2	Birmingham	11 Aug
9:14.25	Paul Northrop		15.01.70	14h2	Birmingham	11 Aug
9:14.3	Andy Fooks		26.04.75	2	Wigan	24 Jun
9:14.58	Justin Reid		26.09.69	4	Dublin (S), IRE	19 Aug
	(40)					
9:14.8	Jeremy Bradley		5.02.77	3	Peterborough	8 Jul

9:15.0	Keith Hood		13.09.72	2	Glasgow (S)	10 Sep
9:15.72	Richard Williams	U20	22.10.81	3	Bath	16 Sep
9:17.24	Andy Williams		21.01.77	4	Eton	6 May
9:17.77	Daniel Yates	U20	7.06.81	3	Bedford	26 Aug
9:17.82	Wayne Dashper		19.10.74	2	Aldershot	5 Jul
9:19.39	Tony Forrest		22.12.76	5	Bedford	28 May
9:19.64	Jason Humm		11.01.71	5	London (He)	6 Aug
9:20.3	Mike Jubb		20.06.70	1	Cleckheaton	3 Jun
9:20.89	Rod Leach		29.05.72	15h2	Birmingham	11 Aug
(50)						
9:21.91	Darius Burrows		8.08.75	3	Bedford	19 Aug
9:22.94	Stephen Murphy	U20	6.01.83	4	Bedford	26 Aug
9:23.39	Andrew Lemoncello	U20	12.10.82	5	Bedford	26 Aug
9:24.0	Kevin Sheppard	U23	21.01.79	1	Aldershot	21 Jun
9:24.1	Mike Hutchinson		5.10.65	6	Enfield	24 Jun
9:25.09	Pat Miller		21.02.67	4	Eton	6 May
9:26.1	Carl Warren		28.09.69	2	Cudworth	22 Jul
9:26.6	Frank McGowan		23.08.70	1	Grangemouth	30 Apr
9:27.03	Andrew Thomas	U20	29.01.81	6	Bedford	26 Aug
9:27.2	Grant Ritchie	U20	25.12.81	2	Glasgow	29 Jul
(60)						
9:27.6	John Brown		2.02.69	1	Cudworth	1 Jul
9:27.9	Francis Malone-Lee	U23	3.03.80	2	Oxford	21 May
9:27.9	Kevin Usher		3.11.65	2	Luton	3 Jun
9:28.6	Jermaine Mays	U20	23.12.82	2	Luton	22 Jul
9:29.11	James Williams	U20	17.07.82	7	Bedford	26 Aug
9:29.14	Andrew Lingard	U20	12.09.81	8	Bedford	26 Aug
9:29.2	Stephen Bazell		1.02.74	4	Jarrow	5 Aug
9:29.4	Chris Smale		10.10.63	2	Luton	9 Sep
9:29.70	Anno Drent		15.08.71	7	Eton	6 May
9:29.7	Kevin Murphy		6.04.74	2	Eton	23 Jul
(70)						
9:29.9	Richard Harris		16.08.71	2	Darlington	9 Jul

Additional Under 20 (1 - 10 above)

9:30.5	Mark Griffith	25.11.81	6	Enfield	23 Jul
9:30.7	John Rice	29.08.81	2	Blackpool	20 May
9:31.2	James Bailey	1.10.82	2	Cudworth	28 Aug
9:35.95	David Ragan	26.03.83	1	Derby	3 Sep
9:38.6	Bruce Raeside	2.12.81	3	Derby	9 Jul
9:42.6	John Halligan	4.05.83	2	Cleckheaton	10 Sep
9:56.4	Abdi Ali	26.12.82	1	Kingston	11 Jun
9:56.9	Mark Harris	2.06.82	2	London (TB)	5 Aug
9:58.2	Chris Hearn	26.06.82	3	Welwyn	22 Jul

Foreign

9:12.48	*Rudi Van Grot (HOL)*	*29.11.74*	*5*	*Stoke-on-Trent*	*30 Apr*

60 METRES HURDLES - Indoor

7.53	Tony Jarrett	13.08.68	2	Ghent, BEL	26 Feb
	7.58		1	Glasgow	5 Mar
	7.61		4s1	Ghent, BEL	26 Feb
	7.62		3r2	Budapest, HUN	4 Feb
	7.62		5	Ghent, BEL	11 Feb
	7.63		3h2	Ghent, BEL	11 Feb
	7.65		1	Birmingham	30 Jan
	7.68		4h4	Ghent, BEL	25 Feb
	7.80		1h1	Birmingham	30 Jan

7.59	Colin Jackson		18.02.67	1h1	Chemnitz, GER	18 Feb
	7.59			2	Chemnitz, GER	18 Feb
	7.60			4	Birmingham	20 Feb
	7.62			2	Glasgow	5 Mar
7.68	Damien Greaves		19.09.77	5s2	Ghent, BEL	26 Feb
	7.71			6	Ghent, BEL	11 Feb
	7.72			1	Birmingham	8 Jan
	7.76			2	Birmingham	30 Jan
	7.76			3	Stockholm, SWE	17 Feb
	7.77			1	Glasgow	23 Jan
	7.77			h	Halle, GER	26 Jan
	7.77			2h2	Ghent, BEL	25 Feb
	7.79			4h2	Ghent, BEL	11 Feb
	7.80			5	Halle, GER	26 Jan
	7.80			1h3	Birmingham	30 Jan
	24 performances to 7.80 by 3 athletes					
7.87	Martin Nicholson		9.12.70	2h3	Birmingham	30 Jan
7.93	Mensah Elliott		29.08.76	4	Birmingham	30 Jan
7.94	Liam Collins	U23	23.10.78	2h1	Birmingham	30 Jan
7.95	Chris Baillie	U20	21.04.81	1	Birmingham	5 Feb
7.96	Dominic Bradley		22.12.76	1	Birmingham	15 Jan
8.03	Duncan Malins	U23	12.06.78	1	Birmingham	17 Feb
8.05	Mike Robbins		14.03.76	2h1	Houston, USA	18 Feb
(10)						
8.06	Nathan Palmer	U20	16.06.82	2	Cardiff	26 Feb
8.09	Mohammed Sillah-Freckleton	U23	11.09.80	1	Bedford	22 Jan
8.09	Neil Owen		18.10.73	2h2	Birmingham	30 Jan
8.10	Jamie Quarry		15.11.72	4h1	Birmingham	30 Jan
8.10	Allan Scott	U20	27.12.82	2h2	Birmingham	5 Feb
8.12	Robert Newton	U20	10.05.81	2	Birmingham	5 Feb
8.16	Nick Cooper		4.02.77	4h3	Birmingham	30 Jan
8.18	Dominic Girdler	U20	6.03.82	4h2	Birmingham	30 Jan
8.20	Martyn Hendry		10.04.75	2h2	Glasgow	23 Jan
8.21	Tony Gill		19.09.77	2	Sheffield	23 Jan
(20)						
8.27	Andy Turner	U23	19.09.80	4h2	Birmingham	15 Jan
8.33	Dwayne Stoddart	U23	29.12.80	6h1	Birmingham	15 Jan
8.36	Luke Gittens	U20	4.01.81	2	Cardiff	19 Feb
8.37	Richard Hunter		12.01.71	1H	Birmingham	23 Jan
8.37	Ian Cawley	U23	21.11.78	7h1	Birmingham	30 Jan
8.47	Simon Hunt	U20	22.07.81	2h2	Glasgow	12 Mar

Hand Timing

8.3	Dwayne Stoddart	U23	(8.33i)	1r2	London (CP)	5 Feb
8.4	Paul Crossley	U23	30.03.79	4	Glasgow	12 Mar
8.4	Fyn Corcoran	U23	17.03.78	6	Glasgow	12 Mar

Foreign

8.4 i	*Pascal Renaud (FRA)*		*20.04.70*	*1h2*	*London (Ha)*	*9 Jan*
8.44 i	*Trevor McGlynn (IRE)*	*U23*	*6.06.78*	*5*	*Cardiff*	*26 Feb*

60 METRES HURDLES - Men Under 20 (3'3") Indoors

7.92	Chris Baillie	21.04.81	1	Glasgow	20 Feb
7.95	Allan Scott	27.12.82	1	Glasgow	13 Feb
8.06	Dominic Girdler	6.03.82	1	Birmingham	13 Feb

60 METRES HURDLES - Men Under 17 (3'0") Indoors

8.10	Edward Dunford	15.09.84	1	Birmingham	5 Feb
8.32	Matthew Roberts	8.07.84	2	Birmingham	5 Feb
8.42	Peter Middleton	27.01.84	3	Birmingham	5 Feb

75 METRES HURDLES - Under 13

11.98 w	Chris Douglas	2.12.87	P	Grangemouth	3 Sep
	12.71		1	Grangemouth	13 May
12.0	Daniel Davis		1	London (BP)	19 Aug
12.7	Stuart Todd	4.09.87	1	Ayr	4 Jun
12.8	Guy Stroud	9.08.88	1	Carn Brea	6 Aug
12.8	Grant Jeffrey		1	Glasgow (S)	20 Aug
12.87 w	Ross Finlayson	26.09.87	P	Grangemouth	22 Sep
	12.9		1h1	Dunfermline	3 Sep
12.9	Wayne Hunt	25.09.87	1	Salisbury	10 Sep

80 METRES HURDLES - Under 13

12.7	Daniel Davis		1	London (TB)	17 Sep
13.0	Vito Tomasi	17.01.88	1A1	Kingston	30 Jul
13.2	Aundre Goddard	21.04.88	1B1	Kingston	30 Jul
13.4	Wayne Hunt	25.09.87	1	Yate	20 Aug
13.4	Oliver McNeillis	24.11.87	P	Exeter	24 Sep
13.5	Jason Briggs	8.10.87	2	Kingston	30 Jul
13.55	Andrew Hill	3.12.87	1	Tamworth	28 Aug
13.6	Calvin Selby	9.09.87	1	Ilford	6 Aug
13.8	Marc Soame	16.10.87	1	Watford	10 Sep

80 METRES HURDLES - Under 15

11.1		Sean Ashton	20.09.85	1	Leicester	10 Jun
		11.16 w 2.3		1	Sheffield	8 Jul
		11.52 1.4		1h1	Sheffield	7 Jul
11.15	2.0	Matthew Hansford	20.02.86	1P1	Birmingham	16 Sep
11.21	0.2	Richard Alexis-Smith	13.02.87	1	Sheffield	30 Jul
11.22	0.2	Fola Orlonishe	14.07.86	2	Sheffield	30 Jul
11.38	2.0	Nathaniel Simpson	15.09.85	2P1	Birmingham	16 Sep
11.43	-0.5	Chris Musa	5.12.86	2	London (He)	20 Aug
11.49 w	2.3	Edward Walsh	21.10.85	3	Sheffield	8 Jul
		11.72 -0.4		2h2	Sheffield	7 Jul
11.66	-0.5	Andrae Davis	27.09.85	3	London (He)	20 Aug
11.71	0.2	Jordan Fleary	1.12.85	3	Sheffield	30 Jul
11.75	0.2	Martin Pang	13.03.86	4	Sheffield	30 Jul
	(10)					
11.78 w	3.2	Andrew Johnson	13.05.86	1	Birmingham	2 Sep
		12.1		1	Crawley	23 Jul
11.80 w	3.8	Louis Moore	8.09.85	1P2	Birmingham	16 Sep
		11.95 -2.5		1P	Stoke-on-Trent	18 Jun
11.82		Phillip Brown	10.11.85	1	Grangemouth	5 Aug
11.87 w	3.8	Kevin Sempers	24.11.85	2P2	Birmingham	16 Sep
		11.89 0.2		6	Sheffield	30 Jul
11.89 w	2.3	Matthew Springett	12.01.86	6	Sheffield	8 Jul
		12.03 -1.0		2h3	Sheffield	7 Jul
11.9		Martin Wright		1	Stoke-on-Trent	23 Jul
11.9 w		Ian Byrne	12.05.86	3	Exeter	17 Jun
		12.04 0.2		7	Sheffield	30 Jul
11.91 w?		Barry O'Brien	21.04.86	2	Grangemouth	5 Aug
		12.04 0.2		7	Sheffield	30 Jul
11.93 w	3.2	James Dunford	14.01.86	2	Birmingham	2 Sep
		12.1 -0.7		1	Leamington	13 May
11.97 w	2.3	Jonathan Grimwade	15.04.86	8	Sheffield	8 Jul
		12.0		2	Kingston	10 Jun
		12.08 -0.4		4h2	Sheffield	7 Jul
	(20)					
12.00 w	2.3	William Fleckney	19.10.85	4	Watford	28 May
12.00 w	3.2	Ben Carne	16.06.86	3	Birmingham	2 Sep
12.00 w	2.5	Michael Newton	3.04.86	1	Birmingham	3 Sep

12.0		Patrick Halcrow		9.01.86	1P	Corby	25	Jun
12.0		Michael Cox		15.01.86		Basildon	23	Jul
12.0		C. Holden			1	Leeds	23	Jul
12.04	1.2	Adam Booth		22.10.85	1P3	Birmingham	16	Sep
12.06		Ben Boyles		19.02.86	1	Bedford	15	Jun
12.07		Euron Roberts		18.11.85	1	Carmarthen	1	Jul
12.09 w	2.5	Ryan McNamara		17.06.86	3	Birmingham	3	Sep
	(30)							
12.1		Daniel Cooper		4.09.85	3	Kingston	10	Jun
12.1		Craig Hale		18.12.85	1	Barking	10	Sep

100 METRES HURDLES - Under 17 (3'0")

13.18	1.5	Edward Dunford		15.09.84	2	Sheffield	30	Jul
13.29 w	2.5	Peter Middleton		27.01.84	1	Sheffield	7	Jul
		13.49 1.0			1h1	Sheffield	7	Jul
13.38	1.5	Kenneth Frempong		17.07.84	3	Sheffield	30	Jul
13.59	1.0	Greg Smith		29.01.84	1h3	Sheffield	30	Jul
13.66	0.6	Anthony Bibby		12.03.85	1	Birmingham	3	Sep
13.78	1.5	Robin Smith		11.09.83	5	Sheffield	30	Jul
13.79	0.9	Ross Tressider		8.11.83	2	Watford	27	May
13.80	1.5	Andrew Hopkinson		20.09.83	6	Sheffield	30	Jul
13.90	1.0	Adam Crickmore		26.01.84	2h3	Birmingham	30	Jul
13.9		Richard Myers		21.12.83	1	Chester-le-Street	2	Jul
		14.01 w 2.5			6	Sheffield	8	Jul
	(10)							
13.94	-0.7	Stephen Alexander		6.10.84	1	Cudworth	19	Aug
14.10 w	2.2	Darren Ho		20.03.85	4O1	Sheffield	30	Jul
14.1		Ramon Durrani		9.10.83	1r2	London (WP)	4	Jun
14.1		Daniel Leonard		3.01.84	2O	Rugby	25	Jun
14.1 w		Mark Orpe		11.10.84	3	Derby	17	Jun
14.1 w?		Alec Porter		21.12.84				
		14.14			4	Blackpool	15	Jul
14.11	1.0	Matthew Thompson		29.12.84	2	Grangemouth	25	Jun
14.17	-0.7	Ben Manchester		1.04.85	3	Cudworth	19	Aug
14.17	1.1	Suote Nyamanyo		3.10.84	1r2	Birmingham	3	Sep
14.18	-0.4	David Hughes		31.05.84	4O1	Birmingham	17	Sep
	(20)							
14.2		Matthew Walden		30.11.83	1m2	Barnsley	30	Apr
14.2		James Francis-Famous		14.12.83	1	Woodford	4	Jun
14.2		Matthew McGowan		2.09.83	1r2	Bath	4	Jun
14.2		James Gahagon		14.01.84	1	Basildon	10	Jun

Unconfirmed

14.05		Ben Manchester		1.04.85	h	Cudworth	19	Aug

110 METRES HURDLES - Under 20 (3'3")

13.96 w	3.8	Dominic Girdler		6.03.82	1	Sheffield	8	Jul
		14.20 -2.3			1	Edinburgh	13	Aug
14.12	-0.3	Robert Newton		10.05.81	1	Birmingham	10	Sep
14.20	-1.6	Allan Scott		27.12.82	1	Grangemouth	17	Jun
14.46 w	3.8	John Holtby		27.03.82	2	Sheffield	8	Jul
		14.88 0.5			3	Watford	2	Jul
14.65	1.5	Matthew Colton		5.11.82	1	Watford	28	May
14.66	1.5	Alex Zulewski		6.06.82	2	Watford	28	May
14.80		Nathan Palmer		16.06.82	1	Carmarthen	1	Jul
15.01	-0.3	Isaac McCalla		28.03.82	2	Birmingham	10	Sep
15.07	-0.3	Edward Dunford	U17	15.09.84	3	Birmingham	10	Sep
15.08		Paul Tohill		9.10.82	1	Antrim	10	Jun
	(10)							
15.09	0.8	Tristan Anthony		16.12.82	h	London (He)	20	Aug

15.15 w	3.8	Richard Baderin	25.03.83	5	Sheffield	8 Jul
		15.31 0.5		5	Watford	2 Jul
15.16	1.5	Steve Green	15.01.83	4	Watford	28 May
15.16	1.5	Dominic Saban	27.02.82	3	Watford	28 May
15.22	-0.6	Liam Lucas	15.12.82	2	London (He)	20 Aug
15.36		Luke Gittens	4.01.81	2	Carmarthen	1 Jul
15.43	-0.6	Russell Billingham	13.10.81	3	London (He)	20 Aug
15.46		Chris Hunter	3.03.81	1	Gateshead	13 May

Hand Timing

13.9		Chris Baillie	21.04.81	1	Wakefield	16 Jul
14.1		Robert Newton	(14.12)	2	Wakefield	16 Jul
14.1	1.2	Nathan Palmer	(14.80)	1	Wrexham	18 Jul
14.8	1.2	Luke Gittens	(15.36)	3	Wrexham	18 Jul
14.9		Simon Bannister	16.04.81	1	Ware	22 Jul
15.0	1.2	Paul Tohill	(15.08)	4	Wrexham	18 Jul
15.0 w	3.0	Richard Baderin	(15.31)	1	Blackpool	10 Jun
		15.2		1	Cleckheaton	27 May
15.1		Nick Edwards	22.03.81	1	Worcester	16 Jul
15.2		Louis Evling-Jones	20.06.83	1r2	Ware	16 Jul
15.4	1.2	Guy Dunlop	28.07.83	5	Wrexham	18 Jul
15.4		James Peet	2.12.82	1	Banbury	10 Sep
15.4		Russell Billingham	(15.43)	2	Banbury	10 Sep
15.5		Lolimar Pagkatipunan	17.11.82	2	London (Ha)	18 Jun

110 METRES HURDLES

13.10	1.4	Colin Jackson	18.02.67	1	Leverkusen, GER	20 Aug
		13.20 -0.1		1	Chemnitz, GER	22 Jul
		13.27 0.6		1h1	Chemnitz, GER	22 Jul
		13.27 0.3		1q4	Sydney, AUS	24 Sep
		13.28 0.1		1h2	Leverkusen, GER	20 Aug
		13.28 0.6		5	Sydney, AUS	25 Sep
		13.29 2.0		3	Gateshead	28 Aug
		13.33 0.2		3	Monaco, MON	18 Aug
		13.34 0.1		3s2	Sydney, AUS	25 Sep
		13.38 -0.8		1h6	Sydney, AUS	24 Sep
		13.45 -1.0		1	Dortmund, GER	8 Jul
		13.54 -2.3		1	Birmingham	13 Aug
		13.65 -3.2		1	Glasgow (S)	2 Jul
		13.76 -2.0		1h3	Birmingham	13 Aug
13.53	2.0	Tony Jarrett	13.08.68	6	Gateshead	26 Aug
		13.61 0.2		4	London (CP)	5 Aug
		13.64 0.5		2	Karlstad, SWE	23 Aug
		13.73 0.2		8	Monaco, MON	18 Aug
		13.78 -2.3		2	Birmingham	13 Aug
		13.79 -0.6		1h2	Birmingham	13 Aug
		13.81 1.7		2h2	Budapest, HUN	22 Jul
13.62	1.3	Damien Greaves	19.09.77	1	Loughborough	30 Jul
		13.75 1.8		1	Bedford	4 Jun
		13.77 -0.9		1h1	Birmingham	13 Aug
		13.80 1.9		2r2	Dormagen, GER	24 Jun
		13.80 1.4		4	Gateshead	16 Jul
		13.85 -2.3		3	Birmingham	13 Aug
		13.89 1.8		1	Loughborough	21 May
		13.89 0.6		3h1	Budapest, HUN	22 Jul
		13.91 2.0		8	Gateshead	28 Aug
		13.95		3	Rhede, GER	23 Jun
		13.97 1.1		1h1	Loughborough	30 Jul
		13.98 -0.4		2r1	Dormagen, GER	24 Jun

13.82	1.3	Mensah Elliott		29.08.76	2	Loughborough	30 Jul
		13.91 -0.9			2h1	Birmingham	13 Aug
		13.92 1.0			1h2	Loughborough	30 Jul
13.84	1.4	Chris Baillie	U20	21.04.81	1	Bedford	27 Aug
		13.86 0.3			4s2	Santiago, CHI	19 Oct
		13.95 1.8			2h2	Santiago, CHI	18 Oct
13.93	0.9	Paul Gray		25.05.69	1	Dublin (S), IRE	29 Jul
13.93	1.5	Neil Owen		18.10.73	1	London (He)	6 Aug
13.95	1.4	Robert Newton	U20	10.05.81	2	Bedford	27 Aug
		42 performances to 14.00 by 8 athletes					
14.05	0.4	Mike Robbins		14.03.76	2	Natchitoches, USA	16 May
14.05	1.8	Liam Collins	U23	23.10.78	4	Bedford	4 Jun
	(10)						
14.08	1.4	Matt Douglas		26.11.76	1rB	London (He)	6 Aug
14.10	0.4	Duncan Malins	U23	12.06.78	1	Bedford	1 Jul
14.18	1.8	Martin Nicholson		9.12.70	4	Loughborough	21 May
14.29	1.0	Dominic Bradley		22.12.76	2h2	Loughborough	30 Jul
14.30	1.4	Dominic Girdler	U20	6.03.82	3	Bedford	27 Aug
14.36	1.8	Allan Scott	U20	27.12.82	5	Bedford	4 Jun
14.38	0.6	Jamie Quarry		15.11.72	4D1	Arles, FRA	4 Jun
14.40	-0.9	Tony Gill		19.09.77	4h1	Birmingham	13 Aug
14.45	1.4	Nathan Palmer	U20	16.06.82	4	Bedford	27 Aug
14.53	-1.4	Dean Maccy		12.12.77	8D4	Sydney, AUS	28 Sep
	(20)						
14.55	0.9	Noel Levy		22.06.75	3	Dublin (S), IRE	29 Jul
14.59	0.4	Dwayne Stoddart	U23	29.12.80	3	Bedford	1 Jul
14.67	1.8	Greg Dunson		2.12.63	4	Solihull	29 Jul
14.72	-0.9	Perry Batchelor		11.12.75	5h1	Birmingham	13 Aug
14.77	0.4	Andy Turner	U23	19.09.80	5	Bedford	1 Jul
14.78	0.4	Ian Cawley	U23	21.11.78	6	Bedford	1 Jul
14.79	0.9	Paul Crossley	U23	30.03.79	1	Bedford	20 Aug
14.86	1.3	Lee Tindal	U23	19.02.80	4	Loughborough	30 Jul
14.88	1.4	Luke Gittens	U20	4.01.81	7	Bedford	27 Aug
14.89	1.5	Paul Hibbert		31.03.65	5	London (He)	6 Aug
	(30)						
15.03	1.5	John Holtby	U20	27.03.82	3D	Val de Reuil, FRA	13 Aug
15.09		Richard Hunter		12.01.71	1	Gateshead	13 May
15.11		Oke Odudu		24.10.76	3	Aldershot	16 Jul
15.12	0.0	Duncan Mathieson		8.03.69	2D3	Arles, FRA	4 Jun
15.18	-2.1	Simon Hunt	U20	22.07.81	2h1	Stoke-on-Trent	30 Apr
15.19	-1.4	Tony Brannen		16.09.68	3h3	Stoke-on-Trent	30 Apr
15.21	-2.1	Bill Wynn		15.02.73	3D1	Stoke-on-Trent	30 Jul
15.22		John Monds	U23	24.03.80	2r2	Loughborough	30 Jul
15.25	-1.5	Kirk Harries		7.08.74	6	Eton	6 May
15.25	-1.2	Barry Thomas		28.04.72	3D1	Logrono, SPA	20 Aug
	(40)						
15.26	2.0	Mark Sweeney		26.02.77	1D5	Waterford, IRE	3 Sep
15.28	1.8	Paul Gilding		2.10.75	7	Brighton	18 Jun
15.31	1.7	Edward Dunford	U17	15.09.84	5h1	Bedford	27 Aug
15.33	0.4	Chris Low	U23	24.04.80	3	Glasgow	29 Jul
15.36	-1.2	Matthew Butler	U23	4.04.80	3h2	Stoke-on-Trent	30 Apr
15.36	0.1	Chris Hough	U20	5.12.81	2	Cudworth	13 May
15.40		Gary Myles		3.02.63	3r2	Loughborough	30 Jul
15.40	0.5	Paul Jones	U23	11.04.78	4D	Val de Reuil, FRA	13 Aug
15.40	0.9	Clarence Allen		1.04.64	3	Bedford	20 Aug
15.47	0.0	Fyn Corcoran	U23	17.03.78	5D3	Arles, FRA	4 Jun
	(50)						
15.48	-2.5	Paul Tohill	U20	9.10.82	4	Antrim	31 Jul
15.49	0.2	Anthony Sawyer	U23	29.04.80	2D	Gateshead	23 Jul
15.51	-0.6	Robert Lewis	U23	2.09.78	4	Getafe, SPA	9 Sep
15.56	-2.1	Richard Sear	U23	21.08.79	4h1	Stoke-on-Trent	30 Apr

15.62	2.0	Alex Kruger		18.11.63	3D1	Stoke-on-Trent	30	Jul
15.63		Martin Taylor	U20	31.01.82	3D4	Hexham	21	May
15.65		Chin Nwokoro		13.03.77	1	Bellville, RSA	18	Mar
15.69		Sean Saxon		11.12.71	1	Tamworth	28	Aug

Wind Assisted

13.64	3.8	Greaves		(13.62)	1	Bedford	19	Aug
		13.66 3.6			1r2	Bedford	11	Jun
13.69	3.8	Mensah Elliott		(13.82)	2	Bedford	19	Aug
		13.99 3.0			1h1	Brighton	18	Jun
13.85	2.1	Baillie	U20	(13.84)	1r3	Bedford	11	Jun
13.87	3.4	Neil Owen		(13.93)	1h2	Brighton	18	Jun
		13.89 3.8			3	Bedford	19	Aug
		13.96 5.1			1	Wigan	24	Jun
		13.97 3.6			3r2	Bedford	11	Jun
		13.99			1r1	Brighton	18	Jun
		10 performances to 14.00 by 4 athletes						
14.08	3.4	Duncan Malins	U23	(14.10)	2h2	Brighton	18	Jun
14.14	2.2	Martin Nicholson		(14.18)	1	Bedford	28	May
14.15	2.2	Dominic Bradley		(14.29)	2	Bedford	28	May
14.34	2.2	Nathan Palmer	U20	(14.45)	3	Bedford	28	May
14.51	4.9	Dwayne Stoddart	U23	(14.59)	3h1	Bedford	28	May
14.52	3.4	Noel Levy		(14.55)	3h2	Brighton	18	Jun
14.62	3.8	Greg Dunson		(14.67)	5	Bedford	19	Aug
14.66	2.4	Perry Batchelor		(14.72)	2h2	Bedford	28	May
14.86	4.9	Luke Gittens	U20	(14.88)	4h1	Bedford	28	May
14.92	3.8	Anthony Southward		31.01.71	6	Bedford	19	Aug
14.95	4.9	Richard Hunter		(15.09)	4h1	Bedford	28	May
15.17	5.1	John Monds	U23	(15.22)	7	Wigan	24	Jun
15.19	3.0	Paul Gilding		(15.28)	4h1	Brighton	18	Jun
15.19	3.1	Mark Sweeney		(15.26)	1D4	Jarrow	25	Jun
15.34	2.6	Isaac McCalla	U20	28.03.82	5h2	Bedford	27	Aug
15.43	2.8	Alexis Sharp		31.10.72	4r2	Enfield	6	Aug
15.45	3.2	Sean Saxon		(15.69)	3	Bedford	5	Aug
15.57	2.4	Nigel Taylor		12.06.69	6h2	Bedford	28	May
15.58	3.2	John McIlwham		29.02.72	4	Bedford	5	Aug
15.58	2.6	James Tattershall	U20	25.11.81	6h2	Bedford	27	Aug
15.63	2.4	Dave Savage		13.11.72	3r2	London (He)	8	Jul
15.68	3.0	Anthony Bliss		7.03.70	5h1	Brighton	18	Jun

Hand Timing

13.7	0.8	Mensah Elliott		(13.82)	2	Vittel, FRA	2	Sep
13.8	0.8	Neil Owen		(13.93)	3	Vittel, FRA	2	Sep
13.8 w	2.4	Jarrett		(13.53)	1	Enfield	6	Aug
13.9 w	2.4	Paul Gray		(13.93)	2	Enfield	6	Aug
		4 performances to 13.9 by 4 athletes including 2 wind assisted						
14.2	1.5	Dominic Bradley		(14.29)	1	Cudworth	22	Jul
14.6		Mohammed Sillah-Freckleton	U23	11.09.80	1	Crawley	23	Apr
14.6 w	2.5	Perry Batchelor		(14.72)	2	Rugby	23	Jul
14.7		Paul Gripton		9.11.76	1	Nuneaton	20	May
14.8		Mark Sweeney		(15.26)	2	Philadelphia, USA	22	Apr
14.8		Tristan Anthony	U20	16.12.82	1	Ware	3	Sep
14.8 w	2.5	Tony Brannen		(15.19)	3	Rugby	23	Jul
14.9 w	2.4	Anthony Southward		(14.92w)	4	Enfield	6	Aug
		15.1 1.1			5	Enfield	24	Jun
15.0		Dave Sweetman		27.01.71	1	Stretford	28	Jun
15.1	1.0	Lloyd Cowan		8.07.62	1rB	Enfield	24	Jun
15.1		Andrew David		9.09.69	1	Welwyn	22	Jul

15.1 w	2.1	Martyn Hendry		10.04.75	7	Peterborough	8 Jul
		15.3			1	Grangemouth	27 Aug
15.2		Bill Wynn		(15.21)	1	Brighton	3 Jun
15.2	-1.0	Andrew Lewis		9.03.68	2rB	Peterborough	8 Jul
15.2		Clarence Allen		(15.40)	2	Welwyn	22 Jul
15.3		Mike Mason		16.06.77	1	Guildford	3 Jun
15.3		Shaun Robson	U23	21.06.80	1m2	Newport	11 Jun
15.3		Martin Taylor	U20	(15.63)	1	Glasgow (S)	11 Jun
15.3		Chris Low	U23	(15.33)	1	Coatbridge	18 Jun
15.3		Mark Roberts		1.09.69	1	Eton	5 Aug
15.4		Richard Sear	U23	(15.56)	1	Abingdon	13 May
15.4		Tom Rawson		6.02.76	1	Luton	18 Jun
15.4		Gareth Evans		28.05.77	2	Cosford	21 Jun
15.4		Richard Scott		14.09.73	2	Stretford	28 Jun
15.4		Alex Zulewski	U20	6.06.82	2	Erith	5 Aug
15.4 w		Tim Tomkinson		31.10.68	1	Blandford	19 Jul
15.5	-0.7	John Heanley	U23	25.09.80	1r2	Watford	20 May
15.5 w	2.5	Nigel Taylor		(15.57w)	6	Rugby	23 Jul
		15.6 -0.8			2	Sheffield (W)	24 Jul
15.5 w	2.5	Sean Saxon		(15.69)	7	Rugby	23 Aug
15.5 w	2.4	Chris Hodson	U23	11.11.80	6	Enfield	6 Aug
15.6		Chin Nwokoro		(15.65)	2	Stellenbosch, RSA	15 Mar
15.6		Scott Exley	U23	9.02.78	1	Bournemouth	14 May
15.6		Mareac Anestic		29.01.72	1	Cleckheaton	11 Jun
15.6		Andi Ball	U20	29.11.82	1	London (TB)	17 Jun
15.6		Nigel Hayman		25.09.74	1	Basildon	24 Jun
15.6	1.5	Dave Savage		(15.63w)	4	Cudworth	22 Jul
15.6		Chris Sleeman	U23	20.03.80	1	Portsmouth	5 Aug
15.6		Matthew Colton	U20	5.11.82	1r2	Woodford	5 Aug
15.6		James Parker	U23	29.09.80	2	London (TB)	16 Aug
15.6 w	2.4	Ayo Falola		29.07.68	7	Enfield	6 Aug

Foreign

14.71 w	*3.4*	*Pascal Renaud (FRA)*		*20.04.70*	*4h2*	*Brighton*	*18 Jun*
		14.91 1.8			*5*	*Brighton*	*18 Jun*
14.8		*Cornell Collins (JAM)*	*U23*	*21.10.80*	*2*	*London (Cr)*	*27 Aug*
		15.57 0.5			*7*	*Dublin (S), IRE*	*20 Aug*
15.0		*Jerome Birot (FRA)*		*28.04.74*	*1*	*Andover*	*24 Jun*
15.17	*1.4*	*Sanusi Turay (SLE)*		*14.04.68*	*3r2*	*London (He)*	*6 Aug*
15.2		*Saulius Vysniakas (LIT)*	*U23*	*1.07.79*	*1*	*Swindon*	*22 Jul*
15.22	*0.3*	*Stephen McDonnell (IRE)*	*U23*	*24.07.80*	*3*	*Derby*	*3 Sep*
15.4 w	*2.5*	*Franck Desailly (FRA)*		*20.01.73*	*5*	*Rugby*	*23 Jul*

200 METRES HURDLES

25.2	Oke Odudu		24.10.76	1	Oxford	21 May
25.4	Gavin Hodgson	U23	1.02.78	1	Cambridge	8 May

300 METRES HURDLES

34.59	Chris Rawlinson	19.05.72	1	Loughborough	30 Jul
	35.68		1	Gold Coast (S), AUS	15 Sep
35.25	Matt Douglas	26.11.76	2	Loughborough	30 Jul
36.12	Tony Borsumato	13.12.73	2	Gold Coast (S), AUS	15 Sep
36.47	Noel Levy	22.06.75	4	Loughborough	30 Jul

400 METRES HURDLES

48.22	Chris Rawlinson	9.05.72	1	Milan, ITA	7 Jun
	48.22		2	Lausanne, SWZ	5 Jul
	48.35		2	Monaco, MON	18 Aug
	48.52		4	Rome, ITA	30 Jun
	48.68		1	Walnut, USA	16 Apr
	48.84		1	Gateshead	15 Jul
	48.95		1	Birmingham	13 Aug
	49.11		3	London (CP)	5 Aug
	49.12		1	Glasgow (S)	2 Jul
	49.25		6s2	Sydney, AUS	25 Sep
	49.62		8	Brussels, BEL	25 Aug
	49.99		5	Oslo, NOR	28 Jul
	50.53		6	Doha, QAT	5 Oct
	50.54		1h3	Birmingham	12 Aug
	51.30		1h5	Sydney, AUS	24 Sep
49.26	Matt Douglas	26.11.76	2	Rovereto, ITA	30 Aug
	49.38		1	Bedford	19 Aug
	49.53		1	Gold Coast (RB), AUS	17 Sep
	49.53		6s3	Sydney, AUS	25 Sep
	49.62		3h7	Sydney, AUS	24 Sep
	49.65		4	Glasgow (S)	2 Jul
	49.89		3	Birmingham	13 Aug
	49.98		1	Eton	6 May
	50.39		7	London (CP)	5 Aug
	50.40		1	London (He)	6 Aug
	50.46		1h2	Birmingham	12 Aug
	51.10		1	Liege, BEL	27 May
	51.24		1	Stoke-on-Trent	30 Apr
	51.32		3	Loughborough	21 May
49.68	Tony Borsumato	13.12.73	5	Glasgow (S)	2 Jul
	49.71		2	Birmingham	13 Aug
	49.84		1	Floro, NOR	8 Jun
	49.95		2r3	Budapest, HUN	22 Jul
	50.06		2	Gold Coast (RB), AUS	17 Sep
	50.17		1r1	Riga, LAT	22 Jun
	50.44		1h1	Birmingham	12 Aug
	50.73		5h6	Sydney, AUS	24 Sep
	50.81		8	London (CP)	5 Aug
	51.22		1	Bedford	29 May
	51.28		2	Loughborough	21 May
50.09	Du'aine Thorne-Ladejo	14.02.71	1rB	London (He)	6 Aug
	50.34		1	Solihull	29 Jul
	50.97		2	Vittel, FRA	2 Sep
	51.43		1	London (He)	8 Jul
50.11	Gary Jennings	21.02.72	2	Celle Ligure, ITA	27 Jun
	50.39		1	Andorra, AND	4 Jun
	50.60		2	Braga, POR	21 Jun
	51.08		5	Birmingham	13 Aug
	51.09		3	London (He)	6 Aug
	51.10		1	Loughborough	21 May
	51.22		2h2	Birmingham	12 Aug
	51.42		2	Eton	6 May
50.52	Paul Hibbert	31.03.65	1	Vittel, FRA	2 Sep
	50.83		2h3	Birmingham	12 Aug
	50.95		4	Birmingham	13 Aug
	51.07		2	London (He)	6 Aug
	51.32		1rB	Loughborough	21 May
	51.32		2	Bedford	19 Aug
	51.39		2	Bedford	29 May
	51.47		6	Dublin (S), IRE	29 Jul

51.09	Richard McDonald	U23	11.01.80	2	Tonsberg, NOR	22 Aug
	51.33			2rB	Braga, POR	21 Jun
	51.47			4	Loughborough	21 May
51.16	Matt Elias	U23	25.04.79	1r2	Riga, LAT	22 Jun
51.18	Paul Gray		25.05.69	5	Dublin (S), IRE	29 Jun
	51.26			4	Ljubljana, SLO	25 Jul
51.29	Robert Lewis	U23	2.09.78	2	Liverpool	22 Jul
	(10)					
51.49	Dave Savage		13.11.72	2	Solihull	29 Jul
51.49	James Hillier	U23	3.04.78	6	Birmingham	13 Aug
	69 performances to 51.50 by 12 athletes					
51.58	Noel Levy		22.06.75	7	Dublin (S), IRE	29 Jul
51.95	Eddie Betts		18.02.71	4h2	Birmingham	12 Aug
52.26	Remi Edu	U23	14.12.78	3	Stoke-on-Trent	30 Apr
52.39	Steve Surety	U23	18.02.80	4	Solihull	29 Jul
52.5	Jeffrey Christie	U20	24.09.82	1	Coventry	16 Jul
	52.72			1	Derby	3 Sep
52.64	Ian Neely		29.12.74	3	Eton	6 May
52.7	Lawrence Lynch		1.11.67	1	Wigan	20 May
	55.66			3h2	Bedford	29 May
52.7	Richard Scott		14.09.73	2	Wigan	20 May
	53.91			1h3	Brighton	17 Jun
	(20)					
52.71	Barry Middleton		10.03.75	5	London (He)	6 Aug
52.83	Andrew Bargh		21.08.76	7h2	Birmingham	12 Aug
53.0	Chris Sleeman	U23	20.03.80	1	Oxford	28 Jun
	53.94			3s1	Stoke-on-Trent	29 Apr
53.06	Nange Ursell	U20	1.10.81	2	Bath	16 Sep
53.07	Glenn Gray		21.04.68	2rB	London (He)	8 Jul
53.12	Tony Williams		1.05.72	7r1	Eagle Rock, USA	13 May
53.2	John McIlwham		29.02.72	2	Derby	9 Jul
	53.52			1	Cudworth	19 Aug
53.2	Stephen Murphy	U20	10.02.82	2	Edinburgh	20 Aug
	53.37			2	Vilvoorde, BEL	6 Aug
53.23	Leon McRae	U23	3.11.80	3rB	London (He)	8 Jul
53.4	Mark Nitsch	U23	3.03.78	2	Peterborough	8 Jul
	54.09			4h3	Birmingham	12 Aug
	(30)					
53.49	Bradley Yiend	U23	25.10.80	5	Solihull	29 Jul
53.67	David Brackstone	U20	13.03.82	1	Watford	2 Jul
53.7	Gavin Hodgson	U23	1.02.78	2	Oxford	28 Jun
	55.23			7	Stoke-on-Trent	30 Apr
53.79	Howard Moscrop	V40	16.12.57	1	Bedford	30 Jul
53.8	Stephen Pratt		14.07.76	1	Peterborough	28 Aug
	54.18			1r2	Enfield	6 Aug
53.81	John Bell		10.09.73	5h1	Birmingham	12 Aug
53.9	Mark Wiscombe		25.01.74	1	St. Ives	24 Jun
	54.18			5	Bedford	1 Jul
53.93	Paul Crossley	U23	30.03.79	1	Bedford	20 Aug
54.01	Richard Castillo	U20	3.12.81	2h1	Sheffield	7 Jul
54.02	Gareth Rees	U20	15.01.82	3h1	Bedford	26 Aug
	(40)					
54.11	Steve Green	U20	15.01.83	2	Watford	2 Jul
54.18	Lee Wiscombe	U23	12.07.80	5	Bedford	1 Jul
54.3	Paul Beaumont		27.03.63	1	Aldershot	21 Jun
	55.33			2	Aldershot	5 Jul
54.38	Greg Dunson		2.12.63	2	Aldershot	28 Jun
54.39	David O'Leary	U23	3.08.80	6	Bedford	1 Jul
54.4	Joel Hopkins		24.11.77	1	Enfield	13 May
54.4	Ben Caldwell	U20	3.03.82	2	Cudworth	1 Jul
	54.67			3h3	Sheffield	7 Jul

Perf	Name	Age	DOB	Pos	Venue	Date
54.4	Matt Kloiber		22.11.71	2	Enfield	20 Aug
	54.94			2	Enfield	6 Aug
54.41	Andrew Bennett	U20	30.09.82	3h1	Sheffield	7 Jul
54.52	Drew Hall	U20	31.08.81	2h2	Bedford	26 Aug
	(50)					
54.58	Alex Zulewski	U20	6.06.82	1h3	Bedford	26 Aug
54.67	Martin Thomas	U23	21.09.78	3h2	Bedford	1 Jul
54.7	David Gifford		9.03.73	1	Grimsby	14 May
	55.27			h	Grantham	18 Jun
54.74	Douglas Thom		13.04.68	4rB	London (He)	8 Jul
54.79	Richard Smith	U20	12.10.82	4h3	Sheffield	7 Jul
54.8	Derek Paisley		1.12.73	3	Cudworth	22 Jul
54.82	Dale Garland	U23	13.10.80	6	Stoke-on-Trent	30 Apr
54.9	Chris Herring	U20	3.03.81	1	Darlington	9 Jul
	56.57			1	Gateshead	14 May
54.95	Shaun Robson	U23	21.06.80	4h2	Bedford	1 Jul
55.0	Howard Frost	U20	9.12.81	1	Catford	5 Aug
	55.32			4h1	Sheffield	7 Jul
	(60)					
55.04	Austin Ferns	U20	12.01.81	6	Loughborough	21 May
55.05	Carl McMullen	U23	9.11.79	4	Aldershot	16 Jul
55.15	Livio Salvador-Aylott		18.07.73	3	Enfield	6 Aug
55.19	Simon Wilson		30.04.74	1	London (CP)	13 May
55.2	Andrew Kennard		2.01.66	2	Enfield	13 May
55.2	Michael George		4.07.72	2	Watford	20 May
	55.50			3h1	Brighton	17 Jun
55.24	Jon Goodwin		22.09.76	3	Glasgow (S)	29 Jul
55.26	Gary Stevenson	U23	12.09.79	2	Antrim	20 Jun
55.3	Paul Gripton		9.11.76	1	Redditch	14 May
55.3	Paul Armstrong	U23	20.10.79	1	Coatbridge	18 Jun
	(70)					
55.41	Sean Reidy	U20	27.01.81	4h2	Bedford	26 Aug
55.5	Gavin Stephens		12.09.77	1	Woodford	24 Jun
55.52	John Squirrell		16.12.75	2	London (CP)	13 May
55.56	Andrew Dean	U23	30.06.78	3	Stoke-on-Trent	17 Jun
55.68	Robert Gascoigne		5.10.74	4h1	Grantham	18 Jun
	May have been faster					
55.7	Matt Dewsberry	U20	9.10.81	1	Bristol	20 May
	56.14			5h3	Sheffield	7 Jul
55.7	John Heanley	U23	25.09.80	1	Eton	22 Aug
55.7	James Lee	U23	6.02.79	1	Cleckheaton	10 Sep
55.72	Daniel Armstrong	U20	28.10.81	5h1	Sheffield	7 Jul
55.77	Chris Woods	U23	27.01.80	1h1	Stoke-on-Trent	29 Apr
	(80)					
55.77	Lee Tindal	U23	19.02.80	3	Portsmouth	13 May
55.8	Stephen Pratt		6.02.71	3	Enfield	24 Jun
55.8	Ben Hooper	U20	10.09.82	2	Exeter	16 Jul
	56.93			5h2	Sheffield	7 Jul
55.8	Jon Cuff	U23	30.03.80	1	Cheltenham	26 Jul
55.82	Ian Monaghan	U20	6.11.81	2h1	Stoke-on-Trent	29 Apr
55.9	Neil Scrivener	U23	18.09.80	1	Hayes	24 Jun
55.95	Tim Lang		8.12.73	2rB	Enfield	6 Aug
56.00	Richard Gawthorpe	U20	28.01.81	4h1	Stoke-on-Trent	29 Apr
56.0	Michael Noyce		31.10.77	1	Hayes	24 Jun

Additional Under 20 (1 - 21 above)

Perf	Name	DOB	Pos	Venue	Date
56.02	Nathan Jones	31.10.82	1	Carmarthen	1 Jul
56.09	James Nasrat	10.01.83	2	Carmarthen	1 Jul
56.2	Nick Edwards	22.03.81	1	Bath	14 May
	56.73		3	Aldershot	5 Jul

56.30	Russell Billingham		13.10.81	3h2	Sheffield	7 Jul
56.3	Ian Palmer		22.11.81	2	Exeter	17 Jun
	56.62			2	London (He)	20 Aug
56.4	Scott McKinlay		11.04.83	1	Grangemouth	17 Jun
56.43	Andy Clements		28.11.82	4h2	Sheffield	7 Jul
56.65	Keith Baldwin		2.03.81	2	Grangemouth	14 May
56.77	Andrew Griffiths		26.09.81	3	Carmarthen	1 Jul
(30)						
56.89	Martin Taylor		31.01.82	3	Grangemouth	14 May
56.9	Andrew Fleet		2.12.82	2	Dumfries	13 Aug
57.0	Adam D'Arcy		25.05.82	1	Tamworth	23 Apr
57.0	Vernon Small		1.01.82	1	Enfield	13 May

Under 17

57.6	Mark Winship		29.09.83	1	Enfield	16 Jul
57.9	Tom Carey		26.02.84	1	Stevenage	3 Jun

Foreign

53.31	*Stephen McDonnell (IRE)*	*U23*	*24.07.80*	*8*	*Dublin (S), IRE*	*29 Jul*
55.0	*Cornell Collins (JAM)*	*U23*	*21.10.80*	*2*	*London (TB)*	*5 Aug*

400 METRES HURDLES - Under 17

53.84	Rhys Williams		27.02.84	1	Grangemouth	5 Aug
55.75	Mark Winship		29.09.83	2	Sheffield	30 Jul
56.61	Robert Ayres		12.11.83	1h1	Sheffield	7 Jul
56.70	Mark Garner		2.11.83	1h2	Sheffield	7 Jul
56.7	Ross Tressider		8.11.83	1	Basildon	10 Jun
	57.49			5h1	Sheffield	7 Jul
56.79	Oliver Teasel		24.04.84	2h2	Sheffield	7 Jul
56.91	Matthew Hawkins		17.12.83	4	Sheffield	30 Jul
56.99	Matthew Williams		31.01.84	2	Blackpool	15 Jul
57.09	Neil Burnside		7.08.84	1	Grangemouth	25 Jun
57.16	Callum McKay		17.02.85	3h1	Sheffield	7 Jul
(10)						
57.25	Tom Carey		26.02.84	4h1	Sheffield	7 Jul
57.28	Peter Middleton		27.01.84	1	Gateshead	14 May
57.3	Patrick Collins		4.02.85	1	Middlesbrough	17 Jun
	57.78			3h2	Sheffield	7 Jul
57.59	Sean Sykes		13.10.83	6h1	Sheffield	7 Jul
57.78	Liam McDermid		23.11.84	4	Blackpool	15 Jul
58.0	Daniel Bray		6.09.83	1	Hayes	23 Jul
58.3	Craig Cannon		6.05.84	3	Solihull	28 May
	58.50			5h2	Sheffield	7 Jul
58.43	Michael Skilling		18.05.84	3	Grangemouth	17 Jun
58.56	Michael Bool		10.11.83	2	Carmarthen	1 Jul
58.63	Rhodri Scanlon		22.08.84	3	Carmarthen	1 Jul
(20)						
58.7	Andrew Hopkinson		20.09.83	1	Lancaster	30 Apr
58.7	Mark Orpe		11.10.84	1	Stoke-on-Trent	23 Jul
58.8	Oliver Brewer		14.09.83	2	Lancaster	30 Apr
58.8	Craig MacKay		30.10.84	1	Dunfermline	7 May
58.9	David Shaw		13.06.84	2	Glasgow (S)	20 Aug

overage

58.08	Kenny Elliott	U20	5.07.83	4	Grangemouth	5 Aug

HIGH JUMP

2.25 i	Ben Challenger	U23	7.03.78	4	Birmingham	20 Feb
	2.24 i			3=	Wuppertal, GER	4 Feb
	2.22			1	Birmingham	13 Aug
	2.20			9	Oslo, NOR	28 Jul
	2.20			7=	Stockholm, SWE	1 Aug
	2.20			1	Bedford	19 Aug
	2.19 i			3	Birmingham	30 Jan
	2.18 i			8	Stockholm, SWE	17 Feb
	2.16 i			14=Q	Ghent, BEL	26 Feb
	2.15 i			7=	Ghent, BEL	11 Feb
	2.15 i			7	Birmingham	24 Jun
	2.15			5	Caorle, ITA	8 Jul
	2.15			6=	Gateshead	15 Jul
	2.15			9	London (CP)	5 Aug
	2.15			27=Q	Sydney, AUS	22 Sep
2.25 i	Dalton Grant		8.04.66	3	Glasgow	5 Mar
	2.23			1	Luton	9 Sep
	2.20 i			10	Arnstadt, GER	28 Jan
	2.20 i			14	Balingen, GER	30 Jan
	2.20 i			5=	Birmingham	20 Feb
	2.20 i			6	Birmingham	24 Jun
	2.18			1	Peterborough	28 Aug
	2.15			1	Birmingham	16 Aug
	2.15			1	Watford	17 Sep
2.22	Danny Graham	U23	3.08.79	1	Watford	20 May
	2.16 i			1	Sheffield	22 Jan
	2.15 i			2=	Nenagh, IRE	13 Feb
	2.15			1	Liverpool	13 May
	2.15			1=	Loughborough	21 May
2.20 i	Robert Mitchell	U23	14.09.80	1	Birmingham	16 Jan
	2.20			2	Bedford	19 Aug
	2.19			1	Bedford	1 Jul
	2.15			1	Eton	6 May
	2.15			1	Bedford	29 May
	2.15			1	London (BP)	4 Jun
	2.15			1	Cwmbran	17 Jun
	2.15			1=	London (He)	6 Aug
2.19 i	Stuart Ohrland		6.09.75	1	Birmingham	30 Jan
	2.18 i			1	Cardiff	26 Feb
	2.17 i			1	Bedford	23 Jan
	2.17			3	Birmingham	13 Aug
	2.17			1	Vittel, FRA	2 Sep
	2.15 i			3	Birmingham	16 Jan
2.16 i	Andrew Penk	U23	19.09.78	1	Cardiff	20 Feb
	2.05			1	Connah's Quay	13 May
2.15	James Brierley		31.07.77	1	Telford	13 May
	2.15			2	Bedford	29 May
2.15	Luke Crawley	U20	5.09.81	1	Bedford	27 Aug
2.15	Chuka Enih-Snell	U17	2.03.84	1	Abingdon	10 Sep
	49 performances to 2.15 by 9 athletes including 20 indoors					
2.14 i	Jamie Russell	U20	1.10.81	1H	Vittel, FRA	18 Mar
	2.12			1D	Val de Reuil, FRA	12 Aug
(10)						
2.12	Dan Turner	U23	27.11.78	6=	Birmingham	13 Aug
2.12	Ian Holliday		9.12.73	9	Birmingham	13 Aug
2.10 i	Tony Gilhooly		26.03.76	1	Glasgow	15 Jan
	2.05			1	Grangemouth	14 May
2.10 i	Rob Brocklebank		12.10.76	2	Sheffield	22 Jan
	2.08			1	Grantham	18 Jun

2.10 i	Colin McMaster	U23	15.01.80	3	Glasgow	23 Jan
	2.05			2	Grangemouth	14 May
2.10	Robert Paul	U23	12.11.80	1	London (Cr)	13 May
2.10	Chris Hindley		21.01.76	1	Nottingham	13 May
2.10	Richard Aspden		15.10.76	2=	Brighton	18 Jun
2.10	Brian Hall	U20	17.11.82	1	Blackpool	18 Jun
2.10	Chris Giblin	U20	20.06.81	2	Watford	2 Jul
	(20)					
2.10	Darryl Stone	U20	6.06.83	2	Sheffield	8 Jul
2.10	Martin Aram	U17	2.12.83	1	Tullamore, IRE	23 Jul
2.09	Sam Hood	U17	17.10.83	3	Bedford	27 Aug
2.09	Dean Macey		12.12.77	3D	Sydney, AUS	27 Sep
2.08	Andrew Lowe		6.03.76	1	Stretford	8 Aug
2.07	Martin Lloyd	U23	18.06.80	1	Dartford	8 Jul
2.07	Chris Petts	U23	22.01.80	1	Salisbury	22 Jul
2.07	Stanley Osuide		30.11.74	10	Birmingham	13 Aug
2.05 i	James Hardie	U20	16.04.82	1	Birmingham	8 Jan
	2.05			1	Edinburgh	11 Aug
2.05 i	Matt Little	U20	22.07.83	5	Birmingham	16 Jan
	1.96			1	London (He)	13 May
	(30)					
2.05 i	Steve Bonnett	U23	13.07.78	1	Birmingham	13 Feb
2.05 i	Dan Plank	U20	27.04.82	2	Birmingham	13 Feb
2.05	Simon Thomas	U20	4.03.81	2	Stoke-on-Trent	30 Apr
2.05	Simon Bannister	U20	16.04.81	6	Bedford	29 May
2.05	Colin Bent		12.04.70	1	Aldershot	5 Jul
2.05	Mark Smith		14.09.74	3	Enfield	6 Aug
2.03 i	Mike Robbins		14.03.76	6=	Houston, USA	19 Feb
	2.03			6	Natchitoches, USA	16 May
2.03 i	Mark Crowley	U17	15.11.83	2	Nenagh, IRE	1 Apr
	2.01			1	Watford	7 May
2.03	Dominic Girdler	U20	6.03.82	1	Loughborough	13 May
2.02 i	Robert Toms	U23	7.08.80	3	Cardiff	12 Mar
	2.00			4	Watford	20 May
	(40)					
2.02	Alex Kruger		18.11.63	1D	Stoke-on-Trent	29 Jul
2.02	Kevin Wilson	U20	28.09.82	1	Portsmouth	5 Aug
2.01 i	Daniel Leonard	U17	3.01.84	1	Bedford	25 Mar
	2.01			1O	Rugby	25 Jun
2.01	Kim Harland	U20	21.02.82	1	Carmarthen	1 Jul
2.01	Matthew Ostridge	U20	23.02.83	4	Sheffield	8 Jul
2.01	Paul Tohill	U20	9.10.82	1	Dublin, IRE	30 Sep
2.00 i	Khaled El Sheikh	U23	26.07.78	4	Birmingham	8 Jan
	2.00			3	Stoke-on-Trent	30 Apr
2.00 i	Stuart Livingstone	U23	29.08.79	4	Glasgow	23 Jan
	1.95			4	Enfield	24 Jun
2.00 i	Mark Elliott	U23	12.08.80	5	Glasgow	23 Jan
	1.95			5	Stoke-on-Trent	30 Apr
2.00	Gareth Dyball	U20	16.03.81	1	Woodford	22 Apr
	(50)					
2.00	Geoff Parsons		14.08.64	1	Enfield	6 May
2.00	Chris Hunter	U20	3.03.81	1	Gateshead	13 May
2.00	Mike Leigh		14.12.77	2	Watford	20 May
2.00	Mark Latham		13.01.76	3	Watford	20 May
2.00	Gareth Moir	U23	17.12.80	1	Southend	3 Jun
2.00	Simon Whittingham	U23	18.09.78	1	Guildford	3 Jun
2.00	Peter Watson	U20	30.06.81	1	Harrow	18 Jun
2.00	John Wallace		9.10.68	4	Sheffield (W)	24 Jun
2.00	Mark Sweeney		26.02.77	1D	Jarrow	24 Jun
2.00	Theo Casey	U17	3.06.84	1	Barking	3 Jul
	(60)					

2.00	Bomene Barikor	U20	22.05.82	1=	Peterborough	8	Jul
2.00	Darragh Murphy		20.01.74	5	Peterborough	8	Jul
2.00	Martyn Bernard	U17	15.12.84	1	York	16	Jul
2.00	Chris Binns	U20	7.05.82	1	Bolton	16	Jul
2.00	Peter Fisher	U20	14.02.82	1	Reading	16	Jul
2.00	Adam Gallie	U17	5.11.84	1	Stoke-on-Trent	23	Jul
2.00	Jason McDade	U23	3.04.80	4	Enfield	6	Aug
2.00	Julian Harrison		4.08.76	1	Wakefield	17	Sep
2.00	Shane Booth	U20	16.01.82	2	Wakefield	17	Sep
1.99 i	Mark Bidwell	U17	4.09.84	1	Cardiff	26	Feb
	1.95			2	Cleckheaton	27	May
	(70)						
1.99	Gary Maitland	U20	16.07.81		-, USA	1	Apr
1.99	Gavin Fordham	U23	1.02.79	1D	Watford	23	Sep
1.98	James Wild	U20	1.10.82	1	Cudworth	16	Apr
1.98	Daniel Crake	U20	21.12.82	1	Carlisle	13	May
1.98	Greg Goodrem	U17	14.09.83	1	Chelmsford	13	May
1.98	Chris France	U17	29.01.84	1	Telford	10	Jun
1.98	Andrew McFarlane	U20	28.02.83	1	Cleckheaton	10	Jun
1.98	Tom Salter	U20	7.01.83	1	Cannock	10	Jun
1.98	David Etheridge	U20	17.09.82	6	Sheffield	8	Jul
1.98	Duncan McInnes	U23	1.05.78	1	Glasgow	16	Jul
	(80)						
1.98	Craig Lewis		5.03.77	1	Inverness	27	Aug
1.97	Brendan McConville	U23	3.01.79	2D	Jarrow	24	Jun
1.96 i	Gavin Fisher		18.11.77	6	Cardiff	12	Mar
	1.95			6	Loughborough	21	May
1.96	Marc Ladrowski	U23	13.07.79	1	Exeter	13	May
1.96	Mark Beer	U23	28.02.80	2	Derby	5	Aug
1.96	Andrew Reeves	U20	10.09.81	8=	Bedford	27	Aug
1.96	Edward Dunford	U17	15.09.84	3D	Waterford, IRE	2	Sep
1.96	Paul Gilding		2.10.75	1D	Crawley	9	Sep
1.95 i	Duncan Mathieson		8.03.69	1=H	Birmingham	22	Jan
1.95 i	N. Watson			2	Birmingham	26	Jan
	(90)						
1.95 i	Ryan Westaway	U20	2.03.83	9=	Birmingham	5	Feb
1.95	Aaron Robb		24.04.76	1	Coatbridge	30	Apr
1.95	Rowan Griffiths		16.01.75	7	Eton	6	May
1.95	James Hart	U20	4.04.82	1	Redditch	13	May
1.95	Matt Ledger	U20	23.11.81	1	Nottingham	13	May
1.95	Tom Parsons	U17	5.05.84	1	Leamington	13	May
1.95	Daniel Gilbert	U20	1.03.81	1	Portsmouth	14	May
1.95	Richard Edden	U23	15.05.78	2	Oxford	20	May
1.95	Greg Beacom	U23	26.02.78	1	Basingstoke	11	Jun
1.95	Ian Massey		9.09.76	1	Bolton	11	Jun
	(100)						
1.95	Chris Oakes		19.10.70	D	Aldershot	21	Jun
1.95	James Alix	U20	24.12.81	1	Coventry	16	Jul
1.95	James Leaver		15.09.75	1	Exeter	16	Jul
1.95	Calvin Hall	U17	15.11.83	2	Derby	23	Jul
1.95	Trevor McSween		27.10.66	1	Aldershot	26	Jul
1.95	Tom Vanhinsbergh	U23	28.12.78	2	Bedford	5	Aug
1.95	Paul Graham	U23	8.10.78	6	Enfield	6	Aug
1.95	Duncan Wheatley	U20	9.06.81	1	Dumfries	13	Aug
1.95	Mark Ovens			3	Luton	9	Sep
1.95	Camara Stewart	U17	11.09.83	3	Birmingham	10	Sep

Additional Under 17 (1 - 15 above)

1.94	Jamie Creighton	15.09.83	1	Stretford	4	Jun
1.93	Colin Bailey	15.11.83	1	Blackpool	10	Jun
1.91	Peter Burn	3.01.84	1	Gateshead	14	May

1.91	Stephen Alexander		6.10.84	2	Stretford	4 Jun
1.91	Iain Ramsay		10.09.83	1	Glasgow	20 Aug
	(20)					
1.90	Bertram Nnanyere		26.09.83	1	Oxford	21 May
1.90	Nick Dance		27.09.83	3	Watford	27 May
1.90	Ewan Graham		3.09.84	2	Basildon	10 Jun
1.90	Philip Taylor		6.02.84	1	Cannock	10 Jun
1.90	David Collard		21.01.85	2	Grangemouth	25 Jun
1.90	Michael Knott			2	Carmarthen	1 Jul
1.90	Ricardo Prevost	U15	31.10.85	1	Sheffield	7 Jul
1.90	Mark Latham		13.05.85	1	Bebington	23 Jul
1.90 i	Richard Blair		15.09.84	1	Glasgow	14 Dec

Additional Under 15 (1 above)

1.83	Louis Moore		8.09.85	1P	Birmingham	16 Sep
1.82	Howard Gale		23.09.85	1	Bedford	7 Aug
1.81	Daniel Campbell		24.02.86	2	Sheffield	7 Jul
1.80	Onose Okojie		19.09.85	1	London (BP)	10 Jun
1.80	Michael Baines		1.11.85	1	Birmingham	3 Sep
1.79	Daniel Segerson		17.09.85	1	Sheffield	29 Jul
1.79	Kevin Sempers		24.11.85	1	Scunthorpe	28 Aug
1.78	Mathew Chetwynd		20.12.85	1	Leamington	14 May
1.78	Adrian Pettigrew		12.11.86	2	London (BP)	10 Jun
	(10)					
1.78	Adam Booth		22.10.85	1	Jarrow	23 Jul
1.76	Corey Searles		18.12.85	2	Enfield	10 Jun
1.76	Chris Kirk			2	Cudworth	19 Aug
1.75	Farron Paul		3.10.85	1	London (He)	30 Apr
1.75	Joel Grant Jones		21.11.85	2	Eton	4 Jun
1.75	Ben Viggars		24.10.85	1	Cudworth	10 Jun
1.75	Simon Dewsbury		2.12.85	1	Exeter	17 Jun
1.75	Lewis Johnson			1P	Wrexham	24 Jun
1.75	Chris Boyd		21.11.85	5	Sheffield	7 Jul
1.75	Steven Bourne		6.09.85	6	Sheffield	7 Jul
	(20)					
1.75	D. Obuquai			1	London (BP)	29 Jul
1.75	Ross Fairgrieve		20.09.85	1	Reading	30 Jul
1.75	Adam Napier		30.09.85	1	Basildon	30 Jul
1.75	Gary Martin		13.09.85	4=	London (He)	20 Aug
1.75	Pierre Wynter		13.01.86	4=	London (He)	20 Aug
1.75	Darren Steadman		26.01.87	1	Watford	10 Sep

Overage

1.75 i	James Stevenson	U17	6.10.85	1	Cardiff	9 Dec

Under 13

1.60	Nick Fladgley	23.11.87	1	Kingston	30 Jul
1.60	Marc Soame	16.10.87	1	King's Lynn	20 Aug
1.55	David Shields		1	Antrim	27 May
1.55	Andrew Allan	9.04.88	1	Grangemouth	6 Aug
1.55	Robbie Grabarz	3.10.87	1	Bedford	6 Aug
1.53	John Abbott	12.12.87	1	Sandown IOW	4 Sep
1.52	M. McCrea		2	Antrim	27 May
1.51	Ashley Hamilton	11.06.88	P	Crawley	10 Sep
1.51	Lewis Robson	9.01.88	P	Hexham	24 Sep
1.50	Oliver McNeillis	24.11.87	1	Stretford	24 Apr

Foreign

2.28 i	*Brendan Reilly (IRE)*	*23.12.72*	*1*	*Reykjavik, ISL*	*5 Mar*
	2.24		*7*	*London (CP)*	*5 Aug*

2.19 i	*Samson Oni (NIG)*	*U20*	*25.06.81*	*2*	*Birmingham*	*30 Jan*
	2.15			*4*	*London (He)*	*6 Aug*
2.00	*Olu Robbin-Cocker (SLE)*		*27.11.75*	*4*	*Peterborough*	*8 Jul*
2.00	*Reg Stasaitis (LIT)*		*6.04.67*	*1*	*Hayes*	*19 Jul*
2.00	*Mark Mandy (IRE)*		*19.11.72*	*10*	*London (He)*	*6 Aug*
1.95	*Gintaras Varanauskas (LIT)*		*17.04.72*	*1*	*London (TB)*	*6 May*
1.95	*Joe Naughton (IRE)*		*17.10.74*	*4*	*Enfield*	*23 Jul*

POLE VAULT

5.55	Paul Williamson		16.06.74	1=jo	Modesto, USA	13 May
	5.51			1=	Irvine, USA	7 May
	5.50 i			1	Cardiff	6 Feb
	5.40 i			9Q	Ghent, BEL	25 Feb
	5.40 i			1	Cardiff	12 Jul
	5.40			1	Enfield	23 Jul
	5.40			8	London (CP)	5 Aug
	5.40			2	Birmingham	13 Aug
	5.30 i			2	Birmingham	29 Jan
	5.30			1	Bedford	19 Aug
	5.20 i			1	Bedford	22 Jan
	5.20 i			1	Cardiff	12 Feb
	5.20			1	Bedford	28 May
	5.20			4	Arles, FRA	4 Jun
	5.20			3	Bedford	11 Jun
5.55	Kevin Hughes		30.04.73	16=Q	Sydney, AUS	27 Sep
	5.50 (cleared 5.60 deemed to be voltz)			1	Birmingham	13 Aug
	5.45			1	Southend	29 Jul
	5.22			2	Dormagen, GER	24 Jun
	5.20 i			8	Halle, GER	26 Jan
	5.20			2=	Somero, FIN	9 Jul
	5.20			6=	Cuxhaven, GER	19 Jul
5.40	Tim Thomas		18.11.73	1	Bedford	11 Jun
	5.40			6	Gateshead	16 Jul
	5.32 i			1	Cardiff	26 Feb
	5.30 i			1	Cardiff	16 Aug
	5.30			1	Bedford	20 Aug
	5.22 i			1	Cardiff	19 Feb
	5.20			4	Caorle, ITA	8 Jul
	5.20			9	London (CP)	5 Aug
	5.20			5	Birmingham	13 Aug
	5.20			2	Bedford	19 Aug
5.40	Nick Buckfield		5.06.73	1	Stoke-on-Trent	2 Aug
5.35 i	Ben Flint	U23	16.09.78	1	Birmingham	29 Jan
	5.30			3	Birmingham	13 Aug
	5.25			1	Bedford	1 Jul
	5.20			2	Bedford	11 Jun
	5.20			1	Wigan	24 Jun
5.21	Matt Belsham		11.10.71	3	Irvine, USA	7 May
	5.20			1	Palo Alto, USA	13 May
	5.20			1	London (He)	6 Aug
	5.20			4	Birmingham	13 Aug
5.20	Mark Davis		1.03.77	1	Bristol	20 May
5.20	Ian Tullett		15.08.69	2	London (He)	6 Aug
	44 performances to 5.20 by 8 athletes including 11 indoors					
5.10 i	Scott Simpson	U23	21.07.79	1	Birmingham	13 Feb
	4.90			2	Derby	3 Sep
5.10	Tom Richards	U23	13.11.78	1	Peterborough	13 May
(10)						
5.10	Mike Barber		19.10.73	3	Bedford	19 Aug
5.00	Christian Linskey	U23	14.06.80	8=	Arles, FRA	4 Jun

5.00	Matt Weaver		14.11.73	1	Oxford	28 Jun
5.00 i	Christian North		2.02.74	2	Cardiff	16 Aug
	4.90			1	Yate	20 Aug
5.00 i	Ashley Swain	U23	3.10.80	3	Cardiff	16 Aug
	4.90			4=	Bedford	19 Aug
4.95	Mark Grant		17.05.71	1	Luton	13 May
4.90	Rufus Cooper	U23	24.02.79	1	Loughborough	10 May
4.90	Mark Beharrell	U20	10.01.81	3	Stoke-on-Trent	2 Aug
4.90	Leigh Walker		17.08.77	1	Bedford	5 Aug
4.81	Andrew Penk	U23	19.09.78	1	Newport	13 May
	(20)					
4.80 i	Chris Type	U20	5.10.81	1	Cardiff	23 Jan
4.80	Richard Smith	U20	17.01.81	3=	Bedford	28 May
4.80	Dean Mellor		25.11.71	2	Cudworth	22 Jul
4.80	Dean Macey		12.12.77	20D	Sydney, AUS	28 Sep
4.75	Gavin Showell		29.09.72	1	Tamworth	28 Aug
4.70 i	Martin Densley	U20	1.05.81	1	Bedford	22 Jan
	4.60			1	Enfield	13 May
4.70 i	Paul Jones	U23	11.04.78	1H	Birmingham	23 Jan
	4.65			10=D	Arles, FRA	4 Jun
4.70 i	Rob Thickpenny		17.07.76	4	Cardiff	6 Feb
	4.62			11	Long Beach, USA	15 Apr
4.70	Barry Thomas		28.04.72	1=D	Esbjerg, DEN	2 Jul
4.70	Cameron Johnston	U20	22.10.82	1	Sheffield	8 Jul
	(30)					
4.65 i	Dominic Shepherd		11.12.76	3=H	Vittel, FRA	19 Mar
4.65	Alan Richardson	U20	15.01.81	1	Cudworth	19 Aug
4.60 i	Bob Kingman		21.02.73	1	Birmingham	17 Feb
	4.50			1	London (Elt)	3 Jun
4.60	Jamie Quarry		15.11.72	4	Loughborough	21 May
4.60	Warren Jousiffe		27.05.77	3	London (BP)	4 Jun
4.60	Steve McLennan	U23	17.11.78	1	Eton	5 Aug
4.55	Alexis Sharp		31.10.72	14=D	Arles, FRA	4 Jun
4.50	Andrew Wake		14.09.68	1	Gateshead	13 May
4.50	Matthew Buck		5.04.74	3=	Wigan	20 May
4.50	Egryn Jones		1.11.71	1	Cwmbran	17 Jun
	(40)					
4.50	Paul Stevens	U17	15.11.83	1	Sheffield	8 Jul
4.50	Stephen Day	U20	10.02.82	4	Enfield	23 Jul
4.50	Tom Benn	U23	20.04.80	3	Horsham	20 Aug
4.46 i	Paul Thomas	U23	1.10.80	1	Horsham	30 Jan
	4.20			8	Eton	8 May
4.45	Neil Young		20.02.77	1	Belfast	8 Jul
4.45	Chris Mills		12.11.75	1	Hoo	5 Aug
4.40 i	Gareth Lease		14.11.77	6	Cardiff	12 Feb
	4.20			1	Cardiff	13 May
4.40 i	Alex Kruger		18.11.63	4	Birmingham	13 Feb
	4.40			2	Cardiff	8 Jul
4.40 i	Chris Wills		18.05.76	5	Birmingham	13 Feb
4.40 i	Ian Noble		2.04.77	3=	Wakefield	19 Feb
	(50)					
4.40	Iain Black		18.09.70	3	Enfield	24 Jun
4.40	Adam Davis		19.11.72	4	Aldershot	16 Jul
4.40	Mark Christie	U17	11.09.84	1	Bebington	23 Jul
4.32 i	Allan Williams	V45	30.05.53	1	Birmingham	26 Feb
4.30	Chris Boundy	U23	25.12.79	2	Gateshead	13 May
4.30	Steve Brown	U20	20.03.82	1	Chelmsford	13 May
4.30	Tim Holsgrove	U20	11.12.82	1	Derby	17 Jun
4.30	Brendan McConville	U23	3.01.79	1	Antrim	19 Jul
4.30	Tony Brannen		16.09.68	3	Jarrow	5 Aug
4.30	Glyn Price		12.09.65	4	Jarrow	5 Aug

Mark	Name	Age	DOB	Pos	Venue	Date
4.30	Chris Tremayne	U17	11.11.84	1	Birmingham	3 Sep
4.25	Olly Mahoney	U17	21.10.83	2	Sheffield	8 Jul
4.25	Alan Jervis	U17	27.07.84	3	Sheffield	8 Jul
4.21	Gerald Manville	U23	21.12.78	2	Bedford	5 Aug
4.20 i	Ian McKenzie	U20	3.07.81	1	Glasgow	20 Feb
	4.20			2	London (He)	7 May
4.20	Dave Gordon		20.03.68	7	Eton	6 May
4.20	Kevin Tufton	U23	30.04.80	1	Kingston	11 Jun
4.20	Simon Lewis	U20	14.01.83	2	Derby	17 Jun
4.20	Daniel Broadhead	U20	19.04.82	2	Derby	18 Jun
4.20	Jason O'Hara		28.10.76	8	London (He)	8 Jul
	(70)					
4.20	Jamie Webb		18.12.75	1	Brighton	8 Jul
4.20	Adam Walker	U23	16.11.79	2	Derby	9 Jul
4.20	Jason Fry	U20	6.01.83	1	London (Ha)	22 Jul
4.20	Douglas Graham		1.01.77	2	Glasgow (S)	29 Jul
4.20	Garry Chiles		15.05.66	2B	Stoke-on-Trent	2 Aug
4.20	Richard Hurren	U17	24.09.83	6	Vilvoorde, BEL	6 Aug
4.20	Anthony Southward		31.01.71	4=	Enfield	6 Aug
4.20	James Wright	U20	2.04.82	1D	Waterford, IRE	3 Sep
4.20	John Hutchinson	U20	3.05.82	1	Birmingham	10 Sep
4.15	Jamie Cole	U20	22.05.81	1	Derby	10 Sep
	(80)					
4.10 i	Robert Gardner	U23	23.12.78	3B	Birmingham	16 Jan
4.10 i	David Bonsall		2.06.71	3	Horsham	30 Jan
4.10 i	Neil Price	U23	15.05.80	1B	Cardiff	6 Feb
	4.10			1	Exeter	16 Jul
4.10 i	Andy Buchanan		12.09.70	2B	Cardiff	6 Feb
	4.10			1	Guildford	3 Jun
4.10	Keith Hatton	V40	19.10.55	1	Enfield	3 Jun
4.10	Steve Bonnett	U23	13.07.78	14D	Esbjerg, DEN	2 Jul
4.10	Anthony Sawyer	U23	29.04.80	2D	Gateshead	23 Jul
4.10	Ian Bowley	U20	14.11.81	3	Bedford	5 Aug
4.10	Steve Garland		12.01.73	4	Bedford	5 Aug
4.10	Alex Bale	U17	1.12.83	3	Cudworth	19 Aug
	(90)					
4.10	Paul Miles	U23	14.09.80	2	Tamworth	28 Aug
4.10 i	Matthew Peerless	U20	3.12.82	2	Glasgow	25 Oct
4.05	Ekakier Benjamin	U17	4.12.84	6	Sheffield	8 Jul
4.05	Brian Hughes		6.01.70	3D	Stoke-on-Trent	30 Jul

Additional Under 17 (1 - 8 above)

Mark	Name	Age	DOB	Pos	Venue	Date
4.00 i	Mike Cross		19.12.83	1	London (CP)	19 Feb
	3.90			1	London (CP)	13 May
3.90	Greg Dillow		16.06.84	1	London (Cr)	4 Jun
	(10)					
3.90	Mark Harvey		2.07.84	1	Newport	28 Aug
3.90	Paul Walker		15.08.85	2	Newport	28 Aug
3.80 i	Michael Parker		29.10.83	2	Wakefield	19 Feb
3.72	Keith Thomas		15.11.83	1	Tamworth	28 Aug
3.70 i	Tom McDowell		11.02.85	1	Birmingham	9 Jan
	3.65			1	Bath	13 May
3.70	Ricky Hallam		17.01.85	3	Stoke-on-Trent	13 May
3.70	Joel Ward-Davies		9.02.84	1	Hereford	13 May
3.70	Steven Lewis	U15	20.05.86	1	Sheffield	29 Jul
3.70	Matthew Dorrian		24.03.84	1	Grangemouth	6 Sep
3.70	Russell Thompson		9.09.83	1	Banbury	10 Sep
	(20)					
3.70	Alistair Brown		14.02.84	2	Grangemouth	10 Sep
3.60	Ben Jackson		22.11.84	2	London (BP)	22 Jul

Additional Under 15 (1 above)

3.40	Keith Higham		7.11.85	1	Blackpool	10 Sep
3.20	Mark Laws		29.09.85	1	Gateshead	13 May
3.20	Chris Wilson		23.09.85	3	High Wycombe	5 Aug
3.20	Michael Johnson		25.09.85	1	Lincoln	5 Sep
3.10	Laurence Steele		24.04.86	1	Lancaster	13 May
3.10	Paul Yeomans		9.10.85	1	Watford	28 Jun
3.01	Michael Cox		15.01.86	1	Basildon	23 Jul
3.00	Luke Cutts	U13	13.02.88	1	Cudworth	13 May
3.00	Richard Curran		19.09.85	7	Sheffield	7 Jul
(10)						
3.00	Martin Vincent		12.04.86	1	Bedford	4 Sep
3.00 i	Scott Costello		9.06.87	1	Cardiff	9 Dec
2.95	Ben Hood		11.11.85	1	Hull	13 May
2.90	Steve Davies		9.11.86	1	Yate	20 Aug
2.90	Tom Davies		9.11.86	1	Banbury	10 Sep
2.85	Ryan Saunders		10.01.86	2	Hull	13 May
2.85	Michael Finch		11.01.86	8	Sheffield	7 Jul

Additional Under 13 (1 above)

2.10	Jamie Clark		11.05.88	1	Corby	22 Aug
2.00	James Wilton		1.09.87	1	Carn Brea	10 Jun
2.00	Gary Forfar		7.10.87	1	Grangemouth	6 Sep

Subsequently Suspended

4.80 i	Mike Edwards ¶		19.10.68	11=	Birmingham	29 Jan

Foreign

4.80 i	*Jerome Birot (FRA)*		*28.04.74*	*2*	*Birmingham*	*8 Jan*
	4.80			*1*	*Bath*	*14 May*
4.45	*Peter McLoughlin (IRE)*		*18.05.77*	*2*	*Belfast*	*8 Jul*
4.20	*Dylan McDermott (IRE)*		*1.12.70*	*1*	*Bromley*	*6 May*
4.20	*Dirk Feil (GER)*		*9.03.65*	*2*	*Gateshead*	*23 Jul*
4.10	*Joe Naughton (IRE)*		*17.10.74*	*5*	*Watford*	*20 May*
4.10	*Matt Pilborough (USA)*	*U23*	*10.07.79*	*1*	*Telford*	*9 Sep*

LONG JUMP

8.05 w	3.5	Nathan Morgan		U23	30.06.78	1	Ljubljana, SLO	25 Jul
		8.00	1.3			1	Getafe, SPA	9 Sep
		7.98	1.8			2	Budapest, HUN	22 Jul
		7.97	1.1			1	Loughborough	30 Jul
		7.97 w	3.2			2	Arles, FRA	3 Jun
		7.90	-0.3			1	Vittel, FRA	2 Sep
		7.85 w	2.4			2	Bedford	19 Aug
		7.81	0.9			4	Gothenburg, SWE	3 Aug
		7.76	1.7			*	Bedford	19 Aug
		7.57	0.4			7	Gateshead	15 Jul
		7.54 w	3.1			2	London (He)	6 Aug
		7.48	-1.0			2	London (He)	8 Jul
7.92 w	4.4	Darren Ritchie			14.02.75	1	Cudworth	28 Aug
		7.90				1	Bedford	19 Aug
		7.88	1.6			1	Bedford	20 Aug
		7.84	1.5			2	Birmingham	12 Aug
		7.81	0.5			1	London (He)	6 Aug
		7.80	1.1			1	Glasgow (S)	29 Jul
		7.70 w	3.0			1	Bedford	11 Jun
		7.68	1.9			1	Riga, LAT	22 Jun
		7.65	2.0			*	Bedford	11 Jun
		7.60	0.4			1	London (He)	8 Jul
		7.60	0.3			Q	Birmingham	11 Aug
		7.59	0.9			5	Budapest, HUN	22 Jul

7.89	1.2	George Audu		18.01.77	1	Birmingham	12 Aug
		7.75 1.8			3	Bedford	19 Aug
		7.63 1.0			2	Bedford	20 Aug
		7.56 w 5.1			1	Wigan	24 Jun
		7.55 0.5			Q	Birmingham	11 Aug
7.86 w	2.6	Steve Phillips		17.03.72	1	Bedford	29 May
		7.81 w 2.5			1	Rugby	23 Jul
		7.79 -0.5			1	Leamington	14 May
		7.63 1.4			*	Rugby	23 Jul
		7.63 0.0			2	Glasgow	29 Jul
		7.62			1	Welwyn	1 May
		7.61			1	Crawley	24 Jun
		7.60 w 2.1			2	Bedford	11 Jun
		7.58 i			1	Glasgow	23 Jan
		7.55 1.8			4	Bedford	19 Aug
		7.52 1.0			*	Bedford	11 Jun
		7.51 i			2	Birmingham	30 Jan
		7.50			1	Blackpool	20 May
		7.46 i			1	Cardiff	6 Feb
7.83	1.1	Phillips Idowu	U23	30.12.78	2	Ljubljana, SLO	25 Jul
		7.62 0.3			1	London (BP)	4 Jun
7.77	-0.5	Dean Macey		12.12.77	1D	Sydney, AUS	27 Sep
		7.69 1.2			1	Enfield	6 Aug
7.66 w	4.1	Dominique Richards	U23	12.09.79	2	Bedford	29 May
		7.35 -0.1			6	Liverpool	22 Jul
7.64 w	2.4	Chris Davidson		4.12.75	1	Loughborough	21 May
		7.58 w 2.4			1	Eton	23 Jul
		7.54 1.4			5	Bedford	19 Aug
		7.51 1.5			*	Eton	23 Jul
		7.50 0.6			*	Loughborough	21 May
		7.46 1.4			3	London (He)	6 Aug
		7.46 1.6			3	Vittel, FRA	2 Sep
		7.45 0.3			1	Dublin (S), IRE	29 Jul
7.62	1.2	Julian Flynn		3.07.72	2	Loughborough	30 Jul
		7.47 1.6			6	Bedford	19 Aug
7.62	0.3	Chris Tomlinson	U20	15.09.81	Q	Santiago, CHI	21 Oct
		7.59 1.1			1	Bedford	27 Aug
		7.57 i			1	Birmingham	30 Jan
		7.48 i			1	Birmingham	5 Feb
		7.47 i			3	Neubrandenburg, GER	4 Mar
	(10)						
7.58		Essop Merrick		24.05.74	1	Enfield	24 Jun
7.58 w		Gary Smith		20.02.71	1	London (PH)	6 May
		7.08			1	Luton	13 May
7.57 w	2.2	Stuart Wells	U23	26.07.79	1	Chelmsford	14 May
		7.51 1.0			*	Chelmsford	14 May
7.55	1.0	Tony Malcolm		15.02.76	1	Cwmbran	18 Jun
7.48	-0.5	Darren Thompson	U23	6.11.79	3	Birmingham	12 Aug
		7.45 1.9			3	Loughborough	30 Jul
7.47	1.9	Martin Taylor	U20	31.01.82	2	Bedford	27 Aug
7.46	1.9	Jonathan Moore	U17	31.05.84	1	Sheffield	30 Jul
		7.45			1	Cheltenham	21 May
73 performances to 7.45 by 17 athletes including 14 wind assisted and 6 indoors							
7.42 w	2.9	Jamie Quarry		15.11.72	4D	Arles, FRA	3 Jun
		7.27			2	Peterborough	8 Jul
7.41 wA		Sam Nash		22.10.71	3	Vygieskraal, RSA	15 Jan
		6.96 1.3			*	Enfield	23 Jul
7.41 w	3.9	Gareth Brown		2.09.73	2	Cwmbran	18 Jun
		7.05			1	Swindon	22 Jul
	(20)						
7.38	0.5	Andrew Lewis		9.03.68	1	Diekirch, LUX	5 Aug

7.38 w		Paul Ralph		16.12.67	2	Cudworth	22 Jul
		7.25			3	Enfield	24 Jun
7.37	1.9	Mark Awanah	U20	23.09.82	3	Bedford	27 Aug
7.35 w	3.4	Levi Edwards	U23	23.11.80	3	Bedford	29 May
		7.27 1.7			*	Bedford	29 May
7.33	1.6	David Mountford	U20	23.06.82	4	Bedford	27 Aug
7.31		Andre Fernandez	U23	2.03.80	1	London (Cr)	27 Aug
7.30	1.3	Michael Nesbeth	U23	1.03.79	3	Bedford	20 Aug
7.29	1.3	Leigh Smith	U20	24.09.82	1	Eton	6 May
7.28		Joe Sweeney		17.07.65	1	Eton	13 May
7.26		Femi Akinsanya		29.11.69	1	Peterborough	28 Aug
	(30)						
7.25		Carl McMullen	U23	9.11.79	1	Aldershot	21 Jun
7.25 w	2.1	Simon Roper	U23	20.09.79	1	Cudworth	19 Aug
		7.21			1	Derby	5 Aug
7.24	0.1	Julian Golley		12.09.71	2	Eton	6 May
7.24 w	2.2	Mark Lawrence		26.01.71	2	Bedford	5 Aug
		6.97			1	Derby	9 Jul
7.23		Stewart Faulkner		19.02.69	1	Birmingham (Un)	22 Jul
7.21	1.9	Jordon Lau	U17	23.09.83	1	Sheffield	8 Jul
7.21	1.5	Onen Eyong	U17	18.02.85	2	Sheffield	30 Jul
7.18 w	3.4	Dave Ashton		24.01.70	2	Cudworth	28 Aug
		7.11			4	Enfield	24 Jun
7.17	1.8	Adam Potter	U23	12.04.80	2	Bath	16 Sep
7.16		Andy Turner	U23	19.09.80	1	Loughborough	14 Jun
	(40)						
7.16 w	3.1	Andrew Thomas		9.02.74	3	Cwmbran	18 Jun
		7.13			1	Newport	11 Jun
7.15	1.7	Tom Roe	U20	25.06.82	6	Bedford	27 Aug
7.14 i		Steven Shalders	U20	24.12.81	1	Cardiff	19 Feb
		6.90			1	Neath	5 Apr
7.13	1.6	Nick Thomas	U23	4.04.79	2	Chelmsford	14 May
7.13	0.3	Brian Robinson	U23	3.09.80	4	Bedford	1 Jul
7.12 i		Duncan Mathieson		8.03.69	1H	Birmingham	22 Jan
		6.91 0.5			3	Watford	20 May
7.12	1.9	Jon French		11.12.75	2	Watford	20 May
7.10	1.3	Alex Hall	U20	2.02.82	3	Sheffield	7 Jul
7.09		Dale Garland	U23	13.10.80	1	St. Peter Port GUE	31 Aug
7.09 w	4.5	Henry Edun		6.02.73	2	Enfield	23 Jul
		6.94			5	Enfield	6 Aug
	(50)						
7.09 w	2.6	James Leaver		15.09.75	8	Bedford	19 Aug
		6.94 1.9			*	Bedford	19 Aug
7.08		Kris Davies	U20	30.10.81	1	Newport	11 Jun
7.07		Stefan Rose		7.04.75	1	Portsmouth	13 May
7.07		Neil Barton	U23	18.07.80	1	Welwyn	22 Jul
7.04 w	2.8	Paul Tuohy	U20	18.03.81	Q	Stoke-on-Trent	30 Apr
		6.88 1.9			6	Loughborough	21 May
7.04 w		John Donnelly	U23	11.09.79	4	Wigan	24 Jun
7.02	-0.6	Barrington Williams	V40	11.09.55	3	Glasgow	29 Jul
7.02 w		Marlon Lewis	U17	7.09.83	1	Blackpool	15 Jul
		6.99 0.7			8	Bedford	27 Aug
7.01 i		Nick Dowsett	U23	24.11.78	1	Cardiff	12 Mar
		6.95			4	Enfield	6 Aug
7.01	1.1	Olu Baptiste			6	Bedford	1 Jul
	(60)						
7.01 w		Mark Bushell		22.10.76	5	Wigan	24 Jun
		7.00			2	Portsmouth	13 May
7.00		Andrew Morley			2	Exeter	16 Jul
6.99		Andrew Delafield	U23	19.03.80	1	Cudworth	14 May
6.99	1.0	Steve Bonnett	U23	13.07.78	7D	Arles, FRA	3 Jun

6.98	1.3	Barry Thomas		28.04.72	16D	Arles, FRA	3	Jun
6.98		Dan Plank	U20	27.04.82	1	Nuneaton	11	Jun
6.98	1.5	James Morris	U23	2.12.79	6	Cwmbran	18	Jun
6.98		Craig Elder	U20	22.05.82		Liverpool	18	Jun
6.98		Gareth Davies		11.05.71	2	Oxford	28	Jun
6.98		Grant Stirling		18.03.75	1	Brighton	8	Jul
	(70)							
6.95		Dave Butler	U23	9.12.78	1	Swindon	16	Apr
6.94		Louis Evling-Jones	U20	20.06.83	1	Grantham	10	Jun
6.94 w	2.8	Dean Goulding		14.06.75	4	Grantham	18	Jun
6.93 i		Willie Stark		11.03.77	1	Glasgow	16	Jan
6.93		Manny Nsudoh		8.04.72	3	Crawley	24	Jun
6.90		Jamie Russell	U20	1.10.81	1	Barnsley	10	Jun
6.90		Nathan Douglas	U20	4.12.82	1	Harrow	18	Jun
6.89	1.2	Alexis Sharp		31.10.72	29D	Arles, FRA	3	Jun
6.84 i		James Gilbert		9.11.74	4	Glasgow	23	Jan
6.84		Alvin Walker		30.04.65		Aldershot	5	Jul
	(80)							
6.82	1.3	Garry Carbon	U20	20.01.81	2	Watford	2	Jul
6.81 i		Allan Scott	U20	27.12.82	1	Glasgow	27	Jan
6.81		Jermaine Bernard	U17	1.12.84	1	Ipswich	9	Apr

Additional Under 17 (1 - 5 above)

6.78		Edward Dunford		15.09.84	1	Leamington	10	Jun
6.76		Chuka Enih-Snell		2.03.84	1	Abingdon	10	Sep
6.76 w	2.3	David Hughes		31.05.84	1O	Birmingham	16	Sep
6.71 w	2.3	Adam Ruffels		3.04.84	1	Watford	28	May
		6.52 1.8			*	Watford	28	May
6.70 w	2.7	Ryan James		10.05.85	6	Sheffield	30	Jul
		6.54			1	Leamington	13	May
	(10)							
6.68 w	4.2	Richard Burslem		4.01.84	4	Sheffield	8	Jul
		6.52			3	Wakefield	16	Jul
6.67		Gary Wilson	U15	18.09.85	1	Bedford	27	Aug
6.65		Bernard Yeboah	U15	7.01.86	2	Bedford	27	Aug
6.64		Matthew Walden		30.11.83	1	Scunthorpe	5	Aug
6.63		Matthew Hulyer		20.06.84	1	Bromley	19	May
6.63		Adam Gallagher		23.03.84	1	Horsham	17	Jun
6.62	1.2	Richardo Childs		9.10.84	7	Sheffield	30	Jul
6.61		Matthew Clay		9.06.84	1	Cudworth	13	May
6.60	1.7	Adrian Dillon		10.09.83	6	Sheffield	8	Jul
6.57		Philip Greenland		10.10.84	1	London (WF)	10	Sep
	(20)							
6.57 w	3.6	Richard Askew		26.04.84	7	Sheffield	8	Jul
		6.55 0.4			*	Sheffield	8	Jul
6.54		Jason Comissiong		7.09.83	1	Hastings	5	Aug
6.53 w		Lewis Cheung		12.12.83	1	Derby	17	Jun
6.51		Mitchell Wilkin	U15	6.12.85	1	Bedford	6	Aug
6.51 w	3.4	Kevin Thompson		24.10.83	2	Birmingham	3	Sep
6.50		Matt Barclay		1.11.84	1	Crawley	25	Mar

Additional Under 15 (1 - 3 above)

6.45 w	2.6	Louis Moore		8.09.85	1P	Stoke-on-Trent	17	Jun
		6.34 1.4			1P	Birmingham	16	Sep
6.39		Phillip Murphy		29.09.85	1	Dartford	23	Sep
6.36 w		Alistair Hinze		25.09.85	1	London (Cr)	13	May
		6.21 i			1	Bedford	22	Jan
		6.20 -1.9			3	Sheffield	7	Jul
6.29		Ashley George		23.05.86	1	Kingston	15	Jul
6.28		John Fletcher		15.07.86	1	Cleckheaton	10	Jun
6.18		Matthew Hansford		20.02.86	1P	Yeovil	24	Jun

6.18		William Fleckney		19.10.85	2	Bedford	6	Aug
6.12	1.3	Andrae Davis		27.09.85	2P	Birmingham	16	Sep
6.07 w	5.3	Chinedum Onuha			3P	Birmingham	16	Sep
6.05		Paul Twidale		30.09.86	7	Bedford	27	Aug
6.05		David Hughes		31.10.85	2	Watford	17	Sep
6.04		Martin Pang		13.03.86	1	Leamington	10	Jun
5.99		David Smy		3.03.86	1	Barking	10	Sep
5.98		Mathew Chetwynd		20.12.85	2P	Rugby	24	Jun
5.96		Dwayne Galloway		22.01.86	1	Derby	17	Jun
5.95		A. Lake			1	Nelson	3	Sep
5.92		James Stevenson		6.10.85	1	Exeter	17	Jun
	(10)							
5.90		Ryan Shaw		30.12.86	1	Chelmsford	15	Jun
5.90	1.4	Graham Jackson		12.11.85	1	Cudworth	19	Aug

Overage

6.46 i		Louis Moore	U17	(6.45w)	1P	Glasgow	9	Dec
5.90 i		Peter Warke	U17	22.05.86	3P	Glasgow	9	Dec

Under 13

5.28		Darryl Thomas		23.11.87	1	Enfield	13	May
5.19		Thomas Sandys		21.09.87	1	Crawley	15	Jun
5.17 w	2.6	Yinca Casal		24.09.87	1	Birmingham	3	Sep
5.16		Andre Campbcll		18.07.88	1	Enfield	21	May
5.16		Marwan Goodridge		5.09.87	1	Basildon	23	Jul
5.11		Vito Tomasi		17.01.88	1	St. Peter Port GUE	1	Oct
5.07		Bruce Tasker		2.09.87	1	Neath	27	May
5.06		Steven Horsburgh		11.11.87	1	Hexham	27	Aug
5.05		Anthony Timms		4.03.88	1	Cudworth	23	Jul
5.05		James Hoad		1.02.88	1	Enfield	20	Aug

Foreign

7.55 w		*Gareth Devlin (IRE)*		*2.06.76*	*1*	*Cudworth*	*22*	*Jul*
		7.22 0.3			*1*	*Dublin (S), IRE*	*20*	*Aug*
7.20		*Gary Munroe (CAN)*		*12.04.69*	*1*	*Berlin, GER*	*10*	*May*
7.02		*Reg Stasaitis (LIT)*		*6.04.67*	*1*	*Portsmouth*	*8*	*Jul*
6.87		*Desmond Kapofu (ZIM)*	*U23*	*6.02.78*	*1*	*Eton*	*6*	*May*

TRIPLE JUMP

17.71	0.2	Jonathan Edwards		10.05.66	1	Sydney, AUS	25	Sep
		17.62 1.4			1	Leverkusen, GER	20	Aug
		17.48 0.6			1	Gateshead	28	Aug
		17.36 0.2			1	Zurich, SWZ	11	Aug
		17.34 0.2			1	London (CP)	5	Aug
		17.32 1.2			1	Yokohama, JPN	9	Sep
		17.23 1.5			1	Fana, NOR	27	Jun
		17.20 1.8			1	Tallahassee, USA	13	May
		17.12 0.9			1	Doha, QAT	5	Oct
		17.11 0.0			1	Tel Aviv, ISR	23	Jul
		17.08 0.7			Q	Sydney, AUS	23	Sep
		16.81 -0.6			4	Rome, ITA	30	Jun
17.31 w	4.4	Larry Achike		31.01.75	1	Gateshead	15	Jul
		17.30 1.0			Q	Sydney, AUS	23	Sep
		17.29 0.5			5	Sydney, AUS	25	Sep
		17.16 0.3			1	Zagreb, CRO	3	Jul
		17.03 -0.8			2	London (CP)	5	Aug
		16.99 w 2.2			2	Stockholm, SWE	1	Aug
		16.91 1.2			*	Gateshead	15	Jul
		16.83 1.4			2	Birmingham	13	Aug
		16.78 0.4			2	Fana, NOR	27	Jun
		16.76 0.8			1	Melbourne, AUS	2	Mar

(Achike)		16.75 1.4			*	Stockholm, SWE	1 Aug
		16.66 1.1			1	Hobart, AUS	30 Jan
		16.58 1.6			1	Adelaide, AUS	8 Mar
		16.56 0.7			2	Brisbane, AUS	11 Feb
		16.56 0.7			2	Yokohama, JPN	9 Sep
		16.53 0.1			Q	Sydney, AUS	25 Feb
		16.53 0.8			3	Gateshead	28 Aug
		16.49 0.2			3	Doha, QAT	5 Oct
		16.44 0.3			5	Berlin, GER	1 Sep
		16.39 1.3			3	St. Petersburg, RUS	17 Jun
		16.28 w 2.3			3	Sydney, AUS	27 Feb
		16.26 0.1			*	Sydney, AUS	27 Feb
		16.26			1	Luton	3 Jun
17.12	-0.6	Phillips Idowu	U23	30.12.78	Q	Sydney, AUS	23 Sep
		17.08 0.0			6	Sydney, AUS	25 Sep
		17.05 0.4			1	Budapest, HUN	22 Jul
		16.87 1.8			1	Birmingham	13 Aug
		16.83 0.6			2	Gateshead	28 Aug
		16.71 w 2.5			2	Bedford	11 Jun
		16.70 w 3.1			3	Fana, NOR	27 Jun
		16.57 0.5			1	Brighton	18 Jun
		16.52 1.6			*	Fana, NOR	27 Jun
		16.32 1.1			1	Liege, BEL	28 May
		16.23 1.6			*	Bedford	11 Jun
16.95	0.0	Julian Golley		12.09.71	2	Zagreb, CRO	3 Jul
		16.82 2.0			1	Bedford	11 Jun
		16.56 i			1	Birmingham	29 Jan
		16.48 i			Q	Ghent, BEL	26 Feb
		16.47 i			6	Stuttgart, GER	6 Feb
		16.47 1.0			4	Yokohama, JPN	9 Sep
		16.38 1.0			4	Birmingham	13 Aug
		16.36 w 2.1			2	Brighton	18 Jun
		16.29 0.8			1	Loughborough	21 May
		16.27 i			1	Glasgow	23 Jan
		16.25 0.9			4	Gateshead	28 Aug
		16.24 1.4			1	Enfield	13 May
		16.24 0.7			6	London (CP)	5 Aug
16.40	1.4	Francis Agyepong		16.06.65	3	Birmingham	13 Aug
		16.38 0.8			1	London (He)	6 Aug
		16.29 -0.2			3	Brighton	18 Jun
16.40 w	4.5	Femi Akinsanya		29.11.69	1	Enfield	6 Aug
		16.18 1.6			*	Enfield	6 Aug
16.37 w	3.2	Tosin Oke	U23	1.10.80	1	Liverpool	22 Jul
		16.04 0.2			2	Loughborough	21 May
16.31	1.4	Nick Thomas	U23	4.04.79	2	Liverpool	22 Jul
		16.27 i			2	Birmingham	29 Jan

66 performances to 16.20 by 8 athletes including 8 wind assisted and 5 indoors

16.02	0.1	Jonathan Moore	U17	31.05.84	1	Edinburgh	13 Aug
15.99	-1.3	Steven Shalders	U20	24.12.81	10	Santiago, CHI	20 Oct
	(10)						
15.97	0.6	Tayo Erogbogbo		8.03.75	5	Birmingham	13 Aug
15.70	0.6	Tosi Fasinro		28.03.72	7	Birmingham	13 Aug
15.59 w		Jon Hilton		11.01.74	1	Cudworth	22 Jul
		15.42 1.0			*	Bedford	11 Jun
15.56 w	5.5	Charles Madeira-Cole		29.11.77	2	Wigan	24 Jun
		15.38 0.5			1	Cwmbran	18 Jun
15.31 i		Chris Tomlinson	U20	15.09.81	1	Birmingham	5 Feb
		15.15 1.0			5	Bedford	28 May
15.31 w	2.6	Mike McKernan	U23	28.11.78	3	Bedford	28 May
		15.07 0.0			1	Solihull	29 Jul

15.25	0.0	Jon Wallace	U23	1.01.79	1	Eton	6 May
15.18	0.8	Nathan Douglas	U20	4.12.82	2	Bath	16 Sep
15.14	2.0	Martin Rossiter		4.09.69	6	Bedford	28 May
15.11		Joe Sweeney		17.07.65	1	Eton	13 May
	(20)						
15.09		Malwyn Gordon	U20	29.04.82	1	Birmingham (Un)	22 Jul
15.04 w		Paul Ralph		16.12.67	2	Cudworth	22 Jul
		14.57			3	Enfield	24 Jun
14.98		Philip Ferdinand	U20	18.11.82	1	Dumfries	13 Aug
14.97	1.0	Ezra Clarke		9.12.74	3	Solihull	29 Jul
14.85	0.0	Alex Hall	U20	2.02.82	1	London (Cat)	5 Aug
14.83 w	2.9	Rez Cameron	V40	18.05.60	3	Bedford	19 Aug
		14.07 1.0			*	Bedford	19 Aug
14.76	1.0	Marvin Bramble		10.06.77	3	Enfield	6 Aug
14.70 i		Michael Nesbeth	U23	1.03.79	1	London (CP)	15 Jan
		14.15			1	Eton	11 Jun
14.69		Alvin Walker		30.04.65	1	Aldershot	5 Jul
14.61 w	2.7	Delroy Hulme		14.09.72	3	Rugby	23 Jul
	(30)						
14.61 w	2.5	Paul Weston		6.10.67	5	Bath	16 Sep
		14.60			1	Gloucester	26 Aug
14.59		Keith Newton		12.12.68	1	Welwyn	22 Jul
14.57		Sayo Ojo	U23	9.05.80	2	Wigan	20 May
14.57		John Donnelly	U23	11.09.79	1	Belfast	20 May
14.50		Ruddy Farquharson		26.03.61	1	Cosford	21 Jun
14.46 w	4.0	Jason Comissiong	U17	7.09.83	2	Sheffield	29 Jul
		14.11 0.3			3	Sheffield	7 Jul
14.44	1.3	Stuart Richmond		11.04.69	6	Irvine, USA	7 May
14.41	0.9	Kevin Thompson	U17	24.10.83	2	Sheffield	7 Jul
14.39		Steve Phillips		17.03.72	1	Blackpool	20 May
14.39		Dave McCalla		23.05.73	3	Aldershot	5 Jul
	(40)						
14.24	2.0	John Naylor	U23	19.04.78	2	Derby	3 Sep
14.22	1.5	Adam Potter	U23	12.04.80	6	Bath	16 Sep
14.20		Mark Lawrence		26.01.71	1	Bedford	5 Aug
14.20 w		Alan Saulters	U20	29.01.83	2	Wrexham	18 Jul
		14.08 0.7			4	Edinburgh	13 Aug
14.19 w	2.6	Dave Emanuel		27.12.66	8	London (He)	8 Jul
14.18 w	2.3	Dan Adejuwon		27.11.76	1	Jarrow	6 Aug
14.17		Semi Majekodunmi	U20	29.06.83	1	Exeter	17 Jun
14.15		Stuart Ohrland		6.09.75	3	Eton	23 Jul
14.12 i		Junior Lewis		19.03.66	2	Bedford	23 Jan
		14.10			1	Welwyn	21 Apr
14.11		Steven Frost	U20	4.01.81	3	Cwmbran	18 Jun
	(50)						
14.11		Tim Medcalf	U23	19.02.79	1	Horsham	8 Jul
14.09 w	4.2	Peter Favell	U20	16.03.82	2	Cudworth	19 Aug
		14.07			1	Nottingham	13 May
14.08	0.8	Paul Revell	U23	18.11.80	3	Cudworth	19 Aug
14.07		Adam Zeller	U20	6.06.81	1	London (Ha)	8 Jun
14.03	1.4	Gary White	U17	16.06.85	4	Sheffield	7 Jul
14.02 i		Kori Stennett		2.09.76	2	Birmingham	13 Feb
14.01 i		Steven Alvey	U23	8.05.80	1	Cardiff	5 Feb
14.01 i		James Etchells	U23	15.10.80	3	Cardiff	12 Mar
13.99		Sam Bobb		29.08.75	1	Bromley	6 Mar
13.99		Martin Ohrland	U23	19.11.79	2	Chelmsford	13 May
	(60)						
13.99		Adam Ireland	U23	5.10.78	1	Oxford	20 May
13.99		Peter Belmore	U20	18.09.81	2	Exeter	17 Jun
13.96		Matthew Delicate	U20	7.02.82	1	Carmarthen	10 Jun
13.96		Simon Roper	U23	20.09.79	1	Derby	5 Aug

13.94		Shane Mott		23.05.73	1	Oxford	6 May
13.94		Denis Costello		3.12.61	2	Sheffield	24 Jun
13.92	0.4	Michael Murray	U23	8.12.79	2	Watford	20 May
13.92		M. Reid	U23		1	Reading	22 Jul
13.91		Manny Nsudoh		8.04.72	1	Bedford	20 Aug
13.90		Matt Randall		28.04.70	2	Welwyn	22 Jul
	(70)						
13.89		Andrew Medcalf	U20	11.05.83	1	Crawley	14 May

Additional Under 17 (1 - 4 above)

13.80		Daniel Bray	6.09.83	1	Watford	21 May
13.80		Anthony Nelson	14.09.84	1	Kingston	10 Jun
13.77 i		Lee Harris	23.11.83	1	Cardiff	20 Feb
13.77	-1.5	Chris Alexis	29.12.84	5	Sheffield	7 Jul
13.69		Jerome Osbourne	28.08.84	1	London (WP)	4 Jun
13.61 w		Lewis Cheung	12.12.83	1	Derby	17 Jun
	(10)					
13.56	1.6	Dennis Fennemore	19.06.84	6	Sheffield	29 Jul
13.55 w	3.2	Matthew Walden	30.11.83	2	Cleckheaton	27 May
		13.51		1	Hull	13 May
13.50 i		Edward Dunford	15.09.84	2	Birmingham	6 Feb
		13.47		1	Gloucester	6 May
13.48		Richard Blair	15.09.84	1	Grangemouth	14 May
13.47 i		Matthew Thurgood	29.12.83	3	Birmingham	6 Feb
13.42	0.7	Andrew Harris	21.09.83	7	Sheffield	29 Jul

Under 15

13.18 w	2.7	Joleon Duvigneau	12.12.85	1	Sheffield	8 Jul
		12.81 0.3		2	London (He)	20 Aug
13.04 w	2.4	Graham Jackson	12.11.85	2	Sheffield	8 Jul
		12.85		1	Middlesbrough	17 Jun
12.87	0.2	Ross Fairgrieve	20.09.85	1	London (He)	20 Aug
12.67 w	3.8	Eugene Dixon	14.12.85	4	Sheffield	8 Jul
		12.41		1	Derby	17 Jun
12.40		Andrew Nicholson	25.03.86	1	Crawley	10 Jun
12.38 w	2.2	Daniel Crow	18.03.86	5	Sheffield	8 Jul
		12.01 1.5		3	Sheffield	29 Jul
12.36 w		Lewis Johnson		1	Carmarthen	1 Jul
		12.34		1	Barry	10 Jun
12.32		Ryan Phelps	16.09.85	2	Derby	17 Jun
12.32	1.2	Jonathan Hawkes	16.07.86	6	Sheffield	8 Jul
12.30 w		Euron Roberts	18.11.85	2	Carmarthen	1 Jul
	(10)					
12.28		Ashley Morris	12.02.86	1	Telford	10 Jun
12.26		Simon Farenden	6.10.85	1	Nottingham	13 May
12.23		Andrew Reilly	26.10.85	1		10 Jun
12.08		Ian Miller	9.01.87	3	Derby	17 Jun
12.07	1.9	Steve Harding	14.12.85	8	Sheffield	8 Jul
12.00		Craig Phillips		3	Carmarthen	1 Jul

Foreign

15.73 w	*3.2*	*Farel Mepandy (CGO)*	*U23*	*27.12.79*	*5*	*Angers, FRA*	*30 Jul*
		15.54 i			*3*	*Birmingham*	*29 Jan*
		15.45 0.9			*3*	*Bondoufle, FRA*	*16 Jul*
15.54	*1.7*	*Desmond Kapofu (ZIM)*	*U23*	*6.02.78*	*2*	*Bedford*	*28 May*
15.35		*Reg Stasaitis (LIT)*		*6.04.67*	*1*	*London (Cr)*	*27 Aug*
14.39 w	*2.1*	*Michael McDonald (IRE)*		*24.08.65*	*9*	*Bedford*	*28 May*
		14.31 i			*1*	*Nenagh, IRE*	*13 Feb*
		14.24 0.5			*2*	*Dublin (S), IRE*	*20 Aug*
14.17 w	*2.6*	*Michael Corrigan(IRE)*		*1.12.77*	*3*	*Stoke-on-Trent*	*29 Apr*
14.12		*Gareth Devlin (IRE)*		*2.06.76*	*1*	*Dublin (S), IRE*	*16 Jul*

SHOT

20.57 i	Mark Proctor		15.01.63	1	Birmingham	17 Feb
	20.11			1	V R de S Antonio, POR	25 Mar
	19.77 i			1	Birmingham	26 Jan
	19.42 i			10	Ghent, BEL	26 Feb
	19.15 i			2	Glasgow	5 Mar
	19.14			1	Bedford	20 Aug
	19.04			1	Cosford	21 Jun
	18.69			1	Ipswich	14 May
	18.55			1	Loughborough	21 May
	18.49			31Q	Sydney, AUS	22 Sep
	18.13			1	Aldershot	5 Jul
	17.96			1	Wigan	24 Jun
	17.93			1	Bedford	19 Aug
	17.79			1	Berlin, GER	10 May
19.72	Mark Edwards		2.12.74	1	Brighton	16 Aug
	19.66			1	Corby	11 Jun
	19.66			1	Stretford	11 Jul
	19.55			1	Stretford	25 Jul
	19.32			1	Loughborough	13 May
	19.15			1	Stretford	30 May
	19.09			1	Loughborough	10 May
	19.07			1	Stretford	8 Aug
	19.05			1	Birmingham (Un)	22 Jul
	18.89			1	Corby	5 Aug
	18.80			1	Tamworth	24 Jun
	18.26			4B	Halle, GER	27 May
	17.97			3	Loughborough	21 May
18.79	Steph Hayward		30.07.74	1	Grangemouth	6 Sep
	18.38			1	Bedford	4 Jun
	18.31			1	Grangemouth	23 Aug
	18.30 i			1	Grangemouth	12 Feb
	18.28 i			1	Cardiff	26 Feb
	18.24			1	Birmingham	13 Aug
	18.23			1	Cudworth	28 Aug
	18.22			1	Grangemouth	24 May
	18.19 i			1	Glasgow	23 Jan
	18.06			2	Loughborough	21 May
	17.98			1	Bedford	28 May
	17.92 i			5	Glasgow	5 Mar
	17.87			3	Kiev, UKR	18 Jun
	17.82			1	Grangemouth	14 May
	17.67 i			1	Birmingham	29 Jan
	17.60 i			1	Glasgow	15 Jan
18.10	Emeka Udechuku	U23	10.07.79	2	Getafe, SPA	9 Sep
	17.95			1	Enfield	6 Aug
	17.90 i			2	Cardiff	26 Feb
	17.82			2	Bedford	20 Aug
	17.81			2	Bedford	19 Aug
	17.81 i			1	London (CP)	16 Dec
	17.74			1	Brighton	17 Jun
	17.66			1	Bedford	1 Jul
	17.65			1	Loughborough	14 Jun
	17.60			1	London (Cr)	27 Aug
17.81	Lee Newman		1.05.73	1	Birmingham (Un)	25 Jul
17.50	David Readle	U23	10.02.80	2	Carbondale, USA	25 Mar
	55 performances to 17.50 by 6 athletes including 12 indoors					
17.16	David Condon		11.04.72	1	Ashford	5 Aug
17.04 i	Scott Rider		22.09.77	1	London (Ha)	9 Jan
	17.04			2	Enfield	6 Aug

16.95	Gary Sollitt		13.01.72	3	Bedford	19	Aug
16.69	Greg Beard	U20	10.09.82	2	Dudingen, SWZ	30	Sep
	(10)						
16.55	Bruce Robb		27.07.77	2	Grangemouth	14	May
16.30	Lyndon Woodward	U23	22.11.80	1	Stoke-on-Trent	17	Jun
16.22	Neil Elliott		10.04.71	1	Luss	19	Jul
16.20	Iain McMullan	U23	15.06.78	7	Birmingham	13	Aug
16.15	Guy Marshall ¶		24.09.71	3	Bedford	11	Jun
15.96	Bruce Aitken		11.12.70	1	Nethybridge	12	Aug
15.94	Paul Reed		2.06.62	1	Middlesbrough	1	Jul
15.81	Bill Fuller		19.10.76	1	Kingston	8	Jul
15.69	Graeme Allan	U23	24.09.80	1	Bathgate	27	May
15.59	Nick Owen	U23	17.07.80	2	London (Cr)	14	May
	(20)						
15.57 i	Mark Leitch		17.11.68	1	London (CP)	20	Feb
	14.58			1	Bournemouth	8	Jul
15.50	Denzil McDonald		11.10.65	2	Chelmsford	13	May
15.44	Adam Major	U20	2.11.81	2	Bedford	26	Aug
15.29	Perriss Wilkins		12.12.69	1	Nuneaton	20	May
15.22	Simon Fricker		14.07.75	1	Bath	28	Aug
15.19	Andrew Rollins	U23	20.03.78	1	Stretford	16	May
15.11	Phil Adams		3.11.71	6	Bedford	28	May
15.09	Steve Whyte		14.03.64	1	Luton	14	May
15.06	David Lovett	U23	13.09.78	4	Glasgow (S)	20	Jul
15.00	Scot Thompson	U20	10.08.81	3	Bath	16	Sep
	(30)						
14.97	Mark Davies		10.01.71	1	Portsmouth	5	Aug
14.94 i	Scott Hayes		4.01.73	2	London (CP)	15	Jan
	14.84			1	Havering	12	Mar
14.90	George Baker		14.08.76	1	Abingdon	13	May
14.85	Mark Wiseman		9.02.69	2	Aldershot	5	Jul
14.84	Morris Fox		30.04.63	2	Stoke-on-Trent	17	Jun
14.84	Tony Zaidman		18.03.62	1	London (Ha)	22	Jul
14.75 i	Rob Earle		15.09.60	3	London (Ha)	9	Jan
	13.82			3	Chelmsford	13	May
14.75 i	John Nicholls		1.09.65	2	Blackpool	16	Jan
	14.74			1	Bebington	5	Aug
14.65 i	Willie Falconer	U23	20.12.78	4	Glasgow	23	Jan
	14.57			1	Grangemouth	14	May
14.62	Dean Macey		12.12.77	15D	Sydney, AUS	27	Sep
	(40)						
14.59	Andy Turner		29.08.63	1	Cwmbran	18	Jun
14.58	Robert Russell		5.08.74	1	Lancaster	2	Jul
14.50	Bryan Kelly		29.12.73	1	Blackpool	10	Sep
14.45	Justin Bryan		16.08.69	2	Cwmbran	17	Jun
14.41	Craig Rogers		14.02.76	2	Cudworth	22	Jul
14.36 i	Iain Styles		2.10.75	4	Cardiff	11	Mar
	14.28				New Haven, USA	8	Apr
14.36	Robert Morris	U20	20.02.82	1	Dartford	24	Jun
14.35	Matthew Twigg		18.07.69	1	Corby	14	May
14.32	Graham Sinclair		21.05.73	1	Enfield	3	Jun
14.32	Daniel Brunt		23.04.76	1	Cudworth	19	Aug
	(50)						
14.32	Jason Young		18.07.69	2	Dunoon	26	Aug
14.29 i	Simon Armstrong		29.05.62	2	Cardiff	4	Mar
	14.02			2	London (Elt)	3	Jun
14.28 i	Paul Corrigan		19.01.66	3	Blackpool	16	Jan
	13.83			1	Gateshead	14	May
14.25	Andrew Wain		2.06.65	1	Peterborough	28	Aug
14.24	Guy Perryman	V40	2.11.58	2	Enfield	3	Jun
14.23 i	Ian Lindley	V40	3.12.55	1	Birmingham	26	Feb
	13.76			1	Cudworth	13	May

14.22 i	Jonathan Ward		25.11.65	4	Birmingham	16 Jan
	13.64			1	Ashford	21 Jun
14.19	Neil Griffin	V50	28.05.48	1	High Wycombe	13 May
14.17	Gregor Edmunds		25.04.77	3	Dunoon	26 Aug
14.11	Peter Beaton		5.04.72	3	Grangemouth	24 May
	(60)					
14.11	Alex Kruger		18.11.63	9D	Arles, FRA	3 Jun
14.01	Glen Smith		21.05.72	7	Bedford	19 Aug
14.00	Tony Norman		5.07.63	1	London (TB)	5 Aug
13.96	Wayne Clarke		24.12.75	2	Cudworth	19 Aug
13.91 i	Andrew Lewis		9.03.68	3	Eton	19 Mar
	13.37			4	Enfield	23 Jul
13.91	Mark MacDonald	V40	2.12.59	1	Berwick	6 Aug
13.89	Barry Thomas		28.04.72	2	Watford	20 May
13.80	Fraser Ewen	U23	1.10.80	2	Bathgate	17 May
13.80	Francis Brebner		27.11.65	1	Inverness	22 Jul
13.80	Brett Heath		6.01.75	1	Yeovil	22 Jul
	(70)					
13.79	Colin Smith	V40	11.09.57	2	Bedford	30 Jul
13.77 i	Jamie Quarry		15.11.72	1	Birmingham	17 Feb
13.76	Gareth Cook		20.02.69	3	London (Cr)	14 May
13.76	Tony Quinn	U20	19.01.81	1	Antrim	10 Jun
13.75	Mike Small	V45	31.03.54	1	Burton	10 Sep
13.73	Manjit Singh Randhawa	U23	19.10.80	6	Stoke-on-Trent	30 Apr
13.73	Tom Dobbing		5.02.73	1	Hayes	19 Jul
13.71	Graeme Stark		12.10.63	2	Cudworth	14 May
13.61	Greg Richards	V40	25.04.56	1	Portsmouth (RN)	8 Jul
13.59	John Painter ¶	V40	12.06.58	3	Bedford	30 Jul
	(80)					
13.58	Anthony Southward		31.01.71	6	Enfield	6 Aug
13.58	David Horne		9.03.68	1	Drumnadrochit	26 Aug
13.57	Carl Saggers	U17	20.09.83	6	Enfield	24 Jun
13.56	John Holtby	U20	27.03.82	1D	Val de Reuil, FRA	12 Aug
13.55	Nick Vince	U20	29.01.82	4	Bedford	26 Aug
13.51	Neil McLellan	U23	10.09.78	2	Great Yarmouth	6 May
13.49	Mark Quigley		6.11.74	11	London (He)	6 Aug
13.45	Gary Herrington		31.03.61	2	Blackpool	20 May
13.44	Ashley Ward		1.08.64	3	Blackpool	20 May
13.43	Dominic Chapman		10.02.72	1	Milton Keynes	6 May
	(90)					
13.42	Marcus Gouldbourne	U20	12.06.81	1	Wakefield	16 Apr
13.42	Brett Marsh		20.01.76	1	Par	8 Jul
13.41 i	Hamish Davidson	V45	25.05.54	1	Glasgow	11 Mar
13.36	Clayton Turner		9.01.68	1	Horsham	8 Jul
13.34	Simon Williams	U23	5.10.80	2	London (TB)	5 Aug
13.34	Rafer Joseph		21.07.68	1	Hoo	5 Aug
13.31	Alun Williams		22.06.62	3	Cosford	21 Jun
13.31	Martin Wilson		3.03.71	1	Lancaster	9 Jul

Additional Under 20 (1 - 8 above)

13.28	Derrick Squire	U17	7.12.83	5	Bedford	26 Aug
13.25	Richard Oparka		28.07.82	5	Glasgow	29 Jul
	(10)					
13.20	David Dawson	U17	3.02.84	2	Exeter	24 Jun
13.07	Leslie McIntosh		25.02.81	1	Liverpool	15 Apr

Drugs disqualification

19.71 i	Carl Myerscough ¶	U23	21.10.79	1	Lincoln, USA	12 Feb

Foreign

16.57	*Fale Seve (SAM)*		*12.05.77*	*1*	*Peterborough*	*8 Jul*
15.30 i	*Tony Soalla-Bell (SLE)*		*3.10.76*	*1*	*London (CP)*	*15 Jan*
	15.16			*11*	*Birmingham*	*13 Aug*
14.10	*Jeroen Westmeijer (HOL)*		*5.07.70*	*2*	*Bromley*	*6 May*
13.95	*Kevin Brown (JAM)*		*10.09.64*	*5*	*Liege, BEL*	*28 May*

SHOT - Under 20 - 6.25kg

17.30	Greg Beard		10.09.82	1	London (He)	20 Aug
16.58	Adam Major		2.11.81	1	London (Ha)	18 Jun
16.28	Scot Thompson		10.08.81	1	Birmingham	10 Sep
15.99	Robert Morris		20.02.82	2	Watford	2 Jul
14.92	Carl Saggers	U17	20.09.83	3	London (He)	7 May
14.77	Derrick Squire	U17	7.12.83	1	Cannock	18 Jun
14.76	Tony Quinn		19.01.81	1	Antrim	10 Jun
14.58	David Dawson	U17	3.02.84	3	London (He)	20 Aug
14.50	Nick Vince		29.01.82	2	Grangemouth	25 Jun
14.31	Paul Archer		7.10.81	2	Sheffield	7 Jul
	(10)					
14.29	John Holtby		27.03.82	1	Scunthorpe	10 Jun
14.24	Edward Reid		22.07.81	1	Loughborough	12 Jul
14.23	Adam Beauford		24.10.81	1	Exeter	17 Jun
14.21	Richard Oparka		28.07.82	3	Grangemouth	25 Jun
14.10	Liam McCaffrey		29.05.81	1	Wrexham	18 Jul
14.02	Tony Smith		11.01.83	1	Dartford	18 Jun
13.99	James Rumbold		4.11.81	4	London (He)	20 Aug
13.98	Chris Orr		20.06.83	1	Cleckheaton	27 May
13.95	Andy Frost		17.04.81	1	Portsmouth	7 May
13.70	Marcus Gouldbourne		12.06.81	1	Cudworth	13 May
	(20)					
13.68	Deane Garrard		19.05.82	3	Sheffield	7 Jul
13.58	David Roberts		16.07.82	1	Cwmbran	17 Jun
13.58	David Onwubalili		5.12.82	5	London (Ha)	18 Jun
13.58 i	Grant Sprigings		26.11.82	1	London (CP)	16 Dec
13.53 i	Stuart Millar		9.03.83	1	Cheltenham	29 Apr

SHOT - Under 17 - 5kg

17.61	Derrick Squire		7.12.83	1	Blackpool	15 Jul
17.34	Carl Saggers		20.09.83	1	Sheffield	30 Jul
16.99	Nsa Harrison		27.11.83	1	Derby	17 Jun
16.92	David Dawson		3.02.84	1	Exeter	27 Jun
15.30	Chris Levett		30.11.83	2	Worcester	10 Jun
15.22 i	Garry Hagan		21.11.84	2	Cardiff	26 Feb
	14.99			1	Grangemouth	25 Jun
15.18	Richard Trimmer		7.09.83	1	Bournemouth	21 May
15.18	Edward Dunford		15.09.84	1O	Rugby	27 Jun
15.16	Peter Cranfield		26.09.84	1	Liverpool	10 Jun
14.95	Sam Westlake		14.09.83	1	London (CP)	9 Apr
	(10)					
14.87	Martin Aram		2.12.83	1	Lancaster	13 May
14.74 i	Dale Hewitson		11.09.84	1	Gateshead	21 Dec
	14.42			1	Gateshead	25 Jun
14.65	Stuart Semple		3.11.83	1	Horsham	17 Jun
14.51	Michael Mogford		19.09.83	1	Carmarthen	1 Jul
14.43	Carl Fletcher		24.09.83	1	Stretford	10 Jun
14.42 i	Andrae Davis	U15	27.09.85	1	London (CP)	16 Dec
14.39 i	Tony Gallagher		16.10.84	2	Cardiff	9 Dec
	13.98			5	Sheffield	7 Jul
14.19	Kyle Stevens		3.06.85	3	London (WF)	17 Sep
14.13	Tom Bivins		18.11.83	1	Loughborough	13 May
14.04	Ramji Nyirenda			2	Carmarthen	1 Jul
14.00 i	Matthew Thompson		29.12.84	1	Glasgow	11 Mar

SHOT - Under 15 - 4kg

16.11	Andrae Davis		27.09.85	1	Sheffield	29	Jul
15.06	Simon Bissell		25.12.85	1	Wigan	20	Aug
14.93	Bill Walter		11.10.85	1	Brighton	3	Jul
14.74	Samuel Clague		26.02.86	2	Sheffield	29	Jul
14.73	Alistair McDiarmid		16.10.85	1	Inverness	9	Jul
14.71	Jacob Babb		7.12.85	1	Yeovil	28	Aug
14.69	Greg Finlay		31.10.85	1	Carmarthen	1	Jul
14.55	Ben Lawrence		13.04.86	2	Sheffield	8	Jul
14.49	Richard May		10.12.85	1	Cudworth	3	Sep
14.27 i	Chris Gearing		30.09.86	1	London (CP)	16	Dec
	13.66			1		18	Jul
(10)							
14.22	Simon Cooke		3.10.85	2	London (He)	20	Aug
14.18	Gareth Williams		7.10.85	3	Exeter	17	Jun
14.02	Daniel Hepplewhite		2.09.86	1	London (WP)	23	Jul
14.01	Ross Zeraffa		2.11.85	3	Sheffield	8	Jul
14.01	Jason Joseph		27.11.85	4	Sheffield	29	Jul
13.99	William Caldeira		16.09.85	2	Crawley	23	Jul
13.96	John Rambotas		20.12.85	Q	Sheffield	8	Jul
13.89	Jamie Pritchard		25.09.85	2	Carmarthen	1	Jul
13.85	Matthew Corrigan		1.12.85	2	Cudworth	19	Aug
13.73	Chris Harrison		19.09.85	1	Blackpool	10	Jun
(20)							
13.64	Charles Allen		15.12.85	1	Scunthorpe	10	Jun
13.55	Fraser Johns		24.09.85	1	Carn Brea	10	Jun
13.49	Jared Carty		25.09.85	Q	Sheffield	8	Jul
13.28	Damien Hines		6.09.85	1	Cleckheaton	3	Sep
13.24	David Price		12.01.87	2	Newport	28	Aug
13.19	Andrew Thomas		14.06.86	1	Solihull	28	May
13.14	Emeka Obanye		18.11.85	Q	Sheffield	8	Jul
13.14	Andrew Bennett		19.12.85	1	Bournemouth	13	Aug
13.06	Matthew Woolley		6.05.86	1	Mansfield	25	Aug
13.05	Richard Parker		21.11.86	2	Cannock	10	Jun

SHOT - Under 13 - 3.25kg

12.40	Shane Birch		22.10.87	1	Basildon	23	Jul
12.25	Brendan Hall		5.09.87	1	Tipton	24	Sep
11.59	Matthew Evans		9.09.88	1	Carmarthen	6	Aug
11.56	Steve McManus		22.09.87	1	Watford	10	Sep
11.32	Oliver King		20.12.87	2	Kingston	30	Jul
11.20	Adam Akehurst		13.09.87	1	Horsham	20	Aug

Overage

12.47 i	Shane Birch	U15	22.10.87	1	Cardiff	17	Dec

DISCUS

65.08	Bob Weir		4.02.61	1	Bedford	19	Aug
	63.65			1	Loughborough	30	Jul
	63.58			1	Helsingborg, SWE	10	Aug
	62.13			1	Birmingham	12	Aug
	61.87			1	Helsingborg, SWE	6	Aug
	61.51			3	Helsingborg, SWE	5	Aug
	61.17			1	Hayes	19	Jul
	61.02			1B	Budapest, HUN	22	Jul
	60.78			4	Gateshead	16	Jul
	60.18			1	The Hague, HOL	22	Aug
	60.05			2	Palo Alto, USA	17	Jun
	60.01			28Q	Sydney, AUS	24	Sep

(Weir)	59.60			6	Budapest, HUN	22	Jul
	59.14			3	Glasgow (S)	2	Jul
	58.78			1	London (He)	8	Jul
	58.30			2	Helsingborg, SWE	9	Jul
64.65	Perriss Wilkins		12.12.69	1	Redditch	22	Jul
	60.21			1	Nuneaton	20	May
	60.02			1	Yate	5	Aug
	59.06			1	Abingdon	13	May
	58.42			1	London (Cr)	27	Aug
63.08	Glen Smith		21.05.72	1	Watford	9	Aug
	62.92			1	Arles, FRA	3	Jun
	62.68			1	Irvine, USA	7	May
	61.92			1	Istanbul, TUR	24	Jun
	61.80			7	Salinas, USA	23	May
	61.62			4A	Modesto, USA	13	May
	61.60			1	Solihull	29	Jul
	61.15			8	Halle, GER	27	May
	60.84			2	Birmingham	12	Aug
	60.41			5	Helsingborg, SWE	5	Aug
	60.22			1	Loughborough	14	Jun
	60.18			2	Leuven, BEL	17	Jun
	59.97			3	Brasschaat, BEL	15	Aug
	59.46			2	Salon-de-Provence, FRA	1	Jun
	59.22			1	London (He)	6	Aug
	58.72			3	Loughborough	30	Jul
	58.58			7	Budapest, HUN	22	Jul
	58.33			4	Gold Coast (RB), AUS	10	Sep
	58.30			5	Gold Coast (RB), AUS	17	Sep
62.07	Emeka Udechuku	U23	10.07.79	2	Bedford	19	Aug
	61.91			1	Getafe, SPA	9	Sep
	59.58			3	Birmingham	12	Aug
	59.55			1	Enfield	6	Aug
	58.84			3B	Halle, GER	27	May
	58.83			2	Loughborough	30	Jul
	58.33			1	Bedford	20	Aug
	47 performances to 58.00 by 4 athletes						
57.44	Lee Newman		1.05.73	3	Bedford	19	Aug
57.14	Mark Proctor		15.01.63	1	Wigan	24	Jun
54.11	Paul Reed		2.06.62	1	Jarrow	11	Jun
53.93	Peter Gordon	V45	2.07.51	1	Macclesfield	16	Jun
53.31	Bruce Robb		27.07.77	3	Loughborough	21	May
53.28	Abi Ekoku		13.04.66	6	Birmingham	12	Aug
	(10)						
53.00	Neville Thompson	V45	28.03.55	1	London (BP)	19	Jul
52.81	Scott Rider		22.09.77	2	Enfield	6	Aug
52.49	Denzil McDonald		11.10.65	4	London (He)	6	Aug
52.42	Gary Herrington		31.03.61	3	Bedford	28	May
51.28	Adam Major	U20	2.11.81	1	Birmingham	10	Sep
51.03	Scott Hayes		4.01.73	4	Eton	6	May
51.02	Leith Marar		7.11.68	1	Kingston	19	Mar
50.22	David Lovett	U23	13.09.78	1	Portsmouth (RN)	8	Jul
50.07	Scot Thompson	U20	10.08.81	1	Bedford	27	Aug
49.77	Luke Rosenberg	U23	29.06.80	1	Loughborough	10	May
	(20)						
49.63	Alexis Sharp		31.10.72	3	Enfield	6	Aug
49.26	Robert Russell		5.08.74	2	Grantham	18	Jun
48.74	Matthew Twigg		18.07.69	2	Corby	14	May
48.72	Nick Woolcott		7.04.61	3	Enfield	24	Jun
48.56	Andrew Rollins	U23	20.03.78	1	Stretford	11	Jul
48.14	Mark Quigley		6.11.74	8	London (He)	6	Aug

48.01	Michael Jemi-Alade		13.10.64	6	Enfield	6	Aug
47.94	Daniel Brunt		23.04.76	3	Grantham	18	Jun
47.90	Greg Beard	U20	10.09.82	3	Bedford	27	Aug
47.37	Simon Fricker		14.07.75	9	Bedford	19	Aug
	(30)						
47.30	Mark Davies		10.01.71	1	London (WP)	8	Jul
47.26	Neil Elliott		10.04.71	2	Coatbridge	18	Jun
46.74	John Moreland	V40	13.09.58	2	Stoke-on-Trent	18	Jun
46.64	Andrew Brittan		17.01.67	3	Bedford	20	Aug
46.41	Robert Morris	U20	20.02.82	4	Bedford	27	Aug
46.39	Mark Wiseman		9.02.69	1	Tamworth	24	Jun
46.38	Simon Williams	U23	5.10.80	2	Aldershot	28	Jun
46.24	Mark Edwards		2.12.74	1	Corby	5	Aug
46.08	Rafer Joseph		21.07.68	1	Hoo	5	Aug
45.72	David Readle	U23	10.02.80	4	Carbondale, USA	25	Mar
	(40)						
45.64	Ian Taylor		2.07.67	2	Telford	9	Sep
45.62	Jeff Clare		21.03.65	2	Stretford	8	Aug
45.57	Andy Turner		29.08.63	3	Bath	16	Sep
45.47	Graeme Allan	U23	24.09.80	2	Stretford	5	Aug
45.44	Neil Griffin	V50	28.05.48	1	Watford	20	May
45.08	Andy Kruszewski	V40	7.04.59	5	London (Cr)	27	Aug
44.92	Ali Bajwa		13.06.71	5	Grantham	18	Jun
44.83	Morris Fox		30.04.63	2	Watford	20	May
44.74	Bryan Kelly		29.12.73	2	Bebington		Aug
44.64	Ali Morganella		28.05.77	6	Grantham	18	Jun
	(50)						
44.62	Gareth Cook		20.02.69	1	London (Cr)	13	May
44.56	Steph Hayward		30.07.74	9	London (He)	6	Aug
44.55	Jonathan Ward		25.11.65	4	Sydney, AUS	23	Oct
44.53	Steven Hale		20.04.77		Birmingham (Un)	22	Jun
44.50	Brett Heath		6.01.75	1	Woodford	29	Apr
44.40	Paul Head		1.07.65	10	London (He)	6	Aug
44.29	Steve Whyte		14.03.64	1	Luton	13	May
44.21	Ashley Ward		1.08.64	4	Bedford	5	Aug
43.81	Allan Brassington	U20	27.09.81	5	Bedford	27	Aug
43.62	James Rumbold	U20	4.11.81	3	Welwyn	22	Jul
	(60)						
43.57	Greg Richards	V40	25.04.56	1	London (WL)	24	Jun
43.40	Nick Owen	U23	17.07.80	1	Kingston	17	May
43.39	Niklas Iliffe	U20	6.03.81	6	Bedford	27	Aug
43.38	Justin Bryan		16.08.69	2	Newport	28	Jun
43.37	Dean Macey		12.12.77	12D	Sydney, AUS	28	Sep
43.33	Alan Rudkin	U23	5.11.78	10	Enfield	24	Jun
43.33	David Abernethy	V40	5.09.55	1	Lancaster	2	Jul
43.29	Edward Reid	U20	22.07.81	1	Loughborough	12	Jul
43.22	Neil Sougrin		14.05.71	2	Enfield	13	May
43.14	Richard Healey	V45	17.11.54	3	Portsmouth	8	Jul
	(70)						
43.10	Felice Miele	U20	24.11.81	1	Enfield	3	Jun
42.82	Mike Small	V45	31.03.54	1	Ewell	10	Jun
42.72	Iain Styles		2.10.75	4	Stoke-on-Trent	17	Jun
42.72	Simon Read		24.06.70	4	Welwyn	22	Jul
42.64	Gary Parsons		17.05.71	1	Thurrock	3	Jun
42.61	John Little	V45	14.04.53	1	Burton	10	Sep
42.54	Marcus Gouldbourne	U20	12.06.81	1	Wigan	6	May
42.37	Craig Burrows		8.08.74	1	Wigan	22	Apr
42.27	John Parkin	U23	23.02.79	2	Warrington	16	Jul
42.17	Anthony Southward		31.01.71	2	Cudworth	22	Jul
	(80)						

42.08	Andrew Wain		2.06.65	2	Peterborough	22 Jul
41.94	Alex Kruger		18.11.63	3	Jarrow	6 Aug
41.90	Andrew Flint		9.11.76	2	Hastings	5 Aug
41.78	Simon Armstrong		29.05.62	2	Basildon	24 Jun
41.78	Steven Lloyd		20.03.74	1	Carlisle	5 Aug
41.74	Rob Earle		15.09.60	2	Ewell	10 Jun
41.68	Paul Howard		19.10.66	1	London (WL)	3 Jun
41.47	Tony Brannen		16.09.68	2	Stafford	11 Jun
41.40	Chris Howe		17.11.67	9	Enfield	5 Aug
41.32	Simon Bates		21.12.76	1	Macclesfield	10 Jun
(90)						
41.29	Willie Falconer	U23	20.12.78	1	Grangemouth	14 May
41.22	Nick Crimmen		15.07.65	2	Cleckheaton	11 Jun
41.16	Tony Smith	U20	11.01.83	2	Thurrock	3 Jun
41.10	Malcolm Fenton	V40	12.02.56	1	Ipswich	5 Aug
40.86	Guy Marshall ¶		24.09.71	1	Hull	14 May
40.79	Alun Williams		22.06.62	2	Aldershot	5 Jul
40.69	Craig Rogers		14.02.76	3	Cudworth	22 Jul
40.50	Ewart Hulse		21.01.62	2	Colwyn Bay	14 May
40.49	Terry Gyorffy		28.01.65	4	Aldershot	28 Jun
40.48	Graham Holder		16.01.72	2	Barking	12 Mar
(100)						
40.47	John Painter ¶	V40	12.06.58	1	King's Lynn	13 May
40.43	Martin Wilson		3.03.71	3	Wigan	6 May
40.43	A. Mills			1	Tipton	22 Jul
40.42	Adam Davis		19.11.72	2	Cosford	21 Jun
40.39	Richard Czernik		12.08.72	1	Gloucester	3 Jun
40.34	Nick Vince	U20	29.01.82	1	Grangemouth	16 Jul
40.32	Ben Walker	U23	8.06.78	2	Ware	3 Sep
40.30	Barry Thomas		28.04.72	5	Enfield	24 Jun
40.27	Iain Park		16.07.74	11	Enfield	24 Jun
40.23	Craig Munden		24.12.76	4	Feltham	6 May
(110)						
40.19	Philip Scowcroft		25.01.71	4	Stretford	16 May
40.14	Guy Perryman	V40	2.11.58	1	Bury St. Edmunds	8 Jul
40.13	Chris Orr	U20	20.06.83	3	Carlisle	5 Aug
40.10	Daniel Greaves	U20	4.10.82	1	Burton	20 May
40.03	Maurice Hicks		1.01.70	12	London (He)	6 Aug
40.01	James Taylor	U20	24.04.82	1	Darlington	9 Jul

Foreign

62.10	*Kevin Brown (JAM)*		*10.09.64*	*1*	*Ipswich*	*3 Aug*
50.69	*Fale Seve (SAM)*		*12.05.77*	*2*	*Enfield*	*24 Jun*
46.40	*Garry Power (IRE)*		*1.09.62*	*1*	*Hastings*	*24 Jun*
41.40	*Libor Krten (CZE)*		*26.02.73*	*3*	*London (WP)*	*8 Jul*
40.03	*Sascha Marchetto (SWZ)*		*11.01.73*	*1*	*Edinburgh*	*22 Apr*

DISCUS - Under 20 - 1.75kg

55.16	Adam Major	2.11.81	1	Birmingham	10 Sep
53.62	Scot Thompson	10.08.81	1	London (He)	7 May
51.26	Greg Beard	10.09.82	1	London (He)	20 Aug
50.44	Robert Morris	20.02.82	2	London (He)	20 Aug
49.59	Niklas Iliffe	6.03.81	1	Loughborough	8 Apr
49.40	Felice Miele	24.11.81	1	Enfield	13 May
48.83	Allan Brassington	27.09.81	1	Cannock	10 Jun
48.23	James Rumbold	4.11.81	1	Exeter	17 Jun
46.59	Edward Reid	22.07.81	2	Watford	2 Jul
46.33	Josh Lamb	14.04.83	1	Crawley	10 Jun
(10)					
46.15	Daniel Greaves	4.10.82	1	Welwyn	1 May

45.37	David Onwubalili		5.12.82	5	Enfield	16 Jul
45.27	Chris Orr		20.06.83	1	Cleckheaton	27 May
44.72	Daniel Lethbridge		1.04.81	4	London (He)	7 May
44.42	Tony Smith		11.01.83	1	Erith	7 May
44.25	Carl Saggers	U17	20.09.83	1	Stadskanal, HOL	1 Jul
43.97	Marcus Gouldbourne		12.06.81	1	Cudworth	13 May
43.95	James Taylor		24.04.82	2	Cudworth	13 May
43.31	Richard Oparka		28.07.82	1	Dundee	24 May
42.34	Peter Favell		16.03.82	8	Sheffield (W)	8 Jul
	(20)					
42.30	Stephen Ashton	U17	21.03.84	2	Dumfries	13 Aug
41.85	Grant Myerscough		3.04.83	2	Cleckheaton	27 May
41.64	Roger Bate		16.01.83	1	Stretford	5 Sep
41.60	Daniel Brandwood		1.10.82	1	Derby	18 Jun
41.50	Philip Titmus		12.11.81	2	Exeter	17 Jun

overage

41.88	Scott Jenns	U23	13.12.80	1	Derby	16 Jul

DISCUS - Under 17 - 1.5kg

53.69	Carl Saggers		20.09.83	1	London (WF)	17 Sep
48.24	Garry Hagan		21.11.84	2	Sheffield	30 Jul
47.60	Glenn Williams		24.03.85	2	Blackpool	15 Jul
47.55	Gareth Bull		3.03.85	3	Sheffield	30 Jul
46.40	Tom Bivins		18.11.83	4	Sheffield	30 Jul
45.89	Chris Levett		30.11.83	4	Blackpool	15 Jul
45.63	Sam Westlake		14.09.83	1	Exeter	17 Jun
45.62	Stephen Ashton		21.03.84	2	Birmingham	3 Sep
45.46	Stuart Semple		3.11.83	2	Sheffield (W)	7 Jul
45.24	Derrick Squire		7.12.83	1	Solihull	28 May
	(10)					
43.85	Robert Jukes		18.09.83	1	Hoo	23 Jul
43.46	Robert Eggleton		13.02.84	1	Stoke-on-Trent	2 Aug
43.42	Leslie Richards		29.03.85	1	Liverpool	21 May
42.90	Martin Aram		2.12.83	1	Wigan	25 Jun
42.85	Ross Elliott		6.09.83	1	Jarrow	13 Aug
42.69	Simon Bissell	U15	25.12.85	1	Lancaster	13 May
42.10	David Dawson		3.02.84	1	Bath	4 Jun
42.04	Simon Bulley		19.09.84	6	Sheffield	30 Jul
41.97	Nick Humphreys		24.12.83	2	Derby	17 Jun
41.40	Edward Dunford		15.09.84	3	Solihull	28 May
	(20)					
41.34	Steven Marlow		13.12.84	3	Watford	28 May
41.29	Tony Gallagher		16.10.84	1	Liverpool	2 Jul
40.81	Ben Kelsey		23.09.84	1	Oxford	11 Jun
40.68	Paul Farley		1.12.84	3	Portsmouth	13 May
40.58	Peter Cranfield		26.09.84	2	Stretford	4 Jun
40.48	Peter Hughes		12.12.83	2	Colwyn Bay	3 Sep
40.27	Michael Whitten		30.09.83	1	Cleckheaton	16 Jul

DISCUS - Under 15 - 1.25kg

49.10	Simon Bissell	25.12.85	1	Burnley	27 Aug
48.48	Simon Cooke	3.10.85	1	Sheffield (W)	8 Jul
47.57	Kieran O'Keefe	19.03.86	2	Sheffield (W)	8 Jul
47.05	Alistair McDiarmid	16.10.85	1	Grangemouth	6 Sep
46.55	Andrew Thomas	14.06.86	1	Birmingham	2 Sep
46.35	Bobby Lockwood	1.02.86	1	Hoo	23 Jul
45.08	Sam Herrington	2.10.86	3	Sheffield (W)	8 Jul
42.54	Lewis Williamson	7.09.85	1	Stretford	4 Jun
42.41	Ian Callahan		1	Stretford	10 Jun
41.89	Lance Symester	5.07.86	5	Sheffield (W)	8 Jul

41.57	Greg Finlay	31.10.85	6	Sheffield	29 Jul
41.11	Andrew Roberts	24.10.85	6	Sheffield (W)	8 Jul
40.12	Samuel Clague	26.02.86	7	Sheffield	29 Jul
39.85	Matthew Corrigan	1.12.85	2	Cudworth	19 Aug
39.42	Ryan Cassidy	12.12.85	2	Birmingham	3 Sep
38.59	James Green	28.11.85	1	Liverpool	21 May
38.47	Damien Hines	6.09.85	1	Cudworth	13 May
38.22	Nnamdi Efobi	14.09.86	3	Birmingham	3 Sep
38.05	David Price	12.01.87	1	Colwyn Bay	3 Sep
37.98	Asandro McLeod	15.09.85	1	Woodford	4 Jun
(20)					
37.71	Daniel Hepplewhite	2.09.86	2	Exeter	17 Jun
37.32	L. Ashman		2	London (BP)	10 Jun
37.28	Jamie Pritchard	25.09.85	1	Worcester	4 Jun
37.22	Ben Lawrence	13.04.86	4	Birmingham	3 Sep
	42.62 unconfirmed		1	Sutton Coldfield	2 Jul
37.20	Jared Carty	25.09.85	2	Woodford	4 Jun

DISCUS - Under 13 - 1kg

31.58	Shane Birch	22.10.87	1	Tonbridge	8 Aug
27.18	Matthew Evans	9.09.88	1	Carmarthen	30 Jul
26.69	Paul Martin	28.01.88	1	Bromley	9 Jul
26.64	Kenneth Robertson	6.04.88	1	Grangemouth	17 Sep
26.58	Alistair Boyle	27.05.88	1	Grangemouth	6 Aug
26.43	Anthony Timms	4.03.88	1	Cleckheaton	3 Sep
25.72	Luke Cutts	13.02.88	1	Scunthorpe	27 Aug

HAMMER

75.94	Mick Jones	23.07.63	1	Crawley	6 Sep
	74.98		1	Crawley	11 Jul
	74.89		1	London (Col)	30 Apr
	74.39		1	Eton	6 May
	74.37		4	Vittel, FRA	2 Sep
	73.86		1	Crawley	14 May
	73.57		1	Bedford	4 Jun
	73.47		1	Crawley	9 Apr
	73.38		6	Halle, GER	27 May
	73.37		1	Liege, BEL	28 May
	73.21		1	Lewes	20 Jun
	72.87		1	Bedford	20 Aug
	72.65		1	Crawley	25 Mar
	72.52		1	Perivale	5 Mar
	72.51		1	London (He)	8 Jul
	72.08		1	Loughborough	30 Jul
	71.54		1	London (He)	6 Aug
	71.51		1	Birmingham	13 Aug
	71.09		1	Enfield	20 Aug
	70.43		1	Wigan	24 Jun
	69.99		1	Bedford	19 Aug
71.76	William Beauchamp	9.09.70	1	North Wembley	23 Apr
	70.75		2	London (Col)	30 Apr
	70.37		1	Enfield	13 May
	67.57		3	Loughborough	21 May
	67.16		2	Perivale	5 Mar
70.90	Paul Head	1.07.65	1	Bedford	29 May
	70.79		Q	Bedford	29 May
	69.63		2	Birmingham	13 Aug
	69.49		2	London (He)	8 Jul
	69.46		6	Vittel, FRA	2 Sep
	69.42		2	Wigan	24 Jun

(Head)	68.92			1	Enfield	30 Jul
	68.89			1	Chelmsford	13 May
	68.63			2	Eton	6 May
	68.50			2	Bedford	19 Aug
	68.36			2	London (He)	6 Aug
	68.23			7B	Budapest, HUN	22 Jul
	68.22			1	Solihull	29 Jul
	67.89			1	London (Cr)	23 Aug
	67.75			7	Gateshead	16 Jul
70.33	John Pearson		30.04.66	2	Loughborough	30 Jul
	69.49			1	Birmingham (Un)	22 Jul
	68.40			1	Loughborough	13 May
	68.36			1	Loughborough	24 May
	68.18			2	Dublin (S), IRE	29 Jul
	68.18			1	Corby	5 Aug
	68.07			1	Stretford	11 Jul
	67.91			1	Loughborough	4 Jun
	67.66			2	Loughborough	21 May
	67.52			1	Yeovil	28 Aug
	67.50			1	Stretford	25 Jul
	67.22			3	Birmingham	13 Aug
69.38	Mike Floyd		26.09.76	1	Grantham	18 Jun
	68.18			1	Loughborough	21 May
	67.71			2	Bedford	29 May
	67.29			3	Loughborough	30 Jul
	67.13			1	Stretford	5 Sep
68.02	David Smith		2.11.74	1	Wakefield	16 Apr
	67.69			1	Cleckheaton	24 Sep
	67.01			3	Bedford	29 May
	61 performances to 67.00 by 6 athletes					
65.22	Simon Bown		21.11.74	1	London (WL)	3 Sep
65.09	Russell Devine		24.04.68	1	Melbourne, AUS	16 Mar
64.47	Steve Pearson	V40	13.09.59	1	Stoke-on-Trent	18 Jun
64.39	Craig Ellams		24.11.72	1	Worcester	19 Aug
	(10)					
63.60	Shane Peacock		5.03.63	3	Grantham	18 Jun
63.01	Matthew Bell	U23	2.06.78	2	Stoke-on-Trent	18 Jun
62.92	Chris Howe		17.11.67	1	Enfield	6 Aug
62.86	Iain Park		16.07.74	2	Enfield	6 Aug
61.44	Graham Holder		16.01.72	1	Cwmbran	18 Jun
60.92	Paul Barnard		27.07.72	5	London (Col)	30 Apr
60.61	Steve Sammut		3.05.67	1	Aldershot	16 Jul
60.58	Rob Careless		7.09.74	1	Nottingham	2 Apr
60.53	Chris Walsh	U23	1.10.78	1B	Derby	3 Sep
60.47	Glen Kerr		27.10.74	1	Bedford	10 May
	(20)					
60.14	Rob Earle		15.09.60	3	Enfield	30 Jul
60.05	David Allan		17.10.70	4	Loughborough	21 May
59.75	Malcolm Fenton	V40	12.02.56	1	Ipswich	30 Jul
59.72	Mark Miller		10.11.71	3	Enfield	6 Aug
59.24	Kevin Davies	U23	11.01.78	1	Leichlingen, GER	22 Oct
59.10	Gareth Cook		20.02.69	1	London (Cr)	14 May
58.76	Wayne Clarke		24.12.75	1	Peterborough	28 Aug
58.75	Andy Frost	U20	17.04.81	2	Derby	3 Sep
58.31	Graeme Allan	U23	24.09.80	1	Cleckheaton	23 Dec
58.22	Chris Black	V50	1.01.50	2	Grendon Hall	1 Oct
	(30)					
57.80	Steve Minnikin		4.01.72	1	Cudworth	13 May
57.64	Matthew Sutton	U20	8.09.81	3	Loughborough	14 Jun
56.95	Adrian Palmer		10.08.69	2	Cwmbran	18 Jun
56.91	Stuart Thurgood		17.05.76	4	Chelmsford	13 May

56.69	Anthony Swain		17.01.75	7	Solihull	29	Jul
56.50	Ross Thompson	U20	7.12.81	1	Cleckheaton	10	Sep
56.36	David Little	U20	28.02.81	3	Derby	3	Sep
56.07	David Robinson	U23	12.01.78	1	Gateshead	9	Jul
55.21	Dave Smith		21.06.62	6	Grendon Hall	30	Sep
55.00	Steve Whyte		14.03.64	5	Enfield	23	Jul
	(40)						
54.79	Calum Bruce		28.02.75	2	Pitreavie	13	Jun
54.76	Tim Wurr	U23	1.03.79	2	Stoke-on-Trent	30	Apr
53.78	Peter Gordon	V45	2.07.51	2	Jyvaskyla, FIN	9	Jul
53.50	Paul Dickenson	V50	4.12.49	2	Bromley	8	Jul
53.36	Maurice Hicks		1.01.70	1	Exeter	16	Jul
53.31	Ali Bajwa		13.06.71	3	Gateshead	26	Aug
53.19	Bill Fuller		19.10.76	1	Hayes	24	Jun
53.19	John Urquhart		14.11.77	10	London (He)	8	Jul
53.17	Peter Field	U20	21.05.82	5	Derby	3	Sep
53.07	Ron James	V40	20.09.59	1	London (PH)	6	May
	(50)						
52.94	Adam Beauford	U20	24.10.81	2	Exeter	16	Jul
52.70	Carl Saggers	U17	20.09.83	2	Enfield	3	Jun
52.66	Peter Fuller	U23	30.04.78	1	London (TB)	17	Jun
52.58	Mark Sheridan		17.06.70	2	Crawley	13	May
52.22	Nigel Winchcombe	V40	10.12.59	1	Grantham	14	May
52.09	Leslie McIntosh	U20	25.02.81	1	Stoke-on-Trent	25	Jun
51.85	David Nicholl		16.09.69	5	Glasgow	29	Jul
51.81	Wayne Gibson		25.02.76	6	Middlesbrough	15	Jul
51.71	Russell Payne		11.09.60	4	Peterborough	27	Aug
51.66	Chris Adams	U20	18.07.81	2	London (Col)	30	Apr
	(60)						
50.88	Andrew Benn		2.09.77	3	Bromley	6	May
50.82	Scott Thompson		29.09.74	2	Cleckheaton	10	Aug
50.53	Ewart Hulse		21.01.62				
50.34	Steve McEvoy		23.05.63	1	Hoo	5	Aug
50.22	Greg Beard	U20	10.09.82	2	London (WL)	30	Jul
50.19	Mark Proctor		15.01.63	2	Aldershot	5	Jul
50.13	Andy Turner		29.08.63	1	Bournemouth	8	Jul
50.11	Timmon Whitehead	U20	20.04.82	2	Southend	3	Jun
50.11	Tom Dempsey	U17	15.12.83	6	Derby	3	Sep
50.02	Ross Blight		28.05.77	3	Cwmbran	18	Jun
	(70)						
49.95	John Owen		28.10.64	2	Rugby	23	Jul
49.69	Alan James		26.03.62	8	Grendon Hall	30	Sep
49.65	Robert Taylor	U23	9.06.80	2	Wakefield	17	Sep
49.57	Eric Kerr		9.12.64	2	Perivale	5	Aug
49.43	Bob Weir		4.02.61	13	London (He)	8	Jul
49.08	Bruce Shepherd		20.03.67	3	Inverness	22	Jul
48.94	Mike Small	V45	31.03.54	1	Portsmouth	26	Aug
48.53	Alan Woods	V45	27.03.51	1	Bedford	29	Jul
48.17	Simon Gate	U20	21.09.82	7	Derby	3	Sep
47.98	Rafer Joseph		21.07.68	2	Hoo	5	Aug
	(80)						
47.96	John Parkin	U23	23.02.79	2B	Manchester	8	Sep
47.85	Nick Fogg	U23	24.03.78	5	Hayes	19	Jul
47.80	Gavin Cook		30.03.70	5	London (WL)	3	Sep
47.72	Kenneth Smith		10.05.64	1	Rugby	20	May
47.70	Jimmy Summers		7.10.65	1	London (Ha)	22	Jul
47.66	Ashley Slater	U20	23.09.81	2	Colwyn Bay	22	Apr
47.37	Martin Roberts	V40	1.03.60	3	Stoke-on-Trent	13	May
47.33	Colin Smith	V40	11.09.57	1	London (Nh)	24	Jun
47.29	Mark Roberson		21.03.75	1	Hayes	5	Aug
47.23	Daniel Gamester	U23	29.04.78	7	Enfield	23	Jul

47.07	Chris James	U20	9.12.82	1	Milton Keynes	6 May
47.06	Darren Kerr		6.10.69	4	Luton	13 May
46.89	Jason Kingwell		8.10.70	2	London (Nh)	24 Jun
46.87	Christopher Snook	U23	6.06.79	5	Loughborough	14 Jun
46.85	Daniel Martin	U20	9.03.82	1	Portsmouth	8 Jul
46.80	Matt Spicer		18.05.71	6	Corby	5 Aug
46.79	Michael Madden		13.09.65	1	Par	8 Jul
46.79	Brett Marsh		20.01.76	1	Eton	5 Aug
46.69	Wesley Clarke		31.12.63	1	London (TB)	5 Aug
46.28	Chris Melluish	V55	15.07.44	2	Feltham	3 Jun
	(100)					
45.83	Gary Herrington		31.03.61	3	Corby	11 Jun
45.72	Stuart Capeling	V45	31.12.51		Hoo	24 Jun
45.71	Neil Bulman		7.09.77	1	Darlington	9 Jul
45.57	Graeme Mackay	U23	4.10.80	2	Cambridge	4 Nov
45.51	Kirk Capeling	U23	27.02.80	3	Crawley	25 Mar

Downhill

60.90	Steve Sammut		3.05.67	1	Haslemere	13 Jun
55.44	Maurice Hicks		1.01.70	1	Haslemere	8 Aug

Foreign

62.87	*John Osazuwa (NIG)*	*U20*	*4.05.81*	*1*	*Derby*	*3 Sep*
58.61	*Phil Spivey (AUS)*		*15.05.61*	*2*	*Stretford*	*28 Jun*
55.37	*Fale Seve (SAM)*		*12.05.77*	*4*	*Enfield*	*24 Jun*
46.31	*Eduardo Reina (HON)*		*9.12.68*	*1*	*Cambridge*	*4 Nov*

HAMMER - Under 20 - 6.25kg

63.20	Nick Williams		2.02.82	1	Bebington	18 Jun
62.65	Peter Field		21.05.82	1	Sheffield (W)	7 Jul
62.53	David Little		28.02.81	1	Middlesbrough	15 Jul
61.64	Matthew Sutton		8.09.81	1	Stoke-on-Trent	4 Jun
61.39	Ross Thompson		7.12.81	1	Wakefield	23 Apr
61.23	Andy Frost		17.04.81	1	Sandown IOW	20 Jun
59.22	Adam Beauford		24.10.81	3	Sheffield (W)	7 Jul
59.04	Carl Saggers	U17	20.09.83	1	London (He)	20 Aug
58.71	Chris Adams		18.07.81	2	Dumfries	13 Aug
56.52	Timmon Whitehead		20.04.82	3	London (Ha)	28 May
	(10)					
56.30	Ashley Slater		23.09.81	1	Telford	23 Apr
55.56	Leslie McIntosh		25.02.81	1	Liverpool	13 May
52.75	Tom Dempsey	U17	15.12.83	1	Rugby	13 Aug
52.57	Kamran Khan	U17	2.10.83	3	Birmingham	10 Sep
52.46	Simon Gate		21.09.82	3	Watford	2 Jul
52.40	Daniel Martin		9.03.82	2	London (He)	20 Aug
51.88	John Hay		4.06.83	1	Corby	10 Jun
51.00	Chris James		9.12.82	2	London (He)	7 May
50.37	Adam Major		2.11.81	4	Birmingham	10 Sep
50.30	Derrick Squire	U17	7.12.83	1	Stoke-on-Trent	5 Mar
	(20)					
50.27	James Nunan	U17	16.09.83	1	Bath	14 May
50.00	Marc Landon		9.11.81	3	Solihull	27 May
48.88	Scot Thompson		10.08.81	5	Birmingham	10 Sep

Downhill

59.39	Timmon Whitehead		20.04.82	1	Haslemere	9 May
54.34	Daniel Martin		9.03.82	2	Haslemere	9 May

Foreign

64.56	*John Osazuwa (NIG)*		*4.05.81*	*1*	*Birmingham*	*10 Sep*

HAMMER - Under 17 - 5kg

68.27	Carl Saggers		20.09.83	1	Brighton	17 Jun
60.92	Derrick Squire		7.12.83	2	Birmingham	3 Sep
60.81	Tom Dempsey		15.12.83	1	Loughborough	10 Sep
60.09	Kamran Khan		2.10.83	3	Birmingham	3 Sep
59.93	James Nunan		16.09.83	1	Bath	4 Jun
56.92	Matthew Frampton		10.04.84	1	London (WP)	23 Jul
55.39	Richard Greene		11.10.84	1	Enfield	13 May
54.82	Paul Farley		1.12.84	3	Brighton	17 Jun
54.58	Simon Bissell	U15	25.12.85	1	Colwyn Bay	3 Sep
54.28	Peter Cranfield		26.09.84	1	Liverpool	13 May
	(10)					
52.81	Chris Mason		6.04.84	1	Middlesbrough	10 Jun
52.80	Glenn Williams		24.03.85	1	Carmarthen	1 Jul
51.60	Laurence Harwood		9.03.85	1	Sandown IOW	26 Jul
51.57	James Grindle		8.01.84	2	Carmarthen	1 Jul
51.19	Michael Jones		12.12.84	1	Worcester	10 Jun
50.93	Tom Bivins		18.11.83	1	Loughborough	30 Aug
50.65	James Forde		10.04.85	7	Sheffield	30 Jul
50.31	Nick Edwards		22.03.84	5	Birmingham	3 Sep
50.28	Paul Nash		13.02.84	1	Leamington	10 Jun
50.23	Reece Drury		2.11.83	1	Hull	13 May
	(20)					
49.55	Robert Mungham		1.12.84	1	Eton	10 Jun
49.27	Richard Sealy		26.11.84	2	Enfield	10 Jun
49.21	Ashley Smith		21.02.84	2	Newport	10 Sep
48.81	Daniel Boneham		9.12.83	1	Bingham	2 Jul
48.71	George Perkins		17.10.83	1	Cleckheaton	4 Jun
48.64	David Dawson		3.02.84	2	Bath	4 Jun
48.10	Kevin Deacon		25.02.84	1	London (Nh)	27 Aug
47.97	Ian Knowles			3	Stretford	4 Jun
47.92	Stephen Ashton		21.03.84	2	Gateshead	21 May
47.47	Andrew Smith		2.10.84	1	Gateshead	14 May
	(30)					
47.21	John Fyvie		23.01.84	1	Aberdeen	30 Jul

HAMMER - Under 15 - 4kg

59.07	Simon Bissell	25.12.85	1	Middlesbrough	15 Jul
53.92	Gordon Grierson	12.10.85	1	Stoke-on-Trent	30 Sep
53.76	Jason Joseph	27.11.85	2	Birmingham	3 Sep
53.04	Alistair McDiarmid	16.10.85	1	Grangemouth	17 Jun
51.11	Kieran O'Keefe	19.03.86	1	Loughborough	30 Aug
48.58	James Green	28.11.85	2	Sheffield (W)	7 Jul
47.33	Ben Lawrence	13.04.86	2	Worcester	19 Aug
46.75	Christian Alessi	28.01.86	1	Cleckheaton	24 Sep
46.63	Jamie Pritchard	25.09.85	1	Cardiff	12 Jul
46.55	John Honey	6.02.86	1	Cardiff	30 Apr
	(10)				
46.39	Matt Watts	1.11.85	4	Birmingham	3 Sep
45.83	Charles Handley	18.01.86	1	Cleckheaton	10 Jun
45.12	Robert Dudman	9.06.86	2	Stoke-on-Trent	9 Sep
44.29	Fraser Campbell	30.05.86	2	Grangemouth	9 Jul
44.28	Charles Hogarth	11.02.86	2	Cleckheaton	24 Sep
43.53	Peter Beckett	10.02.86	2	Brighton	18 Jun
43.03	M. Coverington		1	Guildford	12 Sep
42.51	Peter Downing	21.01.86	1	Exeter	27 Jun

HAMMER - Under 13 - 3.25kg

35.22	Sean Lewis	10.09.87	1	Stoke-on-Trent	29 Sep
25.88	Scott Church	17.05.88	1	Sandown IOW	28 Aug

JAVELIN

89.85	Steve Backley		12.02.69	2	Sydney, AUS	23 Sep
	86.70			1	Birmingham	13 Aug
	85.84			2	London (CP)	5 Aug
	83.74			Q	Sydney, AUS	22 Sep
	82.19			1	Glasgow (S)	2 Jul
	82.13			1	Gateshead	28 Aug
85.09	Nick Nieland		31.01.72	2	Birmingham	13 Aug
	82.51			5	Oslo, NOR	28 Jul
	82.33			5	London (CP)	5 Aug
	82.12			13Q	Sydney, AUS	22 Sep
	81.25			2	Gateshead	28 Aug
	80.90			4	Halle, GER	27 May
	80.20			2	Budapest, HUN	22 Jul
	79.46			4	Glasgow (S)	2 Jul
	78.48			1	Loughborough	21 May
83.71	Mick Hill		22.10.64	1	Cape Town, RSA	31 Mar
	83.06			2	Gold Coast (RB), AUS	17 Sep
	82.42			1	Gold Coast (RB), AUS	10 Sep
	82.29			1	Rovereto, ITA	30 Aug
	82.24			Q	Sydney, AUS	22 Sep
	81.07			7	London (CP)	5 Aug
	81.00			11	Sydney, AUS	23 Sep
	80.28			3	Birmingham	13 Aug
	80.24			5	Gateshead	16 Jul
	79.90			3	Glasgow (S)	2 Jul
	79.36 A			6	Pretoria, RSA	24 Mar
	79.25			4	Ventspils, LAT	17 Jun
	79.00			3	Gateshead	28 Aug
	78.85 A			5	Pietersburg, RSA	18 Mar
	78.61			2	Fana, NOR	27 Jun
	78.59			5	Tartu, EST	11 Jun
	78.44			9	Stockholm, SWE	1 Aug
79.40	Mark Roberson		13.03.67	1	Bedford	19 Aug
	76.10			4	Birmingham	13 Aug
	74.70			5	Budapest, HUN	22 Jul
	74.56			4	Fana, NOR	27 Jun
	74.50			2	Vittel, FRA	2 Sep
	73.70			6	Gateshead	28 Aug
	73.62			1	Bedford	29 May
78.24	David Parker	U23	28.02.80	1B	Halle, GER	27 May
	77.30			2	Bedford	19 Aug
	76.60			2	Karlstad, SWE	18 Jun
	76.31			1	Getafe, SPA	9 Sep
	75.94			Q	Stoke-on-Trent	1 May
	75.12			1	Eton	6 May
75.37	Stuart Faben		28.02.75	1	Torrevieja, SPA	22 Apr
	75.30			3	Bedford	19 Aug
	74.67			2	Eton	6 May
	73.60			5	Birmingham	13 Aug
	73.29			1	London (He)	8 Jul
73.56	Dan Carter	U23	15.04.80	1	Bath	16 Sep
	51 performances to 73.28 by 7 athletes					
71.79	Phill Sharpe	U20	6.03.81	1	Bedford	27 Aug
68.91	Gary Jenson		14.02.67	1	Southend	3 Jun
68.34	Michael Allen	U23	7.03.80	1	Belfast	8 Jul
(10)						
68.27	Neil McLellan	U23	10.09.78	2	Bedford	1 Jul
67.48	Keith Beard		8.11.61	1	Delft, HOL	17 Sep
65.49	Tim Kitney	U23	26.04.80	1	Catford	5 Aug

65.35	Stefan Baldwin		26.04.70	2	Enfield	24 Jun
65.18	Jonathan Lundman	U20	7.12.81	2	Bedford	27 Aug
65.05	Nigel Bevan		3.01.68	4	Eton	6 May
64.33	Paul Cooper		4.12.76	2	Enfield	6 Aug
64.30	Stuart Loughran		19.02.76	5	Dublin (S), IRE	29 Jul
64.25	Mike Tarran	U23	10.12.80	5	Eton	6 May
63.88	Jon Wilkinson		17.02.62	1	Telford	9 Sep
	(20)					
63.66	Sam Armstrong		17.02.74	1	Glasgow (S)	11 Jun
63.57	Simon Carter		5.03.75	1	London (CP)	14 May
63.29	Kevin Murch	V40	11.11.58	2	Derby	9 Jul
63.23	Tom Dobbing		5.02.73	1	Glasgow	28 Jul
63.22	Ian Burns		20.09.77	1	Grantham	18 Jun
63.18	David McKay	U23	22.09.80	2	Grantham	18 Jun
63.15	Simon Bennett		16.10.72	1	Exeter	16 Jul
63.10	Dwayne Marsden		25.10.73	1	Basildon	3 Jun
62.71	Gerard Plunkett	U23	30.06.80	3	Bedford	1 Jul
62.63	Matthew Allison		26.02.73	2	Solihull	29 Jul
	(30)					
62.50	Trevor Ratcliffe		9.03.64	1	Ware	3 Sep
62.02	Tim Eldridge		15.03.76	Q	Stoke-on-Trent	1 May
62.01	David Sketchley		25.02.76	3	Eton	23 Jul
61.85	Derek Hermann	U23	7.04.79	4	Bath	16 Sep
61.68	Jonathan Clarke		20.11.67	1	Watford	20 May
61.27	Stephen Melber	U23	26.02.79	1	Oxford	28 Jun
61.02	Chris Hough	U20	5.12.81	1	Wakefield	16 Apr
60.94	Steve Jamieson	U23	4.02.79	1	Loughborough	10 May
60.86	Wesley Smith	U23	26.02.79	6	London (He)	6 Aug
60.63	Robert Charlesworth	U23	25.03.79	10	Bedford	29 May
	(40)					
60.54	Anthony Lovett	U20	20.09.82	1	Birmingham	10 Sep
60.38	Dean Macey		12.12.77	13D	Sydney, AUS	28 Sep
60.03	Tony Smith	V40	17.05.58	1	Basildon	3 Jun
59.95	Jeremy Smyth	U23	11.08.78	1	Kirkwall	2 Sep
59.37	Andy Hayward		26.10.74	2	Cudworth	13 May
59.36	Livon Houslin		2.11.60	7	Eton	6 May
59.36	Glyn Amos	V40	30.03.58	3	Carlisle	5 Aug
59.32	Phil Parry		4.10.65	4	Enfield	24 Jun
59.19	Alex Kruger		18.11.63	1D	Stoke-on-Trent	30 Jul
58.91	Ben Saville		10.11.77	4	Stoke-on-Trent	1 May
	(50)					
58.81	James Turner	U20	12.08.83	3	Bedford	27 Aug
58.78	Scott Moir	U23	17.12.80	1	Great Yarmouth	13 Aug
58.76	Ken Hayford		10.03.63	1	London (Elt)	3 Jun
58.75	Steven Cotton	U23	8.02.79	5	Bath	16 Sep
58.73	James Apps	U23	29.04.80	1	Bromley	6 May
58.67	Carl Convey	U20	15.10.82	4	Bedford	27 Aug
58.50	Tim Phillips	U23	13.01.79	3Q	Stoke-on-Trent	1 May
58.48	Rhys Williams	U20	4.10.81	1	Neath	4 Jun
58.34	Peter Fraser	U23	28.01.78	1	Glasgow (S)	16 Jul
58.31	Tony Norman		5.07.63	2	Woking	6 May
	(60)					
58.29	Stuart Walker	U23	22.09.78	1	Cudworth	2 Jul
58.05	Paul Howard		19.10.66	1	Woodford	24 Jun
57.74	Barry Thomas		28.04.72	3D	Logrono, SPA	20 Aug
57.64	Emeka Udechuku	U23	10.07.79	Q	Stoke-on-Trent	1 May
57.64	Jim McFarlane	U23	16.06.79	2	Oxford	20 May
57.29	Matthew Dingley	U20	12.01.83	3	Sheffield	8 Jul
56.84	Andrew Gallagher	U20	15.02.83	3	Antrim	20 Jun
56.84	Eric Workman	U20	2.03.83	4	Sheffield	8 Jul
56.70	Landley Darlington		19.01.77	2	Loughborough	10 May

56.61	Chris Boundy	U23	25.12.79	1	London (B)	10 Sep
	(70)					
56.48	Alan van der Merwe	U17	5.01.84	6	Bath	16 Sep
56.47	Kevin Ricketts		29.06.76	2	Aldershot	5 Jul
56.26	Daniel Gilligan	U23	12.05.79	2	London (CP)	14 May
56.07	John Mitchell	U20	13.05.81	4	Glasgow	28 Jul
55.92	David Harding	U23	8.11.80	3	Oxford	20 May
55.72	B. French			1	Inverness	10 Sep
55.71	Rhys Taylor	U20	25.09.82	1	Carmarthen	10 Jun
55.68	Richard Lainson	U20	5.11.81	1	Basingstoke	11 Jun
55.64	Rob Laing		30.07.66	4	Solihull	29 Jul
55.60	Jeremy Goldsmith		6.12.73	2	Cosford	15 Apr
	(80)					
55.32	James Everard	U20	16.05.81	1	Abingdon	10 Sep
55.12	Ben Lloyd	U23	1.04.79	1	Oxford	20 May

Additional Under 20 (1 - 14 above)

54.94	James Roden	24.11.81	1D	Birmingham	17 Sep
54.22	Craig Guest	25.10.82	1	Grantham	10 Jun
54.03	Tim Louth		2	Grantham	10 Jun
54.02	Ian West	23.03.83	1	Crawley	10 Jun
53.90	Martin Taylor	31.01.82	6	Glasgow (S)	28 Jul
53.75	Sam Goddard	4.01.83	1	Hoo	12 Apr

Foreign

72.29	*Petri Matakainen (FIN)*		*3.04.75*	*1*	*Wigan*	*24 Jun*
60.95	*Ben Houghton (IRE)*	*U23*	*6.08.80*	*1*	*Carlisle*	*5 Aug*
59.98	*Leon Karagiounis*		*15.10.75*	*3*	*Derby*	*9 Jul*
58.04	*Demetrio Barros*		*29.06.71*	*1*	*London (PH)*	*8 Jul*
57.95	*Bekele Toia (ETH)*		*10.01.70*	*1*	*Yeovil*	*22 Jul*
57.19	*Andrew van Huyssteen (RSA)*		*17.02.77*	*1*	*London (TB)*	*26 Aug*
56.04	*Ashraf Radwan (EGY)*			*1*	*Sutton*	*26 May*

JAVELIN - Under 17 - 700g

59.92	James Deacon-Brown	26.05.84	1	Jarrow	10 Jun
59.83	Alan van der Merwe	5.01.84	1	Exeter	29 Aug
58.79	Lee Doran	5.03.85	1	Blackpool	15 Jul
58.69	Mark Lindsay	5.11.84	2	Sheffield	29 Jul
56.79	Kunal Kapadia	30.09.83	1	London (Col)	30 Apr
56.54	Michael Whitten	30.09.83	1	Birmingham	2 Sep
55.23	Mike Groves	21.03.84			
54.59	Sean Carson	13.04.84	1	Ayr	14 Jun
54.47	Stephen Adams	4.01.84	1	Ipswich	17 Jun
54.16	Jonathan Harvey	12.09.83	1	London (WF)	17 Sep
	(10)				
53.85	Mike Cross	19.12.83	1	Tonbridge	4 Jun
52.98	Andy Robinson	5.09.84	6	Sheffield	7 Jul
52.97	Aaron Cramp	29.02.84	2	Watford	27 May
52.95	Edward Dunford	15.09.84	1D	Waterford, IRE	3 Sep
52.77	Jamie Davies	10.11.83	5	Blackpool	15 Jul
52.72	David Turner	4.07.84	1	Blackpool	10 Jun
52.58	Richard Andrews	13.01.84	7	Sheffield	7 Jul
52.12	Andrew Ormesher	29.05.85		Blackpool	10 Sep

JAVELIN - Under 15 - 600g

54.11	Thomas Rees	9.03.86	1	Grangemouth	5 Aug
53.93	Farron Paul	3.10.85	1	London (Ha)	9 Apr
47.54	Callim McDonald	30.04.86	2	Sheffield	7 Jul
46.00	Richard Atkinson	29.09.85	2	Grangemouth	5 Aug
45.87	James Docking	19.11.86	1	Exeter	17 Jun

45.11	Philip Mann	25.10.85	3	Sheffield	7 Jul
44.98	Marc Miles	14.09.85	1	Norwich	17 Jun
44.95	Jonathan Winspeare	18.10.85	4	Sheffield	7 Jul
44.80	Mark Laws	29.09.85	1	Birmingham	2 Sep
44.75	Roy Chambers	9.02.86	2	Bedford	27 Aug
(10)					
44.07	Peter Taylor	19.11.85	1	London (He)	20 Aug
43.61	Allandre Johnson	8.12.85	1	Watford	27 May
43.49	Sam Kelvey	12.07.86	2	Birmingham	2 Sep
43.39	Andrew Field	20.09.85	1	Bournemouth	13 May
43.10	James Dunford	14.01.86	1	Stoke-on-Trent	23 Jul
43.03	Simon Cooke	3.10.85	1	Brighton	2 Jul

JAVELIN - Under 13 - 400g

40.91	Adam Akehurst	13.09.87	1	Kingston	30 Jul
38.36	Joel Gebbie		1	Ashford	17 Jun
37.90	Josh Stannard	15.10.87	1	Bath	4 Sep
37.59	Daniel Peatroy	9.03.88	2	Kingston	30 Jul
36.90	Stuart Harvey	2.09.87	1A	Erith	6 Aug
36.20	Mark Rumble	10.07.88		Oxford	11 Jun
35.18	Stuart Heale		1	Exeter	21 May
34.72	David Harrison	17.10.88	3	Kingston	30 Jul
34.30	Chris Matthews	25.05.88	1	Brighton	6 Jul

DECATHLON

8567	Dean Macey				12.12.77	4	Sydney, AUS			28 Sep
	10.81/-1.1	7.77/-0.5	14.62	2.09	46.41	14.53/-1.4	43.37	4.80	60.38	4:23.45
7667	Jamie Quarry				15.11.72	10	Arles, FRA			4 Jun
	10.83/1.9	7.42w/2.9	13.15	1.87	49.30	14.38/0.6	39.32	4.45	48.92	4:29.67
7407	Barry Thomas				28.04.72	4	Logrono, SPA			20 Aug
	11.44/0.1	6.98/0.9	13.74	1.93	50.92	15.25/-1.2	39.63	4.60	57.74	4:47.02
	7209					17	Arles, FRA			4 Jun
	11.26w/3.4	6.98/1.3	13.46	1.87	52.24	15.31/0.0	39.32	4.55	52.47	4:46.93
	7121					7	Esbjerg, DEN			2 Jul
	11.22w/2.9	6.68/0.4	13.35	1.92	51.97	15.60/0.2	35.04	4.70	52.58	4:47.16
7133	Alexis Sharp				31.10.72	20	Arles, FRA			4 Jun
	11.02/1.9	6.89/1.2	11.81	1.93	51.34	15.90/0.0	44.84	4.55	53.81	5:15.76
7071	Paul Jones			U23	11.04.78	22(2)	Arles, FRA			4 Jun
	11.17w/2.1	6.71/0.6	11.82	1.81	50.20	15.87/0.0	37.88	4.65	47.86	4:31.39
	7002 w					1	Waterford, IRE			3 Sep
	11.28W/4.2	6.58	11.62	1.81	50.64	15.42/2.0	36.67	4.60	50.20	4:36.1
	6948					4	Val de Reuil, FRA			13 Aug
	11.41/-0.5	6.57/1.5	11.80	1.82	50.43	15.40/0.5	35.44	4.45	49.03	4:42.36
	6930					11	Esbjerg, DEN			2 Jul
	11.49/1.6	6.70/0.6	11.97	1.77	50.40	15.95/0.0	38.22	4.60	51.77	4:43.49
6975	Alex Kruger				18.11.63	1	Stoke-on-Trent			30 Jul
	11.62w/2.4	6.87/1.6	13.58	2.02	54.05	15.62/1.6	41.52	4.25	50.19	5:01.7
	6499					25	Arles, FRA			4 Jun
	11.67w/2.7	6.66/1.8	14.11	1.99	54.19	15.67/0.9	40.99	4.25	48.88	6:24.66
6862 w	Mark Sweeney				26.02.77	2	Waterford, IRE			3 Sep
	11.63W/4.2	6.40	12.94	1.99	50.90	15.26/2.0	39.28	3.70	51.46	4:50.2
	6752					1	Jarrow			25 Jun
	11.79/1.8	6.24/1.0	12.18	2.00	50.58	15.19w/3.1	38.18	3.80	50.53	4:53.21
	6652					2	Stoke-on-Trent			30 Jul
	11.67w/2.4	6.41/1.7	12.39	1.93	51.39	15.30/-2.0	36.13	3.55	49.80	4:44.26
	6499					2	Stoke-on-Trent			18 Jun
	11.99/-4.1	6.12w/2.1	11.68	1.99	50.55	15.73/-1.4	35.20	3.80	48.96	4:53.64
6761	Fyn Corcoran			U23	17.03.78	29(5)	Arles, FRA			4 Jun
	11.37/0.4	6.85/0.9	12.43	1.78	50.72	15.47/0.0	35.24	3.45	52.31	4:33.22

6754 Steve Bonnett U23 13.07.78 16 Esbjerg, DEN 2 Jul
11.41/1.8 6.55/0.7 11.11 1.92 49.92 15.76/1.6 35.76 4.10 43.15 4:36.84
6458 7 Arles, FRA 4 Jun
11.22w/3.4 6.99/1.0 12.25 1.93 50.30 16.26/0.7 38.82 nhc 48.14 4:26.76
6720 w Brendan McConville U23 3.01.79 3 Waterford, IRE 3 Sep
11.65W/4.2 6.51 11.37 1.96 51.37 15.86/2.0 31.80 4.10 47.96 4:27.8
6561 32(6) Arles, FRA 4 Jun
11.59w/2.7 6.46/1.1 11.04 1.93 51.62 16.16/-1.0 32.59 3.95 46.11 4:29.88
(10)
6696 w Bill Wynn 15.02.73 4 Waterford, IRE 3 Sep
11.38W/4.2 6.38 10.59 1.84 52.05 15.29/2.0 34.59 4.00 54.38 4:36.6
6652 1 Stoke-on-Trent 18 Jun
11.90/-2.4 6.71w/2.9 11.62 1.84 51.51 15.49/-1.4 36.54 3.80 52.50 4:41.52
6563 3 Stoke-on-Trent 30 Jul
11.43w/2.4 6.57w/2.8 10.73 1.75 52.13 15.21/-2.0 33.64 3.85 52.16 4:38.23
6680 Anthony Sawyer U23 29.04.80 1 Gateshead 23 Jul
11.33/1.5 6.59w/2.5 12.95 1.88 51.31 15.49/0.2 32.31 4.10 42.00 4:46.32
6622 8 Val de Reuil, FRA 13 Aug
11.28/-0.5 6.39/1.6 12.48 1.82 50.72 15.59/0.4 36.35 4.05 43.56 4:54.51
6425 3 Stoke-on-Trent 18 Jun
11.54/-2.4 6.28w/3.4 11.46 1.90 51.22 15.72/-1.4 34.02 3.90 40.41 4:46.64
6563 John Heanley U23 25.09.80 9 Val de Reuil, FRA 13 Aug
11.68/-0.2 6.73/1.3 9.27 1.82 50.78 15.87/-0.8 32.87 4.05 48.19 4:25.80
6476 4 Stoke-on-Trent 30 Jul
11.66w/2.4 6.75/1.8 9.19 1.81 51.77 15.94/2.0 28.42 4.05 51.67 4:25.17
6560 Steve Garland 12.01.73 2 Jarrow 25 Jun
11.37/1.6 6.22w/2.3 10.68 1.82 49.72 16.02/1.8 35.24 4.00 42.92 4:29.73
6540 Scott Exley U23 9.02.78 1 Enfield 30 Jul
11.01w/2.2 6.75/1.5 11.72 1.80 50.28 15.68/1.1 37.48 3.60 36.70 4:49.45
6471 John Holtby U20 27.03.82 6 Val de Reuil, FRA 13 Aug
11.32/1.2 6.48/1.5 13.56 1.61 49.78 15.03/1.5 31.79 3.45 47.10 4:48.50
6470 Martin Taylor U20 31.01.82 3 Hexham 21 May
11.29/1.8 6.59/-1.0 11.11 1.76 51.01 15.63/1.3 33.25 3.40 51.36 4:38.23
6436 Kevin Ricketts 29.06.76 1 Aldershot 22 Jun
11.1w 6.39 11.78 1.86 52.5 16.0 33.53 3.60 52.68 4:48.0
34 performances to 6400 by 18 athletes including 5 wind assisted
6388 Jamie Russell U20 1.10.81 7 Val de Reuil, FRA 13 Aug
11.83/1.0 6.50/1.0 9.90 2.12 50.56 17.14/0.6 29.69 3.75 35.80 4:18.28
6302 Adrian Hemery U20 6.08.82 1 Gateshead 23 Jul
11.60/1.5 6.36/0.6 11.97 1.82 51.79 16.40/0.2 32.94 3.60 45.89 4:41.20
(20)
6244 Alex Gibson 3.11.77 1 Watford 24 Sep
11.23/-0.4 6.77/1.8 11.83 1.78 49.98 17.18/0.9 33.78 3.00 47.84 4:54.17
6220 Dominic Chapman 10.02.72 5 Stoke-on-Trent 18 Jun
11.64/-4.1 6.47w/3.3 12.72 1.72 51.68 16.98/-1.4 34.55 3.80 47.48 4:59.41
6178 Eric Scott 20.01.72 2 Enfield 30 Jul
11.40/1.7 6.65w/2.7 11.25 1.89 52.33 16.39/1.1 26.30 3.80 43.10 4:58.85
6146 Louis Evling-Jones U20 20.06.83 2 Watford 24 Sep
11.82/-0.2 6.58w/2.5 9.90 1.96 50.40 15.95/-0.4 30.24 3.10 40.66 4:43.28
6113 Richard Czernik 12.08.72 5 Stoke-on-Trent 30 Jul
11.47w/2.4 6.25/1.2 11.86 1.78 52.19 16.57/-2.0 38.69 3.05 43.82 4:50.71
6105 Brian Hughes 6.01.70 6 Stoke-on-Trent 30 Jul
11.76w/4.0 6.34/1.8 8.82 1.81 52.58 15.96/-1.4 32.03 4.05 44.71 4:51.36
6091 Gavin Fordham U23 1.02.79 2 Watford 24 Sep
11.76/0.0 6.37/1.4 9.73 1.99 53.40 16.96/-0.4 30.54 4.00 48.21 5:08.10
6079 Gerard Plunkett U23 30.06.80 1 Rotherham 10 Sep
12.1 6.22 11.78 1.91 54.5 16.6 36.10 3.55 49.14 4:48.1
6048 Dale Garland U23 13.10.80 1 St. Peter Port GUE 17 Sep
6026 James Wright U20 2.04.82 1 Waterford, IRE 3 Sep
11.52w/3.5 6.38 8.82 1.72 52.10 15.93/1.9 27.38 4.20 45.41 4:57.8
(30)

6000 Steve Hughes U20 25.02.82 2 Stoke-on-Trent 30 Jul
11.68w/2.9 6.08/1.5 10.81 1.75 54.21 16.32/1.5 33.71 3.85 42.74 4:46.86
5943 Richard Hunter 12.01.71 3 Gateshead 23 Jul
11.93/1.1 6.33w/2.1 10.51 1.70 52.41 15.44/0.2 34.34 3.60 34.70 4:48.17
5832 Adam Davis 19.11.72 1 Aldershot 1 Aug
11.5 6.23 12.95 1.72 55.3 17.3 36.24 4.00 48.02 5:39.7
5801 Nick Owen U23 17.07.80 1 Crawley 10 Sep
11.9 6.30 14.41 1.60 55.8 16.8 34.80 3.70 49.10 5:18.9
5763 Geoff Ingram 31.01.68 10 Waterford, IRE 3 Sep
11.84w/3.7 6.11 10.63 1.69 54.41 16.58/1.9 28.70 3.60 49.27 4:54.5
5700 Mark Roberts 1.09.69 2 Crawley 10 Sep
12.3 5.92 10.28 1.72 53.5 16.0 30.86 3.50 47.79 4:46.5
5641 Chris Oakes 19.10.70 2 Aldershot 22 Jun
11.4w 6.38 11.40 1.95 56.9 16.3 35.87 3.30 19.23 4:59.0
5639 Paul Gilding 2.10.75 2 Crawley 10 Sep
11.9 6.68 10.76 1.96 54.4 15.6 26.62 3.00 35.70 5:15.3
5587 Chris Hunter U20 3.03.81 1 Hexham 24 Sep
11.76/0.5 6.46 8.93 1.81 52.50 15.92/0.4 25.87 3.20 32.01 4:56.65
5577 Gerald Manville U23 21.12.78 3 Aldershot 22 Jun
11.7w 6.39 9.69 1.80 55.1 18.2 28.12 4.00 39.48 4:54.0
(40)
5547 Ashley Pritchard U23 14.07.79 8 Stoke-on-Trent 30 Jul
11.91w/4.0 5.68/0.9 7.77 1.72 54.58 16.67/-1.4 29.22 3.75 43.08 4:39.06
5527 Frank Chapman 17.01.70 5 Aldershot 1 Aug
12.2 5.78 11.43 1.75 55.0 16.4 36.16 3.60 36.09 5:06.1
5479 Ben Roberts U23 15.01.80 1 Wrexham 25 Jun
11.8w/2.8 6.44/1.4 13.16 1.90 56.23 16.06/1.0 34.00 3.50 41.13 dnf
5423 Obie Matthews U23 20.12.80 9 Stoke-on-Trent 30 Jul
12.10w/4.0 5.95/1.8 10.34 1.69 56.08 17.62/-1.4 30.16 3.85 38.66 4:54.80
5388 Gurmukh Sahans U23 8.10.78 3 Crawley 10 Sep
12.1 5.92 11.04 1.69 54.7 17.1 33.10 2.70 47.05 4:53.4
5360 Paul Tohill U20 9.10.82 4 Waterford, IRE 3 Sep
11.92w/2.5 6.32 8.70 1.93 53.78 16.04/1.7 19.00 2.90 31.86 4:53.2
5294 w Clint Barrett 21.11.77 3 Watford 24 Sep
12.69/-0.5 5.75W/5.1 8.95 1.72 54.29 17.45/0.0 32.34 2.80 42.01 4:27.78
5293 Sam Allen U23 26.10.78 6 Jarrow 25 Jun
12.06/1.3 5.94/1.8 9.75 1.67 53.19 17.96/1.5 30.96 2.90 45.51 5:01.63
5284 Nicholas Walker 24.02.64 2 Colwyn Bay 3 Sep
12.17 6.00 11.45 1.54 54.60 18.34 33.97 3.60 38.19 5:08.42
5162 Daniel Armstrong U20 28.10.81 4 Stoke-on-Trent 30 Jul
11.78w/2.9 5.85/0.6 7.96 1.72 52.19 16.28/1.5 28.33 nhc 40.33 4:38.11
(50)
5125 Paul Torry U20 17.10.82 5 Stoke-on-Trent 30 Jul
11.81w/2.9 5.86/1.6 9.33 1.72 53.43 18.22/1.5 28.42 2.75 31.73 4:43.19
5112 w Daniel Elias U20 25.12.82 4 Watford 24 Sep
11.90/0.0 6.08W/5.0 7.35 1.84 54.50 17.64/0.0 28.76 3.40 37.52 5:36.70
5034 Matthew Peerless U20 3.12.82 3 Hexham 24 Sep
12.63/0.5 5.40 10.07 1.69 57.75 16.91/0.4 28.92 4.00 36.57 5:22.84
5025 Tom Elvin U20 10.02.81 4 Hexham 24 Sep
12.39/0.5 5.92 9.79 1.78 55.83 18.08/0.4 27.38 3.20 33.32 5:01.75
5020 Chris Low U23 24.04.80 9 Waterford, IRE 3 Sep
11.89w/3.7 5.97 9.30 1.72 53.99 15.75/1.9 30.85 2.40 39.98 6:11.6
4955 Nick Caplan U23 23.12.79 7 Jarrow 25 Jun
12.30/1.3 5.37/1.7 9.36 1.73 54.70 18.32w/2.6 24.06 2.90 37.88 4:38.04
4952 Simon Bull U20 29.09.82 5 Waterford, IRE 3 Sep
11.74w/2.5 5.70 11.65 1.66 57.67 18.69/1.7 34.74 2.20 43.86 5:22.4

During Double Decathlon

5226 DD Peter Coates 21.03.68 3 Hexham 24 Sep
12.28/-0.3 6.06/0.2 9.17 1.68 56.61 17.63/-0.4 28.01 3.42 39.69 4:45.89

Foreign

6011 Cathal McGinley (IRE) U23 16.08.79 4 Jarrow 25 Jun
11.96/1.8 6.14/1.2 12.01 1.85 54.54 16.30w/2.6 33.52 3.40 41.83 4:39.77

DECATHLON - Under 20 with Under 20 Implements

6412 Jamie Russell 1.10.81 1 Rotherham 10 Sep
11.8 6.41 10.75 2.12 51.0 17.0 34.52 3.75 36.86 4:24.0
6181 Alex Zulewski 6.06.82 1 Birmingham 17 Sep
11.66/1.5 6.53w/3.2 9.47 1.76 51.03 15.23/-0.8 30.88 3.70 42.62 4:49.16
6102 John Dickinson 27.01.83 1 Enfield 30 Jul
11.59/1.3 6.52 10.30 1.83 52.17 16.74/0.5 34.50 3.50 40.48 4:44.00
6047 Howard Frost 9.12.81 2 Enfield 30 Jul
11.41/1.3 6.47 9.63 1.65 50.32 15.97w/2.7 33.06 3.70 34.94 4:44.30
5803 James Wright 2.04.82 4 Birmingham 17 Sep
11.61w/2.7 6.09w/2.5 9.18 1.61 53.05 15.75/-0.8 28.11 4.00 42.08 4:52.84
5774 Chris Dack 28.11.82 5 Birmingham 17 Sep
11.44/1.5 6.57w/3.7 12.49 1.88 57.65 15.58/-0.8 34.50 2.50 44.34 5:32.83
5752 Daniel Brandwood 1.10.82 6 Birmingham 17 Sep
11.31/1.5 6.19w/3.4 11.68 1.58 50.39 17.40/-0.2 40.34 3.30 28.84 5:05.31
5730 James Roden 24.11.81 7 Birmingham 17 Sep
11.81w/2.9 5.61w/2.3 11.29 1.82 55.81 16.59/-0.2 32.40 2.70 54.94 4:47.27
5640 w Daniel Armstrong 28.10.81 8 Birmingham 17 Sep
11.88w/2.4 6.05W/4.1 10.48 1.70 53.15 16.14/-0.8 28.65 2.80 43.61 4:40.88
5533 * Birmingham 17 Sep
5.54/1.8
5597 Paul Tohill 9.10.82 1 Antrim 2 Jul
11.8 6.39 10.02 1.91 54.4 15.4 23.15 2.80 41.36 4:57.0
(10)
5566 Nathan Jones 31.10.82 1 Wrexham 25 Jun
11.4w/3.2 6.06w/2.3 11.67 1.57 51.92 15.92/1.0 31.43 2.90 35.01 5:01.62
5546 Andy Clements 28.11.82 3 Eton 25 Jun
11.9/0.3 6.00 9.53 1.63 51.6 15.9/0.6 35.69 2.50 37.91 4:34.3
5530 w Carl Marchment 30.12.82 9 Birmingham 17 Sep
11.78w/2.7 6.07W/4.1 9.80 1.76 53.52 16.49/-1.5 31.80 3.00 39.88 5:05.25
5527 * Birmingham 17 Sep
6.04w/3.8
5453 Daniel Elias 25.12.82 11 Birmingham 17 Sep
11.91/1.5 6.27w/2.5 8.80 1.76 56.07 16.76/-1.5 29.19 3.80 38.78 5:12.64
5443 Chris Gunn 13.09.82 1 Rugby 25 Jun
12.4 5.73 10.60 1.78 56.4 16.6 33.22 3.50 42.46 4:55.9
5404 Steve Hughes 25.02.82 4 Hexham 21 May
11.93/0.8 5.61 9.81 1.75 54.42 17.31/-0.1 30.14 3.40 39.54 4:52.54
5358 Andrew Johnson 10.09.81 4 Eton 25 Jun
11.9/1.3 5.90 10.86 1.72 54.4 16.8 30.70 3.10 43.05 5:12.6
5335 Matt Peleszok 17.10.81 1 Cannock 25 Jun
11.4 6.08 12.76 1.53 54.0 20.3 32.88 2.80 44.31 4:42.2
5302 Simon Bull 29.09.82 2 Wrexham 25 Jun
11.6w/3.2 5.85/-0.7 11.69 1.78 57.00 17.36/1.0 38.45 1.80 45.53 5:10.56
5291 Ryan Westaway 2.03.83 2 Yeovil 25 Jun
12.4 6.56 9.65 1.89 56.0 16.3 31.59 2.80 35.05 5:15.1
(20)
5258 Wilby Williamson 8.08.81 2 Antrim 2 Jul
11.8 5.33 10.41 1.70 53.8 15.8 29.44 2.40 45.51 5:06.0
5222 Wayne Balsdon 14.01.83 12 Birmingham 17 Sep
11.80/1.5 6.14w/2.7 10.34 1.76 53.24 17.82/-0.2 26.51 2.50 31.91 4:46.88
5215 Richard Townsend 1.03.82 2 Rugby 25 Jun
11.7 5.68 9.39 1.63 53.2 18.4 32.04 2.90 44.49 4:49.9
5107 Tim Howell 6.12.82 3 Cannock 25 Jun
12.0 5.68 9.32 1.65 55.1 15.5 32.40 2.70 36.86 5:12.8

5072 Frazer Benzie 4.08.83 1 Grangemouth 3 Sep
12.53/-1.1 5.40/1.6 10.52 1.68 56.53 19.02/0.4 34.24 3.40 43.13 5:01.33

5056 Lee Middleton 15.04.82 13 Birmingham 17 Sep
12.41/1.5 5.77w/2.3 9.99 1.73 57.95 16.70/-1.5 33.79 3.00 36.48 5:17.75

DECATHLON - Under 17 with Under 17 Implements

6712 Edward Dunford 15.09.84 1 Waterford, IRE 3 Sep
11.42w/2.3 6.56 14.49 1.96 54.04 13.63/1.9 40.99 3.20 52.95 5:10.1

OCTATHLON - Under 17

5420 Edward Dunford 15.09.84 1 Stoke-on-Trent 18 Jun
13.68/-4.8 6.58/1.8 47.54 53.58 1.92 39.30 13.38 4:55.40 (b)

4916 Robin Smith 11.09.83 2 Birmingham 17 Sep
6.05w/3.3 31.33 41.72 52.75 13.88/-0.6 1.84 11.68 4:51.88 (a)

4894 Matthew Walden 30.11.83 3 Birmingham 17 Sep
6.44w/3.2 32.81 36.27 54.10 14.63/-0.4 1.84 12.33 4:45.09 (a)

4885 David Hughes 31.05.84 4 Birmingham 17 Sep
6.76w/2.3 29.45 41.16 52.79 14.18/-0.6 1.75 11.38 4:54.89 (a)

4807 Xavier Andre 15.07.85 5 Birmingham 17 Sep
6.10w/3.8 30.55 45.49 53.45 15.03/-1.1 1.81 11.48 4:46.43 (a)

4618 Colin Bailey 15.11.83 3 Stoke-on-Trent 18 Jun
14.90/-4.8 6.17w/3.0 40.25 55.84 1.92 30.08 10.73 5:00.91 (b)

4618 Matthew Clay 9.06.84 1 Rotherham 10 Sep
16.4 6.61 11.19 53.1 26.28 1.86 41.33 4:51.9 (d)

4578 Ross Tressider 8.11.83 1 Corby 25 Jun
5.71 36.03 37.24 52.7 13.9 1.73 10.22 5:06.0 (a)

4525 Stephen Alexander 6.10.84 4 Stoke-on-Trent 18 Jun
14.19/-4.8 6.46w/2.3 29.58 52.74 1.77 23.72 10.82 4:54.41 (b)

4481 Oliver Bournat 4.12.84 1 Enfield 30 Jul
5.71/1.1 15.77/0.9 34.56 56.35 1.69 13.42 31.95 4:36.61 (c)

(10)

4450 Chris Awde 14.02.85 1 Watford 24 Sep
15.03/-0.7 34.52 6.20/1.0 54.15 1.73 9.48 33.77 4:57.60 (e)

4443 Leighton Ballantine 27.01.84 1 Yeovil 25 Jun
6.26 31.01 42.48 55.0 14.7 1.65 10.74 5:08.2 (a)

4416 w Jason Hill 27.09.83 6 Birmingham 17 Sep
5.95W/4.1 34.91 38.88 56.27 14.83/-0.4 1.60 11.05 4:56.30 (a)
4396 * Birmingham 17 Sep
5.86w/3.3

4392 Michael Dyer 27.09.84 7 Birmingham 17 Sep
5.90w/2.4 31.03 43.18 55.45 15.35/-1.1 1.69 10.19 4:55.64 (a)

4350 Philip Taylor 6.02.84 3 Cannock 25 Jun
5.88 30.44 45.54 57.6 15.3 1.84 12.24 5:33.4 (a)

4343 Barrie Prowse 2.03.85 2 Enfield 30 Jul
5.67/1.7 16.05w/2.5 35.95 54.10 1.78 9.85 24.35 4:24.35 (c)

4285 Mark Garner 2.11.83 3 Rugby 25 Jun
5.56 24.20 35.41 54.2 14.7 1.71 11.01 4:46.2 (a)

4260 Robert Miller 20.01.84 1 Grangemouth 3 Sep
5.95w/2.6 24.76 44.86 53.90 15.27/-0.9 1.55 9.86 4:53.27 (a)

4254 Thomas Williams 11.03.84 4 Rugby 25 Jun
5.70 28.13 41.00 55.1 15.3 1.66 9.65 4:45.6 (a)

4250 Malcolm Hawkins 17.12.83 9 Birmingham 17 Sep
5.84w/3.5 24.41 39.13 54.04 16.09/-0.6 1.57 9.84 4:25.11 (a)

(20)

4247 Rupert Gardner 9.10.84 3 Enfield 30 Jul
5.52/1.3 15.10w/2.5 25.27 53.29 1.72 10.13 26.32 4:31.84 (c)

4223 Thomas Jennings 27.01.85 1 Hexham 24 Sep
5.49 29.77 38.95 56.66 14.98/-0.6 1.73 12.08 5:20.1 (a)

4203 Dean Sinclair 17.12.84 2 Eton 25 Jun
5.94 20.87 31.82 52.5 14.6w/3.1 1.75 8.79 4:37.3 (a)

During Decathlon

5537	Edward Dunford		15.09.84		Waterford, IRE	3 Sep
	13.63/1.9 6.56 52.95 54.04 1.96 40.99 14.49 5:10.1 (b)					

Order of Events
a) LJ, DT, JT, 400m, 100mH, HJ, SP, 1500m
b) 100mH, LJ, JT, 400m, HJ, DT, SP, 1500m
c) LJ, 100mH, JT, 400m, HJ, SP, DT, 1500m
d) 100mH, LJ, SP, 400m, DT, HJ, JT, 1500m
e) 100mH, JT, LJ, 400m, HJ, SP, DT, 1500m

PENTATHLON - Under 15

3281	Andrae Davis		27.09.85	1	Birmingham	16 Sep
	11.68/2.0 15.76 6.12/1.3 1.68 2:12.45					
3001	Louis Moore		8.09.85	2	Birmingham	16 Sep
	11.80w/3.8 11.66 6.34/1.4 1.83 2:25.87					
2928	Matthew Hansford		20.02.86	1	Yeovil	24 Jun
	11.4 11.57 6.18 1.70 2:21.4					
2755 w	Nathaniel Simpson		15.09.85	4	Birmingham	16 Sep
	11.38/2.0 9.38 5.42W/4.6 1.68 2:13.95					
	2735			*	Birmingham	16 Sep
	5.32w/2.8					
2738	Mathew Chetwynd		20.12.85	5	Birmingham	16 Sep
	12.36w/3.1 8.98 5.81w/4.0 1.74 2:15.13					
2719 w	Craig Glanville		21.09.86	6	Birmingham	16 Sep
	12.56W/4.3 9.98 5.80w/3.1 1.50 2:06.66					
2710	James Dunford		14.01.86	1	Nuneaton	25 May
	11.9 12.00 5.35 1.69 2:21.9					
2695	Kevin Sempers		24.11.85	7	Birmingham	16 Sep
	11.87w/3.8 10.50 5.35w/2.3 1.74 2:24.65					
2667	Chris Chase		15.11.85	1	Eton	25 Jun
	13.6/0.1 8.65 5.89 1.69 2:07.4					
2653	Adam Booth		22.10.85	1	Rotherham	10 Sep
	12.1 10.11 5.28 1.70 2:15.9					
(10)						
2609	Daniel Ashcroft		23.11.85	1	Hemel Hempstead	16 Jul
	13.9 11.34 5.65 1.68 2:15.9					
2607	Charles Allen		15.12.85	1	York	25 Jun
	12.9 12.59 5.53 1.51 2:17.0					
2565	Ryan Shaw		30.12.86	2	Enfield	30 Jul
	12.24 10.93 5.82 1.41 2:18.69					
2563	Onose Okojie		19.09.85	10	Birmingham	16 Sep
	12.93/1.8 11.25 5.48w/3.6 1.77 2:30.69					
2524	Patrick Halcrow		9.01.86	2	Corby	25 Jun
	12.0 11.16 5.20 1.63 2:25.5					
2506	William Fleckney		19.10.85	3	Corby	25 Jun
	12.2 8.91 6.11 1.63 2:29.5					
2503	Chris Vernon		29.11.85	11	Birmingham	16 Sep
	13.18w/2.8 10.47 5.25w/3.9 1.56 2:13.93					
2502	Martin Pang		13.03.86	1	Rugby	24 Jun
	12.1 11.51 5.99 1.60 2:40.6					

Overage

2651	Steven Cavanagh	U17	9.07.85	1	Antrim	2 Jul
	13.0 12.72 5.39 1.73 2:24.2					

DOUBLE DECATHLON

12409	John Heanly	U23	25.09.80	1	Hexham	24 Sep

100m 12.16, LJ 6.63, 200mH 26.7, SP 9.14, 5000m 17:35.64, 800m 2:06.52, HJ 1.86
400m 55.25, HT 20.44, 3000mSt 11:21.03, 110mH 16.71, DT 30.79, 200m 23.94, PV 4.02,
3000m 10:29.9, 400mH 60.13, JT 47.25, 1500m 4:45.82, TJ 13.04, 10000m 40:46.8

2000 Metres Walk Under 13 - Track

10:43.3	Derry Brown		12.03.89	2	Bebington	4	Nov
11:06.7	Mark Hambridge		18.02.89	2	Bromsgrove	15	Oct
11:08.4	Simon Hambridge		18.02.89	3	Bromsgrove	15	Oct
11:14.4	Lewis Hayden		10.08.89	3	Bebington	4	Nov

Overage

10:42.7	Nick Ball	U15	29.04.88	1	Bebington	4	Nov

3000 Metres Walk - Track

11:58.0	Andi Drake		6.02.65	1	Rugby	1	Jul
	11:59.96			1	Bedford	29	May
12:03.12 i	Martin Bell		9.04.61	2	Birmingham	29	Jan
12:07.54	Matthew Hales	U23	6.10.79	1	Solihull	29	Jul
	12:13.84			2	Bedford	29	May
12:10.08 i	Andy Penn		31.03.67	3	Birmingham	29	Jan
	12:30.52			3	Bedford	29	May
12:16.7	Jamie O'Rawe		3.02.73	1	Ilford	6	Aug
12:23.2	Steve Partington		17.09.65	1	Douglas IOM	29	Jul
12:29.90	Andrew Parker	U17	10.12.83	1	Watford	2	Jul
12:33.31	Dom King	U20	30.05.83	2	Watford	2	Jul
12:40.00 +	Darrell Stone		2.02.68	m	Birmingham	12	Aug
12:48.19 i	Lloyd Finch	U17	23.10.83	2	Birmingham	6	Feb
	12:49.49			1	Blackpool	15	Jul
(10)							
12:56.0	Don Bearman		16.04.66	2	Rugby	1	Jul
12:58.8	Andy O'Rawe		8.09.63	2	Chelmsford	14	May
13:05.18	Cameron Smith	U17	17.01.84	2	Derby	3	Sep
13:05.7	Dan King	U20	30.05.83	2	Woodford	17	Jul
13:17.7	Guy Jackson		10.01.71	2	Leamington	14	May
13:22.96	James Davis	U17	10.10.84	3	Blackpool	15	Jul
13:25.25	Andrew Goudie	U23	4.10.78	5	Bedford	29	May
13:26.3	Darren Thorn		17.07.62	3	Leamington	14	May
13:29.6	Gary Witton		25.08.73	1	Stretford	28	Jun
13:32.4	Noel Carmody	V40	24.12.56	2	Stretford	28	Jun
(20)							
13:33.73 i	Nathan Adams	U20	14.04.82	4	Birmingham	6	Feb
	13:46.2			1	Cudworth	13	May
13:45.4	Jimmy Ball		17.02.63	2	Portsmouth	13	May
13:47.1	Peter Kaneen		12.07.61	2	Douglas IOM	29	Jul
13:48.01 i	Scott Taylor	U23	28.07.78	8	Birmingham	29	Jan
13:48.1	Dave Staniforth	V40	15.11.59	3	Stretford	28	Jun
13:49.6 i	Colin Bradley	V40	2.02.56	1	Birmingham	26	Feb
13:50.0	Dave Turner	V40	20.10.57	2	Cudworth	13	May

Additional Juniors

14:09.93	Luke Finch	U15	21.09.85	1	Sheffield	30	Jul
14:11.46 i	Neil Bates	U17	5.04.84	6	Birmingham	6	Feb
	14:16.6			2	Douglas IOM	8	Jul
14:46.81	Luke Davis	U15	30.08.86	2	Sheffield	30	Jul

5000 Metres Walk (U23 and Junior) - Track

20:06.66	Matthew Hales	U23	6.10.79	3	Vittel, FRA	2	Sep
21:25.17 i	Dom King	U20	30.05.83	3	Neubrandenburg, GER	4	Mar
	22:22.45			5	Vittel, FRA	2	Sep
22:23.45 i	Lloyd Finch	U17	23.10.83	5	Neubrandenburg, GER	4	Mar
22:39.26	Andrew Goudie	U23	4.10.78	6	Vittel, FRA	2	Sep
22:48.91	Andrew Parker	U17	10.12.83	1	Sheffield	31	Jul
23:21.71	Dan King	U20	30.05.83	1	Birmingham	16	Sep

23:36.76	James Davis	U17	10.10.84	2	Birmingham	16 Sep
23:45.94	Nathan Adams	U20	14.04.82	3	Birmingham	16 Sep
23:48.30	Cameron Smith	U17	17.01.84	2	Sheffield	31 Jul
25:08.9	Neil Bates	U17	5.04.84	1	Douglas IOM	7 Jun

No judge

21:18 +	Chris Maddocks	V40	28.03.57	1m	Plymouth	9 Jan
21:20 +	Steve Hollier		27.02.76	2m	Plymouth	9 Jan

10000 Metres Walk - Track

43:12.85	Matthew Hales	U23	6.10.79	1	Birmingham	12 Aug
43:30.50	Steve Partington		17.09.65	2	Birmingham	12 Aug
43:54.49	Jamie O'Rawe		3.02.73	3	Birmingham	12 Aug
44:29.51	Chris Cheeseman	V40	11.12.58	4	Birmingham	12 Aug
45:36.3	Dom King	U20	30.05.83	1	Bebington	4 Nov
45:52.7	Don Bearman		16.04.66	2	Bebington	4 Nov
46:08.0	Gareth Brown		10.05.68	1	Horsham	29 Jan
46:37.46	Andrew Goudie	U23	4.10.78	6	Liverpool	22 Jul
47:23.0	Jimmy Ball		17.02.63	2	Horsham	29 Jan
47:47.95	Andrew Parker	U17	10.12.83	5	Birmingham	12 Aug
(10)						
48:14.9	Dan King	U20	30.05.83	2	Ilford	25 Jul
48:39.4	Peter Kaneen		12.07.61	3	Bebington	4 Nov
49:01.1	Nathan Adams	U20	14.04.82	4	Bebington	4 Nov
49:38.77	Thomas Taylor	U20	30.01.81	5	Bedford	27 Aug

No judge

42:57 +	Steve Hollier		27.02.76	1m	Plymouth	9 Jan
42:58 +	Chris Maddocks	V40	28.03.57	2m	Plymouth	9 Jan

10000 Metres Walk - Road

41:25 +	Andi Drake		6.02.65	m	Eisenhuttenstadt, GER	17 Jun
	41:26			1	East Molesey	9 Jan
42:11	Chris Cheeseman	V40	11.12.58	2	East Molesey	9 Jan
42:18 +	Steve Hollier		27.02.76	2	Douglas IOM	19 Feb
42:22 +	Darrell Stone		2.02.68	m	Leamington	23 Apr
43:10 +	Chris Maddocks	V40	28.03.57	3	Douglas IOM	19 Feb
	44:53 +			m	Eisenhuttenstadt, GER	17 Jun
43:12	Jamie O'Rawe		3.02.73	3	East Molesey	9 Jan
43:48	Andy Penn		31.03.67	1	Leamington	4 Mar
	44:26 +			4m	Douglas IOM	19 Feb
44:21	Steve Partington		17.09.65	1	Douglas IOM	12 Nov
	44:53 +			5m	Douglas IOM	19 Feb
44:53	Don Bearman		16.04.66	1	Bexley	9 Dec
45:03	Dom King	U20	30.05.83	27	Eisenhuttenstadt, GER	17 Jun
(10)						
45:12	Matthew Hales	U23	6.10.79	4	East Molesey	9 Jan
45:20	Thomas Taylor	U20	30.01.81	5	Leamington	23 Apr
45:20	Lloyd Finch	U17	23.10.83	6	Leamington	23 Apr
45:29	Gareth Brown		10.05.68	5	East Molesey	9 Jan
46:03	Andy O'Rawe		8.09.63	2	Leicester	3 Sep
46:08	Mark Easton		24.05.63	7	East Molesey	9 Jan
46:46	Andrew Parker	U17	10.12.83	11	Leamington	23 Apr
47:15	Karl Atton		14.09.71	4	Leicester	3 Sep
47:17	Jimmy Ball		17.02.63	8	East Molesey	9 Jan
47:32	Michael Kemp	U23	23.12.79	2	Birmingham	22 Jan
(20)						
47:40	Dan King	U20	30.05.83	3	Dartford	7 May
47:44	James Davis	U17	10.10.84	9	East Molesey	9 Jan
47:56	Graham White	V40	28.03.59	2	Portsmouth	1 May

20 Kilometres Walk- Road

1:25:56	Andi Drake		6.02.65	2	Dublin, IRE	8 Apr
1:27:08	Darrell Stone		2.02.68	1	Holme Pierrepoint	12 Mar
1:27:38	Chris Maddocks	V40	28.03.57	2	Douglas IOM	19 Feb
	1:31:10			18	Leamington	23 Apr
	1:31:39			50	Eisenhuttenstadt, GER	17 Jun
1:28:47	Andy Penn		31.03.67	2	Holme Pierrepoint	12 Mar
	1:29:24			3	Douglas IOM	19 Feb
	1:30:26			17	Leamington	23 Apr
	1:33:10			51	Eisenhuttenstadt, GER	17 Jun
1:30:54	Mark Easton		24.05.63	1	Leamington	13 Feb
1:30:56	Jamie O'Rawe		3.02.73	6	Dublin, IRE	16 Jul
1:31:14	Steve Partington		17.09.65	4	Douglas IOM	19 Feb
1:31:50	Matthew Hales	U23	6.10.79	3	Holme Pierrepoint	12 Mar
	1:31:57			20	Leamington	23 Apr
1:32:33	Don Bearman		16.04.66	5	Douglas IOM	19 Feb
1:32:43	Gareth Brown		10.05.68	5	Holme Pierrepoint	12 Mar
(10)						
1:34:23	Andy O'Rawe		8.09.63	1	Basildon	27 May
1:35:35	Tim Watt		19.09.66	5	Manassas, USA	2 Apr
1:38:21	Allan King	V40	3.12.56	2	Leamington	13 Feb

Track - No judge

1:27:04	Chris Maddocks	V40	28.03.57	1=	Plymouth	9 Jan
1:27:04	Steve Hollier		27.02.76	1=	Plymouth	9 Jan

30 Kilometres Walk

2:20:04 +	Chris Maddocks	V40	28.03.57	1m	Sint-Oedenrode, BEL	12 Mar
2:22:08 +	Andi Drake		6.02.65	4m	Leamington	23 Apr
2:31:18 +	Chris Cheeseman	V40	11.12.58	13m	Leamington	23 Apr
2:31:26 +	Steve Hollier		27.02.76	14m	Leamington	23 Apr
2:36:38 +	Tim Watt		19.09.66	15m	Leamington	23 Apr

35 Kilometres Walk

2:46:26 +	Andi Drake		6.02.65	6m	Leamington	23 Apr
2:51:20	Chris Cheeseman	V40	11.12.58	1	Dartford	6 May
2:53:10	Don Bearman		16.04.66	2	Dartford	6 May
2:55:59	Gareth Brown		10.05.68	3	Dartford	6 May
2:56:42 +	Steve Hollier		27.02.76	13m	Leamington	23 Apr

50 Kilometres Walk- Road

3:57:10	Chris Maddocks	V40	28.03.57	1	Sint-Oedenrode, BEL	12 Mar
4:07:18	Steve Hollier		27.02.76	28	Eisenhuttenstadt, GER	18 Jun
	4:15:18			9	Leamington	23 Apr
4:07:33	Mark Easton		24.05.63	2	Sint-Oedenrode, BEL	12 Mar
4:13:07	Chris Cheeseman	V40	11.12.58	6	Dublin, IRE	15 Jul
	4:17:57			10	Leamington	23 Apr
	4:23:19			43	Eisenhuttenstadt, GER	18 Jun
4:21:23	Darrell Stone		2.02.68	1	London (VP)	9 Sep
4:23:18	Tim Watt		19.09.66	11	Leamington	23 Apr
4:27:23	Gareth Brown		10.05.68	2	London (VP)	9 Sep
	10 performances to 4:30:00 by 7 athletes					
4:32:42	Don Bearman		16.04.66	3	London (VP)	9 Sep
4:50:47	Peter Kaneen		12.07.61	4	London (VP)	9 Sep
4:51:31	Mike Smith		20.04.63	5	London (VP)	9 Sep
(10)						
4:52:15	Chris Berwick	V50	1.05.46	6	London (VP)	9 Sep
4:56:59	Dave Turner	V40	20.10.57	1	Bradford	29 May
4:58:06	Martin Fisher		27.09.62	2	Bradford	29 May

4 x 100 METRES

38.35	National Team		2	Gateshead	28 Aug
	(D.Chambers, D.Campbell, M.Devonish, J.Gardener)				
38.41	National Team		1	Gateshead	15 Jul
	(C.Malcolm, D.Campbell, M.Devonish, D.Chambers)				
39.05	National Junior Team	U20	1	Santiago, CHI	22 Oct
	(T.Edgar, D.Grant, T.Benjamin, M.Lewis-Francis)				
39.07	National Team		2	Glasgow (S)	2 Jul
	(C.Browne, D.Campbell, M.Devonish, D.Chambers)				
39.14	National Junior Team	U20	1h1	Santiago, CHI	22 Oct
	(T.Edgar, D.Grant, T.Benjamin, M.Lewis-Francis)				
39.19	National 'B' Team		3	Gateshead	28 Aug
	(A.Condon, I.Mackie, J.Golding, C.Malcolm)				
39.49	National Team		4	Villeneuve d'Ascq, FRA	17 Jun
	(D.Campbell, M.Devonish, J.Golding, D.Chin)				
39.61	National Under 23 Team	U23	1	Liverpool	22 Jul
	(C.Malcolm, J.Barbour, J.Stewart, J.Skeete)				
39.71	National Junior Team	U20	2	Grosseto, ITA	7 Oct
	(T.Edgar, D.Grant, T.Benjamin, M.Lewis-Francis)				
39.74	National Junior Team	U20	1	Bedford	11 Jun
	(T.Benjamin, B.Lewis, D.Grant, M.Lewis-Francis)				
39.86	National Under 23 Team	U23	1	Getafe, SPA	9 Sep
	(N.Thomas, N.Morgan, J.Stewart, J.Barbour)				
39.91	M. McFarlane's Team		2	Bedford	11 Jun
	(J.Fergus, -, -, -)				
40.10	National Junior Team	U20	1	Loughborough	21 May
	(T.Benjamin, B.Lewis, D.Grant, M.Lewis-Francis)				
40.16	National Junior Team	U20	1	Bath	16 Sep
	(D.Grant, T.Edgar, T.Benjamin, M.Lewis-Francis)				
40.17	England		3	Budapest, HUN	22 Jul
	(A.Condon, M.Devonish, A.Jarrett, C.Browne)				
40.25	National Junior Team	U20	1	Derby	3 Sep
	(T.Benjamin, B.Lewis, D.Grant, M.Lewis-Francis)				
40.26	England		1	Vittel, FRA	2 Sep
	(J.Fergus, C.Browne, J.Stewart, J.Barbour)				
40.32	All Stars		2	Fullerton, USA	27 Apr
	(A.Patrick, M.Devonish, J.Regis, L.Cowan)				
40.42	Scotland		2	Loughborough	21 May
	(J.Oparka, J.Skeete, B.Doyle, I.Mackie)				
40.58	Sale Harriers Manchester		1	Bedford	4 Jun
	(L.Collins, D.Money, J.Stewart, A.Condon)				
40.76	National Team		2	Dortmund, GER	8 Jul
	(,,,D.Chambers)				
40.8	Birchfield Harriers		1	Cudworth	22 Jul
	(D.Bradley, J.John, B.Lewis, M.Lewis-Francis)				
40.88	Birchfield Harriers		1	Bedford	19 Aug
	(D.Bradley, J.John, B.Lewis, M.Lewis-Francis)				
40.90	Loughborough University		3	Loughborough	21 May
	(T.Barton, M.Woodhouse, A.McFarlane, J.Stewart)				
40.90	Belgrave Harriers		2	Liège, BEL	27 May
	(D.Chin, E.Newell, A.Walcott, D.Campbell)				
40.90	Shaftesbury Barnet Harriers		2	Bedford	19 Aug
	(J.Fergus, L.Davis, A.Knight, A.Fugallo)				
40.9	Cardiff AAC		1	Peterborough	8 Jul
	(K.Williams, D.Turner, D.Papura, T.Benjamin)				
40.94	England U19 team	U19	1	Edinburgh	13 Aug
	(M.Miah, D.Grant, T.Edgar, T.Abeyie)				
41.0	Blackheath Harriers		1	Enfield	24 Jun
41.0	Blackheath Harriers		2	Peterborough	8 Jul
	(D.Burley, J.Barbour, M.Champion, A.Lashore)				

Additional National Team

41.22	Wales (K.Williams, D.Turner, D.Papura, M.Elias)		2	Bath	16 Sep

Additional Club Teams (1 - 7 above)

41.05	Newham & Essex Beagles		1	London (He)	8 Jul
41.1	Enfield & Haringey AC		2	Enfield	24 Jun
41.16	Woodford Green & Essex Ladies		2	Bedford	4 Jun
41.32	Border Harriers		2	Wigan	24 Jun
41.74	Brunel West London		2	Stoke-on-Trent	1 May
41.9	Swansea H		1rB	Newport	11 Jun
41.9	Windsor Slough & Eton AC		3	Eton	23 Jul
41.91	Belgrave Harriers	U20	1	Birmingham	10 Sep
41.92	Team Solent		4	London (He)	6 Aug
41.93	Puma TVH		5	London (He)	6 Aug
42.0	Cambridge University		1	Oxford	20 May
42.0	Harrow AC		4	Peterborough	8 Jul
42.05	Birchfield Harriers	U20	2	Birmingham	10 Sep
42.1	Trafford AC		3	Enfield	24 Jun
42.2	Notts AC		1	Crawley	24 Jun

Additional Under 20 Teams (1 - 8 above)

41.21	National Junior 'B' Team		3	Bedford	11 Jun
41.57	South of England		1	Watford	2 Jul
42.08	Scotland		1	Nicosia,CYP	27 May

Additional Under 20 National Teams

43.28	Wales	U19	3	Edinburgh	13 Aug
44.24	Northern Ireland	U19	4	Edinburgh	13 Aug

Additional Under 20 Club Teams (1 - 2 above)

43.0	Woodford Green & Essex Ladies		1	Erith	7 May
43.4	Sale Harriers Manchester		2	Wakefield	16 Jul
43.9	Notts AC		3	Wakefield	16 Jul
44.1	Coventry Godiva Harriers		1	Tamworth	23 Apr
44.24	Croydon Harriers	U17	1	Birmingham	3 Sep
44.3	George Watson's College		1	Glasgow (S)	10 Jun
44.4	Peterborough AC		1	Ware	16 Jul
44.59	Harrow AC		4	Birmingham	10 Sep

Under 17 Teams (1 above)

43.05	England Schools		1	Blackpool	15 Jul
43.31	Surrey Schools		1h3	Sheffield	9 Jul
43.51	London Schools		1	Sheffield	9 Jul
43.57	Middlesex Schools		2	Sheffield	9 Jul
43.59	Hampshire Schools		3	Sheffield	9 Jul
43.70	West Midlands Schools		1h2	Sheffield	9 Jul
44.16	Scotland Schools		2	Blackpool	15 Jul
44.28	Humberside Schools		6	Sheffield	9 Jul
44.51	Wales Schools		3	Blackpool	15 Jul

Under 17 Club Teams (1 above)

44.7	Ayr Seaforth AAC		1	Dumfries	28 May
44.78	Enfield & Haringey AC		2	Birmingham	3 Sep
44.9	Liverpool Harriers AC		1	Ormskirk	2 Jul
45.0	Blackheath Harriers		1	Barking	3 Jul
45.09	Mandale H		3	Birmingham	3 Sep
45.1	Scunthorpe & District AC			Derby	10 Sep
45.47	Harrow AC		1	Birmingham	2 Sep
45.5	Liverpool Pembroke Sefton		1	Stretford	4 Jun

45.7	Trinity School		1	Oxford	11 May
45.7	Aldershot Farnham & D AC		2	Croydon	4 Jun
45.7	Birchfield Harriers		1	Sutton Coldfield	2 Jul

Under 15 Teams

45.25	London Schools		1	Sheffield	9 Jul
45.55	Cambridgeshire Schools		2	Sheffield	9 Jul
45.83	Hampshire Schools		3	Sheffield	9 Jul
45.93	Middlesex Schools		4	Sheffield	9 Jul
46.26	Devon Schools		5	Sheffield	9 Jul
46.3	Lewisham Schools		1	London (BP)	10 Jun
46.3	Staffordshire Schools		1	Derby	17 Jun
46.41	Kent Schools		6	Sheffield	9 Jul
46.48	Birchfield Harriers		1	Birmingham	2 Sep
46.5	Blackheath Harriers		1	Erith	10 Sep

Additional Under 15 Club Teams (1 - 2 above)

46.8	Belgrave Harriers		1	Barking	3 Jul
46.9	Enfield & Haringey AC		2	Barking	3 Jul
46.9	Cambridge Harriers		2	Erith	10 Sep
46.92	Croydon Harriers		1	Birmingham	3 Sep
47.0	Havering Mayesbrrok AC		1	Barking	3 Jul
47.1	Woodford Green & Essex Ladies		2	Barking	3 Jul
47.3	City of Stoke AC		1	Stoke	23 Jul
47.3	Gateshead Harriers & AC		1	Middlesbrough	25 Jul

Under 13 Club Teams

50.7	Sale Harriers Manchester		1	Lancaster	30 Apr
51.6	Hallamshire Harriers		1	Leeds	23 Jul
51.73	Croydon Harriers		1	Birmingham	3 Sep
52.0	Liverpool Harriers AC		1	Ormskirk	2 Jul
52.2	Enfield & Haringey AC		1	Barking	3 Jul
52.71	Harrow AC		1	Birmingham	2 Sep
53.48	Gateshead Harriers		2	Birmingham	2 Sep
53.5	Blackheath Harriers		1	Barking	3 Jul
53.51	Shaftesbury Barnet Harriers		4	Birmingham	3 Sep
54.1	Chelmsford AC		1	Watford	9 Jul

4 x 200 METRES

1:27.87 i	Brunel University		1	Birmingham	17 Feb
1:28.83 i	Loughborough University		1r1	Cardiff	12 Mar
1:29.14 i	Bath University		2r1	Cardiff	12 Mar
1:30.45 i	Birmingham University		3	Birmingham	17 Feb
1:30.5	Herne Hill Harriers		1	London (TB)	2 Aug
1:30.65 i	Wales		1	Cardiff	4 Mar
1:30.81 i	Army		4	Birmingham	17 Feb
1:31.14 i	South West		2	Cardiff	4 Mar
1:31.8	Cambridge University		1	Cambridge	5 Mar
1:32.4	Epsom & Ewell Harriers		1	London (TB)	16 Aug
1:32.46 i	UWIC		1r2	Cardiff	12 Mar
1:32.65 i	St Mary's University		2r2	Cardiff	12 Mar

Under 20 Team

1:33.9	Harrow School		1	Oxford	11 May

Under 17 Club Teams

1:34.11 i	England Schools	U16	1	Cardiff	26 Feb
1:34.32 i	Scotland Schools	U16	2	Cardiff	26 Feb
1:34.74 i	Ayr Seaforth AAC		1h1	Glasgow	19 Mar
1:36.7	Trinity School		1	Oxford	11 May

Under 15 Teams

1:42.02 i	Giffnock North AAC		1	Glasgow	19 Mar
1:42.50	North Down AC		1	Antrim	19 Aug
1:42.7	Croydon Harriers		1	Walton	18 Jun
1:43.6	Mansfield		1	Mansfield	18 Jun

Under 13 Teams

1:55.9	Croydon Harriers		11	Walton	18 Jun
1:57.90 i	Victoria Park AAC		h	Glasgow	19 Mar
1:57.90 i	Falkirk Victoria Harriers		1h3	Glasgow	19 Mar

4 x 400 METRES

3:01.22	National Team		6	Sydney, AUS	30 Sep
	(J.Deacon 45.63, D.Caines 44.65, I.Thomas 45.26, J.Baulch 45.68)				
3:01.35	National Team		2s2	Sydney, AUS	29 Sep
	(J.Deacon 45.97, D.Caines 44.84, I.Thomas 45.83, J.Baulch 44.71)				
3:04.35	National Team		2h1	Sydney, AUS	29 Sep
	(J.Deacon 46.34, D.Caines 44.86, J.Baulch 46.32, I.Thomas 46.83)				
3:05.24	National team		2	Gateshead	16 Jul
	(R.Knowles 47.39, S.Baldock 45.42, C.Rawlinson 45.87, J.Baulch 46.56)				
3:07.36	National Under 23 Team	U23	1	Liverpool	22 Jul
3:08.02	National Under 23 Team	U23	1	Getafe, SPA	9 Sep
	(A.Buckley, M.Elias, R.Lewis, D.Naismith)				
3:08.03	England		1	Loughborough	21 May
	(E.White 47.7, A.Borsumato 46.4, M.Brown 46.4, J.Deacon 46.8)				
3:08.38 i	National Team		3	Glasgow	5 Mar
	(E.White 48.85, P.Slythe 46.26, D.Caines 45.82, R.Knowles 47.45)				
3:08.59	Newham & Essex Beagles		1	London (He)	8 Jul
	(P.Slythe, D.Naismith, M.Brown, I.Thomas)				
3:08.74	Newham & Essex Beagles		1	Bedford	19 Aug
	(M.Afilaka, D.Naismith, P.McBurney, M.Brown)				
3:08.89	Birchfield Harriers		1	Wigan	24 Jun
	(R.Knowles, G.Djan, D.Caines, D.Ladejo 45.82)				
3:08.93	England		1	Vittel, FRA	2 Sep
	(D.Naismith, R.Knowles, A.Buckley, D.Ladejo)				
3:09.79 i	National Team		4	Ghent, BEL	27 Feb
	(E.White 47.83, P.Slythe 47.43, D.Naismith 47.29, R.Knowles 47.24)				
3:10.53	Scotland		2	Loughborough	21 May
	(B.Middleton, S.Scott, R.McDonald, C.Philp)				
3:10.98	Sale Harriers Manchester		2	Wigan	24 Jun
	(A.Buckley, B.Middleton, A.Borsumato, T.Comyn IRE)				
3:11.20	Belgrave Harriers		1	Liège, BEL	28 May
	(M.Parper, A.Walcott, M.Douglas, S.Baldock)				
3:11.33	Belgrave Harriers		1	Eton	6 May
	(R.David, A.Walcott, T.Lerwill, M.Parper)				
3:11.51	Newham & Essex Beagles		2	Eton	6 May
	(M.Brown, M.Afilaka, A.Donaldson, N.Jennings)				
3:11.94	Border Harriers		3	Eton	6 May
	(A.Mitchell, N.Carlisle, B.Forbes, S.Scott)				
3:11.94	British Universities		3	Loughborough	21 May
	(N.Jennings, W.Martin, I.Deeth, A.Buckley)				
3:12.31	Team Solent		4	Eton	6 May
	(A.Bargh, W.Martin, P.Brend, L.Fairclough)				
3:12.50	Birchfield Harriers		2	Bedford	19 Aug
	(B.Yiend, B.Donkin, R.Knowles, P.Hibbert)				
3:12.69	National Junior Team	U20	2	Grosseto, ITA	7 Oct
	(L.Bryan, R.Nicholls, J.Christie 47.3 M.Bradbury)				
3:12.70	National Junior Team	U20	4	Loughborough	21 May
	(S.Tunnicliffe, L.Holehouse, S.Ellis, L.Bryan)				
3:12.83	Loughborough P & P		5	Loughborough	21 May

3:13.51	Puma TVH		2	London (He)	8 Jul
	(E.Betts, G.Gray, A.Lustgarten, P.Octave)				
3:13.52	Team Solent		3	London (He)	8 Jul
	(J.Goodwin, P.Brend, L.Fairclough, W. Martin)				
3:13.81	Puma TVH		5	Eton	6 May
	(Fernandez, K.Bentham, P.Octave, Williams)				
3:14.03	Newham & Essex Beagles		1	London (He)	6 Aug
	(Griffiths, M.Brown, P.McBurney, N.Jennings)				
3:14.43	North		1	Solihull	29 Jul
3:14.55	Belgrave Harriers		3	Wigan	24 Jun
	(Aspen, M.Douglas, Levy, G.Dearman)				
3:14.60	Team Solent		3	Bedford	19 Aug
	(L.Fairclough, A. MacLean, W.Martin, J.Parker)				
3:14.69	Sale Harriers Manchester		4	London (He)	8 Jul
	(R.Fanning IRE, R.Palmer, B.Middleton, A.Buckley)				
3:14.71	Sale Harriers Manchester		1	Cudworth	28 Aug
3:14.92	Puma TVH		2	London (He)	6 Aug
	(K.Bentham, G.Gray, A.Lustgarten, P.Octave)				
3:14.94	Loughborough Un		1	Stoke-on-Trent	1 May
	(J.Edwards 47.5 anchor)				

Additional Club Teams (1 - 8 above)

3:15.13	Brunel West London University	2	Stoke-on-Trent	1 May
3:15.14	Trafford AC	4	Bedford	19 Aug
3:15.61	Bath University	3	Stoke-on-Trent	1 May
3:15.88	Enfield & Haringey AC	1	Enfield	6 Aug
3:16.26	Blackheath Harriers	2	Enfield	6 Aug
3:16.80	Woodford Green & Essex Ladies	3	Enfield	6 Aug
3:17.1	City of Stoke AC	1	Sheffield	24 Jun
3:17.8	Oxford University	1	Oxford	20 May
3:18.10	Shaftesbury Barnet Harriers	5	London (He)	6 Aug
3:18.23	Worthing Harriers	1	Bedford	20 Aug
3:18.70	Bolton United Harriers	2	Bedford	20 Aug
3:18.8	Liverpool Harriers AC	1	Watford	20 May

Additional Under 20 Teams (1 - 2 above)

3:15.98	National Junior Team		1	Bath	16 Sep
3:17.10	England	U19	2	Edinburgh	13 Aug
3:18.33	North of England		1	Watford	2 Jul
3:18.44	Scotland	U19	3	Edinburgh	13 Aug
3:18.58	South of England		2	Watford	2 Jul
3:18.76	Scotland		1	Nicosia, CYP	20 May
3:18.88	Wales	U19	4	Edinburgh	13 Aug
3:20.89 i	National Team		2	Neubrandenburg,GER	4 Mar

Under 20 Club Teams

3:21.0	Shaftesbury Barnet Harriers	1	London (He)	7 May
3:21.14	Notts AC	1	Birmingham	10 Sep
3:21.56	Belgrave Harriers	2	Birmingham	10 Sep
3:21.84	Enfield & Haringey AC	3	Birmingham	10 Sep
3:23.13	Birchfield Harriers	5	Birmingham	10 Sep
3:23.3	Bolton United Harriers	1	Blackpool	18 Jun
3:29.0	Liverpool Harriers AC	2	Wakefield	16 Jul
3:29.9	Sale Harriers Manchester	3	Wakefield	16 Jul
3:31.2	Gloucester AC	1	Neath	7 May
3:31.3	Aldershot Farnham & District AC	1	Portsmouth	7 May

Under 17 Teams

3:21.39	England Schools	1	Blackpool	15 Jul
3:28.07	Scotland Schools	2	Blackpool	15 Jul
3:29.3	Hertfordshire	1	London (WF)	17 Sep

3:29.73	Enfield & Haringey AC		1	Birmingham	3 Sep
3:30.0	Derby & County AC		1	Stoke	23 Jul
3:30.99	Croydon Harriers		2	Birmingham	3 Sep
3:31.29	Mandale H & AC		3	Birmingham	3 Sep
3:31.87	Blackheath Harriers		1	Birmingham	2 Sep
3:32.2	Middlesbrough & Cleveland AC		1	Middlesbrough	25 Jul

Additional Under 17 Club Teams (1 - 6 above)

3:32.5	Ayr Seaforth AAC		1	Ayr	4 Jun
3:33.4	Notts AC		1	Derby	4 Jun
3:33.4	Middlesex		2	London (WF)	17 Sep
3:33.5	Gateshead Harriers & AC		2	Middlesbrough	25 Jul
3:33.8	Wirral AC		1	Stretford	4 Jun

Under 15 Teams

3:44.10	Croydon Harriers		1	Birmingham	3 Sep
3:44.4	Liverpool Pembroke & Sefton H&AC		1	Gateshead	21 May
3:44.8	Torfaen AC		1	Stoke-on-Trent	23 Jul
3:45.90	Mandale H & AC		2	Birmingham	3 Sep
3:46.21	Harrow AC		1	Birmingham	2 Sep
3:46.26	Sale Harriers Manchester		3	Birmingham	3 Sep
3:47.14	Blackheath Harriers		2	Birmingham	2 Sep
3:47.17	Enfield & Haringey AC		4	Birmingham	3 Sep
3:48.20	Liverpool Harriers AC		5	Birmingham	3 Sep
3:48.84	Wirral AC		3	Birmingham	2 Sep

Under 13 Team

4:34.3	Blackheath Harriers		1	Bromley	9 Jul

3 x 800 METRES

Under 13 Teams

7:36.27	Kilbarchan AC		1	Glasgow (S)	29 Jul
7:37.8	Invicta East Kent AC		1	Erith	10 Sep
7:40.57	City of Edinburgh AC		2	Glasgow (S)	29 Jul
7:44.72	Giffnock AAC		3	Glasgow (S)	29 Jul
7:46.7	Blackheath Harriers		2	Erith	10 Sep
7:49.2	Medway AC		2h1	Erith	10 Sep
7:52.3	Barnidiston Prep School		1	Bury St Edmunds	29 Sep
7:56.3	Bexley AC		3h1	Erith	10 Sep
8:05.2	GEC Avionics AC		2h2	Erith	10 Sep

4 x 800 METRES

7:38.86	St. Malachy's NI	U20	1	Philadelphia, USA	Apr
7:56.5	Sunderland H	U20	1	Middlesbrough	25 Jul
7:57.0	Chester-le-Street AC	U20	2	Middlesbrough	25 Jul
7:59.2	Cambridge University		1	Cambridge	5 Mar
8:00.2	Oxford University		2	Cambridge	5 Mar

Best Age Group Teams

8:52.8	Macclesfield AC	U17	1	Warrington	11 Jul
9:07.3	St Columb's College	U15	1	Belfast	22 Apr
10:53.3	Vale Royal AC	U13	1	Warrington	20 Jun

4 x 1500 METRES

16:48.9	Cambridge University		1	Cambridge	5 Mar
17:04.7	Oxford University		2	Cambridge	5 Mar

2000 LISTS - WOMEN

60 METRES - Indoors

7.24	Marcia Richardson	10.02.72	5	Birmingham	20 Feb
	7.25		1	Birmingham	29 Jan
	7.26		4s1	Ghent, BEL	27 Feb
	7.27		1h4	Birmingham	29 Jan
	7.27		5h1	Ghent, BEL	11 Feb
	7.27		8	Ghent, BEL	27 Feb
	7.28		1s2	Birmingham	29 Jan
	7.29		2	Glasgow	5 Mar
	7.33		2s1	Birmingham	15 Jan
	7.34		4h1	Ghent, BEL	26 Feb
	7.35		3	Birmingham	15 Jan
	7.43		1h1	Birmingham	15 Jan
7.30	Joice Maduaka	30.09.73	6s2	Ghent, BEL	27 Feb
	7.31		1s1	Birmingham	15 Jan
	7.32		2	Birmingham	15 Jan
	7.33		1h3	Birmingham	15 Jan
	7.34		1h1	Birmingham	29 Jan
	7.34		1s1	Birmingham	29 Jan
	7.34		2	Birmingham	29 Jan
	7.36		5h3	Ghent, BEL	26 Feb
	7.36		4	Glasgow	5 Mar
	7.38		8	Birmingham	20 Feb
	7.39		3	Stockholm, SWE	17 Feb
	7.43		6h2	Ghent, BEL	11 Feb
7.32	Diane Allahgreen	21.02.75	1	Birmingham	15 Jan
	7.34		1s2	Birmingham	15 Jan
	7.37		1h7	Birmingham	15 Jan
	7.38		1h5	Birmingham	29 Jan
	7.38		2s1	Birmingham	29 Jan
	7.38		5	Birmingham	29 Jan
	7.45		1	Sheffield	23 Jan
7.35	Stephi Douglas	22.01.69	4	Erfurt,GER	2 Feb
	7.42		1	Sindelfingen, GER	22 Jan
	7.43		3s2	Birmingham	29 Jan
	7.43		h	Erfurt,GER	2 Feb
	7.44		1	Furth, GER	16 Jan
	7.44		6h2	Stuttgart, GER	6 Feb
7.36	Janine Whitlock	11.08.73	3	Birmingham	29 Jan
	7.40		2h4	Birmingham	29 Jan
	7.43		3s1	Birmingham	29 Jan
7.37	Christine Bloomfield	12.02.68	2s2	Birmingham	15 Jan
	7.37		4	Birmingham	29 Jan
	7.38mx			Birmingham	8 Jan
	7.39		1h2	Birmingham	15 Jan
	7.40		2s2	Birmingham	29 Jan
	7.42		1h3	Birmingham	29 Jan
	7.44		4	Birmingham	15 Jan
7.39	Catherine Murphy	21.09.75	3s1	Birmingham	15 Jan
	7.43		3h1	Birmingham	29 Jan
	7.44		4s1	Birmingham	29 Jan
7.39	Zoe Wilson	28.08.76	2h2	Birmingham	29 Jan
	7.41		1	Cardiff	26 Feb
	52 performances to 7.45 by 8 athletes				
7.46	Sarah Oxley/Reilly	3.07.73	7	Birmingham	29 Jan
7.52	Shani Anderson	7.08.75	3s2	Birmingham	15 Jan
(10)					

7.52	Vernicha James	U17	6.06.84	1U17	Birmingham	30 Jan
7.52	Donna Maylor	U20	20.05.82	3r2	Neubrandenburg, GER	4 Mar
7.54	Susan Burnside	U23	3.02.80	1	Glasgow	23 Jan
7.56	Emma Whitter	U23	20.07.80	6s1	Birmingham	29 Jan
7.57	Jo Hill		11.02.73	2h3	Birmingham	29 Jan
7.60	Katherine Endacott	U23	29.01.80	2h5	Birmingham	29 Jan
7.61	Angharad James	U23	7.04.79	1	Cardiff	4 Mar
7.62	Ann Danson		4.05.71	5s1	Birmingham	15 Jan
7.62	Vicky Day/Ward		19.06.72	3h1	Birmingham	29 Jan
7.63	Donna Fraser		7.11.72	3h1	Cardiff	6 Feb
	(20)					
7.64	Ellena Ruddock		23.02.76	4h3	Birmingham	29 Jan
7.65	Simmone Jacobs		5.09.66	1h4	Birmingham	15 Jan
7.65	Jade Johnson	U23	7.06.80	5h1	Birmingham	29 Jan
7.66	Lowri Jones	U20	22.07.83	1	Cardiff	20 Feb
7.67	Sabrina Scott	U23	2.06.79	1	Bedford	22 Jan
7.68	Jemma Sims	U17	2.05.85	1	Birmingham	12 Feb
7.68	Donita Benjamin		7.03.72	1	Birmingham	17 Feb
7.69	Clova Court	V35	10.02.60	3	Birmingham	8 Jan
7.69	Sarah Claxton	U23	23.09.79	3h2	Birmingham	15 Jan
7.70	Rachael Kay	U23	8.09.80	6h1	Birmingham	29 Jan
	(30)					
7.71	Danielle Selley	U17	19.12.83	1rB	Cardiff	4 Mar
7.72	Siobhan McVie	U17	6.07.84	2	Birmingham	5 Feb
7.73	Gemma Ryde	U20	23.06.83	1	Glasgow	20 Jan
7.73	Melanie Purkiss	U23	11.03.79	2	Glasgow	23 Jan
7.74	Susie Williams		2.06.77	3	Bedford	22 Jan

Additional Under 17 (1 - 4 above)

7.76	Emma Bailey	25.07.84	2	Birmingham	12 Feb
7.84	Samantha Gamble	27.03.84	2	Cardiff	19 Feb
7.86	Laura Cunningham	14.02.85	1	Glasgow	27 Jan
7.88	Carolyn McKenna	4.05.84	3	Glasgow	27 Jan
7.88	Kerry Everall	29.02.84	3	Birmingham	12 Feb
7.89	Katherine Jones	21.01.85	2h4	Birmingham	5 Feb
	(10)				
7.89	Georgette Perry	10.12.83	4	Birmingham	12 Feb
7.91	Eleanor Caney	28.05.84	3	Birmingham	30 Jan
7.92	Kara Dunn	12.10.84	2	Cardiff	26 Feb
7.94	Kimberley Velvick	3.01.85	2h2	Birmingham	5 Feb
7.95	Charli Croll	25.10.84	1	Bedford	22 Jan
7.96	Natalie Watson	5.07.84	2	Birmingham	8 Jan
7.97	Yasmine Meite	6.09.84	3h5	Birmingham	5 Feb
7.98	Vicky Griffiths	9.10.84	2h1	Birmingham	5 Feb
7.98	Gemma Winstone	18.11.84	2h1	Cardiff	19 Feb
7.98	Natasha Cross	13.11.84	2	Cardiff	17 Dec
	(20)				
7.99	Natalie Plateau	19.10.84	3h4	Birmingham	5 Feb

Overage

7.86	Melinda Cooksey	19.05.84	1	Cardiff	17 Dec

Under 15

7.75	Amy Spencer	19.09.85	1	Birmingham	5 Feb

Hand Timing

7.5	Vernicha James	U17	(7.52)	1r2	London (CP)	12 Jan
7.6	Simmone Jacobs		(7.65)	2	London (Ha)	9 Jan
7.6	Sabrina Scott	U23	(7.67)	2	London (CP)	19 Feb
7.8	Kimberley Velvick	U17	(7.94)	1	Eton	17 Dec
7.9	Titi Ameobi	U17	20.11.84	1	Jarrow	8 Jan
7.9	Yasmine Meite	U17	(7.97)	2	Jarrow	8 Feb

JONATHAN EDWARDS. Gold at last.

DWAIN CHAMBERS. So close to a medal.

MARK LEWIS-FRANCIS. The Future!

DARREN CAMPBELL. Much improved for an unexpected Silver.

CHRISTIAN MALCOLM. A good year, disappointing Olympics.

DANIEL CAINES. Raw talent.

CHRIS RAWLINSON. Great start to the year, a little flat at the end.

LARRY ACHIKE. British 2nd, Olympic 4th.

PHILLIPS IDOWU. British 3rd, Olympic 6th.

STEVE BACKLEY. A man, a javelin, a flame.

DEAN MACEY. Fought to the end.

CHRIS MADDOCKS. Hero!

KATHARINE MERRY. 2nd British woman under 50 seconds.

DONNA FRASER & KATHY FREEMAN. Third British woman under 50 seconds (with a famous Australian).

KELLY HOLMES. The biggest smile in Sydney.

HAYLEY TULLETT. A greatly improved runner.

PAULA RADCLIFFE. The agony!

PAULA RADCLIFFE. The ecstasy!

Foreign

7.60		*Leanne O'Callaghan*		*15.07.74*	*3h4*	*Birmingham*	*29 Jan*

Outdoors

7.42	0.2	Sarah Wilhelmy	U23	2.02.80	3	Gold Coast (S), AUS	15 Sep
7.45	0.2	Dianne Allahgreen		21.02.75	4	Gold Coast (S), AUS	15 Sep
7.5 mx		Janine Whitlock		11.08.73		Stretford	5 Mar

75 METRES - Under 13

9.7		Carley Wenham	14.03.88	1	Worthing	12 Jul
9.98	1.4	Jenny Igbokwe		1	Birmingham	3 Sep
10.0		Stacey Simpson	25.01.88	1	Dumfries	7 May
10.0		Natalie Pearson	7.06.88	1	Hull	21 May
10.0		Jane Chadwick	15.09.87	1	Wigan	2 Jul
		10.01 1.4		2	Birmingham	3 Sep
10.0		Laura Cox	21.01.88	1	Cheltenham	2 Jul
10.07	1.4	Lauren Duncan	21.03.88	3	Birmingham	3 Sep
10.1		Kayleigh Modeste		1	Coventry	21 May
10.1		Jessica Taylor	27.06.88	1	Rotherham	21 May
10.1		Louise Shaw		2	Wigan	2 Jul
	(10)					
10.1		Chloe Gale	24.02.88	T	Ashford	16 Sep

100 METRES

11.34	1.7	Shani Anderson	7.08.75	1	Nitra, SVK	26 Aug
		11.50 1.1		1inv	Bedford	20 Aug
		11.52 1.9		1	Loughborough	30 Jul
		11.55 -0.9		3	Budapest, HUN	22 Jul
		11.55 -1.9		5h6	Sydney, AUS	22 Sep
		11.57 1.3		1	Solihull	5 Aug
		11.59 -0.2		6	Gateshead	28 Aug
		11.60 1.2		5r2	Budapest, HUN	22 Jul
		11.60 1.2		5r1	Gold Coast (RB), AUS	17 Sep
11.35	2.0	Marcia Richardson	10.02.72	2	Bedford	4 Jun
		11.38 1.1		1r3	Bedford	11 Jun
		11.41 -2.2		1	Birmingham	12 Aug
		11.43 0.9		1	Fullerton, USA	27 Apr
		11.45 -0.5		1s2	Birmingham	12 Aug
		11.47 -0.8		2h1	Budapest, HUN	22 Jul
		11.53 -0.9		2	Budapest, HUN	22 Jul
		11.53 -0.2		5	Gateshead	28 Aug
		11.54 1.1		8	London (CP)	5 Aug
		11.55 0.2		1h1	Birmingham	11 Aug
		11.62 -1.5		4h7	Sydney, AUS	22 Sep
11.42	0.4	Joice Maduaka	30.09.73	1rB	Linz, AUT	8 Aug
		11.44 -0.9		1	Budapest, HUN	22 Jul
		11.46 1.2		1h2	Budapest, HUN	22 Jul
		11.46 -0.5		2s2	Birmingham	12 Aug
		11.47 1.0		3	Baton Rouge, USA	15 Apr
		11.47 -2.2		2	Birmingham	12 Aug
		11.48 1.7		2	Ljubljana, SLO	25 Jul
		11.51 0.9		5h1	Sydney, AUS	22 Sep
		11.52 0.2		1h4	Birmingham	11 Aug
		11.57 1.2		3	Fana, NOR	27 Jun
11.43	1.0	Donita Benjamin	7.03.72	1h5	Birmingham	11 Aug
		11.50		1r2	Dublin (S), IRE	29 Jul
		11.52 1.0		1	Vittel, FRA	2 Sep
		11.56 -2.2		5	Birmingham	12 Aug
		11.60 -1.5		2s1	Birmingham	12 Aug
		11.64 1.1		2inv	Bedford	20 Aug

11.44	0.8	Sam Davies	U23	20.09.79	1h2	Birmingham	11 Aug
		11.47 -2.2			3	Birmingham	12 Aug
		11.51 -0.1			5h1	Leverkusen, GER	20 Aug
		11.55 2.0			4	Bedford	4 Jun
		11.55 -0.5			3s2	Birmingham	12 Aug
		11.56 1.2			2	Fana, NOR	27 Jun
		11.61 0.0			1	Solihull	29 Jul
		11.63 1.6			1	Loughborough	21 May
		11.63 1.7			2s2	Bedford	29 May
		11.63 -1.2			1rB	Liverpool	22 Jul
11.49	0.7	Sarah Wilhelmy	U23	2.02.80	1r2	Gold Coast (RB), AUS	17 Sep
		11.53 0.0			1	Bridgetown, BAR	25 Jun
11.52	1.1	Abi Oyepitan	U23	30.12.79	2r3	Bedford	11 Jun
		11.53 1.4			1	Glasgow (S)	8 Jul
		11.58 -0.2			1	Liverpool	22 Jul
11.55	0.0	Amanda Forrester	U23	29.09.78	1	Getafe, SPA	9 Sep
		11.59 -0.2			2	Liverpool	22 Jul
11.57	1.7	Donna Fraser		7.11.72	1s2	Bedford	29 May
		11.59 1.1			4r3	Bedford	11 Jun
11.58	1.2	Christine Bloomfield		12.02.68	4h2	Budapest, HUN	22 Jul
		11.59 1.0			2	Vittel, FRA	2 Sep
		11.60 0.0			1	Vaxjo, SWE	29 Aug
		11.64 0.3			1	Enfield	6 Aug
		11.64 1.0			2h5	Birmingham	11 Aug
		11.65 1.4			3r1	Irvine, USA	7 May
		11.66 1.7			4	Ljubljana, SLO	25 Jul
		11.66 -1.7			1h2	Gothenburg, SWE	3 Aug
		11.66 -0.5			1	Gothenburg, SWE	3 Aug
	(10)						
11.66	0.9	Zoe Wilson		28.08.76	2	Fullerton, USA	27 Apr
		65 performances to 11.66 by 11 athletes					
11.68	2.0	Catherine Murphy		21.09.75	6	Bedford	4 Jun
11.72	1.9	Donna Maylor	U20	20.05.82	1	Grosseto, ITA	7 Oct
11.74	1.1	Felicia Louisy		17.05.74	1ro	Brighton	17 Jun
11.76		Simmone Jacobs		5.09.66	1=r1	Eagle Rock, USA	13 May
11.77	-1.5	Ellena Ruddock		23.02.76	4s1	Birmingham	12 Aug
11.79	1.2	Susie Williams		2.06.77	4	Brighton	17 Jun
11.80	0.3	Diane Allahgreen		21.02.75	2	Enfield	6 Aug
11.81	1.1	Sabrina Scott	U23	2.06.79	2ro	Brighton	17 Jun
11.81	0.8	Melanie Purkiss	U23	11.03.79	3h2	Birmingham	11 Aug
	(20)						
11.83	1.7	Kelly Thomas	U20	9.01.81	1	Bath	16 Sep
11.85	1.4	Vernicha James	U17	6.06.84	2	Bedford	11 Jun
11.85	1.2	Jo Hill		11.02.73	5	Brighton	17 Jun
11.85	0.3	Emma Whitter	U23	20.07.80	1h3	Bedford	1 Jul
11.88	1.6	Susan Burnside	U23	3.02.80	5	Loughborough	21 May
11.88	1.4	Rachel King		11.05.76	4	Haapsalu, EST	20 Jun
11.88	0.8	Sharon Williams		20.05.70	4h2	Birmingham	11 Aug
11.89	1.4	Gemma Ryde	U20	23.06.83	3	Bedford	11 Jun
11.90	1.7	Angharad James	U23	7.04.79	4s2	Bedford	29 May
11.90	-1.6	Helen Roscoe	U23	4.12.79	1	Shanghai, CHN	25 Jun
	(30)						
11.92	1.1	Michelle Turner		25.12.77	3ro	Brighton	17 Jun
11.93	1.9	Nicole Crosby		23.10.76	1	Cudworth	13 May
11.93	1.7	Katherine Endacott	U23	29.01.80	2	Bath	16 Sep
11.97	1.7	Natalie Hynd/Beattie	U23	30.01.78	5s2	Bedford	29 May
11.98	-0.6	Sharon Allen		23.10.68	5	Modesto, USA	13 May
11.98		Stephi Douglas		22.01.69	2	Stuttgart, GER	22 Jun
12.00	1.3	Danielle Norville	U20	18.01.83	3	Watford	2 Jul
12.00	0.3	Danielle Selley	U17	19.12.83	1	Sheffield	29 Jul
12.00	1.3	Janine Whitlock		11.08.73	3	Solihull	5 Aug

12.02	1.2	Amy Spencer	U15	19.09.85	1	Sheffield	29	Jul
	(40)							
12.04	1.6	Yvette Henry		8.06.73	4	Stoke-on-Trent	29	Apr
12.06	1.0	Kelly Sotherton		13.11.76	5h5	Birmingham	11	Aug
12.09		Kate Denham	U23	18.03.80	1	Watford	7	Jun
12.09	-1.0	Jade Johnson	U23	7.06.80	2h1	Bedford	1	Jul
12.10	-1.6	Clare Russell	U20	11.11.81	1h2	Sheffield	7	Jul
12.10	1.0	Emily Freeman	U23	24.11.80	6h5	Birmingham	11	Aug
12.10	-0.1	Jeanette Kwakye	U20	20.03.83	2h3	Bedford	26	Aug
12.11	-1.7	Jenny Meadows	U20	17.04.81	1	Marsa, MLT	27	Apr
12.11	1.6	Janette Niccolls		7.09.76	5	Stoke-on-Trent	29	Apr
12.11	1.2	Juliet Adeloye	U15	13.06.86	2	Sheffield	29	Jul
	(50)							
12.12	1.4	Victoria Barr	U20	14.04.82	5	Bedford	11	Jun
12.14	1.9	Maria Bolsover	U23	5.06.80	2	Cudworth	13	May
12.15	1.4	Jenni Stoute	V35	16.04.65	8r1	Irvine, USA	7	May
12.15	0.3	Jemma Sims	U17	2.05.85	2	Sheffield	29	Jul
12.18	0.3	Jade Lucas-Read	U17	17.01.84	3	Sheffield	29	Jul
12.18	1.2	Amalachukwu Onuora	U15	16.03.86	3	Sheffield	29	Jul
12.21	1.3	Kara Dunn	U17	12.10.84	2s2	Sheffield	7	Jul
12.22	0.3	Amina Ceesay	U23	19.11.79	5h3	Bedford	1	Jul
12.22		Tracy Joseph		29.11.69	3	Aldershot	16	Jul
12.22	-0.2	Heather McKay	U20	5.09.81	3s1	Bedford	26	Aug
	(60)							
12.23	0.3	Helen Frost		12.03.74	4	Alicante, SPA	6	May
12.24	0.7	Emma Bailey	U17	25.07.84	1h2	Sheffield	29	Jul
12.24	0.2	Kirstie Taylor		10.01.75	4h4	Birmingham	11	Aug
12.25	0.7	Louise Hazel	U15	6.10.85	1	Sheffield	8	Jul
12.26	-0.6	Lesley Owusu	U23	21.12.78	6	Los Angeles, USA	1	Apr
12.26	1.6	Rebecca White	U23	5.06.80	6	Stoke-on-Trent	29	Apr
12.26	-1.9	Kim Rothman	V35	6.09.64	2rB	Eton	6	May
12.27	0.7	Lucy Evans	U20	2.10.82	1h1	Sheffield	7	Jul
12.27	1.5	Charli Croll	U17	25.10.84	2h1	Sheffield	29	Jul
12.27	1.5	Kimberley Velvick	U17	3.01.85	3h1	Sheffield	29	Jul
	(70)							
12.27	1.9	Shereen Charles	U17	27.10.84	3s1	Sheffield	29	Jul
12.28	-0.2	Ann Danson		4.05.71	4	Eton	6	May
12.28	-1.9	Liz Fairs		1.12.77	3B	Eton	6	May
12.28	0.7	Rachel Redmond	U20	7.12.81	2h1	Sheffield	7	Jul
12.28	2.0	Rebecca Sweeney	U17	9.02.85	1	Birmingham	3	Sep

Unconfirmed

11.71		Sharon Allen		23.10.68		Piscataway, USA	9	Jul

Additional Under 17 (1 - 10 above)

12.30	1.3	Melinda Cooksey	19.05.84	3s2	Sheffield	7	Jul
12.36	0.9	Georgette Perry	10.12.83	2h3	Sheffield	29	Jul
12.38	1.3	Sarah Blackwell	1.10.84	1h2	Sheffield	7	Jul
12.38	-0.4	Cherie Pierre	15.05.84	5h1	Bedford	26	Aug
12.39	1.3	Titi Ameobi	20.11.84	5s2	Sheffield	7	Jul
12.39	0.9	Kathryn Evans	1.03.84	3h3	Sheffield	29	Jul
12.42	1.9	Sara Whigham	7.10.83	6s1	Sheffield	29	Jul
12.45	1.3	Tamsin Lees	24.04.84	6s2	Sheffield	7	Jul
12.47	1.9	Carolyn McKenna	4.05.84	7s1	Sheffield	29	Jul
12.47	2.0	Vicky Griffiths	9.10.84	2	Birmingham	3	Sep
	(20)						
12.51	0.7	Natalie Watson	5.07.84	3h4	Sheffield	29	Jul
12.53	1.3	Laura Heslop	12.11.83	7s2	Sheffield	7	Jul
12.56	-1.7	Laura Cunningham	14.02.85	1	Grangemouth	25	Jun
12.56	0.9	Amy Woodman	1.11.84	4h3	Sheffield	29	Jul
12.57	1.9	Louisa Wells	30.12.84	8s1	Sheffield	29	Jul
12.57	0.7	Jemma Walker	17.09.83	5h2	Sheffield	29	Jul

Wind Assisted

11.29	4.7	Marcia Richardson		(11.35)	1s1	Bedford	29 May
		11.39 3.2			1	Bedford	29 May
		11.45			1h1	Bedford	29 May
		11.47 2.8			7	Gateshead	15 Jul
11.45	3.2	Donna Fraser		(11.57)	2r1	Azusa, USA	8 Apr
		11.51 3.2			2	Bedford	29 May
		11.53			2h1	Bedford	29 May
		11.57 2.6			3inv	Bedford	19 Aug
11.49	4.7	Ellena Ruddock		(11.77)	2s1	Bedford	29 May
		11.66 3.2			4	Bedford	29 May
11.49	2.6	Christine Bloomfield		(11.58)	1inv	Bedford	19 Aug
11.52	4.7	Zoe Wilson		(11.66)	3s1	Bedford	29 May
		11.52 4.7			1r1	Bedford	11 Jun
11.53	3.0	Davies	U23	(11.44)	1r2	Bedford	11 Jun
		11.60 3.0			7rB	Gateshead	15 Jul
		11.62 3.2			3	Bedford	29 May
		11.63 2.8			1h3	Bedford	29 May
11.57	2.6	Benjamin		(11.43)	2inv	Bedford	19 Aug
11.59	2.9	Simmone Jacobs		(11.76)	1	Dudelange, LUX	27 May
11.66	4.7	Helen Roscoe	U23	(11.90)	2	Bedford	11 Jun
		20 performances to 11.66 by 9 athletes					
11.74	4.7	Janine Whitlock		(12.00)	4s1	Bedford	29 May
11.76	2.6	Kelly Thomas	U20	(11.83)	5inv	Bedford	19 Aug
11.80	4.7	Nicole Crosby		(11.93)	3r1	Bedford	11 Jun
11.85	3.0	Jade Johnson	U23	(12.09)	3r2	Bedford	11 Jun
11.87		Angharad James	U23	(11.90)	3h1	Bedford	29 May
11.88	4.4	Danielle Selley	U17	(12.00)	1	Blackpool	15 Jul
11.89	2.2	Clare Russell	U20	(12.10)	1	Sheffield	8 Jul
11.92		Natalie Hynd/Beattie	U23	(11.97)	4h1	Bedford	29 May
11.92	2.2	Danielle Norville	U20	(12.00)	2	Sheffield	8 Jul
11.96	2.2	Sharon Allen		(11.98)	4h2	Modesto, USA	13 May
11.99	3.2	Jemma Sims	U17	(12.15)	1s2	Sheffield	29 Jul
12.02	2.8	Vicky Day/Ward		19.06.72	1r2	Azusa, USA	8 Apr
12.03	3.0	Emily Freeman	U23	(12.10)	4r2	Bedford	11 Jun
12.04	4.7	Karlene Palmer	U23	23.10.80	6r1	Bedford	11 Jun
12.05	4.7	Catriona Slater		27.01.77	7s1	Bedford	29 May
12.07	2.2	Rachel Redmond	U20	(12.28)	3	Sheffield	8 Jul
12.08	2.5	Heather McKay	U20	(12.22)	1	Nicosia, CYP	27 May
12.08	2.9	Kirstie Taylor		(12.24)	4h4	Brighton	17 Jun
12.08	2.2	Karen Oughton	U20	26.01.83	4	Sheffield	8 Jul
12.09	3.6	Jade Lucas-Read	U17	(12.18)	3	Sheffield	8 Jul
12.09	3.6	Kara Dunn	U17	(12.21)	2	Sheffield	8 Jul
12.12	3.2	Emma Bailey	U17	(12.24)	2s2	Sheffield	29 Jul
12.13	3.0	Maria Bolsover	U23	(12.14)	5r2	Bedford	11 Jun
12.14	2.2	Rebecca Bird	U20	7.01.83	5	Sheffield	8 Jul
12.16	2.9	Clare Milborrow		10.01.77	5h4	Brighton	17 Jun
12.16	3.6	Melinda Cooksey	U17	(12.30)	5	Sheffield	8 Jul
12.17	3.6	Georgette Perry	U17	(12.36)	6	Sheffield	8 Jul
12.17	2.2	Anisha Barnaby	U20	9.07.83	6	Sheffield	8 Jul
12.18	4.7	Julia White	U23	2.05.79	6r1	Bedford	11 Jun
12.22	2.6	Fiona Westwood	U20	27.02.81	6inv	Bedford	19 Aug

Additional Under 17 (1 - 7 above)

12.24	3.2	Kathryn Evans	(12.39)	4s2	Sheffield	29 Jul
12.26	3.7	Titi Ameobi	(12.39)	1	Birmingham	2 Sep
12.30	3.0	Cherie Pierre	(12.38)	2	Watford	28 May

12.32	3.1	Sarah Blackwell		(12.38)	4s1	Sheffield	7	Jul
12.42	4.4	Jemma Walker		(12.57)	5	Blackpool	15	Jul
12.43	4.4	Laura Cunningham		(12.56)	6	Blackpool	15	Jul
12.47	3.0	Vicki Cooney		2.11.84	1r2	Birmingham	3	Sep
12.48	3.1	Louisa Wells		(12.57)	7s1	Sheffield	7	Jul
12.53	3.1	Eve Serrao		11.12.84	8s1	Sheffield	7	Jul
12.54	3.0	Rhiannon Burdon		29.10.83	4	Watford	28	May
12.54	3.7	Natasha Cross		13.11.84	2	Birmingham	2	Sep
12.55	3.2	Amy Woodman		(12.56)	7s2	Sheffield	29	Jul

Hand Timing

11.3 w	3.0	Shani Anderson		(11.34)	1	Bedford	19	Aug
11.3 w	3.0	Richardson		(11.35)	2	Bedford	19	Aug
11.4 w		Donita Benjamin		(11.43)	1	Blandford	19	Jul
11.4 w	3.0	Sam Davies	U23	(11.44)	3	Bedford	19	Aug
		11.6			1h2	Leamington	13	May
		5 performances to 11.6 by 4 athletes						
11.7 w	3.0	Janine Whitlock		(12.00)	4	Bedford	19	Aug
11.8		Kim Wall	U20	21.04.83	1	London (He)	30	Jul
11.9		Melanie Roberts	U23	2.03.78	1	Burnley	27	Aug
11.9		Katherine Endacott	U23	(11.93)	1	Exeter	2	Sep
11.9 w	2.8	Danielle Norville	U20	(12.00)	1	Rugby	23	Jul
11.9 w	2.2	Jenny Meadows	U20	(12.11)	2	Stoke-on-Trent	6	Aug
		12.1			2	Wakefield	16	Jul
12.0		Victoria Barr	U20	(12.12)	1	Rotherham	4	Jun
12.0		Kirstie Taylor		(12.24)	1	Bournemouth	24	Jun
12.0 w		Melinda Cooksey	U17	(12.30)	1	Tipton	9	Apr
		12.1			1	Tipton	23	Jul
12.0 w		Rachel Redmond	U20	(12.28)	1	Derby	17	Jun
12.0 w	2.9	Kelly Sotherton		(12.06)	2	Cudworth	22	Jul
12.0 w	3.0	Ann Danson		(12.28)	7	Bedford	19	Aug
12.1		Sarah Tomlins	U20	5.04.82	1	Carshalton	29	Apr
12.1		Sara Todd	U23	3.11.79	1	Jarrow	7	May
12.1		Leonie Lightfoot	U20	8.02.82	1	Macclesfield	13	May
12.1		Jemma Sims	U17	(12.15)	1	Nottingham	14	May
12.1	-1.0	Amina Ceesay	U23	(12.22)	3=h1	Brighton	17	Jun
12.1	1.9	Catriona Slater		(12.05w)	4h2	Brighton	17	Jun
12.1	1.0	Janette Niccolls		(12.11)	5h3	Brighton	17	Jun
12.1		Syreena Pinel	U23	13.01.79	2	Stoke-on-Trent	25	Jun
12.1		Jacqui Agyepong		5.01.69	2	London (He)	15	Jul
12.1		Julie Pratt	U23	20.03.79	1rB	Horsham	15	Jul
12.1		Ruth McMenemy		12.04.70	1	Bromley	15	Jul
12.1		Sarah Claxton	U23	23.09.79	2	Colchester	15	Jul
12.1		Petrina Alleyne	U20	10.07.81	1	Reading	16	Jul

Unconfirmed

11.8		Kirstie Taylor		10.01.75	1	Colchester	15	Jul

Additional Under 17

12.2		Tamsin Lees		(12.45)	1	Exeter	10	Jun
12.2		Kerry Everall		29.02.84	1	Yate	10	Jun
12.2		Georgette Perry		(12.36)	1r2	Derby	17	Jun
12.2		Eleanor Caney		28.05.84	1	Banbury	10	Sep
12.2 w	3.6	Titi Ameobi		(12.39)	1	Cudworth	20	Aug
		12.3			1	Rotherham	4	Jun
12.3		Siobhan McVie		6.07.84	1	Dumfries	7	May
12.3		Sarah Blackwell		(12.38)	3	Derby	17	Jun
12.3		Lindsey Winter		19.03.84	2	Oxford	15	Jul
12.3		Monique Parris		28.01.84	3	Oxford	15	Jul

12.3		Cherie Pierre	(12.38)	3	London (He)	30 Jul
12.4		Louisa Wells	(12.57)	2	Bury St. Edmunds	6 Jun
12.4		Rhiannon Burdon	(12.54w)	1	Bournemouth	16 Jul
12.4		Bernice Wilson	21.04.84	1	Grantham	16 Jul
12.4		Natalie Watson	(12.51)	1	Sutton Coldfield	23 Jul
12.4		Cara Roberts	24.05.85	2	Exeter	24 Sep
12.4		Nichola Nutting	14.09.84	2	Tipton	24 Sep
12.4 w		Gemma Winstone	18.11.84	1	Cardiff	11 May

Additional Under 15 (1 - 4 above)

12.3		Lauren Webb	17.11.85	1	Crawley	23 Apr
12.3		Jemma Thake	17.12.85	1	Bury St. Edmunds	6 Jun
		12.32 1.2		4	Sheffield	29 Jul
12.3		Faye Harding	7.09.85	1	Warrington	20 Aug
12.32	0.7	Kadi-Ann Thomas	10.02.86	3	Sheffield	8 Jul
12.39	1.2	Christina Clubley	4.11.85	6	Sheffield	29 Jul
12.4 w	2.9	Nicola Gossman	4.11.86	1	Grangemouth	11 Jun
		12.51		1	Grangemouth	21 Jun
	(10)					
12.46		Louise Dickson	4.09.86	1	Inverness	9 Jul
12.5		Sinead Johnson	24.12.86	1	Telford	10 Jun
		12.57 0.7		4	Sheffield	8 Jul
12.5		Lanre Atljosan	17.10.86	1	London (WL)	24 Jun
		12.51 1.4		2s1	Sheffield	7 Jul
12.5		Alexandra Barton	14.09.85	1	Cheltenham	2 Jul
12.5		Tamara Doherty	15.11.85	1	Glasgow (S)	20 Aug
		12.51		2	Inverness	9 Jul
12.52	1.2	Denae Matthew	3.04.87	7	Sheffield	29 Jul
12.56	1.8	Charlene Lashley	1.09.85	h	Watford	27 May
12.56		Pamela Paterson	26.10.85	3	Inverness	9 Jul
12.56 w	2.5	Lauren Dickson	2.04.86	3h4	Sheffield	29 Jul
		12.59 1.2		8	Sheffield	29 Jul
12.59	1.0	Michelle Nash	19.03.87	3h1	Sheffield	29 Jul
	(20)					
12.59 w	2.5	Laura Jones	4.02.86	4h4	Sheffield	29 Jul
		12.6		1	Hemel Hempstead	12 Aug
12.6	1.0	Gemma Nicol	27.07.86	1	Glasgow (S)	30 Apr
		12.65		1h1	Inverness	9 Jul
12.6		Hayley Allerston	13.04.86	1	Hull	7 May
12.6		Charlotte Beckett	4.01.86	1	High Wycombe	13 May
12.6	0.6	Katie Flaherty	1.10.85	1	Chelmsford	14 May
12.6		Jemma Butler	17.06.87	2	Derby	17 Jun
12.6		Louise Morgan	8.09.85	1	Great Yarmouth	18 Jun
12.6		Kessia Sherliker	9.11.85	2	Eton	2 Jul
12.6		Sally Irwin	12.10.85	4	Eton	2 Jul
12.6		Sophie Newington	15.09.85	1	Brecon	12 Jul
	(30)					
12.6		Kimberley Wainwright	18.01.86	1	Cudworth	16 Jul

Under 13

12.6 w		Carley Wenham	14.03.88	1	London (CP)	9 Apr
		12.9		1	Crawley	23 Apr
12.8		Natalie Pearson	7.06.88	1	Cudworth	16 Jul
12.9	0.8	Stacey Simpson	25.01.88	1r1	Glasgow (S)	30 Apr
		13.08 1.6		1h2	Inverness	9 Jul
12.9		Emma Wood		1	Jarrow	3 May
		13.12		1h1	Gateshead	13 May
12.9		Kelly Fairweather	5.03.88	2r1	Oxford	15 Jul
12.9		Elizabeth Sandall	11.09.87	1	Worcester	15 Jul
12.9		Maria Hanshaw		2	London (CP)	9 Apr
		13.0 -1.0		2r1	Kingston	30 Jul

13.0		Jane Chadwick		15.09.87	1	Wigan	11 Jun
		13.07 -0.4			3	Wigan	25 Jun
13.0		Laura Cox		21.01.88	1	Tipton	25 Jun
13.1		Donna Campbell		15.02.88	1h1	Glasgow (S)	7 Jun
	(10)						
13.1		Amy Harris		14.09.87	1	Redditch	11 Jun
13.1		Kim Skinner		21.09.87	1	Grangemouth	15 Jul
13.1	-1.0	Lauren Duncan		21.03.88	3r1	Kingston	30 Jul
13.1		Emma Baker		22.09.88	1r3	Exeter	3 Sep
13.2		Chloe Walcott		29.01.88	1r1	Carshalton	17 Jun
13.2		Lyndsey Fairweather		5.03.88	2r2	Havering	24 Jun
13.2		Aisha McIntosh		5.01.88		Basingstoke	2 Sep

Foreign

11.45 w	*3.7*	*Sarah Oxley/Reilly (IRE)*		*3.07.73*	*3*	*Lapinlahti, FIN*	*16 Jul*
		11.49 1.2			*1*	*Brighton*	*17 Jun*
		Became Irish upon her marriage in March 2000					
11.91 w		*Leanne O'Callaghan*		*15.07.74*	*2*	*Tullamore, IRE*	*8 Jul*
		11.96			*3r2*	*Dublin (S), IRE*	*29 Jul*

150 METRES - Under 13

19.2		Laura Cox		21.01.88	1	Carmarthen	21 May
19.2		Stacey Simpson		25.01.88	1	Ayr	4 Jun
19.3		Natalie Pearson		7.06.88	1	Hull	21 May
19.6		Carley Wenham		14.03.88	1	Crawley	21 May
19.7		Jane Chadwick		15.09.87	1r1	Wigan	2 Jul
		19.78 1.0			1r1	Birmingham	3 Sep
19.7		Leanne Finlay		14.10.87	1	Norwich	23 Jul
19.8		Amy Harris		14.09.87	2	Carmarthen	21 May
19.9		Kayleigh Modeste			1	Coventry	21 May
19.9		Chloe Gale		24.02.88	1h	Dartford	24 Sep
20.0		Karen Prytz		9.12.87	2	Ayr	4 Jun
	(10)						
20.0		Lauren Duncan		21.03.88	1	Eton	3 Jul
20.0		Kelly Fairweather		5.03.88	1	Horsham	20 Aug

Unconfirmed distance

18.9		Natalie Burleigh			1r2	Liverpool	23 Jul
19.1		Jenny Igbokwe			1r1	Liverpool	23 Jul
19.3		Sarah Schofield			2r2	Liverpool	23 Jul
19.4		Natalie Downey			2r1	Liverpool	23 Jul

200 METRES

22.76	-1.0	Katharine Merry		21.09.74	2	Barcelona, SPA	25 Jul
		23.17 0.3			1	Bedford	4 Jun
		23.22 -1.0			1	Loughborough	21 May
23.06	0.4	Sam Davies	U23	20.09.79	5	Gateshead	28 Aug
		23.20 -0.3			7q2	Sydney, AUS	27 Sep
		23.31 0.3			2	Liverpool	22 Jul
		23.36 0.5			5h6	Sydney, AUS	27 Sep
		23.42 -1.0			2	Birmingham	13 Aug
		23.47 -1.1			1h4	Birmingham	12 Aug
		23.68 -0.7			4	Riga, LAT	22 Jun
23.08	-0.5	Donna Fraser		7.11.72	1r2	Budapest, HUN	22 Jul
		23.14 -0.3			6	Gateshead	16 Jul
		23.15 1.2			1r1	Fullerton, USA	27 Apr
		23.19 -1.0			2	Thessaloniki, GRE	30 Aug
		23.29 0.5			3r1	Irvine, USA	7 May
		23.31 i			2	Birmingham	20 Feb
		23.36 i			1	Birmingham	5 Feb

(Fraser)		23.36 1.9			1inv	Bedford	19 Aug
		23.43 i			2	Birmingham	30 Jan
		23.45 i			1s3	Birmingham	30 Jan
		23.51 1.8			1r3	Bedford	11 Jun
		23.63 i			1	Cardiff	6 Feb
23.17	0.7	Joice Maduaka		30.09.73	3	Linz, AUT	8 Aug
		23.27 0.4			1	Ljubljana, SLO	25 Jul
		23.36 -0.5			5h7	Sydney, AUS	27 Sep
		23.44 -0.7			3	Riga, LAT	22 Jun
		23.52 i			3r1	Ghent, BEL	11 Feb
		23.57 0.6			3r3	Budapest, HUN	22 Jul
		23.57 -0.2			7q1	Sydney, AUS	27 Sep
		23.58 i			3h4	Ghent, BEL	25 Feb
		23.62 i			1s2	Birmingham	30 Jan
		23.63 i			4s3	Ghent, BEL	25 Feb
		23.65 i			3	Birmingham	30 Jan
		23.67 -1.0			4	Birmingham	13 Aug
		23.71 -1.2			2s2	Birmingham	13 Aug
23.20	1.9	Shani Anderson		7.08.75	3	Gold Coast (RB), AUS	10 Sep
		23.36 1.2			1h2	Birmingham	12 Aug
		23.43 1.9			2inv	Bedford	19 Aug
		23.49 -0.5			3r2	Budapest, HUN	22 Jul
		23.51 1.4			1	Solihull	5 Aug
		23.53 -1.0			3	Birmingham	13 Aug
		23.54 -1.1			1s1	Birmingham	13 Aug
		23.72 0.5			5r1	Irvine, USA	7 May
23.26	-0.6	Sarah Wilhelmy	U23	2.02.80	1r1	Dublin (S), IRE	29 Jul
		23.29 0.4			7	Gateshead	28 Aug
		23.39 -1.0			1	Birmingham	13 Aug
		23.61 0.0			2	Bridgetown, BAR	25 Jun
		23.62 -1.2			1s2	Birmingham	13 Aug
		23.73 0.0			1h1	Birmingham	12 Aug
23.31 i		Christine Bloomfield		12.02.68	1	Birmingham	30 Jan
		23.40 i			1s1	Birmingham	30 Jan
		23.62 -3.3			1	Bedford	20 Aug
		23.67 0.8			1	Vittel, FRA	2 Sep
		23.73 0.2			1rB	Enfield	6 Aug
23.46 i		Catherine Murphy		21.09.75	2	Birmingham	5 Feb
		23.57 i			1s1	Birmingham	16 Jan
		23.57 i			2h1	Ghent, BEL	25 Feb
		23.59 2.0			5r4	Walnut, USA	16 Apr
		23.60 i			3s1	Ghent, BEL	25 Feb
		23.73 i			3	Birmingham	20 Feb
		23.74 1.2			4r1	Fullerton, USA	27 Apr
		23.75 i			2	Cardiff	6 Feb
23.49 i		Vernicha James	U17	6.06.84	1	Birmingham	30 Jan
		23.59 1.6			2s2	Santiago, CHI	20 Oct
		23.62 2.0			1	Sheffield	8 Jul
		23.65 1.6			1	Grosseto, ITA	7 Oct
23.53	1.2	Marcia Richardson		10.02.72	2r1	Fullerton, USA	27 Apr
		23.67 1.8			2r3	Bedford	11 Jun
	(10)						
23.57	0.4	Jenni Stoute	V35	16.04.65	3	Ljubljana, SLO	25 Jul
		23.75 0.6			6r3	Budapest, HUN	22 Jul
		70 performances to 23.75 by 11 athletes including 19 indoors					
23.83	0.3	Melanie Purkiss	U23	11.03.79	4	Liverpool	22 Jul
23.85 i		Stephi Douglas		22.01.69	1	Furth, GER	16 Jan
		24.15 -0.4			1	Stuttgart, GER	22 Jun
24.04	0.0	Kim Wall	U20	21.04.83	3q1	Santiago, CHI	19 Oct
24.08	1.2	Emma Whitter	U23	20.07.80	2h1	Brighton	18 Jun

24.09 i		Zoe Wilson		28.08.76	1h5	Birmingham	30	Jan
		24.17 1.2			6r1	Fullerton, USA	27	Apr
24.09		Susie Williams		2.06.77	1	Aldershot	16	Jul
24.11	0.3	Susan Burnside	U23	3.02.80	5	Bedford	4	Jun
24.13	1.5	Lesley Owusu	U23	21.12.78	4r2	Lincoln, USA	7	May
24.13	1.5	Sinead Dudgeon		9.07.76	1h2	Glasgow (S)	29	Jul
	(20)							
24.14	0.5	Helen Frost		12.03.74	2	Alicante, SPA	6	May
24.20 i		Vicky Day/Ward		19.06.72	3h3	Birmingham	30	Jan
		24.30 0.5			2rB	Loughborough	21	May
24.26	-0.6	Kerry Jury		19.11.68	1H3	Logrono, SPA	19	Aug
24.27	1.1	Ellena Ruddock		23.02.76	2	Solihull	29	Jul
24.29	1.7	Eleanor Caney	U17	28.05.84	1	Sheffield	30	Jul
24.31	1.4	Amy Spencer	U15	19.09.85	1s1	Sheffield	8	Jul
24.32	-1.7	Jenny Meadows	U20	17.04.81	1	Marsa, MLT	27	Apr
24.32	0.1	Kelly Thomas	U20	9.01.81	2	Bath	16	Sep
24.34	0.9	Victoria Barr	U20	14.04.82	2	Watford	2	Jul
24.34	-0.1	Denise Lewis		27.08.72	6H4	Sydney, AUS	23	Sep
	(30)							
24.37	1.2	Felicia Louisy		17.05.74	3h1	Brighton	18	Jun
24.37		Sabrina Scott	U23	2.06.79	2	Aldershot	16	Jul
24.38 i		Lowri Jones	U20	22.07.83	4	Neubrandenburg, GER	4	Mar
24.38		Nicole Crosby		23.10.76	1	Cudworth	13	May
24.38		Emma Ania	U23	7.02.79	4r4	Iowa, USA	20	May
24.41	1.0	Helen Roscoe	U23	4.12.79	2h2	Bedford	1	Jul
24.43 i+		Simmone Jacobs		5.09.66	1	Birmingham	29	Jan
24.46	-3.0	Syreena Pinel	U23	13.01.79	2	Stoke-on-Trent	18	Jun
24.47	-1.4	Janine Whitlock		11.08.73	2	Solihull	5	Aug
24.48	0.1	Sarah Still		24.09.75	1H4	Waterford, IRE	2	Sep
	(40)							
24.48	0.8	Kelly Sotherton		13.11.76	1H5	Waterford, IRE	2	Sep
24.50 i		Michelle Thomas		16.10.71	2s2	Birmingham	16	Jan
24.50	1.8	Abi Oyepitan	U23	30.12.79	6r3	Bedford	11	Jun
24.51	-0.6	Lisa Miller	U20	13.01.83	1	London (He)	20	Aug
24.55	0.5	Natalie Hynd/Beattie	U23	30.01.78	3rB	Loughborough	21	May
24.55	0.7	Emily Freeman	U23	24.11.80	4h3	Birmingham	12	Aug
24.56	0.8	Danielle Selley	U17	19.12.83	1h2	Sheffield	30	Jul
24.58	1.2	Jo Hill		11.02.73	7r1	Fullerton, USA	27	Apr
24.59		Gemma Ryde	U20	23.06.83	1	Vilvoorde, BEL	6	Aug
24.61	1.2	Kate Denham	U23	18.03.80	5h1	Brighton	18	Jun
	(50)							
24.63	1.7	Jemma Sims	U17	2.05.85	3	Sheffield	30	Jul
24.65	1.8	Melanie Wilkins		18.01.73	1r2	Fullerton, USA	27	Apr
24.71	0.7	Sarah Tomlins	U20	5.04.82	2	Sheffield	8	Jul
24.72	-0.8	Julie Hollman		16.02.77	2H5	Waterford, IRE	2	Sep
24.76	1.8	Sharon Allen		23.10.68	8h1	Modesto, USA	13	May
24.76	0.6	Liz Fairs		1.12.77	1rB	Solihull	5	Aug
24.79	0.5	Claire McGilp	U23	25.07.78	6	Potchefstroom, RSA	14	Feb
24.84	-0.8	Janette Niccolls		7.09.76	2	Bedford	20	Aug
24.85	0.6	Natalie Watson	U17	5.07.84	1h1	Sheffield	7	Jul
24.85	0.3	Melinda Cooksey	U17	19.05.84	1h3	Sheffield	30	Jul
	(60)							
24.86	-1.1	Xanine Powell	U23	21.05.79	5h4	Birmingham	12	Aug
24.91	0.0	Nicole Bowring		27.01.74	5h1	Birmingham	12	Aug
24.92	-1.4	Keri Maddox		4.07.72	3	Solihull	5	Aug
24.93 i		Samantha Gamble	U17	27.03.84	1	Birmingham	6	Feb
24.95		Vicki Jamison		19.05.77	5	Antrim	31	Jul
24.98	0.9	Danielle Freeman	U23	11.02.80	2H3	Arles, FRA	3	Jun
24.98	1.0	Angharad James	U23	7.04.79	3h2	Bedford	1	Jul
24.98	0.3	Kimberley Velvick	U17	3.01.85	2h3	Sheffield	30	Jul
24.98	0.6	Karlene Palmer	U23	23.10.80	3rB	Solihull	5	Aug

24.98	-0.6	Katie Flaherty	U15	1.10.85	1	London (He)	20	Aug
	(70)							
24.99	1.6	Natasha Danvers		19.09.77	2r2	Tempe, USA	18	Mar
24.99	0.3	Amina Ceesay	U23	19.11.79	6h1	Bedford	1	Jul
25.05	0.0	Nicola Gautier	U23	21.03.78	3H	Schwyz/Ibach, SWZ	1	Jul
25.06	0.4	Kathryn Evans	U17	1.03.84	2h1	Sheffield	30	Jul
25.06	-0.2	Jemma Thake	U15	17.12.85	1s2	Sheffield	30	Jul
25.07	0.3	Roseline Addo	U23	7.06.80	2h1	Boone, USA	21	Apr
25.08 i		Clova Court	V40	10.02.60	s	Birmingham	16	Jan
25.08	1.2	Karen Gear	U23	30.09.79	4h2	Birmingham	12	Aug
25.08	-0.6	Natasha Cross	U17	13.11.84	3	London (He)	20	Aug
25.09	0.2	Lesley Clarkson	U20	18.07.82	2	Grangemouth	25	Jun
	(80)							
25.10	2.0	Kessia Sherliker	U15	9.11.85	1s2	Sheffield	8	Jul
25.11		Maria Bolsover	U23	5.06.80	3	Cudworth	13	May
25.11	1.2	Heather Brookes	U20	17.07.81	5rB	Glasgow (S)	8	Jul
25.15	0.6	Michelle Pierre		30.09.73	4rB	Solihull	5	Aug
25.15	-0.8	Ruth McMenemy		12.04.70	3	Bedford	20	Aug
25.16	0.7	Rachael Harris	U20	17.07.82	3	Sheffield	8	Jul
25.17	2.0	Rhiannon Burdon	U17	29.10.83	4	Sheffield	8	Jul
25.17	0.2	Ruth Watson	U23	29.11.79	2rB	Enfield	6	Aug
25.18 i		Katherine Endacott	U23	29.01.80	4h2	Birmingham	30	Jan
25.19 i		Natalie Smellie	U20	16.01.82	2r1	Birmingham	16	Jan
	(90)							
25.19	0.4	Alanna Wain	U17	27.04.85	3h1	Sheffield	30	Jul
25.19	2.0	Titi Ameobi	U17	20.11.84	1	Birmingham	2	Sep
25.20 i		Sarah Zawada	U20	9.04.82	3	Birmingham	6	Feb
25.20	1.2	Kirstie Taylor		10.01.75	6h1	Brighton	18	Jun
25.20	-3.4	Louise Whitehead		26.03.75	2	Cwmbran	18	Jun
25.20	2.0	Charlotte Beckett	U15	4.01.86	2s2	Sheffield	8	Jul
25.21	1.4	Juliet Adeloye	U15	13.06.86	3s1	Sheffield	8	Jul
25.23	0.4	Charli Croll	U17	25.10.84	4h1	Sheffield	30	Jul
25.23	1.1	Jemma Walker	U17	17.09.83	1	Grangemouth	5	Aug
25.24mx	0.2	Leigh Newton	U23	13.01.78	1	Stretford	11	Jun
	(100)							
25.25	0.7	Lisa Trotman	U20	6.12.82	4	Sheffield	8	Jul
25.25	2.0	Kerry Everall	U17	29.02.84	5	Sheffield	8	Jul
25.25	2.0	Kimberley Matthews	U17	22.03.84	6	Sheffield	8	Jul
25.26 i		Helen Thieme	U20	28.09.81	1	Birmingham	12	Feb
25.26	-1.1	Nicola Sanders	U20	23.06.82	h	London (He)	20	Aug
25.26	0.7	Liza Parry	U17	24.10.84	1H	Birmingham	16	Sep
25.27 i		Carey Easton	U23	16.11.79	2	Glasgow	16	Jan
25.27	-0.8	Fiona Harrison	U20	30.11.81	2H1	Watford	23	Sep

Additional Under 17 (1 - 18 above)

25.39	0.8	Jackie Scott	31.01.85	2	Grangemouth	25	Jun
25.39		Sarah Quinn	22.03.84	2	Belfast	8	Jul
	(20)						
25.40	1.6	Rebecca Sweeney	9.02.85	1	Birmingham	3	Sep
25.49	1.6	Vicky Griffiths	9.10.84	2	Birmingham	3	Sep
25.57	-4.3	Sara Whigham	7.10.83	3	Grangemouth	17	Jun
25.58	-0.7	Sian Scott	20.03.84	2h	London (He)	20	Aug
25.59	-4.3	Lorna Johnston	20.12.83	4	Grangemouth	17	Jun

Unconfirmed

23.63	Sharon Allen	23.10.68	Miami, USA	18	Jun

Wind Assisted

23.08	2.3	Fraser	(23.08)	1	Azusa, USA	8	Apr
23.23	2.4	Sinead Dudgeon	(24.13)	1	Glasgow (S)	29	Jul
23.27	3.7	Anderson	(23.20)	1	Bedford	19	Aug

23.33	2.5	Maduaka		(23.17)	2	Fana, NOR	27	Jun
23.48	2.9	Catherine Murphy		(23.46i)	1	Long Beach, USA	15	Apr
		23.72	2.6		1=	Jona, SWZ	16	Jul
23.65	2.5	Davies	U23	(23.06)	3	Fana, NOR	27	Jun
23.72	2.6	Stoute	V35	(23.57)	1=	Jona, SWZ	16	Jul
23.74	5.2	Zoe Wilson		(24.09i)	1h2	Bedford	28	May
		9 performances to 23.75 by 8 athletes						
23.83	2.2	Emma Ania	U23	(24.38)	4r1	Coral Gables, USA	1	Apr
23.90	3.2	Susie Williams		(24.09)	2	Bedford	28	May
24.00	2.3	Emma Whitter	U23	(24.08)	2	Brighton	18	Jun
24.01	3.6	Denise Lewis		(24.34)	2H3	Talence, FRA	29	Jul
24.06	2.7	Felicia Louisy		(24.37)	1h1	Bedford	28	May
24.11	2.4	Helen Frost		(24.14)	1r2	Bedford	11	Jun
24.12	2.4	Vicky Day/Ward		(24.20i)	2r2	Bedford	11	Jun
24.22	2.4	Jo Hill		(24.58)	2	Glasgow (S)	29	Jul
24.24	3.2	Amy Spencer	U15	(24.31)	1	Sheffield	8	Jul
24.26	2.8	Diane Allahgreen		21.02.75	2	Enfield	6	Aug
24.26	3.7	Ellena Ruddock		(24.27)	2	Bedford	19	Aug
24.32	2.7	Syreena Pinel	U23	(24.46)	2h1	Bedford	28	May
24.35	2.4	Gemma Ryde	U20	(24.59)	3	Glasgow (S)	29	Jul
24.41	3.7	Heather Brookes	U20	(25.11)	3	Bedford	19	Aug
24.50	w?	Nicole Bowring		27.01.74	2	London (CP)	13	May
24.53	2.4	Lisa Vannet		8.11.74	4	Glasgow (S)	29	Jul
24.53	2.7	Helen Thieme	U20	(25.26i)	1rB	Grosseto, ITA	7	Oct
24.60	2.7	Angharad James	U23	(24.98)	5h1	Bedford	28	May
24.61	w?	Xanine Powell	U23	(24.86)	3	London (CP)	13	May
24.65	3.7	Liz Fairs		(24.76)	4	Bedford	19	Aug
24.67	3.8	Sarah Tomlins	U20	(24.71)	3h2	Brighton	18	Jun
24.70	4.3	Leigh Newton	U23	(25.24mx)	5h3	Bedford	28	May
24.72	2.4	Ruth McMenemy		(25.15)	6	Glasgow (S)	29	Jul
24.73	4.3	Kim Rothman	V35	6.09.64	6h3	Bedford	28	May
24.77	2.1	Catriona Slater		27.01.77	4h3	Brighton	18	Jun
24.77	2.2	Heather McKay	U20	5.09.81	5	Bedford	27	Aug
24.79	3.8	Janette Niccolls		(24.84)	4h2	Brighton	18	Jun
24.81	2.1	Amina Ceesay	U23	(24.99)	5h3	Brighton	18	Jun
24.88	2.4	Elizabeth Williams		2.06.77	6r2	Bedford	11	Jun
24.92	2.2	Danielle Norville	U20	18.01.83	7	Bedford	27	Aug
24.94	5.2	Victoria Shipman		31.03.77	6h2	Bedford	28	May
24.94	3.7	Karlene Palmer	U23	(24.98)	7	Bedford	19	Aug
25.01	2.7	Roseline Addo	U23	(25.07)	6	Boone, USA	22	Apr
25.01	3.2	Kessia Sherliker	U15	(25.10)	2	Sheffield	8	Jul
25.22	2.6	Nicola Sanders	U20	(25.26)	2h2	Watford	27	May
25.27	2.7	Laura Watkins	U20	1.01.82	7h1	Bedford	28	May
25.28	3.0	Suzanne McGowan	U23	13.04.78	4h1	Glasgow (S)	29	Jul

Additional Under 17

25.51	2.8	Cherie Pierre		15.05.84	1h1	Watford	27	May

Hand Timing

23.6 i	Bloomfield		(23.31i)	1=	Birmingham	16	Jan
23.6 i	Murphy		(23.46i)	1=	Birmingham	16	Jan
23.7 i	Maduaka		(23.17)	3	Birmingham	16	Jan
23.7	Fraser		(23.08)	1	London (Cr)	24	Jun
	4 performances to 23.7 by 4 athletes including 3 indoors						
23.9	Amanda Forrester	U23	29.09.78	1	Stoke-on-Trent	25	Jun
24.2	Ellena Ruddock		(24.27)	2	Leamington	13	May

24.5		Louise Whitehead		(25.20)	2	Stoke-on-Trent	6 Aug
24.6		Kim Goodwin		16.05.70	1	Lancaster	13 May
24.6		Janette Niccolls		(24.84)	1	Luton	11 Jun
24.6 w	2.5	Danielle Norville	U20	(24.92w)	4	Rugby	23 Jul
		24.9			1	Yate	25 Jun
24.7		Helen Thieme	U20	(25.26i)	1	Nottingham	13 May
24.7	-0.4	Claire Johnson-Cole	U20	21.08.83	3	Leamington	14 May
24.7	-0.4	Sonia Rice	U20	8.01.81	4	Leamington	14 May
24.7		Elizabeth Williams		(24.88w)	1	Brighton	15 Jul
24.8	-1.9	Catriona Slater		(24.77w)	1	Chelmsford	14 May
24.8		Amina Ceesay	U23	(24.99)	1	Eton	11 Jun
24.8		Heather Brookes	U20	(25.11)	2	Wakefield	16 Jul
24.8 w	3.0	Aileen McGillivary		13.08.70	1	Grangemouth	11 Jun
24.9		Leigh Newton	U23	(25.24mx)	2	Lancaster	13 May
24.9		Victoria Shipman		(24.94w)	1	Nottingham	13 May
24.9		Kim Rothman	V35	(24.73w)	1	Kingston	20 May
24.9		Lisa Vannet		(24.53w)	1	Coatbridge	21 May
24.9		Heather McKay	U20	(24.77w)	1	Coatbridge	21 May
24.9		Bianca Liston	U23	28.05.78	1	Basildon	24 Jun
24.9		Ruth McMenemy		(25.15)	1	Bromley	15 Jul
24.9		Linda Staines	V35	26.12.63	1	Derby	6 Aug
24.9 w		Donna Porazinski	U20	28.01.81	1	Newport	11 Jun
25.0		Laura Watkins	U20	(25.27w)	1	Telford	23 Apr
25.0		Claire Rooney	U20	23.08.83	2r1	Coatbridge	21 May
25.0		Sharon Wilson		27.10.74	2r2	Coatbridge	21 May
25.0	1.7	Nicola Sanders	U20	(25.26)	3	Watford	28 May
25.0		Rachael Sutton	U20	28.08.83	1	Banbury	10 Sep
25.0		Rachael Harris	U20	(25.16)	2	Derby	17 Jun
25.0 w	3.2	Stephanie Johnston	U20	9.10.81	4	Cudworth	22 Jul
25.0 w	2.1	Katherine Livesey	U23	15.12.79	1H	Des Moines, USA	28 Apr
25.1		Helen Williams		2.06.77	1	Eton	11 Jun
25.1		Kerry Everall	U17	(25.25)	1	Derby	17 Jun
25.1		Rebecca Bird	U20	7.01.83	2	Yate	25 Jun
25.1		Michelle Turner		25.12.77	1	Oxford	15 Jul
25.1		Yvette Henry		8.06.73	3	Stoke-on-Trent	6 Aug
25.1		Sarah Godbeer		10.06.77	1	Hemel Hempstead	12 Aug
25.1 w		Rosie Thorner		7.08.67	2	Newport	11 Jun
25.1 w	2.5	Emma Symonds		5.06.77	6	Rugby	23 Jul
25.1 w?		Danielle Halsall	U20	27.06.81	2	Dumfries	13 Aug

Additional Under 17

25.3	2.9	Lara Carty	7.03.84	1	Chelmsford	1 May
25.4	0.5	Cherie Pierre	(25.51w)	1	Watford	27 May
25.5		Vicki Cooney	2.11.84	1	Eton	2 Jul
25.5		Michelle Webster	18.04.85	1	Bedford	6 Aug

Additional Under 15 (1 - 6 above)

25.50 w	2.3	Lauren Webb	17.11.85	4	Watford	28 May
		25.67 2.0		5s2	Sheffield	8 Jul
25.5		Caroline Nelson	1.07.86	1	Stockport	7 May
25.58	1.1	Amalachukwu Onuora	16.03.86	2h2	Sheffield	30 Jul
25.6		Leah Dunkley	11.11.85	2	Stockport	7 May
	(10)					
25.6		Louise Hazel	6.10.85	1	Peterborough	23 Jul
25.6		Faye Harding	7.09.85	1	Wrexham	28 Jul
25.61 w	2.7	Tamara Doherty	15.11.85	1	Inverness	9 Jul
		25.69 -0.2		4s2	Sheffield	30 Jul
25.64	2.0	Lia Tappin	9.01.87	4s2	Sheffield	8 Jul

25.64 w	4.6	Gemma Nicol	27.07.86	1h2	Inverness	9	Jul
		25.7		1	Dunfermline	7	May
		26.02 1.1		2h3	Sheffield	30	Jul
25.65	1.4	Leah Caddick	1.06.86	4s1	Sheffield	8	Jul
25.7		Christina Clubley	4.11.85	1	Barnsley	2	Jul
		25.93 -0.2		5s2	Sheffield	30	Jul
25.7		Kadi-Ann Thomas	10.02.86	2	Guildford	23	Jul
25.76	0.5	Kimberley Wainwright	18.01.86	2h1	Sheffield	7	Jul
25.8		Louise Dickson	4.09.86	2	Dunfermline	7	May
		25.98 w 2.7		3	Inverness	9	Jul
		26.08 0.5		1r1	Birmingham	3	Sep
	(20)						
25.8 w	2.8	Nicola Gossman	4.11.86	1	Grangemouth	11	Jun
		26.06 0.3		1r2	Grangemouth	16	Jun
25.82	1.8	Kiri Burbidge	2.10.85	3h4	Sheffield	7	Jul
25.83	1.7	Jenny Christie	28.09.85	3h1	Sheffield	30	Jul
25.83 w	4.6	Eleanor Richardson	1.07.86	2h2	Inverness	9	Jul
25.88 i		Heather Jones	10.09.86	1	Cardiff	9	Dec
25.9		Laura Jones	4.02.86	1	Milton Keynes	6	Aug
		26.26 1.1		4h2	Sheffield	30	Jul
25.99	1.9	Charlotte Featherstone	30.09.85	4h3	Sheffield	7	Jul

Under 13

26.51	-0.1	Jane Chadwick	15.09.87	5	Wigan	25	Jun
26.7		Carley Wenham	14.03.88	1	Crawley	31	May
26.7		Kelly Fairweather	5.03.88	1r1	Havering	24	Jun
26.8		Laura Cox	21.01.88	1	Tipton	25	Jun
26.8	-1.7	Maria Hanshaw		1r1	Kingston	30	Jul
27.0		Elizabeth Sandall	11.09.87	1	Worcester	15	Jul
27.0		Chloe Gale	24.02.88	1r2	London (Elt)	2	Sep
27.0		Louise Shaw		1	Wakefield	17	Sep
27.1 w	5.1	Stacey Simpson	25.01.88	1	Grangemouth	11	Jun
		27.2		1	Ayr	16	Apr
		27.37 -2.5		2h1	Grangemouth	16	Jun
27.2		Natalie Pearson	7.06.88	1	Cudworth	9	Sep
	(10)						
27.2 w		Joedy Platt	27.11.87	2	London (CP)	9	Apr
		27.4 1.2		1	Exeter	14	May
27.3		Amy Harris	14.09.87	1	Redditch	11	Jun
27.3	-0.8	Lauren Duncan	21.03.88	1r2	Kingston	30	Jul
27.3	-0.4	Lyndsey Fairweather	5.03.88	1r3	Kingston	30	Jul
27.5		Lisa Lanini	9.10.87	1	Deeside	13	May
27.5 w		Chloe Walcott	29.01.88	3	London (CP)	9	Apr

Foreign

23.12	*-0.5*	*Sarah Oxley/Reilly (IRE)*	*3.07.73*	*2r2*	*Budapest, HUN*	*22*	*Jul*
24.50	*5.2*	*Leanne O'Callaghan (IRE)*	*15.07.74*	*4h2*	*Bedford*	*28*	*May*
		24.8		*1*	*Thurrock*	*15*	*Jul*
		24.87 i		*2h2*	*Birmingham*	*30*	*Jan*
		25.09 1.2		*5h2*	*Birmingham*	*12*	*Aug*
25.24	*0.6*	*Margaret Veldman (HOL)*	*7.06.74*	*5rB*	*Solihull*	*5*	*Aug*

300 METRES

35.71	Donna Fraser		7.11.72	1	Gateshead	28	Aug
36.00	Katharine Merry		21.09.74	2	Gateshead	28	Aug
37.48	Catherine Murphy		21.09.75	7	Gateshead	28	Aug
37.55	Helen Frost		12.03.74	8	Gateshead	28	Aug
37.59	Jenni Stoute	V35	16.04.65	1	Loughborough	30	Jul
37.79	Shani Anderson		7.08.75	2	Loughborough	30	Jul
37.80	Natasha Danvers		19.09.77	3	Gold Coast (S), AUS	15	Sep

Under 17

38.19	Eleanor Caney	28.05.84	1	Nantes, FRA	22	Jul
38.90	Liza Parry	24.10.84	3	Blackpool	15	Jul
39.36	Olivia Hines	19.10.83	3	Sheffield	29	Jul
39.48	Rebecca Sweeney	9.02.85	2h3	Sheffield	7	Jul
39.57	Sian Scott	20.03.84	1	Watford	28	May
39.58	Alanna Wain	27.04.85	3	Sheffield	8	Jul
40.06	Bernice Wilson	21.04.84	2h2	Sheffield	7	Jul
40.15	Amanda Walters	18.04.84	2h1	Sheffield	7	Jul
40.2	Jemma Simpson	10.02.84	1	Exeter	17	Jun
40.22 i	Samantha Gamble	27.03.84	1	Birmingham	5	Feb
(10)						
40.3	Karen Boyle	25.03.84	1	Coatbridge	27	Aug
	40.61		2	Grangemouth	5	Aug
40.7	Joanne Erskine	28.05.85	1r2	Glasgow	10	Sep
40.71	Victoria Finn	3.02.84	3h2	Sheffield	7	Jul
40.81	Vicky Tunaley	4.06.84	3h1	Sheffield	7	Jul
40.81	Rachel Thomas	19.01.85	4h3	Sheffield	7	Jul
40.9	Rebecca Leitch	12.11.84	1	Templemore, Derry	6	May
	40.99		2	Antrim	17	Jun
40.9	Lorna Johnston	20.12.83	1	Grangemouth	17	Jun
	41.00		1	Inverness	10	Sep
40.91	Kayleigh Friobyo	16.08.85	4h2	Sheffield	7	Jul
41.0	Natalie Street	8.11.83	1	Chelmsford	13	May
	41.56		5h1	Sheffield	7	Jul
41.0	Donna Chatting	30.10.83	3h3	Sheffield	29	Jul
	41.16		5h2	Sheffield	7	Jul
(20)						
41.1	Sam Aspen	27.10.83	4h3	Sheffield	29	Jul
	41.23		6h2	Sheffield	7	Jul
41.1	Kathryn Evans	1.03.84	1	Aberdeen	13	Aug
41.2	Kim Searle	27.12.83	2	Wigan	2	Jul
	41.48		1h3	Wigan	25	Jun
41.2	Charli Croll	25.10.84	1	Norwich	23	Jul
41.29	Lucy Sings	9.07.85	5h3	Sheffield	7	Jul
41.3	Jackie Scott	31.01.85	1	Dundee	23	Apr
41.3	Lauren Caple	7.03.85	2	Stafford	2	Jul
	41.37		4h1	Sheffield	7	Jul
41.4	Emily Parker	7.11.84	2	London (Cr)	14	May
41.5	Kay Sheedy	14.10.84	1	Lancaster	14	May
41.5	Marilyn Okoro	23.09.84	1	London (TB)	21	May
(30)						
41.5	Laura Ellis	4.03.85	2	Grangemouth	17	Jun
41.53	Vicki Cooney	2.11.84	3	Birmingham	3	Sep

400 METRES

49.72	Katharine Merry	21.09.74	3	Sydney, AUS	25	Sep
	50.05		1	Nice, FRA	8	Jul
	50.28		1	Nuremberg, GER	25	Jun
	50.32		2s1	Sydney, AUS	24	Sep
	50.45		3	London (CP)	5	Aug
	50.50		1q2	Sydney, AUS	23	Sep
	50.56		5	Brussels, BEL	25	Aug
	50.72		1	Helsinki, FIN	15	Jun
	50.99		1	Glasgow (S)	2	Jul
	51.61		1h5	Sydney, AUS	22	Sep
49.79	Donna Fraser	7.11.72	4	Sydney, AUS	25	Sep
	50.21		4s2	Sydney, AUS	24	Sep
	50.77		3q4	Sydney, AUS	23	Sep
	50.94		1	Birmingham	13	Aug

(Fraser)	51.06			7	London (CP)	5 Aug
	51.62			3r2	Walnut, USA	16 Apr
	51.71			2	Budapest, HUN	22 Jul
	51.78			2	Gateshead	15 Jul
	51.79			4	Oslo, NOR	28 Jul
	52.00			4	Bratislava, SVK	22 Jun
	52.17			4	Glasgow (S)	2 Jul
	52.33			3h8	Sydney, AUS	22 Sep
	52.94			1h2	Birmingham	12 Aug
51.50	Allison Curbishley		3.06.76	2	Birmingham	13 Aug
	51.96			1	Glasgow (S)	29 Jul
	52.04			1	Lignano, ITA	5 Aug
	52.20			4h6	Sydney, AUS	22 Sep
	52.50			7q3	Sydney, AUS	23 Sep
	53.12			1h3	Birmingham	12 Aug
52.40	Helen Frost		12.03.74	1r2	Gold Coast (RB), AUS	17 Sep
	52.54			4	Riga, LAT	22 Jun
	52.62			1	Solihull	5 Aug
	53.28			1	Bedford	19 Aug
	53.33			3	Birmingham	13 Aug
	53.40			2h2	Birmingham	12 Aug
	53.42			2	Fana, NOR	27 Jun
52.71	Sinead Dudgeon		9.07.76	2r1	Gold Coast (RB), AUS	17 Sep
	52.78			6	Glasgow (S)	2 Jul
52.72	Catherine Murphy		21.09.75	3r2	Gold Coast (RB), AUS	17 Sep
	52.82			1	Bedford	20 Aug
	53.30			2r1	Azusa, USA	8 Apr
53.02	Lesley Owusu	U23	21.12.78	1h1	Columbia, USA	20 May
	53.06			4	Columbia, USA	21 May
	53.08			2	Bedford	20 Aug
	53.13			1h3	Durham NC, USA	1 Jun
	53.30			8	Durham NC, USA	3 Jun
	53.47			1	Lincoln, USA	13 May
53.24	Dawn Higgins		10.12.75	1	Jona, SWZ	16 Jul
53.37	Louise Whitehead		26.03.75	1	Cwmbran	18 Jun
53.41	Jenni Stoute	V35	16.04.65	1h1	Birmingham	12 Aug
	53.42			2	Jona, SWZ	16 Jul
	51 performances to 53.5 by 10 athletes					
53.58	Vicky Day/Ward		19.06.72	3	Claremont, USA	14 Apr
53.84	Jenny Meadows	U20	17.04.81	1	Mannheim, GER	12 Aug
53.86	Lisa Miller	U20	13.01.83	6s1	Santiago, CHI	18 Oct
53.98	Michelle Pierre		30.09.73	6r1	Dublin (S), IRE	29 Jul
54.00	Heather Brookes	U20	17.07.81	2	Mannheim, GER	12 Aug
54.01	Linda Staines	V35	26.12.63	3h1	Birmingham	12 Aug
54.03	Karen Gear	U23	30.09.79	1	Bedford	1 Jul
54.06	Mary McClung		19.12.71	2	Glasgow (S)	29 Jul
54.08	Vicki Jamison		19.05.77	3	Glasgow (S)	29 Jul
54.41	Kim Wall	U20	21.04.83	3	Bath	16 Sep
	(20)					
54.61	Helen Thieme	U20	28.09.81	2	Loughborough	21 May
54.68 i	Michelle Thomas		16.10.71	1	Birmingham	12 Feb
54.72	Kim Goodwin		16.05.70	1	Grantham	18 Jun
54.77	Shani Anderson		7.08.75	2	Eagle Rock, USA	13 May
54.80	Lesley Clarkson	U20	18.07.82	4rB	Budapest, HUN	22 Jul
54.8	Aileen McGillivary		13.08.70	1	Coatbridge	16 Jul
	55.33			1h2	Glasgow (S)	29 Jul
54.83	Elizabeth Williams		2.06.77	4h1	Birmingham	12 Aug
54.93	Keri Maddox		4.07.72	1	Glasgow (S)	8 Jul
55.07	Carey Easton	U23	16.11.79	7	Riga, LAT	22 Jun
55.19	Emma Davies	U23	9.10.78	4	Haapsalu, EST	20 Jun

55.2	Jo Fenn		19.10.74	2rB	Liverpool	7 May
	55.72			4	Brighton	18 Jun
55.2	Tracey Duncan	U23	16.05.79	2	Peterborough	9 Jul
	56.18			3	Enfield	6 Aug
55.31	Samantha Singer	U20	8.05.82	3	Watford	2 Jul
55.4	Nicole Bowring		27.01.74	3	London (Cr)	27 Aug
	55.49			4h3	Birmingham	12 Aug
55.41	Rebecca Lyne	U20	4.07.82	1	Cudworth	13 May
55.42 i	Louretta Thorne		6.05.77	1	Birmingham	8 Jan
55.43	Leigh Newton	U23	13.01.78	5	Solihull	29 Jul
55.46	Melanie Purkiss	U23	11.03.79	2rB	Bath	16 Sep
55.54	Sally Evans		14.05.75	3	Solihull	5 Aug
55.58	Kathryn Bright/Sage		27.03.76	3	Loughborough	21 May
	(40)					
55.6	Hannah Wood	U20	17.11.81	1	Leamington	13 May
	56.06			7h1	Birmingham	12 Aug
55.6	Claire Raven		15.06.72	3	Peterborough	9 Jul
	55.61			2	Enfield	6 Aug
55.61	Claire McGilp	U23	25.07.78	5	Rustenberg, RSA	22 Jan
55.67	Alison Thorne		25.09.72	2	Eton	6 May
55.68	Gaby Howell	U20	25.01.82	3	Brighton	18 Jun
55.69	Susan Hendry		30.06.76	4	Solihull	5 Aug
55.70	Katie Jones		4.01.77	3	Grantham	18 Jun
55.80	Roseline Addo	U23	7.06.80	3r2	Raleigh, USA	31 Mar
55.8	Donna Porazinski	U20	28.01.81	2	Bath	9 Jul
	56.00			2	Derby	3 Sep
55.8	Jane McKay		22.04.77	3	Coatbridge	16 Jul
	55.82			3rB	Loughborough	21 May
	(50)					
55.83 i	Kelly Sotherton		13.11.76	2	Cardiff	4 Mar
	57.10			3h2	Bedford	29 May
55.83	Lynsey Munnoch	U20	24.10.81	5	Glasgow (S)	29 Jul
55.88	Ruth Watson	U23	29.11.79	5h1	Birmingham	12 Aug
55.9	Jennie Matthews	V35	3.07.62	1	Stretford	28 Jun
	57.19			5	Enfield	6 Aug
55.94	Lisa Vannet		8.11.74	1rB	Enfield	6 Aug
56.02	Jennifer Culley		4.03.75	5h3	Birmingham	12 Aug
56.02	Olivia Hines	U17	19.10.83	1	Bedford	20 Aug
56.05	Lois Cresswell	U20	12.01.81	2	Stoke-on-Trent	1 May
56.1	Joy Wright		22.06.75	2	London (Cr)	13 May
56.11	Zoe Arnold		10.11.76	2	Belfast	8 Jul
	(60)					
56.25	Lisa Whigham	U23	14.08.80	3	Stoke-on-Trent	1 May
56.25	Rachel Newcombe		25.02.67	5	Cwmbran	18 Jun
56.3	Lorraine Phillips		27.01.75	1	Basingstoke	11 Jun
56.37 i	Simmone Jacobs		5.09.66	3h1	Birmingham	29 Jan
56.40	Rosie Thorner		7.08.67	1	Stoke-on-Trent	18 Jun
56.48	Nicola Sanders	U20	23.06.82	6	Bedford	11 Jun
56.5	Natalie Smellie	U20	16.01.82	1	London (He)	30 Jul
	56.72			1	Bedford	29 Apr
56.55 i	Rebecca Scotcher	U20	2.07.82	1h1	Birmingham	6 Feb
	57.0			1	Norwich	17 Jun
56.57	Amanda Pritchard	U23	18.03.80	2	Derby	3 Sep
56.60	Sharon Allen		23.10.68	3h4	Birmingham	12 Aug
	(70)					
56.6	Susie Williams		2.06.77	1	Walton	31 May
56.6	Ellie Childs	U20	26.05.83	2	Ware	2 Sep
56.67	Nusrat Ceesay	U20	18.03.81	2	Bedford	20 Aug
56.7	Joanne McDougall	U23	23.08.79	2	Liverpool	14 May
	56.95			4h2	Bedford	1 Jul
56.7	Jennifer Ward	U23	22.09.78	4	Coatbridge	16 Jul

56.74 i	Emma Ania	U23	7.02.79	4r2	Minneapolis/St Paul, USA	27Feb
56.75	Danielle Halsall	U20	27.06.81	3	Shanghai, CHN	25 Jun
56.76	Alice Butler		27.07.73	2	Cudworth	13 May
56.76	Dawn Wilson	U20	16.12.81	1	London (He)	20 Aug
56.8	Lucy Chaffe	U23	25.03.79	3	Liverpool	7 May
(80)						
56.8	Heather McKay	U20	5.09.81	2	Coatbridge	21 May
56.8	Sharon Williams		20.05.70	1	Eton	23 Jul
56.9	Alison Currie		15.07.68	4	Glasgow (S)	30 Apr
56.9	Diana Bennett/Norman		14.06.74	4	London (Cr)	13 May
56.9	Felicia Louisy		17.05.74	1	Luton	14 May
56.9	Sharon Semper		26.11.68	1	Portsmouth	20 May
	57.09 i			5h1	Birmingham	29 Jan
56.93	Claire Gibson	U20	25.12.82	1	Grangemouth	13 May
57.0	Michele Gillham		8.10.74	3rB	Liverpool	7 May
57.0	Sandra Leigh		26.02.66	1	Basildon	24 Jun
	57.06			6	Brighton	18 Jun
57.04	Susan Bovill	U20	6.05.82	1	Watford	28 May
(90)						
57.06	Paula Fryer		14.07.69	1	Cudworth	20 Aug
57.1	Jeina Mitchell		21.01.75	1	London (Cr)	24 Jun
57.12	Anita Eagland		29.09.72	3	Cudworth	20 Aug
57.2	Claire Robinson	U23	18.01.78	1	Philadelphia, USA	22 Apr
	57.37			3s1	Stoke-on-Trent	30 Apr
57.28	Lorna Scott	U23	27.07.78	3rB	Glasgow (S)	8 Jul
57.3	Rachael Kay	U23	8.09.80	2	Rugby	9 Jul
57.33 i	Lindsey Singer	U20	4.06.83	3	Birmingham	12 Feb
57.4	Jo Owbridge	U20	19.01.82	1	Hull	4 Jun
	57.46			2	Cleckheaton	27 May
57.4	Karen Storey		8.11.68	2	Cannock	9 Sep
57.4	Lorna Johnston	U17	20.12.83	1	Aberdeen	13 Sep
(100)						
57.44	Elaine Wells	U23	30.05.78	1	Crawley	13 May
57.44	Lynne Fitzpatrick	U20	21.08.81	6h2	Glasgow (S)	29 Jul
57.5	Sarah Smith		18.08.76	4rB	Liverpool	7 May
57.5	Sarah Tomlins	U20	5.04.82	2	Basildon	24 Jun

Additional Under 17 (1 - 2 above)

57.57	Jill Lando	2.09.84	3	Edinburgh	13 Aug
57.69	Rebecca Leitch	12.11.84	2	Wrexham	18 Jul
57.7	Marilyn Okoro	23.09.84	3	London (He)	30 Jul
57.8	Lisa Dobriskey	23.12.83	4	Norwich	13 Aug
58.1	Jemma Simpson	10.02.84	1	Carn Brea	14 May
58.1	Charlotte Best	7.03.85	1	Bromley	15 Jul
58.5	Natalie Christmas	9.04.84	1	Crawley	19 Jul
58.54	Vicky Tunaley	4.06.84	2	London (He)	20 Aug
(10)					
58.9	Sian Scott	20.03.84	1	Bournemouth	12 Aug

Relay first leg

53.2	Natasha Danvers		19.09.77	Sydney, AUS	30 Sep
54.04	Kim Wall	U20	21.04.83	Santiago, CHI	22 Oct

Unconfirmed

54.85	Sharon Allen	(56.60)	Miami, USA	11 Mar

Foreign

55.27	*Mari Bjone (NOR)*		*11.09.70*	*1*	*Long Beach, USA*	*15 Apr*
56.17	*Michelle Carey (IRE)*	*U20*	*20.03.81*	*2*	*London (BP)*	*4 Jun*
56.5	*Sarah Oxley/Reilly (IRE)*		*3.07.73*	*6*	*Antrim*	*31 Jul*

600 METRES

1:26 +e	Kelly Holmes		19.04.70	m	Sydney, AUS	25 Sep
1:27.18	Diane Modahl		17.06.66	2	Gold Coast (RB), AUS	17 Sep
1:31.58 i	Christa Salt	V35	17.06.64	1	Basel, SWZ	1 May

Under 13

1:37.3	Lisa Lanini		9.10.87	1	Wigan	19 Mar
1:42.4	Stephanie Bloor			1	Hull	16 Apr
1:43.7	Charlotte Browning		8.10.87	1	Eton	17 Sep
1:44.2	Megan Foley		14.04.88	1	Basildon	10 Jun
1:44.4	Hannah Jones		9.06.88	1	Aldershot	1 Jul
1:45.1	Claire Alexander			1	Bournemouth	
1:45.3	Carolyn Plateau		22.08.88	1	Bracknell	25 Mar
1:46.4	Cecilia Savundra		29.12.87	1	Guildford	6 Aug
1:46.8	Laura Hunt			2	Bracknell	25 Mar
1:46.8	Rachel Tovey		17.10.87	1	Guildford	6 Aug

Foreign

1:31.34 i	*Mari Bjone (NOR)*		*11.09.70*	*1*	*Birmingham*	*17 Feb*

800 METRES

1:56.80	Kelly Holmes		19.04.70	3	Sydney, AUS	25 Sep
	1:58.45			2s2	Sydney, AUS	23 Sep
	2:00.35			3	Gateshead	28 Aug
	2:00.53			1	Rovereto, ITA	30 Aug
	2:01.76			1h4	Sydney, AUS	22 Sep
	2:02.08			1	Birmingham	13 Aug
	2:03.26			1	Karlstad, SWE	23 Aug
	2:04.10			1h1	Birmingham	12 Aug
2:00.53	Diane Modahl		17.06.66	3	Jena, GER	3 Jun
	2:02.41			5h5	Sydney, AUS	22 Sep
	2:02.73 mx			1	Stretford	5 Sep
	2:03.13			3	Kassel, GER	7 Jun
	2:03.94			10	Gateshead	28 Aug
	2:04.16			10	Leverkusen, GER	20 Aug
2:01.06	Tanya Blake		16.01.71	4	Leverkusen, GER	20 Aug
	2:02.47			1r2	Budapest, HUN	22 Jul
	2:02.56			6	Palo Alto, USA	1 Jul
	2:02.92			2	Ljubljana, SLO	25 Jul
	2:04.69			1	Eagle Rock, USA	13 May
	2:04.71			4	Gateshead	15 Jul
2:01.25	Hayley Tullett		17.02.73	1r1	Budapest, HUN	22 Jul
	2:01.53			6	Gateshead	28 Aug
	2:02.92			1	Malmo, SWE	7 Aug
2:03.48 mx	Kelly Caffel	U23	10.02.79	1	Watford	30 Aug
	2:04.35			1	Watford	6 Sep
2:03.75	Helen Pattinson		2.01.74	9	Gateshead	28 Aug
	2:04.27			10	Jena, GER	3 Jun
	2:05.0 mx				Stretford	8 Aug
2:03.78 mx	Alex Carter	U23	1.04.80	1	Stretford	5 Sep
	2:05.48			2	Liverpool	22 Jul
2:03.92	Mary McClung		19.12.71	2r1	Budapest, HUN	22 Jul
2:04.07	Emma Davies	U23	9.10.78	2	Gothenburg, SWE	3 Aug
	2:04.42			4	Namur, BEL	18 Aug
	2:04.44			3	Riga, LAT	22 Jun
	2:04.54			1	Getafe, SPA	9 Sep
	2:05.04			1	Basel, SWZ	11 Jun
2:04.15	Jeina Mitchell		21.01.75	8	Rieti, ITA	3 Sep
	2:04.24			2	Tartu, EST	11 Jun
	2:04.74			8	Rovereto, ITA	30 Aug

2:04.19	Jo Fenn		19.10.74	4r2	Budapest, HUN	22	Jul
2:04.58	Claire Raven		15.06.72	6	Dublin (S), IRE	29	Jul
	40 performances to 2:05.05 by 12 athletes						
2:05.10	Jennifer Ward	U23	22.09.78	1	Glasgow (S)	3	Sep
2:05.27	Rebecca Lyne	U20	4.07.82	2	Manchester	14	Jun
2:05.60	Rachel Newcombe		25.02.67	5	Riga, LAT	22	Jun
2:05.75 mx	Lorraine Phillips		27.01.75	2	Watford	30	Aug
	2:07.85			1	Brighton	18	Jun
2:06.02	Emma Ward	U20	2.01.82	1	Solihull	29	Jul
2:06.38	Joanna Ross	U20	18.02.81	3	Glasgow (S)	3	Sep
2:06.56	Christa Salt	V35	17.06.64	1	Diekirch, LUX	2	Jul
2:06.72	Jemma Simpson	U17	10.02.84	3	Solihull	19	Aug
(20)							
2:07.07	Sally Evans		14.05.75	3	Cardiff	5	Jul
2:07.1	Charlotte Moore	U17	4.01.85	1	Bournemouth	12	Aug
2:07.14	Sarah Knights		25.02.67	4h1	Birmingham	12	Aug
2:07.54	Sonya Bowyer		18.09.72	5	Loughborough	21	May
2:07.7	Susan Hendry		30.06.76	3	Glasgow (S)	29	Jul
2:07.71	Paula Fryer		14.07.69	2	Watford	22	Jul
2:07.83	Danielle Thornal		9.08.75	8r1	Dedham, USA	3	Jun
2:07.88	Alice Butler		27.07.73	1	Stretford	30	May
2:08.1	Rhonda Munnik		26.03.74	2	London (Cr)	27	Aug
2:08.15	Natalie Lewis	U20	25.05.82	5	Cardiff	5	Jul
(30)							
2:08.51	Susan Scott		26.09.77	2	Grangemouth	14	May
2:08.6	Sophie Morris/Alford		5.12.75	1	Eton	30	Apr
2:08.71	Lorna Scott	U23	27.07.78	6	Cardiff	5	Jul
2:08.77	Shirley Griffiths		23.06.72	1	Stretford	8	Aug
2:08.80	Zoe Jelbert	U17	21.01.84	2	Watford	28	May
2:08.8 mx	Lucy Vaughan		20.04.69	1	Watford	20	Sep
	2:09.22			2	Watford	6	Sep
2:08.95	Kerry Smithson		13.09.76	1	Stretford	27	Jun
2:09.08	Sarah Bouchard		23.10.74	2	Stretford	30	May
2:09.11	Bev Blakeman		4.04.74	1	Stretford	25	Jul
2:09.14	Sue Lamb		24.03.70	2	London (BP)	25	Jun
(40)							
2:09.23	Kelly McNeice	U23	17.06.78		Dublin, IRE	16	Jul
2:09.26	Michelle Mann/Brooks		6.02.77	3	Lincoln, USA	7	May
2:09.3	Claire Gibson	U20	25.12.82	5	Glasgow (S)	29	Jul
2:09.50	Kate Reed	U20	28.09.82	5	Glasgow (S)	3	Sep
2:09.54	Diana Bennett/Norman		14.06.74	3	Brighton	18	Jun
2:09.58	Tanya Baker		23.11.74		Palo Alto, USA	26	Jul
2:09.67	Ellen O'Hare	U23	4.02.78	1	Watford	13	Jul
2:09.71	Celia Brown		22.01.77	2	Stoke-on-Trent	17	Jun
2:09.72	Liz Yelling		5.12.74	3	Watford	6	Sep
2:09.78	Emma Brady		3.01.74	2	Stretford	22	Aug
(50)							
2:09.80	Vicki Andrews		31.08.69	3	Stretford	30	May
2:09.8	Debbie Sullivan		24.01.72	1	Milton Keynes	2	Sep
2:09.87	Lisa Dobriskey	U17	23.12.83	2	Watford	2	Jul
2:10.0	Pauline Thom		2.08.70	1	Antrim	1	Jul
2:10.1	Louise Damen	U20	12.10.82	1	Bournemouth	13	May
2:10.1	Faye Fullerton	U17	31.05.84	1	Chelmsford	14	May
2:10.2	Rachel Buller		31.08.76	4	Loughborough	10	May
2:10.27	Rachel Felton	U23	27.06.79	2	Bedford	19	Aug
2:10.5	Dianne Henaghan		6.08.65	1	Jarrow	31	May
2:10.56	Lucy Chaffe	U23	25.03.79	3	Jona, SWZ	16	Jul
(60)							
2:10.6	Karen Johns	U23	18.08.80	1	Jarrow	23	Jul
2:10.70	Jill Lando	U17	2.09.84	2	Blackpool	15	Jul
2:10.7	Joy Wright		22.06.75	1	London (TB)	5	Jul

2:10.7	Jenny Meadows	U20	17.04.81	3	Rugby	9	Jul
2:10.71 i	Hayley Cole		1.11.77	3h1	Lievin, FRA	18	Feb
2:10.75 mx	Victoria Lawrence		9.06.73	3h1	Stretford	13	Jun
2:10.89	Louise Whittaker	U20	29.11.82	1rB	Stretford	25	Jul
2:10.89	Hayley Beard	U15	2.12.85	1	Sheffield	30	Jul
2:10.95	Kim Heffernan		20.12.66	1rB	Solihull	19	Aug
2:11.00 i	Iona McIntyre	U20	14.03.83	1	Glasgow (S)	16	Jan
(70)							
2:11.0	Sarah Simmons		12.01.75	1	Ashford	7	May
2:11.02	Kathryn Bright/Sage		27.03.76	3rB	Cardiff	5	Jul
2:11.05	Charlotte Cutler		16.10.72	2rB	Solihull	19	Aug
2:11.10	Pauline Powell		17.05.73	3	Stretford	11	Jul
2:11.1	Nikki Daniels	U20	25.08.82	2	Ashford	7	May
2:11.1 mx	Sarah Alt/Heath	V35	4.01.62	2	Watford	20	Sep
	2:11.84			3h3	Brighton	17	Jun
2:11.16	Julie McDevitt		15.03.73	5	Grangemouth	14	May
2:11.19	Vicky Rolfe	U23	27.08.80	4rB	Cardiff	5	Jul
2:11.29 i	Emily Hathaway	U23	22.12.79	5	Birmingham	30	Jan
2:11.35	Hayley Parkinson-Ovens		5.12.75	6	Grangemouth	14	May
(80)							
2:11.38	Ellie Childs	U20	26.05.83	5	Watford	6	Sep
2:11.52	Charlotte Best	U17	7.03.85	1	Sheffield	30	Jul
2:11.54	Leah Harris	U20	24.02.82	1	Sheffield	8	Jul
2:11.6	Lucy Doughty		1.05.71	1	Gloucester	1	Jul
2:11.7	Andrea Whitcombe		8.06.71	1	Oxford	15	Jul
2:11.72	Maria Sharp		8.12.73	5	Watford	2	Aug
2:12.0	Maxine Baker		15.12.70	1	Coventry	30	Apr
2:12.0	Michelle Thomas		16.10.71	1	Stoke-on-Trent	25	Jun
2:12.0	Claire Martin		12.07.76	1	London (TB)	16	Aug
2:12.02	Sarah Pickering	U17	26.10.83	3	Blackpool	15	Jul
(90)							
2:12.04	Faith Aston		26.11.75	1rC	Manchester	14	Jun
2:12.1	Angela Newport		21.10.70	5	Loughborough	10	May
2:12.16	Jenny Mockler	U20	28.08.82	2rB	Stretford	25	Jul
2:12.20	Denise Lewis		27.08.72	1H	Talence, FRA	30	Jul
2:12.2	Philippa McCrea	U23	1.03.78	1	Cudworth	22	Jul
2:12.2	Sarah Bull		4.06.75	1	Loughborough	22	Aug
2:12.30 i	Joanne Colleran		1.09.72	h	Birmingham	15	Jan
2:12.3	Caroline Swinbank		16.06.75	2	Rugby	23	Jul
2:12.45	Catherine Riley	U20	4.06.82	4	Stretford	30	May
2:12.48	Lisa Samuels	U20	24.09.81	1	Watford	28	May
(100)							
2:12.6	Helen Bebbington	U23	25.11.80	5	Solihull	19	Jul
2:12.69 i	Wendy Davis	U23	7.11.79	2	Lexington, USA	5	Feb
2:12.7	Heidi Smith		20.05.74	1	Deeside	4	Jun
2:12.71	Ruth Vlassak		24.11.61	3	Bedford	30	Aug
2:12.75	Caroline Walsh	U23	29.04.80	2	Watford	7	Jun
2:12.76	Tina Brown		22.08.76	3rC	Manchester	14	Jun
2:12.8	Suzanne Owen	U23	5.05.79	1	Stoke-on-Trent	13	May
2:12.94	Charlene Snelgrove	U20	6.05.82	3h2	Sheffield	7	Jul

Additional Under 17 (1 - 8 above)

2:13.41	Donna Riding	28.11.83	4rC	Manchester	14	Jun
2:13.6	Kim Searle	27.12.83	3h3	Sheffield	29	Jul
(10)						
2:13.84	Jessica Nugent	27.08.84	9	Watford	30	Aug
2:14.02	Marilyn Okoro	23.09.84	2	Birmingham	10	Sep
2:14.16	Lucy Jones	30.11.83	8rB	Solihull	19	Aug
2:14.54	Kaye Kirkham	19.10.84	3rB	Stretford	25	Jul
2:14.58	Nisha Desai	5.08.84	1h1	Sheffield	7	Jul
2:15.0	Adele Bevan	26.03.84	3h4	Watford	27	May
2:15.48	Nicola Gundersen	26.02.85	3h1	Sheffield	7	Jul

2:15.5	Ruth Chadney		20.04.85	1	Bournemouth	14 May
2:15.74 i	Olivia Hines		19.10.83	2	Birmingham	5 Feb
	2:16.5			1	London (CP)	2 Jul
2:15.8	Stacey Ward		16.01.85	2=rC	Watford	22 Jul
	(20)					
2:15.9	Bryony Frost		21.02.84	2	Horsham	17 Jun
2:16.0	Sally Oldfield		25.06.84	4rC	Watford	22 Jul
2:16.09	Phillipa Aukett		9.09.84	4h1	Sheffield	7 Jul
2:16.3	Danielle Woods		2.10.84	1	Stretford	14 May
2:16.3	Elizabeth Brathwaite		10.04.85	1	Watford	14 May
2:16.3	Lisa Cater		16.01.84	2	Stoke-on-Trent	18 Jun
2:16.38	Jennifer Tunstill		16.05.84	1	Stretford	5 Sep
2:16.63	Rebecca Smith		17.10.83	1	Cudworth	13 May
2:16.69	Sarah Holah		9.12.84	7rB	Stretford	8 Aug
2:16.69	Chloe Wilkinson		16.12.84	4	London (He)	20 Aug
	(30)					
2:16.7	Claire Robson		9.01.84	2	Chester-le-Street	7 May
2:16.7	Hayley South		17.11.83	2	London (CP)	2 Jul
2:16.73	Jennifer Main		26.01.84	2rB	Glasgow	3 Sep

Additional Under 15 (1 above)

2:13.01	Rachael Thompson	15.11.85	3	Stretford	22 Aug
2:13.18	Lynsey Jepson	12.01.87	1	Solihull	28 May
2:13.37	Faye Harding	7.09.85	2	Sheffield	30 Jul
2:13.89	Katrina Wootton	2.09.85	3	Sheffield	30 Jul
2:14.0	Emma Hopkins	16.09.86	1	Cudworth	9 Sep
2:15.91	Victoria Clews	21.01.87	9	Watford	6 Sep
2:16.22	Sara Luck	18.11.86	2h3	Sheffield	30 Jul
2:16.4	Rachael Nathan	27.04.86	2	Cudworth	9 Sep
2:16.4	Melissa Wall	10.04.86	2	Barking	10 Sep
	(10)				
2:16.46	Lauren Cunningham	22.08.87	2	Watford	28 May
2:16.83	Charlotte Moss	7.11.85	2h2	Sheffield	7 Jul
2:16.9	Michelle Jessop	21.09.85	1r1	Thurrock	25 Jun
2:16.92	Charlotte Jackson	31.10.85	3	Sheffield	8 Jul
2:16.99	Jenna Hill	16.10.85	6r2	Stretford	25 Jul
2:17.1	Emma Hunt	25.04.86		Guildford	23 Jul
2:17.40	Claire Wilson	7.11.85	2	Glasgow (S)	2 Jul
2:17.4	Danielle Barnes	8.10.85	1r1	Exeter	29 Aug
2:17.80	Lyndsey Freel	23.09.85	1	Antrim	17 Jun
2:18.2	Natalie Bass	3.12.85	4	Solihull	24 May
	(20)				
2:18.4	Laura Finucane	3.08.86	1	Stretford	23 Jul
2:18.68	Sarah Shuttleworth	16.08.86	6	Sheffield	30 Jul
2:18.7	Kelly Rodmell	26.11.85	1	Wigan	2 Jul
2:19.0	Anna Warne	17.11.85	3	Loughborough	14 May

Under 13

2:16.1	Lisa Lanini	9.10.87	1	Wrexham	5 Aug
2:19.89	Charlotte Browning	8.10.87	2	Watford	30 Aug
2:23.7	Megan Foley	14.04.88	2	Milton Keynes	2 Sep
2:23.72	Stephanie Bloor		7	Wigan	25 Jun
2:24.0	Stephanie Lyall	3.02.89	1	Glasgow (S)	10 Sep
2:25.6	Carolyn Plateau	22.08.88		Bournemouth	12 Aug
2:25.97	Claire Alexander		1	Portsmouth	14 May
2:26.5	Katherine Uphill	19.02.88	1		
2:26.8	Natalie Real	14.11.87	1	Bournemouth	14 May
2:26.9	Stephanie Cooper		1	Northampton	3 Jul

Foreign

2:09.69	*Dorita Harmse (RSA)*		*28.09.73*	*1*	*Bedford*	*20 Aug*
2:11.02	*Carolina Nylen (SWE)*	*U23*	*15.09.79*	*4rB*	*Manchester*	*14 Jun*

1000 METRES

2:45.83	Christa Salt	V35	17.06.64	1	Langenthal, SWZ	1 Jun

Under 13

3:06.4	Charlotte Browning		8.10.87	1	Guildford	6 Aug
3:11.7	Carolyn Plateau		22.08.88	1	Reading	28 Aug
3:13.1	Hannah Jones		9.06.88	2	Guildford	6 Aug
3:14.3	Rachel Tovey		17.10.87	1	Woking	4 Jun
3:14.6	India Lee		31.05.88	2	Aldershot	1 Jul
3:14.9	Danielle Christmas		21.12.87	1	Crawley	28 Aug

1200 METRES - Under 13

3:49.1	Megan Foley		14.04.88	1	London (Nh)	2 Jul
3:50.9	Charlotte Browning		8.10.87	1	Horsham	4 Jul
3:51.3	Stephanie Bloor			1	Wigan	2 Jul
3:53.6	Natalie Real		14.11.87	1	Eton	2 Jul
3:55.5	Carolyn Plateau		22.08.88	1	Guildford	23 Jul
3:55.7	Lisa Lanini		9.10.87	1	Deeside	23 Jul
3:57.6	Stephanie Cooper			1	Nuneaton	2 Jul
3:58.8	Hayley Cannon			1	Bebington	2 Jul
3:59.4	Laura Quine			1r1	Liverpool	23 Jul
4:00.1	Katharine Barker			2	Bebington	2 Jul
	(10)					
4:00.2	Lauren Houlihan		14.12.87	1	Norwich	23 Jul
4:00.3	Lyndsey Barr		19.01.88	2	Norwich	23 Jul
4:00.94	Aveen O'Reilly		23.09.88	2	Birmingham	2 Sep
4:02.0	Emily Pidgeon		1.06.89	1	Swindon	23 Jul
4:02.0	Maria Williamson		7.09.87	1	Yate	23 Jul
4:02.1	Kirsten Berryman			2	Guildford	23 Jul

1500 METRES

4:01.23	Hayley Tullett		17.02.73	7	Oslo, NOR	28 Jul
	4:05.19			3	Nice, FRA	8 Jul
	4:05.34			3s1	Sydney, AUS	28 Sep
	4:05.52			4	Berlin, GER	1 Sep
	4:06.44			1	Birmingham	13 Aug
	4:09.23			1	Lucerne, SWZ	27 Jun
	4:10.58			3h3	Sydney, AUS	27 Sep
	4:16.90			1h2	Birmingham	12 Aug
4:04.82	Helen Pattinson		2.01.74	2	Barcelona, SPA	25 Jul
	4:06.27			5	Nice, FRA	8 Jul
	4:07.61			13	Brussels, BEL	25 Aug
	4:08.80			6h1	Sydney, AUS	27 Sep
	4:09.60			9s2	Sydney, AUS	28 Sep
	4:10.33			4	Kassel, GER	7 Jun
	4:10.54			2	Dessau, GER	31 May
	4:11.40			2	Birmingham	13 Aug
	4:12.05			1	Glasgow (S)	2 Jul
	4:12.05			1	Gateshead	16 Jul
	4:13.98			4	Seville, SPA	9 Jun
4:05.35	Kelly Holmes		19.04.70	4s1	Sydney, AUS	28 Sep
	4:08.02			7	Sydney, AUS	30 Sep
	4:10.38			3h2	Sydney, AUS	27 Sep
4:10.22	Kelly Caffel	U23	10.02.79	6	Leverkusen, GER	20 Aug
	4:13.23			1	Liverpool	22 Jul
	4:14.40			10	London (CP)	5 Aug
	4:14.91			3	Glasgow (S)	2 Jul
	4:15.29			3	Birmingham	13 Aug
	4:17.67			1	Brighton	18 Jun
	4:18.14			4	Manchester	14 Jun

4:11.45	Paula Radcliffe		17.12.73	11	Barcelona, SPA	25 Jul
4:14.41	Diane Modahl		17.06.66	8	Dessau, GER	31 May
	4:18.36 mx				Stretford	16 May
4:15.28	Angela Newport		21.10.70	2	Manchester	14 Jun
	4:19.48			5	Glasgow (S)	2 Jul
4:15.46	Kathy Butler		22.10.73	8	Eugene, USA	24 Jun
	4:17.28			1	Glasgow (S)	29 Jul
	4:18.47			2	Des Moines, USA	29 Apr
	4:19.78			9	Raleigh, USA	17 Jun
4:16.75	Liz Yelling		5.12.74	1	Watford	30 Aug
	4:17.50			2	Solihull	19 Aug
4:17.45	Amanda Parkinson		21.07.71	5	Watford	22 Jul
	4:19.68			4	Birmingham	13 Aug
	4:19.70			2h2	Birmingham	12 Aug
	(10)					
4:17.98	Alex Carter	U23	1.04.80	3	Manchester	14 Jun
	4:19.87			3	Cardiff	5 Jul
4:18.04	Dianne Henaghan	V35	6.08.65	7	Watford	22 Jul
	4:19.63			2	Loughborough	21 May
4:18.32	Kerry Smithson		13.09.76	1	Cardiff	5 Jul
4:18.42	Susan Scott		26.09.77	8	Watford	22 Jul
	4:18.63			5	Manchester	14 Jun
	4:18.73			2	Glasgow (S)	29 Jul
4:18.48	Joanne Colleran		1.09.72	1	Solihull	29 Jul
4:19.51	Andrea Whitcombe		8.06.71	2	Brighton	18 Jun
	4:19.61			10	Watford	22 Jul
	4:19.67			2	Solihull	29 Jul
4:19.70	Emma Ward	U20	2.01.82	3h2	Birmingham	12 Aug
4:19.71	Lucy Wright		17.11.69	3	Solihull	19 Aug
	57 performances to 4:20.0 by 18 athletes					
4:20.07	Jeina Mitchell		21.01.75	3	Solihull	29 Jul
4:20.16	Shirley Griffiths		23.06.72	1	Glasgow (S)	3 Sep
	(20)					
4:20.35	Sharon Morris		5.07.68	3	Brighton	18 Jun
4:21.67	Tara Krzywicki		9.03.74	4	Loughborough	21 May
4:21.68	Ellen O'Hare	U23	4.02.78	3	Glasgow (S)	29 Jul
4:21.77	Ann Griffiths		20.08.65	1	Eton	6 May
4:21.88	Catherine Berry		8.10.75	2	Atlanta, USA	19 May
4:21.97	Bev Jenkins		6.02.70	2	Stretford	8 Aug
4:22.19	Sue Lamb		24.03.70	7	Manchester	14 Jun
4:22.30	Maria Sharp		8.12.73	5	Cardiff	5 Jul
4:22.41	Michelle Mann/Brooks		6.02.77	5	Columbia, USA	21 May
4:22.52	Claire Martin		12.07.76	7	Birmingham	13 Aug
	(30)					
4:22.75	Lucy Doughty		1.05.71	6	Cardiff	5 Jul
4:22.93	Gillian Palmer	U23	30.12.80	4	Glasgow (S)	29 Jul
4:22.97	Pauline Thom		2.08.70	3	Bedford	29 May
4:23.15	Tanya Baker		23.11.74		Palo Alto, USA	29 Jul
4:23.38	Louise Damen	U20	12.10.82	6	Loughborough	21 May
4:23.52	Jo Wilkinson		2.05.73	5h2	Birmingham	12 Aug
4:23.6	Sarah Bull		4.06.75	2	Bedford	23 Aug
4:23.61	Charlotte Moore	U17	4.01.85	1	Blackpool	15 Jul
4:23.72	Michelle Wannell		12.07.67	7	Cardiff	5 Jul
4:23.74 mx	Sarah Bouchard		23.10.74	1	Stretford	22 Aug
	(40)					
4:23.83	Sarah Simmons		12.01.75	4	Bedford	29 May
4:23.96	Zoe Jelbert	U17	21.01.84	4	Solihull	19 Aug
4:24.00	Zahara Hyde Peters	V35	12.01.63	5	Solihull	29 Jul
4:24.18	Rachel Newcombe		25.02.67	2	Watford	30 Aug
4:24.28	Christa Salt	V35	17.06.64	1	Basel, SWZ	3 Jun
4:24.47	Maxine Baker		15.12.70	7	Loughborough	21 May

4:24.52	Debbie Gunning		31.08.65	5	Solihull	19	Aug
4:25.2	Hayley Yelling		3.01.74	1	Rugby	9	Jul
4:25.50	Dorothea Lee		28.07.77	3rB	Watford	22	Jul
4:25.5	Caroline Walsh	U23	29.04.80	1	Watford	28	Jun
(50)							
4:25.59	Debbie Sullivan		24.01.72	5	Watford	30	Aug
4:25.6	Hayley Haining		6.03.72	1	Grangemouth	2	Aug
4:26.11 i	Emma Davies	U23	9.10.78	3	Birmingham	16	Jan
4:26.2	Jennifer Ward	U23	22.09.78	1	Coatbridge	27	Aug
4:26.50	Catherine Dugdale		29.11.74	8	Cardiff	5	Jul
4:26.63	Jane Potter	U20	24.10.81	4	Stretford	8	Aug
4:26.74	Sarah Knights		25.02.67	7	Watford	30	Aug
4:26.78	Suzanne Owen	U23	5.05.79	1rB	Manchester	14	Jun
4:26.86	Emma Brady		3.01.74	8	Budapest, HUN	22	Jul
4:26.96 mx	Penny Thackray		18.08.74	4	Stretford	27	Jun
(60)							
4:26.99	Juliet Potter	U20	24.10.81	5	Stretford	8	Aug
4:27.48	Julie Mitchell		3.10.74	3	Grantham	18	Jun
4:27.73 i	Esther Evans		22.12.73	1	Cardiff	4	Mar
	4:30.85			7h1	Birmingham	12	Aug
4:28.10	Lisa Dobriskey	U17	23.12.83	1	London (CP)	14	May
4:28.1	Faye Fullerton	U17	31.05.84	1	Chelmsford	1	May
4:28.28 mx	Liz Proctor		31.10.72	1	Stretford	16	May
	4:33.47			3rB	Manchester	14	Jun
4:28.45	Jilly Ingman	U23	17.08.78	6	Bedford	4	Jun
4:29.02 i	Sarah Salmon		9.09.74	2	Cardiff	4	Mar
	4:31.35			1	Adelaide, AUS	18	Nov
4:29.02	Hayley Parkinson-Ovens		5.12.75	8	Bedford	29	May
4:29.20	Tanya Blake		16.01.71		Fullerton, USA	17	Jun
(70)							
4:29.37	Jessica Nugent	U17	27.08.84	4	Bedford	26	Aug
4:29.70	Wendy Farrow		25.12.71	9	Solihull	15	Aug
4:29.76 i	Val Bothams		19.03.75	3	Cardiff	26	Feb
	4:31.88			2	Stoke-on-Trent	1	May
4:30.06	Philippa McCrea	U23	1.03.78	6	Solihull	29	Jul
4:30.41	Jemma Simpson	U17	10.02.84	2	London (CP)	5	Aug
4:30.52	Vicky Rolfe	U23	27.08.80	3	Bedford	1	Jul
4:30.87	Charlotte Dale	U17	23.03.84	1	Sheffield	30	Jul
4:31.00	Sonia Thomas	U23	16.05.79	4	Bedford	1	Jul
4:31.12	Karen Hind	U23	31.01.79	5	Grantham	18	Jun
4:31.17	Kerrie Nott		28.02.74	11	Solihull	19	Aug
(80)							
4:31.28	Collette Fagan	U20	6.06.82	7	Glasgow (S)	29	Jul
4:31.30	Sally Oldfield	U17	25.06.84	2	Sheffield	30	Jul
4:31.3	Vicki Andrews		31.08.69	4	Loughborough	10	May
4:31.55	Helen Zenner	U20	15.08.82	1rC	Watford	22	Jul
4:32.0	Katrina Wootton	U15	2.09.85	1	London (TB)	15	Jul
4:32.04	Karen Montador	U23	14.05.79	2	Grangemouth	13	May
4:32.20	Tina Brown		22.08.76	7	Solihull	29	Jul
4:32.24	Amber Gascoigne	U23	5.09.79	13	Solihull	19	Aug
4:32.30	Lisa Webb		9.10.65	8	Brighton	18	Jun
4:32.39	Katy Smith	U20	5.08.81	3	Watford	2	Jul
(90)							
4:32.45 mx	Jenny Heath		22.12.77	2	Stretford	25	Jul
4:32.49	Jessica Woolley	U23	19.01.80	14	Solihull	19	Aug
4:32.6	Emma Ford		16.02.77	4	Liverpool	7	May
4:32.6	Kate Reed	U20	28.09.82	1	Wolverhampton	20	Aug
4:32.86	Jennifer Pereira	U17	8.08.85	5	London (CP)	5	Aug
4:32.87	Amy Waterlow	U23	29.07.78	7	Stretford	8	Aug
4:33.0	Louise Whittaker	U20	29.11.82	1	Rugby	23	Jul
4:33.6	Helen Bebbington	U23	25.11.80	3	Leamington	13	May

4:33.69 mx	Ruth Eddy	9.07.75	1r3	Watford	26 Jul
4:33.8	Kathryn Waugh	20.02.73	1	Jarrow	8 Jul
	(100)				
4:33.86	Pauline Powell	17.05.73	6	Grantham	18 Jun

Additional Under 17 (1 - 9 above)

4:34.01	Hannah Whitmore	24.02.84	1rB	Solihull	19 Aug
	(10)				
4:35.78	Freya Murray	20.09.83	3	Sheffield	30 Jul
4:37.48	Bryony Frost	21.02.84	2	Watford	28 May
4:39.56	Chloe Wilkinson	16.12.84	3	Watford	28 May
4:39.6	Stacey Ward	16.01.85	1	Basildon	10 Jun
4:41.23	Kathryn Frost	21.02.84	6rC	Watford	22 Jul
4:41.29	Eleanor Stevens	29.06.84	6	Sheffield	30 Jul
4:42.08	Lucy Thomas	2.11.84	3	Ljubljana, SLO	23 Sep
4:42.18	Rosie Smith	28.06.85	7	Sheffield	30 Jul
4:42.19	Lisa Cater	16.01.84	9	Bedford	26 Aug
4:42.31	Kate Buchan	18.10.84	8	London (CP)	5 Aug
	(20)				
4:42.6	Sonia Clark	1.04.84	1	Cannock	30 Jul
4:43.1	Charlotte Wickham	21.06.85	1	Middlesbrough	17 Jun
4:43.78	Sarah Pickering	26.10.83	9	London (CP)	5 Aug
4:44.59	Claire Robson	9.01.84	1	Gateshead	14 May
4:44.95	Stacey Kirby	19.09.83	5h1	Sheffield	29 Jul
4:45.32	Claire Brodie	1.06.85	9	Sheffield	30 Jul
4:45.5	Ruth Chadney	20.04.85	1	Exeter	30 May
4:45.89	Carolyn Boosey	11.10.84	3	Watford	9 Aug
4:45.9	Stephanie Campbell	14.02.85	1	Belfast	11 May
4:46.07	Kaye Kirkham	19.10.84	3	Wigan	25 Jun
	(30)				
4:46.16	Laura Kenney	27.06.85	1h1	Sheffield	7 Jul
4:46.27	Lucy Flanner	9.07.84	4	Solihull	28 May
4:46.4	Jill Lando	2.09.84	2	Grangemouth	7 Jun
4:46.56	Lucy Jones	30.11.83	5	Solihull	28 May
4:46.63	Samantha Marshall	26.08.85	2	Grangemouth	25 Jun

Additional Under 15 (1 above)

4:34.2	Melissa Wall	10.04.86	2	London (TB)	15 Jul
4:35.77	Danielle Barnes	8.10.85	2r2	Solihull	19 Aug
4:39.0 mx	Rachael Nathan	27.04.86	3	Stretford	3 Sep
4:40.5	Emma Hunt	25.04.86	1	Watford	28 Jun
4:41.6	Lynsey Jepson	12.01.87	1	Loughborough	14 May
4:42.2	Emma Hopkins	16.09.86	1	Tamworth	20 Aug
4:42.42	Kiera Vogel	31.05.86	5	Sheffield	8 Jul
4:43.50	Jenna Hill	16.10.85	7r4	Watford	22 Jul
4:43.7	Gemma Turtle	15.05.86	2	Watford	28 Jun
	(10)				
4:44.65	Lyndsey Freel	23.09.85	4	Sheffield	29 Jul
4:44.83	Leonie Smith	20.12.86	4	Watford	28 May
4:45.75	Cheryl Guiney	24.09.85	1	Antrim	19 Aug
4:46.46	Rachel Deegan	10.01.86	2	Wigan	25 Jun
4:46.6	Natalie Bass	3.12.85	2	Cudworth	9 Sep
4:46.81	Hannah England	6.03.87	5	Watford	28 May
4:46.81	Helen Glover	17.06.86	5h1	Sheffield	7 Jul
4:47.4	Hayley Beard	2.12.85	3	Watford	28 Jun
4:47.96	Nicola Bartholomew	23.10.86	5	Sheffield	29 Jul
4:48.0	Claire Wilson	7.11.85	1	Grangemouth	17 Jun
	(20)				
4:48.2	Cheryl Hammond	13.07.87	1	Watford	31 May
4:49.61	Stephanie Wilson	18.10.86	7	Sheffield	29 Jul
4:50.21	Charlotte Moss	7.11.85	7	Watford	9 Aug

4:50.22	Isabella Stoate	16.07.86	6	Watford	28 May
4:50.3	Lauren Cunningham	22.08.87	1	Welwyn	1 May
4:50.3	Michelle Jessop	21.09.85	1	High Wycombe	13 May

Under 13

4:47.25 mx	Charlotte Browning	8.10.87	1r5	Watford	6 Sep
4:55.4	Megan Foley	14.04.88	2	Bromley	15 Jul
4:58.7	Natalie Real	14.11.87	2r1	Kingston	30 Jul
4:59.84 i	Emily Pidgeon	1.06.89	1	Cardiff	9 Dec
	5:07.70		11	Solihull	19 Aug
5:00.12	Hannah Jones	9.06.88	1	Portsmouth	14 May
5:00.2	Lisa Lanini	9.10.87	1	Bebington	12 Jul
5:00.7	Emma Nesbitt		1	Gateshead	25 Jun
5:01.89	India Lee	31.05.88	2	Portsmouth	14 May
5:03.5	Carolyn Plateau	22.08.88	4r1	Enfield	8 Apr
5:03.6	Charlie Gaspar	7.09.87		Worthing	12 Aug
(10)					
5:04.40	Gillian Moss		1r2	Watford	9 Aug
5:05.6	Danielle McCann		1	Lancaster	14 May
5:05.69	Aveen O'Reilly	23.09.88	1	Antrim	17 Jun
5:05.97	Charlotte Aberdeen	10.03.88	3r2	Watford	26 Jul
5:06.96	Claire Alexander		3	Portsmouth	13 May
5:07.06	Emma Pollant	4.06.89	2r6	Watford	6 Sep
5:07.1	Lyndsey Barr	19.01.88	1r2	Kingston	30 Jul
5:07.6	Lauren Houlihan	14.12.87	3r1	Kingston	30 Jul
5:07.8	Stephanie Cooper		1	Corby	14 May

Foreign

4:28.36	*Dorita Harmse (RSA)*	*28.09.73*	*1*	*Watford*	*7 Jun*
4:30.88 mx	*Charlotte Templeton (AUS)*	*25.01.70*	*1*	*Watford*	*6 Sep*
	4:33.7		*2*	*London (Cr)*	*27 Aug*

1 MILE

4:26.50 i	Hayley Tullett	17.02.73	5	Stuttgart, GER	6 Feb
4:42.07 i	Tanya Baker	23.11.74	2	University Park, USA	12 Feb

2000 METRES

5:43.22 +	Paula Radcliffe	17.12.73	1m	Gateshead	28 Aug
5:44.4 +e	Joanne Pavey	20.09.73	5m	Gateshead	28 Aug
5:52.8 +	Hayley Tullett	17.02.73	m	Gateshead	15 Jul

3000 METRES

8:28.85	Paula Radcliffe	17.12.73	4	Zurich, SWZ	11 Aug
	8:36.11		3	Gateshead	28 Aug
	8:52.0 +		5m	London (CP)	5 Aug
	9:01.99 +		1m	Sydney, AUS	30 Sep
	9:02.09 +		1m	Birmingham	13 Aug
8:36.70	Joanne Pavey	20.09.73	4	Gateshead	28 Aug
	8:53.7 mx		1	Solihull	19 Jul
	8:57.00 mx		2	Cardiff	5 Jul
	8:59.2 +e		m	Sydney, AUS	25 Sep
	9:02.6 +		2m	Birmingham	13 Aug
	9:06 +e		m	London (CP)	5 Aug
	9:19.3 +		3mh1	Sydney, AUS	22 Sep
8:45.39	Hayley Tullett	17.02.73	3	Gateshead	15 Jul
	8:54.63 i		3	Erfurt, GER	2 Feb
	8:55.31 i		7	Ghent, BEL	27 Feb
	9:00.62 i		5h2	Ghent, BEL	25 Feb

8:57.75 mx	Sarah Young/Wilkinson		2.01.70	1	Stretford	27 Jun
	9:04.05 mx			1	Stretford	30 May
	9:12.03			8	Gateshead	28 Aug
	9:16.0 +e			m	London (CP)	5 Aug
9:02.67 mx	Amanda Parkinson		21.07.71	1	Stretford	22 Aug
	9:12.75 mx			1rB	Stretford	27 Jun
9:02.88 mx	Hayley Yelling		3.01.74	4	Cardiff	5 Jul
	9:11.20			1	Manchester	14 Jun
	9:12.4 +			7m	Gateshead	16 Jul
	9:18.9 +e			4m	London (BP)	25 Jun
9:05.86 mx	Angela Newport		21.10.70	1	Stretford	25 Jul
	9:08.46			6	Gateshead	28 Aug
9:09.18	Helen Pattinson		2.01.74	1	Loughborough	21 May
9:11.4 mx	Liz Yelling		5.12.74	1	Watford	2 Aug
	9:19.98			2	Solihull	29 Jul
9:12.45 mx	Andrea Whitcombe		8.06.71	1	Watford	12 Jul
	9:14.2 mx			1	Brighton	16 Aug
	9:16.2 +e			2m	London (BP)	25 Jun
(10)						
9:12.64	Bev Hartigan		10.06.67	2	Manchester	14 Jun
9:13 +e	Birhan Dagne	U23	8.04.78	m	London (CP)	5 Aug
9:13.8	Sonia McGeorge	V35	2.11.64	1	Brighton	15 Jul
9:16.02	Bev Jenkins		6.02.70	3	Manchester	14 Jun
	9:17.12 mx			2	Stretford	25 Jul
9:16.12	Gillian Palmer	U23	30.12.80	4	Manchester	14 Jun
	9:16.31			2	Loughborough	21 May
	9:18.64			2	Liverpool	22 Jul
9:16.42	Jilly Ingman	U23	17.08.78	5	Manchester	14 Jun
9:16.89 i	Zahara Hyde Peters	V35	12.01.63	1	Birmingham	22 Jan
	9:38.1 mx				Solihull	19 Jul
	9:46.0			2	Basingstoke	11 Jun
9:17.42 mx	Joanne Colleran		1.09.72	3	Stretford	25 Jul
	9:21.26 i			2	Birmingham	22 Jan
	9:28.84			7	Brunswick, USA	1 Jul
9:18.59	Karen Hind	U23	31.01.79	6	Manchester	14 Jun
9:19.10	Tara Krzywicki		9.03.74	1	Solihull	29 Jul
(20)						
9:19.31	Lucy Wright		17.11.69	2	Stretford	23 Aug
	48 performances to 9:20.0 by 21 athletes including 5 indoors					
9:22.68 i	Sarah Bull		4.06.75	3	Birmingham	22 Jan
9:22.68	Dianne Henaghan		6.08.65	7	Manchester	14 Jun
9:23.9	Lucy Elliott		9.03.66	1	Watford	7 Jun
9:24.81	Michelle Mann/Brooks		6.02.77	2	Columbia, USA	19 May
9:25.01	Amy Waterlow	U23	29.07.78	4	Loughborough	21 May
9:25.2 imx	Sheila Fairweather		24.11.77	1	Glasgow	15 Nov
	9:29.98 i			3	Cardiff	12 Mar
9:25.38	Catherine Berry		8.10.75	3	Durham NC, USA	8 Apr
9:26.1	Andrea Green		14.12.68	1	Ashford	17 Sep
9:26.31 i	Katie Skorupska	U23	3.11.78	1	Cardiff	12 Mar
	9:34.6				Malakoff, FRA	16 May
(30)						
9:27.36 i	Emma Ford		16.02.77	2	Cardiff	12 Mar
	9:35.46 mx			3	Stretford	27 Jun
	9:42.39			13	Manchester	14 Jun
9:27.63	Emma Ward	U20	2.01.82	1	Solihull	27 May
9:27.75 i	Sarah Salmon		9.09.74	4	Birmingham	22 Jan
	9:48.91 mx				Sydney, AUS	29 Jul
9:28.68	Sharon Morris		5.07.68	8	Manchester	14 Jun
9:30.13	Jane Potter	U20	24.10.81	1	Bedford	27 Aug
9:30.66 mx	Caroline Walsh	U23	29.04.80	1	Watford	26 Jul
9:31.01	Michelle Wannell		12.07.67	1	Street	1 May

9:31.93	Heather Heasman/Knight	V35	27.09.63	9	Manchester	14	Jun
9:32.11	Collette Fagan	U20	6.06.82	3	Grosseto, ITA	7	Oct
9:32.38 i	Shirley Griffiths		23.06.72	5	Birmingham	22	Jan
	9:37.5			1	Cudworth	22	Jul
(40)							
9:32.73	Tanya Baker		23.11.74	5r3	Raleigh, USA	1	Apr
9:33.09 mx	Alison Wyeth	V35	26.05.64	5	Stretford	25	Jul
9:33.4	Debbie Gunning	V35	31.08.65	1	Eton	11	Jun
9:34.9 mx	Charlotte Dale	U17	23.03.84	1	London (Cr)	16	Jul
	9:35.25			1	Solihull	19	Aug
9:35.25	Henrietta Freeman	U20	12.07.83	3	Bedford	27	Aug
9:35.52	Courtney Birch	U17	5.10.84	1	Blackpool	15	Jul
9:36.2	Debbie Sullivan		24.01.72	1	Milton Keynes	2	Sep
9:36.5	Louise Damen	U20	12.10.82	1	Basingstoke	11	Jun
9:36.57 mx	Laura Carney		4.10.75	1	Stretford	25	Jul
9:36.98	Juliet Potter	U20	24.10.81	4	Bedford	27	Aug
(50)							
9:37.0 mx	Jo Wilkinson		2.05.73	1	Watford	30	Aug
	9:48.87			1	Bedford	30	Apr
9:37.54 i	Zoe Jelbert	U17	21.01.84	1	Birmingham	5	Feb
9:37.6	Sarah Simmons		12.01.75	1	Redruth	20	May
9:38.67	Ann MacPhail		3.05.70	12	Manchester	14	Jun
9:38.84	Sue Lamb		24.03.70	1	Solihull	5	Aug
9:41.3	Carolina Weatherill		13.05.68	2	Watford	28	Jun
9:41.83 mx	Jenny Heath		22.12.77	4	Stretford	27	Jun
9:42.3	Faye Fullerton	U17	31.05.84	1	Erith	7	May
9:42.52	Ann-Marie Hutchinson		21.08.77	3	Bath	16	Sep
9:43.4	Penny Thackray		18.08.74	1	Sheffield	15	Apr
(60)							
9:44.54	Kerry Smithson		13.09.76	1	Eton	6	May
9:44.65	Susan Harrison		6.08.71	1	Ghent, BEL	8	Jul
9:44.74 mx	Beth Allott		9.02.77	1	Stretford	13	Jun
9:45.85	Sally Oldfield	U17	25.06.84	2	Blackpool	15	Jul
9:46.4	Sonia Thomas	U23	16.05.79	1	Jarrow	2	Aug
9:47.8	Louise Kelly	U23	20.09.80	1	Peterborough	13	May
9:48.07	Louise Brown	U23	6.05.78	14	Manchester	14	Jun
9:48.45	Catherine Dugdale		29.11.74	2	Street	1	May
9:48.97	Lisa Webb		9.10.65	3	Solihull	5	Aug
9:49.1 mx	Susan Miles	U20	1.11.81	3	Watford	30	Aug
	9:56.80			2	Enfield	29	Jul
(70)							
9:49.32	Ruth McKean		13.04.76	8	Loughborough	21	May
9:49.7	Louise Watson		13.12.71	2	London (Cr)	27	Aug
9:50.1	Charlotte Moore	U17	4.01.85	1	Watford	10	May
9:50.52	Julie O'Mara		11.02.76	15	Manchester	14	Jun
9:52.1	Clare Pauzers	V35	2.08.62	1	London (TB)	16	Aug
9:52.12 mx	Vicky Pincombe		19.06.73	7	Cardiff	5	Jul
9:52.4	Maria Sharp		8.12.73	1	Enfield	13	May
9:53.00 i	Christa Salt	V35	17.06.64	3	Ludwigshafen, GER	9	Jan
9:53.12 mx	Jenny Clague		6.08.73	2	Stretford	8	Aug
9:53.5	Sarah Bradbury	V35	25.02.63	1	London (ME)	24	Jun
(80)							
9:53.6	Meredith Pannett		13.06.71	1	Kingston	19	Mar
9:54.08 i	Lucy Doughty		1.05.71	2	Cardiff	4	Mar
9:54.3	Sue Aperghis		16.03.70	1	Eton	22	Aug
9:55.5	Lynn Williams		6.02.72	1	Horsham	9	Jul
9:55.53 mx	Grace Greenhalgh	U23	17.01.78	2r2	Watford	12	Jul
	9:58.55			3	Bedford	1	Jul
9:56.2	Hayley Parkinson-Ovens		5.12.75	1	Grangemouth	24	May
9:56.27 mx	Susie Rutherford	U23	26.02.79	3	Stretford	25	Jul
9:56.69	Helen Zenner	U20	15.08.82	1	Enfield	29	Jul

9:58.17	Sarah Davey	U23	13.10.78	8	Gainesville, USA	25	Mar
9:58.3	Rebecca Wade	U23	11.06.80	2	Philadelphia, USA	22	Apr
(90)							
9:58.6 mx	Chloe Wilkinson	U17	16.12.84	4	Watford	30	Aug
	10:04.5			1	Watford	10	Jun
9:58.7	Kerrie Nott		28.02.74	1	Hoo	15	Jul
9:58.89	Devina Manship-Jones		12.12.69	1	Hastings, NZL	4	Nov
9:58.9	Sue Reinsford		24.03.69	1	Luton	11	Jun
9:59.02	Helen Lawrence		3.12.76	2	Cudworth	20	Aug
9:59.8	Bronwen Cardy-Wise	V45	26.01.52	1	Redditch	30	Apr
9:59.9	Sarah Jones		1.01.75	1	Warrington	20	Jun

Additional Under 17 (1 - 7 above)

10:04.4	Jennifer Pereira	8.08.85	1	Portsmouth	12	Aug
10:05.6	Jessica Nugent	27.08.84	2	Watford	10	May
10:08.40	Kathryn Frost	21.02.84	1	Sandown IOW	25	Jul
(10)						
10:13.4	Sonia Clark	1.04.84	1	Wakefield	16	Jul
10:15.1	Freya Murray	20.09.83	1	Grangemouth	17	Jun
10:15.68	Laura Burgoine	28.01.85	7	Sheffield	8	Jul
10:23.6	Amie Booth	19.10.84	1	Watford	7	Jun
10:23.6	Eleanor Stevens	29.06.84	1	Sutton Coldfield	23	Jul
10:24.4	Genevieve Gardener	3.09.84	1	London (He)	15	Jul
10:25.2	Alexa Joel	19.09.83	2	London (TB)	15	Jul
10:25.26	Briony Curtis	25.03.85	3	Blackpool	15	Jul
10:25.85	Ruth Proctor	4.05.84	8	Stretford	8	Jul
10:25.96	Bryony Frost	21.02.84	3	Watford	2	Jul
(20)						
10:26.3	Lisa Knight	31.01.85	1	Coventry	21	May
10:26.8	Stacey Ward	16.01.85	2	London (TB)	21	May
10:27.08	Charlotte Wickham	21.06.85	1	Cleckheaton	27	May
10:27.42	Abigail Wilshire	24.02.84	7	Street	1	May
10:33.0 mx	Ruth Waller	6.03.84	1	Stretford	16	May
10:38.46	Louisa Chown	27.07.84	1	Watford	12	Jul
10:38.63mx	Liz Spencer	25.04.85	4	Stretford	8	Aug
10:40.7	Rebecca Sanders	15.07.85	1	Warley	11	Jun
10:41.9	Carolyn Boosey	11.10.84	1	Watford	15	Jul
10:42.30	Donna Daly	25.11.83	4	Cleckheaton	27	May

Foreign

9:22.51	*Giovanna Arici (ITA)*	*24.06.74*	*1*	*Turin, ITA*	*27*	*May*
9:31.9	*Stephanie Van Graan (RSA)*	*4.02.77*	*2*	*Watford*	*7*	*Jun*
9:36.51	*Kelley Wilder (USA)*	*30.07.71*	*11*	*Manchester*	*14*	*Jun*

5000 METRES

14:44.36	Paula Radcliffe	17.12.73	2	London (CP)	5	Aug
	15:05.48		1	Birmingham	13	Aug
	15:05.70 +		1m	Sydney, AUS	30	Sep
14:58.27	Joanne Pavey	20.09.73	12	Sydney, AUS	25	Sep
	15:08.82		2h1	Sydney, AUS	22	Sep
	15:18.51		10	London (CP)	5	Aug
	15:21.15		2	Birmingham	13	Aug
15:32.62	Andrea Whitcombe	8.06.71	2	London (BP)	25	Jun
	16:15.82		15h2	Sydney, AUS	22	Sep
15:36.27	Hayley Yelling	3.01.74	6	Gateshead	16	Jul
	15:42.93		4	London (BP)	25	Jun
	15:50.41		3	Birmingham	13	Aug
	15:59.53		14	London (CP)	5	Aug
	16:09.54		3	Solihull	19	Aug
	16:12.6 +e		5m	Watford	22	Jul

15:36.35	Birhan Dagne	U23	8.04.78	12	London (CP)	5 Aug
	16:12.2 +e			3	Watford	22 Jul
15:40.85	Sarah Young/Wilkinson		2.01.70	4	Stretford	11 Jul
	15:41.75			13	London (CP)	5 Aug
	16:12 +e			2m	Watford	22 Jul
15:42.22	Kathy Butler		22.10.73	4r2	Walnut, USA	14 Apr
	15:45.14			2	Long Beach, USA	18 Mar
15:48.50	Angela Newport		21.10.70	1	Solihull	19 Aug
	16:16.56			10	Birmingham	13 Aug
15:56.58	Gillian Palmer	U23	30.12.80	4	Birmingham	13 Aug
	16:08.54			2	Solihull	19 Aug
	16:19.17			1	Bedford	28 May
15:56.64	Amanda Parkinson		21.07.71	5	Stretford	11 Jul
(10)						
16:00.97	Catherine Berry		8.10.75	5	Birmingham	13 Aug
	16:18.07			8	Durham NC, USA	2 Jun
	16:19.44			14	Palo Alto, USA	5 May
	16:28.24			5r2	Raleigh, USA	31 Mar
16:01.96	Dianne Henaghan		6.08.65	6	Stretford	11 Jul
16:02.48	Tara Krzywicki		9.03.74	6	Birmingham	13 Aug
	16:10.95			4	Solihull	19 Aug
16:02.97	Lucy Wright		17.11.69	7	Birmingham	13 Aug
	16:08.49			7	Stretford	11 Jul
16:03.75	Liz Yelling		5.12.74	6	London (BP)	25 Jun
	16:15.38			9	Birmingham	13 Aug
	16:16 +e				Watford	22 Jul
16:05.80	Karen Hind	U23	31.01.79	8	London (BP)	25 Jun
16:07.51	Debbie Sullivan		24.01.72	8	Birmingham	13 Aug
16:10.25	Jilly Ingman	U23	17.08.78	9	London (BP)	25 Jun
16:21.39	Bev Jenkins		6.02.70	8	Stretford	11 Jul
	16:26.24			11	Birmingham	13 Aug
16:27.7	Andrea Green		14.12.68	1	Tonbridge	8 Aug
(20)						
16:28.81	Lucy Elliott		9.03.66	2	Dudelange, LUX	27 May
16:29.62	Sarah Bradbury	V35	25.02.63	2	Bedford	28 May
16:29.8	Hayley Haining		6.03.72	1	Glasgow (S)	29 Jul
	49 performances to 16:30.0 by 23 athletes					
16:32.13	Michelle Wannell		12.07.67	10	Stretford	11 Jul
16:32.33	Joanne Colleran		1.09.72	13	Birmingham	13 Aug
16:32.73	Susan Harrison		6.08.71	14	Birmingham	13 Aug
16:35.50	Michelle Mann/Brooks		6.02.77	7	Des Moines, USA	29 Apr
16:35.68	Penny Thackray		18.08.74	1	Glasgow (S)	8 Jul
16:36.71	Louise Watson		13.12.71	5	Solihull	19 Aug
16:37.09	Amy Waterlow	U23	29.07.78	15	Birmingham	13 Aug
(30)						
16:37.18	Henrietta Freeman	U20	12.07.83	6	Solihull	19 Aug
16:37.66	Ruth Brown	U23	9.04.80	3	Stoke-on-Trent	29 Apr
16:38.48	Sheila Fairweather		24.11.77	4	Stoke-on-Trent	29 Apr
16:40.37	Zahara Hyde Peters	V35	12.01.63	17	Birmingham	13 Aug
16:42.8	Louise Kelly	U23	20.09.80	2	Oxford	20 May
16:47.44	Collette Fagan	U20	6.06.82	1	Bath	16 Sep
16:47.54	Debbie Gunning		31.08.65	11	London (BP)	25 Jun
16:50.6	Katie Skorupska	U23	3.11.78		Levallois-Perret, FRA	19 Apr
16:52.67	Sarah Davey	U23	13.10.78	13r2	Raleigh, USA	31 Mar
16:55.91	Jo-Anne Newcombe	V35	20.02.65	2	Glasgow (S)	8 Jul
(40)						
17:08.62	Jo Wilkinson		2.05.73	12	London (BP)	25 Jun
17:08.7	Morag McDonnell		27.08.73	2	Glasgow	29 Jul
17:13.0	Jenny Clague		6.08.73	1	Peterborough	9 Jul
17:16.7	Allison Higgins		8.04.72	3	Glasgow	29 Jul
17:18.5	Ruth McKean		13.04.76	2	Peterborough	9 Jul

17:19.66	Julie O'Mara		11.02.76	3	Glasgow (S)	8	Jul
17:22.0	Chris Howard		9.11.70	2	Stretford	28	Jun
17:23.23	Kate Burge		15.10.72	2	Stoke-on-Trent	18	Jun
17:24.63	Lisa Webb		9.10.65	7	Bedford	28	May
17:25.69	Angie Joiner		14.02.69	4	Glasgow (S)	8	Jul
(50)							
17:25.96	Louise Brown	U23	6.05.78	13	Stretford	11	Jul
17:27.44	Clare Pauzers	V35	2.08.62	9	Bedford	28	May
17:28.57	Lisa Mawer		22.05.68	3	Grantham	18	Jun
17:30.1	Lisa Towns	U23	19.04.79	4	Glasgow (S)	29	Jul
17:30.46	Heather Heasman/Knight	V35	27.09.63	4	Grantham	18	Jun

Foreign

16:36.7	*Kelley Wilder (USA)*		*30.07.71*	*1*	*Oxford*	*20*	*May*

10000 METRES

30:26.97	Paula Radcliffe		17.12.73	4	Sydney, AUS	30	Sep
	32:34.73			6h2	Sydney, AUS	27	Sep
32:30.4	Birhan Dagne	U23	8.04.78	2	Watford	22	Jul
	33:35.15			8rB	Lisbon, POR	1	Apr
32:34.7	Sarah Young/Wilkinson		2.01.70	4	Watford	22	Jul
32:52.5	Hayley Yelling		3.01.74	5	Watford	22	Jul
33:07.9	Liz Yelling		5.12.74	8	Watford	22	Jul
	33:11.84			24	Lisbon, POR	1	Apr
33:10.89	Tara Krzywicki		9.03.74	23	Lisbon, POR	1	Apr
33:49.8	Bev Jenkins		6.02.70	9	Watford	22	Jul
	10 performances to 34:30.0 by 7 athletes						
34:30.9	Debbie Sullivan		24.01.72	10	Watford	22	Jul
34:37.3	Bronwen Cardy-Wise	V45	26.01.52	11	Watford	22	Jul
34:39.8 mx	Andrea Green		14.12.68	1	London (Cat)	14	Jun
(10)							
34:56.04	Sheila Fairweather		24.11.77	1	Stoke-on-Trent	1	May
35:05.85	Zahara Hyde Peters	V35	12.01.63	27	Walnut, USA	14	Apr
35:07.36	Sarah Davey	U23	13.10.78	4	Philadelphia, USA	27	Apr
35:21.9	Jo-Anne Newcombe	V35	20.02.65	12	Watford	22	Jul
35:45.7	Susan Harrison		6.08.71	14	Watford	22	Jul
35:57.15	Devina Manship-Jones		12.12.69	6	Melbourne, AUS	4	Dec
36:58.19	Alison Fletcher	V35	8.06.61	4	Jyvaskyla, FIN	8	Jul

Foreign

35:22.5	*Teresa Duffy (IRE)*		*6.07.69*	*13*	*Watford*	*22*	*Jul*

5 KILOMETRES ROAD

15:53	Sarah Young/Wilkinson		2.01.70	1	Timperley	10	May
16:00	Bev Hartigan		10.06.67	1	Stevenage	28	May
16:07	Angela Newport		21.10.70	1	Ringwood	5	Mar
16:10	Debra Curley		20.09.71	1	Chester	12	May
16:17	Kathy Butler		22.10.73	7	Providence, USA	17	Sep
16:25	Zahara Hyde Peters	V35	12.01.63	1	Cardiff	27	Jul
16:26	Catherine Berry		8.10.75	10	Providence, USA	17	Sep
16:30	Amy Waterlow	U23	29.07.78	2	Stevenage	28	May
16:30	Bronwen Cardy-Wise	V45	26.01.52	1	Gloucester	15	Jun
16:33	Lucy Wright		17.11.69	2	Bath	26	Mar
(10)							
16:35	Amanda Allen/Wright		14.07.68	2	Gloucester	15	Jun
16:37	Amanda Parkinson		21.07.71	1	Manchester	8	Apr
16:38	Dianne Henaghan		6.08.65	1	Washington	29	Mar
16:40	Jenny Heath		22.12.77	2	Chester	12	May
16:42	Lucy Elliott		9.03.66	1	Lisburn	22	Oct
16:44	Louise Damen	U20	12.10.82	1	Boscombe	20	Oct

16:45	Sarah Bentley		21.05.67	3	Timperley	10 May
16:47	Kim Fawke/Elliott		2.07.75	1	Birmingham	10 Aug
16:49	Sharon Hatch	V35	5.09.64	2	Lisburn	21 Oct
16:50	Sharon Murphy		31.03.76	3	Stevenage	28 May
	(20)					
16:50	Sue Reinsford		24.03.69	1	Luton	27 Aug
16:50	Marian Sutton	V35	7.10.63	1	Birmingham	29 Oct
16:51	Jane Riley		26.03.69	1	West Cheshire	25 Aug
16:52	Michelle Wannell		12.07.67	3	Bath	26 Mar
16:54	Bev Jenkins		6.02.70	2	Manchester	8 Apr
16:54	Amy Stiles		6.02.75	1	Winchester	20 Jul
16:55	Jude Craft		13.08.72	1	Charndon	19 Jul
16:56	Annie Emmerson		10.05.70	1	London (HP)	29 Dec
16:58	Sarah Salmon		9.09.74	4	Bath	26 Mar
16:58	Caroline Walsh	U23	29.04.80	3	Lisburn	22 Oct
	(30)					
16:59	Jayne Spark		16.09.70	1	Warrington	5 Jul
16:59	Meryl Dodd		12.04.69	1	Sunderland	19 Jul
16:59	Clare Martin		14.09.74	1	Telford	2 Aug
16:59	Wendy Jones	V35	10.03.62	1	Severn	17 Aug

5 MILES ROAD

25:04	Paula Radcliffe		17.12.73	1	Loughrea, IRE	15 Oct
	26:42 +			1m	South Shields	22 Oct
26:09	Liz Yelling		5.12.74	1	Ruislip	5 Mar
26:15	Amanda Allen/Wright		14.07.68	1	Wolverhampton	10 Dec
26:29	Sarah Young/Wilkinson		2.01.70	1	Alsager	6 Feb
26:29	Hayley Haining		6.03.72	6	Balmoral	22 Apr
26:44	Birhan Dagne	U23	8.04.78	2	Welwyn	24 Apr
	26:52			8	Balmoral	22 Apr
26:45	Hayley Yelling		3.01.74	7	Balmoral	22 Apr
26:51	Lucy Wright		17.11.69	2	Alsager	6 Feb
26:57	Sarah Bentley		21.05.67	3	Alsager	6 Feb
26:57	Lucy Elliott		9.03.66	3	Welwyn	24 Apr
	(10)					
27:09	Andrea Whitcombe		8.06.71	1	London (FP)	5 Mar
27:09	Bev Hartigan		10.06.67	10	Balmoral	22 Apr
27:14	Katie Skorupska	U23	3.11.78	11	Balmoral	22 Apr
27:21	Andrea Green		14.12.68	3	Loughrea, IRE	15 Oct
27:22	Sharon Morris		5.07.68	2	Ruislip	5 Mar
27:30	Kate Burge		15.10.72	1	Long Eaton	11 Jun
27:32	Michelle Wannell		12.07.67	6	Welwyn	24 Apr
27:34	Jilly Ingman	U23	17.08.78	13	Balmoral	22 Apr
27:34	Claire Naylor		18.04.71	2	Long Eaton	11 Jun
27:37	Tara Krzywicki		9.03.74	14	Balmoral	22 Apr
	(20)					
27:37	Sue Reinsford		24.03.69	1	Blisworth	18 Aug
27:45	Kim Fawke/Elliott		2.07.75	1	Coventry	23 Apr
27:46	Nikki Lee/Nealon		27.02.68	1	Corby	9 May
27:49	Gillian Palmer	U23	30.12.80	15	Balmoral	22 Apr
27:49	Lynne MacDougall	V35	18.02.65	2	Glasgow	12 Nov
27:50	Penny Thackray		18.08.74	1	Leeds	19 Nov
27:52	Ann MacPhail		3.05.70	16	Balmoral	22 Apr
27:54	Heather Heasman/Knight	V35	27.09.63	6	Alsager	6 Feb
27:55	Wendy Farrow		25.12.71	2	Wolverhampton	10 Dec
27:57	Lisa Mawer		22.05.68	7	Welwyn	24 Apr
	(30)					
27:58	Lindsay Cairns/McMahon		1.06.71	1	Irvine, USA	19 May

Foreign

27:50	*Teresa Duffy (IRE)*		*6.07.69*	*1*	*Navan*	*5 Jul*

10 KILOMETRES ROAD

32:50 +	Paula Radcliffe		17.12.73	1m	South Shields	22	Oct
	33:14 +			1m	Veracruz, MEX	12	Nov
32:55	Hayley Yelling		3.01.74	1	Poole	4	Jun
	33:05			1	Totton	9	Apr
33:10	Liz Yelling		5.12.74	2	Bradford	10	Sep
33:20	Sarah Young/Wilkinson		2.01.70	3	Bradford	10	Sep
	33:24			1	London (SP)	3	Sep
33:22	Lynne MacDougall	V35	18.02.65	1	Leeds	3	Dec
	33:51			1	Dewsbury	13	Feb
33:27	Birhan Dagne	U23	8.04.78	2	Swansea	24	Sep
	33:36			1	Belfast	16	Apr
	33:59			4	Ratingen, GER	2	Jan
33:31	Penny Thackray		18.08.74	2	Leeds	3	Dec
33:36	Marian Sutton	V35	7.10.63	9	Cape Elizabeth, USA	5	Aug
33:38	Hayley Haining		6.03.72	3	Leeds	3	Dec
	33:44			4	Glasgow	14	May
33:41	Andrea Green		14.12.68	3	Swansea	24	Sep
(10)							
33:43	Amanda Parkinson		21.07.71	1	Clitheroe	31	Dec
33:44	Lucy Elliott		9.03.66	1	Eastleigh	19	Mar
33:45	Bev Hartigan		10.06.67	4	Leeds	3	Dec
33:54	Susan Scott		26.09.77	1	Troon	10	May
33:59	Bev Jenkins		6.02.70	1	Stretford	5	Mar
	22 performances to 34:00 by 15 athletes						
34:10 +	Sue Reinsford		24.03.69	1m	Bristol	8	Oct
	34:11			2	Dewsbury	13	Feb
34:11	Kathy Butler		22.10.73	8	Chula Vista, USA	15	Oct
34:12	Karen Hind	U23	31.01.79	5	Leeds	3	Dec
34:13	Kate Burge		15.10.72	1	Chelmsley Wood	25	Jun
34:14	Jilly Ingman	U23	17.08.78	1	Swansea	26	Mar
(20)							
34:15	Amy Waterlow	U23	29.07.78	1	Warrington	20	Aug
34:18	Debbie Percival	V35	22.04.62	1	Brighton	19	Nov
34:18	Amanda Allen/Wright		14.07.68	1	Telford	17	Dec
34:20	Gillian Palmer	U23	30.12.80	5	Glasgow	14	May
34:21	Sarah Bradbury	V35	25.02.63	1	Yateley	5	Jul
34:22	Debra Curley		20.09.71	6	Bradford	10	Sep
34:25	Bronwen Cardy-Wise	V45	26.01.52	1	Newport	15	Jul
34:28	Devina Manship-Jones		12.12.69	3	Eastleigh	19	Mar
34:28	Sarah Bentley		21.05.67	2	Swansea	26	Mar
34:28	Angie Mudge		8.07.70	1	Alexandria	25	Jun
(30)							
34:30	Claire Naylor		18.04.71	1	Lichfield	26	Mar
34:32	Angela Newport		21.10.70	6	Leeds	3	Dec
34:34	Lisa Mawer		22.05.68	1	Leeds	30	Apr
34:35	Beth Allott		9.02.77	2	Manchester	5	Mar
34:38	Debra Robinson		31.01.68	7	Leeds	3	Dec
34:39	Pauline Powell		17.05.73	2	Clitheroe	31	Dec
34:40	Sheila Fairweather		24.11.77	1	Dumbarton	9	Jun
34:41	Nikki Lee/Nealon		27.02.68	1	Rothey	20	Jun
34:47	Jo Thompson	V40	30.10.58	3	Swansea	26	Mar
34:47	Susan Harrison		6.08.71	1	Milton Keynes	4	Jul
(40)							
34:49	Jenny Heath		22.12.77	4	Manchester	5	Mar
34:49	Ann MacPhail		3.05.70	4	Swansea	26	Mar
34:51	Michelle Wannell		12.07.67	4	Eastleigh	19	Mar
34:51	Heather Heasman/Knight	V35	27.09.63	5	Swansea	26	Mar
34:53	Trudi Thomson	V40	18.01.59	1	Grangemouth	13	Feb
34:55	Lucy Wright		17.11.69	1	Basingstoke	15	Oct

34:57	Cathy Newman	V35	12.02.62	1	Greenwich	5	Mar
34:59	Louise Damen	U20	12.10.82	1	Poole	26	Dec

Foreign

34:43	*Teresa Duffy (IRE)*		*6.07.69*	*4*	*Dublin, IRE*	*11*	*Jun*

10 MILES ROAD

51:41 +	Paula Radcliffe		17.12.73	1m	South Shields	22	Oct
54:52	Sue Reinsford		24.03.69	1	Chiswick	2	Apr
55:05	Marian Sutton	V35	7.10.63	3	Park Forest, USA	4	Sep
	55:33			10	Flint, USA	26	Aug
55:10 +	Liz Yelling		5.12.74	1	Stroud	22	Oct
55:57	Andrea Green		14.12.68	1	Erewash	20	Aug
56:22	Trudi Thomson	V40	18.01.59	2	Ballycotton, IRE	12	Mar
56:35	Angie Joiner		14.02.69	1	St. Albans	16	Jan
56:42	Cecilia Greasley	V40	23.01.58	1	Whitby Heath	9	Apr
56:49	Claire Naylor		18.04.71	1	Holme Pierrepoint	3	Jun
57:00	Bev Jenkins		6.02.70	3	Erewash	20	Aug
(10)							
57:01	Hayley Tullett		17.02.73	2	Portsmouth	26	Nov
57:03	Birhan Dagne	U23	8.04.78	3	Portsmouth	26	Nov
57:05	Andrea Whitcombe		8.06.71	1	Epsom	19	Nov
57:06	Debbie Percival	V35	22.04.62	4	Portsmouth	26	Nov
57:24	Susan Harrison		6.08.71	4	Erewash	20	Aug
57:37	Lynne MacDougall	V35	18.02.65	1	Carlisle	18	Nov
57:41	Kate Burge		15.10.72	1	Leyland	28	May
57:54	Sharon Dixon		22.04.68	1	Woking	5	Mar
57:56	Julie O'Mara		11.02.76	5	Erewash	20	Aug
58:01	Louise Watson		13.12.71	1	Twickenham	24	Sep
(20)							
58:08	Michelle Wannell		12.07.67	5	Ballycotton, IRE	12	Mar
58:10	Jo-Anne Newcombe	V35	20.02.65	6	Erewash	20	Aug
58:15	Heather Heasman/Knight	V35	27.09.63	1	Pocklington	20	Feb
58:15	Vicky Pincombe		19.06.73	7	Portsmouth	26	Nov
58:18	Julie Briggs		13.03.69	2	Woking	5	Mar
58:20	Annie Emmerson		10.05.70	2	Twickenham	24	Sep
58:22	Louise Copp	V35	13.09.63	1	Newport	27	May
58:22	Beth Allott		9.02.77	7	Erewash	20	Aug
58:26	Angela Allen		23.09.67	3	Woking	5	Mar
58:27	Jo Wilkinson		2.05.73	2	Welwyn	3	Sep
(30)							
58:39	Bernadette Walters	V35	15.02.63	2	Newport	27	May
58:50	Frances Gill	V40	13.01.60	3	Newport	27	May
58:55	Alison Wyeth	V35	26.05.64	8	Erewash	20	Aug

Downhill

56:16	Sandra Branney	V45	30.04.54	1	Motherwell	9	Apr
56:47	Marlene Gemmell		21.06.72	2	Motherwell	9	Apr
57:52	Claire Couper		11.03.75	3	Motherwell	9	Apr

Foreign

55:56	*Teresa Duffy (IRE)*		*6.07.69*	*1*	*Ballycotton, IRE*	*12*	*Mar*

HALF MARATHON

1:07:07	Paula Radcliffe		17.12.73	1	South Shields	22	Oct
	1:09:07			1	Veracruz, MEX	12	Nov
1:12:31	Liz Yelling		5.12.74	1	Stroud	22	Oct
1:13:28	Andrea Green		14.12.68	1	Bristol	8	Oct
1:13:40	Beth Allott		9.02.77	1	Wilmslow	26	Mar
1:14:21	Sue Reinsford		24.03.69	2	Bristol	8	Oct
	1:14:52			6	Glasgow	20	Aug

1:14:23	Birhan Dagne	U23	8.04.78	1	Reading	12 Mar
	1:14:29			5	South Shields	22 Oct
1:14:33	Sarah Young/Wilkinson		2.01.70	1	Manchester	24 Sep
1:14:50	Lynne MacDougall	V35	18.02.65	3	Reading	12 Mar
1:15:14	Angie Joiner		14.02.69	4	Reading	12 Mar
1:15:35	Kate Burge		15.10.72	2	Wilmslow	26 Mar
	(10)					
1:15:45	Louise Watson		13.12.71	7	South Shields	22 Oct
1:15:49	Vicky Pincombe		19.06.73	4	Bristol	8 Oct
1:15:52	Annie Emmerson		10.05.70	1	Wokingham	13 Feb
1:15:55	Helen Purdy		5.10.75	1	Bath	19 Mar
1:16:07	Michaela McCallum		2.06.66	2	Dolo, ITA	9 Apr
1:16:15	Michelle Dillon		24.05.73	2	Stroud	22 Oct
1:16:16	Sharon Dixon		22.04.68	5	Bristol	8 Oct
1:16:21	Jo-Anne Newcombe	V35	20.02.65	6	Bristol	8 Oct
1:16:26	Ann MacPhail		3.05.70	8	Glasgow	20 Aug
1:16:41	Claire Naylor		18.04.71	1	Worksop	29 Oct
	(20)					
1:16:47	Alison Wyeth	V35	26.05.64	16	Lisbon, POR	26 Mar
1:16:58	Jo Thompson	V40	30.10.58	3	Bath	19 Mar
1:17:02	Sally Goldsmith	V35	18.01.61	1	Verona, ITA	19 Mar
1:17:03	Angela Allen		23.09.67	2	Helsby	23 Jan
1:17:06	Marian Sutton	V35	7.10.63	5	San Diego, USA	13 Aug
1:17:20	Amy Stiles		6.02.75	9	South Shields	22 Oct
1:17:24	Debra Robinson		31.01.68	2	Worksop	29 Oct
1:17:25	Lynn Williams		6.02.72	8	Bristol	8 Oct
1:17:50	Cathy Newman	V35	12.02.62	1	Taunton	9 Apr
1:17:51	Frances Gill	V40	13.01.60	4	Bath	19 Mar
	(30)					
1:17:55	Ruth Pinkvance	V35	29.09.61	9	Bristol	8 Oct
1:18:02	Jackie Newton	V35	28.08.64	2	Helsby	23 Jan
1:18:04	Julie O'Mara		11.02.76	11	South Shields	22 Oct
1:18:16	Trudi Thomson	V40	18.01.59	1	Valladolid, SPA	14 May
1:18:21	Sue Dolan	V35	25.01.61	3	Wilmslow	26 Mar
1:18:24	Samantha Bretherwick		16.04.69	2	Lake Vyrnwy	17 Sep
1:18:25	Louise Copp	V35	13.09.63	5	Bath	19 Mar
1:18:25	Zahara Hyde Peters	V35	12.01.63	11	Bristol	8 Oct
1:18:29	Tracy Brindley		25.08.72	1	Clydebank	12 Mar
1:18:30	Tina Oldershaw		13.05.67	2	Paddock Wood	26 Mar
	(40)					
1:18:30	Chaanah Patton		22.02.72	12	South Shields	22 Oct

Foreign

1:14:51	*Teresa Duffy (IRE)*		*6.07.69*	*1*	*Omagh*	*1 Apr*

MARATHON

2:33:41	Sue Reinsford		24.03.69	3	Rotterdam, HOL	16 Apr
	2:36:57			13	Berlin, GER	10 Sep
2:34:33	Marian Sutton	V35	7.10.63	26	Sydney, AUS	24 Sep
2:38:32	Lynne MacDougall	V35	18.02.65	20	London	16 Apr
2:39:01	Alison Wyeth	V35	26.05.64	21	London	16 Apr
2:40:39	Trudi Thomson	V40	18.01.59	22	London	16 Apr
	2:45:35			6	Stockholm, SWE	3 Jun
	2:49:37			5	Dublin, IRE	30 Oct
2:40:51	Jo Lodge		6.01.68	23	London	16 Apr
2:42:25	Michaela McCallum		2.06.66	1	Copenhagen, DEN	21 May
	2:42:44			3	Padua, ITA	30 Apr
2:42:44	Shona Crombie/Hick		1.06.71	1	Manchester	8 Oct
2:43:54	Anne Buckley		20.06.67	1	Hamilton, NZL	1 Jan
2:44:07	Angie Joiner		14.02.69	24	London	16 Apr
	(10)					

2:45:10	Mandy Spink	V35	12.01.65	1	Nottingham	24	Sep
2:46:16	Jo-Anne Newcombe	V35	20.02.65	25	London	16	Apr
	2:46:42			2	Florence, ITA	26	Nov
2:46:30	Sharon Dixon		22.04.68	26	London	16	Apr
	2:49:54			6	Dublin, IRE	30	Oct
2:46:32	Sandra Branney	V45	30.04.54	23	Boston, USA	17	Apr
2:47:44	Kathy Charnock	V35	4.07.62	2	Manchester	8	Oct
2:47:48	Amy Stiles		6.02.75	3	Florence, ITA	26	Nov
2:47:49	Gillian Horovitz	V45	7.06.55	25	Boston, USA	17	Apr
	2:48:17			19	New York, USA	5	Nov
2:48:59	Lisa Knights		12.07.71	2	Glasgow	20	Aug
2:49:19	Louise Watson		13.12.71	27	London	16	Apr
2:49:43	Sue Dolan	V35	25.01.61	29	London	16	Apr
	27 performances to 2:50:00 by 20 athletes						
2:51:01	Aileen Brown	V35	29.07.65	24	Berlin, GER	10	Sep
2:51:18	Polly Rogers-Dixon		5.04.67	31	London	16	Apr
2:52:04	Jackie Hargreaves		30.07.65	33	London	16	Apr
2:52:07	Megan Clark		31.07.73	34	London	16	Apr
2:52:26	Debra Robinson		31.01.68	35	London	16	Apr
2:53:01	Gill O'Connor	V35	24.09.61	37	London	16	Apr
2:53:11	Louise Copp	V35	13.09.63	38	London	16	Apr
2:53:37	Samantha Bretherwick		16.04.69	3	Manchester	8	Oct
2:53:41	Jessica Draskay		8.09.77	30	London	16	Apr
2:53:47	Christine Double	V35	10.06.64	40	London	16	Apr
	(30)						
2:53:54	Angela Allen		23.09.67	4	Manchester	8	Oct
2:54:03	Sally Goldsmith	V35	18.01.61	1	Bovolone, ITA	26	Mar
2:54:21	Anne Roden	V50	9.10.46	36	Boston, USA	17	Apr
2:54:37	Katrina White		20.02.70	41	London	16	Apr
2:55:02	Zoe Lowe		7.07.65	42	London	16	Apr
2:56:27	Helen Maskrey		23.09.67	43	London	16	Apr
2:56:31	Alison Fletcher	V35	8.06.61	8	Venice, ITA	22	Oct
2:56:40	Teresa Scully	V35	1.10.61	44	London	16	Apr
2:56:48	Joanne McColgan		26.11.69	45	London	16	Apr
2:56:58	Jane Boulton	V40	2.04.56	46	London	16	Apr
	(40)						
2:57:06	Lisa Godding-Feltham		24.11.69	47	London	16	Apr
2:57:17	Clare Pauzers	V35	2.08.62	48	London	16	Apr
2:57:17	Adele Gerrard	V40	24.11.59	8	Dublin, IRE	30	Oct
2:57:34	Paula Craig		2.07.73	49	London	16	Apr
2:57:51	Rachel Weston		12.07.71	50	London	16	Apr
2:58:02	Nikki Haines		30.11.71	51	London	16	Apr
2:58:21	Lesley Whiley	V40	14.05.60	1	New Forest	10	Sep
2:58:25	Beverley Wilson		26.03.67	52	London	16	Apr
2:58:40	Helen Barber		13.12.67	5	Manchester	8	Oct
2:59:31	Sarah Campbell		31.10.74	3	Glasgow	20	Aug
	(50)						
2:59:47	Joy Noad	V40	10.07.59	1	Abingdon	22	Oct
3:00:00	Sarah Ing	V35	10.11.63	54	London	16	Apr
3:00:10	Libby Jones	V35	25.04.61	55	London	16	Apr
3:00:33	Ruth Kingsborough		25.10.67	3	Hamilton, NZL	1	Jan
3:00:44	Amanda Yorwerth		18.05.67	1	Leeds	14	May
3:00:53	Veronique Binglow		11.06.65	57	London	16	Apr
3:00:53	Andrea Paolillo	V35	22.06.64	43	Chicago, USA	22	Oct
3:01:01	Janice Moorekite	V40	1.05.57	58	London	16	Apr
3:01:24	Alison Vuagniaux	V35	31.05.60	59	London	16	Apr
3:01:25	Toni McIntosh	U23	26.11.79	4	Glasgow	20	Aug
	(60)						
3:01:46	Sue Martin-Clarke	V40	13.09.55	60	London	16	Apr
3:02:03	Suzanne Wood		22.04.65	61	London	16	Apr
3:02:04	Sue Becconsall	V40	13.06.59	1	Leyland	2	Jan

3:02:10	Vicki Perry	V40	25.11.57	62	London	16	Apr
3:02:29	Anne-Marie Richards	V35	15.01.61	64	London	16	Apr
3:02:36	Jane Lansdown		24.01.68	65	London	16	Apr
3:02:38	Elinor Rest		27.04.72	66	London	16	Apr
3:02:39	Lisa Vanska		8.10.66	67	London	16	Apr
3:02:47	Jenny Gray	V35	21.06.60	68	London	16	Apr
3:02:49	Emma Latto		16.01.69	69	London	16	Apr
	(70)						
3:02:50	Louise Rosindale	V40	30.11.55	70	London	16	Apr
3:03:03	Wendy Edwards	V35	17.07.61	71	London	16	Apr
3:03:06	Christine Naylor	V45	22.10.54	72	London	16	Apr
3:03:18	Barbara Harries	V40	27.02.58	73	London	16	Apr
3:03:23	Clare Aquilina	V40	5.03.60	74	London	16	Apr
3:03:24	Susanna Harrison	V35	25.01.63	75	London	16	Apr
3:03:52	Rachael Beck		12.08.69	76	London	16	Apr
3:04:03	Sandra Bower	V35	12.11.60	1	Luton	3	Dec
3:04:09	Jacky Tyler	V40	7.12.57	77	London	16	Apr
3:04:21	Kate Jenkins		26.03.74	1	Elgin	3	Sep
	(80)						
3:04:27	Marilyn Gradden	V35	26.01.61	78	London	16	Apr
3:04:33	Sue Cariss	V50	17.11.49	6	Manchester	8	Oct
3:04:41	Sheila Macpherson			5	Glasgow	20	Aug
3:04:45	Andrea Dennison	V35	22.04.63	2	Nottingham	24	Sep
3:04:46	Chris Howard		9.11.70	6	Glasgow	20	Aug
3:04:57	Judy Brown	V45	27.10.54	80	London	16	Apr
3:05:03	Tracy Owen	V35	29.04.64	81	London	16	Apr
3:05:03	Juliette Clark	V35	22.04.64	54	New York, USA	5	Nov
3:05:07	Kay Leigh	V35	3.12.60	82	London	16	Apr
3:05:17	Julia Myatt			7	Manchester	8	Oct
	(90)						
3:05:24	Holly May		23.09.77	83	London	16	Apr
3:05:27	Lindsay Gannon		29.08.66	11	Washington, USA	22	Oct
3:06:04	Wendy Rothenbaugh	V35	30.03.64	85	London	16	Apr
3:06:05	Zoe Hannam		26.11.68	2	Abingdon	22	Oct
3:06:07	Kath Kaiser	V45	24.08.51	57	New York, USA	5	Nov
3:06:24	Marion Rayner	V50	14.01.50	86	London	16	Apr
3:06:27	Elizabeth Lumber		10.08.66	87	London	16	Apr
3:06:28	Michelle Rideout		17.03.68	88	London	16	Apr
3:06:40	Sally Keigher		1.08.71	1	Sheffield	16	Apr
3:06:54	Michelle Birdsall		5.08.73	89	London	16	Apr
	(100)						
3:06:55	Ruth Whitehead		14.01.72	3	Nottingham	24	Sep
3:07:02	Victoria Barrett	V35	7.11.64	90	London	16	Apr

Foreign

2:37:36	*Teresa Duffy (IRE)*		*6.07.69*	*2*	*Dublin, IRE*	*30*	*Oct*

100 KILOMETRES - Road

9:00:15	Jackie Leak	V35	19.10.60	1	Edinburgh	9	Jul
9:04:29	Hilary Walker	V45	9.11.53	20	Winschoten, NED	9	Sep
	9:06:56					30	Apr
	9:31:09				Edinburgh	9	Jul
9:20:44	Victoria Musgrove	V40	6.09.56	2	Edinburgh	9	Jul
9:23:09	Carol Cadger	V45	14.09.50	3	Edinburgh	9	Jul
9:44:19	Sharon Gayter	V35	30.10.63	23	Winschoten, NED	9	Sep

24 HOURS - Road (km)

191.386	Sharon Gayter	V35	30.10.63		Apeldoorn, NED	3	Jun
177.100	Patricia Thwaites				Doncaster	28	May
176.285	Sandra Brown	V50	1.04.49		Doncaster	28	May
	176.036			14	Uden, HOL	22	Oct
156.171	Thelma Thevent-Smith			2	London (TB)	8	Oct

2000 METRES STEEPLECHASE (2'6" barriers)

6:36.02	Jayne Spark		16.09.70	1	Stretford	8 Aug
	6:47.30			1	Stretford	27 Jun
6:37.69	Tara Krzywicki		9.03.74	1	Gateshead	26 Aug
6:57.42	Clare Martin		14.09.74	2	Stretford	8 Aug
7:15.48	Jane Pidgeon	V35	23.01.64	3	Stretford	8 Aug
7:16.99	Paula Gowing	U23	31.05.78	2	Loughborough	21 May
7:31.65	Cicely Hall	U23	12.10.78	2	Gateshead	26 Aug
7:32.48	Sarah Jackson		14.12.77	3	Loughborough	21 May
7:36.24	Emma Hudson	V35	4.02.65	4	Stretford	8 Aug
7:42.06	Alison Hurford	V35	11.10.60	5	Stretford	8 Aug
7:43.55	Samantha Marshall	U17	26.08.85	1	Grangemouth	6 Sep
(10)						
7:48.60	Rebecca Lindsay	U23	20.11.80	3	Stoke-on-Trent	29 Apr

3' barriers

6:36.49	Tara Krzywicki		9.03.74	1	Loughborough	21 May

3000 METRES STEEPLECHASE

10:08.11	Tara Krzywicki		9.03.74	1	Stretford	5 Sep

60 METRES HURDLES - Indoors

7.99	Diane Allahgroon		21.02.75	1h3	Ghent, BEL	26 Feb
	8.04			5	Ghent, BEL	26 Feb
	8.05			3	Glasgow	5 Mar
	8.07			5h2	Lievin, FRA	13 Feb
	8.14			7	Birmingham	20 Feb
	8.20			5h1	Ghent, BEL	11 Feb
	8.24			1	Birmingham	30 Jan
	8.28			1h1	Birmingham	30 Jan
	8.34			1h1	Birmingham	15 Jan
	8.36			1	Sheffield	23 Jan
	8.37			1	Birmingham	15 Jan
	8.42			1	Birmingham	8 Jan
8.29	Melanie Wilkins		18.01.73	2	Birmingham	30 Jan
	8.29			1	Cardiff	26 Feb
	8.37			8	Birmingham	20 Feb
	8.38			5h2	Ghent, BEL	11 Feb
	8.49			1h3	Birmingham	15 Jan
	8.49			3	Birmingham	15 Jan
	8.50			2h1	Birmingham	30 Jan
8.40	Clova Court	V35	10.02.60	3	Birmingham	30 Jan
	8.47			1h3	Birmingham	30 Jan
8.42	Jacqui Agyepong		5.01.69	2	Birmingham	15 Jan
	8.43			2h1	Birmingham	15 Jan
8.43	Sarah Claxton	U23	23.09.79	1h2	Birmingham	30 Jan
	8.54			5	Birmingham	30 Jan
8.43	Julie Pratt	U23	20.03.79	4	Birmingham	30 Jan
	8.44			2h2	Birmingham	30 Jan
	8.54			4	Birmingham	15 Jan
	8.55			2h3	Birmingham	15 Jan
8.50	Danielle Freeman	U23	11.02.80	1P	Vittel, FRA	19 Mar
8.51	Kerry Jury		19.11.68	3h2	Birmingham	30 Jan
8.54	Bianca Liston	U23	28.05.78	1	Cardiff	12 Mar
8.55	Rachel King		11.05.76	2	Cardiff	26 Feb
(10)						
8.57	Clare Milborrow		10.01.77	3h1	Birmingham	15 Jan
	34 performances to 8.59 by 11 athletes					
8.62	Helen Worsey	U20	29.08.82	4r2	Neubrandenburg, GER	4 Mar
8.65	Tamsin Stephens	U23	2.08.80	1	Glasgow	23 Jan

8.65	Nicola Gautier	U23	21.03.78	3P	Vittel, FRA	19 Mar
8.73	Katy Sketchley		9.07.73	2	Glasgow	23 Jan
8.78	Kay Reynolds		15.09.67	1P	Bedford	15 Jan
8.78	Sarah Porter	U23	11.12.79	4	Cardiff	12 Mar
8.80	Sara McGreavy	U20	13.12.82	1	Birmingham	13 Feb
8.82	Anne Hollman		18.02.74	3P	Birmingham	23 Jan
8.82	Lowri Roberts	U20	9.10.81	2	Cardiff	12 Feb
	(20)					
8.82	Kelly Sotherton		13.11.76	1P	Cardiff	5 Mar
8.82	Claire Pearson	U23	23.09.78	5	Cardiff	12 Mar
8.83	Leanne Buxton	U23	27.05.78	4P	Birmingham	23 Jan
8.83	Lynne Fairweather	U23	15.01.80	1	Glasgow	14 Dec
8.84	Sarah Still		24.09.75	1P	Glasgow	12 Mar
8.85	Julie Hollman		16.02.77	5P	Birmingham	23 Jan
8.87	Zoe McKinnon	U20	8.09.81	2	Birmingham	5 Feb
8.87	Jackie Brett		5.07.65	2	Cardiff	4 Mar
8.88	Alyssa Fullelove	U20	16.09.81	1	Glasgow	20 Feb
8.88	Julia Bennett		26.03.70	P	Vittel, FRA	19 Mar
	(30)					
8.90	Ruth Dales	U23	29.10.80	7	Cardiff	12 Mar
8.92	Diana Bennett/Norman		14.06.74	6P	Birmingham	23 Jan
8.93	Grace Smith	U20	30.01.82	4	Birmingham	5 Feb
8.94	Lorna Silver		10.01.74	5h3	Birmingham	30 Jan
8.94	Katherine Livesey	U23	15.12.79	P	Ames, USA	26 Feb
8.96	Katherine Porter	U20	19.08.82	6	Birmingham	5 Feb
8.97	Natalie Murray		24.03.76	2	Sheffield	23 Jan

hand timing

8.5	Claxton	U23	(8.43i)	1	London (CP)	8 Jan

60 METRES HURDLES - Under 17 (2' 6" Barriers)

8.61	Symone Belle		12.11.84	1	Birmingham	5 Feb
8.69	Gemma Fergusson		20.08.84	1h2	Birmingham	5 Feb
8.74	Cathy Crawford		17.12.84	2	Cardiff	26 Feb
8.80	Justine Roach		21.12.84	1h1	Birmingham	12 Feb
8.99	Sarah Gallaway		14.11.84	3P	Glasgow	9 Dec
9.01	Melissa Harris		20.10.83	2	Birmingham	12 Feb
9.06	Catriona Pennet		10.10.83	5	Birmingham	5 Feb
9.07	Jenni Lloyd		12.05.84	3	Birmingham	12 Feb
9.08	Melanie Canning		19.05.85	3	Bedford	22 Jan
9.08	Chanelle Garnett		16.08.85	2h3	Birmingham	5 Feb
	(10)					
9.1	Gemma Bennett		4.01.84	1r2	London (CP)	5 Feb
9.15	Stacie Barnett		9.10.84	2h4	Birmingham	5 Feb
9.18	Lindsey Winter		19.03.84	3h1	Birmingham	5 Feb
9.19	Aisha Myton		3.01.84	4	Bedford	22 Jan
9.20	Sian Scott		20.03.84	3h4	Birmingham	5 Feb
9.22	Aileen Wilson		30.03.84	1P	Birmingham	22 Jan
9.29	Rebecca Mitchell		10.12.83	3	Glasgow	20 Feb

overage

8.83	Catriona Pennet	U20	10.10.83	1P	Glasgow	9 Dec
8.85	Lara Carty	U20	7.03.84	2P	Glasgow	9 Dec
9.23	Hannah Barnes	U20	2.06.84	6P	Glasgow	9 Dec
9.28	Helen Davies	U20	24.03.84	8P	Glasgow	9 Dec

Under 15

9.07	Amy Beighton		6.03.86	1	Birmingham	5 Feb

70 METRES HURDLES - Under 13

11.32	w 2.7	Joanne Baker	15.10.87	1r1	Birmingham	3	Sep
		11.5		1	Wigan	19	Mar
11.4		Faye Richold	24.10.87	1	Barking	10	Sep
11.50		Nafalya Francis	21.04.89	1	Tamworth	28	Aug
11.5		Jodie Bacon		1	Bebington	28	Aug
11.5		Joanna Kirby	26.10.87	2	Bebington	28	Aug
11.6		Clare Rogers	22.05.88	1	Bury St. Edmunds	20	Aug
11.7		Emily Bonnett	22.09.87	1	Crawley	21	May
11.7		Amy Harrats	9.10.87	1r1	Coatbridge	27	Aug
11.7		Stephanie Peaston		2r1	Coatbridge	27	Aug
		11.89 w 2.7		2r1	Birmingham	3	Sep
11.7		Natalie Doyle	5.01.89	1	Grangemouth	17	Sep
	(10)						
11.77		Ashley Austin	29.09.87	1	Inverness	9	Jul
11.8		Claire Alexander		2	Crawley	21	May
11.8		Kaylee Price		1	Walton	1	Jul
11.8		Clare Cooper		1	Perivale	23	Jul
11.8	-2.8	Hannah Olson	29.01.88	1r3	Kingston	30	Jul
11.8		Alison Bennett	12.04.88	1	Banbury	23	Sep

75 METRES HURDLES - Under 15

11.06	1.5	Jessica Ennis	28.01.86	1h1	Sheffield	30	Jul
11.06	0.6	Phyllis Agbo	16.12.85	1P1	Birmingham	17	Sep
11.1		Heather Jones	10.09.86	1	Sheffield	30	Jul
		11.19 1.5		2h1	Sheffield	30	Jul
11.18	1.5	Leah McGuire	30.01.87	1	Sheffield	8	Jul
11.20	1.2	Louise Hazel	6.10.85	2	London (He)	20	Aug
11.25	w 2.3	Maria Garavand	30.06.86	1r1	Birmingham	3	Sep
		11.5		1	King's Lynn	14	May
		11.77 -0.8		4h3	Sheffield	7	Jul
11.28	1.5	Emma Makin	12.10.85	2	Sheffield	8	Jul
11.3		Lisa McManus	3.01.86	1		10	Jun
		11.32 1.5		4	Sheffield	8	Jul
11.3		Katey Read	20.03.86	P	Cannock	25	Jun
		11.34 1.5		5	Sheffield	8	Jul
11.4	2.0	Amy Beighton	6.03.86	1r1	Peterborough	31	May
		11.61		1	Solihull	28	May
	(10)						
11.4		Samantha Day	8.02.86	1	Peterborough	23	Jul
		11.51 1.5		7	Sheffield	8	Jul
11.46	1.8	Louise Massingham	28.02.87	2	Watford	28	May
11.5		Carly Dean	14.10.85	1	London (He)	15	Jul
		11.51 1.5		8	Sheffield	8	Jul
11.5		Claire Sargent	11.03.86	1	Bromley	15	Jul
11.5		Nicola Robinson	16.04.86	2	Grantham	23	Jul
11.56	1.5	Gemma Werrett	15.03.86	5h1	Sheffield	30	Jul
11.60	1.5	Stacy Flint	18.10.85	6h1	Sheffield	30	Jul
11.6		Lucy Fisher	27.09.85	P	Cannock	25	Jun
11.6		Lois Rudkin	25.02.86	1	Wigan	2	Jul
11.6		Anna Conolly	19.04.86	7	Sheffield	30	Jul
		11.65 w 3.4		3h2	Sheffield	30	Jul
	(20)						
11.67	w 2.3	Pamela Paterson	26.10.85	3r1	Birmingham	3	Sep
		11.8		2	Coatbridge	16	Jul
11.68	w 3.4	Samantha Britton	12.09.86	5h2	Sheffield	30	Jul
		11.7		1	Barnsley	2	Jul
11.70	w 4.7	Hannah Mathieson	28.10.85	2	Inverness	9	Jul
		11.8		1	Coatbridge	16	Jul
11.73		Stephanie Madgett	22.02.87	h	Watford	28	May

11.75	0.8	Emma Perkins	4.09.85	P	Birmingham	17 Sep
11.75 w		Kelly Marshall	8.01.86	3	Inverness	9 Jul
		11.8		P	Rugby	25 Jun

80 METRES HURDLES - Under 17

11.18 w	2.2	Symone Belle	12.11.84	1	Sheffield	8 Jul
		11.20 0.2		1	Sheffield	30 Jul
11.3		Sian Scott	20.03.84	1	Bournemouth	12 Aug
		11.52 w 2.2		1	Birmingham	2 Sep
11.33		Gemma Fergusson	20.08.84	1	Gateshead	14 May
11.39 w	2.2	Hannah Elwiss	8.12.84	2	Sheffield	8 Jul
		11.58 1.3		2	Blackpool	15 Jul
11.4	1.5	Chanelle Garnett	16.08.85	2h2	Sheffield	30 Jul
		11.52 w 2.2		1H	Birmingham	16 Sep
		11.57 0.2		3	Sheffield	30 Jul
11.5		Justine Roach	21.12.84	1	Leicester	10 Jun
		11.78		1	Solihull	27 May
11.6 w	3.0	Holly Ferrier	13.07.84	2	Peterborough	31 May
		11.61 w 2.2		4	Sheffield	8 Jul
		11.77 -1.3		1h3	Sheffield	7 Jul
11.62 w	2.2	Gemma Bennett	4.01.84	5	Sheffield	8 Jul
		11.7		1	London (MF)	24 Jun
		11.81 -1.3		3h3	Sheffield	7 Jul
11.65 w	2.2	Lara Carty	7.03.84	2H	Birmingham	16 Sep
		11.8 -0.1		1	Chelmsford	14 May
		11.89 1.4		1h2	Watford	28 May
11.67 w	2.2	Sarah Allsopp	13.10.84	6	Sheffield	8 Jul
		11.82 0.2		6	Sheffield	30 Jul
	(10)					
11.7		Melanie Canning	19.05.85	2	Enfield	14 May
		11.74 w 2.7		3	Watford	28 May
		11.80 0.2		5	Sheffield	30 Jul
11.7 w	3.7	Catriona Pennet	10.10.83	1	Grangemouth	11 Jun
		11.8		1	Coatbridge	27 Aug
		11.84 0.9		2	Grangemouth	25 Jun
11.77	0.2	Jenni Molloy	23.09.83	4	Sheffield	30 Jul
11.8		Lindsey Winter	19.03.84	1	Exeter	10 Jun
		12.03 w 2.7		5	Watford	28 May
		12.07 -0.9		4h2	Sheffield	7 Jul
11.8		Rebecca Mitchell	10.12.83	1	Dublin (S), IRE	24 Jun
		11.94 1.3		4	Blackpool	15 Jul
11.81 w	2.2	Danielle Fawkes	11.08.85	8	Sheffield	8 Jul
		11.93 -0.9		1h2	Sheffield	7 Jul
11.9		Lucy Hunt	4.04.84	1	Cheltenham	10 Jun
11.9		Emily Parker	7.11.84	1	Carshalton	17 Jun
11.9		Joanne Erskine	28.05.85	5h2	Sheffield	30 Jul
		12.08 0.2		7	Sheffield	30 Jul
11.91 w	2.4	Laura Baxter	19.10.84	1	Cudworth	20 Aug
		12.03 0.0		1h1	Cudworth	20 Aug
	(20)					
11.92 w	2.7	Sarah Gallaway	14.11.84	4	Watford	28 May
		12.01 1.4		3h2	Watford	28 May
11.97	-1.4	Melissa Harris	20.10.83	3h1	Sheffield	7 Jul
11.99 w	2.4	Gemma Dooney	12.05.84	2	Cudworth	20 Aug
12.0		Katherine Dawson	22.03.85	1	Bromley	4 May
12.0		Leyna Hird	4.02.84	2	Exeter	13 May
12.0		Louise Toward	27.03.84	1	Lancaster	14 May
12.0		Rachel Leaver	4.09.84	2	London (ME)	24 Jun
12.0		Stacie Barnett	9.10.84	2	Peterborough	23 Jul
12.0		Clare Robinson	15.10.83	1	Ipswich	6 Aug

100 METRES HURDLES

13.11	1.1	Diane Allahgreen		21.02.75	5h4	Sydney, AUS	25	Sep
		13.15 -1.1			1	Dublin (S), IRE	29	Jul
		13.18 1.2			1	Enfield	6	Aug
		13.22 0.6			8q3	Sydney, AUS	25	Sep
		13.24 -2.1			1	Birmingham	12	Aug
		13.26 0.2			4h1	Leverkusen, GER	20	Aug
		13.30 0.0			1	Ljubljana, SLO	25	Jul
		13.30 -0.6			1h2	Birmingham	12	Aug
		13.36 -0.7			2	Riga, LAT	22	Jun
		13.36 -0.4			1rC	Lausanne, SWZ	5	Jul
		13.45 -1.2			4	Glasgow (S)	2	Jul
		13.46 1.5			4h1	St. Petersburg, RUS	18	Jun
		13.49 0.7			3	Karlstad, SWE	23	Aug
		13.63 -1.8			6	Tartu, EST	11	Jun
		13.63 -2.2			1	Budapest, HUN	22	Jul
13.13	1.6	Keri Maddox		4.07.72	1	Loughborough	21	May
		13.15 0.2			4	Gateshead	16	Jul
		13.24 -1.2			3	Glasgow (S)	2	Jul
		13.24 0.3			1	Glasgow (S)	8	Jul
		13.26 -1.6			1	Solihull	5	Aug
		13.52 -1.8			1	Stoke-on-Trent	18	Jun
13.13	1.0	Denise Lewis		27.08.72	1H3	Talence, FRA	29	Jul
		13.23 0.3			2H4	Sydney, AUS	23	Sep
		13.49 1.2			2	Dudelange, LUX	27	May
		13.56 0.3			2	Glasgow (S)	8	Jul
13.17	1.7	Melanie Wilkins		18.01.73	1	Brighton	18	Jun
		13.23 1.6			2	Loughborough	21	May
		13.28 0.8			1h1	Brighton	18	Jun
		13.32 0.9			1h3	Birmingham	12	Aug
		13.35 -2.1			2	Birmingham	12	Aug
		13.39 -1.6			2	Solihull	5	Aug
		13.42 0.0			1	Basel, SWZ	12	Jun
		13.42 0.6			4	Vittel, FRA	2	Sep
		13.45 1.6			1	Fullerton, USA	27	Apr
		13.47 0.1			5h2	Leverkusen, GER	20	Aug
		13.59 0.0			2h	Basel, SWZ	12	Jun
13.20	0.6	Natasha Danvers		19.09.77	2	Los Angeles (Ww), USA	6	May
		13.38 2.0			2h3	Austin, USA	21	Apr
		13.38 1.1			2	Bedford	19	Aug
		13.45 0.3			2	Los Angeles, USA	1	Apr
13.40	1.7	Julie Pratt	U23	20.03.79	2	Brighton	18	Jun
		13.41 0.9			1h2	Brighton	18	Jun
		13.43 1.1			1h1	Birmingham	12	Aug
		13.45 1.6			3	Loughborough	21	May
		13.49 -1.1			1	Getafe, SPA	9	Sep
		13.50 -0.4			1	Bedford	1	Jul
		13.56 -0.3			4	Liverpool	22	Jul
		13.57 -2.1			3	Birmingham	12	Aug
		13.58 1.2			2	Enfield	6	Aug
13.49	1.9	Liz Fairs		1.12.77	1	Loughborough	30	Jul
		13.57 1.1			2h1	Birmingham	12	Aug
13.51	-0.6	Rachel King		11.05.76	2h2	Birmingham	12	Aug
		13.56 0.1			3	Gava, SPA	28	May
		13.58 -2.1			4	Birmingham	12	Aug
13.52	1.9	Bianca Liston	U23	28.05.78	2	Loughborough	30	Jul
		13.58 -2.1			5	Birmingham	12	Aug
		13.63 1.3			1	Solihull	29	Jul
13.55	1.1	Clova Court	V40	10.02.60	3	Bedford	19	Aug
	(10)							

13.62	1.8	Danielle Freeman	U23	11.02.80	2H3	Arles, FRA	3 Jun
		59 performances to 13.64 by 11 athletes					
13.67	-0.3	Sarah Claxton	U23	23.09.79	5	Liverpool	22 Jul
13.89	0.2	Helen Worsey	U20	29.08.82	2	Bath	16 Sep
13.91	0.8	Clare Milborrow		10.01.77	3h1	Brighton	18 Jun
13.92	-0.3	Kerry Jury		19.11.68	1H3	Logrono, SPA	19 Aug
13.93	1.6	Tamsin Stephens	U23	2.08.80	5	Loughborough	21 May
13.94	1.7	Katy Sketchley		9.07.73	6	Brighton	18 Jun
14.01	1.9	Sara McGreavy	U20	13.12.82	5	Loughborough	30 Jul
14.04	0.5	Fiona Harrison	U20	30.11.81	1	Watford	2 Jul
14.13	1.1	Lorna Silver		10.01.74	4h1	Birmingham	12 Aug
	(20)						
14.15	1.6	Katherine Livesey	U23	15.12.79	1H	Columbia, USA	21 May
14.15	1.7	Kelly Sotherton		13.11.76	1H5	Arles, FRA	3 Jun
14.19	0.0	Nicola Gautier	U23	21.03.78	H	Schwyz/Ibach, SWZ	1 Jul
14.19	0.8	Anne Hollman		18.02.74	1H1	Stoke-on-Trent	29 Jul
14.23	1.1	Alyssa Fullelove	U20	16.09.81	2h1	Bedford	27 Aug
14.25	1.0	Lauren McLoughlin	U20	8.09.82	2	Edinburgh	13 Aug
14.47	1.9	Lowri Roberts	U20	9.10.81	8	Loughborough	30 Jul
14.54	0.8	Diana Bennett/Norman		14.06.74	2H6	Arles, FRA	3 Jun
14.54	0.8	Samantha Male		11.04.76	5h1	Brighton	18 Jun
14.55		Sara Todd	U23	3.11.79	1	Gateshead	22 Jul
	(30)						
14.55	-0.3	Julie Hollman		16.02.77	5H3	Logrono, SPA	20 Aug
14.55	1.9	Kate Brewington	U20	15.10.81	1H3	Waterford, IRE	2 Sep
14.56	-1.5	Leanne Buxton	U23	27.05.78	5	Stoke-on-Trent	1 May
14.56	1.3	Katherine Porter	U20	19.08.82	1	Watford	28 May
14.56	-0.4	Claire Pearson	U23	23.09.78	5	Bedford	1 Jul
14.57	0.8	Liz Patrick		29.08.77	6h1	Brighton	18 Jun
14.58	-1.5	Sarah Porter	U23	11.12.79	6	Stoke-on-Trent	1 May
14.60	-1.8	Grace Smith	U20	30.01.82	1	Birmingham	10 Sep
14.67	1.7	Julia Bennett		26.03.70	3H5	Arles, FRA	3 Jun
14.74	1.1	Paula Hendriks	U20	25.01.83	4H1	Val de Reuil, FRA	12 Aug
	(40)						
14.76	1.7	Kirsty Roger	U23	24.03.78	4H5	Arles, FRA	3 Jun
14.78	1.3	Charmaine Johnson	V35	4.06.63	1H7	Arles, FRA	3 Jun
14.80	1.7	Rebecca Jones	U20	17.01.83	5H5	Arles, FRA	3 Jun
14.83	0.7	Lara Carty	U17	7.03.84	1H2	Val de Reuil, FRA	12 May
14.86	-4.0	Katie Jones		4.01.77	2	Grantham	18 Jun
14.90	0.8	Sarah Still		24.09.75	5H1	Stoke-on-Trent	29 Jul
14.93	0.5	Hannah Stares	U23	13.11.78	1H1	Enfield	29 Jul
14.95	-1.0	Zoe McKinnon	U20	8.09.81	1	Crawley	13 May
14.95	0.9	Sharon Price		10.12.75	3	Ghent, BEL	8 Jul
14.96		Amy Teale	U20	30.12.82	2	Cleckheaton	27 May
	(50)						
14.99	1.6	Sian Polhill-Thomas	U20	4.06.83	1r2	Loughborough	30 Jul
15.00	1.6	Rebecca Foster		14.04.71	1H2	Hexham	21 May
15.02	1.1	Vicky Williams	U20	11.04.81	5h1	Bedford	27 Aug
15.05	1.2	Gillian Stewart	U23	21.01.80	5	Enfield	6 Aug
15.07	-2.0	Clare Wise		22.08.69	4	Portsmouth	13 May
15.08	0.5	Stefanie Pullinger	U20	3.04.83	5	Watford	2 Jul
15.09	-2.6	Belinda Samuels	U23	29.11.78	3h2	Stoke-on-Trent	30 Apr
15.09	0.7	Laura Turner	U20	12.08.82	3h1	Sheffield	7 Jul
15.11	0.7	Wendy Davidson	U20	14.10.82	2H	Stoke-on-Trent	29 Jul
15.14	1.9	Natalie Butler	U23	25.11.78	5h2	Brighton	18 Jun
	(60)						
15.15	1.6	Michala Gee		8.12.75	2H2	Hexham	20 May
15.15	1.6	Michelle Debono		1.05.72	2r2	Loughborough	30 Jul
15.16	-2.7	Sarah Richmond		6.01.73	2	Grangemouth	13 May
15.24		Rebecca Mitchell	U17	10.12.83	1	Belfast	8 Jul
15.27	-1.6	Emma Reid	U20	5.01.81	1h1	Grangemouth	25 Jun

15.28	0.8	Chloe Cozens	U23	9.04.80	6H6	Arles, FRA	3 Jun
15.28	0.7	Jemma Scott	U20	14.03.83	3H	Stoke-on-Trent	29 Jul
15.38	0.9	Orla Bermingham		7.10.75	6h2	Brighton	18 Jun
15.38	-1.4	Gemma Bennett	U17	4.01.84	3	Bedford	20 Aug

Wind Assisted

13.19	3.7	Natasha Danvers		(13.20)	7	Austin, USA	22 Apr
		13.23 3.3			1h1	Eugene, USA	20 May
		13.27 3.5			2	Eugene, USA	21 May
13.27	5.1	Wilkins		(13.17)	1h1	Bedford	28 May
		13.38 3.4			1	Bedford	28 May
13.28	3.3	Julie Pratt	U23	(13.40)	1r2	Bedford	11 Jun
13.58	3.3	Liston	U23	(13.52)	2r2	Bedford	11 Jun
		13.61 2.2			1h1	Loughborough	30 Jul
13.61	3.5	Clare Milborrow		(13.91)	1h2	Bedford	28 May
13.64	3.0	Allahgreen		(13.11)	2	Fana, NOR	27 Jun
		10 performances to 13.64 by 6 athletes					
13.76	2.5	Helen Worsey	U20	(13.89)	1	Bedford	27 Aug
13.78	2.9	Kerry Jury		(13.92)	4H2	Arles, FRA	3 Jun
13.88	2.5	Sara McGreavy	U20	(14.01)	2	Bedford	27 Aug
13.89	3.3	Tamsin Stephens	U23	(13.93)	5r2	Bedford	11 Jun
13.96	5.1	Leanne Buxton	U23	(14.56)	2h1	Bedford	28 May
13.96	3.5	Kay Reynolds		15.09.67	3h2	Bedford	28 May
14.07	3.4	Alyssa Fullelove	U20	(14.23)	3r1	Bedford	11 Jun
14.12	5.1	Anne Hollman		(14.19)	4h1	Bedford	28 May
14.14	2.9	Nicola Gautier	U23	(14.19)	6H2	Arles, FRA	3 Jun
14.14	2.5	Lauren McLoughlin	U20	(14.25)	3	Bedford	27 Aug
14.18	3.4	Claire Pearson	U23	(14.56)	4r1	Bedford	11 Jun
14.36	4.6	Samantha Male		(14.54)	3h3	Bedford	28 May
14.39	2.5	Grace Smith	U20	(14.60)	5	Bedford	27 Aug
14.40	2.2	Lowri Roberts	U20	(14.47)	4h1	Loughborough	30 Jul
14.48	3.0	Julie Hollman		(14.55)	2H5	Waterford, IRE	2 Sep
14.50	5.1	Belinda Samuels	U23	(15.09)	5h1	Bedford	28 May
14.65	3.5	Rebecca Jones	U20	(14.80)	5h2	Bedford	28 May
14.73	2.3	Sarah Still		(14.90)	1H4	Waterford, IRL	2 Sep
14.81	2.5	Vicky Williams	U20	(15.02)	8	Bedford	27 Aug
14.91	3.1	Stefanie Pullinger	U20	(15.08)	4	Sheffield	8 Jul
14.96	5.1	Joanne Suddes		27.01.77	6h1	Bedford	28 May
15.05	3.3	Jemma Scott	U20	(15.28)	1H2	Waterford, IRE	2 Sep
15.10	3.0	Chloe Cozens	U23	(15.28)	4H5	Waterford, IRE	2 Sep

Hand Timing

13.2	1.1	Maddox		(13.13)	1	Bedford	19 Aug
		13.5			1	Loughborough	24 May
13.4	1.1	Pratt	U23	(13.40)	1	Chelmsford	13 May
13.4		Bianca Liston	U23	(13.52)	1	London (He)	15 Jul
13.5		Jacqui Agyepong		5.01.69	2	London (He)	15 Jul
		5 performances to 13.5 by 4 athletes					
14.1	1.0	Jackie Brett	V35	5.07.65	1	Bedford	30 Jul
14.2		Sarah Porter	U23	(14.58)	1	Philadelphia, USA	22 Apr
14.2 w	2.5	Katie Jones		(14.86)	1	Cudworth	28 May
14.4		Kay Reynolds		(13.96w)	2	Guildford	29 Apr
14.5	1.1	Julie Hollman		(14.55)	3	Chelmsford	13 May
14.7		Zoe McKinnon	U20	(14.95)	2	Carshalton	29 Apr
14.7		Sarah Richmond		(15.16)	2	Coatbridge	21 May
14.7		Laura Turner	U20	(15.09)	1	Harrow	18 Jun
14.7	0.4	Gillian Stewart	U23	(15.05)	3	Cudworth	22 Jul

14.7		Donna-Louise Hutt		6.06.72	1	Rugby	22	Aug
14.8		Natalie Butler	U23	(15.14)	2	Kingston	20	May
14.8	-2.1	Susan Jones	U23	8.06.78	1	Rugby	9	Jul
14.8		Sharon Price		(14.95)	1	Wolverhampton	20	Aug
14.8 w	2.1	Elaine Donald		30.04.74	3	Glasgow (S)	30	Apr
14.9		Sian Polhill-Thomas	U20	(14.99)	1	Liverpool	15	Apr
14.9		Clare Wise		(15.07)	3	Carshalton	29	Apr
14.9		Marie Major		4.05.74	2	Bournemouth	20	May
14.9		Michala Gee		(15.15)	2	Rotherham	4	Jun
14.9	2.0	Joanne Suddes		(14.96w)	2	Grangemouth	11	Jun
14.9		Stefanie Pullinger	U20	(15.08)	1	Barking	24	Jun
14.9		Debbie Robson		12.07.76	2	Stoke-on-Trent	25	Jun
14.9	0.6	Emma Reid	U20	(15.27)	3	Glasgow (S)	29	Jul
14.9		Hannah Stares	U23	(14.93)	3	Wolverhampton	20	Aug
14.9		Gowry Retchakan/Hodge	V40	21.06.60	1	Hoo	2	Sep
15.0		Gemma Fergusson	U17	20.08.84	1	Cudworth	16	Apr
15.0	-1.3	Belinda Samuels	U23	(15.09)	1	Stoke-on-Trent	13	May
15.0		"Jay" Peet		4.12.71	2	Yate	25	Jun
15.0		Nusrat Ceesay	U20	18.03.81	3	London (He)	15	Jul
15.1	1.0	Wendy Laing	V35	29.12.62	2	Bedford	30	Jul
15.1		Justine Roach	U17	21.12.84	1	Loughborough	10	Sep
15.1 w	2.5	Jocelyn Harwood	V40	21.11.57	3	Cudworth	28	Aug
15.2		Rebecca Wright		20.12.77	3	Oxford	28	Jun
15.2		Ulrike Jones		1.03.73	1	Middlesbrough	1	Jul
15.2		Leyna Hird	U17	4.02.84	2	Oxford	15	Jul
15.2		Orla Bermingham		(15.38)	1	Basingstoke	2	Sep

Additional Under 17

15.3	Lucy Hunt	4.04.84	1	Worcester	16	Jul
15.5	Stacie Barnett	9.10.84	1	Luton	18	Jun
15.6	Rachel Brenton	18.01.85	1r2	Basingstoke	2	Sep
15.7	Jenni Molloy	23.09.83	1r2	Exeter	16	Jul

Foreign

14.22 A	*1.2*	*Vanessa Maganini (RSA)*	*U20*	*26.10.81*	*2*	*Pietersburg, RSA*	*15*	*Apr*
		14.40 1.9			*7*	*Loughborough*	*30*	*Jul*

300 METRES HURDLES - Under 17

42.6	Sian Scott	20.03.84	1	Bournemouth	10	Jun
	43.12		2	Sheffield	30	Jul
42.68	Gemma Dooney	12.05.84	1	Blackpool	15	Jul
43.32	Symone Belle	12.11.84	1	Watford	27	May
43.72	Jenni Molloy	23.09.83	3	Sheffield	30	Jul
43.73	Sarah Gallaway	14.11.84	3	Sheffield	8	Jul
43.82	Natalie Christmas	9.04.84	4	Sheffield	8	Jul
43.84	Natalie Kydd	27.06.84	4	Sheffield	30	Jul
44.28	Natalie Mills	29.05.85	1h2	Sheffield	7	Jul
44.3	Gemma Fergusson	20.08.84	2	Cleckheaton	21	May
44.41	Helen Davies	24.03.84	2	Grangemouth	5	Aug
(10)						
44.55	Justine Roach	21.12.84	1	Colwyn Bay	2	Sep
44.74	Emily Parker	7.11.84	2	Watford	27	May
45.02	Joanne Erskine	28.05.85	6	Sheffield	30	Jul
45.09	Georgina Roberts	9.07.84	6	Sheffield	8	Jul
45.30	Laura Raven	12.03.85	3h3	Sheffield	7	Jul
45.3	Rebecca Mitchell	10.12.83	1	Antrim	27	May
45.6	Chanelle Garnett	16.08.85	2	Bournemouth	12	Aug
45.7	Catriona Pennet	10.10.83	1	Aberdeen	2	Jul
	45.75		3	Grangemouth	17	Jun

45.8	Gemma Bennett	4.01.84	1	London (Nh)	2	Jul
45.90	Faith Cripps	23.09.83	5h3	Sheffield	7	Jul
(20)						
45.9	Mhairi Walker	20.01.84	2	Coatbridge	27	Aug
46.08	Rebecca Geary	2.05.84	2h1	Sheffield	7	Jul
46.08	Rebecca Moss	19.06.84	3h1	Sheffield	7	Jul
46.1	Lynsey Harley	2.04.85	1	Pitreavie	14	Apr
	46.87		4	Grangemouth	17	Jun
46.2	Leyna Hird	4.02.84	2	Exeter	24	Jun
	46.83		4h1	Sheffield	7	Jul
46.3	Natalie Strain	31.01.84	2	Antrim	27	May
46.3	Gemma Tune	28.02.84	1	London (CP)	2	Jul
46.32	Angela Shearer	18.01.85	3	Grangemouth	25	Jun
46.38	Stephanie Little	18.10.83	4h2	Sheffield	30	Jul
46.40	Anwen Rees	14.07.85	7	Blackpool	15	Jul
(30)						
46.4	Sian Davies	16.02.85	1r2	Coventry	21	May
	46.58		4h2	Sheffield	7	Jul
46.5	Sarah Calcott	29.06.84	2r2	Coventry	21	May
	46.93		5h1	Sheffield	7	Jul
46.55	Claire Webber	13.12.83	4	Grangemouth	25	Jun
46.6	Laura Flegg	7.11.83	1	Exeter	13	May
46.6	Mieke Howell	6.10.84	1	Crawley	10	Jun
46.61	Charlotte Martin	12.08.85	5h2	Sheffield	7	Jul

Senior mixed race

40.58	Sinead Dudgeon	9.07.76	1	Gold Coast (S), AUS	15	Sep
40.90	Keri Maddox	4.07.72	3	Gold Coast (S), AUS	15	Sep

400 METRES HURDLES

54.95	Natasha Danvers	19.09.77	3s1	Sydney, AUS	25	Sep
	55.00		8	Sydney, AUS	27	Sep
	55.26		1	Durham NC, USA	2	Jun
	55.34		2	Birmingham	12	Aug
	55.62		4	London (CP)	5	Aug
	55.68		3h2	Sydney, AUS	24	Sep
	55.93		3	Budapest, HUN	22	Jul
	56.46		1	Eugene, USA	21	May
	56.58		5	Gateshead	28	Aug
	56.71		2	Walnut, USA	16	Apr
	56.88		1h2	Durham NC, USA	31	May
	56.91		7	Nice, FRA	8	Jul
	57.00		1	Los Angeles, USA	1	Apr
	57.32		1	Los Angeles (Ww), USA	6	May
	58.48		1h1	Eugene, USA	20	May
55.22	Keri Maddox	4.07.72	1	Birmingham	12	Aug
	55.46		3	Hania, GRE	14	Jun
	55.70		1	Riga, LAT	22	Jun
	56.04		4	Gateshead	28	Aug
	56.20		1	Bedford	4	Jun
	56.36		4	Gateshead	15	Jul
	57.35		1	Bedford	29	May
	57.44		5h5	Sydney, AUS	24	Sep
	57.62		2	Loughborough	21	May
	57.89		1h1	Bedford	29	May
55.45	Sinead Dudgeon	9.07.76	1	Budapest, HUN	22	Jul
	55.56		5	Nice, FRA	8	Jul
	55.74		3	Birmingham	12	Aug
	55.92		5	Hania, GRE	14	Jun
	56.60		7	London (CP)	5	Aug

(Dudgeon)	56.88			1	Loughborough	21 May
	57.02			2	Kalamata, GRE	4 Jun
	57.79			1	Bedford	11 Jun
	57.82			4h1	Sydney, AUS	24 Sep
57.92	Tracey Duncan	U23	16.05.79	2	Dublin (S), IRE	29 Jul
	58.22			4	Liverpool	22 Jul
	58.27			4	Birmingham	12 Aug
	58.43			1	Loughborough	30 Jul
58.3	Gowry Retchakan/Hodge	V40	21.06.60	1	Hoo	2 Sep
	39 performances to 58.5 by 5 athletes					
58.75	Katie Jones		4.01.77	3	Dublin (S), IRE	29 Jul
59.14	Jennie Matthews	V35	3.07.62	6	Birmingham	12 Aug
59.68	Nicola Sanders	U20	23.06.82	1	Bedford	27 Aug
60.08	Celia Brown		22.01.77	2	Dudelange, LUX	27 May
60.37	Rachael Kay	U23	8.09.80	2	Bedford	1 Jul
	(10)					
60.61	Clare Wise		22.08.69	2	Solihull	5 Aug
60.76	Anya Hutchinson		16.07.77	3	Stoke-on-Trent	30 Apr
60.85	Nusrat Ceesay	U20	18.03.81	4h2	Birmingham	11 Aug
60.86	Hannah Wood	U20	17.11.81	2	Bedford	27 Aug
60.9	Michele Gillham		8.10.74	1rB	Liverpool	7 May
61.17	Alison Currie		15.07.68	2	Eton	6 May
61.17	Donna Porazinski	U20	28.01.81	1	Cwmbran	17 Jun
61.38	Rebecca Wright		20.12.77	3	Solihull	5 Aug
61.60	Kate Williams		10.11.77	5h1	Birmingham	11 Aug
62.0	Helen Thieme	U20	28.09.81	2	Liverpool	18 Jun
	62.62			1	Ljubljana, SLO	23 Sep
	(20)					
62.13	Cicely Hall	U23	12.10.78	1	Getafe, SPA	9 Sep
62.2	Anne Hollman		18.02.74	2	Liverpool	7 May
62.23	Leanne Buxton	U23	27.05.78	7	Bedford	4 Jun
62.3	Kim Heffernan		20.12.66	1	Portsmouth	12 Aug
62.40	Tamsin Stephens	U23	2.08.80	2r3	Loughborough	30 Jul
62.60	Emma Reid	U20	5.01.81	1	Grangemouth	25 Jun
62.70	Christine Amede	V35	7.08.63	4	Eton	6 May
62.7	Julia Bennett		26.03.70	3	Enfield	23 Jul
	62.77			1	Bedford	20 Aug
62.74	Claire Brason	U20	16.03.83	2	Watford	2 Jul
62.9	Hannah Stares	U23	13.11.78	1	Wolverhampton	20 Aug
	(30)					
63.07	Sara Todd	U23	3.11.79	4	Solihull	29 Jul
63.1	Susie Williams		2.06.77	1	Brighton	15 Jul
63.1	Gemma Dooney	U17	12.05.84	1	Dumfries	13 Aug
63.14	Judith Owen		20.06.71	1	Aldershot	28 Jun
63.15	Sian Scott	U17	20.03.84	5	Bath	16 Sep
63.18	Charlotte Randall	U23	10.05.80	2h2	Brighton	17 Jun
63.32	Wendy Davidson	U20	14.10.82	4	Edinburgh	13 Aug
63.35	Jo Mahony		22.10.76	1rB	Eton	6 May
63.5	Carey Easton	U23	16.11.79	1	Glasgow (S)	30 Apr
63.6	Sandra Leigh		26.02.66	3	Enfield	20 May
	(40)					
63.62	Sara McGreavy	U20	13.12.82	1	Solihull	28 May
63.73	Karen Lowe	U20	3.05.82	4	Sheffield	8 Jul
63.77	"Jay" Peet		4.12.71	4h1	Bedford	29 May
63.9	Claire Heafford	U20	9.07.81	2	Guildford	12 Aug
	63.95			4h1	Bedford	26 Aug
64.0	Tanya Wilkinson		1.04.70	3	Bedford	6 Aug
64.08	Danielle Codd	U23	17.02.79	2	Grantham	18 Jun
64.09	Katherine Livesey	U23	15.12.79	6	Los Angeles, USA	1 Apr
64.1	Louise Aylwin	U23	8.04.80	1	Walton	20 May
	65.96			5h1	Brighton	17 Jun

64.15	Niki Pocock	U23	9.05.79	5	Eton	6	May
64.3	Ruth Brereton	U20	26.06.81	1	Basingstoke	2	Sep
	65.07			4h3	Brighton	17	Jun
(50)							
64.4	Ruth Thompson		7.06.76	1	Bolton	11	Jun
64.4	Natalie Christmas	U17	9.04.84	1	Bromley	15	Jul
64.5	Sarah Smith		18.08.76	2rB	Liverpool	7	May
	64.85			3h3	Brighton	17	Jun
64.68	Kelly Weall	U23	30.11.78	5	Bedford	1	Jul
64.8	Samantha Watts	U20	13.10.81	1	Liverpool	10	Jun
	65.11			5	Sheffield	8	Jul
65.0	Jackie Noblet	U23	19.04.79	1	Lancaster	14	May
	65.42			4h1	Bedford	1	Jul
65.1	Helen Walker	U23	12.10.80	3rB	Liverpool	7	May
65.33	Kerry Mitchell	U20	23.06.81	4	Tullamore, IRE	23	Jul
65.41	Jacqueline Elliott	U23	13.09.78	3	Gateshead	14	May
65.46	Michelle Mcbride		19.06.68	1	Aldershot	21	Jun
(60)							
65.5	Heather Myers	V35	5.12.64	1rB	London (ME)	24	Jun
	65.63			5h3	Brighton	17	Jun
65.55	Natalie Strain	U17	31.01.84	5	Edinburgh	13	Aug
65.56	Dyanna Clarke	V40	27.02.58	3	Bedford	20	Aug
65.6	Elizabeth Fox	U23	13.02.80	2	Oxford	20	May
65.6	Lindsay Yellop	U23	18.08.78	1	Bury St. Edmunds	4	Jun
65.63	Sarah Beevers		18.11.76	5	Solihull	5	Aug
65.7	Kirsty Mayhead	U23	17.02.78	1	Kingston	20	May
65.87	Megan Freeth	U20	1.02.82	6	Edinburgh	13	Aug

Additional Under 17 (1 - 4 above)

66.2	Georgina Roberts		9.07.84	1	Cleckheaton	2	Jul
66.4	Kristy Wilson		2.08.84	4	Enfield	20	May
	67.64			3	London (He)	20	Aug
67.1	Jasmine Ronan		24.07.84	1	Deeside	23	Apr
67.5	Leyna Hird		4.02.84	2	Exeter	16	Jul
67.5	Sarah-Jane Pickett		24.10.84	1	Bournemouth	16	Jul
67.52	Rebecca Mitchell		10.12.83	3	Belfast	20	Aug
(10)							
67.87	Lisa Murphy		15.04.84	1r2	Birmingham	10	Sep

Foreign

58.12	*Mari Bjone (NOR)*		*11.09.70*	*2*	*Oslo, NOR*	*8*	*Jul*
61.07	*Michelle Carey (IRE)*	*U20*	*20.03.81*	*2*	*Dublin, IRE*	*20*	*Aug*
63.7	*Jeannette Vandenbulk (CAN)*		*14.03.77*	*1*	*Eton*	*11*	*Jun*
	64.09			*2*	*Crawley*	*14*	*May*
65.11	*Geraldine Finnegan (IRE)*		*14.10.65*	*1*	*Belfast*	*8*	*Jul*
65.50	*Catherine Bacon (NZL)*		*25.11.69*	*6*	*Eton*	*6*	*May*

HIGH JUMP

1.93	Susan Jones	U23	8.06.78	1	Vittel, FRA	2	Sep
	1.90			1	Liverpool	22	Jul
	1.89			1	Bedford	4	Jun
	1.89			2	Somosko, HUN	17	Jun
	1.89			1	Bedford	20	Aug
	1.88			1	Bedford	19	Aug
	1.87			1	Loughborough	21	May
	1.86			4	Birmingham	12	Aug
	1.86			2	Getafe, SPA	9	Sep
	1.85			1	Rugby	9	Jul
	1.85			6=	Malmo, SWE	7	Aug

1.93	Michelle Dunkley	U23	26.01.78	2	Vittel, FRA	2	Sep
	1.90			1	Enfield	6	Aug
	1.89			1	Bedford	1	Jul
	1.89			2	Birmingham	12	Aug
	1.89			1	Getafe, SPA	9	Sep
	1.85			1	Loughborough	30	Jul
	1.84			3=	Bedford	19	Aug
	1.83			1	Loughborough	14	Jun
1.89	Jo Jennings-Steele		20.09.69	1	Birmingham	12	Aug
	1.88			1	Glasgow (S)	2	Jul
	1.86			3	Gateshead	16	Jul
	1.85 i			3	Cardiff	13	Feb
	1.85			1	Corby	11	Jun
	1.85			2	Rugby	9	Jul
	1.85			5	Budapest, HUN	22	Jul
	1.85			2	Bedford	20	Aug
	1.85			3	Vittel, FRA	2	Sep
	1.84			3=	Bedford	19	Aug
	1.83 i			1	Cardiff	6	Feb
	1.83 i			3	Cardiff	26	Feb
1.88	Lee McConnell	U23	9.10.78	2	Bedford	19	Aug
	1.86			3	Birmingham	12	Aug
	1.84			2=	Loughborough	21	May
	1.84			1	Solihull	5	Aug
	1.83			1	Glasgow (S)	29	Jul
	1.83			3	Getafe, SPA	9	Sep
1.86 i	Dalia Mikneviciute		5.09.70	1	Birmingham	16	Jan
	1.86			3	Bedford	4	Jun
	1.85			2	Loughborough	30	Jul
	1.84			2=	Loughborough	21	May
	1.83 i			1	London (CP)	12	Feb
	1.83 i			1	Cardiff	26	Feb
	1.83			1	Enfield	23	Jul
1.85 i	Julia Bennett		26.03.70	1P	Birmingham	23	Jan
	1.83 i			2	Cardiff	26	Feb
	1.83 i			1P	Vittel, FRA	19	Mar
	1.83			1H	Arles, FRA	3	Jun
1.85 i	Julie Crane		26.09.76	2	Cardiff	13	Feb
	1.83 i			2	Cardiff	6	Feb
	1.82			1	Cwmbran	17	Jun
1.85	Debbie Marti		14.05.68	1	Brighton	17	Jun
	1.85			3	Glasgow (S)	2	Jul
	1.84			1	Luton	11	Jun
1.84	Denise Lewis		27.08.72	1H	Talence, FRA	29	Jul
1.83 i	Rebecca Jones	U20	17.01.83	1P	Neubrandenburg, GER	4	Mar
	1.83			1=H	Arles, FRA	3	Jun
	(10)						
1.83	Aileen Wilson	U17	30.03.84	1	Sheffield	8	Jul
	1.83			Q	Santiago, CHI	18	Oct
	58 performances to 1.83 by 11 athletes including 12 indoors						
1.82	Lea Haggett/Goodman		9.05.72	4	Bedford	11	Jun
1.81 i	Julie Peacock		19.08.70	1	Bedford	23	Jan
	1.65			10	Solihull	5	Aug
1.81	Hazel Melvin		19.11.73	2	Solihull	5	Aug
1.79	Kerry Jury		19.11.68	1H	Watford	23	Sep
1.78	Natasha Danvers		19.09.77	2	Los Angeles (Ww), USA	6	May
1.78	Julie Hollman		16.02.77	1H	Stoke-on-Trent	29	Jul
1.78	Stephanie Higham	U17	26.12.83	1	Sheffield	30	Jul
1.78	Gillian Black	U23	27.10.79	8	Birmingham	12	Aug
1.77	Claire Wright	U17	9.09.83	1	Liverpool	23	Jul

1.76	Chloe Cozens	U23	9.04.80	9	Bedford	11 Jun
1.75 i	Natalie Clark	U20	4.09.82	1	Birmingham	15 Jan
	1.75			1	Cleethorpes	23 Apr
1.75 i	Samantha Adamson	U20	27.03.82	2P	Neubrandenburg, GER	4 Mar
	1.75			1	Watford	10 Jun
1.75	Lindsey-Ann McDonnell	U23	13.08.79	1	Exeter	13 May
1.75	Sarah White	U23	25.12.80	1	Portsmouth	13 May
1.75	Gayle O'Connor	U23	24.08.79	1	Bolton	11 Jun
1.75	Lesley Buchanan	U20	25.11.81	1	Coatbridge	16 Jul
1.74	Cathy Young	U20	14.03.82	1	Norwich	17 Jun
1.73	Rachel Young	U20	15.05.83	2	Hull	13 May
1.73	Diana Bennett/Norman		14.06.74	1	Woodford	24 Jun
	(30)					
1.73	Ceri Stokoe	U20	19.04.82	1	Newport	16 Jul
1.72 i	Kelly Sotherton		13.11.76	1P	Cardiff	5 Mar
	1.70			2	Eton	6 May
1.72	Laura White	U23	5.09.79	1	Lancaster	14 May
1.72	Danielle Freeman	U23	11.02.80	13H	Schwyz/Ibach, SWZ	1 Jul
1.71 i	Judith Payne	U23	7.07.80	2=	Cardiff	12 Mar
	1.70			7	Bedford	19 Aug
1.71 i	Kirsty Roger	U23	24.03.78	1P	Glasgow	12 Mar
1.71	Jessica Ennis	U15	28.01.86	1	Cudworth	10 Jun
1.71	Alex Selwyn	U17	20.09.83	2	Sheffield	8 Jul
1.70 i	Natalia Norford	U20	29.09.82	5	Birmingham	8 Jan
	1.70			1	Bedford	29 Apr
1.70 i	Sophie McQueen	U20	3.12.81	2=	Sheffield	22 Jan
	1.70			3	Cleethorpes	23 Apr
	(40)					
1.70 i	Sonia Crawley	U17	7.12.83	3	Birmingham	6 Feb
	1.68			1	Leamington	13 May
1.70 i	Antonia Bemrose	U23	3.09.79	2	Cardiff	5 Mar
	1.65			2	Stoke-on-Trent	29 Apr
1.70	India Hadland	U17	7.01.85	2	Bracknell	30 Apr
1.70	Denise Gayle	U23	11.09.79	1	Enfield	13 May
1.70	Katherine Livesey	U23	15.12.79	3H	Columbia, USA	19 May
1.70	Becky Mawer	U17	31.01.84	1	Derby	18 Jun
1.70	Jenny Brown	V40	21.05.59	1	Jyvaskyla, FIN	12 Jul
1.70	Claire Dewsbury	U17	16.01.84	1	Eton	23 Jul
1.70	Tracy Joseph		29.11.69	2	Eton	23 Jul
1.70	Kathy Pritchett	U17	11.04.84	4	Sheffield	30 Jul
	(50)					
1.70	Natalie Hulse	U20	2.12.82	2	Stoke-on-Trent	6 Aug
1.70	Laura Redmond	U20	19.04.81	3=H	Val de Reuil, FRA	12 Aug
1.70	Hollie Lundgren	U15	10.10.85	1	London (He)	20 Aug
1.70	Fiona Harrison	U20	30.11.81	2H	Watford	23 Sep
1.68 i	Jemma Scott	U20	14.03.83	1=P	Glasgow	12 Mar
	1.65			2	Grangemouth	13 May
1.68 i	Wendy Davidson	U20	14.10.82	1=P	Glasgow	12 Mar
1.68 i	Nicola Gautier	U23	21.03.78	3=P	Vittel, FRA	19 Mar
1.68	Jennifer Glaysher	U20	3.05.83	2	Cudworth	16 Apr
1.68	Rachel Martin	U23	9.09.78	1	Stoke-on-Trent	29 Apr
1.68	Sharon Woolrich		1.05.76	1	Portsmouth	12 Aug
	(60)					
1.68	Rebecka Bell	U15	1.12.85	1	Great Yarmouth	13 Aug
1.68	Susannah Green	U20	5.12.81	1	Birmingham	10 Sep
1.68	Emma Perkins	U15	4.09.85	1P	Crawley	10 Sep
1.67 i	Anne Hollman		18.02.74	5P	Birmingham	22 Jan
	1.65			19H	Arles, FRA	3 Jun
1.67	Emma Morris	U15	21.02.86	2	Sheffield	7 Jul
1.66	Rachel Brenton	U17	18.01.85	1	Enfield	8 Apr
1.66	Claire Lidster	U20	26.10.81	1	Watford	28 May

1.66	Helen Cooper	U20	20.06.83	1	Derby	17 Jun
1.66	Vicki Allan	U15	31.12.85	1	Grangemouth	21 Jun
1.66	Helen Smith	U17	9.10.84	1	Basildon	1 Jul
	(70)					
1.66	Laura O'Sullivan	U20	30.07.82	6=	Sheffield	8 Jul
1.66	Sarah Still		24.09.75	3=H	Waterford, IRE	2 Sep
1.65 i	Danielle Parkinson	U20	2.09.81	5	Sheffield	22 Jan
	1.65			1H	Cannock	24 Jun
1.65 i	Jenny Reader		23.12.77	2=	Bedford	23 Jan
1.65 i	Hannah Keight	U17	22.06.85	5	Birmingham	6 Feb
	1.65			2	Leamington	13 May
1.65 i	Kerry Saunders		28.03.77	1	Birmingham	12 Feb
	1.65			1	Nuneaton	30 Apr
1.65 i	Claire Everett	U23	25.06.79	1	Birmingham	17 Feb
1.65 i	Catriona Christie	U17	26.04.85	1	Cardiff	26 Feb
1.65	Danielle Humphreys	U17	16.05.84	1	Telford	23 Apr
1.65	Laura Freeman	U23	22.04.78	3	Coventry	30 Apr
	(80)					
1.65	Sarah Humberstone	U20	6.07.81	4	Hull	13 May
1.65	Staci Stewart	U15	20.09.85	1	Grangemouth	14 May
1.65	Carmilla Carmichael	U23	1.12.79	2	Oxford	20 May
1.65	Sandra Alaneme	U15	7.01.86	1	Watford	28 May
1.65	Catherine Howe	U17	12.12.84	1	Basildon	10 Jun
1.65	Amy Clayton	U17	8.01.84	2	Derby	17 Jun
1.65	Mary Onianwa	U20	20.01.81	1	Andover	24 Jun
1.65	Ursula Fay		23.09.67	1	Belfast	8 Jul
1.65	Henrietta Paxton	U17	19.09.83	3	Exeter	16 Jul
1.65	Dawn Walker	U17	29.09.83	1	Stretford	6 Aug
	(90)					
1.65	Helen Brown	U17	27.12.84	1	London (He)	20 Aug
1.65	Stacy McGivern		14.12.76	1	King's Lynn	20 Aug
1.65 i	Phyllis Agbo	U17	16.12.85	2P	Glasgow	9 Dec
	(1.60	U15		P	Eton	25 Jun)

Additional Under 17 (1 - 20 above)

1.64	Danielle Clear	5.10.83	1	Norwich	17 Jun
1.64	Lara Carty	7.03.84	7=H	Val de Reuil, FRA	12 Aug
1.63 i	Olivia Ross-Hurst	10.12.83	2P	Birmingham	22 Jan
1.63	Jennie Woods	28.01.84	1	Liverpool	14 May
1.63	Elinor Carlisle	3.10.84	1=H	Yeovil	24 Jun
1.63	Catriona Forrest	25.08.84	1	Eton	17 Sep
1.62	Georgina Hayward	15.09.83	1	Crawley	20 May
1.62	Jodie Brockbank	1.10.84	2	Crawley	20 May
1.62	Charlotte Gonella	20.01.85	1	Ayr	15 Jun
1.62	Rachel Cannister	11.10.84	1	Nuneaton	17 Jun
	(30)				
1.62	Stephanie Dalton	8.02.84	1H	York	24 Jun

Additional Under 15 (1 - 9 above)

1.64	Carly Prangnell	4.03.86	1	Sandown IOW	16 Jul
1.62	Lucy Howes	27.06.86	1	Harrow	2 Sep
	(10)				
1.61	Sheena Robertson	8.01.87	1	Portsmouth	10 Jun
1.61	Sophie Upton	18.09.85	1	Derby	17 Jun
1.61	Caya Langlands	8.09.85	4	Sheffield	7 Jul
1.61	Layla Hawkins	3.09.86	P	Enfield	30 Jul
1.61	Montell Douglas	24.01.86	1	Birmingham	2 Sep
1.61	Rachel Culshaw	11.08.86	P	Birmingham	17 Sep
1.60 i	Jade Halket	5.05.86	2	Glasgow	30 Jan
1.60	Tanya Brook	20.02.87	1	Leeds	16 May
1.60	Lanre Atijosan	17.10.86	1	London (BP)	10 Jun

1.60	Sally Peake	8.02.86	1	Carmarthen	1 Jul
(20)					
1.60	Eleri George	25.02.86	2	Carmarthen	1 Jul
1.60	Rachel Spencer	19.08.86	2	Inverness	9 Jul
1.60	Elen Davies	24.04.86	2	Sheffield	29 Jul
1.60	Nadine Simpson	28.02.86	1	Guildford	12 Aug
1.60	Laura Pitts	9.01.86	1	Exeter	29 Aug
1.60	Lucy McManus	2.03.87	1	Kingston	9 Sep
1.60	Stephanie Pywell	12.06.87	1	Cudworth	9 Sep

Under 13

1.56	Natasha Speight	9.09.87	1	Nottingham	16 Apr
1.50	Jessica Horler	9.06.88	1	Cudworth	16 Jul
1.50	Rachel Hamilton	18.10.87	1	Eton	17 Sep
1.48	Lauren Barnes	24.09.87	1	Guildford	6 Aug
1.45	Hannah Weekes		1	Kingston	30 Jul
1.45	Hannah Olson	29.01.88	1	Guildford	12 Aug
1.44	Rachael MacKenzie	23.12.87	1	Inverness	10 Sep
1.43	Claire Linskill	12.01.88	1	Exeter	23 Jul
1.43	Isaura Collyer	21.10.87	1	Corby	30 Jul
1.43	A. Askew		1	Cleckheaton	3 Sep
(10)					
1.43	Dominique Blaize	3.10.87	2	Kingston	9 Sep
1.43	A. Grady		1	Cudworth	9 Sep

Foreign

1.75	*Niina Masalin (FIN)*	*3.01.77*	*5*	*Solihull*	*5 Aug*

POLE VAULT

4.35	Janine Whitlock	11.08.73	2=	Prague, CZE	5 Jun
	4.31 i		2	Birmingham	20 Feb
	4.30 i		3=	Stuttgart, GER	6 Feb
	4.30 i		Q	Ghent, BEL	25 Feb
	4.30 i		5	Ghent, BEL	27 Feb
	4.30		6	Linz, AUT	8 Aug
	4.30		5	Gold Coast (RB), AUS	17 Sep
	4.22 i		5	Stockholm, SWE	17 Feb
	4.21		3	Gateshead	28 Aug
	4.20 i		1	Birmingham	30 Jan
	4.20		12	Athens, GRE	28 Jun
	4.15 i		2	Halle, GER	26 Jan
	4.15		1	Bedford	11 Jun
	4.15		1	Bedford	19 Aug
	4.15		20Q	Sydney, AUS	23 Sep
	4.14 i		4=	Birmingham	24 Jun
	4.12 i		5	Budapest, HUN	4 Feb
	4.11 i		2	Vienna, AUT	1 Feb
	4.10 i		1	Birmingham	15 Jan
	4.10		2	Osaka, JPN	13 May
	4.10		5	Jena, GER	3 Jun
	4.10		4	Gateshead	15 Jul
	4.10		1	Birmingham	12 Aug
	4.01		1	Loughborough	21 May
	4.00 i		3	Cologne, GER	11 Jan
	4.00 i		1	Wakefield	19 Feb
	4.00		8=	Milan, ITA	7 Jun
	4.00		7=	Chemnitz, GER	22 Jul
	3.95		9	Nuremberg, GER	25 Jun
	3.90		1	Eton	6 May

4.20	Irie Hill			16.01.69	1	Stoke-on-Trent	6 Aug
	4.10				2	Munich, GER	2 Jul
	4.10 i				1	Cardiff	16 Aug
	4.02				2	Regensburg, GER	7 Jul
	4.01 i				1	Dortmund, GER	5 Mar
	4.00				2	Melbourne, AUS	10 Jan
	4.00				1	Melbourne, AUS	15 Jan
	4.00				3	Budapest, HUN	22 Jul
	4.00				2	Birmingham	12 Aug
	4.00				1	Cheltenham	17 Aug
	3.96 i				5=	Birmingham	20 Feb
	3.95 i				2	Birmingham	30 Jan
	3.90 i				1	Munich, GER	6 Feb
	3.90 i				1	Ewell	14 Feb
	3.90				1	Meilen, SWZ	24 Jun
	3.90				2	Loughborough	30 Jul
	3.90				1	Stretford	8 Aug
	3.80 iA				9	Reno, USA	21 Jan
	3.75 i				1	Birmingham	12 Feb
	3.75				1	Melbourne, AUS	9 Mar
	4.13 irr	(market place)			2	Jockgrim, GER	19 Jul
4.15	Rhian Clarke			19.04.77	1	Austin, USA	7 Apr
	4.11				1	Houston, USA	6 Jul
	4.00				2	Austin, USA	22 Apr
	4.00				7	Durham NC, USA	2 Jun
	4.00				1	Enfield	6 Aug
	3.97				2	Houston, USA	22 Jun
	3.92				1	Houston, USA	1 Apr
	3.91 i				1	Gainesville, USA	2 Mar
	3.90 i				10	Fayetteville, USA	10 Mar
	3.90				2	Houston, USA	6 May
	3.85 i				1	Houston, USA	5 Feb
	3.80				6	Budapest, HUN	22 Jul
	3.80				6	Birmingham	12 Aug
	3.77				10	Gothenburg, SWE	3 Aug
4.04	Lucy Webber			5.02.72	1	Horsham	15 Jul
	4.00 i				1	Bedford	22 Jan
	3.90				7	Azusa, USA	8 Apr
	3.90				1	Stoke-on-Trent	2 Aug
	3.82				8	Irvine, USA	7 May
	3.80				3	Bedford	11 Jun
	3.80				2	Enfield	6 Aug
	3.80				4=	Birmingham	12 Aug
4.00	Alison Davies		V35	6.04.61	3	Birmingham	12 Aug
	3.95				1	Bedford	29 May
	3.90				3	Eton	6 May
	3.80 i				2	Bedford	22 Jan
	3.80 i				3	Birmingham	30 Jan
	3.80				4	Bedford	11 Jun
	3.80				1	Ashford	9 Sep
3.90	Ellie Spain		U20	23.08.82	2	Eton	6 May
3.90	Tracey Bloomfield		U23	13.09.79	3	Bedford	4 Jun
	3.90				2	Bedford	11 Jun
	3.80				1	London (Cr)	13 May
	3.80				1	Guildford	24 Jun
	3.80				1	Bedford	1 Jul
	3.80				2	Liverpool	22 Jul
	3.80				1	Solihull	29 Jul
	3.80				4=	Birmingham	12 Aug
	3.80				1	London (Cr)	27 Aug

89 performances to 3.75 by 7 athletes including 27 indoors

3.71 A	Allie Murray-Jessee		13.01.67	2	El Paso, USA	15 Apr
	3.60			5	Tucson, USA	21 Apr
3.70	Emma Hornby		12.12.73	2	Stoke-on-Trent	18 Jun
3.70	Liz Hughes		9.06.77	1	Southend	29 Jul
	(10)					
3.65 i	Lindsay Hodges	U20	21.09.82	2	Birmingham	6 Feb
	3.40			1	Yeovil	29 Apr
3.60	Clare Ridgley		11.09.77	1	Peterborough	9 Jul
3.55	Gael Davies	U23	5.02.79	1	Wolverhampton	20 Aug
3.51	Fiona Harrison	U20	30.11.81	2	Alfaz del Pi, SPA	29 Apr
3.50	Nicole Green		28.01.77	6=	Papakura, NZL	26 Jan
3.50	Paula Wilson		20.11.69	1	Coventry	30 Apr
3.50	Larissa Lowe	V35	19.08.63	4	Leuven, BEL	17 Jun
3.50	Hilary Smith		28.02.76	1	Cheltenham	26 Jul
3.50	Linda Stanton		22.06.73	1	Gateshead	26 Aug
3.50	Helen Roscoe	U23	4.12.79	4	Getafe, SPA	9 Sep
	(20)					
3.45	Noelle Bradshaw	V35	18.12.63	1	Abingdon	2 Sep
3.41 i	Louise Gauld	U23	24.08.80	1	Grangemouth	2 Aug
	3.30			3	Nicosia, CYP	28 May
3.40	Ruth Anness	U23	3.10.78	1	Gateshead	22 Jul
3.40	Becky Ridgley	U23	26.02.80	1	Portsmouth	12 Aug
3.35	Kirsty Maguire	U20	5.07.83	1	Grangemouth	25 Jun
3.30 i	Laura Patterson	U20	31.01.81	1	Bedford	22 Jan
	3.30			1	Watford	28 May
3.30 i	Maria Newton		22.07.66	1	London (CP)	12 Feb
	3.30			1	Bromley	23 Apr
3.30	Eugenie Lewis		10.10.74	2	Bromley	29 Apr
3.30	Gillian Cooke	U20	3.10.82	5	Enfield	6 Aug
3.25 i	Anna Leyshon	U23	19.01.80	2	Cardiff	16 Aug
	3.20			1	Stoke-on-Trent	6 Aug
	(30)					
3.25 i	Catherine MacRae	U23	1.01.79	2	Eton	17 Dec
	3.20			2	Stoke-on-Trent	6 Aug
3.20	Kate Alexander		28.04.74	6	Eton	6 May
3.20	Kate Rowe	U23	13.09.78	2	Peterborough	14 May
3.20	Kate Dennison	U17	7.05.84	1	Blackpool	15 Jul
3.20	Janet Vousden		25.11.68	6	Enfield	6 Aug
3.20	Kath Callaghan	U23	11.04.80	1	Bournemouth	12 Aug
3.20	Helen Webb	U23	14.04.80	3	Tamworth	28 Aug
3.20	Natalie Olson	U15	9.05.86	5	Ashford	9 Sep
3.15	Caroline Nutt	U20	17.06.83	1	Hull	6 Aug
3.10	Donna Hunter	U20	9.10.81	1	Grangemouth	10 May
	(40)					
3.10	Dawn-Alice Wright		20.01.76	1	Corby	13 May
3.10	Jacqueline Marshall	U23	20.07.79	2	Coatbridge	27 Aug
3.10	Hannah Olson	U13	29.01.88	6=	Ashford	9 Sep
3.10	Caroline Smith	U20	31.07.83	1	Banbury	10 Sep
3.06	Sam Preston	U20	15.11.81	1	Cannock	9 Sep
3.05 i	Jayne Collins	U23	27.03.80	4	Birmingham	12 Feb
3.05	Amy Rennison	U20	15.06.83	3	Sheffield	7 Jul
3.05 i	Helen Carney	U23	27.03.79	3	Eton	17 Dec
	2.80			1	London (TB)	20 May
3.00	Emily Morris	U20	30.09.82	1	Grimsby	14 May
3.00	Zoe Parsons	U20	11.02.83	1	Reading	20 May
	(50)					
3.00	Zoe Brown	U17	15.09.83	2	Blackpool	15 Jul
3.00	Kim Rothman	V35	6.09.64	4	London (He)	15 Jul
3.00	Kim Hobbs	U23	12.12.78	2	Gateshead	22 Jul
2.90 i	Buffy Beckingsale	U23	20.03.80	6	Cardiff	12 Mar
	2.70			1	Corby	11 Jun

2.90	Samantha Penney	U23	6.10.79	1	Crawley	13 May
2.90	Jo Hughes		7.02.71	1	Chelmsford	14 May
2.90	Nathalie Warren	U20	28.08.81	2	Walton	20 May
2.90	Jenny Cunnane/Wood	V40	23.02.57	1	Cleckheaton	11 Jun
2.90	Jemma Harding	U23	15.02.79	1	Watford	14 Jun
2.90	Judy Turton	U17	26.05.84	3	Blackpool	15 Jul
	(60)					
2.90	Carys Holloway	U20	23.07.82	1	Connah's Quay	19 Aug
2.90	Leasa Williams	U17	10.05.84	8	Ashford	9 Sep
2.90 i	Kim Skinner	U13	21.09.87	1	Grangemouth	10 Dec
	2.80			1	Grangemouth	24 May
2.85	Nikki Witton		30.09.72	4	Telford	9 Sep
2.80 i	Samantha Joseph		11.09.70	6=	Birmingham	15 Jan
2.80 i	Joanne Cozens	U23	9.04.80	6=	Birmingham	15 Jan
2.80 i	Julie Hynan	U23	23.05.80	10	Birmingham	15 Jan
	2.80			1	Macclesfield	14 May
2.80	Fiona Peake		31.05.77	1	Woking	29 Apr
2.80	Alison Lister	U23	18.06.80	5	Stoke-on-Trent	29 Apr
2.80	Rebecca Lumb		7.04.77	2	Cudworth	13 May
	(70)					
2.80	Tracy Morris		25.12.69	3	Leamington	14 May
2.80	Penny Hall		13.01.77	3	London (BP)	4 Jun
2.80	Tracey Hare	U20	9.03.82	1	Ashford	24 Jun
2.80	Michelle Ball	U20	9.05.83	7	Sheffield	7 Jul
2.80	Kate Williams	U17	10.05.84	2	Barking	16 Jul
2.80	Sarah Hartley	U20	4.05.81	1	Cleckheaton	13 Aug
2.80	Lindsey Johnson	U20	3.12.81	3	Cudworth	20 Aug
2.80	Debbie Martin	U23	30.11.79	2	Wolverhampton	20 Aug
2.75 i	Anna Watson	U20	30.04.82	4	Glasgow	23 Jan
	2.70			1	Inverness	14 May
2.75	Amie Everitt	U23	1.11.78	1	Worthing	12 Aug
	(80)					
2.70	Lorna Bayley	U17	6.07.85	1	Crawley	25 Mar
2.70	Helen Croskell		22.11.72	1	Ware	29 Apr
2.70	Sharon Beattie		26.11.72	2	Bath	9 Jul
2.70	Rachel Fairless	U20	19.03.82	7	Peterborough	9 Jul
2.70	Claire Holmes	U17	11.08.85	1	Stretford	11 Jul
2.70	Rebekah Telford		4.11.76	1	Stretford	11 Jul
2.70	Chissie Head	U23	18.12.79	4	Stoke-on-Trent	6 Aug
2.70	Katherine Lacey	U23	6.07.78	1	Loughborough	22 Aug
2.70	Jocelyn Hird	U17	3.12.83	1	Abingdon	2 Sep
2.70	Janet Lyon	V35	12.03.62	1	Aberdeen	9 Sep
	(90)					
2.70	Sara Nichols	U20	9.06.83	2	Watford	17 Sep
2.65	Jenny Cuthbertson	U17	11.06.84	1	Cudworth	20 Aug
2.60 i	Ann Wainwright	V45	26.10.54	1	Birmingham	26 Feb
	2.60			4	Ashford	7 May
2.60	Michelle McMahon	U20	29.08.83	2	Glasgow (S)	30 Apr
2.60	Cariann Cutts	U17	1.02.85	4	Cudworth	13 May
2.60	Lucy Newman	U20	2.03.83	1	Crawley	13 May
2.60	Susan Williams	U23	20.01.79	1	Deeside	13 May
2.60	Holly Cooper	U17	28.01.84	1	Eton	14 May
2.60	Karen Crooks		15.01.75	2	Cardiff	4 Jun
2.60	Lucy Howcroft	U20	23.04.82	1	Enfield	10 Jun
	(100)					
2.60	April Harwood	U20	11.09.82	1	Stafford	18 Jun
2.60	Tara Mooney	U17	1.10.84		Antrim	20 Jun
2.60	Gemma Dowsett	U17	3.02.84	2	Newport	16 Jul
2.60	Louise Hart	U20	27.05.83	2	Guildford	12 Aug
2.60	Julie Butterworth	U20	25.02.82	1	Hull	13 Aug
2.60	Kelly Scrambler	U23	21.11.79	4	Birmingham	20 Aug
2.60	Angie Nichols	U17	22.09.84	3	London (WF)	17 Sep

Additional Under 15 (1 above)

2.40	Catherine McGhee		11.09.85	2	London (He)	20 Aug
2.20	Nadine Simpson		28.02.86	3	London (He)	20 Aug

Additional Under 13 (1 - 2 above)

2.20	Nicola Hewitt		11.12.87	1	Hull	17 Sep

Foreign

3.10	*Shirley Buchanan (IRE)*		*20.01.73*	*6=*	*Ashford*	*9 Sep*

LONG JUMP

6.69	-0.4	Denise Lewis		27.08.72	1H	Talence, FRA	30 Jul
		6.56 w 2.8			1	Glasgow (S)	8 Jul
		6.48 0.8			3H	Sydney, AUS	24 Sep
		6.39 0.9			2	Amsterdam, HOL	15 Jul
6.59	0.1	Jo Wise		15.03.71	13Q	Sydney, AUS	27 Sep
		6.45 1.9			5	Budapest, HUN	22 Jul
		6.44 1.8			1	Birmingham	13 Aug
		6.39 w 3.7			7	Malmo, SWE	7 Aug
		6.36 -0.3			9	Monaco, MON	18 Aug
		6.21 1.0			*	Malmo, SWE	7 Aug
6.58	1.4	Jade Johnson	U23	7.06.80	1	Arles, FRA	4 Jun
		6.53 1.8			4	Budapest, HUN	22 Jul
		6.48 0.6			1	Bedford	1 Jul
		6.46 i			1	Birmingham	30 Jan
		6.36 w 2.2			3	Ljubljana, SLO	25 Jul
		6.35 0.7			1	Riga, LAT	22 Jun
		6.34 -0.4			2	Birmingham	13 Aug
		6.32 1.9			*	Ljubljana, SLO	25 Jul
		6.29 w 2.1			3	Falkoping, SWE	15 Aug
		6.24 i			3	Glasgow	5 Mar
6.51	1.3	Julie Hollman		16.02.77	1H	Waterford, IRE	3 Sep
		6.32 w			1	Rugby	23 Jul
		6.21 1.3			*	Rugby	23 Jul
6.45 w	2.2	Sarah Claxton	U23	23.09.79	1	Bedford	11 Jun
		6.44 1.7			1	Bedford	19 Aug
		6.41 w 3.5			7	London (CP)	5 Aug
		6.35 w?			1	Colchester	15 Jul
		6.27 1.2			2	Bedford	1 Jul
		6.26 1.3			4	Birmingham	13 Aug
		6.23 1.6			1	Getafe, SPA	9 Sep
		6.20 1.8			1	Bedford	29 May
6.45 w	2.4	Donita Benjamin		7.03.72	1	Eton	23 Jul
		6.28 w 2.4			3	Birmingham	13 Aug
		6.28 w 3.3			2	Bedford	19 Aug
		6.26 1.6			*	Bedford	19 Aug
		6.26 w 2.4			2	Glasgow (S)	8 Jul
		6.24 2.0			*	Eton	23 Jul
6.37 w	3.4	Tracy Joseph		29.11.69	2	Eton	23 Jul
		6.16			1	Portsmouth	14 May
6.32		Joyce Hepher	V35	11.02.64	1	London (Cr)	27 Aug
		6.25			1	Luton	11 Jun
		6.24			1	London (CP)	14 May
		6.24			1	Huntingdon	24 Jun
		6.21 1.3			7	Budapest, HUN	22 Jul
6.32 w	5.7	Ann Danson		4.05.71	1	Grantham	18 Jun
		6.31 w 2.2			2	Bedford	11 Jun
		6.23 w 4.0			3	Glasgow (S)	8 Jul
		6.21 i			2	Birmingham	30 Jan
		6.21 1.0			3	Bedford	19 Aug
		6.20 w 3.2			2	Rugby	23 Jul

6.24 w	3.1	Kelly Sotherton		13.11.76	1	Cudworth	22 Jul
		6.09 1.5			1	Stoke-on-Trent	18 Jun
50 performances to 6.20 by 10 athletes including 3 indoors and 18 wind assisted							
6.19	-0.3	Kim Rothman	V35	6.09.64	1	Biella, ITA	9 Sep
6.15	0.7	Zainab Ceesay	U17	27.10.83	1	Bedford	20 Aug
6.12		Andrea Coore		23.04.69	1	Peterborough	9 Jul
6.11		Symone Belle	U17	12.11.84	1	London (WF)	17 Sep
		6.07 1.2			2	Grosseto, ITA	7 Oct
6.06 w?		Jackie White/Spargo		12.01.71	3	Rugby	23 Jul
		6.03 2.0			*	Rugby	23 Jul
6.04		Julia Bennett		26.03.70	1	London (Cr)	14 May
6.02 w?		Joanna Trotman	U23	5.10.80	1	Hemel Hempstead	12 Aug
		5.65			5	London (Cr)	14 May
6.02	1.5	Fiona Westwood	U20	27.02.81	5	Bedford	19 Aug
6.02 w	3.9	Debbie Harrison	U23	13.11.78	3	Bedford	11 Jun
		5.85 1.9			5	Solihull	5 Aug
5.96 w	3.4	Anna-Maria Thorpe		15.07.71	1	Enfield	23 Jul
		5.94 1.6			2	Bedford	20 Aug
	(20)						
5.93 i		Ruth Irving		20.07.74	1	Jarrow	10 Dec
5.92		Rachel Hogg	U20	11.06.82	1	Carlisle	10 Jun
5.89	0.8	Syreena Pinel	U23	13.01.79	3	Eton	6 May
5.88		Lucy Atunumuo	U23	4.11.80	2	London (Cr)	14 May
5.88	-0.3	Danlelle Freeman	U23	11.02.80	14H	Arles, FRA	4 Jun
5.88 w	3.0	Fiona Harrison	U20	30.11.81	1	Sheffield	8 Jul
		5.75 0.5			2	Cleckheaton	27 May
5.87		Gemma Holt		20.12.72	1	Carshalton	29 Apr
5.87 w	5.0	Rebecca White	U23	5.06.80	3	Grantham	18 Jun
		5.85			1	Wakefield	16 Jul
5.83	0.9	Karlene Turner	U17	9.01.85	1	Sheffield	7 Jul
5.83 w	3.0	Elaine Smith	U20	16.05.83	2	Sheffield	8 Jul
		5.75 0.3			3	Bath	16 Sep
	(30)						
5.83 w		Nadia Williams	U20	17.11.81	1	Hayes	19 Jul
		5.70			1	Woodford	24 Jun
5.82 i		Sarah Still		24.09.75	1P	Glasgow	12 Mar
		5.73			1	Grangemouth	11 Jun
5.80	1.2	Sarah Wellstead	U23	22.10.79	4	Bedford	1 Jul
		5.80 w?			3	London (Cr)	14 May
5.80 w?		Lara Richards	U20	7.03.83	1	Cwmbran	18 Jun
		5.75 i			2	Cardiff	26 Feb
		5.75			2	Sarajevo, BSH	4 Jun
5.79 i		Kerry Jury		19.11.68	5	Birmingham	30 Jan
		5.78 w 4.0			5	Grantham	18 Jun
		5.71 0.1			5H	Logrono, SPA	20 Aug
5.76 w	3.1	Siobhan McVie	U17	6.07.84	1	Grangemouth	5 Aug
		5.67 0.6			*	Grangemouth	5 Aug
5.75 i		Emma Hughes	U23	15.09.80	2	Birmingham	9 Jan
		5.66 w 2.1			3	Stoke-on-Trent	30 Apr
		5.59 2.0			*	Stoke-on-Trent	30 Apr
5.75		Danielle Humphreys	U17	16.05.84	1	Stoke-on-Trent	13 Aug
5.74		Rosie Curling	U23	5.09.80	2	Oxford	28 Jun
5.74 w	4.1	Michala Gee		8.12.75	7	Grantham	18 Jun
		5.64			1	Lancaster	7 May
	(40)						
5.73		Sonia Crawley	U17	7.12.83	1	Solihull	28 May
5.73 w		Diana Bennett/Norman		14.06.74	1	London (TB)	15 Jul
		5.70 i			7	Birmingham	30 Jan
		5.57 -0.3			30H	Arles, FRA	4 Jun
5.72 w?		Janine Whitlock		11.08.73	4	Eton	23 Jul
		5.71 1.6			6	Glasgow	8 Jul

5.71		Chanelle Garnett	U17	16.08.85	2	Basingstoke	2 Sep
5.71 w	3.3	Ellie Darby	U15	20.12.85	1	Sheffield	8 Jul
		5.56			1	Stoke-on-Trent	13 May
5.70	0.4	Nicola Gautier	U23	21.03.78	21H	Arles, FRA	4 Jun
5.70	0.6	Kate Brewington	U20	15.10.81	4	Bedford	20 Aug
5.69 i		Sabrina Scott	U23	2.06.79	8	Birmingham	30 Jan
5.69		Katie Richardson	U20	12.09.82	1	Cleckheaton	11 Jun
5.69 w	2.8	Cathryn Dale		31.05.77	4	Stoke-on-Trent	18 Jun
		5.66			1	Rugby	9 Jul
	(50)						
5.68	1.5	Sarah Humphreys	U17	16.10.84	2	Sheffield	7 Jul
5.67	2.0	Henrietta Paxton	U17	19.09.83	3	Sheffield	7 Jul
5.66		Adele Forester		27.03.76	3	Liverpool	7 May
5.66 w	3.0	Rebecca Jones	U20	17.01.83	9	Bedford	29 May
		5.65 1.1			22H	Arles, FRA	4 Jun
5.66 w	3.7	Aimee Cutler	U20	7.10.81	2	Cwmbran	18 Jun
		5.57 i			1	Cardiff	19 Feb
		5.56 1.3			5	Bath	16 Sep
5.66 w	3.1	Lucy Butler	U20	18.11.81	5	Sheffield	8 Jul
		5.59			1	Hexham	10 Jun
5.65	0.9	Liz Patrick		29.08.77	7	Solihull	5 Aug
5.64		Gemma Jones	U23	25.02.79	2	Cwmbran	18 Jun
5.64	1.0	Amy Woodman	U17	1.11.84	5	Sheffield	7 Jul
5.64 w	3.1	Belinda Samuels	U23	29.11.78	4	Stoke-on-Trent	30 Apr
		5.61			1	Stoke-on-Trent	13 May
	(60)						
5.63 i		Vicky O'Brien	U20	15.11.82	2	Birmingham	5 Feb
5.63 i		Katherine Livesey	U23	15.12.79	P	Ames, USA	25 Feb
		5.51 -1.1			6H	Columbia, USA	20 May
5.63	0.3	Kirsty Roger	U23	24.03.78	23H	Arles, FRA	4 Jun
5.62		Stacy McGivern		14.12.76	1	Peterborough	28 Aug
5.61 w	5.4	Mary Devlin	U23	14.09.79	3	Tullamore, IRE	23 Jul
5.59	0.8	Jenny Kelly		20.06.70	27H	Arles, FRA	4 Jun
5.59		Kate Evans		4.02.74	2	Rugby	9 Jul
5.59		Monique Parris	U17	28.01.84	1	Oxford	15 Jul
5.58		Helen Armishaw	U23	4.10.80	1	Rotherham	4 Jun
5.58		Samantha Henderson	U17	27.09.83	1	Braintree	12 Aug
	(70)						
5.58 w	3.3	Paula Hendriks	U20	25.01.83	6	Sheffield	8 Jul
		5.53			1H	Rugby	25 Jun
5.57 w	3.8	Sarah Lane	U20	24.11.82	3	Cwmbran	18 Jun
5.56		Cara Roberts	U17	24.05.85	1	Bournemouth	10 Jun
5.55		Vicky Griffiths	U17	9.10.84	1	Liverpool	15 Apr
5.55	-0.2	Wendy Davidson	U20	14.10.82	1H	Stoke-on-Trent	30 Jul
5.54		Stacey Martin	U20	6.08.82	1	Neath	5 Apr
5.54		Mandy Crompton	U20	25.03.82	1	Cudworth	6 Aug
5.54	-0.5	Chloe Cozens	U23	9.04.80	2H	Watford	24 Sep
5.53		Laura Betts	U17	6.11.84	1	Bromley	23 Apr
5.52		Gemma Fergusson	U17	20.08.84	1	Hexham	10 Jun
	(80)						
5.52 w		Emily Parker	U17	7.11.84	1	Guildford	27 May
		5.48			1	Carshalton	17 Jun
5.52 w	3.6	Debbie Marti		14.05.68	5	Enfield	23 Jul
5.51	1.3	Pam Anderson		16.10.76	1	Grangemouth	14 May
5.51		Danielle Parkinson	U20	2.09.81	1H	Cannock	25 Jun
5.51		Michaela Paul	U20	27.10.81	3	Hoo	15 Jul
5.51		Laura Redmond	U20	19.04.81	2	Wakefield	16 Jul
5.51		Banke Olofinjana		14.05.72	1	London (FP)	12 Aug
5.50		Kerry Saunders		28.03.77	1	Nuneaton	30 Apr
5.50		Nikki Gilding		16.05.72	1	Brighton	15 Jul
5.50		Hannah Lloyd	U23	14.11.78	1	Sandown IOW	4 Sep

Additional Under 17 (1 - 17 above)

Mark	Wind	Name		DOB	Pos	Venue	Date
5.47		Carly Robson		5.12.83	1	Welwyn	5 May
5.47		Michelle Johansen		1.02.84	1	Abingdon	10 Jun
5.45 w	2.4	Hannah Barnes		2.06.84	1H	Stoke-on-Trent	18 Jun
		5.38			1	Cudworth	10 Jun
	(20)						
5.43 i		Joanne Nicoll		27.12.84	2	Cardiff	26 Feb
5.41		Katy Benneworth		5.10.84	1	Bromley	11 Jun
5.41	0.9	Lara Carty		7.03.84	9H	Val de Reuil, FRA	13 Aug
5.41		Emma Wooff		21.05.85	1	Wigan	26 Aug
5.41 w	2.4	Sarah Gallaway		14.11.84	4	Watford	28 May
		5.37			1	Portsmouth	1 May
5.40		Joanne Pybus		18.12.84	1	Middlesbrough	10 Jun
5.39 i		Laura Paterson		8.09.83	2	Glasgow	27 Jan
		5.35			1	Glasgow	30 May
5.37		Sian Briggs		17.07.84	1	Nottingham	14 May
5.37		Louise Toward		27.03.84	1H	Cannock	25 Jun
5.36		Rachel Brenton		18.01.85	1	London (TB)	26 Aug
	(30)						
5.35 i		Cathy Wilson		29.08.84	3	Glasgow	20 Feb
5.35		Amy Protheroe		3.03.84	1	Neath	6 May
5.35		Vicky Lambert		20.11.84	1	Cudworth	13 May

Additional Under 15 (1 above)

Mark	Wind	Name		DOB	Pos	Venue	Date
5.43		Louise Hazel		6.10.85	1	Peterborough	23 Jul
5.40		Sally Peake		8.02.86	1	Lancaster	7 May
		5.16 -0.6			2	Bedford	27 Aug
5.34		Jessica Ennis		28.01.86	P	Stoke-on-Trent	18 Jun
5.32		Helena Carter		17.05.86	1	York	10 Jun
5.30		Elen Davies		24.04.86	1	Hertford	6 Aug
5.29		Angela Barratt		25.12.85	1	Oxford	15 Jul
5.29 w	2.6	Ashleigh Wicheard		20.07.86	3	Sheffield	8 Jul
		5.06			3	Exeter	17 Jun
5.28		Leah McGuire		30.01.87	1	Norwich	17 Jun
5.27		Tamara Doherty		15.11.85	1	Glasgow (S)	20 Aug
	(10)						
5.25	1.3	Georgina Shaw		13.03.86	6	Sheffield	8 Jul
5.25		Kiri Burbidge		2.10.85	1	Bournemouth	12 Aug
5.25 w	3.8	Martha Allbutt		27.12.85	5	Sheffield	8 Jul
		5.21			1	Cannock	7 May
5.23		Denae Matthew		3.04.87	2	Peterborough	23 Jul
5.23	0.6	Aimee Palmer		7.11.86	1	Bedford	27 Aug
5.21		Sophie Newington		15.09.85	2	Carmarthen	1 Jul
5.20	-2.0	Phyllis Agbo		16.12.85	P	Birmingham	17 Sep
5.20 w	2.8	Jade Halket		5.05.86	1	Grangemouth	16 Jun
		5.17 1.7			*	Grangemouth	16 Jun
5.18 w	3.2	Rachel Spencer		19.08.86	1	Inverness	9 Jul
		5.16 1.7			2	Grangemouth	16 Jun
5.17		Katie Flaherty		1.10.85	1	Norwich	23 Jul
	(20)						
5.16 w	3.5	Frances Noble		2.05.86	8	Sheffield	8 Jul
		5.07			3	Lancaster	7 May
5.16 w	3.8	Naida Bromley		27.09.86	7	Sheffield	8 Jul
		5.11			1	Cleckheaton	10 Jun
5.15		Kelly Parkinson		18.03.86	1	Exeter	17 Jun

Overage

Mark	Wind	Name		DOB	Pos	Venue	Date
5.17 i		Emma Perkins	U17	4.09.85	P	Glasgow	9 Dec

Under 13

4.92		Emma Bonny		9.09.87	1	Cambridge	25 Jun
4.91		Amy Harris		14.09.87	1	Banbury	10 Sep
4.81		Saskia Kalmeijer			1	Abingdon	17 Sep
4.78		Aisha McIntosh		5.01.88	3	Basingstoke	2 Sep
4.75		Lauren Duncan		21.03.88	1	Guildford	6 Aug
4.73		Lauren Walton		1.09.87	1	Sutton	17 Jun
4.73		Natalie Brooks			1	Cudworth	16 Jul
4.71		Rachel Conway		30.09.87	1	Brecon	9 Jul
4.71		Alison Bennett		12.04.88	1		12 Aug
4.71		Claire Linskill		12.01.88	3	Exeter	2 Sep
	(10)						
4.69		Faye Richold		24.10.87	1	Kingston	30 Jul
4.69		Chloe Gale		24.02.88	1	Dartford	12 Aug

Foreign

6.03 w	*4.6*	*Margaret Veldman (HOL)*		*7.06.74*	*2*	*Grantham*	*18 Jun*
		5.94 1.1			*1*	*Solihull*	*5 Aug*

TRIPLE JUMP

14.29	-0.4	Ashia Hansen		5.12.71	Q	Sydney, AUS	22 Sep
		14.11 i			2	Birmingham	24 Jun
		13.44 0.4			11	Sydney, AUS	24 Sep
14.14 w	3.9	Michelle Griffith		6.10.71	1	Ljubljana, SLO	25 Jul
		13.71 1.0			1	Solihull	5 Aug
		13.67 -0.8			1	Birmingham	12 Aug
		13.64 1.1			2	Budapest, HUN	22 Jul
		13.63 1.6			1	Bedford	19 Aug
		13.62 1.2			1	Bedford	20 Aug
		13.54 -0.1			6	Bratislava, SVK	22 Jun
		13.54 i			6	Birmingham	24 Jun
		13.52 1.0			1	Brighton	17 Jun
		13.50 1.9			7	Gateshead	15 Jul
		13.49 w 2.2			1	Vittel, FRA	2 Sep
		13.45 w 2.4			1	Bedford	11 Jun
		13.41 0.3			2	Gateshead	28 Aug
		13.29			1	Glasgow (S)	8 Jul
		13.16 1.3			*	Bedford	11 Jun
13.66 w	3.8	Connie Henry		15.04.72	3	Ljubljana, SLO	25 Jul
		13.52 0.9			2	Sydney, AUS	19 Feb
		13.48 1.5			2	Brisbane, AUS	11 Feb
		13.45 -0.4			2	Sydney, AUS	26 Feb
		13.39 w 3.2			2	Adelaide, AUS	8 Mar
		13.31 -0.8			5	Budapest, HUN	22 Jul
		13.17 1.0			Q	Sydney, AUS	24 Feb
		13.15			1	London (He)	15 Jul
		13.14 1.2			8	Bratislava, SVK	22 Jun
		13.10 0.0			2	Dolenjske, SLO	25 Jun
13.14 w		Debbie Rowe		8.09.72	1	Cudworth	22 Jul
		12.97 1.2			*	Cudworth	22 Jul
13.04 w		Kate Evans		4.02.74	1	Rugby	23 Jul
		12.87 1.7			*	Rugby	23 Jul

30 performances to 13.00 by 5 athletes including 2 indoors and 7 wind assisted

12.92	0.8	Liz Patrick		29.08.77	2	Solihull	5 Aug
12.83	1.1	Anna-Maria Thorpe		15.07.71	1	Loughborough	21 May
12.64	1.7	Jodie Hurst		21.06.77	2	Rugby	23 Jul
12.52	0.5	Leandra Polius	U23	14.05.80	1	Bedford	1 Jul
12.47		Caroline Stead		14.09.71	1	Basingstoke	2 Sep
	(10)						
12.24	0.0	Rebecca White	U23	5.06.80	3	Solihull	5 Aug

12.22	0.3	Angela Williams	U20	13.05.81	1	Bath	16 Sep
12.12	1.4	Julia Johnson	U23	21.09.79	3	Loughborough	21 May
12.07 w	3.9	Susan Furlonger	U20	30.09.81	3	Nicosia, CYP	27 May
		11.44 i			1	Birmingham	16 Jan
		11.28 1.2			3	Vilvoorde, BEL	6 Aug
12.06 w		Nikki Barr		26.04.70	2	Cudworth	22 Jul
		11.97 1.8			1	Glasgow (S)	29 Jul
12.03 w	4.8	Jo Morris		16.10.77	6	Bedford	28 May
		11.97			1	Basildon	24 Jun
11.98 w	3.0	Rachel Peacock	U20	18.05.82	1	Bedford	27 Aug
		11.79 0.5			2	Watford	2 Jul
11.94 w	2.8	Natalie Brant	U20	11.12.82	2	Bedford	27 Aug
		11.78 1.2			*	Bedford	27 Aug
11.93	1.1	Sharon Oakes	U20	26.08.82	2	Edinburgh	13 Aug
11.88	-1.1	Emily Parker	U17	7.11.84	1	Sheffield	7 Jul
	(20)						
11.86	1.3	Rebecca Bates	U20	16.05.82	2	Sheffield	8 Jul
11.84	1.8	Rachel Kirby		18.05.69	2	Enfield	6 Aug
11.84 w	3.7	Lisa Holmes		21.11.75	2	Grantham	18 Jun
		11.63 -0.6			4	Solihull	29 Jul
11.83	-0.3	Carly Robson	U17	5.12.83	2	Sheffield	7 Jul
11.82 w		Stacy McGivern		14.12.76	3	Rugby	23 Jul
		11.64 1.2			2	Enfield	6 Aug
11.81		Joanne Stanley		30.03.77	1	Gateshead	14 May
11.80 w	4.4	Michala Gee		8.12.75	3	Grantham	18 Jun
		11.43			2	Rotherham	4 Jun
11.78		Cathryn Dale		31.05.77	1	Coventry	30 Apr
11.78	0.7	Rachel Hogg	U20	11.06.82	4	Loughborough	21 May
11.78	-0.2	Mary Devlin	U23	14.09.79	2	Belfast	8 Jul
	(30)						
11.75 w		Marcia Walker		27.05.70	2	Hayes	19 Jul
		11.66			5	Glasgow	8 Jul
11.66		Rebecca Shiel	U20	16.01.82	1	Jarrow	10 Jun
11.66	1.1	Gillian Cooke	U20	3.10.82	4	Edinburgh	13 Aug
11.64		Kelly Brow	U23	24.09.78	1	Cleckheaton	11 Jun
11.64	1.7	Julia Straker	U20	25.11.82	3	Glasgow	29 Jul
11.62 i		Lara Richards	U20	7.03.83	2	Cardiff	4 Mar
		11.53			2	Coventry	30 Apr
11.61	0.6	Hazel Carwardine	U23	6.11.80	2	Bedford	1 Jul
11.61	-1.2	Aisha Myton	U17	3.01.84	2	Sheffield	30 Jul
11.61	1.3	Katharine Streatfield	U20	28.07.83	6	Bedford	27 Aug
11.58 i		Linsi Robinson	U17	9.01.84	1	Birmingham	6 Feb
		11.26			2	Leamington	14 May
	(40)						
11.58	1.2	Evette Finikin	V35	25.09.63	3	Eton	6 May
11.56		Azaria Francis	U20	12.04.83	1	Kingston	10 Jun
11.55 w	2.3	Nina Ezeogu	U20	11.10.82	7	Bedford	27 Aug
		11.37			1	Enfield	12 Aug
11.53		Judy Kotey	U23	20.05.80	1	Hastings	24 Jun
11.50		Hannah Moody	U23	26.07.79	3	Stoke-on-Trent	1 May
11.50	-0.6	Michelle Johansen	U17	1.02.84	2	London (He)	20 Aug
11.49 i		Michaela Paul	U20	27.10.81	8	Birmingham	29 Jan
		11.27			2	Eton	30 Apr
11.44		Sarah Wellstead	U23	22.10.79	2	Carshalton	29 May
11.43 w	2.2	Jenny Brown	V40	21.05.59	2	Jyvaskyla, FIN	13 Jul
		11.40 1.6			1	Bedford	30 Jul
11.41 w	2.6	Sarah Hunter	U23	19.05.78	6	Bedford	19 Aug
		11.25 1.6			6	Solihull	5 Aug
	(50)						
11.38		Charmaine Turner	U20	5.12.81	1	Abingdon	2 Sep
11.36		Kerry Saunders		28.03.77	1	Stoke-on-Trent	13 May

11.35		Sarah Roberts	U23	25.06.78	1	Yate	20 Aug
11.33		Nikki Gilding		16.05.72	4	London (Cr)	27 Aug
11.30		Helen Williams	U20	13.01.83	1	Derby	17 Jun
11.29		Rachel Brenton	U17	18.01.85	1	Oxford	14 May
11.28		Kimberley Goodall	U17	5.10.83	1	Guernsey	2 Jul
11.28 w	2.2	Gemma Holt		20.12.72	4	Enfield	23 Jul
		11.23			1	Hoo	15 Jul
11.27 i		Alison Rough	U20	1.06.83	8	Birmingham	5 Feb
11.26	-0.3	Alison McAllister	U17	26.02.85	5	Sheffield	7 Jul
	(60)						
11.26		Sarah Strevens	U20	7.10.81	5	London (He)	15 Jul
11.25 w	2.5	Katherine Silto	U20	12.08.83	7	Sheffield	8 Jul
		11.19 1.9			*	Sheffield	8 Jul
11.20		Gemma Sharples	U20	4.08.83	2	Macclesfield	14 May
11.18		Janice Pryce	V40	2.09.59	2	Bedford	30 Jul
11.18	1.3	Katie Jones		4.01.77	7	Bedford	19 Aug
11.17		Natasha Brunning		10.03.73	1	Birmingham	15 Aug
11.14		Stephanie Higham	U17	26.12.83	1	Middlesbrough	17 Jun
11.13		Sally Ash	U23	4.11.80	1	Loughborough	8 Apr
11.13		Alison Croad	U20	10.06.82	1	Exeter	17 Jun
11.13		Becky Ridgley	U23	26.02.80	2	Horsham	15 Jul
	(70)						
11.13		Sara Barry	U20	8.06.83	1	Yate	13 Aug
11.13		Hannah Lloyd	U23	14.11.78	1	Milton Keynes	2 Sep
11.12	0.7	Stacey Savage	U17	30.12.84	8	Sheffield	7 Jul
11.12 w	3.8	Debbie Harrison	U23	13.11.78	7	Solihull	5 Aug
11.10	1.2	Catriona Christie	U17	26.04.85	9	Sheffield	7 Jul
11.08		Zoe McKinnon	U20	8.09.81	1	Crawley	13 May
11.08		Andrea Hall		28.01.77	2	Ware	3 Sep
11.07		Catherine Barnes		28.09.77	1	Hayes	24 Jun
11.07		Sian Jones	U20	20.01.83	4	Rugby	9 Jul
11.07		Michelle Doherty	U17	24.09.84	1	Antrim	22 Jul
	(80)						
11.06	0.6	Fiona Hutchison		18.01.77	7	Eton	6 May
11.06 w	2.4	Jenny Eagen	U17	15.05.84	Q	Sheffield	7 Jul
		10.87			1	Bournemouth	10 Jun
11.03		Rachael Burns	U20	5.08.83	2	Derby	17 Jun
11.02		Maurine Okwue	U23	13.05.78	4	Eton	30 Apr
11.02		Kosnatu Abdulai	U17	8.02.85	3	Ware	3 Sep
11.02 w		Caroline Marsden	U20	1.06.82	1	Cardiff	21 Jun
11.01		Katryna Euridge	U20	22.05.83	3	Carshalton	29 Apr

Additional Under 17 (1 - 14 above)

10.97	0.8	Samantha Henderson	27.09.83	6	Bedford	20 Aug
10.96		Ceri Jones	29.07.84	1	Carmarthen	1 Jul
10.96		Lucy Hunt	4.04.84	1	Worcester	16 Jul
10.93		Emma Wooff	21.05.85	1	Wigan	26 Aug
10.92 i		Laura Paterson	8.09.83	1	Glasgow	20 Feb
		10.70		1	Grangemouth	25 Jun
10.87 w	3.6	Laura Betts	6.11.84	2	Watford	28 May
		10.83 1.4		*	Watford	28 May
	(20)					
10.84 i		Elizabeth Webb	16.12.83	1	Cardiff	20 Feb
		10.77		2	Carmarthen	1 Jul
10.84	1.1	Joanne Reade	28.11.84	6	Sheffield	30 Jul
10.82		Jocelyn Braidy	13.02.84	1	Bournemouth	14 May
10.82		Diana Osagede	18.01.85	2	Basingstoke	2 Sep
10.79		Jennifer Wright	21.09.83	1	Eton	10 Jun
10.76 w	2.8	Claire Baker	13.08.84	7	Sheffield	30 Jul
		10.67		1	Worcester	10 Jun
10.74	2.0	Gemma Tune	28.02.84	Q	Sheffield	7 Jul
10.72		Caron Leckie	23.11.84	7	Blackpool	15 Jul
10.66		Francis Okeke	10.05.84	2	Portsmouth	20 May

Foreign

12.02 w 4.2	*Cathriona Hannafin (IRE)*		*19.09.72*	*2*	*Kerry*	*11 Jun*
	11.99			*1*	*Cardiff*	*4 Jun*
11.30 i	*Bettina Lotsch (GER)*		*7.09.77*	*2*	*Cardiff*	*12 Mar*
	11.19			*1*	*Oxford*	*20 May*
11.07	*Lydia Saka-Nakagirl (SWE)*	*U23*	*20.01.79*	*6*	*London (He)*	*15 Jul*

SHOT

18.30 i	Judy Oakes	V40	14.02.58	1	Birmingham	30 Jan
	18.22			1	Feltham	2 Sep
	18.16			1	Bedford	19 Aug
	18.12 i			1	London (CP)	20 Feb
	18.08			3	Gateshead	16 Jul
	17.99			1	Arles, FRA	4 Jun
	17.92			2	Gold Coast (RB), AUS	17 Sep
	17.91			1	Birmingham	12 Aug
	17.87			1	Brighton	18 Jun
	17.81			2	Glasgow (S)	2 Jul
	17.81			13Q	Sydney, AUS	27 Sep
	17.79			1	Loughborough	21 May
	17.77			1	Solihull	29 Jul
	17.67			1	London (Cr)	13 May
	17.66 i			1	London (CP)	12 Feb
	17.66			1	Eton	11 Jun
	17.65 i			1	London (CP)	15 Jan
	17.28			1	London (Cr)	24 Jun
	17.25 i			13Q	Ghent, BEL	25 Feb
	17.25			1	London (Cr)	20 May
16.40	Julie Dunkley	U23	11.09.79	2	Birmingham	12 Aug
	16.19			1	Getafe, SPA	9 Sep
	16.13 i			1	Bedford	23 Jan
	16.05			1	Woodford	24 Jun
	16.05			1	London (He)	15 Jul
	15.99			3	Vittel, FRA	2 Sep
	15.96			1	Bedford	1 Jul
	15.96			4	Glasgow (S)	2 Jul
	15.96			3	Liverpool	22 Jul
	15.88			3	Arles, FRA	4 Jun
	15.87			1	London (CP)	14 May
	15.87			1	Glasgow (S)	8 Jul
	15.85			2	Brighton	18 Jun
	15.78			2	Bedford	19 Aug
	15.55			1	Eton	6 May
	15.51			1	Dudelange, LUX	27 May
16.09	Jo Duncan		27.12.66	1	Peterborough	9 Jul
	16.00			3	Birmingham	12 Aug
	15.92			1	Bedford	29 May
	15.92			2	Woodford	24 Jun
	15.84			3	Brighton	18 Jun
	15.67			1	Chelmsford	14 May
15.62 i	Philippa Roles	U23	1.03.78	2	Birmingham	30 Jan
	14.84			1	Bath	16 Sep
15.55	Denise Lewis		27.08.72	1H	Sydney, AUS	23 Sep
	15.50			6	Glasgow (S)	2 Jul
15.51	Christina Bennett	U23	27.02.78	1	Portsmouth	29 Apr
	46 performances to 15.50 by 6 athletes including 7 indoors					
15.45 i	Maggie Lynes	V35	19.02.63	3	Birmingham	30 Jan
	14.73			2	Eton	11 Jun
15.44	Vickie Foster		1.04.71	1	Bath	14 May
15.09	Nicola Gautier	U23	21.03.78	1H	Schwyz/Ibach, SWZ	1 Jul

14.90	Eva Massey	U23	22.12.80	1	Dublin (S), IRE	19	Aug
	Competed in Euro Cup for IRE, but was ill-advised - wants to stay British						
	(10)						
14.60 i	Eleanor Gatrell		5.10.76	6	Birmingham	30	Jan
	14.42			1	Eton	11	Jun
14.38	Tracy Axten	V35	20.07.63	4	Eton	6	May
14.30	Alison Grey		12.05.73	1	Grangemouth	13	May
13.98	Claire Smithson	U20	3.08.83	1	Watford	27	May
13.97	Jenny Kelly		20.06.70	3H	Arles, FRA	3	Jun
13.78	Natasha Smith		6.06.77	1	Ashford	7	May
13.77	Emma Merry		2.07.74	3	Solihull	29	Jul
13.73	Debbie Callaway	V35	15.07.64	7	Eton	6	May
13.70	Carol Bennett/Marshall		11.01.77	1	Cudworth	20	Aug
13.38	Kara Nwidobie	U20	13.04.81	1	Derby	3	Sep
	(20)						
13.27	Charmaine Johnson	V35	4.06.63	1H	Portsmouth	1	May
13.27	Debbie Woolgar	V35	10.03.65	1	Crawley	13	May
13.03	Mhairi Walters	U20	19.06.81	2	Bedford	27	Aug
13.01	Clova Court	V40	10.02.60	1	Redditch	13	May
12.91 i	Helen Wilding		25.10.76	2	Blackpool	16	Jan
	12.47			2	Liverpool	14	May
12.90	Rebecca Peake	U20	22.06.83	3	Bedford	27	Aug
12.72	Charlotte Spelzini	U20	7.01.83	1	Norwich	17	Jun
12.71 i	Cathy-Ann Hill		4.05.77	1	Cardiff	4	Mar
	12.33			3	Kingston	20	May
12.66	Carol Parker		22.09.69	3	Rugby	23	Jul
12.66	Lesley Brannan		13.09.76	1	Connah's Quay	29	Jul
	(30)						
12.65	Lorraine Shaw		2.04.68	8	Solihull	5	Aug
12.64	Julie Hollman		16.02.77	3H	Logrono, SPA	19	Aug
12.62	Amy Wilson	U23	31.12.80	1	Ipswich	15	Jul
12.55	Joanne Street	U20	30.10.82	5	Solihull	29	Jul
12.53	Chloe Cozens	U23	9.04.80	1	Loughborough	24	May
12.53	Emma Carpenter	U20	16.05.82	1	Exeter	17	Jun
12.52	Belinda Heil	U20	8.03.82	1	Kingston	10	Jun
12.46	Angela Lambourn		9.04.66	1	Corby	11	Jun
12.38 i	Navdeep Dhaliwal		30.11.77	4	Cardiff	26	Feb
	11.89			1	Glasgow	29	Jul
12.35	Sharon Gibson	V35	31.12.61	1	Loughborough	22	Aug
	(40)						
12.21	Vikki Shepherd	U23	26.01.80	1	Wakefield	16	Apr
12.19	Irene Duffin	V35	10.08.60	3	Carshalton	29	Apr
12.17	Joan MacPherson	U23	18.09.80	1	Derby	3	Sep
12.14	Lorraine Henry		16.09.67	2	Corby	11	Jun
12.13 i	Julia Bennett		26.03.70	2P	Vittel, FRA	18	Mar
	11.86			4	London (Cr)	13	May
12.10	Shelley McLellan	U20	21.03.83	1	London (WL)	15	Jul
12.05	Louise Finlay	U17	2.10.83	1	Grangemouth	5	Aug
11.99 i	Joanna Bennett	U20	6.08.83	4	Birmingham	6	Feb
	11.81			4	Watford	27	May
11.97	Clover Wynter-Pink		29.11.77	1	Eton	30	Apr
11.96 i	Shaunette Richards	U20	15.08.83	1	Birmingham	15	Jan
	11.52			1	Birmingham	10	Sep
	(50)						
11.95	Jenny Grimstone	U23	30.04.79	1	Ware	2	Sep
11.94	Kate Morris	U20	18.01.83	6	Bedford	27	Aug
11.86 i	Alyson Hourihan	V35	17.10.60	2	Cardiff	20	Feb
	11.65			1	Cardiff	13	May
11.83	Catherine Garden	U23	4.09.78	1	Glasgow (S)	30	Apr
11.83	Danielle Freeman	U23	11.02.80	15H	Schwyz/Ibach, SWZ	1	Jul
11.79	Claire Everett	U23	25.06.79	4	Stoke-on-Trent	6	Aug

11.78	Kerry Jury		19.11.68	3H	Watford	23	Sep
11.77	Elaine Cank	U23	5.12.79	1	Cosford	16	Apr
11.77	Lesley-Ann Roy	U20	3.01.82	1	Coatbridge	21	May
11.75	Emma Morris	U20	25.01.82	4	Sheffield	8	Jul
	(60)						
11.73	Anne Hollman		18.02.74	3H	Waterford, IRE	2	Sep
11.72	Esther Augee	V35	1.01.64	4	Liverpool	7	May
11.71	Sharon Wray	U20	8.10.82	1	Telford	13	May
11.70	Gillian Stewart	U23	21.01.80	5	Liverpool	7	May
11.70	Kelly Sotherton		13.11.76	4H	Waterford, IRE	2	Sep
11.69	Sarah McGrath		22.12.72	1	Cambridge	16	Apr
11.69	Donna Maylor	U20	20.05.82	1	Wakefield	16	Jul
11.63	Elizabeth Bowyer	U20	8.09.81	1	Liverpool	10	Jun
11.63	Nicola Dudman	U17	5.10.83	1	Welwyn	2	Sep
11.62	Joanne Holloway		10.05.76	8	Bedford	19	Aug
	(70)						
11.61	Frances Miller	U17	26.12.84	1	Inverness	23	Apr
11.60	Manndy Laing	V40	7.11.59	2	Liverpool	14	May
11.59	Angharad Lloyd	U23	11.09.80	1	Neath	4	Jun
11.59	Leah Lackenby/Weatheritt		18.09.74	3	Cudworth	20	Aug
11.58	Julie Lavender		9.11.75	1	Chester-le-Street	7	May
11.56	Laura Redmond	U20	19.04.81	2	Grangemouth	25	Jun
11.50	Somma Power	U17	18.08.85	2	London (TB)	15	Jul
11.48	Faye Brennan	U17	13.05.84	1	Horsham	17	Jun
11.47	Diana Bennett/Norman		14.06.74	2	Guildford	12	Aug
11.45 i	Rebecca Roles	U23	14.12.79	1	Cardiff	23	Jan
	(80)						
11.43 i	Fran Wilkins	U23	15.01.79	4	Cardiff	11	Mar
11.43	Eleanor Garden		20.11.76	5	Enfield	6	Aug
11.40	Gemma Avil	U17	8.03.84	1	Abingdon	13	May
11.40	Paula Hendriks	U20	25.01.83	1H	Birmingham	16	Sep
11.37	Laura Douglas	U20	4.01.83	1	Wrexham	4	Jun
11.33	Jolene Marshall	U17	22.10.83	1	London (Cr)	23	Jul
11.32	Noelle Bradshaw	V35	18.12.63	3	Aldershot	16	Jul
11.31	Karen Smith	U23	25.12.78	2	Reading	20	May
11.30	Claire Archer		30.09.76	2	Jarrow	7	May
11.28	Belinda Samuels	U23	29.11.78	1	Stoke-on-Trent	13	May
	(90)						
11.20	Charlotte Rees	U17	14.06.84	1	Swansea	12	Apr
11.20	Katie Halford	U20	4.10.82	1	Exeter	16	Apr
11.15	Rebecca Chamberlain	U23	7.09.79	1	Bournemouth	13	May

Additional Under 17 (1 - 8 above)

11.08	Alison Rodger	29.10.84	3	Blackpool	15	Jul
11.01 i	Shelley Moles	31.10.83	1	Birmingham	6	Feb
	10.39		2	Basildon	10	Jun
	(10)					
10.97	Lydia Morgan	1.09.83	5	Sheffield	30	Jul
10.95	Caroline Barrett	16.09.83	1	Hull	17	Sep
10.89	Tanya Hunt	14.09.83	1	Salisbury	15	Jul
10.81	Claire Parkin	26.02.84	2	Grangemouth	17	Jun
10.77 i	Alana Smith	18.01.85	2	Glasgow	20	Feb
10.73	Kerri Fardoe	22.11.83	5	Sheffield	7	Jul
10.71	Kerry Elliott	17.05.85	1	Gateshead	14	May
10.59	Candace Schofield	3.11.84	1H	Eton	24	Jun
10.56	Nicola Gore	17.11.84	1	Wrexham	2	Jul
10.56	Sarah Beer	29.04.84	1	Portsmouth	23	Jul
	(20)					
10.48	Jessica Weir	3.10.84	1	Exeter	17	Jun
10.46	Danielle Hall	27.11.84	1	London (B)	15	Jul
10.36	Laura Fox	25.10.84	1	Bromley	23	Apr
10.32	Cherie Pierre	15.05.84	2	London (He)	30	Jul

SHOT - Under 15 - 3.25kg

11.64	Hayley Hood	12.09.85	1	Rotherham	4	Jun
11.57	Lucy Sutton	29.08.86	1	Sheffield	29	Jul
11.45	Sally Hinds	2.02.86	1	Birmingham	2	Sep
11.38	Iyesha Tomlinson	19.02.86	1	London (He)	20	Aug
11.34	Dani Wheeler	12.10.85	1	Sheffield	7	Jul
11.34	Emma Shaw	19.09.86	1	Cudworth	20	Aug
11.30	Phyllis Agbo	16.12.85	2	London (He)	20	Aug
11.11	Clare Robertson	17.08.86	1	Cannock	10	Jun
11.10	Debbie Collinson	23.10.85	1	Hull	17	Sep
10.85	Nimi Iniekio	25.10.86	1	Bromley	29	Apr
	(10)					
10.84	Rachael Atkinson	20.12.85	1	Stretford	10	Jun
10.84	Lucy Fisher	27.09.85	1	Macclesfield	10	Jun
10.83	Lauren Therin	19.01.86	2	Sheffield	29	Jul
10.80	Christina Carding	26.02.87	1	Basingstoke	7	May
10.80	Chloe Edwards	12.05.87	3	London (He)	20	Aug
10.63	Hayley Bryan	4.03.86	1	Banbury	10	Sep
10.62	Louise Watton	30.10.86	1	Abingdon	2	Sep
10.60	Amy Davis	28.01.86	1	Antrim	23	Jul
10.58	Ashleigh Palmer-Johnson	19.09.86	1	Portsmouth	12	Aug
10.57	Kate Butters	25.07.86	P	Crawley	10	Sep
	(20)					
10.55	Clare Palmer	30.12.85	4	London (He)	20	Aug
10.53	Eshere Singh	15.07.87	1	Exeter	2	Sep

SHOT - Under 13 - 2.72kg

11.42	Candee Rhule	16.09.87	1	London (BP)	29	Jul
10.72	Kayleigh Southgate	15.01.88	1	Birmingham	3	Sep
10.30	Rebecca Hall	15.09.88	1	King's Lynn	20	Aug
9.52	Lauren Davies	21.09.87	1	Bournemouth	7	May
9.50	Susan Bissell		1	Wigan	20	Aug
9.24	April Derbyshire	2.04.88	1	Kingston	30	Jul
9.13	C. Harrison		2	Cudworth	9	Sep
9.09	Laura Teasdale	12.06.88	P	Rotherham	10	Sep
9.07	Diane Pedgrift	10.05.88	1	Coatbridge	16	Jul
9.03	A. Graham		1	Grove Park	10	Jun
	(10)					
9.03	Claire Daubney		2	Birmingham	3	Sep
9.02	Y. Ejoh		2	London (WL)	20	Jun

Overage

10.01 i	Loise Ali	U15	2.03.88	1	Cardiff	17	Dec
9.56 i	Lauren Davies	U15	21.09.87	2	Cardiff	9	Dec

DISCUS

59.03	Shelley Drew	8.08.73	1	Birmingham	13	Aug
	57.79		1	Loughborough	30	Jul
	57.43		3	Arles, FRA	3	Jun
	57.28		1	Solihull	29	Jul
	57.03		1	Bedford	20	Aug
	56.94		6	Walnut, USA	16	Apr
	56.90		3	Lancaster, USA	13	Apr
	56.56		1	Bedford	19	Aug
	56.09		1	Birmingham (Un)	25	Jul
	55.66		1	Bedford	29	May
	55.25		1	Loughborough	21	May
	55.04		1	Barking	2	Apr
	54.75		1	Bedford	11	Jun
	54.07		7	Gateshead	28	Aug
	52.74		8	Gateshead	15	Jul

57.04	Philippa Roles	U23	1.03.78	1	Rugby	23 Jul
	56.35			2	Dublin (S), IRE	29 Jul
	55.87			1	Gloucester	26 Aug
	55.59			3	Loughborough	30 Jul
	55.48			1B	Halle, GER	27 May
	55.44			1	Getafe, SPA	9 Sep
	55.39			1	Liverpool	22 Jul
	54.74			2	Birmingham	13 Aug
	54.56			2	Bedford	19 Aug
	54.21			1	Eton	6 May
	53.85			8	Gateshead	28 Aug
	53.41			3	Loughborough	21 May
	52.76			2	Bedford	20 Aug
	52.75			1	Stoke-on-Trent	30 Apr
	52.71			1	Solihull	5 Aug
	52.20			1	Glasgow (S)	8 Jul
	52.05			1	Bath	16 Sep
55.60	Emma Merry		2.07.74	2	Loughborough	30 Jul
	54.50			2	Loughborough	21 May
	53.73			1	Coventry	30 Apr
	53.69			2	Rugby	23 Jul
	53.08			1	Rugby	22 Aug
	53.03			2	Bedford	29 May
	53.00			3	Birmingham	13 Aug
	52.97			2	Solihull	29 Jul
	52.72			1	Loughborough	10 May
52.34	Debbie Callaway	V35	15.07.64	3	Bedford	29 May
52.21	Emma Carpenter	U20	16.05.82	1	Exeter	17 Jun
52.19	Claire Smithson	U20	3.08.83	1	Grosseto, ITA	7 Oct
	44 performances to 52.00 by 6 athletes					
51.72	Tracy Axten	V35	20.07.63	4	Bedford	29 May
49.82	Judy Oakes	V40	14.02.58	2	Eton	11 Jun
49.77	Lorraine Shaw		2.04.68	2	Gloucester	26 Aug
49.25	Vickie Foster		1.04.71	1	Bournemouth	20 May
(10)						
49.10	Joanna Bradley	U23	23.08.79	1	Enfield	6 Aug
48.84	Nicola Talbot		17.02.72	6	Bedford	19 Aug
47.79	Alison Grey		12.05.73	6	Birmingham	13 Aug
47.72	Eva Massey	U23	22.12.80	2	Antrim	31 Jul
46.85	Rebecca Roles	U23	14.12.79	2	Stoke-on-Trent	30 Apr
45.87	Susan Freebairn	V35	22.08.65	1P	Hexham	24 Sep
45.60	Eleanor Garden		20.11.76	3	Enfield	6 Aug
45.58	Joan MacPherson	U23	18.09.80	1	Basildon	24 Jun
45.30	Joanne Street	U20	30.10.82	3	Sheffield	7 Jul
45.29	Susan Backhouse	U23	6.12.78	2	Loughborough	14 Jun
(20)						
44.43	Elaine Cank	U23	5.12.79	2	Derby	3 Sep
43.46	Sarah Symonds/Nickelson		28.12.73	1	Braintree	12 Aug
43.32	Rebecca Hardy		11.11.68	1	Hayes	24 Jun
42.70	Donna Williams	U23	7.10.78	1	Stretford	14 May
42.25	Hannah Corneby	U20	22.01.81	3	Watford	2 Jul
42.00	Sharon Andrews		4.07.67	4	Enfield	6 May
41.94	Carly Burton	U23	14.10.80	1	Ware	2 Sep
41.72	Maggie Lynes	V35	19.02.63	3	Eton	11 Jun
41.46	Candie Lintern	U20	5.02.82	4	Sheffield	7 Jul
41.10	Laura Wood	U23	31.10.78	8	Bedford	19 Aug
(30)						
40.92	Joanne John	U23	12.11.80	1	Enfield	13 May
40.71	Tasha Saint-Smith		20.12.75	2	Abingdon	2 Sep
40.70	Julie Dunkley	U23	11.09.79	2	London (He)	15 Jul
40.64	Ellisha Dee	U17	24.10.84	1	Sheffield	8 Jul

40.51	Andrea Jenkins		4.10.75	1	Ware	3	Sep
40.50	Claire Cameron	V40	3.10.58	1	Jyvaskyla, FIN	10	Jul
40.42	Angela Mitchell		17.08.65	7	Brighton	18	Jun
40.27	Amanda Sheppard		26.02.68	1	Cleckheaton	11	Jun
40.24	Alyson Hourihan	V35	17.10.60	2	Cardiff	4	Jun
40.21	Joanne Jackson	V35	16.04.63	2	Chelmsford	13	May
	(40)						
40.03	Christina Bennett	U23	27.02.78	2	Woodford	24	Jun
39.99	Claire Moore	U20	29.03.82	5	Sheffield	7	Jul
39.93	Lorraine Henry		16.09.67	3	Ashford	7	May
39.93	Navdeep Dhaliwal		30.11.77	5	Glasgow (S)	29	Jul
39.77	Helen Wilding		25.10.76	10	Eton	6	May
39.74	Carol Bennett/Marshall		11.01.77	4	Ashford	7	May
39.73	Kelly Ricketts		24.01.76	1	Deeside	19	Aug
39.62	Laura Douglas	U20	4.01.83	1	Wrexham	16	Jul
39.57	Eleanor Gatrell		5.10.76	5	Eton	11	Jun
39.56	Catherine Lane		18.11.76	6	Stoke-on-Trent	30	Apr
	(50)						
38.90	Kelly Mellis	U23	4.12.79	2	Hayes	24	Jun
38.80	Belinda Heil	U20	8.03.82	2	London (Cr)	20	May
38.79	Kara Nwidobie	U20	13.04.81	1	Cleckheaton	27	May
38.63	Angela Lockley	U17	7.10.84	2	Sheffield	8	Jul
38.58	Katie Halford	U20	4.10.82	4	Bath	16	Sep
38.54	Lesley Bryant	V40	12.04.56	1	Grantham	14	May
38.47	Lucy Nesbitt	U17	6.09.84	3	Sheffield	8	Jul
38.41	Mhairi Walters	U20	19.06.81	2	Grangemouth	6	Sep
38.39	Julie Robin		16.01.77	2	Aldershot	16	Jul
38.28	Suzanne Last		11.01.70	1	Hoo	2	Sep
	(60)						
38.18	Amie Hill	U23	9.09.80	2	Enfield	8	Apr
38.17	Carol Parker		22.09.69	4	Rugby	23	Jul
37.92	Laura Fox	U17	25.10.84	2	Ware	2	Sep
37.87	Catherine Garden	U23	4.09.78	4	Grangemouth	11	Jun
37.52	Kim Rawling	U20	22.07.83	1	Carn Brea	6	Aug
37.40	Vicci Scott	U23	21.09.80	1	Wakefield	17	Sep
37.33	Donna Calvert	U23	26.06.79	2	Wakefield	17	Sep
37.23	Jane Ramage		7.01.72	4	Loughborough	14	Jun
37.17	Emma Forrester	U17	2.12.83	4	Sheffield	8	Jul
37.04	Fay Champion		27.09.66	3	Bath	14	May
	(70)						
36.93	Debbie Woolgar	V35	10.03.65	2	Portsmouth	29	Apr
36.92	Sandra Terry		28.04.69	3	Woodford	24	Jun
36.85	Karen Heweth	V40	29.11.59	1	Leeds	3	Sep
36.84	Kirsty Male	U20	7.07.82	7	Glasgow (S)	29	Jul
36.70	Lynsey Knott	U23	30.05.79	4	Aldershot	28	Jun
36.59	Irene Duffin	V35	10.08.60	5	Woodford	24	Jun
36.42	Emma Kirby	U20	11.11.81	1	Eton	14	May
36.41	Fallon Harrison	U17	1.05.85	5	Sheffield	8	Jul
36.40	Janine Crosby	U23	17.01.79	2	Cudworth	13	May
36.40	Ffion Jones	U20	19.07.83	4	Edinburgh	13	Aug
	(80)						
36.38	Lauren Therin	U15	19.01.86	1	London (He)	20	Aug
36.33	Evette Peever	U20	31.12.82	2	Derby	17	Jun
36.29	Vicky Gorton		9.05.77	2	Stretford	23	Apr
36.27	Carys Parry	U20	24.07.81	1	Cardiff	13	May
36.20	Anwen James	U20	17.02.81	6	Rugby	9	Jul
36.20	Michelle Wallace		1.11.72	1	Loughborough	22	Aug
36.02	Lydia Morgan	U17	1.09.83	2	Sheffield	30	Jul
35.99	Zoe Bridger		4.03.76	1	Erith	15	Jul
35.98	Raelene Cowie	U20	17.11.82	1	Stretford	10	Jun
35.96	Tracy Shorts		4.11.72	1	Nuneaton	30	Apr

Additional Under 17 (1 - 7 above)

35.72	Candace Schofield	3.11.84	1	Worthing	29 May
35.48	Danielle Hall	27.11.84	1	London (B)	15 Jul
35.44	Caroline Jones	30.04.84	1	Watford	10 Jun
	(10)				
35.40	Michelle Borthwick	28.04.84	1	Watford	28 May
35.33	Ruth Morris	17.10.83	4	Blackpool	15 Jul
35.01	Gemma Avil	8.03.84	1	Bournemouth	18 Jun
34.81	Donna Swatheridge	4.03.85	6	Sheffield	8 Jul
34.71	Alana Smith	18.01.85	1	Birmingham	3 Sep
33.92	Emily Oliver	8.02.84	6	Sheffield	30 Jul
33.75	Candice Francis	7.02.85	1	Wakefield	16 Jul
33.59	Caroline Barrett	16.09.83	3	Lincoln	13 Aug
33.51	Nicola Dudman	5.10.83	2	Luton	7 May
33.49	Coralie Hancock	1.03.85	2	Milton Keynes	2 Sep
	(20)				
33.48	Kirsty Walters	6.09.84	1	East Kilbride	14 Jun
33.33	Louise Finlay	2.10.83	5	Blackpool	15 Jul
32.32	Kirsty Billin	24.05.85	1	Crawley	28 Aug

Additional Under 15 (1 above)

33.98	Iyesha Tomlinson	19.02.86	1	Bedford	29 Apr
33.96	Hayley Hood	12.09.85	1	Birmingham	3 Sep
33.33	Christina Carding	26.02.87	1	Sheffield	29 Jul
32.36	Dominique Lord	8.04.87	1	Banbury	10 Sep
31.74	Hollie Redman	12.12.85	1	Braintree	12 Aug
31.52	Sarah Davies	13.03.86	1	London (He)	15 Jul
31.44	Lucy Sutton	29.08.86	1	Oxford	14 May
31.36	Melanie Harrison	27.11.85	1	Barking	11 Jun
30.74	Eshere Singh	15.07.87	1	Exeter	2 Sep
	(10)				
30.45	Rachael Atkinson	20.12.85	1	Stretford	14 May
30.45	Kimberley Silk	26.03.86	1	London (B)	15 Jul
30.29	Alex Merrill	12.05.86	1	Rotherham	4 Jun
29.89	Katia Lannon	14.09.85	2	Stretford	14 May
29.47	Laura Chalmers	1.05.86	1	Grangemouth	17 Jun
29.24	Louise Watton	30.10.86	1	Southend	12 Aug
28.78	Chloe Edwards	12.05.87	1	St. Ives	10 Jun
28.57	A. Howard		1	Scunthorpe	27 Aug
28.48	Alex Kay		2	Cudworth	20 Aug
28.41	Amanda Moodie	11.09.85	1	Grangemouth	11 Jun
	(20)				
28.36	Gemma Llewelyn	23.04.87	3	Birmingham	3 Sep

Under 13

23.48	Kathy Harriman	13.11.87	1	Leicester	23 May

Foreign

37.73	*Alison Moffitt (IRE)*	*6.10.69*	*2*	*Eton*	*23 Jul*

DISCUS - Under 13 - 0.75kg

34.80	Rebecca Saunders	8.02.88	1	Ashford	28 Aug
28.38	Rebecca Hall	15.09.88	1	Grimsby	24 Sep
27.50	Chloe Beckett	10.06.88	1	Cleckheaton	12 Aug
26.10	Bethany Staniland	10.05.88	1	Warrington	20 Aug
25.20	Anna Griffiths	28.12.87	1	Wigan	11 Jun
24.90	Vicky Doran	17.04.88	1	Carlisle	19 Aug
24.15	Laura Teasdale	12.06.88	2	Wigan	20 Aug
23.91	Claire Williams	29.09.87	1	Carmarthen	30 Jul
23.31	Hannah Cameron	3.03.88	1	Grangemouth	2 Aug
23.31	Cecilia Savundra	29.12.87	1	Eton	17 Sep

HAMMER

67.44	Lorraine Shaw		2.04.68	5	Gateshead	15	Jul
	66.87			2	Budapest, HUN	22	Jul
	66.85			1	Birmingham	12	Aug
	66.21			1	Germiston, RSA	26	Feb
	66.19			1	Solihull	5	Aug
	65.75			1	London (BP)	4	Jun
	65.65			1	London (Col)	30	Apr
	65.64			1	Port Elizabeth, RSA	25	Feb
	65.51			1	Gold Coast (S), AUS	15	Sep
	65.23			3	Szombathely, HUN	23	Jul
	65.20			1	Eton	6	May
	65.03			2	Stellenbosch, RSA	18	Feb
	65.00			7	Halle, GER	27	May
	64.94			1	Perivale	5	Mar
	64.87			1	Bath	14	May
	64.81			1	Bedford	11	Jun
	64.67			2	Loughborough	21	May
	64.28			1	Bedford	19	Aug
	64.27			1	Dublin (S), IRE	29	Jul
	64.27			9	Sydney, AUS	29	Sep
	63.93			1	Lewes	20	Jun
	63.21			Q	Sydney, AUS	27	Sep
	62.53			1	Glasgow (S)	8	Jul
	56.38 (5 kg hammer)			1	Gloucester	26	Aug
63.96	Lyn Sprules		11.09.75	1	Bedford	20	Aug
	63.35			2	Solihull	5	Aug
	63.34			5	Budapest, HUN	22	Jul
	62.71			1	Bedford	4	Jun
	62.48			2	Birmingham	12	Aug
	62.47			1	Enfield	13	May
	62.17			2	Eton	6	May
	62.10			3	Dublin (S), IRE	29	Jul
	61.43			1	Feltham	9	Apr
	61.06			2	Bedford	11	Jun
	60.98			3	Loughborough	21	May
	60.76			3B	Halle, GER	27	May
	59.27			3	Bedford	19	Aug
	59.16			1	London (He)	15	Jul
	58.60			1	Hayes	19	Jul
	56.95			2	Glasgow (S)	8	Jul
	56.67			1	Brighton	17	Jun
63.61	Liz Pidgeon		27.04.77	1B	Halle, GER	27	May
	62.27			1	Enfield	6	Aug
	62.09			2	Bedford	20	Aug
	61.39			1	Liverpool	7	May
	61.26			3	Vittel, FRA	2	Sep
	60.88			1	Chelmsford	14	May
	60.44			1	London (Cr)	27	Aug
	60.33			4	Dublin (S), IRE	29	Jul
	60.32			2	Bedford	19	Aug
	60.12			2	London (Col)	30	Apr
	60.01			5	Szombathely, HUN	23	Jul
	59.95			3	Birmingham	12	Aug
	59.42			7	Budapest, HUN	22	Jul
	58.52			1	Woodford	24	Jun
	57.59			1	Peterborough	9	Jul
58.83	Suzanne Roberts	U23	19.12.78	1	Getafe, SPA	9	Sep
	58.11			4	Birmingham	12	Aug
	57.36			4	Bedford	19	Aug

(Roberts)	57.35			1	Cudworth	28 Aug
	57.07			2	Liverpool	22 Jul
	56.52			4	Vittel, FRA	2 Sep
	56.16			1	Grantham	18 Jun
	56.11			1	Cudworth	20 Aug
57.09	Rachael Beverley	U23	23.07.79	3	Eton	6 May
	56.99			4	Loughborough	21 May
	56.40			2	Getafe, SPA	9 Sep
	56.20			1	Stoke-on-Trent	26 Apr
55.74	Sarah Moore		15.03.73	1	Cardiff	12 Jul
	68 performances to 56.00 by 6 athletes plus 1 with 5kg hammer					
55.62	Diana Holden		12.02.75	5	Loughborough	21 May
55.57	Zoe Derham	U23	24.11.80	1	Worcester	19 Aug
55.10	Mhairi Walters	U20	19.06.81	1	Nicosia, CYP	27 May
54.68	Esther Augee	V35	1.01.64	2	Enfield	6 Aug
	(10)					
54.15	Sarah Harrison	U23	1.03.79	4	Stellenbosch, RSA	18 Feb
53.80	Carys Parry	U20	24.07.81	14Q	Santiago, CHI	17 Oct
53.74	Christina Bennett	U23	27.02.78	3	Bedford	20 Aug
52.47	Vicci Scott	U23	21.09.80	3	Enfield	6 Aug
52.12	Ann Gardner		11.10.68	1	Loughborough	22 Aug
51.86	Lesley Brannan		13.09.76	3	Cwmbran	17 Jun
51.54	Lucy Marshall	U20	28.11.81	3	Derby	3 Sep
50.94	Catherine Garden	U23	4.09.78	4	Bedford	1 Jul
50.42	Katy Lamb	U20	21.08.82	1	London (He)	20 Aug
50.33	Andrea Jenkins		4.10.75	1	Luton	14 May
	(20)					
49.68	Suzanne Last		11.01.70	11	Birmingham	12 Aug
48.66	Karen Chambers		31.08.68	2	Manchester	8 Apr
48.63	Laura Douglas	U20	4.01.83	2	Edinburgh	13 Aug
48.31	Helen Wilding		25.10.76	1	Cleckheaton	1 Jul
48.12	Marina Semenova	V35	12.07.64	13	Birmingham	12 Aug
47.98	Philippa Roles	U23	1.03.78	3	Cardiff	12 Jul
47.89	Helen Taylor	U20	19.07.82	1	Cleckheaton	24 Sep
47.62	Nicola Dudman	U17	5.10.83	6	Bedford	11 Jun
47.38	Belinda Heil	U20	8.03.82	3	Watford	2 Jul
47.33	Shirley Webb	U20	28.09.81	2	Sheffield	7 Jul
	(30)					
47.10	Julie Lavender		9.11.75	1	Sunderland	20 Aug
47.08	Irene Duffin	V35	10.08.60	2	Enfield	20 May
46.99	Janet Smith	V35	7.10.64	7	Bedford	19 Aug
46.57	Helen Arnold	U23	5.10.78	1	Portsmouth	14 May
46.48	Jean Clark		5.10.68	4	Liverpool	7 May
46.39	Karen Bell	U20	18.06.82	2	Grangemouth	25 Jun
46.01	Janette Brown		19.02.73	3	Middlesbrough	15 Jul
45.90	Joanne John	U23	12.11.80	1	Enfield	12 Aug
45.61	Fiona Whitehead		31.05.70	1	Portsmouth	20 May
44.02	Vickie Foster		1.04.71	1	Exeter	16 Jul
	(40)					
43.64	Diane Smith	V35	15.11.60	1	Grimsby	14 May
43.34	Julie Dunkley	U23	11.09.79	5	Woodford	24 Jun
43.32	Claire Pardo	U20	9.08.81	1	Guildford	12 Sep
43.21	Paula Peaty		30.05.66	2	Chelmsford	14 May
43.19	Frances Miller	U17	26.12.84	3	Glasgow (S)	30 Apr
42.97	Lynsey Selbie	U20	9.03.83	3	Derby	6 Aug
42.88	Joanne Holloway		10.05.76	2	Abingdon	2 Sep
42.69	Katie Horne	U23	23.05.79	6	Stoke-on-Trent	29 Apr
42.62	Laura Perry		4.06.75	1	Redditch	27 Aug
42.43	Charlotte Spelzini	U20	7.01.83	1	St. Ives	10 Jun
	(50)					
42.32	Kelly Ricketts		24.01.76	2	Newport	28 Aug

42.18	Madelaine Robinson	U20	13.10.81	1	Middlesbrough	15	Jul
42.02	Emma King	U20	25.07.81	1	St. Peter Port GUE	9	Jul
41.81	Cassie Wilson		24.09.77	2	Cudworth	13	May
41.78	Maysoon Elkhawad		27.02.77	1	Bedford	10	May
41.71	Lindsey Jones		8.09.77	2	Wakefield	16	Apr
41.22	Faye Blacktin	U20	5.11.81	2	Ware	2	Sep
40.99	Joanne Harding	V35	12.04.64	1	Stretford	2	Apr
40.97	Joan MacPherson	U23	18.09.80	4	Bath	9	Jul
40.83	Debbie Callaway	V35	15.07.64	2	Bournemouth	20	May
	(60)						
40.83	Helen Gilbert	U20	1.03.82	2	Peterborough	28	Aug
40.74	Cathy-Ann Hill		4.05.77	4	Kingston	20	May
40.72	Kirsty Walters	U17	6.09.84	3	Blackpool	15	Jul
40.63	Sara-Jane Cattermole		29.01.77	1	Perth	13	Feb
40.54	Anna Howard	U20	18.07.83	2	Bromley	29	Apr
40.48	Eleanor Gatrell		5.10.76	5	Woking	20	Aug
40.21	Verina Horner		15.09.72	3	Cleckheaton	11	Jun
40.21	Karen Ainsley	U23	24.06.80	1	Telford	9	Sep
40.20	Jenny Foster		6.09.77	2	Stretford	8	Aug
40.12	Emma Carpenter	U20	16.05.82	1	Exeter	30	May
	(70)						
40.09	Natasha Smith		6.06.77	1	Barking	24	Jun
40.00	Rachael Cox	U23	27.06.80	2	Birmingham	20	Aug
39.74	Jenny Earle	V40	28.11.58	1	Ewell	12	Aug
39.51	Laura Wood	U23	31.10.78	4	Stretford	8	Aug
39.38	Carly Burton	U23	14.10.80	5	Enfield	6	Aug
39.35	Kim Rawling	U20	22.07.83	1	Carn Brea	6	Aug
39.34	Siobhan Hart		15.06.75	1	Enfield	20	Aug
39.32	Marian James/Routledge		9.05.71	2	Sutton Coldfield	26	Aug
39.22	Jennifer Ayero	U23	13.09.79	2	Stevenage	2	Sep
39.15	Lucy Nesbitt	U17	6.09.84	1	Cudworth	20	Aug
	(80)						
39.07	Sarah Morgan	U17	9.05.84	1	Wigan	25	Jun
39.02	Karen Moody		20.07.67	1	Tamworth	28	Aug
38.84	Natasha Forgie	U17	12.05.84	1	Dartford	24	Sep
38.65	Sarah Symonds/Nickelson		28.12.73	2	Oxford	15	Jul
38.64	Melissa Ashley		17.03.77	2	Guildford	24	Jun
38.64	Jenny Cunnane/Wood	V40	23.02.57	1	Cleckheaton	5	Jul
38.51	Sue Lawrence		25.11.70	2	Thurrock	15	Jul
38.50	Paula Coombs		31.12.69	2	London (TB)	20	May
38.44	Catherine Lane		18.11.76	1	Ilford	2	Sep
38.36	Louise Finlay	U17	2.10.83	1	Cwmbran	17	Jun
	(90)						
38.32	Sarah Drake	U17	13.08.85	1	Cleckheaton	24	Sep
38.29	Zoe Parsons		15.11.69	4	Stoke-on-Trent	6	Aug
38.14	Angela Lockley	U17	7.10.84	1	Stretford	27	Jun
38.04	Hannah Lia	U17	15.11.84	2	Newport	28	Aug
37.90	Claire Fawkes		24.10.77	1	Enfield	12	Aug
37.86	Tracy Shorts		4.11.72	2	Nuneaton	30	Apr
37.71	Kirsty Perrett		17.03.76	3	Gateshead	14	May
37.63	Lynette Bristow		17.11.77	1	Stourport	20	Aug
37.51	Noelle Bradshaw	V35	18.12.63	3	Bournemouth	20	May
37.22	Anna Town		22.04.75	1	London (PH)	15	Jul
	(100)						
37.20	Evaun Williams	V60	19.02.37	4	Enfield	12	Aug
37.16	Paula Cooper		6.08.75	4	Lancaster	7	May

Additional Under 17 (1 - 10 above)

37.09	Emily Oliver	8.02.84	1	Ashford	13	Aug
35.68	Susan McKelvie	15.06.85	3	Grangemouth	17	Jun
35.30	Nicola Jenkins	6.02.84	1	Erith	7	May

34.90	Ruth Morris		17.10.83	3	Newport	28 Aug
34.34	Bethan Lishman		15.11.83	8	Middlesbrough	15 Jul
33.39	Sarah Dobriskey		13.08.85	1	Ashford	21 Jun
33.08	Laura Allan		11.02.85	4	Coatbridge	27 Aug
32.71	Kathryn Evans		1.03.84	3	Inverness	14 May
32.69	Helen Ephgrave		29.10.84	2	Basingstoke	2 Sep
31.49	Claire Stewart		14.10.83	2	Elgin	1 Jan
	(20)					
31.33	Suzanne Frost		27.09.84	1	Exeter	23 Sep
30.95	Angela Farmer		27.03.85	4	Birmingham	10 Sep
30.71	Louise Bennett		11.01.84	3	Erith	7 May
30.61	Leona Wilson		23.05.85	2	Grangemouth	13 May
30.59	Emma Murdoch		26.03.84	1	Inverness	17 Sep
30.42	Laura Mackenzie		9.11.83	2	Inverness	17 Sep

Downhill

46.30	Fiona Whitehead		31.05.70	1	Haslemere	9 May

Light

45.27	Frances Miller	U17	26.12.84	1	Inverness	22 Jul

Foreign

55.50	*Olivia Kelleher (IRE)*		*9.10.75*	*1*	*Sydney, AUS*	*20 Feb*

HAMMER - Under 15 - 3.25kg

40.54	Laura Chalmers		1.05.86	1	Inverness	9 Jul
39.75	Shaeleen Bruce		3.11.86	2	Inverness	9 Jul
38.32	Sarah Holt		17.04.87	1	Middlesbrough	15 Jul

JAVELIN

58.54	Karen Martin		24.11.74	1	Aldershot	5 Jul
	58.07			1	Bedford	4 Jun
	57.75			2	Birmingham	12 Aug
	57.31			1	Derby	6 Aug
	55.73			2B	Halle, GER	27 May
	55.30			1	Nottingham	13 May
	54.74			2	Bedford	19 Aug
	54.62			1	Cosford	16 Apr
	54.23			2	Karlstad, SWE	18 Jun
	53.68 A			1	Pretoria, RSA	24 Mar
	53.41 A			2	Pietersburg, RSA	13 Mar
	52.31			1	Loughborough	21 May
58.45	Kelly Morgan	U23	17.06.80	1	Birmingham	12 Aug
	57.99			1	Solihull	5 Aug
	57.18			1	Bedford	19 Aug
	55.44			2	Getafe, SPA	9 Sep
	54.96			1	Vittel, FRA	2 Sep
	53.41			1	Bedford	20 Aug
57.19	Lorna Jackson		9.01.74	1	Peterborough	9 Jul
	53.57			1	Grangemouth	14 May
	53.48			1	Glasgow (S)	29 Jul
	53.38			1	Coatbridge	16 Jul
	53.19			1	Bedford	28 May
54.58	Goldie Sayers	U20	16.07.82	Q	Santiago, CHI	19 Oct
	53.79			1	Grosseto, ITA	7 Oct
	52.69			2	Bedford	4 Jun
53.06	Shelley Holroyd		17.05.73	1	Liverpool	7 May
	52.10			2	Peterborough	9 Jul
52.20	Jenny Kemp	U23	18.02.80	Q	Stoke-on-Trent	29 Apr
	52.13			3	Bedford	4 Jun
	30 performances to 52.00 by 6 athletes					

51.79	Chloe Cozens	U23	9.04.80	1H	Waterford, IRE	3 Sep
51.22	Kirsty Morrison		28.10.75	1	Ashford	7 May
51.13	Denise Lewis		27.08.72	3	Bedford	19 Aug
48.77	Linda Gray		23.03.71	1	Belfast	8 Jul
	(10)					
48.24	Tammie Francis	U23	14.11.78	1	Portsmouth	29 Apr
48.00	Sharon Gibson	V35	31.12.61	1	Solihull	29 Jul
47.57	Amy Harvey	U20	23.04.82	3	Grosseto, ITA	7 Oct
46.81	Noelle Bradshaw	V35	18.12.63	4	Bedford	19 Aug
46.66	Katie Amos	U23	13.11.78	4	Ljubljana, SLO	25 Jul
46.02	Clova Court	V40	10.02.60	8	Birmingham	12 Aug
45.84	Suzanne Finnis	U20	12.08.83	1	Woodford	24 Jun
45.24	Samantha Redd	U17	16.02.84	1	Watford	27 May
43.82	Katherine Evans		19.11.77	3	Stoke-on-Trent	30 Apr
43.79	Joanne Bruce	U23	26.10.78	4	Stoke-on-Trent	30 Apr
	(20)					
43.70	Chissie Head	U23	18.12.79	1	Great Yarmouth	13 Aug
43.46	Katy Watts	U20	25.03.81	Q	Stoke-on-Trent	29 Apr
43.44	Lucy Stevenson		30.01.73	2	Eton	6 May
43.41	Melanie Burrows		7.08.76	1	Reading	20 May
43.11	Charlotte Rees	U17	14.06.84	1	Newport	28 Aug
42.95	Wendy Newman		31.08.71	2	Woodford	24 Jun
42.73	Carol Wallbanks	U20	9.12.82	1	Carlisle	10 Jul
42.62	Louise Smith		11.07.77	2	Reading	20 May
42.51	Jennifer Ayero	U23	13.09.79	1	London (Cr)	27 Aug
42.19	Paula Blank/Collis		13.12.77	7	Bedford	28 May
	(30)					
41.99	Sarah Ellis	U17	27.10.83	2	Watford	27 May
41.98	Lucy Rann	U23	5.09.80	1	Sandown IOW	4 Sep
41.82	Jenny Grimstone	U23	30.04.79	4	Bedford	1 Jul
41.73	Nicola Gautier	U23	21.03.78	12H	Arles, FRA	4 Jun
41.62	Katie Granger		31.03.75	1	Exeter	24 Jun
41.62	Georgina Hogsden	U20	23.11.81	1	Basingstoke	2 Sep
41.48	Cathy Edgar	U23	27.02.80	1	Antrim	20 Jun
41.47	Jo Chapman	U17	10.01.85	1	London (He)	20 Aug
41.34	Janine King		18.02.73	4	Bedford	19 Aug
41.17	Michelle Lonsdale	U20	29.10.81	1	Cannock	30 Jul
	(40)					
41.11	Alison Siggery	U17	14.09.83	1	Grangemouth	5 Aug
41.09	Liz Pidgeon		27.04.77	4	London (Cr)	27 Aug
40.98	Lisa Fryer	U17	30.05.84	2	Antrim	20 Jun
40.89	Emily Skucek	U20	24.09.81	1	Wrexham	18 Jul
40.71	Rebecca Foster		14.04.71	5H	Hexham	21 May
40.67	Anne Hollman		18.02.74	2H	Waterford, IRE	3 Sep
40.45	Emma Rich		14.05.77	8	Stoke-on-Trent	30 Apr
40.37	Vicky James	U20	13.05.81	1	Bath	14 May
39.89	Catherine O'Halloran	U20	17.09.81	1	Cleckheaton	27 May
39.74	Rachel Dunn	U20	14.11.82	3	London (He)	20 Aug
	(50)					
39.57	Helen Potter		25.06.74	1	Stretford	28 Jun
39.55	Louise Matthews	U17	27.10.83	1	London (Nh)	27 Aug
39.54	Rebecca Bartlett	U17	7.03.85	1	Solihull	28 May
39.43	Danielle Freeman	U23	11.02.80	Q	Stoke-on-Trent	29 Apr
39.40	Lucy Newman	U20	2.03.83	4	Watford	28 May
39.17	Amber Jackson	U20	29.11.82	1	Ware	16 Jul
39.11	Joanne Harding	V35	12.04.64	5	Eton	23 Jul
39.00	Siona Kelly		19.04.74	1	Stockport	7 May
38.67	Kathryn Redd	U20	8.06.82	5	Sheffield	8 Jul
38.56	Anyha Kerr	U23	10.04.80	1	Bath	14 May
	(60)					
38.47	Helen Davis	U17	31.01.85	2	London (WF)	17 Sep
38.40	Vicki Hemmings		4.06.74	1	Aldershot	21 Jun

38.39	Colette Doran	U17	20.09.83	1	Carlisle	19 Jul
38.36	Helen Mounteney	U17	24.09.84	4	Ljubljana, SLO	23 Sep
38.28	Claire Bennett	U20	4.02.83	1	Cannock	18 Jun
38.21	Diana Bennett/Norman		14.06.74	4	Bedford	20 Aug
38.14	Natasha Campbell	U20	6.08.82	1	Bromley	23 Apr
38.06	Natalie Butler	U23	25.11.78	1	Oxford	14 May
38.06	Laura Smith	U17	21.01.84	1	Carlisle	10 Jun
37.94	Hayley Boddey	U20	14.02.83	1	Derby	10 Jun
	(70)					
37.88	Tammy Carless		10.01.77	1	Barking	2 Apr
37.87	Nicky Rolfe		19.08.69	3	Basingstoke	11 Jun
37.86	Clare Lockwood	U23	7.10.79	3	Derby	3 Sep
37.82	Vanessa Stennett		3.06.69	4	Eton	11 Jun
37.65	Roz Gonse	U20	1.03.82	1H	Birmingham	17 Sep
37.64	Kate Grainger	U17	17.02.84	5	Nicosia, CYP	27 May
37.62	Kathryn Stringer	U20	24.09.81	1	Cleethorpes	23 Apr
37.52	Carol Costelloe		14.01.76	2	Stretford	28 Jun
37.45	Laura Bolton	U23	22.01.79	1	Plymouth	15 Jul
37.43	Susan Theobald	U20	4.03.83	1	Ipswich	29 May
	(80)					
37.38	Debbie Woolgar	V35	10.03.65	1	Crawley	14 May
37.36	Lauren Therin	U15	19.01.86	1	Watford	27 May
37.26	Gillian Stewart	U23	21.01.80	1	Glasgow (S)	30 Apr
37.25	Emma Thornton	U20	27.11.82	1	Bolton	7 May
37.20	Danielle Mansfield	U20	18.05.82	2	Chelmsford	14 May
37.19	Nicola Rich	U20	23.02.83	1	Exeter	17 Jun
37.06	Paula Hendriks	U20	25.01.83	2H	Birmingham	17 Sep
37.01	Jo Davis		23.06.73	2	Neath	20 Aug

Additional Under 17 (1 - 13 above)

36.86	Candace Schofield	3.11.84	2	Ilford	2 Sep
36.85	Tanya Hunt	14.09.83	1	London (PH)	29 Apr
36.55	Eloise Manger	6.01.85	1	Lancaster	14 May
36.25	Sarah Garrard	13.05.84	1	London (Cr)	10 May
35.90	Jennifer Leng	1.02.84	1	Blackpool	10 Jun
35.54	Elizabeth Dunn	5.01.85	2	Norwich	17 Jun

Additional Under 15 (1 above)

36.03	Kelly-Jane Berry	23.04.87	1	Yeovil	28 Aug
35.98	Debbie Collinson	23.10.85	1	Jarrow	24 Jun
35.61	Louise Watton	30.10.86	1	Exeter	17 Jun
34.84	Christine Lawrence	4.04.86	1	Bedford	27 Aug
34.16	Joanna Blair	1.03.86	3	Sheffield	8 Jul
34.09	Lark Hanham	25.10.85	1	Yate	10 Jun
33.94	Venetia Ellis	15.09.85	1	London (Cr)	14 May
32.81	Hayley Thomas	16.12.86	1	Chelmsford	1 May
32.16	Rebecca Clutterbuck	13.05.86	6	Sheffield	8 Jul
	(10)				
32.02	Abby Wildbore	12.09.85	7	Sheffield	8 Jul
31.66	Heather Nelson	7.01.86	1	York	10 Jun
31.55	Samantha Case	5.01.86	1	Guildford	12 Aug
31.41	Ashleigh Critchfield	2.03.86	2	Basildon	10 Jun
30.88	Natalie Griffiths	22.04.86	5	Bedford	26 Aug
30.88	Natonia Hagan	6.08.86			
30.82	Alex Oglethorpe	4.09.85	1	Horsham	17 Jun
30.60	Melanie Harrison	27.11.85	2	Chelmsford	1 May
30.52	Hannah Lishman	5.10.85	9	Sheffield	8 Jul
30.19	Cara Marsden	22.05.86	1	Colwyn Bay	3 Sep

Foreign

45.85	*Alison Moffitt (IRE)*	*6.10.69*	*1*	*Belfast*	*20 May*
39.01	*Katrina Campbell (IRE)*	*8.03.72*	*Q*	*Stoke-on-Trent*	*29 Apr*

JAVELIN - Under 13 - 400 grams

30.25	Emma Smith		1	Woodford	19 Jul
28.98	Vicky Doran	17.04.88	1	Carlisle	27 May
28.04	Larnaca Panayiotou	5.02.88	1	Tamworth	28 Aug
27.29	Emma Gray	17.04.88	1	Kirkwall	2 Sep
27.19	Claire Lyne-Ley	14.03.88	1	Exeter	26 Sep
25.71	Lucy Baggley		1	Colwyn Bay	22 Apr
25.36	Joedy Platt	27.11.87	1	Plymouth	27 May
25.26	Ashley Austin	29.09.87	1	Glasgow	5 Sep
24.90	Bethany Staniland	10.05.88	1	Warrington	20 Aug
24.87	Laura Carr	18.02.89	1	Exeter	3 Sep
	(10)				
24.50	Chloe Beckett	10.06.88	1	Wakefield	17 Sep
24.25	C. Smith		1	Macclesfield	14 May

HEPTATHLON

6831	Denise Lewis			27.08.72	1	Talence, FRA		30 Jul
	13.13/1.0	1.84	15.07	24.01w/3.6	6.69/-0.4	49.42	2:12.20	
	6584				1	Sydney, AUS		24 Sep
	13.23/0.3	1.75	15.55	24.34/-0.1	6.48/0.8	50.19	2:16.83	
5735	Kerry Jury			19.11.68	2	Logrono, SPA		20 Aug
	13.92/-0.3	1.77	11.58	24.26/-0.6	5.71/0.1	34.33	2:14.89	
	5667				9	Schwyz/Ibach, SWZ		2 Jul
	13.93/0.4	1.78	11.40	24.62/-1.0	5.70/-1.7	34.29	2:16.93	
	5638				13	Arles, FRA		4 Jun
	13.78w/2.9	1.77	10.87	24.34w/2.7	5.58/0.3	35.95	2:18.90	
5685	Julie Hollman			16.02.77	3	Logrono, SPA		20 Aug
	14.55/-0.3	1.74	12.64	24.81/-0.6	6.06w/2.6	32.16	2:15.46	
	5622				1	Waterford, IRE		3 Sep
	14.48w/3.0	1.60	12.55	24.72/-0.8	6.51/1.3	31.80	2:18.61	
	5560				1	Stoke-on-Trent		30 Jul
	14.64/0.8	1.78	12.15	25.37/1.4	5.87/-0.8	32.33	2:17.22	
5644	Danielle Freeman			U23 11.02.80	12	Arles, FRA		4 Jun
	13.62/1.8	1.71	11.48	24.98/0.9	5.88/-0.3	35.42	2:19.14	
	5442				14	Schwyz/Ibach, SWZ		2 Jul
	13.91/-0.5	1.72	11.83	25.02/-0.3	5.37/-1.2	38.14	2:26.12	
	5014				6	Val de Reuil, FRA		13 Aug
	14.18/-0.6	1.67	11.38	25.56/0.3	4.76/0.4	33.43	2:25.53	
5602	Nicola Gautier			U23 21.03.78	15	Arles, FRA		4 Jun
	14.14w/2.9	1.59	13.69	25.25/1.8	5.70/0.4	41.73	2:20.12	
5538	Julia Bennett			26.03.70	19	Arles, FRA		4 Jun
	14.67/1.7	1.83	11.61	25.85/1.4	5.91/0.6	34.57	2:21.32	
	5444				13	Schwyz/Ibach, SWZ		2 Jul
	15.13/0.0	1.81	11.60	26.18/0.0	5.98/1.9	35.43	2:22.55	
5428	Kelly Sotherton			13.11.76	20	Arles, FRA		4 Jun
	14.15/1.7	1.68	10.64	24.54/1.3	6.03/-0.4	27.11	2:17.37	
	5411				2	Waterford, IRE		3 Sep
	14.25w/3.0	1.66	11.70	24.48/-0.8	6.04/1.2	28.13	2:23.04	
	5388				2	Stoke-on-Trent		30 Jul
	14.32/0.8	1.69	10.84	24.63/1.4	5.91/0.2	27.17	2:17.24	
5308	Diana Bennett/Norman			14.06.74	23	Arles, FRA		4 Jun
	14.54/0.8	1.71	11.23	26.71/1.4	5.57/-0.3	34.75	2:14.11	
5279	Fiona Harrison			U20 30.11.81	11	Santiago, CHI		21 Oct
	14.34/-0.9	1.68	10.11	25.49/-0.2	5.69/-0.3	32.82	2:17.84	
	5250				2	Watford		24 Sep
	14.18/0.4	1.70	9.83	25.27/-0.8	5.59/-0.1	32.37	2:20.71	
5257	Chloe Cozens			U23 9.04.80	1	Watford		24 Sep
	15.30/0.4	1.70	12.40	26.39/-0.8	5.54/-0.5	45.52	2:32.43	
	5246				3	Waterford, IRE		3 Sep
	15.10w/3.0	1.63	12.31	27.01/-0.8	5.41/0.3	51.79	2:30.60	

(Cozens) 5205 4 Val de Reuil, FRA 13 Aug
15.55/0.7 1.64 12.22 26.98/0.4 5.30/0.8 51.67 2:27.20
5098 28 Arles, FRA 4 Jun
15.28/0.8 1.71 12.49 26.94/1.4 5.23/0.6 41.67 2:29.96
(10)
5186 Rebecca Jones U20 17.01.83 25 Arles, FRA 4 Jun
14.80/1.7 1.83 10.57 26.00/1.0 5.65/1.1 33.45 2:33.28
5173 Katherine Livesey U23 15.12.79 6 Columbia, USA 20 May
14.15/1.6 1.70 10.41 25.80/0.9 5.51/-1.1 30.80 2:22.13
5079 4 Des Moines, USA 28 Apr
14.3w/2.3 1.69 9.93 25.0w/2.1 5.40/1.2 29.60 2:21.41
5151 Anne Hollman 18.02.74 27 Arles, FRA 4 Jun
14.20/1.3 1.65 11.58 25.60/1.3 5.31/-0.3 37.04 2:30.74
5028 3 Stoke-on-Trent 30 Jul
14.19/0.8 1.63 10.77 26.24/1.4 5.33/0.2 37.05 2:30.45
5028 4 Waterford, IRE 3 Sep
15.16w/2.3 1.60 11.73 26.25/0.1 5.41w/3.4 40.67 2:29.53
5014 Sarah Still 24.09.75 5 Waterford, IRE 3 Sep
14.73w/2.3 1.66 9.45 24.48/0.1 5.68/0.6 20.86 2:18.59
31 performances to 5000 points by 14 athletes
4998 Paula Hendriks U20 25.01.83 1 Birmingham 17 Sep
15.11/1.6 1.60 11.40 26.19/0.7 5.30/0.0 37.06 2:23.29
4961 Charmaine Johnson V35 4.06.63 31(20)Arles, FRA 4 Jun
14.78/1.3 1.62 12.99 26.45/1.0 5.25/-0.1 33.17 2:30.93
4954 Laura Redmond U20 19.04.81 1 Waterford, IRE 3 Sep
15.37/1.9 1.66 11.18 26.15/0.7 5.38/2.0 33.35 2:24.83
4921 Kirsty Roger U23 24.03.78 33 (8) Arles, FRA 4 Jun
14.76/1.7 1.62 10.86 27.01/1.0 5.63/0.3 29.54 2:22.89
4736 Kate Brewington U20 15.10.81 2 Waterford, IRE 3 Sep
14.55/1.9 1.60 9.07 26.43/0.7 5.42/1.3 34.63 2:35.34
4679 Rebecca Foster 14.04.71 6 Hexham 21 May
15.00/1.6 1.48 10.56 26.78/0.2 5.21 40.71 2:33.96
(20)
4588 Samantha Adamson U20 27.03.82 1 Eton 25 Jun
15.5/-0.4 1.75 10.02 26.0/-0.2 4.85 29.40 2:34.7
4557 Roz Gonse U20 1.03.82 4 Waterford, IRE 3 Sep
15.47w/3.3 1.54 9.40 25.98/0.7 5.34w/2.3 32.81 2:34.56
4553 Hannah Stares U23 13.11.78 1 Enfield 30 Jul
14.93/0.5 1.56 9.31 25.94/1.6 5.03/1.9 31.02 2:32.36
4538 Lara Carty U17 7.03.84 10 Val de Reuil, FRA 13 Aug
14.83/0.7 1.64 7.80 26.52/0.3 5.41/0.9 27.08 2:32.82
4506 Belinda Samuels U23 29.11.78 1 Stoke-on-Trent 18 Jun
15.46/-3.4 1.58 10.68 26.25/-0.7 5.13/0.1 31.51 2:40.87
4502 Sarah Godbeer 10.06.77 1 Exeter 1 Jun
15.3 1.60 9.85 25.4 5.06 27.15 2:33.8
4501 Claire Everett U23 25.06.79 6 Stoke-on-Trent 30 Jul
16.15w/3.0 1.60 11.69 27.41/0.6 5.23/0.3 25.60 2:26.82
4418 Clare Milborrow 10.01.77 1 Crawley 10 Sep
14.4 1.60 8.49 25.6 5.46 22.28 2:43.7
4353 Jemma Scott U20 14.03.83 3 Stoke-on-Trent 30 Jul
15.28/0.7 1.60 8.60 27.33/0.8 5.28/1.1 25.40 2:32.52
4347 Wendy Davidson U20 14.10.82 4 Stoke-on-Trent 30 Jul
15.11/0.7 1.48 9.32 25.77/0.8 5.55/-0.2 20.20 2:36.73
(30)
4336 Danielle Parkinson U20 2.09.81 1 Cannock 25 Jun
15.7 1.65 8.67 26.2 5.51 29.04 2:50.7
4286 Amanda Wale 14.10.70 1 Gateshead 23 Jul
15.73/1.9 1.54 8.78 27.36w/2.3 5.14/1.7 27.02 2:27.66
4276 Natalie Hulse U20 2.12.82 2 Stoke-on-Trent 18 Jun
16.59/-3.4 1.58 8.78 27.16/-0.7 5.42w/3.2 27.98 2:33.02

4112 Jenny Truelove U20 19.01.81 2 Enfield 30 Jul
15.77/0.5 1.59 8.97 27.30/1.2 5.33w/2.2 21.55 2:44.06
4110 Cathy Young U20 14.03.82 1 Corby 25 Jun
16.5 1.65 9.46 28.1 4.92 24.23 2:30.6
4056 Jenny Kelly 20.06.70 40 Arles, FRA 4 Jun
dnf 1.50 13.97 26.43/1.0 5.59/0.8 30.91 2:32.42
4051 Sara Todd U23 3.11.79 2 Jarrow 25 Jun
15.22/1.2 1.38 8.58 26.07/0.4 4.92 23.56 2:35.45
4047 Stephanie Little U20 5.11.81 6 Waterford, IRE 3 Sep
16.00w/3.3 1.45 9.00 27.83/0.7 4.82/1.7 30.85 2:33.51
4034 Vicky Williams U20 11.04.81 3 Stoke-on-Trent 18 Jun
15.62/-3.4 1.49 7.84 27.14/-0.7 5.29w/2.7 27.37 2:46.03
4022 Rachael Harris U20 17.07.82 5 Birmingham 17 Sep
15.34/1.6 1.54 6.72 25.20w/2.5 4.75/-0.2 16.98 2:33.62
(40)
4019 Sara Barry U20 8.06.83 1 Yeovil 25 Jun
15.5 1.51 8.70 27.0 5.21 23.34 2:43.3
4019 Jenny Pacey U20 5.02.83 6 Birmingham 17 Sep
15.91/2.0 1.54 9.73 27.39w/3.4 4.68/-1.2 22.48 2:35.37
3987 Grace Smith U20 30.01.82 2 Cannock 25 Jun
15.1 1.41 8.97 27.1 5.34 25.55 2:49.0
3956 Laura Curtis U20 2.05.81 3 Jarrow 25 Jun
16.75w/3.2 1.50 10.46 28.13/1.5 4.76 23.95 2:31.78
3946 w Alex Hewett U20 10.09.82 8 Birmingham 17 Sep
17.60W/5.4 1.51 9.67 28.21/0.8 4.63/1.4 35.14 2:35.41
3809 2 Eton 25 Jun
18.5/-0.4 1.57 9.26 28.7/-0.2 4.73 34.34 2:37.1
3918 Jacqueline Elliott U23 13.09.78 7 Hexham 21 May
17.39/1.6 1.39 8.29 26.37/0.2 4.96 22.16 2:21.49
3911 Megan Freeth U20 1.02.82 2 Wrexham 25 Jun
15.90w/3.5 1.52 8.28 26.67/-1.7 4.92/1.0 20.32 2:39.42
3885 Lucy Butler U20 18.11.81 1 Hexham 21 May
15.9/1.2 1.45 8.71 27.3 5.27 23.08 2:43.93
3870 Judith Butler U23 5.10.79 7 Stoke-on-Trent 30 Jul
16.77w/3.0 1.48 7.94 27.70/0.6 5.18/0.4 22.57 2:33.33
3819 Lisa Biscoe U20 13.01.83 9 Birmingham 17 Sep
17.12/1.0 1.60 7.73 27.78w/2.5 4.93/-0.7 20.18 2:34.44
(50)
3812 Teresa Mainstone U20 13.07.81 4 Stoke-on-Trent 18 Jun
18.11/-3.4 1.49 8.66 28.67/-0.7 5.00w/2.1 31.97 2:35.01

HEPTATHLON - Under 17

4395 Lara Carty 7.03.84 1 Birmingham 17 Sep
11.65w/2.2 1.60 7.81 26.32/0.7 5.10/0.4 28.02 2:35.17
4338 Hannah Barnes 2.06.84 1 Stoke-on-Trent 18 Jun
12.38/-1.1 1.44 8.03 26.19/-1.3 5.45w/2.4 29.74 2:29.88
4338 Sarah Gallaway 14.11.84 1 Eton 25 Jun
12.3/0.1 1.54 9.18 26.3/1.0 5.06 23.77 2:25.5
4322 Louise Toward 27.03.84 1 Cannock 25 Jun
12.3 1.46 9.89 26.7 5.37 28.50 2:34.7
4254 Samantha Backwell 4.02.85 1 Yeovil 25 Jun
13.1 1.60 7.51 27.3 5.03 27.36 2:19.9
4247 Danielle Fawkes 11.08.85 2 Cannock 25 Jun
12.0 1.55 8.14 26.1 5.24 20.87 2:32.4
4240 Stephanie Dalton 8.02.84 1 York 25 Jun
12.8 1.62 9.03 27.3 5.15 23.89 2:30.5
4227 Chanelle Garnett 16.08.85 5 Birmingham 17 Sep
11.52w/2.2 1.51 7.80 26.06w/2.3 5.32/1.3 17.17 2:32.15
4213 Olivia Ross-Hurst 10.12.83 6 Birmingham 17 Sep
12.47w/2.7 1.57 8.12 26.68/0.7 5.20/-0.3 22.00 2:30.36

4200	Henrietta Paxton	19.09.83	2	Yeovil	25 Jun
	12.4 1.63 7.98 27.3 5.49 23.88 2:41.3				
	(10)				
4162	Emily Parker	7.11.84	2	Eton	25 Jun
	12.2/0.1 1.54 5.80 25.8/1.7 5.35 20.67 2:28.5				
4104	Liza Parry	24.10.84	9	Birmingham	17 Sep
	13.42/0.6 1.45 8.80 25.26/0.7 4.98/-0.3 21.06 2:26.81				
4063	Kimberley Goodall	5.10.83	12	Birmingham	17 Sep
	13.26/0.6 1.45 8.34 27.03/2.0 5.12/-0.1 27.28 2:29.08				
4034	Carly Robson	5.12.83	3	Eton	25 Jun
	12.5/0.1 1.51 8.46 27.4/1.7 4.96 24.63 2:32.9				
4028	Faith Cripps	23.09.83	1	Rugby	25 Jun
	12.5 1.45 8.00 27.2 5.22 25.59 2:34.3				
4001	Rachel Brenton	18.01.85	13	Birmingham	17 Sep
	12.36/1.2 1.63 6.97 27.09w/3.5 5.15/-0.9 22.07 2:45.36				
3992	Anna Clayton	20.03.85	14	Birmingham	17 Sep
	12.23w/3.5 1.54 8.12 26.56/2.0 4.71/0.7 23.65 2:40.93				
3972	Sarah Walsh	28.01.85	16	Birmingham	17 Sep
	13.60w/3.5 1.57 7.78 27.13/2.0 4.98/-0.3 22.38 2:30.28				
3963	Rachel Thomas	19.01.85	3	York	25 Jun
	12.3 1.44 8.05 26.3 4.87 19.16 2:29.7				
3928	Hayley Goodall	20.09.84	1	Ashford	17 Sep
	12.6/0.2 1.57 7.00 27.5/2.0 4.74 22.27 2:29.6				
	(20)				
3902	Gemma Tune	28.02.84	18	Birmingham	17 Sep
	13.31w/3.5 1.48 8.94 27.05/2.0 4.97/-0.2 18.91 2:31.45				
3885	Laura Taylor	22.04.84	19	Birmingham	17 Sep
	12.43w/2.3 1.51 8.16 27.50/2.0 4.79/0.2 18.84 2:32.71				
3883	Adele Oliver	5.10.84	3	Stoke-on-Trent	18 Jun
	13.64/-1.1 1.56 8.47 27.21/-1.3 5.11w/3.0 17.64 2:35.01				
3863	Sarah Henderson	27.09.83	6	Eton	25 Jun
	13.1/1.5 1.60 7.67 26.8/0.1 5.05 20.86 2:46.6				
3860	Gemma Evans	9.09.84	4	Yeovil	25 Jun
	12.6 1.48 8.83 27.7 4.94 26.60 2:47.0				
3847	Hayley Jasper	1.05.84	2	Corby	25 Jun
	13.1 1.49 8.10 27.2 4.50 24.90 2:30.7				
3846	Jade Weekes	15.11.84	2	Ashford	17 Sep
	12.6w/2.7 1.51 8.76 27.6/2.0 4.42 28.66 2:42.8				

PENTATHLON - Under 15

3236	Emma Perkins	4.09.85	1	Crawley	10 Sep
	5.07 11.9 10.15 1.68 2:37.4				
3207	Louise Hazel	6.10.85	1	Birmingham	17 Sep
	5.20/-3.6 11.48/0.6 9.74 1.52 2:29.40				
3172	Faye Harding	7.09.85	1	Hexham	27 Aug
	5.06 11.9 8.37 1.51 2:17.7				
3109	Jessica Ennis	28.01.86	1	Stoke-on-Trent	18 Jun
	5.34 11.68/-3.2 7.92 1.69 2:45.95				
3062	Phyllis Agbo	16.12.85	3	Birmingham	17 Sep
	5.20/-2.0 11.06/0.6 10.46 1.55 2:54.44				
2936	Hollie Lundgren	10.10.85	1	Enfield	30 Jul
	5.14/1.8 12.47/1.7 9.19 1.61 2:47.38				
2890	Layla Hawkins	3.09.86	2	Enfield	30 Jul
	5.11w/2.1 12.59/0.8 8.23 1.61 2:43.78				
2879	Rachel Spencer	19.08.86	1	Dundee	17 Sep
	4.99 12.5 7.83 1.51 2:30.9				
2861	Jade Halket	5.05.86	1	Glasgow (S)	10 Jun
	4.98 12.3 6.62 1.56 2:32.2				
2857	Jenny Christie	28.09.85	4	Birmingham	17 Sep
	4.57/-0.1 12.47/0.8 8.61 1.55 2:31.73				

2800	Lucy Fisher	27.09.85	1	Cannock	25 Jun
	5.01 11.6 10.52 1.46 2:59.0				
2799	Emma Morris	21.02.86	1	York	25 Jun
	4.40 12.6 6.49 1.65 2:30.2				
2799	Stacy Flint	18.10.85	1	Hexham	23 Sep
	5.09 12.2 7.28 1.51 2:39.52				
2793	Nadine Simpson	28.02.86	6	Birmingham	17 Sep
	4.61/-1.2 12.34/0.7 8.35 1.52 2:34.78				
2787	Elen Davies	24.04.86	2	Wrexham	24 Jun
	5.01 12.3 7.21 1.56 2:42.30				
2776	Rachel Culshaw	11.08.86	7	Birmingham	17 Sep
	4.34/-1.9 12.37/0.8 6.60 1.61 2:29.52				
2769	Gemma Nicol	27.07.86	2	Grangemouth	3 Sep
	4.68 12.44/-1.7 8.32 1.48 2:33.47				
2767	Juliet Adeloye	13.06.86	4	Eton	25 Jun
	4.98 12.8/-2.0 7.99 1.48 2:35.4				
2757	Jenny Bliss	6.07.86	5	Eton	25 Jun
	4.66 12.2/-2.0 7.20 1.42 2:25.2				
2751	Naida Bromley	27.09.86	2	York	25 Jun
	4.96 12.8 9.18 1.44 2:39.0				
	(20)				
2729	Samantha Day	8.02.86	3	Cannock	25 Jun
	4.60 11.6 8.69 1.46 2:43.6				
2719	Nicola Martell	20.09.85	1	Chelmsford	1 May
	4.75 12.4 8.46 1.48 2:40.3				
2699	Donna Creighton	20.09.85	1	Yeovil	25 Jun
	4.73 13.0 7.67 1.50 2:33.9				
2692	Rachel Gibbens	31.01.86	10	Birmingham	17 Sep
	4.43/-2.8 12.44/-0.5 7.47 1.49 2:31.04				
2689	Jemma Garrett	21.09.85	3	York	25 Jun
	4.67 13.2 7.81 1.47 2:30.0				
2682	Helen Morton	17.09.85	4	Enfield	30 Jul
	4.86/1.8 12.02/1.7 6.93 1.46 2:39.42				
2658	Amelia Vaughan	26.05.86	2	Yeovil	25 Jun
	4.53 13.1 7.88 1.47 2:30.7				
2656	Helena Carter	17.05.86	4	York	25 Jun
	5.01 12.4 5.73 1.50 2:38.6				
2625	Amy Fozzard	20.04.86	5	York	25 Jun
	4.54 12.5 8.55 1.38 2:34.2				
2618	Emma Smith	14.09.85	3	Corby	25 Jun
	4.50 12.7 6.97 1.45 2:30.1				
	(30)				
2592	Stephanie Madgett	22.02.87	8	Eton	25 Jun
	5.14 11.9/-1.7 8.59 1.36 2:56.3				
2590	Amy Forsyth	16.10.85	1	London (TB)	24 May
	4.34 12.3 8.91 1.45 2:43.2				

Irregular events

2903	Gemma Nicol	27.07.86	1	Dunfermline	1 Jun
	7.38 26.0 12.5 4.72 2:32.4			(SP, 200, 75HG, LJ, 800)	

PENTATHLON - Under 13

2379	Anna Griffiths	28.12.87	1	Manchester (BHC)	16 Apr
	4.26 12.2 8.74 1.39 2:42.9				
2319	Hannah Weekes		1	Hemel Hempstead	16 Jul
	4.29 13.0 6.68 1.45 2:39.2				
2291	Carly Sharp	7.09.87	1	Grangemouth	3 Sep
	4.17 12.53 6.07 1.42 2:36.26				
2286	Emily Bonnett	22.09.87	1	Hemel Hempstead	16 Jul
	4.09 12.5 7.18 1.33 2:33.5				
2241	Chelsea Bearman		1	Crawley	10 Sep
	4.23 12.1 6.68 1.35 2:42.4				

2213	Claire Soutar		26.04.88	1	Dundee	17 Sep
	3.66 12.8 6.17 1.38 2:36.9					
2191	Kim Skinner		21.09.87	2	Grangemouth	3 Sep
	4.39 12.88 7.46 1.36 2:49.97					
2142	Danielle Christmas		21.12.87	2	Crawley	10 Sep
	3.99 13.1 6.62 1.26 2:30.6					
2100	Danielle Thomas			1	Carlisle	15 Jul
	4.00 13.1 7.72 1.33 2:54.9					
2060	Bethany Staniland		10.05.88	2	Hexham	20 May
	3.97 13.81 7.15 1.18 2:35.0					
	(10)					
2000	Claire Alexander			1	Portsmouth	1 May
	3.54 12.4 5.23 1.33 2:37.7					

2000 METRES WALK - Track - Under 13

11:15.0	Rebecca Mersh		28.01.89	1	Bebington	4 Nov
11:19.3	Sarah Bowling		19.03.88	2	Bebington	4 Nov
11:33.7	Fiona McGoram		10.11.88	4	Bebington	4 Nov
11:47.0	Jade Edgington		8.02.89	2	Rugby	1 Jul
11:56.13	Hayley Repton		23.05.88	2	Birmingham	23 Sep

3000 METRES WALK - Track

12:50.61	Lisa Kehler		15.03.67	1	Solihull	29 Jul
	12:59.0			1	Rugby	1 Jul
	13:17.79 +			1m	Birmingham	13 Aug
13:58.96	Catherine Charnock		3.05.75	3	Vittel, FRA	2 Sep
14:07.8	Sharon Tonks		18.04.70	1	Leamington	13 May
	14:17.50 i			2	Birmingham	29 Jan
	14:24.11			2	Solihull	29 Jul
14:08.52	Niobe Menandez		1.09.66	4	Vittel, FRA	2 Sep
14:10.9 +	Sara-Jane Cattermole		29.01.77	1m	Murdoch, AUS	23 Jul
	14:12.70 mx			1	Perth, AUS	13 Feb
	14:29.2			1	Perth, AUS	2 Feb
14:29.37 i	Nicola Phillips	U20	23.04.83	4	Neubrandenburg, GER	4 Mar
	15:36.88			1	London (He)	20 Aug
14:30.3	Kate Horwill		26.01.75	2	Redditch	13 May
14:37.4	Wendy Bennett		21.12.65	3	Redditch	13 May
14:49.6	Sally Warren	U23	29.01.78	1	Brighton	17 Jun
15:05.69	Sophie Hales	U17	30.03.85	1	Blackpool	15 Jul
	(10)					
15:10.7	Lisa Crump		30.03.76	1	Cudworth	13 May
15:13.68	Nikki Huckerby	U23	27.02.78	2	Derby	3 Sep
15:18.5	Jane Kennaugh		26.01.73	1	Douglas IOM	8 Jul
15:39.0	Jo Hesketh		16.06.69	1	London (Cr)	27 Sep
15:46.72	Laura Fryer	U17	3.12.83	3	Blackpool	15 Jul
15:57.2	Bridget Kaneen		15.08.65	2	Douglas IOM	8 Jul
16:00.2	Natalie Evans	U17	15.11.83	2	Birmingham	16 Sep
16:01.9	Nicky Reynolds	U17	24.06.85	2	Bromsgrove	15 Oct
16:08.88	Claire Reeves	U17	31.07.84	3	London (He)	20 Aug
16:10.3 i	Carolyn Watson	V35		1	Birmingham	26 Feb
	(20)					
16:12.0	Natalie Geens	U17	27.12.84	5	Rugby	1 Jul
16:15.5	Katie Stones	U15	22.11.85	1	Bebington	4 Nov
16:17.70	Ann Lewis	V50	29.12.47	1	Bedford	24 May
16:20.8	Bryna Chrismas	U15	18.06.86	2	Bebington	4 Nov

Foreign

15:33.2	*Sigrun Sangvik (NOR)*	*V40*	*5.02.57*	*1*	*Bromley*	*12 Jul*

5000 METRES WALK - Track

22:22.94 +	Lisa Kehler		15.03.67	1m	Birmingham	13 Aug
24:22.84	Niobe Menandez		1.09.66	1	Dublin (S), IRE	19 Aug
24:38.4	Kim Braznell	V40	28.02.56	1	Solihull	11 Jun
25:11.3	Sally Warren	U23	29.01.78	4	Liverpool	22 Jul
25:33.09	Nikki Huckerby	U23	27.02.78	5	Liverpool	22 Jul
25:49.32	Sharon Tonks		18.04.70	1	Birmingham	23 Sep
26:09.3	Liz Corran	V40	23.09.55	1	Douglas IOM	7 Jun
26:15.1	Kate Horwill		26.01.75	1	Bebington	4 Nov
26:26.0	Jane Kennaugh		26.01.73	2	Bebington	4 Nov
26:33.5	Bridget Kaneen		15.08.65	2	Douglas IOM	7 Jun
(10)						
26:54.67	Sophie Hales	U17	30.03.85	4	Bedford	27 Aug
27:13.02	Nicola Phillips	U20	23.04.83	1	Birmingham	16 Sep
27:13.27	Jo Hesketh		16.06.69	2	Enfield	30 Jul
27:24.39	Karen Ratcliffe	V35	1.06.61	2	Birmingham	23 Sep

Additional Under 17 (1 above)

27:24.88	Natalie Evans		15.11.83	1	Sheffield	30 Jul
27:38.4	Natalie Geens		27.12.84	1	Bebington	4 Nov
28:32.66	Claire Reeves		31.07.84	6	Bedford	27 Aug
28:59.3	Nicky Reynolds		24.06.85	3	Bebington	4 Nov
29:15.05	Laura Fryer		3.12.83	3	Enfield	30 Jul

Foreign

27:08.35	*Sigrun Sangvik (NOR)*	*V40*	*5.02.57*	*1*	*Enfield*	*30 Jul*

Road

23:24 +	Lisa Kehler		15.03.67	m	Eisenhuttenstadt, GER	17 Jun
	23:31			1	Birmingham	22 Jan
	23:37 +			17=m	Leamington	23 Apr
23:32 +	Sara-Jane Cattermole		29.01.77	1m	Murdoch, AUS	23 Jul
	23:53 +			1m	Perth, AUS	9 Jul
24:05 +	Niobe Menandez		1.09.66	m	Eisenhuttenstadt, GER	17 Jun
	24:19			1	London (VP)	9 Sep
24:44	Lisa Crump		30.03.76	1	Tamworth	3 Dec
24:58	Wendy Bennett		21.12.65	1	Worcester	12 Jun
24:59	Sharon Tonks		18.04.70	2	Worcester	12 Jun
25:21	Kate Horwill		26.01.75	1	Worcester	21 Oct
25:33	Nicola Phillips	U20	23.04.83	1	Bexley	12 Feb
25:44	Sophie Hales	U17	30.03.85	1	Bexley	18 Mar
25:54	Liz Corran	V40	23.09.55	1	Isle of Man	30 Jan
(10)						
26:11	Bryna Chrismas	U15	18.06.86	2	Tamworth	3 Dec
26:24 +	Catherine Charnock		3.05.75	24=m	Leamington	23 Apr
26:29	Katie Ford	U20	21.10.81	6	Sheffield	15 Apr
26:29	Katie Stones	U15	22.11.85	3	Tamworth	3 Dec
26:34 +	Jane Kennaugh		26.01.73	26=m	Leamington	23 Apr
26:35	Natalie Geens	U17	27.12.84	4	Tamworth	3 Dec
26:43	Laura Fryer	U17	3.12.83	2	Bexley	18 Mar
26:47	Claire Reeves	U17	31.07.84	3	Bexley	18 Mar
26:54	Natalie Evans	U17	15.11.83	2	Worcester	21 Oct
26:57	Bridget Kaneen		15.08.65	2	Isle of Man	30 Jan
(20)						
27:05	Jo Hesketh		16.06.69	5	London (TH)	9 Sep
27:11	Nicky Reynolds	U17	24.06.85	2	Birmingham	16 Dec

10000 METRES WALK - Track

45:09.57	Lisa Kehler		15.03.67	1	Birmingham	13 Aug
54:53.35	Nikki Huckerby	U23	27.02.78	2	Birmingham	13 Aug
55:59.54	Kate Horwill		26.01.75	3	Birmingham	13 Aug
56:34.13	Jo Hesketh		16.06.69	4	Birmingham	13 Aug

10000 METRES WALK - Road

46:30 +	Lisa Kehler		15.03.67	m	Eisenhuttenstadt, GER	17 Jun
	46:42			1	Leicester	3 Sep
	46:51 +			37m	Sydney, AUS	28 Sep
	47:23 +			15m	Leamington	23 Apr
47:47	Sara-Jane Cattermole		29.01.77	1	Murdoch, AUS	23 Jul
	48:05			1	Perth, AUS	9 Jul
	48:48			1	Perth, AUS	7 May
	47:28 + (90 metres Short)			1	Perth, AUS	4 Jun
49:11 +	Niobe Menandez		1.09.66	m	Eisenhuttenstadt, GER	17 Jun
	50:08 + (Note - no judges)			1	Plymouth	9 Jan
	50:48 +			19m	Leamington	23 Apr
49:46	Sharon Tonks		18.04.70	1	Tamworth	3 Dec
49:50	Lisa Crump		30.03.76	2	Tamworth	3 Dec
	12 performances to 51:00 by 5 athletes					
51:36	Nicola Phillips	U20	23.04.83	8	Leamington	23 Apr
52:20	Kim Braznell	V40	28.02.56	2	Leicester	3 Sep
52:37	Sally Warren	U23	29.01.78	2	Dartford	7 May
53:22	Kate Horwill		26.01.75	3	Tamworth	3 Dec
53:35	Jane Kennaugh		26.01.73	1	Douglas IOM	27 Jul
54:15	Nikki Huckerby	U23	27.02.78	3	Dartford	7 May
54:51	Claire Reeves	U17	31.07.84	1	Nottingham	11 Mar
54:59	Jo Hesketh		16.06.69	2	East Molesey	9 Jan
55:54	Bridget Kaneen		15.08.65	1	Isle of Man	18 May
55:54	Liz Corran	V40	23.09.55	2	Isle of Man	18 May
56:07	Katie Ford	U20	21.10.81	2	Nottingham	11 Mar
57:42	Karen Ratcliffe	V35	1.06.61	4	Leicester	3 Sep

20 KILOMETRES WALK

1:33:57	Lisa Kehler		15.03.67	23	Eisenhuttenstadt, GER	17 Jun
	1:35:35			14	Leamington	23 Apr
	1:37:47			33	Sydney, AUS	28 Sep
	1:39:28			1	Holme Pierrepoint	11 Mar
1:36:40	Sara-Jane Cattermole		29.01.77	1	Perth, AUS	4 Mar
	1:37:31			1	Perth, AUS	23 Jan
	1:39:56			1	Murdoch, AUS	9 Jul
	1:41:55			1	Perth, AUS	28 Oct
	1:48:43			21	Leamington	23 Apr
	1:35:52 180 metres Short			1	Perth, AUS	4 Jun
1:43:18	Niobe Menandez		1.09.66	46	Eisenhuttenstadt, GER	17 Jun
	1:44:55			2	Holme Pierrepoint	11 Mar
	1:45:48			19	Leamington	23 Apr
1:46:24	Kim Braznell	V40	28.02.56	50	Eisenhuttenstadt, GER	17 Jun
	1:48:14			3	Holme Pierrepoint	11 Mar
1:49:19	Sharon Tonks		18.04.70	22	Leamington	23 Apr
	1:49:51			4	Holme Pierrepoint	11 Mar
	1:42:10 short			1	Yverdon, SWZ	6 Aug
	16 performances to 1:50:00 by 5 athletes					
1:50:13	Jane Kennaugh		26.01.73	1	Isle of Man	18 May
1:51:25	Nikki Huckerby	U23	27.02.78	23	Leamington	23 Apr
1:52:37	Sally Warren	U23	29.01.78	26	Leamington	23 Apr
1:54:21	Bridget Kaneen		15.08.65	4	Douglas IOM	19 Feb
1:54:46	Kate Horwill		26.01.75	6	Holme Pierrepoint	11 Mar
(10)						
1:55:33	Jo Hesketh		16.06.69	9	Holme Pierrepoint	11 Mar
1:56:27	Liz Corran	V40	23.09.55	5	Douglas IOM	19 Jul

4 x 100 METRES

43.19	National Team		5s2	Sydney, AUS	29	Sep
	(J.Maduaka, M.Richardson, S.Davies, S.Anderson)					
43.26	National Team		4h2	Sydney, AUS	29	Sep
	(J.Maduaka, M.Richardson, S.Wilhelmy, S.Anderson)					
43.92	England		1	Budapest, HUN	22	Jul
	(C.Bloomfield, M.Richardson, J.Maduaka, S.Anderson)					
44.29	England		1	Dublin, IRE	29	Jul
	(D.Allahgreen, M.Purkiss, D.Benjamin, S.Wilhelmy)					
44.38	National Team		2	Gold Coast (RB), AUS	17	Sep
44.52	Birchfield Harriers		1	Bedford	4	Jun
	(D.Maylor, S.Davies, Z.Wilson, K.Merry)					
44.65	National Team		2	Glasgow (S)	2	Jul
	(Z.Wilson, S.Anderson, S.Davies, J.Maduaka)					
44.93	England		2	Vittel, FRA	2	Sep
	(A.Forrester, M.Purkiss, D.Benjamin, C.Bloomfield)					
45.21	Shaftesbury Barnet Harriers		2	Bedford	4	Jun
	(C.Pierre, S.Anderson, S.Jacobs, C.Murphy)					
45.27	National Under 23 Team	U23	1	Getafe, SPA	9	Sep
	(A.Forrester, M.Purkiss, H.Roscoe, E.Whitter)					
45.43	National Junior Team	U20	3	Grosseto, ITA	7	Oct
	(D.Selley, K.Thomas, D.Maylor, V.James)					
45.46	National Junior Team	U20	2	Liverpool	22	Jul
	(D.Maylor, V.Barr, K.Ryde, V.James)					
45.70	England		1	Loughborough	21	May
	(A.Oyepitan, S Williams, J.Pratt, S.Davies)					
45.74	Windsor Slough & Eton AC		1	Bedford	19	Aug
	(C.Court, J.Hill, D.Benjamin, M.Richardson)					
45.77	National Junior Team	U20	2	Loughborough	21	May
	(D.Maylor, V.Barr, K.Wall, V.James)					
45.86	National Junior Team	U20	1	Bath	16	Sep
	(D.Selley, K.Thomas. E.Caney, V.James)					
45.87	Scotland		3	Loughborough	21	May
	(J.Hill, N.Hynd, S.Burnside, S.Dudgeon)					
45.89	National Junior Team	U20	1	Derby	3	Sep
	(D.Selley, K.Thomas, E.Caney, D.Maylor)					
45.95	British Universities		4	Loughborough	21	May
	(B.Liston, A.James, Z.Wilson, A.Forrester)					
46.15	Birchfield Harriers		1	Eton	6	May
	(D.Maylor, S.Pinel, Z.Wilson, K.Merry)					

Additional National Team

47.32	Wales	4	Budapest, HUN	22	Jul

Additional Club Teams (1 - 3 above)

46.44	Woodford Green & Essex Ladies	1	Enfield	6	Aug
46.51	Loughborough University	5	Loughborough	21	May
46.82	Team Solent	4	Bedford	4	Jun
46.93	Sale Harriers Manchester	3	Bedford	19	Aug
46.96	Edinburgh Woollen Mill	5	Bedford	4	Jun
46.96	Trafford AC	4	Bedford	19	Aug
47.06	Wakefield Harriers	4	Solihull	5	Aug
47.4	City of Stoke AC	1	Stoke-on-Trent	25	Jun
47.84	Liverpool Harriers AC	2	Enfield	6	Aug
48.0	Coventry Godiva Harriers	3	Peterborough	9	Jul
48.0	Rugby AC	2	Rugby	23	Jul
48.2	Cardiff AAC	1	Cannock	9	Sep
48.5	Wigan and District H & AC	1	Rugby	9	Jul
48.6	Ealing Southall & Middlesex	1	Woodford	24	Jun
48.7	Herne Hill Harriers	1	Kingston	11	Jun

48.7	Peterborough AC		3	Rugby	23 Jul
48.9	Newham & Essex Beagles		3	Eton	23 Jul

Additional Under 20 Teams (1 - 5 above)

46.59	South of England		1	Watford	2 Jul
47.01	England Schools	U17	1	Blackpool	15 Jul
47.12	North of England		2	Watford	2 Jul
47.25	England	U19	1	Edinburgh	13 Aug
47.45	Wales	U19	2	Edinburgh	13 Aug
47.94	Scotland		3	Vilvoorde, BEL	6 Aug
48.65	Scotland	U19	5	Edinburgh	13 Aug
49.29	Northern Ireland	U19	6	Edinburgh	13 Aug
50.0	Welsh Schools		1	Connah's Quay	18 Jul
51.5	Northern Ireland AF		4	Connah's Quay	18 Jul

Under 20 Club Teams

49.2	Herne Hill Harriers	U17	1	London (CP)	3 Jul
49.4	Sale Harriers Manchester		1	Dumfries	13 Aug
49.45	Birchfield Harriers		1	Birmingham	10 Sep
49.5	Blackheath Harriers		1	Bromley	7 May
49.5	Woodford Green & Essex Ladies		1	London (He)	30 Jul
49.6	Rugby AC		1	Coventry	16 Jul
49.8	Basildon AC		2	London (He)	30 Jul
49.9	Coventry Godiva Harriers		2	Coventry	16 Jul
49.9	Trafford AC		1	Derby	10 Sep
50.0	Wigan and District H & AC		3	Wakefield	16 Jul
50.1	Edinburgh Woollen Mill		2	Dumfries	13 Aug

Additional Under 17 Teams (1 - 2 above)

47.8	Middlesex		1	London (WF)	17 Sep
48.03	Devon Schools		1h1	Sheffield	9 Jul
48.13	Essex Schools		1	Sheffield	9 Jul
48.20	London Schools		2	Sheffield	9 Jul
48.38	West Midlands Schools		3	Sheffield	9 Jul
48.9	Lincolnshire Schools		1		17 Jun
49.04	Merseyside Schools		1h3	Sheffield	9 Jul
49.3	Worcestershire		1	Banbury	10 Sep
49.59	Scotland Schools		3	Blackpool	15 Jul
50.62	Wales Schools		4	Blackpool	15 Jul
50.98	Wales	U16	2	Grangemouth	5 Aug

Additional Under 17 Club Teams (1 above)

49.5	Ealing Southall & Middlesex AC		1	London (Nh)	2 Jul
49.6	Wolverhampton & Bilston AC		1	Sutton Coldfield	23 Jul
49.69	Sale Harriers Manchester		1	Birmingham	3 Sep
49.7	Wigan & District Harriers & AC		1	Wigan	2 Jul
49.7	Dudley & Stourbridge Harriers		2	Sutton Coldfield	23 Jul
49.9	Windsor Slough & Eton AC		1	Eton	3 Jul
50.27	Herne Hill Harriers	U15	1	London (BP)	4 Jun
50.36	Liverpool Harriers AC		3	Birmingham	3 Sep
50.4	Bournemouth AC		1	Guildford	23 Jul

Additional Under 15 Teams (1 above)

49.38	London Schools		1	Sheffield	9 Jul
49.42	Buckinghamshire Schools		1h2	Sheffield	9 Jul
49.42	Greater Manchester Schools		2	Sheffield	9 Jul
50.48	Merseyside Schools		4	Sheffield	9 Jul
50.5	Bromley Ladies		1	Erith	10 Sep
50.7	Birchfield Harriers		1	Stoke-on-Trent	25 Jun
50.70	Humberside Schools		5	Sheffield	9 Jul
50.96	Cheshire Schools		2h1	Sheffield	9 Jul
51.07	Gloucestershire Schools		2h3	Sheffield	9 Jul

Additional Under 15 Club Teams (1 - 3 above)

51.2	Pitreavie AAC		1	Glasgow (S)	20 Aug
51.2	Milton Keynes AC		1	Barking	10 Sep
51.25	Edinburgh Woollen Mill		1	Birmingham	3 Sep
51.3	Wigan & District Harriers & AC		1	Cleckheaton	21 May
51.3	Basildon AC		2	Barking	10 Sep
51.5	Tipton Harriers		1	Tipton	25 Jun
51.5	Cannock & Stafford AC		2	Stafford	2 Jul

Under 13 Teams

52.6	Surrey		1r1	Kingston	30 Jul
53.6	Kent		2r1	Kingston	30 Jul
53.9	Ashford AC		1	Erith	10 Sep
54.1	Sussex		3r1	Kingston	30 Jul
54.2	Berkshire		4r1	Kingston	30 Jul
54.3	Birchfield Harriers		1	Stafford	2 Jul
54.6	Wigan & District Harriers & AC		1	Cleckheaton	21 May
54.8	Sutton & District AC		1	Kingston	9 Sep
54.8	South Yorkshire		1	Cudworth	9 Sep
54.9	Liverpool Harriers AC		1	Blackpool	21 May
54.9	Middlesex		1r2	Kingston	30 Jul

4 x 200 METRES

1:39.72 i	Midlands		1	Cardiff	4 Mar
1:41.03 i	Loughborough University		1r1	Cardiff	Mar
1:43.75 i	South West		2	Cardiff	4 Mar
1:44.00 i	Scotland Schools	U16	2	Cardiff	26 Feb
1:44.51 i	Birmingham University		2	Birmingham	17 Feb
1:45.09 i	England Schools	U16	3	Cardiff	26 Feb
1:45.85 i	Cardiff AAC		1	Cardiff	26 Jan
1:45.99 i	Brunel University		3r1	Cardiff	Mar
1:46.13 i	UWIC		4r1	Cardiff	Mar
1:46.4	Millfield School	U20	1	Oxford	11 May

Additional Under 17 Teams (1 - 2 above)

1:48.51 i	Ayr Seaforth AAC		1	Glasgow	19 Mar
1:49.3	Aberdeen AAC		1	Dundee	28 May
1:49.6	Leicestershire	U15	1	Cudworth	9 Sep
1:49.7	Nottinghamshire	U15	2	Cudworth	9 Sep
1:49.7	Warwickshire	U15	3	Cudworth	9 Sep
1:49.7	Blackheath Harriers		1	Erith	10 Sep
1:49.7	Bromley Ladies	U15	1	Erith	10 Sep
1:50.00 i	Giffnock North AAC		2	Glasgow	19 Mar

Additional Under 15 Teams (1 - 4 above)

1:51.98 i	Giffnock North AAC		1h3	Glasgow	19 Mar
1:52.3	Medway AC		2	Erith	10 Sep
1:52.5	Banchory Stonehaven		1	Aberdeen	30 Jul
1:52.7	Lagan Valley AC		1	Belfast	22 Apr
1:52.7	GEC Avionics		3	Erith	10 Sep
1:52.8	Ashford AC		4	Erith	10 Sep

Under 13 Teams

1:57.46 i	Ayr Seaforth AAC		h	Glasgow	19 Mar
2:00.50 i	Giffnock North AAC		2	Glasgow	19 Mar
2:03.72 i	Whitemoss AAC		h	Glasgow	19 Mar
2:04.3	Grimsby Harriers		1	Hull	15 Jul
2:05.36 i	Central		h	Glasgow	19 Mar
2:06.65	Inverness HAC		1	Inverness	30 Jul

4 x 400 METRES

3:25.28	National Team		1h2	Sydney, AUS	29	Sep
	(H.Frost 52.5, D.Fraser 50.4, A.Curbishley 51.6, K.Merry 50.8)					
3:25.67	National Team		6	Sydney, AUS	30	Sep
	(N.Danvers 53.14, D.Fraser 50.30, A.Curbishley 52.46, K.Merry 49.77)					
3:28.12	National Team		3	Gateshead	16	Jul
	(N.Danvers 53.1, S.Dudgeon 52.1, A.Curbishley 51.95, D.Fraser 51.05)					
3:33.82	National Junior Team	U20	1	Santiago, CHI	22	Oct
	(K.Wall 54.04, J.Meadows 53.07, H.Thieme 53.18, L.Miller 53.53)					
3:38.38	National Junior Team	U20	2h1	Santiago, CHI	21	Oct
	(H.Brookes 56.37, J.Meadows 54.22, H.Thieme 53.70, L.Miller 54.09)					
3:38.63	Scotland		1	Loughborough	21	May
	(J.McKay 56.3, M.McClung 53.4, A.Currie 56.2, S.Dudgeon 52.8)					
3:38.95	National Junior Team	U20	2	Loughborough	21	May
	(L.Clarkson, J.Meadows, H.Wood, H.Thieme)					
3:38.99	National Junior Team	U20	1	Grosseto, ITA	7	Oct
	(K.Wall, H.Brookes, H.Thieme, L.Miller)					
3:39.08	England		3	Loughborough	21	May
	(K.Gear, V.Day, H.Frost, E.Williams)					
3:39.54 i	National Team		4	Glasgow	5	Mar
	(V.Day 57.47, M.Pierre 54.64, D.Fraser 53.76, M.Thomas 53.67)					
3:39.98	National Junior Team	U20	1	Derby	3	Sep
	(K.Wall 55.6, H.Brookes 57.2, L.Miller 53.7, J.Meadows 53.5)					
3:41.62	National Under 23 Team	U23	1	Getafe, SPA	9	Sep
	(R.Watson, L.Newton, L.McConnell, K.Gear)					
3:42.4	Woodford Green & Essex Ladies		1	Peterborough	9	Jul
3:42.72	South		1	Solihull	29	Jul
3:42.87	Loughborough University		4	Loughborough	21	May
	(R.Watson, M.Bjone NOR, Carey, L.Cresswell)					
3:43.16	National Junior Team	U20	1	Bath	16	Sep
	(K.Wall, H.Thieme, L.Miller, J.Meadows)					
3:44.03	Birchfield Harriers		1	Eton	6	May
	(L.Singer, K.Sotherton, H.Thieme, K.Merry)					
3:44.10	Shaftesbury Barnet Harriers		1	Dudelange, LUX	27	May
	(C.Brown, S.Jacobs 54.0, S.Anderson, C.Murphy)					
3:44.13	Woodford Green & Essex Ladies		1	Enfield	6	Aug
	(J.Stoute 53.4 anchor)					
3:44.14	Sale Harriers Manchester		1	Bedford	19	Aug
	(P.Fryer, H.Brookes, S.Evans, K.Maddox)					
3:44.28 i	National Junior Team	U20	1	Neubrandenburg, GER	4	Mar
	(J.Meadows, L.Clarkson, H.Wood, H.Thieme)					
3:44.99	British Universities		5	Loughborough	21	May
	(Rowbottom, S.Whigham, T.Duncan, K.Bright)					
3:45.17	Loughborough University		1	Stoke-on-Trent	1	May
3:45.19	National Under 23 Team	U23	3	Liverpool	22	Jul

Additional National Team

3:57.41	Wales	4	Bath	16	Sep
	(K.Bright, K.Martin, E.Mardle, E.Brady)				

Additional Club Teams (1 - 5 above)

3:47.07	Windsor Slough & Eton AC	1	Solihull	5	Aug
3:47.5	Edinburgh Woollen Mill	2	Peterborough	9	Jul
3:48.40	City of Glasgow AC	3	Glasgow (S)	8	Jul
3:50.07	Trafford AC	3	Bedford	19	Aug
3:50.4	Basingstoke & Mid Hants AC	1	Eton	23	Jul
3:51.5	Peterborough AC	3	Peterborough	9	Jul
3:51.86	Coventry Godiva Harriers	3	Enfield	6	Aug
3:52.81	Newham & Essex Beagles	1	Bedford	20	Aug
3:53.5	Wigan and District H & AC	1	Stoke-on-Trent	6	Aug

3:54.64	Sale Harriers Manchester	U20	1	Birmingham	10 Sep
3:55.06	Liverpool Harriers AC		4	Enfield	6 Aug
3:55.40	Brunel West London University		2	Stoke-on-Trent	1 May
3:55.4	Wigan and District H & AC	U20	2	Wakefield	16 Jul
3:56.9	Shaftesbury Barnet Harriers	U20	1	London (He)	30 Jul
3:57.1	Epsom & Ewell Harriers		2	Enfield	23 Jul
3:57.23	Wakefield Harriers		6	Eton	6 May
3:57.6	City of Norwich AC		2	Stoke-on-Trent	6 Aug

Additional Under 20 Teams (1 - 7 above)

3:45.78	England	U19	1	Edinburgh	13 Aug
3:48.12	Scotland		1	Nicosia,CYP	28 May
	(L.Clarkson, C.Gibson, E.Reid, S.McGrenaghan)				
3:48.26	South of England		1	Watford	2 Jul
	(K.Wall, L.Singer, R.Brereton, N.Sanders)				

Additional Under 20 National Teams

3:56.19	Scotland	U19	4	Edinburgh	13 Aug
4:01.7	Northern Ireland AF		1	Connah's Quay	18 Jul
4:03.99	Wales	U19	5	Edinburgh	13 Aug

Additional Under 20 Club Teams (1 - 3 above)

3:59.5	Basildon AC		2	London (He)	30 Jul
4:01.8	Trafford AC		1	Derby	10 Sep
4:02.6	Kilbarchan AC		1	Ayr	16 Apr
4:03.06	Birchfield Harriers		2	Birmingham	10 Sep
4:05.7	Aldershot Farnham & District AC		1	Abingdon	10 Sep
4:06.1	Bromley Ladies		2	Abingdon	10 Sep
4:08.75	City of Norwich AC		3	Birmingham	10 Sep

Under 17 Team

4:20.6	Hertford & Ware AC		1	Welwyn Garden City	1 May

3 x 800 METRES

7:04.6	Medway AC	U17	1	Erith	10 Sep
	(K.Buchan, J.Pereira, G.Marrs)				
7:07.8	Vale Royal AC		1	Warrington	11 Jul
7:08.1	Lagan Valley AC	U15	1	Belfast	22 Apr
7:19.0	Warrington AC		2	Warrington	11 Jul
7:19.0	Macclesfield AC		3	Warrington	11 Jul
7:19.34	Pitreavie AC	U15	1	Glasgow (S)	29 Jul

Additional Under 17 Teams (1 - 3 above)

7:28.10	Pitreavie AC	U15	2	Glasgow (S)	29 Jul
7:29.4	Bromley Ladies	U15	1	Erith	10 Sep
7:31.6	Macclesfield AC		1	Warrington	11 Jul
7:32.3	Vale Royal AC	U15	1	Warrington	11 Jul
7:33.57	City of Glasgow AC	U15	3	Glasgow (S)	29 Jul

Additional Under 15 Teams (1 - 6 above)

7:38.36	City of Glasgow AC		4	Glasgow (S)	29 Jul
7:42.7	Ashford AC		2	Belfast	22 Apr

Under 13 Teams

8:05.79	City of Edinburgh AC		1	Glasgow (S)	29 Jul
8:07.8	Lagan Valley AC		1	Belfast	22 Apr
8:10.8	Medway AC		1	Erith	10 Sep

4 x 1500 METRES

20:42.01	Ashford AC	U20	3	London (BP)	25 Jun
	(L.Dobriskey, K.Fawke, R.Dyer, L.Fawke)				

MENS INDEX

ARCHER Paul Nicholas U20 7.10.81, Blackh : SPJ - 14.31
ARMSTRONG Daniel U20 28.10.81, Border : 400H - 55.72, Dec - 5162, DecJ - 5640w/5533
ARMSTRONG Paul U23 20.10.79, Pitreavie : 400H - 55.3 (54.78-99)
ARMSTRONG Ryan U17 11.07.85, Liverpool H : 1.5kSt - 4:34.52
ARMSTRONG Samuel 17.02.74, Bord/Law & D : JT - 63.66 (65.31-98)
ARMSTRONG Simon John 29.05.62, B'ournm : SP - 14.29i/14.02 (16.52-90), DT - 41.78 (50.22-92)
ARRAND Andrew 20.01.66, Blackheath : 5k - 14:36.9, HMar - 1:06:14, Mar - 2:24:40 (2:23:36-98)
ARRIDGE Mark 25.09.72, Tipton : Mar - 2:33:48
ASHBY Thomas U13 12.11.87, Harmeny : 400 - 61.4
ASHCROFT Daniel U15 23.11.85, Harrow : PenB - 2609
ASHE Richard 5.10.74, Thames Valley : 800 - 1:50.36 (1:49.38-96), 1500 - 3:41.30 (3:41.2-90)
ASHMAN L. U15, London Schools : DTB - 37.32
ASHTON David 24.01.70, Trafford : LJ - 7.18w/7.11
ASHTON Sean U15 20.09.85, Leics Cor : 80HB - 11.1/11.16w/11.52
ASHTON Stephen U17 21.03.84, Sale : DTJ - 42.30, DTY - 45.62, HTY - 47.92 (48.68-99)
ASKEW Richard U17 26.04.84, Derby & Co : LJ - 6.57w/6.55
ASPDEN Richard William 15.10.76, Belgrave : HJ - 2.10 (2.17i-99/2.16-95)
ATKINSON Jamie U17 12.02.84, Sevenoaks : 800 - 1:57.10, 1500 - 4:06.74
ATKINSON Jason U15 28.10.85, Torfaen : 800 - 2:02.38ioa/2:02.66
ATKINSON Richard U15 29.09.85, Lagan V : JTB - 46.00
ATTON Karl Ronald 14.09.71, Roadhogs : 10kWR - 47:15 (45:40-89)
AUDU George 18.01.77, Thames Valley : LJ - 7.89
AWANAH Mark U20 23.09.82, Blackheath : LJ - 7.37
AWDE Christopher U17 14.02.85, WG & Ex L : OctY - 4450
AYRES Robert U17 12.11.83, Charnwood : 400HY - 56.61

BABB Jacob U15 7.12.85, Wessex & Bath : SPB - 14.71
BACKLEY Stephen James 12.02.69, Camb H : JT - 89.85 (91.46-92)
BADDELEY Andrew James U20 20.06.82, Wir : 800 - 1:51.92, 1500 - 3:46.36
BADERIN Richard Adekunmi U20 25.03.83, Wirral : 110HJ - 15.0w/15.15w/15.2/15.31
BAILEY Colin U17 15.11.83, Burnley : HJ - 1.93, OctY - 4618
BAILEY Edward U17 14.02.84, City of Stoke : 800 - 1:58.6
BAILEY James U20 1.10.82, Sale : 2kSt - 6:12.0, 3kSt - 9:31.2
BAILEY Matthew Robert Darren U20 16.02.81, Barnsley : 800 - 1:54.36
BAILEY Stuart U23 6.08.78, Sale : 800 - 1:49.46
BAILLIE Christopher U20 21.04.81, VPAAC/Bir : 100 - 10.7 (10.90w/10.96-99), 60H - 7.95i (7.94i-99), 60HJ - 7.92i, 110HJ - 13.9 (13.57-99), 110H - 13.84
BAINES Michael U15 1.11.85, Liverpool H : HJ - 1.80
BAINS Peter U15 3.10.85, Derby & Co : 800 - 2:03.3
BAIRD Lawrence W. 14.12.77, Clee/Sheff Un : 200 - 21.64w/21.8/22.20 (21.6w-99, 400 - 48.35i/48.6/48.79 (47.56i-98/47.83-97)
BAJWA Ali 13.06.71, Middlesbro & C : DT - 44.92, HT - 53.31
BAKER George 14.08.76, Newham & Essex B : SP - 14.90 (15.22-97)
BALDOCK Sean Michael 3.12.76, Belgrave : 200 - 21.94w (21.1w-97/21.50i/21.50-99), 300 - 33.56 (32.88-97), 400 - 45.20
BALDWIN Chris U15 10.06.86, Trafford : 400 - 52.9
BALDWIN Keith U20 2.03.81, Inverness : 400H - 56.65
BALDWIN Stefan Mark 26.04.70, Peterbro : JT - 65.35 (72.92-93)
BALE Alex U17 1.12.83, Blackpool : PV - 4.10
BALL Andrew U20 29.11.82, Isle of Wight : 110H - 15.6
BALL James Robert 17.02.63, Steyning : 3kW - 13:45.4 (12:20.0-87), 10kW - 47:23.0 (43:36.0un-87/44:13.4-88), 10kWR - 47:17 (46:17-99)
BALL Nick U13 29.04.88, Steyning : 2kW - 10:42.7oa
BALLANTINE Leighton U17 27.01.84, Swansea : OctY - 4443
BALSDON Wayne U20 14.01.83, Newq & Par : DecJ - 5222
BANGS Neil U23 28.03.80, Thurrock : 800 - 1:52.46, 1500 - 3:49.09
BANNISTER Dominic 1.04.68, Shaft Barnet : 5k - 14:25.0 (13:52.31-97), 10kR - 29:54 (29:39-99), HMar - 1:03:54, Mar - 2:14:39
BANNISTER Simon U20 16.04.81, Peterbro : 110HJ - 14.9, HJ - 2.05 (2.10-99)
BAPTISTE Leon U17 23.05.85, Enf & Har : 200 - 22.6
BAPTISTE Olu, Cambridge Harriers : LJ - 7.01
BARBER Michael W. 19.10.73, Birchfield : PV - 5.10 (5.45-97)
BARBOUR Jonathan U23 3.11.80, Blackheath : 100 - 10.28, 200 - 20.79
BARCLAY Matthew U17 1.11.84, Crawley : LJ - 6.50
BARDEN Spencer Christian 31.03.73, Bel/Loughbro : 1500 - 3:45.90 (3:39.64-98), 5k - 14:02.69 (13:43.84-97)
BARGH Andrew 21.08.76, Team Solent : 400H - 52.83 (52.4-96/52.47-98)

BARIKOR Bomene U20 22.05.82, Blackheath :
HJ - 2.00 (2.03-97)
BARK Thomas U17 18.10.83, Corby :
1.5kSt - 4:36.85 (4:31.09-99)
BARNARD Paul 27.07.72, Birchfield :
HT - 60.92 (62.70-95)
BARNES Alan U23, AF&D/Notts Univ :
5k - 14:40.56
BARRETT Clint 21.11.77, Chelmsford :
Dec - 5294w (5551-99)
BARROS Demetrio 29.06.71, Hounslow/POR :
JT - 58.04 (66.92-93)
BARTON Darren 11.10.69, Morpeth/RAF :
3kSt - 9:12.73 (8:59.60-99)
BARTON Neil U23 18.07.80, Verlea/Man Univ :
LJ - 7.07
BARTON Robert U20 5.11.82, Blackburn :
800 - 1:53.72, 1500 - 3:51.56
BARTON Tim D. 3.10.70, Charnwood :
60 - 6.93i (6.92i-98),
100 - 10.63w/10.84 (10.55w-98/10.67-97)
BARZEY Victor U15 10.01.86, Bexley :
100 - 11.4w, 200 - 22.6w/22.91w/22.94
BATCHELOR Perry 11.12.75, Rugby :
110H - 14.6w/14.66w/14.72 (14.7-99)
BATE Roger U20 16.01.83, Warrington :
DTJ - 41.64
BATES Neil U17 5.04.84, Manx :
3kW - 14:11.46i/14:16.6, 5kW - 25:08.9
BATES Robert U13 29.10.87, Sphinx :
400 - 61.8, 800 - 2:17.8
BATES Simon 21.12.76, Cannock & Stafford :
DT - 41.32
BAULCH James Steven 3.05.73, Cardiff :
200 - 21.33 (20.84-94),
400 - 45.06 (44.57-96)
BAYLEY Tim U20 4.10.81, Belgrave :
400 - 48.92
BAZELL Stephen 1.02.74, City of Stoke :
3kSt - 9:29.2
BEACOM Greg U23 26.02.78, Portsmouth :
HJ - 1.95 (1.95-99)
BEARD Gregory U20 10.09.82, Maidstone :
SP - 16.69, SPJ - 17.30, DT - 47.90,
DTJ - 51.26, HT - 50.22
BEARD Keith Alan 8.11.61, Leiden :
JT - 67.48 (76.10r-91/73.88-90)
BEARMAN Donald J. 16.04.66, Steyning :
3kW - 12:56.0, 10kW - 45:52.7 (45:09.51-99),
10kWR - 44:53, 20kW - 1:32:33,
35kW - 2:53:10, 50kW - 4:32:42
BEASLEY Graham Alexander 24.10.77, Luton/
Brunel Univ : 60 - 6.96i (6.87i-99),
100 - 10.6w/10.61w/10.76 (10.54w/10.70-99),
200 - 21.01w/21.57i/21.6 (21.03-99)
BEATON Peter 5.04.72, Pitreavie :
SP - 14.11 (14.29-94)
BEAUCHAMP William Ronald 9.09.70, TVH :
HT - 71.76 (72.63-99)
BEAUFORD Adam U20 24.10.81, Yeovil Oly :
SPJ - 14.23, HT - 52.94, HTJ - 59.22
BEAUMONT Paul 27.03.63, Belgrave/Army :
400H - 54.3/55.33 (51.23-89)
BECKETT Peter Alistair Cohen U15 10.02.86,
Shaftesbury Barnet : HTB - 43.53
BEDFORD Tom U17 12.12.83, Shaftesbury B :
3k - 8:57.77, 1.5kSt - 4:24.92

BEER Mark U23 28.02.80, Chesterf/Staffs Un :
HJ - 1.96 (1.98-97)
BEEVERS Andrew 3.05.73, Leeds :
5k - 14:38.06, 3kSt - 9:14.01 (9:11.3-99)
BEHARRELL Mark U20 10.01.81, City of Hull :
PV - 4.90 (4.91-99)
BELL John 10.09.73, Newham & Essex B:
400H - 53.81 (53.70-92)
BELL Martin 9.04.61, Cardiff :
3kW - 12:03.12i (11:53.3-95)
BELL Matthew U23 2.06.78, Corby :
HT - 63.01 (63.59-99)
BELL Simon 26.12.66, Cambridge Harriers :
Mar - 2:29:35 (2:25:26-97), 2kSt - 5:45.9,
3kSt - 8:59.63 (8:53.39-96)
BELMORE Peter U20 18.09.81, Somerset Sch :
TJ - 13.99
BELSHAM Matthew 11.10.71, Sale :
PV - 5.21 (5.40i-96/5.35-93)
BENJAMIN Ekakier U17 4.12.84, Notts :
PV - 4.05
BENJAMIN Timothy U20 2.05.82, Cardiff :
60 - 6.75i, 100 - 10.48,
200 - 20.76 (20.60w/20.72-99)
BENN Andrew 2.09.77, Blackheath :
HT - 50.88 (56.86-96)
BENN Thomas U23 20.04.80, Windsor S & E :
PV - 4.50
BENNETT Andrew U15 19.12.85, Soton City :
SPB - 13.14
BENNETT Andrew U20 30.09.82, Havant :
400H - 54.41
BENNETT Christopher U23 18.10.80, Team S :
200 - 22.10 (21.7/21.87-99)
BENNETT Paul 9.08.71, Rotherham :
1500 - 3:49.49 (3:47.9-92), 1M - 4:08.90i
BENNETT Simon 16.10.72, N Devon :
JT - 63.15 (66.58-96)
BENT Colin 12.04.70, Shaftesbury Barnet/RAF :
HJ - 2.05 (2.20-96)
BENTLEY Robin 17.02.65, Wessex & Bath :
Mar - 2:29:28 (2:28:31-99)
BENZIE Frazer U20 4.08.83, Aberdeen :
DecJ - 5072
BERNARD Jermaine U17 1.12.84, Ipswich :
LJ - 6.81
BERNARD Martyn U17 15.12.84, Wakefield :
HJ - 2.00
BERWICK Christopher V50 1.05.46, Leics WC :
50kW - 4:52:15 (4:23:22-86)
BETTS Edward George 18.02.71, TVH :
400H - 51.95 (50.49-97)
BEVAN Nigel Charles 3.01.68, Birchfield :
JT - 65.05 (81.70-92)
BIBBY Anthony U17 12.03.85, Mandale :
100HY - 13.66
BIDWELL Mark U17 4.09.84, Chesterfield :
HJ - 1.99i/1.95 (1.95-99)
BIGNALL Douglas 20.10.74, Enf & Har :
60 - 6.75i (6.7i/6.71i-97),
100 - 10.27wA/10.30A/10.43, 200 - 21.48
BILLINGHAM Russell U20 13.10.81,
City of Plymouth : 110HJ - 15.4/15.43,
400H - 56.30 (55.7-99)
BILTON Darren 9.03.72, City of Hull :
Mar - 2:24:52 (2:21:34-99)
BINNS Christopher U20 7.05.82, Blackpool :
HJ - 2.00

BIRCH Shane U13 22.10.87, Maid & Roch :
SPC - 12.47io/12.40, DTC - 31.58
BIRCHALL Robert 14.06.70, Birchfield :
10k - 30:30.4 (29:17.65-97),
10kR - 29:48 (29:22-97)
BIRCHALL Warren 18.01.65, Stockport :
Mar - 2:29:42
BIROT Jerome 28.04.74, Wessex & Bath/FRA :
110H - 15.0 (14.82-99),
PV - 4.80i/4.80 (5.00-99),
BISHOP Gary 3.08.63, Boxhill :
Mar - 2:29:54 (2:23:59-96)
BISSELL Simon Peter U15 25.12.85, Sale :
SPB - 15.06, DTY - 42.69,
DTB - 49.10, HTY - 54.58, HTB - 59.07
BIVINS Tom U17 18.11.83, Charnwood :
SPY - 14.13, DTY - 46.40, HTY - 50.93
BLACK Christopher Francis V50 1.01.50,
City of Edinburgh : HT - 58.22 (75.40-83)
BLACK Iain Russell 18.09.70, City of Edinb :
PV - 4.40 (4.51-97)
BLACKMAN Gary U23 24.09.80, S & S Heath/
Loughborough Studnts : 3kSt - 9:06.49
BLACKMAN Graham U17 25.03.85, Rushcliffe :
400 - 50.4 (51.71-99)
BLAIR Richard U17 15.09.84, Garscube :
HJ - 1.90i (1.76-99), TJ - 13.48
BLAKE Kevin 29.05.67, Cardiff :
Mar - 2:29:14
BLAKE Stephen U13 29.09.87, AF&D :
3k - 10:24.1
BLENCOWE Martin U15 11.04.86, Belgrave :
100 - 11.5, 200 - 22.43w/22.64
BLIGHT Ross 28.05.77, Cardiff/UWIC :
HT - 50.02
BLISS Anthony 7.03.70, Crawley :
110H - 15.68w (15.1-97/15.37w-98/15.51-97)
BOBB Samuel 29.08.75, Blackheath/Brunel U :
TJ - 13.99 (14.98-97)
BODY Steven 6.01.75, Vauxhall :
1500 - 3:51.42, 1M - 4:07.97, 3k - 8:16.7
BOLT Christopher U23 21.09.80, Bracknell :
800 - 1:50.4 (1:50.1-99), 1500 - 3:42.36,
1M - 4:04.64, 3k - 8:11.8
BONEHAM Daniel U17 9.12.83, Grantham :
HTY - 48.81
BONNETT Stephen U23 13.07.78, C of Stoke/
Staffs Univ : HJ - 2.05i (2.05i-99/2.04-97),
PV - 4.10 (4.20i/4.20-99),
LJ - 6.99 (7.05w/7.01i-99),
Dec - 6754 (7146-99)
BONSALL David 2.06.71, Royal Navy :
PV - 4.10i (4.20i-99)
BOOL Michael U17 10.11.83, Cardiff :
400HY - 58.56
BOOTH Adam Lee U15 22.10.85, Rotherham :
80HB - 12.04, HJ - 1.78, PenB - 2653
BOOTH Shane U20 16.01.82, Barnsley :
HJ - 2.00
BOREHAM James U15 27.11.86, Preseli :
100 - 11.6
BORSUMATO Anthony Patrick 13.12.73, Sale :
400 - 48.17 (46.92-98),
300H - 36.12, 400H - 49.68
BOUCHAMIA Karim U23 14.03.78, TVH/ALG :
800 - 1:52.19, 1500 - 3:43.34 (3:42.8-99),
1M - 4:04.30 (4:01.57-99), 5MR - 23:39
BOUNDY Christopher U23 25.12.79, Gate :
PV - 4.30 (4.50-99), JT - 56.61
BOURNAT Oliver U17 4.12.84, Tonbridge :
OctY - 4481
BOURNE Steven U15 6.09.85, Essex Sch :
HJ - 1.75
BOWDEN Adam U20 5.08.82, Harrow :
800 - 1:54.0, 1500 - 3:53.06,
2kSt - 5:53.1, 3kSt - 9:04.43
BOWDITCH Kristen Robert 14.01.75, N & E B :
1500 - 3:42.59, 3k - 7:52.27,
2M - 8:40.44i, 5k - 13:28.22
BOWLER James U23 2.09.79, Brom & R :
1500 - 3:49.55
BOWLES Ian U17 6.01.84, Bolton :
1.5kSt - 4:28.84
BOWLEY Ian U20 14.11.81, Bedford & Co :
PV - 4.10
BOWLING Luke U20 4.11.81, Peterborough :
100 - 10.8 (10.70w/10.92-98),
200 - 21.68 (21.6-99)
BOWN Simon Paul 21.11.74, Newham & E B :
HT - 65.22 (65.32-99)
BOWRON Lee U15 2.10.85, Ealing,S & Mx :
800 - 1:59.7, 1500 - 4:04.63
BOXELL James U17 21.10.83, Barnsley :
800 - 1:56.5
BOYD Chris U15 21.11.85, Bucks Sch :
HJ - 1.75
BOYLE Alistair U13 27.05.88, Falkirk :
DTC - 26.58
BOYLE Michael V40 29.12.60, Herne Hill :
10k - 31:23.96 (30:42.1-93)
BOYLES Ben U15 19.02.86, Bedford & County:
80HB - 12.06
BRACKSTONE David U20 13.03.82,
C of Stoke : 200 - 21.7w/22.0 (23.02-98),
400 - 49.0/49.19i, 400H - 53.67
BRADBURY Martin U20 20.10.82, Rotherham :
400 - 47.94
BRADLEY Colin V40 2.02.56, Surrey WC :
3kW - 13:49.6i (12:54.8-86)
BRADLEY Dominic 22.12.76, Birchfield :
60 - 6.88i (6.83i-99),
100 - 10.6w/10.77 (10.52w/10.6/10.63-98),
200 - 21.93 (21.7/21.87-99), 60H - 7.96i,
110H - 14.15w/14.2/14.29 (14.07w/14.26-98)
BRADLEY Jeremy 5.02.77, Blackh/Oxford Un :
800 - 1:52.65 (1:51.96-99),
1500 - 3:51.39 (3:50.0-99), 3kSt - 9:14.8
BRADY David 5.07.62, North Belfast :
10k - 31:46.6
BRAMBLE Marvin 10.06.77, Blackheath :
TJ - 14.76 (15.31w-97/15.23-95)
BRANDWOOD Daniel U20 1.10.82, City of Hull :
200 - 22.0w (22.6-99/24.48-97),
DTJ - 41.60, DecJ - 5752
BRANNEN Anthony 16.09.68, CoStoke/Staff U :
110H - 14.8w/15.19 (14.2/14.25w-95/14.35-89),
PV - 4.30 (4.90i/4.80-95), DT - 41.47
BRASIER Samuel Alan Michael U13 5.11.87,
Milton Keynes : 400 - 62.4
BRASSINGTON Allan U20 27.09.81, CoStoke :
DT - 43.81, DTJ - 48.83 (49.56-99)
BRAY Daniel Paul U17 6.09.83, Havant :
200 - 22.6, 400 - 50.33,
400HY - 58.0, TJ - 13.80

BREBNER Francis 27.11.65, SGA (Prof)/ Peterbro : SP - 13.80 (15.28i-97/14.47-99)
BREND Peter A. 2.02.77, Team Solent : 200 - 21.95, 400 - 47.08
BREWER Antony U20 3.06.81, Bracknell : 3k - 8:21.2
BREWER Oliver U17 14.09.83, Bingley : 1.5kSt - 4:28.32, 400HY - 58.8 (58.7/58.81-99)
BRIDGE James U17 28.11.83, Invicta : 200 - 22.21
BRIDLE Matthew 11.08.76, Trafford : 200 - 21.94 (21.41w-93/21.6/21.83-94), 300 - 34.2
BRIERLEY James Richard 31.07.77, Telford : HJ - 2.15 (2.26-96)
BRIGGS Jason U13 8.10.87, Newham & E B : 80HC - 13.5
BRITTAN Andrew John 17.01.67, Cann & Staff : DT - 46.64 (49.76-88)
BRIZZEL Paul 3.10.76, Liverpool H/IRE : 100 - 10.28w/10.35, 200 - 20.54A/20.65
BROADHEAD Daniel U20 19.04.82, Rotherham : PV - 4.20 (4.20i/4.20-98)
BROCKLEBANK Robert J. 12.10.76, Sale : HJ - 2.10i/2.08 (2.16-95)
BROOKS Jerome T. S. 9.08.73, Lond Ire/HW/ Oxford Univ : 3k - 8:16.2, 5k - 14:22.71
BROWN Alistair U17 14.02.84, Inverclyde : PV - 3.70
BROWN Andrew 17.06.77, City of Edinburgh : 800 - 1:50.89
BROWN Derry U13 12.03.89, Steyning : 2kW - 10:43.3
BROWN Gareth James 10.05.68, Steyning : 10kW - 46:08.0 (43:54.25-87), 10kWR - 45:29, 20kW - 1:32:43 (1:30:15-89), 35kW - 2:55:59, 50kW - 4:27:23 (4:27:22-96)
BROWN Gareth 2.09.73, Swindon : LJ - 7.41w/7.05
BROWN John 2.02.69, Salford : 3kSt - 9:27.6 (8:55.6-98)
BROWN Jonathan Michael 27.02.71, Sheffield : Mar - 2:11:17 (2:09:44-99)
BROWN Kevin Dave 10.09.64, Belgrave/JAM : SP - 13.95 (14.73-98), DT - 62.10
BROWN Mark, Clayton-Le-Moors : Mar - 2:32:00
BROWN Mark 3.11.76, Newham & Essex B : 200 - 21.91w (21.6/21.95-99), 300 - 33.81, 400 - 46.54 (46.37-99)
BROWN Phillip U15 10.11.85, North Down : 80HB - 11.82
BROWN Steven U20 20.03.82, Southend : PV - 4.30 (4.61-99)
BROWNE Curtis 11.09.75, Birchfield : 100 - 10.42 (10.38w/10.42-99), 200 - 21.40w/21.63 (21.5/21.54-94)
BRUCE Calum 28.02.75, Pitreavie : HT - 54.79
BRUNT Daniel 23.04.76, Sheffield : SP - 14.32 (14.49-97), DT - 47.94
BRUNT Steve V40 22.07.60, Bristol : Mar - 2:34:11
BRYAN Christopher 12.01.77, Skyrac : 800 - 1:51.60
BRYAN Justin 16.08.69, Torfaen : SP - 14.45 (14.54-99), DT - 43.38 (45.29-98)
BRYAN Lee U20 24.11.81, Coventry Godiva : 200 - 22.0 (22.11w-97/22.18i/22.59-98), 400 - 48.15 (48.13-99)
BUCHANAN Andrew I. 12.09.70, AF&D : PV - 4.10i/4.10 (4.50-94)
BUCK Matthew 5.04.74, WGreen & Ex L : PV - 4.50 (4.60-96)
BUCKFIELD Nicholas Jean 5.06.73, Crawley : PV - 5.40 (5.80-98)
BUCKLEY Adam John U23 6.12.80, Sale/Bath U : 100 - 10.99 (10.8-99), 200 - 21.7 (23.28-97), 400 - 47.04
BUCKLEY Alan 25.10.74, Gateshead : 3k - 8:11.27, 5k - 14:05.74, 5MR - 23:41, 10k - 29:58.72
BUDDEN Nicholas 17.11.75, Norw/Loughbro : 400 - 46.81 (46.34-96)
BULL Gareth U17 3.03.85, Cardiff : DTY - 47.55
BULL Simon U20 29.09.82, Cardiff : Dec - 4952, DecJ - 5302
BULLEY Simon John U17 19.09.84, Wirral : DTY - 42.04
BULMAN Neil Andrew 7.09.77, Mand/Loughbro : HT - 45.71 (49.02-98)
BULSTRIDGE Michael 23.01.73, Birchfield : 5k - 14:44.50 (14:32.72-96)
BURGESS Michael U17 11.05.84, G. Man Sch : 100 - 11.1w
BURLEY Darren U23 13.01.80, Blackheath : 60 - 6.90i, 100 - 10.82 (10.68w-98/10.7db-96), 200 - 21.7w/21.75 (21.50w-96/21.5-99/21.71-98)
BURN Peter U17 3.01.84, Gateshead : HJ - 1.91
BURNS Ian T. 20.09.77, Gateshead : JT - 63.22
BURNS William 13.12.69, Salford : 10kR - 29:31, Mar - 2:15:42
BURNSIDE Neil U17 7.08.84, Ayr Seaforth : 400 - 50.5, 400HY - 57.09
BURROWS Christopher U20 23.11.82, Gate : 800 - 1:53.78
BURROWS Craig 8.08.74, Ilford : DT - 42.37
BURROWS Darius 8.08.75, Birchfield : 1500 - 3:51.88 (3:46.1-96), 3k - 8:03.91 (7:58.7-96), 5k - 14:41.11 (13:50.98-99), 3kSt - 9:21.91 (9:06.9-96)
BURSLEM Richard U17 4.01.84, Sale : LJ - 6.68w/6.52
BURTON Anthony U13 3.02.88, Bournemouth : 200 - 25.5
BUSHELL Mark Anthony 22.10.76, N&EB/Port U : LJ - 7.01w/7.00 (7.51w-96/7.25-95)
BUSS Daniel U17 10.10.83, Belgrave : 100 - 11.0
BUTLER David U23 9.12.78, Charnwood : LJ - 6.95 (7.05-98)
BUTLER Kenny 17.09.63, Army : Mar - 2:24:42
BUTLER Matthew Rhys U23 4.04.80, Cardiff/ UWIC : 110H - 15.36 (15.30-98)
BUTTLER Stephen 20.02.75, Wolves & B : 200 - 22.07db (21.8-93/22.04w/22.06-92)
BUZZA David Edward 6.12.62, Cornwall AC : Mar - 2:21:57 (2:11:06-93)

BYRNE Ian U15 12.05.86, Somerset Sch :
80HB - 11.9w/12.04
BYRNE Joseph U20 1.02.82, East Down :
3k - 8:38.0, 5k - 15:28.00

CADDY Neil 18.03.75, Tipton :
800 - 1:47.89, 1500 - 3:39.03,
1M - 3:58.31 (3:55.84-96)
CAINE Andrew 17.06.77, Tynedale/Loughbro :
1500 - 3:50.87, 3k - 8:16.60, 5k - 14:34.19
CAINES Daniel Stephen U23 15.05.79, Bir/
UW Swansea : 200 - 21.26, 300 - 33.5i+,
400 - 45.37
CAIRNS Steven Mark 3.11.67, Border :
HMar - 1:06:15, 3kSt - 9:03.29 (8:55.2-99)
CALDEIRA William U15 16.09.85, Belgrave :
SPB - 13.99
CALDWELL Benjamin Ian U20 3.03.82, Bolton :
400 - 48.45, 400H - 54.4/54.67
CALLAHAN Ian U15, G. Manchester Sch :
DTB - 42.41
CAMERON Rezlimond V40 18.05.60, TVH :
TJ - 14.83w/14.07 (16.32w-89/16.20-88)
CAMPBELL Andre U13 18.07.88, Enf & Har :
LJ - 5.16
CAMPBELL Daniel U15 24.02.86, Croydon :
HJ - 1.81
CAMPBELL Darren Andrew 12.09.73, Belgrave :
100 - 10.06 (10.04-98), 200 - 20.13
CAMPBELL Fraser U15 30.05.86, Elgin :
HTB - 44.29
CAMPBELL Malcolm 3.01.71, Cambuslang :
10kR - 29:52,
Mar - 2:31:53 (2:21:51-99)
CAMPBELL Paul William Alexander U23 26.03.80,
Mandale/Teeside Univ : 200 - 21.84
CANNON Craig U17 6.05.84, R S Coldfield :
400HY - 58.3/58.50
CAPELING Kirk U23 27.02.80, Medway :
HT - 45.51
CAPELING Stuart V45 31.12.51, Medway :
HT - 45.72
CAPLAN Nick U23 23.12.79, Birmingham Un :
Dec - 4955
CARBON Garry U20 20.01.81, Enf & Har :
LJ - 6.82 (6.86-99)
CARELESS Robert 7.09.74, Charnwood :
HT - 60.58
CAREY Tom U17 26.02.84, Huntingdon :
400 - 51.0, 400H - 57.9, 400HY - 57.25
CARISS Chris 1.03.75, Bingley :
Mar - 2:25:25
CARLETON Jonathan U23 4.11.79, B & A :
100 - 10.72w/10.8/10.98 (10.89-99),
200 - 21.60?/21.66
CARLISLE Nigel 30.12.75, Border/B & Antrim :
400 - 48.81 (48.54-99)
CARMODY Noel Philip V40 24.12.56, Camb H :
3kW - 13:32.4 (12:26.49-91)
CARNE Ben U15 16.06.86, Harrow :
80HB - 12.00w
CARR Gary U20 24.09.82, Ashford :
100 - 10.93, 200 - 22.16
CARSON Sean U17 13.04.84, Ayr Seaforth :
JTY - 54.59
CARTER Daniel W. U23 15.04.80, WG & Ex L :
JT - 73.56
CARTER Ian U17 19.09.83, Jersey :
800 - 1:57.93, 1500 - 4:04.40
CARTER Simon 5.03.75, Maid & R/Read U :
JT - 63.57 (66.37-98)
CARTER Thomas U20 20.08.82, Vale Royal :
800 - 1:54.29, 1500 - 3:55.08
CARTY Jared U15 25.09.85, Harrow :
SPB - 13.49, DTB - 37.20
CASAL Yinca U13 24.09.87, Shaftesbury B :
LJ - 5.17w/4.94
CASEY Theo U17 3.06.84, Croydon :
HJ - 2.00
CASSIDY Ryan U15 12.12.85, Liverpool H :
DTB - 39.42
CASTILLO Richard U20 3.12.81, Notts :
400 - 49.20, 400H - 54.01
CAVANAGH Steven U17 9.07.85, Sparta :
200 - 22.6, PenB - 2651oa
CAVERS David 9.04.63, Border :
Mar - 2:24:50 (2:16:06-98)
CAWLEY Ian U23 21.11.78, Team S/Loughbro :
60H - 8.37i, 110H - 14.78
CHALLENGER Benjamin U23 7.03.78, Bel :
HJ - 2.25i/2.22 (2.30-99)
CHAMBERS Dwain Anthony U23 5.04.78, Bel :
50 - 5.69i+ (5.57+-99),
60 - 6.55i/6.62 (6.41+-99),
100 - 10.08 (9.97-99), 200 - 20.78 (20.68-99)
CHAMBERS Roy U15 9.02.86, Woking :
JTB - 44.75
CHAMPION Michael 3.01.75, Blackheath :
100 - 10.71w/10.81 (10.8-94),
200 - 21.12w/21.3/21.32
CHAPMAN Dominic M. 10.02.72, Worthing :
SP - 13.43, Dec - 6220
CHAPMAN Frank 17.01.70, RAF :
Dec - 5527
CHAPMAN Keith U20 15.02.81, Wirral :
10k - 32:01.2
CHARLESWORTH Robert U23 25.03.79,
Peterborough : JT - 60.63 (60.92-99)
CHARLTON Adam U17 11.05.84, Huntingdon :
100 - 11.1, 200 - 22.46
CHASE Chris U15 15.11.85, Herts Sch :
PenB - 2667
CHASTON Justin Thomas 4.11.68, Belgrave :
5k - 14:04.50 (13:51.86-95),
2kSt - 5:36.6 (5:33.85-92),
3kSt - 8:26.07 (8:23.90-94)
CHATT James U23 11.02.80, Dart/Loughbro :
100 - 10.74 (10.67w-98/10.7-97),
200 - 22.0 (21.63i/21.63w-98/21.7-99/21.76-98
CHEESEMAN Christopher V40 11.12.58,
Surrey WC /Thames H & H :
10kW - 44:29.51 (43:05.11-93),
10kWR - 42:11,
30kW - 2:31:18+ (2:27:11-94),
35kW - 2:51:20, 50kW - 4:13:07 (4:07:49-99)
CHETWYND Mathew John Christopher U15
20.12.85, Nun : HJ - 1.78, LJ - 5.98,
PenB - 2738
CHEUNG Lewis U17 12.12.83, Liverpool H :
LJ - 6.53w, TJ - 13.61w
CHILDS Richardo U17 9.10.84, Brecon :
LJ - 6.62
CHILDS Seriashe U20 2.09.82, Brecon :
100 - 10.84 (10.79w-99)

CHILES Garry 15.05.66, Norwich :
PV - 4.20 (4.35-94)
CHIN Darren U20 30.06.81, Belgrave :
60 - 6.92i (6.83i-99),
100 - 10.63 (10.51-99), 200 - 22.08
CHISHOLM Michael U17 25.02.84, Cambus :
800 - 1:53.48, 1500 - 3:55.79
CHRISTIE Jeffrey U20 24.09.82, Leamington :
400H - 52.5/52.72
CHRISTIE Mark U17 11.09.84, Gateshead :
PV - 4.40
CHURCH Scott U13 17.05.88, Isle of Wight :
HTC - 25.88
CIARAVELLA Simon 24.11.73, WGr & Ex L :
200 - 22.0w (21.87-93),
400 - 48.7/49.05 (47.33-93)
CLAGUE Samuel U15 26.02.86, Reading :
SPB - 14.74, DTB - 40.12
CLARE Jeffrey Mark 21.03.65, Sale :
DT - 45.62 (55.60-88)
CLARK Dean 20.12.73, Hillingdon :
400 - 48.8, 800 - 1:49.24 (1:49.20-99)
CLARK Jamie U13 11.05.88, Corby :
PV - 2.10
CLARKE Ian 6.11.72, Enf & Har :
60 - 6.9i (6.8i/6.88i-98), 100 - 10.6/10.79,
200 - 22.04w/22.13 (22.04w-97)
CLARKE Jonathan 20.11.67, Swansea :
JT - 61.68 (68.74-86)
CLARKE S. Ezra 9.12.74, Belgrave :
TJ - 14.97 (15.75-97)
CLARKE Wayne A. R. 24.12.75, Peterborough :
SP - 13.96, HT - 58.76 (59.86-97)
CLARKE Wesley 31.12.63, Ilford :
HT - 46.69 (48.88-94)
CLAY Matthew U17 9.06.84, Parkside :
LJ - 6.61, OctY - 4618
CLEMENTS Andrew U20 28.11.82, AF&D :
400H - 56.43, DecJ - 5546
COATES Peter 21.03.68, Durham :
Dec - 5226DD (5184-99)
COCKS Iain U15 20.10.85, Croydon :
800 - 2:06.0
COHEN Scott 6.12.64, Leslie Deans RC :
Mar - 2:26:05 (2:18:44-98)
COLE Brian, Royal Navy :
Mar - 2:32:43
COLE Jamie U20 22.05.81, Bolton :
PV - 4.15
COLEMAN Andrew 29.09.74, Enf & Har :
1500 - 3:50.3 (3:50.1-99),
5k - 14:14.3 (14:12.85-99),
5MR - 23:31, 10kR - 29:25, 10MR - 49:02,
HMar - 1:02:28, 3kSt - 8:45.27
COLEMAN Michael U23 14.05.78, Medway :
Mar - 2:29:12
COLEY Alexander U15 8.02.86, Sheffield :
100 - 11.27, 200 - 22.59w/22.9/23.10
COLLARD David U17 21.01.85, C of Glasgow :
HJ - 1.90
COLLINS Cornell U23 21.10.80, HHH/JAM :
110H - 14.8/15.57, 400H - 55.0
COLLINS Joseph U20 28.05.82, Shaft Barnet :
800 - 1:54.4 (1:52.65-99)
COLLINS Liam James O'Neill U23 23.10.78,
Sale : 200 - 22.01 (22.0-98),
60H - 7.94i, 110H - 14.05

COLLINS Patrick U17 4.02.85, Gateshead :
400HY - 57.3/57.78
COLLYMORE Fabian U17 19.10.84, Blackh :
100 - 11.15
COLTHERD Michael U20 28.12.82, Barr & F :
800 - 1:50.31
COLTON Matthew U20 5.11.82, Basildon :
110HJ - 14.65, 110H - 15.6
COMERFORD Nicholas 23.04.66, Cardiff :
10kR - 29:41, 10MR - 48:38
COMISSIONG Jason Kyle U17 7.09.83, TVH :
LJ - 6.54, TJ - 14.46w/14.11
COMPEY Tom U15 21.01.86, Dartford :
3k - 9:36.3
CONAGHAN Steven 18.05.67, Inverclyde :
5MR - 23:45
CONDON Allyn 24.08.74, Sale :
60 - 6.68 (6.64i-98), 100 - 10.42 (10.21-99),
200 - 20.80 (20.53i-98/20.59w-99/20.63-97)
CONDON David Jonathan 11.04.72, S'thend :
SP - 17.16
CONVEY Carl U20 15.10.82, Ipswich :
JT - 58.67
COOK Austin James Gareth 20.02.69, Sut & D :
SP - 13.76 (14.59-90),
DT - 44.62 (49.20-90), HT - 59.10 (67.32-91)
COOK Gavin 30.03.70, Thames Valley :
HT - 47.80 (62.58-88)
COOK Timothy U23 16.10.78, Crawley :
10k - 31:36.97
COOKE Ben U20 10.04.81, Wirral :
800 - 1:53.33
COOKE Simon U15 3.10.85, Chichester :
SPB - 14.22, DTB - 48.48, JTB - 43.03
COOMBES Sam U20 8.08.81, Dartford :
800 - 1:53.2
COOPER Daniel U15 4.09.85, Surrey Sch :
80HB - 12.1
COOPER Nicholas 4.02.77, Belgrave :
60H - 8.16i
COOPER Paul 4.12.76, WGreen & Ex L :
JT - 64.33 (67.03-99)
COOPER Rufus Henry U23 24.02.79, W S & E :
PV - 4.90
COPPIN Glen U20 16.01.83, Havering :
800 - 1:54.25
CORCORAN Fyn U23 17.03.78, Harr/Brun Un :
60H - 8.4i, 110H - 15.47 (15.11w/15.40-99),
Dec - 6761 (7116-99)
COREY Andrew John U20 15.10.81, CoStoke :
400 - 48.0/48.65 (48.53-99)
CORR Kevin U23 17.04.79, Jarrow & Hebb :
800 - 1:51.71
CORRIGAN J. Paul 19.01.66, Morpeth :
SP - 14.28i/13.83 (16.04-89)
CORRIGAN Matthew U15 1.12.85, Border :
SPB - 13.85, DTB - 39.85
CORRIGAN Michael 1.12.77, St. Marys U/IRE :
TJ - 14.17w
COSSINS Daniel U17 22.12.84, Wolves & B :
200 - 22.58
COSTELLO Denis Richard Michael 3.12.61,
Norwich : TJ - 13.94 (15.66-83)
COSTELLO Scott U15 9.06.87, :
PV - 3.00i
COTTON Steven U23 8.02.79, N Devon :
JT - 58.75

COVERINGTON M. U15, Guildford & G :
HTB - 43.03
COWAN Lloyd 8.07.62, WGreen & Ex L :
110H - 15.1 (13.75-94)
COX John 17.09.63, Les Croupiers :
Mar - 2:28:48 (2:27:28-98)
COX Laurence U13 15.03.88, AF&D :
800 - 2:16.5, 1500 - 4:34.6, 3k - 10:10.8
COX Martin, Salford :
5k - 14:15.11
COX Michael U15 15.01.86, Harrow :
80HB - 12.0, PV - 3.01
COYLE William 3.10.62, Shettleston :
10MR - 49:12dh
CRAKE Daniel U20 21.12.82, Border :
HJ - 1.98 (2.00-99)
CRAMP Aaron U17 29.02.84, Basildon :
JTY - 52.97
CRAMPTON Ian 28.01.62, Durham :
Mar - 2:31:05
CRANFIELD Peter U17 26.09.84, Liverpool H :
SPY - 15.16, DTY - 40.58, HTY - 54.28
CRAUFORD Chris J. U20 7.02.81, Enf & Har :
800 - 1:54.42
CRAWFORD Paul U13 4.10.87, Harrow :
100 - 12.46
CRAWLEY Luke U20 5.09.81, Solihull & S H :
HJ - 2.15
CREIGHTON James U17 15.09.83, Liverpool H :
HJ - 1.94 (1.95-99)
CRICKMORE Adam U17 26.01.84, Hereford :
100HY - 13.90
CRIMMEN Nicholas Philip 15.07.65, Spenbro :
DT - 41.22 (46.00-86)
CROASDALE Mark J. 10.01.65, Bing/R Navy :
10MR - 49:07 (49:04-94), Mar - 2:16:02
CROSS Michael U17 19.12.83, Tonbridge :
PV - 4.00i/3.90 (3.90-99), JTY - 53.85
CROSSLEY Paul U23 30.03.79, Luton/Bath U :
60H - 8.4i, 110H - 14.79,
400H - 53.93 (53.62-97)
CROW Daniel P. U15 18.03.86, Notts :
TJ - 12.38w/12.01
CROWLEY Mark U17 15.11.83, St Albans Str :
HJ - 2.03i/2.01
CROWTHER Eric 23.01.75, Salford :
3k - 8:20.24 (8:13.18-98)
CRYER Martyn U20 16.10.81, Blackpool :
3k - 8:22.74, 5k - 14:53.24
CUDDY Grant 6.01.77, Sale :
800 - 1:48.98 (1:47.2-97),
1500 - 3:49.45 (3:44.7-97)
CUFF Jon U23 30.03.80, Gloucester AC :
400H - 55.8 (53.06-99)
CULLEN Keith John 13.06.72, Chelmsford :
5k - 13:47.9 (13:17.21-97),
10k - 28:22.06 (27:50.33-99),
HMar - 1:02:11, Mar - 2:13:37
CUMMINS Daniel Colbert 10.12.76, Brunel U :
100 - 10.91w/10.92
CUNNINGHAM David 24.10.70, Burnley :
10k - 30:12.17
CURRAN Richard U15 19.09.85, Gosforth :
PV - 3.00
CUTTS Luke Arron U13 13.02.88, Barnsley :
PV - 3.00, DTC - 25.72
CZERNIK Richard 12.08.72, Halesowen :
DT - 40.39 (43.49-99), Dec - 6113 (6484-96)

D'ARCY Adam U20 25.05.82, R S C :
400H - 57.0 (56.94-99)
DACK Christopher U20 28.11.82, Donc&Stain :
DecJ - 5774
DAKO Owusu 23.05.73, Sale :
100 - 10.31 (10.17w-98/10.3-97)
DALMEDO Daniel U23 14.03.80, Hill/Staffs U :
3k - 8:20.4
DANCE Nicholas U17 27.09.83, Bracknell :
HJ - 1.90 (1.91-99)
DANIELS Darren 2.09.70, Birchfield :
5k - 14:33.5 (14:24.7-95)
DARBY Brian Roy Senfuma 14.10.72, Cov G :
100 - 10.8, 200 - 21.5,
300 - 34.4, 400 - 47.4/47.99 (47.56-97)
DARLINGTON Landley Sean 19.01.77, Birch/
Loughbro : JT - 56.70 (60.94-97)
DASHPER Wayne 19.10.74, Telford/R Navy :
3kSt - 9:17.82
DATEMA Cor P. 19.09.71, Team Solent/HOL :
1500 - 3:52.63 (3:45.0-98)
DAVENPORT Richard John U15 12.09.85,
Gloucs : 100 - 11.27, 200 - 22.7, 400 - 49.74,
800 - 1:58.65ioa/1:58.69
DAVEY Ian U20 25.10.82, Shildon :
800 - 1:54.4
DAVID Andrew 9.09.69, WGreen & Ex L :
110H - 15.1 (14.83-95)
DAVID Richard 15.08.77, Belgrave :
100 - 10.94, 400 - 49.03 (47.92-99)
DAVIDSON Brian 5.06.64, RRC :
100kR - 7:48:24 (7:25:57-99)
DAVIDSON Christopher 4.12.75, N&EB/Brun U :
LJ - 7.64w/7.54 (7.94w-97/7.90-99)
DAVIDSON Denzil U13 16.09.87, Shaft Barnet :
100 - 12.3, 200 - 25.3
DAVIDSON Hamish M. V45 25.05.54,
SGA (Prof) : SP - 13.41i (17.44-78)
DAVIES Adam Christopher U17 27.07.84,
Gloucs : 400 - 49.97, 800 - 1:55.6
DAVIES Chris U15 7.09.85, Gloucester AC :
400 - 51.1, 800 - 2:00.3
DAVIES Christopher 19.10.76, Telford/Staff U :
1500 - 3:45.24 (3:45.2-99), 1M - 4:08.16,
3k - 7:57.48, 5k - 14:09.89 (14:01.97-99),
5MR - 23:20, 10kR - 29:51
DAVIES Gareth M. 11.05.71, Cardiff :
LJ - 6.98 (7.62w-94/7.22-91)
DAVIES James U17 10.11.83, Dyfed Schools:
JTY - 52.77
DAVIES Kevin U23 11.01.78, Shaft Barn/RAF :
HT - 59.24
DAVIES Kris U20 30.10.81, Cardiff :
LJ - 7.08
DAVIES Mark Howard 10.01.71, Tonbridge :
SP - 14.97 (15.56-92), DT - 47.30 (53.06-92)
DAVIES Matthew 23.07.71, WGreen & Ex L :
1500 - 3:47.28 (3:44.2-96)
DAVIES Stephen U17 16.02.84, Newport :
800 - 1:57.7, 1500 - 4:00.13
DAVIES Steve U15 9.11.86, Yate :
PV - 2.90
DAVIES Tom U15 9.11.86, Telford :
PV - 2.90
DAVIS Adam Gareth 19.11.72, Corby/RAF :
PV - 4.40 (4.70-92), DT - 40.42, Dec - 5832
DAVIS Andrae U15 27.09.85, WGreen & Ex L :
400 - 52.1, 80HB - 11.66, LJ - 6.12,
SPY - 14.42i, SPB - 16.11, PenB - 3281

DAVIS Daniel U13, :
75HC - 12.0, 80HC - 12.7
DAVIS James U17 10.10.84, Portsmouth :
3kW - 13:22.96, 5kW - 23:36.76,
10kWR - 47:44
DAVIS Luke U23 1.01.80, Shaftesbury Barnet :
60 - 6.92i, 100 - 10.53 (10.40w/10.45-97),
200 - 21.74w (21.70-97)
DAVIS Luke U15 30.08.86, Portsmouth :
3kW - 14:46.81
DAVIS Mark Gavin 1.03.77, Corby :
PV - 5.20 (5.20-99)
DAVIS Vincent U20 1.11.81, Sale :
100 - 10.88, 200 - 21.63
DAVOLLS Martin U17 2.09.83, Enf & Har :
200 - 22.2, 400 - 48.8/48.99
DAVOREN Patrick 13.03.72, Phoenix :
800 - 1:51.10, 1500 - 3:43.13 (3:42.3-99),
1M - 4:07.95 (4:02.77-99)
DAVY Nick 26.12.74, Norwich :
800 - 1:52.88 (1:51.9-99)
DAWSON David U17 3.02.84, Exeter :
SP - 13.20, SPJ - 14.58,
SPY - 16.92, DTY - 42.10, HTY - 48.64
DAWSON Nicholas John U23 11.05.78, Bel/
Brunel Univ : 400 - 48.90 (48.2-99)
DAY Stephen U20 10.02.82, Shaft Barnet :
PV - 4.50
DEACON Gareth 8.08.66, Coventry Godiva :
10k - 30:59.8 (30:41.3-94)
DEACON Mark Jared 15.10.75, Morpeth :
100 - 10.92 (10.8-95),
200 - 21.19w/21.52 (21.14-96),
300 - 33.49 (32.78-96), 400 - 45.69
DEACON Kevin U17 25.02.84, Havering :
HTY - 48.10
DEACON-BROWN James U17 26.05.84, Gate :
JTY - 59.92
DEAKIN Robert 21.10.66, Staffs Moorlands :
Mar - 2:23:53
DEAKIN Simon 5.10.77, Leeds :
1500 - 3:50.30
DEAN Andrew U23 30.06.78, Solihull & S H/
Loughbro : 400H - 55.56 (54.76-99)
DEAN Andrew Christopher U17 25.09.83,
Havant : 800 - 1:57.0
DEARMAN Geoffrey Clive 4.08.77, Belgrave/
Brunel Univ : 200 - 21.6 (21.5/22.08i-98),
400 - 45.83
DEASY Colin, Sphinx :
Mar - 2:25:57
DEETH Ian U23 25.06.79, Team Sol/Falkirk/
Brunel Un : 100 - 10.81, 200 - 21.63w/21.94
DELAFIELD Andrew U23 19.03.80, Sheffield :
LJ - 6.99 (7.04-99)
DELBAUGH Phillip G. V40 25.01.60, Hill/RAF :
100 - 10.93
DELICATE Matthew U20 7.02.82,Dyfed Sch :
TJ - 13.96
DEMPSEY Thomas Christopher U17 15.12.83,
Hales : HT - 50.11, HTJ - 52.75, HTY - 60.81
DENMARK Robert Neil 23.11.68, Basildon :
1500 - 3:42.76 (3:37.99-95),
5k - 13:52.06 (13:10.24-92), 10k - 28:03.31,
DENSLEY Martin Richard U20 1.05.81, E,S&M :
PV - 4.70i/4.60 (4.70-98)
DESAILLY Franck 20.01.73, Swansea/FRA :
110H - 15.4w
DEVINE James Russell 24.04.68, Inverness :
HT - 65.09 (66.00-99)
DEVLIN Gareth 2.06.76, Loughbro/Sale/IRE :
LJ - 7.55w/7.22 (7.30-96), TJ - 14.12
DEVONISH Marlon 1.06.76, Coventry Godiva :
60 - 6.71i/6.93, 100 - 10.27 (10.13-98),
200 - 20.59 (20.25-99), 400 - 46.83
DEWSBERRY Matthew U20 9.10.81, Birch :
400H - 55.7/56.14
DEWSBURY Simon U15 2.12.85, Bournem'th :
HJ - 1.75
DIAMOND Quentin 25.09.74, Windsor S & E :
100 - 10.94
DICKENSON Derek Paul V50 4.12.49, Dac & T :
HT - 53.50 (73.20-76)
DICKINSON John U20 27.01.83, Haslemere :
DecJ - 6102
DICKSON Marlon U23 17.11.78, Belgrave :
60 - 6.8i/6.82i,
100 - 10.46w/10.60 (10.46w-99),
200 - 21.36w/21.73i (21.49-98)
DILLON Adrian U17 10.09.83, Wolves & B :
LJ - 6.60
DILLOW Greg U17 16.06.84, Woking :
PV - 3.90
DINGLEY Matthew U20 12.01.83, Birchfield :
JT - 57.29
DIXON Eugene U15 14.12.85, West Mid Sch :
TJ - 12.67w/12.41
DIXON Matthew U23 26.12.78, Sale/LSAC :
800 - 1:49.74, 1500 - 3:39.80,
1M - 4:01.61, 3k - 8:12.68i (8:20.2-99)
DJAN Geoffrey U20 21.07.82, Birchfield :
400 - 47.93
DOBBING Thomas F. 5.02.73, C of Edinburgh/
RAF : SP - 13.73, JT - 63.23 (65.22-93)
DOBBS Graham U17 27.06.84, Cleethorpes :
1.5kSt - 4:29.77
DOCHERTY William U17 2.04.85, Kilbarchan :
1.5kSt - 4:30.33
DOCKING James U15 19.11.86, C of Plymouth :
JTB - 45.87
DONALDSON Alasdair M. 21.06.77, N & E B/
Loughborough Studnts/Pitreavie :
400 - 47.84, 800 - 1:47.32, 1500 - 3:48.78
DONALDSON Andrew U15 23.01.86,
Liv.Pembroke Sefton : 800 - 2:03.85
DONKIN Bradley 6.12.71, Birchfield :
800 - 1:48.72 (1:46.86-98)
DONNELLY Dermot 23.09.70, Annad Str/IRE :
3k - 7:58.03, 5k - 13:56.74 (13:27.63-98),
10k - 29:36.91 (28:32.15-99),
10kR - 29:29 (29:06-98)
DONNELLY John U23 11.09.79, B & Antrim/
Queen's Univ/Border : LJ - 7.04w,
TJ - 14.57 (14.83-99)
DONOGHUE Mark U17 27.09.83,
Liv.Pembroke Sefton : 1.5kSt - 4:29.59
DONOVAN Daniel 8.10.70, Shaftesbury Barn :
100 - 10.6w/10.77 (10.4wdt-99/10.62w-97)
DORAN Lee U17 5.03.85, Carlisle/Aspatria :
JTY - 58.79
DORRIAN Matthew U17 24.03.84, Giffnock :
PV - 3.70
DOSANJH Nathan Luke U23 13.02.79, S& S H/
Loughbro : 800 - 1:51.88, 1500 - 3:47.77
DOUGAL Neil U23 7.03.80, Motherwell :
800 - 1:51.01

DOUGLAS Chris U13 2.12.87, Falkirk :
75HC - 11.98w/12.71
DOUGLAS Matthew 26.11.76, Bel/Brunel Un :
200 - 22.0 (21.68-97), 300 - 34.29 (34.12i-98),
400 - 46.65A (47.5-98/47.64-97), 300H - 35.25,
110H - 14.08 (14.00-99), 400H - 49.26
DOUGLAS Nathan James U20 4.12.82, Ox C :
LJ - 6.90, TJ - 15.18
DOWNES Shane 9.08.66, Army :
Mar - 2:31:26, 100kR - 7:37:36 (6:55:12-95)
DOWNING Peter U15 21.01.86, Brymore Sch :
HTB - 42.51
DOWSE Richard U17 3.01.85, Scunthorpe :
800 - 1:57.43
DOWSETT Nicholas J.E. U23 24.11.78,
WGreen & Ex L/London Univ. :
LJ - 7.01i/6.95 (7.15w-96/7.04i/7.02-97)
DOYLE Brian 12.03.77, C of Edinb/Cumb :
60 - 6.79i (6.79i-99),
200 - 21.15w/21.48i/21.64 (21.60-99)
DRAGUTINOVIC Srdjan 7.08.74, Bristol :
100 - 10.65w (11.22-99)
DRAKE Andrew Paul 6.02.65, Coventry G :
3kW - 11:58.0 (11:31.0-90),
10kWR - 41:25+/41:26,
20kW - 1:25:56 (1:24:53-87),
30kW - 2:22:08+ (2:15:01+-89),
35kW - 2:46:26+ (2:38:01-89)
DRAPER Anthony 23.04.74, Blackheath :
800 - 1:48.78
DRAPER Mark U17 28.06.84, Hounslow :
1500 - 3:59.96, 1M - 4:18.40
DRENT Anno 15.08.71, Shaftesbury Barnet :
3kSt - 9:29.70
DRURY Reece U17 2.11.83, Cleethorpes :
HTY - 50.23
DUBLIN Gavin U17 5.10.83, Croydon :
200 - 22.5, 400 - 49.44
DUDMAN Robert U15 9.06.86, Verlea :
HTB - 45.12
DUFFY Anthony P. V40 26.06.56, Bolton :
Mar - 2:26:38 (2:17:09-89)
DUNFORD Edward James U17 15.09.84, Bir :
60HY - 8.10i, 100HY - 13.18, 110HJ - 15.07,
110H - 15.31, HJ - 1.96, LJ - 6.78,
TJ - 13.50i/13.47, SPY - 15.18,
DTY - 41.40, JTY - 52.95,
DecY - 6712, OctY - 5537+Dec/5420
DUNFORD James Robert U15 14.01.86, Bir :
80HB - 11.93w/12.1 (11.86-99),
JTB - 43.10, PenB - 2710 (2763-99)
DUNLOP Guy U20 28.07.83, Campbell Coll :
110HJ - 15.4
DUNSON Gregory Ian 2.12.63, Army/Shaft B :
110H - 14.62w/14.67 (14.23w-89/14.29-86),
400H - 54.38 (50.88-92)
DURRANI Ramon U17 9.10.83, Herc Wimb :
100HY - 14.1
DUVAL Spencer Gavin 5.01.70, Cann & Staff :
3k - 8:18.47 (8:05.67-95),
HMar - 1:06:10 (1:04:50-97),
2kSt - 5:51.01 (5:33.09-92)
DUVIGNEAU Joleon U15 12.12.85, WG & Ex L :
TJ - 13.18w/12.81
DYBALL Gareth U20 16.03.81, WGreen & Ex L :
HJ - 2.00 (2.00-98)
DYER Michael U17 27.09.84, Berks Sch :
OctY - 4392

EARLE Robert Bernard V40 15.09.60, WG&EL :
SP - 14.75i/13.82 (14.87i-93/14.80-86),
DT - 41.74 (45.12-90), HT - 60.14 (62.60-95)
EAST Michael John U23 20.01.78, Portsmouth :
800 - 1:48.95, 1500 - 3:40.13,
1M - 4:04.65, 3k - 8:04.27,
5k - 14:28.0, 10kR - 29:23
EASTMAN Gavin U23 28.06.80, Enf & Har :
100 - 10.67w/10.7/10.78 (10.6w/10.75-99,
200 - 21.7/22.09
EASTON Mark Jonathan 24.05.63, Surrey WC :
10kWR - 46:08 (40:53-89),
20kW - 1:30:54 (1:24:04-89),
50kW - 4:07:33 (4:03:53-98)
EDDEN Richard A.E. U23 15.05.78, Haslem/
Camb Univ : HJ - 1.95 (1.95-99)
EDGAR Raymond U17 15.05.84, Lanc & Morc :
1500 - 4:01.82, 3k - 8:51.78
EDGAR Tyrone U20 29.03.82, WGreen & E L :
60 - 6.88i, 100 - 10.39,
200 - 21.58w/21.81i (21.55w/21.62-98)
EDMUNDS Cypren 20.06.70, Thames Valley :
200 - 21.84w (20.97-97)
EDMUNDS Gregor 25.04.77, Shettleston :
SP - 14.17
EDU Remi U20 14.12.78, S B/Loughbro :
400H - 52.26 (51.10-99)
EDUN Henry 6.02.73, Enf & Har :
LJ - 7.09w/6.94
EDWARDS Aston U15 29.11.85, Harrow :
400 - 52.9/52.94
EDWARDS Jonathan David 10.05.66, Gate :
TJ - 17.71 (18.43w/18.29-95)
EDWARDS Jonathan U23 6.11.78, Peterbro/
Loughbro : 400 - 47.60
EDWARDS Levi U23 23.11.80, Blackheath :
LJ - 7.35w/7.27
EDWARDS Mark Simon 2.12.74, Charn/Loughbro :
SP - 19.72, DT - 46.24 (46.73-99)
EDWARDS Martin U15 13.10.85, Hallamshire :
1500 - 4:18.56
EDWARDS Michael 19.10.68, Belgrave :
PV - 4.80i (5.64un-99/5.52-93)
EDWARDS Nicholas U20 22.03.81, Gloucs/
Royal Navy : 110HJ - 15.1 (15.1-99),
400H - 56.2/56.73 (55.34-99)
EDWARDS Nicholas U17 22.03.84, Sale :
HTY - 50.31
EDWARDS Noel 16.12.72, Leamington :
800 - 1:50.47 (1:48.58-99)
EFOBI Nnamdi U15 14.09.86, Enf & Har :
DTB - 38.22
EGGLETON Robert U17 13.02.84, C of Stoke :
DTY - 43.46
EKOKU Abi 13.04.66, Belgrave :
DT - 53.28 (60.08-90)
EL SHEIKH Khaled U23 26.07.78, S & S H/
London Univ : HJ - 2.00i/2.00
ELDER Craig U20 22.05.82, Sale Harriers :
LJ - 6.98
ELDRIDGE Timothy 15.03.76, SB/Exeter Univ :
JT - 62.02 (65.93-99)
ELIAS Daniel U20 25.12.82, WGreen & Ex L :
Dec - 5112w, DecJ - 5453
ELIAS Matthew U23 25.04.79, Cardiff/UWIC :
200 - 21.84i/21.96,
400 - 47.25, 400H - 51.16 (50.84-99)

ELLAMS Craig 24.11.72, City of Stoke :
HT - 64.39
ELLERSHAW Philip 9.02.76, Blackpool :
200 - 21.8/22.01w (21.6w-99/22.06-95
ELLINGTON James U15 6.09.85, Belgrave :
100 - 11.32, 200 - 22.46w/22.80
ELLIOTT Kenny U20 5.07.83, Regent House :
400HY - 58.08oa
ELLIOTT Mark U23 12.08.80, C of E/Glas U :
HJ - 2.00i/1.95 (2.00i/2.00-99)
ELLIOTT Mensah Abraham 29.08.76, Blackh :
60H - 7.93i, 110H - 13.69w/13.7/13.82
ELLIOTT Neil 10.04.71, City of Edinburgh :
SP - 16.22, DT - 47.26 (49.15-99)
ELLIOTT Ross U17 6.09.83, Peterlee :
DTY - 42.85
ELLIS Benjamin U20 16.11.81, Winchester :
100 - 10.8, 200 - 21.85
ELLIS James U15 6.09.85, Portsmouth :
1500 - 4:17.2, 3k - 9:23.39
ELLIS Kevin 18.06.76, Peterborough :
60 - 6.89i,
100 - 10.49w/10.7/10.78 (10.7/10.72-99),
200 - 21.87w/21.9 (21.80w/21.9-99/22.87-95)
ELLIS Samuel U20 23.06.82, Barnsley :
200 - 22.0/22.20, 400 - 48.20
ELLWOOD Wayne 26.09.74, Blackpool :
400 - 49.0 (47.50-97)
ELVIN Tom U20 10.02.81, Morpeth :
Dec - 5025
EMANUEL David 27.12.66, Birchfield :
TJ - 14.19w (15.91-91)
EMBLETON Peter V45 16.04.54, Chester Le St :
Mar - 2:27:19 (2:27:07-91)
ENIH-SNELL Chuka U17 2.03.84, Swansea :
HJ - 2.15, LJ - 6.76
ENRIGHT Stephen U17 5.09.84, Halifax :
3k - 8:56.87
EROGBOGBO Temitayo Faruq 8.03.75, Birch :
TJ - 15.97 (16.44w-97/16.32-95)
ERSKINE Craig U17 26.09.83, Dunf & W Fife/
Shaftesbury Barnet : 400 - 50.01 (49.63-99)
ERWOOD Paul Stephen U15 26.03.86,
Vale of Aylesbury : 1500 - 4:20.64
ETCHELLS James R. U23 15.10.80, Copland/
Durham U : TJ - 14.01i (14.34w-99/14.27-98)
ETHERIDGE David U20 17.09.82, Sale :
HJ - 1.98
EVANS Gareth 28.05.77, RAF/Sheffield :
110H - 15.4 (15.3-99/15.37-98)
EVANS Matthew U13 9.09.88, Carmarthen :
SPC - 11.59, DTC - 27.18
EVANS Paul William 13.04.61, Belgrave :
3k - 8:07e+ (7:55.29-96),
5k - 13:56.98 (13:25.38-95),
5MR - 23:49 (22:18sh-97/23:17-99),
10kR - 29:35 (28:13-95),
10MR - 49:21 (46:10+/46:35-97),
HMar - 1:02:58 (1:00:09un-95)
EVERARD James U20 16.05.81, Basildon :
JT - 55.32 (56.22-99)
EVLING-JONES Louis U20 20.06.83, Peterbro :
110HJ - 15.2, LJ - 6.94, Dec - 6146
EWEN Fraser U23 1.10.80, Falkirk :
SP - 13.80
EXLEY Scott U23 9.02.78, Belgrave :
100 - 10.7 (11.51-96),
110H - 15.6 (15.6-98/16.38-96), Dec - 6540
EYONG Onen U17 18.02.85, Belgrave :
LJ - 7.21

FABEN Stuart 28.02.75, Belgrave :
JT - 75.37 (76.66i-96)
FAHEY Thomas U17 27.09.84, Dartford :
3k - 8:58.32
FAIRCLOUGH Lee 23.06.70, Team Solent :
400 - 48.33 (47.2-96/47.30-97)
FAIRGRIEVE Ross U15 20.09.85, Reading :
HJ - 1.75, TJ - 12.87
FALCONER William U23 20.12.78, C of Edinb/
Strathclyde Univ :
SP - 14.65i/14.57, DT - 41.29
FALOLA Ayo 29.07.68, WGreen & Ex L :
60 - 6.89i (6.82i-95),
100 - 10.74 (10.2w-98/10.50-95),
200 - 22.04 (20.93w-95/21.15-91),
110H - 15.6w (14.80-97)
FARAH Mohammed U20 23.03.83, Hounslow :
800 - 1:53.5, 1500 - 3:49.60,
3k - 8:12.53, 5k - 14:05.72, 2kSt - 5:55.72
FARENDEN Simon U15 6.10.85, Chesterfield :
100 - 11.4/11.47, 200 - 22.26w/22.6/22.65,
400 - 52.7, TJ - 12.26
FARLEY Paul Ivor U17 1.12.84, Isle of Wight :
DTY - 40.68, HTY - 54.82
FARMER Matt U17 18.11.84, Crawley :
800 - 1:57.63
FARMER Paul 23.11.77, Luton :
HMar - 1:06:41,
3kSt - 9:09.17 (8:59.01mb/9:01.64-99)
FARQUHARSON Billy 14.04.75, Mansfield :
10MR - 49:31
FARQUHARSON Ruddy Anthony 26.03.61,
Telford/RAF : TJ - 14.50 (15.59w/15.57-85)
FARROW Kevin 8.09.75, Derby & Co :
1500 - 3:47.94, 3k - 8:08.8
FARRUGIA Emmanuel U20 19.07.82, WG&EL :
400 - 49.4 (48.95-99)
FASINRO Ibrahim 'Tosi' 28.03.72, Enf & Har :
TJ - 15.70 (17.30w/17.21-93)
FATIHI Mohammed 16.06.73, TVH/MOR :
3k - 8:03.58, 5KR - 14:15, HMar - 1:06:03
FAULKNER Stewart 19.02.69, Birchfield :
LJ - 7.23 (8.15-90)
FAVELL Peter U20 16.03.82, Chesterfield :
TJ - 14.09w/14.07, DTJ - 42.34 (43.93-99)
FEASEY Terry 5.08.77, Basingstoke & MH :
800 - 1:51.55 (1:50.77-98)
FEASY James U15 11.12.86, Hants S :
100 - 11.6
FEIGHAN Mike 5.11.65, Bideford :
Mar - 2:28:32
FEIL Dirk 9.03.65, Morpeth/GER :
PV - 4.20 (4.40-97)
FELCE Alex U15 11.09.86, Gloucester L :
1500 - 4:19.25i/4:22.97, 3k - 9:22.8
FENNEMORE Dennis U17 19.06.84, Harrow :
TJ - 13.56
FENTON Malcolm Leonard V40 12.02.56, Ips :
DT - 41.10 (47.40-79), HT - 59.75 (62.42-82)
FERDINAND Philip U20 18.11.82, Birchfield :
TJ - 14.98
FERGUS Jason Robert 11.10.73, Shaft Barn :
60 - 6.79i (6.68i-95),
100 - 10.45w/10.58 (10.34w-94/10.4-93/10.44-92),
200 - 21.04i/21.07w/21.25 (20.85w-99/20.91-97)

FERGUSON Martin M. 17.09.64, City of Edin :
10k - 31:35.12 (30:43.6-89),
Mar - 2:32:05 (2:26:45-95)
FERNANDEZ Andre U23 2.03.80, TVH :
200 - 22.12w, 400 - 48.8, LJ - 7.31
FERNS Austin U20 12.01.81, Belgrave :
400H - 55.04 (52.74-99)
FERRIBY Benjamin Bork U13 9.09.87, Chelm :
200 - 25.80
FERRIN John 20.02.67, North Belfast/IRE :
5MR - 23:48, HMar - 1:06:59 (1:03:52-92)
FEWTRELL James U23 22.12.80, Beds & Co :
1500 - 3:51.57
FIELD Andrew U15 20.09.85, Bournemouth :
JTB - 43.39
FIELD Peter U20 21.05.82, City of Stoke :
HT - 53.17, HTJ - 62.65
FIELD Terry 26.11.61, Barnsley :
Mar - 2:27:17
FIELD Tim 30.05.65, Sunderland :
10k - 31:56.0
FIELDING Martin U20 19.05.83, Yate :
5k - 15:34.2
FIFTON Rikki U17 17.06.85, Tower Hamlets :
100 - 10.85, 200 - 22.2 (23.01-99)
FINCH Lloyd U17 23.10.83, Leics WC :
3kW - 12:48.19i/12:49.49 (12:34.98-99),
5kW - 22:23.45i (22:19.11-99),
10kWR - 45:20 (43:38-99)
FINCH Luke U15 21.09.85, Leics WC :
3kW - 14:09.93
FINCH Michael U15 11.01.86, Cleethorpes :
PV - 2.85
FINDLAY Mark¶ U23 20.03.78, Newham & E B :
100 - 10.37drg/10.52w/10.59 (10.35-99),
200 - 21.52 (20.99w-97/21.01-99)
FINDLOW Richard David 4.12.66, Bradford :
5k - 14:36.84 (13:44.58-92),
10k - 29:58.65 (29:32.67-95)
FINILL Chris V40 31.12.58, Harrow :
100kR - 7:22:50
FINLAY Greg U15 31.10.85, Rhondda :
SPB - 14.69, DTB - 41.57
FINLAYSON Ross U13 26.09.87, Lasswade :
400 - 62.8, 800 - 2:17.96, 75HC - 12.87w/12.9
FISH Benjamin U20 21.05.82, Blackburn :
5k - 15:28.6
FISHER Gavin 18.11.77, W Suffolk/Loughbro :
HJ - 1.96i/1.95 (2.00-96)
FISHER Ian 15.09.70, Otley :
HMar - 1:06:35, Mar - 2:20:26
FISHER Martin 27.09.62, York RWC :
50kW - 4:58:06
FISHER Peter U20 14.02.82, V of Aylesbury :
HJ - 2.00
FITZSIMMONS James 20.04.74, Shaft Barnet :
5k - 14:44.66, 10k - 31:10.12, Mar - 2:29:16
FLADGLEY Nick U13 23.11.87, Wimborne :
HJ - 1.60
FLEARY Jordan U15 1.12.85, Carlisle/Asp :
80HB - 11.71
FLECKNEY William U15 19.10.85, Beds & Co :
80HB - 12.00w, LJ - 6.18, PenB - 2506
FLEET Andrew U20 2.12.82, Liverpool H :
400H - 56.9
FLETCHER Carl U17 24.09.83, Wigan :
SPY - 14.43 (15.49-99)
FLETCHER John U15 15.07.86, Wakefield :
LJ - 6.28
FLINT Andrew 9.11.76, Thames Valley :
DT - 41.90
FLINT Benjamin U23 16.09.78, Belgrave :
PV - 5.35i/5.30 (5.40-99)
FLINT Mark A. 19.02.63, Birchfield/RAF :
5k - 14:34.88 (13:54.5-90),
HMar - 1:06:04 (1:01:56-93)
FLOOK Martin U20 20.12.81, Bristol :
800 - 1:52.40
FLOYD Michael Anthony 26.09.76, Sale/
Salford Univ. : HT - 69.38
FLYNN Julian T. 3.07.72, Belgrave :
LJ - 7.62 (7.76w/7.70-99)
FOGG Nicholas U23 24.03.78, Shaft Barnet :
HT - 52.56?/47.85 (49.54-97)
FOLEY Dan U17 11.09.84, Wolves & B :
800 - 1:57.91
FOOKS Andrew 26.04.75, Thames Valley :
3kSt - 9:14.3 (8:56.83-95)
FORBES Brian 6.09.74, Mid Ulster/Border/
QUB/IRE : 400 - 47.8/47.85 (46.84-97)
FORD Antony U20 26.05.83, Blackpool :
3k - 8:28.73
FORDE James U17 10.04.85, Sparkhill :
HTY - 50.65
FORDE Karl U20 15.04.83, Rowheath :
100 - 10.72w/10.84 (10.66w/10.70-99),
200 - 21.9w/22.0 (21.92w/22.47i-99/23.98-97
FORDHAM Gavin James U23 1.02.79,
Bedford & Co/Birm U : HJ - 1.99, Dec - 6091
FORFAR Gary U13 7.10.87, City of Edinburgh :
PV - 2.00
FORREST Anthony 22.12.76, AF&D :
3kSt - 9:19.39
FOSTER William Randolph Garnet V40
9.08.58, Blackheath :
10k - 30:47.7 (29:14.34-96)
FOWLER Justin, V of Aylesbury/Bucks Univ :
10k - 31:59.31
FOWLES Steven James U17 16.05.85, Thurr :
100 - 10.97
FOX Morris 30.04.63, City of Stoke :
SP - 14.84 (14.95-95), DT - 44.83 (46.40-95)
FRAMPTON Matthew U17 10.04.84, Wimborne :
HTY - 56.92
FRANCE Chris U17 29.01.84, Telford :
HJ - 1.98
FRANCIS Nick 29.08.71, Shaftesbury Barnet :
3k - 8:20.80 (8:18.26-99),
5k - 14:19.48 (14:00.14-99),
10k - 31:18.05 (30:40.8-94),
10kR - 29:35
FRANCIS-FAMOUS James U17 14.12.83, Harr :
100HY - 14.2 (13.93-99)
FRANKLIN Andrew U23 13.09.80, Traff/Man U :
3kSt - 9:04.77 (8:55.08mb-99)
FRANKS Thomas U15 8.11.85, Leics Cor :
400 - 52.99
FRASER Peter U23 28.01.78, Aberdeen :
JT - 58.34 (58.95-98)
FRAZER Aaron U17 10.05.84, Sale :
3k - 9:00.3, 2kSt - 6:13.29
FRAZER Thomas U20 10.09.81, St Malachy's :
5k - 15:03.70
FREARY Paul 3.04.68, Belgrave :
5KR - 14:23

FREEMAN Giles U15 19.11.85, Hertford & W : 400 - 53.4
FREMPONG Kenneth U17 17.07.84, Herc W : 100HY - 13.38
FRENCH B., Aberdeen : JT - 55.72
FRENCH Jon 11.12.75, Norwich : LJ - 7.12 (7.38w/7.22-99)
FRICKER Simon David 14.07.75, Team Solent : SP - 15.22 (15.29-96), DT - 47.37 (49.96-97)
FRIEND Andrew U15 2.08.87, AF&D : 3k - 9:36.1
FROST Andrew Derek U20 17.04.81, I of W/ St. Marys : SPJ - 13.95 (14.01-98), HT - 58.75, HTJ - 61.23
FROST Howard U20 9.12.81, Kent : 400H - 55.0/55.32, DecJ - 6047
FROST Russell U23 23.06.80, Kent : 400 - 48.89
FROST Steven U20 4.01.81, Wrexham : TJ - 14.11
FROUD Paul M. 6.04.66, Brighton : Mar - 2:30:21 (2:22:18-94)
FRY Jason U20 6.01.83, Southend : PV - 4.20
FUGALLO Alexander 28.01.70, Shaft Barnet : 100 - 10.8 (10.42w-90/10.5-89/10.60-92), 200 - 21.5/21.60w (21.20w-89/21.2/21.26-90), 400 - 47.15 (46.39-94)
FULFORD Andrew U20 23.06.82, Swindon : 800 - 1:51.26
FULLER Peter John U23 30.04.78, Epsom & E : HT - 52.66 (52.82-99)
FULLER William 19.10.76, Epsom & Ewell : SP - 15.81 (16.36-97), HT - 53.19 (54.20-97)
FYVIE John U17 23.01.84, Banchory : HTY - 47.21

GADD Richard U15 30.07.86, Beds & Co : 100 - 11.6, 200 - 23.21w/23.37
GAHAGON James U17 14.01.84, Southend : 100HY - 14.2
GALE Howard U15 23.09.85, Dacorum & T : HJ - 1.82
GALLAGHER Adam U17 23.03.84, AF&D : LJ - 6.63
GALLAGHER Andrew U20 15.02.83, B & A : JT - 56.84
GALLAGHER Anthony U17 16.10.84, Liv.Pem S : SPY - 14.39i/13.98, DTY - 41.29
GALLAGHER Donal 5.12.72, Sparta : 10k - 31:43.3 (30:52.9-94)
GALLIE Adam U17 5.11.84, Derby & Co : HJ - 2.00
GALLOWAY Dwayne U15 22.01.86, Birchfield : LJ - 5.96
GAMESTER Daniel U23 29.04.78, Havering : HT - 47.23
GARDENER Jason John 18.09.75, Wx & Bath : 60 - 6.48i (6.46i-99), 100 - 10.04w/10.09 (9.98-99)
GARDINER Richard 11.06.73, Cardiff : 10k - 30:43.04
GARDINER Simon U17 14.02.84, Lagan Vall : 100 - 11.1
GARDNER Robert U23 23.12.78, Norwich/ Loughbro : PV - 4.10i (3.70-95)
GARDNER Rupert U17 9.10.84, Milton Keyn : OctY - 4247
GARLAND Dale U23 13.10.80, Guer/Bath Un : 400H - 54.82, LJ - 7.09, Dec - 6048
GARLAND Stephen 12.01.73, Liv.Pembroke S : PV - 4.10 (4.20-99), Dec - 6560 (6676w-99)
GARNER Mark U17 2.11.83, Mansfield : 400HY - 56.70, OctY - 4285
GARRARD Deane U20 19.05.82, Ipswich : SPJ - 13.68 (14.52-99)
GARRETT Lee U23 2.09.78, Mansfield/Staff U : 800 - 1:51.7, 1500 - 3:46.84 (3:44.63-99), 3k - 8:19.47i
GARSIDE Michael U13, : 800 - 2:16.4
GASCOIGNE Robert 5.10.74, Sale : 400H - 55.68 (55.21-97)
GATE Simon U20 21.09.82, Border : HT - 48.17, HTJ - 52.46
GAWTHORPE Richard J. U20 28.01.81, Derby & Co/Oxf Un : 400H - 56.00 (55.6-98)
GAY Richard V50 26.10.50, Beverley : Mar - 2:31:56
GEARING Chris U15 30.09.86, Medway : SPB - 14.27i/13.66
GEARY John U17 30.09.83, Tipton : 1500 - 4:06.25
GEBBIE Joel U13, : JTC - 38.36
GELMAN Bradley U20 18.01.82, Hertford & W : 100 - 10.9 (11.00w-98)
GEORGE Ashley Christian Evan U15 23.05.86, Belgrave : 200 - 23.3, LJ - 6.29 (5.86db-99)
GEORGE Michael 4.07.72, Windsor S & E : 400H - 55.2/55.50 (55.14-99)
GHENT Brendon 7.09.76, Rugby : 60 - 6.87i (6.78i-98), 100 - 10.36w/10.4/10.56 (10.51-99), 200 - 21.0/21.21w/21.24 (21.0/21.01-99)
GIBLIN Christopher U20 20.06.81, Liverpool H : HJ - 2.10 (2.12-99)
GIBSON Alex 3.11.77, Brentwood/Loughbro : Dec - 6244
GIBSON Wayne 25.02.76, Middlesbro & C : HT - 51.81
GIFFORD David 9.03.73, Cleethorpes : 400H - 54.7/55.27 (52.9/53.10-99)
GILBERT Daniel U20 1.03.81, Team Solent : HJ - 1.95
GILBERT James 9.11.74, City of Edinburgh : LJ - 6.84i (7.11-97)
GILBERT Paul U20 21.06.81, Phoenix : 800 - 1:52.96 (1:51.49-99)
GILBY Clive Roger 24.02.66, Belgrave : 800 - 1:52.70 (1:47.33-95)
GILDING Paul 2.10.75, Worthing : 110H - 15.19w/15.28, HJ - 1.96 (2.03i/2.01-93), Dec - 5639
GILHOOLY Anthony 26.03.76, N & Essex B : HJ - 2.10i/2.05 (2.18i-97/2.18-99)
GILL Anthony 19.09.77, Border/Staffs Univ : 100 - 10.84, 60H - 8.21i (8.21i-99), 110H - 14.40 (14.22w/14.29-99)
GILL Jamie U15 29.10.85, Cannock & Stafford : 100 - 11.24, 200 - 23.04
GILL Stephen U17 25.09.84, Middlesbro & C : 400 - 50.71

GILLAM John U17 15.10.84, Oldham & Royton : 1.5kSt - 4:37.03

GILLESPIE Ian 18.05.70, Birchfield : 1500 - 3:46.57 (3:39.8-97), 1M - 4:05.22 (3:57.6-98), 3k - 8:18.91i (7:48.28-97), 2M - 8:49.39i (8:34.5-97), 5KR - 14:04

GILLIGAN Daniel U23 12.05.79, Dartford : JT - 56.26

GIRDLER Dominic Paul U20 6.03.82, Charn : 100 - 10.8w (11.2-98), 60H - 8.18i, 60HJ - 8.06i, 110HJ - 13.96w/14.20, 110H - 14.30, HJ - 2.03

GISBOURNE Steve 24.03.68, Sheffield : 10k - 31:31.8

GITTENS Luke U20 4.01.81, Cardiff : 60H - 8.36i, 110H - 14.86w/14.88, 110HJ - 14.8/15.36 (14.69-98)

GLANVILLE Craig U15 21.09.86, Gateshead : 200 - 23.64, 400 - 51.46, 800 - 2:04.7, PenB - 2719w

GLENNIE Mark U20 19.02.82, Team Solent : 800 - 1:54.1

GLOVER Ross U15 2.11.85, Northampton : 400 - 53.2, 800 - 2:03.9

GODDARD Aundre U13 21.04.88, Reading : 80HC - 13.2

GODDARD Samuel John U20 4.01.83, Padd W : JT - 53.75

GODSELL Joseph U17 27.10.83, Blackheath : 800 - 1:56.65

GOLDING Alexander U20 3.12.81, Mandale : 100 - 10.69w/10.88 (10.67-99)

GOLDING Julian Antonio 17.02.75, Blackheath : 60 - 6.80i, 100 - 10.38 (10.28-97), 200 - 20.64 (20.18-98)

GOLDSMITH Jeremy G. 6.12.73, Team Solent : JT - 55.60 (57.20-93)

GOLLEY Julian Quintin Patrick 12.09.71, TVH : LJ - 7.24, TJ - 16.95 (17.06-94)

GOODALL Liam U17 15.01.84, Northampton : 400 - 50.3 (54.26-98)

GOODLIFFE Nicholas U20 12.05.82, Holmfirth : 1500 - 3:54.89, 3k - 8:33.54, 5k - 14:42.85

GOODREM Greg U17 14.09.83, Southend : HJ - 1.98

GOODRIDGE Marwan U13 5.09.87, Harrow : LJ - 5.16

GOODWIN Jon 22.09.76, Team Sol/St. Marys : 800 - 1:52.3, 400H - 55.24 (52.5/53.14-97)

GOODWIN Robert U17 19.04.84, Grimsby : 800 - 1:57.91

GORDON Alastair U23 16.04.78, Worthing : 200 - 22.09w/22.10 (21.77-98), 400 - 47.98 (48.2-98)

GORDON David 20.03.68, Newham & E B : PV - 4.20 (5.05iun-88/4.85Aun-93/4.75-94)

GORDON Malwyn U20 29.04.82, Bristol : TJ - 15.09 (15.26-99)

GORDON Peter V45 2.07.51, Gateshead : DT - 53.93 (61.62-91), HT - 53.78 (63.20-82)

GORDON Wesley U15 9.11.85, Sunderland : 3k - 9:35.5

GOUDIE Andrew U23 4.10.78, Belgrave : 3kW - 13:25.25 (13:20.95-99), 5kW - 22:39.26, 10kW - 46:37.46

GOUGH S. V40 10.02.56, Royal Navy : Mar - 2:33:12 (2:27:04-93)

GOULD Robert John 16.01.76, Trafford/ Chester U : 3k - 8:19.81i (8:16.4-99), 5k - 14:29.06, 10k - 30:43.63, 10kR - 29:17

GOULDBOURNE Marcus U20 12.06.81, P & B : SP - 13.42, SPJ - 13.70 (14.42i-99), DT - 42.54, DTJ - 43.97

GOULDING Dean 14.06.75, Sheffield : LJ - 6.94w

GOWELL Chris U15 26.09.85, Torfaen : 400 - 53.4, 800 - 2:02.61ioa/2:05.16

GRABARZ Robbie U13 3.10.87, Beds & Co : HJ - 1.55

GRAFFIN Allen Gordon 20.12.77, Tonbridge : 800 - 1:50.1, 1500 - 3:40.14, 1M - 3:59.86, 2k - 5:02.90, 3k - 8:15.44 (8:03.22-98), 5k - 13:41.42, 10kR - 29:35

GRAFFIN Andrew Neill 20.12.77, Tonbridge : 800 - 1:49.1, 1500 - 3:36.18, 1M - 3:56.13, 2k - 5:01.28, 3k - 8:04.63i (8:07.58-99), 5k - 14:06.40, 5MR - 23:39, 10kR - 29:22

GRAHAM Anthony 15.10.63, Tipton : HMar - 1:06:41 (1:04:48-94)

GRAHAM Daniel Alexander U23 3.08.79, Liv H : HJ - 2.22

GRAHAM Douglas 1.01.77, City of Edinburgh : PV - 4.20 (4.26-96)

GRAHAM Ewan U17 3.09.84, Chelmsford : HJ - 1.90

GRAHAM Grant 27.12.72, Motherwell : 800 - 1:50.86 (1:47.85-98)

GRAHAM James U17 10.09.84, Corby : 100 - 11.1 (11.52-99)

GRAHAM Jonathan U17 10.10.83, Gosforth : 1500 - 4:02.4, 3k - 8:53.09

GRAHAM Paul U23 8.10.78, Blackheath : HJ - 1.95 (2.00-97)

GRANT Dalton 8.04.66, WGreen & Ex L : HJ - 2.25i/2.23 (2.37i-94/2.36-91)

GRANT Dwayne U20 17.07.82, Blackheath : 60 - 6.9i/6.97i, 100 - 10.57w/10.61, 200 - 20.88

GRANT JONES Joel U15 21.11.85, Beds & Co : HJ - 1.75

GRANT Mark 17.05.71, Thames Valley : PV - 4.95 (5.10-95)

GRANT Ross U20 28.10.82, Morpeth : 100 - 10.91w

GRAY Glenn 21.04.68, Thames Valley : 400H - 53.07 (52.63-99)

GRAY Paul 25.05.69, Cardiff : 110H - 13.9w/13.93 (13.53-94), 400H - 51.18 (49.16-98)

GREAVES Damien David 19.09.77, N & E B : 60H - 7.68i, 110H - 13.62

GREAVES Daniel U20 4.10.82, Charnwood : DT - 40.10, DTJ - 46.15

GREEN James U15 28.11.85, Liverpool H : DTB - 38.59, HTB - 48.58

GREEN Michael Stephen 12.10.76, Blackburn/ Troy State Un : 1500 - 3:48.14, 3k - 8:17.58 (8:10.57-99), HMar - 1:06:29, 5k - 14:30.34 (14:12.56-99)

GREEN Paul 7.04.72, Sale : HMar - 1:06:43

GREEN Royston U20 4.01.82, Exeter : 800 - 1:53.12

GREEN Steven Christopher U20 15.01.83, Cornwall AC : 110HJ - 15.16, 400H - 54.11

GREENE Richard U17 11.10.84, Enf & Har :
HTY - 55.39
GREENLAND Philip U17 10.10.84, Croydon :
LJ - 6.57
GREGORY Michael 5.11.76, Andover :
1500 - 3:49.13
GRIERSON Gordon U15 12.10.85, W S & E :
HTB - 53.92
GRIFFIN Neil V50 28.05.48, Windsor S & E :
SP - 14.19 (16.06-77), DT - 45.44 (51.66-80)
GRIFFITH Mark U20 25.11.81, Enf & Har :
2kSt - 5:54.4, 3kSt - 9:30.5 (9:22.44-99)
GRIFFITHS Andrew U20 26.09.81, Swansea :
400H - 56.77
GRIFFITHS Rowan 16.01.75, Newham & E B :
HJ - 1.95 (2.00i-97/1.95-99)
GRIME Ian Stuart 29.09.70, Newham & E B :
1500 - 3:45.79 (3:40.1-96),
3k - 8:06.6 (7:55.4-96),
5k - 14:19.56 (13:37.00-97),
10k - 30:58.93 (30:22.88-98),
10kR - 29:21, HMar - 1:05:38
GRIME Peter 8.11.69, Durham Univ :
10k - 31:05.85
GRIMWADE Jonathan U15 15.04.86, Walton :
80HB - 11.97w/12.0/12.08
GRINDLE James U17 8.01.84, Cardiff :
HTY - 51.57
GRIPTON Paul 9.11.76, Bromsgrove & R :
110H - 14.7 (14.59-98), 400H - 55.3
GRISTWOOD William E. V40 20.03.59, E,S&M :
Mar - 2:30:31 (2:25:09-94)
GROVES Michael U17 21.03.84, Torfaen :
200 - 22.07, 400 - 51.0, JTY - 55.23
GUEST Craig U20 25.10.82, Charnwood :
JT - 54.22 (55.17-99)
GUNN Chris U20 13.09.82, Birchfield :
DecJ - 5443
GUNN Luke U17 22.03.85, Derby & Co :
800 - 1:59.0
GYORFFY Terry 28.01.65, Army/Bas & MH :
DT - 40.49

HAGAN Garry U17 21.11.84, Clydesdale :
SPY - 15.22i/14.99, DTY - 48.24
HAINES Alex U20 27.10.82, :
5k - 15:34.0
HALCROW Patrick U15 9.01.86, Thurrock :
80HB - 12.0, PenB - 2524
HALE Craig U15 18.12.85, Hertford & Ware :
80HB - 12.1
HALE Darren V40 2.10.59, Salford :
Mar - 2:29:37 (2:22:09-97)
HALE Steven 20.04.77, Rowheath :
DT - 44.53
HALES Matthew John MacKenzie U23 6.10.79,
Steyning : 3kW - 12:07.54, 5kW - 20:06.66,
10kW - 43:12.85, 10kWR - 45:12 (45:00-99),
20kW - 1:31:50 (1:30:38-99)
HALEY Stuart U17 9.12.84, Gateshead :
100 - 11.07w (11.4-99),
200 - 22.55w (22.93-99)
HALL Alex U20 2.02.82, Cambridge Harriers :
LJ - 7.10 (7.29-99), TJ - 14.85
HALL Brendan Russell U13 5.09.87, Cann & St :
SPC - 12.25
HALL Brian U20 17.11.82, Bolton :
HJ - 2.10
HALL Calvin U17 15.11.83, Birchfield :
HJ - 1.95
HALL Dominic 21.02.71, Highgate Harriers :
800 - 1:49.86 (1:49.1-98)
HALL Drew U20 31.08.81, Birchfield :
400H - 54.52
HALL Jonathon U17 18.11.83, Ayr Seaforth :
400 - 50.92
HALL Samuel Thomas U15 15.10.85, Shaft B :
1500 - 4:18.96, 3k - 9:33.43 (9:13.2-99)
HALL Stuart 21.12.64, Tipton :
HMar - 1:06:54
HALLAM Ricky U17 17.01.85, Tamworth :
PV - 3.70
HALLIGAN John U20 4.05.83, Manx :
3kSt - 9:42.6
HAMBLIN Ben U15 2.11.85, Norwich :
100 - 11.51
HAMBRIDGE Mark U13 18.02.89, Nuneaton :
2kW - 11:06.7
HAMBRIDGE Simon U13 18.02.89, Nuneaton :
2kW - 11:08.4
HAMILTON Ashley Robert U13 11.06.88, Croy :
HJ - 1.51
HANDLEY Charles U15 18.01.86, Wakefield :
HTB - 45.83
HANSFORD Matthew U15 20.02.86, Exeter :
80HB - 11.15, LJ - 6.18, PenB - 2928
HANSON Mark U20 13.05.81, Enf & Har/
Brun U : 100 - 10.90w/10.94 (10.8/10.87-99)
HARDIE James U20 16.04.82, Huntingdon :
HJ - 2.05i/2.05
HARDING David John U23 8.11.80, Hert & W/
Oxford Univ : JT - 55.92
HARDING James U17 8.07.85, Macclesfield :
800 - 1:58.89
HARDING Steve U15 14.12.85, AVON S :
TJ - 12.07
HARLAND Kim U20 21.02.82, Carmarthen :
HJ - 2.01
HARLE Robert Keith U23 1.06.79, St Albans S/
Camb U : 100 - 10.8/10.97, 200 - 21.8/22.07
HARRIES Kirk 7.08.74, Thames Valley :
110H - 15.25 (14.45w-97/14.65-98)
HARRIS Andrew U17 21.09.83, Wessex & Bath :
TJ - 13.42
HARRIS Lee U17 23.11.83, Bristol :
TJ - 13.77i (13.29w/13.18-98)
HARRIS Mark U20 2.06.82, Swindon :
2kSt - 6:14.71, 3kSt - 9:56.9
HARRIS Richard 16.08.71, Rotherham :
3kSt - 9:29.9 (9:27.4-99)
HARRISON Chris U15 19.09.85, Lancs Sch :
SPB - 13.73
HARRISON David U13 17.10.88, Blackheath :
JTC - 34.72
HARRISON Julian 4.08.76, Sheffield :
HJ - 2.00
HARRISON Nsa U17 27.11.83, Worcester :
SPY - 16.99
HART Alistair 25.09.71, Thames H & H :
Mar - 2:31:59
HART Andrew 13.09.69, Coventry Godiva :
800 - 1:46.52 (1:45.71-98),
1500 - 3:51.86 (3:42.0-96),
1M - 4:08.60 (4:01.7-98)
HART James U20 4.04.82, Rowheath :
HJ - 1.95

HART Tom 7.12.77, Windsor S & E/Lancs Un :
10k - 31:33.4
HARVEY Jonathan U17 12.09.83, Braintree :
JTY - 54.16
HARVEY Mark U17 2.07.84, Neath :
PV - 3.90
HARVEY Stuart U13 2.09.87, Blackheath :
JTC - 36.90
HARWOOD Laurence U17 9.03.85, I of Wight :
HTY - 51.60
HARWOOD Paul 19.07.71, AF&D :
Mar - 2:29:39 (2:28:44-99)
HASSAIN Jon U23 16.06.80, Braint/Loughbro :
200 - 22.0, 400 - 49.0/50.51
HASSAN Malcolm Mark U20 27.11.82, Sund :
800 - 1:51.51, 1500 - 3:54.25
HASTEY Rhian U15 5.08.86, Rotherham :
800 - 2:05.00
HATTON Keith V45 19.10.55, Medway :
PV - 4.10
HAUGHIAN Samuel U23 9.07.79, Hounslow :
1500 - 3:49.37 (3:45.23-99),
3k - 8:11.9 (7:57.24-99),
5k - 14:04.85 (13:55.81-99)
HAUGHIAN Tim U15 29.11.86, Hounslow :
3k - 9:00.4
HAWKES Jonathan U15 16.07.86, London Sch :
TJ - 12.32
HAWKEY Terry U17 6.01.84, Dartford :
1500 - 4:06.16
HAWKINS Colin John U17 23.03.84, Derby :
1500 - 4:03.99
HAWKINS Malcolm U17 17.12.83, Stratford :
OctY - 4250
HAWKINS Matthew U17 17.12.83, Stratford :
400HY - 56.91
HAY John David U20 4.06.83, Corby :
HTJ - 51.88
HAYDEN Lewis U13 10.08.89, Nuneaton :
2kW - 11:14.4
HAYES Scott 4.01.73, Thames Valley :
SP - 14.94i/14.84 (16.15i-98/15.62-95),
DT - 51.03 (54.16-97)
HAYFORD Kenneth Nicholas 10.03.63, Camb H :
JT - 58.76 (69.90-87)
HAYMAN Nigel 25.09.74, Bournemouth :
110H - 15.6 (15.2-97/15.33w-99/15.39-97)
HAYWARD Alex U17 29.11.83, WGr & Ex L :
1.5kSt - 4:36.6
HAYWARD Andrew 26.10.74, Rowntrees :
JT - 59.37 (60.96-99)
HAYWARD Stephen William Moore 30.07.74,
Sale/Scottish Borders :
SP - 18.79, DT - 44.56 (47.76-94)
HEAD Paul 1.07.65, Newham & Essex B :
DT - 44.40, HT - 70.90 (74.02-90)
HEALE Stuart U13, :
JTC - 35.18
HEALEY Mark, Lliswerry :
Mar - 2:32:09
HEALEY Richard V45 17.11.54, Portsmouth :
DT - 43.14 (45.50-81)
HEANLEY John U23 25.09.80, Windsor S & E :
110H - 15.5, 400H - 55.7, Dec - 6563
HEARLE Tom 5.06.67, Kilbarchan :
5MR - 23:49
HEARN Christopher U20 26.06.82, Milton K :
3kSt - 9:58.2
HEATH Brett 6.01.75, Havering :
SP - 13.80, DT - 44.50
HEATH David John 22.05.65, Blackheath :
1500 - 3:51.8 (3:41.0-89),
1M - 4:01.06 (3:59.36-89),
5k - 13:57.50 (13:47.95-99), 3kSt - 8:42.04
HEDMAN Graham U23 6.02.79, WGr & Ex L :
100 - 10.8 (10.7w-98/10.8-99/10.83w/10.89-98,
400 - 48.27 (48.1/48.22-99)
HEMERY Adrian U20 6.08.82, Swindon :
Dec - 6302
HEMSTED Joe U15 29.12.85, Woking :
1500 - 4:19.8, 1M - 4:47.0,
3k - 9:29.9
HENDRY Martyn John 10.04.75, C of Edinb :
60H - 8.20i (8.00i-98),
110H - 15.1w/15.3 (14.16-97)
HENNESSY Andrew D. 24.08.77, TVH/
London Univ. : 3k - 8:16.8, 5k - 14:33.68,
2kSt - 5:56.0, 3kSt - 9:01.23 (8:39.71-99)
HENRY Cori 9.12.76, Notts :
100 - 10.8/10.96 (10.5w/10.8-96),
200 - 21.5/21.69w/21.88
(20.8w-96/20.9-99/21.34-96),
400 - 46.83 (46.50-96)
HENRY James U17 31.07.84, Spenborough :
3k - 8:58.60, 1.5kSt - 4:39.57
HENTHORN James 20.02.77, Team Solent :
60 - 6.71i, 200 - 21.21 (20.93-99),
100 - 10.48w/10.52 (10.22w-97/10.39-99)
HEPPLES Stephen David U23 6.01.80, Loftus :
3k - 8:15.40, 5k - 14:26.91
HEPPLEWHITE Daniel U15 2.09.86,
Bournemouth : SPB - 14.02, DTB - 37.71
HERMANN Daniel John U20 3.03.81, Pud & B :
800 - 1:52.99
HERMANN Derek U23 7.04.79, Carmarthen :
JT - 61.85
HERRING Christopher U20 3.03.81, Mandale :
400H - 54.9/56.57 (54.02-99)
HERRINGTON Charles 28.09.71, Belgrave :
10k - 31:00.13 (30:50.1-99)
HERRINGTON Gary Hugh 31.03.61, Rugby :
SP - 13.45 (14.88-98),
DT - 52.42 (56.66-96), HT - 45.83 (50.91-98)
HERRINGTON Samuel Edward U15 2.10.86,
Corby : DTB - 45.08
HEWITSON Dale U17 11.09.84, Elswick :
SPY - 14.74i/14.42
HIBBERD Matthew J. 23.06.73, TVH :
3k - 8:18.25i (8:23.9-95)
HIBBERT Paul N. 31.03.65, Birchfield :
110H - 14.89, 400H - 50.52 (50.52-96)
HICKEY Adam U13 30.05.88, Southend :
400 - 62.8, 800 - 2:14.4,
1500 - 4:29.7, 3k - 9:50.45
HICKS Maurice 1.01.70, Team Sol/Junct 10 :
DT - 40.03 (43.62-92),
HT - 55.44dh/53.36 (56.14-96)
HIGHAM Keith Robert U15 7.11.85, Border :
PV - 3.40
HILL Andrew U13 3.12.87, R Sutton Coldfield :
80HC - 13.55
HILL Jason U17 27.09.83, City of Stoke :
OctY - 4416w/4396
HILL Michael Christopher 22.10.64, Leeds :
JT - 83.71 (86.94-93)

HILL Mick 2.09.75, Tipton :
3k - 8:17.16
HILL Walter V45 19.06.53, Crawley :
24Hr - 216.650km
HILLIER James U23 3.04.78, Birch/Birm U :
400 - 48.8, 400H - 51.49 (51.30-99)
HILTON Jonathan 11.01.74, Sale :
TJ - 15.59w/15.42
HILTON Martin 9.05.75, Leeds/Leeds Univ :
3k - 8:19.75, 5k - 14:41.22
HINDLEY Christopher 21.01.76, Worksop :
HJ - 2.10
HINES Damien U15 6.09.85, Parkside :
SPB - 13.28, DTB - 38.47
HINZE Alistair U15 25.09.85, Herne Hill :
LJ - 6.36w/6.21i/6.20
HO Darren U17 20.03.85, Shettleston :
100HY - 14.10w
HOAD James U13 1.02.88, Enf & Har :
LJ - 5.05
HODGSON Gavin Andrew U23 1.02.78, Bord/
Camb Un : 200H - 25.4, 400H - 53.7/55.23
HODSON Chris U23 11.11.80, Peterborough :
110H - 15.5w (14.9w/15.2-99)
HOGARTH Charles U15 11.02.86, Mandale :
HTB - 44.28
HOLDEN C. U15, Trafford :
80HB - 12.0
HOLDEN Oliver U15 20.05.86, Wells :
3k - 9:16.7
HOLDEN Tom U17 2.02.84, Tipton :
800 - 1:58.6, 1500 - 4:04.39,
1.5kSt - 4:40.3
HOLDER Graham Paul 16.01.72, Shaft Barn :
DT - 40.48 (41.46-99), HT - 61.44 (61.91-99)
HOLEHOUSE Lee U20 23.12.81, Telford :
100 - 10.8w, 200 - 21.7w,
400 - 48.53 (47.74-99)
HOLLADAY Robert 10.01.75, Morpeth :
HMar - 1:05:44
HOLLIDAY Ian 9.12.73, Sale :
HJ - 2.12 (2.16-98)
HOLLIER Steven 27.02.76, Wolves & B :
5kW - 21:20+ (21:27.0-97),
10kW - 42:57+ (45:08.97-98),
10kWR - 42:18+ (42:29-95),
20kW - 1:27:04t (1:28:34-99), 30kW - 2:31:26+,
35kW - 2:56:42+ (2:52:47-99), 50kW - 4:07:18
HOLLOWAY Mark U17 6.10.83, Bracknell :
400 - 50.22
HOLSGROVE Tim U20 11.12.82, Wirral :
PV - 4.30
HOLT Andrew 23.02.64, Verlea :
Mar - 2:30:13 (2:24:26-93)
HOLTBY John U20 27.03.82, City of Hull :
110HJ - 14.46w/14.88, 110H - 15.03,
SP - 13.56, SPJ - 14.29, Dec - 6471
HONEY John U15 6.02.86, Cardiff :
HTB - 46.55
HOOD Ben U15 11.11.85, City of Hull :
PV - 2.95
HOOD Keith 13.09.72, Corstorphine :
3kSt - 9:15.0
HOOD Samuel U17 17.10.83, Cardiff :
HJ - 2.09
HOOPER Benjamin Joseph James U20
10.09.82, Yeovil Oly : 400H - 55.8/56.93

HOPE Steven 8.02.72, Tipton :
HMar - 1:04:50
HOPKINS Joel 24.11.77, Enf & Har :
400H - 54.4
HOPKINSON Andrew U17 20.09.83, Sale :
100HY - 13.80, 400HY - 58.7
HOPSON Luke U15 2.12.85, Birchfield :
800 - 2:02.38
HOPTON Matthew U17 2.03.84, AF&D :
100 - 11.1 (11.18w/11.32-98)
HORN Ian U13 23.09.87, Croydon :
400 - 61.9
HORNE P. David 9.03.68, SGA (Prof) :
SP - 13.58 (13.82-98)
HORSBURGH Ian Joseph U23 10.01.78, CoE :
200 - 21.92 (21.50i/21.5w/21.61-97)
HORSBURGH Steven U13 11.11.87, Gate :
100 - 12.3, LJ - 5.06
HOSKING Gary U15 25.11.85, C of Plymouth :
100 - 11.6, 200 - 23.27
HOUGH Christopher U20 5.12.81, Wakefield :
110H - 15.36, JT - 61.02
HOUGHTON Ben U23 6.08.80, B & A/Gate/IRE :
JT - 60.95 (64.34-97)
HOUSLIN Livon V40 2.11.60, Thames Valley :
JT - 59.36 (63.92-92)
HOWARD Paul 19.10.66, WGreen & Ex L :
DT - 41.68 (44.89-99), JT - 58.05 (65.10-91)
HOWARTH Paul 30.10.77, Wirral :
5k - 14:39.64
HOWE Christopher William 17.11.67, WG&EL/
Loughbro : DT - 41.40 (44.84-90),
HT - 62.92 (66.97-98)
HOWELL Tim U20 6.12.82, City of Stoke :
DecJ - 5107
HUDSPITH Ian 23.09.70, Morpeth :
1500 - 3:48.1 (3:47.6-94),
3k - 8:05.7 (8:03.9-95),
5k - 13:55.54 (13:52.8-97),
10k - 28:50.98 (28:35.11-97),
10kR - 29:24 (28:17sh/29:08RL-96/29:09-97),
HMar - 1:03:19 (1:02:53-96),
Mar - 2:18:40 (2:15:47-99)
HUDSPITH Mark E. 19.01.69, Morpeth :
1500 - 3:48.0, 3k - 8:03.8 (7:58.72-93),
5k - 13:49.37, 10k - 28:43.08,
10kR - 29:23 (29:14-94),
Mar - 2:15:16 (2:11:58-95)
HUGGINS Sam U15 30.11.85, AF&D :
100 - 11.38, 200 - 23.3
HUGHES Andrew 10.07.67, RAF/Shaft Barnet :
60 - 6.94i (6.89i-98), 100 - 10.53w/10.57,
200 - 21.85 (21.3/21.31-98)
HUGHES Brian C. 6.01.70, Trafford :
PV - 4.05 (4.25-94), Dec - 6105
HUGHES David John U15 31.10.85, L Buzzard :
LJ - 6.05
HUGHES David U17 31.05.84, Scunthorpe :
100HY - 14.18, LJ - 6.76w, OctY - 4885
HUGHES Kevin Michael 30.04.73, Enf & Har :
PV - 5.55 (5.61-99)
HUGHES Peter U17 12.12.83, Ynys Mon :
DTY - 40.48
HUGHES Ryan U15 1.11.85, Mandale :
3k - 9:31.8
HUGHES Scott U23 20.11.78, Sale :
800 - 1:52.43 (1:51.8-97), 1500 - 3:49.87

HUGHES Steven U20 25.02.82, Scunthorpe :
Dec - 6000, DecJ - 5404 (5804-99)
HULA Martin 2.01.66, Bristol :
10k - 30:16.84 (30:08.41-95),
10MR - 49:55 (48:09-91)
HULME Delroy 14.09.72, City of Stoke :
TJ - 14.61w (15.50w-91/15.26-90)
HULSE G.Ewart W. 21.01.62, Colwyn Bay :
DT - 40.50 (42.48-97), HT - 50.53 (54.62-91)
HULYER Matthew Joseph Thomas U17
20.06.84, Ashford : LJ - 6.63
HUMM Jason Alex 11.01.71, Shaft Barnet :
3kSt - 9:19.64 (8:49.03-96)
HUMPHREYS Nick U17 24.12.83, Birchfield:
DTY - 41.97
HUMPHRIES Ashley U15 2.01.86, Southend :
1500 - 4:18.8, 3k - 9:03.54
HUNT Simon U20 22.07.81, Sutton & District/
St. Marys Univ : 60H - 8.47i, 110H - 15.18
HUNT Wayne U13 25.09.87, Wessex & Bath :
75HC - 12.9, 80HC - 13.4
HUNTER Christopher U20 3.03.81, Jarr & H :
110HJ - 15.46, HJ - 2.00,
Dec - 5587 (5770-99)
HUNTER Richard Andrew 12.01.71, Morpeth :
60H - 8.37i (8.26i-90), Dec - 5943 (6092-92)
110H - 14.95w/15.09 (14.79w-89/14.8/14.99-95)
HURREN Richard U17 24.09.83, Falkirk :
PV - 4.20
HURST Lee 29.07.72, Belgrave :
1.5kSt - 4:16.57,
3kSt - 8:55.50 (8:48.34-96)
HUSSAIN Bashir 20.12.64, Stockport :
HMar - 1:06:46 (1:03:01-91)
HUTCHINSON Alexander 30.11.75, Bel/CUAC :
1500 - 3:52.63
HUTCHINSON John U20 3.05.82, Enf & Har :
PV - 4.20
HUTCHINSON Michael Innes 5.10.65, Traff :
3kSt - 9:24.1 (8:50.61-92)
HUTT Colin 18.11.66, Bo'ness :
Mar - 2:32:18
HYDE Daniel 5.10.77, Swindon :
10k - 30:37.96
HYDE Tom U17 7.10.83, Bedford & County :
100 - 11.08, 200 - 22.06
HYLTON Mark David 24.09.76, Windsor S & E :
200 - 21.67i (21.04i-97/21.09-95),
400 - 46.24 (45.24-98)
HYMAN Ben 28.08.74, Mansfield :
800 - 1:52.36

IBRAHIM Iskender U15 15.03.86,
N Lond & MH : 800 - 2:05.8, 1500 - 4:17.18
IDDON Christopher U20 8.10.82, Bolton :
400 - 49.1
IDOWU Phillips Olaosebikan U23 30.12.78,
Belgrave/Brunel Univ : LJ - 7.83, TJ - 17.12
IGI Abdi U13 12.12.87, Ealing,Southall & Mx :
800 - 2:16.3, 1500 - 4:33.34
ILIFFE Niklas U20 6.03.81, Charnwood :
DT - 43.39, DTJ - 49.59
INGLE Andrew U23 19.02.80, Bideford :
800 - 1:51.10, 1500 - 3:48.87, 1M - 4:06.7
INGRAM Geoff 31.01.68, RAF/Norwich :
Dec - 5763 (6148-98)
IRELAND Adam U23 5.10.78, Cope/Oxf Univ :
TJ - 13.99

JACKSON Anthony 28.02.67, Shaft B :
10k - 31:53.7 (31:06.73-99)
JACKSON Ben U17 22.11.84, Dacorum & Tring :
PV - 3.60
JACKSON Colin Ray 18.02.67, Brecon :
60H - 7.59i (7.30i-94),
110H - 13.10 (12.8w-90/12.91-93)
JACKSON Darren U23 21.10.78, Enf & Har :
100 - 10.8w (11.0-97/11.20-96),
200 - 21.7 (21.52w/22.24-97)
JACKSON Graham U15 12.11.85, Gateshead :
LJ - 5.90, TJ - 13.04w/12.85
JACKSON Guy 10.01.71, Coventry RWC :
3kW - 13:17.7 (13:04.0-90)
JAMES Alan 26.03.62, Windsor S & E :
HT - 49.69
JAMES Christopher U20 9.12.82, Milton K :
HT - 47.07, HTJ - 51.00
JAMES Donovan U15 30.11.85, Belgrave :
100 - 11.5w, 200 - 23.6
JAMES Ronald V40 20.09.59, Windsor S & E :
HT - 53.07 (68.18-82)
JAMES Ronnie 14.12.64, Cornwall AC :
Mar - 2:31:12 (2:25:33-97)
JAMES Ryan U17 10.05.85, Stratford :
LJ 6.70w/6.61
JAMES Sean U13 8.01.88, Liverpool H :
100 - 12.57
JAMIESON Steven U23 4.02.79, Medway/
Loughbro : JT - 60.94
JARRETT Anthony Alexander 13.08.68,
Enf & Har : 60 - 6.89i (6.73i-98),
200 - 21.69i (20.50-95), 60H - 7.53i (7.42i-95),
110H - 13.53 (13.00-93)
JEFFERIES Robert U23 4.10.79, Derby & Co :
800 - 1:51.41
JEFFREY Grant U13, Dunfermline & W Fife :
75HC - 12.8
JEFFREY Jason U23 16.11.78, Harr/Lond Un :
100 - 10.95
JEMI-ALADE Michael 13.10.64, City of Edinb :
DT - 48.01 (52.38-87)
JENNINGS Gary 21.02.72, Newham & Essex B :
400H - 50.11 (49.82-95)
JENNINGS Neil A. 18.09.77, Mand/Newc Un :
400 - 47.77 (47.46-98)
JENNINGS Thomas U17 27.01.85, Holmfirth :
OctY - 4223
JENNS Scott U23 13.12.80, Tipton :
DTJ - 41.88oa
JENSON Gary 14.02.67, Southend :
JT - 68.91 (79.54r-91/78.54-89)
JERVIS Alan Peter U17 27.07.84, C of Stoke :
PV - 4.25
JOHN Jason 17.10.71, Birchfield :
60 - 6.71i (6.59i-96),
100 - 10.49 (10.08w/10.23-94)
JOHNS Fraser U15 24.09.85, Cornwall AC :
SPB - 13.55
JOHNSON Allandre U15 8.12.85, Herne Hill :
JTB - 43.61
JOHNSON Andrew U20 10.09.81, Hert & W :
DecJ - 5358
JOHNSON Andrew U15 13.05.86, Blackheath :
80HB - 11.78w/12.1
JOHNSON Lewis U15, Derwentside :
HJ - 1.75, TJ - 12.36w/12.34

JOHNSON Michael U15 25.09.85, Grantham :
PV - 3.20
JOHNSON Richard U13 25.10.87, Harrow :
200 - 25.89
JOHNSTON Cameron B. U20 22.10.82, Croy :
PV - 4.70
JOHNSTON Ian James 12.02.68, TVH :
10k - 31:51.89 (31:31.37-99)
JONES Andres 3.02.77, Cardiff :
3k - 7:54.12, 5k - 13:39.43,
10k - 28:00.50, 10kR - 29:19
JONES Ben U15 14.01.86, Wirral :
3k - 9:23.27
JONES Chris U17, Wirral :
1.5kSt - 4:40.43
JONES Colin Maurice 8.04.74, Eryri/Shaft B :
5k - 14:41.24 (14:14.01i/14:15.40-99),
10k - 30:06.17 (30:03.90-99)
JONES David U17 19.02.84, Carmarthen :
1500 - 4:01.83, 3k - 8:40.00
JONES Egryn 1.11.71, Cardiff :
PV - 4.50 (4.90-95)
JONES Gary 6.01.72, Windsor S & E :
60 - 6.91i, 100 - 10.7/10.71w/10.79
(10.6w?-98/10.64w/10.7-97/10.78-99),
200 - 21.6/21.99 (21.83w-97)
JONES Jamie 8.12.71, Overton :
10k - 31:53.0
JONES Matthew U20 10.10.82, City of Stoke :
1500 - 3:52.33, 5k - 14:40.2
JONES Michael David 23.07.63, Belgrave :
HT - 75.94
JONES Michael U17 12.12.84, Hereford :
HTY - 51.19
JONES Nathan U20 31.10.82, Colwyn Bay :
400H - 56.02, DecJ - 5566
JONES Nick 10.07.74, Tipton :
5MR - 23:49 (23:20-99),
10kR - 29:31 (29:27-99),
10MR - 48:49 (48:40-97), HMar - 1:03:12
JONES Paul U23 11.04.78, Colwyn Bay :
110H - 15.40 (15.19w/15.27-99),
PV - 4.70i/4.65 (4.75-99), Dec - 7071
JONES Rhodri 14.08.66, Westbury/Yate :
10k - 31:04.5, 10kR - 29:50, 10MR - 49:39,
HMar - 1:06:27, Mar - 2:18:34
JORDAN Richard V40 14.07.57, Ipswich Jog :
Mar - 2:34:09 (2:29:51-99)
JOSEPH Jason U15 27.11.85, Enf & Har :
SPB - 14.01, HTB - 53.76
JOSEPH Rafer Ernest Lewis 21.07.68, Dac & T :
SP - 13.34 (14.68i-94/14.38-98),
DT - 46.08 (52.00-96), HT - 47.98 (49.41-98)
JOUSIFFE Warren 27.05.77, Windsor S & E :
PV - 4.60 (4.70-96)
JUBB Michael 20.06.70, Derby & Co :
3kSt - 9:20.3 (8:50.37-96)
JUDSON Paul U15 20.06.86, Cannock & Staff :
100 - 11.4w
JUKES Robert U17 18.09.83, Basing & MH :
DTY - 43.85
JULIEN Chris U13 14.09.87, Enf & Har :
100 - 11.86, 200 - 24.28w/25.0

KANEEN Peter 12.07.61, Manx H :
3kW - 13:47.1 (13:14.2-99),
10kW - 48:39.4 (48:26.91-99),
50kW - 4:50:47

KAPADIA Kunal U17 30.09.83, Enf & Har :
JTY - 56.79
KAPOFU Desmond U23 6.02.78, Border/ZIM :
LJ - 6.87 (6.99-99), TJ - 15.54 (16.03-98)
KARAGIOUNIS Leon 15.10.75, Notts/Notts U :
JT - 59.98
KAYES Christopher U17 14.04.84, Liverpool H :
200 - 22.3w?un (23.9w/23.93w-98)
KEAN Alasdair V50 5.11.47, Derby & Co :
Mar - 2:32:15 (2:16:51-83)
KELLIE Peter U17 2.01.84, Gloucester AC :
1.5kSt - 4:30.14
KELLY Bryan 29.12.73, Liverpool H :
SP - 14.50 (15.75-93), DT - 44.74 (46.86-93)
KELLY Craig U17 20.03.84, Wirral :
800 - 1:58.37
KELLY Ian 3.12.64, Bolton :
Mar - 2:33:22 (2:31:37-99)
KELSEY Ben U17 23.09.84, Oxford City :
DTY - 40.81
KELSEY Matthew U15 20.11.85, Havering :
100 - 11.40, 200 - 22.99w/23.1
KELVEY Sam U15 12.07.86, Notts :
JTB - 43.49
KEMP Michael U23 23.12.79, Roadhogs :
10kWR - 47:32 (43:28-97)
KENNARD Andrew 2.01.66, Walton :
400H - 55.2 (53.1-95/53.58-90)
KERR Darren 6.10.69, Bedford & County :
HT - 47.06
KERR Eric 9.12.64, Luton :
HT - 49.57 (54.58-95)
KERR Glen 27.10.74, Bedford & County :
HT - 60.47
KERR John V50 1.06.49, Steel City :
Mar - 2:33:56 (2:31:24-98)
KERRY Robert U23 20.03.80, Cov G/Birm Un :
100 - 10.8/11.13 (10.96?-99)
KESKA Karl 7.05.72, Birchfield :
5k - 13:42.13 (13:23.07-99), 5MR - 22:57,
10k - 27:44.09, HMar - 1:04:07
KHAN Kamran U17 2.10.83, Sale :
HTJ - 52.57, HTY - 60.09
KHAN Safeer U15 1.11.85, Halifax :
1500 - 4:19.92
KING Allan V40 3.12.56, Roadhogs :
20kW - 1:38:21 (1:28:30-85)
KING Daniel U20 30.05.83, Colchester H :
3kW - 13:05.7, 5kW - 23:21.71,
10kW - 48:14.9, 10kWR - 47:40
KING Dominic U20 30.05.83, Colchester H :
3kW - 12:33.31, 5kW - 21:25.17i/22:22.45,
10kW - 45:36.3, 10kWR - 45:03
KING Edward 26.11.75, Sale/Brighton :
800 - 1:49.55 (1:48.00-99), 1k - 2:22.05i,
1500 - 3:44.39i/3:52.48 (3:40.24i/3:43.29-99)
KING Oliver U13 20.12.87, Swindon :
SPC - 11.32
KINGMAN Robert 21.02.73, N & E B/RAF :
PV - 4.60i/4.50 (5.02-94)
KINGWELL Jason 8.10.70, Verlea :
HT - 46.89 (48.38-97)
KINSEY Richard U17 15.10.83, Cardiff :
1500 - 4:01.07, 3k - 8:46.40
KIRK Chris U15, Barnsley :
HJ - 1.76

KIRKWOOD Craig 8.10.74, Tipton/NZL :
1500 - 3:49.83, 3k - 8:01.84, 5k - 13:57.58,
5MR - 23:36 (23:11-99), 10k - 29:58.61,
10kR - 29:44 (29:38-99), HMar - 1:03:43
KITNEY Timothy J. U23 26.04.80, Belgrave :
JT - 65.49 (68.08-98)
KLOIBER Matthew 22.11.71, Trafford :
400H - 54.4/54.94
KNIGHT Andrew G. 26.10.68, Cambridge H :
800 - 1:50.87 (1:48.38-94)
KNIGHTS Christopher U15 17.10.85, Peterbro :
1500 - 4:18.87, 3k - 9:39.8
KNOTT Michael U17, Colwyn Bay :
HJ - 1.90
KNOWLES Ian U17, Liverpool H :
HTY - 47.97
KNOWLES Richard Jonathan 12.11.75, Birch :
200 - 21.16w/21.26i/21.53 (21.1-97/21.24-99),
400 - 46.14 (45.84-97)
KOKAI Amin 5.01.74, Ilford/KEN:
10k - 30:57.1 (30:11.0-94),
HMar - 1:06:43 (1:05:28-94)
KRTEN Libor 26.02.73, Hercules Wimb/CZE :
DT - 41.40 (46.58-96)
KRUGER Alexander Eaton 18.11.63, Sheff :
110H - 15.62 (14.76-95), HJ - 2.02 (2.20-88),
PV - 4.40i/4.40 (4.90-95),
SP - 14.11 (14.76-94),
DT - 41.94 (45.46-96),
JT - 59.19 (60.98-95), Dec - 6975 (8131-95)
KRUSZEWSKI Andrew P. V40 7.04.59,
Enf & Har : DT - 45.08 (51.26-92)

LADROWSKI Marc U23 13.07.79,
City of Plymouth/RAF : HJ - 1.96
LAING Robert Howard 30.07.66, Liverpool H :
JT - 55.64 (67.48-87)
LAINSON Richard T. P. U20 5.11.81,
I of Wight : JT - 55.68 (57.89-98)
LAKE A. U15, Blackburn :
LJ - 5.95
LAMB Josh U20 14.04.83, Crawley :
DTJ - 46.33
LAMBERT Christopher Patrick U20 6.04.81,
Belgrave : 100 - 10.63 (10.31-99),
200 - 21.51 (20.63-99)
LANDON Marc U20 9.11.81, Corby :
HTJ - 50.00
LANE Nathaniel G. 10.04.76, Cardiff/UWIC :
3k - 8:13.39i (8:19.22-99), 5k - 13:58.44,
10k - 29:38.93 (29:01.17-99), HMar - 1:05:40
LANG Tim 8.12.73, Trafford :
400H - 55.95 (55.3/55.53-97)
LASHORE Akinola 28.03.73, Blackheath/
Brunel Univ : 60 - 6.78i (6.77i-98),
100 - 10.38r/10.50 (10.35A-99/10.4-98/10.44-97),
200 - 21.52 (20.99-97)
LASLETT Paul U23 12.05.80, AF&D/UWCN :
800 - 1:52.66
LATHAM Mark 13.01.76, City of Stoke :
HJ - 2.00 (2.12i-98/2.11-94)
LATHAM Mark U17 13.05.85, Liverpool H :
HJ - 1.90
LAU Jordon U17 23.09.83, Chelmsford :
LJ - 7.21
LAWRENCE Ben U15 13.04.86, Cannock & St :
SPB - 14.55, DTB - 42.62un/37.22,
HTB - 47.33
LAWRENCE Mark 26.01.71, Notts/Leeds Univ :
LJ - 7.24w/6.97 (7.33-93),
TJ - 14.20 (14.52-93)
LAWRENCE Tim U17 31.03.84, Derby & Co :
1.5kSt - 4:31.5
LAWS Mark U15 29.09.85, Gateshead :
PV - 3.20, JTB - 44.80
LEACH Rod 29.05.72, AF&D/Army :
10k - 31:33.1, 3kSt - 9:20.89
LEASE Gareth 14.11.77, Cardiff/UWIC :
PV - 4.40i/4.20 (4.40i/4.35-98)
LEAVER James Robert 15.09.75, Team Solent/
Soton Univ : HJ - 1.95 (2.11-95),
LJ - 7.09w/6.94 (7.39w/7.21-98)
LEDGER Matthew U20 23.11.81, Chesterfield :
HJ - 1.95
LEDGERWOOD Daniel U20 24.03.83, AF&D :
3k - 8:26.7
LEE David James 16.09.65, Blackheath :
1.5kSt - 4:18.81, 3kSt - 9:09.0 (8:31.22-92)
LEE James U23 6.02.79, Gate/London Univ :
400H - 55.7
LEE Richard U20 25.12.81, Windsor S & E :
3k - 8:38.87, 5k - 15:12.6
LEES Simon U23 19.11.79, Solihull & S Heath/
Loughbro : 400 - 49.08,
800 - 1:49.26 (1:47.69-98), 1500 - 3:47.31
LEIGH Anthony 27.12.65, City of Stoke :
100 - 10.8/10.99 (10.71w/10.74-97)
LEIGH Michael 14.12.77, Sheffield :
HJ - 2.00 (2.05-98)
LEITCH Mark 17.11.68, Army/Shaftesbury B :
SP - 15.57i/14.58 (14.72-99)
LEMONCELLO Andrew U20 12.10.82, Dunf &
W Fife : 2kSt - 5:59.97, 3kSt - 9:23.39
LEONARD Daniel Jason U17 3.01.84, Milton K :
100HY - 14.1, HJ - 2.01i/2.01
LERWILL Thomas 17.05.77, Belgrave/Bath U :
400 - 49.0 (47.57-95)
LESSING Simon 12.02.71, :
5k - 14:33.69
LETHBRIDGE Daniel U20 1.04.81, Crawley :
DTJ - 44.72 (45.03-99)
LEVETT Christopher U17 30.11.83, Birchfield :
SPY - 15.30, DTY - 45.89
LEVETT William 6.09.75, Vauxhall/Brunel Un :
10k - 30:16.89, 10MR - 49:26
LEVY Noel 22.06.75, Belgrave :
110H - 14.52w/14.55,
300H - 36.47, 400H - 51.58 (50.70-94)
LEWIS Andrew 9.03.68, Harrow :
100 - 10.94 (10.80w/10.89-94),
110H - 15.2 (14.67w/14.8/14.88-94),
LJ - 7.38 (7.54-97),
SP - 13.91i/13.37 (14.10-98)
LEWIS Benjamin U20 6.03.81, Birchfield :
100 - 10.66 (10.66-97),
200 - 21.30w/21.42 (20.80w/21.32-99)
LEWIS Craig 5.03.77, Black Isle :
HJ - 1.98
LEWIS Daniel U17 16.10.83, Shaftesbury B :
1500 - 4:06.7, 3k - 8:46.80,
1.5kSt - 4:22.7
LEWIS James 8.03.69, Swansea/IRE :
10kR - 29:44 (29:22-92), 10MR - 47:57,
Mar - 2:15:07
LEWIS Junior 19.03.66, Verlea :
TJ - 14.12i/14.10 (14.84-96)

LEWIS Marlon U17 7.09.83, Rowheath :
LJ - 7.02w/6.99
LEWIS Robert U23 2.09.78, Bedford & Co :
400 - 47.72, 110H - 15.51 (14.9-99),
400H - 51.29
LEWIS Sean U13 10.09.87, City of Stoke :
HTC - 35.22
LEWIS Simon U20 14.01.83, Rowheath :
PV - 4.20
LEWIS Steven U15 20.05.86, City of Stoke :
PV - 3.70
LEWIS-FRANCIS Mark U20 4.09.82, Birch :
60 - 6.67i, 100 - 10.10
LINDLEY Ian V45 3.12.55, Bingley :
SP - 14.23i/13.76 (17.87i/17.58-81)
LINDSAY Mark Stephen U17 5.11.84, Wake :
JTY - 58.69
LINGARD Andrew U20 12.09.81, Basildon :
2kSt - 6:07.08, 3kSt - 9:29.14
LINSKEY Christian U23 14.06.80, Shaft Barn :
PV - 5.00 (5.21i-99/5.20-98)
LITTLE David Andrew U20 28.02.81, Border :
HT - 56.36, HTJ - 62.53
LITTLE John M. V45 14.04.53, Border :
DT - 42.61 (43.70-95)
LITTLE Matthew U20 22.07.83, Bedford & Co :
HJ - 2.05i/1.96 (1.97-99)
LIVESEY Christopher James U23 8.08.80, Prest/
Providence Un : 800 - 1:51.89, 1M - 4:03.81i
LIVINGSTONE Andrew U13 3.05.88, Thurrock :
1500 - 4:42.4
LIVINGSTONE Stuart U23 29.08.79, C of Edin :
HJ - 2.00i/1.95 (2.08i-97/2.06-98)
LLOYD Ben U23 1.04.79, Oxford Univ :
JT - 55.12
LLOYD Joseph 9.04.73, Swansea :
400 - 48.88 (47.76-96)
LLOYD Mark 28.09.71, Liverpool H :
200 - 21.7w/21.9/22.06 (21.6/21.87-98)
LLOYD Martin Andrew U23 18.06.80, Bexley :
HJ - 2.07 (2.15i/2.15-98)
LLOYD Steven J. 20.03.74, Border :
DT - 41.78 (43.94-94)
LOBB Huw 29.08.76, Bedford & County :
Mar - 2:30:03
LOBO Jason 18.09.69, Belgrave :
800 - 1:47.81 (1:45.82-99),
1500 - 3:46.83 (3:44.06-99)
LOCKWOOD Bobby U15 1.02.86, Camb H :
DTB - 46.35
LOUGHRAN Stuart 19.02.76, Swansea :
JT - 64.30 (68.91-98)
LOUTH Tim U20, Boston AC:
JT - 54.03
LOVETT Anthony U20 20.09.82, Enf & Har :
JT - 60.54
LOVETT David U23 13.09.78, Portsmouth :
SP - 15.06, DT - 50.22
LOW Charles 9.10.74, Shaftesbury Barnet :
3kSt - 8:37.63
LOW Christopher U23 24.04.80, S B/Arbroath :
110H - 15.3/15.33 (14.88-99),
Dec - 5020 (5724w-99/5325-97)
LOWE Andrew 6.03.76, Trafford :
HJ - 2.08
LOWTHER Nigel U20 4.05.83, Medway :
200 - 21.87
LOWTHIAN Ian U23 10.10.80, Liverpool H :
400 - 49.09i/49.1/50.01 (47.11-99)
LUCAS Liam U20 15.12.82, Dartford :
110HJ - 15.22
LUNDMAN Jonathan U20 7.12.81, N & E B :
JT - 65.18
LUSTGARTEN Anders 9.02.74, TVH :
400 - 48.75 (46.93-96)
LYNCH Lawrence 1.11.67, Enf & Har :
400H - 52.7/55.66 (50.05-96)
LYONS Andrew 24.12.69, City of Hull :
10k - 31:23.4 (29:04.05-91)

MACAULAY Donald U17 25.06.84, Nairn :
3k - 9:00.57
MACDONALD Mark W. V40 2.12.59,
SGA (Prof) : SP - 13.91 (15.98-90)
MACDONALD Stewart 10.12.65, Bingley :
Mar - 2:33:16
MACEY Dean 12.12.77, Harrow :
100 - 10.81 (10.65w/10.69-99), 400 - 46.41,
110H - 14.53 (14.35-99), HJ - 2.09 (2.13-95),
PV - 4.80, LJ - 7.77, SP - 14.62 (15.50-99),
DT - 43.37 (47.77-99),
JT - 60.38 (64.03-99), Dec - 8567
MACINTOSH Robin U17 2.03.85, C of Edin :
800 - 1:58.51
MACINTYRE Simon U20 13.10.81, Shett :
1500 - 3:51.86
MACKAY Craig U17 30.10.84, Perth :
400HY - 58.8
MACKAY Graeme D. U23 4.10.80, Chilt/OUAC :
HT - 45.57 (46.68-99)
MACKIE Ian 27.02.75, Pitreavie :
60 - 6.78i (6.73i-97), 200 - 20.68w/20.90,
100 - 10.05w/10.24 (10.00w-98/10.17-96)
MACLEAN Angus U23 20.09.80, Team Solent/
S'ton Univ : 800 - 1:49.82, 1500 - 3:41.19
MADDEN Michael J. 13.09.65, Newq & Par :
HT - 46.79 (55.92-93)
MADDOCKS Christopher Lloyd V40 28.03.57,
Plym'th City W : 5kW - 21:18+ (20:20.0-87),
10kW - 42:58+ (41:06.57-87),
10kWR - 43:10+ (40:17-89),
20kW - 1:27:04t/1:27:38 (1:22:12-92),
30kW - 2:20:04+ (2:11:09-85),
50kW - 3:57:10 (3:51:37-90)
MADEIRA-COLE Charles H. 29.11.77,
Newham & Essex B/Sheffield Univ :
TJ - 15.56w/15.38 (15.82i/15.81w/15.79-98)
MAHONEY Oliver U17 21.10.83, Wirral :
PV - 4.25
MAITLAND Gary U20 16.07.81, Harrow :
HJ - 1.99 (1.99-99)
MAJEKODUNMI Semi U20 29.06.83, Somer :
TJ - 14.17
MAJOR Adam U20 2.11.81, Elgin/Shaft Barn :
SP - 15.44, SPJ - 16.58,
DT - 51.28, DTJ - 55.16, HTJ - 50.37
MAJOR Stuart 5.05.70, S London :
10k - 31:36.35
MALCOLM Anthony 15.02.76, Cardiff/Loughbro :
LJ - 7.55
MALCOLM Christian Sean U23 3.06.79, Card :
60 - 6.65 (6.65i-99),
100 - 10.29 (10.10w/10.12-98), 200 - 20.19
MALIN Darren U17 19.06.85, Annadale Str :
800 - 1:57.02, 1.5kSt - 4:38.1

MALINS Duncan U23 12.06.78, N & E B/
Loughbro : 60H - 8.03i, 110H - 14.08w/14.10
MALONE-LEE Francis U23 3.03.80, Braintree/
Camb Univ : 3kSt - 9:27.9
MALSEED Robert 16.09.71, Chelm/Essex Un :
10k - 31:59.00 (31:04.69-95)
MANCHESTER Benjamin U17 1.04.85, Bingley :
100HY - 14.05un?/14.17
MANDY Mark 19.11.72, Birchfield/IRE :
HJ - 2.00 (2.26i-97/2.25-95)
MANN Philip U15 25.10.85, Barnsley :
JTB - 45.11
MANVILLE Gerald U23 21.12.78, Craw/Army :
PV - 4.21, Dec - 5577 (5599-99)
MARAR Leith A. 7.11.68, Belgrave :
DT - 51.02 (55.68-96)
MARCHETTO Sascha 11.01.73, Aberd'n U/SWZ :
DT - 40.03
MARCHMENT Carl U20 30.12.82, Bas & MH :
DecJ - 5530w/5527
MARLOW Steven U17 13.12.84, Shaft Barnet :
DTY - 41.34
MARSDEN Dwayne 25.10.73, Ealing,S & Mx :
JT - 63.10 (64.38-98)
MARSH Brett 20.01.76, Newquay & Par :
SP - 13.42, HT - 46.79 (47.98-99)
MARSHALL Guy ¶ 24.09.71, City of Hull :
SP - 16.15 (16.65-98), DT - 40.86 (42.55-99)
MARSHALL James U20 6.02.81, Dudley & St :
200 - 22.0/22.20
MARTIN Adam U20 12.10.81, Sale :
200 - 21.89
MARTIN Daniel U20 9.03.82, Southampton C :
HT - 46.85, HTJ - 54.34dh/52.40
MARTIN Gary U15 13.09.85, Invicta :
HJ - 1.75
MARTIN Nathan U17 10.05.84, Shaft Barnet :
100 - 11.59age?, 200 - 22.98age?
MARTIN Paul U13 28.01.88, Invicta :
DTC - 26.69
MARTIN Wayne Daniel 12.08.76, Team Solent/
Brunel U : 200 - 21.9/22.17i (21.9/22.44-97),
300 - 34.64i, 400 - 48.10i/48.21 (48.07-99)
MASON Chris U17 6.04.84, Mandale :
HTY - 52.81
MASON Duncan 8.12.68, Salford :
HMar - 1:05:17, Mar - 2:21:10
MASON Michael 16.06.77, Sutt & D/St. Marys :
110H - 15.3
MASON Richard 25.09.69, Leics Cor :
Mar - 2:27:16
MASSEY Ian 9.09.76, Liverpool H :
HJ - 1.95 (2.10-95)
MATAKAINEN Petri 3.04.75, Sale/FIN :
JT - 72.29
MATHIESON Duncan Graham 8.03.69,
Aberdeen/City of Stoke :
110H - 15.12 (14.81w-93/14.9-90/14.95-91),
HJ - 1.95i (2.07-90), LJ - 7.12i/6.91 (7.62-95)
MATTHEWS Chris U13 25.05.88, Worthing :
JTC - 34.30
MATTHEWS Obie U23 20.12.80, Belgrave :
Dec - 5423
MATTHEWS Owain U20 4.11.81, Vauxhall :
5k - 15:31.68
MAY Paul 31.10.77, Basingstoke & MH :
400 - 48.88
MAY Richard U15 10.12.85, Donc & Stain :
SPB - 14.49

MAYCOCK Robert U20 21.02.81, Sale :
3k - 8:09.67, 5k - 14:37.02
MAYNARD Darrell 21.08.61, Abertillery :
400 - 48.18
MAYO James 24.02.75, Cannock & St/Army :
800 - 1:49.07 (1:48.2-96),
1500 - 3:47.86i (3:44.0-96)
MAYO Thomas 2.05.77, Cannock & Stafford :
800 - 1:50.68 (1:49.1-99),
1500 - 3:44.07 (3:41.2-98),
1M - 4:00.60 (4:00.02-98), 3k - 8:18.55
MAYOCK John Paul 26.10.70, Barnsley :
800 - 1:48.45 (1:47.8-98),
1k - 2:19.20i/2:20.75 (2:18.48-96),
1500 - 3:34.69 (3:31.86-97),
1M - 3:50.61 (3:50.32-96),
2k - 5:02.53i (4:56.75-99),
3k - 7:49.97i (7:43.31i-97/7:47.28-95),
5MR - 23:53
MAYS Jermaine U20 23.12.82, Kent :
800 - 1:53.4, 2kSt - 5:54.08,
3kSt - 9:28.6
MCADOREY John 16.09.74, Liv H/B & A/IRE :
100 - 10.28w/10.52, 200 - 21.21
MCALLISTER Joe U23 23.12.80, Loughbro/
St Malachy's/IRE : 5k - 14:26.41
MCBURNEY Craig 8.09.68, Morpeth/Army :
Mar - 2:25:32
MCBURNEY Paul 14.03.72, N & E B/Lisb/IRE :
100 - 10.8 (10.7dt-90/10.7w-94/10.8-96/10.91-92),
200 - 21.5/21.73 (20.76w-97/20.81-94),
400 - 47.61 (45.85-97)
MCCAFFREY Liam U20 29.05.81, Preseli :
SPJ - 14.10 (15.10-99)
MCCALLA Dave 23.05.73, Coventry G/RAF :
TJ - 14.39 (14.85-98)
MCCALLA Isacc U20 28.03.82, Harrow :
110HJ - 15.01, 110H - 15.34w
MCCALLUM Jonathan 19.11.75, Croydon :
800 - 1:50.40 (1:50.35-99), 1500 - 3:37.75
MCCASH Lee U20 22.10.81, Pendle :
3k - 8:27.1 (8:19.42-99), 5k - 14:42.22
MCCONVILLE Brendan U23 3.01.79, N Down :
HJ - 1.97 (2.02-98), PV - 4.30,
Dec - 6720w/6561
MCCORMICK Nick U20 11.09.81, Tynedale :
800 - 1:52.15, 1500 - 3:45.19, 1M - 4:14.84i
MCCRACK Philip U20 11.03.82, Oadby & W :
1500 - 3:51.8
MCCREA M. U13, :
HJ - 1.52
MCCULLOCH Jacob U13 21.12.87, W S & E :
400 - 61.5, 800 - 2:14.3,
1500 - 4:32.5, 3k - 9:50.7
MCCULLOUGH Alan 9.08.63, North Belfast :
10k - 31:54.4, Mar - 2:29:18
MCDADE Jason U23 3.04.80, WGreen & Ex L :
HJ - 2.00 (2.16i-99/2.15-98)
MCDERMID Liam U17 23.11.84, Victoria P H :
400HY - 57.78
MCDERMOTT Dylan 1.12.70, Epsom & E/IRE:
PV - 4.20 (4.91i-96/4.85-90)
MCDIARMID Alistair U15 16.10.85, Falkirk :
SPB - 14.73, DTB - 47.05, HTB - 53.04
MCDIARMID Scott U23 15.11.80, Pitreavie :
400 - 49.1
MCDONALD Callim U15 30.04.86, Mansfield :
JTB - 47.54

MCDONALD Denzil 11.10.65, Newham & E B : SP - 15.50 (16.10-94), DT - 52.49 (55.04-95)
MCDONALD Michael John Joseph 24.08.65, B & A/Border/Queen's Univ/IRE : TJ - 14.39w/14.31i/14.24 (15.78-94)
MCDONALD Richard U23 11.01.80, Shaft B/ Loughbro : 400H - 51.09 (51.0-99)
MCDONNELL Stephen U23 24.07.80, Cuch/ Liv H/IRE : 110H - 15.22, 400H - 53.31
MCDOUGALL Alan 9.11.75, Medway : 800 - 1:52.24
MCDOWELL Tom U17 11.02.85, Wessex & B : PV - 3.70i/3.65
MCEVOY Stephen 23.05.63, Met. Police : HT - 50.34 (57.14-96)
MCEWAN Greg U20 9.04.81, Shaft Barnet : 400 - 48.92, 800 - 1:51.48
MCFARLAN M. U15, Worthing : 800 - 2:06.0
MCFARLANE Alasdair U23 13.02.78, Grantham : 100 - 10.8/10.83, 200 - 21.9 (23.08w-95/23.16-96)
MCFARLANE Andrew U20 28.02.83, Leeds : HJ - 1.98
MCFARLANE Jim U23 16.06.79, Camb Un : JT - 57.64
MCFARLANE John 9.06.72, Thames H & H : Mar - 2:29:43
MCGINLEY Cathal U23 16.08.79, Dundee U/ IRE : Dec - 6011
MCGLORY Philip U17 2.09.83, Liverpool H : 3k - 8:57.67
MCGLYNN Trevor U23 6.06.78, Sparta/IRE : 60H - 8.44i
MCGOWAN Frank 23.08.70, Shettleston : 3kSt - 9:26.6
MCGOWAN Liam John U17 27.01.84, Gloucs : 400 - 50.80, 800 - 1:55.9
MCGOWAN Matthew U17 2.09.83, Hereford : 100HY - 14.2
MCGURK Ian 17.10.71, City of Edinburgh : 400 - 47.9/49.10 (47.19-98)
MCILROY James 30.12.76, : 800 - 1:45.96 (1:45.32-98)
MCILWHAM John 29.02.72, Blackpool : 110H - 15.58w (15.6-95), 400H - 53.2/53.52 (52.7/52.80-99)
MCINNES Duncan U23 1.05.78, Border/Pitr : HJ - 1.98 (2.05i/2.05-97)
MCINTOSH Leslie U20 25.02.81, Liverpool H : SP - 13.07, HT - 52.09, HTJ - 55.56
MCINTYRE A. U17, Trafford : 200 - 22.6
MCINTYRE Mark 14.10.70, Shaftesbury Barnet : 60 - 6.97i (6.79i-97), 100 - 10.83w/10.95 (10.3w-95/10.60-91)
MCKAY Callum U17 17.02.85, AF&D : 400HY - 57.16
MCKAY David U23 22.09.80, W Cheshire : JT - 63.18
MCKAY Kevin John 9.02.69, Sale : 800 - 1:48.56 (1:45.35-92), 1500 - 3:37.34 (3:34.59-97), 1M - 3:55.07 (3:53.64-94)
MCKEE Paul 15.10.77, Liverpool H/IRE : 200 - 20.87w/21.1/21.20, 400 - 45.92
MCKENNA Andrew David U23 3.01.80, Milt K/ Northampton Un : 10k - 31:15.18
MCKENZIE Ian U20 3.07.81, Inverclyde/Bel/ Glasgow Univ : PV - 4.20i/4.20
MCKERNAN Michael U23 28.11.78, Cov G : TJ - 15.31w/15.07 (15.22-99)
MCKINLAY Scott U20 11.04.83, Pitreavie : 400H - 56.4
MCLEAN Colm U23 7.06.80, St Malachy's/ Loughbro/IRE : 800 - 1:48.53, 1500 - 3:40.42
MCLEAN-FOREMAN Alasdair James U20 10.11.81, Bel : 800 - 1:52.32i (1:53.04-99)
MCLELLAN Neil U23 10.09.78, Steve & NH : SP - 13.51, JT - 68.27
MCLENNAN Stephen U23 17.11.78, Hounslow : PV - 4.60 (4.70-96)
MCLEOD Andrew U15 7.09.85, Giffnock : 3k - 9:31.98
MCLEOD Asandro U15 15.09.85, Blackheath : DTB - 37.98
MCLOUGHLIN Peter 18.05.77, Liv H/Bath U/ IRE : PV - 4.45 (4.60-99)
MCMANUS Steve U13 22.09.87, Colchester H : SPC - 11.56
MCMASTER Colin U23 15.01.80, Law & Dist/ Shaft Barnet : HJ - 2.10i/2.05 (2.15-97)
MCMULLAN Iain U23 15.06.78, Lisb/Loughbro/ Cardiff : SP - 16.20
MCMULLEN Carl U23 9.11.79, Warr/Army : 400H - 55.05 (54.3-97), LJ - 7.25
MCNAMARA Ryan U15 17.06.86, Shaft Barn : 80HB - 12.09w
MCNEILLIS Oliver Frederick U13 24.11.87, Halesowen : 80HC - 13.4, HJ - 1.50
MCQUARRIE David U15 28.11.85, Rowntrees : 3k - 9:31.9 (9:23.1-99)
MCQUEEN Sean U13 28.02.88, Pitreavie : 400 - 62.5
MCRAE Leon U23 3.11.80, Team Solent : 400H - 53.23
MCSHANNOCK Derek U15 2.11.85, Airdrie : 100 - 11.43w/11.54, 200 - 22.99w/23.21
MCSWEEN Trevor C. 27.10.66, Army : HJ - 1.95 (2.01-95)
MEDCALF Andrew Paul U20 11.05.83, E Grin : TJ - 13.89
MEDCALF Timothy James U23 19.02.79, E Grin/Warwick U : TJ - 14.11
MELBER Stephen L. U23 26.02.79, Milton K/ Oxford Univ : JT - 61.27
MELLOR Dean Ashley 25.11.71, Sale : PV - 4.80 (5.30-95)
MELLUISH Christopher Jeremy V55 15.07.44, Cambridge Harriers : HT - 46.28 (62.10-74)
MEPANDY Farel U23 27.12.79, Belgrave/ Loughbro/CGO : TJ - 15.73w/15.54i/15.45
MERRICK Olvin Essop 24.05.74, WG & Ex L : 100 - 10.89, 200 - 22.07, LJ - 7.58 (7.59w-98)
MERRIMAN Alan 26.07.70, WG & Ex L/IRE : 5k - 14:10.9
MIAH Monu U17 10.01.84, WGreen & Ex L : 100 - 10.7/10.79, 200 - 21.31w/21.45
MICHAELSON Thomas U15 3.01.87, Liv H : 1500 - 4:19.68, 3k - 9:22.67
MIDDLETON Barry 10.03.75, Sale/Aberdeen : 200 - 22.10w (21.8-96/22.07i-97/22.40-95, 400 - 48.1/48.53 (47.44i/48.48-97), 400H - 52.71 (51.18-96)

MIDDLETON Darren U23 14.10.80, Barnsley :
800 - 1:52.90
MIDDLETON Lee U20 15.04.82, Hert & Ware :
DecJ - 5056
MIDDLETON Peter Alan U17 27.01.84, N S P :
60HY - 8.42i, 100HY - 13.29w/13.49,
400HY - 57.28
MIELE Felice U20 24.11.81, Enf & Har :
DT - 43.10, DTJ - 49.40
MILES Marc U15 14.09.85, Boston TC :
JTB - 44.98
MILES Mark Thomas 24.03.77, Belgrave :
5k - 14:16.79 (13:56.55-99), 5MR - 23:27
MILES Paul U23 14.09.80, Birchfield :
PV - 4.10 (4.25-98)
MILFORD Shaun 13.07.63, Cornwall AC :
Mar - 2:27:10 (2:25:54-97)
MILLAR Stuart U20 9.03.83, Cheltenham :
SPJ - 13.53i
MILLER Ian U15 9.01.87, West Midland Sch :
TJ - 12.08
MILLER James D. U23 29.03.80, Birc/Wolvs U :
60 - 6.92i, 100 - 10.7w/10.8/10.99 (10.69-99)
MILLER Mark 10.11.71, Enf & Har :
HT - 59.72
MILLER Patrick 21.02.67, Border :
3kSt - 9:25.09 (8:57.47-96)
MILLER Robert U17 20.01.84, Aberdeen :
OctY - 4260
MILLS A., Kettering :
DT - 40.43
MILLS Christopher Leslie 12.11.75, Winchr/
Brunel Un : PV - 4.45
MILLS Joseph 9.07.72, Blackheath :
800 - 1:50.39 (1:50.12-99),
1500 - 3:43.73 (3:42.23-99)
MILTON James U15 26.09.85, Camb & C :
200 - 23.46, 400 - 53.6
MINNIKIN Stephen 4.01.72, Doncaster :
HT - 57.80 (62.20-96)
MITCHELL Andrew U23 30.07.80, Peterbro/
Loughbro : 2kSt - 5:53.5, 3kSt - 9:10.5
MITCHELL Andrew 30.07.76, Kilbarchan/Bord :
200 - 22.0, 400 - 48.47 (47.51-98)
MITCHELL Ian 10.03.76, Longwood :
1500 - 3:47.90 (3:47.3-95),
3k - 8:11.68, 5k - 14:03.30
MITCHELL John U20 13.05.81, St. Andrews U :
JT - 56.07
MITCHELL Mark U13 23.05.88, Forres :
800 - 2:18.47, 1500 - 4:42.9
MITCHELL Robert U23 14.09.80, Shaft Barn :
HJ - 2.20i/2.20
MITCHELL Terrence V40 23.08.59,
Dunf & W Fife : Mar - 2:28:39 (2:17:56-92)
MITCHINSON David U23 4.09.78, N & E B/
Loughbro : 1500 - 3:50.51, 5k - 14:22.64,
3kSt - 8:45.06
MOGFORD Michael U17 19.09.83, Preseli :
SPY - 14.51
MOIR Gareth U23 17.12.80, Ipswich/Bath Un :
HJ - 2.00
MOIR Scott U23 17.12.80, Ipswich :
JT - 58.78
MOISEY Louis U15 9.08.86, Notts :
100 - 11.57w, 200 - 23.53
MONAGHAN Ian U20 6.11.81, Harr/Brunel Un :
400H - 55.82
MONDS John U23 24.03.80, Newham & E B :
110H - 15.17w/15.22 (14.78w/14.9/14.95-99)
MONEY Daniel James 17.10.76, Sale :
60 - 6.86i (6.72i-98),
100 - 10.51w/10.69 (10.16w/10.32-97),
200 - 21.32 (20.75w/20.92-97)
MOORE Colin V40 25.11.60, Bingley :
HMar - 1:06:49 (1:02:06sh-93/1:02:22-85)
MOORE Daniel U20 8.11.81, Blackheath :
2kSt - 6:06.5 (6:04.9-99)
MOORE Jonathan U17 31.05.84, Birchfield :
LJ - 7.46, TJ - 16.02
MOORE Louis Calvin U15 8.09.85, C of Stoke :
80HB - 11.80w/11.95, HJ - 1.83,
LJ - 6.46io/6.45w/6.34, PenB - 3001
MOORE Stephen R. V50 17.12.47, Hert & W/
Keswick : Mar - 2:32:56 (2:27:30-90),
100kR - 7:14:57 (6:43:52-92)
MOORES Paul U17 3.08.84, Tamworth :
1500 - 4:06.6, 3k - 8:44.8, 1.5kSt - 4:28.19
MOORHOUSE Julian 13.11.71, Birchfield :
1500 - 3:43.41, 1M - 4:02.35,
3k - 7:53.11, 5k - 13:42.35
MORAN Anthony U15 8.01.86, Trafford :
1500 - 4:16.11, 3k - 9:10.29
MORANT Martyn U20 26.06.78, Woodcox & B :
400 - 48.5/48.65 (48.38-99)
MORELAND John R. V40 13.09.58, Rugby :
DT - 46.74 (51.76-95)
MORELANDS Stuart U15 16.06.86, Liv H :
800 - 2:04.07
MORETON Andrew U17 1.11.83, Oxford City :
800 - 1:56.3
MORGAN Derek N. 4.04.69, Bristol :
100 - 10.7w/11.24 (10.6-93/10.77-89)
MORGAN Mark 19.08.72, Swansea :
5k - 14:21.9 (13:57.91-99),
5MR - 23:36, 10kR - 29:42 (29:13-99)
MORGAN Nathan U23 30.06.78, Birchfield :
100 - 10.44 (10.38w-99),
LJ - 8.05w/8.00 (8.11-98)
MORGAN-LEE Andrew 1.03.69, Salford :
3k - 8:10.74, 5k - 14:32.47 (14:02.43-99),
3kSt - 8:43.95
MORGANELLA Alessandro 28.05.77, Border :
DT - 44.64
MORLEY Andrew, Exeter :
LJ - 7.00 (7.03w-98)
MORLEY Roger 20.09.77, Bedford & County :
800 - 1:52.69 (1:51.9-99)
MORRIS Ashley U15 12.02.86, Shropshire S :
TJ - 12.28
MORRIS Carl U23 5.05.80, Wells/Exeter Univ :
10k - 31:44.91
MORRIS Greg U17 27.09.83, Grantham :
1.5kSt - 4:39.7
MORRIS James U23 2.12.79, Swansea :
LJ - 6.98
MORRIS Michael 16.07.74, Chester Le Street :
1500 - 3:43.52, 3k - 8:05.74
MORRIS Robert U20 20.02.82, Hertford & W :
SP - 14.36, SPJ - 15.99 (15.99-99),
DT - 46.41, DTJ - 50.44 (50.53-99)
MORRISON Ryan U17 16.12.83, Liverpool H :
100 - 11.1
MOSCROP Howard Wilson V40 16.12.57, Swin :
400H - 53.79 (51.4-84/51.57-82)

MOSES Alister William U23 5.07.78, Reigate : 1500 - 3:47.21, 1M - 4:07.53, 3k - 8:20.8
MOSS Christopher Robert U23 17.06.79, Blackheath/Loughborough Studnts : 800 - 1:47.75, 1500 - 3:47.0
MOSS Damien U20 2.09.82, Northampton : 800 - 1:52.64
MOTT Shane 23.05.73, Chichester : TJ - 13.94 (14.09-96)
MOULTON David U20 7.09.81, Blackh/Bath U : 800 - 1:53.9
MOUNTFORD David U20 23.06.82, C of Stoke : LJ - 7.33
MUIR Andrew C. 20.06.73, Loughborough Col : 10k - 31:07.33
MULVANEY Christopher Shaun U20 5.05.81, Border : 800 - 1:49.86, 1500 - 3:48.13 (3:46.84-99), 1M - 4:10.93, 3k - 8:39.8
MUNDEN Craig 24.12.76, Bournemouth : DT - 40.23 (44.58-99)
MUNGHAM Robert U17 1.12.84, Bracknell : HTY - 49.55
MUNRO Ian U17 5.09.83, Cambuslang : 800 - 1:54.35, 1500 - 3:58.62
MUNROE Gary 12.04.69, N& EB/RAF/CAN : LJ - 7.20 (7.52w?-99/7.27-96)
MURCH Kevin I. V40 11.11.58, Rugby : JT - 63.29 (69.02-89)
MURDOCH Iain U23 10.07.80, Avonside/ Loughbro : 1500 - 3:46.75, 3kSt - 8:42.79
MURDOCH Steven 16.04.61, Border : 10k - 32:01.2 (30:19.1-95)
MURPHY Darragh 20.01.74, Cardiff : HJ - 2.00 (2.11A/2.10-91)
MURPHY Denis U23 14.09.79, Newham & E B/ Loughbro : 800 - 1:52.60
MURPHY Kevin 6.04.74, WGreen & Ex L : 3kSt - 9:29.7
MURPHY Paul U20 30.04.81, Shaftesbury B : 3k - 8:37.61
MURPHY Phillip U15 29.09.85, Dartford : LJ - 6.39
MURPHY Stephen James U20 6.01.83, Shaft B : 1500 - 3:54.00, 3k - 8:21.69, 2kSt - 5:50.6, 3kSt - 9:22.94
MURPHY Stephen U20 10.02.82, C of Edinb : 400H - 53.2/53.37
MURRAY Gary U23 31.01.80, St Malachy's/ Ulst U/Finn V/IRE : 1500 - 3:51.04 (3:49.43-99)
MURRAY Michael U23 8.12.79, Windsor S & E : TJ - 13.92 (14.14i/14.13-99)
MURRAY Thomas 18.05.61, Inverclyde : 5MR - 23:29, 10k - 29:57.58 (29:12.35-94), 10kR - 29:54 (29:09-97), 10MR - 48:47dh (48:15dh-94/48:17-93)
MUSA Christopher U15 5.12.86, Tower Ham : 80HB - 11.43
MUSSETT Adrian 14.04.72, Colchester & T : 5k - 14:19.8 (14:13.7-97), 5MR - 23:49 (23:14-99), 10k - 29:10.86, 10kR - 29:28
MUTAI John 26.05.66, Bromsgrove & R/KEN : HMar - 1:02:34 (1:00:52-99), Mar - 2:13:20
MYERS Richard U17 21.12.83, Tynedale : 100HY - 13.9/14.01w (13.9/14.07-99)
MYERSCOUGH Carl Andrew ¶ U23 21.10.79, Blackpool : SP - 19.71i (19.46-98)
MYERSCOUGH Grant U20 3.04.83, Blackpool : DTJ - 41.85
MYLES Gary 3.02.63, Cannock & Stafford : 110H - 15.40 (14.55-83)

NAISMITH David U23 15.12.79, N & E B : 200 - 21.7/21.76w/22.04i (21.6/22.01-99), 400 - 46.47 (46.27-99)
NAPIER Adam U15 30.09.85, Havering : HJ - 1.75
NASH Kevin 6.02.77, Belgrave : 3kSt - 9:13.69 (8:43.21-96)
NASH Paul U17 13.02.84, Leamington : HTY - 50.28
NASH Robin J. V40 9.02.59, Westbury : Mar - 2:27:16 (2:14:52-94)
NASH Samuel 22.10.71, Thames Valley : LJ - 7.41wA/6.96 (7.01-97)
NASRAT James Thomas U20 10.01.83, Newp : 800 - 1:51.77, 400H - 56.09
NAUGHTON Joe 17.10.74, Havering/IRE : HJ - 1.95 (2.05-97), PV - 4.10 (4.40-99)
NAYLOR Donald E. 5.09.71, Swansea : 1500 - 3:48.7, 5k - 13:58.88, 3kSt - 8:44.03
NAYLOR Jonathan U23 19.04.78, W Cheshire : TJ - 14.24
NEAL Robert U17 14.09.83, Brighton : 1.5kSt - 4:36.4
NEELY Ian 29.12.74, Border : 400H - 52.64 (52.34-98)
NELSON Anthony U17 14.09.84, Croydon : TJ - 13.80
NESBETH Michael U23 1.03.79, Croydon : LJ - 7.30 (7.35i-99), TJ - 14.70i/14.15 (14.83i-99/14.80w/14.79-96)
NEWELL Elisha U23 10.06.79, Belgrave : 100 - 10.91 (10.7w-98)
NEWMAN Lee Jon 1.05.73, Belgrave : SP - 17.81 (18.85-96), DT - 57.44 (60.48-97)
NEWNES James 9.09.67, Salford : HMar - 1:05:50
NEWTON Keith 12.12.68, WGreen & Ex L : TJ - 14.59
NEWTON Michael U15 3.04.86, Sale : 80HB - 12.00w
NEWTON Robert U20 10.05.81, Sale/Bath Un : 60 - 6.86idt, 60H - 8.12i (8.04i-99), 110HJ - 14.1/14.12 (13.90-99), 110H - 13.95 (13.93w-99)
NICHOLL David 16.09.69, Border : HT - 51.85 (57.06-97)
NICHOLLS John S. 1.09.65, Warrington : SP - 14.75i/14.74 (15.98-99)
NICHOLLS Philip U17 29.09.83, Tipton : 1500 - 3:59.7, 3k - 8:37.6
NICHOLLS Russell U20 8.03.83, Enf & Har : 400 - 47.90
NICHOLSON Andrew U15 25.03.86, Sx Sch : TJ - 12.40
NICHOLSON Martin 9.12.70, Birchfield : 60H - 7.87i, 110H - 14.14w/14.18 (13.8/14.14-94)
NICKLESS James U17 27.10.84, Halesowen : 1.5kSt - 4:35.0
NICOLSON Christian 19.09.73, Team Solent : 1500 - 3:44.70, 5k - 13:45.26, 10k - 29:40.17
NIELAND Nicholas 31.01.72, Shaftesbury B : JT - 85.09

NIMMO Thomas 9.05.71, City of Edinburgh :
400 - 48.4 (47.99-92),
800 - 1:49.9 (1:49.0-92)
NITSCH Mark U23 3.03.78, Peterborough :
400H - 53.4/54.09 (53.93-99)
NNANYERE Bertram U17 26.09.83, Croydon :
HJ - 1.90
NOAD Ben 6.05.76, Bristol/Providence Un :
3k - 8:09.49i (8:06.69i-99),
5k - 13:48.98i/13:57.93, 10k - 28:47.94
NOBLE Ian 2.04.77, Trafford :
PV - 4.40i (4.80-99)
NOEL Anthony J. 8.09.63, Cambridge H :
100 - 10.77 (10.5w-99/10.6-98/10.64-99),
200 - 22.12w (21.7-98/21.86-99)
NORMAN Andrew U23 19.08.80, Altr/Hallam U :
1500 - 3:51.94, 5k - 14:32.53, 10k - 31:08.76
NORMAN Anthony Josephus 5.07.63, Woking :
SP - 14.00 (14.94-88), JT - 58.31 (68.74-87)
NORRIS Chris U20 8.10.82, Enf & Har :
2kSt - 6:14.84
NORTH Christian I.R. 2.02.74, Bristol :
PV - 5.00i/4.90 (5.30-99/5.10dhex-98)
NORTH Steffan 19.07.76, Sale :
1500 - 3:51.37
NORTHROP Paul 15.01.70, Enf & Har :
3kSt - 9:14.25 (8:51.25-90)
NORTON Andrew U13 14.12.87, City of Stoke :
100 - 12.5, 200 - 25.3
NOTMAN Lee, Border :
400 - 49.0
NOYCE Michael 31.10.77, Winchester :
2kSt - 5:52.94, 400H - 56.0
NSUDOH Immanuel 8.04.72, Croydon :
LJ - 6.93 (7.14-96), TJ - 13.91 (14.40-93)
NUNAN James U17 16.09.83, Gloucester AC :
HTJ - 50.27, HTY - 59.93
NUTTALL John Barry 11.01.67, Preston :
1500 - 3:47.94 (3:40.6-90),
3k - 7:53.54 (7:36.40-96),
5k - 13:39.02 (13:16.70-95), 5MR - 23:31,
10k - 29:35.48 (28:07.43-95),
10kR - 29:38, 10MR - 49:20, HMar - 1:03:49
NWAOLISE Paul Chukwuemeka 31.05.73,
Morpeth/Teeside Univ :
100 - 10.91w/10.98 (10.73w-98/10.74-99)
NWOKORO Chin 13.03.77, Harr/Camb Univ :
110H - 15.6/15.65
NYAMANYO Suote U17 3.10.84, Mandale :
100HY - 14.17
NYIRENDA Ramji U17, Eryi Schools:
SPY - 14.04

O'BRIEN Anthony 14.11.70, Morpeth :
3k - 8:20.35 (8:19.7-99),
5k - 14:43.5 (14:16.6-95),
HMar - 1:05:50 (1:04:46-96)
O'BRIEN Barry 3.07.76, Gateshead :
400 - 48.5/49.01 (48.0/48.33-99)
O'BRIEN Barry U15 21.04.86, Dunf & W Fife :
80HB - 11.91w?/12.04
O'CALLAGHAN Paul Michael Patrick 1.06.64,
Birchfield/IRE : 10k - 31:54.3,
HMar - 1:05:39, Mar - 2:20:16
O'CONNOR Alastair Paul 22.06.71, Liv H :
1500 - 3:47.68, 3kSt - 8:44.18 (8:42.88-92)
O'DONOVAN Ross U15 12.03.86, TVH :
100 - 11.5/11.52
O'DOWD Matthew 15.04.76, Swind/Loughbro :
1500 - 3:51.62 (3:45.10-99),
5k - 14:03.01 (13:37.00-99), 5MR - 23:21,
10kR - 29:55 (29:32-98)
O'GARA Stephen 3.12.69, Wallsend :
5k - 14:25.3
O'HARA Jason 28.10.76, Shaftesbury Barnet :
PV - 4.20
O'KEEFE Kieran U15 19.03.86, Charnwood :
DTB - 47.57, HTB - 51.11
O'LEARY David U23 3.08.80, Liverpool H :
400H - 54.39 (54.03-99)
O'NEILL Colm U15 7.11.85, St Columbs :
800 - 2:05.00
O'RAWE Andrew 8.09.63, Roadhogs :
3kW - 12:58.8 (12:44.4-98), 10kWR - 46:03,
20kW - 1:34:23 (1:34:05-96)
O'RAWE James 3.02.73, Roadhogs :
3kW - 12:16.7, 10kW - 43:54.49 (43:25.2-96),
10kWR - 43:12, 20kW - 1:30:56 (1:28:46-99)
OAKES Christopher 19.10.70, Army :
HJ - 1.95, Dec - 5641 (5951-97)
OAKES Mark V40 19.11.60, Mornington :
Mar - 2:34:11
OBANYE Emeka U15 18.11.85, Mx Sch :
SPB - 13.14
OBOH Laurence U17 14.05.84, Hounslow :
100 - 10.80, 200 - 21.39w/21.65
OBUQUAI D. U15, Queens Park :
HJ - 1.75
OCTAVE Philip U23 12.06.78, TVH/Reading U :
400 - 47.96 (47.8/47.85-99)
ODUDU Aghogho 24.10.76, Blackburn/Oxf Un :
110H - 15.11, 200H - 25.2 (25.0-97)
ODUNDO-MENDEZ Marimba U15 30.09.86,
AF&D : 200 - 22.99
OGUNYEMI Akeem 4.06.74, Enf & Har :
60 - 6.9i (6.8i/6.82i-98)
OHRLAND Martin U23 19.11.79, Chelmsford :
TJ - 13.99
OHRLAND Stuart 6.09.75, Newham & Essex B :
HJ - 2.19i/2.17 (2.20i-97/2.18-99),
TJ - 14.15
OJO Sayo U23 9.05.80, WGreen & Ex L :
TJ - 14.57 (14.62-99)
OKE Tosin U23 1.10.80, Camb H/Man Univ :
TJ - 16.37w/16.04 (16.57-99)
OKOJIE Onose U15 19.09.85, Thames Valley :
HJ - 1.80, PenB - 2563
OKOTIE Maclean 31.07.69, Thames Valley :
60 - 6.9i/6.97i (6.85i-97),
100 - 10.86 (10.46-98)
OLIVER Geoff V65 8.08.33, :
24HrT - 198.549km (222.720km-94)
OMONUA Samson 16.06.76, Enf & Har :
100 - 10.83 (10.5/10.59-96)
ONI Samson U20 25.06.81, Belgrave/NIG :
HJ - 2.19i/2.15 (2.16-99)
ONIBIJE Fola U17 25.09.84, Ealing,S & Mx :
200 - 21.98
ONUHA Chinedum U15, G. Manchester Sch :
LJ - 6.07w
ONWUBALILI David U20 5.12.82, Belgrave :
SPJ - 13.58, DTJ - 45.37
OPARKA Jonathon U23 27.01.80, Dundee HH/
Border : 60 - 6.84i,
100 - 10.6/10.70 (10.70-99),
200 - 22.0/22.04 (22.0-99)

OPARKA Richard U20 28.07.82, Arbroath :
SP - 13.25, SPJ - 14.21, DTJ - 43.31
OPENSHAW Michael 8.04.72, Chester Le St :
1500 - 3:51.55i (3:39.7-98),
1M - 4:00.77 (3:57.2-98),
3k - 7:55.12, 5k - 13:37.97, 10kR - 29:05
ORLONISHE Fola U15 14.07.86, Tower Ham :
80HB - 11.22
ORMESHER Andrew J. U17 29.05.85, Wigan :
JTY - 52.12
ORPE Mark U17 11.10.84, City of Stoke :
100HY - 14.1w, 400HY - 58.7
ORR Christopher James U20 20.06.83, Border :
SPJ - 13.98, DT - 40.13, DTJ - 45.27
OSAZUWA John U20 4.05.81, Belgrave/NGR :
HT - 62.87, HTJ - 64.56
OSBOURNE Jerome U17 28.08.84, Herne Hill :
TJ - 13.69
OSTRIDGE Matthew U20 23.02.83, Telford :
HJ - 2.01
OSUIDE Stanley 30.11.74, Thames Valley :
HJ - 2.07 (2.15-91)
OTUBAMBO Michael 6.07.73, Enf & Har :
100 - 10.8 (10.7w/10.92-99),
200 - 21.8 (22.06-99)
OUCHE Matthew U17 6.03.85, Newham & E B :
100 - 11.0 (11.44-99)
OUDNEY Graeme U17 11.04.85, Dundee HH :
800 - 1:56.98
OVENS Mark, Swindon :
HJ - 1.95 (1.96-96)
OVERTHROW Stuart 13.06.75, Cheltenham :
800 - 1:51.3 (1:50.16-99),
1500 - 3:50.46 (3:50.23-99)
OWEN John N. 28.10.64, Swansea :
HT - 49.95 (52.96-95)
OWEN Neil James 18.10.73, Belgrave :
60H - 8.09i (7.72i-96),
110H - 13.8/13.87w/13.93 (13.5w-96/13.60-95)
OWEN Nicholas U23 17.07.80, K & P/Brunel U :
SP - 15.59, DT - 43.40, Dec - 5801
OWENS Andrew U15 5.11.85, Liverpool H :
100 - 11.4w, 200 - 23.3w (29.2-97)
OXBOROUGH Wayne 10.11.66, Thames H & H :
Mar - 2:28:36 (2:27:05-99)

PACEY VIGO Kyle U15 10.04.86,
Northants Sch : 200 - 22.99w
PACHTER Daniel U17 24.03.84, Wirral :
400 - 49.40
PAGE Christopher U23 13.11.80, Cardiff :
400 - 47.51
PAGKATIPUNAN Lolimar U20 17.11.82,
Enf & Har : 110HJ - 15.5
PAIN Ashley U13, Tipton :
1M - 5:12.5
PAINTER John James Thomas ¶ V40 12.06.58,
Norwich : SP - 13.59 (16.32i/16.09-89),
DT - 40.47 (50.36-88)
PAINTER Trevor 10.08.71, Trafford :
200 - 22.15 (21.8-94),
400 - 48.52 (47.08-98/47.79A-95)
PAISLEY Derek 1.12.73, Pitreavie :
400H - 54.8 (52.83-94)
PALMER Adrian Mark 10.08.69, Cardiff :
HT - 56.95 (62.56-94)
PALMER Colin 27.07.67, Team Solent/Army :
10k - 31:42.2, 3kSt - 9:04.06 (8:57.4-98)
PALMER Ian U20 22.11.81, Bournemouth :
400H - 56.3/56.62
PALMER Martin 5.04.77, Yate/Chelt & Glos U :
5k - 14:08.26, 10k - 30:15.80
PALMER Nathan U20 16.06.82, Cardiff :
60H - 8.06i, 110HJ - 14.1/14.80 (14.11-99),
110H - 14.34w/14.45
PALMER Ryan U20 21.06.83, Sale :
400 - 49.0
PANG Martin U15 13.03.86, Nuneaton :
80HB - 11.75, LJ - 6.04, PenB - 2502
PAPURA Dominic U20 12.02.81, Cardiff/
Loughbro : 100 - 10.8/10.99, 200 - 21.79
PARK Iain Ross 16.07.74, Harrow/Falkirk :
DT - 40.27 (44.96-98), HT - 62.86 (64.64-98)
PARKER Andrew U23 1.08.80, Swan/UWIC :
60 - 6.96i (6.96i-99),
100 - 10.72w/10.78 (10.7w-98),
200 - 21.6/21.98 (21.4w/21.55w/21.98-98
PARKER Andrew U17 10.12.83, Wolves & B :
3kW - 12:29.90, 5kW - 22:48.91,
10kW - 47:47.95, 10kWR - 46:46
PARKER David U23 28.02.80, S B/Loughbro :
JT - 78.24
PARKER James U23 28.10.79, Team Solent :
800 - 1:49.80
PARKER James U23 29.09.80, Epsom & E :
110H - 15.6
PARKER Michael U17 29.10.83, City of Hull :
PV - 3.80i (3.60-99)
PARKER Richard U15 21.11.86, Cannock & St :
SPB - 13.05
PARKIN John U23 23.02.79, Sale :
DT - 42.27 (46.80-99), HT - 47.96 (51.18-98)
PARKINSON B. U15, Sussex Sch :
800 - 2:06.0
PARPER Michael U23 20.05.78, Belgrave :
200 - 21.94, 400 - 46.91 (46.54-97)
PARR Christopher Daniel U17 13.11.84, Gate :
800 - 1:57.92, 1500 - 4:05.74,
3k - 8:53.05, 1.5kSt - 4:40.5
PARRY Philip John 4.10.65, Harrow :
JT - 59.32 (70.00-94)
PARRY Richard U15 23.05.86, Halesowen :
400 - 52.6
PARSONS Gary 17.05.71, Cambridge & C :
DT - 42.64 (42.95-98)
PARSONS Geoffrey Peter 14.08.64, Lond AC :
HJ - 2.00 (2.31-94)
PARSONS Thomas Martin U17 5.05.84,
Solihull & S Heath : HJ - 1.95
PARTINGTON Stephen Wyand 17.09.65,
Manx H : 3kW - 12:23.2 (11:33.4-95),
10kW - 43:30.50 (41:14.61-95),
10kWR - 44:21/44:53+ (40:40hc-92/40:49-94),
20kW - 1:31:14 (1:24:09sh-94/1:24:18-90)
PASSEY Adrian 2.09.64, Bromsgrove & R :
1500 - 3:47.63 (3:34.50-87),
3k - 7:53.68 (7:48.09-89),
5k - 13:30.67 (13:20.09-97)
PATMORE Stephen U23 9.07.79, City of Hull/
Leeds Poly : 1500 - 3:50.11
PATRICK Adrian Leroy John 15.06.73, WS & E :
100 - 10.48 (10.3/10.38-96),
200 - 21.19w/21.44 (20.62w-95/20.9-96/20.92-99),
300 - 33.84 (32.73-97), 400 - 46.19 (45.63-95)
PATTEN Daniel U15 11.07.86, Thurrock :
3k - 9:16.6

PAUL Farron U15 3.10.85, Enf & Har :
HJ - 1.75, JTB - 53.93
PAUL Robert U23 12.11.80, E & E/St. Marys U :
HJ - 2.10
PAYNE Garry V40 31.01.57, :
Mar - 2:30:55
PAYNE Nigel, Nuneaton :
Mar - 2:33:53
PAYNE Russell H. V40 11.09.60, Birchfield :
HT - 51.71 (56.62-86)
PAYNE Stephen U23 30.01.78, Andover :
100 - 10.8, 400 - 48.31
PAYNE Stephen J. V45 1.12.55, Royal Navy :
Mar - 2:29:36
PAYNE Stewart U20 15.03.82, Sale :
2kSt - 6:07.7 (6:03.99-99)
PEACOCK Shane 5.03.63, Birchfield :
HT - 63.60 (71.60-90)
PEAD Andrew 18.02.66, Stockport :
Mar - 2:33:15
PEARSON John Terry 30.04.66, Charnwood :
HT - 70.33
PEARSON Stephen Gordon V40 13.09.59,
Sale : HT - 64.47 (67.45-98)
PEATROY Daniel U13 9.03.88, Guildford & G :
JTC - 37.59
PEERLESS Matthew U20 3.12.82,
Corstorphine/City of Edinburgh :
PV - 4.10i (4.01-99), Dec - 5034
PEET James U20 2.12.82, Rowheath :
110HJ - 15.4
PELESZOK Matthew Jon U20 17.10.81,
City of Stoke : DecJ - 5335 (5742-99)
PENK Andrew U23 19.09.78, Cardiff :
HJ - 2.16i/2.05 (2.15-97), PV - 4.81
PENN Andrew Shaun 31.03.67, Cov RWC :
3kW - 12:10.08i/12:30.52 (11:35.5-97),
10kWR - 43:48/44:26+ (41:47+-92/42:00-93),
20kW - 1:28:47 (1:23:34-92)
PERKINS George Spanton U17 17.10.83,
Hallamshire : HTY - 48.71
PERRYMAN Guy St. Denis Mansfield V40
2.11.58, Reading :
SP - 14.24 (16.58-89), DT - 40.14 (41.48-85)
PETERS David 30.07.71, Herne Hill :
1500 - 3:50.87
PETROS Daniel U17 8.08.85, Ealing,S & Mx :
400 - 50.75
PETTIGREW Adrian U15 12.11.86, Tower Ham :
HJ - 1.78
PETTS Chris U23 22.01.80, Ashford :
HJ - 2.07
PHELPS Ryan U15 16.09.85, Chessington :
TJ - 12.32
PHILIP Colin U23 8.06.79, City of Edinburgh :
200 - 22.0, 400 - 48.35
PHILLIPS Craig U15, NE Wales Sch :
TJ - 12.00
PHILLIPS Steven 17.03.72, Rugby :
LJ - 7.86w/7.79 (8.07w-99/8.03-98),
TJ - 14.39 (15.47w/15.10-98)
PHILLIPS Timothy P. U23 13.01.79, Brighton/
Brighton Univ. : JT - 58.50 (62.13-98)
PHILPOTT Chris U15 14.12.85, Mandale :
400 - 53.61
PICKERING Lee U17 16.09.83, Bridlington :
3k - 9:00.56 (8:56.31-99)
PICKERING Robert U13 3.11.87, Bridlington :
3k - 9:47.99
PILBOROUGH Matt U23 10.07.79, Halesowen/
Birmingham Univ./USA : PV - 4.10
PILKINGTON Scott U15 27.08.86, Corst :
800 - 2:05.8
PINNOCK Richard 31.10.70, Trafford :
60 - 6.89i,
100 - 10.6w/10.7/10.82w/10.83 (10.70-99/10.7-98)
PLANK Daniel U20 27.04.82, Birchfield :
HJ - 2.05i (2.08i/2.07-99), LJ - 6.98
PLANO Matthew 8.10.76, Trafford/Staffs Univ :
10k - 31:28.7,
3kSt - 9:00.53 (8:54.66-99)
PLATTS Stephen J. 12.03.66, Morpeth :
10k - 31:01.18, HMar - 1:06:35
PLUNKETT Gerard Peter U23 30.06.80,
Hallam : JT - 62.71 (63.02-99),
Dec - 6079 (6587-99)
PORTER Alec U17 21.12.84, Newport :
100HY - 14.1w?/14.14
POTTER Adam Charles U23 12.04.80, Oxf C/
Bath Univ. : 60 - 6.86idt,
200 - 22.0 (23.56-96), 400 - 49.0, LJ - 7.17,
TJ - 14.22 (14.63-99)
POWELL Dalton Hugh 20.08.63, Notts :
200 - 22.0 (21.1dt/21.24w/21.26-92)
POWELL Joelle U13 2.03.88, Bristol :
100 - 12.3, 200 - 24.9
POWER Garry 1.09.62, Herne Hill/IRE :
DT - 46.40 (48.98-86)
PRATT Ross U15 2.06.86, Thurrock :
400 - 53.2
PRATT Stephen 6.02.71, Ealing,S & Mx :
400H - 55.8 (54.15-91)
PRATT Stephen 14.07.76, :
400H - 53.8/54.18
PREVOST Ricardo U15 31.10.85, Harrow :
HJ - 1.90
PRICE David U15 12.01.87, Newport :
SPB - 13.24, DTB - 38.05
PRICE Gareth U23 27.11.79, S B/Loughbro :
1500 - 3:47.82
PRICE Glyn A. 12.09.65, Swansea :
PV - 4.30 (4.80-90)
PRICE Malcolm 18.06.62, Salford :
HMar - 1:06:13 (1:03:38-97)
PRICE Neil U23 15.05.80, Newport :
PV - 4.10i/4.10 (4.20-99)
PRICKETT Edward U20 28.01.83, Reigate :
3k - 8:35.6
PRIDE Simon 20.07.67, Swansea/Keith :
10MR - 49:54, HMar - 1:05:25,
Mar - 2:18:49
PRITCHARD Ashley U23 14.07.79, Macc/
Loughbro : Dec - 5547
PRITCHARD Jamie U15 25.09.85, Cardiff :
SPB - 13.89, DTB - 37.28, HTB - 46.63
PROCTOR Mark Anthony 15.01.63, N & E B/
RAF : SP - 20.57i/20.11 (20.85i-98/20.40-99),
DT - 57.14, HT - 50.19 (53.70-93)
PROPHETT Andrew 10.06.74, City of Stoke :
800 - 1:52.46 (1:51.6-98)
PROUDLOVE Michael 26.01.70, City of Stoke :
HMar - 1:06:11
PROWSE Barrie U17 2.03.85, Cornwall AC :
OctY - 4343

PROWSE Jonathon Richard 15.11.75, Blackpool : 1500 - 3:50.51
PYRAH Jeff 6.07.72, City of Edinburgh : Mar - 2:28:59

QUARRY Jamie Stephen 15.11.72, Harrow/Falkirk :
100 - 10.83 (10.7-97/10.76w-98/10.82-95),
60H - 8.10i (8.10i-97),
110H - 14.38 (14.10-94), PV - 4.60 (4.65-98),
LJ - 7.42w/7.27, Dec - 7667 (7739-99)
SP - 13.77i/13.15 (14.43-97)
QUIGLEY Mark 6.11.74, Border :
SP - 13.49 (14.41-97), DT - 48.14
QUINN Anthony U20 19.01.81, Annadale Str :
SP - 13.76, SPJ - 14.76
QUINN Robert 10.12.65, Kilbarchan :
HMar - 1:06:50

RADWAN Ashraf, Stamford & Deeping/ EGY : JT - 56.04 (57.88-97)
RAESIDE Bruce U20 2.12.81, Notts :
2kSt - 6:00.89, 3kSt - 9:38.6
RAGAN David U20 26.03.83, Basing & MH :
2kSt - 6:13.34, 3kSt - 9:35.95
RAGGETT Glenn U17 3.07.84, AF&D :
3k - 8:48.46
RALPH Paul 16.12.67, Trafford :
LJ - 7.38w/7.25,
TJ - 15.04w/14.57 (15.76w-97/15.67-95)
RAMBOTAS John U15 20.12.85, Bucks Sch :
SPB - 13.96
RAMSAY Iain U17 10.09.83, Inverness :
HJ - 1.91
RAMSEY Chris U17 2.11.84, Sphinx :
1500 - 4:06.85
RANDALL Matthew 28.04.70, WGreen & Ex L :
TJ - 13.90 (15.37-95)
SINGH RANDHAWA Manjit U23 19.10.80, Charn/DMU Leicester : SP - 13.73
RATCLIFFE Trevor 9.03.64, Dacorum & Tring :
JT - 62.50 (66.78-96)
RATHBONE Daniel 9.04.69, Brighton :
Mar - 2:24:02 (2:16:23-97)
RAVEN Gareth 9.05.74, East Cheshire :
1500 - 3:51.12, 3k - 8:14.06, 5k - 14:31.40
RAWLINSON Christopher 19.05.72, Belgrave :
200 - 21.53, 300 - 34.05i, 300H - 34.59,
400H - 48.22 (48.14-99)
RAWSON Tom 6.02.76, Nene Valley H :
110H - 15.4
RAYNER Thomas William U13 26.01.88, Sale :
100 - 12.3, 150 - 18.5, 200 - 24.86w/25.9
READ Simon 24.06.70, Herne Hill :
DT - 42.72
READLE David U23 10.02.80, Belgrave :
SP - 17.50, DT - 45.72
REBOUL Sylvain 4.10.76, Swansea/FRA :
60 - 6.73idt/6.82i, 100 - 10.6,
200 - 21.6/22.08i
REDSHAW Stephen U20 11.11.81, Chest Le St :
800 - 1:52.99
REED Paul 2.06.62, Border :
SP - 15.94 (17.04-88), DT - 54.11 (58.36-99)
REES Gareth U20 15.01.82, Blackpool :
400H - 54.02
REES Martin V45 28.02.53, Neath :
HMar - 1:06:54
REES Thomas U15 9.03.86, Neath :
JTB - 54.11
REES-JONES Steve 24.12.74, Sheffield :
800 - 1:50.21 (1:49.92-97), 1500 - 3:44.93
REESE Ben 29.03.76, Trafford/East Mich Un :
800 - 1:52.53i (1:49.98-97),
1M - 4:01.76i (3:59.82i-97/4:05.39-99)
REEVES Andrew U20 10.09.81, Leamington :
HJ - 1.96
REGIS John Paul Lyndon 13.10.66, Belgrave :
100 - 10.61w/10.64 (10.07w-90/10.15-93),
200 - 21.00i/21.07w/21.30 (19.87A-94/19.94-93),
400 - 49.04 (45.48-93)
REGIS Jonathan U15 7.07.86, Belgrave :
100 - 11.58, 200 - 22.75w/23.34
REID Alan 19.04.66, Peterhead :
100kR - 7:27:24
REID Edward U20 22.07.81, Charnwood :
SPJ - 14.24, DT - 43.29, DTJ - 46.59
REID Graeme U23 14.04.79, Clydes/Iona Coll :
1500 - 3:48.41, 3k - 8:19.08i
REID James 1.01.75, Law & Dist :
Mar - 2:21:15
REID Justin 26.09.69, Willowfield :
10k - 31:42.0, 3kSt - 9:14.58 (8:55.61-92)
REID M. U23, Reading :
TJ - 13.92 (14.33-99)
REID Stewart 15.11.73, Border/Pitreavie :
800 - 1:50.50 (1:50.26-99), 1500 - 3:48.49
REIDY Sean U20 27.01.81, Nene Valley H :
400H - 55.41
REILLY Andrew U15 26.10.85, V of Aylesbury :
TJ - 12.23
REILLY Brendan Anthony John 23.12.72, Bel/IRE : HJ - 2.28i/2.24 (2.32i-94/2.31-92)
REINA Eduardo Enrique 9.12.68, Kent/O Un/ HON : HT - 46.31 (50.96-98)
RENAUD Pascal 20.04.70, Enf & Har/FRA :
60H - 8.4i (8.3i-94/8.34i-97),
110H - 14.71w/14.91 (14.58-92)
RENFREE Andrew James 18.05.75, S Barnet :
1500 - 3:44.88
REVELL Paul U23 18.11.80, Scarborough :
TJ - 14.08 (14.55w/14.25-99)
REY Michael 19.07.68, Windsor S & E :
200 - 22.0 (21.14w-97/21.23-90)
REYNOLDS Christopher U17 23.01.85, WG& EL :
800 - 1:56.2, 1500 - 4:00.67, 3k - 8:53.7
RICE John U20 29.08.81, Liv.Pembroke S :
2kSt - 6:01.16 (5:53.6-99), 3kSt - 9:30.7
RICE Lloyd U17 13.02.85, Bristol :
100 - 11.07
RICHARDS Dominique U23 12.09.79, HHH :
60 - 6.90i (6.83i-99),
100 - 10.70 (10.60w/10.69-99),
200 - 21.40 (21.3-99),
LJ - 7.66w/7.35 (7.52i-99)
RICHARDS Gregory Roy V40 25.04.56, Nth Lond & Mus Hill : SP - 13.61 (15.24-94),
DT - 43.57 (50.66-91)
RICHARDS Henry U20 15.05.81, Charnwood :
60 - 6.93i (6.89i-99),
100 - 10.72w/10.84 (10.69w/10.75-98),
200 - 21.61w/21.9 (21.8/22.38i-99/23.23-96)
RICHARDS Leslie U17 29.03.85, M & C :
DTY - 43.42
RICHARDS Thomas Austin U23 13.11.78, N & E B/CUAC : PV - 5.10 (5.25-99)

RICHARDSON Alan Matthew U20 15.01.81, TVH/Leeds Univ : PV - 4.65
RICHARDSON Mark Austin 26.07.72, W S & E : 400 - 44.72 (44.37-98)
RICHMOND Stuart Anthony 11.04.69, Medway : TJ - 14.44 (15.73-99)
RICKETTS Kevin 29.06.76, Deeside/Army : JT - 56.47, Dec - 6436
RIDER Scott Frederick 22.09.77, Enf & Har : SP - 17.04i/17.04, DT - 52.81
RILEY A. U17, Leics Sch : 100 - 11.1
RILEY Peter U23 6.07.79, Trafford/Iona Col : 3k - 8:15.60, 5k - 13:57.01
RIMMER Michael U15 3.02.86, Liverpool H : 800 - 1:55.56, 1500 - 4:07.8
RITCHIE Darren 14.02.75, Sale/Scot Borders : LJ - 7.92w/7.90 (7.92w-99)
RITCHIE Donald Alexander V55 6.07.44, Forres/Moray RR : 100kR - 7:54:45 (6:18:00sh-78/6:28:11-82), 24Hr - 220.371km (267.543kri-90/234.083km-98)
RITCHIE Grant U20 25.12.81, S B/Arbroath : 2kSt - 6:03.2, 3kSt - 9:27.2
RIXON Dale 8.07.66, Bridgend : HMar - 1:06:56 (1:04:19-94), Mar - 2:23:35 (2:13:41-96)
ROBB Aaron 24.04.76, Shettleston : HJ - 1.95 (2.03-98)
ROBB Bruce 27.07.77, Pitreavie : SP - 16.55, DT - 53.31
ROBBIN-COCKER Olubunmi 27.11.75, Trafford/Dunfermline & W Fife/SLE : HJ - 2.00 (2.05-98)
ROBBINS Michael John 14.03.76, Rotherham/ Univ of Louisiana : 60H - 8.05i, 110H - 14.05 (13.96w-98/14.04-99), HJ - 2.03i/2.03 (2.19i-96/2.17-95)
ROBERSON Mark W. 21.03.75, Milton Keynes : HT - 47.29 (50.30-98)
ROBERSON Mark W. 13.03.67, N & Essex B : JT - 79.40 (85.67-98)
ROBERTS Andrew U15 24.10.85, Liverpool H : DTB - 41.11
ROBERTS Ben U23 15.01.80, Colwyn Bay : Dec - 5479 (6372-99)
ROBERTS Daniel U13 17.02.88, Sale : 1500 - 4:45.6
ROBERTS David U20 16.07.82, Brecon : SPJ - 13.58
ROBERTS Euron U15 18.11.85, Eryri : 80HB - 12.07, TJ - 12.30w
ROBERTS Mark 1.09.69, Kingston & Poly : 110H - 15.3 (15.3-98/15.65-92), Dec - 5700
ROBERTS Martin V40 1.03.60, Cannock & St : HT - 47.37 (53.08-88)
ROBERTS Martin U17 20.09.83, Scunthorpe : 100 - 11.11, 200 - 22.29w/22.40
ROBERTS Matthew U17 8.07.84, Crawley : 60HY - 8.32i
ROBERTSON Alex 6.05.63, Cambuslang : 10MR - 49:27dh
ROBERTSON David T. 11.09.61, Sunderland : Mar - 2:26:09
ROBERTSON Kenneth U13 6.04.88, Falkirk : DTC - 26.64
ROBINSON Andrew U17 5.09.84, Skyrac : JTY - 52.98
ROBINSON Brian U23 3.09.80, Birchfield : LJ - 7.13 (7.60w/7.53-97)
ROBINSON Daniel 13.01.75, Tipton : HMar - 1:06:52
ROBINSON David U23 12.01.78, Gateshead/ Northumbria Univ : HT - 56.07
ROBSON Lewis U13 9.01.88, Gateshead : 800 - 2:15.3, HJ - 1.51
ROBSON Shaun U23 21.06.80, Newport : 110H - 15.3, 400H - 54.95
RODEN James U20 24.11.81, Chorley : JT - 54.94, DecJ - 5730
RODGERS Adam U15 19.01.86, Cambridge H : 400 - 52.5
RODGERS David, Lochaber : Mar - 2:28:53
ROE Thomas U20 25.06.82, Norwich : LJ - 7.15
ROGERS Adam U20 10.04.83, Jarrow & Heb : 200 - 22.08w (21.64-99), 400 - 48.8 (48.85-99)
ROGERS Craig 14.02.76, Birchfield : SP - 14.41 (15.88-97), DT - 40.69
ROGERS Daryl James U15 3.12.85, N & E B : 800 - 2:03.0
ROGERS Jason U17 19.07.84, Ayr Seaforth : 100 - 11.1, 200 - 22.23w/22.58
ROGERS John 30.07.73, Annadale Str/Sale : 800 - 1:49.61, 1500 - 3:46.04
ROLFE Andrew U15 25.10.85, Thurrock : 1500 - 4:19.2, 3k - 9:13.35
ROLLINS Andrew U23 20.03.78, Trafford : SP - 15.19 (15.34-99), DT - 48.56
ROPER Simon U23 20.09.79, Derby & Co : LJ - 7.25w/7.21, TJ - 13.96 (14.47-97)
ROSE Matthew U17 14.09.83, Wirral : 800 - 1:57.84
ROSE Stefan 7.04.75, Team Solent : LJ - 7.07 (7.18-94)
ROSENBERG Luke U23 29.06.80, Harrow/ Loughbro : DT - 49.77 (51.05-99)
ROSSITER Martin R. 4.09.69, Peterborough : TJ - 15.14 (15.53w-99/15.20-97)
ROWE Alex V40 10.04.57, Wesham : Mar - 2:32:04 (2:28:16-99)
ROYDEN Barry Mark 15.12.66, Medway : 5MR - 23:50 (23:42-99), HMar - 1:05:37 (1:02:25-94), Mar - 2:18:54
ROYE Jordan Peter U13 3.11.87, Croydon : 200 - 25.84w/26.5
RUBEN Alan V40 9.03.57, : Mar - 2:33:35 (2:29:54-98)
RUBENIS Richard 10.11.73, Telford : 100 - 10.7/10.75 (10.5w/10.7-94), 200 - 21.88 (21.6-94)
RUDKIN Alan U23 5.11.78, Peterborough : DT - 43.33 (43.84-99)
RUFFELS Adam U17 3.04.84, Tonbridge : LJ - 6.71w/6.52
RUMBLE Mark U13 10.07.88, Oxford City : JTC - 36.20
RUMBOLD James Lee U20 4.11.81, Bournem'th : SPJ - 13.99, DT - 43.62, DTJ - 48.23
RUSBRIDGE Simon U20, Exeter : 800 - 1:54.20

RUSSELL Alaister 17.06.68, Bord/Law & Dist :
10k - 30:33.07 (29:52.16-95)
RUSSELL Jamie U20 1.10.81, Sheffield :
HJ - 2.14i/2.12, LJ - 6.90,
Dec - 6388, DecJ - 6412
RUSSELL Matthew U20 20.01.81, Belgrave :
60 - 6.94i
RUSSELL Robert U20 13.07.82, Central :
5k - 15:12.20
RUSSELL Robert 5.08.74, Sale :
SP - 14.58 (16.77-96), DT - 49.26 (53.76-96)
RUSSELL Tom U15 3.10.85, Cornwall AC :
1500 - 4:18.25
RYDER Sean U13 12.12.87, Cannock & Staff :
1500 - 4:45.0

SABAN Dominic U20 27.02.82, Sutt & D :
110HJ - 15.16 (15.1-99)
SADLER Philip 22.04.77, Havering :
200 - 21.9 (21.7-99/22.43-95),
400 - 49.0 (49.0-99/49.49-95)
SAGGERS Carl Peter Maurice U17 20.09.83,
Enf & Har : SP - 13.57, SPJ - 14.92,
SPY - 17.34, DTJ - 44.25 (44.98-99),
DTY - 53.69, HT - 52.70,
HTJ - 59.04, HTY - 68.27
SAHANS Gurmukh U23 8.10.78, Hounslow :
Dec - 5388 (5750-96)
SALAMI Raymond 11.04.75, Newham & E B :
60 - 6.85i (6.8i/6.82i-97),
100 - 10.68w/10.8
(10.2w/10.59w-99/10.6-96/10.66-99),
200 - 21.8/22.10 (21.44-97)
SALTER Thomas U20 7.01.83, Cannock & St :
HJ - 1.98
SALVADOR-AYLOTT Livio 18.07.73, Harrow :
400H - 55.15
SAMMATER Liban U20 2.11.81, N & E B :
800 - 1:54.4
SAMMUT Steven 3.05.67, Team Solent :
HT - 60.90dh/60.61
SAMPSON Christopher 30.09.75, Morpeth :
3kSt - 9:13.54
SAMUELS Nicholas U20 13.06.81, Blackburn/
Loughbro : 5k - 15:19.29
SAMUYIWA David 4.08.72, Thames Valley :
100 - 10.53w/10.66 (10.2wdt-98/10.4/10.66-97),
200 - 21.43w/21.71 (21.2/21.46-97)
SANDYS Thomas U13 21.09.87, E Grinstead :
LJ - 5.19
SAULTERS Alan U20 29.01.83, Albertville :
TJ - 14.20w/14.08
SAUNDERS Ryan U15 10.01.86, City of Hull :
PV - 2.85
SAVAGE David 13.11.72, Sale :
110H - 15.6/15.63w (15.1w-96/15.34-95),
400H - 51.49 (50.97-96)
SAVILLE Ben 10.11.77, Cleethorpes/Hull Un :
JT - 58.91 (60.60-99)
SAWREY Michael U15 30.05.86, Barrow & F :
800 - 2:05.0
SAWYER Anthony J. U23 29.04.80, WG & E L :
110H - 15.49, PV - 4.10, Dec - 6680
SAXON Sean 11.12.71, Telford :
110H - 15.45w/15.5w/15.69 (15.2-96)
SCANLON Rhodri U17 22.08.84, Carmarthen :
400HY - 58.63
SCANLON Robert 13.04.74, Coventry Godiva :
1500 - 3:47.20 (3:41.3-96)
SCARTH James 3.10.73, Bracknell :
800 - 1:52.51
SCOBIE Duncan 5.07.67, Border :
10k - 31:45.63
SCOTT Allan U20 27.12.82, Whitemoss :
60H - 8.10i, 60HJ - 7.95i, 110HJ - 14.20,
110H - 14.36, LJ - 6.81i (7.07w/6.96i/6.85-98)
SCOTT Darren 7.03.69, Trafford :
100 - 10.8/10.97 (10.5w?-99/10.61w-98/10.74-95),
200 - 21.53w/21.66i/21.7/21.86
(21.0w?-99/21.19w-98/21.3/21.35-95),
400 - 48.76i (48.57i/48.9-98)
SCOTT Eric 20.01.72, Windsor S & E :
Dec - 6178 (6299-92)
SCOTT Michael 4.11.65, Border :
Mar - 2:25:54
SCOTT Richard 14.09.73, WGreen & Ex L :
110H - 15.4,
400H - 52.7/53.91 (52.39-99)
SCOTT Sandy 1.09.76, Shett/Glasgow Univ/
Border : 200 - 22.06w (22.04-99),
400 - 47.94 (47.40-99)
SCOWCROFT Philip 25.01.71, East Cheshire :
DT - 40.19
SCRIVENER Neil U23 18.09.80, Southend :
400H - 55.9
SEALY Richard U17 26.11.84, Hounslow :
HTY - 49.27
SEAR Richard A. U23 21.08.79, Bel/London U :
110H - 15.4/15.56 (14.37-97)
SEARLES Corey U15 18.12.85, Shaft Barnet :
HJ - 1.76
SEGERSON Daniel U15 17.09.85, Swansea :
HJ - 1.79
SELBY Calvin U13 9.09.87, Ilford :
80HC - 13.6
SEMPERS Kevin U15 24.11.85, Scunthorpe :
80HB - 11.87w/11.89,
HJ - 1.79, PenB - 2695
SEMPLE Stuart U17 3.11.83, Basing & MH :
SPY - 14.65, DTY - 45.46
SESAY Mark Gavin 13.12.72, Traff/Loughbro :
400 - 48.86 (46.22-97),
800 - 1:48.55 (1:45.68-99)
SEVE Fale 12.05.77, Cardiff/SAM :
SP - 16.57, DT - 50.69, HT - 55.37
SHALDERS Steven U20 24.12.81, Cardiff :
LJ - 7.14i/6.90 (7.29-99), TJ - 15.99
SHANKEY Mark U17 19.12.84, :
1500 - 4:02.66
SHARP Alexis 31.10.72, Blackheath :
110H - 15.43w (15.21-98), PV - 4.55,
LJ - 6.89 (7.23w-97/7.10-98),
DT - 49.63 (49.65-99), Dec - 7133 (7571-98)
SHARP Stephen 31.12.75, Thames Valley :
800 - 1:51.55, 1500 - 3:43.88 (3:43.42-99),
1M - 4:02.0, 5MR - 23:54 (23:46-99)
SHARPE Phill U20 6.03.81, Border :
JT - 71.79
SHAW David U17 13.06.84, City of Edinburgh :
400HY - 58.9
SHAW Paul U20 7.08.82, Trafford :
5k - 15:31.7
SHAW Ryan U15 30.12.86, WGreen & Ex L :
LJ - 5.90, PenB - 2565

SHEERAN Richard U15 27.11.85, Sale :
400 - 52.20, 800 - 2:00.91
SHEPHERD Alan 28.04.69, Morpeth/Army :
5k - 14:33.86 (14:32.9-97), 5MR - 23:53,
10MR - 49:06, HMar - 1:04:36, Mar - 2:19:29
SHEPHERD Bruce David 20.03.67, Aberdeen :
HT - 49.08 (53.18-96)
SHEPHERD Dominic 11.12.76, City of Stoke :
PV - 4.65i (4.90-94)
SHEPPARD Kevin U23 21.01.79, Army :
2kSt - 5:53.32, 3kSt - 9:24.0
SHERIDAN Mark D. 17.06.70, Crawley :
HT - 52.58 (56.02-91)
SHERMAN Andrew U20 28.09.81, Swindon :
800 - 1:52.23, 1500 - 3:55.12
SHERRATT Jonathan U17 18.10.83, Cann & St :
100 - 11.1
SHIELDS David U13, :
HJ - 1.55
SHONE Matthew 10.07.75, WGreen & Ex L :
800 - 1:49.25 (1:47.99-99), 1500 - 3:51.56
SHOWELL Gavin 29.09.72, Tamworth :
PV - 4.75
SICHEL William Morley V45 1.10.53, Moray RR :
24Hr - 246.704km
SILLAH-FRECKLETON Mohammed U23
11.09.80, Blackheath : 60H - 8.09i,
110H - 14.6 (14.6/14.65-99)
SIMKINS Matthew U20 9.05.82, Solihull & SH :
1500 - 3:53.82
SIMNER Paul U15 13.12.85, Tipton :
1500 - 4:15.51
SIMON Delroy U23 27.11.78, Harrow :
3kSt - 9:00.81
SIMONS Paul 4.04.64, Shaftesbury Barnet :
Mar - 2:29:55 (2:23:49-94)
SIMPKINS Matthew U20 9.05.82, S & S H :
800 - 1:54.47
SIMPSON Jonathan U20 27.05.82, Falkirk/Bel :
400 - 48.86 (48.7-99)
SIMPSON Nathaniel U15 15.09.85, Belgrave :
80HB - 11.38, PenB - 2755w/2735
SIMPSON Neil U17 11.09.83, Blackheath :
400 - 50.51
SIMPSON Scott E. U23 21.07.79, Wx & Bath :
PV - 5.10i/4.90 (5.00-99)
SINCLAIR Dean U17 17.12.84, Harrow :
OctY - 4203
SINCLAIR Graham 21.05.73, Enf & Har :
SP - 14.32
SINCLAIR James U13 22.10.87, Morpeth :
200 - 25.5
SINER Neil U17 27.01.84, Liverpool H :
1500 - 4:06.9
SKEETE John U23 8.09.78, Harrow/Falkirk :
60 - 6.74i, 100 - 10.51 (10.5w-98),
200 - 21.3/21.37w/21.45
SKELTON Matthew 8.11.72, Shaft Barnet :
1500 - 3:51.23 (3:41.8-96),
1M - 4:09.6 (4:05.0-96)
SKETCHLEY David 25.02.76, Team Solent :
JT - 62.01
SKILLING Michael U17 18.05.84, Shettleston :
400HY - 58.43
SKINNER Michael U23 21.11.79, Blackh/
Brun U : 800 - 1:50.79, 1500 - 3:46.66
SLATER Ashley U20 23.09.81, Cannock & St :
HT - 47.66 (50.59-99), HTJ - 56.30 (56.88-99)
SLEEMAN Christopher J. U23 20.03.80,
Tonbridge/Oxford Univ :
110H - 15.6, 400H - 53.0/53.94
SLYTHE Paul J. 5.09.74, Newham & Essex B :
400 - 47.36i/47.53 (45.94-98)
SMALE Chris 10.10.63, City of Hull :
3kSt - 9:29.4
SMALL Mark U15 17.10.85, Birchfield :
100 - 11.49
SMALL Michael V45 31.03.54, Belgrave :
SP - 13.75, DT - 42.82 (45.40-85),
HT - 48.94 (49.98-86)
SMALL Vernon U20 1.01.82, Enf & Har :
400H - 57.0
SMART Michael U15 18.11.85, Harrow :
800 - 2:02.7, 1500 - 4:12.60, 3k - 9:01.80
SMITH Alistair U17 22.02.84, AF&D :
1.5kSt - 4:31.53
SMITH Andrew U17 2.10.84, Middlesbro & C :
HTY - 47.47
SMITH Anthony U20 11.01.83, Thurrock :
SPJ - 14.02, DT - 41.16, DTJ - 44.42
SMITH Ashley U17 21.02.84, Cheltenham :
HTY - 49.21
SMITH Carl Anthony V40 17.05.58,
Shaftesbury B . JT - 00.03 (09.94r-01)
SMITH Cameron U17 17.01.84, Cardiff :
3kW - 13:05.18, 5kW - 23:48.30
SMITH Christopher U23 26.04.79, Liv H :
100 - 10.8, 200 - 22.0, 400 - 48.16
SMITH Colin P. V40 11.09.57, Portsmouth :
SP - 13.79 (15.54-89), HT - 47.33 (48.98-89)
SMITH David 21.06.62, North East SH :
HT - 55.21 (77.30-85)
SMITH David W. 2.11.74, Belgrave :
HT - 68.02 (75.10-96)
SMITH Gary 20.02.71, Luton :
LJ - 7.58w/7.08 (7.49-97)
SMITH Glen Ernest 21.05.72, Birchfield :
SP - 14.01 (14.71-96), DT - 63.08 (65.11-99)
SMITH Gregory U17 29.01.84, Bournemouth :
100HY - 13.59
SMITH Kenneth M. 10.05.64, Tipton :
HT - 47.72 (56.28-85)
SMITH Leigh Matthew U20 24.09.82, Birch :
LJ - 7.29
SMITH Mark 14.09.74, Harrow :
HJ - 2.05 (2.07-91)
SMITH Matthew 26.12.74, Tipton :
1500 - 3:47.36 (3:45.59-97),
3k - 8:06.33i (7:58.15i-98/7:59.23-99),
10kR - 29:36, 3kSt - 8:53.23
SMITH Michael U23 3.06.79, Bolton :
100 - 10.8/10.85
SMITH Michael John 20.04.63, Coventry RWC :
50kW - 4:51:31 (4:09:22-89)
SMITH Richard William U20 17.01.81,
Peterbro : PV - 4.80 (4.90-99)
SMITH Richard U20 12.10.82, Middlesbro & C :
400H - 54.79
SMITH Robert U17 3.03.85, Colchester & T :
400 - 50.04
SMITH Robert U20 3.12.82, Basildon :
800 - 1:54.3, 1500 - 3:53.81, 1M - 4:14.20,
3k - 8:38.3, 2kSt - 6:14.5
SMITH Robin Alistair U17 11.09.83, C of Stoke :
100HY - 13.78, OctY - 4916

SMITH Rory U17 12.12.84, Wirral :
800 - 1:55.90, 1500 - 4:01.28, 3k - 8:59.81
SMITH Roy 5.10.62, Blackheath :
10k - 32:00.3
SMITH Steven 23.10.74, Windsor S & E :
3kSt - 9:05.7
SMITH Wesley U23 26.02.79, Belgrave :
JT - 60.86
SMY David U15 3.03.86, Norwich :
LJ - 5.99
SMYTH Jeremy U23 11.08.78, Orkney Isl :
JT - 59.95
SNOOK Christopher U23 6.06.79, Mand/CUAC :
HT - 46.87 (48.59-98)
SNOW Michael U20 5.09.82, Northampton :
400 - 49.09 (48.69-99)
SNOW Shane 31.10.66, Highgate Harriers :
Mar - 2:26:51
SNOW Tom U15 7.09.85, WGreen & Ex L :
800 - 1:59.2, 1500 - 4:09.08, 3k - 8:53.66
SOALLA-BELL Anthony 3.10.76, S B/SLE :
SP - 15.30i/15.16 (15.89-99)
SOAME Marc U13 16.10.87, Chelmsford :
80HC - 13.8, HJ - 1.60
SOLLITT Gary 13.01.72, Team Solent :
SP - 16.95 (17.29i 99/17.14-97)
SOOS Ricky U20 28.06.83, Mansfield :
800 - 1:51.22, 1500 - 3:47.36, 2kSt - 5:49.9
SOUGRIN Neil 14.05.71, Enf & Har :
DT - 43.22 (47.82-94)
SOUTHWARD Anthony 31.01.71, Trafford :
110H - 14.9w/14.92w/15.1 (14.6w-98/14.69-96),
PV - 4.20 (4.40-96), SP - 13.58 (13.82-96),
DT - 42.17 (43.46-98)
SPEAIGHT Neil Anthony U23 9.09.78, S & NH/
Brunel Univ : 800 - 1:48.74 (1:48.1-99)
SPEAKE William J. 24.01.71, Bilderston B :
Mar - 2:29:09 (2:26:49-94)
SPENCER Robert U17 4.10.83, Skyrac :
1500 - 4:05.0
SPICER Matthew William 18.05.71, Bristol :
HT - 46.80 (60.26jr?-90/59.68-96)
SPIVEY Philip 15.05.61, Belgrave/AUS :
HT - 58.61 (70.94-86)
SPRIGINGS Grant Gerald U20 26.11.82, Bel :
SPJ - 13.58i
SPRINGETT Matthew U15 12.01.86, Tonbridge :
80HB - 11.89w/12.03
SQUIRE Derrick John Preston U17 7.12.83,
Cann & Staff : SP - 13.28, SPJ - 14.77,
SPY - 17.61, DTY - 45.24,
HTJ - 50.30, HTY - 60.92 (60.94-99)
SQUIRRELL John 16.12.75, Belgrave :
400H - 55.52
STAINES Gary Martin 3.07.63, S London :
5MR - 23:47 (22:57+-93)
STAMP Terence 18.02.70, Newham & E B :
60 - 6.88i (6.70i-98),
100 - 10.58w/10.6/10.66 (10.4-97/10.47-95)
STANIFORTH David V40 15.11.59, Sheff RWC :
3kW - 13:48.1 (12:19.0-87)
STANNARD Josh U13 15.10.87, Taunton :
JTC - 37.90
STARBUCK Chris V40 8.12.60, Army :
Mar - 2:29:58 (2:26:21-93)
STARK Graeme 12.10.63, Rotherham :
SP - 13.71 (14.88i-94/14.70-85)
STARK William 11.03.77, Aberdeen :
LJ - 6.93i (7.07w/7.06-95)
STARNES Andrew U15 18.09.85, Camb H :
400 - 53.1
STASAITIS Reginaldas 6.04.67,
N Lond & Mus Hill/LIT : HJ - 2.00 (2.08-84),
LJ - 7.02, TJ - 15.35 (15.62w/15.53-99)
STEADMAN Darren U15 26.01.87, Colch H :
HJ - 1.75
STEBBINGS Simon 23.04.71, Luton :
800 - 1:52.6 (1:49.91-93), 1500 - 3:48.81
STEELE Laurence U15 24.04.86, Blackpool :
PV - 3.10
STEINLE Mark 22.11.74, Blackheath :
5k - 14:04e (13:58.42-99), 10k - 28:04.48,
10MR - 49:52 (48:25-98),
HMar - 1:04:40 (1:02:23-99), Mar - 2:11:18
STENNETT Kori 2.09.76, Cheltenham :
TJ - 14.02i (15.02-94)
STEPHEN Jamie U17 27.09.83, Black Isle :
1.5kSt - 4:37.60
STEPHENS Gavin James 12.09.77, Worthing/
Brunel Univ : 100 - 10.8,
200 - 21.57w/22.00, 400H - 55.5
STEPHENSON Christian 22.07.74, Cardiff :
1500 - 3:48.95 (3:43.85-98), 1M - 4:00.4,
3k - 7:53.23, 3kSt - 8:25.37
STEPHENSON James U17 16.10.84, Millf'ld S :
800 - 1:57.87
STEVENS Kyle U17 3.06.85, Sutton & District :
SPY - 14.19
STEVENS Paul U17 15.11.83, City of Hull :
PV - 4.50
STEVENSON Gary U23 12.09.79, Kilbarchan :
400H - 55.26
STEVENSON James U15 6.10.85, Stroud :
HJ - 1.75io, LJ - 5.92
STEWART Camara U17 11.09.83, Notts :
HJ - 1.95
STEWART Craig U15 24.11.85, Kilbarchan :
800 - 2:02.78
STEWART Glen 7.12.70, RRC :
1500 - 3:46.28 (3:38.66-96),
3k - 7:56.80 (7:55.15-99), 5k - 13:38.37,
10kR - 29:26 (28:52sh-98)
STEWART Henry U17 16.12.83, Liv.Pembr S :
1500 - 4:04.4, 1.5kSt - 4:38.0
STEWART John U23 30.12.79, Sale/Loughbro :
60 - 6.82i, 100 - 10.40 (10.36w-99),
200 - 20.83, 300 - 34.63i (33.93-98),
400 - 48.18i (52.5/52.77-96)
STEWART Jonathan U23 22.05.80, Halifax :
800 - 1:49.53
STICKINGS Nigel 1.04.71, Newham & E B :
60 - 6.93i (6.85i-93),
100 - 10.59 (10.4w-92/10.56w-93),
200 - 21.03w/21.29 (20.84w-93/21.0-92/21.14-93)
STILL Matthew U23 1.12.79, Bas & MH :
400 - 49.04
STIRLING Grant 18.03.75, Tonbridge :
LJ - 6.98
STOBART Christopher U20 27.03.82, Manx :
100 - 10.77 (10.7wdb?-98/10.73w-99)
STOCKS Brett 16.06.74, Sheffield :
1500 - 3:51.32 (3:49.2-99)
STODDART Dwayne U23 29.12.80, W S & E :
60H - 8.3i/8.33i, 110H - 14.51w/14.59

STOKER Chris U17 11.12.83, Sunderland :
800 - 1:57.5
STOKES Stuart 15.12.76, Sale/Edge Hill Un :
1500 - 3:48.27, 3k - 8:20.0 (8:17.0-99),
3kSt - 8:33.61
STONE Darrell Richard 2.02.68, Steyning :
3kW - 12:40.30+ (11:49.0-90),
10kWR - 42:22+ (40:45-89),
20kW - 1:27:08 (1:23:27un-93/1:23:58-96),
50kW - 4:21:23 (4:10:23-90)
STONE Darryl Frank U20 6.06.83, Basildon :
HJ - 2.10
STOPHER Brian U23 8.04.80, AF&D/
St Mark & St John Un : 800 - 1:52.94
STOTT Adrian V45 5.08.54, Sri Chinmoy :
24Hr - 230.667km
STOVES Christopher U17 20.02.84, Lancs & M :
400 - 50.1 (53.04-98), 800 - 1:52.69,
1500 - 3:57.70
STROUD Guy U13 9.08.88, Newquay & Par :
75HC - 12.8
STUART Alan U20 14.08.81, Shettleston :
100 - 10.9, 200 - 21.54, 400 - 48.16
STYLES Iain Bruce 2.10.75, Chelt/Birm Univ. :
SP - 14.36i/14.28, DT - 42.72
SUMMERS James Alexander Edward 7.10.65,
R Navy : HT - 47.70 (58.86un-87/55.78-88)
SURETY Steven Christopher U23 18.02.80,
Basildon/Brunel U : 400 - 49.0, 400H - 52.39
SUTTON Adam C. U20 22.03.81, Preston/
Providence Un : 3k - 8:15.00i
SUTTON Matthew U20 8.09.81, Birchfield :
HT - 57.64, HTJ - 61.64 (64.00-98)
SWAIN Anthony Michael 17.01.75, Bord/Hudd U :
HT - 56.69 (62.88-97)
SWAIN Ashley U23 3.10.80, Team Solent/
Staffs Univ : PV - 5.00i/4.90 (4.90-99)
SWARAY Tyrone 7.11.77, Blackheath :
60 - 6.9i/6.95i (6.9i-98),
100 - 10.94 (10.56-99)
SWEENEY Joe U15 8.10.85, Blackheath :
1500 - 4:20.34
SWEENEY Joseph Leonard 17.07.65, W S & E :
LJ - 7.28 (7.41-87), TJ - 15.11 (16.26-91)
SWEENEY Mark 26.02.77, Notts/Birm Univ. :
110H - 14.8/15.19w/15.26 (15.13w-98),
HJ - 2.00 (2.00i/2.00-97), Dec - 6862w/6752
SWEETMAN David 27.01.71, Charnwood :
110H - 15.0 (14.22w/14.43-98)
SWIFT-SMITH Justin 28.08.74, Shaft Barnet :
800 - 1:48.28 (1:47.9-97), 1500 - 3:42.59,
1M - 4:02.45, 3k - 8:13.32
SYERS Aidan U20 29.06.83, Croydon :
100 - 10.71w/10.89
SYKES Sean U17 13.10.83, Chichester :
400HY - 57.59
SYMESTER Lance U15 5.07.86, Orion :
DTB - 41.89

TABARES Ruben U23 22.10.78, Blackh :
60 - 6.94i, 200 - 21.94i/21.94,
400 - 48.4 (48.01-97)
TALBOT Nicholas P. 14.12.77, Notts/Oxf Univ :
3kSt - 9:13.02 (8:55.59-99)
TANNER Alex U23 29.12.78, Enf & Har :
800 - 1:52.80
TANSER Toby 21.07.68, Sparvagens :
Mar - 2:26:57 (2:18:02-97)
TARGATT Michael U17 1.02.84, Swansea :
1.5kSt - 4:35.39
TARRAN Michael U23 10.12.80, Birchfield :
JT - 64.25
TASKER Bruce U13 2.09.87, Carmarthen :
LJ - 5.07
TATTERSHALL James U20 25.11.81, Roth :
110H - 15.58w
TATTON Allistair U15 9.01.86, Falkirk :
100 - 11.6 (14.22-97)
TAYLOR David William 9.01.64, Blackheath :
10kR - 29:58 (29:02-97),
HMar - 1:05:51 (1:03:24-97),
Mar - 2:22:47 (2:13:27-97)
TAYLOR Gregg 1.08.77, Traff/Chester Un :
800 - 1:50.63, 1500 - 3:44.79
TAYLOR Ian J. 2.07.67, Telford :
DT - 45.64 (49.44-93)
TAYLOR James U20 24.04.82, Hallamshire :
DT - 40.01, DTJ - 43.95
TAYLOR Martin J.M. U20 31.01.82, Vic PAAC :
110H - 15.3/15.63, 400H - 56.89,
LJ - 7.47, JT - 53.90, Dec - 6470
TAYLOR Nigel 12.06.69, Norwich :
110H - 15.5w/15.57w/15.6 (15.6-99)
TAYLOR Paul Thomas 9.01.66, Border :
10kR - 29:45 (27:49RL-96/28:32-94)
TAYLOR Peter U15 19.11.85, Dacorum & Tring :
JTB - 44.07
TAYLOR Philip U17 6.02.84, Cannock & St :
HJ - 1.90, OctY - 4350
TAYLOR Rhys U20 25.09.82, Carmarthen :
JT - 55.71
TAYLOR Richard 5.12.73, Coventry Godiva :
5k - 14:31.29 (13:54.18-99)
TAYLOR Robert Wesley James U23 9.06.80,
Wakefield : HT - 49.65
TAYLOR Scott U23 28.07.78, Leics WC :
3kW - 13:48.01i (13:10.3-98)
TAYLOR Thomas U20 30.01.81, Roadhogs :
10kW - 49:38.77 (45:56.16-98),
10kWR - 45:20 (45:03-98)
TEASEL Oliver James U17 24.04.84,
Chesterfield : 400HY - 56.79
TEDD Phil J.A. 7.11.76, Bingley/Camb Un :
800 - 1:52.8, 1500 - 3:43.54, 1M - 4:07.52
TEJAN COLE Kamil U17 21.01.85, Herne Hill :
200 - 22.51
THACKERY Carl Edward 14.10.62,
Hallamshire : HMar - 1:05:30 (1:01:04-87),
Mar - 2:19:57 (2:12:37-92)
THANDA Lekeladio 'Bob' U15 22.09.85,
Havering : 400 - 52.05
THATCHER Noel 13.05.66, Newham & E B :
10k - 31:50.3
THICKPENNY Robert 17.07.76, Peterborough :
PV - 4.70i/4.62 (4.80-99)
THIE James U23 27.06.78, Cardiff/UWIC :
800 - 1:50.52, 1500 - 3:42.85, 1M - 4:01.7,
3k - 8:16.32i (8:16.12-98)
THOM Douglas 13.04.68, B & A/Border :
400H - 54.74 (52.18-97)
THOMAS Andrew U20 29.01.81, Invicta :
2kSt - 6:03.87 (5:59.62-99), 3kSt - 9:27.03
THOMAS Andrew 9.02.74, Llanelli :
LJ - 7.16w/7.13
THOMAS Andrew U15 14.06.86, Birchfield :
SPB - 13.19, DTB - 46.55

THOMAS Barry V.S. 28.04.72, Sheffield :
110H - 15.25 (14.62w-95/14.81-92),
PV - 4.70 (5.00-92), LJ - 6.98 (7.44-92),
SP - 13.89 (14.06-96), DT - 40.30 (42.21-98),
JT - 57.74 (62.40-97), Dec - 7407 (7766-95)
THOMAS Darryl U13 23.11.87, Ealing,S & Mx :
LJ - 5.28
THOMAS Iwan Gwyn 5.01.74, Newham & E B :
200 - 21.69 (20.87-97), 400 - 45.82 (44.36-97)
THOMAS Joselyn 11.07.71, WG&EL/Army/SLE :
60 - 6.80i (6.77i-98),
100 - 10.8w (10.3w/10.36w-98/10.51-97)
THOMAS Josephus ¶ 11.07.71, WG & Ex L/
Army/SLE : 60 - 6.66ir/6.69i (6.66i-97),
100 - 10.5drg/10.65drg (10.19w-98/10.2-96/10.29-98),
200 - 22.0wdrg (20.49w-98/20.6-96/20.75-97)
THOMAS Julian U15 28.12.86, Birchfield :
200 - 23.38
THOMAS Keith U17 15.11.83, Birchfield :
PV - 3.72
THOMAS Martin U23 21.09.78, Liverpool H :
400H - 54.67 (53.52-97)
THOMAS Nicholas U23 4.04.79, N & E B :
60 - 6.8i/6.86i, 100 - 10.61,
200 - 21.9 (21.97w/22.11-97),
LJ - 7.13 (7.24w-99), TJ - 16.31
THOMAS Paul U23 1.10.80, Team Solent :
PV - 4.46i/4.20 (4.40-99)
THOMAS Simon David U20 4.03.81, Southend/
Camb Univ : HJ - 2.05 (2.10-99)
THOMAS Timothy Paul 18.11.73, Cardiff :
PV - 5.40 (5.40-97)
THOMAS Wayne 21.02.68, Swansea :
Mar - 2:34:13
THOMPSON Anthony 9.11.77, Border :
800 - 1:52.23 (1:49.8-98)
THOMPSON Christopher U20 17.04.81, AF&D :
800 - 1:53.5, 1500 - 3:44.66,
3k - 8:04.93, 5k - 14:06.52,
2kSt - 5:59.1 (5:57.05-98)
THOMPSON Darren U23 6.11.79, Belgrave :
LJ - 7.48 (7.56-98)
THOMPSON Gavin U23 9.04.80, Crawley :
1500 - 3:50.65 (3:47.20-99)
THOMPSON Guy U17 20.09.84, Border :
1500 - 4:06.0
THOMPSON Kevin U17 24.10.83, Liverpool H :
LJ - 6.51w, TJ - 14.41
THOMPSON Matthew U20 20.09.81, Yate :
800 - 1:52.21
THOMPSON Matthew U17 29.12.84, Black I/
N S P : 100HY - 14.11, SPY - 14.00i
THOMPSON Michael 14.09.68, Sunderland :
Mar - 2:27:06 (2:25:22-99)
THOMPSON Neville Leigh V45 28.03.55, S B :
DT - 53.00 (55.68-93)
THOMPSON Ross U20 7.12.81, Gateshead :
HT - 56.50 (57.38-99), HTJ - 61.39 (64.28-99)
THOMPSON Russell U17 9.09.83, Halesowen :
PV - 3.70
THOMPSON Scot William U20 10.08.81, Pitr/
Bel/Bath U : SP - 15.00, SPJ - 16.28,
DT - 50.07, DTJ - 53.62, HTJ - 48.88
THOMPSON Scott 29.09.74, Gateshead :
HT - 50.82 (54.22-94)
THOMSON David V40 18.09.59, Portsmouth :
Mar - 2:29:28 (2:26:02-99)

THORN Darren Michael M. 17.07.62, Cov RWC :
3kW - 13:26.3 (12:15.0-89)
THORNE-LADEJO Du'aine 14.02.71, Birch :
100 - 10.7w/10.92 (10.28w/10.45-98),
200 - 21.67i+ (20.96-93),
400 - 46.4/46.61 (44.66-96), 400H - 50.09
THURGOOD Matthew U17 29.12.83, Verlea :
TJ - 13.47i (13.72w/13.63w?/13.52-99)
THURGOOD Stuart Dennis 17.05.76,
Loughbro/N & E B : HT - 56.91
TICKNER Ben U20 13.07.81, Wells/Okla St Un :
1500 - 3:54.00, 5k - 15:00.16
TICKNER Frank U17 12.10.83, Wells :
3k - 8:56.53
TIETZ Michael 14.09.77, Birchfield :
60 - 6.81i (6.75i-99),
200 - 22.18i (21.40w-99/21.53-98)
TIMMS Anthony U13 4.03.88, Pudsey & Bram :
LJ - 5.05, DTC - 26.43
TINDAL Lee U23 19.02.80, Chich/Chich Univ :
110H - 14.86, 400H - 55.77
TINSLEY Ian U20 23.01.81, Liverpool H :
400 - 48.18
TIPTON Carl 4.02.77, Tipton/Man Univ :
800 - 1:52.34
TITMUS Philip U20 12.11.81, Cheltenham :
DTJ - 41.50
TOBIN Robert John U17 20.12.83, Bas& MH :
200 - 22.1, 400 - 48.22, 800 - 1:54.96
TOBIN Shaun 13.10.62, Swansea :
10k - 31:24.4 (30:23.37-96),
Mar - 2:33:01 (2:21:53-96)
TODD Stuart U13 4.09.87, Victoria Park AAC :
75HC - 12.7
TOHILL Paul U20 9.10.82, Mid Ulster :
110HJ - 15.0/15.08, 110H - 15.48,
HJ - 2.01, Dec - 5360, DecJ - 5597
TOIA Bekele 10.01.70, Hercules Wimb/ETH :
JT - 57.95
TOMASI Vito U13 17.01.88, Guernsey :
400 - 62.2, 80HC - 13.0, LJ - 5.11
TOMKINSON Timothy 31.10.68, Sale/Army :
110H - 15.4w (14.5-92/14.74w-93/14.88-97)
TOMLINSON Christopher U20 15.09.81,
Mandale : 100 - 10.92, LJ - 7.62,
TJ - 15.31i/15.15
TOMPSON Stephen U20 5.12.82, Camb & C :
800 - 1:51.64
TOMS Robert U23 7.08.80, W S & E/UWIC :
HJ - 2.02i/2.00 (2.05-97)
TONNER James 3.06.75, Kilmarnock/Border/
Strathclyde Univ : 3k - 8:18.82i
TORRY Paul U20 17.10.82, Ellon :
Dec - 5125
TOWNSEND Craig U23 1.12.80, Sale :
100 - 10.8w (11.5-97)
TOWNSEND Richard U20 1.03.82, Milton K :
DecJ - 5215
TOYE Simon U15 24.09.85, Thurrock :
400 - 52.36
TREMAYNE Christopher U17 11.11.84,
Cannock & Stafford : PV - 4.30
TRESSIDER Ross U17 8.11.83, Thurrock :
100HY - 13.79, 400HY - 56.7/57.49,
OctY - 4578
TRIGELL Tristan U15 7.12.85, Andover :
100 - 11.5

TRIMMER Richard U17 7.09.83, Bournem'th :
SPY - 15.18
TROMANS Glynn 17.03.69, Coventry Godiva :
3k - 8:05.45 (7:58.31-99),
5k - 13:57.31 (13:44.27-99),
5MR - 23:49 (23:38-99), 10MR - 48:36 (47:25-98),
10k - 29:05.28 (28:21.07-99),
TSHAYE Amanuel U17 15.11.83, Croydon :
800 - 1:58.3
TUFTON Kevin U23 30.04.80, Hav/Brunel Un :
PV - 4.20 (4.20-99)
TULBA Phillip William 20.09.73, Bas & MH/
Loughbro : 800 - 1:49.76 (1:48.31-98),
1500 - 3:43.56 (3:42.3-98),
3k - 8:14.8 (8:06.51i-99)
TULLETT Ian Roger 15.08.69, Belgrave :
PV - 5.20 (5.35-98)
TUNNICLIFFE Simon U20 2.03.83, Nuneaton :
400 - 49.33i/49.4 (48.46-99)
TUOHY Paul U20 18.03.81, Cannock & Staff/
Loughbro : LJ - 7.04w/6.88
TURAY Sanusi 14.04.68, TVH/SLE :
100 - 10.78w/10.81 (10.2w-98/10.24w/10.25-96),
110H - 15.17
TURNBULL Gareth U23 14.05.79, St
Malachy's/Loughborough Studnts/IRE :
800 - 1:48.8 (1:48.57-99/1:55.13un-95),
1500 - 3:39.08, 1M - 3:57.89,
3k - 8:08.03i (8:06.49i/8:09.29-99)
TURNER Andrew 29.08.63, Bournemouth :
SP - 14.59 (14.86i-96/14.74-94),
DT - 45.57 (47.40-95), HT - 50.13 (51.76-96)
TURNER Andrew D. U23 19.09.80, Notts/
Loughbro : 60H - 8.27i, 110H - 14.77,
LJ - 7.16 (7.23w-97)
TURNER Clayton S. 9.01.68, Horsham BS :
SP - 13.36 (15.52-91)
TURNER Clive U17 24.11.84, Enf & Har :
100 - 10.96w/11.10, 200 - 22.5/22.55
TURNER Daniel U23 27.11.78, Team Solent :
HJ - 2.12 (2.15-97)
TURNER David V40 20.10.57, York CIU :
3kW - 13:50.0 (13:25.07-94),
50kW - 4:56:59 (4:45:56-91)
TURNER David James U17 4.07.84, Blackpool :
JTY - 52.72
TURNER Douglas 2.12.66, Cardiff :
100 - 10.53 (10.26w-96/10.40-97),
200 - 20.88w/21.01 (20.36w-97/20.43-96)
TURNER James U20 12.08.83, Nuneaton :
JT - 58.81
TURVILL Steven 17.02.75, Basingstoke & MH :
800 - 1:51.12
TWIDALE Paul U15 30.09.86, Cleethorpes :
400 - 53.03, LJ - 6.05
TWIGG Matthew 18.07.69, Rugby :
SP - 14.35 (15.05-98), DT - 48.74 (49.42-91)
TYDEMAN James U17 4.10.83, Basildon :
800 - 1:58.5, 1500 - 4:03.07
TYPE Christopher U20 5.10.81, Cardiff :
PV - 4.80i (4.70-99)

UDECHUKU Emeka U23 10.07.79, Blackh/
Loughbro : SP - 18.10, DT - 62.07,
JT - 57.64 (61.16-98)
UGONO Uvie U23 8.03.78, WGreen & Ex L :
60 - 6.78i (6.70i-99), 200 - 20.89w/21.08,
100 - 10.36 (10.32w-98)
URQUHART Ronald John 14.11.77, Belgrave :
HT - 53.19 (61.70-98)
URSELL Nangeloum U20 1.10.81, Blackheath :
400H - 53.06 (52.87-99)
USHER Kevin 3.11.65, Hounslow :
3kSt - 9:27.9 (9:03.3-90)
UZOR Reginald U17 19.02.85, London Sch :
100 - 11.1

VAIL Jack U17 30.09.83, Brighton :
1500 - 4:06.69
VALE Matthew U15 3.09.85, Wrexham :
800 - 2:05.4
VAN DER MERWE Alan U17 5.01.84, Exeter :
JT - 56.48, JTY - 59.83
VAN GROT Rudi 29.11.74, Newc Univ/HOL :
3kSt - 9:12.48
VAN HUYSSTEEN Andrew 17.02.77, Wok/RSA :
JT - 57.19
VAN WELL Oliver U15 16.12.85, :
100 - 11.4/11.55, 200 - 23.33
VANDENBERG Adam Philip U17 2.06.84,
AF&D : 800 - 1:56.06, 1500 - 3:59.60
VANDESCHANS Matthew U13, Thurrock :
3k - 10:10.1
VANHINSBERGH Thomas U23 28.12.78,
Crawley : HJ - 1.95 (2.07-97)
VARANAUSKAS Gintaras 17.04.72, S B/LIT :
HJ - 1.95 (2.10-99)
VASS David U15 31.12.85, West Norfolk :
400 - 51.09
VAUX-HARVEY Matthew 30.03.76, Stourport :
5k - 14:13.30 (14:06.99-99),
5MR - 23:56, 10kR - 29:31,
10MR - 49:32, HMar - 1:04:28
VENGDASALAM Natham 11.03.64, Liv.Pem S :
10k - 31:25.2, Mar - 2:25:14
VERNON Chris U15 29.11.85, Nuneaton :
PenB - 2503
VICKERS Gary 26.02.71, Telford :
800 - 1:50.51
VICKERS Peter U17 11.06.84, Mandale :
100 - 11.04
VIGGARS Ben U15 24.10.85, S Yorks Sch :
HJ - 1.75
VINCE Nicholas U20 29.01.82, Falkirk :
SP - 13.55, SPJ - 14.50, DT - 40.34
VINCENT Martin U15 12.04.86, Rugby :
PV - 3.00
VYSNIAKAS Saulius U23 1.07.79, Worth/LIT :
110H - 15.2

WADDINGTON Anthony 30.06.75, Lut :
100 - 10.61 (10.6-99), 200 - 21.68
WADE Thomas U17 31.12.83, Liv.Pemb S :
1.5kSt - 4:32.0
WAIN Andrew 2.06.65, Nene Vallley H :
SP - 14.25 (14.86-99), DT - 42.08
WAKE Andrew 14.09.68, Morpeth :
PV - 4.50 (4.63i/4.50-87)
WALCOTT Andrew 11.01.75, Belgrave :
200 - 21.75w (21.15-96), 400 - 48.53
WALDEN Matthew U17 30.11.83, Scunthorpe :
100HY - 14.2, LJ - 6.64,
TJ - 13.55w/13.51 (13.64w?/13.51-99),
OctY - 4894
WALES Alan U17 7.08.85, Ellon :
1.5kSt - 4:39.68

WALISMBI Geoffrey 27.02.74, Thames Valley :
100 - 10.79w
WALKER Adam U23 16.11.79, Craw/Loughbro :
PV - 4.20 (4.20i-98/4.20-99)
WALKER Alvin 30.04.65, N & E B/Army :
LJ - 6.84 (7.38-97),
TJ - 14.69 (15.71w/15.56-98)
WALKER Ben T. U23 8.06.78, Dacorum & T :
DT - 40.32 (44.26-96)
WALKER John U17 4.03.85, Greenock Glenp :
1.5kSt - 4:39.44
WALKER Leigh 17.08.77, Crawley :
PV - 4.90
WALKER Nicholas O. 24.02.64, Severn :
Dec - 5284 (5510-92)
WALKER Paul 2.12.73, City of Edinburgh :
800 - 1:50.8 (1:46.4-97)
WALKER Paul James U17 15.08.85, Cardiff :
PV - 3.90
WALKER Stuart U23 22.09.78, Derby & Co :
JT - 58.29 (58.94-96)
WALL Terry 12.06.70, Morpeth :
10k - 31:35.3 (29:53.0-97), HMar - 1:06:43
WALLACE John 9.10.68, Morpeth :
HJ - 2.00 (2.16-90)
WALLACE Jonathan U23 1.01.79, Birchfield :
TJ - 15.25 (15.82-98)
WALLING Andrew David 3.04.73, Sale :
800 - 1:52.28 (1:50.6-95), 1500 - 3:47.61
WALMSLEY Dennis 5.09.62, Bourton RR :
Mar - 2:30:34 (2:21:19-95)
WALSH Christopher U23 1.10.78, Shaft Barn :
HT - 60.53
WALSH Edward U15 21.10.85, Belgrave :
80HB - 11.49w/11.72
WALSH Peter U23 5.05.80, Liverpool H :
800 - 1:50.92
WALTER Bill U15 11.10.85, Bournemouth :
SPB - 14.93
WALTERS Lee U15 1.06.86, Leics Cor :
400 - 53.1
WARD Ashley Keith 1.08.64, Crawley :
SP - 13.44 (14.12-92), DT - 44.21 (47.70-82)
WARD Christopher James U17 8.04.84, Wells :
1.5kSt - 4:39.05
WARD Jonathan 25.11.65, Ashford :
SP - 14.22i/13.64, DT - 44.55
WARD Ray 22.08.75, Sheffield :
1500 - 3:50.51
WARD Richard James Stephen U20 5.05.82,
Sutton & District : 800 - 1:52.86,
1500 - 3:49.4, 3k - 8:24.73, 5k - 15:33.00
WARD-DAVIES Joel U17 9.02.84, Hereford :
PV - 3.70
WARDLE Dave 1.10.75, Chester Le Street :
5k - 14:28.47
WARISO Solomon Christopher 11.11.66,
Enf & Har : 200 - 21.7 (20.50-95),
400 - 46.14 (44.68-98)
WARKE Peter U15 22.05.86, Lagan Valley :
400 - 53.41, 800 - 2:02.72, LJ - 5.90io
WARMBY Mark U23 12.12.78, Newham & E B :
3kSt - 9:08.38
WARREN Carl 28.09.69, Birchfield :
5k - 14:42.41 (14:34.1-95), 10kR - 29:13un,
HMar - 1:05:40 (1:04:58-99),
Mar - 2:22:04 (2:20:58-99),
3kSt - 9:26.1 (8:40.74-95)
WATKINS Ben U23 12.11.78, Norwich :
200 - 22.0w/22.14w (21.75-98)
WATKINS Jimmy U20, Somerset Sch :
800 - 1:54.43
WATSON Christopher U20 22.05.83, Vic PAAC :
800 - 1:51.63
WATSON Derek U20 22.05.83, Vic Park AAC :
1500 - 3:52.91
WATSON Garth 20.04.73, Newham & E B :
800 - 1:49.05
WATSON N., RAF :
HJ - 1.95i (1.95-98)
WATSON Peter U20 30.06.81, Oxford City :
HJ - 2.00
WATSON Tim 28.06.73, Havant/Royal Navy :
2kSt - 5:57.10, 3kSt - 9:08.83 (9:04.68-99)
WATT Adam U17 29.10.84, Aberdeen :
1.5kSt - 4:34.0
WATT Timothy James 19.09.66, Steyning :
20kW - 1:35:35, 30kW - 2:36:38+,
50kW - 4:23:18 (4:20:43-95)
WATTS Alistair U15 12.06.86, AF&D :
1500 - 4:20.07
WATTS Matthew U15 1.11.85, Enf & Har :
HTB - 46.39
WEAVER Matthew 14.11.73, Harrow :
PV - 5.00 (5.00-99)
WEBB Jamie 18.12.75, Southend :
PV - 4.20 (4.60-97)
WEBB Philip Stephen U23 17.07.78, Peterbro :
200 - 21.31w/21.6/21.66
(21.01w-97/21.31i/21.4-98/21.44-97)
WEIR Andrew 22.08.67, Thames H & H :
Mar - 2:27:17
WEIR Richard U17 7.08.84, Derby & Co :
800 - 1:57.13
WEIR Robert Boyd 4.02.61, Birchfield :
DT - 65.08, HT - 49.43 (75.08-82)
WELLS Louis U23 6.02.78, Enf & Har :
800 - 1:52.8 (1:51.7-99)
WELLS Stuart U23 26.07.79, Havering :
LJ - 7.57w/7.51 (7.68w-99/7.56-97)
WELSH Graeme 8.10.75, Border :
100 - 10.8/10.86w (10.51w/10.56-98)
WELSH Graham U15 24.09.85, Shettleston :
1500 - 4:17.68
WEST Ian U20 23.03.83, Horsham BS :
JT - 54.02
WESTAWAY Ryan U20 2.03.83, Yeovil Oly :
HJ - 1.95i (1.63-97), DecJ - 5291
WESTLAKE Sam U17 14.09.83, N Devon :
SPY - 14.95, DTY - 45.63
WESTMEIJER Jeroen 5.07.70, E & E/HOL :
SP - 14.10
WESTON Paul 6.10.67, Cardiff :
TJ - 14.61w/14.60 (15.64w-98/15.46-92)
WETHERIDGE Nicholas 11.10.72, Basildon :
1500 - 3:50.0, 1M - 4:08.92, 3k - 7:59.35,
5k - 13:59.28 (13:55.57-99),
5MR - 23:35 (23:21-99),
10kR - 29:21, HMar - 1:04:09
WETHERILL Andrew V40 6.12.57, S-in-Ash :
Mar - 2:24:31
WHALLEY Robert Simon 11.02.68, C of Stoke :
1500 - 3:48.35i (3:40.7-96),
1M - 4:08.41 (4:02.1-92),
3k - 7:53.63i (7:51.4-97),
5k - 14:22.82 (13:41.08-97), 5KR - 14:21

WHEATLEY Duncan U20 9.06.81, Border :
HJ - 1.95 (1.97-97)
WHEELER Craig 14.06.76, Trafford :
1500 - 3:49.68 (3:44.7-99), 5k - 14:42.16,
3kSt - 8:39.72 (8:34.67-99)
WHITBY Benedict 6.01.77, Hounslow :
3kSt - 8:44.68 (8:41.79-98)
WHITE Edward 16.11.73, Sale :
60 - 6.98i (6.88i-99),
200 - 21.20w/21.41 (20.61w-99/21.02-97),
300 - 33.51, 400 - 46.56
WHITE Gary U17 16.06.85, Rugby :
TJ - 14.03
WHITE Graham V40 28.03.59, Brighton :
10kWR - 47:56
WHITE Steffan David 21.12.72, Coventry G :
5k - 14:12.99
WHITEHEAD Lee U17 7.03.84, Oldham & R :
400 - 51.05
WHITEHEAD Timmon U20 20.04.82, G & G :
HT - 50.11, HTJ - 59.39dh/56.52
WHITEMAN Anthony William 13.11.71, S B:
800 - 1:45.81, 1500 - 3:34.93 (3:32.34-97),
3k - 7:58.15i/8:01.0 (7:43.61-98), 5KR - 14:07
WHITTEN Michael U17 30.09.83, Gateshead :
DTY - 40.27, JTY - 56.54
WHITTINGHAM Simon U23 18.09.78, Watford :
HJ - 2.00
WHITTLE Robert U20 14.06.81, Bas & MH :
800 - 1:51.76, 1500 - 3:52.5 (3:50.92-99)
WHYTE Stephen Anthony 14.03.64, TVH :
SP - 15.09 (17.78-89),
DT - 44.29 (50.40-94), HT - 55.00 (67.82-89)
WILD James Gary U20 1.10.82, Wakefield :
HJ - 1.98
WILKIE Jack U17 30.07.84, Blackheath :
100 - 11.1w
WILKIN Mitchell U15 6.12.85, Southend :
LJ - 6.51
WILKINS Perriss 12.12.69, Banbury :
SP - 15.29, DT - 64.65 (66.64-98)
WILKINSON Jonathon 17.02.62, Telford :
JT - 63.88
WILLIAMS Allan Peter V45 30.05.53, Camb H :
PV - 4.32i (5.25-77)
WILLIAMS Alun 22.06.62, Norwich/RAF :
SP - 13.31, DT - 40.79 (43.78-96)
WILLIAMS Andy 21.01.77, Sale :
1.5kSt - 4:18.65, 3kSt - 9:17.24
WILLIAMS Anthony Richard 1.05.72, N & E B :
400 - 48.47 (47.63-98),
400H - 53.12 (49.96-99)
WILLIAMS Barrington Chester V45 11.09.55,
Rugby : LJ - 7.02 (8.05i/8.01-89)
WILLIAMS Devlin U17 8.12.83, Barnet :
100 - 11.03 (10.85w-99)
WILLIAMS Edward 1.10.70, Thames Valley :
400 - 48.6 (46.84-94),
800 - 1:49.45 (1:49.41-96)
WILLIAMS Gareth U15 7.10.85, Devon Sch :
SPB - 14.18
WILLIAMS Glenn David U17 24.03.85, Cardiff :
DTY - 47.60, HTY - 52.80
WILLIAMS James John U20 17.07.82, Cardiff :
2kSt - 6:12.4, 3kSt - 9:29.11
WILLIAMS Kevin S. 15.12.71, Cardiff :
60 - 6.76i (6.63i-97), 200 - 21.57 (21.30-97),
100 - 10.5/10.53 (10.30w/10.34-97)
WILLIAMS Matthew U17 31.01.84, Wolves & B :
400HY - 56.99
WILLIAMS Matthew U13 1.02.89, Aberdare :
1500 - 4:36.2
WILLIAMS Nicholas U20 2.02.82, Trafford :
HTJ - 63.20
WILLIAMS Philip J. U17 28.09.84, Rochdale :
1500 - 4:04.68
WILLIAMS Rhys U17 27.02.84, Bridgend :
400 - 49.87,
400HY - 53.84
WILLIAMS Rhys U20 4.10.81, Neath :
JT - 58.48
WILLIAMS Richard U20 22.10.81, Shaft Barn :
2kSt - 5:52.90, 3kSt - 9:15.72
WILLIAMS Simon David U23 5.10.80,
Bas& MH/Brunel U : SP - 13.34, DT - 46.38
WILLIAMS Thomas U17 11.03.84, Notts :
OctY - 4254
WILLIAMSON Lewis U15 7.09.85, Leeds :
DTB - 42.54
WILLIAMSON Paul Lee 16.06.74, TVH :
PV - 5.55
WILLIAMSON Wilby U20 8.08.81, Lagan V :
DecJ - 5258
WILLIS Peter U20 4.05.82, Windsor S & E :
5k - 15:34.8
WILLS Christopher 18.05.76, Birchfield :
PV - 4.40i (4.80-98)
WILLS Matthew Robert U15 6.02.86, Nuneaton :
800 - 2:05.7
WILSON Alloy U23 25.01.80, Blackheath :
60 - 6.9i (6.93i-98)
WILSON Ben U13 1.07.88, AF&D :
1500 - 4:38.8, 1M - 5:10.7, 3k - 9:59.0
WILSON Ben U13 27.10.87, Mandale :
100 - 12.48
WILSON Chris U15 23.09.85, Enf & Har :
PV - 3.20
WILSON Colin 30.10.77, Ealing,S & Mx :
60 - 6.95i
WILSON Gary U15 18.09.85, Belgrave :
LJ - 6.67
WILSON Kevin U20 28.09.82, Chichester :
HJ - 2.02
WILSON Kirk U15 21.12.85, Morpeth :
1500 - 4:21.95
WILSON Martin 3.03.71, Wigtown :
SP - 13.31 (14.24-90), DT - 40.43 (44.86-91)
WILSON Simon 30.04.74, Medway :
400H - 55.19 (54.9-98/55.03-99)
WILSON Vincent 1.04.73, Morpeth :
800 - 1:52.22 (1:48.68-98),
1500 - 3:45.88 (3:43.38-96)
WILTON James U13 1.09.87, Newquay & Par :
PV - 2.00
WINCHCOMBE Nigel Christopher V40
10.12.59, Lincoln Well :
HT - 52.22 (59.18-88)
WINFIELD Phillip U17 10.02.84, Milton Keynes :
800 - 1:57.37
WINSHIP Mark U17 29.09.83, Enf & Har :
400H - 57.6, 400HY - 55.75
WINSPEARE Jonathan U15 18.10.85,
Middlesbro & C : JTB - 44.95
WISCOMBE Lee U23 12.07.80, Jarrow & H :
400 - 48.80 (48.74-98),
400H - 54.18 (53.92-98)

For brevity in the index the previous age descriptions of the events have been kept. This should not cause any confusion since the age group of each athlete is clearly shown in the new form eg U15 but some examples will clarify this.

A **J** after an event is an Under 20 event eg 110HJ - 110 metres hurdles with 3'3" hurdles

A **Y** or an **I** is an Under 17 event (men and women)
eg 100HY - 100 metres hurdles with 3' 0" hurdles Heptl - Heptathlon with Under 17 implements

A **B** or a **G** is an Under 15 event (men and women) eg JTB - 600 gram Javelin SPG - 3.25kg Shot

A **C** or an **M** is an Under 13 event (men and women) eg SPC - 3.25kg Shot SPM - 2.72kg Shot

WOMENS INDEX

ABDULAI Kosnatu U17 8.02.85, S & NH : TJ - 11.02

ABERDEEN Charlotte U13 10.03.88, AF&D : 1500 - 5:05.97

ADAMSON Samantha U20 27.03.82, Hert & W : HJ - 1.75i/1.75 (1.75-97), Hep - 4588 (4866-99)

ADDO Roseline Emefa Ama U23 7.06.80, Newbury/East Tennessee Univ : 200 - 25.01w/25.07 (24.95w-99), 400 - 55.80

ADELOYE Juliet U15 13.06.86, London Sch : 100 - 12.11, 200 - 25.21, PenG - 2767

AGBO Phyllis U15 16.12.85, Thames Valley : 75HG - 11.06, HJ - 1.65io/1.60, LJ - 5.20, SPG - 11.30, PenG - 3062

AGYEPONG Jacqueline 5.01.69,Shaft Barnet: 100 - 12.1 (11.7-94/11.72w-88/11.81-93), 60H - 8.42i (8.01i-95), 100H - 13.5 (12.90-95)

AINSLEY Karen U23 24.06.80, Rowh/Birm Un: HT - 40.21

ALANEME Sandra U15 7.01.86, Blackheath : HJ - 1.65

ALEXANDER Claire U13, Portsmouth : 600 - 1:45.1, 800 - 2:25.97, 1500 - 5:06.06, 70HM - 11.8, PenM - 2000

ALEXANDER Katherine 28.04.74, Shaft Barn : PV - 3.20 (3.30-96)

ALFORD Sophie 5.12.75, E,S & Mx/ (see MORRIS)

ALI Loise U13 2.03.88, Abertillery : SPM - 10.01io

ALLAHGREEN Diane 21.02.75, Liverpool H : 60 - 7.32i/7.45, 100 - 11.80 (11.6/11.66-99), 200 - 24.26w (24.0w-99/24.81-94), 60H - 7.99i, 100H - 13.11 (12.99-99)

ALLAN Laura U17 11.02.85, Pitreavie : HT - 33.08

ALLAN Vicki U15 31.12.85, Giffnock : HJ - 1.66

ALLBUTT Martha U15 27.12.85, Crewe & N : LJ - 5.25w/5.21

ALLEN Amanda 14.07.68, Birchfield : (see WRIGHT)

ALLEN Angela 23.09.67, Tipton : 10MR - 58:26, HMar - 1:17:03 (1:16:26-98), Mar - 2:53:54

ALLEN Sharon 23.10.68, WGreen & Ex L : 100 - 11.71un/11.96w/11.98, 200 - 23.63un/24.76 (24.20i-97/24.5/24.51-99), 400 - 54.85un/56.60 (54.62i/55.83-97)

ALLERSTON Hayley U15 13.04.86, Hull Ach : 100 - 12.6

ALLEYNE Petrina Louise U20 10.07.81, Read : 100 - 12.1 (12.0w-99/12.17-96)

ALLOTT Elizabeth 9.02.77, Altrincham : 3k - 9:44.74mx (9:54.8-99),10MR - 58:22, 10kR - 34:35 (34:27-99), HMar - 1:13:40

ALLSOPP Sarah U17 13.10.84, Dudley & St : 80HI - 11.67w/11.82

ALT Sarah V35 4.01.62, Shaftesbury Barnet : (see HEATH)

AMEDE Christine F. V35 7.08.63, W S & E : 400H - 62.70 (59.43-98)

AMEOBI Titi U17 20.11.84, Gateshead : 60 - 7.9i, 200 - 25.19 100 - 12.2w/12.26w/12.3/12.39 (12.2w-99)

AMOS Katie U23 13.11.78, Thurr/Gr'wich Un : JT - 46.66 (46.75-99)

ANDERSON Pamela 16.10.76, C of Glasgow : LJ - 5.51 (5.74-94)

ANDERSON Shani 7.08.75, Shaftesbury Barn : 60 - 7.52i (7.48i-99), 100 - 11.3w/11.34, 200 - 23.20, 300 - 37.79,400 - 54.77

ANDREWS Sharon Vivian 4.07.67, WG & Ex L : DT - 42.00 (56.24-94)

ANDREWS Vicki 31.08.69, Wolves & B : 800 - 2:09.80 (2:09.4-95), 1500 - 4:31.3

ANIA Emma Candece U23 7.02.79, S B/Illin U : 200 - 23.83w/24.38 (24.32-95), 400 - 56.74i

ANNESS Ruth Evelyn U23 3.10.78, Bir/Lut U : PV - 3.40

APERGHIS Sue 16.03.70, Wycombe : 3k - 9:54.3

AQUILINA Clare V40 5.03.60, Brighton : Mar - 3:03:23 (2:50:52-91)

ARCHER Claire 30.09.76, Mandale : SP - 11.30 (11.34-96)

ARICI Giovanna 24.06.74, AF&D/ITA : 3k - 9:22.51

ARMISHAW Helen U23 4.10.80, Sale : LJ - 5.58 (5.69w-99/5.63-98)

ARMSTRONG Morwenna U15 23.11.85, Berks Sch : PenG - 2525

ARNOLD Helen Louise U23 5.10.78, Team S : HT - 46.57 (54.72-97)

ARNOLD Zoe 10.11.76, Lagan Valley : 400 - 56.11 (55.98-99)

ASH Sally U23 4.11.80, Norwich/Loughbro : TJ - 11.13 (11.34-99)

ASHLEY Melissa 17.03.77, Thames Valley : HT - 38.64

ASKEW A. U13, Skipton : HJ - 1.43

ASPEN Samantha U17 27.10.83, Bolton : 300 - 41.1/41.23

ASTON Faith 26.11.75, Sale : 800 - 2:12.04 (2:08.2-98)

ATIJOSAN Lanre U15 17.10.86, Southwark : 100 - 12.5/12.51, HJ - 1.60

ATKINSON Emma U13 8.04.88, Wigan : DTM - 23.02

ATKINSON Rachael U15 20.12.85, Wigan : SPG - 10.84, DT - 30.45

ATUNUMUO Lucy U23 4.11.80, Hercules Wim : LJ - 5.88

AUGEE Esther M. V35 1.01.64, WG & Ex L : SP - 11.72 (12.28-99), HT - 54.68 (56.76-93)

AUKETT Phillipa U17 9.09.84, Worthing : 800 - 2:16.09

AUSTIN Ashley U13 29.09.87, C of Glasgow : 70HM - 11.77, JTM - 25.26

AVIL Gemma U17 8.03.84, Oxford City : SP - 11.40,DT - 35.01

AXTEN Tracy V35 20.07.63, Shaftesbury B : SP - 14.38 (15.81-98), DT - 51.72 (58.18-97)

AYERO Jennifer U23 13.09.79, Ealing,S & Mx : HT - 39.22, JT - 42.51

AYLWIN Louise U23 8.04.80, Brack/Exeter U : 400H - 64.1/65.96 (63.99-98)

BACKHOUSE Susan U23 6.12.78, Wakefield/Loughbro : DT - 45.29

BACKWELL Samantha U17 4.02.85, Yeovil O : Hepl - 4254

BACON Catherine 25.11.69, Wakefield/NZL :
400H - 65.50
BACON Jodie U13, Liverpool H :
70HM - 11.5
BAGGLEY Lucy U13, Shrewsbury :
JTM - 25.71
BAILEY Emma Louise U17 25.07.84, North'ton :
60 - 7.76i, 100 - 12.12w/12.24
BAKER Claire U17 13.08.84, Stourport :
TJ - 10.76w/10.67
BAKER Emma U13 22.09.88, C of Plymouth :
100 - 13.1
BAKER Joanne U13 15.10.87, Wigan :
70HM - 11.32w/11.5 (11.63-99), PenM - 1957
BAKER Maxine Claire 15.12.70, Coventry G :
800 - 2:12.0 (2:06.16-92),
1500 - 4:24.47 (4:10.07-92)
BAKER Tanya 23.11.74, Shaftesbury Barnet :
800 - 2:09.58 (2:08.11-98), 1M - 4:42.07i,
1500 - 4:23.15 (4:20.87-97), 3k - 9:32.73
BALL Michelle U20 9.05.83, Blackpool :
PV - 2.80
BARBER Helen 13.12.67, Horsforth :
Mar - 2:58:40
BARKER Katharine U13, Sale :
1200 - 4.00.1
BARNABY Anisha U20 9.07.83, Black/H H H :
100 - 12.17w (12.3/12.31-99)
BARNES Catherine 28.09.77, Winchester :
TJ - 11.07 (11.49-95)
BARNES Danielle U15 8.10.85, Newquay & P :
800 - 2:17.4, 1500 - 4:35.77
BARNES Hannah U17 2.06.84, Sheffield :
60HI - 9.23io, LJ - 5.45w/5.38, Hepl - 4338
BARNES Lauren U13 24.09.87, Windsor S & E :
HJ - 1.48
BARNETT Stacie U17 9.10.84, West Norfolk :
60HI - 9.15i, 80HI - 12.0, 100H - 15.5
BARR Lyndsey U13 19.01.88, Shaftesbury B :
1200 - 4:00.3, 1500 - 5:07.1
BARR Nicola 26.04.70, Edinburgh WM :
TJ - 12.06w/11.97 (12.42w-97/12.27-98)
BARR Victoria U20 14.04.82, Gateshead :
100 - 12.0/12.12 (12.07-99), 200 - 24.34
BARRATT Angela U15 25.12.85, Parkside :
LJ - 5.29
BARRETT Caroline U17 16.09.83, Louth :
SP - 10.95, DT - 33.59
BARRETT Victoria V35 7.11.64, Portsmouth J :
Mar - 3:07:02
BARRY Sara U20 8.06.83, Yate :
TJ - 11.13, Hep - 4019
BARTHOLOMEW Nicola U15 23.10.86, AF&D :
1500 - 4:47.96
BARTLETT Rebecca U17 7.03.85, Telford :
JT - 39.54
BARTON Alexandra U15 14.09.85, Cheltenham :
100 - 12.5 (12.5-99)
BASS Natalie U15 3.12.85, Leamington :
800 - 2:18.2, 1500 - 4:46.6
BATES Rebecca U20 16.05.82, City of Stoke :
TJ - 11.86
BAXTER Laura U17 19.10.84, Scunthorpe :
80HI - 11.91w/12.03
BAYLEY Lorna U17 6.07.85, Sutton :
PV - 2.70
BEARD Hayley U15 2.12.85, Stevenage & NH :
800 - 2:10.89, 1500 - 4:47.4
BEARMAN Chelsea U13, Crawley :
PenM - 2241
BEATTIE Natalie U23 30.01.78, Pitreavie :
(nee HYND)
100 - 11.92w/11.97 (11.82w/11.89-99),
200 - 24.55 (24.49-99)
BEATTIE Sharon 26.11.72, Border :
PV - 2.70
BEBBINGTON Helen U23 25.11.80, R S C :
800 - 2:12.6, 1500 - 4:33.6 (4:29.86-99)
BECCONSALL Sue V40 13.06.59, Todmorden :
Mar - 3:02:04
BECK Rachael 12.08.69, Thames H & H :
Mar - 3:03:52
BECKETT Charlotte U15 4.01.86, Milton K :
100 - 12.6, 200 - 25.20
BECKETT Chloe U13 10.06.88, Wakefield :
DTM - 27.50, JTM - 24.50
BECKINGSALE Elizabeth "Buffy" U23 20.03.80,
Norwich : PV - 2.90i/2.70 (2.90-99)
BEER Sarah U17 29.04.84, Exeter :
SP - 10.56
BEEVERS Sarah 18.11.76, Wakefield :
400H - 65.63 (65.4-99)
BEIGHTON Amy U15 6.03.86, Leics Cor :
60HG - 9.07i, 75HG - 11.4/11.61 (11.59-99)
BELL Karen U20 18.06.82, Edinburgh WM :
HT - 46.39
BELL Rebecka U15 1.12.85, Norwich :
HJ - 1.68
BELLE Symone U17 12.11.84, Tower Hamlets :
60HI - 8.61i, 80HI - 11.18w/11.20,
300H - 43.32, LJ - 6.11
BEMROSE Antonia Marie U23 3.09.79, AF&D/
Coventry Un : HJ - 1.70i/1.65 (1.76-96)
BENJAMIN Dawn Donita 7.03.72, W S & E/
Army : 60 - 7.68i (7.49i-99),
100 - 11.4w/11.43, LJ - 6.45w/6.26
BENNET Jessica U15 28.04.86, Bournemouth :
PenG - 2530
BENNETT Alison L. U13 12.04.88, Dac & Tring :
70HM - 11.8, LJ - 4.71
BENNETT Carol Jane 11.01.77,
C of Hull/Ripon & York U : (see MARSHALL)
BENNETT Christina Jayne U23 27.02.78,
Epsom & Ewell : SP - 15.51 (15.55-99),
DT - 40.03 (42.88-99), HT - 53.74
BENNETT Claire U20 4.02.83, Cannock & St :
JT - 38.28
BENNETT Diana Faye 14.06.74, Epsom & E :
(see NORMAN)
BENNETT Gemma U17 4.01.84, N & Essex B :
60HI - 9.1i (8.80i-99),
80HI - 11.62w/11.7/11.81 (11.72-99),
100H - 15.38, 300H - 45.8
BENNETT Joanna U20 6.08.83, Epsom & E :
SP - 11.99i/11.81
BENNETT Julia Margaret 26.03.70, Epsom & E :
60H - 8.88i (8.83i-98), LJ - 6.04 (6.13i-98),
100H - 14.67 (14.43w-96),
400H - 62.7/62.77 (61.7/61.84-97),
HJ - 1.85i/1.83 (1.92i-90/1.89-94),
SP - 12.13i/11.86 (12.15i-99/12.07-98),
Hep - 5538 (5747w-96)
BENNETT Louise U17 11.01.84, Ilford :
HT - 30.71
BENNETT Wendy V35 21.12.65, Worcester :
3kW - 14:37.4, 5kWR - 24:58

BENNEWORTH Katy U17 5.10.84, Blackheath :
LJ - 5.41
BENTLEY Sarah 21.05.67, Birchfield :
5KR - 16:45 (16:23-99), 5MR - 26:57,
10kR - 34:28 (33:30-96)
BERMINGHAM Orla 7.10.75, WGreen & Ex L :
100H - 15.2/15.38 (13.8w-95/13.87w-94/13.93-95)
BERRY Catherine Ann 8.10.75, K & Poly/
East Tennessee Univ : 1500 - 4:21.88,
3k - 9:25.38, 5k - 16:00.97, 5KR - 16:26
BERRY Kelly-Jane U15 23.04.87, Wessex & B :
JT - 36.03
BERRYMAN Kirsten U13, Milton Keynes :
1200 - 4:02.1
BEST Charlotte U17 7.03.85, Crawley :
400 - 58.1, 800 - 2:11.52
BETTS Laura Nadine U17 6.11.84, Tonbridge :
LJ - 5.53, TJ - 10.87w/10.83
BEVAN Adele U17 26.03.84, Crawley :
800 - 2:15.0
BEVERLEY Rachael Ann U23 23.07.79, Sale/
Loughbro : HT - 57.09 (60.88-99)
BILLIN Kirsty U17 24.05.85, Sutton :
DT - 32.32
BINGLOW Veronique V35 11.06.65, Sutton R :
Mar - 3:00:53
BIRCH Courtney U17 5.10.84, Liv.Pemb Seft :
3k - 9:35.52
BIRD Rebecca U20 7.01.83, Cheltenham :
100 - 12.14w (12.2/12.33-99),
200 - 25.1 (25.00w-98/25.0-99/25.08i/25.30-98)
BIRDSALL Michelle Joanna 5.08.73, Ox C :
Mar - 3:06:54 (2:59:43-99)
BISCOE Lisa U20 13.01.83, Southend :
Hep - 3819
BISSELL Susan U13, Burnley :
SPM - 9.50
BJONE Mari 11.09.70, Sale/Loughbro/NOR :
400 - 55.27 (54.62-99),
600 - 1:31.34i (1:31.30i-99),
400H - 58.12 (57.06-96)
BLACK Gillian Elizabeth U23 27.10.79,
City of Glasgow : HJ - 1.78 (1.83-99)
BLACKTIN Faye U20 5.11.81, Hertford & W :
HT - 41.22
BLACKWELL Sarah U17 1.10.84, Liv. Pemb S :
100 - 12.3/12.32w/12.38
BLAIR Joanna U15 1.03.86, Coventry Godiva :
JT - 34.16
BLAIZE Dominique U13 3.10.87, Kingston & P :
HJ - 1.43, LJ - 4.62
BLAKE Tanya-Gee 16.01.71, Trafford :
800 - 2:01.06 (2:00.10-98),
1500 - 4:29.20 (4:27.59-94)
BLAKEMAN Beverley 4.04.74, Sunderland :
800 - 2:09.11 (2:05.33-98)
BLANK Paula 13.12.77, Verlea :
(see COLLIS)
BLISS Jennifer Anne U15 6.07.86, Brighton :
PenG - 2757
BLOOMFIELD Christine Beverley 12.02.68,
WGreen & Ex L : 60 - 7.37i (7.32i-99),
100 - 11.49w/11.58 (11.32-99),
200 - 23.31i/23.62 (22.85-99)
BLOOMFIELD Tracey U23 13.09.79, Guild & G :
PV - 3.90
BLOOR Stephanie U13, Hull Springhead :
600 - 1:42.4, 800 - 2:23.72, 1200 - 3:51.3
BODDEY Hayley U20 14.02.83, Derby LAC :
JT - 37.94
BODIAM Natalie U13 30.09.87, Elgin :
DTM - 22.90
BOLSOVER Maria Teresa U23 5.06.80, Traff :
100 - 12.13w/12.14 (11.59w-98/11.97-99),
200 - 25.11 (24.39w/24.49-98)
BOLTON Laura Clare U23 22.01.79, Newq & P :
JT - 37.45 (38.15-99)
BONNETT Emily U13 22.09.87, Yeovil Oly :
70HM - 11.7, PenM - 2286
BONNY Emma U13 9.09.87, Havering :
LJ - 4.92
BOOSEY Carolyn U17 11.10.84, V of Aylesb:
1500 - 4:45.89, 3k - 10:41.9
BOOTH Amie U17 19.10.84, Bedford & Co :
3k - 10:23.6
BORTHWICK Michelle U17 28.04.84, B'mouth :
DT - 35.40
BOTHAMS Valerie 19.03.75, City of Glasgow/
Birm Un : 1500 - 4:29.76i/4:31.88 (4:22.7-97)
BOUCHARD Sarah 23.10.74, Salford :
800 - 2:09.08 (2:08.94-93), 1500 - 4:23.74mx
BOULTON Jane V40 2.04.56, Crowborough :
Mar - 2:56:58 (2:52:36-97)
BOVILL Susan U20 6.05.82, Sutton & District :
400 - 57.04 (56.46-99)
BOWER Sandra V40 12.11.60, Thetford :
Mar - 3:04:03 (2:57:56-95)
BOWLING Sarah U13 19.03.88, Sheff RWC :
2kW - 11:19.3
BOWRING Nicole 27.01.74, Bromley :
200 - 24.50w?/24.91 (24.7-98),
400 - 55.4/55.49 (54.87-98)
BOWYER Elizabeth U20 8.09.81, Wirral :
SP - 11.63
BOWYER Sonya 18.09.72, Sale :
800 - 2:07.54 (2:01.67-95)
BOYLE Karen U17 25.03.84, Dunf & W Fife :
300 - 40.3/40.61
BRADBURY Sarah V35 25.02.63, AF&D :
3k - 9:53.5 (9:49.78-95), 5k - 16:29.62,
10kR - 34:21 (33:09sh-96/34:15-95),
BRADLEY Joanna U23 23.08.79, Ashford :
DT - 49.10
BRADSHAW Noelle Elizabeth V35 18.12.63,
AF&D : PV - 3.45 (3.50-98), JT - 46.81
SP - 11.32 (12.26-95), HT - 37.51 (38.82-94)
BRADY Emma Elizabeth 3.01.74, Trafford :
800 - 2:09.78 (2:09.1-97), 1500 - 4:26.86
BRAIDY Jocelyn U17 13.02.84, Bournemouth :
TJ - 10.82
BRANNAN Lesley 13.09.76, Sale/Liv Univ :
SP - 12.66, HT - 51.86
BRANNEY Sandra V45 30.04.54, C of Glasgow :
10MR - 56:16dh (54:05dh-91/55:26-89),
Mar - 2:46:32 (2:35:03-89)
BRANT Natalie V. U20 11.12.82, Epsom & E :
TJ - 11.94w/11.78
BRASON Claire U20 16.03.83, North Shields P :
400H - 62.74
BRATHWAITE Elizabeth U17 10.04.85, Verlea :
800 - 2:16.3
BRAZNELL Kimberley V40 28.02.56, Dud & S :
5kW - 24:38.4 (24:16.4-95),
10kWR - 52:20 (48:36-98),
20kW - 1:46:24 (1:44:29-99)

BRENNAN Faye U17 13.05.84, Worthing :
SP - 11.48
BRENTON Rachel U17 18.01.85, Radley :
100H - 15.6, HJ - 1.66, LJ - 5.36, TJ - 11.29, Hepl - 4001
BRERETON Ruth U20 26.06.81, Herne Hill :
400H - 64.3/65.07 (64.89-99)
BRETHERWICK Samantha 16.04.69, Preseli :
HMar - 1:18:24, Mar - 2:53:37
BRETT Jacquelyn Charis V35 5.07.65, N & P :
60H - 8.87i (8.7i-89/8.75i-87),
100H - 14.1 (13.86-87)
BREWINGTON Katherine Ann U20 15.10.81,
Havering : 100H - 14.55, LJ - 5.70, Hep - 4736
BRIDGER Zoe 4.03.76, AF&D :
DT - 35.99
BRIGGS Julie 13.03.69, Crawley :
10MR - 58:18
BRIGGS Sian U17 17.07.84, Derby LAC :
LJ - 5.37
BRIGHT Kathryn 27.03.76, Newport/Univ
Wales Inst Card : (see SAGE)
BRINDLEY Tracy 25.08.72, City of Glasgow :
HMar - 1:18:29 (1:16:47-97)
BRISTOW Lynette 17.11.77, Worcester :
HT - 37.63
BRITTON Samantha U15 12.09.86, Chesterfield :
75HG - 11.68w/11.7, PenG - 2525
BROCKBANK Jodie U17 1.10.84, East Grin :
HJ - 1.62
BRODIE Claire U17 1.06.85, Annan :
1500 - 4:45.32
BROMLEY Naida U15 27.09.86, Wakefield :
LJ - 5.16w/5.11, PenG - 2751
BROOK Tanya U15 20.02.87, Parkside :
HJ - 1.60
BROOKES Heather U20 17.07.81, Sale :
200 - 24.41w/24.8/25.11, 400 - 54.00,
BROOKS Michelle Louise 6.02.77, Sale/
Univ of Nebraska : 800 - 2:09.26,
1500 - 4:22.41, 3k - 9:24.81, 5k - 16:35.50
BROOKS Natalie U13, Sheffield :
LJ - 4.73
BROOME Louise U13, Exmouth :
PenM - 1945
BROW Kelly U23 24.09.78, Wakefield :
TJ - 11.64
BROWN Aileen V35 29.07.65, Gt Western :
Mar - 2:51:01
BROWN Celia 22.01.77, Shaftesbury Barnet :
800 - 2:09.71, 400H - 60.08
BROWN Helen U17 27.12.84, Thames Valley :
HJ - 1.65
BROWN Janette 19.02.73, Mandale :
HT - 46.01
BROWN Jennifer A. V40 21.05.59, Ashford :
HJ - 1.70 (1.73-89),
TJ - 11.43w/11.40 (11.56-97)
BROWN Judy V45 27.10.54, St Albans Str :
Mar - 3:04:57
BROWN Louise U23 6.05.78, Scarborough :
3k - 9:48.07, 5k - 17:25.96
BROWN Ruth U23 9.04.80, Darlington/
Northumbria Univ : 5k - 16:37.66
BROWN Sandra V50 1.04.49, Surrey WC :
24Hr - 176.285km (194.032km-98)
BROWN Tina 22.08.76, Coventry Godiva :
800 - 2:12.76, 1500 - 4:32.20
BROWN Zoe U17 15.09.83, Ballymena & A :
PV - 3.00
BROWNING Charlotte Lucy U13 8.10.87,
AF&D : 600 - 1:43.7, 800 - 2:19.89, 1k - 3:06.4,
1200 - 3:50.9, 1500 - 4:47.25mx (5:04.5-99)
BRUCE Joanne U23 26.10.78, Woking/
Chichester Coll : JT - 43.79 (47.26-99)
BRUCE Shaeleen U15 3.11.86, Dunf & W Fife :
HTG - 39.75
BRUNNING Natasha 10.03.73, AF&D :
TJ - 11.17 (11.21-99)
BRYAN Hayley U15 4.03.86, South Devon :
SPG - 10.63
BRYANT Lesley Karen V40 12.04.56, Linc W :
DT - 38.54 (55.42-80)
BUCHAN Kate Margaret U17 18.10.84, Med :
1500 - 4:42.31
BUCHANAN Lesley U20 25.11.81, Edinb WM :
HJ - 1.75
BUCHANAN Shirley 20.01.73, AF&D/IRE :
PV - 3.10
BUCKLEY Anne 20.06.67, Salford :
Mar - 2:43:54
BULL Sarah 4.06.75, Derby LAC :
800 - 2:12.2 (2:09.82-96),
1500 - 4:23.6 (4:21.02-98), 3k - 9:22.68i
BULLER Rachel L. 31.08.76, Norwich :
800 - 2:10.2 (2:07.56-98)
BURBIDGE Kiri U15 2.10.85, Bournemouth :
200 - 25.82, LJ - 5.25
BURDON Rhiannon U17 29.10.83, Soton City :
100 - 12.4/12.54w (12.4-99), 200 - 25.17
BURGE Kate 15.10.72, Staffs H :
5k - 17:23.23, 5MR - 27:30,
10kR - 34:13, 10MR - 57:41, HMar - 1:15:35
BURGOINE Laura U17 28.01.85, Bedford & Co :
3k - 10:15.68
BURLEIGH Natalie U13, Southport :
150 - 18.9un
BURLING Vicky U13, Crawley :
PenM - 1953
BURNS Rachael U20 5.08.83, Wigan :
TJ - 11.03
BURNSIDE Susan U23 3.02.80, EWM/Edin U :
60 - 7.54i, 100 - 11.88, 200 - 24.11
BURROWS Melanie 7.08.76, Ashford :
JT - 43.41
BURTON Carly U23 14.10.80, Ashford :
DT - 41.94 (44.37-99), HT - 39.38 (41.16-99)
BUTLER Alice 27.07.73, Wakefield :
400 - 56.76 (55.6/55.81-97),
800 - 2:07.88 (2:04.9mx-97/2:06.8-98)
BUTLER Jemma U15 17.06.87, Birchfield :
100 - 12.6
BUTLER Judith U23 5.10.79, Oadby & W/
Durham Univ : Hep - 3870 (3920-98)
BUTLER Kathy 22.10.73, Hounslow :
1500 - 4:15.46 (4:07.68CAN-97),
5k - 15:42.22 (15:10.69-98), 5KR - 16:17,
10kR - 34:11 (33:01-99)
BUTLER Lucy U20 18.11.81, Gateshead :
LJ - 5.66w/5.59, Hep - 3885
BUTLER Natalie U23 25.11.78, Windsor S & E :
100H - 14.8/15.14 (14.78w/14.89-98),
JT - 38.06
BUTTERS Kate U15 25.07.86, Hastings :
SPG - 10.57

BUTTERWORTH Julie U20 25.02.82, C of Hull :
PV - 2.60 (2.60-99)
BUXTON Leanne U23 27.05.78, Bir/DMU Un :
60H - 8.83i (8.79i-99), 400H - 62.23,
100H - 13.96w/14.56 (13.97-99)

CADDICK Leah U15 1.06.86, Southport :
200 - 25.65
CADGER Carol V50 14.09.50, Perth :
100kR - 9:23:09
CAFFEL Kelly U23 10.02.79, Oxford City :
800 - 2:03.48mp/2:04.35, 1500 - 4:10.22
CALCOTT Sarah U17 29.06.84, Coventry G :
300H - 46.5/46.93
CALLAGHAN Katherine Jane U23 11.04.80,
Hounslow/Brunel Univ : PV - 3.20
CALLAWAY Deborah Ann V35 15.07.64, AF&D :
SP - 13.73 (14.88-93), DT - 52.34 (58.56-96),
HT - 40.83 (44.64-96)
CALVERT Donna U23 26.06.79, Wakefield :
DT - 37.33 (37.53-98)
CAMERON Claire V40 3.10.58, C of Glasgow :
DT - 40.50 (46.34-85)
CAMERON Hannah U13 3.03.88, Penicuik :
DTM - 23.31
CAMPBELL Donna U13 15.02.88, W DUNB :
100 - 13.1
CAMPBELL Katrina 8.03.72, Lisb/QUB U/IRE :
JT - 39.01 (42.13-99)
CAMPBELL Natasha U20 6.08.82, Medway :
JT - 38.14 (39.01-99)
CAMPBELL Sarah 31.10.74, Glasgow Univ :
Mar - 2:59:31
CAMPBELL Stephanie U17 14.02.85, Lagan V :
1500 - 4:45.9
CANEY Eleanor U17 28.05.84, Solihull & S H :
60 - 7.91i, 100 - 12.2, 200 - 24.29, 300 - 38.19
CANK Elaine U23 5.12.79, Telford :
SP - 11.77 (12.57-99), DT - 44.43 (46.40-99)
CANNING Melanie U17 19.05.85, E,S & Mx :
60HI - 9.08i, 80HI - 11.7/11.74w/11.80
CANNISTER Rachel U17 11.10.84, Rotherham :
HJ - 1.62
CANNON Hayley U13, Liverpool H :
1200 - 3:58.8
CAPLE Lauren U17 7.03.85, Derby LAC :
300 - 41.3/41.37
CARDING Christina U15 26.02.87, Bas & MH :
SPG - 10.80, DT - 33.33
CARDY-WISE Bronwen G. V45 26.01.52, B & R :
3k - 9:59.8 (9:29.82-93), 5KR - 16:30,
10k - 34:37.3, 10kR - 34:25 (33:52-87)
CAREY Michelle U20 20.03.81, Loughbro/IRE :
400 - 56.17, 400H - 61.07
CARISS Susan V50 17.11.49, Bingley :
Mar - 3:04:33
CARLESS Tammy 10.01.77, Braintree :
JT - 37.88 (40.57-99)
CARLISLE Elinor U17 3.10.84, Salisbury :
HJ - 1.63
CARMICHAEL Carmilla U23 1.12.79, Ox Univ :
HJ - 1.65
CARNEY Helen U23 27.03.79, Lut/St. Marys U :
PV - 3.05i/2.80
CARNEY Laura 4.10.75, Liverpool H/Liv Univ :
3k - 9:36.57mx (10:22.2-92)
CARPENTER Emma U20 16.05.82, Exeter :
SP - 12.53, DT - 52.21, HT - 40.12
CARR Laura U13 18.02.89, Dorchester :
JTM - 24.87
CARTER Alexandra U23 1.04.80,
Vale Royal/Loughborough Studnts :
800 - 2:03.78mp/2:05.48, 1500 - 4:17.98
CARTER Helena U15 17.05.86, WYorks Sch :
LJ - 5.32, PenG - 2656
CARTY Lara U17 7.03.84, Basildon :
200 - 25.3w (27.78w-97), 60HI - 8.85io,
80HI - 11.65w/11.8/11.89 (11.8/11.88-99),
100H - 14.83, HJ - 1.64 (1.65-99),
LJ - 5.41, Hep - 4538, Hepl - 4395 (4489-99)
CARWARDINE Hazel U23 6.11.80, Bolton :
TJ - 11.61
CASE Samantha U15 5.01.86, Guildford & G :
JT - 31.55
CATER Lisa U17 16.01.84, Mansfield :
800 - 2:16.3 (2:13.53-99),
1500 - 4:42.19 (4:39.12-99)
CATTERMOLE Sara-Jane 29.01.77, C of Edin :
HT - 40.63 (43.30-96),
3kW - 14:10.9+/14:12.70mx/14:29.2,
5kWR - 23:32+, 10kWR - 47:28+sh/47:47,
20kW - 1:35:52sh/1:36:40
CEESAY Amina U23 19.11.79, Newham & E B :
100 - 12.1/12.22 (12.09w/12.20-00),
200 - 24.8/24.81w/24.99 (24.79-99)
CEESAY Nusrat U20 18.03.81, Newham & E B :
400 - 56.67, 100H - 15.0 (14.8-99),
400H - 60.85 (60.53-98)
CEESAY Zainab U17 27.10.83, N & Essex B :
LJ - 6.15
CHADNEY Ruth U17 20.04.85, Bridport R :
800 - 2:15.5, 1500 - 4:45.5
CHADWICK Jane U13 15.09.87, Wigan :
75 - 10.0/10.01, 100 - 13.0/13.07,
150 - 19.7/19.78 (19.7-99), 200 - 26.51
CHAFFE Lucy U23 25.03.79, WGreen & Ex L :
400 - 56.8 (55.8-99/55.93-97),
800 - 2:10.56 (2:09.71-99)
CHALMERS Laura U15 1.05.86, Elgin :
DT - 29.47, HTG - 40.54
CHAMBERLAIN Rebecca U23 7.09.79,
B'mouth : SP - 11.15 (11.46i-98/11.43-99)
CHAMBERS Karen Louise 31.08.68, Sale :
HT - 48.66
CHAMPION Fay 27.09.66, Windsor S & E :
DT - 37.04 (44.64-95)
CHAPMAN Joanna U17 10.01.85, W Suffolk :
JT - 41.47
CHARLES Shereen U17 27.10.84,
Ealing,Southall & Mx : 100 - 12.27
CHARNOCK Catherine 3.05.75, Barrow & F :
3kW - 13:58.96 (13:21.5-99),
5kWR - 26:24+ (23:09-99)
CHARNOCK Kathryn V35 4.07.62, Wigan Ph:
Mar - 2:47:44 (2:47:28-99)
CHATTING Donna U17 30.10.83, Soton City :
300 - 41.0/41.16
CHILDS Ellie Joanne U20 26.05.83, Basildon :
400 - 56.6 (56.5-98), 800 - 2:11.38
CHOWN Louisa U17 27.07.84, Northampton :
3k - 10:38.46
CHRISMAS Bryna U15 18.06.86, Hull Springh :
3kW - 16:20.8, 5kWR - 26:11
CHRISTIE Catriona Rosanna U17 26.04.85,
W S & E : HJ - 1.65i (1.67-99), TJ - 11.10

CHRISTIE Jenny U15 28.09.85, Leamington :
200 - 25.83, PenG - 2857
CHRISTMAS Danielle U13 21.12.87, Crawley :
1k - 3:14.9, PenM - 2142
CHRISTMAS Natalie U17 9.04.84, Crawley :
400 - 58.5, 300H - 43.82, 400H - 64.4
CLAGUE Jennifer 6.08.73, Liverpool H :
3k - 9:53.12mx (9:21.54-93),
5k - 17:13.0 (16:11.61i-92/17:02.53-98)
CLARK Jean 5.10.68, Edinburgh WM :
HT - 46.48 (50.34-97)
CLARK Juliette V35 22.04.64, Belgrave :
Mar - 3:05:03
CLARK Megan 31.07.73, Thames H & H :
Mar - 2:52:07
CLARK Natalie U20 4.09.82, Hull Springhead :
HJ - 1.75i/1.75 (1.76-99)
CLARK Sonia U17 1.04.84, Sale :
1500 - 4:42.6, 3k - 10:13.4
CLARKE Dianne Olivia V40 27.02.58, TVH :
400H - 65.56 (62.9-94/65.33-98)
CLARKE Rhian Clare 19.04.77, WG & Ex L/
Houston University : PV - 4.15
CLARKSON Lesley U20 18.07.82, Inverness :
200 - 25.09 (24.87w-99), 400 - 54.80
CLAXTON Sarah U23 23.09.79, Colc & T :
60 - 7.69i (7.63i-96), 60H - 8.43i/8.5i (8.38i-98),
100 - 12.1 (11.7w-96/11.88w-94/11.9-99/12.19-94),
100H - 13.67 (13.28w-98/13.59-99),
LJ - 6.45w/6.44 (6.56-99)
CLAYTON Amy U17 8.01.84, Shropshire Sch :
HJ - 1.65
CLAYTON Anna U17 20.03.85, West Suffolk :
Hepl - 3992
CLEAR Danielle U17 5.10.83, Ipswich :
HJ - 1.64
CLEWS Victoria U15 21.01.87, Andover :
800 - 2:15.91
CLUBLEY Christina U15 4.11.85, City of Hull :
100 - 12.39,
200 - 25.7/25.93
CLUTTERBUCK Rebecca U15 13.05.86,
Coventry Godiva : JT - 32.16
CODD Danielle U23 17.02.79, Traff/Man Univ :
400H - 64.08
COLE Hayley 1.11.77, Colchester & T :
800 - 2:10.71i (2:12.84-93)
COLLERAN Joanne 1.09.72, Liverpool H :
800 - 2:12.30i (2:06.4-99),
1500 - 4:18.48 (4:15.68i/4:16.24-99),
3k - 9:17.42mx/9:21.26i/9:28.84, 5k - 16:32.33
COLLINS Jayne U23 27.03.80, Birchfield :
PV - 3.05i (3.10-99)
COLLINSON Deborah Joy U15 23.10.85,
Hull Spr : SPG - 11.10, JT - 35.98
COLLIS Paula 13.12.77, Verlea : (nee BLANK)
JT - 42.19 (42.73-99)
COLLYER Isaura U13 21.10.87, Kettering :
HJ - 1.43
CONOLLY Anna R. U15 19.04.86, Telford :
75HG - 11.6/11.65w
CONWAY Rachel U13 30.09.87, Newport :
LJ - 4.71
COOKE Gillian U20 3.10.82, Edinburgh WM :
PV - 3.30, TJ - 11.66
COOKSEY Melinda U17 19.05.84, Tipton :
60 - 7.86io, 100 - 12.0w/12.1/12.16w/12.30,
200 - 24.85
COOMBS Paula 31.12.69, Hastings :
HT - 38.50
COONEY Vicki U17 2.11.84, Windsor S & E :
100 - 12.47w, 200 - 25.5, 300 - 41.53
COOPER Clare U13, Blackheath :
70HM - 11.8
COOPER Helen U20 20.06.83, Blackpool :
HJ - 1.66
COOPER Holly U17 28.01.84, Windsor S & E :
PV - 2.60
COOPER Paula 6.08.75, Rotherham :
HT - 37.16 (37.19-98)
COOPER Stephanie U13, Corby :
800 - 2:26.9, 1200 - 3:57.6, 1500 - 5:07.8
COORE Andrea Anne 23.04.69, Team Solent :
LJ - 6.12 (6.36-98)
COPP Louise V35 13.09.63, Cardiff :
10MR - 58:22, HMar - 1:18:25, Mar - 2:53:11
CORNEBY Hannah E. U20 22.01.81, Can & St/
Birmingham Univ. : DT - 42.25 (42.78-99)
CORRAN Elizabeth M. V45 23.09.55, Manx H :
5kW - 26:09.3 (24:40.91-96),
5kWR - 25:54 (24:51-95),
10kWR - 55:54 (51:37hc-96/51:38-95),
20kW - 1:56:27 (1:47:10-96)
COSTELLOE Carol 14.01.76, Bedford & Co :
JT - 37.52
COUPER Claire 11.03.75, Dunf & W Fife :
10MR - 57:52dh
COURT Clova V40 10.02.60, Windsor S & E :
60 - 7.69i (7.47i-94), 200 - 25.08i (23.57-90),
60H - 8.40i (8.12i-94),
100H - 13.55 (13.04-94),
SP - 13.01 (14.44-97), JT - 46.02
COWIE Raelene U20 17.11.82, Bury :
DT - 35.98
COX Laura Elizabeth U13 21.01.88, Tipton :
75 - 10.0, 100 - 13.0, 150 - 19.2, 200 - 26.8
COX Rachael U23 27.06.80, Birchfield :
HT - 40.00 (41.55-99)
COZENS Chloe U23 9.04.80, Bedford & Co/
Loughbro : HJ - 1.76 (1.80-98),
100H - 15.10w/15.28 (14.78w/15.1-98),
LJ - 5.54 (5.72w-98/5.63-99), SP - 12.53,
JT - 51.79, Hep - 5257 (5358w-98/5283-99)
COZENS Joanne U23 9.04.80, Bedford & Co/
Leeds Poly : PV - 2.80i (2.80-97)
CRAFT Jude 13.08.72, Headington :
5KR - 16:55
CRAIG Paula 2.07.73, St Albans Striders :
Mar - 2:57:34
CRANE Julie 26.09.76, Sale :
HJ - 1.85i/1.82 (1.83-98)
CRAWFORD Catherine Marie U17 17.12.84,
Regent House : 60HI - 8.74i
CRAWLEY Sonia U17 7.12.83, Solihull & S H :
HJ - 1.70i/1.68 (1.70i/1.68-99), LJ - 5.73
CREIGHTON Donna U15 20.09.85, Yeovil Oly :
PenG - 2699
CRESSWELL Lois U20 12.01.81, R Sutton C/
Loughborough Studnts : 400 - 56.05
CRIPPS Faith U17 23.09.83, Milton Keynes :
300H - 45.90, Hepl - 4028
CRITCHFIELD Ashleigh U15 2.03.86, Thurr :
JT - 31.41
CROAD Alison U20 10.06.82, Wimborne :
TJ - 11.13

CROLL Charli U17 25.10.84, Herne Hill :
60 - 7.95i, 100 - 12.27, 300 - 41.2,
200 - 25.23 (25.01w/25.23-99)
CROMBIE Shona 1.06.71, Mornington :
(see HICK)
CROMPTON Mandy U20 25.03.82, Old & R :
LJ - 5.54
CROOKS Karen 15.01.75, Thurrock :
PV - 2.60
CROSBY Janine U23 17.01.79, Bingley :
DT - 36.40 (38.00-98)
CROSBY Nicole 23.10.76, Wakefield :
100 - 11.80w/11.93,
200 - 24.38 (24.3w/24.35-98)
CROSKELL Helen 22.11.72, Tonbridge :
PV - 2.70
CROSS Natasha U17 13.11.84, Swansea :
60 - 7.98i, 100 - 12.54w, 200 - 25.08
CRUMP Lisa Jane 30.03.76, Sheffield RWC :
3kW - 15:10.7 (14:25.09-99),
5kWR - 24:44 (24:20-97), 10kWR - 49:50
CULLEY Jennifer 4.03.75, Belgrave :
400 - 56.02 (54.11-98)
CULSHAW Rachel U15 11.08.86, Wigan :
HJ - 1.61, PenG - 2776
CUNNANE Jennifer V40 23.02.57, Wakefield :
(see WOOD)
CUNNINGHAM Laura U17 14.02.85, Avonside :
60 - 7.86i, 100 - 12.43w/12.56
CUNNINGHAM Lauren Kerry U15 22.08.87,
S & NH : 800 - 2:16.46, 1500 - 4:50.3
CURBISHLEY Allison 3.06.76, Edinburgh WM :
400 - 51.50 (50.71-98)
CURLEY Debra 20.09.71, Wigan Phoenix :
5KR - 16:10, 10kR - 34:22
CURLING Roseanne U23 5.09.80, Bris/CUAC :
LJ - 5.74
CURRIE Alison 15.07.68, City of Glasgow :
400 - 56.9 (55.7/55.98-99),
400H - 61.17 (59.78-97)
CURTIS Briony U17 25.03.85, Banchory :
3k - 10:25.26
CURTIS Laura U20 2.05.81, City of Hull :
Hep - 3956 (4442-99)
CUTHBERTSON Jenny U17 11.06.84, Roth :
PV - 2.65
CUTLER Aimee Louise U20 7.10.81, Cardiff :
LJ - 5.66w/5.57i/5.56 (5.84w/5.77-98)
CUTLER Charlotte 16.10.72, Southend :
800 - 2:11.05
CUTTS Cariann U17 1.02.85, Barnsley :
PV - 2.60 (3.10-99)

DAGNE Birhan U23 8.04.78, WG & Ex L :
3k - 9:13+e (9:21.0-96), 5k - 15:36.35,
5MR - 26:44 (26:36+-99), 10k - 32:30.4,
10kR - 33:27 (33:19-99),
10MR - 57:03 (53:55-98),
HMar - 1:14:23 (1:12:53-99)
DALE Cathryn 31.05.77, Rugby :
LJ - 5.69w/5.66, TJ - 11.78
DALE Charlotte U17 23.03.84, Invicta :
1500 - 4:30.87, 3k - 9:34.9mx/9:35.25
DALES Ruth Marie U23 29.10.80, Wakefield :
60H - 8.90i
DALTON Stephanie U17 8.02.84, Sheffield :
HJ - 1.62, HepI - 4240
DALY Donna U17 25.11.83, Scunthorpe :
3k - 10:42.30
DAMEN Louise U20 12.10.82, Bournemouth :
800 - 2:10.1, 1500 - 4:23.38,
3k - 9:36.5, 5KR - 16:44, 10kR - 34:59
DANIELS Nikki U20 25.08.82, City of Stoke :
800 - 2:11.1
DANSON Ann Elizabeth 4.05.71, Sale :
60 - 7.62i, LJ - 6.32w/6.21i/6.21 (6.38w-94),
100 - 12.0w/12.28 (11.8w-94/11.91-95)
DANVERS Natasha 19.09.77, Shaftesbury B :
200 - 24.99, 300 - 37.80,
400 - 53.2R (52.6R/53.26-98),
100H - 13.19w/13.20 (12.8w-99/13.20-98),
400H - 54.95, HJ - 1.78 (1.82-98)
DARBY Ellie U15 20.12.85, Birchfield :
LJ - 5.71w/5.56
DAUBNEY Claire U13, Cannock & Stafford :
SPM - 9.03
DAVEY Sarah U23 13.10.78, Worth/U N FLO :
3k - 9:58.17, 5k - 16:52.67, 10k - 35:07.36
DAVIDSON Wendy U20 14.10.82, Ellon :
100H - 15.11, 400H - 63.32,
HJ - 1.68i (1.62-99),
LJ - 5.55 (5.66w-99), Hep - 4347
DAVIES Alison V35 6.04.61, Windsor S & E :
PV - 4.00
DAVIES Elen U15 24.04.86, Norwich :
HJ - 1.60 (1.61-99), LJ - 5.30, PenG - 2787
DAVIES Emma J. U23 9.10.78, Andover :
400 - 55.19, 800 - 2:04.07 (2:02.39-98),
1500 - 4:26.11i (4:40.48-95)
DAVIES Gael Iona U23 5.02.79, Gloucester L :
PV - 3.55
DAVIES Helen U17 24.03.84, Colwyn Bay :
60HI - 9.28io, 300H - 44.41
DAVIES Lauren U13 21.09.87, Dorchester :
SPM - 9.56i/9.52, DTM - 22.92
DAVIES Samantha U23 20.09.79, Birchfield :
100 - 11.4w/11.44, 200 - 23.06
DAVIES Sarah U15 13.03.86, Bournemouth :
DT - 31.52
DAVIES Sian U17 16.02.85, Dudley & Stour :
300H - 46.4/46.58
DAVIS Amy U15 28.01.86, Lagan Valley :
SPG - 10.60
DAVIS Helen Marie U17 31.01.85, I of Wight :
JT - 38.47
DAVIS Joanne 23.06.73, Swansea :
JT - 37.01
DAVIS Wendy U23 7.11.79, Lagan V/Ulster U :
800 - 2:12.69i (2:12.24-98)
DAWSON Katherine U17 22.03.85, Bromley :
80HI - 12.0
DAY Samantha U15 8.02.86, Tamworth :
75HG - 11.4/11.51, PenG - 2729
DAY Victoria 19.06.72, WG & Ex L :
(see WARD)
DEAN Carly U15 14.10.85, Bournemouth :
75HG - 11.5/11.51
DEBONO Michelle 1.05.72, Herne Hill :
100H - 15.15
DEE Ellisha U17 24.10.84, Thames Valley :
DT - 40.64
DEEGAN Rachel Sarah U15 10.01.86, Sale :
1500 - 4:46.46
DENHAM Kate U23 18.03.80, T Sol/ Soton I :
100 - 12.09, 200 - 24.61 (24.34w/24.51-97)
DENNISON Andrea M. V35 22.04.63, Bradford :
Mar - 3:04:45

DENNISON Kate U17 7.05.84, Stoke :
PV - 3.20
DERBYSHIRE April Hannah U13 2.04.88, South Devon : SPM - 9.24
DERHAM Zoe U23 24.11.80, Bristol :
HT - 55.57
DESAI Nisha U17 5.08.84, Morpeth :
800 - 2:14.58
DEVLIN Mary U23 14.09.79, Ballymena & A :
LJ - 5.61w (5.58-99), TJ - 11.78
DEVOY Sarah U15 12.01.87, W Cheshire :
PenG - 2525
DEWSBURY Claire U17 16.01.84, B'mouth :
HJ - 1.70
DHALIWAL Navdeep 30.11.77, Shaftesbury B :
SP - 12.38i/11.89 (13.35-98),
DT - 39.93 (43.85-98)
DICKSON Lauren U15 2.04.86, Ayr Seaforth :
100 - 12.56w/12.59
DICKSON Louise U15 4.09.86, Edinburgh WM :
100 - 12.46, 200 - 25.8/25.98w/26.08
DILLON Michelle 24.05.73, Bath Univ. :
HMar - 1:16:15
DIXON Sharon Jane 22.04.68, Parkside :
10MR - 57:54, HMar - 1:16:16,
Mar - 2:46:30,
DOBRISKEY Lisa U17 23.12.83, Ashford :
400 - 57.8, 800 - 2:09.87 (2:08.67-99),
1500 - 4:28.10
DOBRISKEY Sarah U17 13.08.85, Ashford :
HT - 33.39
DODD Meryl 12.04.69, Bingley :
5KR - 16:59
DOHERTY Michelle U17 24.09.84, Sparta :
TJ - 11.07
DOHERTY Tamara U15 15.11.85, W DUNB :
100 - 12.5/12.51, 200 - 25.61w/25.69,
LJ - 5.27
DOLAN Sue V35 25.01.61, Imperial :
HMar - 1:18:21, Mar - 2:49:43 (2:49:21-97)
DONALD Elaine 30.04.74, Thurrock/Vict P H :
100H - 14.8w (14.9/15.26-96)
DOONEY Gemma U17 12.05.84, Wigan :
80HI - 11.99w, 300H - 42.68, 400H - 63.1
DORAN Colette U17 20.09.83, Carlisle/Asp :
JT - 38.39 (39.08-99)
DORAN Vicky U13 17.04.88, Carlisle/Aspatria :
DTM - 24.90, JTM - 28.98
DOUBLE Christine V35 10.06.64, :
Mar - 2:53:47
DOUGHTY Lucy 1.05.71, Bristol :
800 - 2:11.6 (2:10.7-99),
1500 - 4:22.75 (4:21.07-97),
3k - 9:54.08i (9:37.1-97)
DOUGLAS L. Stephanie 22.01.69, Sale :
60 - 7.35i (7.21i-95), 100 - 11.98 (11.27-91),
200 - 23.85i/24.15 (23.17-94)
DOUGLAS Laura U20 4.01.83, Deeside :
SP - 11.37, DT - 39.62, HT - 48.63
DOUGLAS Montell U15 24.01.86, Bromley :
HJ - 1.61
DOWNEY Natalie U13, Southport :
150 - 19.4un
DOWSETT Gemma U17 3.02.84, Medway :
PV - 2.60
DOYLE Natalie U13 5.01.89, Central :
70HM - 11.7

DRAKE Sarah U17 13.08.85, Wakefield :
HT - 38.32
DRASKAY Jessica 8.09.77, East Anglia Univ :
Mar - 2:53:41
DREW Shelley Jean 8.08.73, Sutton & Dist :
DT - 59.03 (60.82-98)
DUDGEON Sinead Marie 9.07.76, Edin WM :
200 - 23.23w/24.13 (23.59-99),
400 - 52.71 (52.05-99),
300H - 40.58mx (46.7-92),
400H - 55.45 (55.24-99)
DUDMAN Nicola Pauline U17 5.10.83, Verlea :
SP - 11.63, DT - 33.51, HT - 47.62
DUFFIN Irene Maria V40 10.08.60, Shaft B :
SP - 12.19 (14.44-90),
DT - 36.59 (44.90-87), HT - 47.08 (50.38-97)
*DUFFY Teresa 6.07.69, WGreen & Ex L/IRE :
5MR - 27:50, 10k - 35:22.5 (33:33.7-97),
10kR - 34:43 (33:34-97), 10MR - 55:56,
HMar - 1:14:51, Mar - 2:37:36*
DUGDALE Catherine 29.11.74, Swansea :
1500 - 4:26.50, 3k - 9:48.45 (9:44.7-99)
DUNCAN Joanne 27.12.66, WGreen & Ex L :
SP - 16.09 (16.12-99)
DUNCAN Lauren U13 21.03.88, Windsor S & E :
75 - 10.07, 100 - 13.1, 150 - 20.0,
200 - 27.3, LJ - 4.75
DUNCAN Tracey Andrea U23 16.05.79, WGreen & Ex L/Brunel Univ :
400 - 55.2/56.18, 400H - 57.92
DUNKLEY Julie U23 11.09.79, Shaftesbury B :
SP - 16.40, DT - 40.70, HT - 43.34
DUNKLEY Leah U15 11.11.85, Barnsley :
200 - 25.6 (25.6-99)
DUNKLEY Michelle Lisa U23 26.01.78, WGreen & Ex L : HJ - 1.93
DUNN Elizabeth U17 5.01.85, Huntingdon :
JT - 35.54
DUNN Kara U17 12.10.84, Ealing,S & Mx :
60 - 7.92i (7.89i-99),
100 - 12.09w/12.21 (12.02w/12.2-99)
DUNN Rachel U20 14.11.82, Huntingdon :
JT - 39.74

EAGEN Jenny U17 15.05.84, Dorset Sch :
TJ - 11.06w/10.87
EAGLAND Anita 29.09.72, Trafford :
400 - 57.12 (56.9-90)
EARLE Jennifer S. V40 28.11.58, Guild & G :
HT - 39.74 (42.49-98)
EASTON Carey U23 16.11.79, Edinburgh WM :
200 - 25.27i (24.56-99),
400 - 55.07 (54.28-98),
400H - 63.5 (61.8/62.82-99)
EDDY Ruth 9.07.75, Colchester H :
1500 - 4:33.69mx (4:28.3-99)
EDGAR Catherine U23 27.02.80, Lagan Val :
JT - 41.48
EDGINGTON Jade U13 8.02.89, Solihull & S H :
2kW - 11:47.0
EDWARDS Chloe U15 12.05.87, Huntingdon :
SPG - 10.80, DT - 28.78
EDWARDS Wendy V35 17.07.61, L Croupiers :
Mar - 3:03:03
EJOH Y. U13, :
SPM - 9.02
ELKHAWAD Maysoon 27.02.77, Chelm/CUAC :
HT - 41.78

ELLIOTT Jacqueline N. U23 13.09.78, Elswick :
400H - 65.41 (64.12-97), Hep - 3918 (4189-98)
ELLIOTT Kerry U17 17.05.85, Gateshead :
SP - 10.71
ELLIOTT Kim 2.07.75, Centurian :
(nee FALKE) 5KR - 16:47, 5MR - 27:45
ELLIOTT Lucy Helen 9.03.66, Shaftesbury B :
3k - 9:23.9 (9:19.2-97), 5KR - 16:42 (15:54-95),
5k - 16:28.81 (15:34.40-97),
5MR - 26:57 (25:54sh-97/26:57-99),
10kR - 33:44 (33:02-98)
ELLIS Laura U17 4.03.85, Falkirk :
300 - 41.5
ELLIS Sarah U17 27.10.83, Havant :
JT - 41.99
ELLIS Venetia U15 15.09.85, Herne Hill :
JT - 33.94
ELLISON Cinnamon U13, Montrose :
PenM - 1903
ELWISS Hannah U17 8.12.84, Preston :
80HI - 11.39w/11.58
ELY Emma U13, East Grinstead :
PenM - 1951
EMMERSON Annie 10.05.70, Stigma Cycles :
5KR - 16:56, 10MR - 58:20, HMar - 1:15:52
ENDACOTT Katherine U23 29.01.80, C of Ply :
60 - 7.60i, 200 - 25.18i (24.57-99),
100 - 11.9/11.93 (11.8w/11.83w/11.89-99)
200 - 25.18i (24.57-99)
ENGLAND Hannah U15 6.03.87, Oxford City :
1500 - 4:46.81
ENNIS Jessica U15 28.01.86, Sheffield :
75HG - 11.06, HJ - 1.71,
LJ - 5.34, PenG - 3109
EPHGRAVE Helen U17 29.10.84, Guild & G :
HT - 32.69
ERSKINE Joanne U17 28.05.85, Dunf & W Fife :
300 - 40.7, 80HI - 11.9/12.08, 300H - 45.02
EURIDGE Katryna U20 22.05.83, Sutton & D :
TJ - 11.01
EVANS Esther 22.12.73, Highgate Harriers :
1500 - 4:27.73i/4:30.85 (4:30.3-96)
EVANS Gemma U17 9.09.84, Yeovil Oly :
Hepl - 3860
EVANS Kate Victoria 4.02.74, Rugby :
LJ - 5.59 (5.60-90), TJ - 13.04w/12.87 (13.03-97)
EVANS Katherine 19.11.77, Cov G/Leeds Un :
JT - 43.82 (45.37-99)
EVANS Kathryn U17 1.03.84, Elgin :
100 - 12.24w/12.39, 200 - 25.06, 300 - 41.1,
HT - 32.71
EVANS Lucy Hannah U20 2.10.82, Sale :
100 - 12.27
EVANS Natalie U17 15.11.83, Wolves & B :
3kW - 16:00.2 (15:41.71-98),
5kW - 27:24.88, 5kWR - 26:54
EVANS Sally 14.05.75, Sale :
400 - 55.54 (55.32-98), 800 - 2:07.07
EVERALL Kerry U17 29.02.84, Yate :
60 - 7.88i, 100 - 12.2, 200 - 25.1/25.25
EVERETT Claire U23 25.06.79, Norw/Brun U :
HJ - 1.65i (1.74i-94/1.71-93),
SP - 11.79 (11.84-97), Hep - 4501 (4759-96)
EVERITT Amie U23 1.11.78, Huntingdon :
PV - 2.75 (2.80-98)
EZEOGU Nina U20 11.10.82, Newham & E B :
TJ - 11.55w/11.37

FAGAN Collette U20 6.06.82, C of Glasgow :
1500 - 4:31.28, 3k - 9:32.11, 5k - 16:47.44
FAIRLESS Rachel U20 19.03.82, Middlesb & C :
PV - 2.70
FAIRS Elizabeth 1.12.77, Traff/Loughbro :
100 - 12.28 (11.9w-98),
200 - 24.65w/24.76, 100H - 13.49
FAIRWEATHER Kelly U13 5.03.88, Parkside :
100 - 12.9, 150 - 20.0, 200 - 26.7
FAIRWEATHER Lyndsey U13 5.03.88,
Parkside : 100 - 13.2, 200 - 27.3
FAIRWEATHER Lynne U23 15.01.80,
Edinburgh WM : 60H - 8.83i (8.75i-96)
FAIRWEATHER Sheila 24.11.77,
City of Glasgow/Glasgow Univ :
3k - 9:25.2imx/9:29.98i (9:23.38-98),
5k - 16:38.48 (16:07.34-98),
10k - 34:56.04 (34:32.70-99),
10kR - 34:40 (34:34-99)
FARDOE Kerri U17 22.11.83, Shrewsbury :
SP - 10.73 (10.82-99)
FARMER Angela U17 27.03.85, Liverpool H :
HT - 30.95
FARROW Wendy 25.12.71, Derby LAC :
1500 - 4:29.70 (4:21.4-96), 5MR - 27:55 (27:53-99)
FAWKE Kim 2.07.75, Centurian :
(see ELLIOTT)
FAWKES Claire 24.10.77, Braintree :
HT - 37.90 (39.96-97)
FAWKES Danielle U17 11.08.85, Barrow & F :
80HI - 11.81w/11.93, Hepl - 4247
FAY Ursula 23.09.67, Lisburn :
HJ - 1.65 (1.84-83)
FEATHERSTONE Charlotte U15 30.09.85,
Medway : 200 - 25.99
FELTON Rachel U23 27.06.79, Shaft Barnet :
800 - 2:10.27
FENN Joanne 19.10.74, WGreen & Ex L :
400 - 55.2/55.72, 800 - 2:04.19
FERGUSSON Gemma U17 20.08.84, NSP :
60HI - 8.69i, 80HI - 11.33,
100H - 15.0 (14.8-99),300H - 44.3, LJ - 5.52
FERRIER Holly U17 13.07.84, Peterborough :
80HI - 11.6w/11.61w/11.77
FINIKIN Evette D. V35 25.09.63, Shaft Barnet :
TJ - 11.58 (13.46-91)
FINLAY Leanne U13 14.10.87, Shaft Barnet :
150 - 19.7
FINLAY Louise U17 2.10.83, Rhondda :
SP - 12.05, DT - 33.33, HT - 38.36
FINN Victoria U17 3.02.84, Shildon :
300 - 40.71
FINNEGAN Geraldine V35 14.10.65, Dunleavy/ IRE : 400H - 65.11
FINNIS Suzanne U20 12.08.83, WG & Ex L :
JT - 45.84
FINUCANE Laura U15 3.08.86, Pendle :
800 - 2:18.4
FISHER Lucy U15 27.09.85, City of Stoke :
75HG - 11.6, SPG - 10.84, PenG - 2800
FITZPATRICK Lynne U20 21.08.81, Falkirk :
400 - 57.44 (57.12-99)
FLAHERTY Katie U15 1.10.85, Basildon :
100 - 12.6 (12.6-99), 200 - 24.98, LJ - 5.17
FLANNER Lucy U17 9.07.84, Sparkhill :
1500 - 4:46.27
FLEGG Laura U17 7.11.83, N Devon :
300H - 46.6

FLETCHER Alison Kay V35 8.06.61, Dulwich R :
10k - 36:58.19 (35:18.59-93),
Mar - 2:56:31 (2:51:54-90)
FLINT Stacy U15 18.10.85, City of Hull :
75HG - 11.60, PenG - 2799
FOLEY Megan Elizabeth U13 14.04.88, Hav :
600 - 1:44.2, 800 - 2:23.7,
1200 - 3:49.1, 1500 - 4:55.4
FORD Emma 16.02.77, Liverpool H :
1500 - 4:32.6 (4:27.90-98),
3k - 9:27.36i/9:42.39 (9:27.01i-98/9:30.83-99)
FORD Katie U20 21.10.81, Sheffield RWC :
5kWR - 26:29 (24:48-98),
10kWR - 56:07 (52:55-98)
FORESTER Adele 27.03.76, Middlesbro & C :
LJ - 5.66 (6.05-94)
FORGIE Natasha U17 12.05.84, Dartford :
HT - 38.84
FORREST Catriona U17 25.08.84, Guild & G :
HJ - 1.63 (1.65-99)
FORRESTER Amanda U23 29.09.78,
City of Stoke/Staffs Univ :
100 - 11.55, 200 - 23.9 (25.02-97)
FORRESTER Emma U17 2.12.83, Telford :
DT - 37.17
FORSYTH Amy U15 16.10.85, S London :
PenG - 2590
FOSTER Jenny 6.09.77, Trafford :
HT - 40.20
FOSTER Rebecca 14.04.71, Wakefield :
100H - 15.00 (14.26w-93/14.8-89/14.91-94),
JT - 40.71 (41.45-99), Hep - 4679 (5165-93)
FOSTER Vickie 1.04.71, AF&D :
SP - 15.44, DT - 49.25, HT - 44.02 (45.46-97)
FOX Elizabeth U23 13.02.80, Oxford Univ :
400H - 65.6
FOX Laura Elizabeth U17 25.10.84, Ashford :
SP - 10.36, DT - 37.92
FOZZARD Amy U15 20.04.86, Wakefield :
PenG - 2625 (2643-99)
FRANCIS Azaria U20 12.04.83, Croydon :
TJ - 11.56
FRANCIS Candice U17 7.02.85, Birchfield :
DT - 33.75
FRANCIS Eden U13 19.10.88, Leics Cor :
DTM - 22.21
FRANCIS Nafalya LeKeziah U13 21.04.89,
Leics Cor : 70HM - 11.50
FRANCIS Tamara U23 14.11.78, B'mouth :
JT - 48.24
FRASER Donna Karen 7.11.72, Croydon :
60 - 7.63i (7.46i-98),
100 - 11.45w/11.57 (11.2wA-98/11.32w-97),
200 - 23.08 (22.90w/22.96i-97),
300 - 35.71, 400 - 49.79
FREEBAIRN Susan V35 22.08.65, C of Glas :
DT - 45.87 (46.70-94)
FREEL Lyndsey U15 23.09.85, Lagan Valley :
800 - 2:17.80, 1500 - 4:44.65
FREEMAN Danielle U23 11.02.80, Leeds/
Bath Univ: 200 - 24.98 (24.87w-99),
60H - 8.50i, 100H - 13.62, HJ - 1.72,
LJ - 5.88 (6.20w/6.15-97),
SP - 11.83, JT - 39.43, Hep - 5644
FREEMAN Emily U23 24.11.80, Wakefield :
100 - 12.03w/12.10 (11.69w/11.83-99),
200 - 24.55 (24.19i-97/24.34-99)
FREEMAN Henrietta U20 12.07.83, Invicta :
3k - 9:35.25, 5k - 16:37.18
FREEMAN Laura U23 22.04.78, Coventry G :
HJ - 1.65 (1.73-96)
FREETH Megan U20 1.02.82, Swansea :
400H - 65.87, Hep - 3911 (4097-99)
FRISBYE Kayleigh U17 16.08.85, Derby LAC :
300 - 40.91
FROST Bryony U17 21.02.84, Isle of Wight :
800 - 2:15.9, 1500 - 4:37.48,
3k - 10:25.96 (10:16.7-99)
FROST Helen Paula 12.03.74, Birchfield :
100 - 12.23 (12.01-99), 200 - 24.11w/24.14,
300 - 37.55, 400 - 52.40
FROST Kathryn U17 21.02.84, Isle of Wight :
1500 - 4:41.23, 3k - 10:08.40
FROST Suzanne Lynette U17 27.09.84,
City of Plymouth : HT - 31.33
FRYER Laura U17 3.12.83, Belgrave :
3kW - 15:46.72 (15:34.53-99),
5kW - 29:15.05 (27:47.9-99), 5kWR - 26:43
FRYER Lisa U17 30.05.84, Lagan Valley :
JT - 40.98
FRYER Paula Tracy 14.07.69, Sale :
400 - 57.06 (54.7-92/55.34-94),
800 - 2:07.71 (1:59.76-91)
FULLELOVE Alyssa U20 16.09.81, Kilbarchan :
60H - 8.88i, 100H - 14.07w/14.23
FULLERTON Faye Alexis U17 31.05.84, Hav :
800 - 2:10.1, 1500 - 4:28.1, 3k - 9:42.3
FURLONGER Susan H. U20 30.09.81,
Oswestry : TJ - 12.07w/11.28 (11.83-99)

GALE Chloe U13 24.02.88, Dartford :
75 - 10.1, 150 - 19.9, 200 - 27.0, LJ - 4.69
GALLAWAY Sarah U17 14.11.84, Havant :
60HI - 8.99i, 80HI - 11.92w/12.01,
300H - 43.73, LJ - 5.41w/5.37, HepI - 4338
GAMBLE Samantha U17 27.03.84, Cardiff :
60 - 7.84i, 200 - 24.93i (24.6w/24.85-99),
300 - 40.22i (40.9-99)
GANNON Lindsay C. 29.08.66, Royal Navy :
Mar - 3:05:27 (2:59:14-99)
GARAVAND Maria U15 30.06.86, Norwich :
75HG - 11.25w/11.5/11.77
GARDEN Catherine U23 4.09.78, Pitreavie :
SP - 11.83 (12.50-97),
DT - 37.87 (42.72-94), HT - 50.94 (54.03-99)
GARDEN Eleanor 20.11.76, Edinburgh WM :
SP - 11.43 (12.60-97), DT - 45.60
GARDENER Genevieve U17 3.09.84, G & G :
3k - 10:24.4
GARDNER Ann 11.10.68, Corby :
HT - 52.12 (55.60-98)
GARNETT Chanelle U17 16.08.85, Herne Hill :
60HI - 9.08i, 80HI - 11.4/11.52w/11.57,
300H - 45.6, LJ - 5.71 (5.74-99), HepI - 4227
GARRARD Sarah U17 13.05.84, S London :
JT - 36.25
GARRETT Jemma U15 21.09.85, Durham :
PenG - 2689
GASCOIGNE Amber U23 5.09.79, Wells :
1500 - 4:32.24 (4:31.47-97)
GASPAR Charlie U13 7.09.87, Milton Keynes :
1500 - 5:03.6
GATRELL Eleanor 5.10.76, Woking :
SP - 14.60i/14.42 (14.68-98),
DT - 39.57, HT - 40.48

GAULD Louise U23 24.08.80, City of Edinb :
PV - 3.41i/3.30 (3.30-99)
GAUTIER Nicola Louise U23 21.03.78, Traff :
200 - 25.05 (24.81-97), 60H - 8.65i (8.65i-98),
100H - 14.14w/14.19 (13.92w/14.07-99),
HJ - 1.68i (1.68-96), LJ - 5.70, SP - 15.09,
JT - 41.73 (44.67-99), Hep - 5602 (5760-99)
GAYLE Denise U23 11.09.79, Barnet :
HJ - 1.70 (1.72-98)
GAYTER Sharon M. V35 30.10.63, N Marske :
100kR - 9:44:19 (8:12:03-95),
24Hr - 191.386km (212.606km-98)
GEAR Karen U23 30.09.79, N Devon :
200 - 25.08 (24.87-99), 400 - 54.03
GEARY Rebecca S. U17 2.05.84, Yeovil Oly :
300H - 46.08
GEE Michala 8.12.75, Rotherham :
100H - 14.9/15.15 (14.55-96),
LJ - 5.74w/5.64, TJ - 11.80w/11.43
GEENS Natalie U17 27.12.84, Solihull & S H:
3kW - 16:12.0 (16:02.06-99),
5kW - 27:38.4, 5kWR - 26:35
GEMMELL Marlene 21.06.72, Strathkelvin :
10MR - 56:47dh
GEORGE Eleri U15 25.02.86, Carmarthen :
HJ - 1.60
GERRARD Adele V40 24.11.59, Lasswade :
Mar - 2:57:17
GIBBENS Rachel U15 31.01.86, Milton K :
PenG - 2692
GIBSON Claire U20 25.12.82, Kilbarchan :
400 - 56.93, 800 - 2:09.3
GIBSON Sharon Angelia V35 31.12.61, Notts :
SP - 12.35 (13.50-82), JT - 48.00 (50.85-99)
GILBERT Helen U20 1.03.82, Grantham :
HT - 40.83
GILDING Nicola 16.05.72, Brighton :
LJ - 5.50 (5.84-89), TJ - 11.33 (11.54-99)
GILL Frances M. V40 13.01.60, Neath :
10MR - 58:50 (57:27-98),
HMar - 1:17:51 (1:17:27-98)
GILLHAM Michele 8.10.74, Ashford :
400 - 57.0 (56.9-99), 400H - 60.9 (60.18-97)
GLAYSHER Jennifer U20 3.05.83, Preston :
HJ - 1.68 (1.74-99)
GLOVER Helen U15 17.06.86, Cornwall AC :
1500 - 4:46.81
GODBEER Sarah 10.06.77, Exeter :
200 - 25.1 (25.26-95), Hep - 4502
GODDING-FELTHAM Lisa 24.11.69, White H :
Mar - 2:57:06 (2:56:50-99)
GOLDSMITH Sally J. V35 18.01.61, Edin WM :
HMar - 1:17:02 (1:13:13-96),
Mar - 2:54:03 (2:34:11-96)
GONELLA Charlotte U17 20.01.85, Ayr Sea :
HJ - 1.62
GONSE Rosalyn U20 1.03.82, Bedford & Co :
JT - 37.65, Hep - 4557
GOODALL Hayley Jane U17 20.09.84, Ashford :
Hepl - 3928
GOODALL Kimberley U17 5.10.83, Guernsey :
TJ - 11.28 (11.44w/11.35-99), Hepl - 4063
GOODMAN Lea Maureen 9.05.72, Croydon
(nee HAGGETT) : HJ - 1.82 (1.92-96)
GOODWIN Kim Louise 16.05.70, City of Hull :
200 - 24.6 (24.25w-96/24.3-99/24.49-96),
400 - 54.72 (54.64-95)
GORE Nicola U17 17.11.84, W Cheshire :
SP - 10.56
GORTON Victoria 9.05.77, Pendle :
DT - 36.29 (38.12-97)
GOSSMAN Nicola U15 4.11.86, C of Glasgow :
100 - 12.4w/12.51 (12.4dt-99),
200 - 25.8w/26.06
GOWING Paula U23 31.05.78, Bris/U of Wales :
2KSTW - 7:16.99 (7:10.77-99)
GRADDEN Marilyn J. V35 26.01.61, E & E :
Mar - 3:04:27 (2:55:59-95)
GRADY A. U13, S Yorks Sch :
HJ - 1.43
GRAHAM A. U13, Essex Sch :
SPM - 9.03
GRAHAM S. U13, Sutton :
200 - 27.6
GRAINGER Kate U17 17.02.84, Inverness :
JT - 37.64 (38.32-99)
GRANGER Katie 31.03.75, Exeter :
JT - 41.62
GRAY Emma U13 17.04.88, Shetland :
JTM - 27.29
GRAY Jenny V40 21.06.60, Vauxhall :
Mar - 3:02:47
GRAY Linda 23.03.71, Peterborough :
JT - 48.77
GREASLEY Cecilia V40 23.01.58, Macc :
10MR - 56:42
GREEN Andrea 14.12.68, Dartford :
3k - 9:26.1, 5k - 16:27.7, 5MR - 27:21,
10k - 34:39.8mx, 10kR - 33:41,
10MR - 55:57, HMar - 1:13:28
GREEN Nicole 28.01.77, Enf & Har :
PV - 3.50 (3.60-99)
GREEN Susannah U20 5.12.81, Liverpool H :
HJ - 1.68 (1.68-99)
GREENHALGH Grace U23 17.01.78, C & T :
3k - 9:55.53mx/9:58.55
GREY Alison Helen 12.05.73, Edinburgh WM :
SP - 14.30 (15.85i/15.69-94),
DT - 47.79 (52.52-94)
GRIFFITH Michelle Amanda 6.10.71, W S & E :
TJ - 14.14w/13.71 (14.08-94)
GRIFFITHS Ann Margaret V35 20.08.65, Sale :
1500 - 4:21.77 (4:07.59-92)
GRIFFITHS Anna Catherine U13 28.12.87,
Hyndburn : DTM - 25.20, PenM - 2379
GRIFFITHS Natalie U15 22.04.86, Carm :
JT - 30.88
GRIFFITHS Shirley 23.06.72, Wakefield :
800 - 2:08.77 (2:07.3-96),
1500 - 4:20.16 (4:14.41i-97/4:15.68-96),
3k - 9:32.38i/9:37.5 (9:23.8-93)
GRIFFITHS Victoria U17 9.10.84, Liverpool H :
60 - 7.98i, 100 - 12.47, 200 - 25.49, LJ - 5.55
GRIMSTONE Jenny U23 30.04.79, Shaft B :
SP - 11.95, JT - 41.82
GUINEY Cheryl U15 24.09.85, Lagan Valley :
1500 - 4:45.75
GUNDERSEN Nicola U17 26.02.85,
Liv.Pembroke Sefton : 800 - 2:15.48
GUNNING Deborah V35 31.08.65, WG & Ex L :
1500 - 4:24.52 (4:12.69-90),
3k - 9:33.4 (9:12.12-94),
5k - 16:47.54 (16:10.08-98)

HADLAND India U17 7.01.85, N Devon :
HJ - 1.70
HAGAN Natonia U15 6.08.86, East Down :
JT - 30.88
HAGGETT Lea Maureen 9.05.72, Croydon :
(see GOODMAN)
HAINES Nikki 30.11.71, Belgrave :
Mar - 2:58:02
HAINING Hayley 6.03.72, City of Glasgow :
1500 - 4:25.6 (4:14.78-99),
5k - 16:29.8 (15:46.05-99), 5MR - 26:29,
10kR - 33:38 (33:25-96)
HALES Sophie Rebecca U17 30.03.85, Stey :
3kW - 15:05.69, 5kW - 26:54.67,
5kWR - 25:44
HALFORD Katie U20 4.10.82, Exeter :
SP - 11.20, DT - 38.58
HALKET Jade U15 5.05.86, Ellon :
HJ - 1.60i/1.58, LJ - 5.20w/5.17,
PenG - 2861
HALL Andrea 28.01.77, Bedford & County :
TJ - 11.08 (11.54-98)
HALL Cicely Jane U23 12.10.78, Norwich :
2KSTW - 7:31.65, 400H - 62.13 (60.83-97)
HALL Danielle U17 27.11.84, Cambridge H :
SP - 10.46, DT - 35.48
HALL Penny 13.01.77, Cardiff :
PV - 2.80 (3.01-99)
HALL Rebecca A. U13 15.09.88, Boston TC :
SPM - 10.30, DTM - 28.38
HALSALL Danielle U20 27.06.81, Liverpool H :
200 - 25.1w?, 400 - 56.75
HAMILTON Rachel U13 18.10.87, Guild & G :
HJ - 1.50
HAMMOND Cheryl-Leigh U15 13.07.87, AF&D :
1500 - 4:48.2
HANCOCK Coralie U17 1.03.85, Soton City :
DT - 33.49
HANHAM Lark U15 25.10.85, Yate :
JT - 34.09
*HANNAFIN Cathriona 19.09.72, Border/IRE :
TJ - 12.02w/11.99 (12.08-99)*
HANNAM Zoe 26.11.68, Bracknell F Runners :
Mar - 3:06:05 (2:59:25-99)
HANSEN Ashia Nana 5.12.71, Shaftesbury B :
TJ - 14.29 (15.16i-98/15.15-97)
HANSHAW Maria U13, Walton :
100 - 12.9w/13.0, 200 - 26.8
HARDING Faye Marie U15 7.09.85, Wrexham :
100 - 12.3, 200 - 25.6,
800 - 2:13.37, PenG - 3172
HARDING Jemma U23 15.02.79, Wycombe/
DMU (Beds) Univ : PV - 2.90 (2.90-99)
HARDING Joanne V35 12.04.64, Trafford :
HT - 40.99, JT - 39.11 (39.39-99)
HARDY Rebecca Jana 11.11.68, Highgate H :
DT - 43.32 (45.20-97)
HARE Tracey U20 9.03.82, Ashford :
PV - 2.80
HARGREAVES Jackie V35 30.07.65, Border :
Mar - 2:52:04
HARLEY Lynsey U17 2.04.85, Pitreavie :
300H - 46.1/46.87
*HARMSE Dorita 28.09.73, Havering/RSA :
800 - 2:09.69, 1500 - 4:28.36 (4:24.17-98)*
HARRATS Amy U13 9.10.87, Ayr Sch :
70HM - 11.7

HARRIES Barbara V40 27.02.58, Cardiff :
Mar - 3:03:18 (3:02:27-94)
HARRIMAN Kathy U13 13.11.87, Charnwood :
DT - 23.48, DTM - 22.64
HARRIS Amy U13 14.09.87, Halesowen :
100 - 13.1, 150 - 19.8, 200 - 27.3, LJ - 4.91
HARRIS Leah U20 24.02.82, Newquay & Par :
800 - 2:11.54
HARRIS Melissa U17 20.10.83, Telford :
60HI - 9.01i (8.98i-99),
80HI - 11.97 (11.8/11.92-99)
HARRIS Rachael U20 17.07.82, Worcester :
200 - 25.0w/25.16 (25.0-99), Hep - 4022
HARRISON C. U13, Coventry Godiva :
SPM - 9.13
HARRISON Deborah U23 13.11.78, Bir/Birm U :
LJ - 6.02w/5.85 (5.89-99), TJ - 11.12w
HARRISON Fallon U17 1.05.85, Chesterfield :
DT - 36.41
HARRISON Fiona Jane U20 30.11.81, Barn :
200 - 25.27 (24.7/24.84-99), 100H - 14.04,
HJ - 1.70 (1.71-99), PV - 3.51 (3.60-98),
LJ - 5.88w/5.75 (5.91w/5.80-99), Hep - 5279
HARRISON Melanie U15 27.11.85, Havering :
DT - 31.36, JT - 30.60
HARRISON Sarah U23 1.03.79, Shaftesbury B :
HT - 54.15 (54.15-99)
HARRISON Susan 6.08.71, Leamington :
3k - 9:44.65 (9:25.5-94), 5k - 16:32.73,
10k - 35:45.7, 10kR - 34:47, 10MR - 57:24
HARRISON Susanna J. V35 25.01.63, Woking :
Mar - 3:03:24
HART Louise U20 27.05.83, Stevenage & NH :
PV - 2.60
HART Siobhan 15.06.75, Enf & Har :
HT - 39.34
HARTIGAN Beverley Marie 10.06.67, Birchfield :
3k - 9:12.64 (9:03.88i-90/9:10.4-92),
5KR - 16:00 (15:49-95), 5MR - 27:09,
10kR - 33:45 (33:02-95)
HARTLEY Sarah Louise U20 4.05.81,
Spenborough : PV - 2.80 (3.15-97)
HARVEY Amy Charlotte Elizabeth U20
23.04.82, Braintree : JT - 47.57
HARWOOD April U20 11.09.82, Rugby :
PV - 2.60
HARWOOD Jocelyn Anne V40 21.11.57, M & C :
100H - 15.1w (13.79-89)
HATCH Sharon V35 5.09.64, Sparta :
5KR - 16:49
HATHAWAY Emily U23 22.12.79, R S C/
Wolvs Univ : 800 - 2:11.29i (2:09.06-99)
HAWKINS Layla U15 3.09.86, Bromley :
HJ - 1.61, PenG - 2890
HAYWARD Georgina U17 15.09.83, E Grin :
HJ - 1.62
HAZEL Louise U15 6.10.85, Peterborough :
100 - 12.25, 200 - 25.6,
75HG - 11.20, LJ - 5.43, PenG - 3207
HEAD Christine U23 18.12.79, Norwich :
PV - 2.70, JT - 43.70
HEAFFORD Claire U20 9.07.81, Epsom & E :
400H - 63.9/63.95
HEASMAN Heather V35 27.09.63,
Altrincham : (see KNIGHT)
HEATH Jennifer 22.12.77, Sale :
1500 - 4:32.45mx, 3k - 9:41.83mx (9:58.1-99),
5KR - 16:40, 10kR - 34:49

HEATH Sarah V35 4.01.62, Shaft Barnet :
(nee ALT)
800 - 2:11.1mx/2:11.84 (2:07.3-80)
HEFFERNAN Kim S. 20.12.66, Medway :
800 - 2:10.95 (2:07.1-87), 400H - 62.3 (61.6-91)
HEIL Belinda U20 8.03.82, Croydon :
SP - 12.52, DT - 38.80, HT - 47.38
HEMMINGS Vicki 4.06.74, Army :
JT - 38.40
HENAGHAN Dianne V35 6.08.65, Morpeth :
800 - 2:10.5 (2:03.1mx/2:05.4-97),
1500 - 4:18.04 (4:16.17-97), 3k - 9:22.68,
5k - 16:01.96, 5KR - 16:38
HENDERSON Samantha U17 27.09.83, Wok :
LJ - 5.58, TJ - 10.97
HENDERSON Sarah U17 27.09.83, Woking :
Hepl - 3863
HENDRIKS Paula U20 25.01.83, Wolves & B :
100H - 14.74, LJ - 5.58w/5.53, SP - 11.40,
JT - 37.06 (38.32-99), Hep - 4998
HENDRY Susan 30.06.76, City of Glasgow :
400 - 55.69, 800 - 2:07.7
HENRY Corinne Cynthia 15.04.72, Shaft B :
TJ - 13.66w/13.52 (13.95-98)
HENRY Lorraine 16.09.67, Norwich :
SP - 12.14 (13.09-88), DT - 39.93 (43.88-90)
HENRY Yvette 8.06.73, Wigan/Sheffield Univ :
100 - 12.04, 200 - 25.1
HEPHER Joyce Elena V35 11.02.64, Bromley :
LJ - 6.32 (6.80w/6.75-85)
HESKETH Joanne 16.06.69, Steyning :
3kW - 15:39.0, 5kW - 27:13.27,
5kWR - 27:05 (26:51-99), 10kW - 56:34.13,
10kWR - 54:59, 20kW - 1:55:33
HESLOP Laura U17 12.11.83, Wirral :
100 - 12.53
HEWETH Karen V40 29.11.59, Hull Achilles :
DT - 36.85 (38.82-93)
HEWETT Alexandra U20 10.09.82, Hillingdon :
Hep - 3946w/3809
HEWITT Nicola Faye U13 11.12.87, Scun :
PV - 2.20
HIBBERT Ashia U15 30.03.86, Rowntrees :
PenG - 2548
HICK Shona 1.06.71, Mornington :
(nee CROMBIE) Mar - 2:42:44
HIGGINS Allison 8.04.72, Kilmarnock :
5k - 17:16.7
HIGGINS Dawn 10.12.75, Cardiff :
400 - 53.24
HIGHAM Stephanie Anne U17 26.12.83, Bord :
HJ - 1.78, TJ - 11.14
HILL Amie U23 9.09.80, Oxford City :
DT - 38.18 (40.72-96)
HILL Cathy-Ann 4.05.77, Team Solent :
SP - 12.71i/12.33 (13.10-96), HT - 40.74
HILL Iris Heidi Alexa 16.01.69, Windsor S & E :
PV - 4.20
HILL Jenna U15 16.10.85, Sale :
800 - 2:16.99, 1500 - 4:43.50
HILL Joanna 11.02.73, Windsor S & E :
60 - 7.57i, 100 - 11.85 (11.67-98),
200 - 24.22w/24.58 (23.62w/23.93-98/24.2-97)
HIND Karen U23 31.01.79, Gate/Leeds Poly :
1500 - 4:31.12, 3k - 9:18.59,
5k - 16:05.80, 10kR - 34:12
HINDS Sally U15 2.02.86, Swansea :
SPG - 11.45

HINES Olivia U17 19.10.83, Herne Hill :
300 - 39.36, 400 - 56.02,
800 - 2:15.74i/2:16.5 (2:12.04-98)
HIRD Jocelyn U17 3.12.83, Wimborne :
PV - 2.70
HIRD Leyna U17 4.02.84, Exeter :
80HI - 12.0 (11.8-99), 100H - 15.2,
300H - 46.2/46.83, 400H - 67.5
HOBBS Kim U23 12.12.78, Middlesbro & C :
PV - 3.00
HODGE Gowry P. V40 21.06.60, Highgate H
(prev RETCHAKAN) :
100H - 14.9 (14.0-92/14.52w-89/14.65-82),
400H - 58.3 (54.63-92)
HODGES Lindsay U20 21.09.82, Yeovil Oly :
PV - 3.65i/3.40 (3.55-99)
HOGG Rachel U20 11.06.82, Trafford :
LJ - 5.92, TJ - 11.78
HOGSDEN Georgina U20 23.11.81, Sutton & D :
JT - 41.62
HOLAH Sarah U17 9.12.84, Pudsey & Bram :
800 - 2:16.69
HOLDEN Diana 12.02.75, AF&D/Brunel Univ :
HT - 55.62 (57.95-98)
HOLDSWORTH Catherine U15 3.01.86, Col H :
PenG - 2568
HOLLMAN Anne Marie 18.02.74, Peterbro :
60H - 8.82i (8.82i-92), 400H - 62.2 (61.13-99),
100H - 14.12w/14.19 (13.98w-99/14.1-96),
HJ - 1.67i/1.65 (1.70-99), SP - 11.73,
JT - 40.67, Hep - 5151 (5259w-99/5258-96)
HOLLMAN Julie Caroline 16.02.77, Peterbro :
200 - 24.72 (24.47w-98), 60H - 8.85i,
100H - 14.48w/14.5/14.55 (14.14w/14.24-98),
HJ - 1.78 (1.81-97), LJ - 6.51,
SP - 12.64, Hep - 5685 (5816w-98)
HOLLOWAY Carys U20 23.07.82, Brecon :
PV - 2.90
HOLLOWAY Joanne 10.05.76, Windsor S & E :
SP - 11.62 (12.02i-96/12.00-98), HT - 42.88
HOLMES Claire U17 11.08.85, Wigan :
PV - 2.70
HOLMES Kelly 19.04.70, Ealing,S & Mx :
600 - 1:26e (1:26.0+-95),
800 - 1:56.80 (1:56.21-95),
1500 - 4:05.35 (3:58.07-97)
HOLMES Lisa 21.11.75, Liverpool H :
TJ - 11.84w/11.63 (11.79-99)
HOLROYD Shelley Ann 17.05.73, WG & Ex L :
JT - 53.06
HOLT Gemma 20.12.72, AF&D :
LJ - 5.87 (6.03A-99/5.99-98),
TJ - 11.28w/11.23 (11.38-99)
HOLT Sarah Joanne U15 17.04.87, Spenbro :
HTG - 38.32
HOOD Hayley Marie U15 12.09.85, Sale :
SPG - 11.64, DT - 33.96
HOPKINS Emma U15 16.09.86, Leics Cor :
800 - 2:14.0, 1500 - 4:42.2
HORLER Jessica U13 9.06.88, Barnsley :
HJ - 1.50
HORNBY Emma 12.12.73, Birchfield :
PV - 3.70 (3.91-98)
HORNE Katherine U23 23.05.79, C of Glas/
Sunderland Univ : HT - 42.69
HORNER Verina 15.09.72, Middlesbro & C :
HT - 40.21

HOROVITZ Gillian P. V45 7.06.55, AF&D :
Mar - 2:47:49 (2:36:52-92)
HORWILL Katherine 26.01.75, Dudley & St :
3kW - 14:30.3 (13:59.89-99),
5kW - 26:15.1 (25:08.24-99),
5kWR - 25:21 (24:37-99),
10kW - 55:59.54 (52:48.5-92),
10kWR - 53:22 (49:38-99),
20kW - 1:54:46 (1:51:38-99)
HOULIHAN Lauren U13 14.12.87, Enf & Har :
1200 - 4:00.2, 1500 - 5:07.6
HOURIHAN Alyson J. V40 17.10.60, Cardiff :
SP - 11.86i/11.65 (12.41-92),
DT - 40.24 (43.58-92)
HOWARD A. U15, Skyrac :
DT - 28.57
HOWARD Anna U20 18.07.83, Oxford City :
HT - 40.54
HOWARD Christine 9.11.70, Matlock :
5k - 17:22.0, Mar - 3:04:46
HOWCROFT Lucy U20 23.04.82, Hillingdon :
PV - 2.60
HOWE Catherine U17 12.12.84, Chelmsford :
HJ - 1.65
HOWELL Gabrielle U20 25.01.82, Shaft Barn :
400 - 55.68 (54.7-98/54.98-99)
HOWELL Mieke U17 6.10.84, Hastings :
300H - 46.6
HOWES Lucy U15 27.06.86, Thurrock :
HJ - 1.62
HUCKERBY Nicola U23 27.02.78, Birchfield :
3kW - 15:13.68 (14:30.94-99),
5kW - 25:33.09 (24:56.69-98),
10kW - 54:53.35, 10kWR - 54:15 (51:07-98),
20kW - 1:51:25 (1:49:12-99)
HUDSON Emma E. V35 4.02.65, Stockport :
2KSTW - 7:36.24
HUGHES Elizabeth 9.06.77, Bromley :
PV - 3.70
HUGHES Emma L. U23 15.09.80, Lut/Bath U :
LJ - 5.75i/5.66w/5.59 (6.14w-99/5.97-98)
HUGHES Johanne 7.02.71, Shaftesbury Barn :
PV - 2.90 (3.13-99)
HULSE Natalie U20 2.12.82, City of Stoke :
HJ - 1.70 (1.70-98), Hep - 4276
HUMBERSTONE Sarah U20 6.07.81, Cleeth :
HJ - 1.65 (1.68-98)
HUMPHREYS Danielle U17 16.05.84, Mansf :
HJ - 1.65 (1.65-99), LJ - 5.75
HUMPHREYS Sarah U17 16.10.84, Border :
LJ - 5.68
HUNT Emma U15 25.04.86, Milton Keynes :
800 - 2:17.1, 1500 - 4:40.5
HUNT Laura U13, Milton Keynes :
600 - 1:46.8
HUNT Lucy U17 4.04.84, Cheltenham :
80HI - 11.9, 100H - 15.3,
300H - 46.96, TJ - 10.96
HUNT Tanya U17 14.09.83, Salisbury :
SP - 10.89, JT - 36.85 (39.35-99)
HUNTER Donna U20 9.10.81, Pitr/Stirling Un :
PV - 3.10
HUNTER Laura U13, South Shields :
PenM - 1909
HUNTER Sarah U23 19.05.78, Shaftesbury B/
Brunel Univ : TJ - 11.41w/11.25
HURFORD Alison J. V40 11.10.60, Bristol :
2KSTW - 7:42.06
HURST Jodie 21.06.77, Sale :
TJ - 12.64
HUTCHINSON Ann-Marie 21.08.77, Neath :
3k - 9:42.52
HUTCHINSON Anya 16.07.77, Notts/Loughbro :
400H - 60.76
HUTCHISON Fiona 18.01.77, City of Glasgow :
TJ - 11.06
HUTT Donna-Louise 6.06.72, Northampton :
100H - 14.7 (14.4-91/14.64-92)
HYDE PETERS Zahara V35 12.01.63, Havant :
1500 - 4:24.00 (4:19.36-93),
3k - 9:16.89i/9:46.0 (9:05.49-91),
5k - 16:40.37 (16:04.12-96), 5KR - 16:25,
10k - 35:05.85 (33:23.25-94),
HMar - 1:18:25 (1:16:33-98)
HYNAN Julie U23 23.05.80, Liverpool H :
PV - 2.80i/2.80 (3.00-99)
HYND Natalie U23 30.01.78, Pitreavie :
(see BEATTIE)

IGBOKWE Jenny U13, Sale :
75 - 9.98, 150 - 19.1un
ING Sarah V35 10.11.63, Swindon :
Mar - 3:00:00
INGMAN Jilly U23 17.08.78, Barnsley :
1500 - 4:28.45 (4:19.3-99),
3k - 9:16.42 (9:12.37mx-99),
5k - 16:10.25 (15:59.00-99),
5MR - 27:34, 10kR - 34:14 (33:57-99)
INIEKIO Nimi U15 25.10.86, Brighton :
SPG - 10.85
IRVING Ruth 20.07.74, Edinburgh WM :
LJ - 5.93i (6.28-98)
IRWIN Sally U15 12.10.85, Reading :
100 - 12.6

JACKSON Amber U20 29.11.82, Verlea :
JT - 39.17
JACKSON Charlotte U15 31.10.85, Portsmouth :
800 - 2:16.92
JACKSON Joanne Elizabeth V35 16.04.63,
Harlow : DT - 40.21 (50.06-89)
JACKSON Lorna J. 9.01.74, Edinburgh WM :
JT - 57.19
JACKSON Sarah 14.12.77, Middlesbro & C/
Liverpool Univ : 2KSTW - 7:32.48
JACOBS Kim Simone Geraldine 5.09.66, S B :
60 - 7.6i/7.65i (7.33i-85),
100 - 11.59w/11.76 (11.18w-97/11.31-88),
200 - 24.43i+ (22.95-96),
400 - 56.37i (55.36-99)
JAMES Angharad U23 7.04.79, Swan/UWIC :
60 - 7.61i, 100 - 11.87w/11.90,
200 - 24.60w/24.98 (24.92-96)
JAMES Anwen U20 17.02.81, Swan/U of Wales :
DT - 36.20 (38.72-99)
JAMES Marian 9.05.71, Hull Spartan :
(see ROUTLEDGE)
JAMES Vernicha U17 6.06.84, Cambridge H :
60 - 7.5i/7.52i, 100 - 11.85,
200 - 23.49i/23.59 (23.48w-99)
JAMES Vicky U20 13.05.81, Cheltenham :
JT - 40.37
JAMISON Victoria Anne 19.05.77, Lagan V :
200 - 24.95 (24.06-98),
400 - 54.08 (52.87R/52.97-98)

JASPER Hayley Laurette U17 1.05.84, Hunt :
Hepl - 3847
JELBERT Zoe U17 21.01.84, Newquay & Par :
800 - 2:08.80, 1500 - 4:23.96,
3k - 9:37.54i (10:11.9-99)
JENKINS Andrea Louise 4.10.75, Bedford & Co :
DT - 40.51, HT - 50.33
JENKINS Beverley 6.02.70, Salford :
1500 - 4:21.97, 3k - 9:16.02,
5k - 16:21.39 (16:08.96-99), 5KR - 16:54,
10k - 33:49.8, 10kR - 33:59, 10MR - 57:00
JENKINS Kate 26.03.74, Carnethy :
Mar - 3:04:21 (2:56:09-99)
JENKINS Nicola U17 6.02.84, Dartford :
HT - 35.30
JENNINGS-STEELE Joanne Loraine 20.09.69,
Rugby : HJ - 1.89 (1.94i-93/1.91-98)
JEPSON Lynsey Rebecca U15 12.01.87,
Leics Cor : 800 - 2:13.18, 1500 - 4:41.6
JESSOP Michelle U15 21.09.85, Milton K :
800 - 2:16.9, 1500 - 4:50.3
JOEL Alexa U17 19.09.83, Basildon :
3k - 10:25.2
JOHANSEN Michelle U17 1.02.84, Oxford C :
LJ - 5.47 (5.54-98), TJ - 11.50
JOHN Joanne E. U23 12.11.80, E, S & Mx/
St. Marys Univ : DT - 40.92, HT - 45.90
JOHNS Karen Lesley U23 18.08.80, Shildon/
Northumbria Univ : 800 - 2:10.6 (2:10.23-99)
JOHNSON Charmaine Rachael V35 4.06.63,
Epsom & Ewell : 100H - 14.78 (14.36-94),
SP - 13.27 (14.29-93), Hep - 4961 (5495-92)
JOHNSON Jade U23 7.06.80, Herne Hill :
60 - 7.65i, LJ - 6.58,
100 - 11.85w/12.09 (11.72w/12.0-98)
JOHNSON Julia U23 21.09.79, Inv/Warwick U :
TJ - 12.12 (12.50-98)
JOHNSON Lindsey U20 3.12.81, Trafford :
PV - 2.80
JOHNSON Sinead U15 24.12.86, Telford :
100 - 12.5/12.57
JOHNSON-COLE Claire U20 21.08.83, Leam :
200 - 24.7 (25.54w-99)
JOHNSTON Lorna U17 20.12.83, Aberdeen :
200 - 25.59, 300 - 40.9/41.00, 400 - 57.4
JOHNSTON Stephanie U20 9.10.81, Barr & F :
200 - 25.0w (26.6-96)
JOINER Angela 14.02.69, Shaftesbury Barnet :
5k - 17:25.69 (16:23.87-99), 10MR - 56:35,
HMar - 1:15:14 (1:13:44-97), Mar - 2:44:07
JONES Caroline U17 30.04.84, Verlea :
DT - 35.44
JONES Ceri U17 29.07.84, Glan-Y-Mor :
TJ - 10.96
JONES Elizabeth V35 25.04.61, Arena :
Mar - 3:00:10 (2:54:03-95)
JONES Ffion U20 19.07.83, Deeside :
DT - 36.40
JONES Gemma U23 25.02.79, Torfaen :
LJ - 5.64 (5.73-97)
JONES Hannah U13 9.06.88, AF&D :
600 - 1:44.4, 800 - 2:27.2,
1k - 3:13.1, 1500 - 5:00.12
JONES Heather U15 10.09.86, Carmarthen :
200 - 25.88i, 75HG - 11.1/11.19
JONES Katherine U17 21.01.85, Cann & St :
60 - 7.89i
JONES Katie 4.01.77, Trafford :
400 - 55.78,
100H - 14.2w/14.86 (14.56w/14.72-98),
400H - 58.75, TJ - 11.18 (11.19-99)
JONES Laura U15 28.09.86, Hertford & Ware :
PenG - 2584
JONES Laura U15 4.02.86, Havering :
100 - 12.59w/12.6, 200 - 25.9/26.26
JONES Lindsey 8.09.77, Wakefield :
HT - 41.71 (49.10-97)
JONES Lowri U20 22.07.83, Cardiff :
60 - 7.66i, 200 - 24.38i (24.56w-98/24.57-99)
JONES Lucy U17 30.11.83, Bristol :
800 - 2:14.16 (2:13.73-99),
1500 - 4:46.56 (4:46.25-99)
JONES Rebecca U20 17.01.83, Wrexham :
100H - 14.65w/14.80, HJ - 1.83i/1.83,
LJ - 5.66w/5.65, Hep - 5186
JONES Sarah 1.01.75, Macclesfield :
3k - 9:59.9 (9:54.1mx-99)
JONES Sian U20 20.01.83, Swansea :
TJ - 11.07
JONES Susan Eva U23 8.06.78, Wigan :
100H - 14.8 (13.95-97), HJ - 1.93
JONES Ulrike 1.03.73, Barrow & Furness :
100H - 15.2
JONES Wendy C. V35 10.03.62, Cirencester :
5KR - 16:59
JOSEPH Samantha 11.09.70, Windsor S & E :
PV - 2.80i (3.10-99)
JOSEPH Tracy Carol 29.11.69, Bas & MH :
100 - 12.22 (11.66w-97/11.79-96),
HJ - 1.70 (1.73-98),
LJ - 6.37w/6.16 (6.44w-97/6.39-98)
JURY Kerry 19.11.68, Wakefield :
200 - 24.26 (23.80w-98/24.12-99), 60H - 8.51i,
100H - 13.78w/13.92 (13.71w-99),
HJ - 1.79 (1.81-97), SP - 11.78 (12.00-98),
LJ - 5.79i/5.78w/5.71 (6.08w-98/5.97-99),
Hep - 5735 (6005w-98/5908-99)

KAISER Kathryn Mary V45 24.08.51,
Valley Str : Mar - 3:06:07 (2:55:03-94)
KALMEIJER Saskia U13, Radley :
LJ - 4.81
KANEEN Bridget V35 15.08.65, Manx H :
3kW - 15:57.2 (15:18.1-99),
5kW - 26:33.5, 5kWR - 26:57,
10kWR - 55:54 (55:06-99), 20kW - 1:54:21
KAY Alex U15, Halifax :
DT - 28.48
KAY Rachael U23 8.09.80, Wigan :
60 - 7.70i (7.65i-99), 400 - 57.3 (56.8-98),
400H - 60.37 (58.91-99)
KEHLER Lisa Martine 15.03.67, Wolves & B :
3kW - 12:50.61, 5kW - 22:22.94+ (21:57.68-90),
5kWR - 23:24+/23:31R (21:55-98),
10kW - 45:09.57, 20kW - 1:33:57,
10kWR - 46:30+/46:42 (45:03-98)
KEIGHER Sally 1.08.71, Stockport :
Mar - 3:06:40
KEIGHT Hannah U17 22.06.85, R S Coldfield :
HJ - 1.65i/1.65
KELLEHER Olivia Maria 9.10.75, WS & E/IRE :
HT - 55.50 (57.53-99)
KELLY Jennifer Angela 20.06.70, Peterbro :
LJ - 5.59 (6.09-93), Hep - 4056 (5826-94),
SP - 13.97 (14.88i-90/14.73-91)

KELLY Louise U23 20.09.80, Barr & F/CUAC :
3k - 9:47.8 (9:28.64-98),
5k - 16:42.8 (16:15.36-98)
KELLY Siona 19.04.74, Barrow & Furness :
JT - 39.00 (40.21-99)
KEMP Jennifer U23 18.02.80, Liverpool H/
DMU (Beds) Univ : JT - 52.20 (52.54-99)
KENNAUGH Jane 26.01.73, Manx H :
3kW - 15:18.5, 5kW - 26:26.0,
5kWR - 26:34+ (24:44-99),
10kWR - 53:35 (51:34-99),
20kW - 1:50:13 (1:48:24-99)
KENNEY Laura U17 27.06.85, R S Coldfield :
1500 - 4:46.16
KERR Anyha U23 10.04.80, Bristol :
JT - 38.56
KING Emma U20 25.07.81, Guern/Brighton U :
HT - 42.02
KING Janine 18.02.73, Trafford :
JT - 41.34
KING Rachel 11.05.76, Cardiff :
100 - 11.88 (11.8w-97), 60H - 8.55i (8.39i-99),
100H - 13.51 (13.44w-98/13.46-99)
KINGSBOROUGH Ruth 25.10.67, Overton :
Mar - 3:00:33 (2:44:33-98)
KIRBY Emma U20 11.11.81, Bracknell :
DT - 36.42
KIRBY Joanna U13 26.10.87, Wirral :
70HM - 11.5
KIRBY Rachel 18.05.69, WGreen & Ex L :
TJ - 11.84 (13.64-94)
KIRBY Stacey U17 19.09.83, Sale :
1500 - 4:44.95
KIRKHAM Kaye U17 19.10.84, Macclesfield :
800 - 2:14.54, 1500 - 4:46.07
KNIGHT Heather V35 27.09.63, Altrincham :
(nee HEASMAN)3k - 9:31.93 (9:16.5mx-98),
5k - 17:30.46 (15:53.84-96),
5MR - 27:54 (26:29-96), 10kR - 34:51 (32:31-94),
10MR - 58:15 (57:15-93)
KNIGHT Lisa U17 31.01.85, Cannock & Staff :
3k - 10:26.3
KNIGHTS Lisa 12.07.71, Sutton-in-Ashfield :
Mar - 2:48:59
KNIGHTS Sarah 25.02.67, Norwich :
800 - 2:07.14, 1500 - 4:26.74
KNOTT Lynsey U23 30.05.79, AF&D :
DT - 36.70
KOTEY Judy U23 20.05.80, St Albans Str :
TJ - 11.53 (12.61w/12.41i/12.33-98)
KRIEHN Rebecca U15 5.12.85, Cornwall AC :
PenG - 2547
KRZYWICKI Tara 9.03.74, Charnwood :
1500 - 4:21.67, 3k - 9:19.10,
5k - 16:02.48 (15:48.1mx/15:53.28-98),
5MR - 27:37 (26:27-99),
10k - 33:10.89 (33:04.55-99), 2kSt - 6:36.49,
2KSTW - 6:37.69, 3kSt - 10:08.11
KWAKYE Jeanette U20 20.03.83, WG & Ex L :
100 - 12.10 (11.8w/11.93w-98)
KYDD Natalie U17 27.06.84, Motherwell :
300H - 43.84

LACEY Katherine U23 6.07.78, Charn :
PV - 2.70
LACKENBY Leah J. 18.09.74, Gate :
(see WEATHERITT)
LAING Manndy June V40 7.11.59, Liv H :
SP - 11.60 (12.42i-83/12.40-81)
LAING Wendy Jean V35 29.12.62, Liv H :
100H - 15.1 (14.14w-93/14.2-81/14.35-86)
LAMB Katy U20 21.08.82, Dartford :
HT - 50.42
LAMB Susan 24.03.70, Sale :
800 - 2:09.14 (2:04.9mx-96/2:05.50-93),
1500 - 4:22.19 (4:11.57-96),
3k - 9:38.84 (9:06.2-92)
LAMBERT Vicky U17 20.11.84, Wakefield :
LJ - 5.35
LAMBOURN Angela Jean 9.04.66, Rugby :
SP - 12.46 (13.75-91)
LANDO Jill U17 2.09.84, Motherwell :
400 - 57.57, 800 - 2:10.70, 1500 - 4:46.4
LANE Catherine 18.11.76, Dacorum & Tring/
Glasgow Univ Cal :
DT - 39.56 (40.72-98), HT - 38.44 (40.73-98)
LANE Sarah E. U20 24.11.82, Swansea :
LJ - 5.57w (5.70w-98/5.59-99)
LANGLANDS Caya U15 8.09.85, Coventry G :
HJ - 1.61
LANINI Lisa Mair U13 9.10.87, Wrexham :
200 - 27.5, 600 - 1:37.3, 800 - 2:16.1,
1200 - 3:55.7 (3:46.4-99), 1500 - 5:00.2
LANNON Katia U15 14.09.85, Manchester :
DT - 29.89
LANSDOWN Jane 24.01.68, Str of Croydon :
Mar - 3:02:36
LASHLEY Charlene U15 1.09.85, W S & E :
100 - 12.56 (12.4-99)
LAST Suzanne F. 11.01.70, Medway :
DT - 38.28 (39.48-98), HT - 49.68
LATTO Emma J. 16.01.69, Herne Hill :
Mar - 3:02:49
LAURIE Bryony U13 1.09.87, Carmarthen :
200 - 27.6w
LAVENDER Julie 9.11.75, Sunderland :
SP - 11.58, HT - 47.10 (51.62-94)
LAWRENCE Christine U15 4.04.86, Ashford :
JT - 34.84
LAWRENCE Helen 3.12.76, Wirral :
3k - 9:59.02
LAWRENCE Susan 25.11.70, Thurrock :
HT - 38.51 (40.58-99)
LAWRENCE Victoria 9.06.73, Edinburgh WM :
800 - 2:10.75mx (2:03.52-96)
LEAK Jackie V40 19.10.60, Chiltern :
100kR - 9:00:15
LEAVER Rachel U17 4.09.84, Portsmouth :
80HI - 12.0
LECKIE Caron U17 23.11.84, Shetland :
TJ - 10.72
LEE Dorothea 28.07.77, Bristol :
1500 - 4:25.50
LEE India A. U13 31.05.88, AF&D :
1k - 3:14.6, 1500 - 5:01.89
LEE Nikki 27.02.68, Huncote :
(see NEALON)
LEES Tamsin U17 24.04.84, Newton Abbot :
100 - 12.2/12.45 (12.2-99/12.35w-98/12.39-99)
LEIGH Kay V40 3.12.60, Todmorden :
Mar - 3:05:07 (3:03:51-98)
LEIGH Sandra Christine 26.02.66, S & NH :
400 - 57.0/57.06 (52.75-91),
400H - 63.6 (61.8-93/63.04-86)
LEITCH Rebecca U17 12.11.84, Lagan Valley :
300 - 40.9/40.99, 400 - 57.69
LENG Jennifer U17 1.02.84, Blackpool :
JT - 35.90

LEWIS Ann V50 29.12.47, AF&D :
3kW - 16:17.70 (15:52.71i/15:55.0-96)
LEWIS Denise 27.08.72, Birchfield :
200 - 24.01w/24.34 (24.10-97),
800 - 2:12.20, 100H - 13.13,
HJ - 1.84 (1.87-99), LJ - 6.69 (6.77w-97),
SP - 15.55 (16.12-99), JT - 51.13,
Hep - 6831
LEWIS Eugenie 10.10.74, Croydon :
PV - 3.30
LEWIS Natalie U20 25.05.82, Cardiff :
800 - 2:08.15
LEYSHON Anna U23 19.01.80, Swan/UWIC :
PV - 3.25i/3.20
LIA Hannah U17 15.11.84, Cardiff :
HT - 38.04
LIDSTER Claire U20 26.10.81, Team Solent :
HJ - 1.66
LIGHTFOOT Leonie U20 8.02.82, C of Stoke :
100 - 12.1 (12.19-99)
LINDSAY Rebecca U23 20.11.80, Birm Univ. :
2KSTW - 7:48.60
LINSKILL Claire U13 12.01.88, N Devon :
HJ - 1.43, LJ - 4.71
LINTERN Candie U20 5.02.82, Crawley :
DT - 41.46 (41.40-99)
LISHMAN Bethan U17 15.11.83, Border :
HT - 34.34
LISHMAN Hannah U15 5.10.85, Gateshead :
JT - 30.52
LISTER Alison U23 18.06.80, Oxford Univ :
PV - 2.80
LISTON Bianca U23 28.05.78, Windsor S & E/
St. Marys Univ : 200 - 24.9 (25.28-96),
60H - 8.54i, 100H - 13.4/13.52
LITTLE Stephanie U20 5.11.81, Newport :
Hep - 4047 (4142-99)
LITTLE Stephanie U17 18.10.83, Dudley & St :
300H - 46.38
LIVESEY Katherine Dawn U23 15.12.79,
Blackpool/Univ of Nebraska :
200 - 25.0w (24.70w/24.78-97), 100H - 14.15,
55H - 8.43i, 60H - 8.94i (8.90i-98),
400H - 64.09, HJ - 1.70 (1.75-96),
LJ - 5.63i/5.51 (5.77-98),
Hep - 5173 (5239w-99/5215-97)
LLEWELYN Gemma U15 23.04.87, Wigan :
DT - 28.36
LLOYD Angharad U23 11.09.80, Carmarthen :
SP - 11.59 (12.01-99)
LLOYD Hannah U23 14.11.78, Havant :
LJ - 5.50, TJ - 11.13
LLOYD Jennifer U17 12.05.84, Tamworth :
60HI - 9.07i
LOCKLEY Angela U17 7.10.84, Trafford :
DT - 38.63 (38.85-99), HT - 38.14
LOCKWOOD Clare U23 7.10.79, Birchfield :
JT - 37.86 (40.21-99)
LODGE Joanna 6.01.68, Hounslow :
Mar - 2:40:51
LONSDALE Michelle U20 29.10.81, Wakefield :
JT - 41.17 (42.68-99)
LORD Dominique U15 8.04.87, Radley :
DT - 32.36
LOTSCH Bettina 7.09.77, Oxford Univ/GER :
TJ - 11.30i/11.19
LOUISY Felicia 17.05.74, Luton :
100 - 11.74, 200 - 24.06w/24.37, 400 - 56.9
LOWE Karen U20 3.05.82, Blackpool :
400H - 63.73 (62.20-99)
LOWE Larissa V35 19.08.63, Windsor S & E :
PV - 3.50
LOWE Zoe A. V35 7.07.65, St Albans Striders :
Mar - 2:55:02 (2:49:28-95)
LUCAS-READ Jade U17 17.01.84, Herc Wim :
100 - 12.09w/12.18
LUCK Sara U15 18.11.86, Havering :
800 - 2:16.22
LUMB Rebecca 7.04.77, Sheffield :
PV - 2.80
LUMBER Elizabeth 10.08.66, Arena :
Mar - 3:06:27
LUNDGREN Hollie U15 10.10.85, St Albans S :
HJ - 1.70, PenG - 2936
LYALL Stephanie Anne U13 3.02.89, Harmeny :
800 - 2:24.0
LYNE Rebecca Louise U20 4.07.82, Hallam :
400 - 55.41, 800 - 2:05.27
LYNE-LEY Claire U13 14.03.88, Exeter :
JTM - 27.19
LYNES Margaret Tracey V35 19.02.63, WG&EL :
SP - 15.45i/14.73 (16.57-94),
DT - 41.72 (44.76-93)
LYON Janet A. V35 12.03.62, Aberdeen :
PV - 2.70

MACDOUGALL Lynne V35 18.02.65,
City of Glasgow : 5MR - 27:49,
10kR - 33:22, 10MR - 57:37 (55:58-98),
HMar - 1:14:50, Mar - 2:38:32
MACKENZIE Laura U17 9.11.83, Inverness :
HT - 30.42
MACKENZIE Rachael U13 23.12.87, Inverness :
HJ - 1.44
MACPHAIL Ann 3.05.70, City of Glasgow :
3k - 9:38.67, 5MR - 27:52,
10kR - 34:49 (34:39-97), HMar - 1:16:26
MACPHERSON Joan U23 18.09.80,
Basingstoke & MH/Brunel Univ :
SP - 12.17, DT - 45.58, HT - 40.97
MACPHERSON Sheila, City of Glasgow :
Mar - 3:04:41
MACRAE Catherine U23 1.01.79, Hounslow :
PV - 3.25i/3.20
MADDOX Keri 4.07.72, Sale :
200 - 24.92 (24.1w-90/24.49-99),
400 - 54.93, 100H - 13.13 (12.95-99),
300H - 40.90mx (42.2-97/43.12-88),
400H - 55.22
MADGETT Stephanie U15 22.02.87, Brack :
75HG - 11.73, PenG - 2592
MADUAKA Joice 30.09.73, WGreen & Ex L :
60 - 7.30i, 100 - 11.42 (11.24-99),
200 - 23.17 (22.83-99)
MAGANINI Vanessa U20 26.10.81, Rug/RSA :
100H - 14.22A/14.40
MAGUIRE Kirsty U20 5.07.83, Edinburgh WM :
PV - 3.35
MAHONY Joanne 22.10.76, Trafford :
400H - 63.35 (59.4/59.46-99)
MAIN Jennifer U17 26.01.84, Inverness :
800 - 2:16.73
MAINSTONE Teresa U20 13.07.81, Worksop :
Hep - 3812 (3985-99)
MAJOR Marie Ann 4.05.74, Basildon :
100H - 14.9 (14.39w/14.4-93/14.69-91)

MAKIN Emma U15 12.10.85, Warrington :
75HG - 11.28
MALE Kirsty U20 7.07.82, Edinburgh WM :
DT - 36.84
MALE Samantha Kate 11.04.76, AF&D :
100H - 14.36w/14.54 (14.25w/14.38-99)
MANGER Eloise U17 6.01.85, Chorley :
JT - 36.55
MANN Michelle Louise 6.02.77, Sale/
Univ of Nebraska : (see BROOKS)
MANSFIELD Danielle U20 18.05.82, Thurrock :
JT - 37.20 (38.32-99)
MANSHIP-JONES Devina 12.12.69, Cov G :
3k - 9:58.89 (9:31.98-92), 10k - 35:57.15,
10kR - 34:28
MARSDEN Cara U15 22.05.86, Horwich :
JT - 30.19
MARSDEN Caroline U20 1.06.82, Cardiff :
TJ - 11.02w
MARSHALL Carol Jane 11.01.77, City of Hull/
Ripon & York Un : (nee BENNETT)
SP - 13.70 (14.24-97), DT - 39.74
MARSHALL Jacqueline U23 20.07.79, EWM/
Edinburgh Univ : PV - 3.10
MARSHALL Jolene U17 22.10.83, Maid & Roch :
SP - 11.33
MARSHALL Kelly U15 8.01.86, Dudley & Stour :
75HG - 11.75w/11.8
MARSHALL Lucy A. U20 28.11.81, Rugby :
HT - 51.54
MARSHALL Samantha U17 26.08.85, Pitreavie :
1500 - 4:46.63, 2KSTW - 7:43.55
MARTELL Nicola U15 20.09.85, Harwich :
PenG - 2719
MARTI Debora Jane 14.05.68, Bromley :
HJ - 1.85 (1.95i-97/1.94-96),
LJ - 5.52w (6.22-96)
MARTIN Charlotte U17 12.08.85, W S & E :
300H - 46.61
MARTIN Claire 12.07.76, Newport :
800 - 2:12.0 (2:10.4-97), 1500 - 4:22.52
MARTIN Clare 14.09.74, Telford :
5KR - 16:59, 2KSTW - 6:57.42
MARTIN Debbie U23 30.11.79, Yate :
PV - 2.80
MARTIN Karen Lesley 24.11.74, Derby LAC :
JT - 58.54 (59.50-99)
MARTIN Rachel U23 9.09.78, Sale/
Crewe & Alsager : HJ - 1.68 (1.76-97)
MARTIN Stacey U20 6.08.82, Newport :
LJ - 5.54
MARTIN-CLARKE Susan J. V45 13.09.55,
Dartford : Mar - 3:01:46 (2:42:32-89)
*MASALIN Niina 3.01.77, Sale/UMIST/FIN :
HJ - 1.75 (1.75-99)*
MASKREY Helen 23.09.67, Belgrave :
Mar - 2:56:27
MASSEY Eva Maria U23 22.12.80, W S & E :
SP - 14.90, DT - 47.72
MASSINGHAM Louise U15 28.02.87, Walton :
75HG - 11.46
MATHIESON Hannah U15 28.10.85, Aberd'n :
75HG - 11.70w/11.8 (11.73-99)
MATTHEW Denae U15 3.04.87, Leics Cor :
100 - 12.52, LJ - 5.23
MATTHEWS Jennifer Ann V35 3.07.62, Ash :
400 - 55.9/57.19 (54.6-88/55.36-84),
400H - 59.14 (57.41-88)
MATTHEWS Kimberley U17 22.03.84, Basildon :
200 - 25.25
MATTHEWS Louise U17 27.10.83, Thurrock :
JT - 39.55
MAWER Lisa 22.05.68, Bingley :
5k - 17:28.57 (17:02.84-94),
5MR - 27:57, 10kR - 34:34
MAWER Rebecca U17 31.01.84, Grimsby :
HJ - 1.70 (1.73-99)
MAY Holly 23.09.77, Hounslow :
Mar - 3:05:24
MAYHEAD Kirsty U23 17.02.78, Epsom & E :
400H - 65.7
MAYLOR Donna U20 20.05.82, Birchfield :
60 - 7.52i, 100 - 11.72 (11.62w-98),
SP - 11.69
MCALLISTER Alison U17 26.02.85, Wolves & B :
TJ - 11.26
MCBRIDE Michelle 19.06.68, Team Sol/Army :
400H - 65.46
MCCALLUM Michaela Jane 2.06.66, :
1HR - 16495m, HMar - 1:16:07,
Mar - 2:42:25 (2:38:28-99)
MCCANN Danielle U13, Preseli :
1500 - 5:05.6
MCCLUNG Mary 19.12.71, Edinburgh WM :
400 - 54.06, 800 - 2:03.92
MCCOLGAN Joanne 26.11.69, McColgan HC :
Mar - 2:56:48
MCCONNELL Lee U23 9.10.78, Shaft Barnet :
HJ - 1.88
MCCREA Philippa U23 1.03.78, Border :
800 - 2:12.2 (2:09.3-96), 1500 - 4:30.06
MCDEVITT Julie 15.03.73, City of Glasgow :
800 - 2:11.16 (2:10.1-97)
MCDONNELL Lindsey-Ann U23 13.08.79,
N Devon : HJ - 1.75 (1.75-99)
MCDONNELL Morag 27.08.73, Saltwell :
5k - 17:08.7
MCDOUGALL Joanne U23 23.08.79, Southport :
400 - 56.7/56.95
MCGEORGE Sonia Marian V35 2.11.64,
Brighton : 3k - 9:13.8 (8:51.33-90)
MCGHEE Catherine U15 11.09.85, Newq & P :
PV - 2.40
MCGILLIVARY Aileen 13.08.70, Edinburgh WM :
200 - 24.8w (23.29-93),
400 - 54.8/55.33 (53.95-98)
MCGILP Claire U23 25.07.78, :
200 - 24.79, 400 - 55.61
MCGIVERN Stacy 14.12.76, Peterborough :
HJ - 1.65, LJ - 5.62,
TJ - 11.82w/11.64 (11.64-95)
MCGORAM Fiona U13 10.11.88, Leics Cor :
2kW - 11:33.7
MCGOWAN Suzanne U23 13.04.78, M'well :
200 - 25.28w (24.79w-95/24.9/24.99-93)
MCGRATH Sarah 22.12.72, Cambridge & C :
SP - 11.69 (12.81-90)
MCGREAVY Sara U20 13.12.82, Leamington :
60H - 8.80i, 100H - 13.88w/14.01, 400H - 63.62
MCGUIRE Leah Christine U15 30.01.87,
Great Yarmouth : 75HG - 11.18, LJ - 5.28
MCINTOSH Aisha U13 5.01.88, Herne Hill :
100 - 13.2, LJ - 4.78, PenM - 1998
MCINTOSH Toni U23 26.11.79, Ayr Seaforth/
Edinburgh Univ : Mar - 3:01:25

MCINTYRE Iona-Eilidh U20 14.03.83, EWM :
800 - 2:11.00i (2:11.2-97)
MCKAY Heather U20 5.09.81, EWM/Heriot W :
100 - 12.08w/12.22 (12.02w-99),
200 - 24.77w/24.9 (24.62-98), 400 - 56.8
MCKAY Jane 22.04.77, City of Glasgow/
Strathclyde Univ : 400 - 55.8/55.82
MCKEAN Ruth 13.04.76, Edinburgh WM :
3k - 9:49.32, 5k - 17:18.5
MCKELVIE Susan U17 15.06.85, Whitemoss :
HT - 35.68
MCKENNA Carolyn U17 4.05.84, Avonside :
60 - 7.88i, 100 - 12.47
MCKINNON Zoe U20 8.09.81, Horsham BS :
60H - 8.87i, TJ - 11.08,
100H - 14.7/14.95 (14.7/14.88-99),
MCLELLAN Shelley U20 21.03.83, S & NH :
SP - 12.10 (12.42-99)
MCLOUGHLIN Lauren U20 8.09.82, Cardiff :
100H - 14.14w/14.25
CAIRNS/MCMAHON Lindsay 1.06.71, Kilm :
5MR - 27:58
MCMAHON Michelle U20 29.08.83, C of Glas :
PV - 2.60 (2.60-99)
MCMANUS Lisa U15 3.01.86, Oadby & Wig :
75HG - 11.3/11.32
MCMANUS Lucy U15 2.03.87, Guildford & G :
HJ - 1.60
MCMENEMY Ruth 12.04.70, Havering :
100 - 12.1, 200 - 24.72w/24.9/25.15
MCNEICE Kelly U23 17.06.78, Lisburn :
800 - 2:09.23 (2:08.58-98)
MCQUEEN Sophie U20 3.12.81, Cleethorpes :
HJ - 1.70i/1.70 (1.75-98)
MCVIE Siobhan U17 6.07.84, Ayr Seaforth :
60 - 7.72i, 100 - 12.3 (13.43-97),
LJ - 5.76w/5.67
MEADOWS Jennifer U20 17.04.81, Wigan :
100 - 11.9w/12.1/12.11, 200 - 24.32,
400 - 53.84, 800 - 2:10.7
MEITE Yasmine U17 6.09.84, Shildon :
60 - 7.9i/7.97i
MELLIS Kelly Ann U23 4.12.79, Belgrave :
DT - 38.90 (44.86-97)
MELVIN Hazel 19.11.73, City of Glasgow :
HJ - 1.81 (1.85-97)
MENANDEZ Niobe J. 1.09.66, Steyning :
3kW - 14:08.52, 5kW - 24:22.84,
5kWR - 24:05+/24:19 (23:47-99),
10kWR - 49:11+ (49:10-99),
20kW - 1:43:18 (1:40:12-99)
MERRILL Alexandra U15 12.05.86, Skyrac :
DT - 30.29 (31.14-99)
MERRY Emma Louise 2.07.74, Rugby :
SP - 13.77, DT - 55.60 (57.75-99)
MERRY Katharine 21.09.74, Birchfield :
200 - 22.76, 300 - 36.00, 400 - 49.72,
MERSH Rebecca U13 28.01.89, Sheff RWC :
2kW - 11:15.0
MIKNEVICIUTE Dalia 5.09.70, Shaftesbury B :
HJ - 1.86i/1.86 (1.89-97)
MILBORROW Clare 10.01.77, Horsham BS :
100 - 12.16w, 50H - 7.2i, 60H - 8.57i,
100H - 13.61w/13.91 (13.89-99), Hep - 4418
MILES Susan U20 1.11.81, Hillingdon :
3k - 9:49.1mx/9:56.80
MILLER Frances U17 26.12.84, Elgin :
SP - 11.61, HT - 45.27lg/43.19
MILLER Lisa U20 13.01.83, Cambridge H :
200 - 24.51, 400 - 53.86
MILLS Natalie U17 29.05.85, Mansfield :
300H - 44.28
MITCHELL Angela V35 17.08.65, Parkside :
DT - 40.42 (42.05-98)
MITCHELL Jeina Sophia 21.01.75, Croydon :
400 - 57.1 (55.9-97),
800 - 2:04.15 (2:03.36-97),
1500 - 4:20.07 (4:19.09-92)
MITCHELL Julie 3.10.74, Jarrow & Hebburn :
1500 - 4:27.48 (4:22.52-97)
MITCHELL Kerry U20 23.06.81, Lisburn :
400H - 65.33
MITCHELL Rebecca U17 10.12.83, Regent H :
60HI - 9.29i (9.25i-99),
80HI - 11.8/11.94 (11.93-99), 100H - 15.24,
300H - 45.3 (45.39-99), 400H - 67.52
MOCKLER Jennifer U20 28.08.82, Sale :
800 - 2:12.16
MODAHL Diane Dolores 17.06.66, Sale :
600 - 1:27.18 (1:22.99+'-89/1:26.18-87),
800 - 2:00.53 (1:58.65-90),
1500 - 4:14.41 (4:12.3-89)
MODESTE Kayleigh U13, Birchfield :
75 10.1, 150 10.0
MOFFITT Alison J. 6.10.69, W S & E/IRE :
DT - 37.73 (47.22-91), JT - 45.85 (47.72-99)
MOLES Shelley U17 31.10.83, Basildon :
SP - 11.01i/10.39 (11.08-99)
MOLLOY Jennifer U17 23.09.83, Bournemouth :
80HI - 11.77, 100H - 15.7, 300H - 43.72
MONTADOR Karen U23 14.05.79, EWM :
1500 - 4:32.04
MOODIE Amanda U15 11.09.85, EWM :
DT - 28.41
MOODY Hannah U23 26.07.79, Skyrac/Birm U :
TJ - 11.50 (11.53-99)
MOODY Karen 20.07.67, Cannock & Stafford :
HT - 39.02
MOONEY Tara U17 1.10.84, Belfast Ladies :
PV - 2.60
MOORE Charlotte U17 4.01.85, Bournemouth :
800 - 2:07.1, 1500 - 4:23.61, 3k - 9:50.1
MOORE Claire U20 29.03.82, Gateshead :
DT - 39.99
MOORE Rebecca U13, Sale :
LJ - 4.60
MOORE Sarah Louise 15.03.73, Bristol :
HT - 55.74 (56.60-97)
MOOREKITE Janice D. V40 1.05.57, Invicta :
Mar - 3:01:01 (2:48:06-95)
MORGAN Kelly U23 17.06.80, Windsor S & E :
JT - 58.45
MORGAN Louise U15 8.09.85, Ipswich :
100 - 12.6
MORGAN Lydia U17 1.09.83, Vale Royal :
SP - 10.97, DT - 36.02
MORGAN Sarah U17 9.05.84, Mandale :
HT - 39.07
MORGAN Victoria U13 25.12.87, Bridgend :
200 - 27.51i
MORRIS Emily U20 30.09.82, City of Hull :
PV - 3.00 (3.00-99)
MORRIS Emma U15 21.02.86, South Shields :
HJ - 1.67, PenG - 2799
MORRIS Emma U20 25.01.82, Wakefield :
SP - 11.75

MORRIS Joanna Elizabeth 16.10.77, W S & E/ Wolvs Univ : TJ - 12.03w/11.97 (12.07w-96)
MORRIS Kate U20 18.01.83, Medway : SP - 11.94
MORRIS Ruth U17 17.10.83, Deeside : DT - 35.33, HT - 34.90
MORRIS Sharon 5.07.68, Hertford & Ware : 1500 - 4:20.35, 3k - 9:28.68 (9:26.6mx-99), 5MR - 27:22
MORRIS Sophie 5.12.75, E,S & Mx/Army : (nee ALFORD) 800 - 2:08.6
MORRIS Tracy 25.12.69, Coventry Godiva : PV - 2.80 (2.90-99)
MORRISON Kirsty 28.10.75, Medway : JT - 51.22 (55.91-99)
MORTON Helen U15 17.09.85, Horsham BS : PenG - 2682
MOSS Charlotte U15 7.11.85, Bedford & Co : 800 - 2:16.83, 1500 - 4:50.21
MOSS Gillian U13, West Norfolk : 1500 - 5:04.40
MOSS Rebecca U17 19.06.84, Bedford & Co : 300H - 46.08
MOUNTENEY Helen U17 24.09.84, Birchfield : JT - 38.36
MUDGE Angela 8.07.70, Carnethy : 10kR - 34:28
MUNNIK Rhonda 26.03.74, Dartford : 800 - 2:08.1
MUNNOCH Lynsey U20 24.10.81, Falkirk : 400 - 55.83
MURDOCH Emma U17 26.03.84, Elgin : HT - 30.59
MURPHY Catherine Ann 21.09.75, Shaft B : 60 - 7.39i (7.85-90), 300 - 37.48, 400 - 52.72, 100 - 11.68 (11.6-96/11.63w-94/11.67-99), 200 - 23.46i/23.48w/23.59 (23.28-99)
MURPHY Lisa U17 15.04.84, Sale : 400H - 67.87
MURPHY Sharon 31.03.76, Shaftesbury Barn : 5KR - 16:50
MURRAY Freya U17 20.09.83, Lasswade : 1500 - 4:35.78, 3k - 10:15.1
MURRAY Natalie 24.03.76, Stockport : 60H - 8.97i (8.67i-98)
MURRAY-JESSEE Alison 13.01.67, C of Glas : PV - 3.71A/3.60 (3.95A-99/3.60-98)
MUSGROVE Victoria V40 6.09.56, Wrexham : 100kR - 9:20:44
MYATT Julia, : Mar - 3:05:17
MYERS Heather Ruth V35 5.12.64, AF&D : 400H - 65.5/65.63 (59.46-94)
MYTON Aisha U17 3.01.84, Herne Hill : 60HI - 9.19i, TJ - 11.61

NASH Michelle U15 19.03.87, Herne Hill : 100 - 12.59
NATHAN Rachael U15 27.04.86, Lincoln Well : 800 - 2:16.4, 1500 - 4:39.0mx
NAYLOR Christine V45 22.10.54, Arena : Mar - 3:03:06
NAYLOR Claire 18.04.71, Sutton-in-Ashfield : 5MR - 27:34, 10kR - 34:30, 10MR - 56:49, HMar - 1:16:41
NEALON Nikki 27.02.68, Huncote : (nee LEE) 5MR - 27:46 (27:27-99), 10kR - 34:41 (34:33-99)
NELSON Caroline U15 1.07.86, Trafford : 200 - 25.5
NELSON Heather U15 7.01.86, W Yorks Sch : JT - 31.66
NESBITT Emma U13, Morpeth : 1500 - 5:00.7
NESBITT Lucy U17 6.09.84, Liverpool H : DT - 38.47, HT - 39.15
NEWCOMBE Helen U13, Devonia AC : 800 - 2:27.9
NEWCOMBE Jo-Anne V35 20.02.65, Shaft B : 5k - 16:55.91 (16:37.16-95), 10k - 35:21.9, 10MR - 58:10 (57:18-97), HMar - 1:16:21 (1:14:54-97), Mar - 2:46:16
NEWCOMBE Rachel 25.02.67, Liverpool H : 400 - 56.25 (55.19-92), 800 - 2:05.60 (2:03.28-98), 1500 - 4:24.18
NEWINGTON Sophie U15 15.09.85, Swansea : 100 - 12.6 (12.56w-99), LJ - 5.21
NEWMAN Catherine Ann Thurlow V35 12.02.62, Exeter : 10kR - 34:57 (34:01-90), HMar - 1:17:50 (1:12:29-90)
NEWMAN Lucy U20 2.03.83, Horsham BS : PV - 2.60 (2.80-99), JT - 39.40
NEWMAN Wendy 31.08.71, WGreen & Ex L : JT - 42.95 (43.17-99)
NEWPORT Angela 21.10.70, Bas & MH : 800 - 2:12.1 (2:03.67-94), 3k - 9:05.86mx/9:08.46, 1500 - 4:15.28 (4:09.29-94), 5k - 15:48.50 (15:43.99-99), 5KR - 16:07, 10kR - 34:32 (33:49-99),
NEWTON Jackie V35 28.08.64, Stockport : HMar - 1:18:02 (1:16:09-97)
NEWTON Leigh U23 13.01.78, Blackpool : 200 - 24.70w/24.9/25.24mx, 400 - 55.43
NEWTON Maria Angela 22.07.66, Ashford : PV - 3.30i/3.30 (3.40-98)
NICCOLLS Janette 7.09.76, TVH/Brunel Univ : 100 - 12.1/12.11 (11.84w/12.0-96/12.04-99), 200 - 24.6/24.79w/24.84
NICHOLS Angela U17 22.09.84, Wycombe : PV - 2.60
NICHOLS Sara U20 9.06.83, Wycombe : PV - 2.70
NICKELSON Sarah Louise 28.12.73, Ox City : (nee SYMONDS) DT - 43.46 (47.50-90), HT - 38.65 (40.58-95)
NICOL Gemma U15 27.07.86, Dunf & W Fife : 100 - 12.6/12.65, 200 - 25.64w/25.7/26.02, PenG - 2903irr/2769
NICOLL Joanne U17 27.12.84, Motherwell : LJ - 5.43i (4.13-97)
NOAD Joy B. V40 10.07.59, Maidenhead : Mar - 2:59:47 (2:52:09-98)
NOBLE Frances U15 2.05.86, Bingley : LJ - 5.16w/5.07, PenG - 2552
NOBLET Jackie U23 19.04.79, Prest/Leeds P : 400H - 65.0/65.42
NORFORD Natalia U20 29.09.82, Bed & Co : HJ - 1.70i/1.70 (1.73-99)
NORMAN Diana Faye 14.06.74, Epsom & E : (nee BENNETT) 400 - 56.9 (56.5-93), 800 - 2:09.54, 60H - 8.92i (8.64i-98), 100H - 14.54 (14.2-99/14.23w/14.38-98), HJ - 1.73 (1.80i/1.79-98), LJ - 5.70i/5.57 (6.08w-98/6.07-97), SP - 11.47 (12.05i-99/12.00-97), JT - 38.21, Hep - 5308 (5555w-98/5550-97)

NORVILLE Danielle U20 18.01.83, Telford :
100 - 11.9w/11.92w/12.00,
200 - 24.6w/24.9/24.92w (24.82w/24.96-99)
NOTT Kerrie 28.02.74, Medway :
1500 - 4:31.17 (4:28.87-99), 3k - 9:58.7
NUGENT Jessica Natalie Rosemary U17
27.08.84, Shaftesbury Barnet : 3k - 10:05.6,
800 - 2:13.84 (2:12.2-99), 1500 - 4:29.37
NUTT Caroline U20 17.06.83, Scunthorpe :
PV - 3.15
NUTTING Nichola U17 14.09.84, Oadby & W :
100 - 12.4
NWIDOBIE Kara U20 13.04.81, Blackpool :
SP - 13.38, DT - 38.79
NYLEN Carolina U23 15.09.79, Loughbro/SWE :
800 - 2:11.02 (2:09.55-99)

O'BRIEN Vicky U20 15.11.82, Inverness :
LJ - 5.63i (5.95w/5.85-99)
O'CALLAGHAN Leanne 15.07.74, Wycom/IRE :
60 - 7.60i, 100 - 11.91w/11.96,
200 - 24.50w/24.8/24.87i/25.09
O'CONNOR Gayle U23 24.08.79, Liverpool H/
Liverpool Univ : HJ - 1.75 (1.75-99)
O'CONNOR Gillian V35 24.09.61, S London :
Mar - 2:53:01
O'HALLORAN Catherine U20 17.09.81, Bing :
JT - 39.89 (40.33-99)
O'HARE Ellen Jane U23 4.02.78, Cirencester/
Oxford Univ : 800 - 2:09.67 (2:06.59-96),
1500 - 4:21.68 (4:20.17-97)
O'MARA Julie 11.02.76, Wakefield :
3k - 9:50.52, 5k - 17:19.66,
10MR - 57:56, HMar - 1:18:04
O'REILLY Aveen U13 23.09.88, Lagan Valley :
1200 - 4:00.94, 1500 - 5:05.69
O'SULLIVAN Laura U20 30.07.82, Liverpool H :
HJ - 1.66 (1.69-99)
OAKES Judith Miriam V40 14.02.58, Croydon :
SP - 18.30i/18.22 (19.36-88),
DT - 49.82 (53.44-88)
OAKES Sharon Elizabeth U20 26.08.82, Med :
TJ - 11.93 (11.60?w-99)
OGLETHORPE Alex U15 4.09.85, Woking :
JT - 30.82
OKEKE Francis U17 10.05.84, Ilford :
TJ - 10.66
OKORO Marilyn U17 23.09.84, Shaftesbury B :
300 - 41.5, 400 - 57.7, 800 - 2:14.02
OKWUE Maurine Inkeira U23 13.05.78, TVH :
TJ - 11.02 (11.58-99)
OLDERSHAW Tina 13.05.67, Paddock Wood :
HMar - 1:18:30
OLDFIELD Sally Grace U17 25.06.84, Kett :
800 - 2:16.0, 1500 - 4:31.30, 3k - 9:45.85
OLIVER Adele U17 5.10.84, Wigan :
Hepl - 3883
OLIVER Emily U17 8.02.84, Blackheath :
DT - 33.92, HT - 37.09
OLOFINJANA Banke 14.05.72, Tower Hamlets :
LJ - 5.51 (5.70-97)
OLSON Hannah U13 29.01.88, Ashford :
70HM - 11.8, HJ - 1.45, PV - 3.10
OLSON Natalie V. U15 9.05.86, Ashford :
PV - 3.20
ONIANWA Mary U20 20.01.81, Hercules Wim :
HJ - 1.65
ONUORA Amalachukwu U15 16.03.86,
Eastbourne AC : 100 - 12.18, 200 - 25.58
OSAGEDE Diana U17 18.01.85, WG& Ex L :
TJ - 10.82
OUGHTON Karen U20 26.01.83, Coventry G :
100 - 12.08w (12.17-99)
OXLEY Sarah E. 3.07.73, Birchfield/IRE :
(see REILLY)
OWBRIDGE Joanne U20 19.01.82, Hull Spr :
400 - 57.4/57.46
OWEN Judith 20.06.71, S London :
400H - 63.14
OWEN Suzanne U23 5.05.79, C of S/ Keele U :
800 - 2:12.8 (2:12.2-99), 1500 - 4:26.78
OWEN Tracy A. V35 29.04.64, Arena :
Mar - 3:05:03 (2:59:53-99)
OWUSU Lesley D. U23 21.12.78, WS&E/Univ
of Nebraska : 200 - 24.13, 400 - 53.02,
100 - 12.26 (11.7w-98/12.10-93)
OYEPITAN Abiodun U23 30.12.79, Shaft B :
100 - 11.52 (11.45w-98),
200 - 24.50 (23.82w/23.98-99)

PACEY Jenny U20 5.02.83, Lincoln Well :
Hep - 4019
PALLANT Emma U13 4.06.89, AF&D :
1500 - 5:07.06
PALMER Aimee U15 7.11.86, Cannock & St :
LJ - 5.23
PALMER Clare U15 30.12.85, Crawley :
SPG - 10.55
PALMER Gillian U23 30.12.80, Edinburgh Un/
EWM : 1500 - 4:22.93, 3k - 9:16.12,
5k - 15:56.58, 5MR - 27:49, 10kR - 34:20
PALMER Karlene J. U23 23.10.80, W S & E/
Loughbro : 100 - 12.04w (11.96w/12.12-97),
200 - 24.94w/24.98 (24.41w/24.42-97)
PALMER-JOHNSON Ashleigh U15 19.09.86,
Windsor S & E : SPG - 10.58
PANAYIOTOU Larnaca U13 5.02.88, Leics Cor :
JTM - 28.04
PANNETT Meredith 13.06.71, Cambridge H/
Dulwich R : 3k - 9:53.6 (9:53.0-99)
PAOLILLO Andrea V35 22.06.64, C of Glasgow :
Mar - 3:00:53 (2:54:27-99)
PARDO Claire U20 9.08.81, Guildford & G/
London Univ : HT - 43.32
PARKER Carol Ann 22.09.69, Coventry G :
SP - 12.66 (14.76i-91/14.71-90),
DT - 38.17 (44.70-89)
PARKER Emily U17 7.11.84, Epsom & Ewell :
300 - 41.4, 80HI - 11.9, 300H - 44.74,
LJ - 5.52w/5.48, TJ - 11.88, Hepl - 4162
PARKIN Claire U17 26.02.84, Edinburgh WM :
SP - 10.81
PARKINSON Amanda 21.07.71, Sale :
1500 - 4:17.45 (4:12.9unmx-95/4:14.19-98),
3k - 9:02.67mx, 5k - 15:56.64,
5KR - 16:37, 10kR - 33:43
PARKINSON Danielle U20 2.09.81, Sale :
HJ - 1.65i/1.65 (1.67-98), LJ - 5.51, Hep - 4336
PARKINSON Kelly U15 18.03.86, Dorset Sch :
LJ - 5.15
PARKINSON-OVENS Hayley 5.12.75, EWM :
800 - 2:11.35 (2:07.99-98),
1500 - 4:29.02 (4:21.27-98),
3k - 9:56.2 (9:45.73-98)

PARRIS Monique U17 28.01.84, Ilford :
100 - 12.3 (12.0-99/12.19-98),
LJ - 5.59 (5.80-98)
PARRY Carys L. U20 24.07.81, Rhondda/
Loughbro : DT - 36.27, HT - 53.80
PARRY Liza Marie U17 24.10.84, Dudley & St :
200 - 25.26, 300 - 38.90, Hepl - 4104
PARSONS Zoe Marie U20 11.02.83, Ashford :
PV - 3.00 (3.10-99)
PARSONS Zoe 15.11.69, Rugby :
HT - 38.29
PATERSON Laura U17 8.09.83, Ayr Seaforth :
LJ - 5.39i/5.35 (5.53w-99/5.35-98),
TJ - 10.92i/10.70 (11.07w/10.98-99)
PATERSON Pamela U15 26.10.85, EWM :
100 - 12.56, 75HG - 11.67w/11.8
PATRICK Elizabeth Sian 29.08.77, Birchfield :
100H - 14.57, LJ - 5.65, TJ - 12.92
PATTERSON Laura Joanne U20 31.01.81,
Wycombe/Staff U : PV - 3.30i/3.30 (3.45-99)
PATTINSON Helen Teresa 2.01.74, Preston :
800 - 2:03.75, 1500 - 4:04.82, 3k - 9:09.18
PATTON Chaanah 22.02.72, Hallamshire :
HMar - 1:18:30
PAUL Michaela U20 27.10.81, Ealing,S & Mx :
LJ - 5.51, TJ - 11.49i/11.27
PAUZERS Clare V35 2.08.62, Herne Hill :
3k - 9:52.1 (9:46.25-96),
5k - 17:27.44 (17:19.19-97),
Mar - 2:57:17 (2:43:27-97)
PAVEY Joanne 20.09.73, Bristol :
2k - 5:44.4+e, 3k - 8:36.70, 5k - 14:58.27
PAXTON Henrietta U17 19.09.83, Salisbury :
HJ - 1.65, LJ - 5.67 (5.75-99), Hepl - 4200
PAYNE Judith A. U23 7.07.80, Wake/CUAC :
HJ - 1.71i/1.70 (1.76-98)
PEACOCK Julie 19.08.70, Shaftesbury Barn :
HJ - 1.81i/1.65 (1.85-94)
PEACOCK Rachel U20 18.05.82, Bournm'th :
TJ - 11.98w/11.79 (12.07w-98)
PEAKE Fiona 31.05.77, Woking :
PV - 2.80 (3.10-96)
PEAKE Rebecca U20 22.06.83, Derby LAC :
SP - 12.90
PEAKE Sally U15 8.02.86, Wirral :
HJ - 1.60, LJ - 5.40
PEARSON Claire U23 23.09.78, Leics Cor/
Loughbro : 60H - 8.82i, 100H - 14.18w/14.56
PEARSON Natalie Grace U13 7.06.88, Hallam :
75 - 10.0, 100 - 12.8, 150 - 19.3, 200 - 27.2
PEASTON Stephanie U13, Edinburgh WM :
70HM - 11.7/11.89w
PEATY Paula 30.05.66, Newham & Essex B :
HT - 43.21
PEDGRIFT Diane U13 10.05.88, Arbroath :
SPM - 9.07
PEET Josephine 4.12.71, Bristol :
100H - 15.0 (14.59-93),
400H - 63.77 (61.00-99)
PEEVER Evette U20 31.12.82, City of Stoke :
DT - 36.33
PENNET Catriona U17 10.10.83, Aberdeen :
60HI - 8.83io/9.06i, 80HI - 11.7w/11.8/11.84,
300H - 45.7/45.75
PENNEY Samantha U23 6.10.79, Haywards H :
PV - 2.90
PERCIVAL Deborah J. V35 22.04.62, Medway :
10kR - 34:18 (33:28-98), 10MR - 57:06

PEREIRA Jennifer U17 8.08.85, Medway :
1500 - 4:32.86, 3k - 10:04.4
PERKINS Emma U15 4.09.85, Worthing :
75HG - 11.75, HJ - 1.68,
LJ - 5.17io, PenG - 3236
PERRETT Kirsty 17.03.76, Middlesbro & C :
HT - 37.71 (39.58-97)
PERRY Georgette U17 10.12.83, Rowheath :
60 - 7.89i, 100 - 12.17w/12.2/12.36
PERRY Laura Helen Susan 4.06.75, Dud & St :
HT - 42.62
PERRY Victoria A. V40 25.11.57, Altrincham :
Mar - 3:02:10 (2:59:30-99)
PHILLIPS Lorraine 27.01.75, Newbury :
400 - 56.3 (56.35-99),
800 - 2:05.75mx/2:07.85
PHILLIPS Nicola U20 23.04.83, Dartford :
3kW - 14:29.37i/15:36.88,
5kW - 27:13.02 (25:11.46-99),
5kWR - 25:33, 10kWR - 51:36
PICKERING Sarah U17 26.10.83, Cann & St :
800 - 2:12.02, 1500 - 4:43.78 (4:39.68-99)
PICKETT Sarah-Jane U17 24.10.84, AF&D :
400H - 67.5
PIDGEON Elizabeth Sarah 27.04.77, WG&Ex L :
HT - 63.61, JT - 41.09 (42.94-99)
PIDGEON Emily Claire U13 1.06.89, Gloucs :
1200 - 4:02.0, 1500 - 4:59.84i/5:07.70
PIDGEON Jane V35 23.01.64, Notts :
2KSTW - 7:15.48
PIERRE Cherie U17 15.05.84, Shaftesbury B :
100 - 12.30w/12.3/12.38 (12.08-99),
200 - 25.4/25.51w (24.99-98),
SP - 10.32 (10.60-99)
PIERRE Michelle 30.09.73, Shaftesbury Barn :
200 - 25.15 (24.4w-96/24.8-95/25.08-99),
400 - 53.98 (52.77-97)
PINCOMBE Vicky 19.06.73, Minehead :
3k - 9:52.12mx, 10MR - 58:15,
HMar - 1:15:49 (1:15:14-98)
PINEL Syreena U23 13.01.79, Birchfield :
100 - 12.1 (12.0w/12.12w-99/12.41-95,
200 - 24.32w/24.46, LJ - 5.89 (6.11-99)
PINKVANCE Ruth V35 29.09.61, Swansea :
HMar - 1:17:55
PITTS Laura U15 9.01.86, Exeter :
HJ - 1.60
PLATEAU Carolyn U13 22.08.88, Radley :
600 - 1:45.3, 800 - 2:25.6, 1k - 3:11.7,
1200 - 3:55.5, 1500 - 5:03.5
PLATEAU Natalie U17 19.10.84, Radley :
60 - 7.99i
PLATT Joedy U13 27.11.87, N Devon :
200 - 27.2w/27.4, JTM - 25.36
POCOCK Nicola U23 9.05.79, AF&D :
400H - 64.15 (63.6-99/64.09-98)
POLHILL-THOMAS Sian U20 4.06.83, Wirral :
100H - 14.9/14.99
POLIUS Leandra U23 14.05.80, N & E B :
TJ - 12.52
PORAZINSKI Donna-Marie U20 28.01.81,
Newport : 200 - 24.9w (25.24-98),
400 - 55.8/56.00 (55.82-98), 400H - 61.17
PORTER Katherine U20 19.08.82, Blackheath :
60H - 8.96i, 100H - 14.56 (14.4/14.41-99)
PORTER Sarah U23 11.12.79, Sutton & Dist/
Birmingham Univ. : 60H - 8.78i (8.77i-99),
100H - 14.2/14.58 (14.1-99/14.12w-98/14.30-99)

POTTER Helen 25.06.74, Trafford :
JT - 39.57
POTTER Jane U20 24.10.81, Charnwood :
1500 - 4:26.63, 3k - 9:30.13
POTTER Juliet U20 24.10.81, Charnwood :
1500 - 4:26.99, 3k - 9:36.98
POWELL Pauline 17.05.73, Blackburn :
800 - 2:11.10, 1500 - 4:33.86 (4:28.54-99),
10kR - 34:39
POWELL Xanine U23 21.05.79, Cambridge H :
200 - 24.61w?/24.86
POWER Somma U17 18.08.85, Basildon :
SP - 11.50
PRANGNELL Carly U15 4.03.86, Isle of Wight :
HJ - 1.64 (1.64-99)
PRATT Julie U23 20.03.79, WGreen & Ex L :
100 - 12.1, 60H - 8.43i (8.37i-99),
100H - 13.28w/13.40 (13.28w/13.40-99)
PRESTON Samantha U20 15.11.81, Cann & St :
PV - 3.06
PRICE Kaylee U13, Walton :
70HM - 11.8, LJ - 4.61
PRICE Sharon 10.12.75, R Sutton Coldfield :
100H - 14.8/14.95 (14.4w-95/14.43w-93/14.61-95)
PRITCHARD Amanda U23 18.03.80, Cardiff :
400 - 56.57 (54.60-97)
PRITCHETT Kathy U17 11.04.84, Wrexham :
HJ - 1.70
PROCTOR Elizabeth 31.10.72, Bolton :
1500 - 4:28.28mx/4:33.47 (4:29.1-99)
PROCTOR Ruth U17 4.05.84, Norwich :
3k - 10:25.85
PROTHEROE Amy U17 3.03.84, Newport :
LJ - 5.35
PRYCE Janice V40 2.09.59, R S Coldfield :
TJ - 11.18
PRYTZ Karen U13 9.12.87, Giffnock :
150 - 20.0
PULLINGER Stefanie U20 3.04.83, Bracknell :
100H - 14.9/14.91w/15.08
PURDY Helen 5.10.75, Pudsey & Bramley :
HMar - 1:15:55
PURKISS Melanie U23 11.03.79, Team Solent/
Loughbro : 60 - 7.73i (7.63i-99),
100 - 11.81 (11.55w/11.76-99),
200 - 23.83 (23.64w/23.80-99),
400 - 55.46 (54.62-99)
PYBUS Joanne U17 18.12.84, Mandale :
LJ - 5.40
PYWELL Stephanie U15 12.06.87, Retford :
HJ - 1.60

QUINE Laura U13, Liverpool H :
1200 - 3:59.4
QUINN Sarah U17 22.03.84, Lisburn :
200 - 25.39

RADCLIFFE Paula Jane 17.12.73,
Beds & Co : 1500 - 4:11.45 (4:05.81-98),
2k - 5:43.22+ (5:39.20-93),
3k - 8:28.85 (8:27.40-99),
5k - 14:44.36 (14:43.54-99),
5MR - 25:04 (24:47-99), 10k - 30:26.97,
10kR - 32:50+ (31:47-97), 10MR - 51:41+,
HMar - 1:07:07
RAMAGE Jane 7.01.72, Border/Nithsdale :
DT - 37.23

RANDALL Charlotte U23 10.05.80, C of Plym/
London Univ : 400H - 63.18
RANN Lucy U23 5.09.80, Isle of Wight :
JT - 41.98 (42.15-99)
RATCLIFFE Karen V35 1.06.61, Cov RWC :
5kW - 27:24.39 (24:12.11-93),
10kWR - 57:42 (48:30-94)
RAVEN Claire Heather 15.06.72, Coventry G :
400 - 55.6/55.61 (53.99-92),
800 - 2:04.58 (2:03.15-97)
RAVEN Laura U17 12.03.85, Cambridge H :
300H - 45.30
RAWLING Kimberley U20 22.07.83, Newq & P :
DT - 37.52, HT - 39.35
RAYNER Marion R. V50 14.01.50, West 4 :
Mar - 3:06:24 (3:03:37-98)
READ Katey U15 20.03.86, Stockport :
75HG - 11.3/11.34
READE Joanne Lesley U17 28.11.84, Rushcl :
TJ - 10.84
READER Jennifer 23.12.77, Southampton City :
HJ - 1.65i (1.73-98)
REAL Natalie U13 14.11.87, Bournemouth :
800 - 2:26.8, 1200 - 3:53.6, 1500 - 4:58.7
REDD Kathryn U20 8.06.82, Brighton :
JT - 38.67
REDD Samantha U17 16.02.84, Brighton :
JT - 45.24
REDMAN Hollie U15 12.12.85, Braintree :
DT - 31.74
REDMOND Laura A. U20 19.04.81, EWM :
HJ - 1.70 (1.66i-98), SP - 11.56, Hep - 4954,
LJ - 5.51 (5.65w/5.52-99)
REDMOND Rachel U20 7.12.81, City of Stoke :
100 - 12.0w/12.07w/12.28 (12.06w/12.21-96)
REED Kate U20 28.09.82, Bristol :
800 - 2:09.50, 1500 - 4:32.6 (4:31.08-99)
REES Anwen U17 14.07.85, Carmarthen :
300H - 46.40
REES Charlotte U17 14.06.84, Neath :
SP - 11.20, JT - 43.11
REEVES Claire U17 31.07.84, Bexley/Dartford :
3kW - 16:08.88 (16:04.64-99),
5kW - 28:32.66 (28:15.16-99),
5kWR - 26:47, 10kWR - 54:51
REID Emma U20 5.01.81, Pitreavie :
100H - 14.9/15.27 (15.04-99),
400H - 62.60
REILLY Sarah E. 3.07.73, Birchfield/IRE :
(nee OXLEY) 60 - 7.46i (still UK),
100 - 11.45w/11.49,
200 - 23.12, 400 - 56.5
REINSFORD Susan 24.03.69, Bedford & Co :
3k - 9:58.9 (9:52.7-87), 5KR - 16:50,
5MR - 27:37 (27:26-99),
10kR - 34:10+/34:11, 10MR - 54:52,
HMar - 1:14:21 (1:13:04-99), Mar - 2:33:41
RENNISON Amy U20 15.06.83, Sale :
PV - 3.05 (3.10-99)
REPTON Hayley U13 23.05.88, Worcester :
2kW - 11:56.13
REST Elinor 27.04.72, Serpentine :
Mar - 3:02:38
RETCHAKAN Gowry P. V40 21.06.60,
Highgate Harriers : (see HODGE)
REYNOLDS Kay Suzzanne 15.09.67, Radley :
60H - 8.78i (8.58i-99),
100H - 13.96w/14.4 (13.9/14.03-99)

REYNOLDS Nicky U17 24.06.85, Birchfield :
3kW - 16:01.9, 5kW - 28:59.3, 5kWR - 27:11
RHULE Candee U13 16.09.87, Southwark :
SPM - 11.42
RICE Sonia U20 8.01.81, Coventry Godiva :
200 - 24.7/25.62
RICH Emma 14.05.77, Yeovil Oly/Loughbro :
JT - 40.45 (41.82-99)
RICH Nicola U20 23.02.83, City of Plymouth :
JT - 37.19 (37.85-99)
RICHARDS Anne-Marie V35 15.01.61, Cardiff :
Mar - 3:02:29
RICHARDS Lara Elesia U20 7.03.83, Newport :
LJ - 5.80w?/5.75i/5.75 (5.82w-99,
TJ - 11.62i/11.53 (11.60w-99)
RICHARDS Shaunette U20 15.08.83, Birchfield :
SP - 11.96i/11.52 (12.98lg/12.48-99)
RICHARDSON Eleanor U15 1.07.86, Wester R :
200 - 25.83w
RICHARDSON Katie U20 12.09.82, Wakefield :
LJ - 5.69
RICHARDSON Marcia Maureen 10.02.72, WS&E :
60 - 7.24i, 100 - 11.29w/11.35,
200 - 23.53 (23.4-93/23.53-95)
RICHMOND Sarah 6.01.73, Pitreavie :
100H - 14.7/15.16 (14.02w/14.2/14.29-94)
RICHOLD Faye Helen U13 24.10.87, Milton K :
70HM - 11.4, LJ - 4.69
RICKETTS Kelly 24.01.76, Deeside :
DT - 39.73 (40.92-98), HT - 42.32
RIDEOUT Michelle 17.03.68, Chichester :
Mar - 3:06:28
RIDGLEY Clare Louise 11.09.77, Team Solent :
PV - 3.60 (3.60-98)
RIDGLEY Rebecca Jane U23 26.02.80, T Sol/
Loughbro : PV - 3.40 (3.50-99),
TJ - 11.13 (11.36w-96/11.24-99)
RIDING Donna U17 28.11.83, Sale :
800 - 2:13.41
RILEY Catherine U20 4.06.82, Trafford :
800 - 2:12.45 (2:09.67-99)
RILEY Jane 26.03.69, Salford :
5KR - 16:51
ROACH Justine U17 21.12.84, Leics Cor :
60HI - 8.80i, 80HI - 11.5/11.78,
100H - 15.1, 300H - 44.55
ROBERTS Cara U17 24.05.85, Bournemouth :
100 - 12.4, LJ - 5.56
ROBERTS Georgina U17 9.07.84, Bingley :
300H - 45.09, 400H - 66.2
ROBERTS Lowri U20 9.10.81, Newport :
60H - 8.82i, 100H - 14.40w/14.47
ROBERTS Melanie U23 2.03.78, Liverpool H :
100 - 11.9 (12.23-98)
ROBERTS Sarah U23 25.06.78, Forr of Dean :
TJ - 11.35
ROBERTS Suzanne U23 19.12.78, Wakefield :
HT - 58.83
ROBERTSON Clare U15 17.08.86, Cann & St :
SPG - 11.11
ROBERTSON Sheena U15 8.01.87, Hamps S :
HJ - 1.61
ROBIN Julie 16.01.77, Edinburgh WM/R Navy :
DT - 38.39 (45.10-94)
ROBINSON Claire U23 18.01.78, Bas & MH/
Birmingham Univ. : 400 - 57.2/57.37
ROBINSON Clare U17 15.10.83, Cambr & C :
80HI - 12.0
ROBINSON Debra 31.01.68, Sutton-in-Ashfield :
10kR - 34:38, HMar - 1:17:24, Mar - 2:52:26
ROBINSON Linsi U17 9.01.84, Nuneaton :
TJ - 11.58i/11.26 (11.43w-99)
ROBINSON Madelaine U20 13.10.81, Border :
HT - 42.18
ROBINSON Nicola Jane U15 16.04.86, Nun :
75HG - 11.5
ROBSON Carly U17 5.12.83, St Albans Str :
LJ - 5.47, TJ - 11.83, Hepl - 4034
ROBSON Claire U17 9.01.84, Teesdale :
800 - 2:16.7 (2:14.49-99),
1500 - 4:44.59 (4:40.45-99)
ROBSON Debbie 12.07.76, Cannock & Staff :
100H - 14.9 (14.91w/14.99-95)
RODEN Anne M. V50 9.10.46, S London :
Mar - 2:54:21 (2:37:37-92)
RODGER Alison U17 29.10.84, Vic Park AAC :
SP - 11.08
RODMELL Kelly U15 26.11.85, Tynedale :
800 - 2:18.7
ROGER Kirsty U23 24.03.78, City of Glasgow :
100H - 14.76 (14.6w-97),
HJ - 1.71i (1.72i-99/1.70-97),
LJ - 5.63, Hep - 4921
ROGERS Clare U13 22.05.88, Cambr & C :
70HM - 11.6
ROGERS-DIXON Polly 5.04.67, Herne Hill :
Mar - 2:51:18
ROLES Philippa U23 1.03.78, Sale/Swan Inst :
SP - 15.62i/14.84 (15.95i-99),
DT - 57.04 (60.00-99), HT - 47.98 (55.09-99)
ROLES Rebecca U23 14.12.79, Rugby/ UWIC :
SP - 11.45i (12.65-99), DT - 46.85 (51.79-99)
ROLFE Nicola 19.08.69, Newbury :
JT - 37.87
ROLFE Vicky U23 27.08.80, Bristol :
800 - 2:11.19 (2:11.05-99), 1500 - 4:30.52
RONAN Jasmine U17 24.07.84, Macclesfield :
400H - 67.1
ROONEY Claire U20 23.08.83, East Kilbride :
200 - 25.0 (25.41-98)
ROSCOE Helen U23 4.12.79, Liv H/Loughbro :
100 - 11.66w/11.90, PV - 3.50,
200 - 24.41 (24.31w-96/24.4-97)
ROSINDALE Louise V45 30.11.55, Baildon :
Mar - 3:02:50
ROSKILLY Abby U13 12.05.88, Milton Keynes :
800 - 2:27.1
ROSS Joanna U20 18.02.81, Vic Park AAC/
Glasgow Univ Cal : 800 - 2:06.38
ROSS-HURST Olivia U17 10.12.83, Hert & W :
HJ - 1.63i (1.63-98), Hepl - 4213
ROTHENBAUGH Wendy V35 30.03.64, Derby :
Mar - 3:06:04
ROTHMAN Kimberly V35 6.09.64, W S & E :
100 - 12.26, 200 - 24.73w/24.9,
PV - 3.00 (3.55-98), LJ - 6.19
ROUGH Alison U20 1.06.83, City of Glasgow :
TJ - 11.27i (11.31w/11.20-99)
ROUTLEDGE Marian 9.05.71, Hull Spartan
(nee JAMES) : HT - 39.32 (39.96-98)
ROWE Deborah 8.09.72, Birchfield :
TJ - 13.14w/12.97
ROWE Kate U23 13.09.78, Peterborough :
PV - 3.20 (3.30-99)
ROY Lesley-Ann U20 3.01.82, Pitreavie :
SP - 11.77 (11.81-99)

RUDDOCK Ellena 23.02.76, Rugby :
60 - 7.64i (7.54i-98),
100 - 11.49w/11.77 (11.63A-99/11.67-98),
200 - 24.2/24.26w/24.27 (23.71-97)
RUDKIN Lois U15 25.02.86, Sale :
75HG - 11.6, PenG - 2512
RUSSELL Clare U20 11.11.81, Oldham & R :
100 - 11.89w/12.10
RUTHERFORD Susannah Rose U23 26.02.79,
Darl/Newc Un : 3k - 9:56.27mx (10:16.57-97)
RYDE Gemma U20 23.06.83, Dunf & W Fife :
60 - 7.73i (7.70i-99), 100 - 11.89,
200 - 24.35w/24.59

SAGE Kathryn 27.03.76, Newp/UWIC :
(nee BRIGHT)
400 - 55.58, 800 - 2:11.02 (2:10.80-93)
SAINT-SMITH Tasha 20.12.75, Enf & Har :
DT - 40.71 (44.68-94)
SAKA-NAKAGIRL Lydia U23 20.01.79,
Windsor S & E/SWE : TJ - 11.07 (11.19-99)
SALMON Sarah 9.09.74, Newquay & Par :
1500 - 4:29.02i/4:31.35 (4:24.00-96),
3k - 9:27.75i (9:40.87-96), 5KR - 16:58
SALT Christa V35 17.06.64, Basel :
600 - 1:31.58i, 800 - 2:06.56 (2:06.15-99),
1k - 2:45.83, 1500 - 4:24.28 (4:22.96-97),
3k - 9:53.00i (9:46.25i-95)
SAMUELS Belinda U23 29.11.78, Bir/Birm U :
100H - 14.50w/15.0/15.09 (14.98-99),
LJ - 5.64w/5.61 (5.62-97), SP - 11.28,
Hep - 4506 (4528-97)
SAMUELS Lisa U20 24.09.81, Stevenage & NH :
800 - 2:12.48 (2:10.84-99)
SANDALL Elizabeth G. U13 11.09.87, Stroud :
100 - 12.9, 200 - 27.0
SANDERS Nicola U20 23.06.82, Wycombe :
200 - 25.0/25.22w/25.26
(24.6/24.64w-98/25.11-97),
400 - 56.48 (55.66-99), 400H - 59.68 (58.96-99)
SANDERS Rebecca U17 15.07.85, Sphinx :
3k - 10:40.7
SANGVIK Sigrun V40 5.02.57, SevenO/NOR :
3kW - 15:33.2, 5kW - 27:08.35
SARGENT Claire U15 11.03.86, Havering :
75HG - 11.5
SAUNDERS Kerry 28.03.77, Derby LAC :
HJ - 1.65i/1.65 (1.73-97), LJ - 5.50,
TJ - 11.36 (11.47w/11.45-97)
SAUNDERS Rebecca U13 8.02.88, Dartford :
DTM - 34.80
SAVAGE Stacey U17 30.12.84, Shaft Barnet :
TJ - 11.12
SAVUNDRA Cecilia U13 29.12.87, AF&D :
600 - 1:46.4, DTM - 23.31
SAYERS Goldie Katherine D. U20 16.07.82,
Peterborough : JT - 54.58
SCHOFIELD Candace U17 3.11.84, Worthing :
SP - 10.59, DT - 35.72, JT - 36.86
SCHOFIELD Sarah U13, Liverpool H :
150 - 19.3un
SCOTCHER Rebecca U20 2.07.82, Peterbro :
400 - 56.55i/57.0 (54.28-99)
SCOTT Jackie U17 31.01.85, Dundee HH :
200 - 25.39, 300 - 41.3
SCOTT Jemma U20 14.03.83, Edinburgh WM :
100H - 15.05w/15.28,
HJ - 1.68i/1.65 (1.70i/1.70-99), Hep - 4353
SCOTT Lorna U23 27.07.78, City of Glasgow :
400 - 57.28, 800 - 2:08.71
SCOTT Sabrina U23 2.06.79, Herne Hill :
60 - 7.6i/7.67i, 100 - 11.81,
200 - 24.37, LJ - 5.69i (5.56-99)
SCOTT Sian U17 20.03.84, Bournemouth :
200 - 25.58, 300 - 39.57, 400H - 63.15,
400 - 58.9 (57.69-99), 60HI - 9.20i,
80HI - 11.3/11.52w, 300H - 42.6/43.12
SCOTT Susan 26.09.77, City of Glasgow :
800 - 2:08.51 (2:07.1mx/2:07.77-98),
1500 - 4:18.42 (4:16.16-99), 10kR - 33:54
SCOTT Victoria Rosemary U23 21.09.80,
Liv H/Liv U : DT - 37.40, HT - 52.47
SCRAMBLER Kelly U23 21.11.79, Birchfield :
PV - 2.60 (2.70-99)
SCULLY Teresa V35 1.10.61, :
Mar - 2:56:40 (2:55:37-99)
SEARLE Kim U17 27.12.83, Hull Springhead :
300 - 41.2/41.48, 800 - 2:13.6
SELBIE Lynsey U20 9.03.83, Border :
HT - 42.97
SELLEY Danielle U17 19.12.83, Preseli :
60 - 7.71i (7.70i-99), 100 - 11.88w/12.00,
200 - 24.56
SELWYN Alex U17 20.09.83, Coventry G :
HJ - 1.71
SEMENOVA Marina V35 12.07.64, Birchfield :
HT - 48.12 (50.04-99)
SEMPER Sharon 26.11.68, Ilford :
400 - 56.9 (55.3/56.32-99)
SERRAO Eve U17 11.12.84, Wimborne :
100 - 12.53w
SHARP Carly U13 7.09.87, Edinburgh WM :
PenM - 2291
SHARP Maria 8.12.73, Thames Valley :
800 - 2:11.72 (2:08.73-95),
1500 - 4:22.30, 3k - 9:52.4
SHARPLES Gemma U20 4.08.83, Liverpool H :
TJ - 11.20
SHAW Emma U15 19.09.86, Skipton :
SPG - 11.34
SHAW Georgina U15 13.03.86, Sale :
LJ - 5.25
SHAW Lorraine A. 2.04.68, Sale :
SP - 12.65 (14.21-94),
DT - 49.77 (55.04-94),
HT - 67.44, HTY - 56.38
SHAW Louise U13, Wakefield :
75 - 10.1, 200 - 27.0
SHEARER Angela U17 18.01.85, Aberdeen :
300H - 46.32
SHEEDY Kay U17 14.10.84, Blackpool :
300 - 41.5
SHEPHERD Victoria U23 26.01.80, Wakefield :
SP - 12.21 (12.35-96)
SHEPPARD Amanda 26.02.68, Wakefield :
DT - 40.27 (42.81-98)
SHERLIKER Kessia U15 9.11.85, Soton City :
100 - 12.6, 200 - 25.01w/25.10
SHIEL Rebecca Ellen U20 16.01.82, Gate :
TJ - 11.66
SHIPMAN Victoria 31.03.77, Coventry Godiva :
200 - 24.9/24.94w (23.87-97)
SHORTS Tracy 4.11.72, Nuneaton :
DT - 35.96 (43.04-96), HT - 37.86 (42.42-96)
SHUTTLEWORTH Sarah U15 16.08.86, Sale :
800 - 2:18.68

SIGGERY Alison U17 14.09.83, Carmarthen :
JT - 41.11
SILK Kimberley U15 26.03.86, Colchester H :
DT - 30.45
SILTO Katherine U20 12.08.83, Swindon :
TJ - 11.25w/11.19
SILVER Lorna Jane 10.01.74, Shaft Barnet :
60H - 8.94i (8.88i-95), 100H - 14.13
SIMMONS Sarah 12.01.75, Hounslow :
800 - 2:11.0 (2:10.2-99),
1500 - 4:23.83 (4:23.76-99), 3k - 9:37.6
SIMPSON Jemma Louise U17 10.02.84,
Newquay & Par : 300 - 40.2, 400 - 58.1,
800 - 2:06.72, 1500 - 4:30.41
SIMPSON Nadine U15 28.02.86, Steve & NH :
HJ - 1.60, PV - 2.20, PenG - 2793
SIMPSON Stacey Louise U13 25.01.88, Ayr S :
75 - 10.0, 100 - 12.9/13.08,
150 - 19.2, 200 - 27.1w/27.2/27.37
SIMS Jemma U17 2.05.85, Notts :
60 - 7.68i, 100 - 11.99w/12.1/12.15, 200 - 24.63
SINGER Lindsey U20 4.06.83, Birchfield :
400 - 57.33i
SINGER Samantha U20 8.05.82, Blackheath :
400 - 55.31
SINGH Eshere U15 15.07.87, Exeter :
SPG - 10.53, DT - 30.74
SINGS Lucy U17 9.07.85, City of Plymouth :
300 - 41.29
SKETCHLEY Katy 9.07.73, Team Solent :
60H - 8.73i (8.44i-97),
100H - 13.94 (13.57w/13.78-98)
SKINNER Kim U13 21.09.87, Falkirk :
100 - 13.1, 200 - 27.6,
PV - 2.90i/2.80, LJ - 4.61, PenM - 2191
SKORUPSKA Katharine Wanda Taylor U23
3.11.78, Edinburgh WM/Oxford Univ :
3k - 9:26.31i/9:34.6 (9:24.26-98),
5k - 16:50.6 (15:55.64-99), 5MR - 27:14
SKUCEK Emily U20 24.09.81, Newport :
JT - 40.89
SLATER Catriona 27.01.77, Chelmsford :
100 - 12.05w/12.1 (12.1-99/12.67-95),
200 - 24.77w/24.8 (24.7/24.82-99)
SMELLIE Natalie U20 16.01.82, WGr & Ex L :
200 - 25.19i (24.81w-98/25.00-97),
400 - 56.5/56.72
SMITH Alana U17 18.01.85, Edinburgh WM :
SP - 10.77i, DT - 34.71
SMITH C. U13, Macclesfield :
JTM - 24.25
SMITH Caroline Jane U20 31.07.83, Radley :
PV - 3.10
SMITH Caroline A.L. U15 15.09.86, Havering :
PenG - 2506
SMITH Diane V40 15.11.60, Hull Achilles :
HT - 43.64 (46.00-96)
SMITH Elaine U20 16.05.83, Mandale :
LJ - 5.83w/5.75
SMITH Emma U13, Braintree :
JTM - 30.25
SMITH Emma Marie U15 14.09.85, W Norfolk :
PenG - 2618
SMITH Grace U20 30.01.82, Sale :
60H - 8.93i, 100H - 14.39w/14.60,
Hep - 3987 (4009-99)
SMITH Heidi 20.05.74, Liv.Pembroke Sefton :
800 - 2:12.7 (2:07.2-98)
SMITH Helen Nicola U17 9.10.84, Basildon :
HJ - 1.66
SMITH Hilary 28.02.76, Halesowen :
PV - 3.50
SMITH Janet Carole V35 7.10.64, W S & E :
HT - 46.99 (50.62-97)
SMITH Karen U23 25.12.78, Ashford :
SP - 11.31 (11.92-97)
SMITH Katy U20 5.08.81, Thurrock/Loughbro :
1500 - 4:32.39
SMITH Laura U17 21.01.84, Border :
JT - 38.06
SMITH Leonie M.E. U15 20.12.86, AF&D :
1500 - 4:44.83
SMITH Louise 11.07.77, Reading :
JT - 42.62
SMITH Natasha 6.06.77, Hounslow :
SP - 13.78 (14.12-97), HT - 40.09 (44.00-98)
SMITH Rebecca U17 17.10.83, Bingley :
800 - 2:16.63
SMITH Rosie U17 28.06.85, Durham :
1500 - 4:42.18
SMITH Sarah 18.08.76, Peterborough :
400 - 57.5,
400H - 64.5/64.85 (63.1-99/63.85-98)
SMITHSON Claire U20 3.08.83, Brighton :
SP - 13.98, DT - 52.19
SMITHSON Kerry 13.09.76, Sale :
800 - 2:08.95 (2:08.4-98/2:09.5mx-96),
1500 - 4:18.32 (4:17.6-98),
3k - 9:44.54 (9:29.0mx-98)
SNELGROVE Charlene U20 6.05.82, Ipswich :
800 - 2:12.94
SOTHERTON Kelly Jade 13.11.76, Birchfield :
100 - 12.0w/12.06 (11.80w/11.85-97),
200 - 24.48 (24.03-97),
400 - 55.83i/57.10 (54.17-97),
60H - 8.82i (8.72i-98), 100H - 14.15,
HJ - 1.72i/1.70 (1.75-97),
LJ - 6.24w/6.09 (6.10-97),
SP - 11.70 (11.84-98), Hep - 5428 (5585-97)
SOUTAR Claire U13 26.04.88, Pitreavie :
PenM - 2213
SOUTH Hayley U17 17.11.83, Norwich :
800 - 2:16.7
SOUTHGATE Kayleigh U13 15.01.88, Diss :
SPM - 10.72
SPAIN Elizabeth U20 23.08.82, Shaft Barnet :
PV - 3.90
SPARGO Jacqueline 12.01.71, Coventry G :
(nee WHITE)
LJ - 6.06w?/6.03 (6.11w-95/6.08-96)
SPARK Jayne Clare 16.09.70, Altrincham :
5KR - 16:59, 2KSTW - 6:36.02
SPEIGHT Natasha U13 9.09.87, Mansfield :
HJ - 1.56
SPELZINI Charlotte U20 7.01.83, Cambr & C :
SP - 12.72, HT - 42.43
SPENCER Amy U15 19.09.85, Wigan :
60 - 7.75i, 100 - 12.02, 200 - 24.24w/24.31
SPENCER Elizabeth U17 25.04.85, Skyrac :
3k - 10:38.63mx
SPENCER Rachel Elizabeth U15 19.08.86,
Banchory : HJ - 1.60, LJ - 5.18w/5.16,
PenG - 2879
SPILLER Beth U13 22.04.88, Rhondda :
DTM - 26.44un/23.02

SPINK Mandy V35 12.01.65, Long Eaton :
Mar - 2:45:10
SPRULES Lyn 11.09.75, Shaftesbury Barnet :
HT - 63.96
STAINES Linda V35 26.12.63, Bas & MH :
200 - 24.9 (23.1/23.51-89),
400 - 54.01 (50.98-91)
STANILAND Bethany U13 10.05.88, Skyrac :
DTM - 26.10, JTM - 24.90, PenM - 2060
STANLEY Joanne Marie 30.03.77, M & C :
TJ - 11.81 (11.90i/11.82w?-99)
STANTON Linda Mary 22.06.73, Sale :
PV - 3.50 (3.72-95)
STARES Hannah U23 13.11.78, Yate :
100H - 14.9/14.93, 400H - 62.9, Hep - 4553
STEAD Caroline 14.09.71, WGreen & Ex L :
TJ - 12.47 (12.67-96)
STENNETT Vanessa 3.06.69, Walton :
JT - 37.82
STEPHENS Tamsin Anne U23 2.08.80, Bir/
Loughbro : 60H - 8.65i,
100H - 13.89w/13.93, 400H - 62.40
STEVENS Eleanor U17 29.06.84, Derby LAC :
1500 - 4:41.29, 3k - 10:23.6
STEVENSON Lucy 30.01.73, Sale :
JT - 43.44 (45.29-99)
STEWART Claire U17 14.10.83, Elgin :
HT - 31.49
STEWART Gillian U23 21.01.80, EWM :
100H - 14.7/15.05 (14.71w-98/14.73-99),
SP - 11.70 (11.72-99), JT - 37.26 (40.78-99)
STEWART Staci U15 20.09.85, C of Glasgow :
HJ - 1.65
STILES Amy 6.02.75, Westbury :
5KR - 16:54, HMar - 1:17:20, Mar - 2:47:48
STILL Sarah 24.09.75, Aberdeen :
200 - 24.48 (24.4-99), 60H - 8.84i,
100H - 14.73w/14.90 (14.61-99),
HJ - 1.66 (1.68-99),
LJ - 5.82i/5.73 (5.85-99), Hep - 5014
STOATE Isabella U15 16.07.86, N Devon :
1500 - 4:50.22
STOKOE Ceri U20 19.04.82, Swansea :
HJ - 1.73
STONES Katie U15 22.11.85, Hull Springhead :
3kW - 16:15.5, 5kWR - 26:29
STOREY Karen 8.11.68, Gateshead :
400 - 57.4
STOUTE Jennifer Elaine V35 16.04.65,
WG & Ex L : 100 - 12.15 (11.63w/11.64-90),
200 - 23.57 (22.73-92),
300 - 37.59 (36.95-91), 400 - 53.41 (51.53-89)
STRAIN Natalie U17 31.01.84, Regent House :
300H - 46.3, 400H - 65.55
STRAKER Julia U20 25.11.82, Morpeth :
TJ - 11.64
STREATFIELD Katharine U20 28.07.83,
Soton City : TJ - 11.61
STREET Joanne U20 30.10.82, Tamworth :
SP - 12.55, DT - 45.30 (45.93-99)
STREET Natalie U17 8.11.83, Hertford & W :
300 - 41.0/41.56 (41.49-99)
STREVENS Sarah U20 7.10.81, N & Essex B :
TJ - 11.26
STRINGER Kathryn U20 24.09.81, Rotherham :
JT - 37.62 (38.13-99)
SUDDES Joanne 27.01.77, Edinburgh WM :
100H - 14.9/14.96w (14.29w/14.4/14.53-99)
SULLIVAN Deborah 24.01.72, Havering :
800 - 2:09.8, 1500 - 4:25.59 (4:21.12-99),
3k - 9:36.2 (9:34.30-97), 5k - 16:07.51,
10k - 34:30.9 (34:30.16-99)
SUTTON Lucy U15 29.08.86, Oxford City :
SPG - 11.57, DT - 31.44
SUTTON Marian R. V35 7.10.63, Tipton :
5KR - 16:50, 10kR - 33:36 (32:38-97),
10MR - 55:05 (52:15-97),
HMar - 1:17:06 (1:09:41-97),
Mar - 2:34:33 (2:28:42-99)
SUTTON Rachael U20 28.08.83, Oxford City :
200 - 25.0
SWATHERIDGE Donna U17 4.03.85,
Basingstoke & MH : DT - 34.81
SWEENEY Rebecca U17 9.02.85, Sale :
100 - 12.28, 200 - 25.40, 300 - 39.48
SWINBANK Caroline 16.06.75, Bristol :
800 - 2:12.3
SYMONDS Emma 5.06.77, Norwich :
200 - 25.1w (24.5-96/24.74w/24.97-95)
SYMONDS Sarah Louise 28.12.73, Oxford C :
(see NICKELSON)

TALBOT Nicola 17.02.72, Birchfield :
DT - 48.84 (54.24-93)
TAPPIN Lia Adina U15 9.01.87, Enf & Har :
200 - 25.64
TAYLOR Helen U20 19.07.82, Wakefield :
HT - 47.89
TAYLOR Jessica R. U13 27.06.88, Rowntrees :
75 - 10.1
TAYLOR Kirstie Louise 10.01.75, Dartford :
100 - 11.8?/12.0/12.08w/12.24 (12.0-99),
200 - 25.20
TAYLOR Laura U17 22.04.84, Radley :
Hepl - 3885 (4029-99)
TEALE Amy U20 30.12.82, N Shields Poly :
100H - 14.96
TEASDALE Laura U13 12.06.88, Wakefield :
SPM - 9.09, DTM - 24.15
TELFORD Rebekah 4.11.76, Trafford :
PV - 2.70 (2.70-99)
TEMPLETON Charlotte 25.01.70, Dul R/AUS :
1500 - 4:30.88mx/4:33.7
TERRY Sandra 28.04.69, Ealing,Southall & Mx :
DT - 36.92 (39.94-98)
THACKRAY Penny D. 18.08.74, Wakefield :
1500 - 4:26.96mx (4:22.4-97),
3k - 9:43.4 (9:23.5mx-96/9:35.76-94),
5k - 16:35.68 (16:16.01-97),
5MR - 27:50, 10kR - 33:31
THAKE Jemma U15 17.12.85, West Suffolk :
100 - 12.3/12.32, 200 - 25.06
THEOBALD Susan U20 4.03.83, Braintree :
JT - 37.43
THERIN Lauren U15 19.01.86, Jersey :
SPG - 10.83, DT - 36.38,
JT - 37.36 (38.01-99)
THEVENT-SMITH Thelma, 26.2 Running Club :
24Hr - 156.171km
THIEME Helen U20 28.09.81, Birchfield :
200 - 24.53w/24.7/25.26i,
400 - 54.61 (54.32-99),
400H - 62.0/62.62 (60.6/62.19-99),
THOM Pauline 2.08.70, Edinburgh WM :
800 - 2:10.0 (2:08.4mx/2:09.06-98),
1500 - 4:22.97 (4:22.31-98)

THOMAS Danielle U13, Barrow & Furness : PenM - 2100
THOMAS Hayley U15 16.12.86, Thurrock : JT - 32.81
THOMAS Kadi-Ann U15 10.02.86, Milton K : 100 - 12.32, 200 - 25.7
THOMAS Kelly U20 9.01.81, Dartf/Loughbro : 100 - 11.76w/11.83, 200 - 24.32
THOMAS Lucy Ann U17 2.11.84, Birchfield : 1500 - 4:42.08
THOMAS Michelle 16.10.71, Birchfield : 200 - 24.50i (23.98-97), 400 - 54.68i (52.47-99), 800 - 2:12.0
THOMAS Rachel U17 19.01.85, Leeds : 300 - 40.81, Hepl - 3963
THOMAS Sonia U23 16.05.79, Sale : 1500 - 4:31.00 (4:28.60-99), 3k - 9:46.4
THOMPSON Joanne Mary V40 30.10.58, City of Bath : 10kR - 34:47 (33:10-93), HMar - 1:16:58 (1:15:51-99)
THOMPSON Rachael U15 15.11.85, Liv H : 800 - 2:13.01
THOMPSON Ruth 7.06.76, Pendle : 400H - 64.4 (65.52-97)
THOMSON Trudi V40 18.01.59, Pitreavie : 10kR - 34:53 (34:46-99), 10MR - 56:22, HMar - 1:18:16 (1:14:34-96), Mar - 2:40:39 (2:38:23-95)
THORNAL Danielle 9.08.75, : 800 - 2:07.83
THORNE Alison 25.09.72, Windsor S & E : 400 - 55.67 (55.11-98)
THORNE Louretta 6.05.77, Wycombe : 400 - 55.42i (54.23-99)
THORNER Rosie 7.08.67, Bristol : 200 - 25.1w, 400 - 56.40 (55.86-95)
THORNTON Emma U20 27.11.82, Bolton : JT - 37.25
THORPE Anna-Maria 15.07.71, TVH : LJ - 5.96w/5.94, TJ - 12.83 (12.84-99)
THWAITES Patricia, Mandale : 24Hr - 177.100km
TODD Sara L. U23 3.11.79, J & H/N'thumbria U : 100 - 12.1 (12.23w-98/12.61-94), 100H - 14.55, 400H - 63.07 (61.57-99), Hep - 4051 (4266-99)
TOMLINS Sarah U20 5.04.82, Horsham BS : 100 - 12.1 (12.57w-98/13.36-97), 200 - 24.67w/24.71, 400 - 57.5
TOMLINSON Iyesha U15 19.02.86, WG & Ex L : SPG - 11.38, DT - 33.98
TONKS Sharon Jayne 18.04.70, Brom & R : 3kW - 14:07.8, 5kW - 25:49.32 (24:20.07-98), 5kWR - 24:59 (24:45-99), 10kWR - 49:46, 20kW - 1:42:10sh/1:49:19
TOVEY Rachel U13 17.10.87, Windsor S & E : 600 - 1:46.8, 1k - 3:14.3
TOWARD Louise U17 27.03.84, Blackpool : 80HI - 12.0, LJ - 5.37, Hepl - 4322
TOWN Anna 22.04.75, Verlea : HT - 37.22
TOWNS Lisa U23 19.04.79, Thames Valley : 5k - 17:30.1 (17:07.46-99)
TROTMAN Joanna U23 5.10.80, Croydon : LJ - 6.02?/5.65
TROTMAN Lisa U20 6.12.82, Trafford : 200 - 25.25
TRUELOVE Jenny U20 19.01.81, Banbury : Hep - 4112
TULLETT Hayley 17.02.73, Swansea : 800 - 2:01.25, 1500 - 4:01.23, 1M - 4:26.50i (4:48.88-95), 2k - 5:52.8+e, 3k - 8:45.39, 10MR - 57:01
TUNALEY Victoria U17 4.06.84, Ipswich : 300 - 40.81, 400 - 58.54
TUNE Gemma U17 28.02.84, Basildon : 300H - 46.3, TJ - 10.74, Hepl - 3902
TUNSTILL Jennifer U17 16.05.84, Park Hill HS : 800 - 2:16.38
TURNER Charmaine U20 5.12.81, W S & E : TJ - 11.38
TURNER Karlene U17 9.01.85, W S & E : LJ - 5.83
TURNER Laura Kate U20 12.08.82, Parkside : 100H - 14.7/15.09
TURNER Michelle 25.12.77, Parkside : 100 - 11.92 (11.9w-99), 200 - 25.1 (25.1-99/25.81-92)
TURTLE Gemma Anne U15 15.05.86, Chilt : 1500 - 4:43.7
TURTON Judy U17 26.05.84, Wycombe : PV - 2.90
TYLER Jacky V40 7.12.57, E Cornwall : Mar - 3:04:09

UPHILL Katherine U13 19.02.88, Bristol : 800 - 2:26.5
UPTON Sophie L. U15 18.09.85, Solihull & S H : HJ - 1.61

VAN GRAAN Stephanie 4.02.77, Shaftesbury Barnet/RSA : 3k - 9:31.9
VANDENBULK Jeannette 14.03.77, Bright/CAN : 400H - 63.7/64.09
VANNET Lisa 8.11.74, Edinburgh WM : 200 - 24.53w/24.9 (24.93-95), 400 - 55.94 (54.54-96)
VANSKA Lisa 8.10.66, East Anglia Univ : Mar - 3:02:39
VAUGHAN Amelia U15 26.05.86, Yeovil Oly : PenG - 2658
VAUGHAN Lucy 20.04.69, Basingstoke & MH : 800 - 2:08.8mx/2:09.22
VELDMAN Margaret 7.06.74, Sale/HOL : 200 - 25.24 (25.15-98), LJ - 6.03w/5.94 (5.94i-98)
VELVICK Kimberley U17 3.01.85, Ashford : 60 - 7.8i/7.94i, 100 - 12.27, 200 - 24.98
VLASSAK Ruth V35 24.11.61, Woking : 800 - 2:12.71 (2:10.9-92)
VOGEL Kiera U15 31.05.86, Liv.Pembroke S : 1500 - 4:42.42
VOUSDEN Janet 25.11.68, Coventry Godiva : PV - 3.20
VUAGNIAUX Alison V40 31.05.60, C of Bath : Mar - 3:01:24

WADE Rebecca U23 11.06.80, Wx & B/ Birmingham Univ. : 3k - 9:58.3
WAIN Alanna U17 27.04.85, City of Stoke : 200 - 25.19 (24.98w-99), 300 - 39.58
WAINWRIGHT Ann V45 26.10.54, C of Stoke : PV - 2.60i/2.60
WAINWRIGHT Kimberley U15 18.01.86, Donc & Stain : 100 - 12.6, 200 - 25.76
WALCOTT Chloe U13 29.01.88, Kingston & P : 100 - 13.2, 200 - 27.5w/27.6

WALDRON Megan U15 4.09.86, Horsham BS :
PenG - 2537
WALE Amanda 14.10.70, Wrexham :
Hep - 4286 (4546-98)
WALKER Dawn U17 29.09.83, Barrow & Furn :
HJ - 1.65 (1.66-98)
WALKER Helen Charlotte U23 12.10.80,
M & C/Sussex Un : 400H - 65.1 (62.92-98)
WALKER Hilary C. V45 9.11.53, Serpentine :
100kR - 9:04:29 (7:50:09-93)
WALKER Jemma U17 17.09.83, Pitreavie :
100 - 12.42w/12.57, 200 - 25.23
WALKER Marcia 27.05.70, Windsor S & E :
TJ - 11.75w/11.66 (11.78-97)
WALKER Mhairi U17 20.01.84, Livingston :
300H - 45.9
WALL Kim U20 21.04.83, Basildon :
100 - 11.8/12.35 (12.13-98),
200 - 24.04, 400 - 54.04R/54.41,
WALL Melissa U15 10.04.86, Basildon :
800 - 2:16.4, 1500 - 4:34.2
WALLACE Michelle 1.11.72, Notts :
DT - 36.20 (41.50-93)
WALLBANKS Carol U20 9.12.82, Border :
JT - 42.73
WALLER Ruth U17 6.03.84, Sale :
3k - 10:33.0mx (10:41.0-99)
WALSH Caroline Elizabeth U23 29.04.80, S B :
800 - 2:12.75, 1500 - 4:25.5 (4:23.35-99),
3k - 9:30.66mx (9:13.4mx/9:20.38-99),
5KR - 16:58
WALSH Sarah U17 28.01.85, Dacorum & Tring :
Hepl - 3972
WALTERS Amanda U17 18.04.84, Wigan :
300 - 40.15
WALTERS Bernadette V35 15.02.63, Cardiff :
10MR - 58:39
WALTERS Kirsty Lynn U17 6.09.84, C of Glas :
DT - 33.48, HT - 40.72
WALTERS Mhairi Lee U20 19.06.81, C of Glas :
SP - 13.03, DT - 38.41, HT - 55.10
WALTON Lauren U13 1.09.87, Guildford & G :
LJ - 4.73
WANNELL Michelle 12.07.67, Exeter :
1500 - 4:23.72 (4:22.33-99),
3k - 9:31.01 (9:27.8-98), 5k - 16:32.13,
5KR - 16:52, 5MR - 27:32,
10kR - 34:51 (34:44-99), 10MR - 58:08
WARD Emma U20 2.01.82, City of Stoke :
800 - 2:06.02, 1500 - 4:19.70, 3k - 9:27.63
WARD Jennifer U23 22.09.78, C of Glasgow :
400 - 56.7 (57.44-99), 800 - 2:05.10,
1500 - 4:26.2 (4:25.8-97)
WARD Stacey U17 16.01.85, Basildon :
800 - 2:15.8, 1500 - 4:39.6, 3k - 10:26.8
WARD Victoria 19.06.72, WG & Ex L :
(nee DAY)
60 - 7.62i, 100 - 12.02w (12.1-93/12.11-98),
200 - 24.12w/24.20i/24.30 (23.84w/24.07-98),
400 - 53.58
WARNE Anna U15 17.11.85, Harborough :
800 - 2:19.0
WARREN Nathalie U20 28.08.81, Walton :
PV - 2.90 (2.90-99)
WARREN Sally U23 29.01.78, Steyning :
3kW - 14:49.6, 5kW - 25:11.3,
10kWR - 52:37 (51:20-98), 20kW - 1:52:37
WATERLOW Amy U23 29.07.78, Sale :
1500 - 4:32.87 (4:25.5mx/4:30.3-99),
3k - 9:25.01 (9:21.55-99),
5k - 16:37.09 (15:57.45-98), 5KR - 16:30,
10kR - 34:15 (33:44-99)
WATKINS Laura U20 1.01.82, Telford :
200 - 25.0/25.27w (25.07-99)
WATSON Anna U20 30.04.82, Inverness :
PV - 2.75i/2.70 (3.03-98)
WATSON Carolyn V35, Dartford :
3kW - 16:10.3i
WATSON Louise Carole 13.12.71, Maid & R :
3k - 9:49.7 (9:16.45-92),
5k - 16:36.71 (15:57.06-95), 10MR - 58:01,
HMar - 1:15:45, Mar - 2:49:19
WATSON Natalie U17 5.07.84, Wolves & B :
60 - 7.96i (7.92i-99),
100 - 12.4/12.51 (12.1-98/12.12w/12.27-99),
200 - 24.85 (24.73w-99)
WATSON Ruth U23 29.11.79, Peterborough :
200 - 25.17 (24.75-98), 400 - 55.88 (55.24-99)
WATTON Louise U15 30.10.86, Wimborne :
SPG - 10.62, DT - 29.24, JT - 35.61
WATTS Katy Louise U20 25.03.81, Bas & MH/
Brunel Univ : JT - 43.46 (45.24-99)
WATTS Samantha U20 13.10.81, Sale :
400H - 64.8/65.11
WAUGH Kathryn 20.02.73, Liverpool H :
1500 - 4:33.8 (4:31.2-96)
WEALL Kelly U23 30.11.78, M & C/Staffs Un :
400H - 64.68 (62.5/63.80-97)
WEATHERILL Carolina 13.05.68, Shaft Barn :
3k - 9:41.3 (9:23.1-95)
WEATHERITT Leah J. 18.09.74,
Gateshead : (nee LACKENBY) SP - 11.59
WEBB Elizabeth U17 16.12.83, Cardiff :
TJ - 10.84i/10.77 (10.91-99)
WEBB Helen Julie U23 14.04.80, Halesowen :
PV - 3.20
WEBB Lauren U15 17.11.85, Sutton & District :
100 - 12.3, 200 - 25.50w/25.67
WEBB Lisa Jane V35 9.10.65, Shaft Barnet :
1500 - 4:32.30 (4:22.9-88),
3k - 9:48.97 (9:11.45-88),
5k - 17:24.63 (16:23.90-88)
WEBB Shirley Catherine U20 28.09.81, NSP :
HT - 47.33
WEBBER Claire U17 13.12.83, Arbroath :
300H - 46.55
WEBBER Lucy Kate 5.02.72, Team Solent :
PV - 4.04
WEBSTER Michelle U17 18.04.85, Beds & Co :
200 - 25.5
WEEKES Hannah U13, Stevenage & NH :
HJ - 1.45, PenM - 2319
WEEKES Jade U17 15.11.84, Dartford :
Hepl - 3846
WEIR Jessica U17 3.10.84, Wilts Sch :
SP - 10.48
WELLS Elaine U23 30.05.78, Craw/Chich Coll :
400 - 57.44 (57.3-97/57.38-98)
WELLS Louisa U17 30.12.84, West Suffolk :
100 - 12.4/12.48w/12.57
WELLSTEAD Sarah U23 22.10.79, Sutton & D :
LJ - 5.80 (5.86-98), TJ - 11.44 (11.63-97)
WENHAM Carley Ann U13 14.03.88, Crawley :
75 - 9.7, 100 - 12.6w/12.9,
150 - 19.6, 200 - 26.7

WERRETT Gemma Elizabeth Harvie U15 15.03.86, Cannock & Staff : 75HG - 11.56
WESTON Rachel 12.07.71, Belgrave : Mar - 2:57:51
WESTWOOD Fiona U20 27.02.81, Wakefield : 100 - 12.22w (13.3-97), LJ - 6.02
WHEELER Dani U15 12.10.85, Dac & Tring : SPG - 11.34
WHIGHAM Lisa U23 14.08.80, Vic Park AAC/ Strathclyde Univ : 400 - 56.25
WHIGHAM Sara U17 7.10.83, Vic Park AAC : 100 - 12.42 (12.4-99), 200 - 25.57
WHILEY Lesley V40 14.05.60, Reading RR : Mar - 2:58:21
WHITCOMBE Andrea 8.06.71, Parkside : 800 - 2:11.7 (2:10.7-96), 1500 - 4:19.51 (4:14.56-90), 3k - 9:12.45mx/9:16.2+e (8:58.59-91), 5k - 15:32.62, 5MR - 27:09, 10MR - 57:05,
WHITE Jacqueline 12.01.71, Coventry G : (see SPARGO)
WHITE Julia U23 2.05.79, Peterborough : 100 - 12.18w/12.49 (12.00w-99/12.0/12.05-97)
WHITE Katrina 20.02.70, Milton Keynes : Mar - 2:54:37
WHITE Laura E. U23 5.09.79, Trafford : HJ - 1.72 (1.75-98)
WHITE Rebecca U23 5.06.80, Sale/Bath Un : 100 - 12.26 (11.45w-98/12.00-97), LJ - 5.87w/5.85, TJ - 12.24
WHITE Sarah U23 25.12.80, Andover : HJ - 1.75
WHITEHEAD Fiona 31.05.70, Havant : HT - 46.30dh/45.61 (52.84-93)
WHITEHEAD Margaret Louise 26.03.75, Swan : 200 - 24.5/25.20 (24.03w-98/24.1-93/24.24-97), 400 - 53.37 (53.34-99)
WHITEHEAD Ruth 14.01.72, Bingley : Mar - 3:06:55 (3:04:59-99)
WHITLOCK Janine 11.08.73, Trafford : 60 - 7.36i/7.5mx, 100 - 11.7w/11.74w/12.00 (11.56-99), 200 - 24.47 (23.30-99), PV - 4.35, LJ - 5.71 (5.94-98)
WHITMORE Hannah U17 24.02.84, Charn : 1500 - 4:34.01
WHITTAKER Louise U20 29.11.82, Sale : 800 - 2:10.89, 1500 - 4:33.0
WHITTER Emma U23 20.07.80, Herne Hill : 60 - 7.56i, 100 - 11.85 (11.74-99), 200 - 24.00w/24.08 (23.73w/24.08-99)
WICHEARD Ashleigh U15 20.07.86, Wilts S : LJ - 5.29w/5.06
WICKHAM Charlotte U17 21.06.85, Gateshead : 1500 - 4:43.1, 3k - 10:27.08
WILDBORE Abby U15 12.09.85, Wilts Sch : JT - 32.02
WILDER Kelley E. 30.07.71, Oxford Univ/USA : 3k - 9:36.51, 5k - 16:36.7
WILDING Helen 25.10.76, Trafford/Liv Univ : SP - 12.91i/12.47 (13.88-95), DT - 39.77 (42.90-95), HT - 48.31
WILHELMY Sarah U23 2.02.80, Southend : 60 - 7.42, 100 - 11.49, 200 - 23.26 (23.20w/23.23-98)
WILKINS Frances U23 15.01.79, Bir/Birm Un : SP - 11.43i (11.75-99)
WILKINS Melanie 18.01.73, Windsor S & E : 200 - 24.65 (24.47w-94), 60H - 8.29i, 100H - 13.17 (13.1-95)
WILKINSON Chloe U17 16.12.84, Shaft Barn : 800 - 2:16.69, 1500 - 4:39.56, 3k - 9:58.6mx/10:04.5
WILKINSON Jo 2.05.73, Bedford & County : 1500 - 4:23.52, 3k - 9:37.0mx/9:48.87, 5k - 17:08.62, 10MR - 58:27
WILKINSON Sarah 2.01.70, Salford : (nee YOUNG) 3k - 8:57.75mx/9:12.03 (9:04.27-98), 5k - 15:40.85, 5KR - 15:53, 5MR - 26:29, 10k - 32:34.7, 10kR - 33:20 (32:45-99), HMar - 1:14:33
WILKINSON Tanya 1.04.70, City of Stoke : 400H - 64.0 (60.2/60.32-98)
WILLIAMS Angela U20 13.05.81, Medway : TJ - 12.22
WILLIAMS Claire U13 29.09.87, Llanelli : DTM - 23.91
WILLIAMS Donna Maria U23 7.10.78, Sale : DT - 42.70 (48.08-96)
WILLIAMS Elizabeth 2.06.77, Walton : 200 - 24.7/24.88w (24.1-99), 400 - 54.83 (54.53-99)
WILLIAMS Evaun V60 19.02.37, Enf & Har : HT - 37.20 (41.90-95)
WILLIAMS Helen 2.06.77, Walton : 200 - 25.1 (24.49w/24.8-98/25.07-95)
WILLIAMS Helen U20 13.01.83, Vale Royal : TJ - 11.30 (11.32w-99)
WILLIAMS Kate U17 10.05.84, Southend : PV - 2.80
WILLIAMS Kathryn S. 10.11.77, Swansea : 400H - 61.60 (60.21-96)
WILLIAMS Leasa U17 10.05.84, Southend : PV - 2.90
WILLIAMS Lynn 6.02.72, Arena/Brighton Un : 3k - 9:55.5 (9:53.8-99), HMar - 1:17:25
WILLIAMS Nadia U20 17.11.81, Shaft Barnet : LJ - 5.83w/5.70
WILLIAMS Sharon Bernadette 20.05.70, Windsor S & E : 100 - 11.88 (11.53-95), 400 - 56.8 (55.33-99)
WILLIAMS Susan U23 20.01.79, Deeside : PV - 2.60 (2.65-98)
WILLIAMS Susan 2.06.77, Walton : 60 - 7.74i (7.60i-98), 100 - 11.79 (11.61w-98), 200 - 23.90w/24.09 (23.59-99), 400 - 56.6, 400H - 63.1 (63.48-99)
WILLIAMS Victoria U20 11.04.81, Yate/UWIC : 100H - 14.81w/15.02 (14.9/14.96-98), Hep - 4034 (4289-98)
WILLIAMSON Maria U13 7.09.87, Leamington : 1200 - 4:02.0
WILSHIRE Abigail U17 24.02.84, Bristol : 3k - 10:27.42
WILSON Aileen J. U17 30.03.84, Peterborough : 60HI - 9.22i (9.05i-99), HJ - 1.83
WILSON Amy U23 31.12.80, Ipswich : SP - 12.62 (13.03-99)
WILSON Bernice U17 21.04.84, Grantham : 100 - 12.4 (12.62w/12.68-98), 300 - 40.06
WILSON Beverley 26.03.67, Cleethorpes : Mar - 2:58:25

WILSON Cassie 24.09.77, Bingley/Loughbro :
HT - 41.81
WILSON Cathy U17 29.08.84, Lagan Valley :
LJ - 5.35i (5.40-99)
WILSON Claire U15 7.11.85, Shetland :
800 - 2:17.40, 1500 - 4:48.0 (4:44.34-99)
WILSON Dawn U20 16.12.81, Bromley :
400 - 56.76
WILSON Kristy U17 2.08.84, Enf & Har :
400H - 66.4/67.64
WILSON Leona U17 23.05.85, Wigtown :
HT - 30.61
WILSON Paula Anneke 20.11.69, Birchfield :
PV - 3.50 (3.80-98)
WILSON Sharon 27.10.74, Dunf & W Fife :
200 - 25.0 (25.77w-96)
WILSON Stephanie U15 18.10.86, Lagan V :
1500 - 4:49.61
WILSON Zoe 28.08.76, Birchfield :
60 - 7.39i, 100 - 11.52w/11.66,
200 - 23.74w/24.09i/24.17 (23.91-99)
WINSTONE Gemma U17 18.11.84, Cardiff :
60 - 7.98i, 100 - 12.4w
WINTER Lindsey U17 19.03.84, Exeter :
100 - 12.3, 60HI - 9.18i,
80HI - 11.8/12.03w/12.07 (11.8/11.93-99)
WISE Clare L. 22.08.69, AF&D :
100H - 14.9/15.07 (14.48-98),
400H - 60.61 (59.07-98)
WISE Joanne 15.03.71, Coventry Godiva :
LJ - 6.59 (6.76-99)
WITTON Nikki 30.09.72, Newp/U Wales Newp :
PV - 2.85
WOOD Emma U13, Mansfield :
100 - 12.9/13.12
WOOD Hannah U20 17.11.81, Solihull & S H :
400 - 55.6/56.06, 400H - 60.86
WOOD Jennifer V40 23.02.57, Wakefield :
(nee CUNNANE)
PV - 2.90 (3.20-97), HT - 38.64 (44.93-98)
WOOD Laura U23 31.10.78, Trafford :
DT - 41.10 (41.28-98), HT - 39.51
WOOD Suzanne V35 22.04.65, Vale Royal :
Mar - 3:02:03
WOODMAN Amy U17 1.11.84, Bristol :
100 - 12.55w/12.56 (12.5/12.53w-99),
LJ - 5.64
WOODS Danielle U17 2.10.84, Liverpool H :
800 - 2:16.3
WOODS Jennie U17 28.01.84, Liverpool H :
HJ - 1.63 (1.66-98)
WOOFF Emma U17 21.05.85, Wigan :
LJ - 5.41, TJ - 10.93
WOOLGAR Deborah Caroline V35 10.03.65,
Worthing : SP - 13.27 (14.18-89),
DT - 36.93 (40.92-91), JT - 37.38 (38.78-99)
WOOLLEY Jessica U23 19.01.80, Bristol :
1500 - 4:32.49
WOOLRICH Sharon 1.05.76, C of Portsmouth :
HJ - 1.68 (1.70-94)
WOOTTON Katrina U15 2.09.85, Bedford & Co :
800 - 2:13.89, 1500 - 4:32.0
WORSEY Helen U20 29.08.82, Leics Cor :
60H - 8.62i, 100H - 13.76w/13.89
WRAY Sharon U20 8.10.82, Oswestry :
SP - 11.71
WRIGHT Amanda 14.07.68, Birchfield :
(nee ALLEN)
5KR - 16:35, 5MR - 26:15 (25:57-96),
10kR - 34:18 (32:46un-96/33:05-92)
WRIGHT Claire U17 9.09.83, Liverpool H :
HJ - 1.77
WRIGHT Dawn-Alice 20.01.76, Coventry G :
PV - 3.10 (3.10-94)
WRIGHT Jennifer U17 21.09.83, Bracknell :
TJ - 10.79
WRIGHT Joy 22.06.75, Herne Hill :
400 - 56.1 (56.96-99), 800 - 2:10.7
WRIGHT Kimberley U13, Dartford :
DTM - 22.35
WRIGHT Lucy 17.11.69, Leeds :
1500 - 4:19.71,
3k - 9:19.31 (9:16.1mx/9:16.93-98),
5k - 16:02.97 (15:59.51-98),
5KR - 16:33, 5MR - 26:51,
10kR - 34:55 (34:19-99)
WRIGHT Rebecca 20.12.77, W S & E/CUAC :
100H - 15.2, 400H - 61.00
WYETH Alison V35 26.05.64, Parkside :
3k - 9:33.09mx (8:38.42-93),
10MR - 58:55 (54:30-98),
HMar - 1:16:47 (1:10:54-98),
Mar - 2:39:01 (2:38:26-99)
WYNTER-PINK Clover 29.11.77, W S & E :
SP - 11.97 (12.08-99)

YELLING Elizabeth 5.12.74, Bedford & Co :
800 - 2:09.72, 1500 - 4:16.75,
3k - 9:11.4mx/9:19.98 (9:15.25-98),
5k - 16:03.75 (15:50.85-98),
5MR - 26:09, 10k - 33:07.9,
10kR - 33:10, 10MR - 55:10+ (55:05-98),
HMar - 1:12:31
YELLING Hayley 3.01.74, Hounslow :
1500 - 4:25.2, 3k - 9:02.88mx/9:11.20,
5k - 15:36.27, 5MR - 26:45 (26:42-99),
10k - 32:52.5, 10kR - 32:55
YELLOP Lindsay Victoria U23 18.08.78, Norw :
400H - 65.6
YORWERTH Amanda E. 18.05.67, St Albans S :
Mar - 3:00:44 (2:54:56-97)
YOUNG Catherine U20 14.03.82, Stam & D :
HJ - 1.74, Hep - 4110 (4418-99)
YOUNG Rachel U20 15.05.83, Grimsby :
HJ - 1.73
YOUNG Sarah 2.01.70, Salford :
(see WILKINSON)

ZAWADA Sarah U20 9.04.82, AF&D :
200 - 25.20i (24.1w/24.20-97/24.4-98)
ZENNER Helen U20 15.08.82, Team Solent :
1500 - 4:31.55, 3k - 9:56.69

AMENDMENTS TO BRITISH ATHLETICS 2000

From Peter Matthews & Martin Rix and others

INTERNATIONAL RESULTS

p.113	World CC Championships: Men 12k correct placings to 35 Cullen, 53 Tromans, 66 Pearson, 74 Stephenson, 93 Bannister
p. 119	IAAF World Youth (U17) Championships at Bydgoszcz
p. 129	GER v GB v POL v FRA U19 at Neubrandenburg, GER
p. 135	UK v USA. Men 4x400: 1 USA 3:04.62
p. 138	Sco PV McGloughlin IRE, NIR HT Healy IRE, NIR W Hep - McAluey competed in Under 17 event, doesn't appear to have been any senior entrants so "vacant title"
p. 139	Mid: JT Mike Tarran 61.87; W HJ Aneska Binks, SP Elaine Cank 10.95, HT Gardner North: 3000SC Berry 9:02.9 and W 5000W Charnock 23:11.7 manual; Dec: Liam Collins 6073 (Garland competed as guest)

MERIT RANKINGS

SP & DT	Remove SP 2nd and DT 6th Myerscough due to drugs ban and move up the rest. add as 12th SP: Guy Marshall, DT: Scott Rider
Dec	Quarry Previous ranking (1998) 1=
Overall	Leading points scorers – women: add 6. Denise Lewis 315

MEN 1999

100m:	10.68w +6.2 Ben Inatimi U17 6.7.83 2 Sheffield 15 Aug Liverpool H
800m:	2:02.72 Murdoch
HJ:	1.95 Edden
PV:	U13: 2.70 Luke Cutts 13.2.88 1 Grantham 24 Jul; Foreign: 4.60 McLaughlin 18.5.77
LJ:	performances: 70 to 7.50, missing marks in 7.49 to 7.45 range; delete 7.29 Reni Edu (was Seni – above), 6.85 Blair 21.6.74; U15: Yeboah 7.1.86
TJ:	15.26 Malwyn Gordon 29.4.82
HT:	55.58 Davies 5 Leichlingen, GER 7 Aug, 50.42 Mark Roberson (Bicester) 21.3.75 1 Salisbury 31 Jul
3000mW:	13:27.9 Adams at Rotherham, 15:43.98 Smith 17.1.84

WOMEN 1999

300m:	38.8i+ M Thomas
Mar:	3:03:46 Denise Dean
PV:	3.13 Jo Hughes 7.2.71
TJ:	Katharine Streatfield
HT:	37.83 Maysoon Elkawed 27.2.77 on 4 Sep (Chelmsford/CUAC)
JT:	44.38 Harvey was new JT, 37.13 old javelin Riordan (not 37.73 new) b. 4.12.76; 35.31/37.06 Mounteney; U17: 35.85 Sonia Green 19.11.83 (move to new JT additional U17 list)
Hep:	Cozens 5201 – add 42.01 JT
Pen U15:	2551 Clayton
50kmW:	5:27:00 Kennaugh at 32.5M = 52.3km.

INDEX

Men	Hayball – BRIDPORT, Taylor, Thomas – Road Hoggs
Women	Benjamin, Donita (correct in lists), Chadney – BRIDPORT, NAISH – delete first entry (300H 45.05)

PREVIOUS ANNUALS

1994:	4x100m: 39.92 team was Gardener, Devonish, Mark, Cameron

Other Publications

Umbra and the NUTS publish other statistical athletic books, currently an All-Time Compilation and Internationals to 1939 are available. NUTS also publish a quarterly statistical review and Umbra can source some ATFS books. Finally, back copies of British Athletics Annuals are available for the last 10 years.

Contact Julie Fletcher at

Umbra Athletics Limited
Unit 1, Bredbury Business Park
Bredbury Park Way
Stockport SK6 2SN
Tel: 0161 406 6320 Fax: 0161 406 6732
e-mail julie@umbra.co.uk